HANDBOOK OF LATIN AMERICAN STUDIES: No. 60

A Selective and Annotated Guide to Recent Publications in Art, History, Literature, Music, and Philosophy

VOLUME 61 WILL BE DEVOTED TO THE SOCIAL SCIENCES: ANTHROPOLOGY, ECONOMICS, GEOGRAPHY, GOVERNMENT AND POLITICS, POLITICAL ECONOMY, INTERNATIONAL RELATIONS, AND SOCIOLOGY

EDITORIAL NOTE: Comments concerning the *Handbook of Latin American Studies* should be sent directly to the Editor, *Handbook of Latin American Studies*, Hispanic Division, Library of Congress, Washington, D.C. 20540.

HANDBOOK OF LATIN AMERICAN STUDIES: NO. 60

HUMANITIES

Prepared by a Number of Scholars
for the Hispanic Division of The Library of Congress

LAWRENCE BOUDON, *Editor*
KATHERINE D. McCANN, *Senior Assistant Editor*
TRACY NORTH, *Assistant Editor and Webmaster*

2005

UNVERSITY OF TEXAS PRESS   *Austin*

International Standard Book Number: 0-292-70608-1
International Standard Serial Number: 0072–9833
Library of Congress Catalog Card Number: 36–32633
Copyright © 2005 by the University of Texas Press.
All rights reserved.
Printed in the United States of America.

Requests for permission to reproduce material
from this work should be sent to:
Permissions, University of Texas Press,
Box 7819, Austin, Texas 78713–7819.

First Edition, 2005

The paper used in the publication meets
the minimum requirements of American National
Standard for Information Sciences—Permanence
of Paper for Printed Library Materials,
ANSI Z39.48–1984. ⊚

DEDICATION

DOLORES MOYANO MARTIN (1935–2003)

Dolores Martin was one of the most extraordinary people I have ever known. Her interests and keen insights ranged far beyond Spanish, English, and American literature and the humanities. When I first met her in the late sixties as a researcher at the Library of Congress, she was looking for materials on Che Guevara. Our conversation rapidly turned from the Argentine revolutionary to Dostoevsky and Russian literature. She had also read Akhmatova, Brodsky, and Aksyionov. I learned that during her childhood in Argentina, Dolores had a Ukranian nanny who introduced her to Russian children's stories. Dolores was fascinated with the parallels between Spanish, Argentine, and Russian culture, and explored the subject in some of her writings. It was this lively intellectual curiousity and her vast mental storehouse of knowledge that never ceased to amaze her friends and coworkers.

Both through her own writing and her editorship of the *Handbook of Latin American Studies,* a major reference source in the field, Dolores was a major contributor to knowledge and interpretation of Latin American culture. She wrote historical articles, literary criticism, political essays, memoirs, and book reviews, as well as short stories and translations of Latin American poetry. Her writings appeared in *The New York Times, Wall Street Journal, The Republic of Letters, The Washingtonian, The Washington Review, The Military History Quarterly,* and various scholarly publications. Her detailed recollections of Ernesto Che Guevara as a boy and young man were published in *The New York Times Magazine* in August 1968, less than a year after his death in Bolivia. *The World & I* (February 1988) published "From El Cid to El Che: The Hero and the Mystique of Liberation in Latin America," which writer-editor Cynthia Grenier described as a "brilliant, penetrating analysis that links Guevara with a long tradition of Hispanic and Latin American history and psychology."

Born in Córdoba, Argentina, to an American mother and Argentine father, Dolores came to the US to study at Vassar College from which she graduated in 1956. Before taking a position at the Library of Congress, Martin worked at the Argentine Embassy, the Inter-American Development Bank, and American University Center for Research in Social Systems. From 1977–1980, she was a consultant to former Representative John Brademas.

Beginning her Library of Congress career in 1970 as assistant editor of the *Handbook of Latin American Studies,* Dolores became editor in 1976. In 1989, under her direction, volume 50 of the *Handbook* was the first Library bibliography to become available electronically. During the 1990s, Dolores and her staff undertook the retrospective conversion of the first 55 volumes of the *Handbook,* now available in a CD-ROM version that is searchable in English and Spanish and on the web (*HLAS Online*), searchable in English, Spanish, and Portuguese. At her initiative, these bibliographic records are also shared with the Research Library Group (RLG). Dolores retired from the Library of Congress in 1999.

Her work with the *Handbook of Latin American Studies* earned her several major awards from professional associations, as well as special recognition by the Library of Congress. She received the Lifetime Achievement Award from the Conference on Latin American History (a section of the American Historical Association) and twice was the recipient of the José Toribio Medina Award from the Seminar on the Acquisition of Latin American Library Materials (SALALM), which named her an honorary member after her retirement. She served on committees of the Latin American Studies Association, SALALM, and was a member of the Washington Literary Society.

Less well known are Dolores' many contributions to the development of the Luso-Hispanic collections at the Library of Congress. She undertook many acquisitions trips to Latin America. Her debriefing sessions to library staff were riveting accounts of scaling the Andes in Bolivia in search of materials about the Ayamaras, exploring the Paraguayan Chaco looking for Guarani tribes, and her unforgettable trip to the Argentine south where she visited a little-known museum whose director's work is part of the Library's collection. She thrilled the old man by presenting him with copies of the bibliographic records for his slender work on the Patagones. Dolores' network of friends and coworkers extended across several continents. She made sure she had contributing editors to the *Handbook* from Japan, China, Poland, Hungary, France, Germany, India and Russia.

Throughout the years, Dolores offered crucial help to an unending stream of scholars and journalists who sought her out for her knowledge of the library's collections and her insight into Latin American culture. She assisted Georgie Ann Geyer with her work on Castro, Jorge Castañeda with his book on Che Guevara, and Jorge Schwartz with Portuguese translations of Borges. She and I recorded for the Library's collections Mario Vargas Llosa, Carlos Fuentes, and Gabriel García Márquez. Dolores wrote superb essays on Hispanic and western culture and a memorable short story for *The Republic of Letters*, a literary journal edited by Saul Bellow. Her lifelong commitment to research and learning were evident upon the occasion of her LC retirement, when she commented that the Library should never become a "homogenized, stratified, corporate entity," but should be like "a giant coral reef with knowledge accumulating through the centuries."

Dolores was a devoted wife to physicist Bill Martin and an extraordinary mother to Eric and Christian Martin. She died just three days before Christian married Carmel Geraghty whom Dolores adored. Dolores was a wonderful friend and colleague for over thirty five years. Her sense of humor and her inimitable ability to tell stories will never be forgotten.

Georgette Magassy Dorn
Chief, Hispanic Division

(Reprinted from *The Gazette*, Vol. 14, No. 32. Washington, DC: Library of Congress, September 19, 2003, p. 3.)

CONTRIBUTING EDITORS

HUMANITIES

Maureen Ahern, *The Ohio State University*, TRANSLATIONS
Severino João Albuquerque, *University of Wisconsin-Madison*, LITERATURE
Félix Angel, *Inter-American Development Bank*, ART
Barbara von Barghahn, *George Washington University*, ART
Clara Bertranou, *Universidad Nacional de Cuyo (Argentina)*, PHILOSOPHY
Dain Borges, *University of California-San Diego*, HISTORY
John Britton, *Frances Marion University*, HISTORY
Francisco Cabanillas, *Bowling Green State University*, LITERATURE
Walter Clark, *University of Kansas*, MUSIC
Don M. Coerver, *Texas Christian University*, HISTORY
Wilfredo Corral, *University of California-Davis*, LITERATURE
Edith B. Couturier, *National Endowment for the Humanities*, HISTORY
Edward Cox, *Rice University*, HISTORY
Sandra Cypess, *University of Maryland*, LITERATURE
Jennifer Eich, *Loyola Marymount University, Los Angeles*, LITERATURE
Darío Euraque, *Trinity College*, HISTORY
César Ferreira, *University of Oklahoma*, LITERATURE
Juan Flores, *Hunter College*, LITERATURE
José Manuel García García, *New Mexico State University*, LITERATURE
Magdalena García Pinto, *University of Missouri, Columbia*, LITERATURE
John D. Garrigus, *Jacksonville University*, HISTORY
Miguel Gomes, *University of Connecticut*, LITERATURE
Gilberto Gómez, *Wabash College*, LITERATURE
Lance R. Grahn, *University of Wisconsin, Stevens-Point*, HISTORY
Michael T. Hamerly, *Independent Consultant, Seattle, Washington*, HISTORY
Robert Haskett, *University of Oregon*, HISTORY
José M. Hernández, *Professor Emeritus, Georgetown University*, HISTORY
Steven Hirsch, *University of Pittsburgh at Greensburg*, HISTORY
Rosemarijn Hoefte, *Royal Institute of Linguistics and Anthropology, The Netherlands*, HISTORY
Joel Horowitz, *Saint Bonaventure University*, HISTORY
Regina Igel, *University of Maryland*, LITERATURE
Erick Langer, *Carnegie Mellon University*, HISTORY
Asunción Lavrin, *Arizona State University at Tempe*, HISTORY
Alfred Lemmon, *Historic New Orleans Collection*, MUSIC
Peter Linder, *New Mexico Highlands University*, HISTORY
Maria Angélica Guimarães Lopes, *University of South Carolina*, LITERATURE
Cristina Magaldi, *Towson University*, MUSIC
Carol Maier, *Kent State University*, TRANSLATIONS

Claire Martin, *California State University, Long Beach*, LITERATURE
Teresita Martínez-Vergne, *Macalester College*, HISTORY
Félix V. Matos-Rodriguez, *Hunter College*, HISTORY
David McCreery, *Georgia State University*, HISTORY
Joan Meznar, *Westmont College*, HISTORY
Elizabeth Monasterios, *State University of New York-Stony Brook*, LITERATURE
Naomi Hoki Moniz, *Georgetown University*, LITERATURE
José M. Neistein, *Brazilian-American Cultural Institute, Washington*, ART
Suzanne B. Pasztor, *University of the Pacific*, HISTORY
Daphne Patai, *University of Massachusetts-Amherst*, TRANSLATIONS
S. Elizabeth Penry, *Fordham University*, HISTORY
Anne Pérotin-Dumon, *Pontificia Universidad Católica de Chile*, HISTORY
Charles Perrone, *University of Florida*, LITERATURE
Guido Podestá, *University of Wisconsin, Madison*, LITERATURE
José Promis, *University of Arizona*, LITERATURE
James Radomski, *California State University, San Bernardino*, MUSIC
Susan E. Ramírez, *Texas Christian University*, HISTORY
Jane M. Rausch, *University of Massachusetts-Amherst*, HISTORY
Oscar Rivera-Rodas, *University of Tennessee, Knoxville*, LITERATURE
Humberto Rodríguez-Camilloni, *Virginia Polytechnic Institute*, ART
Mario A. Rojas, *Catholic University of America*, LITERATURE
Kathleen Ross, *New York University*, TRANSLATIONS
Oscar Sarmiento, *Potsdam College*, LITERATURE
William F. Sater, *California State University, Long Beach*, HISTORY
Flora Schiminovich, *Barnard College/Columbia University*, LITERATURE
Jacobo Sefamí, *University of California-Irvine*, LITERATURE
Susan M. Socolow, *Emory University*, HISTORY
Barbara A. Tenenbaum, *Hispanic Division, The Library of Congress*, HISTORY
Juan Carlos Torchia Estrada, *Consultant, Hispanic Division, The Library of Congress*, PHILOSOPHY
Lilián Uribe, *Central Connecticut State University*, LITERATURE
Thomas Whigham, *University of Georgia*, HISTORY
Steven White, *St. Lawrence University*, LITERATURE
Stephen Webre, *Louisiana Tech University*, HISTORY
Stephanie Wood, *University of Oregon*, HISTORY

SOCIAL SCIENCES

Juan M. del Aguila, *Emory University*, GOVERNMENT AND POLITICS
Benigno E. Aguirre-López, *Texas A&M University*, SOCIOLOGY
G. Pope Atkins, *University of Texas at Austin*, INTERNATIONAL RELATIONS
Melissa H. Birch, *University of Kansas*, ECONOMICS
Jacqueline Braveboy-Wagner, *The City College-CUNY*, INTERNATIONAL RELATIONS
Joyce Baugher, *Tulane University (Doctoral candidate)*, SOCIOLOGY
Luis Réne Cáceres, *Inter-American Development Bank*, ECONOMICS
Roderic A. Camp, *Claremont-McKenna College*, GOVERNMENT AND POLITICS
William L. Canak, *Middle Tennessee State University*, SOCIOLOGY
César Caviedes, *University of Florida*, GEOGRAPHY

Robin M. Wright, *Universidade Estadual de Campinas (Brazil)*, ANTHROPOLOGY
Clarence Zuvekas, Jr., *Consulting Economist, Annandale, Virginia*, ECONOMICS

Foreign Corresponding Editors

Teodoro Hampe-Martínez, *Universidad Pontificia Católica de Lima*, COLONIAL
    HISTORY MATERIALS IN GERMAN AND FRENCH LANGUAGES
Kotaro Horisaka, *Sophia University, Tokyo, Japan*, JAPANESE LANGUAGE
Mao Xianglin, *Chinese Academy of Social Sciences*, CHINESE LANGUAGE
Franz Obermeier, *Universitätsbibliothek Kiel*, GERMAN LANGUAGE
Inge Schjellerup, *Nationalmuseet, Denmark*, DANISH LANGUAGE

Special Contributing Editors

Christel Krause Converse, *Independent Consultant, College Park, Maryland*,
    GERMAN LANGUAGE
Barbara Dash, *Library of Congress*, RUSSIAN LANGUAGE
Georgette M. Dorn, *Library of Congress*, GERMAN AND HUNGARIAN LANGUAGES
Zbigniew Kantorosinski, *Library of Congress*, POLISH LANGUAGE
Vincent C. Peloso, *Howard University*, ITALIAN LANGUAGE
Juan Manuel Pérez, *Library of Congress*, GALICIAN LANGUAGE
Iêda Siqueira Wiarda, *Library of Congress*, SPECIAL MATERIAL IN PORTUGUESE
    LANGUAGE

CONTENTS

HISTORY

LITERATURE

SPANISH AMERICA

MUSIC

PHILOSOPHY: LATIN AMERICAN THOUGHT

INDEX

EDITOR'S NOTE

I. GENERAL AND REGIONAL TRENDS

One unmistakable trend observed in the many chapters that make up Volume 60 is the high quality and quantity of the works reviewed. One contributor after another heaped words of praise on the books and articles he/she annotated. A Mexican historian noted the "ever more sophisticated" (Tenenbaum, p. 211) work being produced. Another historian observed that "one finds works utilizing innovative approaches in almost every category" (Rausch, p. 370). Yet another remarked that there is "an increasing methodological sophistication and an expanding topical reach" (Hirsch, p. 385). Finally, despite his criticism of the inconsistency in historical scholarship on Argentina, one historian quickly added that "often the works being produced are exceptional" (Whigham, p. 415).

Many of the trends noted in Volume 58 continue in the current volume, while new, exciting areas of study also have arisen. One ongoing trend is the focus on regional and local history. Historians in just about every Latin American country are exploring the past in areas outside of the capital cities. Works on Mexico, for instance, shed new light on the history of Jalisco and the western part of that country (item **1220**). In addition, the Revolution and its aftermath are examined in the states of Querétaro (item **1533**), Michoacán (item **1579**), and Durango (item **1601**). Still other works delve into the Reform in Tlaxcala (item **1405**), while Guzmán López looked at the rivalry between Lerdo de Tejada and Iglesias in Guanajuato in the year 1876 (item **1433**).

Regional and local history also thrive elsewhere. In Venezuela, Urdaneta has published a study on the resistance to dictator Juan Vicente Gómez in the state of Zulia (item **2480**). In Argentina, meanwhile, historians are moving away from the focus on Buenos Aires and the Pampas region, examining what was a very different historical experience in the provinces. One locale that received a good deal of attention in this volume is Neuquén, in western Argentina (items **2834** and **2949**). In Peru, studies have proliferated on Ayacucho, Arequipa, and Cuzco, among others. One particularly noteworthy book by Nugent on the political culture in the Chachapoyas region (1885–1930) makes "the case for state-making 'from below'" (Hirsch, p. 385). Finally, economic history works in Brazil examine regions outside of the main export sectors, although studies of coffee in places such as southern Minas Gerais also appeared (item **3236**).

Another trend that continued in this volume is the history of immigration and immigrants. And it occurred not just in countries that experienced huge influxes of immigrants (e.g. Argentina and Brazil), but also in countries that did not, such as Colombia. Two works examined the impact of Syrians and Lebanese on the Chocó (item **2510**) and the Atlantic Coast (item **2502**). Another, by Silva Téllez, takes a look at the legacy of Italian immigration, despite the fact that only a small fraction of the Colombian population can claim to be of Italian origin or descent (item **2539**).

Argentina, of course, is fertile ground for historiographies of immigration and this biennium does not disappoint. One interesting work is Moya's study of what he calls "the invisible immigrants:" (Horowitz, p. 418) the Spanish (item **2945**). His study is noteworthy, in particular, because he is able to portray Spanish immigrants both at the level of the individual and as a group. Similarly, in Peru, scholars are switching their focus to immigrant groups that had been previously understudied—Eastern Europeans, Jews, and Africans. Another trend, the use of photos and paintings, documents the economic and cultural contributions of Chinese immigrants over a span of 150 years (item **2588**). Finally, in the general realm are several works on Jewish immigration. Cohen's work (item **978**) covers the colonial period, while Bokser Liwerant and Gojman de Backal (item **1006**) looked at the 20th century, particularly around the time of World War II.

The study of women continues to attract considerable attention in colonial scholarship. One historian was surprised about the proliferation of works on women in Puerto Rico. She further notes that the research covers a wide range of topics and makes "use of the latest methodological tools in the field" (Martinez-Vergne, p. 268). Likewise, women were an important focus of research in the Anglophone Caribbean. One interesting work, by Hutton, explores the participation of women in the Morant Bay rebellion (item **1961**). In Mexico, on the other hand, one historian expressed concern that works centered on women declined in number over the past several years. Of those published, however, one noteworthy study, by Sefchovich, examined the lives of the wives of Mexican rulers, revealing the changes affecting Mexican women, in general (item **1620**). The opposite trend occurred in Central America, where gender has garnered more attention than in previous years.

A worthwhile new theme in historical research tries to describe the nature of private life (i.e. family, customs, fashion, etc.). Two works, one edited by Devoto and Madero (item **2895**) and another by Cicerchia (item **2818**), cover the topic with regard to Argentina. The four-volume *Historia da vida privada no Brasil* gives us a glimpse into Brazil's culture from the colonial times to the present (*HLAS 58:3177* and items **3277**, **3278**, and **3279**). And Rubial García provides an overview of daily life in 17th-century Mexico City (item **1323**).

Of a related nature is research on cultural history that, in Mexico at least, is receiving new attention. One notable work is a special edition of the *Hispanic American Historical Review* (1999) that was devoted to "Mexico's New Cultural History." It featured articles by Vaughan, Haber, Mallon, Socolow, and Lomnitz, among others, several of which were reviewed in *HLAS 60* (see items **1547, 1561, 1568, 1623**, and **1633**) and in the section on Mexican Post-Revolutionary History). Another contributor noted how scholarship on colonial Bolivia has shifted toward social and cultural history.

The 100th anniversary of the Spanish-American War predictably generated new works on that conflict and its impact on the former Spanish colonies of Cuba and Puerto Rico. But it also produced works that examined the role of Spain in the Americas. For instance, Zea and Magallón edited a book that focused on relations between Spain and its former colonies (item **1102**). Another edited work, by Cortés Zavala, Naranjo Orovio, and Uribe Salas, looks at the larger international context of the war (item **1078**).

The indigenous peoples are once again the focus of research, both in historical and ethnohistorical works. More than two dozen publications were reviewed for the general history section, alone. Among other topics, they examined their social, political, and economic position following the conquest and their interaction with European people and institutions. A much studied and often misunderstood topic, the impact of disease was examined by Cook (item **984**). Similarly, Rodríguez Lorenzo examined the Spanish missionaries and their efforts to educate the indigenous peoples (item **1053**). For Mexico, Tanck Estrada's work on education in the late colonial period is seminal and won the 2000 Howard F. Cline Prize (item **1334**). Two other works on both methods used to convert the indigenous Mexicans to Christianity also stand out: one by Castro Gutiérrez (item **1227**) and the other by Menegus (item **1296**). In Chile, studies explored the historical relationship between the government and the Mapuche (item **2736**), and various aspects of indigenous life (item **2706**).

Research on diplomatic history also was reviewed in this volume, but it did not display the same breadth or scope as in some previous years. In Chile, diplomatic history is "enjoying a revival" (Sater, p. 408). One interesting study, by Rinke, argues that Chile tried to use its ties to Germany to offset US influence (item **2743**). Another, by Fermandois Huerta, focuses on Chile's relations with the US immediately after World War II and contends that its repression of the Communist Party did little good in diplomatic terms (item **2712**).

Slavery continues to get attention in some regions. One contributor described the topic as being a dominant theme in the history of 19th-century Brazil. One notable change is the appearance of works dealing with slavery in areas other than São Paulo and Rio de Janeiro. For instance, Carvalho wrote on Recife (item **3252**) and Lima examined Rio Grande do Sul (item **3293**). In addition, some of the scholarship focused on nontraditional slave activities, such as transportation (item **3251**) and small-scale, nonexport agriculture (item **3300**).

The historiography of the Anglophone Caribbean also focused heavily on slavery and there are several outstanding works reviewed in this volume. One all encompassing work was Craton's *Empire, Enslavement, and Freedom* (item **1942**), which will no doubt fuel further research. He brought together essays published elsewhere, often in resources with little accessibility. Welch, meanwhile, relied on wills, inventories, and contemporary accounts to offer us a glimpse into slaveholding patterns and slave life (item **1908**).

A few other works stand out on their own. Bordi de Ragucci's study of drinking water in Buenos Aires (item **2793**) is hailed as "one of the most creative historical studies to appear of late" (Horowitz, p. 416). Another work is Peard's *Race, Place, and Medicine,* a major study of the history of medical practice in Brazil (item **3313**). Also from Brazil are two noteworthy studies, by Barman and Schwarcz, of Pedro II and his efforts to create and maintain the empire (items **3237**, and **3331**). And while works on Simón Bolívar are hardly scarce and the topic somewhat overstudied, two reviewed in this volume stand out: Vaz analyzes Bolívar's religious beliefs (item **2427**), while Beltrán Salmón examines his communication skills (item **2431**).

Turning now to other disciplines, the field of Art continued to receive scholarly attention, despite the economic realities that adversely affected many museums and galleries, resulting in the smuggling of many works of art. In Colombia, for instance, one now needs the approval of the Ministry of Culture to take any works out of the country. One attempt to inventory art works in Argentina was the *Catálogo de la pintura española en Buenos Aires,* by Fernández García (item **225**), which one contributor called "a revelation" (Angel, p. 21). Another noteworthy work, also from Argentina, documents the history of the Witcomb Gallery, possibly the first commercial gallery in Latin America (1896). At nearly the same time as the release of the movie *Frida,* comes a new book on her husband, *Entre andamios y muros: ayudantes de Diego Rivera en su obra mural* (item **108**), which discusses the contributions by the many artists who assisted him with his murals. Finally, *Cuba siglo XX: modernidad y sincretismo* (item **188**) offers us a historical review of Cuban artwork in the 20th century.

The vast majority of works on Brazilian art reviewed in *HLAS* 60 deal with contemporary visual arts and architecture, marking a shift from past volumes. There were two entries on one of Brazil's most renowned painters, Guignard (items **356** and **351**). Many other artists were the focus of one work each. The avant-garde artist Lygia Clark, described by one contributor as "a seminal presence," (Neistein, p. xx) is the subject of a major exhibition catalog containing articles by renowned art critics as well as examples of her work (item **348**). In sculpture, the work by Vlavianos stands out (item **377**). Lúcio Costa published three books on modern architecture (items **394, 395,** and **402**) and regional architecture also was well represented. Lastly, a noteworthy *Festschrift* on the legacy of noted art historian Robert C. Smith discusses his relationship with the art of Brazil, Portugal, and the US.

A major development in the field of Art in this biennium was the near simultaneous openings of museums containing the *Donación Botero* in Bogotá and Medellín, Colombia. The former is located in a beautiful colonial building across the street from the equally impressive Biblioteca Luis Angel Arango, and contains not only 118 works by Botero, himself, but also about 70 paintings and sculptures by such masters as Corot, Monet, Renoir, Dalí, Picasso, Tamayo, and Moore. It is truly an impressive collection by one of Latin America's most celebrated artists. One can take a virtual tour at *http://www.banrep.gov.co/blaavirtual/donacion/ home.htm.* The smaller collection in Medellín mostly contains Botero's own works.

Works on musicology continue to address the enormous variety of music emanating from Latin America and the Caribbean. In Mexico, two different works appeared on the composer Manuel Ponce. One, by Díaz Cervantes, is a biography (item **4397**), while the other, by Miranda, analyzes his style (item **4408**). Several dictionaries and encyclopedias were published in recent years and were reviewed in this volume. Among them is the impressive *Diccionario de la música española e hispanoamericana,* produced by the Sociedad Española de Autores y Editores (several entries on individual countries, composers, etc. are reviewed here). In addition, *The New Grove Dictionary of Music and Musicians* contained articles on Colombia, Ecuador, Peru, and Venezuela that were reviewed in this volume (items **4457, 4462, 4463,** and **4468**). It also included an article by renowned scholar Béhague on the Afro-Brazilian musical traditions (item **4376**). One contributor reviewed the wealth of online sources for music and musicology in Brazil and the Southern Cone.

Touching on the world of Literature, our contributors noted certain trends that continued and others that are new. One of the latter is the fact that, in Argentina, the literature has come to reflect the crisis that has gripped the country since the late 90s. Not only is it a reflection of the situation, but it acts as a criticism of the ideological, political, and cultural reality of the country. This may explain, in part, the increasing popularity of the historical novel and its appeal to the nostalgia of the past. Nostalgia (so-called "radical nostalgia") (García-García, p. 508) also figures prominently in the literature from Mexico, standing alongside postmodernism as the prevailing trends there. In Colombia, the bankruptcy of noted publisher Tercer Mundo has led to a decrease in the production of Literature, as well as Social Science. Nevertheless, important works appeared in this biennium, including a compilation of short stories by Germán Espinoza (item **3561**).

Meanwhile, Chilean novelist Jorge Edwards won the prestigious Cervantes Award in 1999 for his novel *El sueño de la historia* (item **3637**). Compatriot Isabel Allende published two more novels, *Retrato en sepia* (item **3623**) and the semiautobiographical *Hija de la fortuna* (item **3622**), also reviewed in the Translation section (see *Daughter of Fortune*, item **4274**). In Cuba, noted authors Amelia del Castillo and Mirta Yánez published compilations of their short stories, *De trampas y fantasías* (item **3478**) and *Narraciones desordenadas e incompletas* (item **3532**), repectively. And in Central America, two works stood above the others: Argueta's *Siglo de o(g)ro: bio-novela circular* (item **3433**) and Helen Umaña's *Panorama crítico del cuento hondureño (1881–1999)* (item **3465**).

Mirroring the renewed ties between Spain and Latin America in International Relations and Economics, a new dialogue has emerged between the two in the world of poetry. Two works reviewed in this volume stand in testimony to this trend. Iván A. Schulman and Evelyn Picón Garfield put together a new and expanded edition of *Poesía modernista hispanoamerica y española* (item **3761**), while Consuelo Triviño coordinated *Norte y sur de la poesía iberoamericana: Argentina, Brasil, Colombia, Chile, España, México, Venezuela* (item **3757**).

In the field of Drama, it is heartening to see the continued state and local support for theater despite the economic hardships in much of Latin America. It also is gratifying to know that some of the annual festivals that occur in just about every country of the region remain free, such as the *Festival Internacional de Teatro* in the Dominican Republic. Another encouraging trend is that, in addition to the fact that more plays are being written, many of them are actually making it to the stage.

I will end by dedicating this volume to Dolores Moyano Martin, the longtime Editor of the *Handbook* who passed away in October of 2003. She was the longest serving Editor in the history of the *HLAS* and under her guidance and stewardship the *Handbook* continued to be the most widely respected reference work on Latin America.

II. CLOSING DATE

The closing date for works annotated in this volume was mid-2002. Publications received and cataloged at the Library of Congress after that date will be annotated in the next humanities volume, *HLAS 62*.

III. ELECTRONIC ACCESS TO THE *HANDBOOK*

The *Handbook's* web site, *HLAS Online*, continues to offer, free of charge, access to all bibliographic records corresponding to *HLAS* volumes 1–62. Records that did not appear in a print volume may or may not be annotated, and some records may be in a preliminary editorial stage. The web site also includes a list of *HLAS* subject headings, a list of journal titles and the corresponding journal abbreviations found in *HLAS* records, searchable tables of contents for volumes 51–58 (*http://www.loc.gov/hlas/contents.html*), and introductory essays for volumes 1–49 of *HLAS*. The web address for *HLAS Online* is *http://www.loc.gov/hlas/*. The site is updated weekly.

Online Public Access Catalog

HLAS records from volumes 50 onward may also be searched through the

Library of Congress online catalog. Searches at this site may be limited by language, publication date, and place of publication. The address for the catalog web site is *http://catalog.loc.gov/*. In addition, selected bibliographic records in the Library of Congress' main catalog now contain *HLAS* annotations.

CD-ROM

Volumes 1–55 (1935–96) of the *Handbook* are available on the *Handbook of Latin American Studies: CD-ROM: HLAS/CD (v. 2.0)*. This retrospective version is produced by the Fundación Histórica TAVERA (Madrid) and distributed for them by DIGIBIS. For ordering information, contact DIGIBIS:

DIGIBIS Publicaciones Digitales
Claudio Coello, 123, 4ta,
28006 Madrid SPAIN
Phone: (91) 420–10–74 or (91) 429–80–03
Fax: (91) 429–80–71
http://www.digibis.com/ (home page)

Portals to the World

Users of the *Handbook* may also be interested in an electronic resource available through the Library of Congress—the *Portals to the World*, an ongoing project being carried out by the Area Studies divisions, including the Hispanic Division. *Portals to the World* contains selective Internet links to web sites that provide authoritative, in-depth information about Latin American nations and other countries of the world. Area Specialists and other Library staff choose and annotate the links based on Library of Congress selection criteria. The web address is: *http://www.loc.gov/rr/international/portals.html*.

IV. CHANGES FROM PREVIOUS HUMANITIES VOLUME

Changes in Coverage

The *Handbook* will no longer include a separate chapter on General Spanish American literature. Works of literature will now be assigned to the Contributing Editor responsible for a work's country of publication. Occasional works of literary criticism will be handled similarly. (See Editor's Note, Volume 54, p. xx, for a discussion of current *HLAS* policy on coverage of literary criticism.)

The last decade has seen a nearly overwhelming proliferation of Electronic Resources including CD-ROMS, web sites, geographic information systems, digitized archival collections, and e-journals, along with a growing acceptance of these resources as an effecient means of sharing information with a worldwide audience. Therefore, Electronic Resources will no longer be treated in a separate chapter. Instead Contributing Editors will select and review those Electronic Resources that they have found to be especially useful within their particular fields of study.

History

Dario Euraque from Trinity College took over the general and national chapters on Central America. Félix Matos Rodriguez of Hunter College covered Puerto Rico, while Teresita Martínez-Vergne, Macalaster College, turned her attention from covering Puerto Rico to reviewing works on the Dominican Republic. S. Elizabeth Penry from Fordham University took over the colonial history chapters for Peru and Alto Perú (Bolivia). And Steven Hirsch, of the University of Pittsburgh at Greensburg, assumed responsibility for post-independence Peru.

Literature

For prose fiction of the Hispanic Caribbean, Juan Flores of Hunter College covered Puerto Rico, and Diana Alvarez-Amell, from Seton Hall University, reviewed Cuba and the Dominican Republic. Flora Schiminovich of Barnard College collaborated with Claire Martin, California State University at Long Beach, on the prose fiction of Argentina.

For poetry, Guido Podestá, from the University of Wisconsin at Madison, assumed responsibility for Peru, while Lilián Uribe of Central Connecticut State University coordinated the chapter. Finally, Steven White, St. Lawrence University, joined the team covering translations from the Spanish and the Portuguese.

V. ACKNOWLEDGMENTS

The *Handbook* staff would like to express its sincere thanks to the many people at the Library of Congress who have collaborated on projects, offered advice, and supported the work of the *Handbook*. Those who were instrumental in ensuring that work progressed on a number of projects during the past year were Marla Banks, Ann Della Porta, Erik Delfino, Edmundo Flores, Andy Lisowski, Tony Pierce, Belinda Urquiza, and David Williamson.

HLAS Online is proud to provide OpenURL linking functionality to institutions with compatible software; this accomplishment would not have been possible were it not for the instrumental support of Mary Ambrosio and Barak Stussman, as well as the rest of the LC OpenURL Team: Katherine McCann and Tracy North from *HLAS*, Caroline Arms, Ardie Bausenbach, Ray Denenberg, and Larry Dixson from elsewhere in the Library.

In addition, we are grateful to our Library of Congress managers Deanna Marcum, Carolyn Brown, Beacher Wiggins, and Elgin Reid, and to Hispanic Division Chief Georgette Dorn for their continued support of the *Handbook* and its staff. We would also like to thank the members of the Hispanic Division, interns, and fellows who regularly lend their assistance and expertise to the *Handbook*.

Lawrence Boudon, *Editor*

HANDBOOK OF
LATIN AMERICAN STUDIES:
No. 60

ART

SPANISH AMERICA
Colonial
General, Middle America, and the Caribbean

BARBARA VON BARGHAHN, *Professor of Art History, George Washington University*

THE SCOPE OF SUBJECTS IN *HLAS 60* encompasses a diversity of studies that augment knowledge about the architecture and art of important colonial centers. The works reviewed here provide discussions about the evolution of towns first settled by missionary orders, investigations of archeological data, analyses of lesser-known sites, debates concerning conservation efforts, and examinations of specific colonial works of art.

Current research attests to a continued interest in Spanish America's rich architectural legacy, but the pictorial traditions have not been neglected. In their research on carvings and murals of a precolumbian past, some scholars have explored aspects of postconquest syncretism. Others have either cataloged icons by important mannerist-baroque painters, or delved into subgenre categories of the decorative arts as an attempt to explain probable ornamental sources.

Several new studies have modernized methodological approaches and presented challenging avenues for future investigations concerning the history of urbanization (items **9, 30, 34, 36, 38, 44,** and **45**). Classical and colonial revival in secular monuments (18th–20th centuries) is a subject receiving attention (items **13, 23,** and **28**). Worthy of singular mention is a comprehensive book showing plans and panoramic views of Mexico's cities, with abundant information accompanying the plates (item **33**). Very fine surveys are always welcome (items **10, 25, 29,** and **37**), and the proceedings of a 1994 colloquium produced a fascinating ensemble of essays related to the topography of Mexico City and the transformation of its landscape from the Spanish conquest to the colonial epoch (item **15**).

Of special interest is the focus upon the order of the Friars Minor in New Spain, which embraces such important topics as the growth and complexion of Spanish missions, daily life in the monastery of San Francisco in Querétaro, and the impact of Franciscan spirituality (items **24, 35,** and **52**). Also worthy of note are architectural studies pertaining to Oaxaca, particularly the renovation of Santo Domingo de Guzmán (item **40**). The restoration of the Cathedral of Mexico has yielded significant information (item **14**), but by far the most spectacular publication in this section is a sumptuously illustrated discussion of the Palace of the Archbishop (item **8**). Other texts also address Mexico's precolumbian heritage. Notably, intriguing commentaries accompany works about the Casa del Marqués del Apartado in Mexico City and San Juan de Tlayacápan in Morelos (items **7** and **22**). Even a recent short account about the Basilica of Guadalupe contains relevant material relating ancient female goddesses with the *tilma* of "La Guadalupana" (item **26**).

Of exceptional merit is a publication concerning 17th-century *retablos* in Querétaro (item **39**). Yet another text marks an even more dynamic threshold in defining the stylistic complexion of baroque Mexico. This book centers on the collection of paintings housed in Iowa's Davenport Museum of Art, and its informative entries on colonial titans are accompanied by superb illustrations (item **12**).

By far the most sumptuous edition on Mexican painting reviewed this biennium is a long-awaited monograph on Cristóbal de Villalpando, which does not disappoint and sets a high standard for needed tomes on significant masters (item **18**). As usual, additional entries feature the decorative arts of lacquer, nacre, and embroidery (items **6, 21, 31,** and **32**). Useful additions to the literature on religious art are books on Querétaro sculptures and colonial holy cards (items **6** and **20**).

With respect to art and architecture of Central America and the Caribbean, an important publication on La Merced in Antigua, Guatemala, contains lavish illustrations of its architecture, *retablos,* and treasures (item **52**). Books about colonial Cuba provide invaluable references (items **47, 48,** and **50**). A conference in Cartagena in 1996 yielded important essays about forts of the Caribbean, constituting a significant reference for military architecture (item **49**).

The historical studies included in this section are plentiful and varied in scope, and many editions reflect a greater awareness of the visual impact provided by color plates or sharp b/w photographs. This trend, combined with an apparent commitment to serious analysis of images and ideas, augers well for future publications not only on colonial Mexico, but also on Central America and the Caribbean. A note of appreciation is given to Debra Lavelle, an MA candidate at George Washington University, for her collaboration in the preparation of this chapter.

GENERAL

1   Barroco iberaamericano: de los Andes a las Pampas. A cargo de Ramón Gutiérrez. Barcelona: Lunwerg, 1997. 483 p.: bibl., ill. (some col.), indexes.

Multiauthored encyclopedic volume covers art and architecture of Andean countries. Pays tribute to late art historian Santiago Sebastián López, whose contribution "Pintura y escultura barrocas en Colombia y Venezuela" is included. Clearly intended as a response to Gasparini's controversial groundbreaking study *América, barroca y arquitectura* (see *HLAS 36:270a* and *502*), the indiscriminate use of the stylistic label "baroque" by various authors remains less than satisfactory, notwithstanding Gutiérrez's affirmation in the Epilogue, "América continúa siendo barroca." Chapters are loosely organized by country, often characterized by a synoptic treatment of important subjects such as history of Spanish colonial urbanism, religious art and architecture, and decorative arts. In contrast, includes very little coverage

of civil architecture. Although not integrated with the texts, volume provides a wealth of visual materials such as plans, historic documents, and excellent quality b/w and color photographs. The absence of notes is a definite drawback, but the factual information of the texts and general bibliography make this a valuable reference for future studies. [H. Rodríguez-Camilloni]

2   Bonet Correa, Antonio. Monasterios iberaamericanos. Madrid: Ediciones El Viso, 2001. 415 p.: ill. (chiefly col.), index.

Beautifully illustrated monograph by leading Spanish architectural historian deals with the great complexes of monastic institutions in Latin America, by far the richest legacy of Iberian colonial architecture. Its splendid format meets expectations of the fine quality publications in the series Biblioteca Mundo Hispánico. Introductory chapters discuss the important role that Christianity and the religious orders played in the colonization of the Americas, and how the European evangelical mission received its most tangible expression in magnificent buildings and works of art. South American monastic institutions are well represented with 19 examples in Ecuador, Colombia, Peru, Chile, Bolivia, and Brazil, each treated in a separate chapter. Excellent photographs compliment the highly informative text, full of essential historic data and sensitive analytic observations. An outstanding contribution to the field, even though specialized readers will lament the absence of footnotes and bibliography. [H. Rodríguez-Camilloni]

3   Mesa, José de. La arquitectura del manierismo en América Hispana. (*in* Simposio Panamericano de Historia, *3rd, México, 1995.* Memorias. México: Instituto Panamericano de Geografía e Historia, 1997, p. 395–404, bibl.)

Dean of Bolivian architectural historians discusses the origins of mannerism in 16th-century European art and architecture and its spread to Latin America, predominately in Mexico, Guatemala, Colombia, and Ecuador. Identifies specific examples of key monuments exhibiting manneristic tendencies in each of these countries; and considers the wide circulation of architectural treatises imported from Europe—such as those by Serlio, Vignola, and Villalpando—as important sources of inspiration for architects and builders in America. A good introductory study on the subject, although it could be expanded to include Peru and Bolivia. [H. Rodríguez-Camilloni]

4   Museo Chileno de Arte Precolombino. América precolombina en el arte. Santiago: Museo Chileno de Arte Precolombino: Banco Santiago, 1998. 95 p.: ill. (some col.).

Emphasizing the importance of the various cultural manifestations of precolumbian art, this catalog from the Chilean Museum is a wonderful overview of indigenous art. In addition to the art of South America, the text encompasses examples from Mexico, Central America, and the Caribbean. Splendid illustrations with helpful introductory map divided and labeled by region.

5   Schenone, Héctor H. Iconografía del arte colonial. v. 3, Jesucristo. 1. ed. argentina. Buenos Aires?: Fundación Tarea, 1998. 1 v.: bibl., ill.

Exhaustive study of the iconography of Christ in Latin American colonial art is an important complement to v. 1–2 by the same author (see *HLAS 56:64*). Format again follows closely Louis Réau's *Iconographie de l'art chrétien* (Paris, 1955–59), with a comprehensive listing of representational themes fully described in the main text and accompanied by the identification of specific pictorial and/or sculptural examples with information about their current location. Even though the geographic distribution mainly covers Andean countries, volume also includes Brazil, Central America, Mexico, and the US. Variations of iconographic themes are carefully noted; and some representations are traced back to European models widely circulated through prints in the Spanish and Portuguese American colonies. Unfortunately, the few b/w reproductions of uneven quality are useful only as visual references. Abundant footnotes and a complete biography provide additional guidance for further research. [H. Rodríguez-Camilloni]

MEXICO

6   Anaya Larios, José Rodolfo. El arte virreinal de Querétaro. Querétaro, Mexico: Gobierno del Estado de Querétaro, 1998. 106 p.: bibl., ill. (Historiografía queretana; v. 3)

Concerns mainly devotional sculptures of Querétaro. Although the treatment of the subject appears cursory and the photographs are in b/w, the information presented about specific carvings is a welcome addition to the study of religious icons in New Spain.

7   La antigua Casa del Marqués del Apartado: arqueología e historia. Coordinación de Elsa Hernández Pons. México: Instituto Nacional de Antropología e Historia, 1997. 391 p.: bibl., ill., maps. (Colección científica; 329) (Serie Arqueología)

Consists of synthetic studies and preliminary observations concerning discoveries of precolumbian culture in the Casa del Apartado, the principal façade of which overlooks the excavated ruins of the famed Templo Mayor. Tenochtitlán's Temple of Coatiocalli, dedicated to the worship of diverse Aztec gods—specifically the goddess Cihuacoatl, was the site of a fortified house and tower built by conquistadors. Extending to the Calle de Guatemala, the building was occupied in the 18th century by Don José Francesco de Gagoaga y Arozqueta, viscount of San José and Marquis of Apartador. His architect, Manuel Tolsá, undertook extensive renovations. This book examines the precolumbian treasures found at the Casa del Apartado and contains important photographs and diagrams documenting archeological discoveries.

8   Antiguo Palacio del Arzobispado: Museo de la Secretaría de Hacienda y Crédito Público. Textos de Miguel León Portilla *et al.* México: SHCP Hacienda, 1997. 254 p.: bibl., col. ill.

Beautifully illustrated monograph presents the Palace of the Archbishop in Mexico City, built upon the Temple of Tezcatlipoca, as one of the premier ideological centers of New Spain. The palace was eventually transformed into the present-day New Palace for History and Culture. Maps and engravings generously supplement the unparalleled splendor of the color illustrations. An undeniable scholarly contribution to the study of cultural transformations in Mexico from the precolumbian Aztecs to the colonial epoch.

9   Arquitectura y espacio social en poblaciones purépechas de la época colonial. Dirección general de Carlos Paredes Martínez. Morelia, Mexico: Univ. Michoacana de San Nicolás de Hidalgo, Instituto de Investigaciones Históricas, 1998. 421 p.: bibl., ill. (some col.).

Well-documented studies by different authors examine architectural space, urbanization, and monuments of Michoacán. Includes discussion about art and architecture, detailed line drawings, ground plans of important preconquest and colonial buildings, and maps.

10   Artigas H., Juan B. Chiapas monumental: veintinueve monografías. Granada, Spain: Univ. de Granada, 1997. 276 p.: bibl., ill. (some col.). (Monográfica Arte y arqueología; 35)

Text is divided into 29 essays, each devoted to a particular Mexican monument. Architectural types vary, ranging from churches and convents to pueblos and bridges. Provides an extensive bibliography, good photographs, reconstruction drawings, and floor plans.

11   Avila Hernández, Julieta. El influjo de la pintura china en los enconchados de Nueva España. México: Instituto Nacional de Antropología e Historia, 1997. 93 p.: bibl., col. ill.

Posits the possible influence of Chinese painting on Mexican mother-of-pearl pictures (*enconchados*). Some comparative examples of Asian art are selected to bolster the hypothetical impact of oriental landscape in New Spain due to the "Manila Galleon" trade. Not addressed are Flemish paradigms which were exported and distinguished by panoramic "world landscapes" with fantastic geological formations.

12   Burke, Marcus B. Treasures of Mexican colonial painting: the Davenport Museum of Art collection. Santa Fe, N.M.: Museum of New Mexico Press, 1998. 176 p.: bibl., ill. (chiefly col.), index.

Excellent, informative contribution to the field of Latin American art. This exhibition catalog, the third in a series from the Davenport Museum's permanent collection, is the result of 10 years of exhaustive study. Presents a fine balance between interpretation, stylistic analysis, and factual information. Could be used as a textbook for an introductory course on Mexican painting. The illustrations are of consistently high quality and permit appreciation of the colonial works discussed.

13   La casa de Tezontle: monografía de la casa Zuno. Guadalajara, Mexico: Univ. de Guadalajara, 1998. 78 p.: bibl., ill. (some col.).

Discusses and provides illustrations of the former residence of José Guadalupe Zuno (1891–1980), one of Jalisco's most brilliant scholars. Zuno's house was built in the neocolonial style in 1923 and donated to the Univ. of Guadalajara in 1974.

14   La Catedral de México: problemática, restauración y conservación en el futuro. Recopilación de Martha Fernández. México: UNAM, Instituto de Investigaciones Estéticas, 1997. 189 p.: bibl., ill. (Estudio de arte y estética; 40)

A thorough and well-written investigation of the Cathedral of Mexico City, divided into two parts. Pt. 1 concerns construction problems, architectural losses, mutilations, and alterations over time. Pt. 2 is devoted to restoration and conservation. Includes clear photographs, floor plans, and axial drawings of the Cathedral.

**15   El Centro Histórico, ayer, hoy y
mañana.** Coordinación de Cristina
Barros. México: Instituto Nacional de Antropología e Historia: Depto. del Distrito Federal, 1997. 228 p.: bibl., ill. (Arte y cultura)
    Papers presented during a colloquium
in 1994 sponsored by INAH and CNCA. Offers a synthesis of the topography of Mexico
City, comprising such topics as: the geological substratum upon which the postconquest
urban center rose; the metamorphosis of the
landscape after the *chinampa* model; the
prehispanic structures under the Cathedral;
an ecological study of the environs; and the
evolution of public space from 16th-20th
centuries.

16   Clancy, Flora S. Sculpture in the ancient Maya plaza: the early classic
period. Albuquerque: Univ. of New Mexico
Press, 1999. 169 p.: bibl., ill., index, map.
    A welcome addition to classic Maya
scholarship by one of the specialists in the
field. Examines stelae sculpture and glyphs
from perspectives of composition, carving
techniques, imagery, and texts as related to
the dedication and placement of the monuments in civic plazas. The stelae are examined on both social and historical levels,
including a broad geographic spectrum of
examples. Supplemented with numerous
illustrations and drawings, copious notes,
and a superb bibliography. For archeologist's
comment, see *HLAS 59:134.*

17   Coahuila, inventario artístico. Saltillo,
Mexico: Centro de Estudios Sociales y
Humanísticos, 1998. 303 p.: bibl., ill. (some
col.). (Signos para la memoria; 3)
    A general cultural review of Coahuila,
encompassing architecture, music, literature,
dance, and popular customs. Contains good
historical photographs and color plates.

**18   Cristóbal de Villalpando: ca. 1649–
1714: catálogo razonado.** México: Instituto de Investigaciones Estéticas: Fomento
Cultural BANAMEX: Consejo Nacional para
la Cultura y las Artes, 1997. 444 p., 1 folleto
(15) p.: bibl., ill. (some col.).
    First chronological, comprehensive
examination of Villalpando's career and
works with numerous full-page illustrations and magnificent color details. The
text, which contains a very fine bibliography
and several scaled reconstructions of major
altarpieces, should serve as a prototype for

future monographs on Mexico's premier colonial masters. The informative discussions
of Villalpando's singular baroque style will
provide a solid foundation for further analysis of aspects of his oeuvre, particularly the
complex iconography he selected to accommodate erudite patrons of significant religious institutions.

19   Cruz Aguillón, Raúl. El Zócalo de
Oaxaca y su entorno. Oaxaca de
Juárez, Mexico: Gobierno del Estado de Oaxaca: Ayuntamiento de Oaxaca de Juárez,
1997. 97 p.: bibl., ill. (some col.).
    An interesting text about the Plaza
Principal (*Zócalo*) of Oaxaca and the monuments in its environs. Contains some historical photographs and a brief list of sources.

**De la patria criolla a la nación mexicana,
1750–1860.** See item **1418.**

**20   Devocionario mexicano: pequeños
grabados novohispanos.** México:
Backal Editores, 1998. 163 p.: bibl., ill.
    Contains illustrations of a number of
devotional holy cards printed in the wood
block technique from 18th-19th centuries.
Also provides a list of artists specializing in
this genre. Might be viewed as a useful stylistic parallel to emblematic paintings of
New Spain.

**21   Los enconchados de la conquista
de México: colección del Museo Nacional de Bellas Artes de Argentina.** México:
Museo de El Carmen, 1998. 1 v. (unpaged):
bibl., col. ill.
    Exhibition catalog pertaining to an im-
portant cycle of *enconchados* paintings, one
of which is signed by the late 17th-century
artist Miguel González. Miguel González,
son of Tomás González, worked in Mexico
City with his brother Juan González de Mier.
Their workshop specialized in the technique
of *nácar*. Miguel's 22 episodes of Hernán
Cortés' conquest of Mexico (1519–21) are
based partly upon the chronicle of Bernal
Díaz del Castillo, *Historia verdadera de la
conquista de Nueva Hispania* (1632). The
collection in Argentina comprises nearly the
entire original cycle of 24 works (two panels
are in Madrid).

22   Favier Orendáin, Claudio. Ruinas de
utopía: San Juan de Tlayacápan: espacio y tiempo en el encuentro de dos culturas.
Cuernavaca, Mexico: Gobierno del Estado de

Morelos: UNAM, Instituto de Investigaciones Estéticas: Fondo de Cultura Económica, 1998. 322 p.: bibl., ill., maps.

Addresses the syncretic relationship
between the prehispanic utopia in Morelos at
Tlayacapan and the postconquest structures
and ideologies which evolved upon the foundation of the precolumbian past. Discussing
religious symbolism, the author parallels precolumbian seasonal feasts with the Christian
liturgical calendar.

23   **Fierro Gossman, Rafael R.** La gran cor-
      riente ornamental del siglo XX: una re-
visión de la arquitectura neocolonial en la
ciudad de México. México: Univ. Iberaamericana, 1998. 227 p.: bibl., ill.

Study looks at the continuous style of
neocolonial architecture and ornamentation
in both Mexico and the US during the three
decades following the Mexican Revolution.
Contains a diversity of illustrations and floor
plans.

24   **Fisher, Lewis F.** The Spanish missions
      of San Antonio. San Antonio, Tex.:
Maverick Pub. Co., 1998. 103 p.: bibl., ill.
(some col.), index, maps.

Examines five Spanish missions in San
Antonio from a comprehensive history of
their founding to the decline of the mission
as an integral social and religious center. Essays devoted to 20th-century restorations
precede each chapter. Numerous b/w photographs supplement the text.

25   **Gómez Martínez, Javier.** Historicis-
      mos de la arquitectura barroca novo-
hispana. México: Univ. Iberaamericana,
Depto. de Arte, 1997. 199 p.: bibl., ill.

Discusses distinct architectural styles
as transmitted from European models to
New Spain. Contends that mannerist architectural forms as applied in colonial building were more successfully assimilated
into a Mexican vocabulary than the proto-
Renaissance style, which in Mexico lacked
a classical foundation rooted in the Vitruvian
tradition. Excellent bibliography and distinctive photographs.

26   **Guadalupe: maravilla americana:**
      homenaje a Monseñor Guillermo
Schulenburg Prado. México: Centro de
Cultura Casa Lamm, 1998. 80 p.: bibl., ill.
(some col.).

A brief, well-written and illustrated

account of Guadalupe's famed Basilica and
its treasures. Contains a chapter on the female deities of ancient Mexico and a descriptive catalog of the diverse works of art in the
collection.

27   **Guanajuato.** México: Grupo Editorial
      Proyecció de México, 1998. 269 p.:
bibl., col. ill.

A pictorial resource for the architecture of Guanajuato. Introduction offers an
overview of historical antecedents. Subsequent chapters discuss religious, civil, cultural, and municipal structures. Also looks
at urbanism in Guanajuato.

28   **Hernández, Regina.** Ignacio de Cast-
      era: arquitecto y urbanista de la ciudad
de México 1777–1811. México: Instituto de
Investigaciones Dr. José María Luisa Mora,
1997. 194 p.: bibl., ill.

Study focuses on the neoclassical
structures erected in the late-18th and early-
19th centuries by the master architect Ignacio de Castera. Includes considerations of urban spaces, very good photographs, and a fine
bibliography.

29   **Historia de la arquitectura mexicana.**
      t. 1, Los conceptos de historia y meso-
américa. t. 2, El siglo XVI, el enfrentamiento
de dos mundos. t. 3, Los siglos XVII y XVIII,
el auge del barroco. Guadalajara, Mexico:
Centro Universitario de Arte, Arquitectura y
Diseño: Univ. de Guadalajara, 1998. 3 v.:
bibl., ill., maps.

Brief analysis of basic concepts in
Mexican art and architecture. Vol. 1 encompasses religion, astronomy, and archeology.
Vol. 2 addresses some intriguing topics,
inter alia Hapsburg imperial institutions,
the problem of the late Gothic, the medieval mentality, and Mexican utopias of the
16th century. Vol. 3 explores the 17th- and
18th-century baroque, citing the cathedrals
of Durango, San Cristóbal de las Casas, and
the Cathedral of Zacatecas. Third volume includes an informative essay on the guilds of
masons and architects. Additional illustrations would be welcome in a second edition.

30   **Jiménez, Víctor; Salvador Díaz-Berrio;**
      and **Felipe Solís.** Centros históricos de
México. Prólogo de Enrique Cervantes. Coordinación editorial de Jaime Bali Wuest. México: Banobras, 1998. 143 p.: bibl., ill. (some
col.), maps (some col.).

A finely illustrated overview of the cities of Mexico from the precolumbian period to the 20th century. Focuses on the urbanization of the historic center, with examples including Mexico City, Chihuahua, Veracruz, Tlaxcala, Querétaro, and Morelia.

31   Lacas mexicanas. Textos de Ruth Lechuga *et al.* México: Museo Franz Mayer: Artes de México, 1997. 81 p.: col. ill. (Colección Uso y estilo; 5)

Exhibition catalog moves from the origins and forms of lacquer work to a discussion of the debate over the degree to which European and Oriental artistic influences can be applied. Elegantly illustrated with a thorough bibliography. Includes English translations of the essays.

32   Litto Lecanda, Lilia del. El revestimiento de lo sagrado: la obra del bordador Marcus Maestre en Tepotzotlán. México: Instituto Nacional de Antropología e Historia, 1999. 170 p., 33 p. of plates: bibl., ill. (some col.), map. (Colección Obra diversa)

A significant iconographical study of the components of a chasuble in the Cathedral of Mexico created by the Sevillian Marcus Maestre. Study encompasses liturgical ornamentation of baroque Spain, particularly the materials of embroidery and the techniques of the *gremios* (guilds). Text is supplemented with several documents from the municipal and historical archives of Seville and the Cathedral of Mexico. Very fine color illustrations.

33   Mayer, Roberto L. Poblaciones mexicanas, planos y panoramas, siglos XVI al XIX = Mexican towns, plans and panoramas, 16th to 19th centuries. Contribuciones especiales de Elías A. Trabulse. Recopilación de Mario de la Torre. México: Smurfit Cartón y Papel de México, 1998. 347 p.: col. ill., col. maps.

Comprehensive and richly illustrated study of the plans and views of Mexican cities. Comprises often overlooked details pertaining to cartography and measuring techniques as well as ordinances for dividing cities into quarters. Aerial views consist of spectacular reproductions of paintings and engravings. Wonderful clarity and presentation of plates and well-developed accompanying text.

34   Mijares, Carlos G. San Angel. Mexico: Clío, 1997. 121, 7 p.: bibl., ill. (some col.).

Originally with Tacubaya and San Agustín de las Cuevas, San Ángel was founded in 1529 by the Dominicans and by 1601 the town acquired a hospital built by the Carmelite order. Book provides a history of San Ángel and discusses its evolution from the colonial period through the 19th century. Includes numerous color photographs of the municipal and religious institutions.

35   Montes Bardo, Joaquín. Arte y espiritualidad franciscana en la Nueva España: siglo XVI: iconología del Santo Evangelio. Jaén, Spain: Univ. de Jaén, 1998. 334 p.: bibl., ill., map. (Colección Martínez de Mazas. Serie Estudios)

Formidable, lucid investigation presents the inseparable links between art and spirituality in the Franciscan community of New Spain. In addition to architecture, murals are illustrated in sharp photographs and discussed with a discerning eye for their hagiographic content as well as style. Analysis of Franciscan spirituality merits emulation in future discourses about the impact of religious orders in Mexico.

36   Moya Pérez, Alfonso. Arquitectura religiosa en Jalisco: cinco ensayos. Guadalajara, Mexico: Amate Editorial, 1998. 223 p.: bibl., ill., maps.

Begins with the colonial period, and moves into an examination of 19th-century religious architecture. Each essay is followed by bibliographic references, and abundant maps and photographs are included. An important scholarly investigation of key monuments in Jalisco.

37   Mullen, Robert James. Architecture and its sculpture in viceregal Mexico. Austin: Univ. of Texas Press, 1997. 263 p.: bibl., index, maps.

Impressive work examines the urban phenomenon in Mexico from preconquest to the colonial period. Covers a broad scope of monuments, such as churches, sanctuaries, residences, and frontier missions. Provides a cohesive analysis of buildings and their decoration from 16th-19th centuries. In addition to a general bibliography, each chapter includes suggestions for further reading. Contains a useful glossary of architectural terms.

Provides an excellent foundation for preliminary exposure to the rich architectural heritage of Mexico.

38 Muñoz Balderas, Benjamín Gerardo. Santa Rosa Jáuregui: una semblanza histórica. Mexico: s.n., 1998? 208 p.: bibl., ill., maps.

Contains introductory chapters pertaining to the conquest and origins of Querétaro, and advances to a discussion of the haciendas and ultimately to the inception of Santa Rosa Jáuregui. The town was founded in 1745 in honor of the Dominican tertiary St. Rose of Lima (1586–1617: canonized 1671). The photographs are not exceptional, but the book presents useful historical information and primary documentation.

Museo Nacional de Arte (Mexico). Una ventana al arte mexicano de cuatro siglos: colecciones del Museo Nacional de Arte. See item **141**.

39 Ramírez Montes, Guillermina. Retablos y retablistas: Querétaro en el siglo XVII. México: Gobierno del Estado de Querétaro, 1998. 215 p.: bibl., ill., index. (Colección Historiografía queretana; v. 22)

Iconographical study examines the five significant retables of Santiago de Querétaro, which were executed between 1631–99. Identifies the primary painters, sculptors, and artisans and provides key documents and reconstruction drawings. Also includes an informative iconographical appendix of religious themes, a glossary of technical terms used in the 17th century, charts related to the commissions, and a very good bibliography.

40 Restauración de Santo Domingo de Guzmán, Oaxaca, 1994–1998. México: Instituto Nacional de Antropologia e Historia, 1998. 46 p.: ill. (some col.).

A brief documentary of the restoration of Santo Domingo de Guzmán which includes photographs taken before and after the work was completed. Includes cut-away views and ground plans.

41 San Francisco: un convento y un museo surcando el tiempo. Colaboración de Jorge René Gonzalez M. *et al.* Coordinación editorial y fotografía de José Manuel Rivero Torres. México: Museo Regional de Querétaro, 1997. 192 p.: bibl., ill. (some col.).

Examines the daily life of the Franciscan monks of Querétaro through a discussion of their real property. Addresses aspects of architecture, furnishings, and paintings. Also provides inventories of various topics ranging from architectural projects to lists of kitchen staples. One chapter is devoted to Querétaro's archeological collections of ceramic, jade, and obsidian objects.

42 Serrano Espinoza, Luis Antonio and Juan Carlos Cornejo Muñoz. De la plata, fantasías: la arquitectura del siglo XVIII en la ciudad de Guanajuato. México: Instituto Nacional de Antropología e Historia; Guanajuato, Mexico: Univ. de Guanajuato, 1998. 192 p.: bibl., ill. (Colección Obra diversa)

Modest publication provides useful information concerning 17th- and 18th-century architecture of Guanajuato. Discusses civil architecture, particularly houses, as well as religious institutions in a town noted for its mining of gold and silver. Good historical discussions with b/w photographs, some floorplans, and a very good bibliography. Marks an important advance in the study of regional architecture.

43 Talavera Márquez, Raúl. De casona de bravo a Museo Nishizawa. Toluca, Mexico: Univ. Autónoma del Estado de México, 1997. 97 p.: ill. (some col.).

This text pertains to the restoration of the Casona de Bravo in the city of Toluca and its remodeling into the Museo Nishizawa.

44 Tello Peón, Berta E. Santa María la Ribera. Mexico City: Clió, 1998. 123, 9 p.: bibl., ill. (some col.).

Discusses early development of colonial Santa María la Ribera. Includes a number of 19th-century site plans and documents in color. Historical photographs in both color and b/w and accompanying informative text provide an important contribution to the study of civil architecture.

45 Vázquez Soriano, Mario Armando. Patrimonio arquitectónico y urbano de Nuevo Laredo. Ciudad Victoria, Mexico: Consejo Estatal para la Cultura y las Artes de Tamaulipas, 1997. 89 p.: bibl., ill. (Palabra de papel; 8)

Examines vernacular architecture and includes chapters devoted to the historic center of Nuevo Laredo. Looks at government, local inhabitants, and the tourist industry in relation to public buildings.

46   Villar Rubio, Jesús Victoriano. El Centro Histórico de la ciudad de San Luis Potosí y la obra del ingeniero Octaviano Cabrera Hernández. San Luis Potosí, Mexico: Univ. Autónoma de San Luis Potosí, Facultad de Hábitat, 1998. 373 p.: bibl., ill., maps.

Wide-ranging synthesis of the work of the architectural engineer Cabrera Hernández. Focuses upon his construction between 1905–24. Seeks to explain how he modified the colonial city of San Luis Potosí, and includes a plethora of documents pertaining to the civil architecture in the historical districts. Text is supplemented by historical photographs and good plans, as well as a bibliography and appendix of documents relating to the personal life and career of Cabrera Hernández.

Zalamea Traba, Fernando. Iconos de la ciencia en el arte neogranadino y en el arte novohispano, 1600–1760. See item **62.**

THE CARIBBEAN

47   Carley, Rachel. Cuba: 400 years of architectural heritage. Photography by Andrea Brizzi. New York: Whitney Library of Design, 1997. 224 p.: bibl., col. ill., col. maps, index.

Traces the development of architecture in Cuba from the 16th century to the present day. Comprehensive overview includes splendid photographs and floor plans. Presents information on city planning and the growth of urban centers, and addressses technical aspects of engineering. Chapters are subdivided by type of structure: civic, religious, and domestic. A welcome addition to the literature on Havana.

48   Fernández Santalices, Manuel. Las antiguas iglesias de La Habana: tiempo, vida y semblante. Miami, Fla.: Ediciones Universal, 1997. 184 p.: bibl., ill. (Colección arte)

Beginning with the founding of the first church in Havana, this book traces the architectural development of various ecclesiastical structures within and around the city limits from the 16th-20th centuries. Biblio-

graphic entries follow each essay. A second reprinting would be welcome on a larger scale, accompanied by color plates.

49   Fortificaciones del Caribe: memorias de la reunión de expertos: 31 de julio, 1 y 2 de agosto de 1996, Caragena de Indias, Colombia. Bogotá: Colcultura; s.l.: Patrimonio Mundial; s.l.: UNESCO, 1997. 120 p.: bibl., ill., maps.

Conference proceedings (Cartagena, Colombia, 31 July-2 Aug. 1996) provide an informative study of the forts of the Caribbean. Includes small photographs and significant site map of strongholds. Comprised of general essays on fortifications as well as specific studies pertaining to the Antilles, the Gulf of Mexico, Cuba, the Dominican Republic, the British Caribbean, and Bocachica.

50   Martín Zequeira, María Elena and **Eduardo Luis Rodríguez Fernández.** La Habana: guía de arquitectura = Havana, Cuba, an architectural guide. La Habana: Ciudad de La Habana; Sevilla, Spain: Junta de Andalucía, Consejería de Obras Públicas y Transportes, Dirección General de Arquitectura y Vivienda, 1998. 327 p.: bibl., ill. (some col.), indexes.

This tour of Havana functions as a pictorial guide to the city and its primary architectural monuments. Divided geographically by districts, each with an accompanying historical synopsis, the guide provides succinct entries describing the most popular historical sites.

51   Monte Urraca, Manuel E. del. Mi propuesta. Santo Domingo: Alfa & Omega, 1998. 326 p.

Penetrating work in which the author argues for the restoration of colonial Dominican Republic. Directs attention to key monuments that merit historical preservation.

52   The treasure of La Merced: art and history. Recopilación de Ana María Urruela de Quezada. English translation by Kami Amestoy Lee, with the collaboration of Ana María Urruela de Quezada. Miami, Fla.: Trade Litho, 1997. 240 p.: bibl., col. ill.

Important contribution to the literature on the churches of Antigua, Guatemala. Though focused specifically upon the Mercedarian church of La Merced, the text contains a copious amount of color plates that capture the colonial architecture as well as the retables, paintings, and decorative objects within the religious institution. Also provides an excellent bibliography and pertinent information concerning some of the most significant works of art. A "must have" for scholars of colonial Antigua.

South America

HUMBERTO RODRÍGUEZ-CAMILLONI, *Professor of Architecture and Director, Henry H. Wiss Center for Theory and History of Art and Architecture, Virginia Polytechnic Institute and State University*

WITH FEW EXCEPTIONS, items reviewed for this volume of *HLAS* represent significant contributions to the artistic literature of Spanish colonial South America. Several titles set a high standard of scholarship that will help establish or strengthen solid foundations for future studies in the field. Even though studies on architecture and urbanism still account for the largest number of publications— with those devoted to painting, sculpture, and the decorative arts lagging behind— a more consistent rigor of scholarly research and a variety of methodological approaches rather than standard chronological surveys are more prevalent throughout the field. Reviews of the historiography of colonial art and architecture during the last two decades by several authors confirm this assessment (see items **72, 74,** and **78**).

Religious architecture, in particular, is well represented by a number of beautifully illustrated publications that also exemplify outstanding scholarly research. One example is *Monasterios Iberaamericanos* by Bonet Correa, which offers a comprehensive discussion of the important role that Christianity and the religious orders played in the colonization of the Americas and how the evangelical mission received its most tangible expression in magnificent buildings (item **2**). The work is an excellent addition to the Biblioteca Mundo Hispánico by Editorial El Viso and should be consulted together with Navascués Palacio's *Las catedrales del Nuevo Mundo* (Madrid, 2000) in the same series.

The ongoing inclusion of historic monuments and sites in UNESCO's World Heritage List continues to serve as an impetus for fine publications while helping to promote the restoration and conservation of Latin America's endangered cultural heritage. *The Jesuit Missions of the Guaranis* by Gazaneo et al. documents a model international intervention in Paraguay by UNESCO and ICOMOS (item **57**). In Peru, the recent efforts conducted by the municipal government in Lima to rehabilitate plazas and streets within the historic district with impressive results are fully discussed in *Lima: Centro Histórico* (item **75**). Such initiatives, worthy of emulation, are finally receiving the recognition and dissemination they deserve.

Gisbert and De Mesa's second revised and expanded edition of *Arquitectura andina, 1530–1830* is an exemplary work, representing a lifetime of scholarly research (item **73**). Several of the studies in this classic anthology are of seminal importance in the field. This edition, which includes a previously unpublished chapter on the industrial city of Potosí, Bolivia, makes these long out-of-print studies available to a new generation of readers.

As noted by Gutiérrez in his brief review of the historiography of Peruvian architecture and urbanism during the last two decades, there remain major voids in the study of civil, vernacular, and rural architecture, particularly in remote areas and regions outside principal urban centers (item **74**). These observations would equally apply to the rest of South America. Nevertheless, two recent contributions covering these topics are noteworthy. Item **56** involves important archival and historical archeological research of a house in the city of Old Santa Fé, Argentina; while item **68** is a splendid monograph dealing with the famous Casa del Moral in Arequipa, Peru.

Deluxe multi-authored monumental works on architecture, painting, and sculpture include *Barroco iberaamericano* (item **1**); *Caazapá: las reducciones franciscanas y los Guaraní del Paraguay* (item **55**); *Perú: fe y arte en el Virreynato* (item **80**); and *El barroco peruano* (item **64**). Among these, the latter deserves to be singled out as the most successful attempt at reinterpreting the concept of a "baroque style" as applied to the art and architecture of Spanish colonial Peru. Departing from standard chronological and factual presentations, this book offers a thematic approach using different methods of analysis and interpretation that should serve as inspiration for future studies. The magnificent color photographs, never before reproduced, add immensely to the better appreciation of works discussed in the text.

Banking institutions throughout Latin America continue to sponsor some of the finest publications in the field (items **64, 71,** and **81**). This patronage is of vital importance since the rising costs of lavishly illustrated books in most countries make many publications impossible. Some institutions, such as Peru's Banco del Sur (Bancosur) and Banco de Crédito, have established a record of distinguished series like the Colección Arte y Tesoros del Perú (item **64**). One major drawback of these publications, however, is their limited circulation (typically only among patrons of the respective institutions), thus making them generally inaccessible to academic communities or the public.

A remarkable work devoted to sculpture is Majluf and Wuffarden, *La piedra de Huamanga: lo sagrado y lo profano*, which gives the art of Peruvian alabaster carving the attention it deserves (item **77**). Often categorized as popular art or craft, Huamanga stone sculpture merits recognition as a fine art in its own right, representative of a tradition that originated in the Spanish colonial period and continues today in the central Andes of Peru. By far the most complete study on the subject to date, it significantly expands Stastny's earlier treatment in *Las artes populares del Perú* (see *HLAS 46:316*).

Items **5, 54, 62,** and **70** focus on the iconography of Spanish colonial art. Most welcome here is the third volume of Schenone's *Iconografía del arte colonial*, devoted to the iconography of Jesus Christ (item **5**). A monumental work modeled after Réau's classic *Iconographie de l'art chrétien* (Paris, l955–59), it offers the most complete list of representational themes accompanied by the identification of specific pictorial and/or sculptural examples with information about their location in public and private collections throughout Latin America and the US. Cummins' paper presented at the first Encuentro Internacional de Peruanistas uses an innovative semiotic approach to study early Spanish colonial art in Peru, which leads to a new interpretation that transcends the conventional analysis of problems surrounding indigenous idolatry and the description and iconographic analysis of Christian art (item **70**).

New archival research conducted in Lima (items **76, 83, 84**) and Arequipa (item **63**) has led to the discovery of a wealth of reliable documentation that significantly expands our knowledge of the life and work of architects and artists active during the Spanish colonial period. These primary sources are of critical importance for they permit the identification of the names of individuals associated with the different artistic professions and the extent of their contributions. Remaining questions of attribution for existing works can often also be put to rest; while in other instances the written records are the only remaining testimony of their work. For example, Lohmann Villena's fine research on the Corral de las Comedias in Lima provides detailed descriptions of the physical appearance of an important public building no longer extant as it was restored and partially rebuilt in the mid-17th century (item **76**).

Studies on decorative arts are again few in number, but continue to reflect an increasing interest in colonial silverwork. *La platería en el Perú* by Del Busto Duthurburu is much more than a catalog documenting the Enrico Poli collection in Lima, one of the finest collections in South America (item **66**). The erudite text provides a comprehensive overview of the major centers of production throughout the viceroyalty of Peru, discussing the silversmith guild's organization and identifying artisans active during the time. In turn, *Plata y plateros del Perú* by Carcedo Muro *et al.*, offers a more complete study of Peruvian silver and the art of the silversmith from precolumbian times through the 20th century (item **67**). Much more modest in presentation and scope but also featuring examples of decorative arts are the museum catalogs *Breve catálogo del Museo de Arte Colonial [de Quito]* (item **65**), *Casa Real de la Moneda [de Potosí]* (item **69**), and *Arte del período hispánico venezolano en la hacienda Carabobo* (item **61**).

Another category of titles corresponds to papers presented at international conferences or symposia. As is the case with other disciplines, these events are becoming increasingly important due to the special opportunities they provide for the exchange of ideas among scholars while at the same time helping to minimize the duplication of research efforts. Depending on the themes covered, some of these meetings have also encouraged meaningful and very much needed interdisciplinary collaborations. In chronological order, they include: Segunda Conferencia Internacional de Arqueología Histórica (Santa Fe, Argentina, l995) (item **56**); Tercer Simposio Panamericano de Historia (Mexico City, l995) (items **3** and **63**); Primero Encuentro Internacional de Peruanistas (Lima, l996) (items **70, 72, 74, 78**); The Jesuits II Conference on Cultures, Sciences, and the Arts, 1540–1773, (Boston College, Chestnut Hill, Mass., 2002) (proceedings awaiting publication by Univ. of Toronto Press); and First International Congress on Construction History (Madrid, 2003) (will be reviewed in *HLAS 62*). Participation of both the academic communities and general public in these events provides yet another effective platform for the dissemination of studies on Spanish colonial art and architecture

ARGENTINA, CHILE, PARAGUAY, AND URUGUAY

53 **Abramo, Lívio.** Livio Abramo: 133 obras restauradas. Asunción: Embajada de Brasil; Centro de Artes Visuales, Museo del Barro, 2001. 139 p.: bibl., ill. (some col.).

Lívio Abramo (1903–92) was one of the top Brazilian printmakers in the 20th century. Known and respected by his many disciples as an example of high professional competence and ethical integrity, he became a master of masters. This book celebrates 133 works on paper restored and conserved, all of them belonging to the *Museo del Barro*, in Asunción, Paraguay, repository of the most comprehensive collection of the artist's output. Abramo lived for many years in Asunción and adopted Paraguay as his second country. Includes two excellent essays and many reproductions, but no bibliography. [J. Neistein]

54   Bauzá, Hugo F. Tradición sibilina y las síbalas de San Telmo. Buenos Aires: Fondo Nacional de las Artes, 1999. 75 p.: bibl., col. ill.

Thorough study of the iconography of the sibyls depicted in 12 oil canvases hanging in the sacristy of the church of San Telmo in Buenos Aires. An unusual theme in Spanish colonial art, these female figures from antiquity symbolizing the intuiting of higher truths and prophetic powers appear holding flower-framed vignettes with scenes from the life of Christ. Although unsigned and undated, stylistic analysis reveals these paintings belong to the Altiplano School of Peru and Bolivia and were probably executed during the 18th century. A most likely compositional adaptation from European prints is also proposed. Excellent full-page color reproductions of each painting are included in an appendix preceded by a comprehensive bibliography.

55   Caazapá: las reducciones franciscanas y los Guaraní del Paraguay. Granada, Spain: Diputación Provincial de Granada, 1998. 198 p.: bibl., ill. (some col.), maps.

Important companion to exhibitions of Spanish colonial art from Franciscan mission towns in Paraguay held in 1998 in Santa Fe (Granada) and Seville, Spain. Even though less well-known than their Jesuit counterpart mission towns (*reducciones*), the Franciscan missions initiated by Fray Luis Bolaños in 1580 also covered the vast neotropical region of the Amazon east of Asunción and contributed significantly to the evangelization process that brought a Christian way of life to the Guaraní and other indigenous groups. The 1606 Franciscan foundation of San José de Caazapá, singled out as a model of the Christian community the missionaries hoped to establish throughout the colony, is a principal focus and point of departure for an in-depth discussion of all aspects considered essential for the full spiritual and intellectual development of the Guaraní. The urbanism, architecture, sculpture, and music of Franciscan missions are more specifically addressed in separate chapters by Jorge R. Vera, Francisco Corral, and Luis Szarán. Concludes with a catalog of fine color plates portraying

religious sculptures, liturgical objects, and indigenous crafts featured in the exhibitions.

56   Calvo, Luis María. Familia y ámbito doméstico en Santa Fe la Vieja: la casa de Hernando Arias Montiel. (*América/Santa Fe*, 14, 1998, p. 53–84, bibl., tables)

Good study of Capt. Arias Montiel, his family, and their house in the Spanish colonial city of Old Santa Fe, Argentina, based on original archival research. With painstaking detail, the text discusses the genealogy of the family, their landholdings and occupations, thus providing the most complete picture to date of daily life in the old city. Although Old Santa Fe was abandoned in 1660 and re-founded in a different location (the present Santa Fe), the combination of notarial records preserved in the Depto. de Estudios Etnográficos y Coloniales with the archeological remains at the site allows a better appreciation of the main house, its spatial distribution and typical rammed-earth wall construction. A model of historic research, this work should serve as a solid foundation for future studies.

57   The Jesuit missions of the Guaranis. Publishing director, Manrique Zago. Scientific director, Jorge O. Gazaneo. Photographs by Carlos Mordo. Buenos Aires: M. Zago Ediciones, 1997. 222 p.: bibl., ill. (some col.), maps (some col.). (The humanity's heritage; 2)

Second volume in series compiled by cultural and scientific organization ICOMOS, in collaboration with UNESCO, provides an excellent overview of extant architectural remains and religious art from the 30 Jesuit mission towns founded in Argentina (15), Brazil (7), and Paraguay (8) during the 17th-18th centuries to protect the Guaraní Indians from Portuguese slave trade and depredations of Spanish colonists, and to teach them the arts of a Christian town life. Intended for a broad readership, the multi-authored text focuses on the historic and artistic importance of a rich cultural heritage facing an uncertain future. Their remote location in a vast area of the neotropical region of the Amazon territory, destruction by wars, and centuries of abandonment and neglect have allowed the conservation of only a few ruins of the original 30 missions, and the recovery and proper protection which involve complex and difficult challenges. Spectacular color photographs permit a good appreciation of the extraordinary beauty of the mission churches and their natural settings. Useful annexes include a chronology of the missionary period, a discussion of the photogrammetric technique used for recording the monuments, and the international "Charter for the Protection and Management of the Archaeological Heritage."

Moreno, Carlos. Las cosas de la ciudad y la campaña. See item **2404**.

58   Sustersic, Bozidar Darko; Estela Auletta; and Cristina Serventi.
Crónica del desplome y la reconstrucción de la cúpula de Trinidad. (*Folia Hist. Nordeste,* 13, 1997, p. 23–54)

Thorough compilation of primary and secondary sources document the collapse and reconstruction of the dome of the church in the Jesuit mission town of Trinidad, Paraguay, during the Spanish colonial period. This important work was part of the research preceding the restoration and conservation project initiated in 1981 by ICOMOS and UNESCO (see item **57**). Principal findings clarify many aspects concerning the chronology of the magnificent church, considered the crown jewel of Jesuit mission churches. For example, the date of completion of the reconstructed dome was determined to be 1764, under the direction of the Jesuit Pedro Pablo Danesi. The original structure, constructed of sandstone carefully hewn, has columns and pilasters with capitals decorated with leaves and flowers suggesting Guaraní inspiration. Most noteworthy, however, is the building's frieze brought to life with carved angels playing musical instruments of the period, among them the Paraguayan harp. This and similar publications contribute to the definitive conservation of this historic site.

COLOMBIA AND VENEZUELA

59   Aristizábal Giraldo, Tulio. Iglesias, conventos y hospitales en Cartagena colonial. Fotografías de Juan Diego Duque. Bogotá: Banco de la República; El Ancora Editores, 1998. 154 p.: bibl., col. ill., index.

Handsome survey of Spanish colonial churches, monasteries, and hospitals in Cartagena offers a readable historic narrative without any formal analysis or interpretation. Each monument is covered separately, and is illustrated with a few fine quality color photographs—mostly of exterior views. The bibliography is worth consulting as a guide to other sources for a more in-depth study of the subject. Intended for general public.

60   Caricatura y costumbrismo: José María Espinosa y Ramón Torres Méndez: dos colombianos del siglo XIX. Bogotá: Museo Nacional de Colombia: Ministerio de Relaciones Exteriores de la República de Colombia, 1999. 100 p.: bibl., ill. (chiefly col.).

Color-illustrated and annotated catalog of the exhibition at the *Museo de América* in Madrid, drawn from the collection of the *Museo Nacional de Colombia.* Espinosa and Torres Méndez were two artists who, in the words of Andrés Pastrana Arango (President of Colombia), "bore exceptional witness to the birth of our country: Colombia." [F. Angel]

Morales Folguera, José Miguel. Tunja: Atenas del Renacimiento en el Nuevo Reino de Granada. See item **2157**.

61   Rivas, Jorge. Arte del período hispánico venezolano en la hacienda Carabobo. Caracas: Fundación Cisneros, 2000. 32 p.: bibl., col. ill. (Cuaderno; 00.5)

Handsomely illustrated pamphlet documents a small but significant private collection of Spanish colonial art housed in the Hacienda Carabobo. Individual entries in the catalog provide full captions with name of artist (if known), date, medium, dimensions, and an art historical commentary. Also considers issues of provenance, style, and relationship with contemporary artistic developments in Europe and elsewhere in the continent. Of special interest are several fine examples of Venezuelan furniture, including an armchair of circa 1798 by the famous cabinetmaker José Ramón Cardozo, whose work in the Cathedral of Caracas is well documented.

62   Zalamea Traba, Fernando. Iconos de la ciencia en el arte neogranadino y en el arte novohispano, 1600–1760. (*Quipu/México,* 12:1, enero/abril 1999, p. 69–98, tables)

Weak attempt at adopting Charles Sander Pierce's semiotic typology of *icon, index,* and *symbol* to the study of Spanish colonial art in Colombia and Mexico. Following a lengthy introduction describing the objectives and methodological approach of the study, identifies five major activities as examples of premodern scientific practices in Colombia during the period 1600–1760: astronomic observations; medicine; engineering works; natural history descriptions; and the preparation of handbooks on physics, logic, and mathematics. Less successful is the listing of selected motifs such as specimens of American fauna and flora, which need not be recognized as "scientific icons" each time they appeared in colonial art. The lack of a specific reference to context and the absence of illustrations raise serious questions about the study's conclusion concerning the "characterization of New Granada [Colombia] as an indexical discrete cultural context... as opposed to a similar characterization of New Spain [Mexico], as a symbolically dense cultural context."

BOLIVIA, ECUADOR, PERU

63   Bacacorzo, Gustavo. Mansiones históricas y artísticas de Arequipa. (in Simposio Panamericano de Historia, *3rd, México, 1995.* Memorias. México: Instituto Panamericano de Geografía e Historia, 1997, p. 239–255, bibl.)

Using archival and literary sources, identifies ownership of historic houses in the city of Arequipa dating back to the Spanish colonial period. Historic and descriptive narrative focuses around the Tristán del Pozo Palace of 1738 which was restored and retrofitted as headquarters of Banco Continental in 1976. Although lacking in visual material, footnotes and bibliography list many useful documentary sources not included in item **68.**

64   El barroco peruano. Lima: Banco de Crédito, 2002. 333 p.: bibl., col. ill., index, maps, 1 CD-ROM (4 3/4 in.). (Col. Arte y Tesoros del Perú)

Monumental deluxe anthology of important studies by leading art and architectural historians marks an original contribution to the historiography of Peruvian Spanish colonial art and architecture. Departing from a standard chronological or factual presentation, attempts to reinterpret the concept of a "baroque style" as applied to the art and architecture of Spanish colonial

Peru. Instead, each author follows a thematic approach using a method of analysis and interpretation reflecting the most current research advances in the field. Accordingly, the opening chapter by Mujica Pinilla discusses the concept of "baroque" from a semantic, stylistic, and hermeneutic perspective. Duviols' study examines in detail the iconography of two exceptional artists, Santa Cruz Pachacuti and Guamán Poma de Ayala, whose work reveals how the blending of precolumbian and European cosmologies and religions contributed to shape a distinct Spanish colonial worldview. An excellent chapter by Gisbert discusses ethnic identity among artists in the viceroyalty, considering other artistic representations in light of social milieu of the period and well-established ritual practices. Spanish colonial architecture is best covered in Samanez Argumedo's splendid chapter, a model of morphological analysis. In addition to a comprehensive bibliography, each chapter is accompanied by extensive notes with references to sources for further reading. Beautifully illustrated with spectacular color photos, this book is an outstanding addition to the fine quality publications in the series.

65   Breve catálogo del Museo de Arte Colonial. Revisión de textos de Jorge Luna Yepes *et al.* Fotografía de Patricio Pazán León. Quito: Fundación Amigos del Museo Nacional de Arte Colonial; Casa de la Cultura Ecuatoriana Benjamin Carrion, 1997. 48 p.: col. ill.

Brief but useful trilingual catalog in Spanish, English, and French permits an appreciation of the important collection of Spanish colonial art housed in Quito's Museo Nacional de Arte Colonial. Newly restored following years of gradual deterioration, the building located at the intersection of Cuenca and Mejía streets in the historic center of the city was originally the residence of Don Francisco de Villacís, a wealthy Creole whose fortune helped to finance the construction of the 17th-century chapel bearing his name inside the Spanish colonial church of San Francisco. Catalog describes exhibition halls arranged by chronological order and highlights principal works in each collection. Color plates, generally in small format, vary in quality but serve as a visual reference.

66 Busto Duthurburu, José Antonio del.
La platería en el Perú: dos mil años de arte e historia: colección Enrico Poli. Lima: Banco del Sur del Perú, 1996. 357 p.: bibl., col. ill.

Deluxe publication documents the magnificent Enrico Poli silver collection in Lima, one of the finest collections in South America. The very informative text, divided into 16 chapters, gives a historical background of the development of Peruvian silver from precolumbian to modern times. Pays special attention to major centers of production of Lima, Arequipa, and Cuzco during Spanish colonial period. Most valuable are discussions of silversmiths' guild organization and identification by name of artisans active during the time. Even though not a catalog raisonné *per se,* the beautiful color illustrations with separate descriptive captions make this splendid collection available to a wide range of researchers for the first time. Regrettably, however, the publication does not indicate the actual size of the objects. Expands considerably the corpus of silverwork illustrated in item **67**. Also available in English as *Peruvian silverwork: 2000 years of art and history* (1996).

67 Carcedo Muro, Paloma *et al.* Plata y plateros del Perú. Lima: Patronato Plata del Peru, 1997. 385 p.: bibl., ill. (some col.).

Monumental work with contributions by renowned scholars offers the most complete study on Peruvian silver and the art of the silversmith from precolumbian times through 20th century. Of special interest for the Spanish colonial period is the well-documented chapter, "Platería colonial, un trueque divino" by Francisco Stastny. Spanish techniques of working silver, practiced in Peru since the 16th century, are fully discussed in the chapter "Historia de la tecnología minera en el Perú" by Felipe de Lucio. Fine color reproductions with detailed captions show each piece in exquisite detail, permitting comparative analysis of an impressive corpus from private and public collections especially assembled for this publication. Indispensable reference for future studies on the subject, it is a necessary complement to the Enrico Poli collection catalog (see item **66**).

68 La Casa del Moral: un hito en la historia de Arequipa. Coordinación de Ramón Gutiérrez *et al.* Arequipa, Peru: Bancosur, 1996. 137 p.: bibl., ill. (some col.), maps (some col.).

Elegant multiauthored monograph is devoted to one of the best examples of planiform style civil architecture from the Spanish colonial period in Arequipa. This model study of a single monument is beautifully illustrated with splendid b/w and color photographs, reproductions of historic documents, and plans. Six well-documented chapters cover 18th-century history of the city; biographical data and genealogy of house owners from early 18th century-present; general history of domestic architecture in Arequipa; detailed account of house's history and its place in the development of the city's civil architecture; and restoration and adaptive reuse as a cultural center in 1995 undertaken by present owner, Bancosur, also the sponsor of the publication. Ample footnotes and bibliographic references by chapter serve as a useful guide for further reading.

69 Casa Real de la Moneda (Potosí, Bolivia). La Casa de la Moneda: museum guide. Written by Wilson Mendieta Pacheco *et al.* English translation by Brenda Cobarruvias *et al.* Photographs by Rolando Flores. Potosí, Bolivia: Patrimonio Natural y Cultural de la Humanidad, 1997. 54 p.: col. ill.

Popular guide makes available in English a brief history of the *Casa de la Moneda* (the Mint) of Potosí, and a general description of its museum collections. Designed by Salvador de Villa and built from 1759–73, Potosí's mint is one of the city's most distinguished examples of Spanish colonial civil architecture. Today this magnificent structure houses historical archives and a museum with collections representative of Bolivia's cultural heritage from precolumbian times to the present. Useful as a quick reference to the museum collections, the guide includes color illustrations of selected Spanish colonial paintings, sculptures, altarpieces, silverwork, coins and medals, and furniture.

70 Cummins, Tom. El lenguaje del arte colonial: imagen, ékfrasis e idolatría. (*in* Encuentro Internacional de Peruanistas, *1st, Lima, 1996.* Estado de los estudios histórico-sociales sobre el Perú a fines del siglo XX. Lima: UNESCO; Univ. de Lima; Fondo de Cultura Económica, 1998, v. 2, p. 23–43, facsims.)

Using a semiotic methodology to study early Spanish colonial art in Peru, offers a new interpretation that transcends conventional analysis of problems surrounding indigenous idolatry and the description of iconographic analysis of Christian art. Even though the extent to which the indigenous population understood the visual language of Christian signs and symbols introduced by the Europeans may be questioned, proposes that the true success of the evangelical mission did not consist in the vanishing of the pagan Andean religion, but rather in the modifying of the discourse of its representation. Careful reading of selected primary sources such as *Doctrina cristiana y catecismo para instrucción de los indios* (1584), Francisco de Avila's *La relación. . . acerca de los pueblos de indios de este arzobispado donde se ha descubierto la idolatría* (1611), and Guamán Poma de Ayala's *Nueva corónica y buen gobierno* (1615) provide effective comparisons of literary descriptions and visual images.

71   Giménez-Carrazana, Manuel. Sucre y sus museos de arte. Relación histórico-artística de Manuel Giménez Carrazana. Fotografías de Jaime Cisneros. Edición a cargo de Edgar Bustamante Delgado. La Paz?: Electropaz, 1998. 143 p.: col. ill.

Handsome publication documents the art collection of a Sucre university and the Cathedral of Sucre. Introductory text provides a brief historical account of the development of Sucre as an important religious and cultural center during the Spanish colonial period. The catalog raisonné of the two collections is also included; each work is reproduced in a full-page color illustration with a complete caption identifying the artist (if known), medium, date, and size. In addition, the bilingual English-Spanish text offers a useful art historical commentary on each work. Among the most distinguished artists of the Spanish colonial period represented here are the painters Bernardo Bitti (16th century), Antonio Mermejo (17th century), and Melchor Pérez de Holguín (18th century).

72   Gisbert, Teresa. Arte virreinal: recuento de las últimas investigaciones. (*in* Encuentro Internacional de Peruanistas, *1st, Lima, 1996.* Estado de los estudios histórico-sociales sobre el Perú a fines del siglo XX. Lima: UNESCO; Univ. de Lima; Fondo de Cultura Económica, 1998, v. 2, p. 49–54)

Autobiographical essay by distinguished Bolivian art historian reviews her own research during the last decade. The annotated bibliography highlights her thematic approach to help elucidate a wide range of formal and iconographic issues pertinent to the development of Spanish colonial art and architecture. Among the major works discussed is *Arquitectura andina* (see item 73).

73   Gisbert, Teresa and José de Mesa. Arquitectura andina, 1530–1830. 2da. ed. La Paz: Embajada de España en Bolivia, 1997. 432 p.: bibl., ill. (some col.), indexes.

Revised and expanded second edition of classic anthology of studies on Andean Spanish colonial architecture by renowned Bolivian art historian couple, representing a lifetime of scholarly research. Among the most noteworthy entries are the analytical essays "Serlio y los Esquemas Circulares en América;" "Iglesias Jesuíticas en el Virreinato Peruano;" and "Capillas Abiertas y Capillas de Indios." Several studies, which are of seminal importance in the field, were originally published in professional journals or periodicals of limited circulation and are now out of print. This edition, which includes a previously unpublished chapter on the industrial city of Potosí and several new color photographs, is therefore a most welcome addition to the artistic literature of Spanish colonial South America. Will benefit present and future generations of readers.

74   Gutiérrez, Ramón. Situación de los estudios de historia de la arquitectura y urbanismo en el Perú. (*in* Encuentro Internacional de Peruanistas, *1st, Lima, 1996.* Estado de los estudios histórico-sociales sobre el Perú a fines del siglo XX. Lima: UNESCO; Univ. de Lima; Fondo de Cultura Económica, 1998, v. 2, p. 107–108)

Succinct assessment of historiography of Peruvian architecture and urbanism produced during the last two decades points out major research advances and deficiencies.

With respect to the Spanish colonial period, important contributions in archival research are noted, together with an enrichment of methodological approaches for the analysis and interpretation of monuments and sites. Argues that more scholarly research and attention are needed for regions outside of principal urban centers and rural architecture in general.

75 Lima: Centro Histórico. Lima: Municipalidad Metropolitana de Lima, 1998. 336 p.: col. ill., maps.

Deluxe publication under the auspices of the city's municipal government celebrates the 1992 inclusion of Lima's historic center in UNESCO's World Heritage List. Also includes a well-deserved tribute to city mayor Alberto Andrade Carmona, who was largely responsible for the rehabilitation of plazas and streets within the historic district during the 1990s. Separate chapters are devoted to Lima's urban history, religious architecture, civil architecture, sculpture, painting, and museums, illustrated with abundant color plates of very fine quality. Each chapter highlights Spanish colonial art and architecture, revealing the rich cultural heritage of the former viceregal capital. Text concludes with transcription of Ordinance No. 052–93 concerning the "Patrimonio Cultural, Histórico-Monumental de la Provincia de Lima," an important reference for the delineation of historic districts in other Latin American cities.

76 Lohmann Villena, Guillermo. La reconstrucción del Corral de las Comedias de Lima en 1660. (*Rev. Arch. Gen. Nac./Lima*, 17, mayo 1998, p. 131–150)

Well-documented study by distinguished Peruvian historian expands on his earlier classic study *El arte dramático en Lima durante el Virreinato* (Madrid, 1945). Four fully transcribed notarial records from Archivo General de la Nación shed new light on substantial repairs of Lima's prime Spanish colonial theater (*Corral de las Comedias*) which began following destruction by the 1655 earthquake. The restoration work, involving extensive reconstruction, began in 1660 and was executed by the master carpenter Cristóbal Ortiz and the better-known architect Asensio de Salas. The detailed information contained in these documents, including materials of construction, spatial distribution, and ornamentation, give a good idea of the general appearance of this important public building that is now lost.

77 Majluf, Natalia and **Luis Eduardo Wuffarden.** La piedra de Huamanga: lo sagrado y lo profano. Lima: Museo de Arte de Lima; Banco de Crédito del Perú; Prom Perú, 1998. 170 p.: appendix, bibl., col. ill., index.

The art of *piedra de Huamanga* (Peruvian alabaster) sculpture merits the attention of this very fine publication with erudite texts by two distinguished art historians. Often combined with popular art or craft, Huamanga stone sculpture deserves recognition as a fine art in its own right, representative of a tradition that originated in the Spanish colonial period and continues today, particularly in Ayacucho, in the central Andes of Peru. By far the most complete study on the subject to date, it significantly expands Stastny's earlier treatment in *Las artes populares del Perú* (see *HLAS 46:316*). Here a thematic approach covers well the historic development of the art from 17th-20th centuries with separate chapters addressing such relevant topics as "El Espacio de lo Religioso: Usos de la Talla Colonial"; "Ecos de la Ilustración: Figuras Galantes y Alegorías Clásicas"; and "Costumbrismo y Devoción." The impressive corpus of works from private and public collections reproduced in excellent quality color plates will serve as an indispensable resource for future studies. A useful documentary annex, bibliography, and index complete the study.

78 Mesa, José de. Investigaciones sobre la arquitectura y el arte del Virreinato del Perú realizadas entre 1959 y 1989. (*in* Encuentro Internacional de Peruanistas, 1st, Lima, 1996. Estado de los estudios histórico-sociales sobre el Perú a fines del siglo XX. Lima: UNESCO; Univ. de Lima; Fondo de Cultura Económica, 1998, v. 2, p. 45–48)

Autobiographical essay documenting 30 years of scholarly research on Peruvian art and architecture complements work in the same volume by Teresa Gisbert (see item 72). The author's distinguished professional intervention as restoration architect in the Andean region of Cuzco and Puno between

1972–80, which led to the elaboration of master plans for the restoration and conservation of some 27 Spanish colonial buildings under the auspices of PLAN COPESCO, UNESCO, and Instituto Nacional de Cultura, is also highlighted. Another major contribution in this area is the author's 15-year collaboration with Peruvian architect José Correa Orbegoso in the UNESCO-CRYRZA Mission, which took on the extensive documentation and restoration of several prehistoric and historic buildings in the city of Trujillo and its vicinity following the devastating earthquake of May 31, 1970. The review of important books co-authored with Gisbert includes the classic studies *Holguín y la pintura virreinal en Bolivia* (see *HLAS 42:263*) and *Arquitectura andina* (see item 73).

79   Paniagua Pérez, Jesús. El trabajo de la plata en el sur del Ecuador durante el siglo XIX. León, Spain: Univ. de León, 1996. 184 p.: bibl., ill., index, map.

Unpretentious, well-documented, and easy-to-read study about the development of silverwork after independence in the region of Cuenca. Includes bibliography, few explanatory drawings, and b/w photographic appendix. [F. Angel]

80   Pastor de la Torre, Celso and **Luis Enrique Tord.** Perú: fe y arte en el Virreynato. Córdoba, Spain: Publicaciones Obra Social y Cultural CajaSur, 1999. 312 p.: bibl., col. ill.

Well-documented and illustrated publication is a companion to the special exhibition with the same title held in Córdoba, Spain (1999), under the auspices of Obra Social y Cultural CajaSur. Culminates several years of curatorial work and close collaboration between the Peruvian and Spanish governments to bring together more than 50 Spanish colonial paintings from public and private Peruvian collections representative of the work of the best artists. The principal objective, as stated by Miguel Castillero Gorraiz in the "Presentación," was to introduce to a European audience important works of schools of painting from Lima, Cuzco, Arequipa, and other colonial centers so that the splendor of this rich cultural heritage could

be recognized and better appreciated. To this end, scholarly texts by Pastor de la Torre ("La Evolución Pictórica del Cuzco") and Tord ("Arte y Religión en Virreynato del Perú") trace the historic development of Spanish colonial painting in the Viceroyalty of Peru and provide a critical assessment of the major contributions by artists whose many beautiful works merit not only recognition but also admiration. The full-color reproductions of all the works in the exhibition, including many close-up details, will facilitate comparisons with other works in collections outside of Peru. Also includes an excellent bibliography containing historic sources and most recent research on the subject.

81   Redescubramos Lima: colección graba-dos Antonio Lulli; Galería Municipal Pancho Fierro, Plaza Mayor. Lima: Fondo Pro Recuperación del Patrimonio Cultural de la Nación; Banco de Crédito del Perú, 1997. 51 p.: bibl., ill. (some col.).

Elegant publication sponsored by Banco de Crédito del Perú follows format of *Los Cristos de Lima* (see *HLAS 56:185*) and *Iglesia de San Pedro* (see *HLAS 58:116*) in the same series. The informative text by Ricardo Estabridis Cárdenas titled "Lima a Través del Arte de los Viajeros Extranjeros" provides an essential documentary background for the private collection of prints of Antonio Lulli featured in a special exhibition held at Galería Municipal Pancho Fierro, Plaza Mayor of Lima in 1997. Many of these b/w and color prints dating from the 19th century depict panoramic views, street scenes, and people dressed in typical costumes representing a unique visual record of the late Spanish colonial and early Republican periods. Includes fine quality, small size reproductions of all prints, plus enlargements of selected prints integrated with the text.

82   Rodríguez Camilloni, Humberto. Manuel de Amat y Junyent y la Navona de Lima: un ejemplo de diseño barroco del siglo XVIII en el virreinato del Perú. (*An. Inst. Invest. Estét.*, 74/75, 1999, p. 147–176, ill., photos)

Eulogizes Viceroy Amat y Junyent for the architecture and urbanism that took shape during his reign. Based on archival documents, recreates the works that once embellished the colonial city of Lima. Also investigates certain unassigned works, making possible their attribution to Amat, the enlightened viceroy. Like many intellectuals of his time, Amat saw in Rome an eternal city. Both architect and viceroy, he was influenced by these ideas to transform the "City of Kings" into an eternal city. Inspired by baroque Italian models, the viceroy adapted innovations to the topology and necessities of Peru with a modernizing impulse that was never to be repeated.

83   San Cristóbal Sebastián, Antonio.
Martín Alonso de Mesa y Juan García Salguero en el retablo mayor de La Concepción. (*Rev. Arch. Gen. Nac./Lima*, 17, mayo 1998, p. 91–130)
Exhaustive research in the Archivo General de la Nación in Lima yields the discovery of notarial records documenting the work of sculptors Martín Alonso de Mesa, Juan Martínez de Arrona, and Juan García Salguero in the early 17th-century main altarpiece (*retablo*) of the church of La Concepción. The historic documents, fully transcribed in an appendix, are invaluable for the wealth of information they provide about professional artistic practices during the time, as well as for the details about the design and execution of works often no longer extant. Unfortunately, the author's focus on refuting or discrediting earlier research by other scholars is distracting.

84   San Cristóbal Sebastián, Antonio.
Obras en San Agustín a finales del siglo XVII. (*Rev. Arch. Gen. Nac./Lima*, 16, dic. 1997, p. 191–208, appendices)
In light of archival documentation recently discovered in the Archivo General de la Nación, this work retells history of the 17th-century reconstruction and transformation of the Church of San Agustín in Lima from a single-nave church flanked by crypto-collateral chapels into a three-naved basilica with full transept crowned by a hemispheric dome. Also describes other works carried out in the main cloister and surrounding rooms of the monastery by architect Francisco Jiménez in 1699 in a contemporary notarial act fully transcribed in the documentary appendix. Complemented with a later study by the same author, "Coro, bóvedas y portadas en la iglesia San Agustín," in *Historia y Cultura, Revista del Museo Nacional de Arqueología, Antropología e Historia*, 23, 1999, p. 143–175.

19th and 20th Centuries

FÉLIX ÁNGEL, *Curator, Cultural Center, Inter-American Development Bank*

IN GENERAL, THE REGION IS MAKING A SPECIAL EFFORT to upgrade art institutions, but some countries in particular are transforming their museums in the areas of management, conservation, exhibitions, and educational outreach. This development is relatively new for Latin America and the Caribbean. Art institutions have been accustomed to receiving subsidies from the state, with little involvement from civil society. When the private sector has become proactive—with the best of intentions, one assumes—the potential participation of the middle class has not been taken into account, thereby depriving it of the opportunity to enjoy the practice and appreciation of the arts.

The new directions taken by the world economy have forced us all to reevaluate the concept of sustainability in many ways. Art institutions and museums in general have not escaped the debate; quite the opposite: their effectiveness has been questioned and their societal role scrutinized, since money does not seem to abound these days.

Most countries have made progress in their efforts to determine the kind of resources needed to preserve cultural patrimony. There is, however, still much strategizing and planning to be done to make museums and similar institutions self-sustainable, and at the same time, effective vehicles of social change. Collectors, other than the state, do not trust the fact that they must disclose their holdings; there is a generalized feeling that in doing so the items themselves will be in jeopardy, risking confiscation or additional taxation, and not necessarily for the benefit of the majority. Some of them might be right. Others feel that because of the lack of reasonable legislation and incentives to keep their treasures inside the countries, either for private or public enjoyment, the best way to protect their investment is to dispose of the artworks in the least conspicuous way. That is why, in part, some of those treasures are eventually smuggled out of the country and offered for sale on the international market, with the earnings going into an offshore account.

Due to the economic boom at the end of the 19th and early 20th centuries, Argentina boasts many artistic treasures. *Catálogo de la Pintura Española en Buenos Aires,* by Ana María Fernández García (item **225**), is a good example of taking the first steps to identify the country's resources. The work is a revelation; it documents a wealth of Spanish painting covering nearly six centuries. One wonders how many people are aware that the works are in Argentina. The author states that many more works were not possible to inventory.

Entries such as *Juan Mauricio Rugendas: pintor y dibujante* (item **329**), registering the artist's drawings in the Guita and José Mindlin Collection of Sao Paulo, or *Rafael Troya 1845–1920: el pintor de los Andes ecuatorianos* (item **279**), and *La escultura en Venezuela durante el siglo XIX y la presencia italiana* (item **309**), are symptomatic of the need to be more rigorous in deciding how those art works that are part of the artistic evolution of the countries, molding their cultural identity and creating traditions, can be made more accessible, either by research or display.

The 20th century art collection of Argentine businessman Eduardo Constantini, previously annotated in *HLAS 58* and again now in *Claves del arte latinoamericano* (item **88**), went public in 2001 at MALBA (Museo de Arte Latinoamericano de Buenos Aires). The museum might have been considered an exemplary case of private entrepreneurship where individual vision and everything else is shared with the public at large. The difficulties faced by the beautiful new museum offer hard lessons for similar ventures. Financed by the millionaire himself, the museum fell victim to turbulent economic times only a few months after its glorious inauguration.

The truth is that Argentina has always been a country in which art has had a prominent social and intellectual role. *Memoria de una galería de arte: Archivo Witcomb 1896–1971* (item **234**) documents the history of the Witcomb Gallery, the first commercial art gallery established in Buenos Aires (and probably one of the first in Latin America). The gallery is credited for introducing to Argentina some of the most well-known European artists of the day, and later for promoting some of the most progressive ones, such as with the controversial Pettoruti exhibition of 1924.

As well-known as Argentine 19th and 20th century art may be, *La herencia olvidada: arte indígena de la Argentina* (item **235**) focuses on 12,000 years of esthetic production by Argentina's aboriginal cultures, a subject practically unknown outside archeological or anthropological circles. In a similar vein, *Tableaux Kuna: les molas, un art d'Amerique* (item **178**) is at once a sensible, enjoyable, and revealing book about the traditional weavings of the Cuna Indians from Panama, and attempts to dissect the mola as an object bearing multiple meanings within the context of Cuna culture.

It is now accepted that the US achieved indisputable prominence as a promoter of international visual languages during the second half of the 20th century. *Vanguardia, internacionalismo y política* (item **226**) offers a fascinating profile about the state of the arts in Argentina during the 1960s, a period in which the country achieved unparalleled international prominence through the arts, especially in the US and France. The book reconstructs the conditions and strategies that made it possible for Argentina to achieve a reputation in the US as a country with progressive art, while most of the other countries in South America had to rely on individual figures.

Mexico, as always, continues to produce insightful art publications that confirm the belief of many about how much art matters. What distinguishes Mexico from the rest of Latin America is the devotion with which the intelligentsia, as well as the private sector, dedicate time and resources to increase the collective awareness of the country's artistic achievements, at every level. Good examples to illustrate this point are *Great Masters of Mexican Folk Art* (item **120**); *Misiones culturales: los años utópicos 1920–1938* (item **136**), which focuses on the Vasconcelos era; and *Los ecos de Mathias Goeritz* (item **116**), which analyzes both the historical and critical context of the contribution of the German-born artist to Mexican art.

Art will always reflect society, with its contradictions and assertions. Artists do not work in a vacuum, although characters like Reveron and Andrés de Santamaría may lead us to think the opposite. This biennial brings a new book, *Entre andamios y muros: ayudantes de Diego Rivera en su obra mural* (item **108**), which helps us understand the thematic, esthetic, ideological, and technical contributions of the many artists who assisted Diego Rivera; these artists form the context from which Mexican muralism emerged, and gives due credit to those who were, literally, on the scaffolding making it possible for the Mexican giant to execute many of his magnificent murals.

The reader will also find revealing Venezuela's Galería Nacional *Lewis Brian Adams: retratista del romanticismo paecista* (item **302**), which is carefully researched and worthy of interest, in line with some of the ideas previously expressed.

Throughout the second half of the 20th century, Latin America and the Caribbean witnessed the creation of many biennials, and then saw their disappearance after the corporations that supported them experienced economic trouble. Several biennials and art fairs have resurfaced and changed their scope to mostly local artwork. One can only wonder why more resources are not dedicated to cultural events that advance the arts and in turn help to mobilize other resources that benefit local economies.

That is why it is uplifting to see the catalogs of regional biennials such as the *Bienal del Istmo Centroamericano* (items **86** and **87**), the *Segunda Bienal Iberoamericana de Lima* (item **285**), and the first *Bienal Nacional de Lima* (item **286**). It is going to take a while for Latin America to close the digital divide. Until that happens, biennial events and the publications they generate are of fundamental importance to scholars interested in the development of the visual arts.

Cultural tradition, identity, and customs seem to be in jeopardy in light of new globalization. The discussion is pertinent since some scholars question the authenticity of some modernist movements in Latin America. For example, *Modernidad y postmodernidad* (item **305**) allows for the revision of a decades-old discussion about how much Venezuela, and all of Latin America for that matter, should acknowledge the artistic traditions it developed in the 20th century.

Cuba's pre- and post-revolution art continue to fascinate, regardless of one's political orientation. *Cuba siglo XX: modernidad y sincretismo* (item **188**) is a robust color-illustrated and annotated exhibition catalog with a complete critical and historical revision of 20th century Cuban art. *Por América: la obra de Juan Francisco Elso* (item **200**), is an excellent publication about the work of an artist who tried to overcome the paradoxes of Latin American culture.

GENERAL

85   Arte y utopía en América Latina. Textos de Alberto Híjar *et al.* México: Consejo Nacional para la Cultura y las Artes: Instituto Nacional de Bellas Artes: Centro Nacional de Investigación, Documentación e Información de Artes Plásticas, 2000. 153 p.: bibl., ill. (some col.).

The right of humans to aspire to unrealistic goals is the theoretical premise of the essays by five authors compiled in this volume, as a result of their presentation and discussion at CENIDIAP (National Center for Research, Documentation, and Information of Plastic Arts). The message seems to be that, at the present time, the notion of utopia is indispensable to overcome hopelessness, emptiness, and obligation.

86   Bienal de Pintura del Istmo Centroamericano, *1st, Guatemala, 1998.*
I Bienal de Pintura del Istmo Centroamericano. Asunción, Guatemala: Fundación Paiz, 1998. 60 p.: col. ill.

Color-illustrated catalog of the event celebrated in Guatemala City, after national selections were made separately in Panama, Costa Rica, Honduras, Guatemala, Nicaragua, and El Salvador. Each delegation was composed of six artists. Includes individual essays about each group of participants.

87   Bienal de Pintura del Istmo Centroamericano, *2d, San José, 2000.*
2a Bienal de Pintura del Istmo Centroamericano. San José: Centro Costarricense de Ciencia y Cultura, 2000. 96 p.: col. ill.

Color-illustrated catalog of the event celebrated in San José, Costa Rica, after national selections were made separately in Panama, Costa Rica, Honduras, Guatemala, Nicaragua, and El Salvador. Includes the transcription of the opening remarks made by the three members of the jury in a panel organized simultaneously with the event and essays about the various artistic delegations. See also item **86.**

88   Claves del arte latinoamericano: colección Costantini. Barcelona: Fundación "La Caixa", 1999. 172 p.: bibl., col. ill.

Excellent color-illustrated catalog of the exhibition at Madrid's *Fundación "La Caixa,"* selected from the Latin American art collection of Eduardo Costantini. With few exceptions, the selection focuses on works produced by Latin American modernists between 1920–50. Marcelo E. Pacheco and Juan Manuel Bonet contribute essays, while Luis Monreal presents the exhibit stressing "the need to arrive at a vision of Latin American art that at the same time addresses the regional complexities and its multiple and provocative crossroads" in an international context. Includes short biographies of the artists included.

89   Historia del arte iberaamericano. Recopilación de Ramón Gutiérrez and Rodrigo Gutiérrez Viñuales. Barcelona: Lunwerg, 2000. 394 p.: bibl., ill. (some col.).

General overview of the arts in Spanish and Portuguese America from a markedly Iberian perspective. Covers architecture, urbanism, painting, sculpture, silverwork, and photography through various periods, with emphasis on colonial art. Follows an encyclopedic and regional structure, with many well-selected color illustrations.

90   Horizontes del arte latinoamericano. Recopilación de José Jiménez and Fernando Castro Flórez. Madrid: Tecnos: Generalitat Valenciana, Conselleria de Cultura, Educació i Ciència, Direcció General de Promoció Cultural, Museus i Belles Arts, 1999. 165 p.: bibl., indexes. (Colección Metrópolis)

Edited collection of essays presented by various authors at the symposium *IX Encuentros Internacionales en el Arte Contemporáneo,* as a parallel event with ARCO 97

(Madrid International Art Fair). Topics include transterritorialism in Latin American art, regional criticism, postmodern strategies, and relations between globalization and local contexts.

Modernidad y postmodernidad: espacios y tiempos dentro del arte latinoamericano. See item **305**.

91   Montealegre, Samuel. Percepción estética: ejercicios, reflexiones y ejemplos del percibir, proyectar y actuar estético-artístico. Bogotá: Montealegre Editores, 1998. 174 p.: bibl., ill. (some col.), index.

Four lectures on surface, volume, space, and sound and movement, originally written in Rome in 1981, are united in this volume following their original format and content. The subjects explore the relations between stimulus and physiological and electrochemical reactions, individualizing esthetic effects and revealing techniques and procedures used by artists to obtain them. Concepts are dense and highly speculative, however provoking. To understand them requires the reader to have knowledge of artistic, psychological, and philosophical principles. Illustrated in b/w and color.

92   Pintura del Mercosur: una selección del período 1950–1980. Buenos Aires: Ediciones Banco Velox, 2000. 532 p.: bibl., ill. (chiefly col.).

Heavy volume attempts to give an overview of the development of painting in the four Mercosur countries (Argentina, Brazil, Paraguay, Uruguay) during a 30-year period, with essays written for the occasion and illustrations selected by the publisher. Does not represent a comprehensive view of the subject as stated in the foreword. Illustrations accompanying the essays in the first part of the book are confusing since they lack captions and do not correspond with the discussion. Book's most valuable feature is a catalog of properly identified reproductions in the second part of the book.

93   Pintura, escultura y fotografía en Iberoamérica: siglos XIX y XX. Coordinación de Rodrigo Gutiérrez Viñuales and Ramón Gutiérrez. Madrid: Cátedra, 1997. 547 p.: bibl., ill., indexes. (Manuales arte Cátedra)

Interesting collection of essays on various topics, from landscape and customs to museums and collections, as well as generalized visions about painting, photography, and sculpture in the region from the 19th century through 1995. Illustrated in b/w.

MEXICO

94   Alvide, Gilberto. Antonio Peláez: un homenaje. México: Univ. Autónoma Metropolitana, 2001. 100 p.: col. ill.

Illustrated tribute to the late painter Peláez (1921–94), born in Asturias, who was known for his reclusive low profile. This work accompanied a double exhibition at the Univ. Autónoma Metropolitana, seven years after the painter's death and 20 years after his last solo exhibition. Includes a "critical retrospective" of short essays by prominent Mexican intellectuals, including Nobel Prize winner Octavio Paz.

95   El arte de la cerería en Michoacán. Morelia, Mexico: Fimax Publicaciones, 1999. 163 p.: ill.

Modest, historical account of the use of wax in Michoacán related to the imaging of figures, their symbolism, sociocultural role, and commercialization.

96   El arte en México: autores, temas, problemas. Coordinación de Rita Eder. México: Consejo Nacional para la Cultura y las Artes: Lotería Nacional para la Asistencia Pública: Fondo de Cultura Económica, 2001. 389 p.: bibl., ill. (Biblioteca Mexicana. Serie Arte)

Compilation of essays by nine authors questions indirectly how the history of Mexican art has been written. Intentionally, the selected pieces have in common one thing: their marginality in the "big picture" of the history of art, which in turn raises the question of how that "picture" came about. Intriguing among the essays is Cordero Reiman's revision of George Kluber's methodology for historiography. The book's goal was not to entertain but rather to open windows to alternative analysis of some aspects of Mexican art.

97   Arte moderno y contemporáneo de Chiapas. Coordinación de Roberto Sepúlveda. México: CONECULTA Consejo Estatal para la Cultura y las Artes de Chiapas: CONACULTA, 2000. 365 p.: bibl., ill. (chiefly col.), index.

Broad perspective about the artistic

manifestations (folk arts, music, visual arts, dance, and architectural patrimony) in Chiapas, until recently the poorest state in Mexico. Given the ambitious nature of the publication, design and printing could have been more carefully controlled; however, the content is interesting.

98   (A)salto a la vida cotidiana: murales populares en taludes. México: Consejo Nacional para la Cultura y las Arte: Instituto Nacional de Bellas Artes: Museo Casa Estudio Diego Rivera y Frida Kahlo: Gobierno del Distrito Federal, Delegación Alvaro Obregón; Aguascalientes, Mexico: Instituto Cultural de Aguascalientes: Museo de Arte Contemporáneo No. 8 de Aguascalientes, 2000. 112 p.: bibl., ill. (chiefly col.).

Illustrated history of a project that the Mexican government implemented in cooperation with the civil sector in the Álvaro Obregón neighborhood, located far from Mexico City and known for its large number of displaced people. The project consisted of encouraging the local population to decorate with murals the slopes affected by deforestation and erosion. Interesting experiment with both urban and visual implications.

99   Belaunzarán, Carlos. Carlos Belaunzarán: una mirada. México: Juan Pablo Editores: Casa Lamm: Librería Pegaso, 1998. 70 p.: ill. (some col.).

Color-illustrated catalog of the exhibitions held at Casa Lamm and Librería Pegaso in México City, of recent oils, ink drawings, and watercolors. José María Espinoza, Alfredo Joskowicz, and Alfredo Juan Alvárez offer separate accounts of the artist.

100   Ceja Bravo, L. Armando. Pintores michoacanos contemporáneos: colores y trazos. Morelia, Mexico: Univ. Vasco de Quiroga: Instituto Michoacano de Cultura, 2000. 119 p.: ill. (some col.).

Biographical, illustrated, and annotated compilation of Michoacán painters active in the second half of the 20th century, the most veteran being Alfredo Zalce.

101   Cinco siglos de plástica en Chiapas. Mexico: Centro Cultural de Chiapas Jaime Sabanes, 2000. 429 p.: bibl., ill. (chiefly col.).

Excellent color-illustrated, annotated catalog of an exhibition covering 500 years of artistic expression in Chiapas within major areas of the arts. Worthy effort highlights region's contribution to Mexico's artistic spectrum.

102   50 mujeres en la plastica de México. Textos de Aguedo Lozano et al. México: Instituto de Seguridad y Servicios Sociales de los Trabajadores del Estado: Univ. Autónoma Metropolitana, 1997. 17, 1 p., 25 leaves of plates: bibl.

Color-illustrated catalog of an exhibition at the gallery of the Univ. Autónoma Metropolitana in Mexico City, which included 19th-century women artists. Margarita Herrera introduces the publication with a historic reference to the Women's Pavillion at the commemorative centenary exhibition held in Philadelphia in 1876.

103   La colección Bernard y Edith Lewin: del Museo de Arte del Condado de Los Ángeles: vivencias para ser exhibidas: autobiografía de una galerista Bernard Lewin. Compilación de Juan Coronel Rivera. México: Consejo Nacional para la Cultura y las Artes: Instituto Nacional de Bellas Artes: Museo del Palacio de Bellas Artes, 1998. 155 p.: bibl., ill. (some col.).

Color-illustrated catalog of the 1998 exhibition of 96 works by Mexican artists selected out of more than 2000 pieces collected by Beverly Hills, Calif., art dealer Lewin and now the property of the Los Angeles County Museum of Art, presented at the Museo Palacio de Bellas Artes in Mexico City. Bernard Lewin himself wrote the biographical introduction and included a personal recollection about each of the artists represented. Interesting document by a person with no cultural connection with Mexico (Lewin was born in Germany of Jewish origins), who nevertheless felt deeply touched by its art and made his life as an art dealer.

104   Congreso Internacional de Muralismo, *Antiguo Colegio de San Ildefonoso, Museum, 1998.* Memoria: San Ildefonso, cuna del Muralismo mexicano: reflexciones historiográficas y artisticas. México: Antiguo Colegio de San Ildefonoso, 1999. 357 p.: bibl., ill.

Compilation of most of the papers presented at the symposium on *Muralismo* (Feb. 1998) at the Antiguo Colegio de San Ildefonoso in Mexico City—the cradle of the Mexican Muralist School. Participants analyze various subjects including the legacy of great 20th-century Mexican muralists, the historic roots and artistic significance of *muralismo*, and the importance of *muralismo* as an artistic manifestation in countries such as the US and Spain.

105   Cuevas, José Luis. Animales impuros. México: Impronta Editores, 1998. 192 p.: bibl., ill. (some col.).

Updated edition of catalog of Cuevas' 19 bronze sculptures and 25 engravings presented at the Seville World's Fair in 1992. Book's title takes its name from José-Miguel Ullán, whose equal number of poems are included in this edition. The catalog, originally published in 1992, now includes an introduction by Isaac Masri, as well as new essays about Cuevas' work by Spanish writer Gustavo Martín Garzo and *El País* critic Francisco Calvo Serraller. Includes b/w and color illustrations.

106   Cuevas, José Luis. Cuevario. La enfermedad de Bertha (I-XIV). Colima, Mexico: Museo José Luis Cuevas, 1997. 69 p.: ill. (Colección La mano de Dios; 3)

Collection of 14 articles written between March 10-June 30, 1996, and published in *El Excelsior* in Mexico City, coinciding with Cuevas' wife's discovery that she was ill with breast cancer and that the tumor was malignant. Against this backdrop, Cuevas, in his peculiar style, discusses his many projects and situations. Includes a detachable, unnumbered lithograph of him drawing while his wife is in surgery, and other illustrations on the same theme.

De la patria criolla a la nación mexicana, 1750–1860. See item **1418**.

107   Emerich, Luis Carlos. Francisco Toledo: obra gráfica para Arvil, 1974–2001. Introducción de Carlos Monsiváis. México: Prisma Editorial, 2001. 167 p.: ill. (some col.).

Catalog of five portfolios and a number of individual pieces created by Toledo for the well-known Mexican art gallery, Arvil, in Mexico City. Excellent reproductions make this publication a valuable tool for those interested in researching the graphic work of this Oaxacan master.

108   Entre andamios y muros: ayudantes de Diego Rivera en su obra mural: Consejo Nacional para la Cultura y las Artes, Instituto Nacional de Bellas Artes, Museo Mural Diego Rivera: noviembre-enero, 2001–2002. México: Instituto Nacional de Bellas Artes, 2001. 91 p.: ill. (some col.).

Eduardo Espinosa Campos' titular essay attempts to explain the thematic, esthetic, ideological, and technical contributions of the many artists who collectively form the context within which muralism developed. The publication accompanied the third exhibition thus far (checklist included) of artists who helped Diego Rivera to develop and execute his murals, among them figures of the caliber of Carlos Mérida, Jean Charlot, and Juan O'Gorman. Previous exhibits in Mexico took place in 1967 and 1987. Offers b/w and color illustrations, with biographies of the 32 artists included in the exhibit.

109   Escultura mexicana: de la academia a la instalación. México: Consejo Nacional para la Cultura y las Artes: Instituto Nacional de Bellas Artes: Museo del Palacio de Bellas Artes: Landucci Editores, 2000. 453 p.: bibl., ill. (some col.).

Catalog of the exhibition of 371 works representing a segment of the 650 sculptors active in Mexico in the last 60 years, which appears to prove Monasterios' assertion that Mexicans are sculptors by nature. Gerardo Estrada, however, laments that sculpture in Mexico has not been promoted as much as painting. Several essays contribute to the analysis of the factors that have influenced the development of sculpture in the country. In all, the book represents a fair survey of the activity and work of sculptors in Mexico.

110   Favela Fierro, María Teresa. Francisco Goitia: pintor del alma del pueblo mexicano. Prólogo de Elisa García Barragán. México: Fondo Editorial de la Plástica Mexicana, 2000. 131 p.: bibl., ill. (some col.).

Monograph on the ascetic and eccentric artist analyzes, among other things, the different stages of Goitia's artistic production, with the intention of recovering the "silent" legacy of the Mexican artist "unfairly forgotten by the critics and art promoters," as stated in the prologue. Illustrated in color.

111   El ferrocarril en el arte mexicano: catálogo. México: Ferrocarriles Nacionales de México, 1988. 107 p.: ill. (some col.).

Color-illustrated catalog of the 1998

exhibition held at the Museo Nacional de los Ferrocarriles Mexicanos in Mexico City, which gathered 102 works inspired by the development of the railroad in Mexico. The selection covers as far back as an 1859 composition by Luis Coto y Maldonado, *El tren de la Villa de Guadaloupe.* The essay by curator Sofía Rosales reflects the various themes under which the exhibit was organized.

112 **Francisco Corzas.** México: Bital Grupo Financiero, 2001. 191 p.: bibl., ill. (some col.).

Six essays by different authors reconstruct the personality and life of the late artist (d. 1983), while the selected illustrations, many published for the first time, attest to the expressionistic character of Corzas' early work, the softened tone it acquired toward the end of his career, and his enduring pursuit of the female figure.

113 **Frida Kahlo.** México: Grupo Financiero Bital, 2000. 245 p.: bibl., ill. (some col.).

In the editor's words, this book unites paintings, drawings, and photographs "rarely published all together." Monsiváis' acute essay describes Kahlo's and other people's obsession with her image, thus saving the book from being another coffee-table publication about "the woman whose mask is her true face."

114 **García Barragán, Elisa.** José Agustín Arrieta: lumbres de lo cotidiano. Coyoacán, Mexico: Fondo Editorial de la Plástica Mexicana, 1998. 143 p.: bibl., col. ill.

García Barragán characterizes this study as a "critical recovery" which describes and relates the work of Arrieta—known for his still-life compositions—to other artists of his generation. A chronicler of customs more than a witness of his tumultuous time (1803–74), Arrieta's art embraces 19th-century Mexico, when the country enjoyed opulence and ostentation, even in everyday life. Well illustrated in color.

115 **Geller, Luis.** Alberto Misrachi: una vida dedicada a promover el arte de México. México: Editorial Sylvia Misrachi, SM: Conaculta: INBA, 1998. 201 p.: bibl., ill. (some col.).

Geller has compiled a testimonial book honoring the career of art dealer Misrachi, owner of one of the oldest and most prestigious art galleries in Mexico City.

Includes texts by Geller himself and 48 others, including former president Luis Echeverría, artists Rufino Tamayo and José Luis Cuevas, critic Berta Taracena, and members of the dealer's family. Includes b/w and color illustrations.

116 **Goeritz, Mathias.** Los ecos de Mathias Goeritz: catálogo de la exposición. México: Instituto Nacional de Bellas Artes: Antiguo Colegio de San Ildefonso, 1997. 251 p.: bibl., ill. (some col.).

Catalog of the retrospective exhibition at the Colegio de San Ildefonso of 500 works by the Danzig-born Mexican artist who moved to Guadalajara in 1949, and died in Mexico City in 1990. Provides an excellent overview of the contribution that Goeritz, one of the main protagonists of contemporary art, made to Mexican art, fundamentally changing its course. With plentiful color illustrations and with a biographical summary, the work boasts 14 essays, including one by his longtime friend Ida Rodríguez. Also includes a complete checklist.

117 **González de Noval, María Helena.** Manuel González Serrano: un monólogo apasionado. México: Consejo Nacional para la Cultura y las Artes, Dirección General de Publicaciones, 1998. 44 p.: bibl., col. ill. (Círculo de arte)

Pocket-size illustrated monograph briefly explains the artist's formative years, artistic affiliations, and the main themes he seemed to favor in painting.

González-Esteva, Orlando. Enigma, old friend: the drawings of Juan Soriano. See item **4237**.

118 **González Serrano, Manuel.** Manuel González Serrano: el hechicero. Guadalajara, Mexico: Instituto Cultural Cabañas; México: CONACULTA, INBA, 1998. 95 p.: bibl., ill. (some col.).

Color-illustrated catalog of the exhibition of 117 works at the Instituto Cultural Cabañas in Guadalajara, in tribute to the tormented, self-taught, surreal artist (who died in 1960 at 43 years of age). Teresa del Conde, A. Zamora, and Ricardo Pérez Escamilla attempt, in individual essays, to decipher the personality and work of the artist, also known as "the sorcerer" and "El Nene."

119 Granda, Luis. Luis Granda: diálogo de los videntes = dialogue of the seers. México: Instituto Nacional de Bellas Artes: Fundación Cultural Gallo, 1998. 127 p.: col. ill.

Color-illustrated bilingual catalog of the exhibition of 40 recent paintings by the Madrid-born artist at the Museo del Palacio de Bellas Artes in Mexico City. Mario del Valle introduces the new work of Granda, stating that this exhibit marked a new beginning of the artist's 30-year career.

120 Great masters of Mexican folk art. México: Grupo Financiero Basnamex-Accival: Fomento Cultural Banamex, 1998. 551 p.: bibl., col. ill., index.

English edition of the book documenting the highlights of the Program for Support of Folk Art, sponsored by Fomento Cultural Banamex of Mexico since 1994. The works of 179 artisans were selected for the lavish publication, representing nearly 25 methods, from clay and wood to obsidian and feathers. Photography, layout, and printing are superb, making it an interesting display and promotional publication, as well as an excellent reference for contemporary Mexican crafts, attesting to Mexico's rich multicultural tradition and highly sophisticated craft production. Includes a bibliography and an alphabetical index of artisans.

121 Guajardo, Rosario. Ni soles ni lunas. Monterrey: Museo de Monterrey, 1998. 95 p.: col. ill.

Color-illustrated bilingual catalog of the exhibition of 76 paintings at the Museo de Monterrey, with texts by Agustín Arteaga and Xavier Moyssén L.; the latter explains Guajardo's abstractionism as the result of the newest trend in abstract painting and the human need for abstract thought for the sake of knowledge. Includes a biographical summary of the artist's career.

122 Guerrero, Arturo and Marisa Lara. El oxidado espíritu del siglo: objetos y sujetos en transición. México: Instituto Nacional de Bellas Artes, 1998. 1 v. (unpaged): bibl., col. ill.

Color-illustrated catalog of 58 works by the two artists, exhibited at Museo José Luis Cuevas. Cuevas himself wrote the introduction, calling them "compadres." Germaine Gómez Haro and Hervé-Pierre Lambert present the artists.

123 Hernández, Sergio. El circo. Oaxaca, Mexico: Museo de Arte Contemporáneo de Oaxaca, 1998. 43 p.: bibl., col. ill.

Color-illustrated catalog of the exhibition held in Oaxaca, where the artist was born in 1957. Presentation by Fernando Solana Olivares, and a bilingual essay by Jaime Moreno Villareal. Includes a biographical summary.

124 Huellas del grabado mexicano en el siglo XX. México: Instituto Mexicano del Seguro Social, 1997. 1 v. (unpaged): ill. (some col.).

Catalog of an exhibition at the Centro Médico Nacional in Mexico City (IMSS) that pays tribute to Mexican printmaking and reinforces the values that define Mexico and Mexicans, according to the presentation. Exhibit brought together 406 works from 254 artists (as early as José Guadalupe Posada), shown with several printing presses to enhance the installation.

125 Icaza, Francisco. Francisco Icaza: Pintura: Museo de Arte Moderno, Sala Antonieta Rivas Mercado, del 26 de noviembre al 14 de marzo, México, D.F. México: Instituto Nacional de Bellas Artes, 1998. 40 p.: bibl., col. ill.

Color-illustrated catalog of the exhibition of 47 paintings at the Museo de Arte Moderno in Mexico City, with an interview by Teresa del Conde and biographical outline.

126 Imágenes y colores de Oaxaca. Prólogo de Andrés Henestrosa. Introducción de Alberto Blanco. Oaxaca, Mexico: Gobierno del Estado de Oaxaca: Instituto Politécnico Nacional: Fundación Ingeniero Alejo Peralta y Díaz Ceballos, 1998. 183 p.: col. ill.

Color-illustrated book that accompanied the exhibition of 36 artists in Mexico City, assembled with the idea of disseminating the work of artists from Oaxaca. Blanco introduces the exhibit, and explains the characteristics of Oaxacan painting. Approximately half of the 158 works selected are reproduced in large format, and every artist appears with a biographical summary. Good contemporary reference about the regional "Oaxaca School."

127 Lara Elizondo, Lupina. Visión de México y sus artistas: siglo XX. t. 1, 1901–1950. México: Quálitas Compañía de Seguros, 2000. 1 v.: bibl., ill. (chiefly col.).

Promotional volume in which the insurance company pays tribute to the outstanding work of artists who made a substantial contribution to the artistic history of Mexico during the first half of the 20th century. The first two chapters, by Federico Campbell and Laura Pérez Rosales, analyze the history and trajectory of Mexican art during the time period. The third and final chapter by Lara Elizondo symbolically unites 50 of the most relevant artists, with illustrations of their works, and critical and biographical annotations.

128   Lazo, Rina. Rina Lazo: sabiduría de manos: conversaciones con Abel Santiago. Oaxaca, Mexico: Instituto Oaxaqueño de las Culturas, 1998. 193 p.: ill. (some col.). (Yinchuvi)

Biographical memoir and interview with Guatemalan-born Lazo, who went to Mexico in 1944 on a scholarship to study art. There, by chance, she became one of Diego Rivera's assistants. Later she married Mexican printmaker Arturo Lazo and became an activist in the Communist Party, which she left only to charge against those attacking the Mexican School. Lazo's recollections add one more perspective on the final chapter of the Mexican School, and the changes that Mexican arts and society experienced under the inevitable pressure of more progressive ideas. Includes b/w and color illustrations.

129   Lazos de sangre: retrato mexicano de familia, siglos XVIII y XIX. México: Museo de la Ciudad de México, 2000. 178 p.: bibl., col. ill.

Excellent catalog of the exhibition of 211 works organized around five themes: marriage, maternity, paternity, brotherhood, and family, which provide chronological, stylistic, and sociological perspectives within the historical context of Mexican culture. Beautifully illustrated in color with an essay by Juan Carlos Corrales.

130   Libertad en bronce: Leonora Carrington, José Luis Cuevas, Manuel Felguérez, Gunther Gerzso, Roger von Gunten, Joy Laville, Brian Nissen, Irma Palacios, Vicente Rojo, Juan Soriano, Fernando de Szyszlo. México: Impronta Editores, 1999. 395 p.: ill. (some col.).

Nicely printed, color-illustrated bilingual catalog of the collection of sculptures commissioned from 11 painters. According to Rafael Tovar y de Teresa, the purpose of such a commission was to cross the bridge that joins painting and sculpture, thereby creating a revealing mosaic of Mexico's art during the second half of the 20th century. Different writers, among them Teresa del Conde and Juan García Ponce, introduce each artist.

131   Lindauer, Margaret A. Devouring Frida: the art history and popular celebrity of Frida Kahlo. Hanover, N.H.: Univ. Press of New England, 1999. 218 p.: bibl., ill., index.

Responds to questions raised by idolization of Frida Kahlo's persona after the public's rediscovery of her work in the early 1970s. Considers the way in which Frida—the celebrity—complies with Kahlo, the artist. Interesting view of the reinvented Mexican icon. With few b/w illustrations, good notes, bibliography, and index.

132   Losilla, Edelmira. Breve historia y técnicas del grabado artístico. Xalapa, Mexico: Univ. Veracruzana, 1998. 231 p.: bibl., ill.

Didactic guide on printmaking by the Costa Rican-born artist and former disciple of master woodcutter Francisco Amighetti. Traces geographic development of printmaking, its relationship to the invention of the book and its subsequent evolution, and an examination of the various methods of the craft, Losilla carves a clear picture of the art form. Illustrated in b/w, with examples drawn from the work of Latin American and other artists.

133   Luz Jiménez, símbolo de un pueblo milenario, 1897–1965. México: Consejo Nacional para la Cultura y las Artes: Instituto Nacional de Bellas Artes: Museo Casa Estudio Diego Rivera y Frida Kahlo: Mexic-Arte Museum, 2000. 154 p.: bibl., ill. (some col.).

Catalog of the exhibit of nearly 100 paintings, prints, watercolors, and sketches in a tribute to Julia Jiménez González (known as Luz Jiménez or Doña Luz) who posed as a model for artists such as Rivera, Siqueiros, and Orozco, and whose likeness, poise, and physique was considered by many "the most finished image of the Mexican Indian woman." Twelve essays profile her character and provide a glimpse into the past.

Includes b/w and color illustrations. Complemented with a short bibliography.

134 Manrique, Jorge Alberto. Arte y artistas mexicanos del siglo XX. México: Consejo Nacional para la Cultura y las Artes, Fondo Editorial Tierra Adentro, 2000. 168 p.: bibl., ill. (Lecturas mexicanas. Cuarta serie)

The author himself has selected these essays, written between the 1960s-90s and organized chronologically and thematically, as the most representative of his ideas about Mexican art. Some specifically focus on one artist (Tamayo, Toledo, Rojo, etc.), while others refer to exhibitions and exhibit spaces.

135 Martínez Domínguez, Margarita G. El arte funerario de la Ciudad de México. México: Gobierno del Distrito Federal, 1999. 182 p.: bibl., ill.

As in many countries of the Americas, funerary art has a long tradition in Mexico, dating to prehispanic times. Martínez Domínguez gives a succinct account of the subject, explaining how sociocultural influences changed the perception of death and beliefs about commemorating and celebrating the passing from this world to the unknown. The time frame goes from preclassic period to the popular celebrations of today, touching briefly on the realm of literature. Includes b/w illustrations.

Méndez Sáinz, Eloy. Ciudades y arquitecturas del noroeste mexicano. See item **1575.**

136 Misiones culturales: los años utópicos 1920-1938. México: Consejo Nacional para la Cultura y las Artes: Instituto Nacional de Bellas Artes: Museo Casa Estudio Diego Rivera y Frida Kahlo, 1999. 154 p.: bibl., ill.

Catalog of the exhibition of 145 items at the Museo-Casa-Estudio Diego Rivera and Frida Kahlo, about the "cultural missions" sponsored by José Vasconcelos after he was appointed dean of UNAM by provisional Mexican President Adolfo de la Huerta in June 1920. Vasconcelos launched a national campaign to educate the masses, above all the peasants, with the help of schoolteachers, and later artists, writers, and intellectuals. He was responsible in great part for what is known as the Mexican Cultural Renaissance, a fascinating initiative that transformed Mexico forever. Includes a well-documented and easy-to-read text, illustrated in black and white.

137 Moyssén L., Xavier. La crítica de arte en México, 1896-1921: estudios y documentos. v. 1-2. México: Instituto de Investigaciones Estéticas, UNAM, 1999. 2 v.: bibl., indexes. (Estudios y fuentes del arte en México; 63)

The last 10 years of the Porfiriato and the decade in which the Revolution began and consolidated constitute the historical background of this compilation of art criticism, essays which examine the concept of nationalism. During this time, popular art was appreciated, the colonial legacy was re-evaluated, and the beginnings of a new expression were about to develop. Recommended for those interested in researching Mexican art in depth and expanding its historical perspective.

138 La muerte niña: Museo Poblano de Arte Virreinal, Puebla de los Angeles, mayo a octubre de 1999. Puebla, Mexico: El Museo, 1999. 81 p.: col. ill.

Bilingual color-illustrated catalog of the exhibition of 69 works, mostly painting and some drawing and photography, examining one of the rites fixed in Mexican art from colonial times to today, especially at the popular level. A fascinating but morbid subject, this work informs the world about Mexican culture. The main essay by Gutierre Aceves Piña lends its title to the exhibit and catalog.

139 Los murales del Palacio Nacional. Textos de Raquel Tibol *et al.* México: Instituto Nacional de Bellas Artes: Milan, Italy: Américo Arte Editores, 1997. 216 p.: bibl., col. ill.

Raquel Tibol, Víctor Jiménez, Itzel Rodríguez, and Juan Coronel Rivera joined together in this marvelous, artfully illustrated volume to analyze, interpret, and describe the epic murals of Rivera at the Palacio Nacional, depicting the history of Mexico from the precolonial period to the Revolution. Carlos Fuentes does the honors in his introduction, suggesting that the murals fulfill their purpose despite all that may be objectionable, since Rivera may have achieved the goal of forcing the spectator to formulate the questions and interrogate the work of art instead of the artwork supplying the answers to the public.

140 Museo Chihuahuense de Arte Contemporáneo. Casa Redonda: Museo Chihuahuense de Arte Contemporáneo: Septiembre de 2000. Chihuahua, Mexico: Conaculta, 2000. 202 p.: bibl., ill. (some col.).

Catalog of the inaugural exhibition at the new museum, which presents an institutional memory of the building—the circular, former state house for locomotive maintenance, whose shape explains its nickname. The exhibit is divided into four themes, all associated with the railroad.

141   Museo Nacional de Arte (Mexico).

Una ventana al arte mexicano de cuatro siglos: colecciones del Museo Nacional de Arte. Reedición México: Patronato del Museo Nacional de Arte: El Museo: CONACULTA-INBA, 1999. 120 p.: ill. (some col.).

Color-illustrated and annotated catalog of a temporary exhibition at the Palacio Nacional of the most significant works in Mexico's Museo Nacional de Arte held just before closing for reinstallation. Four centuries were represented in the exhibit, but the 19th century section appears most cohesive and interesting due to the number and quality of the works selected, and their significance in the evolution of Mexican art. For review of first edition, see *HLAS 56:113*.

142   Ocho mujeres en el arte hoy. Textos de Yolanda Andrade *et al.* México: La Sociedad Mexicana de Arte Moderno, 1998. 55 p.: ill. (some col.).

Color-illustrated catalog of the exhibition in Mexico City of the work (sculpture, photography, engraving, painting, video-installation, etc.) of eight women artists. The intention—according to Teresa del Conde, who presents the exhibit—is to compensate for the fact that since 1990, the Museo de Arte Moderno de México has not presented a multidisciplinary genre exhibition. Raquel Serur and Carlos-Blas Galindo contributed essays explaining why many of the feminist issues of the 1970s are still relevant to the exhibitions of female artists.

143   O'Gorman. México: Bital Grupo Financiero, 1999. 291 p.: bibl., ill. (some col.).

Nine authors, including Elena Poniatowska and Ida Rodríguez Prampolini, write about specific aspects of O'Gorman, the artist who best represents the second generation of the Mexican School. Includes a useful, though partial, catalog of O'Gorman's work as a painter, draftsman, muralist, and archi-

tect. Excellent color plates make the extensive volume valuable in the absence of any previous comprehensive or detailed publication about his work.

144   O'Higgins, Pablo. Pablo O'Higgins: los trabajadores de la construcción. Textos introductorios de Luis de Pablo *et al.* Curaduría de Rosa del Carmen Olvera. Textos críticos de Carlos Sansores San Roman. Fotografía de obra de Alberto Morteno. Recopilación de Martha Elena León. México: Instituto del Fondo Nacional de la Vivienda para los Trabajadores, 2000. 142 p.: bibl., ill. (some col.).

Metaphoric monograph on the artist, exclusively centered on the figure of the construction worker, a recurrent theme in the extensive legacy of US-born Paul O'Higgins, an active member of the Mexican School during its second phase. Also includes sketches, drawings, and lithographs presented as the foundation of his mural oeuvre, paralleling the materialization of a building with the role of the construction worker. Well-illustrated and annotated.

145   El origen del reino de la Nueva España, 1680–1750: Museo Nacional de Arte, Universidad Nacional Autónoma de México, Instituto de Investigaciones Estéticas, junio-octubre, 1999: catálogo de exposición. México: Patronato del Museo Nacional de Arte: Banamex: CONACULTA-INBA, 1999. 319 p.: bibl., ill. (chiefly col.). (Los pinceles de la historia)

Companion volume of the exhibition *Los Pinceles de la historia* (Paintbrushes of history), which included 166 works (painting on cloth and furniture, and one sculpture). The show and book focus on the origins and traditions of Mexican art, acknowledging the significance of the colonial legacy in light of circumstances, influences, and cultural objectives, such as the Spanish conquest and evangelization. Illustrated in color and well documented, with a collection of essays on diverse topics by nine authors.

146   Para disfrutar el infinito: homenaje a Arnold Belkin. México: Museo Universitario del Chopo, 1998. 53 p.: ill. (some col.).

Color-illustrated catalog of the exhibition of 86 works in tribute to the Canadian-born artist (who died in 1992), at the Museo Universitario del Chopo, which he directed.

Offers several texts and diary entries, including some related to Nueva Presencia and Los Interioristas, whose manifests he signed.

147 Parra, Tomás. Tomás Parra, tributo a la poesía: Museo de Arte Moderno, Sala José Juan Tablada, del 3 de diciembre de 1998 al 28 de marzo de 1999. México: Sociedad Mexicana de Arte Moderna, 1998. 48 p.: bibl., ill. (some col.).

In this color-illustrated catalog, Teresa del Conde presents Parra's anthology of 53 works, suggesting that if Breton had known Parra, he most likely would have incorporated him as a member of the Surrealist movement. Veronica Volkow and Alfonso Colorado add two different perspectives on the artist's development. Complemented with a biographical summary.

148 Rendón Lozano, Mario. México, vitalidad y raíces: esculturas y dibujos = Mexico, vitality and roots: sculptures and drawings. México: Guernika, 1999. 78 p.: bibl., ill.

Monograph illustrated in b/w on the artist, and catalog of the traveling exhibition presented in Austin, Kingsville, and San Antonio, Texas. Includes complete biographical information and a list of past exhibitions, commissions, and awards. Alberto Híjar Serrano wrote the main text.

149 El retrato novohispano en el siglo XVIII. Puebla de Los Ángeles, Mexico: Museo Poblano de Arte Virreinal, 1999. 183 p.: ill. (some col.).

Color-illustrated exhibition catalog of 63 pieces including portraits of social, clerical, and political figures, as well as historic compositions. Texts by Rogelio Ruiz Gomar, Jaime Moreno Villareal, Eduardo Merlo Juárez, and Iván Escamilla González contribute different perceptions on the theme of portraiture. Catalog complements other publications on portraiture, which in Mexico is second only to religious art.

150 Rivera, Diego. Diego Rivera: arte y revolución. México: Consejo Nacional para la Cultura y las Artes, Instituto Nacional de Bellas Artes; Cleveland: The Cleveland Museum of Art: Ohio Arts Council, 1999. 449 p.: bibl., ill. (chiefly col.).

Catalog of the traveling retrospective, which was the last about the Mexican master in the 20th century, is divided into four thematic nuclei, with a number of essays that cover most aspects of Rivera's work, from his formative years to surrealism in Mexico. Lavishly illustrated in color.

151 Rivera, Diego. Diego Rivera: obra inconclusa. México: Consejo Nacional para la Cultura y las Artes: Instituto Nacional de Bellas Artes: Museo Mural Diego Rivera, 1999. 50 p.: bibl., ill. (some col.).

Color-illustrated catalog of an interesting—although not comprehensive—exhibition that includes unfinished works from various periods of Rivera's vast career. Sheds light on many technical and conceptual aspects of Rivera's art.

152 Rodríguez, Antonio. Rodolfo Morales. Textos de Antonio Rodríguez y María Luisa Mendoza. Fotografía de Pedro Hiriart. México: Fundación Ingeniero Alejo Peralta y Díaz Ceballos, 2000. 249 p.: bibl., col. ill.

Catalog of the exhibition dedicated to the Oaxacan painter presents good color illustrations. In his essay, Rodríguez profiles the human and esthetic dimension of Morales, whose work seems to oscillate between the spontaneous and the metaphysical, never losing a distant stylistic echo of Tamayo's earliest period.

153 Rodríguez Prampolini, Ida. La crítica de arte en México en el siglo XIX. v. 1, Estudio y documentos, 1810–1858. 2. ed. México: UNAM, Instituto de Investigaciones Estéticas, 1997. 1 v.: bibl., indexes. (Estudios y fuentes del arte en México; 16–18)

Second edition of the first vol. of the 1964 original 3-vol. compilation of nearly 700 documents, enhanced with the addition of 16 new articles in vols. 1–2, and 214 news and critiques in vol. 3. According to Rita Eder, this work aims to construct a history of art for a period in the life of the country, and to understand the fundamentals of an artistic production which attempted to respond to the concept of a modern nation.

154 Ruiz Naufal, Víctor M. Francisco Díaz de León: creador y maestro. Aguascalientes, Mexico: Instituto Cultural de Aguascalientes, 1998. 359 p.: bibl., ill. (some col.).

Carlos Monsiváis presents an insightful, well-documented portrait of the life and work of Díaz de León (d. 1975), in a well-compiled volume, nicely illustrated in b/w and color. Highlights the regional importance of this Mexican artist born in Aguascalientes in 1897.

155 Salazar, Ignacio. Sobre la duda. México: Instituto Nacional para la Cultura y las Artes: Instituto Nacional de Bellas Artes: Museo de Arte Moderno, 1999. 129 p.: bibl., col. ill.

Bilingual (English-Spanish) catalog of the exhibition of 38 paintings presented at the Museo de Arte Moderno in Mexico City. Color-illustrated, with an introduction by Teresa del Conde and an interview with the artist conducted by Dutch historian Hanna Van der Hoock. Includes checklist and biographical profile.

156 Salón de Arte Bancomer, 5th, 1999. 99 Salón de Arte Bancomer. México: Fundación Cultural Bancomer, 1999. 136 p.: ill. (some col.).

Color-illustrated catalog of the annual competition sponsored by the Fundación Cultural Bancomer since 1995. The salon is organized to show the extraordinary mobility of the current Mexican art scene due to the "interaction of several generations and tendencies with similarities and differences," in the words of Luis Carlos Emerich, who introduces the exhibit. Fifty-six artists participated, 21 of them as invitees, with works in all types of media.

157 Santiago, Abel. En tinta negra y en tinta roja: Arturo García Bustos, vida y obra. México: Fundación Todos por el Istmo, 2000. 207 p.: ill. (some col.).

Santiago gathers a number of personal impressions collected by García Bustos, printmaker and muralist, throughout his life and work. Illustrated.

158 Santiago, José de. José Chávez Morado: vida, obra y circunstancias. 1. ed., rev. and corr. México: Ediciones La Rana, 2001. 397 p.: bibl., ill. (chiefly col.). (Artistas de Guanajuato)

Descriptive monograph that includes a biographical essay vis-à-vis Chávez Morado's easel work and an analysis of his monumental pieces in the context of contemporary Mexican art. Attempts to help clarify the cultural fabric of postrevolutionary Mexico. Color illustrations and bibliography. The painter himself provided much of the information.

159 Siete escultores: primavera 2000. México: Impronta Editores: Ciudad de México, 2000. 141 p.: ill. (some col.).

B/w and color illustrated catalog, with texts by Alberto Blanco, of the invitational outdoor exhibition of 37 large-scale sculptures by seven artists, along Paseo de la Reforma, in the museum neighborhood of Mexico City's Woods of Chapultepec. The event was complemented with dance, theater, and music, in celebration of the arrival of spring. The exhibit is the second project of Impronta Editores, who in 1999 organized *Libertad en bronce* (see item **130**).

160 Talavera contemporánea. México: Secretaría de Cultura del Estado de Puebla: Univ. de las Américas-Puebla: Uriarte Talavera, 1999. 139 p.: bibl., col. ill.

Color-illustrated catalog of the exhibition at the Centro Cultural San Francisco, in the state of Puebla, Mexico. Includes 136 works executed by a large group of notable contemporary Mexican artists. All works were made using the traditional *talavera* technique (vitreous ceramic), which in Puebla dates back to the 16th century. Includes several essays (with summaries in English) about the rich history of the technique developed in Puebla, and its use by contemporary artists.

161 Tamayo, Rufino. Rufino Tamayo: pintura, dibujo y gráfica: exposición retrospectiva. Bogotá: Museo de Arte Moderno de Bogotá, 2000. 79 p.: ill. (some col.).

Color-illustrated catalog of the retrospective of 31 paintings, 31 drawings, and 30 graphic pieces, the earliest dating from 1926, at the Museo de Arte Moderno de Bogotá (MAMBO). Includes an introduction, three separate essays, and a complete checklist.

162 Tamayo, Rufino. Tamayo. México: Grupo Financiero Bital, 1998. 249 p.: bibl., ill. (some col.).

Official book of the celebration of the 100th anniversary of Tamayo's birth, exquisitely produced. Generously illustrated with a superb selection of the artist's masterpieces (mostly paintings, some drawings and prints) and personal photographs, along with essays by Fernando del Paso, Teresa del Conde, Xavier Moyssén, Juan Coronel Rivera, Ingrid Suckaer, and Robert Valerio. Tamayo himself would have been happy with this kind of celebratory book, one that most artists wish for, but few truly deserve and live to see.

163 Tamayo, Rufino. Tamayo: centenario, 1899–1999. Oaxaca, Mexico: Museo de Arte Contemporáneo de Oaxaca: Instituto de Artes Gráficas de Oaxaca, 1999. 66 p.: bibl., ill. (chiefly col.).

Illustrated catalog of two exhibitions organized in Oaxaca on occasion of the centenary of the artist. "Vivir un siglo" was a biographical and documentary exhibit at the Museo de Arte Contemporáneo de Oaxaca, which included objects and drawings, and "Obra gráfica de Rufino Tamayo" was at the Instituto de Artes Gráficas de Oaxaca.

164 Tamayo, Rufino. Tamayo: paintings and drawings, 1925–1989. Beverly Hills, Calif.: Latin American Masters; México: Galería López Quiroga, 1998? 46 p.: col. ill.

Color-illustrated catalog of the exhibition of Tamayo's small-format works in various media, shown in two galleries: Latin American Masters (Beverly Hills, Calif.) and Galería López Quiroga (Mexico City). Presents 31 pieces illustrated with data, including cover and back cover, but there is no separate checklist. Also includes a biographical outline and a list of selected exhibitions.

165 Tamayo, Rufino. Tamayo, su idea del hombre: Ciudad de México, 26 de agosto-31 de octubre, 1999. México: Consejo Nacional para la Cultura y las Artes: Instituto Nacional de Bellas Artes: Fundación Olga y Rufino Tamayo, Museo de Arte Contemporáneo Internacional Rufino Tamayo, 1999. 91, 9 p.: ill. (some col.).

Color-illustrated catalog of the Tamayo exhibition of 57 superbly selected paintings, honoring the 100th anniversary of the artist's birth. Jaime Moreno Villareal's essay places the exhibit within the context of Tamayo's concern for people and his relation to life and the universe. Includes a complete checklist and chronology of the artist's life.

166 Tibol, Raquel. Hermenegildo Bustos: pintor del pueblo. 1. ed., rev. y corr. México: Ediciones La Rana, 1999. 253 p.: bibl., ill. (some col.). (Artistas de Guanajuato)

Monograph on one of Mexico's most outstanding prerevolutionary popular artists who specialized in portrait painting, supplying the popular demand for photography that

most people at the time could not afford. Illustrated in color with annotations. For review of earlier edition, see *HLAS 54:294.*

167 Torre Villar, Ernesto de la. El arte de ilustrar en México, 1920–1999. México: UNAM, 1999. 364 p.: bibl., ill.

Preface traces the history of printmaking in the West and within Mexico. Torre then offers an overview of the art of illustration through the work of 23 well-known artists who have created an important body of work in this area, covering almost the entire 20th century. Illustrated in b/w, with excellent bibliography.

168 Variantes, ocho pintores: pintores de la ruptura: pintores abstractos de hoy. México: Impronta Editores, 1999. 139 p.: col. ill.

Color-illustrated catalog of the promotional exhibition sponsored by Isaac Masri, a friend of all eight artists, of works executed between 1997–98. The show was organized into two groups by Teresa del Conde with separate essays for each.

169 Villoro, Juan. Manuel Felguérez, el límite de una secuencia. México: Consejo Nacional para la Cultura y las Artes, 1997. 31 p., 32 p. of plates: col. ill. (Círculo de arte)

Pocket-size and rather personal account of the prolific artist, illustrated with some works from the last 15 years.

170 Visiones apocalípticas, cambio y regeneración: siglos XVI al XX. México: Museo Nacional del Virreinato: CONACULTA, INAH, 2000. 179 p.: bibl., ill. (chiefly col.).

Color-illustrated catalog of the exhibition of 60 works inspired by uncertainty about the world's future that is related to millenial concerns and beliefs about humanity's ultimate destiny. Exhibit articulates two main themes: visions of destruction and visions of hope. Covering five centuries, artists include Martín de Vos, Cristóbal de Villalpando, Juan Correa, José Guadalupe Posada, Rufino Tamayo, and Leopoldo Méndez. Contains many annotations, and includes a complete and illustrated checklist and a useful glossary of terms.

171 Williams, Adriana. Covarrubias. Traducción de Julio Colón Gómez. 1. ed. en español. México: Fondo de Cultura

Económica, 1999. 420 p.: bibl., ill. (some col.), index.

Intimate portrait of the Covarrubias couple in the context of Mexico's cultural and intellectual life during the first half of the 20th century, through the sensibility of a woman who apparently sympathizes more with Rose than with Miguel. To a great extent, Williams' account helps us understand the complex and multifaceted personality of the couple. Intentionally or not, *his* personality comes across as more overwhelming than *hers*.

172 **Zenil, Nahum B.** El gran circo del mundo: Museo de Arte Moderno, sala Carlos Pellicer, del 8 de abril al 1 de agosto, México, D.F., 1999. México: Sociedad Mexicana de Arte Moderno, 1999. 47 p.: bibl., ill. (some ill.).

Color-illustrated catalog of the exhibition of 71 objects and bidimensional pieces inspired by the similarities between life and the circus, where funny, cruel, and grotesque situations resemble everyday situations. Teresa del Conde writes a short introduction and Santiago Espinosa de los Monteros contributes an essay. Both add a sharp dimension to the significance of the work of this provocative artist.

CENTRAL AMERICA

173 **Arte naïf Guatemala: pintura maya guatemalteca contemporánea. Versión abreviada. Guatemala:** BANCAFE, 1999. 162 p.: bibl., col. ill., index.

Re-edited and revised version of the 1998 color-illustrated catalog of *Arte naïf Guatemala,* originally published under the sponsorship of UNESCO. Most of the artists belong to communities in Comalapa and Atitlán. Includes an essay by Lucrecia Méndez de Penedo.

174 **Bahamón, Astrid.** Escultura en El Salvador. San Salvador: Somos Editores Libros de Arte, 1999. 103, 5 p.: bibl., ill. (chiefly col.).

Offers an approximation of the development of sculpture in a country where painting has prevailed since the end of the 19th century. Includes a complementary section on nine contemporary artists, introduced by Bélgica Rodríguez. Illustrated in color. Not an exhaustive study.

175 **Becerra, Longino.** Moisés Becerra: un pintor comprometido con su pueblo. Tegucigalpa: Baktun Editorial, 1998. 208 p.: bibl., ill. (some col.).

Monograph on a former employee of the United Fruit Company who, in 1953 at the recommendation of the French Cultural Attaché in Tegucigalpa, received a government scholarship to study in the Academy of Fine Arts in Rome. Mostly biographical, with no critical content. Illustrated.

176 **Cornejo, Jorge A.** La pintura en El Salvador. Presentación de Francisco A. Escobar. San Salvador: Dirección de Publicaciones e Impresos, 1999. 179 p. (Colección Biblioteca Popular; v. no. 53)

Escobar introduces the work of Cornejo as educator and art critic, mainly due to the variety of writings. Although the book lacks structure and intellectual rigor, the obvious connection among the various essays endows the book with interest. In spite of its title, the last essay is dedicated to a sculptor.

177 **Panama contemporáneo: 15 artistas panameños = Contemporary Panama: 15 Panamanian artists.** Textos de Adrienne Samos and Tania Iglesias. Panamá: Museo de Arte Contemporáneo, 2001. 82 p.: bibl., col. ill.

Color-illustrated and annotated catalog of the exhibition originally presented in Italy, organized by the Panamanian Ministry of Foreign Affairs on occasion of the official visit of Panama's President Mireya Moscoso to His Holiness John Paul II. Introduction by curator Carmen Aleman.

178 **Perrin, Michel.** Tableaux Kuna: les molas, un art d'Amérique. Paris: Arthaud, 1998. 204 p.: bibl., col. ill., index, map.

Sensible and unspeculative at the same time, Perrin dissects the mola as an object bearing multiple meanings within the context of Cuna culture, and tries to decipher its enigmatic visual world. Good design and excellent content make this publication both enjoyable and revealing.

179 **Pintura nicaragüense contemporánea: Centre Cultural La Beneficiència, Diputació de València: del 17 de marzo al 3 de mayo de 1998 = Pintura nicaragüenca contemporània: Centre Cultural La Beneficiència, Diputació de València: del 17**

de març al 3 de maig de 1998: **Fernando Saravia** *et al.* Valencia, Spain: Diputación de Valencia, 1997. 127 p.: bibl., ill. (some col.). (Colección Imagen; 52)

Color-illustrated catalog of the exhibition of selected works by 16 artists covering the last 50 years of activity in Nicaragua. Essays by Jana Cazalla and Julio Valle establish the context in which the exhibit should be viewed.

180 Re-visión de un siglo 1897–1997: ciclo de conferencias sobre arte y sociedad. San José: Museo de Arte Costarricense, 1998. 122 p.: bibl., ill. (some col.).

Compiles a series of lectures by eight authors on aspects related to art and society on occasion of the 20th anniversary of the creation of the Museo de Arte Costarricense (MAC). The lectures complemented three major exhibitions organized by the museum to examine pivotal moments in the development of Costa Rican art in the 20th century, including the creation of the Escuela Nacional de Artes Plásticas in 1897.

THE CARIBBEAN

181 Alonso, Alejandro G. La obra escultórica de Rita Longa. La Habana: Editorial Letras Cubanas, 1998. 61 p.: ill. (Artistas cubanos)

Modestly published monograph that pays a personal tribute to Cuba's pioneer female sculptor (b. 1912). Longa started her career influenced by the Deco style, meriting inclusion in the 1937 inaugural exhibition of the Rockefeller Center. After Castro's revolution, she committed her work to the Cuban cause, for which she was generously rewarded. Biographical in character, the book has little historic or critical content. Illustrated in b/w.

182 Alonso, Alejandro G. Sosabravo. La Habana: Editorial Letras Cubanas, 1999. 103 p.: bibl., ill. (some col.). (Artistas cubanos)

Brief monograph on the veteran illustrator and sculptor who received the Cuban Ministry of Culture's highest award in 1997.

183 Arte cubano: más allá del papel. Textos de Llilian Llanes, Antonio Zaya, and José Manuel Noceda. Madrid: Caja Madrid Fundación, 1999. 137 p.: bibl., ill. (some col.).

Color-illustrated and annotated catalog of the Madrid exhibition focusing on artists who utilize paper as a vehicle for expression. According to Llanes, paper has played a major role in the survival of Cuban art during the time the country has been subjected to economic depredation. Includes two additional essays on the subject by Zaya and Noceda, and a biographical profile of the artists in the exhibit.

184 Báez, Myrna. Myrna Báez, una artista ante su espejo = Myrna Báez, an artist and her mirrors. San Juan: Univ. del Sagrado Corazón, 2001. 289 p.: bibl., ill. (some col.), index.

Well-documented, nicely put together bilingual monograph about a figure much admired in her homeland of Puerto Rico. Reasonable quality printing. The three-part book includes two essays on her work, a historical chronology of events tied to her biography, and an illustrated catalog of works. Throughout the book it is clear that Báez's emphasis on the anecdote supersedes pictorial proficiency. Her graphic work is perhaps the strongest and most consistent.

185 Benítez, Adigio. Adigio, o la insurrección del tiempo. Havana: Fondo Cubano de Bienes Culturales, 1998. 60 p.: bibl., ill. (some col.).

Synthetic but complete monograph on the artist, showing his long career and stylistic transformations. Nicely illustrated in b/w and color.

186 Blanco, Dionisio. Dionisio Blanco (Dominican Republic): recent paintings, December 4—December 18. Coral Gables, Fla.: The Embassy, Gallery of International Art, 1998. 1 v. (unpaged): bibl., ill. (some col.).

Catalog of the exhibition of recent paintings, with a presentation by Maria Luisa Borras.

187 Cuatro siglos de pintura puertorriqueña. Puerto Rico: Banco Santander, 1998. 193 p.: bibl., ill. (some col.), index.

With a brief introductory essay, this generously color-illustrated book traces the development of painting in the former Spanish Caribbean colony, from the 16th century anonymous mural of San Telmo at the St. Tomas Church, to the new artists of the 1990s. Commissioned by Banco Santander

Puerto Rico, it includes an index of the artists.

188 Cuba siglo XX: modernidad y sincretismo. Las Palmas de Gran Canaria, Spain: Centro Atlántico de Arte Moderno; Palma, Spain: Fundació "La Caixa"; Barcelona: Centre d'Art Santa Mónica, 1996. 422 p.: bibl., ill. (chiefly col.).

Monumental color-illustrated and annotated catalog of the exhibit organized by the CAAM (Centro Atlántico de Arte Moderno). Curators Borras and Zayas warn that the exhibit is neither revisionist nor a definitive reading of Cuban art, but any exhibit of such magnitude implies an overall review of Cuban art, and the six essays seem to demonstrate just that. The introduction by Angulo González confirms the reappraisal of the scope of 20th century art in Cuba. The exhibit, he affirms, offers the most complete critical and historical revision of contemporary Cuban art to date. The catalog responds to a worthwhile effort.

189 Fifty years - fifty artists: 1950–2000, the School of Visual Arts. Edited by Petrine Archer-Straw. Kingston: Ian Randle Publishers in association with the Edna Manley College of the Visual and Performing Arts, 2000. 210 p.: bibl., ill. (some col.).

Book published to celebrate the 50th anniversary of the School of Visual Arts in Jamaica, which includes the work and biographical profile of 50 graduates in several areas, documenting the historical development of the school from its early beginnings in the 1940s. The selection seems to correspond to the prominence the artists have achieved in Jamaica.

190 Gerón, Cándido. Enciclopedia de las artes plásticas dominicanas: 1844–2000. 4. ed. aum., actualizada y corr. Dominican Republic: Editora Corripio, 2000. 737 p.: bibl., ill. (some col.).

The author refers to this book as a biographical dictionary of "outstanding Dominican painters." The illustrations, however, make unclear the criteria for selection.

191 Gerón, Cándido. Pintura Dominicana: un cuarto de siglo, 1970–1996. Dominican Republic: Editora de Colores, 1998. 188 p.: col. ill.

Not an attempt to synthesize the evolution of Dominican painting after 1970, but rather intended to contextualize some views and stylistic situations, according to author's own words. The text is bilingual (although both the English and Spanish versions could benefit from some editing), complemented with generous illustrations. Lacks a bibliography and index.

192 Hasbún Espinal, Judet. Notas sobre las artes plásticas dominicanas. Santo Domingo: Editora Corripio, 2000. 207 p.: col. ill.

Color-illustrated volume unites 25 previously published articles about early modernists and friends. Artists include Darío Suro, Jaime Colson, Mariano Eckert, Radhamés Mejía, and Dionisio Blanco, to whom the book is dedicated.

Hispanofilia: arquitectura y vida en Puerto Rico, 1900–1950 = Hispanophilia: architecture and life in Puerto Rico, 1900–1950. See item **2063.**

Juan, Adelaida de. José Martí: imagen, crítica y mercado de arte. See item **4670.**

193 Larraz, Julio. Julio Larraz. Buenos Aires: Der Brücke Ediciones, 1998. 30 p.: col. ill. (Colección Cuadernos de arte; 45)

Der Brücke Ediciones 45th color-illustrated monograph from the *Colección Cuadernos de arte* dedicated to the Cuban-born artist, with a bilingual presentation by Edward Shaw entitled "Don Quixote in Wonderland," and a biographical profile.

194 Lucie-Smith, Edward. Albert Huie: father of Jamaican painting. Kingston: Ian Randle Publishers, 2001. 20 p., 69 p. of plates: col. ill.

Monographic approach to the work of the cofounder of the Edna Manley College for the Visual Arts, divided by subjects: landscape, genre scenes, nudes, portraits, and flowers. Born in what the author refers to as a "cultural backwater," Huie is the first Jamaican painter from humble origins to have enjoyed a full professional career. Illustrated.

195 Luis, Carlos M. El oficio de la mirada: ensayos de arte y literatura cubana. Miami, Fla.: Ediciones Universal, 1998. 231 p.: bibl., ill., index. (Colección Arte)

Collection of essays offers a perspective on outstanding artistic and literary figures in Cuba up to the 1950s, such as

Lezama Lima and Carlos Enríquez. Also covers other topics relevant to aspects of Cuban culture and society, such as tobacco labels and ethnicity represented by people of African-descent. Illustrated in b/w.

196 **Martis, Adi** and **Jennifer Smit.** Arte: beeldende kunst van de Nederlandse Antillen en Aruba [Dutch Caribbean art]. Amsterdam: KIT Publishers, Kingston: Ian Randle Publishers, 2002. 142 p.: bibl., ill., map.

Handsome, richly illustrated volume on art history and art in Aruba, Bonaire, Curaçao, St. Maarten, Saba, and St. Eustatius is divided into eight chapters. In Dutch and English the authors describe the first artistic activities on the islands; the institutionalization through cultural centers, museums, galleries, and the Academy of Fine Arts; the primitives; professionalization of Aruban art; developments in the Dutch Windward islands; regional contacts; and recent developments in Curaçao, Bonaire, and Aruba. The last chapters discuss the work of 12 artists from these islands. [R. Hoefte]

197 **Mateo, David.** Incursión en el grabado cubano, 1949–1997. Miramar, Cuba: Artecubano Ediciones, 2001. 182 p.: bibl., col. ill.

Summarizes almost half a century of printmaking and engraving in Cuba. Explains the beginnings and effects of subsequent workshops that, in the 1940s and 1960s respectively, established the foundation for further developments. Includes 90 small illustrations and is complemented with an artists' dictionary of more than 100 artists who have practiced the technique in the country.

198 **Museo Nacional de Bellas Artes (Cuba).** Colección de arte cubano. Coordinador y catalogación de Roberto Cobas Amate. Palma de Mallorca, Spain: "Sa Nostra"; Barcelona: Ambit, 2001. 301 p.: bibl., ill. (chiefly col.).

Color, annotated catalog of selections from the collection of Cuban art in the Museo Nacional de Bellas Artes in Havana, which reopened in 2001 after years of restoration and conditioning. The illustrations are organized in four sections: colonial, turn-of-the-century, modern, and contemporary art. Includes some essays about the history of the collections and the proposal for organization and display of the artworks.

El Palacio Nacional de la República Dominicana: 50 años de su historia y architectura. See item **2087.**

199 **Pérez Cisneros, Guy.** Las estrategias de un criítico: antología de la crítica de arte de Guy Pérez Cisneros. Prólogo de Graciela Pogolotti. Selección y notas de Luz Merino Acosta. La Habana: Letras Cubanas; 2000. 380 p.: bibl.

Art criticism in Cuba before the Revolution of 1958, from the mid-1930s until the early 1950s, can be measured in part by the writings of Pérez Cisneros, who by 1937 had proclaimed the historic importance of Amelia Peláez, Víctor Manuel, Fidelio Ponce, and Carlos Enriquez, among others, in relation to the anachronistic attitude of the general public towards art. This anthology gathers chronicles and criticism, some unpublished, and includes some memorial articles about the author, considered by many "an implicit reference for the critics and historians after him."

200 **Por América: la obra de Juan Francisco Elso.** Textos de Luis Camnitzer *et al.* Recopilación de Rachel Weiss. México: UNAM, Instituto de Investigaciones Estéticas, Dirección General de Artes Plásticas, Coordinación de Difusión Cultural, 2000. 289 p.: bibl., ill. (some col.).

Four excellent essays by Weiss analyze and historically contextualize Elso's contribution to art, including his short but intense career and the complexity of his artistic practice, and elucidate some of his works. Five additional essays by other authors help to define the elusive work and personality of this Cuban artist who tried to overcome the paradoxes of Latin American culture. Illustrated, with a chronology and bibliography.

201 **Poupeye, Veerle.** Caribbean art. New York: Thames and Hudson, 1998. 224 p.: bibl., ill. (some col.), index, map. (World of art)

First book published to date that presents a comprehensive and inclusive view of the arts and artists of the Caribbean from historical and thematic perspectives. Includes descriptions of the diverse colonial origins and ethnic composition of the many countries that form the region. In seven chapters, Poupeye creates a solid framework to discuss the evolution of the arts in the region, while trying to define the meaning of *Caribbean*. With 177 illustrations, 76 of them in color, excellent bibliography, and glossary of terms. Desirable reading for those interested in the subject, and recommended for all persons concerned with modern and contemporary art in the Americas.

202   Les rakaba de l'art: les matériaux de Guyane mis en art: Musée des cultures guyanaises, Cayenne, 4 juin-21 août 1999. Cayenne: Le Musée des Cultures Guyanaises, 1999. 46 p.: ill. (chiefly col.).

Catalog of the exhibit that brought together 36 artists working in a variety of media. Contains biographical data and illustrations. The publication is not particularly impressive, but it is a rare opportunity to see documentation about the work done by artists from this part of the Americas.

203   Rey Yero, Luis and Manuel Echevarría Gómez. Arte cubano del centro de la isla. Sancti Spiritus, Cuba: Ediciones Luminaria, 1997. 110 p.: bibl., ill., index. (Colección Arcada. Ensayo)

Modest booklet divided in three parts, centered on the artistic developments of Sancti Spiritus, a province in the center of the Cuba. The first part offers a panoramic view of the 20th century in Cuba. The second refers to specific artists who have received awards at local competitions in the mid-1980s. The last is dedicated to Óscar Fernández Morera, the most emblematic artist of the area, according to the authors. Poor b/w illustrations.

204   Rodríguez, Mariano. Todos los colores de Mariano. México: Fideicomiso Museo Dolores Olmedo Patiño, 2000. 71 p.: bibl., col. ill.

Color-illustrated catalog of the exhibition in memory of the artist in celebration of the 10th anniversary of his death. Succinctly presents transformation of Mariano's painting through various influences. First impression is that perhaps Mariano's most interesting period was his earliest one. Coba's essay is short and overenthusiastic. Includes chronology.

205   Routté Gómez, Eneid. Conversando con nuestros artistas. Fotografías de Eduardo Firpi. San Juan: Museo de Arte Con-

temporáneo de Puerto Rico, 1999. 125 p.: bibl., ill. (some col.).

Collection of short essays on 23 Puerto Rican artists, based on interviews commissioned from the author by the Museo de Arte Contemporáneo de Puerto Rico. Complemented with b/w photographic portraits by Firpi, and a biographical profile on each of the artists selected.

Rubiera Castillo, Daisy and Raúl Ruiz Miyares. Dos ensayos. See *HLAS 59:5070.*

206   Salon de Arte Cubano Contemporáneo, 2nd, Havana, 1998. Habana vieja. Havana: Centro de Desarrollo de las Artes Visuales, 1998. 176 p.: ill. (some col.), 1 compact disc.

Color-illustrated paper catalog and compact disc, on the second version of the Salon organized under the general theme of "The city, metaphor for the end of a century," presented by Caridad Blanco de la Cruz. Two additional exhibits complemented this event: "De la java al shopping bag," a designer's exhibit around the idea of buying-selling (recurrent actions of every day life), and a solo exhibit of the late artist Santiago Armada (Chego). Includes a biographical index of the participating artists.

207   Simposio Regional "Incidencias de la Cultura Precolombina en el Arte Caribeño Contemporáneo," 1st, Santo Domingo, 1997–98. Presencia de la cultura precolombina en el arte caribeño contemporáneo: textos conferencias presentadas en ocasión del primer Simposio Regional. Edición de Mildred Canahuate. Santo Domingo: Banco Central de la República Dominicana, 1999. 78 p.: bibl., col. ill. (Colección Arawak de investigaciones antropológicas; vol. 1)

Unites papers presented at the three-day regional symposium with Puerto Rican, Uruguayan, Spanish, and Dominican participants, from predominantly anthropological and archeological perspectives.

208   Los Tesoros de la pintura puertorriqueña = Treasures of Puerto Rican painting. Edited by Carmen T. Ruiz de Fischler and Mercedes Trelles. Traducción de Anne Jones. Fotografía de John Betancourt. San Juan: Museo de Arte de Puerto Rico, 2000. 420 p.: bibl., col. ill.

Very good catalog of the exhibition showing selected works from the holdings of 10 major Puerto Rican public collections, several private collections, and the Museé d'Orsay. Provides a look at the evolution of arts, mostly painting, in the country. Osiris Delgado, Trelles Hernández, and Manuel Álvarez Lezama authored the three essays covering a range of pertinent topics, such as art collecting in Puerto Rico, trends and predilections, and the artists who established themselves in the 1990s.

209   Tolentino, Marianne de. Oviedo: un pintor ante la historia. Santo Domingo: Antonia Ocaña, 1999. 200 p.: ill. (some col.).

Laudable, color-illustrated monograph on Ramón Oviedo, who was named "Illustrious master of Dominican painting" by the Dominican Congress in 1997. Tolentino has written this essay in the context of painting in general, the history of the country, and the evolution of Dominican painting. Includes French and English summaries of the main Spanish text, bibliography, and biographical profile.

210   Tufiño, Rafael. Rafael Tufiño, pintor del pueblo: exposición retrospectiva, 6 de julio-7 de octubre de 2001. San Juan: Museo de Arte de Puerto Rico, 2001. 248 p.: bibl., ill. (chiefly col.).

Color, bilingual illustrated catalog of the retrospective of 332 works and 13 books. Tió's biographical and critical essay (probably the most complete to date about the artist) is factual and convincing. Includes chronology and checklist.

211   La vida urbana en la región del Caribe = Urban life in the Caribbean region. Textos de Derek Walcott *et al.* Santo Domingo: Centro Cultural Cariforo de la República Dominicana, 2000. 104 p.: ill. (chiefly col.).

Color annotated catalog of the traveling exhibition organized by the Centro Cultural Cariforo in the Dominican Republic, representing the 15 Caribbean member countries of CARIFORUM (including Puerto Rico) that speak Spanish, French, English, and Dutch. The exhibit included 69 artists, some of regional importance. A rare occasion to see the Caribbean area unified through the arts and a common theme. Texts by Derek Walcott, Gérald Alexis, Veerle Poupeye, and Marianne de Tolentino.

SOUTH AMERICA

Argentina

212   Arte argentino contemporáneo. Santo Domingo: Museo de Arte Moderno, 2000. 64 p.: ill. (some col.).

Catalog of the group exhibition of 31 artists, mostly painters and sculptors, presented by Irma Arestizabal, curator of the collection of Argentina's Foreign Ministry. The majority of artists included are not well known outside Argentina. Good reproductions in color with photos of the artists and biographical sketches.

213   Arte de Cuyo: septiembre-octubre de 1999: Centro Cultural Recoleta, Museo Eduardo Sívori. Buenos Aires: Centro Cultural Recoleta, Museo Municipal de Artes Plásticas Eduardo Sívori, 1999. 201 p.: ill. (some col.).

Color-illustrated catalog of the exhibition sponsored by the government of the City of Buenos Aires, held at the Centro Cultural Recoleta and the Museo Sívori in Buenos Aires, presenting an overview of 20th-century artists from the Cuyo region, particularly from the cities of Mendoza and San Juan. With an introduction by architect Alberto Petrina, a brief chronology of the developments of the arts in the region covering the 19th-20th centuries by Silvia Benchimol, and notes on the exhibition by Andrés Cáceres and Eduardo Peñafort.

214   Artistas argentinos de los '90. Buenos Aires: Fondo Nacional de las Artes, 1999. 234 p.: bibl., ill. (chiefly col.).

Informative book about the various moods and fads of Argentina's art scene in the 1990s. Not intended to canonize or discover the enduring styles, according to authors Gumier Maier and Pacheco. Illustrated in color, with biographical profiles of the nearly 60 artists selected.

215   Bayón, Damián. Art, c. 1920-c. 1980. (*in* Cultural history of Latin America: literature, music, and the visual arts in the 19th and 20th centuries. Edited by Leslie Bethell. New York: Cambridge Univ. Press, 1998, p. 393–454)

Good encyclopedic overview of the state of the arts in Latin America between 1920–80, with emphasis on the main socioartistic events and the most notorious figures.

216 **Benavídez Bedoya, Alfredo.** Benavídez Bedoya. Buenos Aires: Fundación Alberto Elía Mario Robirosa, 1998. 116 p.: ill.

Complete stenographic version of the debate regarding the work of the Argentine engraver Benavídez Bedoya, at the meeting of the International Association of Art Critics at Villa María, Córdoba, Argentina. Azucena Barbagallo served as moderator of the five-person panel that included David Pink, Head curator of the Photography Dept. at the Boston Public Library. High-quality publication illustrated in b/w.

217 **Berní, Antonio.** Antonio Berní. Texto de Fermín Fèvre. Buenos Aires: Banco de Inversión y Comercio Exterior: Manrique Zago y León Goldstein, 1999. 64 p.: bibl., col. ill. (Colección Pintores argentinos)

The collection of color reproductions from Argentine collections is the best feature of this concise, unpretentious profile on the artist.

218 **Casanegra, Mercedes.** Josefina Robirosa. Buenos Aires: Ediciones de Arte Gaglianone, 1997. 205 p.: bibl., ill. (some col.).

Illustrated monograph follows the development of the artist's work. Complemented with an exhibition listing, critical anthology, and a biographical chronology; sponsored by *Telefónica de Argentina*. Illustrated in color and b/w.

219 **Castagnino, Juan Carlos.** Castagnino: otra mirada. Curadora, Martha Nanni. Buenos Aires: FBC Fundación Banco Ciudad: Associación Amigos Centro Cultural Recoleta, 2000. 202 p.: bibl., ill. (some col.).

Catalog of the exhibit sponsored by Fundación Banco Ciudad and curated by Martha Nanni, focusing on lesser-known aspects of the artist's work between 1938 until his death in 1972. Like many of his contemporaries, Castagnino did not find it incompatible to enjoy the benefits of capitalism while declaring himself to be a leftist. Despite the "other look," the social references in his work prevail along with his somewhat anachronistic style, however competent. Contains biographical chronology, numerous quotations from the artist's notebooks, and

intimate photos. Color reproductions of fair quality.

220 **Correas, Nora.** Nora Correas: sumando. Textos de Mercedes Casanegra (entrevista) *et al.* Buenos Aires: Museo Nacional de Bellas Artes, 1999. 96 p.: ill. (chiefly col.).

Color-illustrated catalog of the anthological exhibition covering 1977–98, from works with fibers to sculpture and installation in a variety of materials. The evolution of the artist is clear and consistent. Curator Sacca Abadi summarizes Correas' endeavor as a re-evaluation of the spiritual world.

221 **Deira, Ernesto.** Ernesto Deira: mayo 1998: retrospectiva: obras, 1961–1985. Buenos Aires: Centro Cultural Borges, 1998. 79 p.: col. ill.

Color-illustrated catalog of the retrospective exhibition of 30 paintings at the *Centro Cultural Borges* in Buenos Aires. The small selection presents a clear idea of Deira's evolution as a painter, from his early beginnings as a member of the Other Figuration group (with de la Vega, Noé, and Macció) until 1985, a year before his death in Paris. Includes brief texts by Guillermo Whitelow and the artist.

222 **Delmonte, Alberto.** Alberto Delmonte. Buenos Aires: Arte Argentino Contemporáneo, 1998. 222 p.: bibl., ill. (some col.).

Color-illustrated monograph produced by the artist. Introduction by Guillermo Whitelow; interviews and accolades by several authors.

223 **Desde la otra vereda: momentos en el debate por un arte moderno en la Argentina, 1880–1960.** Coordinación de Diana Beatriz Wechsler. Buenos Aires: Ediciones del Jilguero, 1998. 250 p.: bibl., ill. (Archivos del CAIA; 1)

Several essays describe crucial moments in the debate defining modern art in Argentina, not only in the artistic context, but also the sociocultural and intellectual ones. The papers are part of the research activities that each author is currently developing under grants and subsidies from different institutions. Illustrated in b/w. With good notes and bibliographic references.

224 **Escultura y memoria: 665 proyectos presentados al concurso en homenaje a los detenidos, desaparecidos y asesinados**

por el terrorismo de estado en la Argentina.
Buenos Aires: EUDEBA: Comisión Monumento a las Víctimas del Terrorismo de Estado, 2000. 681 p.: ill.

B/w annotated catalog that inventories entries submitted for Argentina's international contest, 338 of which came from Argentina. The competition's mediocre turnout resulted in the majority of the 665 proposals lacking dignity, imagination, and ingenuity. Anecdotes and literary illustrations outdid by far design, esthetic, urban, and environmental considerations.

225 **Fernández García, Ana María.** Catálogo de pintura española en Buenos Aires. Oviedo, Spain: Univ. de Oviedo, Servicio de Publicaciones; Buenos Aires: Univ. de Buenos Aires, Facultad de Filosofía y Letras, 1997. 223 p.: bibl., ill. (some col.).

Well-documented catalog of current holdings of Spanish paintings in Argentine collections. The works entered the country in great quantities through the port of Buenos Aires between the end of the 19th century and the late 1930s, coinciding with Argentina's golden age. The collected data is amazing in wealth and quality of the works. The catalog, partially illustrated, records 761 entries, although the author states that many more were not possible to inventory. Most entries include bibliographic references. With few exceptions, such as Diego Velásquez, all important Spanish painters from the baroque to the 20th century are represented, such as El Greco, Bartolomé Esteban Murillo, Francisco de Goya, Hermenegildo Anglada Camarasa, and Pablo Picasso.

O fotográfico. See item 385.

226 **Giunta, Andrea.** Vanguardia, internacionalismo y política: arte argentino en los años sesenta. Buenos Aires: Paidós, 2001. 412 p.: bibl., ill., index. (Espacios del saber; 22)

Fascinating examination of the state of the arts in Argentina during the 1960s, a period in which the country achieved an unparalleled international prominence through the arts, especially in the US. Aided by carefully gathered documentation, reconstructs conditions and strategies that made it possible for Argentina's imagery to connect with the international scene.

227 **Gómez de Rodríguez Britos, Marta.** Mendoza y su arte en la década del '20. Mendoza, Argentina: Editorial de la Facultad de Filosofía y Letras de la Univ. Nacional de Cuyo, 1999. 172 p.: bibl., facsims., ill., indexes.

General overview of the state of the visual arts in Mendoza during the 1920s examines the institutions that promoted foreign and local artists whose activity contributed to the local artistic environment.

228 **Kemble, Kenneth.** Kenneth Kemble: la gran ruptura: obras 1956–1963: 11 de noviembre al 13 de diciembre de 1998. Buenos Aires: Centro Cultural Recoleta: Gobierno de la Ciudad de Buenos Aires, 1998. 69 p.: bibl., col. ill.

Catalog of the exhibition at Centro Cultural Recoleta in Buenos Aires, of 55 works covering the years 1956–63 (complemented by four works by other artists). The posthumous show (Kemble died April 30, 1963) was intended to illustrate his (and Alberto Greco's) transplantation to Argentina during the late 1950s, a period of European informalism and US action painting, signaling a rupture with the Buenos Aires avant garde and its dominating geometric trends. This trendsetting activity placed Kemble in a protagonist role as Marcelo E. Pacheco clearly explains in his accompanying essay. Illustrated in color, with complete checklist and exhibition record.

229 **Lecuona, Juan.** Juan Lecuona. Buenos Aires: Diana Lowenstein Fine Arts Ediciones, 1999. 31 p.: bibl., ill. (chiefly col.). (Colección Cuadernos de arte; no. 53)

Brief profile on the abstract painter with good color reproductions and an introduction by Elena Oliveras.

230 **López Anaya, Jorge.** Enio Iommi: escultor. Buenos Aires: Ediciones de Arte Gaglianone, 2000. 159 p.: bibl., ill. (some col.).

Concise color- and b/w-illustrated monograph in which López Anaya characterizes the artist as the first abstract sculptor in Argentina (1945). Defines Iommi's approach to art as an adventure; his work has evolved through the years in a succession of transformations, not all equally successful, but loyal to Apollinaire's idea of perceiving what cannot be seen in order to make it exist.

231 Magariños D., Víctor. Victor Magariños D.: 1924–1993. Buenos Aires: Asociación de Amigos de Víctor Magariños D., 1999. 95 p.: ill. (some col.).

Color-illustrated catalog in chronological sequence, of the 1999 postmortem retrospective exhibition at the Museo Nacional de Bellas Artes, sponsored by the Asociación de Amigos de Víctor Magariños D. Includes a critical essay by Andrea Giunta.

232 Magrini, César. Argentina, su arte ingenuo. Buenos Aires: Ediciones Arte Aldía Internacional, 1998. 129 p.: col. ill.

The publication honoring Osiris Chierico is the result of 10 exhibitions of naïve art organized between 1984–95 by *Galería Hoy en el Arte* in Buenos Aires. Magrini's text explains how the style adopted by the 40 artists represented in the book has come to be known in modern times, but can also be traced to an earlier stage of civilization. Illustrated in color with biographical references about the artists.

233 La memoria del ciudad: Centro Cultural Recoleta, del 12 al 30 de mayo de 1999, sala C. Buenos Aires: Ediciones de Arte Gaglianone, 1999. 78 p.: col. ill.

Catalog of the exhibition of 30 artworks from the collection of *Banco de la Ciudad de Buenos Aires,* at the Centro Cultural Recoleta. Included early, mid- and late 20th century artists such as Fernando Fader and Valentín Thibon de Libian, Jorge de la Vega, Rómulo Maccio, Luis Scafati, and Marcia Schvarts. All works are reproduced in color, with complete description and a short biography of each artist.

234 Memorias de una galería de arte: Archivo Witcomb, 1896–1971. Buenos Aires: Fundación Espigas: Fondo Nacional de las Artes, 2000. 271 p.: bibl., ill. (some col.).

Interesting publication of the Fundación Espigas, documenting the history of the Witcomb Gallery. Originally a photographic studio, it become the first commercial art gallery in Buenos Aires. Witcomb is credited with introducing to Argentina some of the most well-known, turn-of-the-century European artists of the time, in particular the Spanish modernists, as well as for promoting the most progressive Argentine artists, such as with the controversial Pettoruti exhibition in 1924. Illustrated, with many reprints of original catalog texts and documents.

235 Mordo, Carlos. La herencia olvidada: arte indígena de la Argentina. Buenos Aires: Fondo Nacional de las Artes, 2001. 237 p.: bibl., ill. (chiefly col.).

Fascinating visual history with essays covering 12 millennia of esthetic production by Argentina's aboriginal cultures, in the words of Luis Fernando Benedit. Includes rare discussion of the complexities of regional Amerindian culture in the second largest South American country—traditionally considered too European. A topic that merits more research, indeed.

236 Museo Histórico Nacional. Dirección editorial de Manrique Zago. Coordinación general de Juan José Cresto. Textos de Juan J. Cresto *et al.* Buenos Aires: M. Zago Ediciones, 1997. 222 p.: bibl., ill. (some col.), 1 col. map.

Carlos Saúl Menem, then President of Argentina, presented this volume published on the occasion of the 100th anniversary of the creation of the museum, an institution entrusted with "all the historic relics of the Nation and therefore the patrimony that identifies our nationality." Many events related to the history of Argentina are united here in a nicely illustrated volume containing numerous references to art works, furniture, and documents. An informative read.

237 Museo Nacional de Bellas Artes (Buenos Aires). Premios colección Costantini. Buenos Aires: MNBA, Museo Nacional de Bellas Artes, 1999. 173 p.: ill. (chiefly col.).

Color-illustrated catalog of the third exhibition and painting competition sponsored by the patron and collector Costantini. The positive effects in Buenos Aires are evident in the response to the contest since 1997, the impact on the local scene, and the high level demonstrated by Argentine artists. The 11-member jury awarded first and second acquisition prizes, five honorable mentions, and four special jury mentions. Jorge Gluzberg, the director of the museum, introduces the competition as a commitment to Argentine art. See also item **239.**

238 Premios Banco Provincia: grabado '97. Buenos Aires: Banco Provincia, 1997. 58 p.: col. ill.

Illustrated catalog offering a healthy panorama of the state of printmaking in Argentina, which boasts excellent artists dedicated solely to work on this technique. The reproductions attest to the high level of quality achieved by the artists participating in this contest. Images corresponding to prizes and honorable mention winners also include biographical references. However, the publication does not include sufficient data on the reproductions to indicate the techniques utilized or how the different works were executed, which is detrimental to its didactic value.

239 Premios colección Costantini: 68 artistas, 25 críticos. Buenos Aires: MNBA, Museo Nacional de Bellas Artes, 1997. 158 p.: col. ill.

Color-illustrated catalog of the 68 works selected for exhibition (among nearly 800 works submitted) at the Museo Nacional de Bellas Artes in Buenos Aires. Eduardo Costantini sponsored the competition. Jorge Gluzberg, director of the museum, writes in the introduction about the art of collecting. See also item **237**.

240 Premios Fundación Amalia Lacroze de Fortabat. Buenos Aires: Museo Nacional de Bellas Artes, 1999. 160 p.: bibl., ill. (chiefly col.).

Color-illustrated catalog of the annual competition in Buenos Aires sponsored by prestigious collectors and arts patrons. For this occasion 18 sculptors were invited and a jury of seven professionals, among them Jorge Gluzberg, the director of the Museo Nacional, selected 46 painters. Gluzberg also presents the competition as "a symbol of the vitality of the Argentine visual expressions of our time."

241 Quinquela Martín, Benito. Quinquela Martín. Textos de Fermín Fèvre. Buenos Aires: Banco de Inversión y Comercio Exterior: Manrique Zago, León Goldstein, 1999. 56 p.: bibl., col. ill. (Colección Pintores argentinos)

Brief monograph on the artist, mostly useful for the color reproductions of the artist's work and notation of the location of the works in Buenos Aires' collections.

242 Roux, Guillermo. Guillermo Roux: MNBA, Museo Nacional de Bellas Artes, Buenos Aires. Moncalieri, Italy: Edizioni d'Arte Fratelli Pozzo, 1998. 134 p.: bibl., chiefly ill. (some col.).

In this handsome catalog, Jorge Gluzberg, director of the museum, calls for "a double challenge" as he introduces the exhibition of 174 works by the highly technical and sophisticated Argentine veteran, on occasion of the retrospective at the Museo Nacional de Bellas Artes in Buenos Aires. Includes texts by Jorge Romero Brest (1984), Pedro Orgambide (1998), and Mario Corcuera Ibáñez, and a biographical summary, bibliography, and complete checklist of works.

243 Sagastizábal, Tulio de. Tulio de Sagastizábal: pinturas indolentes. Buenos Aires: Der Brücke Ediciones, 1997. 1 v. (unpaged): col. ill. (Colección Cuadernos de arte; 40)

Number 40 of the monographic, color-illustrated booklet series *Cuadernos de arte*, dedicated to Argentine artists. Fabián Lebenglik writes the presentation entitled "Flight towards Paintings." Includes a biographical profile on the artist.

244 Santander, Cristina. Cristina Santander: color & forma antológica: Biblioteca Nacional, del 2 al 26 de junio de 1998: Centro Cultural Borges, del 4 al 29 de junio de 1998. Buenos Aires: Biblioteca Nacional: Centro Cultural Borges, 1998. 1 v. (unpaged): col. ill.

Color-illustrated catalog of the double exhibition of paintings (1985–98) and engravings (1964–97). The anthology of work brings together selections of 25 different series that the artist has developed throughout the years, which Fermín Fèvre uses in his short essay to describe the evolution of the artist's work.

245 Squirru, Rafael F. Geber: townscape = imágenes urbanas. Estudio crítico-biográfico por Rafael Squirru. Buenos Aires: Ediciones Arte al Día, 1997. 119 p.: bibl., ill. (some col.).

Squirru describes this work as a critical and biographical study on the German-born artist who migrated to Buenos Aires in 1941. Illustrated in color with a biographical profile.

246 **Taverna Irigoyen, J.M.** Papel & estampa 2000: el gran libro de los artistas latinoamericanos. Buenos Aires: Grabart Papel & Estampa, 2000. 155 p.: bibl., ill. (chiefly col.).

This color-illustrated catalog of works on paper from nine countries, the majority from Argentina, compiled at the initiative of Ricardo Crivelli, a printmaker himself, is not quite what the title promises. The publication nevertheless provides a perspective on a number of techniques Latin American artists are currently utilizing to produce art using paper. Includes biographical profiles of the artists invited.

247 **Verlichak, Victoria.** El ojo del que mira: artistas de los noventa. Buenos Aires: Proa Fundación, 1998. 207 p.: bibl., ill.

Author states that this selection responds to a personal agenda, motivated by the variety of visual proposals of the artists selected, during the Menem administration. The book, she adds, is not the ending, but only the beginning of the story of the 11 artists who are her subjects. She wrote a similar work on artists of the previous decade called *En la pluma de la mano: artistas de los ochenta* [*In the palm of the hand: artists of the eighties*] (1996).

248 **Whitelow, Guillermo; Fermín Fèvre; and Diana Beatriz Wechsler.** Spilimbergo. Buenos Aires: Fondo Nacional de las Artes, 1999. 237 p.: bibl., ill. (some col.), ports.

Monograph on the artist, with good color and b/w illustrations of selected works (on canvas and paper) grouped thematically, including appendix and chronology. A sober book that puts the work of this Argentine modernist in perspective.

Chile

249 **Abarca, Agustín.** Agustín Abarca: reactivando la memoria entre cielo y tierra. Santiago, Chile: Museo Nacional de Bellas Artes, 1997. 64 p.: bibl., ill. (some col.).

Monograph on the pupil of Fernando Álvarez Sotomayor, who heavily influenced the so-called "1913 generation" in Chile, perpetuating the 19th century Spanish-school painting model at the School of Fine Arts in Santiago. Includes a catalog raisonné and fair color and b/w illustrations.

250 **Cienfuegos Browne, Gonzalo.** Cienfuegos: pintura, gráfica, escultura. Santiago, Chile: Ediciones Tomás Andreu, 1997. 318 p.: ill. (chiefly col.).

Color monograph and catalog, generously illustrated in retrospective fashion, divided in four periods, each introduced by a different writer and focusing on particular aspects of the work of the painter, draftsman, and sculptor.

251 **Gana, Andrés.** Gana Chile: Andrés Gana pinturas, 1991–1998: Museo Nacional de Bellas Artes, 21 de Julio al 16 de Agosto de 1998. Santiago: Museo Nacional de Bellas Artes, 1998. 48 p.: ill. (chiefly col.).

Catalog of the exhibition of paintings at the Museo Nacional de Bellas Artes, with a presentation by Ramón Castillo, curator of the museum, and a summary of transcriptions of conversations held with the artist (b. Santiago, 1950) by Radomiro Spotorno. Illustrated in color, includes a list of past exhibitions.

252 **Matta Echaurren, Roberto Sebastián.** Matta. Barcelona: Fundació Caixa de Catalunya, 1999. 172 p.: bibl., ill. (chiefly col.).

Handsome, color-illustrated catalog of the exhibition at the Museo Nacional Centro de Arte Reina Sofía, with works on paper executed between 1936–45, and works on canvas from 1938–98. These works illustrate Matta's unchallenged contribution to surrealism, his pivotal role in the development of contemporary art, and his marked influence on US abstract expressionism. Introduction by Josefina Alix.

253 **Matta Echaurren, Roberto Sebastián.** Matta: tras las huellas de un gigante = Matta: following the footsteps of a giant. Curadores, Thomas Monahan and Manuel Basoalto. Buenos Aires: Centro Cultural Borges, 1998. 102 p.: col. ill.

Color-illustrated, bilingual catalog of the exhibition of 84 works done between 1943–95 in various media, at Centro Cultural Borges in Buenos Aires. Most of the works came from the private collection of Thomas R. Monahan, who, along with Basoalto, acted as curator of the exhibit. Includes interesting texts previously published by Curtis L. Carter, André Breton, and Octavio Paz, among other authors.

254 Museo de Artes Visuales, Colección Santa Cruz-Yaconi. Museo de Artes Visuales: colección Santa Cruz-Yaconi. Textos de Manuel Santa Cruz and Milan Ivelic. Santiago, Chile: Fundación Cultural Plaza Mulato Gil de Castro, 2001. 169 p.: ill. (chiefly col.), index.

Color-illustrated catalog of the exhibition of a selection of pieces from the corporate collection of Chilean artists housed at the Museo de Artes Visuales in Santiago, which comprises approximately 650 works, representing the second half of the 20th century. The book does not explain any additional criteria used for assembling the collection, but some curatorial work was developed for the exhibition, grouping works by technique and theme.

255 Palmer Trías, Montserrat. N. Antúnez. Santiago: Ediciones ARQ, Escuela de Arquitectura, Pontificia Univ. Católica de Chile, 1997. 219 p.: bibl., ill. (some col.). (Serie Arte. Colección Pintura; v. 1)

The first vol. of the art series published by the School of Architecture of the Pontificia Univ. Católica de Chile is dedicated to the artist who graduated from there as an architect in 1941 and died in 1993. Palmer Trías gathered 10 articles by different authors (six previously published, among the authors are Marta Traba and Jorge Edwards, and a letter from Neruda) which attempt to relate Nemesio Antúnez's work with some crucial moments in his career as a painter. The most revealing and compelling is perhaps his own autobiographical "carta aérea" (airmail letter), illustrated with photographic mementos of his personal and family life. A selection of 239 paintings, prints, and watercolors illustrates the publication.

256 Piemonte, Carmen. Carmen Piemonte Miani: 17 de marzo al 26 de abril de 1998: Museo Nacional de Bellas Artes, Santiago, Chile. Santiago: Museo Nacional de Bellas Artes, 1998. 61 p.: ill. (some col.).

Color-illustrated catalog of the exhibition organized by the Museo Nacional de Bellas Artes, as part of the cycle dedicated to Chilean artists of systematic and extended careers. Includes a summarized autobiography and texts by Ana Helfant and Carolina Abell.

257 Vergara-Grez, Ramon. Vergara-Grez: geometria andina. Santiago, Chile: Museo Nacional de Bellas Artes, 1997. 127 p.: bibl., col. ill., index, port.

Attractive catalog of the 1997 retrospective dedicated to the artist (forerunner of geometric abstraction in Chile) at the Museo de Bellas Artes in Santiago, covering 55 years of artistic activity. The publication unites presentations and commentary by many critics (including several by Argentine Rafael Squirru) and a number by Vergara-Grez himself. Among the works by the artist is the "manifesto" of the group *Rectángulo* he created in 1956, which "interrupted the sentimental history of Chilean painting," according to Milan Ivelic, the museum director. Includes a biographical summary.

Colombia

258 Amaral, Olga de. Olga de Amaral: el manto de la memoria: el hilo en la imagen del tiempo y el tejido de la vida. Textos de Edward Lucie-Smith *et al.* Bogotá: Zona Ediciones, 2000. 221, 2 p.: bibl., ill. (chiefly col.).

In a handsome, color-illustrated book, Juan Carlos Moyano Ortiz approaches the life and work of Amaral, an artist that Lucie-Smith correctly calls "unique among contemporary Latin American artists." Three additional essays complement the publication, which features the artist's thoughts throughout—both smart and sensitive—along with a complete catalog of her works, biography, and bibliography.

259 Arte y violencia en Colombia desde 1948: mayo-junio de 1999, Museo de Arte Moderno de Bogotá. Dirección de Glora Zea. Curación de Álvaro Medina. Bogotá: Museo de Arte Moderno de Bogotá: Grupo Editorial Norma, 1999. 303 p.: bibl., ill. (some col.).

Illustrated catalog (color and b/w) of the exhibition organized by Santafé de Bogotá's Museo de Arte Moderno on the subject of violence, a recurrent theme that "has marked Colombian culture in an indelible way," according to museum director, Gloria Zea. Lists 63 artists with a total of 138 works, from drawing to installation, and from the merely allusive to the testimonial. Eleven authors contributed essays about the relationship between violence and the visual arts, filmmaking, theater, literature, poetry, etc., in the context of Colombian life. The show brought together a significant group of artists. It does not, however, include all those Colombian artists who have developed some interest in the subject.

260 Botero, Fernando. Botero: sculptures. Texts by Jean-Clarence Lambert. Designed and edited by Benjamín Villegas. Bogotá: Villegas Editores, 1998. 1 v. (unpaged): bibl., chiefly ill. (all col.), index.

Beautiful coffee table book printed with the customary high quality of Villegas Editores, the Colombian publishing house. The excellent color plates and artful photography center around the monumental sculpture exhibition the artist has staged in several great cities of the world, among them Paris, Madrid, Florence, Jerusalem, São Paulo, and Buenos Aires.

261 Botero, Fernando. Donación Botero: Museo de Antioquia. Dirección diseño y edición de Benjamín Villegas. Fotografía de Carlos Tobón. Bogotá: Villegas Editores, 2000. 186 p.: bibl., ill. (some col.).

Color-illustrated catalog of the works donated by Botero to the Museo de Antioquia, in Medellín (the artist's hometown), including paintings, drawings, and sculptures, as well as 21 paintings by internationally known artists such as Robert Rauschenberg, Roberto Matta, and Wilfredo Lam. Includes an essay by director Pilar Velilla about the relocation of the institution, and one on the artist's work by Carlos Arturo Fernandez, who explains why Botero's work has always belonged to the city.

262 Corrêa, Carlos Augusto. Conversaciones con Pedro Nel. Prólogo de Miguel Escobar Calle. Medellín, Colombia: Instituto para el Desarrollo de Antioquia, IDEA, 1998. 219 p. (Colección Autores antioqueños; Vol. no. 119)

Presents 30 colloquial conversations between Corrêa and Pedro Nel Gómez, two pivotal figures in the development of Colombian art during the 1930s-40s, revealing the strong personalities of both characters and encapsulating, with judgmental passion, the sociopolitical and cultural context of a turbulent period (1955–72), during which both

artists were ostracized by the "dictatorial regimen of [art critic] Marta Traba." Miguel Escobar Calle calls this book "a document of multiple readings... a delightful book, disconcerting and irreverent."

263 Gaviria Gutiérrez, Jesús. Pedro Nel Gómez: los años europeos. Cronología y bibliografía de Miguel Escobar Calle. Medellín, Colombia: Fondo Editorial Universidad EAFIT, 1999. 126 p.: bibl., col. ill. (Colección El arte en Antioquia ayer y hoy; volumen 6)

Color-illustrated catalog of works executed by Gómez during his stay in Europe (1925–30), mostly in Florence. This time period was part of his formative years, which explains many of his later stylistic traits, and partially served as the foundation of later work.

264 Jaramillo, Carmen María. Alejandro Obregón: el mago del Caribe. Bogotá: Asociación de Amigos del Museo Nacional de Colombia, 2001. 191 p.: bibl., col. ill. (Colecciónes Públicas)

The title of a 1961 painting by the artist gives this book its name, which does justice to Obregón, an artist who transformed the panorama of Colombian painting in the 1950s, bringing to it a contemporary dimension. Jaramillo's judicious study, which includes a chronology and bibliography along with good design and quality printing, is the most serious reference published to date about one of the most important and least understood Latin American artists of the 20th century.

265 Mutis Durán, Santiago. Eduardo Ramírez Villamizar: la belleza del pensamiento. Colombia: Ediciones Jaime Vargas, 2000. 239 p.: bibl., ill. (some col.).

Provides a personal account of the artist and his work, covering the entire evolution of his development as an artist. Well designed and illustrated, the book includes a chronology and detailed bibliography, in addition to an appendix dedicated to the Museo de Arte Moderno Eduardo Ramírez Villamizar, in Pamplona, Colombia, the artist's hometown.

266 Ramírez Villamizar, Eduardo. Ramírez Villamizar, pintor: programa homenajes nacionales: colección exposiciones temporales, arte, historia, ciencia. Bogotá: Museo Nacional de Colombia: Ministerio de Cultura, 1999. 96 p.: bibl., col. ill.

Color-illustrated catalog of the exhibition that focused on Ramírez Villamizar's work as a painter, as part of a series of tributes to national artists, organized by the Museo Nacional de Colombia. Juan Alberto Gaviria introduces the prolific master. Complemented with a biographical chronology, selected bibliography, and exhibition listing.

267 Restrepo, Elkin. José Antonio Suárez Londoño: obra sobre papel. Bibliografía de Miguel Escobar Calle. Bogotá: Fondo Editorial Universidad EAFIT, 1999. 117 p.: bibl., ill. (some col.). (El Arte en Antioquia ayer y hoy; 5)

Poet Elkin Restrepo presents the work of Suárez Londoño in nine pages. The publication has a predominantly visual interest given that the rest of it is dedicated to reproducing the artist's work. Miguel Escobar Calle adds a short bibliography and a biographical profile.

268 Richter, Leopoldo. Leopoldo Richter. Textos de Oscar Collazos. Prólogo de Walter Engel. Investigación, documentación y supervisión de Gisela Richter. Bogotá: Villegas Editores, 1997. 247 p.: bibl., ill. (chiefly col.).

Monograph on the German-born Colombian artist who arrived in Santafé de Bogotá in 1935 and died there in 1984. Benjamin Villegas presents the work of Richter by saying that his singularity sets him apart from the "official catalog" of Colombian artists, making him marginal in several aspects, but not in that which is essential. With texts by Collazos and prologue by Engel, the book accurately profiles one of the most under-appreciated figures in Colombian art. Beautifully illustrated.

269 Robayo Alonso, Alvaro. La crítica a los valores hegemónicos en el arte colombiano. Bogotá: Convento Andrés Bello: Ediciones Uniandes, 2001. 140 p.: bibl., ill. (chiefly col.).

Attempts to demonstrate the existence among Colombian artists of a systematic attitude of resistance through different generations against the values of the establishment and the concentration of power. To this end, selectively analyzes the work of Débora Arango, Beatriz González, Antonio Caro, and María Teresa Hincapié. Illustrated in color and b/w.

270 Rozo, Rómulo. Sincretismo: Consejo Nacional para la Cultura y las Artes, Instituto Nacional de Bellas Artes, Museo del Palacio de Bellas Artes, Museo de Arte Moderno de Bogotá, Ciudad de México, marzo-junio de 1999. México: El Instituto: El Museo de Bellas Artes, 1999. 63 p.: bibl., ill.

B/w illustrated catalog of the exhibition organized to examine the work of the Colombian sculptor (b. 1899) who lived and worked first in Europe and then in Mexico after 1931, where he ultimately died in 1964. Alvaro Medina implies in his essay that the artist's contribution to contemporary sculpture has yet to receive the critical evaluation it deserves. Medina's point becomes more relevant in light of Agustín Arteaga's enthusiastic endorsement and the place he seems to find for Rozo within the mainstream of the Mexican School.

271 Salcedo, Bernardo. Bernardo Salcedo: el universo en caja: Casa Republicana, febrero-junio 2001. Curaduría de María Iovino M. Bogotá: Banco de la República, Biblioteca Luis Angel Arango, 2001. 215 p.: bibl., ill. (some col.).

Catalog of the retrospective exhibition of 116 of Salcedo's works. Includes an interview and chronology, reproducing some texts from past exhibits as well as newspaper clippings. Also includes an essay by curator Iovino M.

272 Salones locales de artes plásticas: Puente Arranda, Bosa, San Cristobal, Barrios Unidos, Martires: noviembre— diciembre, 1998. Bogotá: Alcaldia Mayor, 1998. 58 p.: ill. (chiefly col.).

Visual document about the artworks presented at a number of exhibitions sponsored by the municipality, held at five non-conventional locations in Santafé de Bogotá, with the idea of decentralizing artistic activity while responding to the need of artists who have not had the opportunity to access traditional exhibition spaces.

273 Sanín, Fanny. Fanny Sanín: 1987–1999: color y simetría. Bogotá: Biblioteca Luis Ángel Arango, 2000. 104 p.: bibl., col. ill.

Germán Rubiano Caballero explains the evolution of Sanín's painting on occasion of the exhibit dedicated to the years 1987–99, calling attention to Kandinsky's ideas about characterizing the image, which makes possible the definition and understanding of abstraction. Complemented by María Clara Martínez's detailed annotated biographical chronology and excellent color reproductions.

274 Santa María, Andrés de. Andrés de Santa María (1860–1945): un precursor solitario. Bogotá: Museo Nacional de Colombia, 1998. 96 p.: bibl., ill. (some col.).

Color-illustrated catalog of the traveling exhibition of Colombia's quintessential pioneer of modern art, best described by Federica Palomero as an "independent Latin American." Includes chronology and bibliography.

275 Serrano, Eduardo; Carmen María Jaramillo; and Ana María Lozano. Rafael Echeverri. Bogotá: Panamericana Formas e Impresos, 1999. 151 p.: bibl., ill. (some col.).

Handsome monograph posthumously dedicated by the Museo de Arte Moderno in Bogotá to Echeverri, the geometric abstractionist who died mid-career in 1996. Serrano, Jaramillo, and Lozano provide separate accounts of the artist and his work.

276 Valenzuela, Carlos. Quién es Carlos Valenzuela?: 6 de mayo–27 de junio de 1999: Museo Nacional de Colombia, Ministerio de Cultura. Bogota: Museo Nacional de Colombia, Ministerio de Cultura, 1999. 55 p.: bibl., ill. (chiefly col.). (Colección Exposiciones temporales: arte, historia, ciencia) (Nuevos nombres del pasado)

The provocative title refers to the catalog of the first exhibition organized at the Museo Nacional de Colombia under their "New Names from the Past" program, aimed at reviving appreciation for forgotten figures in the history of Colombian art. According to the essay by Beatriz González, Valenzuela came from a well-to-do family and appeared to have studied in Italy for a while. On his return to Santafé de Bogotá, he enjoyed relative success. He did not need to work to make a living and spent his life dedicated to his art and other personal endeavors.

Ecuador

277 Eros en el arte ecuatoriano. Quito: Banco Central del Ecuador, 1998. 52 p.: col. ill.

Color-illustrated catalog of the exhibition presented at the Museo Nacional de Bellas Artes, in Santiago, Chile, on occasion of the II Summit of Americas in 1998. The selection included Ecuadorian precolumbian, colonial, republican, and contemporary works, under the generic theme of love and sexuality, around which Julio Pazos Barrera wrote the introductory essay.

278 Guayasamín, Oswaldo. Guayasamín. Córdoba, Spain: Diputación de Córdoba, 1997. 92 p.: ill. (some col.).

Color-illustrated catalog of the 1997 exhibition organized by the Diputación de Córdoba (Spain). José Marín-Medina presents the artist and his work. Other texts include the speech by Guayasamín at the Second Latin American Meeting on the Defense of Human Rights, and a chronology of the artist.

279 Kennedy Troya, Alexandra. Rafael Troya 1845–1920: el pintor de los Andes ecuatorianos. Quito: Ediciones del Banco Central del Ecuador, 1999. 128 p.: bibl., ill. (chiefly col.).

The author—a great-grandchild of the artist—who she calls the "forerunner of landscape painting in Ecuador." Although published 22 years after it was begun (as a master degree thesis at Tulane Univ.), very little—if nothing—else has been published in the meantime about the artist and the development of the arts in 19th-century Ecuador. Thus, this work retains its interest due to efforts to clarify the self-taught artist's role in Ecuador, within the context of neoclassical and romantic ideas imported to South America by Europeans and wealthy Creoles alike. More important, however, is the impact that geologist Alphons Stübel and naturalist Wilhem Reiss, who employed Troya to document their studies while traveling throughout South America, had on Troya and his landscape painting. Illustrated in color but without a catalog raisonné.

280 El regreso de Humboldt: exposición en el Museo de la Ciudad de Quito, junio-agosto del 2001. Quito: s.n., 2001. 207 p.: bibl., ill. (chiefly col.), map.

Catalog of the exhibit organized for the 200th anniversary of the arrival of the German scientist (with Aimé Bonpland) in South America. In the words of María Mercedes de Carrión, Humboldt combined curiosity and the rationalist method with romantic passion and a humanistic perspective. Curator Frank Koll superbly highlights the different facets of Humboldt's personality and the influence of his studies. Contains good color reproductions and nearly 20 short essays by different authors about the man and his time.

Paraguay

281 Abramo, Lívio. Arte y artistas de Brasil y Paraguay. Recopilación, introducción y notas de Miguel Angel Fernández. Presentación de Bernardo Pericás Neto. Asunción: El Lector, 1999. 215 p.: ill.

Compilation of texts written by the Brazilian artist who lived in Asunción for the last 30 years of his life, headed the Centro de Estudios Brasileños, and died there in 1992. Abramo is credited with introducing engraving in Paraguay in the 20th century, as well as familiarizing Paraguayans with the work of many Brazilian artists. This is not an exhaustive selection since many other texts known to have been written by Abramo appear to be lost, missing, or unaccounted for.

282 Arte popular del Paraguay. Buenos Aires: Centro Cultural Recoleta, 1999. 51 p.: col. ill.

Color-illustrated catalog of the Buenos Aires exhibition curated by Víctor Casartelli, which gathered an array of contemporary objects in clay and wood, as well as embroidery inspired by colonial and indigenous themes.

283 Soler Núñez, Ignacio. Ignacio Nuñez Soler: Proyecto Cultural Artistas del Mercosur. Textos de Ticio Escobar. Curadoría de Osvaldo Salerno. Asunción: Banco Alemán, 1999. 255 p.: bibl., col. ill., index.

Monograph on the self-taught artist and political anarchist (1891–1983) who considered himself a craftsman, had his first exhibit at age 40, and left an unpretentious body of works related to the times he experienced throughout his life, which he spent entirely in Asunción. Illustrated in color, with some annotations about specific works.

Peru

284 Balbi, Mariella. Szyszlo: travesía. Recopilación de Mariella Balbi. Lima: UPC, 2001. 163 p.: ill. (some col.).

Extensive, color-illustrated book in the format of an interview, published as a tribute to the artist by the Univ. Peruana de Ciencies Aplicadas (UPC). Divided into themes as diverse as love, Indianism, the painter's craft, literature and film, God and death, etc., which, when put together by Balbi, assemble a picture of the artist, his intellectual traits, and personal experience about art and life.

285 Bienal Iberoamericana de Lima, 2nd, Lima, 1999. Lima Bienal Iberoamericana, octubre-diciembre 1999. Lima: Municipalidad Metropolitana de Lima: Bell-South, 1999. 191 p.: col. ill.

Color-illustrated and annotated catalog of the event sponsored by the Municipalidad Metropolitana de Lima, which included some parallel exhibitions (by invitation), panels of discussion, and two retrospective exhibitions dedicated to Peruvian artists. Twenty-one countries from Latin America were represented, as well as Portugal and the US. For review of the 1st Bienal, see *HLAS 58:346.*

286 Bienal Nacional de Lima, 1st, Lima, 1998. Lima Primera Bienal Nacional: salones regionales: julio—agosto 1998. Lima?: Municipalidad Metropolitana de Lima, 1998. 144 p.: col. ill.

Color-illustrated catalog of regional exhibitions and their winners, organized by the Municipalidad Metropolitana de Lima in a decentralized fashion (Arequipa, Ayacucho, Cuzco, Iquitos, Lima, and Trujillo), prior to the 1st International Lima Biennial, with the idea of making national participation more inclusive. The 84 artists selected offer a representative segment of the state of the arts outside the capital city of Peru.

Esteva Grillet, Roldán. Julián Oñate y Juárez (1843–1990 ca): un pintor de ultramar, en el arte latinoamericano del siglo XIX. See item **303**.

287 Fierro, Pancho. Pancho Fierro, 1809?-1879: colecciones del Banco Central de Reserva del Perú y del Museo de Arte de Lima. Bogotá: Biblioteca Luis Ángel Arango; Lima: Museo de Arte de Lima, 1998. 52 p.: bibl., ill. (some col.).

Color-illustrated catalog of an exhibition of 29 watercolors at the Biblioteca Luis Ángel Arango in Santafé de Bogotá. This self-taught mulatto artist's work left a documentary about customs, fashion, and human characters during the first decades of newly independent Peru, and in particular, the city of Lima. José Antonio Melo points out that Fierro's work makes evident the lack of comparative studies among other Latin American artists of the 19th century who were part of the process that defined countries after independence.

288 Gutiérrez, Sérvulo. Sérvulo Gutiérrez: 1914–1961. Lima: Telefónica del Perú, 1998. 382 p.: bibl., ill. (some col.).

Color-illustrated catalog raisonné of 381 works. Elida Román gives a historic interpretation of the life and work of the singular artist, who was initially a boxer, ended up a sculptor and painter, and died engulfed in the bohemian lifestyle he chose to pursue. His expressionistic style was not well understood in Lima, at a time when lyric abstraction was the dominant trend; with complete checklist, which includes lost works.

289 Macera, Pablo and **José Sabogal Wiesse.** Centenario de Don Joaquín López Antay. Lima: Pontificia Univ. Católica del Perú, Instituto Riva Agüero, 1997. 93 p.: ill. (Publicación del Instituto Riva Agüero; no. 167)

Compilation of various texts, some previously published, on occasion of the 100th anniversary of the birthday of the popular artist from Ayacucho, who at one point received Peru's highest art award.

290 Pintura mural peruana, siglo XX: catálogo. v. 1. Lima: Seminario de Historia Rural Andina, UNMSM, 2001. 1 v.: bibl.

Despite its precarious printing quality, uneven content, and lack of illustrations, this catalog is a useful inventory of Peruvian murals that may serve as the foundation for a more detailed study.

291 Sagástegui, Oswaldo. Oswaldo Sagástegui. Lima: Galería de Arte Camino Brent, 1998. 1 v. (unpaged): col. ill.

Critics Josu Iturbe and Elida Román presented the exhibition of recent paintings by the artist—better known for his caricatures and comics—at Galería de Arte Camino Brent in Lima, noting how he distanced himself from his previous work, while maintaining his provocateur style. Illustrated in color.

292 Shinki, Venancio. Shinki: Venancio Shinki retrospectiva, 1960–2000. Miraflores, Peru: Galería ICPNA Miraflores, 2001. 139 p.: bibl., ill. (chiefly col.).

Color-illustrated catalog of the retrospective exhibition covering 40 years of painting, from early abstraction to dreamlike, Hellenistic-inspired compositions. Includes chronology and bibliography.

293 Tello Garust, Guillermo. Pinturas y pintores del Peru. Lima: C & C Servicios Especializados, 1997. 401 p.: ill. (some col.).

Practical dictionary of Peruvian painters, from colonial times to the present. Color-illustrated, although not always with the best selection, and includes the signatures of many of the artists. Useful as a firsthand guide; however, the quality of the edition is not the best.

Uruguay

294 Alpuy, Julio. Retrospectiva. Montevideo: Intendencia Municipal de Montevideo: Club de Arte Contemporáneo: Galería Cecilia de Torres, 1999. 100 p.: ill. (some col.).

Color-illustrated and documented catalog of the exhibition of 116 works covering 1941–99. Cecilia de Torres recreates the artist's journey before settling in New York where he currently resides. Alicia Haber contributes with her own impression on Alpuy's work and its relation to Torres García's ideas and the famous *Taller*. Ronald Christ's interview adds the artist's own invaluable words.

295 Arquitectura y diseño art déco en el Uruguay. Textos de Mariano Arana *et al.* Montevideo: Dos Puntos: Univ. de la República, Facultad de Arquitectura, Instituto de Historia de la Arquitectura, 1999. 139 p.: bibl., ill.

With a prologue and eight brief chapters profusely illustrated in b/w, the authors create a lively memory of the cultural patrimony left by the art deco style in Uruguay, in light of its architectural integrity and historical significance. This solid publication could be the departure for a more elaborate and comprehensive study.

296 Battegazzore, Miguel A. J. Torres García: la trama y los signos. Montevideo: Impr. Gordon, 1999. 272 p.: bibl., ill. (some col.), indexes.

Study on the interpretation of symbolic and compositional structure in the artistic production of the "universal constructivist." In five chapters Battegazzore attempts to discover the essence of Torres García's geometry and meaning of his recurrent use of signs and symbols in relation to cosmic, spiritual, and humanistic orders. Illustrated in color, and b/w, including numerous diagrams and geometric analyses of the master.

297 Kalenberg, Angel. José Gurvich: pero yo voy a pintar. Montevideo: Ediciones J. de Arteaga & G. Tejería Loppacher, 1997. 255 p.: bibl., ill. (some col.).

Insightful biography and critical interpretation of the artist's work. Kalenberg refers to this disciple of Torres García as one of the most significant artists of 20th century Uruguayan art, distinguishing three clear periods in his creative process. Illustrated in color.

298 Lezama Montoro, Arturo. Milo Beretta, 1870–1935. Curaduría de Gustavo Tejería Loppacher. Montevideo: Iocco Rematadores, Departamento de Arte, 1998. 103 p.: ill. (some col.).

Biographical, illustrated catalog of the exhibition of 64 paintings from the collection of Lezama Montoro, the most extensive organized to date in tribute to the artist.

299 Pereda, Raquel. Carlos Alberto Castellanos: imaginación y realidad. Montevideo: Fundación Banco de Boston, 1997? 175 p.: bibl., ill. (some col.).

Color-illustrated monograph on the elusive, stylistically temperamental although predominantly decorative, Uruguayan artist who, like many others of his generation, spent a great deal of time in Spain and traveling throughout Europe, alternating his stays with returns to Montevideo. Seemingly well-produced document with Pereda's characteristic attention to detail, despite the scarce bibliography.

Venezuela

300 Arte y locura: espacios de creación. Caracas: Museo de Bellas Artes, 1997. 384 p.: bibl., ill. (some col.). (Serie Reflexiones en el Museo; no. 3)

Gathers 29 of the 30 papers presented at the seminar on art and madness organized in 1996 by the Museo de Bellas Artes in Caracas. The content is divided in four groups: artistic representation, statements by artists, reflection and theory, and art and psychopathology. Cármen Hernández introduces the main theme with dialogue about madness and its relation to art creation. In color with b/w illustrations and a brief profile about the participants, including several psychiatrists and psychoanalysts, artists, and museum professionals.

301 Benavides, Pablo. Pablo Benavides: por poco tallo el cuadro. Texto general de Juan Calzadilla. Caracas: Armitano Editores, 1999. 240 p.: bibl., ill. (chiefly col.), indexes.

Color-illustrated monograph on the artist, who was a late representative of the second generation of landscape painters in Venezuela. His style was figurative, mildly expressionistic, and perhaps for that reason he was able to join the Association of Independent Artists responsible for the glorification of abstraction in Venezuela. He remained loyal to his favorite subject, however, for the rest of his career.

302 Duarte, Carlos F. Lewis Brian Adams: retratista del romanticismo paecista. Caracas: Galería de Arte Nacional, 1997. 183 p.: bibl., ill. (some col.).

Carefully documented monograph on the life and work of the British painter who appears to have been born in London and settled in Caracas at age 27. Although not a brilliant technician, Adams developed a career in Venezuela as a portrait artist, leaving behind a singular gallery of military, economic, and social personalities of the time, including the "caudillo," Gen. José Antonio Páez. Includes 50 works reproduced in color, identified and annotated; 40 more are listed as missing. Complemented with a chronology of Venezuela's history.

303   Esteva Grillet, Roldán. Julián Oñate y Juárez (1843–1990 ca): un pintor de ultramar, en el arte latinoamericano del siglo XIX. Caracas: Univ. Central de Venezuela, Consejo de Desarrollo Científico y Humanístico, 2000. 318 p.: bibl., ill. (Colección Monografías; no. 64)

Monograph on the Spanish painter who emigrated to Peru where he worked in Lima for about 20 years and later moved to Venezuela. In Caracas he was hired to paint decorations at the Miraflores palace and the Municipal Theater. The book interprets the three environments in which he developed his work and achieved a certain degree of prestige despite lingering shortcomings. Includes chronology, catalog of works on canvas, and bibliography.

304   Michelena, Arturo. Genio y gloria de Arturo Michelena: 1863–1898 en el centenario de su muerte. Caracas: Galería de Arte Nacional, 1998. 147 p.: bibl., ill. (some col.). (Exposición; 194) (Catálogo; 189)

Excellent publication on occasion of the exhibition presented at the Galería de Arte Nacional in Caracas, honoring the 100th anniversary of the death of Michelena (1863–98), the most internationally known academic Venezuelan painter. Luis Pérez Oramas introduces Michelena, followed by an annotated color-illustrated catalog of 45 works most representative of the artist. Complemented with awards, a list of exhibitions, illustrated chronology and bibliography, which together give a comprehensive semblance of the man and his work.

305   Modernidad y postmodernidad: espacios y tiempos dentro del arte latinoamericano. Caracas: Museo Alejandro Otero, 2000. 160 p.: bibl. (Colección Delta Solar; 2)

The articles united here, originally published in El Nacional of Caracas, revolve around the confrontation between Marta Traba and Alejandro Otero, after they first questioned the authenticity of modernist movements in Latin America. Eventually the polemic engulfed other personalities in Venezuela's art scene. To complement the discussion, additional essays have been included to keep alive an issue that for some has already been satisfactorily answered.

306   Pérez Oramas, Luis. Mirar furtivo. Caracas: Consejo Nacional de la Cultura, 1997. 172, 3 p.: bibl., ill. (some col.). (Colección Arte y crítica; no. 2)

Re-edited version of 28 essays previously published by Pérez Oramas in various newspapers and magazines, including El Universal of Caracas. The bulk of the text is divided in two groups of 12 essays each. One group is dedicated to Western art, the other to Latin American and Venezuelan art. Three essays at the beginning of the book and one at the end are more theoretical in nature and function as introduction and coda. Several interesting hypotheses come across in the author's writings, one example is that the so-called crisis of the arts is merely a crisis of interpretation now that the arts have lost their regulated narrative.

307   Salón Nacional de Arte Aragua. *23rd, Maracay, Venezuela, 1998.* Catálogo. Caracas: Consejo Nacional de la Cultura: Maracay: Gobierno de Aragua: Museo de Arte Contemporáneo de Maracay Mario Abreu, 1998. 83 p.: ill. (some col.).

Catalog of the 1998 event held at the Museo de Arte Contemporáneo de Maracay Mario Abreu. The theme for this edition of the salon was "the private self to the collective space where the public lives," according to curator María Luz Cárdenas. Fifty-seven artists participated in three categories (bidimensional, tridimensional, and installation), and eight others displayed their work as special guests. Profusely illustrated, mostly in b/w.

308   Salón Pirelli, Jóvenes Artistas, *3rd, Caracas, 1997.* III Salón Pirelli, Jóvenes Artístas: octubre 1997-enero 1998. Textos de María Luz Cárdenas and Luis Angel Duque. Caracas: Museo de Arte Contemporáneo de Caracas Sofía Imber, 1995. 167 p.: ill. (some col.). (Exposicion; 163) (Catálogo; 130)

Color-illustrated catalog of the III Salón Pirelli, which, in this edition, includes

54 participating artists and three guest artists, all under 35 years of age. The theme of this salon was "Vision." Cárdenas interprets the exhibition according to the artists' proposals, and Duque introduces the concepts in a separate essay. In his words, the artists "intended to create a temporal and collective sculpture integrated by the visual power of the artwork activated by the gaze of the spectator."

309 Silva, Carlos. La escultura en Venezuela en el siglo XIX y la presencia italiana. Caracas: Armitano Editores, 1999. 157 p.: bibl., ill. (some col.).

Color-illustrated study helps us to understand the development of sculpture in Venezuela in the 19th century. During the first half of the century, the traditions inherited from Spain continued, while in the second half, Italian influences, represented by figures such as Tenerani and Tadolini, left their imprint in commemorative, celebra-

tory, and funerary statuary, practiced in Venezuela by Italian immigrant artists like Emilio Gariboldi.

310 Silva, Carlos. Tomás L. Golding. Caracas: Armitano Editores, 1998? 168 p.: bibl., ill. (chiefly col.).

Laudatory monograph about the landscape artist who represents, in Venezuela, a second group of landscape artists after the famous generation of the 1912 Circle of Fine Arts. Illustrated with 131 color plates. Scarce bibliography.

311 Soto, Jesús Rafael. Soto: la poética de la energía. Santiago, Chile: Fundación Telefónica, 1999. 48 p.: ill. (some col.).

Color-illustrated catalog of the artist's exhibition in Chile, with works created between 1985–95. Includes a profile on Soto's artistic career, two texts by Leopoldo Castedo and Marcel Joray, and one by the artist himself.

BRAZIL

JOSÉ M. NEISTEIN, *Executive Director, Brazilian-American Cultural Institute, Washington DC*

THE OVERWHELMING MAJORITY OF THE WORKS selected for this chapter study modern and contemporary arts: painting, sculpture, architecture, design, printmaking, and mixed media. This is a clear indication of the current direction of scholarship, as the selection was proportional to the books and publications received. However, various items included in other periods and areas were no less relevant and attractive, despite their lesser numbers.

Among the reference and theoretical works, De Sant'Anna's multiple-perspective study on the baroque stands out (item **318**). Several new reference works—two of them dictionaries, and the other two bibliographic studies—are also notable (items **313, 315, 316,** and **317**). This section additionally includes a fairly complete overview of the history of art in Brazil (item **314**), and a variety of essays by a large number of authors on the history and theory of contemporary art in Brazil.

The colonial period includes 14 items, several of which are of particular interest. The monograph on Antonio Giuseppe Landi is deserving of special mention (item **320**). The catalog of the baroque exhibition is an encompassing collection of original essays on the topic (item **312**). A speculative book on the nature of the baroque in Brazil is noteworthy (item **324**).

The 19th century is represented by a small number of items, all of them interesting in their own right, since they cover different aspects of the arts in that century. *Viagem ao Brasil...* is a substantial addition to the Brazilian iconography (item **334**). So also is Corrêa do Lago's study, focusing on São Paulo iconography (item **331**). The use of exposed iron structures in Brazilian 19th-century architecture was a major event in the country's modernization. Kühl provides a full account in her work (item **330**).

Works on art of the 20th and 21st centuries make up almost half of the items in this chapter and represent studies of virtually all media, individually studied or considered as a group. Even architecture, a separate section, contains a considerable number of items dedicated to modernity.

Guignard, one of Brazil's most beloved painters, is well deserving of the two in-depth studies reviewed this biennium (items **351** and **356**) and two extensive monographs focus on Lasar Segall (items **338** and **361**). Various classics of Brazilian modernism are represented by one monograph each, all of them commendable: Lívio Abramo (item **53**), Volpi (item **378**), Tarsila (item **375**), Flávio de Carvalho (item **344**), and Vicente do Rego Monteiro (item **380**). Modernists of second and third generations were also included: Anna Letycia (item **360**), Franz Weissmann (item **379**), Fiaminghi (item **342**), Renina (item **359**), and De Fiori (item **350**).

Avant-garde artists are well represented both in monographs, and thematic and summary studies, among them Lygia Clark, a seminal presence (item **348**), Emilie Chamie (item **345**), and more recent artists such as Carmela Gross (item **339**), Rosângela Rennó (item **367**), Leda Catunda (item **347**), Gonçalo Ivo (item **362**), and Tuneu (item **335**). Among the sculptors, Vlavianos is noteworthy (item **377**). Among the studies on artistic movements, it is worth stressing item **351** on the Armorial Movement, item **343** on the most recent tendencies, item **352** about the 1960s, item **337** on constructivism in Brazil, item **346** on international Brazilian art, and item **376** on the currents of three-dimensional art.

As for printmaking, such a relevant segment of Brazilian art, items **355, 363,** and **364** should be mentioned. A special manifestation in the past 60 years has been naïf art, of which item **381** offers an overview.

The photography section has only four items, each one distinctive and relevant: photopictorialism in Brazil (item **386**), photography in Pará (item **387**), theory of photography and history of photography in Brazil and Argentina (item **385**), and photography in Rio Grande do Sul (item **384**).

The vast majority of the items on architecture are also devoted to the 20th century, either as monographs or as group studies. Thus, Costa enters with three monographs (items **394, 395,** and **402**). Regional architecture is well represented here, with in-depth studies and reference works: Curitiba (item **396**), São Paulo's Ramos de Azevedo (item **393**), Porto Alegre (item **406**) and Porto Alegre's Corona (item **392**), Santa Catarina (item **401**), Belo Horizonte (item **388**), and Espírito Santo (item **399**). Vernacular architecture is also present (item **400**). City planning is covered by a few excellent studies, such as one on Salvador (item **397**), and one on city planning issues since World War II (item **404**). Last but not least are topics such as landscape architecture (items **390** and **405**), and Burle Marx (item **389**).

Among the miscellaneous publications, the catalog on Smith stands out (item **411**). Comparative art deco in the New World is of historical interest (item **408**). The Visual Arts Mercosur Biennial concerns art exchanges in South America (item **407**). On the iconography of Rio de Janeiro, item **410** is, and will remain, one-of-a-kind for a long time.

REFERENCE AND
THEORETICAL WORKS

312 **Arte contemporânea brasileira.** Organização de Ricardo Basbaum. Textos de Adriano Pedrosa et al. Rio de Janeiro: Contra Capa: Rios Ambiciosos, 2001. 413 p.: bibl., ill. (Coleção N-Imagem)

Collects a large variety of essays by nearly 30 authors—critics, art historians, curators, artists—who discuss the textures, dictions, fictions, and strategies of contemporary Brazilian art. Historical perspectives and theoretical elaborations are predominant, but polemics also abound. Sources of the included texts are given, and information on the contributors is succintly printed. A wide debate on Brazilian identity in and through art.

313 **Ayala, Walmir.** Dicionário de pintores brasileiros. Ed. rev. e ampliada por André Seffrin. Curitiba, Brazil: Editora UFPR, 1997? 428 p.: ill. (some col.).

Includes painters from all over Brazil who were not included in previous biographical dictionaries. Basic biographical information, conscientious critical approach, and color illustrations make this work a very welcome supplement to the already existing bibliography.

314 **Brazil: body and soul.** Edited by Edward J. Sullivan. Curated by Edward Sullivan et al. New York, N.Y.: Guggenheim Museum, 2001. 600 p.: bibl., col ill.

This monumental catalog of an exhibition first held in Brazil, then in New York (much encompassing albeit in smaller proportions) to celebrate through art the first 500 years of Brazilian history covers virtually all aspects of the arts in Brazil from its origins to contemporary avant-garde. Each profusely illustrated section is introduced by a scholarly essay. The catalog is itelf a wide and broad introduction to the art history of Brazil. This exhibition was the most complete survey of the arts of Brazil ever presented in the US under one roof. Selected bibliography.

315 **Costa, Cacilda Teixeira da.** Livros de arte no Brasil: edições patrocinadas. São Paulo: Itaú Cultural, 2000. 112 p.: bibl., ill. (some col.). (Col. Itaú cultural)

Included in this informative, though unannotated, bibliography are editions sponsored by the private sector in Brazil, which, especially in the past 20 years, has played an important role in the publication of art books in Portuguese, often with translations into English, French, Italian, and German. Includes almost 700 books all focused on Brazilian art. A relevant source for future studies. Bibliography and some b/w illustrations.

316 **Leon, Fernando Ponce de** and **Lúcia Maria Coêlho de Oliveira Gaspar.** História da arte luso-brasileira: guia bibliográfico. Recife, Brazil: Fundação Joaquim Nabuco, Editora Massangana, 1998. 226 p.: bibl. (Série Obras de consulta; n. 18)

This excellent contribution to the field covers: obras de referência e bibliográficas; fonte, teoria, e metodologia; arquitetura e urbanismo; gêneros artísticos; estilos e períodos; monumentos arquitetônicos; artistas—ofícios; índice onomástico; índice de monumentos, localidades e instituições. Nonannotated bibliography.

317 **Rosa, Renato** and **Decio Presser.** Dicionário de artes plásticas no Rio Grande do Sul. Porto Alegre, Brazil: Editora da Univ., Univ. Federal do Rio Grande do Sul, 1997. 439 p.: bibl., ill. (some col.).

In addition to being an invaluable reference work, the dictionary is also a panorama of the arts in Rio Grande do Sul. Lists over 1,500 names of past and current artists. Objective information supplemented with many b/w and color reproductions.

318 **Sant'Anna, Affonso Romano de.** Barroco: do quadrado à elipse. Rio de Janeiro: Rocco, 2000. 281 p.: bibl., ill., maps.

The central theme of this book is the metamorphosis of the renaissance square into the baroque ellipse. Study moves from the palaces and monuments in Rome to the remote villages of Minas Gerais in search of a baroque Weltanschauung, from Bernini to Aleijadinho. More than an art style, the baroque is an encompassing way of looking at life and death and beyond, and nearly everything in between. A brilliant essay, an original contribution. Includes b/w illustrations and bibliographic references.

COLONIAL PERIOD

319 Alvim, Sandra P. de Faria. Arquitetura religiosa colonial no Rio de Janeiro. v. 1, Revestimentos, retábulos e talha. Rio de Janeiro: Editora UFRJ; IPHAN; Prefeitura da Cidade do Rio de Janeiro, 1997. 1 v.: bibl., ill. (some col.). (Risco original)

Minute detailed study includes surface materials (marble, tiles, painting, etc.), typology of altars, typology of wood carvings. Almost 40 churches are analyzed globally. Extensive bibliography, many drawings, plans, and b/w photographs. Technical and esthetic glossary. A relevant addition to the study of religious architecture in colonial Rio de Janeiro. For review of vol. 2, see item **327**.

320 Amazónia Felsínea: António José Landi, itinerário artístico e científico de um arquitecto bolonhês na Amazónia do século XVIII. Textos de Anna Maria Matteucci *et al.* Lisboa: Comissão Nacional para as Comemorações dos Descobrimentos Portugueses, 1999. 299 p.: bibl., ill. (chiefly col.).

An architect from Bologna, Landi (1713–91) worked for the Portuguese recognition mission of the Amazon, for which he produced hundreds of natural history drawings and maps. He designed and built many late baroque-classical buildings in Belém do Pará, of which this book gives full account, while also recounting his accomplishments as a draftsman, engraver, altar designer, ceiling painter, decorative stucco designer and more. This book, one of the best ever published on Landi, covers his production both in Italy and Brazil. Bibliography, chronology, drawings, engravings, and photographs.

321 Azulejos na cultura luso-brasileira. Organização de Dora de Alcântara. Rio de Janeiro: Ministério da Cultura, Instituto do Patrimônio Histórico e Artístico Nacional, 1997? 110 p.: bibl., ill. (some col.). (Edições do Patrimônio)

The long tradition of tile-making from Babylon to the Muslim cultures found in Portugal one of its finest heirs. Most "azulejos" extant in Brazil came from Portugal, mainly in the 17th-18th centuries. The Brazilian production of the past 100 years is modest by comparison. The Museu do Açude possesses excellent collections of "azulejos." The text of the publication is made up of four rather "light" lectures on the subject. Adequate illustrations.

O Brasil e os holandeses, 1630–1654. See item **3149**.

322 Coelho, Gustavo Neiva. O espaço urbano edificado em Vila Boa. (*Estudos/Goiânia*, 28:1, jan./fev. 2001, p. 25–53, bibl., graphs, photos)

Vila Boa was the first capital of Goiás, built beginning in the 1730s by gold prospectors from Minas Gerais. For various reasons it is marked by formal and esthetic differences both in the civil and religious architecture. Article discusses the differences and the common Portuguese heritage of sites in Vila Boa. Bibliographic references.

González de Canales y López Obrero, Fernando. Iconografía española en la defensa hispana de Brasil, 1624–1640. See item **3173**.

323 Ott, Carlos. Atividade artística da Ordem 3a do Carmo da Cidade do Salvador e de Cachoeira, 1640–1900. Salvador, Brazil: Secretaria da Cultura e Turismo do Estado da Bahia, Fundação Cultural: EGBA, 1998. 249 p.: bibl., ill. (Col. Selo Editorial Letras da Bahia; 25)

The third order of the Carmelites was very active in religious architecture and related arts both in Salvador and Cachoeira, Bahia. Ott presents sources for the study of their creative endeavors and interprets them according to a more updated methodology. Bibliography and b/w photos.

324 Sant'Anna, Affonso Romano de. Barroco, alma do Brasil. Fotos de Pedro Oswaldo Cruz. Rio de Janeiro: Comunicação Máxima, 1997? 202 p.: col. ill.

The baroque is understood and described here not only as a period style (1600–1700), but also and, more importantly, as a state of mind that pervaded the history of Brazil from the 16th century to the present: from artistic manifestations to the behavior and identity of the Brazilian people. A personal approach with solid foundations, presents a conception of the baroque as a constant source of esthetic-ideological inspiration in Brazil. Stunning color photographs by Cruz. Chronology but no bibliography. Also available in English: *Baroque, the soul of Brazil* (1998).

325 **Silva, Geraldo Gomes da.** Engenho & arquitetura: tipologia dos edifícios dos antigos engenhos de açúcar de Pernambuco. Recife, Brazil: Editora Fundação Gilberto Freyre: Secretaria de Indústria, Comércio e Turismo, 1997. 135 p.: bibl., ill. (some col.).

Sugarcane plantations and sugar refineries are fundamental for understanding Pernambuco, from mid-16th century to the early 1900s. Dutch painters documented extensively the architecture and landscape of the *engenhos*, from 1630–54. Frans Post above all. Studies the typology of the four buildings that made up the engenhos: the factory, the shanty (slave quarters), the mansion (residence of the lords), and the chapel, all derived from northern Portuguese models. Richly illustrated.

326 **O universo mágico do barroco brasileiro.** Curadoria de Emanoel Araújo. Textos de Orlandino Seitas Fernandes *et al.* São Paulo: FIESP/CIESP/IRS; SESI; SENAI, 1998? 403 p.: bibl., col. maps, ill. (some col.).

The baroque was an explosion of movement, curved lines and ornamentation that sought to induce contemplation of God. But the baroque also celebrated worldly power. In Brazil, the baroque found fertile soil. The major show held at FIESP in São Paulo (1999), of which this book was the catalog, covered virtually all aspects of the baroque in Brazil. Twenty scholars contributed essays. Chronology, selected bibliography, and a wealth of color photographs make this a welcome reference and resource book.

19TH CENTURY

327 **Alvim, Sandra P. de Faria.** Arquitetura religiosa colonial no Rio de Janeiro. v. 2, Plantas, fachadas e volumenes. Rio de Janeiro: Editora UFRJ: IPHAN: Prefeitura da Cidade do Rio de Janeiro, 1999. 1 v.: bibl., ill., photos. (Risco original)

From the 1750s, when Rio de Janeiro became the capital of Brazil, to 1822, when Brazil became independent, Portuguese religious architecture was particularly significant in the city. Most of the churches and chapels survive, but until now a deeper study of their structures, typology, and religious and social meaning was missing. This book

fills the gap. Drawings, plans, and photographs followed by accurate analysis make it a major art historical event. For review of vol. 1, see item **319**.

328 **Diener, Pablo.** Rugendas: 1802–1858. Augsburg: Wissner, 1998. 385 p.: bibl., ill. (some col.).

Second edition of the bilingual, illustrated catalog of the 1998 exhibition presented at the Museo Nacional de Bellas Artes in Santiago de Chile and the Pinacoteca do Estado de São Paulo in Brazil. Diener's careful research about the work of the German artist who traveled through the New World in the 19th century, influenced by the ideas of Alexander von Humboldt, is his doctorate thesis presented at the Faculty of Philosophy of the Univ. of Zurich. Two-thirds of the book is dedicated to the catalog raisonné of the artist's works. This is undoubtedly the most complete document on Rugendas to date and a fundamental resource for those interested in his work and that of the 19th century artists traveling in the Americas in general. [F. Angel]

329 **Diener, Pablo** and **Maria de Fátima Costa.** Juan Mauricio Rugendas: pintor y dibujante. São Paulo: Estação Liberdade Goethe-Institut, 1998. 132 p.: bibl., ill. (some col.).

Spanish (smaller) version of the Diener-Acosta catalog of the exhibition on Rugendas for the presentation at the Museo Nacional de Bellas Artes de Chile, which included drawings from the Colección Guita y José Mindlin, São Paulo, and, for the first time, a group of Rugendas' large oils, besides biographical documents. [F. Angel]

Diener, Pablo and **Maria de Fátima Gomes Costa.** A América de Rugendas: obras e documentos. See item **1084**.

330 **Kühl, Beatriz Mugayar.** Arquitetura do ferro e arquitetura ferroviária em São Paulo: reflexões sobre a sua preservação. Cotia, Brazil: Ateliê Editorial; São Paulo: FAPESP; Governo do Estado de São Paulo, Secretaria de Estado da Cultura, 1998. 436 p.: bibl., ill., maps.

Eager to modernize in the 19th century according to European standards and technologies, Brazil imported the know-how and esthetic of exposed iron structures in industrial, commercial, civilian, private, and public architecture. While focusing on São Paulo railways, an overall picture of Brazil's iron architecture emerges in this work, along with discussions of inspiration found in France, England, Belgium, Italy, and the US. Also concerned with ironwork conservation. Richly illustrated, encompassing bibliography.

331 Lago, Pedro Corrêa do. Iconografia paulistana do século XIX. São Paulo: Metalivros, 1998. 184 p.: bibl., ill. (some col.), col. maps.

A large number of Brazilian and foreign artists produced drawings, watercolors, prints, photographs, and paintings showing the many aspects of life, architecture, and landscape in São Paulo prov. and in the city of São Paulo. Now some of the finest examples are assembled here in book form. Biographical information and extensive captions accompanying color and b/w illustrations make this a welcome addition to Brasiliana.

332 Lopes, Almerinda da Silva. Arte no Espírito Santo do século XIX à Primeira República. Vitória, Brazil: s.n., 1997? 240 p.: bibl., ill. (some col.).

Offers an overview of the arts in the state of Espírito Santo in the 19th century. More than artistic considerations, mainly emphasizes the circumstances and local chronicles about the production of architecture and paintings. Biographies and bibliography round out this effort.

333 Migliaccio, Luciano. Great expectations: Brazilian XIXth century art and the pursuit of a national identity. (*Ciênc. Cult.*, 51:5/6, Sept./Dec. 1999, p. 477–484, bibl.)

Brief history of development of fine arts in 19th-century Brazil. Whereas in the 18th century the Church had been the chief supporter of art, under the Empire the state and private collectors held increasingly important roles. A struggle early in 19th century between traditional art and a new "French" school gave way after 1850 to a surge of Brazilian nativism and an emphasis on the creation of a new nation out of the merging of cultures. [D. McCreery]

334 Wagner, Robert and Júlio Bandeira. Viagem ao Brasil nas aquarelas de Thomas Ender: 1817–1818. v. 1–3. Petrópolis, Brazil: Kapa Editorial, 2000. 3 v. (983 p.): bibl., col. ill., index.

Austrian artist Ender arrived in Rio de Janeiro in Nov. 1817 with Archduchess Leopoldina, and remained for one year, during which time he produced many drawings and watercolors of daily life and the streets, cities, towns, country, landscapes, flora and fauna of Brazil. One of the earliest, largest, and most relevant collections of its kind in the 19th century. These three volumes present, in excellent reproductions, a representative selection of his output.

20TH CENTURY

Abramo, Lívio. Arte y artistas de Brasil y Paraguay. See item **281**.

Abramo, Lívio. Livio Abramo: 133 obras restauradas. See item **53**.

335 Albano, Ana Angélica. Tuneu, Tarsila e outros mestres—: o aprendizado da arte como um rito da iniciação. São Paulo: Plexus, 1998. 189 p.: bibl., ill. (some col.).

The relationship between artists through art works is commonplace in art history, but the initiation process goes far beyond professional relationships. Talented, younger artists learn lessons from the older one(s) and absorb a mature artist's ability to encourage the creative processes of his apprentice. Esthetic and ethical questions mature together. Albano smoothly shows how this process worked between Tuneu and Wesley, Willys and Barsotti, and finally between Tuneu and his disciple Sueli Bonfim. Profusely illustrated with a bibliography and notes.

336 Amaral, Antonio Henrique. Antonio Henrique Amaral: obra em processo. Textos de Edward J. Sullivan, Frederico Morais e Maria Alice Milliet. São Paulo: DBA, 1997. 323 p.: bibl., ill. (some col.), index.

Today Amaral is one of the most prominent living Brazilian painters. Stemming from the painting tradition of Tarsila do Amaral, who having studied with Fernand Léger, searched for an idiomatic Brazilian way of painting, Antonio Amaral blends the pulsating yet disciplined approach with avant-garde and political features. The three excellent introductory texts in this work focus on those different aspects. Plush edition. Amaral is now a relevant name in the international art scene.

337 Arte construtiva no Brasil: coleção Adolpho Leirner = Constructive art in Brazil: Adolpho Leirner collection. Coordenação editorial de Aracy Amaral. São Paulo: Dórea Books and Art: Cia. Melhoramentos de São Paulo, 1998. 363 p.: bibl., ill. (some col.), index.

Constructivism is a relevant segment in Brazilian contemporary art, and this collection may well be the best and most encompassing of its kind. Textile engineer turned art collector Leirner started collecting the art of abstract geometric movements in Brazil of the 1950s when they were outmoded and depreciated on the market in the 1960s. This book became the standard work in the field, and gathers thorough essays by a number of scholars coordinated by Amaral. Chronology (1945–64), biographies, and bibliography round out the book, luxurious otherwise, rich in color illustrations, b/w photographs, and documentation.

338 Bardi, Pietro Maria. Lasar Segall. Reed. São Paulo: Instituto Lina Bo e P.M. Bardi: Imprensa Oficial SP, 2000. 211 p., 3 folded leaves: bibl., ill. (chiefly col.), index.

The first edition of this book was published in 1952. This second edition preserves the original design and essay, with the addition of some documents and texts. Segall (b. Vilna, Lithuania 1891—d. São Paulo, 1957), trained by German expressionists in Dresden, introduced expressionism to Brazil as early as 1913, and became one of the major names in the arts of Brazil. His great themes are drawn from WWI and II, pogroms, portraits, and prostitution life in Rio. Chronology, documentation, photographs, many illustrations, and a bibliography. Edition commemorates the centennial of P.M. Bardi.

339 Belluzzo, Ana Maria de Moraes. Carmela Gross. São Paulo: Cosac & Naify, 2000. 150 p.: bibl., ill. (chiefly col.).

One of the names in evidence in the past 30 years of avant-garde in São Paulo, this monograph includes a selection of works in several media produced by Carmela Gross since the mid-1960s. It captures the poetics of the artist, having the works themselves and their phenomenology as the raw material for speculation. Belluzzo elaborates on Gross' response to the contradictions of art in our times. Chronology, bibliography, and many illustrations.

340 Bracher, Elisa. Madeira sobre madeira. Esculturas de Elisa Bracher. Texto de Rodrigo Naves. Fotografias de João Musa = Wood on wood. Sculptures by Elisa Bracher. Text by Rodrigo Naves. Photographs by João Musa. São Paulo: Cosac & Naify Edições, 1998. 113 p.: ill. (some col.).

Rodrigo Naves introduces Bracher's sculptures, affirming that he is somewhat concerned about how they will be received since contemporary taste is positively adverse to form due to the growing antipathy for "classical" modern art. He adds, however, that he finds the work assertive, powerful, and brawny. Illustrated with color photographs by João Musa. [F. Angel]

341 Brazilian sculpture: an identity in profile = Escultura brasileira: perfil de uma identidade. Idealization and coordination by Elcior Ferreira de Santana Filho. Curation by Emanoel Araujo. Associate curation by Sérgio Pizoli. Texts by Mario de Andrade et al. São Paulo: Associação dos Amigos da Pinateca, 1997. 207 p.: bibl., ill. (some col.).

The exhibition at the Inter-American Development Bank (Washington, 1997) aimed to provide an overview of 20th-century Brazilian sculpture. However incomplete, the assembled examples testified to the quality and variety of Brazilian sculpture. This catalog is a good source of information. Biographies, portraits of the artists, reproductions of the best pieces, and critical texts in Portuguese and English.

342 Cabral, Isabella and M.A. Amaral Rezende. Hermelindo Fiaminghi. São Paulo: Edusp; Imprensa Oficial, 1998. 189 p.: bibl., ill. (some col.). (Artistas brasileiros. Pintura)

One of the masters of Brazilian constructivist painting, Fiaminghi grew up in São Paulo after WWI, became a commercial designer, printer, and printmaker, and evolved into a painter. Mostly a loner with strong ties to constructivism, he had an impact on *concretismo* as it developed in São Paulo in the 1950s. This book is the first full-length portrait of the artist, from his early days among the concretists after having been a representational painter, to his later geometrical and mathematical rituality that integrates Russian supremacists' optical art and Dutch neoplasticism. A consistent researcher of color and light, he created the term *corluz*. Cabral and Rezende combine the artistic biography with theory and many illustrations. Chronology and bibliography included.

343 Canton, Katia. Novíssima arte brasileira: um guia de tendências. São Paulo: Iluminuras, 2001. 198 p.: bibl., ill. (some col.).

An effort to define Brazilian art in the 1990s gathers materials of several exhibitions held at and curated for the Museum of Contemporary Art of the Univ. of São Paulo by Canton. Some 70 artists are discussed according to their expressed and historical orientations. Contemporary heritages were the leitmotif of all these exhibits. Chronology and bibliography. Many b/w and color illustrations and a variety of statements.

344 Carvalho, Flávio de Rezende. Flávio de Carvalho: 100 anos de um revolucionário romântico. Curadoria de Denise Mattar. Realização do Centro Cultural Banco do Brasil e Fundação Armando Alvares Penteado. Rio de Janeiro: Centro Cultural Banco do Brasil; São Paulo: Museu de Arte Brasileira da FAAP, 1999. 127 p.: bibl., ill. (some col.).

The extraordinary personality of Flávio de Carvalho made him a conspicuous, stimulating presence in the modern art scene of Brazil. Born in 1899 in the state of Rio, he studied in France and England (civic engineering) and joined the modernists in São Paulo in 1922. Throughout his long and productive life he created works, statements, and performances of shocking value as a painter, sculptor, architect, choreographer, fashion designer, draftsman, printmaker, and performer. A renaissance man, his prolific output contained personal interpretations of expressionism, cubism, dada, and futurism. This publication celebrated the centennial of his birth with a much encompassing exhibi-

tion. Includes documentation, bibliography, photographs, sources, and texts.

345 Chamie, Emilie. Rigor e paixão: poética visual de uma arte gráfica. São Paulo: Editora SENAC São Paulo, 1998. 1 v. (unpaged): bibl., ill. (some col.).

One of the most inventive members of her generation, for 50 years Chamie has actively introduced and modernized the creative processes of visual communication, which she practices with consummate artistry. The book brings sufficient critical and visual materials to make it clear why she became nationally and internationally recognized. Her output encompasses marks, book covers and layouts, posters, photographs, performing arts design, and more. Chronological and biographical notes. Select bibliography.

346 Chiarelli, Tadeu. Arte internacional brasileira. São Paulo: Lemos Editorial, 1999. 311 p.: bibl., ill. (some col.), index.

Chiarelli is among the most active and creative art critics in Brazil today, in addition to producing stimulating theoretical texts. This book gathers essays on the art history of Brazil, as well as essays on a great variety of Brazilian 20th-century artists. A panoramic view provides an implicit evaluation. One of the essays elaborates on the development of Brazilian national art into a Brazilian international art, attune with the esthetic syntax of art at large today, inserting Brazil in its context. Many reproductions.

347 Chiarelli, Tadeu. Leda Catunda. Contribuições de Lisette Lagnado e Paulo Herkenhoff. Versão para o inglês e revisão de John Norman. São Paulo: Cosac & Naify Edições, 1998. 189 p.: bibl., ill. (chiefly col.).

Text aims at an understanding of Catunda's plastic language, developed in less than 20 years, from 1980s-90s. Essays by Chiarelli, Lagnado, and Herkenhoff highlight Catunda's creativity process and its inherent interaction. "Her earlier works had blotted out the printed images, now her actions highlighted them." The paintbrush and the eye dropper. Pregnant forms. A relevant statement in the contemporary arts of Brazil. Includes a chronology, a bibliography, and excellent reproductions.

348 Clark, Lygia. Lygia Clark: Fundació Antoni Tàpies, Barcelona, 21 octobre-21 décembre 1997; MAC, galeries contemporaines des Musées de Marseille, 16 janvier-12 avril 1998; Fundação de Serralves, Porto, 30 avril-28 juin 1998; Société des Expositions du Palais des Beaux-Arts, Bruxelles, 24 juillet-27 septembre 1998; Paço Imperial, Rio de Janeiro, 8 décembre 1998-28 février 1999. Barcelona: Fundació Antoni Tàpies, 1998. 362 p.: bibl., ill. (some col.).

Written and printed to accompany a major exhibition of a significant avant-garde Brazilian artist, this book-catalog gathers sharp essays by Paulo Herkenhoff, Ferreira Gullar, Guy Brett, and Suely Rolnik. The Lygia Clark (1920–88) show was held in Barcelona, Marseille, Porto, Brussels, and Rio. Texts in Portuguese and French, biography, chronology, bibliography.

349 DaSilva, Orlando. Guido Viaro: alma e corpo do desenho. Curitiba, Brazil: Governo do Paraná, Secretaria de Estado da Cultura, 1997. 290 p.: ill. (some col.).

Bilingual and mostly b/w illustrated book dedicated to the life and work of the centenary of Italian-born artist who moved to Curitiba (State of Paraná) in 1929 and lived there for the rest of his life. A revered local figure, Viaro became a symbol for the arts in Paraná, opened and taught at the first Brazilian art school for children, among other things. Fellow printmaker Orlando DaSilva gives the reader a glimpse of the artist. [F. Angel]

350 De Fiori, Ernesto. Ernesto de Fiori, uma retrospectiva: pintura, desenho e escultura. Curadoria de Mayra Laudanna. Textos de Leon Kossovitch, Mayra Laudanna, and Wolfgang Pfeiffer. São Paulo: Pinacoteca Edições, 1997. 240 p.: bibl., ill. (some col.).

Born in Italy in 1884, De Fiori lived in London, Paris, and Munich, before settling in Brazil in 1936. By then he was an established international name, primarily as a sculptor but also as a painter. He contributed largely to the art scene in Brazil, both as a naturalist and as an expressionist. He died in São Paulo in 1945. This retrospective focused mainly on his production in Brazil. Well-documented catalog, with three excellent essays and many b/w and color reproductions.

351 Didier, Maria Thereza. Emblemas da sagração armorial: Ariano Suassuna e o Movimento Armorial, 1970–76. Recife, Brazil: Editora Universitária UFPE, 2000? 215 p.: bibl.

In Recife in the 1970s, a group of artists and intellectuals discussed Brazilian culture and national identity, under the orientation of novelist and poet Ariano Suassuna, founder and organizer of the Armorial Movement. The idea was to develop a Brazilian art based on its folk roots. Armorial estetics focused on the medieval Iberian influences found in the popular artistic universe of Brazil's Northeast. That movement encompassed virtually all the arts, and this book discusses all that in context, from the surface to the underground. Ideology and politics were important coordinates. Sources and bibliography. Stresses relationship between symbol and reality.

352 Duarte, Paulo Sérgio. Anos 60: transformações da arte no Brasil. Rio de Janeiro: Campos Gerais, 1998. 321 p.: bibl., ill. (some col.).

The 1960s witnessed many changes in Brazil, reflecting the changes in the rest of the world. The arts must be acknowledged as making among the strongest statements of that decade, reflecting urban imperatives, the postconstructivist experimentations, the new representation of art, and a diversity of new paths, including responses to pop art, the years of concrete and neoconcrete art, and ostensible political art. This publication discusses the main manifestations of the period and brings many excellent reproductions. Photographic documentation, biographies, bibliography. A plush, sophisticated edition.

353 Frota, Lélia Coelho. Guignard: arte, vida. Rio de Janeiro: Campos Gerais, 1997. 329 p.: bibl., ill. (some col.).

Guignard is among the most significant 20th-century Brazilian painters, and this book does him justice. Frota's exhaustive biography and critical analysis of Guignard's work may well be the most complete and insightful to date. As background, presents an overview of life in Brazil and its implications in art and the artistic community from the 1930s-60s. A wealth of sources, bibliography, b/w photographs and color reproductions. The book itself is a luxurious edition.

354 Fukushima, Takashi. Tikashi Fukushima. São Paulo: Sociedade Brasileira de Cultura Japonesa: Imprensa Oficial SP, 2001. 223, 31 p.: bibl., ill. (some col.).

Born in Japan, Tikashi Fukushima began as a representational painter, then became a major abstract painter in Brazil from the mid-1950s to the present. Introductory texts, chronology, bibliography, and over 200 illustrations. In Portuguese, English, and Japanese.

355 Gravura: arte brasileira do século XX. São Paulo: Itaú Cultural: Cosac & Naify, 2000. 270 p.: bibl., ill. (some col.), index.

Printmaking only became a legitimate art expression in Brazil in the early part of the 20th century with Carlos Oswald. He was followed by Oswaldo Goeldi, Livio Abramo, and Axl Laskoschek and from the 1940s on, generations of creative printmakers emerged, working in many esthetic directions. This plush edition covers the production of the past 90 years with competent essays and excellent reproductions both in color and b/w. Name index and bibliography. Chapters are organized by subjects, themes, and media.

356 Guignard, Alberto da Veiga. O humanismo lírico de Guignard: 5 de abril a 28 de maio de 2000, Museu Nacional de Belas Artes. Texto de Frederico Morais. Rio de Janeiro: Museu Nacional de Belas Artes, 2000. 287 p.: ill. (some col.).

With over 100 works, this was the largest exhibition of Guignard to date and its catalog is a landmark. The title of the exhibition pinpoints the profile of the artist as a lyric humanist. Beloved by all Brazilians, Guignard is also a benchmark to many artists of several generations. Excellent text and color reproductions. Pertinent captions in both Portuguese and English for all exhibited works. Chronology but no bibliography.

357 Hansen, João Adolfo. Carlos Bracher. São Paulo: Edusp; Imprensa Oficial, 1997. 224 p.: bibl., ill. (some col.). (Artistas brasileiros. Pintura)

Gestural brushwork, bold colors, and an expressionistic vein made Bracher well known in Brazil and abroad. With many reproductions, Hansen offers an exhausting analysis of Bracher's creative process. Focuses on cityscapes of colonial Minas Gerais, Paris, and Rio de Janeiro, still-life architecture, landscapes and portraits.

358 Horta, Arnaldo Pedroso d'. O olho da consciência: juízos críticos e obras desajuizadas: escritos sobre arte. Organização de Vera d'Horta. São Paulo: Imprensa Oficial SP: Edusp: Secretaria de Estado da Cultura, 2000. 406 p.: ill. (some col.), index.

After having been a militant communist, Horta became a democratic socialist, while also developing as an artist and a journalist. His paintings, drawings, and prints are imaginative and austere, both representational and abstract. Self taught, he also remained independent throughout his life (1914–74). His writings on art now have been collected and published by his daughter; they show a different, though no less fascinating, aspect of his personality as he was, in equal proportions, an artist and an intellectual. His writings from newspapers, magazines, and diaries criticize the commercialization of art and the decadence—in his opinion—of the São Paulo Biennial. Art and politics is his favorite subject. Includes many photographs and reproductions of original art works.

359 Katz, Renina. Renina Katz. São Paulo: Edusp, 1997. 274 p.: bibl., col. ill. (Artistas da USP; 6)

Katz is one of the outstanding Brazilian printmakers and a major name in contemporary Brazilian art. Active since the 1940s, first in Rio then in São Paulo, she produces mainly woodcuts, lithographs, drawings, and watercolors. Her itinerary goes from expressionistic b/w woodblock prints to abstraction in space, experimenting with color and transparencies primarily in lithographs in the past 30 years. Includes a biographical-artistic essay by Leonor Amarante, supplemented with theoretical notes, critical excerpts, CV, bibliography, and many color illustrations.

360 Luz, Angela Ancora da. Anna Letycia. São Paulo: Edusp; Imprensa Oficial SP, 1998. 166 p.: bibl., ill. (some col.). (Artistas brasileiros. Artes plásticas)

Anna Letycia is a major presence in Brazil's modern printmaking both as an artist and as a teacher. She also contributed to Brazil's international reputation in the field. This detailed study shows how her life and art are deeply intertwined. Includes a chronology, a bibliography, and excellent reproductions.

361 **Mattos, Cláudia Valladão de.** Lasar Segall. São Paulo: EDUSP, 1997. 192 p.: bibl., ill. (some col.). (Artistas brasileiros. Pintura e escultura)

Segall introduced German expressionism to Brazil and remained one of its proponents on both sides of the Atlantic. This particular monograph emphasizes the links between late romanticism and expressionistic avant-garde. Segall's impact on Brazilian art was seminal and this study does it justice. Richly illustrated with reproductions of drawings, watercolors, paintings and sculptures. Extensive bibliography.

362 **Morais, Frederico.** Gonçalo Ivo. Rio de Janeiro: Salamandra, 1997. 120 p.: chiefly ill. (some col.).

Ivo's painting confirms the great vitality of contemporary Brazilian art. Starting in the early 1980s, his canvasses are often passionate and intense. A prolific artist whose forte is color, he also creates watercolors, objects, and miniatures. He is comfortable with representational modes as well as with abstraction. Morais explores how life and art intertwine in Ivo's output. Chronology. No bibliography. Text in Portuguese and English.

363 **Mostra Rio Gravura, *Rio de Janeiro, 1999*.** Catálogo geral dos eventos. Rio de Janeiro: A Secretaria Municipal de Cultura, 1999. 227 p.: bibl., ill. (chiefly col.).

The exhibition—and its catalog—included masters of European printmakers of the past and Brazilian printmakers of the 20th century up to the latest avant-garde and also scientific engraving. Brief introductions to artists, movements, and themes. Various essays, photographs, reproductions, bibliography. See also item **364**.

364 **Mostra Rio Gravura, *Rio de Janeiro, 1999*.** Gravura moderna brasileira: Acervo Museu Nacional de Belas Artes: 15 de setembro a 12 de outubro de 1999. Rio de Janeiro: Prefeitura do Rio, Secretaria Municipal de Cultura, 1999. 134 p.: ill. (some col.).

Catalog of an exhibition of some of the finest examples in the collection of the Museu Nacional de Belas Artes in Rio. Includes over 100 prints by a virtual who's who of Brazilian 20th-century print-making. Each artist is introduced by a short biography. No bibliography. B/w and color reproductions. See also item **363**.

365 **Parreiras, Antônio.** História de um pintor, contada por ele mesmo: Brasil-França, 1881–1936. Organização do plano geral e preparação do texto crítico sob a orientação e direção de Maximiano de Carvalho e Silva. Com a colaboração de Maria Teresa Kopschitz de Barros. 3a. ed. Niterói, Brazil: Niterói Livros, 1999. 335 p.: ill., index.

Parreiras (1860–1937) was one of the most accomplished Brazilian painters of landscapes and genre, and one of the very few to have written his autobiography. Self-conscious and critical, he provides an account—often caustic—of art, politics, and society in Brazil and Paris, from the 1880s-1930s. He ignored and remained untouched by modernism. Critical text, contemporary reviews. No bibliography. Poor reproductions.

366 **Pellegrini, Aldo** *et al.* Surrealismo e novo mundo. Organização de Robert Ponge com a colaboração de Nara H.N. Machado. Porto Alegre, Brazil: Editora da Univ., Univ. Federal do Rio Grande do Sul, 1999. 334 p.: bibl., ill. (some col.).

Of special interest are the essays by Valentim Facioli, Sergio Lima, and Benjamin Péret on surrealism in Brazil. Notes on the authors, iconographical sources. Bibliographical references, photographs, documents, illustrations.

367 **Rennó, Rosângela.** Rosângela Rennó. São Paulo: Edusp; Imprensa Oficial SP, 1997. 197 p.: bibl., ill. (some col.). (Artistas da USP; 9)

Rennó's raw material is small, anonymous i.d. photographs, mostly of deceased persons. She uses large numbers of these portraits of the unknown, side-by-side, to conjure up the affective memory of our culture; the more images we devour, the more images we forget. Her creative work offers a critique of the relationship between the image and the spectator's shock, between memory and amnesia. Philosophical insights into the symbolic value of photographic language. Includes eye-opening essay on her work by P. Herkenhoff, the artist's biography, and reproductions.

368 **Ribeiro, Marília Andrés.** Neovanguardas: Belo Horizonte, anos 60. Belo Horizonte, Brazil: Editora C/Arte, 1997.

304 p., 24 p. of plates: bibl., ill. (some col.). (História & arte)

In the decade following Guignard's impact on the arts in Minas Gerais, the new avant-garde developed in Belo Horizonte. Its rise marked the waning of many Mineiran traditions. Ribeiro describes the specific movements in Belo Horizonte, after introducing international movements and their impact on Brazil, and, ultimately on Belo Horizonte in the 1960s. Discusses all major trends. Reference sources encompass bibliography, catalogs, newspapers, magazines, and unpublished materials.

369 **Rocha, Glauber** *et al.* Calasans Neto: gravuras. Salvador, Brazil: Governo da Bahia, Secretaria da Cultura e Turismo; Secretaria da Fazenda; Fundação Casa de Jorge Amado, 1998. 119 p.: bibl., ill. (Casa de palavras. Série Desenho)

Anthology of selected texts and poems by various authors, including Vinicius de Moraes and Carlos Drummond de Andrade, and images of Neto's engravings—mostly woodcuts, in the tradition of Brazil's northeastern region. Includes record of exhibitions, illustrated books, and commissions. [F. Angel]

370 **Scaldaferri, Sante.** Os primórdios da arte moderna na Bahia: depoimentos, textos e considerações em torno de José Tertuliano Guimarães e outros artistas. Salvador, Brazil: Fundação Cultural do Estado da Bahia: Governo da Bahia, Secretaria da Cultura e Turismo: Fundação Casa de Jorge Amado, 1998. 180 p.: bibl., ill. (some col.). (Col. Casa de palavras. Série Memória; no. 2)

Book's main topics include academic background, the first manifestations of modern art, *Selva* magazine, the First Group Show of 1944 and the Ultramodern Show, the Second Group Show of 1948 and the Counterexhibition. Provides sources, interviews, and bibliography, as well as many photographs. Reproductions in b/w and some in color.

371 **Um século de história das artes plásticas em Belo Horizonte.** Organização de Marília Andrés Ribeiro e Fernando Pedro da Silva. Belo Horizonte, Brazil: Editora C/Arte; Sistema Estadual de Planejamento, Fundação João Pinheiro, Centro de Estudos

Históricos e Culturais, 1997. 493 p.: bibl., ill. (some col.). (Col. Centenário)

Broad overview of the arts in the past 100 years in the capital of Minas Gerais. Chapters by different scholars cover: artistas populares; Belo Horizonte: arraial e metrópole; emergência do modernismo; Guignard; as gerações pós-Guignard; formação da arte contemporânea; Prospecções: arte nos anos 80. Biographic notes. Profusely illustrated. Elegant edition. Excellent historic and critical texts.

372 **Senise, Daniel.** Daniel Senise. Buenos Aires: Diana Lowenstein Ediciones, 1999. 32 p.: bibl., ill. (some col.). (Col. cuadernos de arte; 54)

Slim biographical and critical profile illustrated with works from 1998–99. One of a series produced by the Argentine commercial gallery. [F. Angel]

373 **Senise, Daniel.** Daniel Senise: ela que não está. Textos de Ivo Mesquita, Dawn Ades, e Gabriel Pérez-Barreiro. São Paulo: Cosac & Naify Edições, 1998. 219 p.: bibl., ill. (some col.).

Color-illustrated 1998 bilingual monograph reproducing a 1994 revised essay by Ivo Mesquita, and two others by Dawn Ades and Gabriel Pérez Barreiro, the latter the most insightful. Includes chronological and biographical profile. [F. Angel]

374 **Sued, Eduardo.** Eduardo Sued: pinturas 1980–1998. Curadoria de Paulo Sergio Duarte. Rio de Janeiro: Centro de Arte Hélio Oiticica, 1998. 96 p.: bibl., ill. (some col.).

A painter of refined geometries and *chromaticism,* Sued occupies a special niche in contemporary Brazilian painting. This catalog offers a glimpse into his mature output, from 1980–98. Two sharp interpretive texts, a good number of color illustrations. In Portuguese and English.

375 **Tarsila.** Tarsila do Amaral: Proyecto Cultural Artistas del Mercosur. Textos de Aracy Amaral. Buenos Aires: Banco Velox, 1998. 225 p.: bibl., ill. (some col.).

Aimed at the Spanish-speaking audiences of Mercosur countries, offers an introduction to the art of Tarsila, her relationship to the avant-garde movements of *Pan Brasil* and *Antropofagia,* her seminal place in 20th-century Brazilian art. Other than photographs, newspaper clippings, memorabilia, and letters, this book also presents almost 50 excellent color reproductions of Tarsila's best paintings, both the well known and unknown. Chronology.

376 Tridimensionalidade na arte brasileira do século XX. Artigos de Annateresa Fabris *et al.* São Paulo: Instituto Itaú Cultural, 1997? 222, 14 p.: bibl., ill. (some col.).

Not all three-dimensional art work being created in recent decades can be classified as "sculpture," as there are other modes of inscribing forms and gestures in space. Here a number of critics and art historians contribute to the better understanding of diversity in Brazil writing about "recontaktalizando a escultura modernista; abstracionismo, concretismo, neoconcretismo e tendências construtivas; das novas figurações às arte conceitual; o tridimensional na arte brasileira dos anos 80 e 90. Book covers relevant segments of Brazilian contemporary art. Biographies, bibliographies, many and excellent reproductions. In Portuguese only.

377 Vlavianos, Nicolas. Vlavianos: a práxis da escultura = The praxis of sculpture. Textos de Walter Zanini and Olívio Tavares de Araújo. Contribuições de Efi Ferentinou *et al.* São Paulo: Editora Globo, 2001. 263 p.: bibl., ill. (some col.).

Combining the esoteric and the primitive, in the past 40 years Vlavianos has become one of the most expressive sculptors in Brazil. Born in Athens in 1929, he lived in Paris in the 1950s where he was strongly influenced by the expressionistic surrealism of Henry Moore, Zadkine and Laszlo Szabo: working with welded iron, stainless steel, brass, bronze, aluminum, and wood, he settled in São Paulo in the 1960s. His sculpture became monumental. This book includes 10 essays on his 50 years of output. Chronology, artist's bio, bibliography, and many excellent illustrations.

378 Volpi, Alfredo. Volpi. Ensaio, coordenação de pesquisa e edição de texto de Sônia Salzstein. Projeto e coordenação geral de Sílvia Roesler. Rio de Janeiro: Campos Gerais, 2000. 323 p.: bibl., ill. (some col.).

Volpi (1896–1988) matured during the era of the representational painting of the "Paulista Artistic Family" in the 1930s-40s, but his entrance into contemporary Brazilian art was a spontaneous occurrence. Though the *concretists* claimed him as one their

own, Volpi always maintained his independence and evolved into one of the most original painters Brazil ever produced. Salzstein covers the artist's journey with sharp insights and a strong critical grasp of his work. Chronology, select bibliography, documentation, and a large and representative selection of color reproductions make this a welcome contribution.

379 Weissmann, Franz. Franz Weissmann: uma retrospectiva. Edição de Martha Spolaor *et al.* Rio de Janeiro: Centro Cultural Banco do Brasil; Museu de Arte Moderna do Rio de Janeiro; São Paulo: MAM, 1998. 260 p.: bibl., ill. (some col.).

Celebrated Austrian-born Brazilian sculptor Weissmann believes that art only exists in the encounter of the individual and the collective in the reality of space, of which the work is the measure. Essays cover the constriction of space, the epic of form, transitive situations, and the poetics of the cube. The highpoints of his work are his monumental geometric-abstract pieces in steel and painted steel. Biography, chronology, bibliography, b/w and color photographs. Texts in Portuguese and English.

380 Zanini, Walter. Vicente do Rego Monteiro: artista e poeta. São Paulo: Empresa das Artes: Marigo Editora, 1997? 437 p.: bibl., ill. (some col.), index.

Sculptor, painter, draftsman, printmaker, illustrator, poet, producer, educator, Monteiro lived between Recife and Paris, and was Brazil's legitimate representative to the School of Paris, of which he was a brilliant member. A pioneer of modern art in Brazil, he also fought consistently for the precedence of national and indigenous themes as sources for the establishment of a Brazilian expression of the visual arts. Zanini does him justice in authoring the most complete, authoritative monograph on the artist to date. A wealth of materials is gathered here: a detailed chronology, biography, and bibliography, including all possible sources. Richly illustrated with reproductions and photographs.

FOLK ART

381 Ardies, Jacques. A arte naïf no Brasil. Textos de Geraldo Edson de Andrade *et al.* São Paulo: Empresa das Artes, 1998. 245 p.: bibl., ill. (some col.).

Since the 1950s Brazil gradually became known abroad as a country with a huge variety of naive artists working in several media. The ones who made an international name for themselves were mainly painters. This book presents almost 80 self-taught painters, their styles, their biographies, and curricula. Nearly 200 high-quality color plates. Bibliography. List of collectors.

382   Arte popular de Alagoas. Pesquisa e organização de Tânia de Maya Pedrosa. Maceió, Brazil: Grafitex, 2000. 218 p.: bibl., ill. (some col.).

Of special interest to this section on folk art is the chapter on the visual arts and most of its manifestations. Presents a variety of articles and essays on the folk arts. Includes illustrations.

383   D'Ambrosio, Oscar. Os pincéis de Deus: vida e obra do pintor naïf Waldomiro de Deus. São Paulo: Editora UNESP: Imprensa Oficial, 1999. 191 p.: bibl., ill. (some col.). (Coleção Studium)

Deus has been painting in São Paulo for almost 40 years, and developed into one of Brazil's outstanding naïf painters. One of his main subjects is the religiosity of the lower classes of Brazilian society. In his canvasses humans live everyday with God, the devil, saints, spirits, and nature. Simplicity and sophistication walk hand-in-hand. Human rights is his other favorite subject. D'Ambrosio gives a full account of Waldomiro's life and work, with a chronology. Bibliography and a good many illustrations.

PHOTOGRAPHY

384   Ensaios (sobre o) fotográfico. Organização de Luiz Eduardo R. Achutti. Porto Alegre, Brazil: Unidade Editorial Porto Alegre, 1998. 126 p.: bibl., ill. (Série Escrita fotográfica)

This collection of 18 original essays covers much of the history of photography in Rio Grande do Sul from the early 1850s—when the first Italian photographers started working there—to the present day, from various perspectives: the pioneers, the modernists, photojournalism, etc. Some theoretical and speculative essays are also included. New technologies and the languages of the new image photography and the real photography and social sciences and humanities,

the photographic glance, etc. Illustration in b/w. Bibliography.

385   O fotográfico. Organização de Etienne Samain. Textos de Jan Baetens *et al.* São Paulo: Editora Hucitec; Brasília, Brazil: CNPq, 1998. 357 p.: bibl., ill. (some col.), maps. (Linguagem e cultura; 29)

A sizable variety of essays on the many aspects of photography selected, organized, and presented by Samain covers topics like image and memory, reconstitution through photography, photography in Brazil and Argentina in the past 150 years, photography and culture, anthropology, ethnography, art, education and theory, and more. Original contributions by creative authors. Open perspectives bring together European and Brazilian historical, esthetical, and philosophical texts. Samain is a Belgian theologian and anthropologist who has been living, working, and teaching in Brazil since 1973, with deep ties to photography.

Levine, Robert M. The Brazilian photographs of Genevieve Naylor, 1940–1943. See item **3291.**

386   Mello, Maria Teresa Bandeira de. Arte e fotografia: o movimento pictorialista no Brasil. Rio de Janeiro: FUNARTE, 1998. 213 p.: bibl., ill., index. (Coleção Luz & reflexão; 7)

In premodernistic Brazil photopictorialism played a role in establishing an esthetic in which photography and art became deeply enmeshed. Artist-photographers decided against objective representation, instead using painterly techniques to explore photography as an art form. Mello researches this little-known chapter of art in Brazil and its relationship to work in the Europe and the US. Includes various indexes, sources, and bibliography.

387   Pará, Brazil (state). Secretaria de Estado da Cultura. Fotografia contemporânea paraense: panorama 80/90. Belém, Brazil: SECULT, 2002. 300 p.: bibl., ill.

With essays by P.C. Fernandes, Rosangela Britto, Mariano Klautan Filho, Rubens Fernandes Junior, Rosely Nakagawa, Patrick Pardini, and Gratuliano Bibas, book introduces almost 40 active photographers in Pará, of at least three generations, of various artistic tendencies. Pará chronology, national chronology, biographies, English summaries, and bibliography. A deluxe edition. A photography book of the highest standards.

CITY PLANNING, ARCHITECTURE, AND LANDSCAPE ARCHITECTURE

388 Arquitetura da modernidade. Organização de Leonardo Barci Castriota. Belo Horizonte, Brazil: Editora UFMG: Instituto de Arquitetos do Brasil-Depto. MG, 1998. 309 p.: bibl., ill. (some col.), maps (some col.).

A publication celebrating Belo Horizonte's centenary and the approximately 6,000 architects who live and work in the city today. To put their creativity in perspective, Castriota organized an anthology of essays by architecture historians, bringing to life the complex background of the city's architecture since its beginnings. The result is a survey of plans, drawings, and photographs. Perhaps the most complete extant work on the topic.

389 Arte e paisagem: a estética de Roberto Burle Marx. Organização de Lisbeth Rebollo Gonçalves. São Paulo: USP/MAC, 1997. 210 p.: ill. (some col.).

Made to accompany a posthumous retrospective of Burle Marx's (1909–94) work, this publication has essays by Lélia Coelho Frota, Giulio G. Rizzo, and Burle Marx himself. Considered the most important landscape architect of Brazil, he was also one of the finest on the international scene. His many projects in Brazil and abroad show how his purely plastic reflection intertwines with the unique usage of tropical and subtropical plants and flowers in his landscaping. He was one of the most creative artists of the second generation of modernists in Brazil. Texts in Portuguese and English, chronology, bibliography, b/w photographs and some in color.

390 Arte pública: trabalhos apresentados nos Seminários de Arte Pública. Realizados pelo SESC e pelo USIS, de 17 a 19 de outubro de 1995 e de 19 a 21 de novembro de 1996, este último com a participação da União Cultural Brasil-Estados Unidos. São Paulo: SESC São Paulo, 1998. 319 p.

City planners, architects, landscape architects, artists, critics, educators, art historians, and other scholars worked together on two seminars (São Paulo, 1995 and 1996) and discussed concerns about dehumanization in major Brazilian and US cities and its impact on the quality of life. One of the main issues given consideration is the place of public art in the midst of contemporary urban chaos. Texts and discussion records are organized by topic.

391 Bienal Internacional de Arquitetura, *3rd, São Paulo, 1997.* 3a. Bienal Internacional de Arquitetura de São Paulo. São Paulo: Fundação Bienal de São Paulo: Instituto de Arquitetos do Brasil, 1997. 363 p.: ill.

Special galleries have been assigned to Vilanova Artigas, Oswaldo Bratke, Rino Levi, Victor Dubugras, Lina Bò Bardi, and R.B. Parker. Main topics of discussion: the search for social and environmental balance; integration of art/city; transformations in Curitiba; urban flux; downtown São Paulo; visions of São Paulo architecture; radiology of Brazilian landscaping; social standing and modern architecture in Brazil; new architecture in Britain, Germany, Holland, Japan, the US, and elsewhere. Large variety of essays, many b/w photographs, plans, drawings, models. No bibliography.

392 Canez, Anna Paula. Fernando Corona e os caminhos da arquitetura moderna em Porto Alegre. Porto Alegre, Brazil: Unidade Editorial Porto Alegre: Prefeitura de Porto Alegre, Secretaria Municipal da Cultura: Faculdades Integradas do Instituto Ritter dos Reis, Faculdade de Arquitetura, 1998. 209 p.: bibl., ill. (Série Escritos de arquitetura; 1)

Master's thesis on Corona, a self-taught architect who contributed largely to changing the face of Porto Alegre from 1928–51 and to modern architecture in that city in general. Analyzes his many projects on the basis of photos, drawings, plans, sketches. Chronology and bibliography.

393 Carvalho, Maria Cristina Wolff de. Ramos de Azevedo. São Paulo: Edusp: FAPESP, 1999. 406 p.: bibl., ill., (some col.). (Artistas brasileiros. Arquitetura)

Revered as the renovator and modernizer of São Paulo in the early 1900s, Azevedo (1851–1928) became a symbol of integrity, hardwork, and progress. This in-depth monograph covers his 19th-century background, his education in Belgium, his role as a professor, and his projects for public buildings, institutional edifices, and residences, in addition to his academic modernity. Plans, elevations, drawings, watercolors, chronology, and bibliography. A valuable contribution.

394   Costa, Lúcio. A arquitetura dos jesuítas no Brasil. *(Rev. Patrim. Hist. Artíst. Nac.,* 26, 1997, p. 105–169, ill., photos)

The brilliant architect and city planner, responsible for the original plans of Brasília, was also a scholar of the history of architecture in Brazil, and a pioneer of the preservation of Brazil's historical and artistic patrimony. In this extensive essay Costa's premise is that the contribution of Jesuits to art in Brazil may not have been the richest, the most beautiful, or the most important in the past, but it may well have been the most significant, linking the Jesuit style in Brazil to the rather sober renaissance composition and not to the exuberant, even extravagant, features of their later period. In fact, baroque is less a single style than a system, a commonwealth of differentiated styles. In Brazil this is particularly evident in the composition of altars, as well as in the façades of churches, and detailed wood carvings.

395   Costa, Lúcio. Lúcio Costa: documentos de trabalho. Organização de José Pessôa. Rio de Janeiro: IPHAN, Ministério da Cultura, 1998. 325 p.: bibl., ill. (some col.), index.

Costa was equally committed to preserving the architecture of the past and supporting that of the present, as both are closely linked, testifying the historical continuity of a culture and civilization. Brazil is a case in point. While working for the Patrimônio Histórico e Artístico Nacional, Costa traveled extensively in Brazil carefully studying all sorts of buildings that deserved preservation, documenting them technically and stylistically. Those visual and written documents are assembled here for future generations of scholars.

396   Dudeque, Irã Taborda. Espirais de madeira: uma história da arquitetura de Curitiba. São Paulo: Studio Nobel, 2001. 437 p.: bibl., ill. (some col.), index, maps.

Curitiba architecture from 1920–90 has been the subject of international interest in recent years, as a result of the city's success as a city planning model for medium-sized modern cities. Architects from all over Brazil created buildings there from the 1960s–90s, but eclecticism, futurism, and European styles can also be found there. Plans, elevations, photographs, and in-depth essays make this the most complete overall study to date. Bibliography.

397   Evolução física de Salvador, 1549 a 1800. Ed. especial. Salvador, Brazil: Fundação Gregório de Mattos; Univ. Federal da Bahia, Centro de Estudos da Arquitetura na Bahia, 1998. 181 p.: bibl., ill. (some col.), maps (some col.).

City planning of Salvador from 1549–1800. Designed by Portugal to be the first capital city of Brazil (1549–1763), city plans evolved over the centuries. This encompassing study covers cartography (and the growth of Salvador), iconography of the different periods, zones developed in each period, comparative demographic and socioeconomic history of each period, architectural monuments of historical and artistic interest, and areas of landscaping interest. Includes maps, elevations, drawings, watercolors, chronology, sources, and a bibliography. This book is the most encompassing of its kind to date.

398   Fábio Penteado: ensaios de arquitetura. Concepção editorial e desenhos de Luiz Antônio Vallandro Keating. Textos de Mônica Junqueira de Camargo, Cecília Scharlach, and José Augusto Lemos. São Paulo: Empresa das Artes Projetos e Edições Artísticas, 1998. 210 p.: bibl., ill. (some col.), maps.

Some of the most daring architects and their representative projects—for Brazil as well as for several other countries—are discussed here in a number of essays. From small residences to high-rises, from commercial and industrial purposes to cultural and governmental, etc., the projects cover the time span from 1948–98. Many plans, drawings, and photographs, bibliographical references, chronology.

Mesquita, Otoni Moreira de. Manaus: história e arquitetura, 1852–1910. See item **3301.**

399   Muniz, Maria Izabel Perini. Cultura e arquitetura: a casa rural do imigrante italiano no Espírito Santo. Vitória, Brazil: EDUFES, 1997. 214 p.: bibl., ill., maps. (Col. Estudos capixabas)

An in-depth monograph about the origins, transplantation, adaptation, and synthesis of rural architecture in Espírito Santo, an original contribution on a state heretofore very little studied by art and architecture historians. Also contributes to a better understanding of the contribution of Italian immigrants to the state. Formal and technical questions are discussed along with the social frame of colonization, coming from Trentino and Veneto. Photographs, plans, drawings, statistics, and bibliography.

400 Oliveira, Adriana Mara Vaz de. Arquitetura como fenômeno cultural: a casa brasileira. (*Estudos/Goiânia*, 28:1, jan./fev. 2001, p. 11–24, bibl.)

Discusses Brazilian vernacular architecture from social and historical perspectives, in terms of culture, society, and epoch, focusing on nonprofessional building. Uses Portuguese vernacular architecture as a point of departure. Bibliographic references.

401 Panorama da arquitetura catarinense.

Idealização e curadoria do projeto de Cristina Maria da Silveira Piazza. Florianópolis, Brazil?: CP Editorial, 2000? 341 p.: col. ill., indexes.

Who's who in contemporary architecture in Santa Catarina. Focusing on younger generations of architects, active in the past 25 years, presented in their various categories: residential, commercial, industrial, government, banks, hospitals, hotels, religious, naval, interior, etc. Projects accompanied by color photographs, plans, sketches, and drawings. Also includes pictures of the architects and their biographies. No bibliography.

402 Peixoto, Elane Ribeiro. Passado & presente: vicissitudes de um arquiteto moderno. (*Estudos/Goiânia*, 28:1, jan./fev. 2001, p. 139–177, bibl., ill., photos)

Lengthy article devoted to the philosophy and the architecture of Lúcio Costa, including his awareness and articulation of his cultural heritage and of the modernity proposed by Le Corbusier, whom Costa met in Rio in 1929. Le Corbusier's ideas about the integration of the arts within a modern approach changed the face of architecture in Brazil through Lúcio Costa. Illustrations and bibliographical references.

403 Puppi, Marcelo. Por uma história não moderna da arquitetura brasileira: questões de historiografia. Campinas, Brazil: Pontes; CPHA/IFCH, 1998. 190 p.: bibl. (Col. Pandora)

This study revolves around Puppi's assertion that there is a discrepency between the value of Brazilian national architecture and the relative lack of interest in researching the history of Brazilian architecture. Most studies focus on the nationalistic interpretation of Brazilian 20th-century architecture. As a consequence, several important periods of the past have been excluded, among them the eclecticism of Rio de Janeiro that Puppi discusses here. Highlights contributions of Lúcio Costa, Paulo Santos, and Yves Bruand. Sources and bibliography.

404 Segawa, Hugo M. Arquiteturas no Brasil, 1900–1990. São Paulo: EDUSP, 1998. 224 p.: bibl., ill., index.

Segawa studies the formation of Brazilian architecture in the 20th century, especially the various approaches to the modern. With the exception of a few remarkable architects and their masterpieces, focuses on the historical perspective and the interdisciplinary implications. City planning is one of the main concerns, particularly after WWII. The concept of modernity in Brazil is complex and controversial. Much space is given to "modernity," as practiced in Brazilian architecture between the world wars. Plans, photographs, bibliography.

405 Visões de paisagem: um panorama do paisagismo contemporâneo no Brasil: Associação Brasileira de Arquitetos Paisagistas = Landscape sights: an exhibition on contemporary landscape architecture in Brazil: Brazilian Association of Landscape Architects. Organização de Guilherme Mazza Dourado. São Paulo: Associação Brasileira de Arquitetos Paisagistas, 1997. 169 p.: ill. (some col.), maps (some col.).

Contemporary landscape architecture is quite differentiated in Brazil. This publication surveys an array of professionals and their main projects in a variety of areas in Brazil. Projects are discussed and illustrated according to landscape of the city, landscape of leisure, landscape of memory, reconstructed landscape, landscape of diversity, landscape of intimacy, and landscape of ideas.

Plans, color photographs, technical information, short biographies, no bibliography.

406 Weimer, Günter. Arquitetura modernista em Porto Alegre: entre 1930 e 1945. Porto Alegre, Brazil: Unidade Editorial Porto Alegre, 1998. 173 p.: bibl., ill. (Série Corona; 1)

This inventory highlights lesser known aspects of modernism in Brazil such as the impact of Berman (Bauhaus) architecture on Porto Alegre before and during WWII, as well as the *Neue Sachlichkeit*, historicism, and eclecticism. The many projects are analyzed based on specially created drawings. Concluding remarks (on the topic of architecture and politics) but no bibliography; only references.

MISCELLANEOUS

407 Bienal de Artes Visuais do Mercosul, *1st, Porto Alegre, Brazil, 1997*. I Bienal de Artes Visuais do Mercosul = I Bienal de Artes Visuales del Mercosur, de 2 de outubro a 30 de novembro de 1997, Porto Alegre, Brasil. Porto Alegre, Brazil: Fundação Bienal de Artes Visuais do Mercosul, 1997? 537 p.: bibl., ill. (some col.).

Participating countries: Argentina, Bolivia, Brazil, Chile, Paraguay, Uruguay, and Venezuela. The most recent tendencies and esthetic trends of the arts in those countries were assembled in an auspicious major event allowing for an exchange among South American artists. Includes biographical information and critical appraisal. Great variety of illustrations. This catalog became instantly a representative source of its kind.

408 Centro de Arquitetura e Urbanismo do Rio de Janeiro. Seminário Internacional. *1st, Rio de Janeiro 1996*. Art déco na América Latina. Rio de Janeiro: Prefeitura da Cidade do Rio de Janeiro, Secretaria Municipal de Urbanismo: Solar Grandjean de Montigny, PUC/Rio, 1997? 229 p.: bibl., ill.

Draws together original studies on art deco by native scholars from several countries: France, the US, Mexico, Cuba, Argentina, Uruguay, Chile, and Brazil; as well as introductory papers of various seminar roundtables, some of them on the regional aspects of art deco in Brazil. The vast majority of the essays underscore either the international features of this style, predominant in the late 1920s, or the national contributions. Illustrations in b/w only.

409 Museu de Arte da Bahia. O Museu de Arte da Bahia. Salvador, Brazil: Museu de Arte da Bahia, 1997. 359 p.: bibl., col. ill.

Established in 1871, the Museu de Arte da Bahia never ceased to develop. Functioning nowadays in the handsome "Palácio da Vitória," the museum houses a rich ethnographic collection, as well as paintings, religious sculpture, porcelains, furniture, silver glass, crystal, numismatic and fashion. A major source for the study of the traditions and history of Bahia, notably of colonial painters, sculptors, and cabinet makers. Many color reproductions and photographs. Extensive descriptions.

410 A paisagem carioca. Curadoria geral de Carlos Martins. Curadoria de Aline Carrer *et al.* Colaboração de Adauto Novaes *et al.*, Museu de Arte Moderna, Rio de Janeiro, 8/8–17/9 de 2000. Rio de Janeiro: Prefeitura do Rio, Secretaria Municipal de Cultura, Secretaria Municipal de Educação: MAM, 2000. 244 p.: chiefly ill.

Organized by the Rio de Janiero Prefeitura and the Museu de Arte Moderna on Brazil's fifth centennial, this exhibition containing art works, films, music, maps, objects, computer images, and multimedia resources celebrates the city of Rio, itself almost 500 years old. The wealth of images, items, and objects set together provide some perspective on the city's history, developments, and transformations, and helps in evaluating its natural, cultural, and urban space as a symbol of Brazil. With the exhibition dismantled (with 1,159 items—it was the largest ever of its kind), what remains is this voluminous publication with 12 scholarly essays, and a wealth of iconographic materials, including paintings, watercolors, and prints by foreign artists who visited Rio over the centuries. Texts in Portuguese and English. Many notes but no bibliography.

411 Robert C. Smith, 1912–1975: a investigação na história de arte. Curadoria de Dalton Sala. Apresentação de Pedro Tamen and Jorge Rodrigues. Textos de António Filipe Pimentel *et al.* = Robert C.

Smith, 1912–1975: research in history of art. Curation by Dalton Sala. Presentation by Pedro Tamen and Jorge Rodrigues. Texts by António Filipe Pimentel *et al.* Lisboa: Fundação Calouste Gulbenkian, Serviço de Belas Artes, Arquivo de Arte, 2000. 451 p.: bibl., ill. (some col.).

The legacy of Robert C. Smith was celebrated in a major exhibition held in Lisbon, the first ever of its kind devoted to an art historian. The catalog published to accompany the exhibition is a landmark in Smith's bibliography, a *Festschrift* that assembles 15 essays by different scholars on Smith's relationship to the art of the US, Portugal, and Brazil. Photographs and illustrations. Bibliography of Smith's works. A memorial to a noted scholar. In Portuguese and English.

412 22 por 22: a Semana de Arte Moderna vista pelos seus contemporâneos. Organização de Maria Eugenia Boaventura. São Paulo: Edusp, 2000. 461 p.: bibl., ill.

Received by many journalists, intellectuals, and critics as alienated artists and contemptible futurist jerks, the participants of the Week of Modern Art in Feb. 1922 had a long but steady path to prove that the 20th century belonged to them and not to their detractors. The many articles and essays gathered here mirror the shock caused by most of the exhibitions. The Week's detractors are long forgotten.

HISTORY

ETHNOHISTORY
Mesoamerica

ROBERT HASKETT, *Professor of History, University of Oregon*
STEPHANIE WOOD, *Assistant Professor of History, University of Oregon*

ETHNOHISTORIANS HAVE BEEN PARTICULARLY PROLIFIC since the publication of *HLAS 58*. As a result, we have dealt with a larger than usual number of individual works. In aggregate, they cover a vast amount of temporal, cultural, and investigatory territory that often defies easy categorization. Entries range from two very useful archival guides (items **564** and **632**), to reissues of enduringly important, classic studies by Spiden (item **621**), Bruman (item **435**), and De Berghes (item **426**).

Ethnohistorians remain determinedly multidisciplinary, which is, of course, one of the strengths of the field. The dividing line between "precontact" and "post-conquest" continues to be blurred in cultural, if not strictly historical, terms, though most of us still tend to package our work with these two fundamental categories in mind. Most of us concentrate on either the Nahuas, particularly the Aztecs, or the Mayas (especially but not exclusively of the Lowlands).

Our field has long been characterized by the use of "ethnohistorical sources," or in other words, pictorial, alphabetic, or even "artistic" records created by indigenous Mesoamericans, which often are used to flesh out or counterbalance archeological or European-authored sources. As James Lockhart once said, to study these societies without recourse to such sources would be akin to investigating the Romans without knowing Latin (for a recent collection of Lockhart's work in the "new philology," see item **548**). For this reason, the "bread and butter" of our field has long been studies, transcriptions, translations, and facsimiles of what can broadly be called "codices," or documents that could fall under the typology of "native tradition." Codices are well represented in *HLAS 60*. As always, most are from the Nahua, Maya, and (at least in the form of pictorials) Mixtec peoples. These documents are sometimes spectacular and always rich in information. Many of them deserve continued analysis, so it follows that some of the noteworthy work contributed here revisits or reinterprets well-known pictorial and alphabetic texts, such as Durand-Forest's investigation of the glyphs of the *Códice Borbónico* (item **470**), Gingerich's revisionist analysis of the *Leyenda de los soles* (item **489**), a new Spanish translation of Chimalpahin's *Third Relation* (item **449**), Prem and Dyckerhoff's examination of different versions of the *Anales de Tlatelolco* (item **582**), a new critical edition of Muñoz Camargo's *Historia* (item **566**), the first-ever publication of Zorita's *Relación de la Nueva España* (item **653;** as opposed to the well-known *Breve Relación*), and others (such as items **516, 541,** and **593**). Several scholars mine these documents for new information, resulting in a number of inventive works, such as an investigation of the representations of salt in precontact-style pictorials (item **591**), a look at remedies for sleep disorders in the *Códice de la Cruz Badiano* (item **643**), and an innovative study of precontact courtship and marriage using Chimalpahin as a source (item **609**).

Yet there seems to be a quickening interest in lesser-known codices, especially postconquest alphabetic texts of the mundane, exemplified by León-Portilla's presentation of a 16th-century Nahuatl letter from a cacique of Soconusco (item **537**), León-Portilla's translation of correspondence from indigenous lords of Mexico City to Philip II (item **539**), Sell's accessible publication of a set of Nahuatl early-17th-century *cofradía* records (item **612**), and Sell and Kellogg's transcription and translation of 16th-century royal ordinances that had been written in Nahuatl (item **614**). Reyes García presents us with a valuable translation and study of the late-16th-century *Anales de Juan Bautista* (item **589**), a little-known text rich with information about indigenous life in this period, an equally significant translation and transcription of the Nahuatl *Historia cronológica de la Noble Ciudad de Tlaxcala*, compiled in the late 17th century by Juan Buenaventura Zapata y Mendoza (item **436**), as well as a fine little collection of transcribed and translated Nahuatl testaments and bills of sale from Cuahuixmatlac, Tlaxcala (item **590**). Four high-quality and highly recommended anthologies, *De tlacuilos y escribanos* (item **466**), *Códices y documentos sobre México: segundo simposio* (item **455**), *Códices y documentos sobre México: tercer simposio international* (item **456**), and *La collection Aubin-Goupil a la Bibliotheque nationale de France*, an issue from the *Journal de la Société des Américanistes* (item **527**) are particularly important for those seeking a deeper understanding of the nature and analysis of documents in the native tradition.

Other scholars have been more concerned with divining the truth about historical records, which are often surrounded by controversy and, really, a certain amount of interpretive mystery. The celebrated Canek Manuscript, which when first described seemed to be a first-hand account of a clerical embassy to the rebel Itza capital in the Petén, has, upon closer inspection, turned out to be a fairly recent forgery (items **526 and 581**). Some may be surprised when two other works of apparently unsullied pedigree are questioned, too, in Restall and Chuchiak's convincing "A Reevaluation of the Authenticity of Fray Diego de Landa's *Relación de las cosas de Yucatán*" (item **588**) and Milbrath's "New Questions Concerning the Authenticity of the Grolier Codex" (item **560**). On the other hand, texts in the related Techialoyan and *títulos primordiales* (primordial titles) genres, once dismissed as outright fakes, have been deservedly receiving more nuanced attention. This biennium, a number of high quality studies have been made available which will help place these valuable records in a more prominent position as legitimate ethnohistorical sources (items **451, 454,** and **649**).

This is a good thing, because there are several studies noted in these pages in which apparent Techialoyans, and especially possible primordial titles, are not recognized as such. Without seeing the documents ourselves, it is of course difficult to come to a completely satisfactory conclusion on this matter, but we might gain even more important insights if such records were held up to a new round of critical and comparative scrutiny (items **464, 630,** and **644**). Some of these suspected Techialoyans/*títulos* (such as item **569**) originate from parts of Mesoamerica that are not normally associated with these genres—Guatemala and the Yucatan, for instance—which may have led them to be unrecognized for what they really are. In fact, as we will see in the works annotated in this chapter, new documentary discoveries outside the Nahua sphere should give us pause, prodding us to rethink our traditional and comfortable assumptions about the spread and scope of particular kinds of documentary forms.

Since a key emphasis in the broad documentary type of "codices" is what we would generally call "history," it is fitting that ethnohistorians have continued to grapple with the issues of historical memory and representations of the past (for instance, see items **420, 580,** and **646**). We are fortunate that three outstanding works of scholarship address these issues, and do so in fresh, innovative, and accessible ways. Enrique Florescano's *Memoria indígena* represents a refinement of his significant earlier work in the area (item **476**), and Hassig's erudite *Time, History, and Belief in Aztec and Colonial Mexico* challenges some of our enduring ideas about Aztec historical thinking (item **499**). Elizabeth Hill Boone's marvelous *Stories in Red and Black,* which systematically and imaginatively examines a range of precontact-style historical genres, deserves a long run as a standard and oft-consulted work in the area (item **429**).

A second enduring area of ethnohistorical interest well represented in *HLAS* 60 is that of the friar-ethnographers, dominated almost as a matter of course by a durable scholarly interest in Fray Bernardino de Sahagún and his extensive textual output (see item **514**). This biennium, the most significant works are undoubtedly Browne's challenging *Sahagún and the Transition to Modernity* (item **434**), the massive anthology entitled *Fray Bernardino de Sahagún y su tiempo* (item **478**), and León-Portilla's more traditional biography, *Bernardino de Sahagún, First Anthropologist* (item **540**), which approach the friar and his work from markedly different perspectives. At the same time, stand-alone studies of some aspect of the Florentine Codex, while present (items **468** and **577**), are not as pervasive as in some past bodies of work we have reviewed. It is heartening to see that Baudot has contributed two significant pieces of scholarship—"Los franciscanos etnógrafos" (item **424**) and "Los precursores franciscanos de Sahagún del siglo XIII al siglo XVI en Asia y América" (item **425**)—which both examine the "old world" roots of later "new world" efforts, and pay attention to other friars like Andrés de Olmos, Martín de la Coruña, and Francisco de las Olmos who are sometimes overshadowed by the larger-than-life figure of Sahagún (see also item **538**).

The very existence of the "friar-ethnographers" seems to prove the truism that it is often impossible to separate the mundane from the sacred in texts in the "native tradition," or those that have sought to recover the Mesoamerican past. So it is fitting that investigations of the sacred continue to occupy the thoughts of many of the scholars whose works are reviewed here. Serious, often innovative studies of the precontact sacred are dominated by the ideologies and practices of the Nahuas, though the Mayas get some attention as well, most notably in López Austin and López Luján's *Mito y realidad de Zuyuá: Serpiente emplumada y las transformaciones mesoamericanas del Clásico al Posclásico* (item **551**), Milbrath's *Star Gods of the Maya* (item **561**), and Schele and Mathews' *The Code of Kings* (item **607;** see also items **483, 622,** and **637**). Numbered among substantial works that concentrate principally on the Nahuas and central Mesoamerica are the praiseworthy anthology edited by Albores and Broda, *Graniceros: Cosmovisión y meteorología indígena de Mesoamérica* (item **492**), Alcina Franch's intriguing study of the *temazcalli* (item **414**), López Austin's evocative *Tamoanchan, Tlalocan: Places of Mist* (item **550**), and Maldonado Jiménez's more regionally focused *Deidades y espacio ritual en Cuauhnáhuac y Huaxtepec* (item **554**). Ritual violence and human sacrifice receive new interpretive attention in Almere Read's insightful

Time and Sacrifice in the Aztec Cosmos (item **586**), Carrasco's stand-out *City of Sacrifice: The Aztec Empire and the Role of Violence in Civilization* (item **439**), and Graulich's "Aztec Human Sacrifice as Expiation" (item **494**). Beyond this, there seems to be an unusually dense grouping of individual deity studies (such as items **521, 556,** and **572**), with López Luján and Vida Mercado's tour-de-force look at Mictlantecuhtli (item **552**) and Nicolson's long awaited *Topiltzin Quetzalcoatl: The Once and Future Lord of the Toltecs* (item **568**) particularly worth noting.

Once the focus shifts to the fate of indigenous spirituality in the colonial era there are a significant number of studies that advance our understanding of the religious dialogue created when Christianity entered indigenous sacred worlds. These include an able translation into English of don Bartolomé de Alva's *A Guide to Confession Large and Small* (item **415**) which is most revealing, especially when paired with Martiarena's explication of indigenous resistance to Christianity as it emerges from the structure of confessional guides, *Culpabilidad y resistencia: ensayo sobre la confesión en los indios de la Nueva España* (item **555**), Sousa's "The Devil and Deviance in Native Criminal Narratives from Early Mexico" (item **620**), and Tavárez's "La idolatría letrada: un análisis comparativo de textos clandestinos rituales y devocionales en comunidades nahuas y zapotecas" (item **625**). Sell and Taylor's presentation of a Nahuatl-language sermon attributed to Juan de Tova, S.J. is commendable (item **613**), as is Wake's "Sacred Books and Sacred Songs from the Former Days: Sourcing the Mural Paintings at San Miguel Arcangel Ixmiquilpan" (item **645**). New studies of indigenous *cofradías* uncovering a wealth of social, cultural, and political details are provided by Amos Megged, "The Religious Context of an 'Unholy Marriage'" (item **557**), and Schroeder, "Jesuits, Nahuas, and the Good Death Society in Mexico City" (item **610**), both of which complement Sell's translation of confraternity records noted above.

Devotional music created for and by indigenous Christians has not received much attention from ethnohistorians, and though several ensembles have produced recordings (accurate or not) of this musical genre (generally without particularly enlightening liner notes or transcriptions of lyrics), none of them has ever been mentioned in these pages. However, thanks to *Estudios de cultura náhuatl* and Cruz, a lucid study of two Nahuatl texts of hymns devoted to the Virgin Mary (including "Yn ilhuicac cihuapille," which elsewhere has been rightly or wrongly linked to the Virgin of Guadalupe), has come to see the light of day (item **460**). We need more of this kind of work, since devotional music likely had as much or more of an impact on indigenous parishioners as the better-known and more often studied theatrical presentations (which were always enlivened with music), sermons, Christian doctrines, and other evangelical texts. The theater of evangelization is not ignored by our authors, however, with Díaz Balsera's "A Judeo-Christian Tlaloc or a Nahua Yahweh?" particularly compelling here (item **422**).

None of this means that lay culture has been neglected by ethnohistorians. Accordingly, another traditional area of interest, studying various aspects of secular life, its intersections with the sacred, and cultural change during both precontact and colonial eras, is still fairly well represented here. For once, however, Maya-centered studies of the colonial era (such as items **446, 463, 587, 603,** and **619**) outnumber those about central Mexicans (for instance, items **500, 596,** and **624**). Most of these make modest though noteworthy contributions, although few could be described as "blockbusters." Jones' admirable work on the conquest of the Itza in 1697, *The Conquest of the Last Maya Kingdom,* is a definite exception to this rule as far as the Maya zone is concerned (item **525**), as is Bos' impeccable look at caciques in the colonial Valley of Toluca, in central Mexico, *The Demise of the Caciques of Atlacomulco, Mexico, 1598–1821* (item **431**). *Lost Shores, Forgotten Peoples: Spanish Explorations of the South East Maya Lowlands* (item **553**), edited and translated by Feldman, presents an array of translated documents related to the Manche Chol and Mopan Mayas and their experience of conquest and foreign colonization, in the process bringing out information about a southeastern Mesoamerican people not always accorded much attention in comparison to other groups.

The numerical weight of Maya-specific studies versus those of central Mesoamericans is reversed as far as the precontact era is concerned. (Good examples of the Maya group are items **437, 469, 518, 602,** and **638**.) Not surprisingly, the Aztecs get considerable attention from high quality scholarship (items **505, 592, 594, 604,** and **636**). Carrasco, Jones, and Sessions' finely crafted anthology, *Mesoamerica's Classic Heritage: From Teotihuacan to the Aztecs* (item **558**), as well as Carrasco and Sessions' deft *Daily Life of the Aztecs: People of the Sun and Earth* (item **441**), and the comprehensive collection of articles edited by Grove and Joyce, *Social Patterns in Pre-classic Mesoamerica* (see *HLAS 59:90*) are especially recommended to our readers. A four-volume assemblage of contributions from a significant number of well-known scholars, *Historia antigua de México,* expanded from a three-volume version published in 1994–95 and put together by Manzanilla and López Luján, will be an especially useful overview resource (item **506**).

Studies of the Mesoamerican calendar are not as numerous as in some past bodies of work reviewed for this section, aside from Durand-Forest's study of the *Códice Borbónico* mentioned above (see items **428, 433,** and **465**). Conversely, interest in women and gender remains high. Most of the studies that came across our desks in this area of inquiry are the result of exceptional scholarship (items **531, 575,** and **595**), and some examine subjects which have received little attention in the past (see Wood in a special edition of *Journal de la Société des américanistes* entitled *La collection Aubin-Goupil,* item **527**). Notable are Gustafson and Trevelyan's highly useful anthology, *Ancient Maya Gender Identity and Relations* focused principally on the classic era (item **416**), the outstanding anthology edited by Klein, *Gender in Pre-hispanic America,* with a number of impressive chapters focused on Mesoamerica (item **484**), Sigal's innovative study of sexuality among the Mayas, *From Moon Goddesses to Virgins* (item **615**), and Joyce's marvelous *Gender and Power in Prehispanic Mesoamerica,* which comprehensively crosses temporal and cultural lines (item **528;** see also Joyce, item **529**). Having said this, it seems to us that more authors are considering gender as part of their analytical methodologies, a hopeful trend which admittedly still has a long way to go.

Another topic that once caught the imagination of more scholars, but which receives only minimal attention here, is land tenure. Of note for the colonial era are Iglesias' "Tierras indias bajo ley española," a careful look at land struggles in Cuautinchan (item **513**); and Palma Murga's "De los usos de la memoria histórica prehispánica sobre la territorialidad en la Guatemala colonial," an investigation of intercommunity conflicts during the 16th- and 17th-centuries (item **576**). The few precontact offerings are dominated by Arnold's challenging analysis of the sacred dimensions of the land in central Mexico, *Eating Landscape* (item **418**).

Arnold's work can also be taken to represent what seems to be a rising interest in topics and issues related to ecology, the environment, and flora and fauna, noting in some cases the sacred implications of latter. Especially valuable are a new edition of *An Aztec Herbal,* edited by Gates (item **461**), and an extremely important collection of documents and articles presenting the life, work, and times of the great "naturalist" (to risk using the term anachronistically) Dr. Francisco Hernández. The latter has been crafted by Varey, Chabrán, Chamberlin, and Weiner in companion volumes entitled *The Mexican Treasury: The Writings of Dr. Francisco Hernández* (item **501**), and *Searching for the Secrets of Nature: The Life and Works of Dr. Francisco Hernández* (item **611**). These extremely useful resources are among just a few works of this type with a "colonial" focus, though Garavaglia's fine article, "Atlixco: El Agua, los Hombres y la Tierra en un Valle Mexicano, Siglos XIV–XVII," is, among other things, an analysis of the impact of introduced European livestock and crops (item **480**). Others, such as Berres (item **427**), Schlesinger (item **608**), and González Torres (item **490**), examine the precontact era Basin of Mexico and the flora and fauna of this region and of the Maya zone. Here is an area of inquiry that can still bear more sustained study, though it is potentially a difficult topic for ethnohistorians to pursue. Yet as is apparent in the work of Arnold and Hernández, the landscape and the living and even inanimate things that inhabited it loomed large in the sacred and secular lives of the Mesoamericans. History is embedded in the landscape in precontact-style pictorials such as the cartographic histories, as it was in colonial-era primordial titles. Murals such as those found at Ixquimilpan present viewers with a swirling mass of vegetation bearing other kinds of figures and messages. Just as in the case of gender, we must constantly challenge ourselves to factor in "the landscape" broadly speaking as we seek to craft meaningful ethnohistorical studies.

If one searches beyond the Nahuas and the southeastern Mayan region, it quickly becomes apparent that other Mesoamerican groups are still being overlooked. In the past this was explained by the "fact" that primary ethnohistorical sources comparable to those associated with the better represented groups were almost nonexistent. However, the research and recent publications of a small number of scholars should be seen as a challenge to this convenient assertion. Three of the more important pieces of scholarship reviewed for this volume of *HLAS* are models of the perceptive analysis of Mixtec-centered ethnohistorical sources, including many written in the indigenous language: Kevin Terraciano's *The Mixtecs of Colonial Oaxaca: Nudzahui History, Sixteenth through Eighteenth Centuries* (item **629**), "The Colonial Mixtec Community" (item **627**), and "Crime and Culture in Colonial Mexico: The Case of the Mixtec Murder Note" (item **628**). Of similar significance is Oudijk's laudable evaluation of postcontact Zapotec records, *Historiography of the Bénizáa: The Postclassic and Early Colonial Periods* (item **573**; see also item **574**). Equally weighty work on Purépecha sources and culture in the postconquest includes Roskamp's *La historiografía indígena de Michoacán: El Lienzo de Jucutácato y los títulos de Carapan* (item **599**; see also items **598** and **600**) and Verástique's *Michoacán and Eden* (item **640**), a new look at Vasco Quiroga's enterprise through an indigenous lens. The Otomí get some attention from Crespo and Cervantes (item **459**), García Castro (item **1250**), and the Huastecs from Escobar Ohmstede (item **472**). Some of these "northerners" were actually Otomí and Tlaxcalan colonists and thus of interest to scholars who study "central Mexicans." Their story, as told in such things as *Miguel Caldera y los tlaxcaltecas en el norte de la Nueva España* (item **559**), is not to be missed.

So we issue a challenge to present and future ethnohistorians, urging them to leave behind archival complacency and venture into some of these newly unfolding areas of investigatory possibility. We would like to applaud the initiative of Reyes, Sullivan, Campbell, Karttunen, and scholars from the University of Leiden (such as

Bos, Oudijk, and Roskamp, who are represented in these pages) who are collaborating with native speakers of indigenous languages, people who can bring vital insight to the reading of precolumbian and colonial texts, even if languages and cultures have evolved considerably in the interim. We are also encouraged by our colleagues both in and outside of Mesoamerica who read the work of all serious contributors to the field regardless of their national origin and first language. We live in a time remote from that of the peoples we are studying. In this sense, most of us are outsiders seeking to gain entry into an often alien world. Maintaining mutual respect, working together, and learning from one another will allow us to achieve our common goals more quickly and more successfully than otherwise. It is our sincere wish that the annotated bibliography which follows will serve these ends.

413 **Aguilera, Carmen.** A sacred song to Xochipilli. (*Lat. Am. Indian Lit.*, 14:1, Spring 1998, p. 54–72)

Interpretation of this song, found in both the *Primeros Memoriales* and the *Códice Florentino* of Sahagún, deduces that Xochipilli symbolized the sun, while the Quetzalcoxcox bird (usually equated with Xochipilli) actually stands for Quetzalcoatl in his guise as the Morning Star. The article ranges much more widely, succinctly discussing ways in which iconographic evidence from other sources supports the thesis presented here.

414 **Alcina Franch, José.** Temazcalli: higiene, terapéutica, obstetricia y ritual en el Nuevo Mundo. Sevilla, Spain: Escuela de Estudios Hispano-Americanos de Sevilla, Consejo Superior de Investigaciones Científicas, 2000. 245 p.: bibl., ill., maps. (Publicaciones de la Escuela de Estudios Hispano-Americanos de la Universidad de Sevilla; 403)

Dense ethnohistorical study of the Mesoamerican *temazcalli*, or sweat bath, that centers on beliefs, attributes, and uses attached to it from precontact to recent times. Concentrates on the past rather than the present; however, presents a broad investigation taking in ideas, practices, and rituals associated with childbirth and health. An important work.

415 **Alva, Bartolomé de.** A guide to confession large and small in the Mexican language, 1634. Edited by Barry D. Sell and John Frederick Schwaller, with Lu Ann Homza. Norman: Univ. of Oklahoma Press, 1999. 184 p.: bibl., index.

Sell and Schwaller present illuminating introductory essays and painstaking translations of the guide, from both its Spanish and Nahuatl texts, which was composed by the mestizo Alva, younger brother of the much better known Don Francisco de Alva Ixtlilxochitl. The text serves as an essential tool for understanding the mind-set of the Spanish clergy of the mature colonial era (as opposed to the early period of the exuberant "spiritual conquest"); the nature of the 17th-century indigenous belief system; and at least some aspects of daily indigenous life. This revealing text not only is concerned with grilling confessants about their adherence to the Ten Commandments and the seven Sacraments, but also is laced with homilies remarking on various beliefs and practices of the indigenous people, and with hypothetical dialogues between confessor and indigenous confessant. Alva frequently pays a good deal of attention to idolatrous practices, sexual deviancy, and other similar matters.

416 **Ancient Maya gender identity and relations.** Edited by Lowell S. Gustafson and Amelia M. Trevelyan. Westport, Conn.: Bergin & Garvey, 2002. 359 p.: bibl., ill., index.

Essential anthology of excellent scholarly articles examines Mayan gender ideologies and practices. Articles are set within broader context of sociocultural history, principally as conditions existed in the classic period. Rather than proposing some kind of artificial unity, the diverse set of contributions reveal a variegated gender landscape sharing some commonalities, but riven by significant differences too, depending on time and space, with some changes observable over time even within the same sociopolitical entity. Individual articles include: Amelia M. Trevelyan and Lowell S. Gustafson, "Introduction;" Marvin Cohodas, "Multiplicity and Discourse in Maya Gender Relations;" Lowell S. Gustafson, "Shared Gender Relations: Early Mesoamerica and the Maya;" Julia A. Hendon, "Household and State in Pre-Hispanic Maya Society: Gender, Identity, and Practice;" Amelia M. Trevelyan and Heather W. Forbes, "The Gendered Architecture of Uxmal;" Lowell S. Gustafson, "Mother/Father Kings;" Karen Bassie-Sweet, "Corn Deities and the Male/Female Principal;" Beatriz Barba de Piã Chán, "The Popol Vuh and the Decline of Maya Women's Status;" María Elena Bernal-García, "A Divine Couple's Gender Roles in the Setting of the Earth at Palenque;" Carolyn E. Tate, "Holy Mother Earth and Her Flowery Skirt: The Role of the Female Earth Surface in Maya Political and Ritual Performance;" F. Kent Reilly, "Female and Male: The Ideology of Balance and Renewal in Elite Costuming among the Classic Period Maya;" and Rosemary A. Joyce, "Desiring Women: Classic Maya Sexualities."

417 **Aramoni Calderón, Dolores.** Las cofradías zoques: espacio de resistencia. (*Anu. Estud. Indíg.*, 7, 1998, p. 89–104)

Well-researched and clearly written, this fine article contains the plausible argument that the Zoques of Chiapas were able to benefit from the existence of *cofradías*. The organization and fellowship of these sodalities allowed them to confront the rigors of colonialism and to maintain to an extent their social structures, community identities, and even a certain amount of cultural continuity from the precontact past.

418 **Arnold, Philip P.** Eating landscape: Aztec and European occupation of Tlalocan. Niwot: Univ. Press of Colorado, 1999. 304 p.: bibl., ill., index. (Mesoamerican worlds)

Hermeneutical study of relationships of humans to the land of central Mexico, examined by means of a dense study of beliefs about Tlaloc, Tlalocan, and the natural world. Thus, religious thought and ritual practices receive sustained attention as author develops what he calls a "hermeneutics of occupation" of the material world. A significant and challenging contribution to the field.

419 *Arqueología Mexicana.* Vol. 4. No. 23, 1997, p. 6–69, bibl., facsims. México: Instituto Nacional de Antropología e Historia, Editorial Raíces.

Glossy, lavishly illustrated edition of this journal contains six short articles written by prominent scholars. Collectively, these works can serve as an accessible introduction to the field of Mesoamerican ethnohistory. Kicked off by Galarza, "Los códices mexicanos," subsequent contributions include Miguel León-Portilla, "Grandes momentos en la historia de los códices;" Luz María Mohar Betancourt, "Tres códices nahuas del México antiguo: Codice Borbónico, Tira de la peregrinación, Matricula de tributos;" María de Los Angeles Ojeda Díaz, "Los códices del Grupo Borgia;" Laura Elena Sotelo Santos, "Los códices mayas" (especially the Madrid, Dresden, and Paris codices); and Perla Valle, "Códices coloniales."

420 **Aveni, Anthony F.** and **Edward E. Calnek.** Astronomical considerations in the Aztec expression of history. (*Anc. Mesoam.*, 10:1, Spring 1999, p. 87–98, bibl., tables)

Skilled researchers chart significance of eclipses in the Aztec construction of history, and more generally of the refiguring in time of events to associate them with significant cosmic events. Though relatively brief, this is a contribution worthy of note. For archeologist's comment, see *HLAS 59:15*.

421 **Ayala, Gabriel de.** Apuntes de los sucesos de la nación mexicana desde el año 1243 hasta el de 1562. (*Estud. Cult. Náhuatl*, 27, 1997, p. 397–404)

Transcription and translation of a brief Nahuatl annal authorized by don Gabriel de Ayala, a noble of Texcoco.

422 **Balsera, Viviana Díaz.** A judeo-christian Tlaloc or a Nahua Yahweh?: domination, hybridity and continuity in the Nahua evangelization theater. (*Colon. Lat. Am. Rev.*, 10:2, Dec. 2001, p. 209–228)

Compelling analysis of ways in which the theater of evangelization was likely transformed from a tool of colonization to an instrument through which indigenous Christians could recover a certain amount of control over their own religiosity, their religious practices, and their ritual space. The author does so by means of an exceptionally well done interpretation of the play *The Sacrifice of Isaac,* noting possible conceptual implications for a Nahua audience of the portrayal of a near human sacrifice in the story. A worthy addition to the growing body of scholarship in this area of inquiry.

Baskes, Jeremy. Indians, merchants, and markets: a reinterpretation of the repartimiento and Spanish-Indian economic relations in colonial Oaxaca, 1750–1821. See item **1214.**

423   Batalla Rosado, Juan José. Nuevas hipótesis sobre la história del *Códice Tudela* o *Códice del Museo de América.* (*Rev. Esp. Antropol. Am.,* 31, 2001, p. 131–163, bibl., facsims.)

Exercising a sound method of detection, author revisits history of this key document before its emergence into public ownership in 1940s. Concentrating on its wanderings in Mexico and Spain before 1800, Batalla finds compelling evidence to suggest that the document was in the hands of Cervantes de Salazar in the 16th century, and that by 1799 had made its way to Spain and was in a collection of materials held by Juan Bautista Muñoz. Batalla voices doubts that the document could have been authored by Fray Andrés de Olmos, and adds a coda to the article in which he critiques a 1980 facsimile edition and a restoration of the codex carried out in 1981.

424   Baudot, Georges. Los franciscanos etnógrafos. (*Estud. Cult. Náhuatl,* 27, 1997, p. 275–307)

Involving piece of scholarship positioning members of the Franciscan order as early ethnographers and tracing their intellectual precursors in the order back to 13th century. At the same time, examines spiritual education and thinking of the Franciscans just prior to, and at the time of, contact with the Western Hemisphere, in a sense expanding on earlier work on this subject produced by such scholars as John Leddy Phelan. Baudot concludes this fine piece by examining the careers of friars Andrés de Olmos, Toribio de Benevente Motolinía, Martín de la Coruña, and Francisco de las Navas, arguing that all of them were active

as "ethnographers" prior to the more famous efforts of Bernardino de Sahagún. See also item **425.**

425   Baudot, Georges. Los precursores franciscanos de Sahagún del siglo XIII al siglo XVI en Asia y América. (*Estud. Cult. Náhuatl,* 32, 2001, p. 159–173)

Brief but illuminating discussion of the rising tradition among Franciscans to observe and understand the human societies that confronted them in their work of evangelization, setting the stage for the appearance of the "ethnographer" Sahagún. See also item **424.**

426   Berghes, Carl de. Descripción de las ruinas de asentamientos aztecas durante su migración al Valle de México, a través del actual Estado Libre de Zacatecas. Compilada tras investigaciones y levantamientos en este lugar y esclarecida por el manuscrito en jeroglíficos aztecas del Museo de México por Carl de Berghes. Traducción, estudio introductorio y notas de Achim Lelgemann. Zacatecas: Gobierno del Estado de Zacatecas, Comité Organizador de los Festejos del 450 Aniversario de la Fundación de Zacatecas, Archivo Histórico del Estado de Zacatecas: Univ. Autónoma de Zacatecas, Facultad de Humanidades: Centro Bancario del Estado de Zacatecas, 1996. 97 p.: bibl., ill. (Colección Joyas bibliográficas zacatecanas; 2)

Spanish translation of a German account published in 1855, recounting the experiences of Berghes as he studied what he believed were settlements established by the Aztecs during their migration from Aztlan to the Valley of Mexico. Includes excellent reproductions of the original's woodcuts and drawings. Interesting and useful artifact from an earlier age of archeological investigation made accessible to a new audience.

427   Berres, Thomas E. Climatic change and lacustrine resources at the period of initial Aztec development. (*Anc. Mesoam.,* 11:1, Spring 2000, p. 27–38, bibl., ill., maps)

Examines climatic changes in the basin of Mexico and their probable impact on the fish and waterfowl that provided sources of food for its human population, covering a span of years from 1150–1200 C.E. Postulates an increase in the carrying capacity of the region during this era.

428 Bill, Cassandra R.; Christine L. Hernández; and **Victoria R. Bricker.** The relationship between early colonial Maya New Year's ceremonies and some almanacs in the *Madrid Codex*. (*Anc. Mesoam.*, 11:1, Spring 2000, p. 149–168, bibl., ill., tables)

New insights into the rendering of New Year's ceremonies in the *Madrid Codex* and their iconographic links to Fray Diego de Landa's account on the same subject.

429 Boone, Elizabeth Hill. Stories in red and black: pictorial histories of the Aztecs and Mixtecs. Austin: Univ. of Texas Press, 2000. 296 p.: bibl., ill., index.

Superb study of forms and nature of precontact historical memory in central Mesoamerica. Author examines a wide range of documentary types, lacing her splendidly written account with critical presentations of representative stories. Discrete genres are discussed in detail; effectively illustrated throughout. One of the best and most important ethnohistorical books reviewed in *HLAS 60*.

430 Borg, Barbara E. Los mayas kaqchikeles de Sacatepéquez y la encomienda de Bernal Díaz del Castillo en Guatemala. (*Mesoamérica/Antigua*, 19:35, junio 1998, p. 155–198, maps, tables)

Carefully researched treatment of the Díaz del Castillo encomienda in Guatemala, brings to light new information about a segment of the indigenous population largely neglected by modern scholars. Deftly employing information gleaned from archival sources, author reconstructs patterns of *congregación* and town formation, *cacique* lineages, commerce and agricultural production, the nature of tribute delivered to Díaz, indigenous support (mainly material) for the resident Dominicans, demographics, and the jurisdictional vagaries of the grant. Much of the focus is on San Juan and San Pedro Sacatepéquez, and the fate of the encomienda under Díaz's sons, particularly his direct heir don Francisco Díaz del Castillo, is examined. Informative maps and tables enhance the article.

431 Bos, Anne. The demise of the caciques of Atlacomulco, Mexico, 1598–1821: a reconstruction. Leiden, The Netherlands: Research School of CNWS, School of Asian, African, and Amerindian Studies, 1998. 333 p.: bibl., ill., map. (CNWS publications, 0925–3084; 68)

Excellent study, based on extensive original archival research, of a process in which the domination of several noble indigenous clans in this Valley of Toluca community slipped over the course of the centuries. Links this demise to shifts in the political, economic, and social power of *caciques*, who gradually lost out to a rising, nonindigenous population of priests, landholders, merchants, and government functionaries, particularly in second half of the 18th century. The evolving character of the community, issues of land tenure, internal political conflicts, and the dimensions of social relations are all given their due.

432 Bricker, Victoria R. The Mayan *uinal* and the Garden of Eden. (*Lat. Am. Indian Lit. J.*, 18:1, Spring 2002, p. 1–20)

Analyzes "Creation of the *Uinal*" text included in the *Book of Chilam Balam of Chumayel* to gauge impact of Christianity on postconquest Mayan religious thought; the *uinal* was one of the two cycles which made up the time unit called the *tzolkin* ("day count"). Finds influence in this text from the Genesis story of creation, as author or authors of the Mayan text recast their own story in light of new religious influences. Appendix includes a transcription and English translation of the salient text.

433 Brotherston, Gordon. Los textos calendáricos inscritos en el Templo del Tepozteco. (*Estud. Cult. Náhuatl*, 28, 1998, p. 77–97, bibl., ill.)

Straightforward analysis of inscriptions featured in article's title, noting their wider implications in terms of precontact religious beliefs and calendrical conventions.

434 Browne, Walden. Sahagún and the transition to modernity. Norman: Univ. of Oklahoma Press, 2000. 271 p.: bibl., index. (Oklahoma project for discourse and theory; 20)

Well-written reevaluation of Sahagún's

life and work questions common interpretations such as depiction of the friar as the "first anthropologist." Browne makes a conscious effort to understand Sahagún within the context of his own time, a period identified here as being between the medieval and the modern, all of which makes this thoughtful book worthy of attention.

435 Bruman, Henry J. Alcohol in ancient Mexico. Foreword by Peter T. Furst. Maps by J. Chase Langford. Salt Lake City: Univ. of Utah Press, 2000. 158 p.: bibl., index, maps, photos.

Long-delayed publication of Bruman's 1940 Berkeley doctoral dissertation, which author augmented and updated periodically over time until his 86th year. The resulting book is an invaluable study of the fermented beverages developed by the precontact Mesoamericans, including pulque of course, but also many other concoctions. Among other things, author notes existence of regional specialization in the production of specific kinds of intoxicating beverages. This is not an artifact of an earlier period of scholarship, but rather a useful study in any age.

436 Buenaventura Zapata y Mendoza, Juan. Historia cronológica de la noble ciudad de Tlaxcala. Transcripción paleográfica, traducción, presentación y notas de Luis Reyes García y Andrea Martínez Baracs. Tlaxcala, Mexico: Univ. Autónoma de Tlaxcala, Secretaría de Extensión Universitaria y Difusión Cultural: Centro de Investigaciones y Estudios Superiores en Antropología Social, 1995. 746 p.: bibl., ill. (Colección Historia: Serie Historia de Tlaxcala; 4)

This is the first published transcription and translation of this significant ethnohistorical source, a set of annals written in Nahuatl by a prominent member of Tlaxcala's late-17th-century indigenous community. The text begins with information about the vicissitudes of the migrating people who eventually founded Tlaxcala, and then follows their historical fortunes through the Spanish invasion and up to 1692. The text is particularly rich in material specific to the 17th century, highlighting the traditional kinds of political, religious, astronomical, and other portentous events that have made Mesoamerican annals famous. For comment

by historian of colonial Mexico, see item *HLAS 58:1105.*

437 Carmack, Robert M. Evolución del reino k'iche' = Kik'ulmatajem le k'iche'aab'. Guatemala: Cholsamaj, 2001. 540 p.: bibl., ill.

This work and Carmack's *Historia social de los k'iche's* (2001), both of which originally appeared in 1979 (see *HLAS 43:843*), include a collection of previously published articles by Carmack which distill his research and insights about the Quiché Mayas, and a study of Utatlán.

438 Carochi, Horacio. Grammar of the Mexican language, with an explanation of its adverbs, 1645. Translated and edited with commentary by James Lockhart. Stanford, Calif.: Stanford Univ. Press; Los Angeles, Calif.: UCLA Latin American Center Publications, 2001. 538 p.: bibl., index. (UCLA Latin American studies; 89) (Nahuatl studies series; 7)

More than a grammar, this monumental work of Nahuatl literature, here offered in English translation for the first time, includes real-life examples of great quality and relevance to ethnohistorians, plus Lockhart's extended commentary. A great companion to Lockhart's *Nahuatl as written* (see item *547*).

439 Carrasco, David. City of sacrifice: the Aztec empire and the role of violence in civilization. Boston, Mass.: Beacon Press, 1999. 279 p.: bibl., ill., index.

Marvelous study of Tenochtitlán, a "city as performance," teasing out the interrelationships of ritual, religion, and power as they were expressed and staged in the Aztec capital. Central to the investigation is the question of sacrifice, or ritual violence, as the key component of this performance. Deserves to become an enduring classic in the literature.

440 Carrasco, David. Uttered from the heart: guilty rhetoric among the Aztecs. (*Hist. Relig./Chicago,* 39:1, Aug. 1999, p. 1–31, facsims.)

Fascinating interpretation of Aztec beliefs and practices related to what we call sin and guilt; in fact, author addresses issue of whether or not it is proper to attribute the concepts to these Mesoamericans. Along the way he deftly recreates for the reader what he believes were Aztec ideas about *tlazolli,* translated by Spaniards as "sin." He relates how this concept, as well as the act of confession to the female deity Tlazolteotl, the "eater of filth," was linked to pervasive ideas about the structure of the cosmos, balance, and duality; to ways in which organs of the body such as the heart and the tongue were related to human behavior; and to the nature of sexual transgressions. An essential piece.

441 Carrasco, David and **Scott Sessions.**
Daily life of the Aztecs: people of the sun and earth. Westport, Conn.: Greenwood Press, 1998. 282 p.: bibl., ill., index, maps. (The Greenwood Press "Daily life through history" series, 1080–4749)
Accessible yet sophisticated treatment, in a way providing an updating of Jacques Soustelle's venerable work (see *HLAS 19:35*). Many aspects of mundane and political life are covered here, but the sacred is appropriately prominent, overtly or otherwise.

442 Carrasco Pizana, Pedro. The Tenochca Empire of ancient Mexico: the triple alliance of Tenochtitlán, Tetzcoco, and Tlacopán. Norman: Univ. of Oklahoma Press, 1999. 560 p.: bibl., index, maps. (The civilization of the American Indian series; 234)
English translation of Carrasco's monumental *Estructura político territorial del imperio tenochca* (see *HLAS 58:475*) has been slightly revised and updated by the author. Continues to offer a first-rate study of the structure and operation of the empire, now made readily accessible to the English-speaking world.

443 Carrillo Vivas, Gonzalo. Atlixco: perfil histórico-cultural. v. 1. Puebla, Mexico: Gobierno del Estado de Puebla, Secretaría de Cultura, 1998. 1 v.: bibl., ill., maps. (Colección Portal poblano; 37)
Interesting little book details precontact and 16th-century history of Atlixco. Unexpected tidbits include a short narrative about the organization of indigenous forces who were intended to join the fray against Francis Drake. Information about monasteries, the cabildo, and other internal matters is included.

444 Caso Barrera, Laura. Religión y resistencia indígena en Yucatán, siglos XVI-XIX. (*CLAHR,* 8:2, Spring 1999, p. 153–184, map)

Well-documented study of, on the one hand, how colonial authorities persisted in using allegations of idolatry to subjugate the Yucatecan Mayas, and on the other, how those same Mayas preserved some of their traditional religious practices and beliefs, often by manipulating Catholic sacred spaces for their own purposes. This able entry into the literature on religious dialogue of the colonial era also examines social dimensions of the situation within indigenous communities.

445 Castellón Huerta, Blas Román. Análisis estructural del ciclo de Quetzalcóatl: una aproximación a la lógica del mito en el México antiguo. México: Instituto Nacional de Antropología e Historia, 1997. 269 p., 2 folded leaves: bibl., ill. (Col. Biblioteca del INAH) (Serie Historia)
Well-mounted structuralist analysis of the Quetzalcoatl "myths," offering some useful interpretations of this enduring subject. Author operates from a solid base of primary and recent secondary literature, all intelligently integrated into his own work. See also items **507, 562,** and **568.**

446 Castillo Canché, Jorge I. Ocioso, pobre e incivilizado: algunos conceptos e ideas acerca del maya yukateko a fines del siglo XVIII. (*Mesoamérica/Antigua,* 21:39, junio 2000, p. 239–254, photo)
Examines ideas of Bernardo Ward who, in his 1762 *Proyecto económico,* argued that the "Indians" should be converted into a basic agricultural workforce. The desire to rationalize production and at the same time reform indigenous humanity was laced with negative characterizations of the Mayas as obstacles to improvement and who, in the name of humanitarianism, could be forced to work. The role of education and involuntary Hispanicization is also examined. Obviously, all of this was a kind of refinement of much older ideas about the character of indigenous peoples, a pernicious attitude that would cause even more mischief in the national period, especially with the rise of the liberal politics of progress.

447 Castro Gutiérrez, Felipe. Migración indígena y cambio cultural en Michoacán colonial, siglos XVII y XVIII. (*CLAHR,* 7:4, Fall 1998, p. 419–440, maps, table)

Charts indigenous migration, seeing it as movement primarily to landed estates in the 17th century, and as labor in copper mines and refineries in the 18th. Seeks especially to understand the process through which migrations came about, considering both voluntary forms (movement away from communities suffering a depletion of their land bases, from excessive tribute obligations, from indebtedness, and even from the threat of criminal prosecution) and more obviously coercive or involuntary types. For historian's comment, see item **1227**.

448 Chance, John K. The noble house in colonial Puebla, Mexico: descent, inheritance, and the Nahua tradition. (*Am. Anthropol.*, 102:3, Sept. 2000, p. 485–502, map)

Chance applies Claude Lévi-Strauss' concept of the "house" to the surviving *tecalli* "noble house" of late-colonial *cacicazgos* in Santiago Tecali, in the Puebla-Tlaxcala valley. Argues that broader and more inclusive "house" concept offers a more useful vehicle for understanding the *tecalli* and noble indigenous efforts to preserve their estates in the face of growing Spanish competition for access to land and other material and human resources, than does reliance on the more limited, kin-based model of lineage used in the past. For a related article dealing with the precontact Mayas, see Gillespie, item **486**.

449 Chimalpahin Cuauhtlehuanitzin, Domingo Francisco de San Antón Muñón. Primer amoxtli libro: 3a relación de las *Différentes histoires originales*. Estudio, paleografía, traducción, notas, repertorio y apéndice por Víctor M. Castillo Farreras. México: UNAM, 1997. 346 p.: bibl., ill. (Serie Cultura Náhuatl. Fuentes; 10)

Welcome translation into Spanish of this key ethnohistorical source, an important body of Chimalpahin's annals, with text running from 1064 (in the European calendar) to 1520. Nahuatl text is presented in parallel with the Spanish translation, and Castillo has provided a detailed and revealing preliminary study of the text.

450 Chinchilla Mazariegos, Oswaldo. Historiografía de los mayas en Guatemala: el pensamiento de Manuel García Elgueta. (*Mesoamérica/Antigua*, 20:38, dic. 1999, p. 55–75, appendix, photo)

Study of the life, work, and times of a late-19th-century Guatemalan liberal investigator who argued in favor of the notion that the ancestors of the present population of Guatemala were responsible for construction of its great archeological sites, including those in the lowlands.

451 Christensen, Alexander F. The Codex of San Cristóbal Coyotepec and its ramifications for the production of Techialoyan manuscripts. (*Estud. Cult. Náhuatl*, 27, 1997, p. 247–266, bibl., facsims., ill., tables)

Author focuses on what he calls "double-register" codices, which have "two scenes painted on each page, one above the other," rather than just a single picture. Considering this type of codex to be a Techialoyan subgenre, Christensen believes that the relationship between text and illustration (or the lack of it) can help us better classify and understand these enigmatic documents more generally. A useful contribution.

452 Christensen, Alexander F. Ethnohistorical evidence for inbreeding among the pre-Hispanic Mixtec royal caste. (*Hum. Biol.*, 70:3, June 1998, p. 563–577, graph, map, tables)

Using codices as sources, author charts evidence for inbreeding from 10th-16th centuries, concentrating on people connected to Lord 8 Deer Jaguar Claw of Tilantongo (1063–1115 CE). Though not written primarily for an audience of humanists or social scientists, article is of significance for ethnohistorians interested in understanding nature and effects of precontact elite marital practices.

453 Cioffi-Revilla, Claudio and **Todd Landman.** Evolution of Maya polities in the ancient Mesoamerican system. (*Int. Stud. Q./Oxford*, 43:4, Dec. 1999, p. 559–598, bibl., graphs, tables)

Ambitious attempt to reevaluate and understand nature of Mayan political development and eventual 9th-century "classic Maya collapse" by applying contemporary political theory and statistical analysis. Drawing data from 72 polities ranging over the entire geographical spread of the Maya zone, authors posit both a revised explanation for the collapse of Mayan states (ultimately, their failure to achieve some kind of pan-Mayan political unity), and a new periodization for Mayan political history. Application of such interpretive tools to what remains a spotty and incomplete record of the past may raise some scholarly eyebrows, as may the political determinism of their explanation for the collapse (they are, after all, political scientists), but this study deserves attention.

454   Códice Techialoyan de San Pedro Tototepec, Estado de México. Estudio Introductorio de Xavier Noguez. Zinacantepec, Mexico: Colegio Mexiquense, 1999. 132 p.: bibl., facsims. (some col.), ill. (some col.), maps.

Noguez returns with another exemplary study and facsimile of this Techialoyan codex, which came to light in 1994 in Tototepec. As an added bonus, this publication includes discussions of the techniques used to restore the document, including various kinds of microscopic and digital methods employed with the paper, texts, and images. A valuable contribution.

455   Códices y documentos sobre México: segundo simposio. v. 1-2. México: Instituto Nacional de Antropología e Historia, Dirección de Estudios Históricos: Dirección General de Publicaciones del Consejo Nacional para la Cultura y las Artes, 1997. 2 v.: ill. (Col. Científica; 356) (Serie Historia)

This commendable two-volume anthology contains 50 articles in English and Spanish by noted scholars covering a wide range of documentary types in the native tradition, featuring codices, principally from Nahua, Mixtec, and Mayan origins. Individual contributions are far too numerous to list here, but it can be said that ethnohistorians will find analyses of such things as the Madrid Codex, the *Códice Xolotl*, the *Códice Azoyú 2*, the *Códice Borbónico*, and several others; Mixtec historical codices; *lienzos*; and several different genres of more mundane postconquest records from the indigenous world. Subjects addressed include calendar studies, deity studies, Nahualism, dynastic history, the sacred, gender and politics, life and culture in postcontact indigenous communities. Aside from the editors themselves, some of the authors are Elizabeth H. Boone, Johanna Broda, Gordon Brotherston, Bruce Byland, Jacqueline de Durand-Forest, Michel Graulich, Doris Heyden, Patrick Johannson K., Ulrich Kohler, Miguel León Portilla, Druzo Maldonado Jiménez, Luz María Mohar Betancourt, Xavier Noguez, Ross Parmenter, Hanns J. Prem, Marc Thouvenot, Rafael Tena, Gabrielle Vail, Perla Valle, and Stephanie Wood. An essential resource.

456   Códices y documentos sobre México: tercer simposio. Coordinación de Constanza Vega Sosa. México: Instituto Nacional de Antropología e Historia, 2000. 631 p.: ill. (Col. Científica; 409. Serie Historia)

Papers from third meeting of international scholars dedicated to the study of records in the native tradition. Covers a good deal of investigatory ground. Too numerous to list individually here, the 35 articles (written in either Spanish or English) include analyses of pictorial codices and alphabetic texts; emphasis ranges from the sacred to the mundane. Contributors bring expertise from many allied fields: Laura Caso Barrera, Gordon Brotherston, Bernd Fahmel Beyer, Elizabeth H. Boone, Byron Harmann, Hermann Lejarazu, María del Carmen Herrera, Patrick Johansson K., Nicholas Johnson, Ulrich Kohler, Patric Lesbre, Druzo Maldonado, Rodrigo Martínez Baracs, Luz María Mohar B., John Monaghan, Federico Navarrete, H.B. Nicholson, Guilhem Olivier, Merideth Paxton, Hanns J. Prem, Eloise Quiñones Keber, Alfredo Ramírez C., Kay Almere Read, Carlos Rincón Mautner, Elke Ruhnau, Ethelia Ruiz M., Susan Spitler, Rafael Tena, Kevin Terraciano, Marc Thouvenot, Gabrielle Vail, Ana Rita Valero de García Lascuráin, Perla Valle, Constanza Vega Sousa, Eleanor Wake, Stephanie Wood, and Keiko Yoneda. A significant resource for ethnohistorians.

457   La conquista del Lacandón. Recopilación, introducción y notas de Nuria Pons Sáez. México: UNAM, Coordinación de Humanidades, 1997. 178 p.: bibl. (Biblioteca del Estudiante Universitario; 122)

Following a well-crafted historical overview covering material from the precontact era to early 18th century, Pons Sáez presents in turn several excerpts from chronologically arranged, Spanish-authored accounts touching on the Lacandon and their contacts and conflicts with the Spanish intruders: Gonzalo Fernández de Oviedo (1535-37); Fray Antonio de Remesal (1619); Antonio de

León Pinelo (mid-17th century); Fray Francisco Ximénez (late-17th century); Juan de Villagutierre Soto-Mayor (1701); and Nicolás de Valenzuela (c. 1700). A useful publication for those seeking early information about this well-known southeastern Mesoamerican group.

458 Cosmovisión, ritual e identidad de los pueblos indígenas de México. Coordinación de Johanna Broda y Félix Báez-Jorge. México: Consejo Nacional para la Cultura y las Artes; Fondo de Cultura Económica, 2001. 539 p.: bibl., ill., index. (Biblioteca mexicana. Serie Historia y antropología)

The majority of the nine articles in the anthology present results of modern ethnographic research, though many look back to the colonial and prehispanic eras in a comparative way. For this reason, the articles will be of some use to the ethnohistorians who consult this guide. Two of the articles, however, are more directly pertinent: Johanna Broda's thoughtful Introduction, which explores a number of relevant general themes of cultural evolution and religious ideology; and Alfred López Austin's insightful "El núcleo duro: la cosmovisión y la tradición mesoamericana."

459 Crespo, Ana María and **Beatriz Cervantes.** El papel de la élite Otomí en el avance hispano hacia el norte de México. (*in* Confronto de culturas: conquista, resistência, transformação. Rio de Janeiro: Expressão e Cultura; São Paulo: Edusp, 1997, p. 79–92, bibl.)

Authors follow fortunes of an Otomí *cacique* named Conin who, after relocating in what became the Querétaro area, received baptism as Don Hernando de Tapia and went on to have a successful career as a military, political, and economic ally of the Spaniards. Three generations of men and women in this family are examined, noting their incomplete but significant Hispanicization and their role in the founding of a convent of nuns and an indigenous hospital in Querétaro.

460 Cruz, Eloy. De como una letra hace la diferencia: las obras en náhuatl atribuidas a Don Hernando Franco. (*Estud. Cult. Náhuatl*, 32, 2001, p. 257–295)

Refreshing change of pace offered by analysis of two polyphonic songs found in the so-called Códice Valdes dated to 1599,

representing the earliest known surviving musical text from New Spain, dedicated to the Virgin Mary (Yn ilhuicac cihuapille . . .). Recordings of performances exist without commentary, making this publication doubly welcome to those interested in recovering the sounds, textures, and meanings of sacred music and their use in evangelization of the indigenous population of Mexico. Facsimiles, transcriptions, and translations are provided.

461 Cruz, Martín de la. An Aztec herbal: the classic codex of 1552. Translation and commentary by William Gates. Introduction by Bruce Byland. Mineola, N.Y.: Dover Publications, 2000. 144 p.: bibl., ill., index.

With its introductory study by Byland, this reprinting of Gates' English-language translation (see *HLAS 5:298*) of the earliest known herbal produced in Mexico is a significant event. The original was written in Nahuatl and has been attributed to Martín de la Cruz, of Mexica ancestry. The location of the Nahuatl text is not known, but a Latin translation, *Libellus de Medicinalibus Indorum Herbis*, was created by Juan Badiano, an indigenous professor at the Colegio de Santa Cruz (the text is also known as the Códice de la Cruz Badiano). Gates published his translation of the Latin text in 1939, and it remains an extremely useful work in its present reproduction.

462 El cuerpo humano y su tratamiento mortuorio. Coordinación de Elsa Malvido, Grégory Pereira y Vera Tiesler. México: Instituto Nacional de Antropología e Historia; Centro Francés de Estudios Mexicanos y Centroamericanos, 1997. 255 p.: bibl., ill. (Col. científica; 344) (Serie Antropología social)

Anthology derives from 1995 international and interdisciplinary meeting in Mexico City focusing on death and its rituals among indigenous peoples. Volume stretches temporally from precolumbian times to present, and geographically from Ayacucho to the US Southwest; but the bulk of the studies are about Mexico. Two of the more ethnohistorical pieces are Mercedes de la Barza, "Ideas nahuas y mayas sobre la muerte;" and Elsa Malvido, "Civilizados o salvajes: los ritos al cuerpo humano en la época colonial mexicana."

463 Dardón Flores, Ricardo Danilo. Los cakchiqueles de Sacatepéquez: historia y vida cotidiana durante la época colonial. (*Estudios/Guatemala,* abril 1998, p. 88–101, bibl.)

Succinct overview of history, social organization, and daily life of this Guatemalan community from eve of the Spanish invasion to independence. Includes some useful details on household organization and religious observances. See also item **464.**

464 Dardón Flores, Ricardo Danilo. Los Sacatepéquez: Chahomá, Cazchiquile, A cahal Guinac; en busca de su memoria histórica. (*Estudios/Guatemala,* agosto 1998, p. 32–51, bibl.)

Using the *Título de los Señores de Jilotepeque* (copy dated 1689, but attributed to 1555) as its centerpiece, article considers such things as precontact migration and the formation of community. Includes a transcription of a Spanish translation of this Cakchiquel text. Useful edition, since it may be in order to compare this purported 16th-century document with the wider corpus of the so-called primordial titles with which the *Título* seems to share certain similarities. See also item **463.**

465 Davoust, Michel. Le serpent Ochcan dans la table d'éclipses solaires et lunaires du Codex de Dresde. (*TRACE/México,* 28, dic. 1995, p. 3–28, bibl., ill., tables)

Richly illustrated and detailed examination of the subject of the title, complemented by clear and useful tables in an appendix.

466 De tlacuilos y escribanos: estudios sobre documentos indígenas coloniales del centro de México. Coordinación de Xavier Noguez and Stephanie Wood. Zamora, Mexico: El Colegio de Michoacán; Zinacantepec, Mexico: El Colegio Mexiquense, 1998. 221 p.: bibl., ill. (Col. Memorias)

Growing out of a panel presented at the 47th meeting of the International Congress of Americanists, this collection of more recently updated scholarly articles contains new interpretations of the well known Códice de Tlaltelolco as well as of postconquest Techialoyan codices (such as the García Granados text) and primordial titles. Its strength lies not only in the careful investigations produced by the contributors, but

also in a thematic and geographic spread that helps us flesh out the nature and variation of these rich and challenging ethnohistorical sources. Contributions include: "El Códice de Tlatelolco: una nueva cronología" by Noguez; "La sección VIII del Códice de Tlatelolco: una nueva propuesta de lectura" by Perla Valle; María Teresa Jarquín's "El Códice Techialoyan García Granados y las congregaciones en el Altiplano Central de México;" "Dominio Tepanceca en el Valle de Toluca" by Rosaura Hernández; "Autenticidad de los glifos toponómicos del círculo de Tepanecayotl del Códice Techialoyan García Granados" by Anton Saurwein; Ursula Dyckerhoff's "Dos títulos de tierras procedentes del Pueblo de Huaquilpan, Estado de Hidalgo;" Robert Haskett's "El legendario Don Toribio en los títulos primordiales de Cuernavaca;" and Wood's "El problema de la historicidad de títulos y los Códices del Grupo Techialoyan." For literature specialist's comment, see item **3363.**

467 Dead giveaways: indigenous testaments of colonial Mesoamerica and the Andes. Edited by Susan Kellogg and Matthew Restall. Salt Lake City: Univ. of Utah Press, 1998. 335 p.: bibl., index, maps.

Well-crafted anthology presents cutting-edge scholarship on interpretation of indigenous language testaments, the majority of which come from Mesoamerica: Sarah Cline, "Fray Alonso de Molina's Model Testament and Antecedents to Indigenous Wills in Spanish America"; Susan Kellogg, "Indigenous Testaments of Early-Colonial Mexico City: Testifying to Gender Differences"; Rebecca Horn, "Testaments and Trade: Interethnic Ties among Petty Traders in Central Mexico (Coyoacan, 1550–1620)"; Stephanie Wood, "Testaments and *Títulos:* Conflict and Coincidence of *Cacique* and Community Interests in Central Mexico"; Kevin Terraciano, "Native Expressions of Piety in Mixtec Testaments"; Matthew Restall, "Interculturation and the Indigenous Testament in Colonial Yucatan"; and Robert M. Hill, "Land, Family, and Community in Highland Guatemala: Seventeenth-Century Cakchiquel Maya Testaments." Many of these articles include transcriptions of parts or all of pertinent texts, and the editors provide excellent introductory and concluding chapters.

La destrucción de las Indias y sus recursos renovables, 1492–1992: dignidad con el pasado y reivindicación con el presente y futuro de los pueblos y las culturas mesoamericanas. See item **869.**

468 **Dibble, Charles E.** Los manuscritos de Tlatelolco y México y el *Códice Florentino.* (*Estud. Cult. Náhuatl*, 29, 1999, p. 27–64, tables)

Systematic, book-by-book comparison of a number of successive versions of Sahagún's corpus of work, noting the derivations from the Florentine Codex.

469 **Drew, David.** The lost chronicles of the Maya kings. Berkeley: Univ. of California Press, 1999. 450 p., 24 p. of plates: bibl., ill. (some col.), index, maps.

Accessible and detailed account of the Mayas (especially the "classic Mayas"), their society, culture, and history; and of the lives and ideas of those who "discovered" them, studied them, and theorized about them. Book's synthesis draws heavily from recent epigraphic and archeological advances. For anthropologist's comment, see *HLAS 59:35.*

470 **Los elementos anexos del Códice Borbónico.** Traducción de Edgar Samuel Morales Sales. México: Univ. Autónoma del Estado de México, Centro de Investigación en Ciencias Sociales y Humanidades, 2000. 308 p., 18 p. of plates: appendix, ill. (some col.).

Fastidious study of each successive glyph of this famous divinatory calendar, noting among other things their form, color(s), and associations with other signs. A full-color facsimile is appended. There is also a separately bound "appendix" with the same facsimile, which is intended to obviate the need to flip back and forth in the main study to find the position of a certain glyph in the original document.

471 **Elferink, Jan G.R.** Aphrodisiac use in Pre-Columbian Aztec and Inca cultures. (*J. Hist. Sex.*, 9:1/2, Jan./April 2000, p. 25–37, tables)

Author sifted through 16th-century chronicles for information about Aztec and Inca aphrodisiac usage in order to advance understanding of this dimension in the history of sexuality in the Americas. Largely descriptive, although Elferink is cognizant of the ecclesiastical filter of the sources.

Empire of sand: the Seri Indians and the struggle for Spanish Sonora, 1645–1803. See item **1367.**

472 **Escobar Ohmstede, Antonio.** De la costa a la sierra: las Huastecas, 1750–1900. México: CIESAS; Instituto Nacional Indigenista, 1998. 253 p.: appendix, bibl., ill. (some col.). (Historia de los pueblos indígenas de México)

Exacting study of the Huasteca from late colonial Bourbon age to end of 19th century. Work emphasizes economic and demographic issues, creating a valuable resource for ethnohistorians by refusing to see achievement of national independence as a stark watershed between two distinct eras. Instead, author exposes the reader to what he sees as an ongoing cultural process, featuring indigenous peoples as actors rather than as objects of events. The selected region, with its principal components in the modern states of Hidalgo and Veracruz, is notable for its ethnic diversity, taking in people of Spanish heritage, Teenek (of the Maya family), Otomí, Nahua, Totonaco, Tepehua, and some Chichimec groups. Seventeen Spanish-language documents about various pueblos from the 1790s forward are included in the appendix. A valuable addition to an excellent series of publications mounted by CIESAS and INI under the editorial direction of Teresa Rojas Rabiela and Mario Humberto Ruz.

473 **Figueras Vallés, Estrella.** Matrimonio nahua-mexica y matrimonio cristiano: reflexiones sobre dos sociedades enfrentadas. (*in* Formas familiares, procesos históricos y cambio social en América Latina. Recopilación de Ricardo Cicerchia. Quito: Ediciones Abya-Yala, 1998, p. 83–95)

Straightforward, if brief, consideration of Spanish attempts to impose their ideas of legitimate marriage on the Nahuas. Author prefaces this analysis with a comparative discussion of indigenous and Spanish marital ideologies, and ends the piece by highlighting cultural difficulties facing the Nahua women and men as they were obliged to comply with foreign imperatives.

474 **Florescano, Enrique.** El canon memorioso forjado por los "títulos primordiales." (*Colon. Lat. Am. Rev.*, 11:2, Dec. 2002, p. 183–230, ill.)

Thoughtful interpretation of the primordial titles genre takes in Techialoyans, *mapas,* and *lienzos* as well, and considers examples not only from Central Mexico but also from Oaxaca and Michoacán. Generously illustrated.

475 Florescano, Enrique. Etnia, estado y nación: ensayo sobre las identidades colectivas en México. México: Aguilar, 1997. 512 p.: ill. (Nuevo siglo)

Explores origins of collective Mexican identity, giving particular attention to indigenous peoples, their histories, and their problematic status today, with proposals for resolving the disintegration of the nation. Devotes large sections to a review of the salient elements in the prehispanic past, indigenous society under Spanish domination, and struggles within the nation-state.

476 Florescano, Enrique. Memoria indígena. México: Taurus, 1999. 403 p.: bibl., ill., indexes. (Pensamiento)

In some ways an updating and expansion of the indigenous-centered core of author's classic *Memoria mexicana* (see *HLAS 52:964*), this excellent book represents his evolving and deepening insights into ways in which Mesoamerican group memories originated and were preserved across time, from the precontact era through the indigenista movement of the Mexican Revolution and beyond. Essential reading.

Florescano, Enrique. The myth of Quetzalcoatl. See item **4336**.

477 Florescano, Enrique. Sobre la naturaleza de los dioses de Mesoamérica. (*Estud. Cult. Náhuatl,* 27, 1997, p. 41–67, bibl., ill., photo)

After presenting a historiographical overview of the evolution of scholarly thinking about the true nature of Mesoamerican divinities, Florescano suggests his own interpretation. As a few other scholars have done, he links his ideas to Durkheim's, and calls on more investigators to do the same.

478 Fray Bernardino de Sahagún y su tiempo. Coordinacion de Jesús Paniagua Pérez y María Isabel Viforcos Marinas. León, Spain: Univ. de León, Secretariado de Publicaciones; Instituto Leonés de Cultura, 2000. 790 p.: bibl., ill., index.

Collection of 45 articles written by prominent scholars (including Miguel León

Portilla, Georges Baudot, and many others) growing out of a 1999 meeting held in León to commemorate 500th anniversary of Sahagún's birth. Begins with works concerned with the Spanish intellectual context of which Sahagún was a product, and follows him as he migrated to New Spain and carried out his enduring life's work. Once again, many articles concern themselves with reconstructing the sociocultural milieu of his adopted home, including the more general enterprise of the Catholic Church and the Franciscan order, as well as with the life and work of the friar himself. Here authors cover a variety of specific topics, from Mictlan to the *Psalmodia Christiana,* from the *huehuetlatolli* to the *Colloquios.* Nearly encyclopedic in scope, this is a very useful resource.

479 Fuentes para la historia india de Coahuila. Coordinación de Carlos Manuel Valdés y Ildefonso Dávila B. Madrid: Fundación Histórica Tavera; Archivo Municipal de Saltillo, 1998. 350 p.: index, maps. (Documentos Tavera; 7)

Valuable annotated guide to documents held in the Archivo Municipal de Saltillo and the Archivo General del Estado de Coahuila. The listed documents date from 1591–1891, with about two-thirds coming from the 19th-century periods of independence struggle and Mexican nationhood. Of the colonial records, the bulk date from the 18th century, though the 17th is represented to some extent, as well (only two documents date from the late 16th century). A substantial number of documents pertain to the activities of Tlaxcalan colonists, and San Estéban de Nueva Tlaxcala is well represented among them. References to the Chichimecs can also be found. A valuable resource. See also items **559, 631,** and **632.**

480 Garavaglia, Juan Carlos. Atlixco: el agua, los hombres y la tierra en un valle mexicano, siglos XIV-XVII. (*in* Tierra, agua y bosques: historia y medio ambiente en el México central. Coordinación de Alejandro Tortolero Villaseñor. México: Centre français d'études mexicaines et centraméricaines; Instituto de Investigaciones Dr. José María Luis Mora; Potrerillos Editores; Guadalajara, Mexico: Univ. de Guadalajara, 1996, p. 69–126, bibl., graphs, maps, tables)

Thoroughly researched study begins with a dose of precontact history, and includes a study of hydraulics, natural vegetation, and agriculture in the area. Focusing on comparisons between Atlixco and Tochimilco, as well as Huejotzingo, the author moves on to chart the changes and conflicts wrought by the introduction of wheat agriculture and Spanish competition for land and resources. For geography specialist's comment, see *HLAS 59:2477*.

García Castro, René. Indios, territorio y poder en la provincia Matlatzinca: la negociación del espacio político de los pueblos otomianos, siglos XV-XVII. See item **1250**.

481 García Quintana, María José. Historia de una *historia*: las ediciones de la *Historia general de las cosas de Nueva España* de Fray Bernardino de Sahagún. (*Estud. Cult. Náhuatl*, 29, 1999, p. 163–188, bibl.)

Another entry into the ever-expanding corpus of work studying the production of the great Franciscan. In this case, the author traces the history of Sahagún's magnum opus in its Spanish-language version from its inception to its relatively recent publications.

482 Garduño, Ana. Conflictos y alianzas entre Tlatelolco y Tenochtitlán, siglos XII a XV. México: Instituto Nacional de Antropología e Historia, 1997. 185 p.: bibl., ill. (Biblioteca del INAH) (Serie historia)

Well-done study of often contentious relationships between these two island *altepetl* from the time of the Aztlán migration to the immediate aftermath of Tenochtitlán's defeat of its rival in 1473. Skillful synthesis of information from a variety of chronicles, and fine balancing of Tlatelocan and Tenochca voices.

483 Garza, Mercedes de la. El perro como símbolo religioso entre los mayas y los nahuas. (*Estud. Cult. Náhuatl*, 27, 1997, p. 111–133, bibl., ill., photos)

Succinct review of Mesoamerican thought about dogs, based on interpretations of a variety of sources.

484 Gender in Pre-Hispanic America: a symposium at Dumbarton Oaks, 12 and 13 October 1996. Edited by Cecelia F. Klein and Jeffrey Quilter. Washington: Dumbarton Oaks Research Library and Collection, 2001. 405 p.: bibl., ill., index, maps.

Masterful anthology of multidisciplinary articles growing out of a 1996 symposium. Over half focus directly on Mesoamerica, including Elizabeth M. Brumfiel's assessment of the strengths and weaknesses of ethnohistorical and archeological sources from which information about gender can be recovered; Louise Burkhart's inquiry into the possibly Christian-influenced lessons about sexual morality and female submission embodied in the *Huehuetlatolli*; Rosemary Joyce's innovative analysis of sex and gender among the Mayas of the classic period; Cecelia Klein's complex study of ways in which Nahua gender ideologies came to terms with "gender-ambiguous" people; Mari Carmen Serra Puch's meticulous reconstruction of "the concept of feminine" as deduced from archeological evidence at the classic-era Tlaxcalan site of Xochitécatl; and Joyce Marcus' thoughtful comparative investigation of ways in which royal women could sometimes break the "glass ceiling" in Mesoamerica and other ancient societies. These excellent contributions are rounded out and complemented by studies of gender in 20th-century Mesoamerica and of gender and more specifically of masculinity in the precontact Andes. Concluding chapters address relevant theoretical issues.

485 Giasson, Patrice. Tlazolteotl, deidad del abono: una propuesta. (*Estud. Cult. Náhuatl*, 32, 2001, p. 135–157)

Ecological interpretation of the functions of Mexica deities, focused here on the example of Tlazolteotl and this goddess' relationships to various natural forces.

486 Gillespie, Susan D. Rethinking ancient Maya social organization: replacing "lineage" with "house." (*Am. Anthropol.*, 102:3, Sept. 2000, p. 467–484)

This author sees Claude Lévi-Strauss' concept of "house" as a more "flexible" interpretive tool for the analysis of precontact Mayan lordly establishments than the more restricted idea of "lineage." As in Lévi-Strauss' model, the noble Mayan "house" encompassed not just lines of directly related kin, but also a whole complex of dependent commoners, lands, and other possessions which in sum total expressed elite status, social, economic, and political power. For a related article applying this model to colonial Puebla, see item **448**.

487 **Gillespie, Susan D.** and **Rosemary A. Joyce.** Deity relationships in Mesoamerican cosmologies: the case of the Maya God L. (*Anc. Mesoam.*, 9:2, Fall 1998, p. 279–296, bibl., facsims., ill.)

Authors challenge scholars to move beyond taxonomic identification of deities, which they argue is fraught with difficulty and imprecision due to a plethora of shared visual characteristics. Instead, through a detailed analysis of Maya Gods L and M, as well as of Bolon Yokte, authors urge that relationships between deities, and between deities and humans such as rulers, be explored in an effort to create a deeper understanding of the roles and meanings of Mesoamerican divinities.

488 **Gilonne, Michel.** La civilisation aztèque et l'aigle royal: ethnologie et ornithologie. Paris: L'Harmattan, 1997. 217 p.: bibl., map. (Collection Recherches et documents. Amériques latines)

Intriguing study of the significance of eagles among the Aztecs, set within a broader context of representations of birds more generally.

489 **Gingerich, Willard.** *Tlamachilliztlatolçaçanilli:* a performance translation of the Náhuatl "Wisdom-Discourse Fables" from the Manuscript of 1558. (*Estud. Cult. Náhuatl*, 28, 1998, p. 159–196, bibl.)

New translation and evaluation of the "Manuscript of 1558," better known as *La leyenda de los soles,* appended to the end of the *Códice Chimalpopoca;* the designation "Wisdom-Discourse Fables" is Gingerich's translation of *tlamachilliztlatolçaçanilli,* a classification found in the document itself. Gingerich discusses ways in which orality and performance might still be recoverable in the prose document, and has structured his translation with this in mind.

490 **González Torres, Yolotl.** Animales y plantas en la cosmovisión mesoamericana. México: Plaza y Valdés Editores; CONACULTA-INAH; Sociedad Mexicana para el Estudio de las Religiones, 2001. 322 p.: bibl., ill.

Collection of 13 articles assesses cosmic significance of plants and animals in the thinking of the precontact Mesoamericans,

principally among the Nahuas and the Mayas, but including such groups as the Huichols as well. Book is divided into two sections: the first deals with flora (maíz, amaranth, the ceiba, and psychoactive plants); the second with fauna (the jaguar, the snake, molluscs, the caiman, and the quetzal, and the deer, among others). Many useful illustrations grace the articles.

491 **Graff, Don** and **Gabrielle Vail.** Censers and stars: issues in the dating of the Madrid Codex. (*Lat. Am. Indian Lit. J.*, 17:1, Spring 2001, p. 58–95)

Sifting through a wealth of iconographic evidence, authors conclude that Madrid Codex was a product of mid-15th century. This solid article is related to ongoing controversies surrounding the authenticity of the four known "preconquest" Mayan screenfolds (Madrid, Dresden, Paris, and Grolier). For new conclusions about the authenticity of the Grolier Codex, see item **560**.

492 **Graniceros: cosmovisión y meteorología indígenas de Mesoamérica.** Coordinación de Beatriz Andrea Albores Zárate y Johanna Broda. Zinacantepec, Mexico: El Colegio Mexiquense; México: Instituto de Investigaciones Históricas, UNAM, 1997. 563 p.: bibl., ill.

Collection of 19 articles from a 1994 symposium sponsored by the Colegio Mexiquense centered around the *graniceros,* specialists in the manipulation of sites connected in some way with the sacred causes of atmospheric phenomena. While many of the individual articles are ethnographic in nature, those under the heading "El culto do la lluvia y los cerros en la Cuenca de México y zonas aledañas" contain fruits of new research into sacred meanings of mountains, caves, and the sky. Pertinent articles include: "Los cerros de Tlacloc" by Gordon Brotherston; "El culto mexica de los cerros de la Cuenca de México" by Broda; "El Monte Tlaloc y el calendario mexica" by Morante López; "El culto a los volcanes en el sur de la Cuenca de México durante el Preclásico" by Aranda Monroy; "Culto en la Cueva de Chimalacatepec, San Juan Tlacotenco, Morelos" by Broda and Druzo Maldonado; "Hacia una arqueoastronomía atmosférica" by Espinosa Pineda; and "Noticias historicas y actuales sobre lugares de culto en la zona del

Ajusco y en El Pedregal de San Angel" by Alejandro Robles.

493 Graulich, Michel. Atamalcualiztli: fiesta azteca del nacimiento de Cinteotl-Venus. (*Estud. Cult. Náhuatl*, 32, 2001, p. 359–370, bibl.)

Succinct study of Atamalcualiztli, translated by the author as the "Feast of Water Tamales," an eight-day festival staged in commemoration of the "transgression" at Tamoanchan and the birth of Centeotl-Venus. Based on a close reading of some of the most important ethnohistorical sources, such as Sahagún, Durán, and the *Códice Telleriano-Remensis.*

494 Graulich, Michel. Aztec human sacrifice as expiation. (*Hist. Relig./Chicago*, 39:4, May 2000, p. 352–372)

Not content with standard explanations, Graulich looks at the complex levels and meanings of sacrificial practices, arguing that ultimately they had to do with the expiation of "sins or transgressions" so that a better afterlife could be achieved. In support, he offers new interpretations of such topics as the story of the creation of the sun and moon, among other myths long thought to justify and explain the necessity of human sacrifice. A serious contribution.

495 Graulich, Michel. Más sobre la Coyolxauhqui y las mujeres desnudas de Tlatelolco. (*Estud. Cult. Náhuatl*, 31, 2000, p. 77–94, bibl.)

Reacting to Cecelia Klein's article "Fighting with Feminity: Gender and War in Aztec Society," (see *HLAS 58:528*), Graulich presents his own interpretations. A contribution to the continuing study and debate over the nature of gender ideologies among the precontact Nahuas.

496 Graulich, Michel. Ritos aztecas: las fiestas de las veintenas. México: Instituto Nacional Indigenista, 1999. 459, 32 p.: bibl., ill. (Fiesta de los pueblos indígenas)

As title of the book implies, work examines *veintenas* festivals of the Aztec ritual year. Each festival is examined separately, and Graulich offers some useful insights into the cosmic and ritual aspects of the precontact Nahua calendar. See also items **499** and **597**.

497 Graulich, Michel. La royauté sacrée chez les aztéques de México. (*Rev. Esp. Antropol. Am.*, 28, 1998, p. 99–117, bibl.)

Author ponders why Aztec rulers never assumed the status of deities themselves, but were rather content to be, and taken as, chief priests who were intermediaries between humanity and the supernatural.

498 Gutiérrez, Oscar R. El reclamo de cacicazgos: una forma de obtener poder y servicios personales. (*Estudios/Guatemala*, abril 1998, p. 102–123, bibl.)

Transcription with commentary of a document connected with the *cacique* Don Juan de Rojas y Cortés, of Santa Cruz del Quiché, dating from last years of the 16th century. The ways in which members of this class achieved and maintained power are apparent in this useful publication.

The lords of Tikal: rulers of an ancient Maya city. See *HLAS 59:175.*

499 Hassig, Ross. Time, history, and belief in Aztec and colonial Mexico. Austin: Univ. of Texas Press, 2001. 235 p.: bibl., ill., index.

This erudite reinterpretation of Aztec calendar and concepts of the past should prompt discussion and rethinking of topics long taken for granted. See also items **496** and **597**.

500 Hassig, Ross. Xicoténcatl: rethinking an indigenous Mexican hero. (*Estud. Cult. Náhuatl*, 32, 2001, p. 29–49)

Moves beyond typical cardboard cutout portrayals of the Tlaxcalan opponent of Cortes—Xicoténcatl the Younger cast as either a hero or villain depending on a particular writer's agenda—to create a more nuanced and compelling portrait of this complex character. Setting Xicotencatl's actions within a context of ongoing internal political struggle in Tlaxcala, author presents a tour de force of perceptive historical reinterpretation.

501 Hernández, Francisco. The Mexican treasury: the writings of Dr. Francisco Hernández. Edited by Simon Varey. Translated by Rafael Chabrán, Cynthia L. Chamberlin, and Simon Varey. Stanford, Calif.: Stanford Univ. Press, 2000. 300 p.: bibl., ill., index.

Translations of significant and representative texts written by Hernández, the chief royal medical officer in New Spain in the 1570s who created a monumental natural history of that region. Extremely useful to interested scholars of Mesoamerican ethnohistory (as well as many others), as are the introductory texts. An important addition to the literature. For more information on the life and work of Hernández, see item **611**.

502 Herren, Angela Marie. Representing and reinventing Doña Marina: images from the *Florentine Codex* and the *Lienzo de Tlaxcala.* (*Lat. Am. Indian Lit. J.*, 16:2, Fall 2000, p. 158–180, ill.)

Herren assesses the depiction of Doña Marina in these two sources, which offer the most extensive representations of this figure from an indigenous point of view. Neither source casts her as what Sahagún's informants described as a "bad noblewoman," and in her role as both translator and aide to Cortés she is bathed in an apparently positive light. Seeing Doña Marina in these documents as an emblem of the indigenous role in the triumph of Christianity and the Spanish more generally, author concludes that the image of this iconized and often demonized figure will continue to be manipulated for partisan ends. Many illustrations of Doña Marina as she appears in both codices are included with the article.

503 Heyden, Doris. La muerte del Tlatoani: costumbres funerarias en el México antiguo. (*Estud. Cult. Náhuatl*, 27, 1997, p. 89–109, bibl., ill.)

Examines descriptions written by Toribio de Benevente Motolinía, Francisco Cervantes de Salazar, Diego Muñoz Camargo, Juan Bautista Pomar, Joseph de Acosta, Antonio de Herrera, Fray Juan de Torquemada, Francisco Javier Clavijero, Fray Bernardino de Sahagún, and Fray Diego Durán to reconstruct and understand funerary practices among the Nahua ruling class in the pre-Christian era.

504 Heyden, Doris. El Templo Mayor de Tenochtitlán en la obra de Fray Diego Durán. México: Instituto Nacional de Antropología e Historia, 2000. 138 p.: appendix, bibl., ill. (some col.). (Col. Obra diversa)

Heyden presents a compilation of the friar's descriptions of the Great Temple, its origin, construction, and rites and beliefs associated with it, drawn from her previous and significant editions of Durán's *History of the Indies of New Spain* (see *HLAS 56:430*) and *Book of the Gods and Rites and the Ancient Calendar* (see *HLAS 34:1036*). All of this is prefaced by a concise discussion of Durán's life, work, and thought. A series of brilliant illustrations, mainly from Durán's work, is appended.

505 Hicks, Frederic. The middle class in ancient Central Mexico. (*J. Anthropol. Res.*, 55:3, Fall 1999, p. 409–427, bibl.)

Hicks believes that while in one sense there were two orders or "estates" in Nahua society based on birth (nobles and commoners), the power wielded within each group varied, propelling some lineages from both estates into an identifiable "middle class." A discussion of specific types and professions within this middle class is offered, and the forms of compensation and privileges extended to them by the upper class (and used to set the middle level apart from both the commoners and the higher elites) are reviewed.

506 Historia antigua de México. v. 1, El México antiguo, sus áreas culturales, los orígenes y el horizonte preclásico. v. 2, El horizonte clásico. v. 3, El horizonte posclásico. v. 4, Aspectos fundamentales de la tradición cultural mesoamericana. México: INAH; UNAM, Coordinación de Humanidades, Instituto de Investigaciones Antropológicas; M.A. Porrúa, 2000. 4 v.: bibl., ill., maps.

Ambitious series of four volumes containing articles on pertinent subjects written by prominent scholars in the field. Volumes follow a standard scheme of periodization. For comments on individual volumes, see *HLAS 57:82, HLAS 57:83,* and *HLAS 58:517.*

Historia general de América Latina. See item **1002.**

507 Históricas. 51, enero/abril 1998. México: UNAM, Instituto de Investigaciones Históricas.

This issue of the journal includes four articles based on scholarly talks given at a 1997 presentation of Enrique Florescano's *El mito de Quetzalcóatl* in Tegucigalpa. The noted scholar provides a semi-autobiographical piece entitled "El mito de Quetzalcóatl," which is followed by Félix Báez-Jorge's "Las máscaras de Quetzalcóatl," Johanna Broda's "Quetzalcóatl y el origen de la agricultura," and Doris Heyden's "Quetzalcóatl como deidad de la vegetación." These articles respond to, critique, or expand on what Florescano has accomplished. For comment on first edition of original monograph, see *HLAS 56:440*. For comment on English-language translation of monograph, see item **4336**. See also items **445, 562**, and **568**.

508 Horcasitas, Fernando and **Alfred E. Lemmon.** El tratado de Santa Eulalia: un manuscrito musical náhuatl. (*Tlalocan/México*, 12, 1997, p. 71–115)

Fascinating reprint of key sections of a 1980 article ("Manuscrito teórico musical de Santa Eulalia: un estudio de un tesoro musical y lingüístico de Guatemala colonial"), with a new English-language introduction bringing the scholarship up to date. The original study, which includes a transcription and translation of the Nahuatl text, considers the ethnohistorical implications of a Nahuatl-language musical text composed around 1607 by means of careful linguistic analysis. The authors link the text to the cultural and linguistic impact of the postconquest migration of Tlaxcalans and other central Mexicans to Guatemala during and after Alvarado's invasion, suggesting as well a previous Nahuatl-speaking presence.

509 Houston, Stephen D. Decorous bodies and disordered passions: representations of emotion among the Classic Maya. (*World Archaeol.*, 33:2, Oct. 2001, p. 202–220)

Examines rare but socioculturally significant depictions of emotion that move beyond the "decorous" and—to modern observers at least—unemotional images of bodily positions and hand gestures typically expressed in painting or carved relief. Houston identifies and assesses the meanings of several different kinds of representation, including horrified captive warriors, figures displaying grief, and individuals engaged in sexual acts, which help strip away this facade of emotional decorum.

510 Ibarra, Laura. La idea mágico-religiosa de la virginidad en el mundo prehispánico. (*Iztapalapa/México*, 19:45, enero/junio 1999, p. 65–78, bibl., photos)

Author seeks to understand why female virginity was so important to the precontact Mesoamericans. Focuses particularly on the Nahuas and uses many friar-authored accounts of prehispanic indigenous thought; however, fails to explore sufficiently the influence of the friars' own sensibilities on their descriptions.

511 Ibarra, Laura. Los sacrificios humanos: una explicación desde la teoria histórico-genética. (*Estud. Cult. Náhuatl*, 32, 2001, p. 341–358)

Author grapples with the logic behind human sacrifice among the Aztecs, offering her own plausible theory. As an example, she describes the rite principally as it was staged in the festival of Ochpaniztli, but in some others as well.

512 Ibarra Rojas, Eugenia. Cristóbal Colón y la etnohistoria de América Central en los albores del siglo XXI. (*Rev. Hist. Am./México*, 124, enero/junio 1999, p. 7–27, bibl.)

Regarding him as a keen and accurate observer of indigenous life and customs, the author recounts Columbus' ideas about the peoples of Española and the Caribbean, as well as the coast of what is now Costa Rica.

513 Iglesias, Miriam. Tierras indias bajo ley española: Cuauhtinchán, Puebla, México; siglo XVI. (*Anu. IEHS*, 13, 1998, p. 215–233, bibl., graph, table)

Informative overview of nature of land disputes in 16th- and early-17th-century Cuauhtinchán. Prefacing her work with a brief discussion of the prehispanic era and its land tenure situation, author devotes most of her attention to land disputes pitting indigenous litigants against one another. Along the way she is able to say something about the structure of Cuauhtinchán's class-based land tenure system as it existed in the Spanish era.

514 Ilarregui, Gladys M. Preguntar y responder en Nueva España: el caso de Tlatelolco y Sahagún. (*Estud. Cult. Náhuatl*, 26, 1996, p. 173–186)

Intelligent analysis of the shaping power of the questions posed by Sahagún to the Tlatelolcans, which of course ultimately came from a Catholic perspective. Also considers the impact of the surrounding matrix of colonialism on the informants, as well as their own cultural transformations.

515 In iihiyo, in itlahtol = Su aliento, su palabra: homenaje a Miguel León Portilla. México: Instituto de Investigaciones Históricas, UNAM; El Colegio Nacional; Instituto Nacional de Antropología e Historia, 1997. 364 p.: bibl., ill.

Twenty-six essays from collaborators, friends, and disciples of eminent ethnohistorian Miguel León Portilla, whose work over the past few decades has considerably elevated global appreciation for the history of the indigenous peoples of Mexico. Included are commentaries on his books, his translation work, his editing of primary sources, his impact on the indigenous world, and his role as a professor, among other themes.

516 Información de 1554 sobre los tributos que los indios pagaban a Moctezuma. Recopilación y paleografía de José Luis de Rojas. México: Ciesas, 1997. 214 p.: bibl., ill.

New analytical study and transcription of a mid-16th-century ethnohistorical source in the Archivo General de Indias (AGI) includes detailed testimonials from six Nahua *principales* given through an interpreter. Their testimonies therefore are recorded in Spanish, but they do preserve some Nahuatl terminology. There are many useful tables, and in one case the localities mentioned in this document are compared with those found in the *Codex Mendoza* and the *Matricula de Tributos*, in three parallel columns.

517 Isaac, Barry L. Cannibalism among Aztecs and their neighbors: analysis of the 1577–1586 *Relaciones Geográficas* for Nueva España and Nueva Galicia provinces. (*J. Anthropol. Res.*, 58:2, Summer 2002, p. 203–224)

Analyzes testimony about the practice of cannibalism found in 40 of the *Relaciones*. While many allegations come from the pens of Spaniards, nearly half of the testimony is provided by indigenous informants. For this reason, Isaac believes that this kind of source can be used to gain a better understanding of actual dimensions of the practice. The practice in rural areas seems to have been very similar to the better-known traditions in large urban areas such as Tenochtitlán. See also item **580**.

518 Izquierdo, Ana Luisa. Acalán y La Chontalpa en el siglo XVI: su geografía política. México: UNAM, 1997. 215 p.: bibl., ill.

Exacting, well-researched reconstruction of Chontal Mayan polities of the late postclassic era, on the eve of the Spanish invasion. By carefully delineating the political, economic, and geographic organizations of Chontal states, author is able to demonstrate that these Mayan peoples had maintained complex organizations in a time traditionally regarded by scholars as a period of cultural decadence.

519 Jansen, Maarten E.R.G.N. Los fundamentos para una "lectura lírica" de los códices. (*Estud. Cult. Náhuatl*, 30, 1999, p. 165–181, bibl.)

Author presents a detailed rebuttal to criticism leveled at his interpretations of codices by Miguel León Portilla (see item **541**).

520 Johansson K., Patrick. Escatología y muerte en el mundo nahuatl precolombino. (*Estud. Cult. Náhuatl*, 31, 2000, p. 149–183, bibl., facsims.)

Intriguing, well-documented examination of what author regards as seamless ideological links between certain bodily functions (ingestion and digestion of foods, production of excrement, and the like) and the decay of cadavers, death, and ultimately regeneration.

521 Johansson K., Patrick. Estudio comparativo de la gestación y del nacimiento de Huitzilopochtli en un relato verbal, una variante pictográfica y un "texto" arquitectónico. (*Estud. Cult. Náhuatl*, 30, 1999, p. 71–111, bibl., facsims.)

Another retelling of this story, but an extremely sophisticated one, which tangles with the complexities implicit in the tale. The comparative nature of the study adds depth and is worth noting, for the author is not content to limit his gaze to a single kind of source. Johansson's "oral" source is Sahagún's *Historia general de las cosas de Nueva España: Florentine Codex*, by virtue of author's position that the text was originally copied from the spoken word. The main pictographic source is the *Códice Borutrini, o Tira de la peregrinación*, and the archeological "text" is the Templo Mayor.

522   Johansson K., Patrick. La fecundación del hombre en el Mictlan y el origen de la vida breve. (*Estud. Cult. Náhuatl*, 27, 1997, p. 69–88, bibl., photos)

Assesses the meanings of the creation of the humanity which would populate the fifth age, based on a close analysis of relevant text from *La leyenda de los soles*.

523   Johansson K., Patrick. La imagen en los codices nahuas: consideraciones semiológicas. (*Estud. Cult. Náhuatl*, 32, 2001, p. 69–124)

Dense analysis of way in which images in several specific genres of pictorial codices were part of the process of communication in precontact Mesoamerica (not including the Maya zone). Another careful and significant contribution by this prolific author.

524   Johansson K., Patrick. *Tlahtoani* y *Cihuacoatl:* lo diestro solar y lo siniestro lunar en el alto mando mexica. (*Estud. Cult. Náhuatl*, 28, 1998, p. 39–75, bibl.)

Intends to establish more clearly the precise relationships between the *Cihuacoatl* and the *Tlahtoani* of the Mexica. To do so, author examines a range of interrelated concepts, such as dualism, gender, thought about the nature of "right" and "left" and their relationships to the sun and the moon, and the character of the goddess Cihuacoatl and her links to the male political figure also known as Cihuacoatl, among others. All of this allows the author to make some intriguing suggestions about the duality of power at the pinnacle of authority in late precontact Mexico.

525   Jones, Grant D. The conquest of the last Maya kingdom. Stanford, Calif.: Stanford Univ. Press, 1998. 596 p.: bibl., ill., index, maps.

Important investigation of the last major Spanish military conquest in Mesoamerica: the destruction of the Itza kingdom in 1697. Jones lays extensive groundwork for understanding both the nature of this indigenous polity and the long run-up to the final Spanish attack. An examination of the tragic and violent events which followed the conquest form a concluding section to this essential book.

526   Jones, Grant D. Revisiting the "Canek Manuscript." (*Anc. Mesoam.*, 10:2, Fall 1999, p. 313–316, bibl.)

Jones reveals the elements that led him to conclude that the "Canek Manuscript" is most likely a 20th-century forgery, prompted by communications from and collaboration with Hanns J. Prem (see item **581**).

527   *Journal de la Société des américanistes.* Vol. 84, No. 2, 1998. La collection Aubin-Goupil a la Bibliotheque nationale de France. Paris: Au siège de la Société.

High quality collection of articles written in French, Spanish, English, and German assessing different strengths of the Aubin-Goupil collection of ethnohistorical documents. Aside from work provided by the editors themselves, contributors include Jacqueline de Durand-Forest, Monique Cohen, Patrick Lesbre, Maarten Jansen, Martine Simonin, José Rubén Romero Galván, Berthod Riese, Perla Valle, and Ethellia Ruiz Medrano. Particularly important for the *HLAS* chapter on ethnohistory are H.B. Nicholson's discussion of the shape of the "native tradition" in pictorials; Susan Spitler's study of the Texcocan *Mapa Tlotzin;* Eloise Quiñones Keber's probing examination of historical paintings produced by the Acolhua creators of the *Mapa Quinatzin* and *Codex Xolotl;* Elke Ruhnau's analysis of ways in which Chimalpahin sought to solidify indigenous Christianity among the readers of his historical work; and Stephanie Wood's evaluation of ways in which pictorials in the collection depict women as town founders and as guardians of community sovereignty.

528   Joyce, Rosemary A. Gender and power in prehispanic Mesoamerica. Austin: Univ. of Texas Press, 2000. 269 p.: bibl., ill., index, map.

Major offering concentrates mainly on the Mayas (preclassic, classic, and postclassic) and the Aztecs. Joyce brings fresh insights about Mesoamerican attitudes toward gender and status by seeking what she calls "gender performances," viewing gender as a kind of activity expressed in bodily adornment and costume, in everyday life as well as in official ritual. For anthropologist's comment, see *HLAS 59:51*.

529 Joyce, Rosemary A. Girling the girl
and boying the boy: the production of
adulthood in ancient Mesoamerica. (*World
Archaeol.*, 31:3, Feb. 2000, p. 473–484)

Author investigates what she calls
"lifecycle transformations" and how they
were effected among the Aztecs, concentrating especially on childhood. By examining a
variety of ethnohistorical sources, Joyce constructs a compelling analysis of different
stages in the process of producing an adult
through gendered rituals, costume and adornment, education, and discipline.

530 Khan, Yasmin and **Robert S. Stone.**
Garcia M8 reviews the conquest of
Mexico. (*Lat. Am. Indian Lit. J.*, 15:1, Spring
1999, p. 64–84)

Preliminary analysis of this colonial-
era manuscript, held in the Nettie Lee Benson Library at the Univ. of Texas at Austin.
While text seems to be an eyewitness account of the arrival of Cortés and the first friars as told by a 16th-century indigenous narrator named Pedro Creyra, authors believe
that the illustrated Spanish-language text actually dates from 18th century and has a
close affinity to the Techialoyan genre without being exactly the same. Points the way to
a larger-scale study of this document.

531 Klein, Cecelia F. The devil and the
skirt: an iconographic inquiry into the
prehispanic nature of the tzitzimime. (*Estud.
Cult. Náhuatl*, 31, 2000, p. 17–62, bibl., ill.)

Exacting and convincing article in
which the author demonstrates how the
Tzitzimime, whom she argues were a group
of female deities, were transformed into
masculine demons and the devil in the postconquest through the influence of Spanish
clergy. She argues that, prior to the arrival of
the Iberian invaders, the Tzitzimime were
thought to have positive as well as negative
qualities. Very well done, and effectively illustrated. The article was published under
the same title in *Ancient Mesoamerica*, 11:1,
Spring 2000, p. 1–26. For archeologist's comment, see *HLAS 59:197.*

532 Köhler, Ulrich. "Debt-payment" to the
gods among the Aztecs: the misrender-
ing of a Spanish expression and its effects.
(*Estud. Cult. Náhuatl*, 32, 2001, p. 125–157)

Author argues that a mistaken translation of the root of the Náhuatl word *nextla-*

hualli (to offer sacrifice) by Rene Simeon led
to an equally mistaken interpretation of the
relationship between humanity and the deities, distorting the true nature of the reciprocal obligations that linked them together in
the cosmos. Köhler's less than diplomatic
critical tone may offend some currently active North American students of the Aztecs,
but scholars should nonetheless pay attention to his argument.

533 Konig, Viola. Lienzo Seler II and the
Coixtlahuaca group of *lienzos*. (*Lat.
Am. Indian Lit. J.*, 18:2, Fall 2002, p. 147–
210, tables)

Detailed comparison between the
Seler and the broader group of texts named in
the title. The study is supported by many
comparative tables.

534 Koontz, Rex; Kathryn Reese-Taylor;
and **Annabeth Headrick.** Landscape
and power in ancient Mesoamerica. Boulder,
Colo.: Westview Press, 2001. 383 p.: bibl.,
ill., index, maps.

Anthology of a dozen scholarly articles
examining Mesoamerican notions of sacred
geography, its expression, and its influence in
the interconnected areas of ritual, politics,
and architecture at selected sites, including
Chichén Itzá, El Tajín, Teotihuacán, Izapa,
and Tenochtitlán.

535 LeCount, Lisa J. Like water for chocolate: feasting and political ritual
among the late classic Maya of Xanantunich,
Belize. (*Am. Anthropol.*, 103:4, Dec. 2001,
p. 935–953)

Using evidence of feasting as it was
depicted on pottery vessels, as well as a
study of the distribution of various types of
crockery in specific residential and official
settings, author reconstructs patterns of consumption of both chocolate beverages and
tamales that can be linked to expressions of
sociopolitical organization. LeCount believes
that chocolate was often consumed by elites
during politically charged rituals, and that it
served to express and preserve power and status. Maintains that feasting in general could
be used to set apart noble patrons from the
majority, as well as to preserve patriarchal relationships. Well-done archeological work
with real ethnohistorical significance.

536 Lengua y etnohistoria purépecha: homenaje a Benedict Warren. Coordinación de Carlos S. Paredes Martínez. Morelia, Mexico: Univ. Michoacana de San Nicolás de Hidalgo, Instituto de Investigaciones Históricas; México: Centro de Investigaciones y Estudios Superiores en Antropología Social, 1997. 378 p.: port. (Encuentros; 2)

Growing out of a colloquium held in Morelia, Michoacán (1994), this useful volume includes many articles of particular interest to linguists. However, in a final section entitled "Historia y Etnohistoria," there are five pieces of potential appeal to ethnohistorians of Mesoamerica, covering the themes of land tenure in precontact Michoacán, an interpretation of the *Lienzo de Jucatacato*, ethnic and social conflict in the colonial era, and impact of the Bourbon reforms on indigenous communities in the region.

537 León-Portilla, Ascensión H. de. Una carta en náhuatl desde el Soconusco, siglo XVI. (*Estud. Cult. Náhuatl*, 31, 2000, p. 236–258)

Study of a letter written c. 1561 by Don Miguel Cortés, a *tlatoani* of Tocantlán (modern Tuzantán). Cortés complained about the excesses of Spanish officials from Guatemala (including the forced sale of goods), stating that his community should really be governed from Mexico. The letter also speaks out against what seem to be the grasping padres dispatched by the bishop of Guatemala. A facsimile, transcription, and translation of the letter are included.

538 León-Portilla, Ascensión H. de. De la palabra hablada a la palabra escrita: las primeras gramáticas de náhuatl. (*Estud. Cult. Náhuatl*, 27, 1997, p. 209–225)

As title suggests, much of this well-written article examines work of the first three friar-linguists of 16th-century Mexico: the Franciscans Andrés de Olmos and Alonso de Molina, and the Jesuit Antonio del Rincón. Prefaced by a discussion of the first documentary fruits of the "conquest of the word" by the friars as they sought to educate themselves so that they would be able to convey the tenets of Christianity in alphabetic Nahuatl. All of this is put in the context of the rise of the vernacular grammar,

initiated by the Spaniard Elio Antonio de Nebrija, a process in which the friars of Mexico were important pioneers.

539 León Portilla, Miguel. La autonomía indígena: carta al Príncipe Felipe de los principales de México en 1554. (*Estud. Cult. Náhuatl*, 32, 2001, p. 235–256)

León Portilla's brief commentary fronts a presentation of a facsimile, transcription, and two translations (one by the author, the other contemporary with the original Nahuatl text) of a letter in which lords of indigenous Mexico City complain about their loss of autonomy (Archivo General de Indias, Seville: Audiencia de México, Legajo 158).

540 León Portilla, Miguel. Bernardino de Sahagun, first anthropologist. Translation by Mauricio J. Mixco. Norman: Univ. of Oklahoma Press, 2002. 333 p.: bibl., ill., index.

Translation of *Bernardino de Sahagún: pionero de la antropología* (México, 1999), presents illuminating biography of this justly celebrated figure, approaching his life through his works. Very useful addition to the corpus of scholarly work centered around Sahagún and his activities as an early "ethnographer."

541 León Portilla, Miguel. El binomio oralidad y códices en Mesoamérica. (*Estud. Cult. Náhuatl*, 27, 1997, p. 135–154, bibl.)

Significant article in which León Portilla suggests new ways of "reading" pictorial manuscripts in the indigenous tradition among the Nahuas, Mixtecs, and Mayas. He recommends comparing them with colonial-era alphabetic texts, which sometimes explain or even relate the stories of the signs. This technique can help to recapture some of the orality and full rhetorical meanings of the codices. For rebuttal of the interpretations presented here, see item **519**.

542 León Rivera, Jorge de. Un arte de la lengua mexicana escrito en Milpa Alta denunciado ante la Inquisición por el Cura de Iztapalpa. (*Estud. Cult. Náhuatl*, 26, 1996, p. 245–252)

Transcription and analysis of a denunciation brought against the Arte de la Lengua Mexicana compiled by the Guardián y Ministro of Milpan, Fray Francisco ávila, alleging that it contained "una proposición herética." The offending text, dealing with the Holy Sacrament, is presented in transcription in parallel with a Spanish translation.

543 Lesbre, Patrick. Coyohua Italatollo: el ciclo de Coyohua. (*Lat. Am. Indian Lit. J.*, 16:1, Spring 2000, p. 47–75)

Examines presentation of Nezahuacóyotl in the *Anales de Cuauhtitlán*, paying particular attention to the role of a figure named Coyohua in the rise of the famous Alcolhua leader. Comparisons are made to information found in the *Códice Xolotl.*

544 Lesbre, Patrick. El Tetzcutzinco en la obra de Fernando de Alva Ixtlilxóchitl: realiza, religión prehispánica y cronistas coloniales. (*Estud. Cult. Náhuatl*, 32, 2001, p. 323–340)

Brief but informative article plays off Alva Ixtlilxóchitl's sanitized description of the "royal gardens" of Texcoco against earlier chroniclers' assertions that the site saw the performance of rites of human sacrifice, assertions apparently confirmed by archeological evidence.

545 Libro di Chilam Balam di Chumayel. Introduzione, traduzione e note di Chiara Bollentini. Roma: Bulzoni, 1998. 126 p.: bibl., ill. (Studi di letteratura ispano-americana; 7)

Italian translation of the well-known source of knowledge about the Maya. Detailed introductory essay sets the work within the context of other known Maya texts of the prehispanic era, reminding readers that this book of "hidden things" was produced by the same culture that produced the greatest number of testimonial texts in the Americas. The translator/editor discusses importance of the Chilam Balam books as sources of Maya thought; discusses the priest Chilam Balam; notes that the Chumayel is the most important of the books; accepts religious quality of the text; and analyzes book's role in the quest to decipher Maya culture. Also notes the difficulty of translating "an allegorical and esoteric" text like this one. Large parts of 18 of the books are translated. Extensive concordances and a bibliography. [V. Peloso]

546 Limón Olver, Silvia. El Dios del Fuego y la regeneración del mundo. (*Estud. Cult. Náhuatl*, 32, 2001, p. 51–68)

Well-written analysis of this deity's attributes, symbols, and rites, as well as of the particular characters and meanings of his associations with the heavens, the earth, and the underworld.

547 Lockhart, James. Nahuatl as written: lessons in older written Nahuatl, with copious examples and texts. Stanford, Calif.: Stanford Univ. Press; Los Angeles, Calif.: UCLA Latin American Center Publications, 2001. 261 p.: index. (UCLA Latin American studies; v. 88) (Nahuatl studies series; 6)

Besides being of great utility for ethnohistorians who would like to consult Nahuatl-language sources, this volume includes some authentic colonial texts in Nahuatl and English side-by-by side, a vocabulary, and an index. Highly recommended. See also item **438.**

548 Lockhart, James. Of things of the Indies: essays old and new in early Latin American history. Stanford, Calif.: Stanford Univ. Press, 1999. 408 p.: bibl., index, map.

While volume is in some ways a retrospective publication of a number of important works by Lockhart which have appeared in print over the years, it also offers some new pieces in which author summarizes scholarly insights he has gained during his career. While not every offering here can be described precisely as "ethnohistory," all provide important contextual and comparative information (especially in terms of the Andean region) for interested specialists. Beyond this, readers will welcome the reappearance of "Double Mistaken Identity: Some Nahua Concepts in Postconquest Guise;" "A Double Tradition: Editing Book Twelve of the Florentine Codex;" "Three Experiences of Culture Contact: Nahua, Maya, and Quechua;" and new articles entitled "Some Unfashionable Ideas on the History of the Nahuatl Language" and "Receptivity and Resistance [for and against Things Spanish]."

549 Longhena, María. Maya script: a civilization and its writing. Translated from the Italian by Rosanna M. Giammanco Frongia. New York: Abbeville Press, 2000. 180 p.: bibl., ill., index, maps.

Richly illustrated summary of current knowledge about meanings of Maya script and what this information has revealed about the nature of that people during the classic period. Examines representative glyphs with political, ritual, and calendrical significance. Highly recommended for classroom use.

550 López Austin, Alfredo. Tamoanchan, Tlalocan: places of mist. Translated by Bernard R. Ortiz de Montellano and Thelma Ortiz de Montellano. Niwot, Colo.: Univ. Press of Colorado, 1997. 379 p.: bibl., ill., index. (Mesoamerican worlds)

Seminal, exacting study of these places of primordial creation and origin. Another superb landmark in this author's quest to achieve an understanding of the Nahua (and by extension, Mesoamerican) view of the cosmos and its intersections with human life, thought, and belief. A highly significant work. For review of original Spanish-language version, see *HLAS 56:489*.

551 López Austin, Alfredo and **Leonardo López Luján.** Mito y realidad de Zuyuá: serpiente emplumada y las transformaciones mesoamericanas del clásico al posclásico. México: Colegio de México: Fideicomiso Historia de las Américas: Fondo de Cultura Económica, 1999. 168 p.: bibl., ill. (Sección de obras de historia) (Serie Ensayos)

Authors pursue what they call the "old problem of Tollan and Quetzalcoatl," seeking to understand origins, meanings, and even political implications of what they see as an enduring Mesoamerican "obsession" with this pairing and the transitions between the so-called "classic" and "postclassic" eras. After developing two interpretive models, they examine examples of this obsession among the cultures of the central highlands, the Yucatán, Oaxaca, Michoacán, and Guatemala; one highlight is their treatment of the enduring conundrum presented by the apparent similarities between Tula and Chichén Itzá. Central to their interpretation is what they call *zuyuano*, a pan-Mesoamerican system of sociopolitical organization linked to beliefs in a unitary place of origin known as Zuyuá.

552 López Luján, Leonardo and **Vida Mercado.** Dos esculturas de Mictlantecuhtli encontradas en el Recinto Sagrado de México-Tenochtitlán. (*Estud. Cult. Náhuatl*, 26, 1996, p. 41–68, bibl., ill., photos)

Spurred on by the recent discovery of two unique sculptures of Mictlantecuhtli in the "Casa de las Aguilas" in the Templo Mayor complex, the authors mount a study which investigates two aspects of this deity: his relationship to death and decay, but also his possible possession of creative powers and influences. In so doing, they also explore the nature of the Nahua concept of Mictlan. For archeologist's comment, see *HLAS 59:210*.

553 Lost shores and forgotten peoples: Spanish explorations of the South East Maya lowlands. Edited and translated by Lawrence H. Feldman. Durham, N.C.: Duke Univ. Press, 2000. 293 p.: bibl., ill., index, maps. (Latin America in translation/en traducción/em tradução)

Excellent collection of translated documents pertaining to the Manche Chol and Mopan Mayan peoples, and their long and relatively little-known history of contact and conflict with Spaniards.

554 Maldonado Jiménez, Druzo. Deidades y espacio ritual en Cuauhnáhuac y Huaxtepec: tlalhuicas y xochimilcas de Morelos, siglos XII-XVI. México: UNAM, Instituto de Investigaciones Antropológicas, 2000. 267 p.: appendix, bibl., ill.

Finely crafted study of the religious ordering of space in what is now the state of Morelos during the precontact era. After reconstructing early history of Cuauhnáhuac (Cuernavaca), Huaxtepec, and their environs in a first chapter, Maldonado systematically discusses the many deities venerated in the era, including those who were said to have founded *altepetl* in the region, as well as sacred spaces of various types in the landscape. An appendix grapples with the confusion over the terms "Tlahuica" and "Tlalhuica," and looks at records of migration that include this group.

555 Martiarena, Oscar. Culpabilidad y resistencia: ensayo sobre la confesión en los indios de la Nueva España. México: Univ. Iberoamericana, Depto. de Historia, 1999. 228 p.: bibl., ill. (Col. Historia cultural)

Worthy study of the program of confession as it involved New Spain's indigenous peoples (especially those of the center). Begins with a useful overview of thought and practices of confession as they developed in Catholic Europe prior to and during occupation of America. A good deal of attention is paid to the confessional texts prepared to assist the clergy as they confronted the indigenous people. A consideration of later-colonial clerical attitudes about indigenous culpability and resistance, as it was expressed in confessional texts and related writings, not surprisingly forms a part of this study.

Marzal, Manuel María. Antropologia indigenista. See *HLAS 59:1017.*

556 **Matos Moctezuma, Eduardo.** Tlaltecuhtli: señor de la tierra. (*Estud. Cult. Náhuatl*, 27, 1997, p. 15–40, ill., photos)

Author turns his attention to representations of Tlaltecuhtli, a lesser-known inhabitant of the Nahua cosmos than Huitzilopochtli, Tlaloc, and others. Matos explores the masculine/feminine nature of Tlaltecuhtli; ponders the significance of this deity; and speculates as to why it does not seem to have been worshiped publicly. Many illustrations enhance the article.

557 **Megged, Amos.** The religious context of an "unholy marriage": elite alienation and popular unrest in the indigenous communities of Chiapa, 1570–1680. (*Ethnohistory/Columbus*, 46:1, Winter 1999, p. 149–173)

The "unholy marriage" was the split between local elites and commoners apparently united in *cofradías*, which the author argues created sociocultural conflict within indigenous communities, while at the same time the confraternities allowed for the preservation of a degree of autonomy. Megged links this situation to what he sees as the breakdown of the old *calpulli* system by the late 1560s and its replacement by the *cofradías*. Discussions of indigenous piety, idolatry, and the effects of epidemic disease are integral parts of this investigation.

558 **Mesoamerica's classic heritage: from Teotihuacan to the Aztecs.** Edited by David Carrasco, Lindsay Jones, and Scott Sessions. Boulder: Univ. Press of Colorado, 2000. 559 p.: bibl., ill., index, maps.

Collectively, the 16 articles assembled in this anthology explore influence of Teotihuacán on contemporary and subsequent Mesoamerican peoples, especially the Aztecs, as title suggests. Too numerous to list individually here, contributors all grapple in their distinctive ways with the same issue: whether or not an underlying, unified, and evolving cultural heritage linked all Mesoamericans across time and space despite their specific observable cultural differences. The anthology develops from symposia held in 1995–96 which brought together archeologists, ethnohistorians, art historians, and many other scholars. An important contribution. For anthropologist's comment, see *HLAS 59:60.*

559 **Miguel Caldera y los tlaxcaltecas en el norte de la Nueva España: IV centenario de la muerte de Miguel Caldera.** Coordinación de Luz Carregha. San Luis Potosí, Mexico: El Colegio de San Luis, 1998. 74 p.: bibl. (Cuadernos del centro)

Collection of short articles growing out of a 1997 event commemorating death of the mestizo Capitán Miguel Caldera, founder of San Luis Potosí. Articles of ethnohistorical interest include Glafira Magaña's "Participación tlaxcalteca en el poblamiento del norte: dos documentos del Archivo del Estado [de Tlaxcala]," which suggests that there is archival evidence that Tlaxcalan colonization efforts may have begun earlier than 1591, the date usually given for the initiation of this program. María Isabel Monroy Castillo, in "La vida cotidiana con los tlaxcaltecas: una aportación a la historiografía de Tlaxcala," charts foundation and elaboration of Tlaxcalan colonies in the region, and discusses as well the role of Diego Muñoz Camargo in the process. See also items **479**, **631**, and **632**.

560 **Milbrath, Susan.** New questions concerning the authenticity of the Grolier Codex. (*Lat. Am. Indian Lit. J.*, 18:1, Spring 2002, p. 50–83)

Milbrath subjects earlier studies of the Codex, and this apparently preconquest Mayan pictorial itself, to rigorous critical scrutiny. In the end, she is forced to conclude that the Grolier was created during the postconquest era, and considers whether it is a sophisticated forgery. To settle this issue definitively, the author calls for more thorough testing of pigments. For a related analysis of the Madrid Codex, see item **491**.

561 **Milbrath, Susan.** Star gods of the Maya: astronomy in art, folklore, and calendars. Austin: Univ. of Texas Press, 1999. 372 p.: appendices, bibl., ill., photos, tables. (The Linda Schele series in Maya and pre-Columbian studies)

Dense, impressively researched study of Mayan astronomy, calendrics, and the sacred. With a wide source base including both information about late 20th-century Mayan beliefs and practices as well as codices in the pictorial tradition, the book ranges across space and time. Opening with a look at the modern situation, subsequent chapters often blend a consideration of the postconquest as well as the prehispanic. Accessible text is supported by numerous illustrations. For archeologist's comment, see *HLAS 59:304*.

562 Monaco, Emanuela. Quetzalcoatl: saggi sulla religione azteca. Roma: Bulzoni, 1997. 243 p.: bibl., ill., index. (Chi siamo; 25)

Scholarly offering on the durable topic of nature, meaning, and significance of this most famous of Mesoamerican deities and beliefs surrounding him. Book is divided into three parts: the first examines the story of Quetzalcoatl and his role in Tollan; the next two examine ways in which the "myth" of Tollan was recorded in a number of different sources and address related cosmogonical/cosmological issues. See also items **445, 507,** and **568.**

563 Morales, Francisco. Los coloquios de Sahagún: el marco teológico de su contenido. (*Estud. Cult. Náhuatl,* 32, 2001, p. 175–188)

Discusses presentation of two key Christian themes in Sahagún's *Coloquios:* the nature of the concept of God, or in other words of divinity; and the nature of the Church itself. Author compares and contrasts the presentation in the *Coloquios* with teachings on these subjects presented in Nahuatl-language catechisms and sermons. As such, this article helps us understand more about the process of evangelization as it was carried out in 16th-century Mexico.

564 Morales, Francisco. Impresos y manuscritos en lenguas indígenas en la antigua biblioteca de San Francisco de México. (*Estud. Cult. Náhuatl,* 26, 1996, p. 365–397)

Important study and listing of a wealth of significant manuscripts held in this library, including many grammars, *vocabularios* and dictionaries, *Doctrinas Christianas,* and other similar works. They range from the well known to the obscure. A welcome resource.

565 Morante López, Rubén B. Las piedras de Xipe y las amenazas del Imperio. (*Estud. Cult. Náhuatl,* 32, 2001, p. 15–28)

Interpretation of two petroglyphs which seem to depict Xipe, one the so-called Piedra de Gigante from Orizaba and the other from Amecameca. Employing ethnohistorical sources such as Durán and Sahagún, the author suggests a common date for the creation of the two, and posits other suggestive links between them. See also item **639.**

566 Muñoz Camargo, Diego. Historia de Tlaxcala: Ms. 210 de la Biblioteca Nacional de París. Paleografía, introducción, notas, apéndices e índices analíticos de Luis Reyes García, con la colaboración de Javier Lira Toledo. Tlaxcala, Mexico: Gobierno del Estado de Tlaxcala; Centro de Investigaciones y Estudios Superiores en Antropología Social, Univ. Autónoma de Tlaxcala, 1998. 435 p.: bibl., indexes. (Col. Historia. Serie Historia de Tlaxcala; 5)

New edition of this important ethnohistorical source is prefaced by a biography of its author, as well as a discussion of the entire body of his work and of the sources he seems to have used for the *Historia.* As an added bonus, Reyes García has appended a "Catálogo" of documents related to Muñoz's family held in the Archivo General del Estado de Tlaxcala, as well as transcriptions of several other texts including testaments of family members. An outstanding presentation.

567 Nash, June. Gendered deities and the survival of culture. (*Hist. Relig. / Chicago,* 36:4, May 1997, p. 333–357)

Analyzes gender dynamics behind precolumbian gods and goddesses across Mesoamerican religions, and explores the evolution of such dynamics following contact with Christianity, including quite recent expressions. Suggests a relationship between religious ideology and the human division of labor, particularly the work of women in the domestic realm, where greater cultural continuity could occur.

568 Nicholson, Henry B. Topiltzin Quetzalcoatl: the once and future lord of the Toltecs. Boulder: Univ. Press of Colorado, 2001. 360 p.: bibl., ill. (some col.), index, map. (Mesoamerican worlds)

Long-awaited, updated publication of

Nicholson's classic 1957 Harvard doctoral dissertation. Consulted by serious scholars for decades, this important work is now made more readily available by this high quality edition. Centerpiece of the work is author's painstakingly systematic and critical examination of both major and minor ethnohistorical sources which provide information about Topiltzin Quetzalcoatl of Tollan. See also items 445, 507, and 562.

Nolasco Armas, Margarita. Conquista y dominación del noroeste de México: el papel de los jesuitas. See item 1382.

569 Okoshi Harada, Tsubasa. Los Xiu del siglo XVI: una lectura de dos textos Mayas coloniales. (*Mesoamérica/Antigua,* 21:39, junio 2000, p. 224–238)

Examines ways in which Xiu lineage sought to survive impositions of the Spanish system during 16th century. Study has two principal sources: a document called "Memoria de la Distribución de los Montes" (1557), and a genealogical tree (c. 1560) found in the "Papeles de los Xiu de Yaxá" (Yucatán), also known as the "Xiu Chronicle." The "Memoria" is in Yucatec, written in European script, and describes the Xiu *montes,* as the name suggests. Okoshi Harada's analysis seems sound as far as it goes, but one hopes for a more extensive new publication of both of these Mayan records, which may be in the works.

570 Olivier, Guilhem. Acercamiento al estudio de los dioses de los mercaderes en el altiplano central de México prehispánico. (*TRACE/México,* 31, junio 1997, p. 35–43, bibl.)

The author seeks a better understanding of deities worshiped by the *pochteca,* such as Yacatecuhtli. Links with more famous divinities—Quetzalcoatl, Tezcatlipoca, and Xiuhtecuhtli—are suggested.

571 Olivier, Guilhem. Huehuecóyotl, "Coyote Viejo," el músico transgresor: ¿Dios de los otomíes o avatar de Tezcatlipoca? (*Estud. Cult. Náhuatl,* 30, 1999, p. 113–132, bibl., ill.)

Olivier dissects what is known about the "Old Coyote" by examining nature of representations in various codices as well as in written text such as those gathered by Sahagún and Durán. Along the way, he draws some intriguing parallels between the nature of Huehuecóyotl, who seems to have been the paramount Otomi deity, and Tezcatlipoca of the Nahuas. See also item 572.

572 Olivier, Guilhem *Tepeyóllotl,* "Corazón de la Montaña" y "Señor del Eco": el dios jaguar de los antiguos mexicanos. (*Estud. Cult. Náhuatl,* 28, 1998, p. 99–141, bibl., ill.)

Well-documented, multifaceted study of what author characterizes as a poorly understood and seldom studied deity. As in his later piece about Huehuecóyotl (see item 571), Olivier argues for many linkages between Tepeyóllotl and Tezcatlipoca, but also identifies shared traits with Tlaloc and even Quetzalcoatl in the course of reconstructing the attributes and character of the "Jaguar God."

573 Oudijk, Michel R. Historiography of the Bènizàa: the postclassic and early colonial periods, 1000–1600 A.D. Leiden, The Netherlands: Research School of Asian, African and Amerindian Studies, Univ. Leiden, 2000. 429 p.: appendices, bibl., ill., maps. (CNWS publications; 84)

Well-written and significant book traces evolution of the Bènizàa (Zapotec) people through an intense interpretation of their "historiography," particularly in terms of their pictorial manuscripts. The quest to recover the orality of these records, aided by recourse to other kinds of alphabetic sources in indigenous as well as Spanish languages, leads author to suggest new ways of interpreting Bènizàa history, and raises many significant questions which should occupy interested researchers for some time to come. Book is not confined to the people still widely known as the Zapotecs, but also considers the Mixtecs in a comparative way with sensitivity shown to regional variations between the Sierras, the Valley of Oaxaca, and the Isthmus of Tehuantepec. Appendices include transcriptions of some of the key documents used in the study, and are followed by an extensive and useful collection of reproductions of select folios from these and others. See also item 574.

574 Oudijk, Michel R. and **Maarten E.R.G.N. Jansen.** Changing history in the Lienzos de Guevara and Santo Domingo Petapa. (*Ethnohistory/Columbus,* 47:2, Spring 2000, p. 281–332)

Compares Zapotec pictorials from neighboring towns, providing glimpses into indigenous views of history and the place of elite families in the local political landscape from before and after the Spanish invasion. They also situate these sources in a larger body of codices and manuscripts from the region of Tehuantepec in an exemplary way. See also item **573**.

575 Overmyer-Velázquez, Rebecca. Christian morality revealed in New Spain: the inimical Nahua woman in Book Ten of the Florentine Codex. (*J. Women's Hist.*, 10:2, Summer 1998, p. 9–38)

Posits certain changes in gender ideology among the Nahuas that came with introduction of Christianity, including a loss of status for women. Explores the good/evil Christian dichotomy as illustrated in "The People" volume of Sahagún's corpus, and displacement of native views of human relationships that were less hierarchical and more complementary.

576 Palma Murga, Gustavo. De los usos de la memoria histórica prehispánica sobre la territorialidad en la Guatemala colonial: el caso de pocomames y kakchiqueles en el valle central de Guatemala, siglos XVI y XVII. (*Estudios/Guatemala*, abril 1998, p. 76–87, bibl.)

Intriguing little study of a land conflict pitting pueblos of Mixco and Santiago Sacatepéquez against Chinautla in 1700, highlighting ways in which, to win their points, all parties invoked (and reinvented) historical memories and traditions stretching back through earlier colonial centuries to the precontact era.

577 Palmeri Capesciotti, Ilaria. La fauna del Libro XI del Códice Florentino de Fray Bernardino de Sahagún: dos sistemas taxonómicos frente a frente. (*Estud. Cult. Náhuatl*, 32, 2001, p. 189–221)

This thoughtful article moves well beyond a simple descriptive rendering of the presentation of fauna in the Codex to consider the complex process through which that presentation was created, as well as the intellectual and cultural influences brought to bear.

578 Pérez-Rocha, Emma. Privilegios en lucha: la información de Doña Isabel Moctezuma. México: Instituto Nacional de

Antropología e Historia, 1998. 289 p.: bibl., ill., index. (Serie Etnohistoria) (Col. Científica; 380)

Transcriptions of records compiled during court proceedings initiated (but certainly not concluded) in 1546 connected with struggle to settle claims to Doña Isabel's properties and privileges as Moctezuma's daughter. Witness testimony, in particular, includes a wealth of valuable ethnohistorical and social information.

579 Pérez-Rocha, Emma and **Rafael Tena.** La nobleza indígena del centro de México después de la conquista. México: Instituto Nacional de Antropología e Historia, 2000. 459 p.: bibl., ill., indexes, tables. (Col. Obra diversa)

Useful and well-mounted collection of transcriptions (and in some cases translations) of 16th-century letters, wills, petitions, *probanzas*, and other kinds of documents pertaining to indigenous nobles, most of them residents of the old Triple Alliance capitals of Mexico City (Tenochtitlán), Tlacopan, and Texcoco. While most of these records were originally written in Spanish, there are some examples in Nahuatl and Latin. Editors provide a useful introduction to the collection including biographical information about those featured in the documents themselves. Workable bibliography is appended to the book, although it lacks references to the many studies of indigenous nobility, politics, and also documentary collections, that have been published outside of Mexico.

580 Pino Díaz, Fermín del. Por la revaloración de una fuente olvidada: la Crónica de Indias. (*Soc. espaces temps*, 1997, p. 639–651)

After informative discussion of the nature and evolution of the analytical discipline of "ethnohistory," in which a kind of comparative "historiography" plays an important role, this brief and accessible article turns to a consideration of cannibalism among the Aztecs in light of the techniques developed by ethnohistorians. Author's discussion is based on an interpretation of key passages from the chronicles of Bernal Díaz del Castillo, López de Gómara, and José de Acosta. See also item **517**.

581 Prem, Hanns J. The "Canek Manuscript" and other faked documents. (*Anc. Mesoam.*, 10:2, Fall 1999, p. 297–311, bibl., ill., map, tables)

Prem deftly exposes four recently concocted documents allegedly relating episodes in colonial Mayan history: "Las memorias de [Gonzalo] Guerrero," "Historias de la conquista del Mayab por Fray Joseph de San Buenaventura," "Historia de la pazificazion de las tierras de los indios Itzaes y las Ganzias de el Tyasal y de todos los pueblos de la laguna en el año 1697," and the "Canek Manuscript." An engaging and informative cautionary tale for serious scholars. For comment on a related article by Prem's collaborator, see item **526**.

582 Prem, Hanns J. and Ursula Dyckerhoff. Los Anales de Tlatelolco: una colección heterogénea. (*Estud. Cult. Náhuatl*, 27, 1997, p. 181–207, bibl., tables)

Careful and detailed examination of well-known alphabetic *anales* from Tlatelolco. Among other things, the authors take issue with traditional attribution of authorship. More importantly, they compare the two existing copies of the *anales*, the older on amate and the more recent on European paper, finding some significant differences as well as similarities between them. Arguing that the *anales* is made up of several related documents, authors believe that each was written by a different author at a different date. Authors then compare some of the contents of the *anales* with similar incidents narrated in other sources, such as the Florentine Codex.

583 Quezada, Sergio. Los pies de la República: los mayas peninsulares, 1550–1750. México: Centro de Investigaciones y Estudios Superiores en Antropología Social: Patronato Indígena, AC, 1997. 263 p.: appendix, bibl., ill. (Historia de los pueblos indígenas de México)

Handsome entry in this high quality series of publications presents a valuable synthetic treatment of the Yucatecan Mayan experience of Spanish invasion and colonialism through middle of 18th century (although emphasis is on the first two centuries of Spanish occupation). Quezada is especially interested in the sacred world, presenting informative discussions of Franciscan-led evan-

gelization, idolatry and resistance, and local religious observance. Also examines Izta resistance, trade, tribute, the dislocations of epidemic disease, and impact of an overly taxing forced labor system. A valuable documentary appendix covers many distinct topics including land issues, the Catholic Church, and the vicissitudes of the wax trade, although only one of these texts is partly in Yucatec Maya.

584 Radding Murrieta, Cynthia. Crosses, caves, and *matachinis:* divergent appropriations of Catholic discourse in northwestern New Spain. (*Americas/Washington*, 55:2, Oct. 1998, p. 177–203)

Applies some elements of methodologies developed by those reexamining the "spiritual conquest" in central Mexico to the Sonoran mission frontier. The significance of Jesuit and Franciscan attitudes towards the Teguime and O'odham peoples (more popularly known as the Opatas, Endeves, and Pimas) is discussed, as is the pedagogical methodology employed by the friars. The nature of the reception of such things by the missionized is seen as a good gauge of the true nature of the entry of Christianity into the indigenous belief systems.

585 Radding Murrieta, Cynthia. Cultural dialogues: recent trends in Mesoamerican ethnohistory. (*LARR*, 33:1, 1998, p. 193–211, bibl.)

Thoughtful, well-crafted review essay examines contributions of a number of important ethnohistorical anthologies, covering economic, agricultural, political, and social topics. Author's detailed, critical discussion creates a revealing and useful resource for interested scholars.

586 Read, Kay Almere. Time and sacrifice in the Aztec cosmos. Bloomington: Indiana Univ. Press, 1998. 331 p.: bibl., ill., index. (Religion in North America)

Intricate and insightful study of practice of human sacrifice among the Aztecs. Author moves well beyond a simple discussion to provide deep analysis of the practice within the matrix of the Aztec belief system. Thus she succeeds in making the whole complex more comprehensible. A significant contribution.

587 Restall, Matthew. The ties that bind: social cohesion and the Yucatec Maya family. (*J. Fam. Hist.*, 23:4, Oct. 1998, p. 355–381, facsim., graphs, tables)

Redefinition of the nature of colonial Mayan social groupings stresses among other things the importance of the extended family and its relationships to the patronymic family group (*chibal*) and to the community (*cah*). This revealing article is based on extensive research in census and notarial records as well as testaments, and ranges across the three main centuries of the colonial era.

588 Restall, Matthew and **John F. Chuchiak.** A reevaluation of the authenticity of Fray Diego de Landa's *Relación de las cosas de Yucatán.* (*Ethnohistory/Columbus*, 49:3, Summer 2002, p. 651–669)

As the result of painstaking textual analysis, including a surprisingly rare consultation of manuscript copy of the *Relación* held by the Real Academia de la Historia, authors conclude that this famous account was not written by Landa himself. Instead, they argue that the work is a compilation, accomplished by several different copyists during late 17th-18th centuries, of information drawn from a much more extensive (and currently lost) *Recopilación* written by the Franciscan in the 16th century, a text kept in Mérida's Franciscan monastery until it was taken to Spain in the 17th century. Authors suggest, moreover, that some of the text contained in the *Relación* comes from other sources, including a lost *Relación* writen by Landa's contemporary Gaspar de Najera and an indigenous associate of Landa's named Gaspar Antonio Chi. For all that, authors continue to view "Landa's" *Relación* as a valuable and authentic resource, just not precisely in the way it has been traditionally accepted. This article will undoubtedly lead to a good deal of rethinking and debate.

589 Reyes García, Luis. Anales de Juan Bautista: ¿cómo te confundes? ¿acaso no somos conquistados? México: Centro de Investigaciones y Estudios, Superiores en Antropología Social; Biblioteca Lorenzo Boturini, Insigne y Nacional Basílica de Guadalupe, 2001. 343 p.: bibl., facsims., ill., indexes.

First-rate commentary, transcription, and translation of the *anales* created by notaries from Mexico City's district of San Juan Moyotlan in late-16th century. Now housed in the Archivo de la Basílica de Guadalupe, the text has some unique and ethnohistorically significant qualities. Written by persons who were not situated professionally at the center of indigenous political power, the *anales* contain more information about daily life, tribute payment, personal service, and the like, than about major political events. This edition includes a readable facsimile of the entire document. An extremely valuable resource.

590 Reyes García, Luis. Documentos históricos Cuahuixmatlac Atetecochco. Tlaxcala, Mexico: Depto. de Filosofía y Letras de la Univ. Autónoma de Tlaxcala, Instituto Tlaxcalteca de la Cultura, Comisión para Escribir la Historia de Cuahuixmatlac, 2001. 50 p., 12 p. of plates: bibl., col. ill.

Useful documentary collection from the Tlaxcalan town of San Bartolomé Cuahuixmatlac includes transcriptions and, where necessary, translations of Spanish and Nahuatl testaments and bills of sale found in the municipal archive dating from 1528–1613. Reyes also describes, and includes color photographs of, several pictorial documents kept in the same repository. Present as well is the fascinating "Anales de Cuahuixmatlac (1528–1997)," a brief record in traditional style created in 2000 by a community elder named Don Martiniano Gutiérrez Meza.

591 Reyes Garza, Juan Carlos. La sal en los códices pictográficos. (*Estud. Cult. Náhuatl*, 31, 2000, p. 185–201, facsims.)

First stage of an investigation into the nature and implications of representations of salt presented with both sacred and mundane associations in a number of different kinds of pictorial records. The relative lack of graphic depictions of salt offers a challenge which this article begins to take up.

592 Ringle, William M.; Tomás Gallareta Negrón; and **George J. Bey.** The return of Quetzalcoatl: evidence for the spread of world religion during the epiclassic period.

(*Anc. Mesoam.*, 9:2, Fall 1998, p. 183–232, bibl., facsim., ill., map, tables)

Provocative and important scholarly work maintains that since supposedly "Toltec" Chichén Itzá actually dates architecturally from the epiclassic, the postclassic influence of Tollan must be reconsidered. For archeologist's comment, see *HLAS 59:78.*

593 Rivera Dorado, Miguel. ¿Influencia del cristianismo en el Popol Vuh? (*Rev. Esp. Antropol. Am.*, 30, 2000, p. 137–162, bibl.)

Considers several key episodes and elements in this well-known text, concluding that there is less Christian influence in the document than some have argued.

594 Rocha, Arturo. Nadie es ombligo en la tierra = Ayac xictli in tlaltícpac; discapacidad en el México antiguo, cultura náhuatl. México: Teletón; Miguel Angel Porrúa, 2000. 187 p.: bibl., col. ill., indexes.

An effort to draw attention away from some of the negative stereotypes about ancient Mexicans and redirect it toward their high moral character, particularly with regard to their treatment of the handicapped.

595 Rodríguez-Shadow, María. La mujer azteca. 3a. ed. Toluca, Mexico: Univ. Autónoma del Estado de México, 1997. 276 p.: bibl., ill. (Col. Historia; 6)

Third edition of this durable investigation of women and gender in the Aztec era. The author presents a revised and augmented first chapter, while the rest of the book is substantively the same as the second edition.

596 Rojas, José Luis de. La moneda indígena y sus usos en la Nueva España en el siglo XVI. México: CIESAS, 1998. 229 p.: bibl. (Historias/CIESAS)

Exacting study, based heavily on archival research, of the "monetary units" in use in central Mexico just prior to and immediately after the Spanish invasion. An important contribution to our knowledge about a subject that is often dealt with in a cursory manner. Rojas presents detailed information about two major forms of exchange: *mantas* and cacao. Different types, values, and regional variations are discussed in their own right and linked as well to social organization, politics, and the changes wrought by the coming of the Spaniards.

597 Romano, Giuliano. I calendari nahuatl. (*Atti Memorie Ateneo Treviso*, 10, 1992/93, p. 115–138, bibl., facsims., tables)

Analysis of the three most prominent Aztec calendars: Tonalpohualli (the religious calendar), Xihuitl (the civic calendar), and Xiuhmolpilli (the astrological calendar). Derived from the pre-existing Texcoco calendar, the Aztec calendar came into use in central Mexico at beginning of 13th century, continuing until mid-16th. Discusses the symbols, periodic divisions, and colors associated with the calendars, and argues that variations in the use of colors, as well as overall use of the calendars, was associated with different geographic locations within the Aztec world. Also discusses Aztec mathematics and the astrological uses of the calendars. Copiously illustrated. See also items **496** and **499**. [V. Peloso]

598 Roskamp, Hans. La heráldica novohispana del siglo XVI: un escudo de armas de Tzintzuntzan, Michoacán. (*in* Esplendor y acaso de la cultura simbólica. Zamora, Mexico: El Colegio de Michoácan, Consejo Nacional de Ciencia y Tecnología, 2002, p. 227–268)

Revealing and well-researched study of a coat of arms assumed by indigenous municipality of Tzintzuntzan in 16th century examines meanings of the incorporated elements in the context of cultural contact, change, and survival. Comparisons are made between this shield and others found in indigenous-authored colonial documents from Michoacán, including several in *lienzos* and other texts from Carapan.

599 Roskamp, Hans. La historiografía indígena de Michoacán: el Lienzo de Jucutácato y los títulos de Carapan. Leiden, The Netherlands: Research School CNWS, School of Asian, African, and Amerindian Studies, 1998. 442 p.: bibl., ill. (CNWS publications, 0925–3084; 72)

Excellent, systematic study goes well beyond historiographic identification to often probing documentary analysis. In the case of the Carapan records, the existence of several related documentary forms (*lienzos*, genealogies, and primordial titles) allows author to chart ways in which various kinds of information about the past, the land, and the sacred were preserved over time and modified to serve particular social and political interests. Documentary appendices, maps, and many useful illustrations add further dimensions to this noteworthy book. See also item **600**.

600 Roskamp, Hans and **Benjamín Lucas.** Uacús Thicátame y la fundación de Carapan: nuevo documento en lengua p'urhépecha. (*Relaciones/Zamora*, 21:82, primavera 2000, p. 159–173)

Transcription, translation, and brief analysis of a primordial title-like document discovered in Tulane's Latin American Library. This is compared to other known indigenous-style documents from Carapan. See also item **599**.

601 Roulet, Eric. Mariano Veitia: une vision nouvelle de l'histoire indienne; la revalorisation du passé indigène en Nouvelle-Espagne au XVIIIéme siécle. (*Estud. Cult. Náhuatl*, 27, 1997, p. 405–417)

Succinct study of *Historia antigua de México* by the *poblano* Creole Mariano de Echeverría y Veitia (1718–80). Echeverría y Veitia was part of the Creole intellectual trend which tended to rehabilitate the precontact indigenous peoples of Mexico, in this case equating them with the Greeks and Romans.

602 Royal courts of the ancient Maya. v. 1, Theories, themes, and comparisons. Boulder, Colo.: Westview Press, 2001. 1 v.: bibl., ill, index, maps.

High quality anthology in which the contributors, benefiting from fairly recent advances in epigraphy, move beyond a concentration on rulers, dynasties, and dehumanized politics. Instead, they try to recapture complexities of what authors call "the court as a group of people," principally during classic era. Editors provide a fine introductory article laying out the rationale for the collection, and pondering the issue of what a "court" actually is. The uniformly excellent articles are as follows: "King's People: Classic Maya Courtiers in a Comparative Perspective" by Takeshi Inomata; "Peopling the Classic Maya Court" by Stephen D. Houston and David Stuart; "Perspectives on Actors, Gender Roles, and Architecture at Classic Maya Courts and Households" by Patricia A. McAnany and Shannon Plank; "Spatial Dimensions of Maya Courtly Life: Problems and Issues" by David Webster; "Court and Realm: Architectural Signatures in the Classic Maya Southern Lowlands" by Simon Martin; "Classic Maya Concepts of the Royal Court: an Analysis of Renderings on Pictorial Ceramics" by Dorie Reents-Budet; a comparative piece contributed by Susan Toby Evans titled "Aztec Noble Courts: Men, Women, and Children of the Palace;" and a set of "Concluding Remarks" provided by Michael D. Coe.

603 Ruz, Mario Humberto. Gestos cotidianos acercamientos etnológicos a los mayas de la época colonial. Campeche, Mexico: Gobierno del Estado de Campeche; Univ. Autónoma del Carmen, 1997. 260 p.: bibl. (Serie Historia. Palo de tinte)

Ruz searches for indigenous voices and perspectives on everyday life under Spanish domination, rereading some traditional sources and seeking new ones. This study includes, for example, ethnological readings of colonial vocabularies of languages such as Tzeltal, Cakchiquel, and Yucateco, among others.

604 Santamarina Novillo, Carlos. La muerte de Chimalpopoca: evidencias a favor de la tesis golpista. (*Estud. Cult. Náhuatl*, 28, 1998, p. 277–316, bibl., ill.)

By painstakingly examining a wide range of available evidence, author argues in favor of the *golpe* thesis, that Chimalpopoca was assassinated at the behest of members of Tenochtitlán's ruling elite, rather than through Tepanec treachery. Santamarina deftly links this thesis with a study of dynastic politics, rules of succession, and familial rivalry.

605 Sautron, Marie. La representación de la amistad entre los antiguos mexicanos: un análisis léxico y semántico a través del corpus poético náhuatl, *Romances de los Señores de la Nueva España*. (*Estud. Cult. Náhuatl*, 31, 2000, p. 259–274, bibl.)

Consideration of the terms and metaphors of friendship found in the texts of Nahuatl songs is supported by transcriptions and translations of key texts.

606 **Schalley, Andrea C.** Das mathematische Weltbild der Maya. Frankfurt; New York: P. Lang, 2000. 296 p.: bibl., ill., index. (Grazer altertumskundliche Studien, 0947-3157; Bd. 6)

A thorough background and familiarity with mathematics, archeology and anthropological studies, field trips, and an extensive bibliography enable the author to take an interdisciplinary approach to her examination of the Mayan use of mathematics for mundane and mythological events as well as for astronomical predictions. Valuable contribution to understanding the highly complex culture and cosmology of the classical Maya. [C. Converse]

607 **Schele, Linda** and **Peter Mathews.** The code of kings: the language of seven sacred Maya temples and tombs. Photographs by MacDuff Everton and Justin Kerr. New York: Scribner, 1998. 431 p.: bibl., ill. (some col.), index, maps.

Engagingly written study based on epigraphic "revolution" fueled by the present authors and other scholars, with the goal of achieving a better understanding of the meanings of Mayan sacred architecture. The seven "temples and tombs" are Toh-Chak-Ich'ak's palace at Tikal, Hanab-Pakal's tomb at Palenque, the Great Plaza of Waxaklahun-Ubah-K'awil at Copan, a Katun-ending commemoration at Seibal, the ballcourt at Chichén Itzá, the Nunnery Quadrangle at Uxmal, and the site of Iximiché, the Kaqchiquel capital. These cases are the subjects of successive chapters, and the book begins with a discussion of the symbolism of pyramids, plazas, and the glyphic texts and decorations that grace them. This symbolism, as well as a wealth of details about how the Mayas planned and built their civil-ceremonial centers, is a constant feature in the balance of the book.

608 **Schlesinger, Victoria.** Animals and plants of the ancient Maya: a guide. Foreword by Carlos Galindo-Leal. Illustrations by Juan C. Chab-Medina. Austin: Univ. of Texas Press, 2001. 371 p.: bibl., ill., maps.

While not intended to be an ethnohistorical study, this well-researched, clearly written, and systematically organized guide to the flora and fauna which would have surrounded the Mayas in the Yucatán Peninsula during the classic era is an invaluable resource. Excellent maps and illustrations are a useful bonus.

609 **Schroeder, Susan.** The first American valentine: Nahua courtship and other aspects of family structuring in Mesoamerica. (*J. Fam. Hist.*, 23:4, Oct. 1998, p. 341-354)

Continuing to mine the rich body of material created by Chimalpahin, the author presents a polished gem of an article examining Nahua thought and teachings about family and marital alliance.

610 **Schroeder, Susan.** Jesuits, Nahuas, and the Good Death Society in Mexico City, 1710-1767. (*HAHR*, 80:1, Feb. 2000, p. 43-77, ill.)

The Congregación de la Buena Muerte was a Jesuit-sponsored *cofradía* linked to their Colegio de San Gregorio, which educated elite indigenous boys. This first-rate study of Spanish and Nahuatl-language records generated by the sodality not only uncovers the purpose, structure, and organizing philosophy of the society, but reveals a wealth of information about daily life, naming patterns, indigenous sociopolitical structures, gender roles, and the shape of Nahua Catholicism. The roots of the Mexico City confraternity are traced back to Rome, where a similar organization was established by the Jesuits in the 16th century. Schroeder also includes some information about the foundation in 1753 of a Jesuit school for indigenous girls, the Colegio de Indias Doncellas de Nuestra Señora de Guadalupe, which was linked to the success of the Society.

611 **Searching for the secrets of nature: the life and works of Dr. Francisco Hernández.** Edited by Simon Varey, Rafael Chabrán, and Dora B. Weiner. Stanford, Calif.: Stanford Univ. Press, 2000. 245 p.: bibl., ill., index.

Companion volume to *The Mexican Treasury* (see item **501**), this book presents a crossdisciplinary anthology of significant articles assessing life, works, cultural context, and influence of Hernández, whose work in natural history (laced with an encounter between 16th-century Christian humanism and the Nahuas' persistently different way of looking at the natural world) remains a landmark in early scientific investigation. The 18 articles are grouped into thematically unified sections, including "The Intellectual Milieu of Hernández," "Medical Knowledge and Practices in New Spain," "The Dissemination of Hernández's Knowledge," and "Continuing Traditions of Mexican Medicine." This high-quality collection will be of great and continuing use to ethnohistorians and scholars in a wide array of other fields.

612 **Sell, Barry D.** Our Lady of Solitude of San Miguel Coyotlan, 1619: a rare set of *cofradía* rules in Nahuatl. (*Estud. Cult. Náhuatl*, 31, 2000, p. 331–389, bibl.)

Brief but illuminating description of the document in question (p. 362–368) is followed by a Nahuatl transcription (p. 369–379) and translation into English (p. 380–389) of this important text, housed in the collection of Berkeley's Bancroft Library.

613 **Sell, Barry D.** and **Larissa Taylor.** "He could have made marvels in this language": a Nahuatl sermon by Father Juan de Tovar, S.J. (*Estud. Cult. Náhuatl*, 26, 1996, p. 211–244, appendix)

Well-considered study of a Nahuatl-language sermon on the Most Holy Sacrament included in the 1624 sermonary compiled by Fray Juan Mijangos. Discusses the structure and context of this work, indicating how it presented its message in a manner that would be comprehensible to a Nahua audience, while also conforming to the dictates of such things as the Council of Trent. A full transcription and translation (into English) of the sermon forms an appendix to the article.

614 **Sell, Barry D.** and **Susan Kellogg.** We want to give them laws: royal ordinances in a mid-sixteenth century Nahuatl text. (*Estud. Cult. Náhuatl*, 27, 1997, p. 325–367, bibl., table)

First-rate study, accompanied by a transcription and English translation, of a set of *ordenanças* issued under Viceroy Don Antonio de Mendoza in June of 1546, and translated into Nahuatl some time later. Sell and Kellogg present an excellent, first-ever analysis of these ordinances, which were intended as a tool to teach (and enforce) good behavior among the Nahuas. The ordinances cover a mix of what we would call "civil" and "religious" themes, ranging from teachings about proper marital practices and Christian beliefs to warnings about the persistence of idolatry,

lessons about the dangers of homosexuality, and crime. An excellent and important work.

La Sierra Gorda: documentos para su historia. See item **1193**.

615 **Sigal, Peter Herman.** From moon goddesses to virgins: the colonization of Yucatecan Maya sexual desire. Austin: Univ. of Texas Press, 2000. 342 p.: bibl., ill., index.

Starting with what author calls the "encoded figures" of the Mayan Moon Goddess and the Virgin Mary, this innovative study examines the intersections of religion, gender, and sexuality among the Mayas, both before and after the Spanish invasion. This important new interpretive work adds new dimensions to scholarship about gender in the field of ethnohistory, examining everything from religion and family to bisexuality and transexuality. For ethnologist's comment, see *HLAS 59:806*.

616 **Simbológicas.** Recopilación de Marie-Odile Marion. México: CONACYT; Plaza y Valdes Editores, 1997. 215 p.: bibl., ill., maps.

Compiled in honor of French scholar Maurice Godelier, this collection of 15 articles (including the text of an interview with Godelier entitled "Simbológica del Cuerpo, Orden Social y Lógica del Poder") stems mainly from a colloquium held in Mexico City in 1996. While some of the contributions are ethnographic, theoretical, or archeological in their foci, others are of ethnohistorical interest and (like all of the included articles) investigate themes of myth, symbolism, and representation.

617 **Smith, Mary Elizabeth.** The Codex López Ruiz: a lost Mixtec pictorial manuscript. Nashville, Tenn.: Vanderbilt Univ., 1998. 282 p.: bibl., ill., maps. (Vanderbilt University publications in anthropology; 51)

Smith seeks to prove that a document described in 1898 by Mariano López Ruiz, a "teacher and poet from Nochixtlán in the Mixteca Alta," was a pictorial genealogical manuscript. By carefully studying original alphabetic glosses in Mixteco reproduced by López, and by comparing the information contained in them with similar data from better known genealogies, Smith is able to reconstruct the pictorial's form and to suggest that the now-lost codex was from the

Tlaxiaco area of the western Mixteca Alta. A facsimilie of López's original article is appended.

Social patterns in pre-classic Mesoamerica: a symposium at Dumbarton Oaks, 9 and 10 October 1993. See *HLAS 59:90*.

618 Solanilla Demestre, Victória. Quetzalcoatl y su proyección en el cristianismo. (*in* Encuentro-Debate América Latina ayer y hoy = Trobada-Debat Amèrica Llatina ahir i avui, *6th, Barcelona, 1997*. Lo que duele es el olvido: recuperando la memoria de América Latina = El que dol és l'oblit: recuperant la memòria d'Amèrica Llatina. Barcelona, Spain: Univ. de Barcelona, 1998, p. 83–91, ill.)

Thoughtful contribution to ongoing discussion of 16th-century Spanish identification of Quetzalcoatl as the apostle Saint Thomas. Examining surviving iconography and textual descriptions of the deity, Solanilla argues essentially that the pairing resulted from efforts of people such as Fray Diego Durán to make sense of the unexpected indigenous cultures encountered as a result of the Spanish invasion. Also shows how and why a Christianized Quetzalcoatl became an important symbol of emerging Creole nationalism.

619 Solís Robleda, Gabriela. El repartimiento de géneros y la sociedad indígena en Yucatán en el siglo XVII. (*Estud. Hist. Novohisp.*, 22, 2000, p. 13–48, bibl.)

Careful study of the forced *repartimiento de géneros*, based on significant archival research, helps illuminate conditions during the still understudied 17th century.

620 Sousa, Lisa. The Devil and deviance in native criminal narratives from early Mexico. (*Americas/Washington*, 59:2, Oct. 2002, p. 161–179, ill.)

This well-crafted article assesses the power of the Devil in the minds of 13 citizens of Nahua, Mixtec, and Zapotec communities who cited diabolical influences as the cause of their wrongdoings. Departs from previous studies of the entry of the European image of the Devil into the belief systems of colonial indigenous societies in that it examines evidence from secular criminal court cases rather than Inquisition or other kinds of ecclesiastical sources. Fits nicely into the ongoing stream of important work investigating the nature of postcontact indigenous religiosity.

621 Spinden, Herbert Joseph. Ancient civilizations of Mexico and Central America. Introduction by Bruce E. Byland. Mineola, N.Y.: Dover, 1999. 287 p.: bibl., ill., index, maps.

Reissue of the 1928 revision of Spinden's classic synthetic work. Fronted by an informative introduction by Byland, this landmark in scholarship about Mesoamerica can still be of use.

622 Šprajc, Ivan. La estrella de Quetzalcóatl: el planeta Venus en Mesoamérica. México: Diana, 1996. 224 p., 32 p. of plates: bibl., ill. (some col.) (Arqueoastronomía)

Wide-ranging inquiry into how and why the Mesoamericans venerated Venus and incorporated the planet into their systems of the cosmos, thought, and constructions of time. While the emphasis is on the Classic Mayas, central Mesoamerica and Oaxaca are accorded some significant attention, as well.

623 Suárez Díez, Lourdes. El comercio de la concha en el mundo prehispánico de Occidente. (*TRACE/México*, 31, junio 1997, p. 7–21, appendices, bibl., maps)

Brief description of caches of shell materials which, like the conch, were used in luxury and ceremonial ways in precontact times, in several different western Mexican locations. Author is able to establish existence of at least 10 trade routes linking this region with other parts of the Pacific Coast as well as the Caribbean.

624 Sullivan, John. Construcción de dos enunciados colectivos en el cabildo de Tlaxcala. (*Estud. Cult. Náhuatl*, 32, 2001, p. 297–322)

Comparison of a set of Spanish voting instructions for indigenous cabildos with the actual process as recovered from the records of two Tlaxcalan sessions preserved in its Actas de Cabildo. Author finds strong evidence that the indigenous councillors did not follow foreign precepts and in fact maintained a good deal of autonomy in the way they conducted political business.

625 Tavárez, David Eduardo. La idolatría letrada: un análisis comparativo de textos clandestinos rituales y devocionales en comunidades nahuas y zapotecas, 1613–1654. (*Hist. Mex./México*, 49:2, oct./dic. 1999, p. 197–252, bibl., graph, maps, tables)

Insightful article represents beginning of an effort to create a comparative analysis of Mesoamerican "idolatrous" texts dating mainly from 17th-century era of extirpations, including well-known *Tratado* by Hernando Ruiz de Alarcón, but also relatively obscure items such as European-style zodiacal texts in Nahuatl and Zapotec ritual manuscripts confiscated or described by ecclesiastical authorities.

626 Tavárez, David Eduardo. Naming the Trinity: from ideologies of translation to dialectics of reception in colonial Nahua texts, 1547–1771. (*Colon. Lat. Am. Rev.*, 9:1, June 2000, p. 21–47, bibl., tables)

Focuses on ways in which the Trinity was described and taught to the Nahuas in evangelical texts from the time of Pedro de Gante through late 18th century, but moves beyond this genre to include such things as Nahuatl testaments and their introductory references to the Trinity. Exacting and revealing work advances our understanding of an extremely complex process of religious indoctrination and dialogue.

627 Terraciano, Kevin. The colonial mixtec community. (*HAHR*, 80:1, Feb. 2000, p. 1–42, ill., photos)

In a major work prefiguring his book (see item **629**), author uses an impressive source base of indigenous and Spanish-language documents to investigate the organization of Nudzahui (Mixtec) communities, particularly the "lordly establishment" (*aniñe*) and the "reciprocal labor and responsibility" system (*tniño*). Terraciano notes what he sees as a significant pattern of gradual decline of the *aniñe* and the persistence of the *tniño* in the Mixteca Alta, in the *alcaldía mayor* of Teposcolula and Yanhuitlan.

628 Terraciano, Kevin. Crime and culture in colonial Mexico: the case of the Mixtec murder note. (*Ethnohistory/Columbus*, 45:4, Fall 1998, p. 709–745, bibl., facsim., map)

A lively and sensitive reading of a unique letter written in Mixtec by a man justifying his murder of his allegedly adulteress wife is the starting point for an excellent study of indigenous attitudes about marital infidelity, crime, punishment, and, ultimately, what might be called "sin." Article is noteworthy as well for its usage of members of an indigenous group and language which remain relatively understudied compared above all with the Nahuas of central Mexico. A transcription and translation of the murder note is included.

629 Terraciano, Kevin. The Mixtecs of colonial Oaxaca: Ñudzahui history, sixteenth through eighteenth centuries. Stanford, Calif.: Stanford Univ. Press, 2001. 528 p.: appendix, bibl., ill., index, maps.

Impressive ethnohistory of the Mixtecs' journey through colonialism, told largely through their own voices as found in pictorial, native-language, and more traditional Spanish-language records. Author concerns himself with socioculturally significant topics such as writing and language, structure of communities, social and gender relations, politics, land tenure, the sacred world, and ethnicity and identity. An appendix offering transcriptions and translations of representative documents is a welcome addition. High quality work deepens our understanding of this significant Mesoamerican group. See also item **627**.

630 Título sobre la fundación de Coatepec de las Bateas. Introducción y notas de Pilar Maynes, Paciano Blancas y Francisco Morales. México: UNAM, Instituto de Investigaciones Históricas, 1995. 63 p., 24 p. of plates: bibl., facsims., ill.

Well-mounted publication of a Nahuatl-language document from the eastern Valley of Toluca, prefaced by a succinct and informative introduction. The editors suggest a link between this document and the Techialoyan manuscripts. The included facsimile and transcript, however, suggest links to the broader *títulos primordiales* (primordial titles) genre, complete with some stylistically typical illustrations. This is a useful edition which includes parallel Nahuatl and Spanish texts.

631 Tlaxcala: historia y democracia. Tlaxcala, Mexico: Gobierno del Estado de Tlaxcala, 2000. 79 p.: bibl., ill. (some col.).

Reproduction, with descriptive commentary, of select panels from the *Lienzo de Tlaxcala* and other pictorial or illustrated colonial-era documents from the *altepetl*. Creates a kind of pictorial narrative history of Tlaxcala from last stages of its independence through the Spanish invasion and up to early 17th century. Of note, in part, because of what the work says about ways in which modern-day Tlaxcalans have assembled a pictorial history of their past, and the things they consider significant and worthy of inclusion. See also items **479, 559,** and **632.**

632   Los tlaxcaltecas en Coahuila. Presentación, compilación y transcripción de Carlos Manuel Valdés y Idelfonso Dávila B. 2. ed. corr. y aum. San Luis Potosí, Mexico: El Colegio de San Luis: Tlaxcala, Mexico: Gobierno del Estado de Tlaxcala, 1999. 325 p.: appendix. (Biblioteca tlaxcalteca. Fuentes documentales)

Collection of transcribed documents traces foundation and later developments of Tlaxcalan colonies, beginning in 1591 and extending into early 19th century. The records are mainly of a political or ecclesiastical nature and often come from the pens of Spaniards, but there is an appendix of documents pertaining more specifically to the internal indigenous community, including two testaments. Each section is preceded by a succinct and informative introduction by the editors. See also items **479, 559,** and **631.**

633   Trejo, Silvia. La imagen del guerrero victorioso en Mesoamérica. (*Estud. Cult. Náhuatl,* 31, 2000, p. 221–236)

Lavishly illustrated discussion of symbolic depiction in myth and art of valor and success in war. Ranges widely across time and space in Mesoamerica, from representations found at places such as Olmec archeological sites through Teotihuacán, Tula, Bonampak, Malinalco, and Tenochtitlán. See also item **645.**

634   Tschohl, Peter. Inhalt und Schema eines verlorenen *Códice Matrícula de Tetzcoco* nach den Lesungen Motolinía, *Memoriales* (1971:803–10) und *Anales de Cuauhtitlan* (1938:1342–51). (*Ibero-Am. Arch.,* 22:3/4, 1996, p. 295–363, bibl., facsims., ill., maps, tables)

Meticulous attempt to reconstruct codex of the title, with an eye to establishing boundaries, administration, and political centers of precontact tribute districts connected with Texcoco.

635   Los últimos reinos mayas. Presentación de Eduardo Matos Moctezuma. Barcelona: Lunwerg, 1998. 240 p.: bibl., ill. (some col.), maps (some col.). (Corpus Precolombino. Sección Las civilizaciones mesoamericanas)

Well-mounted book provides solid overview of current knowledge about the Maya, particularly the postclassic Maya, through articles by well-known contributors. Includes many maps, line drawings, and gorgeous color plates that present views of codices, artifacts, and archeological sites.

636   Umberger, Emily. New blood from an old stone. (*Estud. Cult. Náhuatl,* 28, 1998, p. 241–256, bibl., ill.)

Thought-provoking reinterpretation of meanings of glyphs and figures carved on the Tizoc Stone.

637   Vail, Gabrielle. Kisin and the underworld gods of the Maya. (*Lat. Am. Indian Lit. J.,* 14:2, Fall 1998, p. 167–187)

New interpretation of identities of Gods A and Q, who appear as deities associated with death and sacrifice in the Dresden, Paris, Madrid, and Grolier screenfolds. Vail draws well-supported and suggestive comparisons between these deities and a modern Lacandón god known as Kisin, lord of earthquakes and the underworld.

Vail, Gabrielle. Pre-hispanic Maya religion: conceptions of divinity in the Postclassic Maya codices. See *HLAS 59:316.*

638   Valdés, Juan Antonio; Federico Fashen; and **Héctor L. Escobedo.** Reyes, tumbas y palacios: la historia dinástica de Uaxactún. México: UNAM; Guatemala: Instituto de Antropología e Historia de Guatemala, 1999. 123 p.: bibl., ill., maps. (Cuaderno/Instituto de Investigaciones Filológicas, Centro de Estudios Mayas; 25)

Informative study of the dynastic history of Uaxactún, concentrates mainly on the early and late classic periods. The dynastic implications of relations with Tikal form an important part of the mix here, and the authors develop a clear dynastic sequence for Uaxactún.

639   El Valle de Orizaba: textos de historia y antropología. Recopilación de Carlos Serrano Sánchez y Agustín García Márquez.

México: Instituto de Investigaciones Antropológicas, UNAM; Orizaba, Mexico: H. Ayuntamiento de Orizaba; Museo de Antropología de la Univ. Veracruzana, 1999. 144 p.: bibl., ill., maps. (Cuadernos de divulgación)

Series of articles by contemporary Mexican scholars focused on various aspects of Orizaba's history. Of interest to ethnohistorians of this region are: Rubén B. Morante López's "La Piedra Xipe en Orizaba" (part of this scholar's ongoing work analyzing this monument; see also item **565**); "La industria prehispánica de la obsidiana en la región de Orizaba" by Annick Daneels and Fernando A. Miranda Flores; and "El pueblo de indios de Orizaba, 1531–1821" by Agustín García Márquez (this article largely treats the 16th century).

640 Verástique, Bernardino. Michoacán and Eden: Vasco de Quiroga and the evangelization of western Mexico. Austin: Univ. of Texas Press, 2000. 194 p.: bibl., ill., index, map.

Superb study of Catholic evangelical enterprise among the Purépecha, centered around the programs of Bishop Vasco de Quiroga. The bishop, who has often been effectively sanctified in earlier studies, is here stripped of his idealized persona without being vilified. Instead, the author fashions a compelling examination of the indigenous and Spanish belief systems which came into contact and conflict beginning in the 1520s, with the story of Vasco de Quiroga's utopic initiatives deepened because the Purépechas' role as actors in this drama is given its due. A valuable contribution to newer literature which views the process of religious "conversion" less as a "spiritual conquest" than as an intricate dialogue between different cultural groups and ideologies. Also valuable for its highlighting of role of secular rather than order clergy.

641 Victoria Ojeda, Jorge. El sincretismo religioso como dominio ideológico en el pueblo maya. (*Mesoamérica/Antigua*, 18:34, dic. 1997, p. 341–355, photos)

Suggests that a 16th-century stone cross from town of Maní, Yucatán, presents a syncretic mix of Christian and indigenous imagery, and that it may have been used as a vehicle to smooth the way for Catholic indoctrination.

642 Viesca Treviño, Carlos. *Curanderismo* in Mexico and Guatemala: its historical evolution from the sixteenth to the nineteenth century. (*in* Mesoamerican healers. Austin: Univ. of Texas Press, 2001, p. 47–65)

High-quality discussion of emergence of *curanderismo* in Mexico as an artifact of the Spanish cultural invasion, noting ways in which traditional precontact curing survived both within and on the margins of colonial medical practices. Includes excellent treatment of formally trained indigenous doctors such as Martín de la Cruz of the Colegio de Santa Cruz in Tlatelolco, Mexico; Spanish ideas about the need for indigenous physicians to treat indigenous patients; and growing opposition of European physicians to the activities of their native counterparts. Shows how this world of Spanish-influenced medical practice could intersect with the more "traditional" native methods and beliefs.

643 Viesca Treviño, Carlos and **Andrés Aranda.** Las alteraciones del sueño en el *Libellus de medicinalibus Indorum herbis*. (*Estud. Cult. Náhuatl*, 26, 1996, p. 147–161)

The authors discuss the meanings of the remedies for sleep disorders prescribed in this mid-16th-century work, also known as the Códice de la Cruz Badiano.

644 Villela Flores, Samuel. El *Códice Panel de Chiepetlan* y las migraciones nahuas a la montaña de Guerrero. (*Estud. Cult. Náhuatl*, 26, 1996, p. 133–145, bibl.)

Description and preliminary analysis of a primordial title or Techialoyan-like document discovered during preparations for the celebration of the 500th anniversary of the foundation of San Miguel Chiepetlan, in the Tlapa municipality of Guerrero. The document, which seems to be a later copy of a manuscript written in 1666, concerns migrations and town founding, and is used by the author as the centerpiece of a discussion of this subject. Though named the *Códice Panel de Chiepetlan* because of its association with this town in terms of its discovery, the text (presented as a Nahuatl transcription and Spanish translation) actually seems to deal with localities in what is now the State of Morelos, including Yautepec.

645 Wake, Eleanor. Sacred books and sacred songs from former days: sourcing the mural paintings at San Miguel Arcángel Ixmiquilpan. (*Estud. Cult. Náhuatl*, 31, 2000, p. 95–121, bibl., facsims., ill.)

Intriguing study of famous murals at Ixquimilpan, arguing that precontact-style warrior imagery presented in them is actually a depiction of the text of one or more Nahua "warrior songs" found in such sources as the *Cantares Mexicanos*. Wake believes that murals provide, among other things, graphic evidence for ways in which Nahuas embraced the new Catholic faith and attempted to meld it with their own religious imagery and traditions. Very well done. See also item **633**.

646 Ward, Thomas. Expanding ethnicity in sixteenth-century Anahuac: ideologies of ethnicty and gender in the nation-building process. (*MLN/Baltimore*, 116:2, March 2001, p. 419–452, bibl.)

Ambitious article investigates ways in which ethnicity, gender, and "nation" were understood among the precontact Aztecs and by indigenous and Spanish chroniclers later in 16th century. Ultimately suggests ways in which such "ideologies" affected nascent concepts of the linkage between ethnicity and "Mexican" nationhood that emerged by the mature colonial era. See also item **647**. For literature specialist's comment, see item **3398**.

647 Ward, Thomas. From the "people" to the "nation": an emerging notion in Sahagún, Ixtlilxóchitl, and Muñoz Camargo. (*Estud. Cult. Náhuatl*, 32, 2001, p. 223–234)

Short article charts emergence of a linkage of group identity, lineage, and ethnicity with the European notion of "nation" through the pens of three major chroniclers of Nahua society and culture. See also item **646**.

648 Williams, Barbara J. and **H.R. Harvey.** The Códice de Santa María Asunción—facsimile and commentary: households and lands in sixteenth-century Tepetlaoztoc. Salt Lake City: Univ. of Utah Press, 1997. 422 p.: bibl., ill. (some col.), maps.

Pictorial census and land register, with Nahuatl glosses. In the land register, individuals depicted as a profile head with name glyphs attached are associated with fields of specific types. Very important publication shows the association of land and people and the importance given to the size of plots. Includes descriptions of plot types.

649 Wood, Stephanie. The false Texhialoyan resurrected. (*Tlalocan/México*, 12, 1997, p. 117–140, ill.)

Argues that a recently discovered Techialoyan text is the original Nahuatl version of the "Codice de San Cristóbal y Santa María" (Techialoyan 744 in Donald and Martha Robertson's 1975 catalog—see *HLAS 38:2061*). Long thought to have been destroyed, and dismissed by some as a "false" Techialoyan based on the analysis of a surviving Spanish translation, the present author corrects these mistaken notions by engaging in an exacting comparison with the Spanish and rediscovered Nahuatl texts. The issue of authorship of the document, from Tezcalucan and Chichicaspa in the modern state of Mexico, is also discussed. A transcription of the Nahuatl is included, as well as two color plates of representative folios.

650 Wright, David. El papel de los Otomi en las culturas del altiplano central: 5000 A.C.-1650 D.C. (*Relaciones/Zamora*, 17:72, otoño 1997, p. 225–242)

Careful analysis of the development of Otomi culture from its origins in the preclassic era through mid-colonial period. Argues that the Otomi have been unfairly neglected, emphasizing need to recognize cross-fertilization of Nahua and Otomi cultures that resulted in a relatively uniform, shared culture in this part of Mesoamerica. Wright traces the Otomies' crucial role from possible link between Otopame culture and classic Teotihuacán through their role as Spanish allies in invasion of Mexico and onward to their participation in the consolidation of territory on Chichimec frontier.

651 Zaballa Beascoechea, Ana de. Sahagún y la educación indígena: la explicación de la fe cristiana desde la mentalidad azteca. (*Novahispania/México*, 4, 1998, p. 161–182)

Examining forms of expression in the friar's "Adiciones" and "Apéndice" of the *Postilla*, as well as the *Ejercicio cotidiano*, author suggests topics that Sahagún considered essential for the Nahua audience to comprehend about Christian beliefs, as well as ways in which he employed indigenous terms and turns of phrase to convey these teachings.

652 Zeitlin, Judith Francis. Text and context in the interpretation of Aztec culture and society. (*LARR*, 32:3, 1997, p. 168–186)

Well-considered review essay of recent secondary studies of precontact and conquest-era central Mexico, as well as of a relatively new English-language edition of Zorita's *Life and Labor in Ancient Mexico* (see *HLAS 56:553*). Author does a good job relating what is actually a diverse and not always thematically unified collection of works.

653 Zorita, Alonso de. Relación de la Nueva España: relación de algunas de las muchas cosas notables que hay en la Nueva España y de su conquista y pacificación y de la conversión de los naturales de ella. v. 1–2. 1. ed. en Cien de México. México: CONACULTA, 1999. 2 v.: bibl., index. (Cien de México)

At last, a definitive publication of Zorita's major work, which for a long time has languished in obscurity while his *Breve relación* (see *HLAS 8:3022*) has seen many editions. A biographical study of Zorita and a historiographical discussion of his work introduce present volumes. The *Relación* focuses mainly on central Mexico, and begins with information on Mexico's natural history and the customs of its indigenous inhabitants. Also provides information on precontact social and economic matters, though not as much attention is given to things political. Zorita next treats the Spanish conquest—military and spiritual. A wonderful indexed edition of this valuable ethnohistorical resource.

South America

SUSAN E. RAMÍREZ, *Professor and Neville G. Penrose Chair of History and Latin American Studies, Texas Christian University*

THE BOOKS, ARTICLES, AND CHAPTERS REVIEWED HERE represent an ongoing, progressively constructed discourse about context and meaning. Each generation of scholars, while overlapping and building on the past, finds its own ways of defining and looking at the lives and times of indigenous South Americans. New questions asked of well-known sources and new examinations of accepted interpretations, together with standard questions asked of new "finds" contribute to a constant dialogue and the evolution of ethnohistorical understandings (item **801**). The selection of current research reviewed for *HLAS 60* updates our existing knowledge of the field.

Some traditional studies tease out new insights from standard sources by applying the tools of other or related disciplines (items **718, 774,** and **1858**). An article by linguist Cerrón-Palomino exemplifies such work (item **688**). He reinterpreted the text of a song found in Juan de Betanzos' early chronicle. His analysis of the lyrics and the translation of one word suggest native ideas about victory and defeat in war and the status of women that had not been readily apparent to previous readers. Such investigations are important because they suggest that philology and knowledge of indigenous languages are indispensable tools for doing anthropological history (items **671, 673, 677, 681, 739,** and **760**).

Other authors have found new sources to elucidate and complement the old (item **680**). Some of these sources have been found in local archives, which continue to be rich and underutilized repositories (items **698, 703, 755,** and **821**). In local documentation, one can most readily find the native voice. A few other unknown sources uncovered in studies reviewed here are located in private collections, where access is restricted (item **777**). The most notable example is the "Naples" document that, among other things, suggests that Felipe Guamán Poma de Ayala, a Hispanized native, did not write the *Nueva corónica y buen gobierno,* one of the longest and most accessible of the early 17th-century texts (item **700**). This "discovery" and the debate over its authenticity remind scholars of the importance of questioning the manuscripts, contextualizing them, and knowing the author(s) (items **728** and **761**). By extension, anonymous, undated documents are less reliable than those with provenance.

Still other ethnohistorians have sought new types of sources to complement the paper trail of the past (items **731, 820,** and **827**). Architectural remains are proving to be one source of new information (item **683**). Niles' book (item **772**) and Isabel's article on Incan and earlier ruins show how they reflect state cosmology and served as a stage for state theater. Analogously, on the borders of what is now Paraguay, Brazil, and Argentina, the remains of the *reducciones* demonstrate how the church helped the state colonize space and the indigenous imagination (item **711**). Such resettlement patterns, meant initially to aid conversion, also affected social relations, culture, production, and the indigenous peoples' sense of their past and themselves.

The interpretation of signs and symbols and ritual analysis are also gaining popularity (items **687, 701, 705, 713, 720, 768, 805,** and **812**). Ritual and ceremonial paraphernalia served as pedagogical devices to reiterate fundamental principles of indigenous cosmology. Viewing state (or local) pageantry and theater, like the Inca-sponsored dramas, no doubt bolstered acceptance of the reigning politico-religious myth and helped forge identities. Songs (e.g., the so-called *taquies* of the Incas), to the extent that lyrics can be found (e.g., in chronicles by Betanzos and Guamán Poma), are a possible related avenue into the thoughts, values, and lives of indigenous peoples (item **780**).

A cautionary note regarding the interpretation of architecture, signs, symbols, pageantry, and ritual, without an accompanying and explicating text, is that the interpreter will impose his/her own culturally mediated meaning onto the object. Thus, the challenge is figuring out a way to decenter our understandings. Special attention in these endeavors must be given to provenance, carefully identifying the object of attention according to when (precontact, early, or late contact), under what circumstances, and for what purpose it originated in order to understand more clearly representational significance and meaning. Similarly, where there is a textual guide, investigators must remain cognizant that indigenous peoples had to explain their cultural axioms to their colonizers in a language that was not their own, either directly or through an interpreter. To truly understand what indigenous texts were trying to convey, one must investigate how the speakers expressed concepts without exact Spanish or Portuguese equivalents and remain suspicious of translations. Comparing the written word with the material record and/or the behavior of the actors is one method of verifying meanings and establishing confidence in today's interpretations.

With due caution, architectural remains and iconographical and ritual analysis represent ways of seeking the indigenous voice outside of the written record. These alternative resources help to overcome the fact that most history is written by the victors, and to decenter the dialogue that is the historical process (items **717** and **821**). In practical terms, no one person can be expected to command the disciplines of history, anthropology, archeology, architecture, art history, and linguistics. Therefore, it is incumbent upon the practitioners of our discipline to: 1) familiarize ourselves and our students with the rudiments of additional disciplines; 2) present our findings so that they are accessible to nonspecialists; and 3) further communicate, collaborate, and cooperate among ourselves and our public (items **669** and **813**).

654 Abejez, Luis J. Las crónicas de Indias y el origen humano en América. (*in* Encuentro-Debate América Latina ayer y hoy = Trobada-Debat Amèrica Llatina ahir i avui, 6th, *Barcelona, 1997*. Lo que duele es el olvido: recuperando la memoria de América Latina = El que dol és l'oblit: recuperant la memòria d'Amèrica Llatina. Barcelona, Spain: Univ. de Barcelona, 1998, p. 21–33)

Synthesis of how chroniclers reported on the origin of human life in America. When the chroniclers write about an external origin, they negate the originality of American cultures and unlink the Americans from their lands (arguing that they are invaders, too), thus justifying the idea of reconquest.

655 Abercrombie, Thomas Alan. Pathways of memory and power: ethnography and history among an Andean people. Madison: Univ. of Wisconsin Press, 1998. 603 p.: bibl., ill., index.

Important book on ethnography and history of an Aymara-speaking people in the town of K'ulta on the Bolivian Altiplano. Analyzes the people's ways of remembering, noting that their form of relating their history does not necessarily coincide with Western academic traditions. For ethnologist's comment, see *HLAS 59:1040*.

656 Abou, Sélim. The Jesuit "Republic" of the Guaranis, 1609–1768 and its heritage. Translated by Lawrence J. Johnson. New York: Crossroad Pub. Co.; Paris: UNESCO Pub., 1997. 160 p.: bibl., ill. (some col.), col. maps.

Account of the Jesuit missions to the Guarani between 1606–1768. Text, complemented by evocative color photographs, introduces the missions, organization of the "Jesuit Republic," and the Treaty of Madrid and its consequences (the Guarani War). Final section deals with impact of the Jesuits

and their effect on the ancestors of the people alive today.

Academia Nacional de la Historia (Argentina). Nueva historia de la nación argentina. See item **2345**.

657 Adrián, Mónica. El espacio sagrado y el ejercicio del poder: las doctrinas de Chayanta durante la segunda mitad del siglo XVIII. (*Anuario/Sucre*, 1997, p. 239–255, bibl.)

Carefully researched article on concept of the sacred among the Aymara. Surveys the process of turning a *doctrina*, originally conceived as a demographically defined group of a certain size for conversion purposes, into a geographically delimited area.

658 Alcina Franch, José. El complejo "santuario-mercado-festival" y el origen de los centros ceremoniales en el área andina septentrional. (*Rev. Indias*, 59:215, enero/abril 1999, p. 31–53, graph, tables)

Article studies origins of urbanism in the Andean area. Contends that urbanism takes form in and around a ceremonial center. Inter-ethnic peace is maintained there to encourage pilgrimages and religious observation. Author hypothesizes that such centers offered space in which to exchange products as well.

659 Alcina Franch, José. Las culturas precolombinas de América. Madrid: Alianza Editorial, 2000. 245 p.: bibl., ill., maps. (Libro universitario. Materiales; mt 035)

Survey of prehispanic societies of Latin America back to the paleolithic. Author takes evolutionary approach to the cultures of the peoples of both Mesoamerica and South America. Includes a glossary, chronologies, maps, and bibliography.

660 Aldana Rivera, Susana. Tres temas para una identidad: pautas historiográficas en Piura y Tumbes, Perú. (*Rev.*

Complut. Hist. Am., 23, 1997, p. 23–38, bibl.)

A short article on the formation of a northern regional identity or identities among the Tallan (of Piura) or Tumpi (of Tumbes) peoples. Author highlights prehispanic culture, the formation of cities (especially Piura), mestizaje, and independence as key elements of a regional sense of self.

661 Almeida, Rita Heloísa de. O diretório dos índios: um projeto de "civilização" no Brasil do século XVIII. Brasília: Editora UnB, 1997. 411 p.: bibl., ill. (some col.), maps (some col.).

Originally presented as author's doctoral thesis, this serious book focuses on colonization as a means for civilizing the indigenous peoples. Covers themes such as slavery and good government. One section analyzes a judicial document that regulated the behavior of the colonists in Brazil between 1757–98. The document, aimed at controlling evangelization, addresses populating and defending the territory.

662 Almeida Reyes, Eduardo. Culturas prehispánicas del Ecuador. Quito: Viajes Chasquiñan, 2000. 180 p.: bibl.

Archeological manual on the precolonial peoples of Ecuador written as a university text and based on some standard secondary sources. Chapters cover the peoples of the Archaic period to the invasion of the Incas. Discussion alternates from analysis of sites such as Chobshi, Cubilán, Cotocollao, Alausí, and Catamayo, to characterization of cultures such as the Valdivia, Machalilla, Chorrera, Panzaleo, Huancavilca, Cañari, and Caranquis. A separate chapter deals with the peoples of the Amazon.

Anello Oliva, Giovanni. Historia del reino y provincias del Perú y vidas de los varones insignes de la Compañía de Jesús. See item **2227**.

Apel, Karin. De la hacienda a la comunidad: la sierra de Piura, 1934–1990. See *HLAS 59:1153*.

663 Aráuz, Maritza. Pueblos de indios en la costa ecuatoriana: Jijipapa y Montecristi en la segunda mitad del siglo XVIII. Guayaquil, Ecuador: Archivo Historico del Guayas, 1999. 137 p.: bibl., ill. (Col. A la costa; 1)

A historical ethnography of the coastal peoples of Jijipapa and Montecristi, Ecuador, in the second half of 18th century. Central themes are Andean political economy, regional development, inter-ethnic relations, and changing social stratification within communities. Author determines role of indigenous communities in the social and economic life of the colony. Based on extensive archival research.

664 Areces, Nidia R. Paraguayos, portugueses y Mbayás en Concepción, 1773–1840. (*Mem. Am.*, 8, 1999, p. 11–44, bibl.)

Examines colonization of Concepción (Paraguay) in 1773. Argues that there is no clear-cut and rigid separation between white and indigenous nor between barbarian and civilized. Also discusses the agricultural frontier and the moving warfront, arguing that they were linked by commerce.

665 Arévalo Merejildo-Chaski, James. El despertar del puma: camino iniciático; evidencias astronómicas en los Andes. Cusco, Peru: Imprenta del Centro Bartolomé de Las Casas, 1997. 178 p.: bibl., ill. (some col.).

Purports to deal with astronomy and magic of ancient Andean cultures, including the Inca. Sections discuss the sites of Tawantinsuyu, Chavin de Huantar, Tiwanaku, Cuzco, Quenco, Ollantaytambo, and Machu Picchu. Based on secondary sources and on-the-spot observations.

666 Arqueología, antropología e historia en los Andes: homenaje a María Rostworowski. Recopilación de Rafael Varón Gabai y Javier Flores Espinoza. Lima: Instituto de Estudios Peruanos; Banco Central de Reserva del Perú, 1997. 803 p.: bibl., ill. (some col.). (Serie Historia andina, 1019–4541; 21)

Thick book of articles by leading ethnohistorians in honor of María Rostworowski's 80th birthday. Papers focus on chronicles, metallurgy, quipus, guano, land and tenure, Incas, and the Chavín. Last section includes seven papers on methodology—specifically on cosmology, identity, rites, and merchants and markets.

667 Arquivo Público do Estado do Maranhão (Brazil). Repertório de documentos para a história indígena no Maranhão. São Luís, Brazil: Arquivo Público do Estado de

Maranhão, 1997. 361 p.: bibl. (Série Instrumentos de pesquisa)

Invaluable catalog of primary documents for history of indigenous peoples of Maranhão between 1738–1888. Lists mission records, governmental correspondence, censuses, laws, and maps.

668 Ascher, Marcia and **Robert Ascher.** Mathematics of the Incas: code of the quipu. Mineola, N.Y.: Dover Publications, 1997. 166: bibl., ill.

Book written for the nonspecialist on the Andean quipu, a record-keeping device made up of color-coded and knotted strings, and mathematics. Work is the result of years of study and systematic analysis of about 200 quipus. Authors conclude that Incas developed a form of recording that forces reconsideration of the meaning of *writing* as the term is generally understood today. For comments on previous editions of this work, see *HLAS 44:1572* and *HLAS 45:841.*

669 Assis, Virgínia M. Almoêdo de. Subsídios documentais à pesquisa arqueológica: as missões religiosas em PE, PB e RN. (*in Rev. Arqueol./São Paulo*, 8:2, 1994/95, p. 341–349, bibl.)

A plea for collaboration between historians and archeologists specifically with respect to colonial documents preserved at the Universidade Federal de Pernambuco, which deal with religious missions in Pernambuco, Paraíba, and Rio Grande do Norte.

670 Avellaneda, Mercedes. Orígenes de la alianza jesuita-guaraní y su consolidación en el siglo XVII. (*Mem. Am.*, 8, 1999, p. 173–200, bibl.)

Well-documented study of the founding of Jesuit *reducciones* on the Paraná and Guayra Rivers, which gave a privileged role to the indigenous chiefs. Intertribal wars, colonial exploitation, and subsistence needs were some of the factors that influenced negotiations. *Reducciones* were established in return for freedom from *encomienda* and *mita* obligations. The indigenous quickly learned European military tactics and used them against other indigenous troops as well as the Spanish and Portuguese.

671 Avendaño, Santiago. Usos y costumbres de los indios de la Pampa: segunda parte de las Memorias del ex-cautivo Santiago Avendaño. Recopilación de Meinrado

Hux. Buenos Aires: Elefante Blanco, 2000. 154 p.

A treatise on the belief system of the Ranquel of the Pampas written by a captive who spent seven years in their company in the 1840s. Later he served as official interpreter of the army and as a diplomat. His extensive association with the Ranquel makes his observations on their customs and traditions important and valuable. Work includes parts written in the native language. Part I of the memorias were issued by the same publisher under the title: *Memorias del ex-cautivo Santiago Avendaño, 1834–1874* (1999).

672 Ayala Loayza, Juan Luis. Etnohistoria de Huancané. Lima: Editorial Horizonte, 1998. 284 p.: bibl., ill.

A detailed history of the people of Huancané, depto. of Puno in southern Peru, from 16th-late 20th centuries. Huancané's colonial story is told through its institutions: encomiendas, *repartimientos, reducciones, curacas, caciques, corregimientos,* the Church, and its people. National history is told in short sections on important characters in Huancané's history such as caudillo Andrés Ignacio Qama Condori, Andean rebels Pascual Alarapita and Isidro Mamani, caudillo Juan Bustamante Dueñas, and others.

Bacigalupo, Ana Mariella. "Ngünechen": el concepto de dios mapuche. See *HLAS 59:1096.*

673 Ballón Aguirre, Enrique. Mito y rito: linderos y puentes discursivos en el *Manuscrito de Huarochirí.* (*Anthropol. Dep. Cienc. Soc.*, 15:15, 1997, p. 305–326, bibl., table)

Discursive analysis of contents of the Huarochirí manuscript. Author compares durability of Andean myths as oral ethnic literature with Spanish intolerance for and destruction of symbols of the Quechua belief system.

674 Bastidas Valecillos, Luis. Una mirada etnohistórica a las tierras indígenas de Mérida: el problema en la actualidad. (*Bol. Antropol./Mérida*, 44, sept./dic. 1998, p. 34–59, bibl., map, photos)

Analyzes historical continuities of communal land tenure arrangements around Mérida, Venezuela (specifically the communities of Timotes, Chiguara, Lagunillas, and

Horcaz). Shows how they have been re-dressed in modern legal jargon and guise. Mentions self-development programs and pressures to divide and privatize. See also items **675** and **676**.

675 **Bastidas Valecillos, Luis.** Una mirada etnohistórica a las tierras indígenas de Mérida: época colonial. (*Bol. Antropol./ Mérida*, 41, sept./dic. 1997, p. 46–67, bibl., tables)

Reviews land disputes near Mérida, Venezuela. Cites late 16th- and 17th-century *resguardo* titles and other documents to show differences in access to land and water in communities such as Timotes and Lagunillas. See also items **674** and **676**.

676 **Bastidas Valecillos, Luis.** Una mirada etnohistórica a las tierras indígenas de Mérida: siglo XIX e inicios del XX. (*Bol. Antropol./Mérida*, 43, mayo/agosto 1998, p. 5–51, bibl., maps, table)

Reviewing laws proclaimed in 19th and early 20th centuries concerning indigenous land and tenure, analyzes process of adjudication and division of indigenous reservations in Mérida, Venezuela. Finds that application of these laws produced no positive change in relation to indigenous conception of common property. On the contrary, the laws tried to homogenize a society that was socially and culturally very different. However, indigenous peoples learned to use the republican legal system to defend their common lands, as they did in colonial times as well. See also items **674** and **675**.

677 **Bauer, Brian S.** The sacred landscape of the Inca: the Cusco ceque system. Austin: Univ. of Texas Press, 1998. 249 p.: appendix, bibl., indexes, maps, photos, tables.

Re-examination of the *ceque* system of Cuzco, first described by R. Tom Zuidema over three decades ago (see *HLAS 27:1358*). Author attempts to reconstruct the ritual system, composed of several hundred shrines in and around the city of Cuzco. Using recent archeological and archival research, provides new insights on organization of one of the New World's largest indigenous societies. Text is accompanied by maps, photographs, figures, tables, and an appendix that includes Bernabé Cobo's account of the shrines and suggested glosses of shrine names by Margot Beyersdorff.

678 **Becker, Itala Irene Basile.** O índio kaingáng do Paraná: subsídios para uma etno-história. Colaboração de Luis Fernando da Silva Laroque. São Leopoldo, Brazil: Editora Unisinos, 1999. 344 p.: bibl., ill., maps.

Monograph covers the history of the Kaingang (of the Paraná) from precolonial times to 20th century. Topics covered include the usual descriptions of material culture, sociopolitical organization, and spirituality, as well as language and personality.

679 **Becker, Itala Irene Basile** and **Luís Fernando da Silva Laroque.** Uma etno-história para os índios Kaingáng do Paraná da pré-história ao seculo X. (*Estud. Leopold-enses Sér. Hist.*, 3:1, jan./junho 1999, p. 129–137, bibl., map)

Short article on ethnohistory of the Kaingang peoples of the Paraná from 16th-century contact to the 20th century.

680 **Berg, Hans van den.** *El Eco Guarayo* del padre Bernardino Pesciotti: una revista manuscrita sobre los Guarayos, y las Misiones del Colegio de Propaganda Fide de Tarata, 1896–1918. (*in* Reunión Anual de Etnología, *11th, La Paz, 1997*. Actas. La Paz: Museo Nacional de Etnografía y Folklore (MUSEF); Fundación Cultural, Banco Central de Bolivia, 1997, t. 1, p. 35–59, bibl., table)

Interesting history of a manuscript periodical about life among the Guarayos, first written in 1896 by a Franciscan, Bernardino Pesciotti. In addition to advertisements and editorials, periodical contained historical documents about the missions of the Colegio de Propaganda Fide de Tarata. Pesciotti continued to write *El Eco Guarayo* until shortly before his death. See also item **711**.

681 **Beyersdorff, Margot.** Documentos inéditos para la historia de los pueblos originarios de Oruro. (*Eco Andin.*, 3:6, 1998, p. 7–40, maps)

A welcome addition to published documents on indigenous land holdings in Bolivia. The land titles published here encourage researchers to consider the importance of toponyms, cropping patterns, tenure arrangements, and the difference between Spanish jurisdictional boundaries and ethnic settlement patterns. Multi-ethnic enclaves complicate attempts to delimit cohesive ethnic territories.

Beyersdorff, Margot. Historia y drama ritual en los andes bolivianos, siglos XVI-XX. See *HLAS 59:1046.*

682 Boccara, Guillaume. Análisis de un proceso de etnogénesis: el caso de los Reche-Mapuche de Chile en la época colonial. (*Mem. Am.*, 7, 1998, p. 11–27, bibl.)

Focuses on political, economic, and social transformations among the Reche groups of south-central Chile as a consequence of contact with Hispanic Creoles. Changes in self-perception in the face of the "other" helped forge new identities. The history of the Hispanic-indigenous encounter is an ethnogenetic process that slowly transformed the central Reche groups into the Mapuche ethnicity in second half of 18th century.

683 Bollinger, Armin. Así construían los inkas: apuntes de arquitectura en los andes centrales. Revisión general de Oswaldo Rivera Sundt. Traducción de Rainer B. Podratz. La Paz: Editorial Los Amigos del Libro, 1997. 311 p.: bibl., photos. (Col. Descubra Bolivia)

Useful survey of Inca architecture includes numerous b/w photos. Discusses highways, inns, bridges, irrigation networks, terraces, cities, and fortifications.

684 Busto Duthurburu, José Antonio del. Túpac Yupanqui, descubridor de Oceanía. Lima: Editorial Brasa, 2000. 159 p.: bibl.

Reconstructs the possible explorations in America and Oceanía of the Tenth Inca (Túpac Yupanqui), based largely on chroniclers' reports. After studying wind and wave patterns and other factors, author favors second theater of action.

685 Cahill, David Patrick. After the fall: constructing Incan identity in late colonial Cuzco. (*in* Constructing collective identities and shaping public spheres: Latin American paths. Edited by Luis Roniger and Mario Sznajder. Brighton, England; Portland, Ore.: Sussex Academic Press, 1998, p. 65–99, bibl.)

A well-documented study focusing on the person of Tupac Amaru II and Cuzco indigenous aristocracy. Argues that members of Cuzco elites' ancestral glory and justification of their position was challenged by the parvenu Tupac Amaru's vision of an entirely new community, controlled by the colonized themselves, who would be at liberty to construct a new Incario.

686 Calavia Sáez, Óscar. Los otros quinientos: historia brasileña y etnología indígena. (*Rev. Indias*, 60:218, enero/abril 2000, p. 99–110)

Short, straightforward analysis of the place of the indigenous movement in Brazilian history. Author briefly sketches the historiography of indigenous societies, and contrasts it with the Spanish-American experience.

687 Campana D., Cristóbal and **Ricardo Morales.** Historia de una deidad mochica. Lima: A & B, 1997. 120 p.: bibl., ill. (some col.).

Short book analyzes iconography on the Huaca de la Luna, an impressive pyramid of the Mochica culture. Identifies a recurrent polychrome low-relief face as representation of a primordial ancestor. This ubiquitous symbol appears to suggest divine origin of the ruling elite and justify its power.

688 Cerrón-Palomino, Rodolfo. Tras las huellas del aimara cuzqueño. (*Rev. Andin.*, 17:1, julio 1999, p. 137–161, bibl.)

Linguistic analysis of the languages of southern highland Andes. Concludes that Puquina, the "secret language" of the Incas mentioned by Garcilaso de la Vega and other chroniclers, was a variety of Puquina "transfigured" in Aymara.

689 Chávez Hualpa, Fabiola. Embarazo y parto en los cronistas de los siglos XVI-XVII. (*Anthropol. Dep. Cienc. Soc.*, 15:15, 1997, p. 97–134, bibl.)

A compendium on pregnancy and birthing compiled from the Jesuit Annual Letters in the Archivo Romano de la Sociedad Jesuita, the writings of chroniclers (Santillán, Murúa, Cobo, Ramos Gavilán, etc.), and other primary documents. Topics include abortion, breach birth, the moon, the rainbow, and twins.

690 Choque Canqui, Roberto. Cacicazgo aymara de Pakaxa. (*Estud. Boliv.*, 4, sept. 1997, p. 5–75, bibl., photo)

Comprehensive summary of Aymara-speaking Pakaxa, beginning with waning years of Tiwanaku rule. This well-documented article touches on duality, the *mallku* (lord of vassals), the colonial *curaca*, and kinship. Analysis is based on both secondary and primary (published and unpublished) sources.

691 Comunidades: tierra, instituciones, identitad. Recopilación de Carlos Iván Degregori. Lima: Diakonía; CEPES; Asociación Arariwa, 1998. 225 p.: bibl.

Essays on indigenous communities in Peru, Mexico, Ecuador, Bolivia, and Colombia in second half of 20th century. Themes include land, identity, and community. Shows that conflict over land results in violence and displacement.

692 Congreso Internacional de Etnohistoria, 4th, Lima, 1997. Actas. v. 1–3. Lima: Pontificia Univ. Católica del Perú, Fondo Editorial, 1998. 3 v.: bibl., ill., map.

Invaluable survey of recent research on South American ethnohistory. Vol. 1 covers authority and power, and the economy. Specific topics include iconography, water control, *curacas*, identity, commerce, verticality, *chasquis*, tribute, urban indigenous peoples, *obrajes*, and offshore island resources. Vol. 2 is organized around ethnicity, territoriality, methodology, and Pizarro. Individual contributions include thoughts on *curacas*, *forasteros*, *mitimaes*, inter-ethnic relations, *acllas*, and encomiendas. Vol. 3 covers religion and society. Under these rubrics are papers on Andean gods, *guacas*, the Andean Mass, shamanism, funeral rites, Taqui Oncoy, relations between blacks and indigenous peoples, and Japanese immigrants.

693 Costales Samaniego, Alfredo and **Dolores Costales Peñaherrera.** Historia de Macas en el Departamento del Sur y la República, 1822–1922. Quito?: Casa de la Cultura Ecuatoriana Benjamín Carrión, Núcleo de Morona Santiago, 1998. 192 p.: bibl., ill.

Valuable for the wealth of data on history, geography, and resource base of Macas, a town in Ecuador; work might serve as an example for a study on a more general theme. Specific topics include the Canton of Sungay, Jesuit and Dominican missions, and mestizaje.

694 De hombres, tierras y derechos: la agricultura y la cuestión agraria por los caminos del Descubrimiento. Coordinación de Ramón Vicente Casanova. Mérida,

Venezuela: Instituto Iberoamericano de Derecho Agrario y Reforma Agraria, Univ. de los Andes; Caracas: Monte Avila Editores Latinoamericana, 1997. 181 p.: bibl., index. (Col. Perspectiva actual)

A study of the reciprocal influence of agricultural practices in the New World and Europe since contact. Explores and analyzes exchange of plants (such as wheat, barley, apples, and peaches from Europe and corn, cacao, avocados, and potatoes from America) and animals (e.g., the European horse and the American turkey); ideas about property and corporate and private forms of ownership; and modern agrarian reform. Includes case studies on the Jesuit *reducciones* of Paraguay and peasant communities in Peru.

695 Delgado Morales, Serafín. Etnografía y folklore uru-valluna: carnavales de Oruro, urqupiña de Cochabamba; folklore, institucionalidad e historia, cuentos y leyenda, homenajes y discursos. Cochabamba, Bolivia: S. Delgado Morales, 1999. 331 p.: ill. (some col.).

Collection of writings (articles, chronicles, essays) on folklore and culture of Oruro by an observer and participant. Includes histories of carnival, the Club de Leones, the Colegio Bolívar, and the Club Oruro; an essay on the founding of Cochabamba; and biographies of important local personages.

696 Delrio, Walter Mario. Sobre los elementos de la política mapuche durante la segunda mitad del siglo XVIII. (*in* Congreso Argentino de Americanistas, 2nd, *Buenos Aires, 1997.* Actas. Buenos Aires: Sociedad Argentina de Americanistas, 1998, t. 1, p. 169–188, bibl.)

Relates difficulties of retelling or reconstructing 18th-century history of Araucanía, given the mostly European perspectives of the sources. Author touches on myth of "permanent warfare," tribal politics, status based on merit and prestige, consensus building, redistribution and reciprocity, and exchange.

697 Díaz, Sandra Liliana. Lo diario y lo extraordinario en el entorno material del guarani de las misiones. (*in* Congreso Argentino de Americanistas, 2nd, *Buenos Aires, 1997.* Actas. Buenos Aires: Sociedad Argentina de Americanistas, 1998, t. 2, p. 53–89, bibl.)

Summary of establishment of the Catholic Church in 16th century in area that became the Viceroyalty of Río de La Plata. Includes information on first bishops, *reducciones*, indigenous-religious relations, and conversion. Lacks footnotes.

698 Díaz Rementería, Carlos J. Supervivencia y disolución de la comunidad de bienes indígena en la Argentina del siglo XIX. (*Rev. Hist. Derecho Ricardo Levene*, 30, 1995, p. 11–39)

Lengthy article on land and tenure in 19th-century Argentina, based on primary documents in the archives of Salta, Buenos Aires, Tucumán, Córdoba, and Jujuy. Discusses colonial tenure, alienation and sale of public lands, process of "denunciation," land grants, and emphyteuses.

699 Diez Hurtado, Alejandro. Comunes y haciendas: procesos de comunalización en la Sierra de Piura, siglos XVIII al XX. Piura, Peru: CIPCA; CBC, 1998. 262 p.: bibl., ill. (Archivos de historia andina, 1022–0879; 31)

Exhaustive scholarly study, based on years of archival research, of process of peasant community formation in Peru's northern highlands from late 18th-middle 20th centuries. Analyzes economic, social, and political conditions that gave rise to the particular types of community found in Piura, and internal and external agents involved in formation and transformation of the institution of haciendas.

700 Domenici, Viviano and Davide Domenici. Talking knots of the Inka: a curious manuscript may hold the key to Andean writing. (*Archaeology/New York*, 49:6, Nov./Dec. 1996, p. 50–56, ill., photos)

Short introduction to controversy surrounding the "Naples document" provides a summary of its contents and offers opinions by leading scholars about its authenticity and the reliability of its contents.

701 Eeckhout, Peter. La renarde yunga: une figure symbolique préhispanique. (*Rev. Esp. Antropol. Am.*, 28, 1998, p. 119–149, bibl., map, table)

By studying figure of the fox in central coastal iconography, author explores relationship of Yunga peoples with the highland Yauyos. Prehispanic myths and rites, as well as folklore and customs, reveal antagonism

and complementarity between Peruvian coast and highlands.

Elferink, Jan G.R. Aphrodisiac use in Pre-Columbian Aztec and Inca cultures. See item **471**.

702 Encuentro Taller Latinoamericano de Teología India, *3rd, Cochabamba, Bolivia, 1997.* Sabiduría indígena: fuente de esperanza; teología india. v. 1–2. Puno, Peru: IDEA; Cusco, Peru: IPA; La Paz: CTP, 1998. 2 v.

Presents texts from Encuentro with sessions centered on indigenous spirituality, resistance to neoliberalism, and inter-ethnic dialogue. Participants from Brazil, Colombia, Ecuador, Mexico, Panama, and Chile recount indigenous myths and ceremonies in an effort to create and instill "ecumenical fraternity."

703 Estenssoro Fuchs, Juan Carlos and **Jesús Bustamante.** Falsificación y revisión histórica: informe sobre un supuesto nuevo texto colonial andino. (*Rev. Indias*, 57:210, mayo/agosto 1997, p. 563–578)

Description and analysis of *Historia et rudimenta linguae piruanorum*, a seven-folio manuscript in the possession of Señora Clara Miccinelli, that, among other things, states that the *Nueva corónica y buen gobierno* was not written by Felipe Guamán Poma de Ayala. Authors conclude that the manuscript is not authentic. See also items **765, 777,** and **800.**

704 Faces of pre-Columbian Chile. Illustrations by José Pérez de Arce. Texts by Carlos Aldunate del Solar and Francisco Gallardo Ibañez. Santiago: Banco Santiago; Museo Chileno de Arte Precolombino, 1997. 92 p.: bibl., ill. (some col.), col. map.

Selection of illustrations covers extensive part of Chile's prehistory. The drawings, each prefaced with an explanation about its chronological, geographical, and cultural context and supplemented with photographs, represent different precolumbian periods in various parts of the country.

705 Falchetti, Ana María. El poder simbólico de los metales: la *tumbaga* y las transformaciones metalúrgicas. (*Bol. Arqueol./Bogotá*, 14:2, mayo 1999, p. 53–82, bibl., ill., maps, tables)

Analyzes symbolic meanings of metal,

particularly gold and copper. Concludes that indigenous societies associate the properties of these metals with the transformation, regeneration, and continuity of life. For archeologist's comment, see *HLAS 59:555.*

706 Faulhaber, Priscila. Nos varadouros das representações: redes etnográficas na Amazônia do início do século XX. (*Rev. Antropol./São Paulo*, 40:2, 1997, p. 101–143, bibl.)

Interesting discussion of a group of ethnographers who studied Amazonian peoples at the beginning of 20th century, and of their place in the history of the field. Author finds a relationship between their works even though their personal interactions are largely unknown.

707 Fernández, Jorge. Pichi Painé Gner o los orígenes y el universo de Painé joven, 1820–1830: descubriendo a su probable hermano, el capitán Santiago Lincogur. (*Cuad. Inst. Nac. Antropol. Pensam. Latinoam.*, 18, 1998/99, p. 109–132, bibl., facsim.)

Biography of indigenous chief Painé Guor going back to 1806 when he served the Boroanos and Huilliches of the central Pampas. A brother, Capt. Santiago Lincojur, of military fame, is identified.

708 Fleck, Eliane Cristina Deckmann. A doença e a morte na religiosidade Guarani: elementos para uma história do medo nas reduções jesuítico-guaranis. (*Anais/São Paulo*, 16, 1997, p. 121–125)

Short article on influence of disease and Christian conceptions and rites associated with death on Guarani mythological and magical thought in 17th century. Author quotes extensively from Jesuit annual letters.

709 Freyer, Bärbel. Los chiquitanos: descripción de un pueblo de las tierras bajas orientales de Bolivia según fuentes jesuíticas del siglo XVIII. Traducido del alemán por Dudrun Birk. Santa Cruz, Bolivia: ATLANTIDA, 2000. 121 p.: bibl., ill., maps. (Pueblos indígenas de las tierras bajas de Bolivia; 15)

Compendium on historical ethnography of the Chiquito indigenous group at the time of first contact with the Europeans, drawn from 18th-century Jesuit descriptions. Gives special attention to the spiritual and

material culture; and economic, political, and social organization.

710 Gallegos, Hector. El viejo Perú. Lima?: Colegio de Ingenieros del Perú, 2000. 215 p.: bibl., ill., index. (Col. La ingeniería en el Perú; t. 1)

Compendium on engineering in the ancient Andes, beginning with summary descriptions of the Chavín, Huarí, Tiahuanaco, and Mochica-Chimu. Emphasizes Inca technical accomplishments in agriculture and infrastructure, with a section on construction techniques.

711 García Jordán, Pilar. La invasión simbólica del espacio indígena: una reflexión sobre la apropiación ideológica del espacio en las misiones guarayas. (*in* Encuentro-Debate América Latina ayer y hoy = Trobada-Debat Amèrica Llatina ahir i avui, 6th, Barcelona, 1997. Lo que duele es el olvido: recuperando la memoria de América Latina = El que dol és l'oblit: recuperant la memòria d'Amèrica Llatina. Barcelona: Univ. de Barcelona, 1998, p. 229–243, maps, tables)

Innovative study of a series of maps and plans (dated 1894–1902) used to found missionary towns among the Guarayo. Shows how indigenous space was colonized with the construction of "civilized" space, which supported new work habits and ways to spend leisure time. See also item **680.**

712 Gates Chávez, Carlos. La historia inédita de los chachapoyas: descendientes de los constructores de la fortaleza de Kuélap. Lima: Univ. de San Martín de Porres, Facultad de Turísmo y Hotelería, 1997. 361 p.: bibl., ill. (some col.), maps.

Ethnohistory of the Chachapoya of northern Peru begins with Inca rule. Pt. 1 summarizes what is known about 16th-century history. Remainder focuses on archeological sites such as Kuelap, the tombs of Jucusbamba, and El Gran Pajatén; their tourist potential is also assessed.

713 Gisbert, Teresa. La serpiente Amaru y la conquista del Antisuyo. (*Anuario/Sucre*, 1997, p. 3–18, bibl., photos)

Analyzes iconography of a trunk (*cofre*) in the Casa de Murillo in La Paz. Author hypothesizes that the personage painted on the trunk is Amaro Topa Yupanqui, as lieutenant to Pachacutec and later to Inca

Tupac-Yupanqui. This artifact is testimony to the persistent efforts to preserve prehispanic history after the encounter with the Spanish.

714 González Coll, María Mercedes. Conquista, evangelización y relaciones interétnicas: una visión etnohistórica del problema. (*Cuad. Sur Hist./Bahía Blanca*, 28, 1999, p. 155–172, bibl.)

Summarizes establishment in 16th century of Catholic Church in area that became the Viceroyalty of Río de La Plata. Includes information on missionaries, goals and methods of evangelization, first bishops, *reducciones*, indigenous-religious relations, and conversion. Lacks footnotes.

715 González Lebrero, Rodolfo E. Impacto de la invasión hispana sobre los indígenas rioplatenses, 1580–1640. (*Quinto Sol/Santa Rosa*, 2:2, 1998, p. 111–140, bibl., table)

Investigates encounter between European and indigenous peoples (groups like the Yaro, Minoano, Guenoa, Bohane, Timbú, Carcarañá, Coronda, Quiloaza, and Colastiné) in Río de la Plata region from 1580–1640. Documents how ecosystems were changed, and extent to which indigenous population collapsed. Also discusses realignment of indigenous social structure and changes in settlement patterns.

716 Gorla, Carlos María. La frontera de Patagones en el período 1820–1840. (*Invest. Ens.*, 47, 1997, p. 409–431)

Well-documented article on frontier interaction between settlers and indigenous peoples (Aucas, Chilenos, and Valdivianos) between 1820–40. Details how planned expansion up-river was thwarted.

717 Gregorio-Cernadas, Maximiliano. Crítica y uso de las fuentes históricas relativas a la diplomacia indígena en la Pampa durante el siglo XIX. (*Mem. Am.*, 7, 1998, p. 61–89, bibl.)

Methodological article focuses on inter-ethnic relations on the Pampas and how to analyze them through contemporary—mostly 19th-century—documents. Author proposes ways of evaluation, including a four-fold categorization: 1) documents written by indigenous peoples; 2) documents written by mestizos and whites with direct

first-hand knowledge; 3) criollo testimony, based on brief observations and with the help of intermediaries; and 4) criollo documents based on indirect knowledge.

718 Guarisco Canseco, Claudia. El componente occidental: una lectura de la *Nueva corónica y buen gobierno* de Felipe Guamán Poma de Ayala. (*Allpanchis/Cuzco*, 29:49, primer semestre 1997, p. 11–32, bibl.)

An attempt to understand European or Western ways of thinking as evidenced in the long letter to the king written by a Hispanized Indian at beginning of 17th century. Focuses particularly on a phrase referring to Moors and Jews as a category of marginalized peoples, and to topics that link Guamán Poma's thinking to themes circulating among the Peninuslar intelligentsia such as indigenous peoples as members of an original Christian community, the city as the center of evil, and the spiritual justification of the prevalent social order.

719 Guido Boggiani: fotograf/photographer = Guido Boggiani photographer. Edited by Frič Pavel and Yvonna Fričová. Prague: Titanic, 1997. 137 p.: bibl., ill., photo-CD.

Publishes for the first time a small part of Guido Boggiani's (1861 Omegna, Italy—1901 Gran Chaco) photographic documentation about the Chamacoco. Plates were collected by the Czech ethnologist A.V. Fric between 1904–08 after Boggiani had been killed in the Chaco by the Chamacoco who disapproved of his photographic work. The photo-CD contains a few more items. See also item **744**. [F. Obermeier]

720 Hagen, Adriana von. Nueva iconografía Chachapoya: de la Laguna de los Cóndores. (*Iconos/Lima*, 4, sept. 2000/ feb. 2001, p. 8–16, ill., photos)

Describes mummies and grave goods of burial chambers on the shores of Laguna de los Cóndores in northeastern Peru. Gives particular attention to Chachapoya iconography, both before and after Inca occupacion.

721 Hampe Martínez, Teodoro. La Colección Brüning de documentos para la etnohistoria del Perú: inventario de sus fondos. (*Rev. Arch. Gen. Nac./Lima*, 16, dic. 1997, p. 53–77)

A valuable inventory of the documentation in the Brüning Collection of the Museum für Völkerkunde in Hamburg. Brüning came to Lambayeque, Peru, in late 19th century and stayed until 1925. During his residence, he collected effigy pots from the Mochica and Chimu cultures, and local manuscripts. Author describes 128 of the latter dating from 16th-19th centuries.

722 Herberts, Ana Lucia. Os Mbayá-Guaicurú: história, área e assentamento. (*Estud. Leopoldenses Sér. Hist.*, 3:1, jan./junho 1999, p. 21–42, bibl., map, table)

Examines ethnohistorical records to understand settlement patterns of the Mbaya-Guaycuru in 16th-17th-century Chaco. Focuses on how European contact affected their settlement patterns, their mode of travel (from on foot to on horseback), and their adoption of new cultural elements.

723 Heredia, Edmundo A. Espacios regionales y etnicidad: aproximaciones para una teoría de la historia de las relaciones internacionales de América Latina. Córdoba, Argentina: Alción Editora, 1999. 216 p.: bibl.

Work centers on international relations. Concepts such as "region," "nation," and "ethnicity" are keys for author's discussion of conflict and peace, especially in the Southern Cone.

724 Hernández, Juan Luis. Tumultos y motines: la conflictividad social en los pueblos guaranís da la región misionera, 1768-1799. (*Mem. Am.*, 8, 1999, p. 83–100, bibl.)

Examines social conflict in three Guarani towns in Misiones area, from Jesuit expulsion in 1768 to beginning of Viceroy Avilés' term in 1799. Analyzes different types of community protest, focusing on both elite and indigenous actors. Concludes that Guarani were not indifferent to injustices; that communal society was structured and differentiated; that cabildos and *corregidores* played important roles in conflict resolution; and that *caciques* continued to play a leadership role in the communities.

725 Hinojosa Cuba, Carlos. Las momias de los Incas: el corazón de una tradición. (*Bol. Lima*, 21:116, 1999, p. 30–41, bibl.)

Summarizes Spanish chroniclers' statements about Inca mummies and 19th-20th-century attempts to locate those entombed in the Hospital de San Andres of Lima. Since the Hospital may contain these valuable remains, author advocates sparing the institution from destruction.

726 Historia y etnicidad en el noroeste amazónico. Recopilación de Alberta Zucchi y Silvia Vidal. Caracas: Instituto Venezolano de Investigación Científica; Univ. de Los Andes, 2000. 171 p.: bibl. (Col. Ciencias sociales. Serie Historia)

Collection of essays on the people of the northeastern Amazon. Includes a study of archeological sites along the Orinoco and Negro Rivers; linguistic studies of the Arawaks and Maku; and surveys of 18th-century multi-ethnic confederations.

727 Huertas Vallejos, Lorenzo. Conformación del espacio social en Huamanga, siglos XV y XVI. (*in* Historia, religión y ritual de los pueblos ayacuchanos. Osaka, Japan: National Museum of Ethnology, 1998, p. 7–28, bibl., maps, tables)

Overview of changing occupational patterns of peoples settled around Huamanga in 16th century. Author's analysis reiterates the dispersed and multi-ethnic settlement pattern before the *reducciones* ordered by Viceroy Francisco Toledo.

728 Hyland, Sabine. The imprisonment of Blas Valera: heresy and Inca history in colonial Peru. (*CLAHR*, 7:1, Winter 1998, p. 43–58)

A contribution to the debate over the authenticity of the "Naples document" and the claims that Blas Valera was imprisoned by the Jesuits for idolatry; that the Incas possessed a secret syllabic writing system; and that the Jesuits faked Valera's death so that he could return to Peru to write the *Nueva corónica y buen gobierno* (attributed to Felipe Guamán Poma de Ayala). This study demonstrates that the Jesuits imprisoned Valera for his teachings on Inca language and religion. Author also comments on the production of knowledge showing that Jesuit chroniclers faced constraints and censorship of their work.

729 The Inca world: the development of pre-Columbian Peru, A.D. 1000-1534. Edited by Laura Laurencich Minelli. Color photos by Mireille Vautier. Norman: Univ. of Oklahoma Press, 2000. 239 p.: bibl., ill. (some col.), maps.

Beautifully illustrated text on the Inca

world from 1000–1534, written by leading figures in the field of Andean studies. In addition to such standard Inca topics as the quipu, reciprocity, succession, and resource use, chapters describe provincial chieftainships, the Sican culture, the Chimu state, art and architecture, the jungle, and the Chanca challenge.

730 Intercambio y comercio entre costa, andes y selva: arqueología y etnohistoria de Suramérica. Recopilación de Felipe Cárdenas-Arroyo y Tamara L. Bray. Bogotá: Univ. de Los Andes, Depto. de Antropología, 1998. 345 p.: bibl., ill., index.

Good collection of papers by leading scholars on the political, economic, and ideological interaction among peoples of different ecological zones in the Andes, based on the latest archeological and ethnohistorical evidence. Papers cover ethnicities now within Colombia, Ecuador, Peru, and Argentina, and such specific topics as inter-regional exchange of flora, obsidian, and highly prized seashells; inter-ethnic iconographic borrowings; and ritual relations.

731 Jaramillo E., Luis Gonzalo. Guerra y canibalismo en el Valle del Río Cauca en la época de la conquista española. (*Rev. Colomb. Antropol.*, 32, 1995, p. 41–84, bibl., map)

Well-conceived and reasoned article on warfare and cannibalism among the Anserma, Quimbaya, and Arma peoples in the Cauca Valley. Author criticizes the literal interpretation and acceptance of chroniclers' judgements on these topics, and advocates using chronicler information as an archeological guide with the aim of refining our understanding of indigenous societies.

732 Jecupé, Kaka Werá. A terra dos mil povos: história indígena brasileira contada por um índio. São Paulo: Editora Fundação Peirópolis, 1998. 115 p.: ill. (Série Educação para a paz)

Transcribes oral history of a native Txucarramãe of Brazil, a story passed down from great grandparents to grandparents and parents. His narrative covers such diverse topics as ancestors, art, agriculture, and slavery.

733 Jones, Kristine L. Comparative raiding economies: north and south. (*in* Contested ground: comparative frontiers on the northern and southern edges of the Spanish Empire. Edited by Donna J. Guy and Thomas E. Sheridan. Tucson: Univ. of Arizona Press, 1998, p. 97–114, table)

Wide-ranging article argues that frontier raiding and trading economies involving indigenous peoples and Creoles alike not only facilitated formation of modern ranching industry but also played a central role in state-building process. Author's research covers areas that include present-day Mexico, (parts of the) US, Chile, and Argentina before and after 19th-century independence movements.

734 Jong, Ingrid de. Comunidad nacional, local e indígena: una aproximación histórica al discurso sobre la integración indígena en la pampa bonaerense. (*Mem. Am.*, 7, 1998, p. 117-142, bibl.)

Examines social, racial, and intellectual context in which a Mapuche "Tribu de Coliqueo" lived circa 1938. Shows how "otherness" was constructed; indigenous peoples were defined as a "problem." Solutions emphasized civilization through education. Mestizaje was not envisioned.

735 Juliano, María Dolores. Los mapuches, la más larga resistencia. (*Anu. IEHS*, 11, 1996, p. 303–327, bibl.)

History of Mapuche resistance from 1546–1879 focuses on factors such as armed struggle, political negotiations, commercial transactions, context of resistance (peripheral location and lack of natural resources), and their flexibility and willingness to adopt new technology and cultural forms.

736 Julien, Catherine J. Reading Inca history. Iowa City: Univ. of Iowa Press, 2000. 338 p.: bibl., index.

Scholarly book offers specialists two important contributions: 1) study of meaning and use of the word *capac* in regard to divine Inca kings; and 2) exploration of later texts in attempt to retrieve earlier sources, a method author describes as a kind of archeology of source materials. In so doing, she compares passages from the texts of chroniclers such as Cabello Valboa and Morúa; Betanzos, Cieza, and Cobo; and Sarmiento and Betanzos.

737 Karasch, Mary. Conflito e resistência inter-étnicos na fronteira brasileira de Goiás. (*Rev. SBPH*, 12, 1997, p. 31–49, bibl.)

Examines Brazilian frontier of Goiás, where a colonial power attempted to, but did not succeed in, imposing its European way of life, values, and methods of civilizing and Christianizing on indigenous population. Concludes that the conflict has not been resolved, and that, in last decade of 20th century, the fate of the Goiás frontier, especially in the north, remains to be determined.

738 Kaulicke, Peter. La muerte en el antiguo Perú: contextos y conceptos funerarios; una introducción. *(Bol. Arqueol. PUCP,* 1, 1997, p. 7–54, bibl., facsims., ill.)

Introduction to subject of death and its relevance to history of ancient Peru. Discusses available information (16th-20th centuries) and presents a methodology for analysis and interpretaion followed by a synthesis of the evidence. Illustrations and bibliography will be helpful to anyone working on the topic.

739 Kosel, Ana Carina. Los sermones de Valdivia: distribución de lugares, didáctica y polémica en un testimonio del choque de dos culturas. *(Anu. Estud. Am.,* 54:1, enero/junio 1997, p. 229–244, appendix)

Analyzes texts of the sermons of padre Luis de Valdivia dating from early 17th century. The Jesuit priest used the sermons to pacify and educate the Arucanians of Chile. The goal of writing them was to translate Christian concepts, expropriating words, and impose Spanish culture on the indigenous population.

740 Lane, Kris E. Taming the master: *brujería,* slavery, and the *encomienda* in Barbacoas at the turn of the eighteenth century. *(Ethnohistory/Columbus,* 45:3, Summer 1998, p. 477–507)

Involved story of indigenous resistance to sexual abuse and exploitation in the gold-mining regions of the Audiencia of Quito circa 1700. What began as a tale of witchcraft had far-reaching consequences, as the Audiencia investigated *encomendero* and indigenous interactions and eventually questioned the institution of encomienda itself.

741 Lázaro Avila, Carlos. Las fronteras de América y los "flandes indianos." Madrid: Consejo Superior de Investigaciones Científicas, Centro de Estudios Históricos, Depto. de Historia de América, 1997. 135 p.: appendix, bibl. (Col. Tierra nueva e cielo nuevo; 35)

Well-documented book about wars involving native Americans. Covers the Mixtón War (1540–42); the Chichimeca War (1550–1600); and the hostilities by Chiriguanos, Chaqueños, and Araucanos. Text is accompanied by transcriptions of primary documents as an appendix.

742 Lazzari, Axel. Civilización clemente y condición militar/tourista en *Una excursión a los indios ranqueles:* contribución al estudio de la subalternización étnica de los ranqueles. *(Mem. Am.,* 7, 1998, p. 91–116, bibl.)

Discursive analysis of the voices of Lucio Victorio Mansilla's 1870 book that ultimately shows "Indianism" to be a stain on Argentine national character.

743 Lecoq, Patrice. Algunos apuntes sobre la importancia de las caravanas de camélidos en el desarrollo de la ciudad de Potosí, comienzo del período colonial. *(Yachay/Cochabamba,* 14:26, segundo semestre 1997, p. 173–206, bibl., maps)

Examines changing patterns of exchange in and around the city of Potosí. From exchange of goods among peoples of different ecological niches, a new pattern emerges centered on Potosí's market. Argues that the shift could not have taken place without llama caravans.

744 Leigheb, Maurizio. Lo sguardo del viaggiatore: vita e opere di Guido Boggiani = The glance of the voyager: life and work of Guido Boggiani. Novara, Italy: Interlinea, 1997. 135 p.: bibl., ill. (Le colonne)

Biography of Italian artist, ethnologist, and photographer Guido Boggiani, known for his photographic and ethnographic work on indigenous people in the Chaco such as the Kaduveo and Chamacoco. See also item **719**. [F. Obermeier]

745 León Solís, Leonardo. Guerras pehuenche-huilliche en Araucanía y las Pampas, 1760–1765. *(Historia/Santiago,* 31, 1998, p. 113–145, appendices)

Reviews the first phase of the Pehuenche-Huilliche 18th-century wars in the eastern piedmont of the southern Andes. Covers from 1761, when the Huilliche raided the Pehuenche settlement of Malalhue, to 1765. "To fight to survive, to survive to fight" became the main paradigm of the Pehuenche military ethos. They waged war to defend their land and resources, to bolster their military prestige, and to maintain their traditional way of life.

746 Leoni Pinto, Ramón A. La frontera santiagueña con el indio del Chaco, 1810–1825. (*Folia Hist. Nordeste,* 12, 1996, p. 99–140)

Detailed and well-documented history of a frontier region between 1810–25 that in part compares war against the Spanish and war against indigenous peoples. The latter is judged most destructive. Indigenous territoriality, white-indigenous relations, and assimilation are covered in passing.

747 Lógica mestiza en América. Recopilación de Guillaume Boccara and Sylvia Galindo Godoy. Temuco, Chile: Instituto de Estudios Indígenas, Univ. de La Frontera, 2000. 204 p.: bibl., maps.

Six studies organized around indigenous resistance and adaptation and the construction of identity. Most of the contributors discuss the term mestizaje. Chapter 3 (by José Luis Martínez C.) on *ayllus* is of particular importance for his finding of widely scattered populations sharing a cultural identity. Jacques Poloni-Simard writes on cultural mestizaje, the birth of new social groups, and the possibilities of upward mobility. Other contributors focus on similar and related processes in Patagonia in 18th-19th centuries and Mapuche identity in the city of Santiago.

748 Lorandi, Ana María. De quimeras, rebeliones y utopías: la gesta del Inca Pedro Bohorques. Lima: Pontificia Univ. Católica del Perú, Fondo Editorial, 1997. 357 p., 2 folded leaves of plates: bibl., map.

Serious study of life of Pedro Bohorquez, within context of social expectations and utopian vistas. Focuses on construction of an Inca legacy during first half of 17th century, which Bohorquez used to found a revolutionary movement to reestablish the Tawantinsuyu in Tucumán, Argentina.

749 Loza, Carmen Beatriz. Du bon usage des *quipus* face à l' administration coloniale espagnole, 1550–1600. (*Population/Paris,* 53:1/2, jan./avril 1998, p. 139–159, photo, tables)

History of use of the *quipu* in early

colonial times for administrative and juridical purposes. Documents its acceptance and uses, and the fact that the *quipu* never became a transcultural recording device.

750 Lozada Pereira, Blithz. La visión andina del mundo. (*Estud. Boliv.,* 8, 1999, p. 7–76, bibl., graphs, ill.)

Wide-ranging review of various interpretations of Inca cosmology. Accepts city of Cuzco as planned in the shape of a puma (contrary to Barnes and Slive). Highlights discrepancies among various writers.

751 Maestri Filho, Mário José. Jesuítas e Tupinambas: a catequese impossível. (*in* Confronto de culturas: conquista, resistência, transformação. Rio de Janeiro: Expressão e Cultura; São Paulo: Edusp, 1997, p. 213–228, bibl.)

Conversion of Brazilian indigenous peoples in 16th-17th centuries is focus of this short article on Jesuits. Concludes that initial efforts to convert the indigenous population were not as successful as planned.

Maia, Alvaro. Banco de canoa: cenas de rios e seringais do Amazonas. See item **4161.**

752 Maldi, Denise. De confederados a bárbaros: a representação da territorialidade e da fronteira indígenas nos século XVIII e XIX. (*Rev. Antropol./São Paulo,* 40:2, 1997, p. 183–221, bibl.)

Consideration of "territoriality" and "frontier" as cultural constructions gives special attention to missions as frontier institutions and to attacks by *bandeirantes* that forced the missions to relocate. The problem of how to characterize the "other" (as "nations" or "confederations," "civilized" or not) is also addressed.

753 Mamani Coaquira, Leoncio F. El pueblo aimara y los conflictos con el poder: caso de la zona aimara norte de Puno, 1915–1925. Lima: Editorial Horizonte, 1998. 139 p.: bibl., ill.

Analysis of power relations in Puno, specifically between 1915–25, centering on prov. of Huancané y Moho. Author analyzes this time period to find objectives and gains from confrontations between *latifundistas* and communities. Notes a positive correlation between high prices for regional products and increasing pressure from large landowners to increase their holdings.

754 Mandrini, Raúl J. Las fronteras y la sociedad indígena en el ámbito pampeano. (*Anu. IEHS*, 12, 1997, p. 23–34)

A panoramic review of indigenous-criollo relations in La Plata area emphasizes effect of trade on cross-cultural relations to 1870.

Marberry Rogers, Elizabeth. Ethnicity, property and the state: legal rhetoric and the politics of community in Otavalo, Ecuador. See *HLAS 59:1138.*

755 Martí Mayor, José. El P. José María Vila: misionero y etnólogo. (*Arch. Ibero-Am.*, 57:225/226, 1997, p. 709–729)

Relates story of Padre José María Vila, a Franciscan missionary who lived on the banks of the Ucayali and Amazon Rivers in 19th century, based on his manuscript memoirs. Author accepts that Vila reported on what he himself saw and knew.

756 Martín Rubio, María del Carmen. El mundo andino como paradigma de perseverancia en su ancestral cultura. (*Estud. Hist. Soc. Econ. Am.*, 14, enero/junio 1997, p. 25–43, bibl.)

Taking primary historic documents as main source, attempts to show ways of and motivation for indigenous active resistance against Spanish political and ideological domination. Explains how such resistance lasted until end of viceregal period.

757 Martínez C., José Luis. Papeles distantes, palabras quebradas: las informaciones sobre los lipes en el siglo XVI. (*in* Integración surandina: cinco siglos después. Arica, Chile: Corporación Norte Grande Taller de Estudios Andinos; Antofagasta, Chile: Univ. Católica del Norte de Antofagasta; Cuzco, Peru: Centro de Estudios Regionales Andinos Bartolomé de Las Casas, 1996, p. 229–259, bibl., maps)

Excellent article by well-known author focuses on the Lipes in 16th century. Martínez uses different types of primary documents to show a discourse that defines the Lipes by their silence, and relegates them to a marginal category. For archeologist's review of entire volume, see *HLAS 59:375.*

758 Martinic Beros, Mateo. Dawsonians o Selkkar: otro caso de mestizaje aborigen histórico en Magallanes. (*An. Inst. Patagon. Ser. Cienc. Hum.*, 27, 1999, p. 79–88, bibl., map)

Analyzes contact between Kaweskar (sea hunters) and Selknam (land hunters), arguing that intermarriage among the two groups gave rise to the Selkkar in the Magellan region. Based on writings by missionaries and others going back to late 19th century.

759 Martinic Beros, Mateo. La inmigración chilota en Magallanes: apreciación histórica sobre sus causas, características y consecuencias. (*An. Inst. Patagon. Ser. Cienc. Hum.*, 27, 1999, p. 27–47, appendix, bibl., graphs, photo, tables)

Surveys migration from Chiloé to Magallanes. Migration began to increase in about 1868; leveled off from about 1894–96; and continued to middle of 20th century. Discusses origins of this movement, colonization, characteristics of the migrants, and consequences of the flow.

760 Martinic Beros, Mateo. Las misiones cristianas entre los Aonikenk, 1833–1910: una historia de frustraciones. (*An. Inst. Patagon. Ser. Cienc. Hum.*, 25, 1997, p. 7–25, photos)

Detailed information about efforts of Protestant and Catholic missionaries among the Aonikenk of southern Patagonia between 1833–1910 reveals frustrations based on misunderstandings between the missionaries and the Aonikenk due to lack of fluency in their respective languages.

761 Martins, José de Souza. Um documento falso sobre a conquista do território dos índios Goitacá no século XVII. (*in Rev. Antropol./São Paulo*, 39:2, 1996, p. 141–163, bibl.)

In 1893 a document on 17th-century conquest of the Goitacá was published. In spite of suspicions concerning origins, document has been used by historians and anthropologists as a reliable source of information. Article points out some inconsistencies between styles used in the document and documentary style typical for that period; and, similarly, incongruities between some historical data contained in the document as compared to those obtained from reliable sources. In conclusion, author argues that the document at issue is a 19th-century fake created for the purpose of land appropriation.

Marzal, Manuel María. Antropologia indigenista. See *HLAS 59:1017.*

762 Medinaceli, Ximena. Nombres disidentes: mujeres aymaras en Sacaca, siglo XVII. (*Estud. Boliv.*, 1, 1995, p. 321–342, bibl., map, tables)

Important analysis of personal names based on 1614 census. Findings include: 1) no clear relationship between age and names; 2) a relationship between ecology and naming; and 3) different last names for each family member. Author suggests longitudinal studies of naming to better understand transition from indigenous custom to Spanish practice.

763 Medinaceli, Ximena and **Silvia Arze.** Los mallkus de Charkas: redes de poder en el norte de Potosí, siglos XVI y XVII. (*Estud. Boliv.*, 2, 1996, p. 283–319, bibl., maps, tables)

Well-researched contribution to early history of interaction among indigenous elites of the southern Andes, based on primary and secondary sources. Discusses "ethnic territory," the Charka confederation, and political power of leading 16th-century indigenous authorities.

764 Millones, Luis. Logros y azares de la cristianización colonial: el obispado de Huamanga. (*in* Historia, religión y ritual de los pueblos ayacuchanos. Osaka, Japan: National Museum of Ethnology, 1998, p. 29–49, bibl.)

A history of indigenous religion focuses on the peoples of Huamanga from precolonial times. Discusses Vilcashuaman, the Taki Onqoy movement, conversion, and idolatry. Argues that, by the 18th century, popular religious practices had become mestizoized. See also items **770** and **795**.

765 Los misterios del Lago Sagrado. Editado por Marco A. Ninamango Jurado. Lima: El Autor, 1998. 74 p.: bibl., ill. (some col.).

Slim book aimed at popular audience compiles short excerpts from Spanish chronicles (Felipe Guamán Poma de Ayala, Juan de Betanzos, Pedro Cieza de León, Inca Garcilaso de la Vega, Juan Santa Cruz Pachacuti Yamqui, Antonio de la Calancha) on the gods (e.g., Contici Viracocha, Pachacamac) and myths of ancient Peru. See also items **703**, **777**, and **800**.

766 Molina, Luis E. De los trapiches decimonónicos a los centrales protoindustriales: aproximación histórico-arqueológica a los establecimientos cañeros de la segunda mitad del siglo XIX y primera del XX en Venezuela. (*Bol. Antropol./Mérida*, 45, enero/abril 1999, p. 48–77, bibl., photos)

Survey of Venezuela's sugar industry from second half of 19th century to beginning of 20th century focuses on technological change. Development of modern agroindustrial complexes began in 1940s with government stimulous and incentives.

767 Montes, Aníbal. El Gran Alzamien to Diaguita, 1630–1643. (*Estudios/Córdoba*, 10, julio/dic. 1998, p. 57–70)

Detailed analysis of 17th-century Diaguita rebellion. Presents causes for the war which include harsh treatment related to imposition of colonial institutions such as the encomienda, the *mita,* and the *reducción.* Lacks footnotes.

768 Montoya, Rodrigo. Historia, memoria y olvido en los Andes quechuas. (*Tempo Bras.*, 135, out./dez. 1998, p. 157–180, bibl.)

Discusses possibilities and limits of memory in Quechua-speaking communities. Author's sometimes autobiographical analysis touches on such themes as oral history, inequality of power, ritual, theater, and chroniclers' accounts.

769 Mota, Lucio Tadeu. Os indios Xetá na província paranaense, 1853–1889. (*Pós-Hist.*, 6, 1998, p. 175–189, bibl, ill.)

History of the Guaraní-speaking Heta of Paraná. This group remained hidden in the forests until the middle of the 20th century despite white overtures. They survived until the last refugees were overtaken in 20th century as white farmers replaced forests with pastures and coffee bushes.

770 Mumford, Jeremy. The Taki Onqoy and the Andean nation: sources and interpretations. (*LARR*, 33:1, 1998, p. 150–165, bibl.)

Presents a history of the Taki Onqoy movement in Peru. Some students write that the "dance of disease" movement never existed; others conclude that it has been a political tool in colonial infighting. See also items **764** and **795**.

771 Mundo peruano antiguo: una visión interdisciplinaria; curso virtual de extensión = Ancient Peruvian world: an interdisciplinary view; extension course by Internet. Lima?: Pontificia Univ. Católica del

Perú, Facultad de Letras y Ciencias Humanas; PromPerú, 2000. 177 p.: bibl.

A bilingual text designed to accompany a basic extension course via internet, offered by the Pontificia Universidad Católica del Perú. Chapters cover prehispanic Andean societies, the sacrificial ceremony in Mochica art, languages, prehispanic Andean agriculture, and urban planning.

772 Niles, Susan A. The shape of Inca history: narrative and architecture in an Andean empire. Iowa City: Univ. of Iowa Press, 1999. 336 p.: bibl., ill. (some col.), index.

Study of Inca Huayna Capac's estate and other commemorative monuments. Argues that in royal architecture as in their narratives, Incas shaped historical events, giving material form to claims based on victories in battle, encounters with gods, and deeds of their kings. Proposes a way to "read" the monuments as propaganda designed to enhance the reputation of a king. For archeologist's comment, see *HLAS 59:675.*

773 Nordenskiöld, Erland. The cultural history of the South American Indians. Edited and with an introduction by Christer Lindberg. New York: AMS Press, 1999. 223 p.: bibl., ill. (AMS studies in cultural history; 4)

Translation from the Swedish of a classic work on the geography of human culture in South America. Includes some revisions by author that were made before his untimely death. Contains most of his original sketches, drawn during six years of travel. Topics include agriculture and hunting; food preparation; clothing; communications; and trade, war, and ritual activity.

Nugent, David. Modernity at the edge of empire: state, individual, and nation in the northern Peruvian Andes, 1885–1935. See item **2616.**

Nugent, David. The morality of modernity and the travails of tradition: nationhood and the subaltern in northern Peru. See *HLAS 59:1175.*

774 Olivari Ortega, Jorge. Pachacutec y los lavaderos de oro de Chuquibamba. (*Bol. Lima,* 20:112, 1998, p. 25–36, bibl.)

Summarizes accomplishments of Pachacuti Inca Yupanqui, with a section on gold mining in Chuquibamba. Based on standard chroniclers and *visita* to prov. of León de Huanuco.

775 Oliveira Filho, João Pacheco de. Ensaios em antropologia histórica. Rio de Janeiro: Editora UFRJ, 1999. 269 p.: bibl., maps.

Collection of essays divided into four parts: 1) ethnography of the Tucuna of the Amazon (circa 1991–92); 2) analysis of census data on indigenous peoples; 3) criticisms of sociological theory; and 4) state policy.

776 Orquera, Luis Abel. El consumo de moluscos por los canoeros del extremo sur. (*Relac. Soc. Argent. Antropol.,* 24, dic. 1999, p. 307–327, bibl., tables)

Discusses diet of the Magallanic-Fueguian canoe people and more specifically their consumption of mussels. Shows that time needed for gathering, processing, and consuming mussels is not justified by energy they provide. However, mussels were in fact consumed massively for 6,000 years and constituted an important factor in the decision of habitation location. Concludes that mussels were beneficial for groups adapted to littoral life, not merely as food but as factor in reduction of tension involved in procurement of other resources of higher nutritional value.

777 Ossio A., Juan M. Guamán Poma y Murúa ante la tradición oral andina. (*Iconos/Lima,* 4, sept. 2000/feb. 2001, p. 44–57, bibl., facsims., ill.)

Welcome article compares published letter of Guamán Poma de Ayala with unpublished texts, here identified as the Manuscripts Loyola, Irlandes, and Wellington. Author argues that Guamán Poma's writing is the most indigenous text; the Wellington is the most Europeanized. He also hypothesizes that Guamán Poma came from a family of *quipucamayocs,* and that Guamán Poma and Fray Martín de Murúa knew each other, probably in Cuzco. See also items **703** and **765,** and **800.**

778 A outra margem do ocidente. Organização de Adauto Novaes. Brasília: Ministério da Cultura, FUNARTE; São Paulo: Companhia das Letras, 1999. 525 p.: bibl., col. maps, ill. (some col.), index.

Book of indigenista essays on such themes as the encounter, public policy, memory and history, shamanism, and the demarcation of indigenous lands.

779 Parada Soto, Ana Isabel. Pueblos de Indios de la provincia de Mérida: su evolución, 1558–1657. Mérida, Venezuela: Univ. de Los Andes, Consejo de Publicaciones, Vicerrectorado Académico, 1998. 92 p.: bibl. (Col. Ciencias sociales. Serie Historia)

Slim book focuses on founding and development of *reducciones de indios* in prov. of Mérida between 1558–1657. Personages such as Juan Rodríguez Suárez, Juan de Maldonado, and Gil Naranjo intervene early in the story. Spanish efforts to concentrate indigenous peoples in organized villages was met with resistance by those who continued to insist on returning to their original homes.

780 Paredes, Luis Hugo. Máscaras rituales, máscaras sociales: pasado y presente del afro-uruguayo. (*in* Congreso Argentino de Hispanistas, *4th, Mar del Plata, Argentina, 1995.* La cultura hispánica y occidente: actas. Mar del Plata, Argentina: Facultad de Humanidades, Univ. Nacional de Mar del Plata, 1997?, p. 432–436, bibl.)

Short disposition on the Afro-Uruguayan and the development of "candombe-protesta," a music that is an expression of popular culture.

781 Pease G.Y., Franklin. Cuatro décadas de etnohistoria andina. (*in* Encuentro Internacional de Peruanistas, *1st, Lima, 1996.* Estado de los estudios histórico-sociales sobre el Perú a fines del siglo XX. Lima: UNESCO; Univ. de Lima; Fondo de Cultura Económica, 1998, v. 1, p. 229–240, bibl.)

A welcome overview and synthesis of history of "ethnohistory," starting with Luis E. Valcárcel's work in the 1940s. Mentions contributions by María Rostworowski, John V. Murra, Augusto Cardish, Edmundo Guillén, Waldemar Espinoza, and Juan José Vega. Discusses types of sources and evolving interpretations of them.

782 Peralta Barrera, Napoleón. El país de los muzos. Tunja, Colombia: Academia Boyacense de Historia, 1998. 534 p.: bibl., ill. (some col.), index. (Biblioteca de la Academia Boyacense de Historia. Serie Obras fundamentales; 20)

Long, well-organized book on encounter between Spanish and Muzos, who lived in what is now Dept. de Cundinamarca, Colombia. Based in part on archival research, text is filled with local minutia, highlighting indigenous resistance to invading colonizers who came in search of emeralds. Covers expeditions of Luis Lanchero, Diego de Martínez, Melchor de Valdéz, and Pedro de Ursúa; founding of cities of Tudela, Santísima Trinidad de los Muzos, and Nuestra Señora de la Palma y Ronda; and such colonial institutions as the encomienda, the *resguardos,* the *visita,* and the mission.

783 Perea, Alejandro. Los yanas: cambios y permanencias; de la época prehispánica al siglo XVI. (*Contracorriente/Lima,* 1, nov. 1997, p. 5–26, bibl.)

Surveys situation of the Yana from prehispanic times to 16th century, based (in part) on *visitas* of Sonqo and Huánuco. Discusses inherited status, inequalities among the population, relations between server and authority, and acculturation.

Platt, Tristan. El sonido de la luz: comunicación emergente en un diálogo chamánico quechua. See *HLAS 59:1074.*

784 Poderti, Alicia. Palabra e historia en los Andes: la rebelión del inca Tupac-Amaru y el noroeste argentino. Buenos Aires: Corregidor, 1997. 175 p.: appendix, bibl., ill., maps.

Discusses the 1780 rebellion led by indigenous leader José Gabriel Condorcanqui, better known as Tupac-Amaru II, against higher taxes and other perceived abuses. Author situates resistance at the juncture of complicated inter-ethnic relations, the Bourbon reforms, the political culture of the actors, and resurrection of the image of the Inca. Based mostly on secondary sources. Includes an appendix reproducing primary sources.

785 Poggi, Rinaldo Alberto. Releyendo cartas de Calfucurá. (*Invest. Ens.,* 47, 1997, p. 469–493)

Detailed biography of Argentine *cacique* Juan Calfucurá, based on primary sources. Article recaps his exploits and negotiations with the likes of Rosas, Urquiza, Mitre, and Sarmiento.

786 Polentini Wester, Juan Carlos. El Paí Titi. Lima: Asociación Librería Editorial Salesiana, 1999. 159 p., 12 leaves of plates: ill., maps (some col.).

Recounts a priest's story of his search for Paititi, a refuge and stronghold of the Incas in southern Peru. Includes a map showing its location (near the Chortiari River) and colored images of archeological remains and petroglyphs.

787 Poloni-Simard, Jacques. História de los indios en los Andes, los indígenas en la historiografía andina: análisis y propuestas. *(Anu. IEHS,* 15, 2000, p. 87–100)

Thought-provoking article on diversity of the people subsumed under the category of "Indian" during colonial times. Argues that the category is internally differentiated. Also advocates looking at social relations to approximate the workings of society, assess possibilities of social mobility, and understand better both biological and cultural mestizaje.

788 Poloni-Simard, Jacques. La mosaique indienne: mobilité, stratification sociale et métissage dans le corregimiento de Cuenca, Equateur, du XVIe au XVIIIe siècle. Paris: Editions de l'Ecole des hautes etudes en sciences sociales, 2000. 514 p.: bibl., ill., index, maps. (Civilisations et sociétés; 99)

Detailed history of *corregimiento* of Cuenca during colonial times, based on intensive archival research in Ecuador, Spain, and Colombia. Notable among the topics covered are characterization of 17th-century indigenous (and emerging *casta*) society using notarial records; discussion of emerging real estate market between 1591–1700; and analysis of credit networks among and between indigenous peoples, Spaniards, and *castas.* Author succeeds in nuancing the stereotypical view of indigenous peoples in colonial society. For colonial historian's comment, see item **2210.**

789 Os povos do Alto Xingu: história e cultura. Organização de Bruna Franchetto e Michael J. Heckenberger. Rio de Janeiro: Editora UFRJ, 2000. 493 p.: bibl., ill., maps.

A serious collection of chapters on the history of the people of the Alto Xingu in the state of Mato Grosso, Brazil, over last 1,000 years. Waurá, Mehinako, Yawalapiti, Kuikuro, Kalapalo, Matipu, Nahukwá, Kamayurá, Aweti, and Trumai peoples occupy the Parque Nacional do Xingu, which is conceived of as an intertribal, multilingual soci-ocultural unit. Topics include disease, encounter, marriage as intertribal political alliance, cosmology, ritual, and oral tradition.

790 Prieto, Alfredo and **Rodrigo Cárdenas.** Introduction to ethnical photography in Patagonia = Introducción a la fotografía etnica de la Patagonia. Traducción de Karen Miller y Belinda MacClean. Punta Arenas, Chile: H. Pisano Skarmeta, Editor, 1997. 1 v. (unpaged): bibl.

Bilingual book features b/w photos of indigenous peoples of Patagonia. Most date from the late 19th-early 20th centuries. Photos are organized into groups focusing on housing, dress, ornamentation, and weapons. Accompanying text fails to provide a cultural context.

791 Propuestas para una antropología argentina. v. 5. Buenos Aires: Editorial Biblos, 1999. 1 v.: bibl.

Compiles 20 papers on such varied topics as the penal code as applied to Amerindians, gauchos, at-risk children, regional trade and exchange, social policy, *candombe* in Buenos Aires, the identity of the Toba-taksek of the central Chaco, globalization, Lucio V. Mansilla, and the urban landscape of Buenos Aires. For comment on v. 4, see *HLAS 59:1035.*

792 Pueblos indígenas y originarios de Bolivia: diagnóstico nacional. La Paz: Ministerio de Asuntos Campesinos Pueblos Indígenas y Originarios, 2001. 260 p.: ill.

Government publication offers systematic and panoramic view of the indigenous peoples of Bolivia. Covers social, economic (lands and markets), and historical characteristics. Also contains chapters on legislation and indigenous peoples' demands for future development.

793 Querejazu Lewis, Roy. Incallajta y la conquista incaica del Collasuyu. La Paz; Cochabamba, Bolivia: Editorial Los Amigos del Libro, 1998. 216 p.: bibl., ill. (some col.). (Col. Historia; NA 493)

Serious attempt to write a history of the Colla based on chronicles and secondary sources. Author's hypothesis is that origins of the Inca empire date back to a time when Cuzco was among many local chieftainships subject to and dependent on Jatun Colla. It was Pachacuti Inca Yupanqui who restated the history of the Inca, giving it divine origins.

794 Ramos Gómez, Luis Javier. Algunos datos sobre los abusos e injusticias padecidas en 1737 por los indios de los obrajes de la ciudad de Quito. (*Rev. Esp. Antropol. Am.*, 27, 1997, p. 153–166, bibl.)

Analyzes abuses and injustices suffered by *obraje* indigenous peoples in Audiencia of Quito in 1737. Based on a document (AGI/Audiencia Quito 134) written by don Juan de Lujan, a royal official charged with protecting indigenous peoples. He vainly hoped to implement the protective ordinances of the Viceroy Count of Santisteban. See also item **2217.**

795 Regalado de Hurtado, Liliana. El inca Titu Cusi Yupanqui y su tiempo: los incas de Vilcabamba; y los primeros cuarenta años del dominio español. Lima: Pontificia Univ. Católica del Perú, Fondo Editorial, 1997. 168 p.: appendix, ill. (Biblioteca "Lo que debo saber"; 3, Historia)

Covers interaction between Spanish and Inca peoples during lifetime of Titu Cusi Yupanqui. Discusses organization of the Tawantinsuyu, Manco Capac's resistance to Spanish rule, Vilcabamba, Manco Yupanqui, Sayri Túpac, Christianization, Taki Onqoy, Viceroy Francisco Toledo, and Túpac Amaru. Appendix includes pages from written record left by Titu Cusi Yupanqui. See also items **764** and **770.**

796 Robins, Nicholas A. El mesianismo y la semiótica indígena en el Alto Perú: la gran rebelión de 1780–1781. Traducción de Silvia San Martín y Sergio del Río. Edición revisada por Luz M. Escobar y Aristides Baraya. La Paz: Hisbol, 1998. 219 p.

A translation from English of work on rebellion of Túpac Amaru in 1780–81 in Alto Perú. Explores millenarian aspects of the movement, which aimed at establishing a new order, free of colonial constraints. Also highlights contradictions and opposing forces within the revolutionary sector.

797 Rocca Torres, Luis. Nichoujin: japoneses bajo el sol de Lambayeque. Lima: Univ. Nacional Pedro Ruiz Gallo, Facultad de Ciencias Histórico Sociales y Educación; Asociación Peruano-Japonesa del Perú; Comisión Conmemorativa del Centenario de la Inmigración Japonesa al Perú, 1997. 402 p.: bibl., ill., maps.

Well-documented study of Japanese immigrants who settled in northern Peruvian province in 20th century. Traces group from its origins, emphasizing commercial, political, professional, and cultural contributions. Contains valuable data based on extensive archival research as well as oral history.

798 Rodas Morales, Raquel. Dolores Cacuango. Quito: Sociedad Alemana de Cooperación Técnica, Projecto de Educación Bilingüe Intercultural, 1998. 179 p.: bibl., ill.

Pictorial and testimonial history on leadership of Doña Dolores Cacuango, who was instrumental in founding the first bilingual primary schools for indigenous children in the town of Cayambe, Ecuador. Work is dedicated to her legacy. In telling her story, covers rebellion, indigenismo, agricultural syndicates, the Federación Ecuatoriana de Indios, and agrarian reform.

799 Rodríguez Cuenca, José Vicente. Los chibchas, pobladores antiguos de los Andes orientales: adaptaciones bioculturales. Bogotá: Fundación de Investigaciones Arqueológicas Nacionales; Banco de la República, 1999. 217 p.: bibl., ill. (Fundación de Investigaciones Arqueológicas Nacionales; 71)

Archeologically based study of the Chibcha-speaking peoples of prehispanic Colombia. Examines degree to which these populations adapted to Andean ecosystem by looking at such variables as nutrition and rates of morbidity and mortality.

800 Roel Pineda, Virgilio. Historia de los Incas y de España; grabados de Guamán Poma. Lima?: Herrera Editores, 1998. 164 p.: bibl., ill.

Basic overview of Inca history and culture, illustrated with the drawings of Guamán Poma de Ayala. Author summarizes founding and expansion of Inca hegemony and its major institutions; he then juxtaposes these against European (Spanish, Portuguese, Dutch, English, and French) development to 18th century. See also items **703, 765,** and **777.**

801 Rojas, José Luis de. Acerca de la definición y uso de las fuentes: una perspectiva indígena americana. (*Estud. Hist.*

Soc. Econ. Am., 14, enero/junio 1997, p. 45–58, bibl.)

Methodological statement on the uses and abuses of historical sources by practitioners of three disciplines. Argues that historians should find new sources to complement the traditional archeological, ethnohistorical, and ethnographic sources available.

802 Romero, Mario Diego. Historia y etnohistoria de las comunidades afro-colombianas del Río Naya. Cali, Colombia: Gobernación del Valle del Cauca, Gerencia Cultural, 1997. 139 p.: bibl., ill. (Col. de autores vallecaucanos)

Portrait of an Afro-Colombian community from late 18th century to mid-1990s that lived on land given to Univ. del Cauca in 1827. Includes long quotes from primary documents and a chapter describing folkways.

803 Rostworowski de Diez Canseco, María. History of the Inca realm. Translated by Harry B. Iceland. Cambridge; New York: Cambridge Univ. Press, 1999. 259 p.: bibl., ill., index, maps.

Translation from Spanish of a basic text outlining the author's research and writing on Inca empire as developed over last several decades. Topics include Inca expansion, successions, and socioeconomic structure of the polity. For ethnologist's comment, see *HLAS 59:1185*. For comments on original work, see *HLAS 50:742* and *HLAS 52:682*.

804 Rozo Gauta, José. Alimentación y medicina entre los muiscas. Bogotá: Ediciones Naidí, 1998. 142 p.: bibl., ill., maps. (Col. Estudios culturales CIAM)

Discusses food and health among the Muisca peoples of Colombia. Author uses foods as a way to understand this group's view of the body. Based on manuscript sources, oral histories, and ethnographical and archeological observations.

805 Rozo Gauta, José. Espacio y tiempo entre los muiscas. Bogotá: Editorial El Buho, 1997. 101 p.: bibl., ill.

Short book on Muiscas' concepts of time and space, based on chronicles, grammars, dictionaries, and documents from 16th-17th centuries. Provides analysis of domestic and ritual spaces and different categories of time.

806 Ruiz, Marta. Los inkas: espacio y cultura. Apendice "Los Inkas en Jujuy" de Marta Ruiz y María Ester Albeck. San Salvador de Jujuy, Argentina: Editorial Univ. Nacional de Jujuy, 1998. 209 p.: appendix, bibl., ill., maps. (Col. Arte-ciencia. Serie Jujuy en el pasado)

Basic book written by and for teachers (*docentes*) of prov. of Jujuy, Argentina, about the history of the Incas. Text is based on historical, ethnohistorical, linguistic, and archeological research. Topics include Inca expansion, cultural development, interaction with other groups, and first encounters with the Spanish. Appendix indexes Inca action in Jujuy.

807 Saberes y memorias en los Andes: in memoriam Thierry Saignes. Recopilación y compilación de Thérèse Bouysse-Cassagne. Paris: Institut des hautes études de l'Amérique latine; Lima: Institut français d'études andines, 1997. 434 p.: bibl., ill. (Travaux de l'Institut français d'études andines; 97) (Travaux et mémoires de l'Institut des hautes études de l'Amérique latine; 63)

Collection of articles on the archeology and history of the Andes. Contributions on Chile, Peru, and Bolivia cover Pachacuti, myths, indigenous wills, quipus, textiles, rituals, and maps.

808 Saito, Akira. La conquista de la historia: la extirpación de la idolatría y la transformación de la conciencia histórica en los Andes. (*Anuario/Sucre*, 1997, p. 49–71, bibl.)

Good article discusses changes in consciousness and history brought to Andean communities by Christian evangelization. Focuses on ancestor worship during colonial times and continuities into the present era.

809 Salas, Adela María. Una encomienda de indios chaqueños en el Pago de La Matanza. (*Folia Hist. Nordeste*, 13, 1997, p. 5–21, graph, tables)

Analysis of a 1744 census (*padrón*) of the Pago de La Matanza revealed existence of an encomienda of Malbalae and Mocoví. This encomienda was made up of a group of rebellious indigenous peoples that were given by Gov. Esteban de Urizar to José de Arregui. Arregui moved and settled them in the area.

No trace of this population remained in the *padrón* of 1778.

810 San Roman Bontes, Manuel; Flavia Morello R.; and Alfredo Prieto. Cueva de los Chingues, Parque Nacional Pali Aike, Magallanes, Chile: historia natural y cultural; Pt. I. (*An. Inst. Patagon. Ser. Cienc. Hum.*, 28, 2000, p. 125–146, appendix, bibl., graphs, maps, photos, tables)

Preliminary results of excavations at Chingues Cave show characteristics of animal and human occupations of the site. A bioanthropological study of a human skeleton located nearby is presented in an appendix.

811 Santamaría, Daniel J. Población y economía interna de las poblaciones aborígenes del Chaco en el siglo XVIII. (*ANDES Antropol. Hist.*, 9, 1998, p. 173–195, bibl.)

Study based on archival research reconstructs demographic structure and describes exploitation of natural resources of the Chaco in 18th century. Discusses population trends, epidemics, raiding, abortion and infanticide, environment, migration, and hunting and gathering.

812 Sawyer, Alan Reed. Early Nasca needlework. London: Laurence King in association with Alan Marcuson, 1997. 175 p.: bibl., ill. (some col.), index, col. maps.

Large format highlights striking photographs of ancient mantles, shirts, and ceremonial clothes characteristic of the Nazca culture. Textile iconography is compared to artifacts such as gold masks and pottery to identify deities.

813 Scatamacchia, María Cristina Mineiro. Etno-histórica e interpreteção arqueológica: a documentação textual para o estudo dos grupos Tupi e Guarani. (*Rev. Arqueol. Am./México*, 11, julio/dic. 1996, p. 79–102, bibl.)

A consideration of archeological data and historical texts as ethnohistorical sources (letters, reports, and chroniclers), with specific reference to Tupi and Guarani peoples. Discusses settlement patterns, subsistence, and social organization.

Silva Santisteban, Fernando. Desarrollo político en las sociedades de la civilización andina. See *HLAS 59:1191*.

814 Silva Santisteban, Fernando. Sobre la formación del estado en la civilización andina. (*in* Encuentro Internacional de Peruanistas, 1st, Lima, 1996. Estado de los estudios histórico-sociales sobre el Perú a fines del siglo XX. Lima: UNESCO; Univ. de Lima; Fondo de Cultura Económica, 1998, v. 1, p. 241–252, bibl.)

Broad historical vision of evolution of the Andean state starts with discussion of bands and egalitarian societies; then mentions chieftainships and various phases of state-building, culminating with the Inca.

815 Someda, Hidefuji. El imperio de los Incas: imagen del Tahuantinsuyu creada por los cronistas. Lima: Pontificia Univ. Católica del Perú, Fondo Editorial, 1999. 327 p.: bibl., ill. (some col.), index.

Reviews Spanish chroniclers' image of Incas and their civilization, arguing that indigenous history and culture were quickly reconstructed in the image of the Europeans. Survey begins with writings of Vasco Núñez de Balboa and Pascual de Andagoya. Long quotes from Francisco López de Xerez, Pedro Sancho de la Hoz, Miguel Estete, Agustín de Zárate, Pedro de Cieza de Leon, and Juan Diez de Betanzos are considered.

Soux, María Luisa. La vida cotidiana en las comunidades aymaras: ejercicios metodológico comparativo en fuentes antropológicas e históricas; trabajo de campo y expedientes judiciales. See *HLAS 59:1082*.

816 Stavig, Ward. The world of Túpac Amaru: conflict, community, and identity in colonial Peru. Lincoln: Univ. of Nebraska Press, 1999. 348 p.: bibl., ill., index.

Well-researched book provides historical context for much-studied revolt of Túpac Amaru II. Themes developed include sexual values and marital life; robbers, rustlers, and highwaymen; land and tenure; labor; and rebellion.

817 Stevenson, Christopher M., Joan Wozniak, and Sonia Haoa. Prehistoric agricultural production on Easter Island, Rapa Nui, Chile. (*Antiquity/Cambridge*, 73:282, Dec. 1999, p. 801–812, bibl., maps)

Proposes that lithic mulching on Easter Island was a technological innovation introduced to enhance moisture retention capacity of excessively drained island soils.

Also suggests that the process was incorporated into elite-managed field systems which arose in early 15th century to meet demands for surplus production. This new production strategy is correlated with a sharp rise in the construction of religious structures located in primary centers of island districts. This series of events lends support to a proposed model for the development of island chiefdoms dependent upon a dryland agricultural system.

818 Suescún Monroy, Armando. Derecho y sociedad en la historia de Colombia. v. 1, El derecho Chibcha, siglo IX-siglo XVI. Tunja: Editorial Univ. Pedagógica y Tecnológica de Colombia, 1998. 1 v.: bibl., maps.

Summarizes Chibcha culture from 9th-16th centuries based mainly on secondary sources. Chapters include information on myths, economy, crime, and government.

819 Szemiński, Jan. Las apuestas del Inqa. (*Anuario/Sucre,* 1996, p. 3–18, bibl.)

Excellent article, based (in part) on a 1585 manuscript in the Archivo Nacional de Bolivia, showing that peoples who were incorporated into the Inca empire were considered the booty of the Sun. The *ayllu* game legitimized Incas' redistribution of defeated and captive labor. Concludes that indigenous peoples, not lands, were the prize, despite terminological imprecision in the sources.

820 Tacca, Fernando de. O índio *pacificado:* uma construção imagética da Comissão Rondon. (*Cad. Antropol. Imagem,* 6:1, 1998, p. 81–101, bibl., photos)

Partial analysis of films and photographs made by the Rondon Commission in early 20th century. Shows how photos were used to construct an image of pacified indigenous peoples who were thus ready to be integrated into the nation. The image of civilized indigenous peoples affirmed that they were no longer an obstacle to progress.

821 Tamagnini, Marcela A. Cartas de frontera: el discurso de la alteridad. (*Rev. Univ. Nac. Río Cuarto,* 15:1/2, 1995, p. 95–106, bibl.)

Using documents from archives of the Convent of San Francisco in Río Cuarto, author analyzes 19th-century cross-cultural contact and conflict between Europeans and the Ranquel indigenous group. Her analysis of discourse between the two groups

modifies official history written by 1880s generation.

822 Tantaleán Arbulú, Javier. El circuito macroeconómico incaico. (*Social. Particip.,* 79, sept. 1997, p. 49–65, ill.)

Macroeconomic analysis of Inca economy focuses on accumulation and distribution of surplus as enabling mechanisms for continuing domination.

823 Torres, Mauro. América Latina, dos veces herida en sus orígenes. Bogotá: Ecoe Ediciones, 2001. 177 p.: bibl., ill., map. (Col. Interés general. Area Historia)

Short history of precolonial and colonial America, based on secondary sources. An underlying thesis is that liberty has been lost.

824 Tovar Pinzón, Hermes; Luis Enrique Rodríguez Baquero; and Marta Herrera Angel. Territorio, población y trabajo indígena: Provincia de Pamplona, siglo XVI. Bogotá: Centro de Investigaciones de Historia Colonial, Instituto Colombiana de Cultura Hispánica, y Fondo Mixto de Promoción de la Cultura y las Artes del Norte de Santander, 1998. 144 p.: bibl., ill.

Well-documented, foundational study of indigenous peoples of Norte de Santander region, Colombia, in 16th century. Detailed text discusses Spanish colonial rule and its impact on health and welfare of the population. As in other areas of the Hapsburg Empire, the population collapsed. Indigenous peoples who survived were granted in encomienda and used in the fields and mines. Footnotes will lead readers to the wealth of documents in Colombia's well-organized archives.

825 Untoja Choque, Fernando and Ana A. Mamani Espejo. Pacha en el pensamiento aymara. La Paz: Fondo Editorial de los Diputados, 2000. 127 p.: bibl.

Exploration of multiple meanings of the word *pacha* and the insights it gives into the Aymara and even the Tiahuanacu way of thinking.

826 Urquiza, Lincoln R. Noticias históricas de Ischilín. Córdoba, Argentina: Ediciones La Posta de Córdoba, 1998. 187 p.: bibl., ill., map.

Popular and anecdotal history of town of Deán Funes and its hinterland in north of

Córdoba prov., Argentina, based on both secondary and primary sources (the latter in local archives). Provides historical data from as early as 16th century on ethnohistory and such local personages as Pedro Ladrón de Guevara and José Clemente Villada.

827 Urton, Gary. From knots to narratives: reconstructing the art of historical record keeping in the Andes from Spanish transcriptions of Inka *khipus*. (*Ethnohistory/Columbus*, 45:3, Summer 1998, p. 409–438, bibl.)

Re-evaluation of evidence on quipus. Argues that these knotted string devices recorded more than just numbers. Finds evidence that they represented a system of writing and could be "read" by members of the Inca state bureaucracy.

828 Urton, Gary. Inca myths. Austin: Univ. of Texas Press, 1999. 80 p.: bibl., ill., index, maps. (The legendary past)

Basic collection of Andean myths with overview of Inca culture presented as context and discussion of sources in both written and material form. Includes cosmic origin myths, the origin stories of the Inca state, and detailed summaries of provincial oral traditions.

Urton, Gary and **Primitivo Nina Llanos.** The social life of numbers: a Quechua ontology of numbers and philosophy of arithmetic. See *HLAS 59:1201*.

829 Vanegas Munõz, Sayed Guillermo.
Cuña del mismo palo: participación política de la élite muisca en las instituciones del Nuevo Reino de Granada, siglos XVII y XVIII. Prólogo de Rodrigo Losada Lora. Bogotá: Ediciones Naidí, 1997. 88 p.: bibl., map. (Col. Pedagogía política; 2)

Short book relates how political and religious Muisca elite interacted with royal officials of New Granada in 17th-18th centuries. Elite included *caciques, gobernadores, capitanes, tenientes, alcaldes* and *regidores, alguaciles, fiscales, sacristanes,* and *cantores.* Many spent their time aiding the *corregidores* in implementing local laws.

830 Veniard, Juan María. Las informaciones geográficas de los indígenas de la Patagonia en sus comunicaciones con los españoles: siglo XVIII; análisis y comentarios. (*Invest. Ens.*, 47, 1997, p. 527–550, bibl.)

Analyzes geographical information contained in selected 18th-century accounts of southern Pampas and Patagonia. Concludes that records contain both reliable information—which sometimes is misinterpreted—and unreliable data. Author suggests assessing information in a detailed way, without preconceived ideas and without the idea that our own information is more reliable than that in the reports.

831 A viagem da volta: etnicidade, política e reelaboração cultural no Nordeste indígena. Organização de João Pacheco de Oliveira Filho. Rio de Janeiro: Contra Capa, 1999. 350 p.: bibl., maps. (Territórios sociais; 2)

Collection of eight papers on indigenous peoples of Brazil's Northeast. Focuses on resurgence of identities and traditions among the Kiriri, Pankararu, Tremembé, and others. For ethnologist's comment, see *HLAS 59:962*.

832 Vidal, Silvia M. Liderazgo y confederaciones multiétnicas amerindias en la Amazonia luso-hispana del siglo XVIII. (*Antropológica/Caracas*, 87, 1997, p. 19–45, map, tables)

Analyzes changes experienced by Rio Negro Arawak sociopolitical formations during 18th century. Addresses emergence and extinction of multi-ethnic confederacies under leadership of powerful Baré and Manao warrior chiefs.

833 Vila Mitjá, Assumpció and **Guillermina Ruiz del Olmo.** Información etnológica y análisis de la reproducción social: el caso yamana. (*Rev. Esp. Antropol. Am.*, 31, 2001, p. 275–291, bibl.)

Documents inherent social discrimination against women in Yahgun society. Culture devalues women's worth despite the fact that the social production of men and women is roughly equal.

Walker, Charles. Smoldering ashes: Cuzco and the creation of Republican Peru, 1780–1840. See *HLAS 59:1203*.

834 Wilde, Guillermo. La actitud guaraní ante la expulsión de los jesuitas: ritualidad, reciprocidad y espacio social. (*Mem. Am.*, 8, 1999, p. 141–172, bibl., maps)

Thought-provoking article on expulsion of the Jesuits from *reducciones* in the La

Plata area and its aftermath. Reinterprets relationship between Church and state and, more specifically, argues that arrival of Virrey Bucareli and his relations with the Guarani signaled a return to important ritual and social systems based on reciprocity once lived in the missions.

835 **Zambrano, Marta.** Trabajo precioso, trabajadores despreciables: prácticas conflictivas y consenso epistémico en el discurso colonial. (*Anu. Colomb. Hist. Soc. Cult.*, 25, 1998, p. 5–34)

Very well documented study of labor relations in 16th-17th-century Bogotá. Examines acquiescence, consent, and resistance of the Chibcha to imposition of labor obligations by the powerful invaders, as the Chibcha are transformed into "Indians" and conquerors' preoccupation turns from hoarded gold to tribute.

836 **Zapater Equioíz, Horacio.** Huincas y Mapuches, 1550–1662. (*Historia/ Santiago*, 30, 1997, p. 441–504)

Covers inter-ethnic relations between 1550—the year Pedro de Valdivia crossed the River Bío-Bío for the second time to enter Araucanian territory—and 1662, when the Spanish crown pardoned rebellious indigenous peoples. Author characterizes these relations as pacific or conflictive. Work deals with uprisings, imposition of Hispanic institutions, slavery, racial attitudes, depopulation, and mestizaje.

837 **Zuidema, R. Tom.** Espacio-tiempo en la organización del Cusco: hacia un modelo prehispánico. (*in* Encuentro Internacional de Peruanistas, 1st, Lima, 1996. Estado de los estudios histórico-sociales sobre el Perú a fines del siglo XX. Lima: UNESCO; Univ. de Lima; Fondo de Cultura Económica, 1998, v. 1, p. 253–266, bibl.)

Interesting argument that the *panacas* functioned like age-grades or categories; also discusses their eventual conversion into *ayllus* (kinship groups that had not existed before Spanish arrived).

GENERAL HISTORY

JOHN BRITTON, *Gasque Professor of History, Francis Marion University*

THE LAST DECADE OF THE 20TH CENTURY was characterized by much concern about economic development and the pattern of general studies in Latin American history reflected this world-wide preoccupation. At least 50 articles and books published in the last few years of the century dealt with this issue, from West's study of native American preconquest metallurgy (item **1070**) to Lacoste's review of modern efforts to promote hemispheric economic integration (item **901**). Studies on the colonial period focused on trade, currency, and commodities as exemplified by Luque Talaván's examination of the legal context of commerce (item **1017**) and Woodward's research on the *consulados* of the 18th century (item **1071**). The collection of articles edited by Vila Vilar and Kuethe provided a useful cross-section of colonialist scholarship (item **1051**).

The origins and operations of markets drew much attention in terms of in-depth research as well as in the form of stimulating debates. The group of articles edited by Silva Riquer and Ohmstede examined native American markets from the late colonial era into the 19th century (item **913**). There was a rich variety of perspectives on the roles of prices, trade, and internationalization in the articles by Gálvez Ruiz (item **994**), Salvatore (item **941**), Brown (item **969**), Engerman and Klein (item **875**), and Topik (item **954**). The notion that the 1870–1930 period was crucial in Latin America was reinforced in two edited volumes: one by Cárdenas, Ocampo, and Thorp (item **874**) and a second by Topik and Wells (item **944**). Palacios Rodríguez's monograph also made an important contribution (item **926**). In such an active area, synthesis remains vitally important. Bauer and O'Brien each wrote important, although considerably different, syntheses on economic history (items **847** and **1137**, respectively).

The position of indigenous peoples after the conquest and their complex interactions with European influences and institutions in the colonial era were leading subjects for research, with at least two dozen publications on these topics. The approaches employed were various: Cook examined the impact of disease (item **984**), while Narvaja and Pinotti studied demographics and indigenous identity (item **1026**). Mira Caballos explored the status of native Americans who went to Spain (item **1024**), and Rodríguez Lorenzo summarized Spanish missionaries' educational efforts among indigenous peoples (item **1053**). Jackson contributed a nuanced comparative study of communities in Bolivia and northern New Spain (item **1005**). Two books contain a wealth of information for scholars: the reference work by Magnaghi (item **911**) and Brown's text on social history (item **968**).

The 100th anniversary of the Spanish-American War was the occasion for a surge in publications on this conflict and on Spain's role in Latin America, in general. Political and diplomatic trends over the last half of the 19th century were examined in the works of Fradera (item **1087**), Heredia (item **1089**), and González P. (item **1088**). Adams Fernández provided an analysis of the image of Latin America in the Spanish periodical *La Ilustración Española y Americana* (item **1074**). Reactions to the war in Spain and South America were documented by Filippi (item **1086**), Quijada (item **1106**), and Melgar Bao (item **1099**). Two edited volumes assembled articles on the war and its repercussions. Zea and Magallón concentrated their collection on the relations between Spain and Spanish America (item **1102**), while Cortés Zavala, Naranjo Orovio, and Uribe Salas covered a larger international framework (item **1078**).

The study of the Jewish presence in Latin America also received particular attention. For example, Mario Cohen wrote a general survey of Jews in the Americas in the colonial period (item **978**), while Segal Freilich examined the Jewish *converso* population of the Peruvian Amazon (see item **2630** in the Peruvian History section). Three collections of articles followed different thematic lines: Mario Cohen and Lértora Mendoza emphasized colonial Hispanic America (item **855**); Paolo Bernardini and Norman Fiering included articles on the Jewish role in general European expansion from 1450–1800 (item **1006**); and Bokser Liwerant and Gojman de Backal concentrated on 20th-century themes, particularly immigration and World War II (item **1122**).

A few publications deserve recognition because of special contributions to the field. Two works provided straightforward treatments of sensitive topics: Schoultz and Sagrera took on the challenges of investigating racial prejudice and its impacts on government policies and diplomatic relations in the Americas (see *HLAS 58:815* and **940**, respectively), while Vitale's comprehensive survey is strong on social history and also contains much of value on politics and economics expressed in a well-organized text (item **955**). Altman provided impressive historical depth in her study of immigration from Castile to New Spain from 1560–1620 (item **1211**). Miller's extensive examination of the interaction between the state and intellectuals in the 20th century brought intelligent analysis to an important topic (item **1132**).

GENERAL

838 Aguilar i Lozano, Núria; Mónica Couso Núñez; and Eva María Giménez Freire. Lo pasado, ¡pasado está?: Colón, Cortés, Pizarro; héroes a través del espejo de la historia oficial. (*in* Encuentro-Debate América Latina ayer y hoy = Trobada-Debat Amèrica Llatina ahir i avui, *6th, Barcelona, Spain, 1997.* Lo que duele es el olvido: recuperando la memoria de América Latina = El que dol és l'oblit: recuperant la memòria d'Amèrica Llatina. Barcelona, Spain: Univ. de Barcelona, 1998, p. 381–396, bibl.)

Sometimes revealing and generally interesting observations on the evolution of the historical images of the central trio of the conquest generation in Spanish publications of the 20th century.

Al final del camino. See item 2110.

839 Alía Miranda, Francisco. Fuentes de información para historiadores: obras de referencia y bibliografías. Gijón, Spain: Ediciones Trea, 1998. 177 p.: bibl. (Biblioteconomía y administración cultural; 21)

A basic guide for researchers that includes descriptions of recent reference tools from Spain, the US, and Great Britain, some of which relate to Latin America.

840 América Latina: imagens, imaginação e imaginário. Coordenação de Tânia Maria Tavares Bessone e Tereza Aline P. Queiroz. Rio de Janeiro: Expressão e Cultura; São Paulo: Edusp, 1998. 755 p.: bibl. (América 500 anos; 8)

This volume of 45 scholarly essays is devoted to cultural history in the broadest and best sense of the term. Contributors discuss literature, film, printing, and similar themes spanning six centuries.

841 Anes Alvarez, Gonzalo *et al.* Españoles de ambas orillas: emigración y concordia social. Coordinación de Juan Antonio Escudero. Madrid: Sociedad Estatal Lisboa 98, 1998. 273 p.: bibl., ill.

Thirteen essays address various aspects of emigration to the Americas. Time periods of focus range from the early colonial era to the 20th century. Most articles employ a general approach.

842 Aragonés, Ana María. Migración internacional de trabajadores: una perspectiva histórica. México: UNAM, Campus Acatlán: Plaza y Valdés Editores, 2000. 177 p.: bibl., ill.

Synthesis drawn from published studies of labor migration explained in a global historical context.

843 Atlantic history: history of the Atlantic system 1580–1830. Edited by Horst Pietschmann. Göttingen, Germany: Vandenhoeck & Ruprecht, 2002. 556 p.: bibl., map. (Veröffentlichung der Joachim Jungius-Gesellschaft der Wissenschaften Hamburg; 94)

Proceedings of a conference in Hamburg (1999) mainly focused on the relevance of the concept of "Atlantic system" in historic research. The editor gives an extensive introduction about the notion in recent historic research. [F. Obermeier]

844 Aycart Luengo, Carmen *et al.* Historia de los ferrocarriles de Iberoamérica: 1837–1995. Coordinación de Jesús Sanz Fernández. Madrid: Unión Fenosa: Fundación de los Ferrocarriles Españoles: Ministerio de Fomento: Centro de Estudios y Experimentación Obras Públicas: Centro de Estudios Históricos de Obras Públicas y Urbanismo, 1998. 456 p.: bibl., ill. (some col.).

Well-written general essays by six different authors. Content ranges from prerailroad transportation of the late 1700s to the efforts to privatize rail systems in the late 1900s. Accompanied by excellent maps and charts with an introduction to a complementary CD-ROM.

Baer, Werner and **Joseph L. Love.** Las raíces del retraso económico el Latinoamérica. See *HLAS 59:1226.*

845 Bakewell, Peter John. A history of Latin America: empires and sequels, 1450–1930. Malden, Mass.: Blackwell Publishers, 1997. 520 p., 12 p. of plates: bibl., ill., index, maps. (The Blackwell history of the world)

Colonialists who teach university-level courses will find this textbook to be of much interest with 351 of its 462 pages devoted to the pre-1810 period. Viewed in terms of the author's goals, this book is a lucid, well-informed survey with special attention given to the 16th century.

846 Banko, Catalina. Liberalismo económico, inversiones extranjeras y las reacciones antiimperialistas en América Latina. (*Tiempo Espacio/Caracas*, 15:29/30, 1998, p. 157–191, bibl.)

Interesting preliminary assessment of a very important theme—the anti-imperialist response to the expansion of foreign investments in Latin America in the 19th century.

847 Bauer, Arnold J. Goods, power, history: Latin America's material culture. Cambridge; New York: Cambridge Univ. Press, 2001. 245 p.: bibl., ill., index. (New approaches to the Americas)

This unusually succinct interpretation of Latin American history concentrates on the material goods that formed the basis for culture as well as economics from preconquest to the late 20th century. Examples include textiles, tools, grain crops, beverages, native food preparation, and in the era of globalization, fast food and Coca-Cola.

848 Bernecker, Walther L. and **Thomas Fischer.** Alemania y América Latina en la época del imperialismo 1871–1914. (*Rev. Hist./Heredia*, 33, enero/junio 1996, p. 9–42, tables)

Much-needed synthesis of scholarly publications—mostly in German—on German influence in Latin America through trade, finance, and military missions. Also covers the German rivalry with the US in the Western Hemisphere.

849 Bethencourt, Francisco. La Inquisición en la época moderna: España, Portugal, e Italia, siglos XV-XIX. Madrid: Akal, 1997. 564 p.: bibl., ill., indexes. (Akal universitaria; 195. Serie Historia moderna)

Very broad study that incorporates the Spanish and Portuguese experiences into a larger Mediterranean context. Some comparative value for Latin Americanists.

850 Beyond the ideal: Pan Americanism in Inter-American affairs. Edited by David Sheinin. Westport, Conn.: Greenwood Press, 2000. 225 p.: bibl., index. (Contributions in Latin American studies, 1054–6790; no. 18)

The 14 selections in this anthology designed for the undergraduate classrooom offer high quality historical analyses with a wel-come emphasis on cultural, intellectual, and environmental factors.

851 Blas, Patricio de et al. Historia común de Iberoamérica. Madrid: Editorial EDAF, 2000. 585 p.: bibl., ill., maps. (EDAF ensayo; 2)

A notable attempt to write a synthesis of Latin American history intended for the introductory student. Approximately one-fourth of the text is devoted to indigenous civilizations and one-fourth to the colonial period. The coverage of the national era is mainly thematic with emphases on economics, politics, and culture.

852 Centre de Recherches et d'Etudes sur l'Amérique Ibérique. Colloque International. *Univ. de Liège, 1998.* 1898–1998: fines de siglos historia y literatura hispanoamericanas; actas = 1898–1998: fins de siècles histoire et littérature hispano-américaines: actas. Publiés par Jacques Joset et Philippe Raxhon. Geneva: Librarie Droz, 2000. 190 p.: bibl. (Bibliothèque de la Faculté de philosophie et lettres de l'Université de Liège; fasc. 279)

Cuba and Argentina figure prominently in this highly diverse collection that includes four essays on history and seven on literature.

853 The church in colonial Latin America. Edited by John Frederick Schwaller. Wilmington, Del.: Scholarly Resources, 2000. 252 p.: bibl. (Jaguar books on Latin America; no. 21)

This balanced collection of articles covers both macrohistory in the form of large policy and cultural issues and microhistory through selected studies at the local level.

854 Cifuentes Toro, Arturo. Herencia de mujeres: espacios y vida cotidiana en la conquista y la colonia. Bogotá: Editado por el convenio de CEUDES, Corporación Unidades Democráticas para el Desarrollo, y ASRIO, Asociación Mujeres del Río, 1997–2000. 112 p.: bibl., ill.

Very general treatment of an important topic. Intended for introductory study.

855 Cinco siglos de presencia judia en América: actas del encuentro internacional. Recopilación de Mario E. Cohen and Celina Ana Lértora Mendoza. Buenos Aires: Editorial Sefarad 92, 2000. 542 p.: bibl., ill.

The emphasis is on the colonial period with four of the five sections of this collection covering the themes of the Jewish presence in pre-1492 Spain, the 1492 expulsion, and the subsequent Jewish presence in Hispanic America.

856 Cities of hope: people, protests, and progress in urbanizing Latin America, 1870–1930. Edited by Ronn Pineo and James A. Baer. Boulder, Colo.: Westview Press, 1998. 285 p.: bibl., ill., index, 1 map.

The response of working people to a wide range of urban problems is the unifying theme in this group of nine well-documented articles. The cities covered include Bogotá, Montevideo, Mexico City, Veracruz, Buenos Aires, Valparaíso, Rio de Janeiro, Panama City, and Lima.

857 Clayton, Lawrence A. and **Michael L. Conniff.** A history of modern Latin America. Fort Worth, Tex.: Harcourt Brace College Humanities, 1999. 605 p.: bibl., ill., index.

This college textbook is an outstanding contribution to what is becoming a crowded field. The authors concentrate on the 19th-20th centuries with a balance of political, economic, and social history. This text's strong points include a jargon-free explanation of caudillismo, and perceptive explanations of the arrival of international economic integration in the 19th century and the persistence of populism in the 20th century.

858 Colonial legacies: the problem of persistence in Latin American history. Edited by Jeremy Adelman. New York: Routledge, 1999. 318 p.: bibl., index.

This selection of sophisticated articles combines a healthy mix of primary research and thought-provoking generalizations that, in most cases, coalesce around the task of assessing the weight of the region's colonial past on the modern era. Much of the work here draws from the scholarship of Stanley Stein.

859 El comercio de vinos y aguardientes andaluces con América, siglos XVI-XX. Recopilación de Alberto Ramos Santana y Javier Maldonado Rosso. Cádiz, Spain: Servicio de Publicaciones de la Univ. de Cádiz, 1998. 325 p.: bibl., ill.

Wide-ranging collection of 17 articles on the wine industry, an important but often slighted area in economic history. Includes considerable quantitative material and much archival research.

860 Congreso Internacional de Historia de América, 7th, Zaragoza, Spain, 1996. Ponencias y comunicaciones. v. 1, La corona de Aragón y el Nuevo Mundo: del Mediterráneo a las Indias. v. 2, España en América del Norte. v. 3, La economía marítima del Atlántico: pesca, navegación y comercio. Zaragoza, Spain: Gobierno de Aragón, Depto. de Educación y Cultura; Madrid: Ministerio de Educación y Cultura, 1998. 3 v.: bibl., ill., maps. (Col. Actas; 48–50)

This very large collection of 116 articles is organized into three general categories: Aragon and the New World (vol. 1), Spain in North America (vol. 2), and the maritime economy of the North Atlantic (vol. 3). The thematic emphasis is on the colonial era, but there are several articles on the 19th century. Many of these articles employ research from Spanish archives.

861 Congreso Internacional Nueva España y las Antillas, 1st, Castellón de la Plana, Spain and Benicásim, Spain, 1997. De súbditos del rey a ciudadanos de la nación: Actas. Compilacion del Centro de Investigaciones de América Latina. Contribuciones de Francisco Javier Pizarro et al. Castelló de la Plana, Spain: CIAL, Univ. Jaume I, 2000. 414 p.: bibl. (Col. Humanitats; 1)

Although this collection includes some articles on the colonial period, the emphasis is on Cuba and Mexico in the 19th century. A useful contribution to the history of the emergence of nations and nationality.

862 Congreso Internacional sobre los Dominicos y el Nuevo Mundo, 5th, Querétaro, Mexico, 1995. Los Dominicos y el Nuevo Mundo, siglos XIX-XX: actas. Coordinación de José Barrado Barquilla y Santiago Rodríguez López. Salamanca, Spain: Editorial San Esteban, 1997. 681 p.: bibl., ill. (some col.), index. (Monumenta histórica iberoamericana de la Orden de Predicadores; 13)

The range of this volume extends from 19th-century evangelism to an essay entitled "Chiapas hoy, presencia dominica en tierra de conflicto" by Jorge Rafael Díaz Nuñez. Most of the contributions have footnotes, and the editors have appended a useful name index.

863 Constitucionalismo y orden liberal: América Latina, 1850–1920. Coordinación de Marcello Carmagnani. Torino, Italy: Otto Editore, 2000. 380 p.

This useful collection extends beyond the study of constitutions to examine the nation-state and its role in the administration of justice, the promotion of economic development, census taking (Peru of 1876), and also the effects of politics and the military on governments. Several of the 11 contributions contain primary research and all are thoroughly footnoted.

864 Corbière, Emilio J. La masonería. v. 1, Política y sociedades secretas. Buenos Aires: Sudamericana, 1998. 1 v.: bibl., ill.

This somewhat rambling volume touches few of the general aspects of Masonry; however, most of the text concentrates on the influence of Masonry on Argentine politics from independence to the later half of the 20th century. The author's extensive footnotes will be of interest to the specialist.

865 Cruz, Consuelo. Identity and persuasion: how nations remember their pasts and make their futures. (*World Polit.*, 52:3, 2000, p. 275–312)

This sophisticated article contrasts the development of the political cultures of Costa Rica and Nicaragua by examining the historical evolution of these two nations from the colonial era to the 19th century.

866 Cultura alimentaria Andalucía-América. Compilación de Antonio Garrido Aranda. México: UNAM, 1996. 255 p., 1 leaf of plates: bibl., ill. (Serie Historia General/17)

Six essays present an interesting mix of topics: Muslim influences in Andalucia, royal banquets, reciprocal exchanges between Andalucia and America, the role of fasting, Andalucian cooking and kitchens, and cattle ranching.

867 Dager Alva, Joseph. Una aproximación a la historiografía del siglo XIX: vida y obra de José Toribio Polo, 1841–1918. Lima: Pontificia Univ. Católica del Perú: Banco Central de Reserva del Perú, 2000. 354 p.:

bibl., ill. (Publicación del Instituto Riva-Agüero; 186)

Biographical and bibliographical materials abound in this appreciation of the Peruvian historian.

868 De La Pedraja Tomán, René. Oil and coffee: Latin American merchant shipping from the imperial era to the 1950s. Westport, Conn.: Greenwood Press, 1998. 191 p.: bibl., index. (Contributions in economics and economic history; 206)

Much-needed and well-executed study of a generally neglected topic. The author examines the efforts of individual nations to develop their own merchant lines—especially Brazil, Chile, Mexico, and Argentina. Based on archival research and extensive reading in specialized periodicals. Also see author's continuation of this work, *Latin American Merchant Shipping in the Age of Global Competition*, item **1119**.

869 La destrucción de las Indias y sus recursos renovables, 1492–1992: dignidad con el pasado y reivindicación con el presente y futuro de los pueblos y las culturas mesoamericanas. Obra colectiva, coordinada y presentada por Alejandro Sánchez Vélez. Chapingo, Mexico: Univ. Autónoma Chapingo, Centro de Investigaciones Económicas, Sociales y Tecnológicas de la Agroindustria y la Agricultura Mundial, Dirección de Difusión Cultural, División de Ciencias Forestales, Depto. de Agroecología, 1999. 311 p.: bibl., ill.

Studies in history, climatology, and social science give this collection diversity and chronological range (preconquest to the 1990s).

870 Deutsch, Sandra McGee. Las Derechas: the extreme right in Argentina, Brazil, and Chile, 1890–1939. Stanford, Calif.: Stanford Univ. Press, 1999. 491 p.: bibl., index.

Well-conceived and nicely executed comparative study of rightest movements fills a large gap in the historiography of Latin American politics. The author tends to stress the variety and persistence of rightest manifestations including nationalism, populism, anti-Semitism, militarism, and state-directed repression. The research, as indicated by the footnotes and bibliography, was extensive.

871 Diouf, Sylviane Anna. Servants of Allah: African Muslims enslaved in the Americas. New York: New York Univ. Press, 1998. 254 p.: bibl., index.

An important pioneering study of a previously neglected topic, this book focuses on Brazil and the Caribbean and includes considerable coverage of religion and culture as well as enslavement and labor. Well-written and nicely organized, the text extends from the colonial era into the 20th century.

872 Discriminación y racismo en América Latina. Edición preparada por Ignacio Klich y Mario Rapoport. Con colaboración del Instituto de Investigaciones de Historia Económica Social, Facultad de Ciencias Económicas, U.B.A., Fundación de Investigaciones Históricas, Económicas y Sociales. Buenos Aires: Grupo Editor Latinoamericano, 1997. 475 p.: bibl., 1 map. (Nuevohacer) (Col. Estudios políticos y sociales)

This valuable collection of scholarly articles focuses on the controversies surrounding Jewish refugees and their struggles to find a safe haven in Latin America in the first half of the 20th century. Some essays also deal with the influence of fascism and Nazism in the region. Most articles are thoroughly footnoted.

873 Dunkerley, James. Warriors and scribes: essays on the history and politics of Latin America. London; New York: Verso, 2000. 211 p.: bibl., ill. (Critical studies in Latin American and Iberian cultures)

The essays in this volume cover a wide variety of themes from an extended critical commentary on the writings of René Barrientos, Regis Debray, and Jorge Castañeda to Hollywood's image of Central America in the 1980s to the Latin America career of Francis Burdett O'Connor in the early 1800s. Scholarly depth expressed in lively prose.

874 An economic history of twentieth-century Latin America. v. 1, The export age: the Latin American economies in the late nineteenth and early twentieth centuries. Edited by Enrique Cárdenas, José Antonio Ocampo, and Rosemary Thorp. v. 2, Latin America in the 1930s: the role of the periphery in world crisis. Edited by Rosemary Thorp. Houndsmills, Basingstoke, Hampshire, England; New York: Palgrave; Oxford: in association with St. Antony's College, 2000. 2 v.: bibl., ill., index. (St Antony's series)

The focus is on export economics in the set of 10 essays that make up Vol. I. The introductory contributions by the editors explain the general pattern and precede eight country-by-country analyses and one article on Central America. In general, these contributions strike a healthy balance between narrative and quantification. Vol. II is a reprint of the 1984 edition which emphasizes the 1930s.

875 Engerman, Stanley L. and **Herbert S. Klein.** Prices as a tool of historical analysis. (*Am. Lat. Hist. Econ. Bol. Fuentes*, 5, enero/junio 1996, p. 9–18)

Lucid discussion of the importance of commodity prices as component indicators in rates of growth and in other economic and social phenomena.

876 English-speaking communities in Latin America. Edited by Oliver Marshall. New York: St. Martin's Press, 2000. 387 p.: bibl., index, maps.

Case studies reveal the multiplicity of experiences for British communities in Latin America from the wars for independence of the early 19th century to the Anglo-Argentina conflict of 1982. Based on impressive research.

877 Estudios sobre historia y ambiente en América. v. 1. México: Instituto Panamericano de Geografía e Historia: El Colegio de México, 1999. 1 v.: bibl, ill., index.

This collection of scholarly articles on ecological topics maintains high levels of conceptualization and original research while spanning five centuries. The majority of the contributions deal with the colonial period.

878 Familias iberoamericanas: historia, identidad y conflictos. Coordinación de Pilar Gonzalbo Aizpuru. México: Colegio de México: Centro de Estudios Históricos, 2001. 323 p.: bibl., ill.

This edited volume includes articles that range from domestic slavery in colonial Santo Domingo to the family and socialist education in Mexico in the 1930s.

879 Fazer a América: a imigração em massa para a América Latina. Organização de Boris Fausto. São Paulo: Edusp: Memorial; Brasília: Fundação Alexandre de Gusmão, 1999. 577 p.: bibl., ill.

This volume of 17 articles includes five on Argentina, seven on Brazil, and one each on Uruguay, Chile, Peru, and Cuba, plus a general introductory essay. As a whole, this collection offers some helpful interpretations of 19th- and 20th-century patterns based on extensive surveys of published monographs with some primary research.

880 Fournier García, Patricia. Arqueología del colonialismo de España y Portugal: imperios contrastantes en el Nuevo Mundo. (*Bol. Antropol. Am.*, 32, julio 1998, p. 89–96, bibl., ill., photos)

This stimulating essay indicates that, in spite of significant differences, the two empires left much material evidence of imperial advantages that accrued to both Spain and Portugal.

881 Fróes da Fonseca, Maria Rachel. La construcción de la patria por el discurso científico: México y Brasil, 1770–1830. (*Secuencia/México*, 45, sept./dic. 1999, p. 5–26, bibl., ill.)

An innovative exploration of the connection between scientific writing and the origins of a sense of national identity in late colonial Mexico and Brazil.

882 Gamboa Cáceres, Teresa; Gabriela Morán Leal; and Haydée Ochoa Henríquez. Historia del trabajo en América Latina. (*Tierra Firme/Caracas*, 16:61, enero/marzo 1998, p. 25–57, bibl.)

A general, somewhat abstract commentary that emphasizes the contrasts between "cooperación forzada" as in tribute payment and slavery, "coerción económica" as in peonage, and "cooperación espontánea" as in local cooperatives.

883 Gilderhus, Mark T. The second century: U.S.-Latin American relations since 1889. Wilmington, Del.: Scholarly Resources, 2000. 282 p.: bibl., index. (Latin American silhouettes)

Nicely organized chronological survey that strikes a fine balance between factual detail and meaningful generalization from the pen of a respected specialist in Latin American-US relations. Volume contains carefully balanced coverage of the controversial points surrounding the Panama Canal, Fidel Castro, and Central America in the 1980s. For comment by international relations specialist, see *HLAS 59:4170.*

884 Guerra Vilaboy, Sergio. La historiografía latinoamericana en la coyuntura entre siglos XIX y XX. (*Debates Am.*, 5/6, 1998, p. 19–34)

General discussion of the efforts of such writers as Rufino Blanco Fambona, Justo Sierra, and Laureano Vallenilla Lanz to deal with the events of the 1890s.

885 Guia de fontes portuguesas para a história da América Latina. Instituto dos Arquivos Nacionais/Torre do Tombo. Elaboração de Fernanda Olival *et al.* Lisboa: Comissão Nacional para as Comemorações dos Descobrimentos Portugueses: Fundação Oriente: Impr. Nacional-Casa de Moeda, 1997. 1 v. (Guides to the sources for the history of nations [sic]; 1)

Brazilian foreign relations constitute a central theme in this description of the holdings of the Ministério dos Negócios Estrangeiros and the Instituto dos Arquivos Nacionais. This volume focuses on the archives of consulates and legations in Europe and the US. The last section of this volume includes some private archives from the colonial era.

886 Guy, Donna J. and Thomas E. Sheridan. On frontiers: the northern and southern edges of the Spanish Empire in the Americas. (*in* Contested ground: comparative frontiers on the northern and southern edges of the Spanish Empire. Edited by Donna J. Guy and Thomas E. Sheridan. Tucson: Univ. of Arizona Press, 1998, p. 3–15)

Thoughtful discussion of key social and cultural factors impacting frontier regions.

887 Henderson, Paul. The rise and fall of anarcho-syndicalism in South America, 1880–1930. (*in* Ideologues and ideologies in Latin America. Edited by Will Fowler. Westport, Conn.: Greenwood Press, 1997, p. 11–26)

Excellent brief synthesis of current scholarship on the growth and decline of the movement.

888 **Hernández González, Manuel.** La emigración canaria a América, 1765–1824: entre el libre comercio y la emancipación. La Laguna, Canary Islands, Spain: Centro de la Cultura Popular Canaria, 1996 [i.e. 1997]. 374 p.: bibl. (Taller de Historia; 20)

Detailed examination of the origins and course of Canary Islanders' immigration, especially to Cuba, Puerto Rico, and Venezuela. Based on archival research and published documents. See also item **934**.

889 **Hidden histories of gender and the state in Latin America.** Edited by Elizabeth Dore and Maxine Molyneux. Durham, N.C.: Duke Univ. Press, 2000. 394 p.: bibl., index.

Collection of 12 well-chosen case studies and two informative introductory essays constitutes a major, path-breaking contribution to the study of the relationships between women and the state from the late colonial period to the late 20th century.

890 **História da ciência: o mapa do conhecimento.** Coordenação de Ana Maria Alfonso-Goldfarb e Carlos A. Maia. Rio de Janeiro: Expressão e Cultura; São Paulo: Edusp, 1996. 968 p.: bibl. (América 500 anos; 2)

The colonial period receives heavy emphasis in this collection of 51 essays, most of which are based on published sources and monographs.

891 **História do Cone Sul.** Organização de Amado Luiz Cervo e Mario Rapoport. Brasília: Editora UnB; Rio de Janeiro: Editora Revan, 1998? 334 p.: bibl.

Commendable effort at synthesis extends from 17th century to 20th century and is organized around economic and political trends. Stresses the roles of Brazil and Argentina, and provides an interesting analysis of the connections between the region and world powers.

892 **Historiografía latinoamericana contemporánea.** Coordinación de Ignacio Sosa y Brian Francis Connaughton Hanley. México: UNAM, Centro Coordinador y Difusor de Estudios Latinoamericanos, Dirección General de Asuntos del Personal Académico, 1999. 270 p.: bibl.

Broadly based volume contains eight essays that cover several topics including periodization from the early 1500s to the mid-1900s, urbanization in the Bourbon era, and contemporary trends in Andean and Brazilian history.

893 **Image and memory: photography from Latin America, 1866–1994: FotoFest.** Edited by Wendy Watriss and Lois Parkinson Zamora. Austin: Univ. of Texas Press, 1998. 450 p.: bibl., ill. (some col.), index.

Perceptive essays support the carefully selected, largely historical photographs from 10 countries. The overall impact of text combined with photographic images is very impressive. Extensive footnotes and bibliography.

894 **El indio como sujeto y objeto de la historia latinoamericana, pasado y presente.** Recopilación de Hans-Joachim König. En colaboración con Christian Gros, Karl Kohut y France-Marie Renard-Casevitz. Frankfurt: Vervuert; Madrid: Iberoamericana, 1998. 269 p.: bibl., ill. (Americana Eystettensia: Publikationen des Zentralinstituts für Lateinamerika-Studien der Katholischen Universität Eichstätt. Serie A, Kongressakten = Publicaciones del Centro de Estudios Latinoamericanos de la Universidad Católica de Eichstätt, Serie A; 18)

Collection of well-researched articles extends from the preconquest to the contemporary era with an emphasis on the last decades of the 20th century. Covers political and ecological issues.

895 **La inmigración española en Chile, Brasil y Argentina.** Coordinación general de Hernán A. Silva. México: Instituto Panamericano de Geografía e Historia, 1999. 250 p.: bibl., maps. (Serie Inmigración; v. 8)

Detailed studies concentrate on Argentina with a lesser emphasis on Chile and Brazil. A healthy mix of descriptive narrative and statistics.

896 **Izard, Miquel.** Agresión, rechazo y forja de sociedades alternativas. (*in* Raíces de la memoria: América Latina, ayer y hoy, quinto encuentro debate = Amèrica Llatina, ahir i avui, cinquena trobada debat. Coordinación de Pilar García Jordán *et al.* Barcelona: Univ. de Barcelona, 1996, p. 301–312)

Forcefully argued thought piece on the consequences of imperial conquest.

897 Klein, Herbert S. The Atlantic slave trade. New York: Cambridge Univ. Press, 1999. 234 p.: bibl., ill., maps. (New approaches to the Americas)

A very well informed, remarkably concise synthesis of recent scholarship, covering South America, the Caribbean, and North America. Includes 12-page bibliographic essay.

898 Knight, Alan. Latinoamérica: un balance historiográfico. (*Hist. Graf. / México*, 10, 1998, p. 165–207, bibl.)

Ambitious and well-executed essay that covers major trends in the field including regional/local history, ethno-popular history, and historical theory.

899 Knight, Alan. Pueblo, política y nación, siglos XIX y XX. (*Rev. Hist. / Heredia*, 34, julio/dic. 1996, p. 45–79)

Insightful examination of the concept of nationalism as applied to Latin America.

900 Korol, Juan Carlos and **Enrique Tandeter.** Historia económica de América Latina: problemas y procesos. Buenos Aires: Fondo de Cultura Económica de Argentina, 1999. 117 p.: bibl. (Sección Obras de historia)

Brief essay condenses recent scholarship into a compact text. Specialists may find it too brief, but introductory students will find it helpful. Ample footnotes.

901 Lacoste, Pablo. Las propuestas de integración económica sudamericana: de Diego Portales a Alfredo Palacios, 1830–1939. (*Historia/Santiago*, 32, 1999, p. 103–129)

Explanatory essay on various proposals for economic integration.

902 Langley, Lester D. The Americas in the age of revolution, 1750–1850. New Haven, Conn.: Yale Univ. Press, 1996. 374 p.: bibl., maps.

Stimulating comparative history of three revolutions: British colonists in North America, African slaves in Haiti, and Spanish Americans in South America and Mexico. Skillfully incorporates political, ideological, racial, and class issues.

903 Latin America, history and culture: an encyclopedia for students. Edited by Barbara A. Tenenbaum. New York: Scribner's Sons, Macmillan Library Reference USA, 1999. 4 v.: bibl., ill. (some col.), index, maps (some col.).

Well-organized, convenient summation of current state of knowledge, suitable for university and high school students. Text is strengthened by appropriate illustrations. Cross references and extensive index will be helpful to beginning researchers. High level of scholarly content combined with clear prose free of jargon.

904 Latin American civilization: history and society, 1492 to the present. Edited by Benjamin Keen. 7th ed., rev. and updated. Boulder, Colo.: Westview Press, 2000. 514 p.: bibl.

Most recent edition of this venerable collection intended for the university classroom contains new selections on economic history and Latin American women.

905 Latin American popular culture: an introduction. Edited by William H. Beezley and Linda Ann Curcio. Wilmington, Del.: Scholarly Resources, 2000. 255 p.: bibl.

This sprightly volume presents essays that penetrate deeply into popular culture through explorations of the origins and manifestations of the tango, the calypso, world trade fairs, funerals, and public monuments.

906 Laviña, Javier. Comunidades afroamericanas: identidad de resistencia. (*Bol. Am. /Barcelona*, 38:48, 1998, p. 139–151, bibl.)

Sociology and history combine in this synthesis on social structure, religion, and the onset of rebellion and the creation of cimarron communities.

907 Lavrin, Asunción. Género e historia: una conjunción a finales del siglo XX. (*Nomadías/Santiago*, 1, junio 1999, p. 15–46)

Review of recent publications on gender history with an emphasis on employment, politics, and the role of the state.

908 López, Alfred J. Posts and pasts: a theory of postcolonialism. Albany, N.Y.: SUNY Press, 2001. 285 p.: bibl., index. (SUNY series, explorations in postcolonial studies)

Literature, literary theory, history, philosophy, and anthropology intersect in this nuanced study of several writers and their reflections on the uneven transition from the age of empires to postcolonialism. Concentrates on Joseph Conrad, Franz Fanon, Alejo Carpentier, and Gabriel García Márquez, among others.

Loveman, Brian. For La Patria: politics and the armed forces in Latin America. See *HLAS 59:4186.*

909 Lucena Giraldo, Manuel Las expediciones de límites y la ocupación del espacio americano, 1751–1804. (*Paramillo/San Cristóbal*, 15, 1996, p. 649–669)

Traces various efforts to clarify boundaries between Spanish and Portuguese possessions. Drawn from published sources and some archival records.

910 Magnaghi, Russell M. Herbert E. Bolton and the historiography of the Americas. Westport, Conn.: Greenwood Press, 1998. 227 p.: bibl., ill., index, map. (Studies in historiography; 5)

A welcome review of recent publications relevant to Bolton's approaches to history, covers both the Borderlands area and the larger concept of the history of the Americas, which Magnaghi presents, in part, as comparative history. Also interesting biographical portrait based on research in the Bolton papers.

911 Magnaghi, Russell M. Indian slavery, labor, evangelization, and captivity in the Americas: an annotated bibliography. Lanham, Md.: Scarecrow Press, 1998. 559 p.: bibl. index. (Native American bibliography series; 22)

A useful reference work for beginning and senior scholars. The author has a general section on the "Native Experience" and country-by-country surveys covering both colonial and national periods including studies in Spanish, Portuguese, and English. Includes both subject and author indexes.

912 Marichal, Carlos. Reflexiones sobre el concepto de América Latina. (*Estud. Hombre*, 9, 1999, p. 141–152)

Thoughtful examinations of the origins of the term *Latin America* in the 1860s and also the development of the concept by writers such as José Enrique Rodó and Francisco Bulnes. See also item **930**.

913 Mercados indígenas en México, Chile y Argentina, siglos XVIII-XIX. Coordinación de Jorge Silva Riquer y Antonio Escobar Ohmstede. México: Instituto de Investi-

gaciones Dr. José María Luis Mora: Centro de Investigaciones y Estudios Superiores en Antropología Social, 2000. 211 p.: ill. (Historia económica)

Well-organized set of essays on an important theme in economic and cultural history—the interaction of native Americans and markets. Includes much archival research.

914 Merrell, Floyd. Sobre las culturas y civilizaciones latinoamericanas. Lanham, Md.: Univ. Press of America, 2000. 423 p.: maps.

A survey text for university students in advanced Spanish language classes, this volume emphasizes literature and cultural themes in general, but also includes interesting discussions of crucial political trends.

915 Mesa Redonda sobre Historia de la Medicina Iberoamericana, *Cádiz, Spain, 1993.* Páginas de historia de la medicina hispanoamericana: comunicaciones a la Mesa Redonda sobre Historia de la Medicina Iberoamericana. Coordinación de Antonio Orozco Acuaviva. Cádiz, Spain: Sociedad de Historia de la Medicina Hispanoamericana: Servicio de Publicaciones de la Univ. de Cádiz, 1997. 142 p.: bibl.

Collection of brief, preliminary studies on the history of medicine extending from the colonial era to the 20th century.

916 Meyer, Eugenia. América Latina, ¿una realidad virtual?: a propósito del artículo de Dora Schwarzstein. (*Hist. Antropol. Fuentes Orales*, 16, 1996, p. 141–149)

Precisely focused and sharply worded critique buttressed by extensive footnotes. For historian's comment on original article by Schwarzstein, see *HLAS 58:816.*

917 Mines of silver and gold in the Americas. Edited by Peter Bakewell. Aldershot, Great Britain; Brookfield, Vt.: Variorum, 1997. 420 p.: bibl., ill., index, maps. (An Expanding world; v. 19)

This group of very well-researched articles is drawn from a variety of journals and previously published essay collections to provide a convenient volume of scholarship on this topic. Editor Bakewell's introduction places the topic in the larger context of European expansion quite effectively.

918 Mitos e heróis: construção de imaginários. Organização de Loiva Otero Félix e Cláudio P. Elmir. Contribuções de Adhemar Lourenço da Silva Júnior et al. Porto Alegre, Brazil: Editora da Univ., Univ. Federal do Rio Grande do Sul, 1998. 253 p.: bibl.

Culture and politics intersect in these 12 scholarly articles that deal mostly with the mythical and heroic elements in the development of national culture, especially in Brazil.

919 Mörner, Magnus. The characteristics of Latin America within global history. (in Between national and global history. Edited by Stein Tonnesson et al. Helsinki: FHS, 1997, p. 115–127)

Mörner explicates seven large generalizations about the region. A valuable exercise that includes provocative analyses of the Iberian colonial empires as well as current economic trends. Also published in Spanish in the journal Historia y Sociedad (Medellín), 5, dic. 1998, p. 135–148.

920 Mott, Luiz Roberto de Barros. Etnohistoria de la homosexualidad en América Latina. (Hist. Soc./Medellín, 4, dic. 1997, p. 123–144)

Pioneering overview of a topic of increasing interest. Based on an extensive survey of relevant scholarly publications.

921 Movimientos estudiantiles en la historia de América Latina. v. 1–2. México: Centro de Estudios sobre la Univ., UNAM: Plaza y Valdés Editores, 1999. 2 v.: bibl. (Col. Historia de la educación. Serie mayor)

Although these 14 articles span four centuries, all but two deal with the national period and five focus on Argentina. In general, these articles are well-documented with stimulating analyses, especially the work of María Cristina Vera de Flachs on the faculty of the Univ. de Córdoba in the half-century before 1918 and Monica Rein on Argentine universities and Peronism.

922 Navarro, Marysa and Virginia Sánchez Korrol, with Kecia Ali. Women in Latin America and the Caribbean: restoring women to history. Bloomington: Indiana Univ. Press, 1999. 128 p.: bibl., maps. (Restoring women to history)

A highly competant survey based on an extensive reading of recently published monographs. Covers the precolumbian, colo-

nial, and national periods and includes social, economic, and political factors. Useful as a much-needed synthesis and also as a classroom text.

923 Negrín Fajardo, Olegario. La influencia pedagógica española en Iberoamérica: estudios sobre historia de la educación contemporánea. Madrid: Univ. Nacional de Educación a Distancia, 1999. 379 p.: bibl. (Aula abierta)

This study explores educational theory and practice in Costa Rica, Cuba, and Colombia in the late 19th and early 20th centuries to a large extent through the work of the brothers Valeriano and Juan Fernández Ferraz. Drawn mainly from published works, but includes some private correspondence.

924 Um olhar sobre o passado: história das ciências na América Latina. Organização de Silvia F. de M. Figueirôa. Tradução de Beatriz Mattos Marchesini. Campinas, Brazil: Editora Unicamp; São Paulo: Imprensa Oficial SP, 1999 (2000 printing). 282 p.: bibl. (Pesquisas)

Useful collection of 10 essays on a subject that is in need of serious scholarly work. The range of these essays extends from the colonial period to the 20th century. Specific topics include botany, geology, and mathematics.

925 On earth as it is in heaven: religion in modern Latin America. Edited by Virginia Garrard-Burnett. Wilmington, Del.: Scholarly Resources, 1999. 251 p.: bibl. (Jaguar books on Latin America; no. 18)

Valuable collection places religion in the appropriate social and ideological contexts including 19th-century church-state rivalry, "folk Catholicism," liberation theology, and Protestant missionary work. The editor's introduction and bibliographical essay are especially helpful for students and senior scholars alike.

926 Palacios Rodríguez, Raúl. Redes de poder en el Perú y América, 1890–1930. Lima: Univ. de Lima, Fondo de Desarrollo Editorial: Instituto de Estudios Histórico-Marítimos del Perú: Fondo de Cultura Económica S.A., 2000. 465 p.: bibl., ill. (Col. Biblioteca Universidad de Lima)

Excellent scholarly synthesis that examines the displacement of British economic influence in Latin America by the US in general terms with Peru serving as a case study. Emphasizes the consolidation of US influence under the Peruvian presidency of Augusto Leguia in the 1920s.

927 Para una historia de América. v. 1, Las estructuras. México: Colegio de México, Fideicomiso Historia de las Américas: Fondo de Cultura Económica, 1999. 570 p.: bibl., ill., (some col.) maps (some col.). (Serie Américas) (Sección de obras de historia)

Five extended interpretive essays offer thoughtful generalizations in the areas of historical geography, economic history, and social history, and on the themes of material culture and Westernization.

928 Paz Sánchez, Manuel de and Manuel Hernández González. La América española, 1763–1898: cultura y vida cotidiana. Madrid: Editorial Sintesis, 2000. 270 p.: ill. (Historia de España 3er. milenio; 22)

A substantial survey text that emphasizes the diffusion of ideas during the Enlightenment, as well as daily life in cities and the countryside.

929 La prosa no ficcional en Hispanoamérica y en España entre 1870 y 1914. Compilación de Aldo Albònico y Antonio Scocozza. Caracas: Monte Avila Editores Latinoamericana; Instituto di Studi Latinoamericani; Pagani, Italy: Alcaldía de Pagani: Caracas: Fundación La Casa de Bello, 2000. 438 p.: bibl. (Estudios. Serie Literatura)

Culture, politics, and nationalism are the emergent themes in this exemplary collection in the field of intellectual history. Among the essayists featured are José Ingenieros, Manuel González Prada, Manuel Ugarte, and José Vasconcelos.

930 Quijada, Mónica. Sobre el origen y difusión del nombre *América Latina:* o una variación heterodoxa en torno al tema de la construcción social de la verdad. (*Rev. Indias,* 58:214, sept./dic. 1998, p. 595–616)

Historically grounded observations on the origins of the term *Latin America,* with an emphasis on the 1850s and concern about US expansionism. See also items **912** and **4612.** For philosophy specialist's comment, see item **4609.**

931 Raízes da América Latina. Coordenação de Francisca L. Nogueira de Azevedo e John Manuel Monteiro. Rio de Janeiro: Expressão e Cultura; São Paulo: Edusp, 1996. 598 p. (América 500 anos; 5)

This book of essays extends its coverage from the colonial era into the 19th century. Most of the essays are based on published monographs rather than primary research and, as a whole, offer a sampling of themes in political, economic, and social history.

932 Reconstructing criminality in Latin America. Edited by Carlos A. Aguirre and Robert Buffington. Wilmington, Del.: Scholarly Resources, 2000. 273 p.: bibl. (Jaguar books on Latin America; 19)

Extensive chronological coverage of the social, political, and legal ramifications of criminality is one of the strong points of the selections in this volume, all of which are based on sound scholarship. An informative bibliographical essay and filmography are included.

933 Revolution and revolutionaries: guerrilla movements in Latin America. Edited by Daniel Castro. Wilmington, Del.: SR Books, 1999. 273 p.: bibl. (Jaguar books on Latin America; no. 17)

An extensive yet coherent selection of primary documents and scholarly analyses prefaced by an intelligent introduction. Ranges from Tupac Amaru to the Sendero Luminoso and the Zapatistas of the 1990s.

934 Rodríguez Mendoza, Félix. Estudio de una cadena migratoria a América: Icod de Los Vinos, 1750–1830. La Laguna, Canary Islands, Spain: Centro de la Cultura Popular Canaria, 1998. 259, 30 p.: port. (Taller de Historia; 23)

Detailed examination of migration including causes, finances, and destinations (especially Cuba, Venezuela, and Louisiana). Strong on research in local (Canary Island) archives. See also item **888.**

935 Rosoli, Gianfausto. Iglesia, ordenes y congregaciones religiosas en la experiencia de la emigración italiana en América Latina. (*Anu. IEHS,* 12, 1997, p. 223–247)

Careful, well-conceived longitudinal examination of the place of Italians in Latin American Catholicism. Relies heavily on published works in Italian, Spanish, and Portuguese.

936 Routes to slavery: direction, ethnicity, and mortality in the transatlantic slave trade. Edited by David Eltis and David Richardson. London; Portland, Ore.: Frank Cass, 1997. 151 p.: bibl., ill., index. (Studies in slave and post-slave societies and cultures)

Impressive research and scholarly analysis provide the foundations for these seven essays that utilize the slave trade data in the Du Bois Institute with focal points on Jamaica and colonial Louisiana.

937 Rueda Hernanz, Germán. Españoles emigrantes en América, siglos XVI-XX. Con la colaboración de Consuelo Soldevilla. Madrid: Arco Libros, 2000. 94 p.: bibl., maps. (Cuadernos de historia; 82)

Broad overview of immigration patterns with good balance between colonial and postindependence periods. More statistical than narrative with an impressive scholarly bibliography.

938 Ruiz Acosta, María José. Hispanoamérica en la prensa sevillana: el reflejo público de una crisis, 1898–1914. Sevilla, Spain: Area de Cultura, Ayuntamiento de Sevilla, 1997. 335 p.: bibl.

This well-researched study provides an important perspective on the coverage of South America by Sevilla's press (mainly newspaper) during a critical period. Includes discussion of migration, economic contacts, and the expanding role of the US.

939 Ruiz-Peinado Alonso, José Luis. Insurrecciones negras. (*in* Encuentro-Debate América Latina ayer y hoy = Trobada-Debat Amèrica Llatina ahir i avui, *6th, Barcelona, Spain, 1997.* Lo que duele es el olvido: recuperando la memoria de América Latina = El que dol és l'oblit: recuperant la memòria d'Amèrica Llatina. Barcelona, Spain: Univ. de Barcelona, 1998, p. 191–208, bibl.)

Slave uprisings in Brazil's Bahia placed within the larger framework of African and African-American uprisings in Latin America in general.

940 Sagrera, Martín. Los racismos en las Américas: una interpretación histórica. Madrid: IEPALA, 1998. 384 p.: bibl.

The extensive examination of racism and racial attitudes spans half a millennium with emphasis on the 19th-20th centuries. The author's command of published writing from the nations of the Americas and Europe brings considerable weight to his analysis.

Approximately one-third of the text concerns the interaction of the US and Latin America.

941 Salvatore, Ricardo Donato. The strength of markets in Latin America's sociopolitical discourses, 1750–1850: some preliminary observations. (*Lat. Am. Perspect.*, 26:1, Jan. 1999, p. 22–43, bibl.)

Valuable interpretive essay on discussions and policy decisions regarding the role of the market in Latin America, with special attention to the Bourbon era and the 19th century.

942 Sandoval Rodríguez, Isaac. Historia e historiografía en América Latina. Santa Cruz, Bolivia: Sirena color, 1999. 187 p.: bibl.

This approach to Latin American historiography is mainly concerned with the political history of Bolivia and Venezuela in the national period and the implications of the new economic history.

943 Saturno Canelón, Jesús. Barberos y sucesores: medio milenio de odontología en Iberoamérica. Odontología tradicional en una zona rural venezolana: estudio de casos por Neizer Toro de Vieira. Caracas: Monte Avila Editores Latinoamericana, 1996. 303 p.: bibl., ill.

Two different but related studies make up this volume. The first is a very general history of dentistry in Latin America with emphasis on the influence of US medical practices and on public health issues. The second is a case study from the state of Guarico in Venezuela that explores the practice of folk medicine (much of the information is from interviews).

944 The second conquest of Latin America: coffee, henequen, and oil during the export boom, 1850–1930. Edited by Steven C. Topik and Allen Wells. Austin: Univ. of Texas Press, 1998. 271 p.: bibl., ill., index, map. (ILAS critical reflections on Latin America series)

One of the best collections of thematic readings published in recent years, this volume contains specialized studies of key export products as well as multinational corporate structures. Beginning students and experienced scholars alike will benefit from the trenchant introductory and concluding essays. Includes a helpful 15-page bibliography. For international relations specialist's comment, see *HLAS 59:4207.*

945 Sherman, John W. Latin America in crisis. Boulder, Colo.: Westview Press, 2000. 217 p.: bibl., index, maps.

This compact introductory text is intended for university classrooms. The author openly states that he has adopted a provocative approach, providing students with a challenging leftist perspective.

946 Skidmore, Thomas E. Studying the history of Latin America: a case of hemispheric convergence. (*LARR*, 33:1, 1998, p. 105–127, bibl.)

This review of major Latin American history textbooks in English, Spanish, and Portuguese published from the 1950s-1990s provides trenchant observations on ideology as well as historiography.

947 Strange pilgrimages: exile, travel, and national identity in Latin America, 1800–1990's. Edited by Ingrid Elizabeth Fey and Karen Racine. Wilmington, Del.: Scholarly Resources, 2000. 258 p.: bibl., ill. (Jaguar books on Latin America; 22)

This exceptionally valuable reader contains a collection of articles on the responses of Latin American intellectuals to their travels in foreign lands and their related quests for their own national identity.

948 Sustentos, aflicciones y postrimerías de los indios de América. Recopilación de Manuel Gutiérrez Estévez. Madrid: Casa de América, 2000. 468 p.: bibl. (Diálogos amerindios)

This collection of scholarly articles and essays spans the centuries from the pre-columbian epoch to the present. Most of the contributions have footnotes and/or bibliography. In addition to the topics mentioned in the title, this volume has a section on religion, especially evangelism, in the 20th century.

949 Symposium Internacional de Historia de la Masonería Española, 8th, Barcelona, 1997. La masonería española y la crisis colonial del 98. v. 1–2. Zaragoza, Spain: Centro de Estudios Históricos de Masonería Española, Univ. de Zaragoza, 1999. 2 v. (1174 p.): bibl., ill., 1 map, music.

About half of the 63 articles in this collection deal with the crises of the Spanish colonial system in the 1890s, including some interesting work on masonry in Cuba and the Philippines. Most of the articles are foot-

noted. This volume has neither an introduction nor a concluding essay.

950 Tabanera, Nuria. Conmemoración e historiografía: los estudios sobre emigración española a América Latina en el Quinto Centenario. (*Estud. Migr. Latinoam.*, 13:38, abril 1998, p. 3–15)

Explanation of the lack of development in the field of immigration studies in Spain in the 20th century.

951 Tabanera, Nuria; Joan del Alcázar; and Gonzalo Cáceres. Las primeras democratizaciones en América Latina: Argentina y Chile, 1880–1930. Valencia, Spain: Tirant lo Blanch: Univ. de Valencia, 1997. 232 p.: bibl. (Estudios iberoamericanos. Historia; 1)

The three authors of this well-written study provide an effective synthesis of the political and cultural environments in which democratization appeared in these two countries. The coverage of Chile extends to the revival of authoritarianism in the 1927–1931 era. Thoroughly footnoted, based mainly on published monographs.

952 Taboada, Hernán. Un orientalismo periférico: viajeros latinoamericanos, 1786–1920. (*Estud. Asia Afr.*, 33:2, mayo/agosto 1998, p. 285–305)

Important pioneering examination of Latin American travelers to the Orient. Based largely on published travel accounts.

953 Topik, Steven. Coffee anyone?: recent research on Latin American coffee societies. (*HAHR*, 80:2, May 2000, p. 225–266)

Perceptive historiographical essay that emphasizes the importance of and difficulties involved in generalizations about the economics and sociology of coffee production.

954 Topik, Steven. The construction of market society in Latin America: natural process or social engineering. (*Lat. Am. Perspect.*, 26:1, Jan. 1999, p. 3–21, bibl.)

This introductory essay to a thematically organized issue of the journal *Latin American Perspectives* is also an insightful analysis of the limited impact of the free market and neoclassical economics in Latin America history.

Torres, Mauro. América Latina, dos veces herida en sus orígenes. See item **823**.

955 Vitale, Luis. Historia social comparada de los pueblos de América Latina. v. 1, Pueblos originarios y colonia. v. 2, Independencia y formación social republicana, siglo XIX. v. 3, Del nacionalismo al neoliberalismo, 1900–1990. Punta Arenas, Chile: Comercial Atelí: Ediciones Plaza, 1998–99. 3 v.: bibl.

Respected Chilean historian Vitale has produced an impressive synthesis of Latin American history that centers on social structure and ethnic groups, but also gives appropriate attention to international conflicts in the 19th-20th centuries, the women's movement, the rise of Marxism, daily life and popular culture, and a critical assessment of neoliberalism in the last decade of the 20th century.

COLONIAL

956 Alberro, Solange. Aculturación de españoles en la América colonial. (*Anu. Estud. Soc.*, 95, 1996, p. 11–37)

Subjective essay on the response of the Spanish nation to native American culture. Suggestive observations but lacks footnotes and bibliography.

957 Alvar, Manuel. Los otros cronistas de Indias. Madrid: Agencia Española de Cooperación Internacional: Ediciones de Cultura Hispánica, 1996. 117 p.: bibl. (Historia)

Interesting selections exerpted from 650 letters written from America by a socially diverse group of correspondents. Selections arranged topically with commentary on each letter by Alvar.

958 Álvarez Peláez, Raquel. Felipe II, la ciencia y el Nuevo Mundo. (*Rev. Indias*, 59:215, enero/abril 1999, p. 9–30)

Focus is on navigation, mining, and natural sciences in the late 1500s. Based on published sources and monographs.

959 Andrés-Gallego, José. Esquilache y el pan, 1766. New Orleans, La.: Univ. Press of the South, 1996. 238 p.: bibl. (Iberian studies; 1)

Imperial policy, economics, and sociology are intertwined in this examination of food shortages and popular protest in the 1760s. Includes considerable archival research.

960 Angulo Morales, Alberto. La influencia del tabaco americano en la España del Antiguo Regimén, siglos XVI-XVII. (*Iberoamericana/Tokyo*, 21:1, primer semestre 1999, p. 45–68, bibl.)

A very general overview of the consumption of tobacco and the government's role in its production and sale.

961 Assadourian, Carlos Sempat. Hacia la *sublimis deus:* las discordias entre los dominicos indianos y el enfrentamiento del franciscano Padre Tastera con el Padre Betanzos. (*Hist. Mex./México*, 47:3, enero/marzo 1998, p. 465–536, appendix)

Extensive examination of the clerical discussion of the nature of native Americans with considerable attention to the observations of Betanzos. Also includes the text of the 1532 Betanzos memorial to the Council of the Indies.

962 Barros Franco, José Miguel. La incursión de Richard Hawkins en Hispanoamérica y su epílogo. (*Rev. Hist. Nav.*, 17:65, 1999, p. 63–77)

Historical sketch of Hawkins' activities on the west coast of South America in the 1590s.

963 Bataillon, Marcel. La América colonial en su historia y literatura. v. 1. Lima: Pontificia Univ. Católica del Perú, Fondo Editorial, 1998. 1 v.: bibl.

A convenient collection of several of Bataillon's less accessible writings. Includes a 30-page introduction by Mercedes Lopez-Baralt and a 65-page chronological bibliography.

964 Batllori, Miguel. Iberoamèrica: del descobrimento a la independèndencia. Edició a cura d'Eulàlia Duran i Josep Solervicens. Pròleg de Pere Grases. València, Spain: Tres i Quatre, 1999. 543 p.: bibl. (Obra completa; 14) (Biblioteca d'estudis i investigacions; 31)

Religion and the movements for independence are emphasized in this survey of the colonial period. Includes a 134-page annotated bibliography.

965 Bernabéu Albert, Salvador and **Manuel Lucena Giraldo.** Recordando a Francisco de Solano. (*Rev. Indias*, 57:209, enero/abril 1997, p. 7–19)

Respectful tributes to the prolific Spanish Latin Americanist, including bibliographical commentary.

966 Bohn Martins, Maria Cristina. Entre a diversão e a doutrinação: as festas na Hispano-América colonial. (*Estud. Ibero-Am./Porto Alegre*, 25:1, junho 1999, p. 93–112)

Interpretive essay on the social and cultural functions of festivals in the colonial era.

967 Brading, D.A. Patriotism and the nation in colonial Spanish America. (*in* Constructing collective identities and shaping public spheres: Latin American paths. Edited by Luis Roniger and Mario Sznajder. Brighton, England; Portland, Ore.: Sussex Academic Press, 1998, p. 13–45, bibl.)

An impressive examination of the many manifestations of patriotism (as distinct from full-blown nationalism) in the colonial era.

968 Brown, Jonathan C. Latin America: a social history of the colonial period. Fort Worth, Tex.: Harcourt College Publishers, 2000. 495 p.: bibl., ill., maps.

This exceptionally well-written survey provides exactly what the title promises by drawing from recently published scholarly monographs. Includes an interesting section on social change in the 1700s.

969 Brown, Kendall W. El estudio de la historia de los precios en la América española colonial: metodología y oportunidades. (*Am. Lat. Hist. Econ. Bol. Fuentes*, 5, enero/junio 1996, p. 19–30)

Exploration in quantitative methodology based on extensive examination of recent publications in the field.

970 Calvo, Thomas. Santuarios y devociones: entre dos mundos, siglos XVI-XVIII. (*in* Coloquio de Antropología e Historia Regionales, *17th, Zamora, Mexico, 1995*. La Iglesia Católica en México. Zamora, Mexico: El Colegio de Michoacán; México: Secretaría de Gobernación, Subsecretaría de Asuntos Jurídicos y Asociaciones Religiosas, Dirección General de Asuntos Religiosos, 1997, p. 365–379)

Discussion of the transfer from Spain to the Americas of the religious practices and values associated with *marianismo*.

971 Cañizares-Esguerra, Jorge. How to write the history of the New World: histories, epistemologies, and identities in the eighteenth-century Atlantic world. Stanford, Calif.: Stanford Univ. Press, 2001. 468 p.: bibl., ill. (some col.), maps. (Cultural sitings)

This penetrating examination of 18th-century historiography probes the works of writers on both sides of the Atlantic. Prominent issues include the image of native American civilizations.

972 Cañizares-Esguerra, Jorge. New World, new stars: patriotic astrology and the invention of Indian and Creole bodies in colonial Spanish America, 1600–1650. (*Am. Hist. Rev.*, 104:1, Feb. 1999, p. 33–68, facsims., plates)

A stimulating examination of colonial astronomy and astrology and their roles in the attempts by Spaniard and Creole to explore the differences between the populations in the New World and in Europe.

973 Las casas de moneda en los reinos de Indias. v. 1, Las cecas indianas en 1536–1825. v. 2, Cecas de Fundaciones Temprana. Madrid: Museo Casa de la Moneda, 1996–97? 2 v.: bibl., ill.

These volumes cover in impressive depth the establishment of mints and the evolution of metallic currency in the Spanish Empire. Topics include the administration and the technical operations of the mints. Vol. 2 features individual studies of mints in Mexico City, Santiago, Lima, and Potosí. Extensive archival research. Complete work contains 3 vols.

974 Ceballos Gómez, Diana Luz. Gobernar las Indias: por una historia social de la normalización. (*Hist. Soc./Medellín*, 5, dic. 1998, p. 149–195, ill., map)

A general discussion of the origins and use of power within the Spanish colonial political system drawing heavily from social science concepts as well as published historical studies. Provocative approach that may inspire some debate.

975 Cervera Pery, José. La Casa de Contratación y el Consejo de Indias: las razones de un superministerio. Madrid: Ministerio de Defensa, 1997. 188 p.: bibl., ill. (Colección Aula de navegantes)

Institutional study that emphasizes the diversification of functions of the Casa. Mainly a synthesis of previous publications.

976 Chocano Mena, Magdalena. La América colonial, 1492–1763: cultura y vida cotidiana. Madrid: Editorial Síntesis, 2000. 287 p.: bibl. (Historia de España, 3er. milenio; 19)

Well-organized survey text addresses issues relating to material inequity, gender, and the family.

977 Clément, Jean-Pierre and Raúl Rodríguez Nozal. L'Espagne apothicaire de l'Europe: l'exploitation médico-commerciale des ressources végétales américaines a la fin du XVIII siècle. (*Bull. hisp./Bordeaux,* 98:1, 1996, p. 137–159)

The interaction of botany, pharmacology, and commercial monopoly are emphasized in this insightful essay in medical history. Considerable attention given to quinine.

978 Cohen, Mario Eduardo. América colonial judía. Buenos Aires: Centro de Investigación y Difusión de Cultura Sefardí, 2000. 203 p.: bibl., ill. (some col.), maps (some col.).

Thoughtfully organized survey text supported by extensive footnotes and a bibliography. Well-written. Also includes British North America.

979 Colonial lives: documents on Latin American history, 1550–1850. Edited by Richard E. Boyer and Geoffrey Spurling. New York: Oxford Univ. Press, 2000. 368 p.: bibl., ill., maps.

Nicely integrated set of articles focuses on the social and economic aspects of ordinary folk in the colonial era. This book includes footnotes for each article and is intended for university courses.

980 Colonial Spanish America: a documentary history. Edited by Kenneth Mills and William B. Taylor. Wilmington, Del.: Scholarly Resources, 1998. 372 p.: ill., index.

Designed as a university textbook, this edited volume combines excerpts from primary sources and scholarly articles. Well-chosen illustrations are accompanied by editorial explanations that connect them to larger historical themes. A promising approach to undergraduate education.

Colonialism past and present: reading and writing about colonial Latin America today. See item **3361**.

981 Las colonias del Nuevo Mundo: discursos imperiales. Compilación de Carmen Perilli. San Miguel de Tucumán, Argentina: Instituto Interdisciplinario de Estudios Latinoamericanos, Univ. Nacional de Tucumán, 1999. 282 p.: bibl., maps. (Estudios coloniales)

Diverse collection of articles and thought pieces covering not only imperial/political aspects of the colonial period, but also social and cultural history.

982 Congreso Internacional Las Sociedades Ibéricas y el Mar a Finales del Siglo XVI, *Lisbon, Portugal, 1998.* Congreso Internacional. t. 6, Las Indias. Spain: Los Centenarios de Felipe II y Carlos V; Lisboa: Pabellón de España, Expo '98, 1998. 1 v.: bibl., ill., maps.

Wide range of topics from navigation to art history. Most of Vol. 6 deals with the Spanish colonial system. Emphasis is on economic issues, such as mining, trade, and piracy. The color illustrations in the catalog portion are especially vivid.

983 La conquête de l'Amérique espagnole et la question du droit. Textes réunis par Carmen Val Julián. Fontenay-aux-Roses, France: ENS éditions, 1996. 144 p.: bibl. (Feuillets de l'ENS Fontenay/Saint-Cloud, 1254–9878)

Six thoughtful scholarly articles explore the legal and moral questions surrounding the Spanish conquest.

984 Cook, Noble David. Born to die: disease and New World conquest, 1492–1650. Cambridge; New York: Cambridge Univ. Press, 1998. 261 p.: bibl., ill. (New approaches to the Americas)

Effective synthesis of scholarly works on the spread of European diseases in the Americas. The prose is measured and understated, but the overall impact of this book is compelling.

985 Crónicas de Indias: antología. Recopilación de Mercedes Serna. Madrid: Cátedra, 2000. 527 p.: bibl. (Letras hispánicas; 483)

An interesting anthology drawn from the writings of the chroniclers.

986 **De Cesare, Michele.** El debate sobre el "indio" y las instituciones españolas en el Nuevo Mundo. Salerno, Italy: Edizioni del paguro, 1999. 131 p.: bibl. (Mare occidentale; 2)

Brief, well-organized summary of a familiar topic: the status and treatment of indigenous peoples under Spanish colonial rule. Based on secondary sources.

987 **Deans-Smith, Susan.** Culture, power, and society in colonial Mexico. (*LARR*, 33:1, 1998, p. 257–277)

Unusually penetrating review essay that expands upon the diverse but interrelated themes of symbolism-ideology, gender, race, the law, and the Church.

988 **Deveau, Jean-Michael.** European slave trading in the eighteenth century. (*Diogenes/Oxford*, 45:3, 1997, p. 49–74)

Succinct evaluation of the role of European nations and the US in the slave trade, and a trenchant analysis of the relationship between the slave trade and capitalism.

989 **Domínguez Ortiz, Antonio.** Estudios americanistas. Madrid: Real Academia de la Historia, 1998. 350 p.: bibl. (Clave historial; 7)

Convenient republication of a dozen of the author's articles on a variety of topics in colonial history.

990 **Domínguez Ortiz, Antonio.** La sociedad americana y la corona española en el siglo XVII. Spain: M. Pons: Asociación Francisco López de Gómara, 1996? 193 p.: bibl. (La corona y los pueblos americanos; 7)

Thematic social history that, in spite of its brevity, provides a commendable survey of topics such as nobles and encomenderos, the Church, the condition of indigenous peoples, mestizos, and African-Americans, as well as various roles of the colonial government.

991 **Entre dos mundos: fronteras culturales y agentes mediadores.** Coordinación de Berta Ares Queija y Serge Gruzinski. Sevilla, Spain: Escuela de Estudios Hispano-Americanos, Consejo Superior de Investigaciones Científicas, 1997. 450 p.: bibl. (Publicaciones de la Escuela de Estudios Hispano-Americanos de Sevilla; 388)

Social and cultural perspectives predominate in this well-conceived collection

of articles that strikes a reasonable balance of archival research and textual explication. Themes include mestizaje, missionary work, and art history.

992 **The faces of honor: sex, shame, and violence in colonial Latin America.** Edited by Lyman L. Johnson and Sonya Lipsett-Rivera. Albuquerque: Univ. of New Mexico Press, 1998. 250 p.: bibl., ill., maps. (Diálogos)

An engaging and exceptionally well-focused collection of essays explores the often-neglected concept of honor in the colonial era. This book has much of value on gender, the family, and general social history.

993 **Fajardo Ortiz, Guillermo.** Los caminos de la medicina colonial en Iberoamérica y las Filipinas. México: UNAM, Coordinación de Humanidades, Facultad de Medicina, 1996. 171 p.: bibl.

Useful synthesis based on published documents and monographs. Includes 27-page bibliographical essay.

994 **Gálvez Ruiz, María Angeles.** La fiscalidad y el mercado interno colonial en la historiografía americanista. (*Anu. Estud. Am.*, 55:2, julio/dic. 1998, p. 653–675)

An extensive review of major scholarly publications is the foundation for this examination of an important but often elusive and controversial economic topic.

995 **Garcés, Carlos Alberto.** El cuerpo como texto: la problemática del castigo corporal en el siglo XVIII. San Salvador de Jujuy, Argentina: Editorial Univ. de Jujuy, 1999. 238 p.: bibl.

Based on archival research in Argentina and Bolivia and inspired by the writing of Foucault, this innovative and disturbing monograph probes some of the darker recesses of the colonial legal system.

996 **García Bernal, Manuela Cristina.** Las élites capitulares indianas y sus mecanismos de poder en el siglo XVII. (*Anu. Estud. Am.*, 57:1, enero/junio 2000, p. 89–110)

Extensive examination of criollo elite participation in local government and bureaucratic politics. Based on published works.

997 **González Casasnovas, Ignacio.** Documentación eclesiástica para la historia iberoamericana en archivos españoles: nuevos instrumentos de investigación, 1990–1997. (*Rev. Complut. Hist. Am.*, 24, 1998, p. 271–287, bibl.)

This descriptive listing of documents in Spanish archives will be of much interest to specialists in church history.

998 **Grunberg, Bernard.** Les noirs et l'Inquisition en Amérique hispanique, XVIe-XVIIe siècles: problèmes d'interprétation à travers quelques publications récentes. (*in* Esclavages: histoire d'une diversité de l'océan Indien à l'Atlantique sud. Coordination de Katia de Queiros Mattoso. Paris: Harmattan, 1997, p. 143–153, table)

Brief synthesis based on published monographs describes the experience of blacks with the Inquisition.

999 **Gutiérrez Carbó, Arturo S.** Los 7/8 del témpano: lo sumergido del proceso descubridor de América por Europa 1492–1503. (*Rev. Hist. Am./México*, 121, 1996, p. 59–81, bibl., maps, table)

A well-organized but rather mechanistic examination of the growth of knowledge about America among learned observers in Europe.

1000 **Gutiérrez Escudero, Antonio.** Acerca del proyectismo y del reformismo borbónico en Santo Domingo. (*Temas Am.*, 13, 1997, p. 17–30)

Thoroughly researched overview of Bourbon reforms, especially in the areas of agriculture, mining, ship construction, and trade.

1001 **Herzog, Tamar.** *A stranger in a strange land:* the conversion of foreigners into members in colonial Latin America. (*in* Constructing collective identities and shaping public spheres: Latin American paths. Edited by Luis Roniger and Mario Sznajder. Brighton, England; Portland, Ore.: Sussex Academic Press, 1998, p. 46–64, bibl.)

This examination of naturalization policies in Spanish America includes some archival research as well as a survey of published monographs. Also provides a comparative study of the policies as practiced in Spanish America and in Spain.

1002 **Historia general de América Latina.** v. 1, Las sociedades originarias. v. 2, El primer contacto y la formación de nuevas sociedades. Madrid: Editorial Trotta; Paris: Ediciones UNESCO, 1999–2000. 2 v.: ill., maps.

These two volumes contain 45 articles that cover a wide range of topics in the colonial era from the origins of European expansionism to epidemic diseases, slavery, and mestizaje to the organization of the colonial governments and the colonial economy. Many of these articles rely on primary research. The editors and authors gave considerable attention to effective generalizations on large themes.

1003 **Horna, Hernán.** La indianidad = The indigenous world before Latin Americans. Introduction by Jane Rausch. Princeton, N.J.: Markus Wiener Publishers, 2001. 179 p.: bibl., ill., index, maps.

English translation of the author's *La indianidad antes de la independencia latinoamerica* (1999) is a somewhat unconventional thought piece on the character of indigenous societies before, during, and after the Spanish invasion, highlighting Mesoamerica and the Americas. [R. Haskett/S. Wood]

Ibsen, Kristine. Women's spiritual autobiography in colonial Spanish America. See item 1172.

1004 **Instituto Internacional de Historia del Derecho Indiano. Congreso. *11th*, Buenos Aires, Argentina, 4 al 9 de septiembre de 1995.** Actas y estudios. Buenos Aires: Instituto de Investigaciones de Historia del Derecho, 1997. 4 v.: bibl.

Impressive scholarship highlights this extensive collection. Focuses on southern South America, but New Spain, Puerto Rico, Caracas, and the Philippines are included along with some interesing general essays.

1005 **Jackson, Robert H.** Race, caste, and status: Indians in colonial Spanish America. Albuquerque: Univ. of New Mexico Press, 1999. 162 p.: bibl.

Jackson's in-depth research on native American communities in the Valle Bajo of Bolivia, and in Sonora and Baja California in northwestern New Spain, serve as the foundation for this perceptive study of status and identity.

1006 The Jews and the expansion of Europe to the west, 1450 to 1800. Edited by Paolo Bernardini and Norman Fiering. New York: Berghahn Books, 2001. 582 p.: bibl., ill., maps. (European expansion and global interaction; v. 2)

This thick, well-edited volume testifies to the Jewish presence in intellectual and cultural history as well as in commerce. Commendable quality of research in these 25 articles.

1007 Keen, Benjamin. Essays in the intellectual history of colonial Latin America. Boulder, Colo.: Westview Press, 1998. 256 p.: bibl., index.

A convenient collection of 11 of Keen's essays originally published between 1959–94. Includes some of his sparring with Lewis Hanke. The author has revised some of the essays. Much historiographical value.

1008 Labastida, Jaime. Una jornada de trabajo de Alexander von Humboldt: su método científico. (*Cuad. Am./México,* 13:76, julio/agosto 1999, p. 44–52)

Brief commentary on Humboldt's use of the scientific method.

1009 Lane, Kris E. Pillaging the empire: piracy in the Americas, 1500–1750. Armonk, N.Y.: M.E. Sharpe, 1998. 251 p.: bibl. (Latin American realities)

Well-written synthesis that captures the excitement of an inherently interesting topic. Heyn, Hawkins, Drake, Morgan, and Teach emerge within their appropriate historical contexts including imperial defensive strategies. Suited for the university classroom and general readership.

1010 Langenscheidt, Adolphus. Los hornos para la metalurgia del plomo en América, siglos X a XVII. (*Quipu/México,* 12:2, mayo/agosto 1999, p. 231–250, facsims., ill.)

Informative study of the development of lead mining and metallurgy in both Mesoamerica and the Andes. The bulk of the article deals with the precontact era, giving attention to mining techniques and the methods used to smelt the ore. The ways in which indigenous techniques were incorporated into colonial smelting practices are also discussed, as are more technical aspects of the process. [R. Haskett/S. Wood]

1011 Lenkersdorf, Gudrun. La carrera por las especias. (*Estud. Hist. Novohisp.,* 17, 1997, p. 13–30, bibl.)

Solidly researched examination of the impact of the spice trade on some of the early Portuguese and Spanish voyages to the Americas.

1012 Levaggi, Abelardo. Un derecho matrimonial indiano para protestantes. (*Jahrb. Gesch. Staat Wirtsch. Ges. Lat.am.,* 33, 1996, p. 129–138)

Includes "La Real Instrucción del 30 Noviembre de 1792" and Levaggi's analysis of this document as an indication of Spain's attitude toward Protestants in the late colonial era.

1013 Levaggi, Abelardo. Los tratados con los indios en la época borbónica: reafirmación de la política de conquista pacífica. (*in* Congreso del Instituto Internacional de Historia del Derecho Indiano, *11th,* *Buenos Aires, 1995.* Actas y estudios. Buenos Aires: Instituto de Investigaciones de Historia del Derecho, 1997, v. 2, p. 103–118)

Archival research supports this cogent examination of an important aspect of Spanish colonial policy toward native American communities.

1014 Lira Montt, Luis. El estatuto de limpieza de sangre en el derecho indiano. (*in* Congreso del Instituto Internacional de Historia del Derecho Indiano, *11th,* *Buenos Aires, 1995.* Actas y estudios. Buenos Aires: Instituto de Investigaciones de Historia del Derecho Indiano, 1997, v. 4, p. 31–47)

Competent, straightforward legal history.

Lockhart, James. Of things of the Indies: essays old and new in early Latin American history. See item **548.**

1015 Lucena Salmoral, Manuel. El derecho de coartación del esclavo en la América española. (*Rev. Indias,* 59:216, mayo/agosto 1999, p. 357–374)

Archival sources undergird this study of the legal problems surrounding slaves' exercise of their right to purchase their freedom.

1016 Lucena Salmoral, Manuel. La instrucción sobre educación, trato y ocupaciones de los esclavos de 1789; una prueba del poder de los amos de esclavos frente a la debilidad de la Corona española. (*Estud. Hist. Soc. Econ. Am.*, 13, 1996, p. 155–178)

Extensive research in the Archivo General de Indias forms the basis for this fine article on legal and social history of slavery in colonial Latin America.

1017 Luque Talaván, Miguel. La avería en el tráfico marítimo-mercantil indiano: notas para su estudio, siglos XVI-XVIII. (*Rev. Complut. Hist. Am.*, 24, 1998, p. 113–145)

Well-organized article on the historiography, etiology, and history of the administrative aspects of this specific area in maritime law. Extensive footnotes.

1018 MacLeod, Murdo J. Self-promotion: the *relaciones de méritos y servicios* and their historical and political interpretation. (*CLAHR*, 7:1, Winter 1998, p. 25–42)

MacLeod discusses these documents as sources for social, economic, and political analysis. A valuable exploration in historiography.

1019 Malagón Barceló, Javier and **Manuel Díaz-Marta Pinilla.** El reino de Toledo en el poblamiento y ordenación del nuevo mundo. Toledo, Spain: Institución Provincial de Investigaciones y Estudios Toledanos, 1996. 200 p.: bibl., ill. (Serie Ia.- Monografías; 41)

A strong biographical approach characterizes these two essays, which discuss viceroy Francisco de Toledo and Father Diego de Landa.

1020 Mariluz Urquijo, José María. El agente de la administración pública en Indias. Buenos Aires: Instituto Internacional de Historia del Derecho Indiano: Instituto de Investigaciones de Historia del Derecho, 1998. 490 p.: bibl.

Institutional study of Spanish colonial officials that includes such topics as selection, remuneration, and removal from service. Based on archival research and published monographs.

1021 Mena García, María del Carmen. Sevilla y el abasto de víveres a las flotas de indias: la armada de Castilla del Oro en 1514. (*in* Raíces de la memoria: América Latina, ayer y hoy, quinto encuentro debate = Amèrica Latina, ahir i avui, cinquena

trobada debat. Coordinación de Pilar García Jordán *et al*. Barcelona: Univ. de Barcelona, 1996, p.147–159, tables)

In-depth case study of the provisioning of a 1514 fleet reinforced by three detailed charts that include quantity, price, and place of origin of the key commodities.

1022 Las minas hispanoamericanas a mediados del siglo XVIII: informes enviados al Real Gabinete de Historia Natural de Madrid. Contribuciones de Isabel Galor *et al*. Madrid: Iberoamericana; Frankfurt: Vervuert, 1998. 244 p.: bibl., maps. (Veröffentlichungen aus dem Deutschen Bergbau-Museum Bochum; 65) (Berliner Lateinamerika-Forschungen, 10)

Contains 13 documents from the 1750s accompanied by thorough introductory commentaries, useful editorial annotations, and an extensive bibliography.

1023 Mira Caballos, Esteban. La Armada Guardacostas de Andalucía y la defensa de la Carrera de Indias, 1521–1555. Prólogo por Adolfo L. González Rodríguez. Sevilla, Spain: Muñoz Moya Editor, 1998. 104 p.: bibl. (Colección Biblioteca americana)

Precisely focused institutional study based on archival sources. Examines in considerable detail the finances, ships, armaments, and crews.

1024 Mira Caballos, Esteban. Indios americanos en el Reino de Castilla: 1492–1550. (*Temas Am.*, 14, 1998, p. 1–8, tables)

Primary research provides the information for the central theme of this balanced article on indigenous peoples that includes both descriptive narrative and quantitative analysis.

1025 Montané Martí, Julio C. El mito conquistado: Alvar Núñez Cabeza de Vaca. Hermosillo, Mexico: Univ. de Sonora, 1999. 559 p.: bibl., maps. (Colección Alforja del tiempo; 4)

Editorial footnotes and textual explication enhance this publication of the essential documents related to the story of Cabeza de Vaca. A useful chronological bibliography is also included.

1026 Narvaja, Benito R. and **Luisa V. Pinotti.** Violencia, población e identidad en la colonización de América hispánica:

las secuelas demográficas de la conquista. Buenos Aires: Univ. de Buenos Aires, Ofio cina de publicaciones del CBC, 1996. 84 p.: bibl., ill.

Brief, pointed summation of the demography of the conquest accompanied by an interesting attempt to define native American identity in terms of linguistic factors and census material.

1027 Navarro García, Luis. La crisis del reformismo borbónico bajo Carlos IV. (*Temas Am.*, 13, 1997, p. 1–16)

General study that emphasizes the role of Floridablanca, based mainly on published sources.

1028 Normas y leyes de la ciudad hispanoamericana. v. 1, 1492–1600. v. 2, 1601–1821. Madrid: Consejo Superior de Investigaciones Científicas, Centro de Estudios Históricos, 1996. 2 v.: bibl. (Biblioteca de historia de América; 13, 16)

This publication of 192 documents is especially suitable for undergraduate research projects and will also be of help to more advanced students.

1029 Olaechea, Juan Bautista. Gregorio XIII, Felipe II y el mestizaje indiano: calumnia de un franciscano americano contra el rey de España. (*Arch. Ibero-Am.*, 58:230, mayo/agosto 1998, p. 337–352)

The controversies surrounding the entry of mestizos into the priesthood provide the main theme in this well-written article. Based on scholarly monographs and published documents.

1030 Olaechea, Juan Bautista. Una reina contra el sistema: Isabel la Católica y la esclavitud de los indios. (*Arbor/Madrid*, 160:629, mayo 1998, p. 133–170)

Well-argued position paper based on published scholarly works.

1031 El oro y la plata de las Indias en la época de los Austrias. Madrid: Fundación ICO, 1999. 797 p.: bibl., col. ill.

Large, heavily illustrated tome on an exposition in Madrid that includes 41 essays, some of which have considerable scholarly value. The emphasis is on mining and metallurgy, and the photographs of gold and silver items will be of value to those interested in art, as well as those studying economic history and the history of technology.

1032 Ots, Mauricio Valiente. El tratamiento de los no-españoles en las ordenanzas municipales indianas. (*Estud. Hist. Soc. Econ. Am.*, 13, 1996, p. 47–58)

Well-researched and precisely focused legal-administrative study.

1033 Peña Saavedra, Vicente. Indianos precursores de la filantropía docente en Galicia, 1607–1699. (*Rev. Indias*, 59:216, mayo/agosto 1999, p. 375–389, tables)

Detailed archival research is the basis for this examination of philanthropic enterprise.

Pensamiento europeo y cultura colonial. See item **4604**.

1034 Pérez de Tudela y Bueso, Juan. De guerra y paz en las Indias. Madrid: Real Academia de la Historia, 1999. 408 p.: bibl. (Clave historial; 23)

This collection of six of the author's previously published articles concentrates on events in 17th-18th century Brazil, Argentina, and Peru.

1035 Pérez Fernández, Isacio. Bartolomé de las Casas, viajero por dos mundos: su figura, su biografía sincera, su personalidad. Cuzco, Peru: Centro de Estudios Regionales Andinos "Bartolomé de las Casas," 1998. 191 p.: bibl. (Archivos de historia andina, 1022–0879; 30)

An interpretive study that attempts to bring some insights to the immense Las Casas historiography by focusing on the personality of the famous Dominican. Absence of scholarly apparatus will frustrate serious students.

1036 Pérez Samper, María de los Angeles. España y América: el encuentro de dos sistemas alimentarios. (*in* Raíces de la memoria: América Latina, ayer y hoy, quinto encuentro debate = Amèrica Latina, ahir i avui, cinquena trobada debat. Coordinación de Pilar García Jordán et al. Barcelona: Univ. de Barcelona, 1996, p. 171–187)

Interesting discussion of the 1490s and early 1500s that employs numerous quotations from the chroniclers.

1037 Pieper, Renate. Die Vermittlung einer neuen Welt: Amerika im Nachrichtennetz des Habsburgischen Imperiums 1493–1598 ["Mediation" of a New World: America in the Habsbourg Empire's news network]. Mainz, Germany: Verlag P. von Zabern, 2000. 354 p.: bibl., ill., index, maps. (Veröff-entlichungen des Instituts für Europäische Geschichte Mainz; 163)

Source-based study showing how the information about America was propagated in the 16th-century European communication system. Focusing on certain periods (Columbus, Vespucci, etc.) and the spreading of European knowledge about them, the author also keeps in mind the importance of American gold and trading products in Europe. [F. Obermeier]

1038 Piossek Prebisch, Teresa. La antropofagia en América en tiempos de la conquista. (*Rev. Hist. Am./México,* 123, 1998, p. 7–24, bibl.)

Attempts to create an objective discussion of various forms of cannibalism practiced by peoples such as the Aztecs, the Caribbean islanders, and others at the time of the Spanish invasion. [R. Haskett/ S. Wood]

1039 Piqueras Céspedes, Ricardo. Episodios de hambre urbana colonial: las hambrunas de La Isabela, 1494, Santa María La Antigua del Darién, 1514 y Santa María del Buen Aire, 1536. (*Bol. Am./Barcelona,* 38:48, 1998, p. 211–223, bibl.)

Useful comparative study of three early Spanish settlements that experienced difficulties in food supply. Drawn from published sources.

1040 Piqueras Céspedes, Ricardo. Resistencia a la conquista: la guerra del hambre. (*in* Raíces de la memoria: América Latina, ayer y hoy, quinto encuentro debate = Amèrica Llatina, ahir i avui, cinquena trobada debat. Coordinación de Pilar García Jordán *et al.* Barcelona: Univ. de Barcelona, 1996, p. 329–340)

The author places unusually heavy emphasis on the drive for material sustenance as a motive for the Spanish in their campaigns against the native Americans.

1041 Poole, Stafford. The politics of *limpieza de sangre:* Juan de Ovando and his circle in the reign of Philip II. (*Americas/Washington,* 55:3, Jan. 1999, p. 359–389)

Interpretive examination of the origins, impact, and eventual circumvention of this requirement for government positions. Emphasis on the role of Jewish conversos.

1042 Portugal, Ana Raquel Marques da Cunha Martins. A inquisição espanhola e a bruxaria andina: evangelização e resistência. (*Rev. Hist. Reg.,* 4:2, inverno 1999, p. 9–34, bibl.)

Sociology, textual criticism, and history combine effectively in this study of the interaction of the Inquisition and native practices in the 16th-17th centuries.

1043 Prieto Lucena, Ana María. El esclavo negro en la América virreinal. (*in* De puntillas por la historia. Coordinación de Luis Palacios Bañuelos. Córdoba, Spain: Servicio de Publicaciones, Univ. de Córdoba, 1997?, p. 211–234)

Useful sociological profiles drawn from published scholarly works.

1044 Puig-Samper, Miguel Angel. Humboldt, un prusiano en la corte del rey Carlos IV. (*Rev. Indias,* 59:216, mayo/agosto 1999, p. 329–355, appendices)

New archival research supports this study of Humboldt's preparations for his trip to America.

1045 Raminelli, Ronald. Viagens e inventários: tipologia para o período colonial. (*Hist. Quest. Debates,* 17:32, jan./junho 2000, p. 27–46)

Discusses variety of ways in which travel accounts can be used by historians, especially as they produce "inventories" of space, local customs, and the environment. [J. Meznar]

1046 Ramos, Demetrio. El problema de las delimitaciones oceánicas: Tordesillas y su fin. (*Jahrb. Gesch. Staat Wirtsch. Ges. Lat.am.,* 33, 1996, p. 9–25)

Thoughtful analysis of the philosophical origins and political role of the Tordesillas Agreement extending from the 1490s to the 18th century.

1047 Ramos, Elvira. La posesión de la encomienda y otros rituales coloniales españoles en las provincias americanas. (*Bol. Antropol./Mérida,* 46, mayo/agosto 1999, p. 22–38, bibl.)

A brief examination of the use of ritual in the establishment of Spanish authority in the Americas.

1048 Ramos Sosa, Rafael. La fiesta barroca en Ciudad de México y Lima. (*Historia/Santiago*, 30, 1997, p. 263–286, photos)

Art history and religious history are appropriately combined in this essay on the strength and longevity of baroque forms in popular celebrations. The author brings a sophisticated esthetic sense to this evaluative essay.

1049 Real Academia de la Historia (Spain). Servicio de Cartografía y Bellas Artes. Cartografía histórica de América: catálogo de manuscritos, siglos XVIII-XIX. Recopilación de Carmen Manso Porto. Madrid: Real Academia de la Historia, Servicio de Cartografía y Bellas Artes, 1997. 175 p.: bibl., ill. (some col.), maps (some col.).

Profusely illustrated volume also includes detailed descriptions of the maps. Useful for researchers in history and historical geography.

1050 Reding Blase, Sofia. Párrocos y misioneros: precursores coloniales del pensamiento antropológico latinoamericano. Obispado de Choluteca, Honduras: Ediciones Subirana, 1999. 211 p.: bibl. (Colección Rafael Heliodoro Valle; no. 2)

Well-organized discussion of the perception of native Americans among Hispanic writers.

1051 Relaciones de poder y comercio colonial: nuevas perspectivas. Recopilación de Enriqueta Vila Vilar y Allan J. Kuethe. Índices preparado por Ana Isabel Martínez Ortega. Sevilla, Spain: Escuela de Estudios Hispano-Americanos: Texas Tech Univ., 1999. 319 p.: bibl. (Publicaciones de la Escuela de Estudios Hispano-Americanos de Sevilla; 394)

Well-written articles cover consulados, family networks, private companies, and government regulations. Extensive footnoting indicates considerable archival research.

1052 Río Moreno, Justo L. del and **Lorenzo E. López y Sebastián.** Hombres y ganados en la tierra del oro: comienzos de la ganadería en Indias. (*Rev. Complut. Hist. Am.*, 24, 1998, p. 11–45, bibl., graphs, tables)

Helpful synthesis on cattle ranching, an important topic in economic history.

1053 Rodríguez Lorenzo, Sergio. Un capítulo de la historia de la escritura en América: la enseñanza de las *primeras letras*

a los indios en el siglo XVI. (*Anu. Estud. Am.*, 56:1, enero/junio 1999, p. 41–64)

Surveys the educational methods employed in the teaching of literacy to native Americans. Includes some primary research.

1054 Sánchez Gómez, Julio; Guillermo Mira Delli-Zotti; and **Rafael Dobado.** La savia del imperio: tres estudios de economía colonial. Salamanca, Spain: Ediciones Univ. de Salamanca, 1997. 495 p.: bibl., ill. (Acta Salmanticensia. Estudios históricos & geográficos; 102)

Three lengthy essays deal with mining and metallurgy, the Royal Bank of San Carlos de Potosí and mining in Alto Perú, and the quicksilver monopoly in New Spain. All three essays incorporate extensive archival research.

1055 Sanchiz Ochoa, Pilar. El trabajo de la mujer en América. (*in* Jornadas de Estudios Históricos, 7th, *Salamanca, Spain, 1995*. El trabajo en la historia: Séptimas Jornadas de Estudios Históricos organizadas por el Departamento de Historia Medieval, Moderna y Contemporánea de la Univ. de Salamanca. Salamanca, España: Univ. de Salamanca, 1996, p. 252–263)

Pioneering, preliminary survey that concentrates on colonial Guatemala as a case study.

1056 Sanz Tapia, Angel. Aproximación al beneficio de cargos políticos americanos en la primera mitad del siglo XVIII. (*Rev. Complut. Hist. Am.*, 24, 1998, p. 147–176, graphs, tables)

Descriptive essay with strong quantitative content provides an evaluation of Spain's efforts to generate revenue by the sale of government offices.

1057 Seibold, Jorge R. La Sagrada Escritura en la primera evangelización americana: el Sermonario del Padre Valdivia y el teatro bíblico indiano. (*Stromata/San Miguel*, 53:3/4, julio/dic. 1997, p. 251–276)

Clearly drawn portrait of religious conversion experience connected with popular theater. Based largely on published sources.

1058 Sin, crimes, and retribution in early Latin America: a translation and critique of sources—Lope de Aguirre, Francisco de Carvajal, Juan Rodríguez Freyle. Translated by Felix Jay. Lewiston, N.Y.: E. Mellen

Press, 1999. 367 p.: bibl., map. (Latin American studies; v. 4)

This selection of documents contains images of three exceptionally violent individuals. The editors' brief introductions provide literary and historical orientation.

1059 Slatta, Richard W. Spanish colonial military strategy and ideology. (*in* Contested ground: comparative frontiers on the northern and southern edges of the Spanish Empire. Edited by Donna J. Guy and Thomas E. Sheridan. Tucson: Univ. of Arizona Press, 1998, p. 83–96)

Excellent interpretive essay that focuses on the shortcomings of Spanish military policies toward native Americans.

1060 Socolow, Susan Migden. The women of colonial Latin America. Cambridge: New York: Cambridge Univ. Press, 2000. 237 p.: bibl., ill., index. (New approaches to the Americas)

General synthesis of recent research in the vital area of women in Latin America. Covers elite as well as poor women, castas as well as Indians, Iberian as well as African contexts. Follows a mixed chronological and balanced thematic approach, including women in precolumbian societies, conquest and civilization, marriage, religious women, labor, slavery, deviance, and late-18th century reforms. Informative, effective, and readable. [A. Lavrin]

1061 Tabaco y economía en el siglo XVIII. Recopilación de Agustín González Enciso y Rafael Torres Sánchez. Pamplona, Spain: Ediciones Univ. de Navarra, 1999. 496 p.: bibl., ill. (Histórica)

Interrelated set of scholarly articles, with an impressive overview by González Enciso, provides a coherent view of the economics of tobacco production. Articles cover Peru, the Philippines, Mexico, and Cuba. Over half of the contributions deal with Spain. Articles demonstrate archival research and make use of statistical analysis.

1062 Tejera Gaspar, Antonio. Los cuatro viajes de Colón y las Islas Canarias, 1492–1502. Gomera, Canary Islands, Spain: Cabildo de La Gomera, 1998. 167 p.: bibl., ill. (some col.), maps (some col.).

Nicely illustrated and well-organized volume recounting the voyages of Columbus is based on published documents and secondary material.

1063 Torres Aguilar, Manuel. Algunos aspectos del delito de bigamia en la Inquisición de Indias. (*Rev. Inquis.*, 6, 1997, p. 117–138)

Extensive research supports this article that ably combines gender issues with religious and legal history.

1064 Transgressions et stratégies du métissage en Amérique coloniale. Travaux réunis et présentés par Bernard Lavallé. Paris: Presses de la Sorbonne nouvelle, 1999. 248 p.: bibl.

Eleven studies based heavily on archival research approach mestizaje from several angles, including the roles of the frontier, the Catholic Church, and the colonial elite.

1065 Twinam, Ann. Public lives, private secrets: gender, honor, sexuality, and illegitimacy in colonial Spanish America. Stanford, Calif.: Stanford Univ. Press, 1999. 458 p.: bibl., index, maps.

This innovative study of illegitimacy among the Spanish-American elite sheds light on the internal dynamics of family life in the colonial era, as well as on the court system, colonial politics, and social values (particularly the concept of honor). Based on commendable multi-archival research and a firm command of the relevant social science literature.

1066 Valenzuela Márquez, Jaime. Notas sobre la imagen del rey en América colonial: una aproximación a través de la palabra escrita. (*Mapocho/Santiago*, 46, segundo semestre 1999, p. 221–228)

Preliminary study of royal images based on published monographs.

1067 Vega, Garcilaso de la. Comentarios reales. Recopilación, selección, introducción y notas de Mercedes Serna. Madrid: Editorial Castalia, 2000. 493 p.: bibl., ill. (Clásicos Castalia; 252)

This convenient paperback edition includes an extensive, well-footnoted introduction by the editor.

1068 Verdesio, Gustavo. Forgotten conquests: rereading New World history from the margins. Philadelphia: Temple Univ. Press, 2001. 216 p.: bibl.

A close analysis of colonial-era texts that describe the gradual European occupation of the part of South America just north of the Río de la Plata. Scholarly approach that includes considerable commentary on native Americans.

1069 Weber, David J. Borbones y *bárbaros:* centro y periferia en la reformulación de la política de España hacia los indígenas no sometidos. (*Anu. IEHS,* 13, 1998, p. 147–171)

Extending from northern New Spain to Chile, this nuanced study emphasizes innovations in trade and treaties in Spain's dealings with various independent native American groups, but also points out provincial perspectives and priorities in frontier areas. Based on a thorough review of recent scholarship in English and Spanish.

1070 West, Robert C. Aboriginal metallurgy and metalworking in Spanish America: a brief overview. (*in* Mines of silver and gold in the Americas. Edited by Peter Bakewell. Aldershot, Great Britain; Brookfield, Vt.: Variorum, 1997, p. 41–56, bibl., facsims., map)

Well-constructed synthesis of archeology and history emphasizes the relatively sophisticated metallurgy of preconquest native Americans. Based on published scholarly works.

1071 Woodward, Ralph Lee. The new *consulados de comercio* in the Spanish empire, 1778–1829. (*SECOLAS Ann.,* 31, Nov. 1999, p. 5–24)

This article on economic history is thoroughly grounded in archival research and benefits from the author's impressive command of the secondary literature.

1072 Yaqouti, Hamid. Christophe Colomb: une historiographie vivante, 1492–1992. (*Rev. hist./Paris,* 608, oct./déc. 1998, p. 765–793, graphs, tables)

Innovative computer analysis of a portion of the huge Columbus historiography focusing on Spain, France, Italy, and Portugal.

INDEPENDENCE AND 19TH CENTURY

1073 Los abolicionistas españoles: siglo XIX. Recopilación de Enriqueta Vila Vilar y Luisa Vila Vilar. Madrid: Ediciones de Cultura Hispánica, 1996. 151 p.: bibl. (Antología del pensamiento político, social y económico español sobre América Latina; 4)

A varied collection of abolitionist doc-

uments including essays, poetry, speeches, and legislation. Emphasizes Puerto Rico and Cuba.

1074 Adams Fernández, Carmen. La América distorsionada: una visión española de finales del siglo XIX. Oviedo, Spain: Univ. de Oviedo, 1999. 341 p.: bibl., ill., 1 map.

Based on the influential Spanish periodical *La Ilustración Española y Americana* during the years 1875–1900, this scholarly study offers a valuable perspective on the anticolonial struggle in Cuba and the war between Spain and the US. Also provides a broad panorama of the era, including Spanish immigration to Argentina, Cuba, and other Latin America nations and the emergence of major Spanish American cities. Thoroughly footnoted.

Aggarwal, Vinod K. Debt games: strategic interaction in international debt rescheduling. See *HLAS 59:4146.*

1075 Allendesalazar, José Manuel. Apuntes sobre la relación diplomática hispanonorteamericana, 1763–1895. Madrid: Ministerio de Asuntos Exteriores, 1996. 221 p.: bibl., ill., index. (Biblioteca diplomática española. Estudios; 14)

Interesting survey of key episodes in Spanish-US relations, including much material on the southeastern Borderlands and the Caribbean. Drawn from published monographs.

The allure of the foreign: imported goods in postcolonial Latin America. See *HLAS 59:4147.*

1076 Arciniegas Duarte, Orlando. El inicio de las negociaciones entre España y los nuevos estados americanos: la misión de Mariano Montilla, 1834. (*Estud. Hist. Soc. Econ. Am.,* 14, enero/junio 1997, p. 135–150, bibl.)

Archival research undergirds this valuable study of Montilla, who represented Venezuela and opened the way for other Spanish American diplomats in Madrid.

1077 Cañizares-Esguerra, Jorge. Entre el ocio y la feminización tropical: ciencia, élites y estado-nación en Latinoamérica, siglo XIX. (*Asclepio/Madrid,* 50:2, 1998, p. 11–31)

Broadly conceived study primarily

concerned with the gap between elite and subaltern groups in Latin American society, and the impact on the elite groups of Anglo-European perceptions of weaknesses in Latin American culture.

1078 El Caribe y América Latina: el 98 en la coyuntura imperial. v. 1–2. Morelia, Mexico: Instituto de Investigaciones Históricas, Univ. Michoacana de San Nicolás de Hidalgo: Instituto Michoacano de Cultura, Gobierno del Estado de Michoacán; Spain: Consejo Superior de Investigaciones Científicas; Río Piedras: Univ. de Puerto Rico, Recinto de Río Piedras, 1998–99. 2 v.: bibl., ill.

The geographical extent of this set of essays and scholarly articles runs from the Philippines to Gibraltar, but the focus is on Cuba, Puerto Rico, and the repercussions of the Spanish American War on Latin America. Some of the articles are based on archival work so that these two volumes have a varied research base including Spain, the US, Puerto Rico, and Germany.

1079 Carmagnani, Marcello. Elites políticas, sistemas de poder y gobernabilidad en América Latina. (*Metapolítica/ México*, 2:5, enero/marzo 1998, p. 7–16)

A thought piece that deals with the issues of stability and centralization in 19th-century Latin America.

1080 Centeno, Miguel Angel. Blood and debt: war and taxation in nineteenth-century Latin America. (*Am. J. Sociol.*, 102:6, May 1997, p. 1565–1605, graphs, tables)

Well-made argument that wars did not produce powerful central governments in Latin America as contrasted with the experience of Western Europe.

Coerver, Don M. and **Linda Biesele Hall.** Tangled destinies: Latin America and the United States. See *HLAS 59:4158.*

1081 Colmenares, Germán. Las convenciones contra la cultura: ensayos sobre la historiografía hispanoamericana del siglo XIX. 4. ed. Colombia: Univ. del Valle: Banco de la República: Colciencias: TM Editores, 1997. 136 p.: bibl. (Obra completa/Germán Colmenares; 7)

A penetrating examination of the emergence of national identity and the recog-

nition of symbolic heroes within the context of 19th-century historical writing.

1082 Coronas Gonzalez, Santos M. La América Hispana: de la libertad económica a la libertad política, 1765–1810. (*in* Congreso del Instituto Internacional de Historia del Derecho Indiano, *11th, Buenos Aires, 1995.* Actas y estudios. Buenos Aires: Instituto de Investigaciones de Historia del Derecho Indiano, 1997, v. 1, p. 339–359)

Focuses on politics and policies in Spain during this crucial period. Based on published documents and monographs.

1083 Díaz-Trechuelo Spínola, María Lourdes. Bolívar, Miranda, O'Higgins, San Martín: cuatro vidas cruzadas. Madrid: Encuentro Ediciones, 1999. 246 p.: bibl. (Ensayos; 146) (Historia)

Brief, well-organized treatment of the leading figures of the independence era in Spanish South America with emphasis on the personalities of the quartet named in the title and the points of intersection of their lives.

1084 Diener, Pablo and **Maria de Fátima Gomes Costa.** A América de Rugendas: obras e documentos. São Paulo: Estação Liberdade; Livraria Kosmos Editora, 1999. 166 p.: bibl., ill. (some col.).

A biographical sketch, critical commentary, and reproduced documents accompany well-chosen illustrations, many of which are in color.

1085 Farcau, Bruce W. The Ten Cents War: Chile, Peru, and Bolivia in the War of the Pacific, 1879–1884. Westport, Conn.: Praeger, 2000. 214 p.: bibl., index.

A nicely organized and detailed narrative of the military and diplomatic history of a conflict that is often overlooked outside South America. Farcau is even-handed in his treatment of the three belligerents, drawing from works published in all three countries, as well as studies in English.

1086 Filippi, Alberto. España 1898; "la pérdida del Imperio": para una arqueología de un mito historiográfico y de sus usos ideológico-políticos. (*in* Latinoamérica entre el Mediterráneo y el Báltico. México: Instituto Panamericano de Geografía e Historia, Fondo de Cultura Económica, 2000, p. 77–96)

A stimulating survey of the decline of Spain's imperial power in the 19th century, refuting the myth that the opposite was true.

1087 Fradera, Josep Maria. Gobernar colonias. Barcelona: Ediciones Península, 1999. 152 p.: bibl. (Historia, ciencia, sociedad; 282)

Contains five of the author's articles on particular aspects of 19th-century Spanish colonial history. In general, these essays set Spain's policies in the context of the late century surge of European imperialism and provide an interpretation of Spanish colonial reform in Cuba, Puerto Rico, and the Philippines. Well-footnoted with some primary research.

1088 Gouvêa, Maria de Fátima Silva. Revolução e independências: notas sobre o conceito e os processos revolucionários na América Espanhola. (*Estud. Hist./Rio de Janeiro*, 10:20, 1997, p. 275–294, bibl.)

Historiographical study of some of the leading publications on the age of revolution and Spanish America's place within that context. Includes works by historians Palmer, Guerra, Pons, and Bushnell.

1089 Heredia, Edmundo A. El imperio del guano: América Latina ante la guerra de España en el Pacífico. Córdoba, Argentina: Alción, 1998. 246 p.: bibl.

Archival research in Spain, Peru, and Argentina provides a solid foundation for this examination of Spain's campaign on the Pacific coast of South America and its repercussions throughout the hemisphere.

1090 Heredia, Edmundo A. Los vencidos: un estudio sobre los realistas en la guerra de independencia hispanoamericana. Córdoba, Argentina: Programa de Historia de las Relaciones Interamericanas CIFFYH, Univ. Nacional de Córdoba, 1997. 211 p.: bibl.

Archival research in Spain and in Mexico, Argentina, and other Latin American countries buttresses this study of the fate of royalists. Encompasses emigration, loss of property, and the postwar years.

1091 Hermann, Christian. La politique de la France en Amérique latine, 1826–1850: une rencontre manquée. Bordeaux, France: Maison des pays ibériques, 1996. 308 p.: bibl. (Coll. de la Maison des pays ibériques, 0296–7588; 67)

Valuable work based on archival research and a thorough review of secondary sources fills a gap in the history of the Americas. Presents much information on France's response to US expansion into Texas and California and the British-French involvements in La Plata.

1092 Hernández González, Manuel. El Observador español en Londres, un periódico fernandino contra la emancipación americana. (*Rev. Indias*, 59:216, mayo/agosto 1999, p. 439–454)

Capable historical analysis of the futile propaganda efforts of a Spanish review published in London from 1819–20.

1093 La huella de Humboldt. Compilación de Leopoldo Zea y Mario Magallón Anaya. México: Instituto Panamericano de Geografía e Historia: Fondo de Cultura Económica, 2000. 141 p.: bibl., ill. (Col. Latinoamérica fin de milenio; 14) (Tierra firme)

An introduction to Humboldt in Latin America containing five stimulating essays that establish the context of his journey. Also provides commentary on the journey.

Langer, Erick D. The Eastern Andean frontier (Bolivia and Argentina) and Latin American frontiers: comparative contexts, 19th and 20th centuries. See item **2667**.

1094 Lewis, James E. The American Union and the problem of neighborhood: the United States and the collapse of the Spanish empire, 1783–1829. Chapel Hill: Univ. of North Carolina Press, 1998. 315 p.: bibl.

Provides a significant new interpretation of the discussion among US political leaders from Jefferson to Clay concerning the dissolution of the Spanish Empire. Lewis concentrates on the proposals for a loose union of independent nations in the Western Hemisphere. Based on extensive research in US archives.

1095 López-Ocón, Leoncio. La formación de un espacio público para la ciencia en la América Latina durante el siglo XIX. (*Asclepio/Madrid*, 50:2, 1998, p. 205–225)

Focuses on the growth of periodicals devoted to scientific topics, but concludes that the status of science and technology in Latin America was fragile at the close of the 19th century.

Luna, Félix. La emancipación argentina y americana. See item **2922**.

1096 Magical sites: women travelers in 19th century Latin America. Edited by Marjorie Agosín and Julie H. Levison. Buffalo, N.Y.: White Pine Press, 1999. 234 p.: bibl.

The interaction of foreign visitors with Latin American society and culture and the difficulties of travel in the region are central themes in this nicely edited volume.

1097 Martínez, Carmen Pumar. 1898 en el contexto del intervencionismo norteamericano en Hispanoamérica. (*Estud. Hist. Soc. Econ. Am.*, 13, 1996, p. 253–261, bibl.)

Study of US expansionism in the Western Hemisphere attempts to link the Monroe Doctrine and Manifest Destiny with the events of 1898.

1098 Martínez, Frédéric. L'idéal de l'immigration européenne dans la Colombie du XIXe siècle: du rêve civilisateur à la peur de la subversion. (*Bull. Inst. fr. étud. andin.*, 25:2, 1996, p. 233–268, bibl.)

A detailed examination of the goals and frustrations of Colombia's plans to stimulate immigration as a case study of Latin American immigration policies. Based on a healthy mixture of primary sources and scholarly monographs.

1099 Melgar Bao, Ricardo. Las ideologías radicales frente a la guerra y la identidad: anarquistas y socialistas latinoamericanos. (*in* Latinoamérica entre el Mediterráneo y el Báltico. México: Instituto Panamericano de Geografía e Historia, Fondo de Cultura Económica, 2000, p. 125–150, bibl.)

Survey of published works assesses the impact of the Spanish American War (1898) on Spanish socialist and anarchist thought.

1100 Mellafe R., Rolando and **María Teresa González Pardo.** Breve historia de la independencia latinoamericana: la formación de las nacionalidades. Santiago, Chile: Editorial Universitaria, 1997. 237 p.: bibl., ill. (Col. El saber y la cultura. Temas de historia)

University-level survey text that emphasizes demography, economics, geography, and the organization of the first governments.

1101 Mendizábal, Francisco Javier de. Guerra de la América del Sur, 1809–1824. Estudio preliminar de Ramón Gutiér-

rez. Buenos Aires: Academia Nacional de la Historia, 1997. 205 p.: bibl., ill. (Biblioteca de publicaciones documentales; t. 19)

Publication of the 1824 manuscript with an 8-page introduction by Gutiérrez. Several editorial footnotes add explanatory value.

1102 1898: ¿desastre o reconciliación? Compilación de Leopoldo Zea y Mario Magallón. México: Instituto Panamericano de Geografía e Historia: Fondo de Cultura Económica, 2000. 178 p.: bibl. (Colección Latinoamérica fin de milenio; 6)

Edited volume places a well-conceived emphasis on the cultural and political interactions of Spain and the Spanish American nations in the context of the events of 1898.

1103 Mörner, Magnus. Viajeros e inmigrantes europeos como observadores intérpretes de la realidad latinoamericana del siglo XIX. (*in* Observation and communication: the construction of realities in the Hispanic world. Edited by Johannes-Michael Scholz and Tamar Herzog. Frankfurt: Vittorio Klosermann, 1997, p. 415–430)

Astute commentary on the social and cultural origins of travelers and immigrants, their readership, and their descriptions of Latin America.

1104 Orbigny, Alcide Dessalines d'. Alcide d'Orbigny: á la découverte des nouvelles républiques sud-américaines. Sous la direction de Philippe de Laborde Pédelahore. Préface de Yves Laissus. Biarritz, France: Atlantica, 2000. 400 p.: ill. (some col.), col. map. (Transhumances)

Handsome edition that includes vivid illustrations and seven informative essays by scholars.

1105 Pueblos, comunidades y municipios frente a los proyectos modernizadores en América Latina, siglo XIX. Recopilación de Antonio Escobar Ohmstede, Romana Falcón, y Raymond Buve. San Luis Potosí, Mexico: El Colegio de San Luis, A.C., 2002. 283 p. (CEDLA Latin American Studies; 88)

Collection of 12 essays (one in Portuguese) on 19th-century modernization processes in Mexico, Brazil, Nicaragua, Argentina, Bolivia, Colombia, and Latin America in general. Volume is divided into three parts discussing the process of nation building, the question of nationalism and identity, and paradoxes and answers of modernization.

Publication is the result of a conference held in Oporto, Portugal (1999) on social, economic, political, and ethnic aspects of the creation of modern nation states in Latin America. [R. Hoefte]

1106   Quijada, Mónica. Latinos y anglo-sajones: el 98 en el fin de siglo sudamericano. (*Hispania/Madrid,* 57:196, 1997, p. 589–609)

Impressive analysis of the Latin American response to the war between Spain and the US. Emphasis on books and articles published in Argentina and Uruguay.

1107   Rodríguez O., Jaime E. The independence in Spanish America. Cambridge; New York: Cambridge Univ. Press, 1998. 282 p.: bibl., index, maps. (Cambridge Latin American studies; 84)

Perceptive and well-written synthesis of the causes and outcomes of the independence movements. Focuses on political and ideological causative factors and the centers of "civil war" in America. Extensive footnotes will be of value to specialists. For review of original Spanish-language version, see *HLAS 58:1016.*

1108   State and society in Spanish America during the Age of Revolution. Edited by Victor M. Uribe-Uran. Wilmington, Del.: Scholarly Resources, 2001. 282 p.: bibl. (Latin American silhouettes)

Intended as a collection of readings for the undergraduate classroom, this volume also contains an historiographically important evaluation of the extent to which this period saw meaningful social and economic changes.

1109   Tenorio-Trillo, Mauricio. Argucias de la historia: siglo XIX, cultura y "América Latina." México: Paidós, 1999. 280 p.: bibl. (Inicios en las ciencias sociales; 3)

A thoughtful and thought-provoking re-examination of the 19th century that focuses on Latin America and the US as interpreted through recent innovative approaches in cultural history.

1110   United States-Latin American relations, 1850–1903: establishing a relationship. Edited by Thomas M. Leonard. Tuscaloosa: Univ. of Alabama Press, 1999. 303 p.: bibl.

Exceptionally well-coordinated group of articles covers a critical period in US-Latin American relations. Examines the forces within Latin American nations that influenced policy toward hemispheric neighbors and toward the US, as well as the determining factors in policy formulation in Washington. The 11 authors are specialists in their areas. For comment by international relations specialist, see *HLAS 59:4214.*

1111   Vergara Quiroz, Sergio. Mujeres en la independencia de América: fuentes documentales para su estudio. (*in* Simposio Panamericano de Historia, *3rd, México, 1995.* Memorias. México: Instituto Panamericano de Geografía e Historia, 1997, p. 405–417)

Pathbreaking study of five types of documents available for research on the roles of women. Names several archives and published collections of documents and discusses their content.

1112   The Wars of Independence in Spanish America. Edited by Christon I. Archer. Wilmington, Del.: Scholarly Resources, 2000. 338 p.: bibl. (Jaguar books on Latin America; no. 20)

Thirteen well-selected articles plus an insightful introduction by Archer make for a volume appropriate for the university classroom.

1113   Women through women's eyes: Latin American women in nineteenth-century travel accounts. Edited by June E. Hahner. Wilmington, Del.: SR Books, 1998. 184 p.: bibl., ill. (Latin American silhouettes)

Well-chosen selections from the pens of 19th-century travelers provide an arresting panorama of social portraits that includes washerwomen, market women, house servants, and the wives and offspring of wealthy male landowners. For review of one chapter on upperclass women in Lima, see *HLAS 59:1020.*

20TH CENTURY

Aggarwal, Vinod K. Debt games: strategic interaction in international debt rescheduling. See *HLAS 59:4146.*

The allure of the foreign: imported goods in postcolonial Latin America. See *HLAS 59:4147.*

1114 América Latina: história, crise e movimento. Contribuções de Antônio Ozaí da Silva *et al.* Organização de Paulo Barsotti e Luiz Bernardo Pericás. Santo André, Brazil: Núcleo Emancipação do Trabalho; São Paulo: Xamã, 1999. 222 p.: bibl. (Biblioteca América livre)

A provocative collection of essays by leftist scholars and activists with a focus on Brazil.

1115 Austin, Robert. Popular history and popular education: el Consejo de Educación de Adultos de América Latina. (*Lat. Am. Perspect.*, 26:4, July 1999, p. 39–68, bibl., tables)

An engaging and pointed examination of the growing influence of CEAAL in the 1990s with an emphasis on feminism and the Zapatistas.

1116 Beezley, William H. and Colin M. MacLachlan. Latin America: the peoples and their history. Fort Worth, Tex.: Harcourt Brace College Publishers, 2000. 302 p.: bibl., ill., index, maps.

This relatively short college textbook claims social, cultural, and economic history as its central points. The authors effectively employ this approach in their analyses of several themes: US-Latin American relations, popular religion, and popular culture.

1117 Bertocchi Morán, Alejandro Nelson. El Graf Spee en la trampa de Montevideo. Buenos Aires: Ayer y Hoy Ediciones, 1998. 111 p.: bibl., ill. (some col.), maps. (Estudios militares breves)

Diplomatic and political ramifications of the arrival and destruction of the German battleship are discussed in this brief book. No footnotes and a one page bibliography.

1118 Che Guevara and the FBI: the U.S. political police dossier on the Latin American revolutionary. Edited by Michael Ratner and Michael Steven Smith. Melbourne; New York: Ocean Press, 1997. 233 p.: ill.

Reproduction of Federal Bureau of Investigation (FBI) records that also included reports from the Central Intelligence Agency (CIA) and other government bureaus. Editorial annotations and introductory essays are sympathetic to Guevara.

Coerver, Don M. and Linda Biesele Hall. Tangled destinies: Latin America and the United States. See *HLAS 59:4158.*

1119 De La Pedraja Tomán, René. Latin American merchant shipping in the age of global competition. Westport, Conn.: Greenwood Press, 1999. 198 p.: bibl. (Contributions in economics and economic history, 0084–9235; no. 209)

Documents the frustrated efforts by several Latin American nations to create their own merchant shipping industries in the half century after WWII and the ultimate triumph of privatization. A continuation of the author's earlier book, *Oil and Coffee* (see item **868**).

Dent, David W. The legacy of the Monroe Doctrine: a reference guide to U.S. involvement in Latin America and the Caribbean. See *HLAS 59:4161.*

1120 Devés V., Eduardo. El pensamiento nacionalista en América Latina y la reivindicación de la identidad económica, 1925–1945. (*Historia/Santiago*, 32, 1999, p. 43–75)

Interesting examination of the emergence of nationalist thought including Raul Scalabrini Ortiz, José Vasconcelos, Victor Raul Haya de la Torre, and Vicente Saenz.

1121 Díaz Lovera, Armando. Nixón en la geografía del hambre. Caracas: A. Díaz Lovera, 1999. 212 p.: ill.

This critique of US policy toward Latin America during the Cold War focuses on Richard Nixon's 1958 trip to Venezuela. Valuable as an expression of opinion, but not as a scholarly work.

1122 Encuentro y alteridad: vida y cultura judía en América Latina. Coordinación de Judit Bokser Liwerant y Alicia Gojman de Backal. Compilación de Hellen B. Soriano. México: UNAM; Jerusalem: Univ. Hebrea de Jerusalén; México: Asociación Mexicana de Amigos de la Univ. de Tel Aviv: Fondo de Cultura Económica, 1999. 758 p.: bibl. (Tierra firme)

Outstanding group of specialized articles focuses on the 20th century with an emphasis on migration from Europe to Latin America, the era of WW II, and Jewish communities and the development of a sense of cultural identity. High quality research and extensive documentation.

1123 Fermandois Huerta, Joaquín. Interpretación histórica de las relaciones hispano-chilenas: el sentido de una pregunta. (*Estud. Int./Santiago*, 32:127/128, sept./dic. 1999, p. 36–54)

A political-legal-historical commentary inspired by the recent case of Augusto Pinochet. Thoughtful discussion, but not footnoted.

1124 Fox, Arturo A. Latinoamérica: presente y pasado. Upper Saddle River, N.J.: Prentice Hall, 1998. 392 p.: bibl., ill., maps.

History textbook intended for students of intermediate Spanish at the university level. Good coverage of the colonial period and the 20th century, but tends to slight the 19th century. Emphasizes literature and cultural themes. Excellent organization.

1125 Graham-Yooll, Andrew. Pequeñas guerras británicas en América Latina. Buenos Aires: Editorial de Belgrano, 1998. 368 p.: bibl.

Fast-paced survey of the British use of military force in Latin America from the wars of independence to the Anglo-German blockade of Venezuela in 1902 to the Falklands/Malvinas conflict of 1982. A translation of the 1983 English edition (*Small Wars You May Have Missed*).

1126 Hansis, Randall. The Latin Americans: understanding their legacy. New York: McGraw-Hill Co., 1997. 359 p.: bibl., ill., maps.

Well-written college textbook stresses social, cultural, and economic themes breaking with traditional chronological/political history survey texts. The author's organization is both perceptive and challenging. Includes helpful footnotes and an instructor's bibliography.

Huggins, Martha K. Political policing: the United States and Latin America. See *HLAS* 59:4176.

Klaiber, Jeffrey L. The church, dictatorships, and democracy in Latin America. See *HLAS* 59:3043.

1127 Latin America: politics and society since 1930. Edited by Leslie Bethell. Cambridge; New York: Cambridge Univ. Press, 1997. 496 p.: bibl.

This volume consists of chapters from *The Cambridge History of Latin America: Latin America since 1930. Economy, Society, and Politics*, pt. 2, v. 6. The thematic connections among the essays on democracy, the left, the military, urban labor, and rural mobilizations make this a useful grouping of readings. Based on a thorough command of the published scholarship. Also published in Spanish as *Historia de América Latina: política y sociedad desde 1930* (1997).

1128 Lozano, Daniel and **Lola Delgado.** Historias de ultramar: aventuras y desventuras de los españoles de hoy en América Latina. Barcelona: Ediciones Península, 1999. 362 p.: ill. (Atalaya; 32)

Interesting mixture of contemporary travel accounts with biographical sketches that are often combined in ways that characterize a particular country. Includes the Caribbean, Mexico, Central America, and South America.

1129 Lucchini, Cristina *et al.* Industrialismo y nacionalidad en Argentina y el Brasil, 1890–1950. Buenos Aires: Ediciones del Signo con Fundación Simón Rodríguez, 2000. 153 p.: bibl. (Colección MERCOSUR)

Government policies and macroeconomic perspectives are the main focal points in these five essays that help to place in context the early 20th-century problems of these two nations.

1130 Maloof, Judy. Voices of resistance: testimonies of Cuban and Chilean women. Lexington: Univ. Press of Kentucky, 1999. 267 p.: bibl., ill.

Presents the personal accounts of six Cuban and seven Chilean women who were active in major political movements in their respective countries. This study is largely based on interviews, but the author also provides informative introductory essays to establish the historical contexts.

1131 Maza Zavala, Domingo Felipe. La vida económica en Hispanoamérica. Caracas: Academia Nacional de la Historia de Venezuela, 1996. 344 p.: bibl., ill. (some col.). (Historia general de América; 25. Período nacional)

Chronologically organized survey text emphasizes 19th-century British economic imperialism, 20th-century US economic imperialism, and the problems of peripheral capitalism through both centuries. The text concludes in 1989 and thereby lacks coverage of the crucial 1990s.

1132 Miller, Nicola. In the shadow of the state: intellectuals and the quest for national identity in twentieth-century Spanish America. London; New York: Verso, 1999. 342 p.: bibl., index. (Critical studies in Latin American and Iberian cultures)

Excellent analysis of the containment of intellectuals by the state in modern Spanish America. Miller concentrates on the nations of Mexico, Argentina, Peru, Cuba, and Chile and individuals such as José Vasconcelos, Manuel Ugarte, and José Martí as well as the Uruguayan José Enrique Rodó. Chapter 5, "From Ariel to Caliban: Anti-Imperialism among Spanish American Intellectuals," is an especially stimulating contribution on a topic that is sometimes undervalued.

1133 Mitchell, Nancy. The danger of dreams: German and American imperialism in Latin America. Chapel Hill: Univ. of North Carolina Press, 1999. 323 p.: bibl. ill., maps.

Sophisticated assessment of German involvement in the Venezuelan crisis of 1902–03 and the Huerta imbroglio in Mexico, as well as German migration to Brazil in the early 20th century. Based mainly on US and German sources, renders a realistic assessment of the rather limited German government intentions in the region.

1134 Morata y Salmerón, Alfonso M. Fuga del quinto infierno: Franco, Castro, Allende, Videla, Pinochet; la página no escrita de la historia. Madrid?: Grupo Editorial M & G Difusión, 1999. 816 p.: bibl., ill.

First person account of struggles against dictatorships of both right and left from Franco's Spain of the 1930s to Pinochet's Chile of the 1980s. Valuable as a primary source to be used in conjunction with other documents and relevant monographs.

1135 Nacionalismo e internacionalismo en la historia de las ciencias y la tecnología en América Latina. Recopilación de Luis Carlos Arboleda y Carlos Osorio. Cali, Colombia: Univ. del Valle, 1997. 440 p.: ill.

This collection of 29 scholarly essays and articles offers more coverage on science and academic research than on applied technology. Contains some impressive work on medical history.

1136 Notable twentieth-century Latin American women: a biographical dictionary. Edited by Cynthia Margarita Tompkins and David William Foster. Westport, Conn.: Greenwood Press, 2000. 357 p.: bibl., ill.

Convenient collection of 72 biographical entries including bibliographies. Emphasis on women active in politics, human rights, and culture.

1137 O'Brien, Thomas F. The century of U.S. capitalism in Latin America. Albuquerque: Univ. of New Mexico Press, 1999. 199 p.: bibl., ill. index. (Diálogos)

This intriguing synthesis brings together cultural and economic factors to provide the reader with a provocative but non-polemical examination of a topic of considerable relevance to contemporary economic trends. O'Brien's command of the scholarly literature is impressive. For international relations specialist's comment, see *HLAS 59:4194.*

1138 Populism in Latin America. Edited by Michael L. Conniff. Tuscaloosa: Univ. of Alabama Press, 1999. 251 p.: ill.

Editor Conniff's second book of essays on populism reflects the revival of this phenomenon in the 1990s. All 10 essays have a sense of history in that they explore the connections of the recent upsurge in populism to the "classic era" of Juan and Evita Perón, Getulio Vargas, and Lázaro Cárdenas.

1139 Rabe, Stephen G. The most dangerous area in the world: John F. Kennedy confronts Communist revolution in Latin America. Chapel Hill: Univ. of North Carolina Press, 1999. 257 p.: bibl.

This perceptive analysis of President Kennedy's policy toward Latin America deals with the purposes and impact of the Alliance for Progress within the larger context of the Cold War. In addition to coverage of the ill-fated programs for economic development and social change, devotes much attention to interventionist policies and counterinsurgency programs, thereby showing that Latin America was a major arena for covert and overt conflict. For comment by international relations specialist, see *HLAS 59:4200*.

1140 Rolland, Denis. Mémoire et imaginaire de la France en Amérique latine: la commémoration du 14-Juillet, 1939–1945. Paris: Harmattan, 2000. 187 p.: bibl., ill. (some col.). (Recherches, Amériques latines)

Traces the large presence of French cultural influences in Latin America through commemorations of Bastille Day in various countries, from Mexico to Argentina, not only in the 1939–45 period but in the early 20th century as well. Much of the discussion of this annual event is based on research in French diplomatic archives.

1141 Schmitz, David F. Thank God they're on our side: the United States and right-wing dictatorships, 1921–1965. Chapel Hill: Univ. of North Carolina Press, 1999. 394 p.: bibl.

Well-researched, critical assessment of the US government's support of conservative dictators in Latin America extends from the Nicaraguan crises of the 1920s-30s to the Good Neighbor Policy of the 1930s, WWII, and, most extensively, the Cold War. The author focuses on policy formulation in the context of US politics and geopolitical goals.

1142 Ward, John. Latin America: development and conflict since 1945. London; New York: Routledge, 1997. 127 p.: bibl., ill., index, map. (The making of the contemporary world)

This succinct synthesis of recent economic, social, and political trends contains a judicious rendering of the issues surrounding neoliberalism.

1143 Wasserman, Claudia. A manutenção das oligarquias no poder: as transformações econômico-políticas e a permanência dos privilegios sociais. (*Estud. Ibero-Am. / Porto Alegre*, 24:2, dez. 1998, p. 51–70)

Historiographical treatment of recent studies of Latin American oligarchies with stress on their persistence in the face of change.

1144 Wright, Thomas C. Latin America in the era of the Cuban Revolution. Rev. ed. Westport, Conn.: Praeger, 2001. 229 p.: bibl., maps.

Revisions of this commendable text concentrate on the fragility of democratization in the 1990s. For international relations specialist's comment on first edition (1991), see *HLAS 55:3881*.

MEXICO
General and Colonial Period

ASUNCIÓN LAVRIN, *Professor of History, Arizona State University at Tempe*
EDITH B. COUTURIER, *Independent Scholar, Washington DC*

THIS CHAPTER OF *HLAS 60* contains more reviews than usual owing to the transition to a new editor at the *Handbook* and changes in the production process. The General Section covers works that either stride between colonial and independence eras, or cover the complete span of Mexican history. This section also includes archival guides. The Colonial General and Colonial North sections include reviews of monographs and articles of a shorter span and are bound by chronological and geographical boundaries.

The publication of two new histories of Mexico and a revised edition of another indicate a renewed interest in synthesis and incorporation of new forms of analysis and interpretation. (See *The Oxford History of Mexico*, edited by Meyer and Beezley (2000); *El Gran Pueblo: A History of Greater Mexico*, by MacLachlan and Beezley (1999); and *Mexico: From Montezuma to NAFTA, and Beyond*, by Suchlicki (item **1194**).) The production of local and regional guides to archival sources as well as the publication of research resources continue apace. Jalisco and western Mexico are examined under the intellectual scrutiny of the Colegio de Jalisco and the French Center of Mexican and Central American Studies (e.g., see item **1220**). These institutions maintain a high standard of historical research and publication. Noteworthy is the second volume of the annotated guide to the Inquisition edited by Agueda Méndez (item **1152**).

The bulk of historiographical production focuses on the central core areas of the Viceroyalty, with limited output for southern Mexico or the Yucatán. A revisionist study of the *repartimiento* in Oaxaca by Baskes is one of the most challenging works on southern Mexico, focusing on the textile industry and indigenous revolts (item **1214**). Viqueira (items **1203** and **1346**) and Grijalva (item **1168**) also contribute productive academic research on southern Mexico.

The evangelization of indigenous peoples, including both methods of conversion and their results, remains an intriguing theme of investigation and debate. Castro Gutiérrez's multifaceted works on Michoacán (items **1226** and **1227**), and Menegus' research on indigenous groups deserve praise (item **1296**), while García Castro's new work on the Otomis brings that neglected group into focus (item **1250**). The most impressive book on colonial Indians is the comprehensive demographic study of late-18th century education by Tanck Estrada, winner of the 2000 Howard F. Cline Prize (item **1334**). The conveyance of Christianity, the assimilation of its message, and the significance of popular interpretations of religion keep historians and ethnohistorians searching for nuances as they question and revise what were assumed to be well-established truths. Brading's scrutiny of the Virgin of Guadalupe and her rise as an object of worship adds fuel to this always appealing topic (item **1151**). On the other hand, examinations of 17th-century beliefs and expressions of piety by Rubial García unfold a rich panorama of a colonial society fixated on the worship of saints and relics (items **1321** and **1322**).

Colonial society and colonial elites are well represented in a group of works covering a broad spectrum of topics. Altman revisits the immigration process and settlement patterns from a social viewpoint (item **1211**); a work edited by Castañeda focuses attention on the political elites of peripheral areas (item **1231**); Díaz Cruz analyzes the social and religious hierarchies of Mayas in Chiapas (item **1239**); Zárate aptly explores the attitudes of the nobility regarding death (item **1354**); while Rubial García offers a comprehensive and extremely readable overview of daily life in 17th-century Mexico City (item **1323**).

Issues of women and gender continue to be treated discretely, mostly in articles (see, for example, item **1186**). Work on nuns links women to the Church and underlines the importance of the only significant corporate presence in colonial female life. Some of the works reviewed for *HLAS 60* also introduce the topic of spirituality (items **1172, 1243, 1267,** and **1286**). In a category of its own is Gonzalbo's study of women and family, the product of many years of archival research (item **1256**), which effectively combines the sensitivity for the human aspects of personal relations with statistical data. Her latest edited work on Latin American families contains essays on Mexican family history throughout the 20th century (item **878**).

Credit, agricultural production, regional economy, and industrial development are represented by some important works such as Cervantes Bello on regional economy (item **1230**) and Wobeser on chantries (item **1352**). Revisionist views on trade, commerce, and agricultural production by Ouweneel and Studnick-Gizbert indicate that economic historians continue a lively exchange of opinions on this staple branch of history (items **1185** and **1333,** respectively).

A beautiful three-volume collection on Mexican history, profusely illustrated with the best expression of national painters, rises above the usual standard for coffee table books. One volume addresses daily life while the others, companion volumes to an exhibition bearing the suggestive name "Paintbrushes of History," consist of thoughtful, well-written essays that draw heavily from history and propose a fresh perspective on the visual representation of key themes and events of national life from the 16th century through 1860 (items **145, 1418,** and *Pintura y vida cotidiana en México, 1650–1950* (1999)).

Three subjects, especially important for the history of northern New Spain, have emerged since we reviewed books and articles for *HLAS 58:* the history of Saltillo, ethnohistory, and the role of the Jesuits. On Saltillo, three works deserve mention: De la Teja's "St. James at the Fair" (item **1392**); Offutt's *Saltillo, 1770–1810: Town and Region in the Mexican North* (item **1384**); and Garza Martínez and Pérez Zevallos' publication of the cabildo records of that city (item **1377**).

The outstanding works in ethnohistory include Radding's chapter, "The Colonial Pact and Changing Ethnic Frontiers in Highland Sonora, 1740–1840" (item **1387**), and a number of works on the Tlaxcalans and their role both in relation to other indigenous groups as well as with Spaniards and mestizos. The works of Sego (item **1391**) and Cavazos Garza (items **1360** and **1361**) are of special interest. Also commendable is the work by Sheridan on the Seri Indians, which analyzes the conflicts of nomadic versus sedentary indigenous peoples (item **1367**). Jackson's edited collection of essays by leading North American scholars of the region, *New Views of Borderlands History* (item **1381**), indicates the increasing maturity and sophistication of research into this aspect of the history of northern New Spain.

On the Jesuits, the works of Hausberger are especially worthy of note. His work on the daily life of Jesuits in the northwest is of special interest because of the details it reveals about frontier conditions for missionaries (item **1374**). Nolasco Armas' work on Jesuits in the Northwest should also be mentioned (item **1382**), as well as the work by Messmacher on Jesuits in Baja California (item **1380**).

Another noteworthy piece is Del Río's examination of the insanity of José de Gálvez during his inspection of Sonora (item **1389**). In addition, Basques in the northwest emerge in the edited collection by Olveda (item **1341**), complementing a three-volume work on *Vascos en las regiones de México, siglos XVI a XX,* edited by Garritz, which is the product of papers from four conferences and includes a number of essays about the north (item **1200**).

Increasing attention to the field has been enhanced by works too numerous to be included in this section. North American and central Mexican historians working on the history of indigenous peoples in the north, as well as the increasing dominance of the north by the military; missionaries; indigenous groups from central Mexico; and white, mestizo, and Afro-Mexican settlers, add increasing information and sophistication to the written history of the region.

This section was completed with the collaboration of Patricia Harms and Brian E. Cassity.

GENERAL

1145 **Aguilar-Robledo, Miguel.** Ganadería, tenencia de la tierra e impacto ambiental en una región fronteriza de la Nueva España: la jurisdicción de la Villa de Santiago de los Valles de Oxitipia, 1527–1921. (*Estud. Geogr./Madrid,* 59:230, enero/marzo 1998, p. 5–34, bibl., map, table)

Study of the cattle industry in San Luis Potosí and the jurisdiction of Valles, Huasteca area, largely on the colonial period, despite the article's title. Underlines the importance of cattle raising in the area and disputes thesis that cattle had a negative impact on the environment. For geography specialist's comment, see *HLAS 59:2467*. [AL]

1146 Archivo General de Notarías (Mexico). Catálogo de protocolos de la notaría no. 1 de Texcoco. v. 2, 1617–1640. Mexico: Gobierno del Estado de México, Secretaría General de Gobierno, Sub-Secretaría "B" de Gobierno, Dirección General del Registro Público de la Propiedad, 1998. 1 v.: bibl., ill., indexes.

Useful annotated catalog of all entries of the notarial records for Tlaxcala between 1617–40. Onomastic index and glossary. [AL]

1147 Benavides, Adán. Archival investigations for Mission Nuestra Señora de los Dolores de los Ais, San Augustine County, Texas: a catalog of documents and maps of the Mission Dolores de los Ais historical materials collection. Austin: Texas Dept. of Transportation, Environmental Affairs Division, Archeological Studies Program, 1998. 252 p.: bibl., maps. (Report; no. 11)

Important contribution to the study of the 18th-century Spanish presence in Texas. A model guide to all the documentary evidence about one mission, albeit one that failed. Summaries of the contents of the principal collections of documents suggest future study on questions of conversion, Indian-Spanish relations, imperial policies, etc. Concluding appendix summarizes the issues. [EBC]

1148 Biblioteca Nacional de Antropología e Historia (Mexico). Fondo conventual de la Biblioteca Nacional de Antropología e Historia. v. 7, pt. 2. México: Instituto Nacional de Antropología e Historia: UNAM, 1997. 1 v.: indexes. (Colección Fuentes) (Serie Catálogos)

One of series of catalogs for the conventual libraries of Mexico City. The 12 volumes in the series cover the holdings of the most important convents as well as the cathedral library. Carefully crafted. Useful for intellectual historians, historians of education, church historians, and others. [AL]

1149 Blanco, Mónica Alejandra; Alma Parra; and Estela Ruiz Medrano. Breve historia de Guanajuato. México: Colegio de México, Fideicomiso Historia de las Américas: Fondo de Cultura Económica, 2000. 290 p.: bibl., maps. (Serie Breves historias de los estados de la República Mexicana)

One in a series of histories of the states of Mexico. Follows an established pattern that includes precolumbian populations, as well as economic and political issues throughout the last 500 years. Readable and informative. [AL]

1150 Blázquez Domínguez, Carmen. Breve historia de Veracruz. México: Colegio de México, Fideicomiso Historia de las Américas: Fondo de Cultura Económica, 2000. 203 p.: bibl., maps. (Serie Breves historias de los estados de la República Mexicana)

Surveys the history of the state of Veracruz as part of the series covering the general history of all Mexican states. This volume is strong in the colonial period but weak on 20th century coverage. [AL]

1151 Brading, D.A. Mexican Phoenix: Our Lady of Guadalupe—image and tradition, 1531–2000. New York: Cambridge Univ. Press, 2001. 444 p.: bibl., facsims., index.

Meticulous study of the evolution of the image and history of the worship of Guadalupe, from the 16th through the late-20th century. Using a broad range of printed sources, this appealing work deals with the many controversial issues surrounding this figure, which only began to become a national icon in the 18th century. Also studies the problems surrounding Juan Diego's figure. Readable and very well researched. [AL]

1152 Catálogo de textos marginados novo-hispanos: Inquisición, siglo XVII: Archivo General de la Nación (México). Recopilación de María Agueda Méndez *et al.* Mexico: Colegio de México, Centro de Estudios Lingüísticos y Literarios: Archivo General de la Nación: Fondo Nacional para la Cultura y las Artes, 1997. 741 p.: indexes.

Sequel to catalog of forbidden texts of the 18th century. Excellent source for research on a variety of causes and people subjected to the scrutiny of the Inquisition. Given the Inquisition's interest in unorthodox materials and forms of behavior, the catalog offers researchers a key to a body of evidence unlike any other: writings by religious and lay persons, censured sermons, blasphemous poetry, erroneous forms of prayers, divination practices, conjures, etc. Several indexes help the reader locate materials by first line of text, type of criminal process, name, or location. A list of the beleaguered authors completes the guide material. Highly recommended source. [AL]

1153 Catolicismo social en México: teoría, fuentes e historiografía. t. 1. México: Academia de Investigación Humanística, 2000. 1 v.: bibl.

Eight essays preceded by an Introduction, written by nine specialists, on the topic of Church-state relations and the meaning of the social teachings of the Church. All essays deal with the topic of "social Catholicism," or the role that the Catholic Church had in the reshaping of the concepts of "moral society" and "just society" during the formation of the nation. Covering the period between the late 18th-late 19th centuries, this volume analyzes the theme from theoretical, historical, and legal viewpoints. Thorough and commendable work. [AL]

1154 Chilcuautla: reflejo de la historia de México; Valle del Mezquital, Hidalgo. Coordinación de Verónica Kugel y Pedro Gabriel Martínez. Chilcuautla, Mexico: Parroquia Santa María Asunción, 1998. 244 p.: bibl., ill. (some col.), maps (some col.).

Celebration of the local scene, and especially the role of the Church in the life of the town, this book includes some colonial information, but is mainly about more contemporary times. Some useful ethnographic information is included. [R. Haskett/ S. Wood]

1155 Cien años de Daniel Cosío Villegas. Recopilación de Fernando Vizcaíno. México: Clío, 1999. 487 p.: bibl., ill. (some col.), index. (Obras completas de Daniel Cosío Villegas)

A collection of essays by various historians and intellectuals appraising the work of Cosío Villegas. Additional letters and a list of his articles in journals and newspapers complete the volume. [AL]

1156 Comercio marítimo colonial: nuevas interpretaciones y últimas fuentes. Coordinación de Carmen Yuste. México: Instituto Nacional de Antropología e Historia, 1997. 202 p.: bibl. (Biblioteca del INAH) (Serie Historia)

Anthology of works on Mexican colo-

nial trade is the result of a seminar offered by the Instituto Nacional de Antropología e Historia in 1993. Reexamines our knowledge of Mexican trade, offering the Mexican perspective on key areas of national and regional commerce. Covers 17th-18th centuries. [AL]

1157 Dávalos, Marcela. Basura e Ilustración: la limpieza de la Ciudad de México a fines del siglo XVIII. México: Instituto Nacional de Antropología e Historia: Depto. del Distrito Federal, 1997. 159 p.: bibl., maps. (Arte y cultura)

Novel combination of urban and public health history. Discusses contemporaneous theories connecting climate, cleanliness, and human health, and studies the various efforts made to solve the problem of garbage disposal in the city of Mexico. Focuses on late 18th and early 19th centuries. [AL]

1158 Enciclopedia de Quintana Roo. Dirección de Juan Angel Xacur Maiza; Coordinacion de la investigación de María Cecilia Lavalle Torres; Dirección editorial de María Eugenia Varela Carlos. México: J.A. Xacur Maiza, 1998. 10 v.: ill., maps.

Detailed 10-volume encyclopedia on the state of Quintana Roo including flora, fauna, major civilizations, biographies of hundreds of people who lived in or visited the state, from presidents of Mexico to school teachers. Abundantly illustrated, including Maya stelae. Last volume is bibliography. [EBC]

1159 Encuentro de Historiografía, 1st, Univ. Autónoma Metropolitana. Unidad Azcapotzalco, 1996. Memorias. Coordinación de Saúl Jerónimo Romero y Carmen Valdez Vega. Azcapotzalco, Mexico: Univ. Autónoma Metropolitana Azcapotzalco, 1997. 432 p.: bibl. (Colección Memorias)

Collection of 22 essays on the historiography of key themes in Mexican history, i.e., colonial history, history of indigenous rebellions, elites, labor, education. Each essay has its own bibliography. The attempt is more philosophical than exhaustive. Although quality and coverage are uneven, it signals process of self-analysis by the younger generation. Lacks index and general bibliography. [AL]

1160 Foster, Lynn V. A brief history of Mexico. New York: Facts on File, 1997. 276 p.: bibl., ill., index, maps.

Survey of Mexican history from the precolumbian era until the mid-1990s, based predominantly on secondary sources. Designed to provide contrast and a deeper understanding of the varied human responses to historical events. The first six chapters focus on the precontact and colonial periods. [P. Harms]

1161 Gruzinski, Serge. Histoire de Mexico. Paris: Fayard, 1996. 454 p.: bibl., ill., index. (Histoire des grandes villes du monde)

Literary, lyrical, and architectural history of Mexico City begins with the contemporary city, compares it with other cities, and observes that the city of the 1950s appears as a lost paradise. Also includes a description of the Porfirato, the mestizo city, and the Aztec city. Part of a series on the great cities of the world. [EBC]

1162 Guedea, Virginia. El proceso de independencia novohispano: algunas consideraciones sobre su estudio. (*Históricas/ México,* 50, sept./dic. 1997, p. 3–15)

Historiographical survey of the works devoted to the independence of Mexico, reviewing those published between 1987–97. [AL]

1163 Hamnett, Brian R. A concise history of Mexico. New York: Cambridge Univ. Press, 1999. 336 p.: bibl., ill. (Cambridge concise histories)

Discusses such themes as indigenous communities and culture; colonial conquest and the institution of Hispanic law, politics, religion, custom, and commerce; independence from Spain and postrevolutionary politics; nationalism; and relations with the US, including NAFTA, immigration, and drug trafficking. Compact and readable. [B. Cassity]

1164 Harris, Max. Aztecs, Moors, and Christians: festivals of reconquest in Mexico and Spain. Austin: Univ. of Texas Press, 2000. 309 p.: bibl., ill., index.

The drama of Moors and Christians begins with a description of two modern evocations of these events, then returns to medieval Spain for the original dramas, and then to 16th-century Mexico and Europe. Concludes with late 20th-century performances. Opines that these dramas of conquest had a hidden agenda for the expression of dissent

as well as hope for an eventual victory of the conquered. [EBC]

1165 Hernández Chávez, Alicia. México: breve historia contemporánea. México: Fondo de Cultura Económica, 2000. 530 p.: index, maps. (Colección Popular; 580)

Compact pocket book covers Mexico's history. Aimed at general readers, work is a masterpiece of synthesis. Attempts a balanced approach of themes related to the colonial period, but leans mostly toward political history, especially after independence. [AL]

1166 Hernández Rodríguez, Rosaura. Toluca, 1603: vista de ojos. Zinacantepec, Mexico: El Colegio Mexiquense: H. Ayuntamiento de Toluca, 1997. 182 p.: bibl., maps. (Fuentes para la historia del Estado de México; 5)

A 1603 inquiry into the territorial limits of the lands of the Marquisate of the Valley originally belonging to Hernán Cortes. Questionnaire drafted by the authorities addressed mostly indigenous witnesses who provided a wealth of information on the territory. Recording the indigenous voice, this document becomes a source of information for ethnographers as well as historians. [AL]

1167 Historia e historias: cincuenta años de vida académica del Instituto de Investigaciones Históricas. Entrevistas con Guadalupe Borgonio et al. Presentación por Gisela von Wobeser. Introducción por Salvador Rueda. Coordinación de Alicia Olivera. Entrevistas por Salvador Rueda y Laura Espejel. México: UNAM, Instituto de Investigaciones Históricas, 1998. 243 p.: ill.

Collection of essays by 12 Mexican historians who recollect their apprenticeships at the Instituto de Investigaciones Históricas in Mexico City. [AL]

1168 Historia general del Estado de México. v. 1, Geografía y arqueología coordinación de Yoko Sugiura Yamamoto. v. 2, Epoca prehispánica y siglo XVI coordinación de Rosaura Hernández Rodríguez. v. 3, La época virreinal coordinación de María Teresa Jarquín Ortega. v. 4, Independencia, reforma e imperio coordinación de Gerald L. McGowan. v. 5, República restaurada y Porfiriato coordinación de Manuel Miño Grijalva. v. 6, De la Revolución a 1990 coordinación de Luis Jaime Sobrino. México: Gobierno del Estado de México: Colegio Mexiquense, 1998. 6 v.: bibl., ill., maps.

An impressive 6-volume history of the state of Mexico that should be emulated by other states. Chronologically and thematically organized, it runs from precolumbian times to 1990, and consists of 16–20 essays in each volume authored by the best historians of Mexico and the region. Written for the general public, the essays do not underestimate the readers' intelligence. Profusely illustrated and handsomely bound, these books are attractive and informative. [AL]

1169 Historia y cultura obrera. Compilación de Victoria Novelo. México: Instituto Mora: CIESAS, 1999. 307 p.: bibl. (Antologías universitarias.)

Anthology of eight articles on labor history (European and Mexican) preceded by a historiographical essay by compiler Novelo. Mexican articles from the Porfiriato to the present. Sociological slant predominates. [AL]

1170 Historias y procesos: el quehacer de los historiadores en la Universidad Michoacana. Coordinación de José Alfredo Uribe Salas, María Teresa Cortés Zavala, and Alonso Torres Aburto. Morelia, Mexico: Escuela de Historia, Instituto de Investigaciones Históricas, Univ. Michoacana de San Nicolás de Hidalgo: Instituto Michoacano de Cultura, Gobierno del Estado de Michoacán, 2000. 346 p.: bibl. (Colección Historias y procesos; 1)

This volume contains 19 essays produced by the School of History of the Univ. Michoacana de San Nicolás de Hidalgo, representing a selection of topics chosen by graduates. Studies are divided into three groups: cultural history and education, politics and power, and economic and social history. All deal with Mexico, except one on Chile. [AL]

1171 Historiografía michoacana: acercamientos y balances. Coordinación de Gerardo Sánchez Díaz and Ricardo León Alanís. Morelia, Mexico: Univ. Michoacana de San Nicolás de Hidalgo, Instituto de Investigaciones Históricas: Morevallado Editores, 2000. 282 p.: bibl., ill., maps.

Useful collection of essays on the historiography of Michoacán, from prehispanic times to the 20th century. Six of the 17 articles focus on colonial historians, mostly ecclesiastical. Good balance between studies of personal historians and general historiography make this a useful bibliographic tool. [AL]

1172 Ibsen, Kristine. Women's spiritual autobiography in colonial Spanish America. Gainesville: Univ. Press of Florida, 1999. 202 p.: bibl., index.

Critical literary analysis of the spiritual autobiography genre as a form of self-representation. Visionary, mystical, and mundane experiences come out of the pages of the diaries of nuns. Ibsen covers writings of nuns from Chile, Colombia, Mexico, and Peru, mostly straddling the 17th-18th centuries—the golden age of spiritual writings. Important study for historians, demonstrating the usefulness of an interdisciplinary and comparative view of religious women writers as historical actors. For literature specialist's comment, see item **3370**. [AL]

1173 Identidad y prácticas de los grupos de poder en México, siglos XVII-XIX: seminario de formación de grupos y clases sociales. Coordinación de Rosa María Meyer Cosío. México: Instituto Nacional de Antropología e Historia, 1999. 276 p.: bibl., ill. (Colección científica; 398) (Serie Historia/Instituto Nacional de Antropología e Historia)

Fourteen essays discuss the history of social elites and identities of groups in power, emanating from research groups at INAH. Topics include: control of the credit market, textile entrepeneurs, the Consulados of Mexico and Veracruz, and colonial confraternities. These works aim to clarify how such groups exercised or represented power. [AL]

1174 Indice de documentos virreinales de San Luis Potosí existentes en el Archivo General de la Nación. Organización de José Antonio Rivera Villanueva. San Luis Potosí, Mexico: Colegio de San Luis, 1999. 171 p. (Colección Investigaciones)

Survey of all items in the Indios and Tierras section of the Archivo General (National Archives), pertaining to the history of San Luis Potosí. Uses archives' cd-rom. Covers 16th-19th centuries. [AL]

1175 La industria mexicana y su historia: siglos XVIII, XIX, XX. Coordinación de María Eugenia Romero Sotelo. México: Facultad de Economía, Univ. Nacional Autónoma de México, 1997. 494 p.: bibl.

Anthology of six essays on the history of Mexican industry. One essay on the colonial period is followed by six on the 19th and 20th centuries. Informative and useful, this text is a reference work that fulfills its goal of creating a general history on the subject. [AL]

1176 Iturriaga de la Fuente, José N. Viajeros extranjeros en San Luis Potosí. San Luis Potosí, Mexico: Editorial Ponciano Arriaga, Gobierno del Estado de San Luis Potosí, 2000. 403 p.: bibl. (Colección Ciencias sociales)

Excerpts from the works of 41 travelers to San Luis Potosí from the 16th to the end of the 20th century collected by an author with a special interest in travel literature. Major emphasis is the 19th century. Includes much ethnographic information, as well as descriptions of the city and surrounding countryside. [EBC]

1177 Kuri Camacho, Ramón. La Compañía de Jesús: imágenes e ideas: la axiología jesuita, Juan de Palafox y Mendoza y otros estudios novohispanos. México: Instituto Nacional de Antropología e Historia: Benemérita Univ. Autónoma de Puebla: Univ. Autónoma de Zacatecas, 1996. 303 p.: bibl. (Colección Lafragua)

Collection of essays illuminating Jesuit philosophy and discourse demonstrates the adaptability of their philosophy to political circumstances and daily needs. Also includes essays on other topics. [AL]

1178 Langue, Frédérique. La historiografía mexicanista y la hacienda colonial: balances y reconsideraciones. (*Secuencia/México,* 42, sept./dic. 1998, p. 65–116, bibl., facsims.)

Study of the historiography of the Mexican hacienda, in which the author reviews several aspects of the economy and social features of haciendas. [AL]

1179 Lizama Quijano, Jesús and **Daniela Traffano.** El Archivo Histórico de la Arquidiócesis de Oaxaca: una memoria que se exclaustra. Oaxaca, Mexico: Archivo Histórico de la Arquidiócesis de Oaxaca; Fondo Estatal para la Cultura y las Artes, 1998. 76 p.: bibl., graph, music, tables. (Cuadernos de Historia Eclesiástica; 1)

Explains the structure of the ecclesiastical curia and the history of the ecclesiastical cabildos, and describes the resources available for research at the archives of the Archdiocesis of Oaxaca. Useful guide. [AL]

1180 Marín Bosch, Miguel. Puebla neocolonial, 1777–1831: casta, ocupación y matrimonio en la segunda ciudad de Nueva España. Zapopan, Mexico: Colegio de Jalisco; Puebla, Mexico: Instituto de Ciencias Sociales y Humanidades, BUAP, 1999. 244 p.: bibl., ill.

Using a broad sample of Pueblan society, this demographic analysis focuses on race, marriage, and birth, and provides occupational categories. Intensely researched, this general picture of Pueblan population in the last years of the colony and the beginning of republican life provides valuable information on changes in racial categorization and the general trends of mestizaje and the dilution and/or preservation of some racial groups. [AL]

1181 Mercado interno en México: siglos XVIII-XIX. Coordinación de Jorge Silva Riquer y Jesús López Martínez. México: Instituto Mora, El Colegio de Michoacán, El Colegio de México, Instituto de Investigaciones Históricas-UNAM, 1998. 226 p.: bibl., ill. (Lecturas de historia económica mexicana)

Anthology of published articles on the internal market in Mexican history. Looks at impact of supply and demand on the rest of the economy. [AL]

1182 Mott, Margaret. The rule of faith over reason: the role of the Inquisition in Iberia and New Spain. (*J. Church State,* 40:1, Winter 1998, p. 57–81)

Revisionist interpretation of the Inquisition's social role. Using sources and arguments valid for the 16th-17th centuries, Mott underlines the institution's task of containing the influence of the devil in this world and maintaining the law under a patrimonial state based on faith. [AL]

1183 Los occidentes de México, siglos XVI-XIX: el archivo, instrumento y vida de la investigación histórica. Compilación de Celina Guadalupe Becerra J. Guadalajara,

Mexico: Editorial CUCSH, Univ. de Guadalajara, 1997. 566 p.: bibl., ill.

Papers presented in a regional conference of historians. Some of the essays are useful guides to the holdings of local and regional archives; others illustrate how to put the archives to use. The inclusion of short and shallow pieces leads to uneveness in the overall quality, but on the whole a useful reference work. [AL]

1184 Olmedo Gaxiola, Regina. Catálogo de documentos históricos del Archivo General Agrario. México: Registro Agrario Nacional: Centro de Investigaciónes y Estudios Superiores en Antropología Social, 1998. 226 p.: bibl., ill. (Colección Agraria)

Guide to the documents under the custody of the Archivo General Agrario, which keeps documents registered up to 1915, and the Archivo General de la Nación. Largely related to native land ownership. [AL]

1185 Ouweneel, Arij. Ciclos interrumpidos: ensayos sobre historia rural mexicana, siglos XVIII-XIX. Zinacantán, Mexico: El Colegio Mexiquense, 1998. 444 p.: bibl., maps.

Collection of eight essays by Dutch economic historian, largely dealing with the late colonial period. Eclectic selection of topics, such as local governments, collection of tithes, and indigenous self-government. Some essays are highly theoretical and quantitative. Challenges established assumptions of economic historians. [AL]

1186 Penyak, Lee. Safe harbors and compulsory custody: *casas de depósito* in Mexico, 1750–1865. (*HAHR*, 79:1, Feb. 1999, p. 83–99, table)

Studies the process of *depósito* (the placement of a woman in safe keeping during a legal suit) in the late colonial and early republican period. Interprets *depósito* as a form of control of female sexuality. [AL]

1187 Pérez Toledo, Sonia. Artesanos y gremios de la ciudad de México, 1780–1842. (*Hist. Graf./México*, 6, 1996, p. 55–85, tables)

Study of the artisans and tradesmen in the period of transition from late colonial to independence and early republican life. Quantitative reconstruction, focusing on spa-

tial distribution, number of men engaged in work, and corporative survival. [AL]

1188 Pietschmann, Horst. Dinero y crédito en la economía mexicana a finales del periodo colonial, 1750–1810: reflexiones sobre el estado actual de las investigaciones. (*Históricas/México*, 47, sept./dic. 1996, p. 27–51, map)

Surveys the state of the art historiography on credit, regions, and financial sources using some key works up to the beginning of the 1990s. [AL]

1189 Procesos rurales e historia regional: sierra y costa totonacas de Veracruz. Coordinación de Victoria Chenaut. México: CIESAS, 1996. 223 p.: bibl., maps.

Collected essays address the history and social features of the Totonac area of coastal Veracruz. Essays cover a wide range of topics such as popular mythology, the dynamics of popular markets, and popular rebellion. While there is no uniting theme, essays do gather significant information. [AL]

1190 Querétaro: interpretaciones de su historia: cinco ensayos. Coordinación de Lisette Griselda Rivera Reynaldos y Martín Pérez Acevedo. Morelia, Mexico: Univ. Michoacana de San Nicolás de Hidalgo, Instituto de Investigaciones Históricas, 1998. 238 p.: bibl., ill. (Estudios de historia mexicana; 5)

Anthology of five essays on the history of Querétaro's water supply and sewage, population growth, 19th century political history, financial work, daily life and recreation. [AL]

Roland, Ana Maria. Fronteiras da palavra, fronteiras da história: contribuição à crítica da cultura do ensaísmo latino-americano através da leitura de Euclides da Cunha e Octavio Paz. See item **4762.**

1191 El rostro colectivo de la nación mexicana. Coordinación de María Guadalupe Chávez Carbajal. Morelia, Mexico: Univ. Michoacana de San Nicolás de Hidalgo, Instituto de Investigaciones Históricas, 1997. 335 p.: bibl., ill. (Encuentros; 1)

Part of the project to study the "third root" of the Mexican nation, the African. Presents a collection of 19 essays in honor of Gonzalo Aguirre Beltrán, from the fifth meeting of Afro-Mexican scholars (Michoacán, 1995). Topics include inter-ethnic relations; sources for the examination of Afro-Mexican studies; and the presence of African culture in history, music, and even baseball. [AL]

1192 Roulet, Eric. L'histoire ancienne du Mexique selon Mariano Veitia, XVIIIe siècle. Préface de Jacqueline de Durand-Forest. Paris: Harmattan, 2000. 238 p.: bibl., ill., index. (Collection Recherches et documents. Amériques latines)

Historiographical study of colonial historian of Mexican antiquities, Mariano Veitia. Underlines his contribution as an early enlightened connoisseur of Aztec history. Well crafted and balanced. [AL]

1193 La Sierra Gorda: documentos para su historia. v. 1–2. México: Instituto Nacional de Antropología e Historia, 1996–97. 2 v.: ill. (Colección científica; 339–340)

Provides an extensive collection of documents and older secondary sources about the Sierra Gorda, as well as results of modern archeology. Addresses vexing question concerning where the zone of sedentary peasant farmers—which characterized Mesoamerica—ended, and where the Sierra Gorda—in which hunter-gatherers predominated—began. Includes materials from 16th century to the present. [EBC]

1194 Suchlicki, Jaime. Mexico: from Montezuma to NAFTA, and beyond. With a new preface by the author. 1st pbk. ed. New Brunswick, NJ: Transaction Publishers, 2000. 241 p.: bibl., ill., index, 1 map.

Revised paperback edition of survey of Mexican history. Largely political and economic emphasis. Stronger for postindependence period. Compact and readable for the general public. [AL]

1195 Thompson, Angela Tucker. Family and social change in the city of mines: Guanajuato, Mexico, 1760–1870. (in Formas familiares, procesos históricos y cambio social en América Latina. Recopilación de Ricardo Cicerchia. Quito: Ediciones Abya-Yala, 1998, p. 113–129)

Uses Guanajuato as a case study to argue that increased educational facilities between 1760–1870 gave women a public voice to improve life for their families and commu-

nities in the 19th century. They also became agents for some state goals, such as public health and public education of women. [AL]

1196 Thompson, Angela Tucker. Imagining how to live during 101 years of change: family strategies and children in Guanajuato, Mexico, 1766 to 1867. (Popul. Fam./São Paulo, 2, 1999, p. 113–140, bibl., tables)

Imaginative exercise in historical reconstruction of the meaning of education and economic potential of children in Guanajuato, a mining town suffering considerable changes in its economy. Author has teased information from difficult sources to examine family strategies for, and expectations involved in, educating their children. [AL]

1197 Tortolero, Alejandro. Presentación: historia, espacio y medio ambiente en el México Central. (in Tierra, agua y bosques: historia y medio ambiente en el México central. Coordinación de Alejandro Tortolero. México: Centre français d'études mexicaines et centraméricaines; Instituto de Investigaciones Dr. José María Luis Mora; Potrerillos Editores; Guadalajara, Mexico: Univ. de Guadalajara, 1996, p. 9–48, maps, table)

Ecological study examines the use of geographical space in central Mexico mainly since the 19th century. Focuses on the centrality of Mexico City and its control over its rural surroundings and resources. [AL]

1198 Tuñón, Julia. Mujeres en México: recordando una historia. 1. ed. en Regiones. México: CONACULTA, 1998. 214 p.: bibl., ill. (Regiones)

Brief general survey of the history of women in Mexico begins with Mexican women in Central Mexico and ends in the late 1980s. Follows traditional coverage of social and political issues featured in secondary sources. Basic bibliography is largely in Spanish. Intended for general readers and undergraduate students. For comment on translation of this work, see item 4346. [AL]

1199 Valenzuela Arce, José Manuel. Impecable y diamantina: la deconstrucción del discurso nacional. Tijuana, Mexico: Colegio de la Frontera Norte; Tlaquepaque, Mexico: ITESO, 1999. 284 p.: bibl.

Discusses formation of a credible national identity, or "imagined community," for Mexico, a national project that began to take shape in the 16th century. Focuses on the postindependence period and analyzes those texts relevant to understanding the "national character" as it was defined by dominant intellectuals. Women and indigenous discourses receive special attention. Enticing interpretation. [AL]

1200 Los vascos en las regiones de México, siglos XVI a XX. v. 1–3. México: UNAM, Instituto de Investigaciones Históricas; Spain: Ministerio de Cultura del Gobierno Vasco; S.l.: Instituto Vasco-Mexicano de Desarrollo, 1996–97. 3 v.: bibl., ill., index, maps.

Papers from four congresses on the history of the Basque community in Mexico. Each volume covers all regions and time periods. Essays are of uneven value, but are of special note for the depth of their research. Includes works by Heriberto Moreno García, María Teresa Huerta, and Mario Cerutti. Many contributors have their work represented in more than one volume. Northern regions receive special emphasis. [EBC]

1201 Vázquez Mantecón, María del Carmen. La palabra del poder: vida pública de José María Tornel, 1795–1853. México: UNAM, 1997. 224 p.: bibl., ill. (some col.), index, col. map. (Serie Historia moderna y contemporánea; 27)

Examines the first turbulent decades of Mexican independence through the political writings of a criollo, José María Tornel y Mendívil. A public servant and key postindependence leader, Tornel's vision for an independent Mexico created both allies and political enemies. [AL]

1202 Vicios públicos, virtudes privadas: la corrupción en México. Coordinación de Claudio Lomnitz. México: CIESAS: M.A. Porrúa, 2000. 291 p.: bibl.

Collection of essays by historians, ethnographers, and sociologists aimed at placing the meaning of corruption within a historical framework and tracing its evolution in Mexican society. Essays discuss the historical transformation of the discourses on corruption, administrative and political corruption, and the relationship between corruption and political representation. Covers

Mexican history from the colonial period through the 20th century. [AL]

1203 Viqueira, Juan Pedro. Éxitos y fracasos de la evangelización en Chiapas, 1545–1859. (*in* Coloquia de Antropología e Historia Regionales, *17th, Zamora, Mexico, 1995.* Iglesia Católica en México. Zamora, Mexico: El Colegio de Michoacán; México: Secretaría de Gobernación, Subsecretaría de Asuntos Jurídicos y Asociaciones Religiosas, Dirección General de Asuntos Religiosas, 1997, p. 69–98, bibl.)

Surveys the history of the evangelization in Chiapas, pointing to the inherent difficulties of the task, the influence of the Dominican order, the failure to truly Christianize the region which retained a large measure of its indigenous beliefs. Viqueira succinctly describes the diffusion of Protestantism, explaining that there are at least three forms of worship in Chiapas. Supported in part by the archival sources, this is a solid and pithy synthesis of the subject. [AL]

1204 Yucatán en el tiempo: enciclopedia alfabética. v. 1–3. Mérida, Mexico: Inversiones Cares, 1998-. 3 v.: ill. (some col.).

Thorough and well-prepared encyclopedia of Yucatecan history. The organization is onomastic and thematic. The essays are well documented and the coverage is complete. An excellent working tool. [AL]

COLONIAL
General

1205 Abadie-Aicardi, Aníbal. Contexto socio-cultural de la condición de pobreza y el beneficio de pobreza en la Universidad de México, 1553–1700. (*Jahrb. Gesch. Staat Wirtsch. Ges. Lat.am.*, 33, 1996, p. 99–128)

Examines access to university education for poor and relatively poor students in New Spain in the 16th-17th centuries. [AL]

1206 Aceves Pastrana, Patricia. La red científica en el área farmacéutica, química y metalúrgica en la Nueva España de finales del siglo XVIII. (*in* História da ciência: o mapa do conhecimento. Coordenação de Ana Maria Alfonso-Goldfarb e Carlos A. Maia. Rio de Janeiro: Expressão e Cultura; São Paulo: Edusp, 1996, p. 745–771)

Study of pharmaceutical, chemical, and metallurgical knowledge in the late-colonial period based on the works and treatises of contemporary authors. [AL]

1207 Aguirre Salvador, Rodolfo. El ascenso de los clérigos de Nueva España durante el gobierno del arzobispo José Lanciego y Eguilaz. (*Estud. Hist. Novohisp.*, 22, 2000, p. 77–110, bibl., tables)

Study of the system of appointment and promotion of the clergy in New Spain in the first quarter of the 18th century. Posits that Lanciego y Eguilaz, archbishop of Mexico was very favorable to the appointment of American-born clergy. [AL]

1208 Alba Pastor, María. Criollismo y contrarreforma: Nueva España entre 1570 y 1630. (*Ibero-Am. Arch.*, 22:3/4, 1996, p. 247–266)

Interpretive essay seeks to establish the roots of the word "criollo" as it was created, rejected, and then, eventually accepted by mid-17th century. [AL]

1209 Alberro, Solange. Barroquismo y criollismo en los recibimientos hechos a don Diego López Pacheco Cabrera y Bobadilla, virrey de Nueva España, 1640: un estudio preliminar. (*CLAHR*, 8:4, Fall 1999, p. 443–460)

Analyzes the meaning of the public performances celebrated at the 1640 reception of Viceroy Marquis of Villena, which mixed all ethnic groups and made use of multiple arts media. Of special interest is the fact that it was written about, and that the indigenous peoples became distinctively "Mexican" although the festivities attempted to express all cultural and ethnic elements. Author sees in such expressions an incipient manifestation of national identity. [AL]

1210 Alfaro Ramírez, Gustavo Rafael. ¿Quién encarceló al alguacil mayor de Puebla?: la vida, los negocios y el poder de Don Pedro de Mendoza y Escalante, 1695–1740. (*Estud. Hist. Novohisp.*, 17, 1997, p. 31–62, table)

Life and deeds of Pedro de Mendoza y Escalante, an Asturian who settled in Puebla achieved success as a meat provider for the city. Having signed a *poder* to marry a 12-year old in Spain, he became a bigamist when he married in Puebla. Entertaining reading and useful approach to personal history as emblematic of provincial colonial elite. [AL]

1211 Altman, Ida. Transatlantic ties in the Spanish empire: Brihuega, Spain, and Puebla, Mexico, 1560–1620. Stanford, Calif.: Stanford Univ. Press, 2000. 262 p.: bibl., ill., index, maps.

Traces the lives and deeds of approximately 800 migrants from the town of Brihuega (Spain) to Puebla (New Spain) between 1560–1620. Focuses on the daily lives of the migrants, their relationships, and conflicts. Dwells on how families separated, relocated, and reconfigured themselves through marriage and family life. Also deals with their activities in textiles, trade, and landownership. Their public and private lives are part of the history of late-16th century transatlantic migration and its impact on the formation of urban societies. [AL]

1212 Arias, Patricia and Rodolfo Fernández. Toluquilla y los Echauri: hacienda, familia y región en el sur de Jalisco, 1764–1853. (*Estud. Hombre*, 6, 1997, p. 159–181, tables)

Three closely studied testaments support this work on the evolution of a family in southern Jalisco that, in a modest way, captures the human interests of the family members throughout a century. [AL]

Arrom, Silvia Marina. Containing the poor: the Mexico City Poor House, 1774–1871. See item **1399.**

Astigueta, Bernardo P. Filósofos humanistas novohispánicos. See item **4628.**

1213 Báez-Jorge, Félix. Entre los naguales y los santos: religión popular y ejercicio clerical en el México indígena. Xalapa, Mexico: Univ. Veracruzana, 1998. 268 p.: bibl., ill. (Biblioteca/Universidad Veracruzana)

Drawing upon previously published works and Antonio Gramsci's model of hegemony, argues that indigenous popular religion emerged in a dialectical relationship to the religious and cultural hegemony of the Spaniards. The cult of saints represents the manifestation of the social effects and expression of resistance, utilizing both orthodox Catholicism and prehispanic Nahua visions of the cosmos. [P. Harms]

1214 **Baskes, Jeremy.** Indians, merchants, and markets: a reinterpretation of the repartimiento and Spanish-Indian economic relations in colonial Oaxaca, 1750–1821. Stanford, Calif.: Stanford Univ. Press, 2000. 305 p.: bibl., ill., index, maps.

Well-researched book focuses on the notorious commercial *repartimiento de efectos*, or sale of goods by local Spanish officials to the indigenous people, rather than the tribute labor system of the same name. This is a revisionist approach; the author rejects the old idea that the *repartimiento* was a coerced system fastened on the indigenous by a powerful and corrupt colonial state. A wealth of information about the structure of the region's cochineal trade is found here, forming an integral part of the study. [R. Haskett/ S. Wood]

1215 **Bechtloff, Dagmar.** Las cofradías en Michoacán durante la época de la colonia: la religión y su relación política y económica en una sociedad intercultural. Versión al español de Joaquín Francisco Zaballa Omaña. 1. ed. en español. Zinacantepec, Mexico: Colegio Michoacán: Colegio Mexiquense, 1996. 405 p.: bibl.

Translation of a study originally published in Hamburg, Germany (1992). Thorough and useful examination of confraternities in Michoacán in the last quarter of the 18th century, based on archival research. Provides sample data of foundations, ethnic composition, properties and their administration. A documentary annex and numerous tables strengthen this work. [AL]

1216 **Berthe, Jean-Pierre; Thomas Calvo; and Agueda Jiménez Pelayo.** Sociedades en construcción: la Nueva Galicia según las visitas de oidores, 1606–1616. Guadalajara, Mexico: Univ. de Guadalajara, Coordinación Editorial; México: Centre Français d'Études Mexicaines et Centraméricaines, 2000. 375 p.: bibl., indexes, maps. (Colección de documentos para la historia de Jalisco; 6)

Three co-authors provide critical introductions to colonial reports of three royal representatives relative to their visits to the rural jurisdiction of New Galicia at the beginning of the 17th century. Royal bureaucrats were charged with investigating and resolving problems between colonial authorities and indigenous groups in the areas of government, crime, agriculture, mining, and customs. Transcribes original sources and provides important data on labor, salaries, social mores, indigenous-Spanish relations, and details of local historical value. Commendable publication. [AL]

Beuchot, Mauricio. Escolástica y humanismo en Fray Julián Garcés. See item **4629**.

Beuchot, Mauricio. The history of philosophy in colonial Mexico. See item **4630**.

1217 **Boyer, Richard E.** Cast [sic] and identity in colonial Mexico: a proposal and an example. Storrs, Conn.: Center for Latin American & Caribbean Studies, Univ. of Connecticut; Providence, R.I.: Center for Latin American Studies, Brown Univ.; Amherst, Mass.: Latin American Studies Program, Univ. of Massachusetts, 1997. 20 p.: bibl. (Occasional paper/Latin American Studies Consortium of New England; no. 7)

Preview of Boyer's *Lives of the Bigamists* (see *HLAS 56:1125*). Argues for the ambiguity of racial identity in colonial Mexico and accommodation and resistance on racial typing. [P. Harms]

1218 **Brading, D.A.** Profecía, autoridad y religión en Nueva España. (*in* Coloquio de Antropología e Historia Regionales, *17th, Zamora, Mexico, 1995*. La Iglesia Católica en México. Zamora, Mexico: El Colegio de Michoacán; México: Secretaría de Gobernación, Subsecretaría de Asuntos Jurídicos y Asociaciones Religiosas, Dirección General de Asuntos Religiosas, 1997, p. 21–38)

Using three criteria developed by Cardinal John Henry Newman in 1877, Brading studies the meaning of Bartolomé de Las Casas, Bishop Juan de Palafox, and the priest Miguel Sánchez within the history of the mid-17th century apparition of the Virgin of Guadalupe. The three men represent the doctrinal, the hierarchical, and the worshipful natures of the Catholic Church. [AL]

1219 **Brescia, Michael M.** Material and cultural dimensions of episcopal authority: Tridentine donation and the Biblioteca Palafoxiana in seventeenth-century Puebla de los Angeles, Mexico. (*CLAHR*, 8:2, Spring 1999, p. 207–227)

Founded in mid-17th century, Bishop Palafox's library was created to support the education of the elite. Brescia explores the cultural and material ramifications of the foundation using the document of donation. [P. Harms]

1220 Calvo, Thomas. Por los caminos de Nueva Galicia: transportes y transportistas en el siglo XVII. Guadalajara, Mexico: Univ. de Guadalajara; Mexico: Centre Français d'Études Mexicaines et Centraméricaines, 1997. 190 p.: bibl., maps. (Colección de documentos para la historia de Jalisco; 5)

Argues that the transportation system of 17th century New Galicia reflects a microcosm of society. The roadways and those who traveled upon them influenced economic progress, connected urban and rural areas, and contributed to the existing social hierarchy. Based on archival research. [P. Harms]

1221 Cárdenas, Alejandra. Hechicería, saber y transgresión: afromestizas ante la Inquisición—Acapulco, 1621–1622. Chilpancingo, Mexico: Impr. "Candy", 1997. 134 p.: bibl., ill., maps.

Following French tradition of microhistory, studies the lives and times of three Afro-Mexicans from Acapulco brought to the Inquisition on charges of prostitution and witchcraft. [AL]

1222 Cárdenas Gutiérrez, Salvador. Razón de estado y emblemática política en los impresos novohispanos de los siglos XVII y XVIII. (*Relaciones/Zamora*, 18:71, verano 1997, p. 61–99, ill.)

Study of the emblems of royal power and their ability as symbols of royal and ecclesiastical power to legitimize the state's interests. Focuses on several means of expression, such as imprints, celebrations, and triumphal arches. [AL]

1223 Castañeda Delgado, Paulino and Isabel Arenas Frutos. Un portuense en México: don Juan Antonio Vizarrón, arzobispo y virrey. El Puerto de Santa María, Spain: Ayuntamiento de El Puerto de Santa María, 1998. 323 p.: bibl., ill. (some col.). (Biblioteca de temas portuenses; 7)

This volume contains two works on Vizarrón. Castañeda studies him as an archbishop, and Frutos examines his administration as Viceroy. Combined, they provide a satisfactory portrait of the man, his times, and his performance as the highest authority

in mid-18th century New Spain. Based on archival sources. [AL]

1224 Castañeda García, Carmen. Bienes, libros y escritos de Domingo Lázaro de Arregui. (*Estud. Hombre*, 6, 1997, p. 101–119)

To the personal information on the life of well-known 17th-century author, Castañeda adds data on his books while recalling contributions by herself and other historians. All of them yield a quite satisfactory personal profile of Arregui. [AL]

1225 Castellanos, Ana María de la O. La hacienda de San Clemente: un retrato de la oligarquía regional. (*Estud. Jalisc.*, 35, feb. 1999, p. 5–20)

Examines the 400-year history of Hacienda San Clemente situated between Guadalajara and the Pacific Coast. Good example of microhistory focusing on productivity, ownership, and workers. [P. Harms]

1226 Castro Gutiérrez, Felipe. Conflictos y fraudes electorales en los cabildos indígenas de Michoacán colonial. (*JILAS/Bundoora*, 4:2, Dec. 1998, p. 41–68, appendix)

Argues that indigenous cabildo electoral practices are part of a tradition. Michoacán communities adopted Spanish cabildo, but used it to ensure their own local interests. In the process, new groups acceded to power while elections channeled local tensions. Novel analysis supported by archival research. [AL]

1227 Castro Gutiérrez, Felipe. Migración indígena y cambio cultural en Michoacán colonial, siglos XVII y XVIII. (*CLAHR*, 7:4, Fall 1998, p. 419–440, maps, table)

Tarascan migration to the northern mines began in mid-16th century and ended by the 1680s, shifting to the agricultural south. A fierce competition for labor and a scarcity of communal lands seemed to have caused these shifts, according to Castro Gutiérrez, who elaborates on the nuances of this situation throughout the 18th century. For ethnohistorian's comment, see item **447**. [AL]

1228 Castro Rivas, Jorge A.; Matilde Rangel López; and Rafael Tovar Rangel. Desarrollo socio demográfico de la ciudad de Guanajuato durante el siglo XVII: investigación histórica. Guanajuato, Mexico: Univ. de Guanajuato, 1999. 88 p.: bibl., ill. (some col.), maps.

Quantitative analysis of the population of Guanajuato in the 17th century using baptismal, marriage, and death records reveals the peculiar traits of this mining town. Offers information on labor groupings, landownership, town personalities, and the incorporation of the indigenous groups to a Spanish-speaking community. [AL]

1229 **Ceballos-Escalera Gila, Alfonso.** Una navegación de Acapulco a Manila en 1611: el cosmógrafo mayor Juan Bautista de Labaña, el inventor Luis Fonseca Coutinho, y el problema de la desviación de la aguja. (*Rev. Hist. Nav.*, 17:65, 1999, p. 7–42, bibl., map)

Makes a case for recognizing Portuguese and Spanish navigators of the Manilla Galleon route, who, in the late-16th century, began attempting to resolve the problem of magnetic deviation in the long trek between the Philippines and the New World. [AL]

1230 **Cervantes Bello, Francisco Javier.** Crisis agrícola y guerra de independencia en el entorno de Puebla: el caso de San Martín y sus cercanías, 1800–1820. (*Estud. Hist. Novohisp.*, 20, 1999, p. 107–133, graphs, map, tables)

Using the figures of the *diezmo* (tithes), reconstructs the state of agriculture in the Puebla area, noting that lack of labor, lack of demand, and debts affected production negatively afer 1813, especially for the small landowner. [AL]

1231 **Círculos de poder en la Nueva España.** Coordinación de Carmen Castañeda García. México: CIESAS: M.A. Porrúa, 1998. 239 p.: bibl.

Anthology of nine essays on the political elites of the peripheral areas of New Spain. Each author selected his or her vision of the elites. Thus there are studies of one single individual or groups of people and their social and political activities. Despite the diversity of approaches, this work is commendable both for renewing the study of elites in Mexico and for the historical strength of its contributions. [AL]

1232 **Contreras Sánchez, Alicia del C.** Algunas fuentes de precios de los colorantes, 1750–1802. (*Am. Lat. Hist. Econ.*

Bol. Fuentes, 5, enero/junio 1996, p. 39–50, tables)

Study of the fluctuations in the price of dyes. Proposes that price information is key to assess impact on producers and consumers of the product. [P. Harms]

1233 **El crédito en Nueva España.** Coordinación de María del Pilar Martínez López-Cano y Guillermina del Valle Pavón. México: Instituto Mora, El Colegio de Michoacán, El Colegio de México, Instituto de Investigaciones Históricas-UNAM, 1998. 243 p.: bibl. (Lecturas de historia económica mexicana)

Anthology of previously published works on credit, largely focusing on the 18th century. Useful introductory essay of a historiographical nature. [AL]

Crespo, Ana María and **Beatriz Cervantes.** El papel de la élite Otomí en el avance hispano hacia el norte de México. See item **459.**

1234 **Cruz Velázquez, Romeo.** El hospital de San Juan de Montes Claros en la época borbónica: Veracruz, 1760–1800. (*Entorno Urbano*, 2:3, enero/junio 1996, p. 83–102, bibl., tables)

Describes the penury, unsanitary conditions and maladministration of the hospital under the care of the order of San Hipólito. Of interest for public health history and the politics of hospital administration in the city of Veracruz. [AL]

1235 **Cuenya, Miguel Ángel.** De la metrópoli a la Puebla de los Angeles: un acercamiento al estudio de la migración española en el siglo XVIII. (*Entorno Urbano*, 2:3, enero/junio 1996, p. 7–38, bibl., facsim., maps, tables)

One fourth of the population of Puebla came from Spain, mostly from Castile and Andalusia. Study surveys that migration in the 18th century. Tables are the best part of the work. [AL]

1236 **Cuenya, Miguel Ángel.** Peste en una ciudad novohispana: el matlazahuatl de 1737 en la Puebla de los Angeles. (*Anu. Estud. Am.*, 53:2, 1996, p. 51–70, maps, tables)

Study of the character and demographic impact of the epidemic of *matlazahuatl* in the city of Puebla. Provides number of deaths according to gender and race. [AL]

1237 **De Rueda Iturrate, Carlos José.** Envío de misioneros franciscanos a Nueva España, 1790–1830. (*Arch. Ibero-Am.*, 57:225/226, 1997, p. 421–432, graphs, tables)

Explores the geographical origins and the destination of Franciscans arriving in Mexico between 1790–1830. Combines statistical analysis with narrative history. [P. Harms]

1238 **Delgado Aguilar, Francisco Javier.** Subdelegados en Aguascalientes a fines del siglo XVIII: la aplicación de la Ordenanza de Intendentes. (*Caleidoscopio/ Aguascalientes*, 3:5, enero/junio 1999, p. 35–79)

Details the problem subdelegates had with local authorities and other members of the bureaucracy in the enforcement of the laws and the exercise of their power. In Aguascalientes the cabildo functioned without subdelegados between 1799–1803 and 1805–09, proving the desire of many communities to maintain their autonomy. [AL]

1239 **Díaz Cruz, Manuel J.** La élite indígena colonial de la alcaldía mayor de Chiapas, México. (*Bol. Am./Barcelona*, 49, 1999, p. 81–101, bibl., map, table)

Useful methodic analysis of the social and religious hierarchy of the colonial Maya communities in Chiapas. [AL]

1240 **Díaz del Castillo, Bernal.** Historia verdadera de la Conquista de la Nueva España. v. 1. Madrid: Dastin, 2000. 1 v.: bibl., 1 map. (Crónicas de América; 2- Historia)

Extensive introduction analyzes the manuscripts on which the various editions of Bernal Díaz are based, the literary significance of the book, and the author's intent. Finds literary relationship with Cervantes' *Don Quixote*. [EBC]

1241 **Enciso Contreras, José.** Trabajadores indios del valle de Tlaltenango, Zacatecas, en las Salinas Viejas de Santa María en el siglo XVI. (*Estud. Hist. Novohisp.*, 18, 1998, p. 31–67, tables)

Provides useful details on labor recruitment for the salt mines in Zacatecas among the indigenous population of a town near Guadalajara, 14 days away from the mines. Furnishes information on salaries, diseases, labor, and impact personal lives and homes. [AL]

1242 **Escamilla González, Francisco Iván.** Inmunidad eclesiástica y regalismo en Nueva España a fines del siglo XVIII: el proceso de Fray Jacinto Miranda. (*Estud. Hist. Novohisp.*, 19, 1999, p. 47–68, bibl.)

Interesting study of a Mercedarian friar tried for murder in late colonial Mexico. It tested the regalist policies developed by Charles III and Charles IV restricting the ecclesiastical *fueros*. While the case was effectively deterred by the Archbishop, it gave the Audiencia the opportunity to make a case for the restriction of religious privileges. [AL]

1243 **La escritura femenina en la espiritualidad barroca novohispana: siglos XVII y XVIII.** Edición de Asunción Lavrin y Rosalva Loreto L. Puebla, Mexico: Univ. de las Américas; México: Archivo General de la Nación, 2002. 273 p.: bibl.

This edited collection of five spiritual autobiographies, biographies, and letters contains explanatory introductions. The nuns lived and wrote in Puebla, Querétaro, and Mexico City in the 17th-18th centuries. The texts inform us about mysticism, education, and daily life in colonial convents. This book also informs us about the history of postreformation Catholicism. [EBC]

1244 **Fee, Nancy H.** La entrada angelopolitana: ritual and myth in the viceregal entry in Puebla de Los Angeles. (*Americas/Washington*, 52:3, Jan. 1996, p. 283–320)

Elaborate description of all aspects of the preparation and execution of fiestas for the welcome of the viceroys in Puebla. Explains the emblematic meaning of the arches, the writings to memorialize the visits, etc. The fiestas attempted to demonstrate the prestige of the city. [AL]

1245 **Fernández Bulete, Virgilio.** La desconocida *relación de gobierno* del Duque de Alburquerque, Virrey de Nueva España. (*Anu. Estud. Am.*, 55:2, julio/dic. 1998, p. 677–702)

The Duque of Alburquerque left two accounts of his administration (1653–60) which have recently been discovered. One is extremely short and the second is 20 folios long, containing a more informative overview of his government. Both are reproduced in this work, which also provides a brief account of his activities in New Spain. [AL]

1246 **Ferrer Muñoz, Manuel.** Las comunidades indígenas de la Nueva España y el movimiento insurgente, 1810–1817. (*Anu. Estud. Am.*, 56:2, julio/dic. 1999, p. 513–538)

Surveys the literature of the independence movement to assess the contribution of indigenous peoples to the wars and the opinion held about their participation by contemporaries and modern historians. [AL]

1247 **Flores Clair, Eduardo.** Los créditos del Tribunal de Minería de Nueva España, 1777–1823. (*Ibero-Am. Arch.*, 24:1/2, 1998, p. 3–30, bibl., graphs, table)

Surveys the credit resources and the lending pattern of the powerful Tribunal de Minería in the last 50 years of the viceregal period. Organized as a corporation in 1776, its funds came from taxes on minting. Between 1777–1823, this "bank" made 500 loans worth over 10 million pesos. This careful study follows its lending policies and concludes that a great deal of speculation prevailed and that the Crown abused its rights to borrow. Based on archival sources, this is a commendable contribution. [AL]

1248 **Flores Padilla, Georgina.** Las crónicas jesuitas en relación con el Colegio de San Pedro y San Pablo, 1573–1597. (*in* Historia y universidad: homenaje a Lorenzo Mario Luna. México: UNAM, Centro de Estudios sobre la Univ. y Facultad de Filosofía y Letras; Instituto Dr. José María Luis Mora, 1996, p. 307–327)

Comparative study of the different Jesuit chronicles aiming at clarifying the history of the foundation and development of the Colegio de San Pedro y San Pablo in the 16th century. [AL]

1249 **Francois, Marie.** *Prendas* and *pulperías:* the fabric of the neighborhood credit business in Mexico City, 1780s–1830s. (*Estud. Hist. Novohisp.*, 20, 1999, p. 67–106, tables)

Socioeconomic study of small businesses (*pulperías*) in late colonial Mexico City. Supported by official census data and archival sources, this study shows that the *pulperías* acted as pawnshops. Also describes the nature of their merchandise and the extent of their profits. [AL]

1250 **García Castro, René.** Indios, territorio y poder en la provincia Matlatzinca: la negociación del espacio político de los pueblos otomianos, siglos XV-XVII. México: CONACULTA-INAH, 1999. 519 p.: bibl., ill. (2 folded). (Historias CIESAS)

In-depth study of the Otomi Indians in the 16th century with an overview of the fate of this area during the rest of the colonial era. Dwells on lordship, conquest, encomienda, conversion, assimilation of Spanish institutions, etc. Nearly half the work is devoted to appendixes that provide synthetic and useful information. Based on archival research. Commendable work. [AL]

1251 **García León, Antonio.** Economía y vida cotidiana en el Veracruz del siglo XVII: 1585–1707. (*Bol. Am./Barcelona*, 38:48, 1998, p. 29–45)

Charmingly written, this article traces the history of the city of Veracruz, as the center of voluminous legal and illegal trade and the meeting place of different races and cultures, where Crypto-Jews, Africans, Spaniards, and Indians created a true biological and cultural melting pot. [AL]

1252 **Giraudo, Laura.** Conquista y constitución: el paseo del real pendón en la ciudad de México, 1809–1818. (*Estud. Ibero-Am./Porto Alegre*, 25:1, junho 1999, p. 7–21)

Analysis of the symbolic meaning of the ritual of exhibiting the royal mace under the auspices of the Mexico City *ayuntamiento* in the last days of the Viceroyalty. Playing a role in a dispute with the Indians, and restored for a few years, it disappeared in 1815. [AL]

Gómez, Fernando. Experimentación social en los albores coloniales de la modernidad: el deseo utópico-reformista de Vasco de Quiroga, 1470–1565. See item **4637.**

1253 **Gómez, Fernando.** The legal reformation of Indian subjectivities: Quiroga's *Información en derecho*, 1535. (*Rev. Hist. Am./México*, 122, 1997, p. 25–107)

Examines the legality of colonization through the figure of Vasco de Quiroga and his 1535 treatise, *Información en derecho* which challenged the validity of the Spanish presence and suggested internal reforms. [P. Harms]

1254 **Gómez Alvarez, Cristina and Francisco Téllez Guerrero.** Un hombre de estado y sus libros: el obispo Campillo, 1740–1813. Puebla, Mexico: Benemérita Univ. Autónoma de Puebla, Instituto de

Ciencias Sociales y Humanidades, 1997. 205 p.: bibl., ill., index.

The library of Manuel Ignacio González del Campillo, Bishop of Puebla from 1803–13, is inventoried in this volume. The book is organized into two parts: pt. 1, the shorter section, examines the bishop himself, while pt. 2, the more extensive section, explores his collection of printed materials. [P. Harms]

1255 Gonzalbo, Pilar. Educación y vida cotidiana en la Nueva España según la historiografía contemporánea. (*in* Historia y universidad: homenaje a Lorenzo Mario Luna. México: UNAM, Centro de Estudios sobre la Univ. y Facultad de Filosofía y Letras; Instituto Dr. José María Luis Mora, 1996, p. 291–305, bibl.)

Makes a case for historians to consider all aspects of daily life as part of the history of education. Uses texts of Christian indoctrination, sermons, theater, confessionals, etc., to show how they taught modes of social conduct that were part of the informal education of most people. [AL]

1256 Gonzalbo, Pilar. La familia novohispana y la ruptura de los modelos. (*Colon. Lat. Am. Rev.,* 9:1, June 2000, p. 7–19, bibl., tables)

Interpretive essay in which the author argues that there were many models of families in New Spain. Discusses illegitimacy and marriage rates among the different ethnic groups to define nuances in the family formation process and suggest a trend towards legitimization of families among all races in the late-18th century. [AL]

1257 Gonzalbo, Pilar. Familia y orden colonial. México: El Colegio de México, Centro de Estudios Históricos, 1998. 316 p.: bibl., ill.

Colonial authorities envisioned the life of their subjects in one way and people acted in opposing ways. The numbers of children born out of wedlock, concubinage, numbers of unrelated residents in one household, secular women living in convents, vows of chastity ignored, and abuse of workers and slaves leads the author to conclude that a parallel order was constructed by residents. Meticulous research in primary and secondary sources. [EBC]

1258 González Fasani, Ana Mónica. Problemática del clero en el México del siglo XVII: aproximaciones a un texto de Juan de Palafox y Mendoza. (*in* Vida pública y vida privada: actas de las primeras jornadas de historia argentina y americana; Buenos Aires, 5 al 7 de junio de 1996. Buenos Aires: Facultad de Filosofía y Letras de la Pontificia Univ. Católica Argentina Santa María de los Buenos Aires, 1996, p. 183–200, bibl.)

Analysis of a letter from Palafox to Innocent X challenging the validity of the Jesuits' presence in New Spain as a disruptive element in need of discipline and reform. Extensive quotations from the original with some commentary on the conflict between the regular and the secular clergy. [P. Harms]

1259 González González, Enrique and **Víctor Gutiérrez Rodríguez.** Los consiliarios en el surgimiento de la Real Universidad de México, 1553–1573. (*in* Historia y universidad: homenaje a Lorenzo Mario Luna. México: UNAM, Centro de Estudios sobre la Univ. y Facultad de Filosofía y Letras; Instituto Dr. José María Luis Mora, 1996, p. 339–390, tables)

Prospographic study of the student representatives in the governing board of the Real Univ. de México. [AL]

1260 González Rodríguez, Jaime. Circuitos de comunicación social en Nueva España: el caso de la política lingüística. (*Mar Oceana,* 3, 1999, p. 17–46, tables)

Informative review of the language policies of the Spanish Crown throughout the colonial period. Faced with the dilemma of catechisms in either native languages or Spanish, the Church and the Crown followed a meandering path in the 16th century, favoring one or the other. Eventual adoption of a mixed approach prevailed through much of the colonial period, using Nahuatl as the official indigenous language alongside Spanish. Well-crafted article. [AL]

González Rodríguez, Jaime. Lecturas e ideas en Nueva España. See item **4639**.

1261 González Sánchez, Isabel. Haciendas, tumultos y trabajadores: Puebla-Tlaxcala, 1778–1798. México: Instituto Nacional de Antropología e Historia, 1997. 181 p.: bibl. (Colección Fuentes) (Serie Manuales)

Looking into archival sources, author hopes to prove that the treatment of the peones in late-18th century haciendas was inequitable and abusive at times, even though the laborers sometimes challenged their status in the form of small local revolts. Uses testimonies from four haciendas in the vicinity of Puebla. Includes useful documentary appendix. [AL]

1262 Grajales Porras, Agustín and José Luis Aranda Romero. Niños abandonados e hijos naturales en la ciudad de Puebla a mediados del siglo XVII. (*Novahispania/México*, 3, 1998, p. 209–226, graphs, tables)

Statistical demographic study of abandoned and illegitimate children in the city of Puebla in mid-17th century. Both conditions were high among all races of the population. [AL]

1263 Grande, Carlos. Sinaloa en la historia. v. 1, Sinaloa indígena. Sinaloa colonial. 1a coedición UAS-Gobierno del Estado de Sinaloa. Culiacán Rosales, Mexico: Univ. Autónoma de Sinaloa: Gobierno del Estado de Sinaloa, 1998. 1 v.: bibl., ill., maps. (Colección 125 aniversario)

In this first of two volumes, Grande focuses on the cultural history of indigenous and colonial Sinaloa. Relying primarily on secondary sources, this 665 p. volume explores significant historical events as well as Sinaloa's geography, climate, and populations. [P. Harms]

1264 Grunberg, Bernard. L'inquisition apostolique au Mexique: histoire d'une institution et de son impact dans une société coloniale, 1521–1571. Paris: L'Harmattan, 1998. 236 p.: bibl., ill., map. (Collection Recherches Amériques latines)

Follows the establishment and activities of the apostolic Inquisition, when the institution was dominated by powerful individual archbishops, and acted as the moral and religious watchguard of nascent Mexico. Based on archival sources, this work is a compact survey of the topic. [AL]

1265 Guedea, Virginia. The first popular elections in Mexico City, 1812–1813. (*in* Origins of Mexican national politics, 1808–1847. Wilmington, Del.: SR Books, 1997, p. 39–63)

Revision and translation of a 1991 article on the first popular elections in Mexico City. [AL]

1266 Guerra, Francisco. Origen y efectos demográficos del tifo en el México colonial. (*CLAHR*, 8:3, Summer 1999, p. 273–319, facsims.)

Survey of the origin and demographic effects of typhus on both the Spanish and indigenous population. Also studies lifestyles and concludes that Spaniards were more resistant to the disease largely as a result of different hygienic conditions. [P. Harms]

1267 Gunnarsdóttir, Ellen. The convent of Santa Clara, the elite and social change in eighteenth century Querétaro. (*J. Lat. Am. Stud.*, 33:2, May 2001, p. 257–290, graphs, tables)

Deftly investigates the changing role that the convent played in the society and economy of Querétaro. Families affirmed their status by placing daughters in Santa Clara, borrowing money, and participating in extravagant celebrations of holy days. Later in the 18th century, nuns came from different sections of the Bajio and varied social classes, and the economy depended less upon Santa Clara as a source of capital and status. The secularization of society and increasing role of peninsular merchants debilitated the convent. [EBC]

1268 Gutiérrez Zamora, Angel Camiro. El origen del guadalupanismo: fue Montúfar, y no Zumárraga, el padre de la devoción a la Virgen de Guadalupe. México: EDAMEX, 1996. 211 p.: bibl., ill.

General history of the origins of worship of the Virgin of Guadalupe. Posits that Archibishop Fr. Alonso de Montúfar was the "father" of the worship since he openly supported it against the wishes of the Franciscans. Montúfar's plan was to remove the Indians from under the influence of the orders and bring them into the secular church. [AL]

1269 Guzmán, Nuño de. Proceso, tormento y muerte del Cazonzi, último Gran Señor de los tarascos. Introducción, versión paleográfica y notas de Armando M. Escobar Olmedo. Morelia, Mexico: Frente de Afirmación Hispanista, A.C., 1997. 215 p.: bibl., indexes.

Complete transcription of two archival sources dealing with the judgement and death of the Puérepecha leader Cazonzi. They are Legajo 2205 (Section Justice) of the Archives of the Indies (Seville)—previously unpublished, and Legajo 108–6 of the same section—first published in 1952. Useful for historians of the period. [AL]

1270 Haslip-Viera, Gabriel. Crime and punishment in late colonial Mexico City, 1692–1810. Albuquerque: Univ. of New Mexico Press, 1999. 205 p.: bibl., index, maps.

Focuses on late 18th-century urban crime committed by the poor in the city of Mexico. Underlines socioeconomic background of petty criminals, attitudes about crime, and means to control it. Broad sociological base complemented by numerous tables and a readable text. [AL]

1271 Hausberger, Bernd. La Nueva España y sus metales preciosos: la industria minera colonial a través de los *libros de cargo y data* de la Real Hacienda, 1761–1767. Frankfurt: Vervuert Verlag; Madrid: Iberoamericana, 1997. 323 p.: bibl., graphs, tables.

Significant work on the 18th-century mining boom in 10 centers utilizing and analyzing the plethora of quantitative evidence. Includes questions of technology, capital formation, entreprenuers, and labor. [EBC]

1272 Higgins, Antony. Constructing the criollo archive: subjects of knowledge in the *Bibliotheca mexicana* and the *Rusticatio mexicana*. West Lafayette, Ind.: Purdue Univ. Press, 2000. 283 p.: bibl., index. (Purdue studies in Romance literatures; v. 21)

Studies how criollos sought to "articulate a body of practical and theoretical knowledge of their environment and the history of its inhabitants with a view to constructing themselves a position and space of authority within colonial society." The *Biblioteca mexicana* allows its author, Juan José de Eguiara y Eguren, to catalog and interpret information. *Rusticatio mexicana* allows its author, Rafael Landívar, to detail the features that distinguish New Spain. [AL]

1273 Historia de Chilpancingo. Chilpancingo, Mexico: Asociación de Historiadores de Guerrero: H. Ayuntamiento de Chilpancingo: Gobierno del Estado de Guerrero: Univ. Autónoma de Guerrero, 1999. 307 p.: bibl., ill., maps.

These collected essays focus on the history of Chilpancingo, in the state of Guerrero, where Morelos held his 1813 congress.

While the work covers the city's entire history, the first chapters focus on its precolonial roots and the colonial era. One chapter analyzes the establishment of the 1813 congress. All contributors integrate both primary and secondary sources in their analysis. [P. Harms]

1274 Historia y arte en un pueblo rural: San Bartolomé (hoy Valle de Allende, Chihuahua). Coordinación de Clara Bargellini. México: UNAM, Instituto de Investigaciones Estéticas, 1998. 342 p.: bibl., ill., index, maps. (Estudios y fuentes del arte en México; 61)

Interdisciplinary study of a small town in Chihuahua. Combined effort by urban, social, and art historians provides in-depth examination of the birth of the town in an oasis. Town's urban development and the development of a parish rich in worship treasures are carefully studied. Demonstrates the advantages of multiple perspectives when doing microhistory projects. [AL]

Hurtado López, Juan Manuel. La evangelización en la obra y pensamiento de Vasco de Quiroga. See item **4640**.

1275 Ilarione, da Bergamo, fra. Daily life in colonial Mexico: the journey of Friar Ilarione da Bergamo, 1761–1768. Translated from the Italian by Williams J. Orr; edited by Robert Ryal Miller and William J. Orr. Norman: Univ. of Oklahoma Press, 2000. 240 p.: bibl., facsims., maps, photos. (The American exploration and travel series; v. 78)

First translation into English of a diary of a mid-18th century Capuchin monk who stayed five years in Mexico. While not offering much new factual information, it still provides many interesting details about daily life in late colonial Mexico. [AL]

Imágenes de los inmigrantes en la ciudad de México, 1753–1910. See item **1438**.

1276 Indios y franciscanos en la construcción de Santiago de Querétaro, siglos XVI y XVII. Contribuciones de José Antonio Cruz *et al.* Santiago de Querétaro, Mexico: Gobierno del Estado de Querétaro, Archivo Histórico del Estado, 1997. 284 p.: bibl.

Five essays on 16th-17th century Querétaro. Based on key archival sources, each essay attempts to enrich our knowledge of the role of Franciscans and indigenous elites in the life of the city. No central theme connects the essays. [AL]

1277 Inquisición novohispana. v. 1–2. México: UNAM, Instituto de Investigaciones Antropológicas: Univ. Autónoma Metropolitana, 2000. 2 v.: bibl., ill., maps.

Comprehensive study of the Inquisition in its multiple functions and forms of influence. Includes 46 essays covering such topics as indigenous peoples, medicine, literature, censorship of books, and popular religiosity. Ranging from traditional to newer interpretations, the various works provide a wealth of information about the relationship of the institution with the people it was assumed to have controlled. [AL]

1278 Jiménez Abollado, Francisco L. Implantación y evolución de la encomienda en la provincia de Tabasco, 1522–1625. (*Anu. Estud. Am.*, 57:1, enero/junio 2000, p. 13–39)

Surveys adoption of encomienda in Tabasco, the coastal southwest, a region hostile to any Spanish enterprise. Consequently, most Spaniards living there relied on encomiendas throughout the 16th century. The declining Indian population encouraged many encomenderos to transfer ownership to others so that by the beginning of the 17th century, available encomiendas had been concentrated in the hands of a few. [AL/B. Cassity]

1279 Jiménez Pelayo, Agueda. Una visión sobre la esclavitud en la Nueva Galicia a fines del periodo colonial. (*Estud. Hombre*, 6, 1997, p. 145–158, table)

Useful profile of the African and mixed ancestry population of New Galicia, based on two censuses and different archival sources. Provides information on the purchase and sale of slaves, manumission, and prices, numbers of blacks vs. mulattoes, and the final census of 1813–14. Table based on the 1789–1913 census. [AL]

1280 Jocotitlán. Coordinación de Rosaura Hernández Rodríguez. Jocotitlán, Mexico: Municipio de Jocotitlán; Zinacantepec, Mexico: Colegio Mexiquense, 2000. 217 p.: bibl., ill., maps. (Cuadernos municipales; 14)

Interdisciplinary anthology focuses on the municipality of Jocotitlán, a region of rich archeological sites. Includes chapters on archeology and family and on caciques in the 17th century. The last four chapters focus on contemporary historical events. [P. Harms]

1281 Katzew, Ilona. Algunos datos nuevos sobre el fundador de la Real Academia de San Carlos, Jerónimo Antonio Gil. (*Mem. Mus. Nac. Arte,* 7, 1998, p. 31–65, bibl., ill., plates)

Personal data on the life and family life of engraver Jerónimo Antonio Gil, who died in 1798 and who taught at the art academy of San Carlos. The inclusion of his will and inventory are useful. [AL]

1282 Krippner-Martínez, James. Rereading the conquest: power, politics, and the history of early colonial Michoacán, Mexico, 1521–1565. University Park: Pennsylvania State Univ. Press, 2001. 222 p.: bibl., ill., index.

Revisionist view of 16th-century Michoacán argues in a series of essays that Nuño de Guzmán was made the villain of the conquest in order to make other conquerors and settlers appear in a more favorable light. Indicates that Vasco de Quiroga shared many ethnocentric and patriarchal traits with Nuño de Guzmán. He owned slaves, believed that Indians were natural slaves, and was a harsh and blunt man. Heroic image of Quiroga appeared only in the 18th century. [EBC]

1283 Lameiras, Brigitte Boehm de and **Margarita Sandoval Manzo.** La transformación cultural de un paisaje palustre: tiempos largos en la Ciénega de Chapala. (*Estud. Hombre,* 10, 1999, p. 81–123, bibl., maps)

Ecological history of property in the swamp region of Chapala, Guadalajara. Intense struggles for land between nonindigenous and indigenous peoples runs through 21st century. Highlights ownership and production. [AL]

1284 Landavazo Arias, Marco Antonio. La fidelidad al rey: donativos y préstamos novohispanos para la guerra contra Napoleón. (*Hist. Mex./México,* 48:3, enero/ marzo 1999, p. 493–521, bibl.)

Argues that Ferdinand VII was a popular king whose capitivity triggered numerous cash gifts and loans during the war with Spain. [AL]

1285   Larkin, Brian. The splendor of worship: baroque Catholicism, religious reform, and last wills and testaments in eighteenth-century Mexico City. (*CLAHR*, 8:4, Fall 1999, p. 405–442, tables)

Three archbishops of Mexico in the 18th century discouraged the use of highly decorated and elaborate images of saints, and sought to simplify and reform the practice of heavily decorating churches. Author examined 960 wills from plague years of 1696, 1737, 1779, and 1813, and concludes that episcopal reforming efforts failed to discourage testators from leaving substantial bequests for the decoration of churches. In fact, a surge in such pious practices occurred in 1779, at the height of episcopal reforming efforts. Women remained more faithful to baroque piety than did men. [EBC]

1286   Lavrin, Asunción. La escritura desde un mundo oculto: espiritualidad y anonimidad en el Convento de San Juan de la Penitencia. (*Estud. Hist. Novohisp.*, 22, 2000, p. 49–76, bibl.)

The journal of a nun directed to her spiritual director or confessor reveals some of her interior life in addition to the 18th-century spirituality of an enclosed woman. Aspects of the intellectual life of the convent—both the opportunities for expression and the limitations of a spiritual life—appear in the analysis of this document. Finds that Jesus and the angels do not treat the nun as an ignorant person but rather as a wise woman. The document provides new intellectual visions of woman as protagonist. [EBC]

1287   Lavrin, Asunción. Indian brides of Christ: creating new spaces for indigenous women in New Spain. (*Mex. Stud.*, 15:2, Summer 1999, p. 225–260)

Analysis and narration of the changing attitudes of white elites toward the Indian nobility and Indian women over three centuries. Discusses the actions of Indian women who came to epitomize the highest spiritual state among the elites of 18th-century New Spain. These changing attitudes made possible the establishment of three convents for Indian women. Illuminates issues of class, race, and religion over three centuries while telling a compelling story. [EBC]

1288   Lipsett-Rivera, Sonya. The intersection of rape and marriage in late-colonial and early-national Mexico. (*CLAHR*, 6:4, Fall 1997, p. 559–590, appendix, tables)

On the basis of extensive archival research and published accounts of Nahuatl society, concludes that the legal and practical relationship between rape and marriage was derived from Spanish law and not from indigenous antecedents. Extensive examination of judicial cases from 1720–1856 records ages and races of victims and the resolution of the cases. [EBC]

1289   López Castillo, Gilberto. El Palmito de Verde: una hacienda ganadera en la costa de Sinaloa. (*Estud. Jalisc.*, 35, feb. 1999, p. 49–63)

Chronological study of an important hacienda in Sinaloa belonging to the Marquis of Panuco, Francisco Xavier Vizcarra. Traces its formation and development as a grain and cattle center. [P. Harms]

1290   Luque Alcaide, Elisa. Agustin de Hipona en Juan de Grijalba. (*in* Tempus Implendi Promissa. Homenaje al Prof. Dr. Domingo Ramón-Lissón. Pamplona, Spain: Eunsa, 2000. p. 729–746)

Analysis of the theological influence of St. Augustin in Juan de Grijalba's *Chronicle of the Order of St. Augustin in New Spain*, which also includes the history of the Order in the Philippines. Luque shows how Grijalba followed Augustinian interpretation of history as a providential event planned by God. [AL]

1291   Luque Alcaide, Elisa. La evangelización americana en Pedro de Feria y el III Concilio Provincial Mexicano. (*Annu. Hist. Concil./Paderborn*, 31:1, 1999, p. 145–165)

Analysis of the *Memorial* to the Third Mexican Council by Bishop of Chiapas, Pedro de Feria. According to Luque Alcaide, the bishop's writing reflected an older "missional" form of evangelization out of touch with the newer spirit of Trent. [AL]

1292   Luque Alcaide, Elisa. Paternidad de Dios en el Catecismo Zapoteco de Pedro de Feria. (*in* Dios y Padre Nuestro Senor Jesucristo. Coordinación de Jose Luis Illanes *et al.* Pamplona, Spain: Publicaciones de la Univ. de Navarra, 2000, p. 165–182)

Careful analysis of Feria's explanation

of the concept of God as One, Father of All, merciful and the source of salvation, to his Zapotec neophytes. Also shows how he stressed the theory of unity of all humanity. Useful guide to key theological concepts of early evangelizer. [AL]

1293 Maldonado Polo, J. Luis. De California a El Petén: el naturalista riojano José Longinos Martínez en Nueva España. Logroño, Spain: Gobierno de La Rioja, Instituto de Estudios Riojanos, 1997. 194 p.: bibl., col. ill., col. maps. (Ciencias de la tierra; 20)

Itinerary of the life and work of a distinguished scientist of the late 18th century. Discusses his influence as a collector, preserver, and cataloger of the flora and fauna of Mexico and Guatemala. Good illustrations. [AL]

1294 María de San José, Madre. A wild country out in the garden: the spiritual journals of a colonial Mexican nun. Selected, edited, and translated by Kathleen A. Myers and Amanda Powell. Bloomington: Indiana Univ. Press, 1999. 386 p.: bibl., ill., index, maps.

Lively and detailed account of life of Madre María de San José (1656–1719) offers a "rare and vivid glimpse" of complex society of colonial Mexico, and of how class, race, and gender "helped shape the roles people played in society and the ways in which they contributed to community belief and identity." Collaboration of two major Hispanic scholars has produced a rich volume setting a high-water mark for editing unpublished colonial texts. Introductory study and incisive discussion of translation issues precede Pt. 1, "The Translated Selections," edited from among the 2,000 pages of Madre María's writing over three decades (1656–1717). Pt. 1 includes chapters about her long struggle to enter the Augustinian convent; the early years at Santa Mónica in Puebla; and her new foundation in Oaxaca. Pt. 2, by the joint editors, focuses on the nun's world, gender, tradition, and autobiographical spiritual writings. Appendices offer chronologies, an outline of the contents of Madre María's 12 journals, a glossary, and an extensive bibliography. This scholarly tour-de-force provides a wealth of hitherto unknown and unavailable writing, in combination with brilliant scholarship and a stunning translation. An essential source for the study of writing by religious women in colonial Mexico. Highly recommended for classroom and research use alike. For colonial literary specialist's review, see item **3411**. [M. Ahern]

1295 Martínez Ferrer, Luis. Las ordenes mendicantes y el sacramento de la confesión en Nueva España, siglo XVI. (*Rev. Complut. Hist. Am.*, 24, 1998, p. 47–68)

Using the chronicles of the mendicant orders, surveys the pedagogical methods used to teach the sacrament of confession, and describes how the Indians responded to indocrination. Focuses on the method and form, strictly from a missionary's point of view. [AL]

1296 Menegus Bornemann, Margarita. El gobierno de los indios en la Nueva España, siglo XVI: señores o cabildo. (*Rev. Indias*, 59:217, sept./dic. 1999, p. 599–616)

Analysis of the historical discussion over the recognition of the indigenous lords by members of the Church and Crown. Accepted at the municipal level, changes introduced throughout the 16th century caused the ascent of commoners and the decline in power of the traditional indigenous elites. Clear and useful synthesis of the debate. [AL]

1297 Michoacán en la década de 1580: relaciones. Estudio introductorio y recopilación de J. Benedict Warren. Morelia, Mexico: Univ. Michoacana de San Nicolás de Hidalgo, Instituto de Investigaciónes Históricas, 2000. 125 p.: bibl. (Col. Nuestras raíces; 6)

Introduces two important documents for the history of the church in Michoacán in the 16th century. One by Juan de Medina Rincón, a Spanish Augustinian bishop, and the second by Diego Muñoz, a Creole Franciscan. Both contain information on the members of the orders and the administration of ecclesiastical affairs. [AL]

1298 Monroy, María Isabel and Tomás Calvillo Unna. Breve historia de San Luis Potosí. México: El Colegio de México, Fideicomiso Historia de las Américas: Fondo de Cultura Económica, 1997 (1999 printing). 335 p.: bibl., maps. (Serie Breves historias de los estados de la República Mexicana) (Sección de obras de historia)

Part of a series on histories of Mexican states, this book focuses on both the colonial and modern eras of San Luis Potosí. Utilizing both primary and secondary sources, the first five chapters focus on the precolonial and colonial experience. Includes geographic and cultural information, as well as an annotated bibliography. [P. Harms]

1299 Montanos Ferrin, Emma. Felipe II y la Universidad de México. (*in* Congreso del Instituto Internacional de Historia del Derecho Indiano, *11th, Buenos Aires, 1995.* Actas y estudios. Buenos Aires: Instituto de Investigaciones de Historia del Derecho Indiano, 1997, v. 1, p. 385–430)

Argues that the reorganization of the university in Mexico City in the 1580s reflected current European and Spanish trends toward centralization and control, ending medieval freedoms. [AL]

1300 Moreno Martínez, Alida Genoveva.

Notas sobre los indios y las haciendas trigueras de Guadalajara durante los siglos XVII y XVIII. (*Estud. Hombre,* 10, 1999, p. 185–201)

Study of Indian labor allocations (repartimiento) in late-17th century Guadalajara. This labor system lasted through the mid-18th century, mostly to the economic benefit of the civil and ecclesiastical elite. [AL]

1301 Native resistance and the Pax Colonial in New Spain. Edited by Susan Schroeder. Lincoln: Univ. of Nebraska Press, 1998. 223 p.: bibl., index, maps.

Spanning the entire colonial period, these collected essays explore indigenous resistance to Spanish control throughout New Spain. Based on primary sources, the six essays contradict the opinion that the colonial era was a peaceful one. Rather, indigenous groups responded to local conditions in ways most advantageous to the preservation of their own societies. [P. Harms]

1302 Ngou-Mve, Nicolás. El cimarronaje como forma de expresión del África bantú en la América colonial: el ejemplo de Yangá en México. (*Am. Negra,* 14, dic. 1997, p. 27–51, bibl.)

Argues that palenques and quilombos, towns founded by runaway slaves, are symbols of freedom and explain the survival of the Africa bantu culture on the American continent. [AL]

1303 Obregón, Baltasar de. Historia de los descubrimientos de Nueva España. Estudio introductorio, recopilación y glosario de Eva María Bravo García. Sevilla, Spain: Ediciones Alfar, 1997. 286 p.: bibl. (Colección Alfar universidad; no 90. Serie "Ediciones, textos y documentos")

This edited volumes of Obregón's 1584 work provides valuable 16th-century historical and linguistic information. Obregón's work presents the discovery and conquest of New Spain from the perspective of a first generation criollo. [P. Harms]

1304 Olveda, Jaime. El mayorazgo de los Gómez Parada. (*Estud. Hombre,* 10, 1999, p. 167–183, graph, map)

Survey of the mayorazgo Gómez Parada, one of the most important in Guadalajara, underlining the strategies used to construct and enhance their elite social and economic status. [AL]

1305 Pazos Pazos, María Luisa Julia. El Ayuntamiento de la Ciudad de México en el siglo XVII: continuidad institucional y cambio social. Sevilla, Spain: Diputación Provincial de Sevilla, 1999. 442 p.: bibl., ill. (some col.). (Nuestra América; 6)

Thorough study of the Cabildo as an institution and as a venue for expressing social status. Examines the internal structure, the daily business of government, financial resources, relations with other administrative institutions, and the human element that formed its body throughout the century. Resulting from a doctoral dissertation, this work leaves little ground uncovered as it makes use of a broad range of archival sources. [AL]

1306 Peñaflores, René Amaro and **Isabel Jiménez Maldonado.** La protoindustrialización en el México colonial: el caso de la producción textil doméstica en Ozumba, 1780–1810. (*Iztapalapa/México,* 18:43, enero/junio 1998, p. 253–278, bibl., facsims., maps, tables)

Studying the late colonial textile industry, authors argue the existence of an economic process of protoindustrialization. Highlights input by women and families in the indigenous town of Ozumba. [P. Harms]

1307 Pérez Rosales, Laura. Agraviados y ofendidos: notas sobre los registros oficiales de inconformidad social en la Nueva España durante el siglo XVIII. (*Hist. Graf. / México*, 13, 1999, p. 17–44)

By searching through many sections of the AGN such as Correspondencia de Virreyes, Minería, and General de Parte, documents the incidence of riots, rebellions, and peaceful protests throughout the 18th century. Concludes that during the latter half of the century, active social discontent increased by 144 percent because of the Bourbon reforms, including the tobacco monopoly, taxation, mine labor, etc. Indicates that authorities dealt with these incidents both harshly and through negotiations. [EBC]

1308 Picó, Fernando. Los pequeños y medianos productores agrícolas del bajío en la época del virreinato: Irapuato en los siglos XVII y XVIII. (*Relaciones/Zamora*, 18:72, otoño 1997, p. 87–137, tables)

Thorough study of small land ownership in central Mexico (Irapuato). Focuses on one in-depth family case study, but also includes materials on ownership in several social sectors, concluding that small owners were a sector of the economy, but not a social class. [AL]

1309 Pietschmann, Horst. Mexiko zwischen Reform und Revolution: vom bourbonischen Zeitalter zur Unabhängigkeit = Mexico between reform and revolution: from the Bourbon-time to independence. Herausgegeben von Jochen Meissner, Renate Pieper und Peer Schmidt. Stuttgart, Germany: F. Steiner, 2000. 299 p.: bibl., ill., maps. (Beiträge zur Kolonial- und Überseegeschichte, 0522–6848; 80)

Collection of articles by leading German specialist on Mexican history from 1750–1825, published on occasion of his 60th birthday. [F. Obermeier]

1310 Pineda Mendoza, Raquel. Origen, vida y muerte del acueducto de Santa Fe. México: UNAM, Instituto de Investigaciones Estéticas, 2000. 281 p.: bibl., ill., map. (Estudios y fuentes del arte en México; 55)

Meticulous study of the construction of the Santa Fe Aqueduct that provided water to the city of Mexico in the 16th century and was destroyed in the 19th century. Offers important information on the designer Miguel Martínez and on the workers who constructed the aqueduct. [AL]

1311 Pita Moreda, María Teresa. Mujer, conflicto y vida cotidiana en la ciudad de México a finales del período Español. Comunidad de Madrid: Dirección General de la Mujer, Consejería de Sanidad y Servicios Sociales, 1999. 246 p.: bibl.

Surveys some aspects of women's history in the late colonial period. Focuses on conjugal conflicts at a personal level, and the operating judicial apparatus in charge of resolving them. Based on archival research and secondary sources, this is a serious attempt at synthesizing while using personal vignettes retrieved from primary sources. [AL]

1312 Poblett Miranda, Martha. Narraciones chiapanecas. v. 1, Viajeros extranjeros en los siglos XVI-XIX. v. 3, Viajeros extranjeros en Palenque, siglos XVIII y XIX. Tuxtla Gutiérrez, Mexico: Libros de Chiapas, 1999-. 2 v.: ill., indexes, maps. (Historia e historiografía)

Contains seven accounts of travel through the state of Chiapas between 1586–1896. Travelers include religious men, scientists, and administrators. Antonio de Ciudad Real, Antonio Vazquez de Espinosa, and Thomas Gage traveled during the colonial period. [P. Harms]

1313 Poncio de León, Carlos A. Interpretación económica del último período colonial mexicano. (*Trimest. Econ.*, 65:257, enero/marzo 1998, p. 99–125, bibl., graphs, tables)

Revisionist interpretation of the correlation between silver prices, productivity, and economic crisis in the late colonial period. Highly technical. [AL]

1314 Ragon, Pierre. Evangelización, matrimonio cristiano y poder de los caciques en el Valle de México, siglo XVI. (*in* Coloquio de Antropología e Historia Regionales, *17th, Zamora, Mexico, 1995.* Iglesia Católica en México. Zamora, Mexico: El Colegio de Michoacán; México: Secretaría de Gobernación, Subsecretaría de Asuntos Jurídicos y Asociaciones Religiosos, Dirección General de Asuntos Religiosas, 1997, p. 49–68, table)

Discusses how indigenous leaders had problems assimilating the concept of Christian marriage in the 16th century, and how some used marriage to empower themselves against superficially converted leaders. Christian marriage eventually served to legalize unions and opened an avenue of social mobility for lower class *macehuales* as well as opportunistic leaders. [AL]

1315 Ragon, Pierre. El Niño Jesús de Azoyú. (*TRACE/México*, 34, déc. 1998, p. 64–73, map)

Detailed examination of late-18th century inquisitorial inquiry into the cult of a miraculous statue of baby Jesus. An interesting case because this cult took root among the largely African population of the tropical lowlands of Guerrero. The unorthodox nature of the miracles—of a sexual nature—contributed to the denunciation of the parish priest. [AL]

1316 Ramírez González, Clara Inés. La autoridad papal en la Real Universidad de México: el conflicto con los jesuitas en el siglo XVI. (*in* Historia y universidad: homenaje a Lorenzo Mario Luna. México: UNAM, Centro de Estudios sobre la Univ. y Facultad de Filosofía y Letras; Instituto Dr. José María Luis Mora, 1996, p. 413–434)

Describes the struggle over degree granting between the Real Univ. de México and Jesuit colleges. Jesuits and Dominican colleges tried to break the university's monopoly. [AL]

1317 Recéndez Guerrero, Emilia. Zacatecas: la expulsión de la Compañía de Jesús (y sus consecuencias). Zacatecas, Mexico: Instituto Zacatecano de Cultura: Univ. Autónoma de Zacatecas, 2000. 176 p.: bibl., 1 map.

Regional study of the expulsion of the Jesuits in the state of Zacatecas based on primary sources from Chile, the Archivo General de la Nación (Mexico), and archives in Zacatecas and Guadalajara, Mexico. Statistical analysis evaluates the monetary impact of the expulsion and traces the subsequent destination of the Jesuits' wealth. [P. Harms]

1318 Reyes, Juan Carlos. Hacienda de San José del Trapiche, Colima: resumen de una historia larga. (*Estud. Jalisc.*, 35, feb. 1999, p. 21–38, maps, tables)

Chronological history of Hacienda San José del Trapiche dating back to 1524, and officially registered in 1643. Focuses on production and administration. [P. Harms]

1319 Rípodas Ardanaz, Daisy. Dos advocaciones indianas en la Andalucía dieciochesca: la peregrina de Quito y el crucifijo de Ixmiquilpan. (*in* Congreso Argentino de Americanistas, *3rd, Buenos Aires, 1999.* Actas. Buenos Aires: Sociedad Argentina de Americanistas, 2000, t. 1, p. 207–216, ill.)

Traces the round-trip from Spain to the Americas and back of two devotional icons. Of interest to cultural historians. Provides more information on the Quiteño image than on the Mexican crucifix. [AL]

1320 Romero Sotelo, María Eugenia. El mercurio y la producción minera en la Nueva España, 1810–1821. (*Hist. Mex. / México*, 48:3, enero/marzo 2000, p. 349–377, bibl., tables)

Studies the production and distribution of mercury during the tumultuous years of rebellion prior to independence. Underlines that the Crown yielded its monopoly of distribution, but not of production, which after independence would pass to powerful merchants. [AL]

1321 Rubial García, Antonio. Cuerpos milagrosos: creación y culto de las reliquias novohispanas. (*Estud. Hist. Novohisp.*, 18, 1998, p. 13–30)

Posits that the worship of relics that began in the late 16th century responded to the new needs of a more diverse population, the existence of idolatry, and the slow down of evangelization due to wars with Indians in northern New Spain. From the late 17th century onwards, relics of local male and female venerables performed the purpose of validating the New World's faith and true Christianity. Rubial notes the many exercises in exhumation and the meaning of such rites in creating local pride. Most such acts were forgotten in the 19th century. [AL]

1322 Rubial García, Antonio. Monjas y mercaderes: comercio y construcciones conventuales en la ciudad de México durante el siglo XVII. (*CLAHR*, 7:4, Fall 1998, p. 361–385)

Traces the connection between enriched merchants and religious piety expressed in the patronage of female convents. Demonstrates the colonial search for salvation through nuns' prayers and the desire to be remembered. Uses the city of Mexico as a testing ground and enumerates all the pious deeds—mostly repairing convents, building, or enriching churches. [AL]

1323 Rubial García, Antonio. La plaza, el palacio y el convento: la ciudad de México en el siglo XVII. 1. ed. en Sello Bermejo. México: Consejo Nacional para la Cultura y las Artes, 1998. 168 p.: bibl. (Sello Bermejo)

Historical overview of daily life in 17th-century Mexico, covering themes as diverse as street life, popular religiosity, markets, fiestas, rebellions, etc., to create a "live" urban history with peoples as actors. Written with grace and erudition, this book reminds the reviewer of Irving Leonard's style and interests. [AL]

1324 Sales Colín, Ostwald. El movimiento portuario de Acapulco: un intento de aproximación, 1626–1654. (*Rev. Complut. Hist. Am.*, 22, 1996, p. 97–119, bibl., tables)

Traces the movement of ships in mid-17th century Acapulco to argue the existence of well-known contraband traffic and corroborate the dismissal of trade with the Philippines. [AL]

1325 Salvucci, Richard J. and **Richard L. Garner.** An exchange on the eighteenth-century Mexican economy. (*Americas/Washington*, 54:1, July 1997, p. 109–123)

Two economic historians discuss the merits of their own interpretation of late-18th century Mexico. Response to two book reviews. [AL]

1326 Sánchez Gómez, Julio and **Renate Pieper.** ¿Tras las huellas de un espejismo?: la minería en Nueva España y Europa central en la segunda mitad del siglo XVIII. (*Jahrb. Gesch. Lat.am.*, 37, 2000, p. 49–72, graphs)

Comparative study of mining in Mexico and Europe with interesting data about productivity. Reveals that the European mines—held as a model for New Spain—were less efficient than their American counterparts. [AL]

1327 Scharrer Tamm, Beatriz. Azúcar y trabajo: tecnología de los siglos XVII y XVIII en el actual estado de Morelos. Mexico: CIESAS: Instituto de Cultura de Morelos: Miguel Angel Porrua, 1997. 214 p.: bibl., ill., maps.

Utilizing hacienda records from the state of Morelos, this book explores the technological innovations in the cultivation of sugar from the late 16th century-18th century. The work pays attention to the contribution of laborers, both free and slave, and to the increased sophistication of cane sugar production. [P. Harms]

1328 Schwaller, John Frederick. Don Bartolomé de Alva. (*in* Simposio Panamericano de Historia, *3rd, México, 1995.* Memorias. México: Instituto Panamericano de Geografía e Historia, 1997, p. 125–141)

Biographical sketch of the younger brother of Fernando de Alva Ixtlixochitl, who was an able translator of golden age literary Spanish works into Nahuatl, and the author of a Confessional (1634). Member of a distinguished mestizo family, Bartolomé was a priest and Schwaller analyzes his nahuatl confesionario as well as his methods of translation. [AL]

Sefchovich, Sara. La suerte de la consorte: las esposas de los gobernantes de México; historia de un olvido y relato de un fracaso. See item **1620.**

1329 Seminario de Historia Colonial de Michoacán, *Morelia, Mexico, 1997.* Historia y sociedad: ensayos del Seminario de Historia Colonial de Michoacán. Coordinación de Carlos Paredes Martínez. Morelia, Mexico: Univ. Michoacana de San Nicolás de Hidalgo, Instituto de Investigaciones Históricas; México: Centro de Investigaciones y Estudios Superiores en Antropología Social, 1997. 391 p.: bibl., ill., maps. (Encuentros; 3)

Ten essays on colonial Michoacán on themes such as demography, local economy, the Enlightenment and local politics, agrarian conflict, and art and religion. All essays are well crafted and based on primary sources. [AL]

Sluyter, Andrew. The ecological origins and consequences of cattle ranching in sixteenth-century New Spain. See *HLAS 59:2520.*

1330 Sola Corbacho, Juan Carlos. Los comerciantes mexicanos frente a la muerte, 1765–1800. (*Rev. Complut. Hist. Am.*, 25, 1999, p. 167–194, tables)

Analyzes over 300 wills of late 18th-century merchants in Mexico City. A structural analysis permits a definition of the features of the wills, and reveals key aspects in the written form of wills, disposition of properties, and choice of executors and beneficiaries. As expected, church and family featured significantly in the wills. [AL]

1331 Stein, Stanley J. Francisco Ignacio de Yraeta y Azcárate, almacenero de la ciudad de México, 1732–1797: un ensayo de microhistoria. (*Hist. Mex./México*, 50:3, enero/marzo 2001, p. 459–512, bibl.)

Follows the life and career of this well-known Basque merchant. Explains the operation of his business network and business philosophy, as well as his goals as an entrepreneur. Underlines his activities in the broader world of North Atlantic and Pacific trade. [AL]

1332 Stein, Stanley J. Tending the store: trade and silver at the Real de Huautla, 1778–1781. (*HAHR*, 77:3, Aug. 1997, p. 377–407)

Fascinating article on the structure of small merchant business in late colonial New Spain. Focus on a merchant's business—Juan Thomas de Mendiburu's store in Huautla. Brings daily operations into focus. Based on extensive correspondence of the merchant and his associate. [AL]

1333 Studnicki-Gizbert, Daviken. From agents to consulado: commercial networks in colonial Mexico, 1520–1590 and beyond. (*Anu. Estud. Am.*, 57:1, enero/junio 2000, p. 41–68, graphs, tables)

Characterizes the relationship between members of the merchant class in New Spain and Seville as one of interaction rather than subordination due to the difficulty of 16th-century transatlantic communication, local control of goods and credit, local circulation of coin and the protection of the Mexico City consulado. [B. Cassity]

1334 Tanck Estrada, Dorothy. Pueblos de indios y educación en el México colonial, 1750–1821. México: El Colegio de México, Centro de Estudios Históricos, 1999. 665 p., 2 folded leaves of plates: bibl., index, maps.

Massive, thorough study of the indigenous communities in the last decades of the viceregal period. Begins with an assessment of the income of the communities and their administration. Then looks at the establishment of schools and the education they pro-

vided, but this is not the central theme of the book, despite its title. The focus on confraternities and their political maneuvers in the last colonial years makes this work an impressive study of the Indian communities as financial and political entities. [AL]

1335 Timmer, David E. Providence and perdition: Fray Diego de Landa justifies his inquisition against the Yucatecan Maya. (*Church Hist.*, 66:3, Sept. 1997, p. 477–488)

By examining 16th-century ideas on millennialism, Timmer's revisionist essay on Yucatan's Bishop Landa explains his personality, ideas, and actions, as a response to contemporary fears of the fragility of Christianity in Europe and the New World. [AL]

1336 Torales Pacheco, María Cristina. Ilustrados en la Nueva España: los socios de la Real Sociedad Bascongada de Amigos del País. México: Univ. Iberoamericana, Depto. de Historia, 2001. 527, 16 p. of plates: bibl., col. ill., index.

Surveys history of one of the most productive groups in colonial New Spain. Basques organized the Amigos del País as a fulfillment of Enlightenment principles of education. It became closely linked with the clergy, especially the Jesuits. The society provided a method of promoting Basque uniqueness, while fostering their advancement within colonial society. Thorough and well-documented work by accomplished historian. [B. Cassity]

Torchia-Estrada, Juan Carlos. Los estudios de filosofía (Artes) en el siglo XVI: México y Perú. See item **4620.**

Torre Villar, Ernesto de la. El deceso de Felipe II: sus repercusiones en Nueva España. See item **3414.**

1337 Torre Villar, Ernesto de la. Don Juan de Palafox y Mendoza, pensador político. México: UNAM, Instituto de Investigaciones Jurídicas, 1997. 108 p. (Serie C—Estudios históricos; 66)

Competent and incisive analysis of Juan de Palafox's treatise on government, *Historia real sagrada, Luz de príncipes y súbditos.* A perfect expression of his regalist position, this work was intended as a guide for rectitude and honesty in the government, much needed commodities in the Spanish government. Torre Villar eulogizes Palafox as a thinker and as a man of his times, leaving little margin for critical appraisal of this controversial figure. For philosophy specialist's comment, see item **4650**. [AL]

1338 Traslosheros H., Jorge E. Los motivos de una monja: Sor Feliciana de San Francisco, Valladolid de Michoacán, 1632–1655. (*Hist. Mex./México*, 47:4, abril/junio 1998, p. 735–763, bibl.)

Multilayered analysis of the many interests involved in a power struggle over the forced internment of a Spanish woman in the convent of Santa Catarina de Sena in Valladolid in the 17th century. She ultimately professed as a nun of her own will. [AL]

Tutino, John. The revolution in Mexican independence: insurgency and the renegotiation of property, production, and patriarchy in the Bajío, 1800–1855. See item **1484**.

1339 Uriega Ponce de León, María de los Angeles and **Antonio Escobar Ohmstede.** La estructura socioeconómica de la jurisdicción de Tacuba en las postrimerías del siglo XVIII: el padrón militar de 1792. (*Entorno Urbano*, 2:3, enero/junio 1996, p. 39–82, bibl., graphs, map, tables)

Analyzes the military census of 1792 against the background provided by other late-18th century census records. Going beyond individual data such as race and civil status, stresses economic activities, occupational categories, and the political and economic meaning of the location (Tacuba) in the interpretation. [AL]

1340 Valle Pavón, Guillermina del. Intereses del Consulado de Comerciantes en la reconstrucción de las calzadas de la ciudad de México, siglo XVIII. (*Entorno Urbano*, 2:4, julio/dic. 1996, p. 7–24, bibl., table)

Study of the construction and improvement of major roads to and from Mexico City in the 18th century. Argues that the commercial interests of the Consulado provided the impetus for the creation and maintenance of highways. [P. Harms]

1341 Los vascos en el noroccidente de México, siglos XVII-XVIII. Coordinación de Jaime Olveda. Zapopan, Mexico: Colegio de Jalisco, 1998. 197 p.: bibl.

A collection of essays about Basques in Mexico includes materials about various aspects of their lives in Colima, Guadalajara, Baja California, Sinaloa, Aguascalientes, and other regions. Essays discuss how the chief leaders of the settlement of western Mexico such as Ibarra and Urdiñola made it possible for Basques to become the elite population of the region. [EBC]

1342 Velazco, Salvador. Historiografía y etnicidad emergente en el México colonial: Fernando de Alva Ixtlilxochitl, Diego Muñoz Camargo y Hernando Alvarado Tezozomoc. (*Mesoamérica/Antigua*, 20:38, dic. 1999, p. 1–32, facsims., tables)

Brief but informative essay on the writings of three of the most important historians of indigenous Mexico. Velazco maintains that they were not "mestizo" writers. Each one understood their ethnicity differently and wrote from a different cultural perspective. Alva Ixtlilxochitl identified as Indian, Muñoz Camargo identified as Spanish, and Alvarado Tezozomoc as a Christian noble speaking to others like him in the middle ground of the two cultures. Velazco argues for the adoption of transculturation as a means of interpreting the works of these men. [AL]

Verástique, Bernardino. Michoacán and Eden: Vasco de Quiroga and the evangelization of western Mexico. See item **640**.

1343 Villavicencio Rojas, Josué Mario. Mercedes reales y posesiones: cacicazgo de Tecomaxtlahuaca, 1598–1748. Puebla, Mexico: Benemérita Univ. Autónoma de Puebla, Instituto de Ciencias Sociales y Humanidades, Dirección General de Fomento Editorial; México: Consejo Nacional para la Cultura y las Artes, 2000. 396 p.: bibl., facsims., maps.

Complete transcription of previously unknown titles of properties to colonial cacicazgos in the Oaxaca area. Of interest to historians of Indian communities. The delimitation of land properties in the 20th century is based on documents such as these. [AL]

1344 Vinson, Ben. Bearing arms for his majesty: the free-colored militia in colonial Mexico. Stanford, Calif.: Stanford Univ. Press, 2001. 304 p.: bibl., ill., index, maps.

Using material about Puebla, Yucatán, and Veracruz, reveals unsuspected aspects of military history as well as the role of castas in New Spain from the late 17th century to 1793. Free-colored men were attracted to the militia by immunity from tribute payment and fuero rights rather than by material rewards. Foreign born men of color, especially from Cuba, served as officers until 1793 when peninsular inspectors were named. [EBC]

1345 Vinson, Ben. Race and badge: free-colored soldiers in the colonial Mexican militia. (*Americas/Washington*, 56:4, April 2000, p. 471–496)

Investigates the issue of racial identity among the offspring of Afro-Mexicans through the study of the militia for free-coloreds, which began taking shape in the 16th century. Argues that despite restrictions in their free status in the late-18th century, many in this group of men had confidence in their racial status. Well-reseached article. [AL]

1346 Viqueira, Juan Pedro. Indios rebeldes e idólatras: dos ensayos históricos sobre la rebelión india de Canuc, Chiapas, acaecida en el año 1712. México: Ciesas, 1997. 213 p., 6 folded leaves of plates: bibl., maps.

Two essays on the 1712 Indian rebellion in Chiapas, not the contemporary turmoil. One essay underlines the variety of peoples and towns involved, and the meaning of their geographical location in the revolt. A second essay explores Catholic worship and beliefs among the indigenous and the coexistence of Christian and precolumbian religions. [AL]

1347 Warren, J. Benedict. Testamento del Obispo Vasco de Quiroga: edición facsimilar con otros documentos. Morelia, Mexico: Fimax Publicaciones, 1997. 91 p.: facsims.

Facisimile edition of Vasco de Quiroga's last will and several other documents of interest. Ably paleographed, this face-to-face pagination of the original and the printed transcription makes it a useful paleographic exercise for the reader. [AL]

1348 Warren, J. Benedict. Vasco de Quiroga en América. Morelia, Mexico: Fimax Publicistas, 1998. 147 p.: indexes, photo.

Transcription and introductory study of two litigations which Vasco de Quiroga conducted in Spanish Oran prior to his trip

to Mexico. Adds to our knowledge of Vasco's character. [AL]

1349 Warren, J. Benedict. Vasco de Quiroga y sus pueblos hospitales de Santa Fe. Morelia, Mexico: Univ. Michoacana de San Nicolás de Hidalgo, 1997. 235 p.: bibl., index, tables.

Revised Spanish edition of the original work (1965) in English (see *HLAS 28:574* for review of original work). Author has updated materials and added a documentary appendix. [AL]

1350 Wobeser, Gisela von. El error de Humboldt: consideraciones en torno a la riqueza del clero novohispano. (*Secuencia/México*, 42, sept./dic. 1998, p. 49–64, bibl., facsims.)

Shows how Alexander von Humboldt misinterpreted his sources in the evaluation of the wealth of the church in Mexico. Whereas his sources stated endowment of pious deeds, he used real property and also assumed that capital destined to the same purpose were mortgages in favor of the clergy. Humboldt's figures on this topic are rendered useless. [AL]

1351 Wobeser, Gisela von. La función social y económica de las capellanías de misas en la Nueva España del siglo XVIII. (*Estud. Hist. Novohisp.*, 16, 1996, p. 119–138, tables)

Introductory study on the meaning of chantries in the spiritual and worldly economy of New Spain. General survey based on archival sources. [AL]

1352 Wobeser, Gisela von. Vida eterna y preocupaciones terrenales: las capellanías de misas en la Nueva España, 1700–1821. México: UNAM, 1999. 283 p.: bibl. (Serie historia novohispana; 64)

Comprehensive and well-researched study of chantries in New Spain, from the mid-colonial period through independence. Defines their main features, their economic meaning, the founders and their motivations, and their spiritual "purchase." Appendixes listing all the chantries founded in New Spain (possibly only the central areas), masses celebrated in 1821, the income of chantries and real estate income in 1822, and the patrons and the priests endowed with them are positively daunting in scope and very useful. [AL]

1353 Yáñez Rosales, Rosa H. Las cofradías indígenas de Tlajomulco, siglos XVII y XVIII. (*Estud. Hombre*, 6, 1997, p. 121–143, tables)

Describes the Indian confraternities in one district of New Galicia (Jalisco), providing data on their common features, such as institutions, and their economic holdings, especially cattle. [AL]

1354 Zárate Toscano, Verónica. Los nobles ante la muerte en México: actitudes, ceremonias y memoria, 1750–1850. México: Centro de Estudios Históricos, El Colegio de México: Instituto de Investigaciones Dr. José María Luis Mora, 2000. 484 p.: bibl., ill.

Death and how the Mexican nobility faced it are the main themes of this well-researched book. Based on 303 wills, author analyzes the sources and the structure of the nobility before she delves into the rituals of death. Following the wording of the wills, she looks into the nature of piety and the ceremonies surrounding burial. Quantification of many of the general features of the nobility adds a touch of social science to this essay. Commendable work. [AL]

NORTH

1355 Adams, David Bergen. At the lion's mouth: San Miguel de Aguayo in the defense of Nuevo León, 1686–1841. (*CLAHR*, 9:3, Summer 2000, p. 324–346, maps)

Explains that Nuevo León remained north of the perimeter of presidios along the 18th-century frontier. Describes the local efforts to protect the growing settlements from the raids and the increasing population pressure of indigenous groups. San Miguel de Aguayo was crucial to the defense and had been established by the descendants of the original Tlaxcalan communities to the west. [EBC]

1356 Arredondo López, María Adelina. Andanzas de un pueblo en pos de su escuela, Chihuahua, 1779–1820. (*Hist. Mex./México*, 49:4, abril/junio 2000, p. 549–592, bibl.)

History of the first public educational institution in Chihuahua illustrates how Enlightenment ideals permeated middling and artisan groups through their support of a

school assisted by the ayuntamiento and attended by students of different social groups. [EBC]

1357 Baroni Boissonas, Ariane. Formación de la propiedad y comunidades indígenas en Ures de 1770 a 1860. (*in* Simposio de Historia y Antropología de Sonora, 22nd, Hermosillo, Mexico, 1997. Memorias. Hermosillo, Mexico: Univ. de Sonora, Depto. de Historia y Antropología, 1998, p. 313–345, bibl., graphs, maps)

Detailed study of the processes by which Indians in a Sonora community lost their lands to men with abundant resources and high political positions. [EBC]

1358 Benedict B., H. Bradley. La administración de temporalidades y haciendas en Chihuahua colonial, 1767–1820. México: Casa Londres, 1998. 212 p.: bibl., index.

Examines the results of the expropriation Jesuit possessions in Chihuahua where the documentation was most complete. Provides insights into the royal administration of the goods, profits obtained by the Crown, and the fate of those who purchased the haciendas. Provides information on the workings of government and the history of the hacienda system. [EBC]

1359 Castañeda, Antonia I. Engendering the history of Alta California, 1769–1848: gender, sexuality, and the family. (*Calif. Hist.*, 76:2/3, Summer/Fall 1997, p. 230–259, ill., map, photos)

Recounts the efforts to hispanicize Upper California by encouraging mestizo family immigration and unions of soldiers with indigenous women. After the North American conquest, women resisted these efforts. Evidence is anecdotal. [EBC]

1360 Cavazos Garza, Israel. Haciendas y ganados en el Nuevo Reino de León: siglos XVII y XVIII. (*Humanitas/Monterrey*, 26, 1999, p. 441–461, bibl.)

Wealth of the soil in Nuevo León for livestock in the 17th-18th centuries led to enormous flocks of animals and large land grants to support them. Debts often were paid with animals rather than silver. Damage to the soil done by livestock destroyed a flourishing economy during the 19th century. Traces of the livestock culture remain in vocabulary, food, clothing, and the shells of the large hacienda buildings. [EBC]

1361 Cavazos Garza, Israel. El Nuevo Reino de León y Monterrey: a través de 3,000 documentos (en síntesis) del Ramo Civil del Archivo Municipal de la Ciudad, 1598–1705. Monterrey, Mexico: Congreso del Estado de Nuevo León, 1998. 501 p.

Continuation of immense work of cataloging and summarizing the documents from the Monterrey archives which the author began in 1964. This collection from the *ramo civil* includes wills, land grants, *visitas*, ecclesiastical materials, residencias, and materials presented in disputes over properties. [EBC]

1362 Constructores de la nación: la migración tlaxcalteca en el norte de la Nueva España. Textos de Israel Cavazos Garza *et al.* Presentación de María Isabel Monroy Castillo. San Luis Potosí, Mexico: Colegio de San Luis; Tlaxcala de Xicohténcatl, Mexico: Gobierno del Estado de Tlaxcala, 1999. 141 p.: bibl., maps. (Biblioteca tlaxcalteca)

Series of articles about the experiences and role of the Tlaxcalans in the establishment of the Spanish presence in northern New Spain. Finds influence on language and popular culture as well as on the history of the villages established by the Tlaxcaltecans and the relations between the Tlaxcaltecans and nomadic Indians. [EBC]

1363 The Coronado expedition to Tierra Nueva: the 1540–1542 route across the Southwest. Edited by Richard Flint and Shirley Cushing Flint. Introduction by Carroll L. Riley and historiographical chapters by Joseph P. Sánchez. Niwot, Colo.: Univ. Press of Colorado, 1997. 442 p.: bibl., ill., index.

Revised and edited collection of papers and ancillary documents from a 1992 conference on the Coronado expedition. Utilizes archeological, linguistic, and anthropological research on 16th century explorers. [EBC]

1364 Cutter, Charles R. The administration of law in colonial New Mexico. (*J. Early Repub.*, 18:1, Spring 1998, p. 99–115, facsims.)

Summary of a larger study, *The Legal Culture of Northern New Spain, 1700–1810* (1995). Argues that Anglo-Americans ignored the legal traditions of former Spanish colonies because the laws were not administered by lawyers. Proves that Hispanic officials, without legal training, used Spanish compilations of laws to settle disputes and punish malefactors. These decisions, based on these laws, emphasized community comity and social equilibrium. [EBC]

1365 de Groof, Bart. Encuentros discordantes: expectativas y experiencias de los jesuitas belgas en el México del siglo XVII. (*Hist. Mex./México*, 47:3, enero/marzo 1998, p. 537–569, bibl.)

Description and analysis of the attitudes of the 17th century Flemish Jesuits on the evangelization of the indigenous peoples of northern Mexico. Dwells on expectations and motivations for undertaking this task, the manner in which they carried out their evangelization, and their opinions of indigenous peoples. Fine analysis of the mental and intellectual world of the missionaries. [AL]

1366 Deeds, Susan M. Indigenous rebellions on the northern Mexican mission frontier: from first-generation to later colonial responses. (*in* Contested ground: comparative frontiers on the northern and southern edges of the Spanish Empire. Edited by Donna J. Guy and Thomas E. Sheridan. Tucson: Univ. of Arizona Press, 1998, p. 32–51)

A comparison of two indigenous rebellions illuminates varying frontier conditions in time and space. Fragility of resources and epidemics brought about both rebellions, but one had messianic qualities while the other prefigured 19th-century indigenous responses. Both exploited divisions among Jesuits, government, and settlers. [EBC]

1367 Empire of sand: the Seri Indians and the struggle for Spanish Sonora, 1645–1803. Compiled and edited by Thomas E. Sheridan. Tucson: Univ. of Arizona Press, 1999. 493 p.: bibl., ill., index, maps.

Collection of documents on the Seri Indians of Sonora with informative introductions. Notes that until the Seri Indians were defeated, the Spanish could not undertake a successful campaign against the Apaches. Growth of the settled populations by the end of the 18th century weakened the Seris, but remnants of them survive until this day. [EBC]

1368 **Espinosa Morales, Lydia.** El convento franciscano de San Andrés en la ciudad de Monterrey. (*Humanitas/Monterrey*, 24, 1997, p. 449–482)

Overview of the history of the principal church in Monterrey from its foundation in the early 17th century until 1918. Emphasizes decoration and material construction of the church, its patrons, cofradías, and the activities of the Third Order of Franciscans. Lacks analysis, but provides extensive data. [EBC]

1369 **Font, Pedro.** Diario íntimo. Y, Diario de fray Tomás Eixarch. Edición, transcripción, introducción, notas y apéndices de Julio César Montané Martí. Hermosillo, Mexico: Univ. de Sonora; México: Plaza y Valdés Editores, 2000. 524 p.: bibl., index.

This work explores the diary of Franciscan Fr. Pedro Font during his journey through Sonora in the late 18th century (1777). Exceptional for its rich narrative and detailed accounts of indigenous culture. Montané Martí includes another Franciscan travel account along the Colorado River. [P. Harms]

1370 **Frank, Ross.** From settler to citizen: New Mexican economic development and the creation of Vecino society, 1750–1820. Berkeley: Univ. of California Press, 2000. 329 p.: bibl., ill., index, maps.

Analyzes economic changes and the growing strength of the "vecino" population over the settled indigenous peoples. A combination of the Bourbon reforms, small-pox epidemic, raids by Apaches and Comanches, and growth of a nonindigenous population weakened the Pueblos and laid the basis for the transformation of settler to vecino society. [EBC]

Fuentes para la historia india de Coahuila. See item **479.**

1371 **González Claverán, Virginia.** Sanidad, hospital y botica en el Puerto de San Blas, 1779–1792. (*in* Simposio Panamericano de Historia, *3rd, México, 1995.* Memorias. México: Instituto Panamericano de Geografía e Historia, 1997, p. 433–455, appendices)

Spanish expansion to the north in the 18th century turned San Blas into an essential port for ships plying the coast of North America. Its reputation as an insalubrious place led the viceroys to attempt to establish and supply a pharmacy. Difficulties in obtaining a pharmacist and acquiring medicines partially defeated these efforts. [EBC]

1372 **Gradie, Charlotte May.** The Tepehuan Revolt of 1616: militarism, evangelism and colonialism in seventeenth century Nueva Vizcaya. Salt Lake City: Univ. of Utah Press, 2000. 238 p.: bibl., index, 1 map.

Carefully drafted study of an indigenous revolt on the northern frontier. Places the Tepehuan in geographical and historical context, and studies the worldview of their Jesuit evangelizers to understand how the sources of the "dominant" affect the historical image of the rebels. Concludes that the revolt was an effort of the Tepehuan to regain some traits of their own culture. [AL]

1373 **Hall, Thomas D.** The Río de la Plata and the Greater Southwest: a view from world-system theory. (*in* Contested ground: comparative frontiers on the northern and southern edges of the Spanish Empire. Edited by Donna J. Guy and Thomas E. Sheridan. Tucson: Univ. of Arizona Press, 1998, p. 150–166)

Brings new perspectives to familiar materials on the relationships between Spanish authorities, missionaries, and nomadic peoples. [EBC]

1374 **Hausberger, Bernd.** La vida cotidiana de los misioneros jesuitas en el noroeste novohispano. (*Estud. Hist. Novohisp.*, 17, 1997, p. 63–106, bibl.)

Lengthy article summarizes a 1995 German monongraph, *Jesuiten aus Mitteleuropa im kolonialen Mixiko: e. Bio-Bibliographie*. Describes the difficulties and pleasures of everyday life of Jesuit missionaries in the 17th-18th centuries. While evangelizing the Indians, the Jesuits lacked essentials, such as soap and candles, and faced challenges in traveling from one mission to another and learning unrelated languages. Also discusses their friendships. Examines the reciprocal influences of the Indians on the Jesuits. Reactions of the Jesuits varied from depression at their isolation to enthusiasm for the region as reflected in scientific studies. Describes the importance of individual reactions to their situation. [EBC]

1375 **Kelsey, Harry.** Juan Rodríguez Cabrillo. 1st. paperback ed. San Marino, Calif.: Huntington Library, 1998. 261 p.: bibl., facsims., ill., index.

Meticulously documented biography of the man who led the first European voyages to Upper California. Includes an account of Cabrillo's career in Guatemala as well as his early life. Pleasingly written. [EBC]

1376 **Lazcano Sahagún, Carlos.** La primera entrada: descubrimiento del interior de la antigua California. Ensenada, Mexico: Fundación Barca: Museo de Historia de Ensenada: Seminario de Historia de Ensenada, 2000. 390 p.: bibl., ill., index, maps. (Colección de documentos sobre la historia y la geografía del Municipio de Ensenada; no. 3)

Traces late 17th and 18th century explorations of Baja California through the routes that united the missions. Annotated publication provides, in one place, eight accounts of the European exploration of Baja California. [EBC]

1377 **Libro del cabildo de la villa de Santiago del Saltillo, 1578–1655.** Paleografía, introducción y notas de Valentina Garza Martínez y Juan Manuel Pérez Zevallos. Tlalpan, Mexico: Centro de Investigaciones y Estudios Superiores en Antropología Social; México: Archivo General de la Nación; Saltillo, Mexico: Archivo Municipal de Saltillo, 2002. 452 p.: bibl., index.

Elegant publication of a significant primary source for the history of northern New Spain. Contains materials about elections, appointments, Indian-white relations, financial questions, etc. Valuable appendices identify settlers, officials, and land grants. [EBC]

1378 **Martínez Saldaña, Tomás.** La diáspora tlaxcalteca: colonización agrícola del norte mexicano. 2. ed. Tlaxcala, Mexico: Tlaxcallan, Ediciones del Gobierno del Estado de Tlaxcala, 1998. 170, 3 p.: bibl., ill., maps.

Study of the fate of the 400 Tlaxcalans who left their native lands to colonize the north. Treats the mixing of cultures, the loss of life, and survival techniques of hunting and gathering peoples. [EBC]

1379 **McDonald, Dedra S.** Incest, power, and negotiation in the Spanish colonial borderlands: a tale of two families. (CLAHR, 6:4, Fall 1997, p. 525–557)

Recounts the history of two cases of incest in the early 19th century, drawing conclusions about family relationships based on a sensitive reading of the documents. [EBC]

1380 **Messmacher, Miguel.** La búsqueda del signo de dios: ocupación jesuita de la Baja California. México: Fondo de Cultura Económica, 1997. 418 p.: bibl., ill., maps. (Sección de obras de historia)

Containing abundant quotations from printed primary sources, this detailed study includes comparative materials about the Jesuits in Paraguay. Also considers viewpoints and activities of missionaries and indigenous peoples, the habitat, and the 18th-century history of the peninsula. [EBC]

1381 **New views of borderlands history.** Edited by Robert H. Jackson. Albuquerque: Univ. of New Mexico Press, 1998. 250 p.: bibl., ill., index.

Five North American interpreters of the borderlands, including Florida and Louisiana, collaborate on bringing together recent research in an expanding field. Articles by Susan Deeds, Ross Frank, Jesús F. de la Teja, Patricia Wickman, as well as Robert Jackson. [EBC]

1382 **Nolasco Armas, Margarita.** Conquista y dominación del noroeste de México: el papel de los jesuitas. México: Instituto Nacional de Antropología e Historia, 1998. 126 p., 1 folded leaf of plates: bibl., maps. (Serie historia/Instituto Nacional de Antropología e Historia) (Colección científica; 361)

Combining the history of the indigenous peoples of the Northwest with the arrival of the Jesuits after 1594; cumulates the materials about each mission and the names of missionaries around 1765 and concludes that only 20 percent of the Jesuits served in missions, while the other Jesuits dedicated themselves to education. [EBC]

1383 **Nugent, Daniel.** Two, three, many barbarisms?: the Chihuahuan frontier in transition from society to politics. (*in* Contested ground: comparative frontiers on the northern and southern edges of the Spanish Empire. Edited by Donna J. Guy and Thomas E. Sheridan. Tucson: Univ. of Arizona Press, 1998, p. 182–199)

History and analysis of the fate of the military colonies granted lands in the colonial period to defeat the Apaches. These inhabitants became the new "barbarians," whose land was appropriated by wealthy entrepreneurs. [EBC]

1384 Offutt, Leslie Scott. Saltillo, 1770–1810: town and region in the Mexican north. Tucson: Univ. of Arizona Press, 2001. 277 p.: bibl., index, maps.

Describes how Mexico City's merchants dominated Saltillo because of the annual fair. After 1630, finds widespread fragmentation of haciendas which became independent small holdings. Later, in the 1780s, concentration of land resumed. Also examines the cabildo and its officers, and discusses the production of the Tlaxcalan Indian community. [EBC]

1385 Osante, Patricia. Presencia misional en Nuevo Santander en la segunda mitad del siglo XVIII: memoria de un infortunio. (*Estud. Hist. Novohisp.*, 17, 1997, p. 107–135)

Describes the work of the Franciscan Colegio de Propaganda Fide de Zacatecas between 1749–66 in conflict with the colonizing enterprise of José de Escandón. Aligned with the Viceroy Revilla Gigedo and his representatives, Escandón sought to put an end to the missionary prerogatives of the Franciscans and to prevent a replication of the power of the Jesuits who often resisted the demands for indigenous labor. The fact that the hunting and gathering peoples of the frontier failed to become rooted in the missions helped the civil authorities in their goal. [EBC]

1386 Pazos Pazos, María Luisa Julia. De los hombres y mujeres gallegos en la vida minera de Zacatecas. (*Semata*, 11, 1999, p. 153–168)

While Basques and Catalans were the ethnic groups that dominated immigration into Zacetecas, Galicians and Asturians also played an important role. Documents how Galicians could begin as muleteers, enter commerce, buy property, and begin to accumulate enough money to invest in mines. [EBC]

1387 Radding Murrieta, Cynthia. The colonial pact and changing ethnic frontiers in Highland Sonora, 1740–1840. (*in* Contested ground: comparative frontiers on the northern and southern edges of the Spanish Empire. Edited by Donna J. Guy and Thomas

E. Sheridan. Tucson: Univ. of Arizona Press, 1998, p. 52–66)

Analysis of Sonoran indigenous groups that maintained their ethnic and village identities through the mid-19th century by participating in the militia. Corporate Indian communities lost lands because of the increasing mestizo population. [EBC]

1388 Reyes Costilla, Nora and Martín González de la Vara. El demonio entre los marginales: la población negra y el pacto con el demonio en el norte de Nueva España, siglos XVII y XVIII. (*CLAHR*, 10:2, Spring 2001, p. 199–221)

Using Inquisition cases and secondary sources involving Afro-Mexicans, concludes that Afro-Mexicans were isolated from their families and acted as individuals in pacts with the devil. Some repented, turning themselves into the Inquisition and receiving mild sentences. [EBC]

1389 Río, Ignacio del. Autoritarismo y locura en el noroeste novohispano: implicaciones políticas del enloquecimiento del visitador general José de Gálvez. (*Estud. Hist. Novohisp.*, 22, 2000, p. 111–138, bibl.)

Focuses on Gálvez' mission to the north and finds that he had had a similar attack of insanity in the Caribbean Islands before the Sonora incident. Opines that it might have been caused by malaria. Those who attempted to describe his madness were punished. [EBC]

1390 Romero de Terreros Castilla, Juan M. San Saba, misión para los Apaches: el plan terreros para consolidar la frontera norte de Nueva España; lección de ingreso como Amigo de Número leída el día 28 febrero de 2000. Palabras de recepción por D. Eric Beerman. Madrid: Delegación en Corte, Real Sociedad Bascongada de los Amigos del País, 2000. 143 p.: bibl., ill.

Account of the ill-fated Franciscan mission on the Texas frontier between 1756–58. [EBC]

1391 Sego, Eugene B. Aliados y adversarios: los colonos tlaxcaltecas en la frontera septentrional de Nueva España. San Luis Potosí, Mexico: Colegio de San Luis; Tlaxcala de Xicohténcatl, Mexico: Gobierno del Estado de Tlaxcala; San Luis Potosí, Mexico: Centro de Investigaciones Históricas de San

Luis Potosí, 1998. 311 p.: bibl., maps. (Colección Investigaciones)

Recruitment of Tlaxcalans from the end of the 16th century throughout the 18th century followed government realization that peace was cheaper than war. Law suits testify to the continuing sense of identity and privilege of Indian colonizing groups along the northern frontier. Detailed and competent study of this aspect of the settlement of northern New Spain. [EBC]

1392 Teja, Jesús F. de la. St. James at the fair: religious ceremony, civic boosterism, and the commercial development on the colonial Mexican frontier. (*Americas/Washington*, 57:3, Jan. 2001, p. 395–416)

Emphasizes the connections between the preparations for the annual fair, the celebration of a feast day, and the establishment of a powerful merchant community in Saltillo during the 18th century. [EBC]

Los tlaxcaltecas en Coahuila. See item **632.**

1393 Valdés, Carlos Manuel. Sociedad y delincuencia en el Saltillo colonial. Saltillo, Mexico: Archivo Municipal de Saltillo, 2002. 126 p.: bibl.

Based on archival sources, seeks to understand and illuminate the crises of ordinary people, who appear as people in trouble with the law in the Saltillo colonial records. [EBC]

1394 Valdés Dávila, Alma Victoria. ¿Para garantizar la vida después de la muerte?: legados piadosos al doblar del siglo XVIII. (*Hist. Graf./México*, 10, 1998, p. 37–66)

Study of testamentary pious deeds in the town of San Esteban de la Nueva Tlaxcala (next to Saltillo on the northern frontier), mostly left by Spanish and criollo inhabitants between 1800–05. Dwells on chantries, donations for confraternities, legacies for the benefit of the soul, and similar pious ends. [AL]

Independence, Revolution, and Post-Revolution

BARBARA A. TENENBAUM, *Mexican Specialist, Hispanic Division, Library of Congress; Editor in Chief, Encyclopedia of Latin American History and Culture*
DON M. COERVER, *Professor of History, Texas Christian University*
SUZANNE B. PASZTOR, *Associate Professor of History, University of the Pacific*

INDEPENDENCE TO REVOLUTION

SCHOLARLY WRITING ON MEXICAN HISTORY from 1810–1910 continues to push forward on new topics while developing innovative approaches to both old and new concerns. Although the field is becoming ever more sophisticated, it has yet to adopt fully the ideological debates that so affect international scholarship today. The biennium saw two magnum opus from major scholars, Hart on the US in Mexico (item 1434) and Van Young on the independence insurgency (item 1486). Researchers are working on uncovering health and medical topics; among the scholars reviewed here are López Ramos on press coverage of medical articles (item 1444), López Sánchez on women's health care (item 1445), Urbán Martínez on pharmacies (item 1485), Agostoni on doctors trying to defend "orthodox" medicine against *curanderos* (item 1395), Piccato on Porfirian views of the causes of aberrant behavior (item 1467), and Santoyo on the development and acceptance of a "Sanitary Code" for Mexico City (item 1474).

The influence of cultural topics has spread ever-wider; especially noteworthy is the study by Lau Jaiven of Gen. Manuel Barrera, an *empresario de espectáculos* like hot-air balloons (item **1441**). Two different authors look at the newspapers of Mexico City at the beginning of the 20th century: Garrido (item **1476**) and Pérez-Rayón Elizundia (item **1466**). Two works examine different aspects of culture within the publishing industry: Torre Rendón on illustrated magazines (item **1481**) and Ortiz Gaitán on advertising (item **1463**). To date, Mexican historians have not yet gravitated to the more theoretical aspects of the cultural discussion, but *HLAS* *62* may indicate otherwise.

Politics, as ever, continues to fascinate, but approaches to it have become much more subtle and thought-provoking. Some researchers continued the trend noted in *HLAS 58* by concentrating on the relationship between individual regions and the national government; for example, Buve tracing the Reform in Tlaxcala (item **1405**), Gutiérrez Grageda looking at elections in Querétaro before and during the Porfiriato (item **1432**), Guzmán López investigating the rivalry between Lerdo de Tejada and Iglesias in 1876 Guanajuato (item **1460**), and Altable Fernández revealing how fragmented centralization really was in Baja California (item **1396**). Others focused on statecraft with Craib's essay leading the way on mapping in 1857 (item **1415**), Mayer Celis on statistics and government planning (item **1451**), and Maurer on how the Porfirian state concentrated banking institutions so efficiently that the revolutionaries could not (or would not) dislodge them (item **1450**).

Scholars published innovative studies on a wide array of topics. Contreras Delgado traced the development of a mining camp in Coahuila to its current function supplying housing to maquila workers (item **1411**), while both Arrom (item **1399**) and Blum (item **1403**) looked at the relationship between poverty and charity. The French intervention attracted some well-designed studies; eg., Meyer on the French soldiers who went to Mexico (item **1455**), with Duncan (item **1420**) and Pani (item **1465**) analyzing how Maximilian tried to Mexicanize his empire, Sausi Garavito on Mexico's finances during the 1750–1860 period (item **1417**), and Ullman's new translation of the memoirs of Maximilian's personal physician, Dr. Samuel Basch (item **1401**). Although scholars en masse did not latch onto the thread mentioned in *HLAS 58* of looking at immigrants, Schell writes on the US trade diaspora helping Mexico achieve its "defensive modernization" (item **1475**), while Villaverde García relates Galician migration and contributions (item **1488**), and Salazar Anaya compiles a quasi-reference work on immigration to Mexico City (item **1438**). [BT]

REVOLUTION AND POST-REVOLUTION

An especially notable development in the field of Mexican history is the continuing emergence of cultural history as an identifiable subfield. Although the contours of the "new cultural history" began to appear nearly a decade ago, the task of revealing the cultural change that occurs amid more general or macrolevel historical developments is attracting more scholars. In 1999, a special edition of the *Hispanic American Historical Review* was devoted to "Mexico's New Cultural History." In it, articles by Vaughan (item **1633**), Haber (item **1547**), Mallon (item **1568**), Socolow (item **1623**), and Lomnitz (item **1561**) assess the usefulness of cultural history and demonstrate that this approach has generated both optimism and pessimism among historians.

Recent studies within the cultural history domain include three articles by Bliss examining the effect of post-Revolution reform efforts on notions of gender, sexuality, motherhood, and fatherhood (items **1504, 1505,** and **1506**), and Piccato's study of the relationship between reformism and Mexico City's urban poor (item **1597**). The issues of culture and modernity inform Pilcher's book-length study of Cantinflas (item **1598**) and Macías González's examination of the murder trial of "Miss Mexico 1928" (item **1566**).

Although there was a decline in the production of histories focused specific-ally on women during the last biennium, three studies examine women's political involvement in Mexico during and after the Revolution: Vatsala Kapur's examina-tion of women's role in the PAN and PRD (item **1555**), Agustín Vaca's exploration of the role of women in the Cristero Rebellion (item **1631**), and Benedikt Behrens' interesting investigation into the role played by women in a Veracruz rent control movement (item **1502**). Another notable study is Sara Sefchovich's examination of the wives of Mexican rulers, whose lives reveal changes for Mexican women in general (item **1620**).

The history of agrarian reform has attracted a handful of scholars. Ginzberg has produced two works on the agrarian program of Veracruz leader Adalberto Te-jada (items **1538** and **1539**), and Brewster explores the efforts of a Puebla cacique to negotiate demands for land reform (item **1515**). Chassen de López details an agrar-ian struggle between indigenous peoples and mestizos in Oaxaca (item **1522**), Ale-jos García underscores the ethnic component of land struggles in Chiapas (item **1495**), and Castellanos provides a detailed study of the agrarian struggle in the state of Mexico (item **1520**). Finally, Henderson uses the story of Rosalie Evans in his well-researched account of agrarian reform in Puebla (item **1549**).

Several scholars produced works on Mexican diplomatic history during the last biennium, with US-Mexican relations continuing to attract the most attention. Mark Anderson explores American press images of Mexico during the Revolution (item **1498**), and Morris studies more current Mexican press portrayals of the US (item **1584**). Solórzano Ramos examines the Rockefeller Foundation's campaign against yellow fever in 1920s Mexico (item **1624**), Paz explores the impact of World War II on security concerns of the two countries (item **1596**), and Griswold del Castillo probes the Mexican response to the Zoot Suit Riots in Los Angeles (item **1543**). Mexican relations with Spain during the Spanish Civil War and the issue of Spanish exiles are the topics of works by Ferrer Rodríguez (item **1530**), Matesanz (item **1570**), MacGregor (item **1565**), and Katz (item **1557**).

There was continued interest in regional history, especially for the 1910–20 time period. García Ugarte describes the diversity of interests affecting the Revolu-tion in Querétaro (item **1533**), while Mijangos Díaz examines political forces oper-ating in Michoacán in the first decade of the Revolution (item **1579**). Martínez Guzmán and Chávez Ramírez provide a detailed account of revolutionary activities in Durango between 1914–20 (item **1569**), while Plascencia de la Parra analyzes the de la Huerta rebellion of 1923–24 on a regional basis (item **1601**). Lorey's examina-tion of the border region emphasizes the boom-bust economic cycle and social de-velopments in the area (item **1563**).

Several notable miscellaneous works appeared in this biennium. The highly anticipated study of Pancho Villa and *villismo* by Katz will be a reference point for future scholars of the Revolution (item **1556**). Benjamin provides an important ex-amination of the development and the various representations of the "Revolution-ary Tradition" (item **1503**). Henderson's study of the "Porfirian Progressive," León de la Barra, offers excellent insights into the difficulties of the transition from the Porfiriato to the Madero administration (item **1548**). Niblo examines the official switch by the government from traditional revolutionary themes to a "new vision of modernity" in the 1940s (item **1587**). [DC and SP]

INDEPENDENCE TO REVOLUTION

1395 Agostoni, Claudia. Médicos científicos y médicos ilícitos en la ciudad de México durante el porfiriato. (*Estud. Hist. Mod. Contemp. Méx.*, 19, 1999, p. 13–31)

Interesting look at officially sanctioned medicine and medicine considered "alternative" to use a modern term. Faced with the problem of both *curanderos* and licensed doctors who were completely unqualified, professional doctors tried to combat these "charlatans" by banding together in professional societies and writing newspaper articles against ads promising phony herbal cures.

1396 Altable Fernández, María Eugenia. Autonomía y centralización en el México del siglo XIX: el caso de Baja California. (*Secuencia/México*, 41, mayo/agosto 1998, p. 5–22, bibl., facsims.)

Shows how Baja California was able to retain substantial freedoms despite the power of the *jefes políticos* dispatched from Mexico City beginning in 1871. Attributes this phenomenon to the state's location as an entrepot for the country with the outside commercial world.

1397 *The Americas: a Quarterly Review of Inter-American Cultural History.* Vol. 53, No. 4, April 1997. Washington: The Catholic Univ. of America.

Issue devoted entirely to Caste War and its aftermath, with groundbreaking essays by Angel (see item **1398**) and Rugeley (see *HLAS 58:1345*).

1398 Angel, Barbara. Choosing sides in war and peace: the travels of Herculano Balam among the Pacíficos del Sur. (*Americas/Washington*, 53:4, April 1997, p. 525–549, ill.)

Describes situation in the Puuc or Sierra region of southern Yucatán after the Caste War as each side tried to keep its followers loyal. Shows that some peasants, very aware of the political ideas surrounding them, successfully managed to follow a peaceful path that was neither Creole nor rebel.

1399 Arrom, Silvia Marina. Containing the poor: the Mexico City Poor House, 1774–1871. Durham, N.C.: Duke Univ. Press, 2000. 398 p.: bibl., ill., index.

Well-conceived study of Mexico City's Hospicio de Pobres from its inception in 1774 to its official demise in 1871. Argues that combination of financial constraints and rapid abandonment of original Bourbon intent of eradicating street begging subverted the experiment almost from the beginning. Important contribution.

1400 Ascencio Ceseña, José Rafael. Magdalena, Jal. después de la Reforma y antes del Porfiriato, 1860–1875. Guadalajara, Mexico: Ediciones Cuéllar, 2001. 168 p.: bibl., ill., maps.

Invaluable resource for scholars searching for demographic information about towns in Jalisco during this period. Provides census data and town documents covering up to the year 1875.

1401 Basch, Samuel. Recollections of Mexico: the last ten months of Maximilian's Empire. Edited and translated by Fred D. Ullman. Wilmington, Del.: Scholarly Resources, 2001. 278 p.: ill., map. (Latin American silhouettes)

Excellent intimate account of the last months of Maximilian's life, as told by his doctor and friend. Editor has enriched his translation with additional historical notes, illustrations, and maps.

1402 Benavides H., Artemio. El general Bernardo Reyes: vida de un liberal porfirista. Monterrey, Mexico: Ediciones Castillo, 1998. 399 p.: bibl., ill., index.

Good biographical study of one of the most important figures in the late Porfiriato era. Makes use of extensive collection of letters beginning in 1885. Ends abruptly in 1913 without much assessment of the significance of Gen. Reyes.

1403 Blum, Ann S. Conspicuous benevolence: liberalism, public welfare, and private charity in Porfirian Mexico City, 1877–1910. (*Americas/Washington*, 58:1, July 2001, p. 7–38)

Discusses impact of liberalism on Porfirian position regarding limited role of the state in helping those in need. Clearly shows that wealthy Mexicans had begun to donate philanthropically as individuals, wresting charity away somewhat from the hands of the clergy. Also describes feminization of private and public efforts to alleviate poverty.

1404 Bobadilla González, Leticia. La Revolución cubana en la diplomacia, prensa y clubes de México, 1895–1898: tres visiones de una revolución finisecular. México: Secretaría de Relaciones Exteriores, 2001. 260 p.: bibl., ill., indexes.

Valuable contribution to diplomatic and military history of Cuba, Mexico, and the US. Author uses archival material and newspapers to show how Cuban-born Andrés Clemente Vázquez—and others—stirred up support for his native country in his adopted home.

1405 Buve, Raymundus Thomas Joseph. Impacto y resistencia frente a los proyectos modernizadores: Tlaxcala en los años de la Reforma. (*Hist. Graf./México*, 13, 1999, p. 45–68)

Author sees Reform laws as having the most impact of any process in Mexico during period. Poses fundamental question whether struggles in Tlaxcala represented ideological battles or long-standing feuds. Shows how various local factions in Tlaxcala used national ideology to retain or gain power for themselves.

1406 Carballo, Alfonso. La conversión de 1846 de la *deuda inglesa* y la guerra de intervención estadounidense. (*Estud. Filos. Hist. Let.*, 50/51, otoño/invierno 1997/98, p. 27–57, bibl., graphs)

Looks at the Mexican government's struggle to maintain its sovereignty and keep its moneylenders in check during the war with the US. Shows the involvement of British consular representatives in the heat of negotiations. For review of entire journal, see item **1424.**

Cárdenas, Enrique. A macroeconomic interpretation of nineteenth-century Mexico. See *HLAS 59:1451.*

1407 Cerutti, Mario. Propietarios, empresarios, y empresa en el norte de México: Monterrey de 1848 a la globalización. México: Siglo Veintiuno Editores, 2000. 262 p.: bibl., ill., map.

Emphasizes growth of strong familial organizations in Mexican northeast and development of two different economies characterized by slower internal traditional methods and rapid external efficiency. Challenges Mexico-centric explanations with fruitful comparisons with Bilbao and northern Italy.

1408 Cerutti, Mario and **Miguel A. González Quiroga.** El norte de México y Texas, 1848–1880: comercio, capitales y trabajadores en una economía de frontera. México: Instituto Mora, 1999. 190 p.: bibl., maps.

Continuation of their *Frontera e historia económica: Texas y el Norte de México (1850–1865)* (1993). Displays unusual and penetrating understanding of the southern US as well as Mexico. González Quiroga's section on Mexican workers in the US represents a real breakthrough.

1409 Charnay, Désiré. Voyage au Mexique: 1858–1861. Présentation et commentaires de Pascal Mongne. Paris: Ginkgo, 2001. 355 p.: bibl., ill., map. (Col. Mémoires d'homme)

Excellent introduction to the French archeologist through his first work on Mexico. Mongne supplies a lengthy foreword, but neglects any explanatory footnotes. Should be read together with the excellent study by Clementina Díaz y de Ovando on the reaction to Charnay's wish to ship Mexican artifacts home in 1880 as per previous agreement (see *HLAS 54:1356*).

1410 El conservadurismo mexicano en el siglo XIX. Coordinación de Will Fowler y Humberto Morales Moreno. Puebla, Mexico: Benemérita Univ. Autónoma de Puebla; Gobierno del Estado de Puebla, Secretaría de Cultura; Scotland, U.K.: Saint-Andrews Univ., 1999. 338 p.: maps.

Collection of essays considers Mexican conservatism as a political philosophy. Although good companion to both small and large studies of social and economic issues for the period, most contributions concern the period 1821–67.

1411 Contreras Delgado, Camilo. Espacio y sociedad: reestructuración espacial de un antiguo enclave minero. México: El Colegio de la Frontera Norte; Plaza y Valdés Editores, 2002. 191 p.: bibl., maps.

Groundbreaking study of transformation of space over time. Focuses on coal mining area of Minas de Barroterán in Múzquiz, Coahuila, that changed from a supply town for a mining camp to one supplying housing for maquila workers at close of 20th century. Provides excellent supporting documentation including maps. Should function as a model for such in-depth studies.

1412 **Corvera Poiré, Marcela.** La Provincia de San Diego de México en los siglos XIX y XX. (*Arch. Ibero-Am.*, 57:225/226, 1997, p. 451–470)

Relates how Franciscan Order in Mexico handled numerous complaints from the public and from its own leadership, ranging from wearing of shoes (instead of sandals) and excessive drinking. Also discusses how expulsion of Spaniards in 1827 and later Church-state struggles had a major impact on the order, leading to its suppression in 1908.

1413 **Corzo González, Diana.** La conformación de una política exterior mexicana en torno al Corolario Roosevelt a la Doctrina Monroe, 1904–1906. (*Secuencia/México*, 48, sept./dic. 2000, p. 183–194, bibl.)

Author uses Limantour archives in CONDUMEX to reveal that, as part of the Roosevelt Corollary to the Monroe Doctrine, US was prepared to support Mexico in annexation of Central America and parts of the Caribbean. Tries to show how Mexico's reluctance to seize the opportunity affected US understanding of the Latin American situation.

1414 **Costeloe, Michael P.** Mariano Arista and the 1850 presidential election in Mexico. (*Bull. Lat. Am. Res.*, 18:1, Jan. 1999, p. 51–70, bibl., tables)

Claims the election of Arista in 1850 was "the first genuinely contested presidential election since independence." Provides in-depth analysis of political fights following the war with the US, but gives other factors short shrift.

1415 **Craib, Raymond B.** A nationalist metaphysics: state fixations, national maps, and the geo-historical imagination in nineteenth-century Mexico. (*HAHR*, 82:1, Feb. 2002, p. 33–68)

Fascinating and innovative analysis of the making of the Mexican state through study of the role of members of the Sociedad Mexicana de Geografía y Estadística. Discusses García Cubas' mapping of a nation-state prior to its creation, and his *inchoate indigenismo* in 1857. Recommended.

1416 **Cunningham, Michele.** Mexico and the foreign policy of Napoleon III. Houndmills, England; New York: Palgrave, 2001. 251 p.: bibl., index, maps.

Well-researched account of French Empire in Mexico largely from French sources. Strongly biased in favor of Emperor Napoleon III. Strangely, author omits Barker's classic study (see *HLAS 42:2171*) in bibliography.

1417 **De colonia a nación: impuestos y política en México, 1750–1860.** Recopilación de Carlos Marichal y Daniela Marino. México: El Colegio de México, Centro de Estudios Históricos, 2001. 279 p.: ill.

Eight excellent essays on significant aspects of fiscal policy and results during the period. Includes Monica Gómez on the findings of TePaske and Klein, a first time look at the finances of the French Empire by Rhi Sausi Garavito, and an excellent introduction by Marichal. Highly recommended.

1418 **De la patria criolla a la nación mexicana, 1750–1860.** México: Banamex; México: Patronato del Museo Nacional de Arte; UNAM, Instituto de Investigaciones Estéticas; México: CONACULTA, INBA, 2000. 311 p.: bibl., ill. (chiefly col.). (Los pinceles de la historia)

Catalog for an exhibit held at Museo Nacional de Arte from Nov. 2000-March 2001. Contains thought-provoking essays by Fausto Ramírez (on paintings reflecting the conservative project and those depicting national beginnings), Esther Acevedo (on the gap between the "allegorical tradition and narrative history," and from independence to the intervention), as well as essays on new topics such as how satire reflects political projects and lithography as an instrument of nationalism. Especially good for finding illustrations for lectures or monographs.

1419 **Delgado Aguilar, Francisco Javier.** Jefaturas políticas: dinámica política y control social en Aguascalientes, 1867–1911. Aguascalientes, Mexico: Gobierno del estado de Aguascalientes; Univ. Autónoma de Aguascalientes, 2000. 325 p.: bibl., ill.

Examines role of *jefes políticos* in the state of Aguascalientes, concentrating on years 1874–81. Shows how the *jefes* had so little power that when their opponents replaced them, they behaved similarly. Once situation had clarified, the *jefes* ran everything down to meddling in individual lives.

1420 **Duncan, Robert H.** Embracing a suitable past: independence celebrations under Mexico's Second Empire, 1864–6. (*J. Lat. Am. Stud.*, 30:2, May 1998, p. 249–277)

Details how Emperor Maximilian tried

to manipulate the Sept. 15–16 independence festivities for imperial advantage. Shows how he preferred to present himself as a supporter of liberal culture almost from the beginning, even embracing Morelos and Guerrero, and distancing himself from the conservatives who had summoned him.

1421 Duval Hernández, Dolores. Luis de la Rosa y el paso interoceánico en Tehuantepec, 1849–1852. México: Instituto Mora, 2000. 66 p.: bibl. (Perfiles. Historia diplomática)

Analyzes the career of Rosa, who served as Mexican Minister Plenipotentiary to the US from 1848–52, with regard to issue of a transatlantic canal through Tehuantepec. Includes detailed biography of Rosa as well as accounts of his diplomatic maneuvers among the various actors.

1422 En la cima del poder: elites mexicanas, 1830–1930. Coordinación de Graziella Altamirano. México: Instituto Mora, 1999. 272 p.: ill.

Valuable collection of six essays about Mexican elites during extremely complicated period in national history. Half of the book is devoted to studies on Durango, while the other looks at Mexico City. Does not have the variety or the novelty of the original stab at this question: *Formación y desarrollo de la burguesía en México, siglo XIX*, edited by Ciro Cardoso (1978).

1423 Escamilla García, Ana Paula. Los paseos dominicales en Toluca durante el porfiriato. Toluca, Mexico: Univ. Autónoma del Estado de México, 2001. 190 p.: bibl., ill. (Col. Tesis universitarias; 4)

Fascinating *licenciatura* thesis for UAEM's Facultad de Turismo relates how residents of Toluca enjoyed their Sunday day off during the Porfiriato. Focuses on the concept and practice of recreation with the clear purpose of finding many more ways to entice visitors to that city.

Espacios en disputa: México y la independencia de Cuba. See item **1952.**

1424 *Estudios: Filosofía, Historia, Letras.* No. 50/51, otoño/invierno 1997/98. El Tratado de Guadalupe Hidalgo: ciento cincuenta años después. México: Instituto Tecnológico Autónomo de México, División Académica de Estudios Generales y Estudios Internacionales, Depto. Académico de Estudios Generales.

Issue contains seven essays on the Mexican-American War and its aftermath. Considers interesting subjects not yet tackled elsewhere, including Evgeni Dik on "La posición rusa." Curiously, article by Velasco on Mexican opinion during the disaster doesn't cite the very important chapters in Charles Hale's *Mexican Liberalism in the Age of Mora* (see *HLAS 36:2026*).

1425 Figueroa Esquer, Raúl. La guerra de corso de México durante la invasión norteamericana, 1845–1848. México: Instituto Tecnológico Autónomo de México, 1996. 188 p.: bibl.

Timely study of the war with Mexico focuses on sea vessels and battles. Interestingly, author cites Mexico's diplomatic isolation as one of the reasons for its defeat on all fronts.

1426 Fregoso Génnis, Carlos. El *Despertador Americano*: primer periódico insurgente de América. Guadalajara, Mexico: Univ. de Guadalajara, 2001. 213 p.: bibl., ill. (Rectoría general)

Author rebels against the common trend of using this first insurgent newspaper as a source rather than as an important subject in itself. Nevertheless, attempt falls short because some of the most important interpretations by Archer, Guedea, and Rodríguez are missing from the discussion. Part of a larger work, which hopefully will use a wider selection of secondary studies.

Fuentes para la historia india de Coahuila. See item **479.**

1427 Gamboa Ojeda, Leticia. La urdimbre y la trama: historia social de los obreros textiles de Atlixco, 1899–1924. Presentación de Bernardo García Díaz. México: Fondo de Cultura Económica; Benemérita Univ. Autónoma de Puebla, 2001. 425 p.: bibl., ill. (Sección de obras de historia)

Making excellent use of municipal archive of the town of Atlixco and sources from textile owners, author skillfully melds social and political history to produce a well-rounded portrait of textile workers and their families from the apogee of the Porfiriato to end of the Obregón presidency. While too limited to be a "Making of the Mexican Working Class," it is a worthy contribution to the topic.

1428 García Hermosillo, Luz Delia. El retrato de angelitos: magia, costumbre y tradición. Guanajuato, Mexico: Presidencia Municipal de Guanajuato, Dirección Municipal de Cultura, 2001. 163 p.: bibl., ill. (Vida y tradiciones de Guanajuato)

Discussion of "angelitos" (small children who have died) in the city of Guanajuato, based on collection of famed photographer Romualdo García housed in the regional museum there. Combines photos with statistical data and interviews about modern practices with regard to this sad phenomenon. Not as beautifully produced as work described in *HLAS 56:1364*, but equally fascinating.

1429 García Luna Ortega, Margarita. Los orígenes de la industria en el Estado de México, 1830–1930. Toluca, Mexico: Instituto Mexiquense de Cultura, 1998. 111 p.: bibl., ill.

What looks like a picture book turns out to be an interesting study of the industrialization of Mexico state, combining the best information from basic economic history with interesting illustrations. Proves the value of the "industrial archeology" taking place in various states.

1430 Gómez Serrano, Jesús. Haciendas y ranchos de Aguascalientes: estudio regional sobre la tenencia de la tierra y el desarrollo agrícola en el siglo XIX. Aguascalientes, Mexico: Univ. Autónoma de Aguascalientes; Fomento Cultural Banamex, 2000. 514 p.: bibl., ill., indexes.

Thorough study of landholding in a small and neglected state. Contrary to findings of earlier historians, author sees a substantial growth of middle-class landholding and strong tendency throughout the century for haciendas to break up rather than stay intact. Important contribution to literature on landholding before the Revolution.

1431 Gurza Lavalle, Gerardo. Una vecindad efímera: los Estados Confederados de América y su política exterior hacia México, 1861–1865. México: Instituto Mora, 2001. 150 p.: bibl., index. (Historia internacional)

Well-researched look at Confederate foreign policy with respect to Mexico. Matías Romero, the Juárez regime's ambassador to US, brilliantly capitalized on Confederacy's support of slavery to the detriment of its relations with its southern neighbor. It is a

pity author didn't begin his study of the South and Mexico with the relationship with the first US representative, Joel Poinsett from South Carolina.

1432 Gutiérrez Grageda, Blanca Estela. Consolidación del régimen gonzalista queretano. (*Auriga/Querétaro*, 13, enero/junio 1998, p. 135–157)

Fascinating account of how liberalism fared in the state of Querétaro following execution there of Emperor Maximilian. Author shows that elections were rigged and state and national constitutions modified both prior to and after rise of Porfirio Díaz. Originally voters were coerced to vote correctly through judicious appearance of troops nearby; later elections during the Porifiriato offered voters a single, preapproved choice. Recommended.

1433 Guzmán López, Miguel Angel. La participación del gobierno del estado de Guanajuato en el movimiento decembrista de 1876. Guanajuato, Mexico: Ediciones La Rana, 1999. 184 p.: bibl. (Nuestra cultura)

Interesting contribution to Perry (see *HLAS 42:2229*) and others on political battle between Sebastián Lerdo de Tejada and José María Iglesias in 1876. Good example of how regional history can contribute to national political history and vice versa.

1434 Hart, John Mason. Empire and revolution: the Americans in Mexico since the Civil War. Berkeley: Univ. of California Press, 2002. 677 p., 8 p. of plates: appendices, bibl., ill., index, map.

Most ambitious book of its kind yet to appear. Concerns mostly period prior to 1940. Appendices of US landownership and banking syndicates are invaluable. Highly recommended. See also item 1475.

1435 Hernández Montemayor, Laura. Guadalupe Mainero: gobernador de Tamaulipas; vida y obra, 1856–1901. Ciudad Victoria, Mexico: Instituto Tamaulipeco para la Cultura y las Artes, 2001. 305 p.: bibl., ill., maps.

Fancy biography of Mainero, governor of Tamaulipas, contains facsimiles of important documents of a crucial period in that state bordering the US, including information about the term of Manuel González (1880–84) and the Porfirian state at its apogee.

1436 Ibarra Bellon, Araceli. El comercio y el poder en México, 1821–1864: la lucha por las fuentes financieras entre el estado central y las regiones. México: Fondo de cultura económica; Guadalajara: Univ. de Guadalajara, 1998. 622 p.: bibl., ill., indexes.

Excellent in-depth study of how Mexicans worked to fund national and state governments. Also discusses findings in terms of the many-faceted explanations of Mexican "instability." Late author's "mapas cognitivos" of weakness of the Mexican state are a gem. Highly recommended.

1437 Illades, Carlos. Estudios sobre el artesanado urbano en el siglo XIX . 2. ed. corr. y aum. México: Univ. Autónoma Metropolitana, Unidad Iztapalapa, Miguel Angel Porrúa, 2001. 246 p.: bibl. (Biblioteca de signos; 15)

This re-edition with additions to author's *Estudios sobre el artesanado urbano del siglo XIX* (1997) is a guidebook to the study of urban artisans in general and textile artisans in particular. Includes thoughtful look at origins of the textile industry with a discussion of role and significance of Estevan de Antuñano. Also discusses work of E.P. Thompson. Indispensable for any study of 19th-century artisanry in Mexico as well as a good starting point when looking at this phenomenon in other Latin American countries.

1438 Imágenes de los inmigrantes en la ciudad de México, 1753–1910. Coordinación de Delia Salazar Anaya. México: Plaza y Valdés Editores; CONACULTA/INAH, 2002. 250 p., 15 p. of plates: bibl., ill., maps. (Historia)

Collection of six groundbreaking essays on a recently discovered subject. Despite title, authors present only demographic and sociological information here. In effect, essays represent an atlas of foreign immigration to Mexico City. Recommended.

1439 Krippner-Martínez, James. Invoking "Tata Vasco": Vasco de Quiroga, 18th-20th centuries. (*Americas/Washington,* 56:3, Jan. 2000, p. 1–28)

Stimulating look at how Vasco de Quiroga (known as "Tata Vasco") has been mythologized over subsequent centuries during which life and deeds of the real historical figure have been lost. Excellent deconstruction of the myth process and a good start for those who would want to look at more contemporary figures separate and apart from their myth.

1440 Kuntz Ficker, Sandra. Economic backwardness and firm strategy: an American railroad corporation in nineteenth-century Mexico. (*HAHR,* 80:2, May 2000, p. 267–298, maps)

Excellent examination of experience of US-financed Mexican Central Railway Co. as it faced challenges in expanding for greater market share. Ultimately, its growth came at a very high price, propelling Treasury Minister Limantour to buy the line and others to preempt bankruptcy and possible sale to foreign investors. Important contribution.

1441 Lau Jaiven, Ana. Primeras ascensiones en globo en la ciudad de México: un empresario de espectáculos, 1833–1835. (*Secuencia/México,* 46, enero/abril 2000, p. 21–35, bibl., ill.)

Study of Gen. Manuel Barrera, impresario of spectacular events in early republican Mexico. Whether it be cockfights, bullfights, or balloons in the air, Barrera was part of the action. New way of looking at very complex period.

1442 Lenz, William E. Identity in John Lloyd Stephens's *Incidents of Travel in Central America, Chiapas, and Yucatan.* (*in* Travel culture: essays on what makes us go. Edited by Carol Traynor Williams. Westport, Conn.: Praeger, 1998, p. 79–87, bibl.)

A look at Stephens and his construction of an American identity abroad, focusing on his 1841 book. Stephens felt superior to most of what he surveyed, but was quite gifted in his tales of Catholic and bloodthirsty Central America designed to be read by groups of Protestant Americans who longed to travel themselves. Very interesting on topics of sex and race and on Stephens' idea of carting off Maya ruins to the US as the British had done in Greece.

1443 Liehr, Reinhard. Andrés Torres, comerciante y empresario de Puebla: entre el mercado interno mexicano y la economía atlántica, 1830–1877. (*Anu. Estud. Soc.,* 96, 1997, p. 157–186, apendices, bibl., tables)

In-depth study of Torres, a wholesale and retail merchant from Puebla, and his family. Shows how early business centered around buying and selling grain, fueling trade in textiles and part ownership of factories until his death, when his affairs were continued by his nephew.

1444 López Ramos, Sergio. Prensa, cuerpo y salud en el siglo XIX mexicano: 1840–1900. México: Miguel Angel Porrúa; CEAPAC, 2000. 353 p.: bibl.

Intensive study of 19th-century press and how it treated health issues. More interested in psychological aspects than issues of cultural history. A must read for social historians of the period 1840–1900.

1445 López Sánchez, Oliva. Enfermas, mentirosas y temperamentales: la concepción médica del cuerpo femenino durante la segunda mitad del siglo XIX en México. México: CEAPAC; Plaza y Valdés Editores, 1998. 165 p.: bibl.

Relates how medical profession and science in general looked at women in 19th-century Mexico. Using medical records and various other sources, shows that Mexican doctors avoided using painkillers during childbirth and contributed to society-wide view of women as fundamentally sickly and temperamental. Interesting contribution to women's history.

1446 Macías Richard, Carlos. El territorio de Quintana Roo: tentativas de colonización y control militar en la selva maya, 1888–1902. (*Hist. Mex./México*, 49:1, julio/sept. 1999, p. 5–54, bibl., map)

Important contribution to several fields including economic development, regional and national politics, and relations between Yucatán and the soon-to-be created territory of Quintana Roo. Posits that Mexican leaders of colonization projects were "capitalistas de vanguardia."

1447 Macías Zapata, Gabriel Aarón. La península fracturada: conformación marítima, social y forestal del Territorio Federal de Quintana Roo, 1884–1902. México: CIESAS; Univ. de Quintana Roo; M.A. Porrúa Grupo Editorial, 2002. 332 p.: bibl., maps. (Col. Peninsular. Serie Estudios)

Shows process of making Quintana Roo a territory separate from the rest of the Yucatán peninsula. Describes resistance of indigenous inhabitants to military and civilian encroachment, and how Mexico created a firmer buffer to foreign interests in British Honduras.

1448 Maria y Campos, Alfonso de. José Yves Limantour: el caudillo mexicano de las finanzas, 1854–1935. México: Grupo Condumex, 1998. 222 p.: ill.

Thought-provoking and sympathetic full-scale biography of one of the most important figures in Mexican history. Contains rare, previously unavailable material about Limantour and complements nicely the recently opened archives at CONDUMEX. Highly recommended.

1449 Marti, Judith. Nineteenth-century views of women's participation in Mexico's markets. (*in* Women traders in cross-cultural perspective: mediating identities, marketing wares. Edited by Linda J. Seligmann. Stanford, Calif.: Stanford Univ. Press, 2001, p. 27–44)

Interesting examination of widow market vendors' petitions for reduction of fees submitted in Guadalajara during the Porfiriato. Argues that these women, far from being as vulnerable as they claimed, were instead able to muster the well-connected on their behalf and were in some cases able to write their own petitions.

1450 Maurer, Noel. The power and the money: the Mexican financial system, 1876–1932. Stanford, Calif.: Stanford Univ. Press, 2002. 250 p.: bibl., ill., index. (Social science history)

Argues that Porfirian state concentrated banking in a few powerful financial institutions to maintain private property rights of potential creditors who would also benefit from economic development. The system worked so well that even the Revolution was unable to dislodge it. Recommended. See also item **1571.**

1451 Mayer Celis, Leticia. Entre el infierno de una realidad y el cielo de un imaginario: estadística y comunidad científica en el México de la primera mitad del siglo XIX. México: Colegio de México, Centro de Estudios Históricos, 1999. 188 p.: bibl., ill., maps.

Important contribution to the histories of both science and statecraft as the two blended to make statistics an important and legitimate tool for government planners. Also comments on creation and function of learned societies and libraries. Highly recommended.

1452 Melzer, Richard. Governor Miguel Otero's War: statehood and New Mexican loyalty in the Spanish-American War. (*CLAHR*, 8:1, Winter 1999, p. 79–103, facsims.)

Focuses on question of whether *hispanos* of the still-territory of New Mexico would show themselves to be loyal to Spain or to US in 1898. Despite Governor Otero's repeated statements praising the loyalty of his constituents, there were many examples of at best divided feelings and a lower level of enlistment in US army in part because of Otero's reliance on the Anglo community.

1453 The Mexican economy, 1870–1930: essays on the economic history of institutions, revolution, and growth. Edited by Jeffrey Bortz and Stephen H. Haber. Stanford, Calif.: Stanford Univ. Press, 2002. 348 p.: bibl., ill., index. (Social science history)

Collection of 10 essays focusing mostly on detailing the domestic economic policy of the Porfiriato, firing yet another salvo at exclusively political interpretations. Based on articles by Beatty, Kuntz Ficker, Marichal, Riguzzi, and others, volume argues that the period saw development of a crony capitalism that allowed the regime to maintain itself politically and that permitted economic growth.

1454 México, Francia: memoria de una sensibilidad común, siglos XIX-XX. Coordinación de Javier Pérez Siller. Puebla, Mexico: Benemérita Univ. Autónoma de Puebla; San Luis Potosí, Mexico: Colegio de San Luis; México: CEMCA, 1998. 445 p.: bibl., ill., index, maps.

Brings together 12 essays exulting the positive influence of France in Mexico. Covers French views of Mexico prior to the intervention, its influence in Mexico to 1910, and some regional perspectives from Puebla and San Luis Potosí. Should be read in conjunction with Díaz y de Ovando's *Memoria de un debate* (see *HLAS 54:1356*) for contrasting picture.

1455 Meyer, Jean A. Yo, el francés: la intervención en primera persona; biografías y crónicas. México: Tusquets Editores, 2002. 467 p.: bibl., ill., maps. (Tiempo de memoria)

Tour de force by author uniquely qualified to write this book. Breathes life into a dusty episode and puts it under a microscope from all angles, annotated by Meyer's historical perspective. Portraits of various members of the French invading force are spellbinding. Terrific accomplishment.

1456 Meyer Cosío, Francisco Javier. Querétaro árido en 1881: una visita gubernamental a Tolimán, Colón y Peñamiller. Querétaro, Mexico: Univ. Autónoma de Querétaro, 2001. 67, p.: bibl., maps. (Serie humanidades)

Author collected several reports written by *Prefecto* Antonio María de la Llata on his visits to Tolimán, Colón, and Peñamiller in 1881. Work has multiple historical uses including comparison with reports of Bourbon officials, insights on how Mexico City sought to exercise regional control, problems of the Mexican countryside, etc.

1457 Mora-Torres, Juan. The making of the Mexican border. Austin: Univ. of Texas Press, 2001. 346 p.: bibl., index.

Study focuses on development of state of Nuevo León and its capital Monterrey, rather than on entire border. Examines transition between creation of the frontier in 1848 and its emergence as a border by 1910, emphasizing role of the centralizing Porfirian state and spread of the capitalist economy throughout the region.

1458 Moreno García, Heriberto. Diez estampas de vida social zamorana en tiempos de Don Porfirio. (*Estud. Michoac.*, 7, 1997, p. 65–90, photo)

Author cleverly uses judicial proceedings to create pictures of everyday life in Zamora, Michoacán. Shows that trade was often affected by flooding; *hacendados* had almost absolute control over their workers; medical doctors were sued over pills that didn't work; machos drank too much, and seduced and abandoned women; and families went to the theater.

1459 Moya López, Laura A. *México, su evolución social*, 1900–1902; aspectos teóricos fundamentales. (*Sociológica/México*, 14:41, sept./dic. 1999, p. 127–156, bibl., tables)

Delves into the methodology, sociology, and philosophy implicit in the group production of *México, su evolución social*. Reminds readers how novel these ideas were in late 19th century. Shows how authors followed Comte's and John Stuart Mill's concepts of progress rather than those of Spencer.

1460 Muñoz Mata, Laura. Geopolítica, seguridad nacional y política exterior: México y el Caribe en el siglo XIX. México: Instituto Mora; Morelia, Mexico: Instituto de Investigaciones Históricas, Univ. Michoacana de San Nicolás de Hidalgo, 2001. 194 p.: bibl., maps. (Alborada latinoamericana; 14)

Good overview of how the Caribbean was seen by Mexican policymakers during the 19th century. Chapter 5, on how Mexico sought to use the Spanish-American War to its advantage, deserves wide reading.

1461 O'Dogherty Madrazo, Laura. Los *laicos* como instrumento de influencia eclesial: la arquidiócesis de Guadalajara durante el porfiriato. (*Hist. Graf./México*, 14, 2000, p. 81–103, map)

Interesting article on how Church hierarchy managed to recoup its influence after triumph of secular liberalism. By focusing on outreach to the laity in archdiocese of Guadalajara, author establishes a model for historians to use elsewhere in the republic.

1462 Olveda, Jaime. Guadalajara: abasto, religión y empresarios. Zapopan, Mexico: Colegio de Jalisco; H. Ayuntamiento de Guadalajara, 2000. 192 p.: bibl.

Collection of seven previously published essays by one of the foremost historians of Guadalajara. Covers economic, religious, and cultural aspects of Mexico's second largest city. Essay on the Basque Cofradía de la Virgen de Aránzazu is a standout.

1463 Ortiz Gaitán, Julieta. Arte, publicidad y consumo en la prensa: del porfirismo a la posrevolución. (*Hist. Mex./México*, 48:2, oct./dic. 1998, p. 411–435, bibl., ill.)

Discusses role of advertising in Mexican newspapers and magazines, given that the number of subscriptions tended to fluctuate. Indicates that postrevolutionary print media switched its focus from French styles to US trends—particularly with Hollywood influence, and that advertisements were often drawn by some of the best artists in the country. Includes interesting illustrations.

1464 Padilla Arroyo, Antonio. Los jurados populares en la administración de justicia en México en el siglo XIX. (*Secuencia/México*, 47, mayo/agosto 2000, p. 137–170, bibl., ill.)

Illustrates difficulties in establishing a functioning and permanent local judiciary. Author is concerned more with intellectual history of the movement than with its popular use. Discusses how through entire 19th century and into 20th it was difficult to enact a penal code and to find judges to enforce it. Very good on the prevalence of French thought on the debate.

1465 Pani, Erika. Para mexicanizar el Segundo Imperio: el imaginario político de los imperialistas. México: Colegio de México, Centro de Estudios Históricos: Instituto de Investigaciones Dr. José María Luis Mora, 2001. 444 p.: bibl.

Excellent salvo in the battle to understand full complexity of the Mexican past. Examines conservative forces in Mexico that first led to the Second Empire and then tried mightily to sustain it. Highly recommended.

1466 Pérez-Rayón Elizundia, Nora. México 1900: percepciones y valores en la gran prensa capitalina. México: Univ. Autónoma Metropolitana, Unidad Azcapotzalco; M.A. Porrúa Grupo Editorial, 2001. 399 p.: bibl., ill.

By focusing on four important dailies (*El Imparcial, Diario del Hogar, El Tiempo, El País*), author looks at "mentalités" and weight of tradition at a key turning point in the Western world. Finds the Porfiriato much more diverse than its name would suggest, and that belief in the wonders of science was shared fairly broadly.

1467 Piccato, Pablo. "El Chalequero," or the Mexican Jack the Ripper: the meanings of sexual violence in turn-of-the-century Mexico City. (*HAHR*, 81:3/4, Aug./Nov. 2001, p. 623–651, ill., tables)

Using case of the "Mexican Jack the Ripper," author presents Porfirian views on rape, sanity, the hereditary factors that cause aberrant behavior, criminology, and the characteristics of the "macho."

Planes políticos, proclamas, manifiestos y otros documentos de la independencia al México moderno, 1812–1940. See item **1600**.

1468 Porfiriato y revolución en Durango. Coordinación de Gloria Estela Cano Cooley y Mario Cerutti. Durango, Mexico: I.I.H., Univ. Juárez del Estado de Durango; Gobierno del Estado de Durango, 1999. 286 p.: bibl., maps.

Collection of seven essays on state of Durango ranging from property-holding to water rights to culture and *maderismo* by Mexican and US historians. Includes article by the late David Walker on the state after the Revolution. Good addition to literature on neglected state.

1469 Riguzzi, Paolo. El surgimiento de la integración económica entre México-Estados Unidos: los años cruciales, 1878–1887. Zinacantepec, Mexico: Colegio Mexiquense, 2000. 25 leaves: bibl. (Documentos de investigación/El Colegio Mexiquense; 53)

Makes controversial and surprising argument that close ties between Mexico and the US were not inevitable. Explains that because the US never really coordinated its investments and trade in Mexico, it allowed its southern neighbor to remain independent enough to pursue national goals. Recommended.

1470 Rojas, Rafael. Retóricas de la raza: intelectuales mexicanos ante la Guerra del 98. (*Hist. Mex./México,* 49:4, abril/junio 2000, p. 593–629, bibl.)

Author looks at "la guerra de los discursos" concerning Mexico's position in the Spanish-American War. Contrasts pro-US stance argued by Francisco Bulnes, who saw in the northern neighbor a good model for Latin America, with that of Francisco Gamboa, whose pro-Spanish attitude was a more conservative version of the Spanish "Generation of 1898." Contends that the war produced a hardening of attitudes in Mexico.

1471 Román Jáquez, Juana Gabriela. Del Aguanaval a Sierra Mojada: el conflicto de límites entre Durango y Coahuila, 1845–1900. Saltillo, Mexico: Ceshac, 2001. 124 p.: bibl., maps. (Cuadernos del Ceshac)

Worthy companion to O'Gorman's study of Mexican territorial limits (see *HLAS 30:1154*). Good in-depth look at the conflicting claims of two frontier states, emphasizing the obvious: that the struggle was more political than geographical. Also shows how the central authority muddied up the waters as well.

1472 Sáez Pueyo, Carmen. Justo Sierra: antecedentes del partido único en México. México: UNAM, Facultad de Ciencias Políticas y Sociales; M.A. Porrúa Grupo Editorial, 2001. 321 p.: bibl., index.

Fresh look at Sierra as political thinker and politician. Argues that many Mexican leaders like Sierra had high hopes for a single unified party (like the PRI), but that the idea proved unworkable as Don Porfirio aged and a growing number of critics and potential successors emerged.

1473 Salinas Sandoval, María del Carmen. Política interna e invasión norteamericana en el Estado de México, 1846–1848. Zinacantepec, Mexico: El Colegio Mexiquense, 2000. 217 p.: bibl., maps.

Work started as part of a project headed by Josefina Zoraida Vázquez on individual states during war with the US. Includes mainly political and fiscal archival data, but worthy contribution to history of state of Mexico and impact of the war on its development.

1474 Santoyo, Antonio. De cerdos y de civilidad urbana: la descalificación de las actividades de la explotación porcina en la Ciudad de México durante el último tercio del siglo XIX. (*Hist. Mex./México,* 47:1, julio/sept. 1997, p. 69–102, bibl.)

Discussion of how to clean up Mexico City finally resulted in a "Sanitary Code" published in 1891. Problem noted as far back as 1756, as some tried to get *zahurdas* banned from the capital. The animals were finally expelled from the city during end of 19th-beginning of 20th century.

1475 Schell, William. Integral outsiders: the American colony in Mexico City, 1876–1911. Wilmington, Del.: SR Books, 2001. 274 p.: bibl., ill., index. (Latin American silhouettes)

Argues that Americans in Mexico formed a "trade diaspora" of expatriate cross-cultural brokers that Díaz employed to enable his strategy of "defensive modernization," defined as every advantage annexation would provide without its penalties. His is a controversial argument; see item **1434** for example.

1476 Se acaba el siglo, se acaba—: el paso del siglo XIX al XX en la prensa de la ciudad de México. Recopilación y presentación de Felipe Garrido. Colaboración de Alejandro García. México: CONACULTA, 2000. 438 p.: index. (Lecturas mexicanas. Cuarta serie)

Collection of approximately 200 articles from Mexican press, mostly from Mexico City, written in 1899–1900, giving a wonderful and sometimes amusing look at how Mexicans understood the turn of the century. Excellent for social and cultural history, and good classroom material.

Sefchovich, Sara. La suerte de la consorte: las esposas de los gobernantes de México; historia de un olvido y relato de un fracaso. See item **1620.**

1477 Sifuentes Espinoza, Daniel. Historia del agua en Nuevo León, siglo XIX: compilación y selección de documentos para el estudio del agua en Nuevo León. Monterrey, Mexico: Univ. Autónoma de Nuevo León, Centro de Información de Historia Regional, 2002. 297 p.: bibl., indexes. (Serie Testimonios; 5)

A compilation of documents relating to water rights and water use in Nuevo León during 19th century, with brief historical introduction by the editor.

1478 Super, John C. *Rerum Novarum* in Mexico and Quebec. (*Rev. Hist. Am./ México*, 126, enero/junio 2000, p. 63–84)

Looks at papal encyclical *Rerum Novarum* as it was understood in Mexico and Quebec. Refers to two subsequent encyclicals, *Au Milieu des Sollicitudes* (1892) and *Graves de Communi Re* (1901), that underscored differences between social and Christian democracy. Asserts that in Quebec, unlike Mexico, the Church became part of the identification of nationality. The Mexicans, instead, saw the Church as one of the strongest voices against liberalism, culminating in the formation of the Partido Católico Nacional in 1911. Argues that studying Catholic social movements without reference to Catholicism itself is easier, but much less rewarding.

1479 Tecuanhuey Sandoval, Alicia. La resistencia pasiva: modalidad de defensa de los poblanos en tiempos de la invasión estadunidense, mayo de 1847. (*Anu.*

Estud. Soc., 96, 1997, p. 265–286, graph, tables)

Author contends that *poblanos* did not collaborate with US occupiers, but resisted passively by directing funds to the maintenance of the basic institutions of nation, state, and city. Uses state budgetary figures to determine that expenses usually reserved for war went to political organizations instead.

1480 Terrazas y Basante, María Marcela. Inversiones, especulación y diplomacia: las relaciones entre México y los Estados Unidos durante la dictadura santannista. México: UNAM, 2000. 292 p.: bibl. (Serie Historia moderna y contemporánea; 35)

Interesting look at internal political considerations in Mexico and the US, coupled with the international perspective, and as capitalized on by *agiotistas* and *especuladores*. Unusual for its sensitivity to the internal political concerns of the US at the time.

1481 Torre Rendón, Judith de la. Las imágenes fotográficas de la sociedad mexicana en la prensa gráfica del porfiriato. (*Hist. Mex./México*, 48:2, oct./dic. 1998, p. 343–373, bibl., ill.)

Author looks at illustrated magazines from 1890–1910 intended expressly to civilize the masses. For example, many included sports sections; and to promote progress, there were frequent portraits of political figures like Limantour and Ramón Corral as well as coverage of upper-class women's beneficent groups.

1482 Townsend, Mary Ashley. Here and there in Mexico: the travel writings of Mary Ashley Townsend. Edited by Ralph Lee Woodward, Jr. Tuscaloosa: Univ. of Alabama Press, 2001. 332 p.: index.

The Porfiriato's answer to Fanny Calderón de la Barca, Mary Ashley Townsend, "the poet laureate of New Orleans," traveled to Mexico several times in last decades of 19th century. She left an unfinished manuscript of her impressions of everything from the pastimes of the wealthy to pulque manufacture that has been very ably edited by Woodward. Recommended.

1483 Trujillo Bolio, Mario A. Protesta y resistencia de los trabajadores textiles en el Valle de México y su relación con los circuitos comerciales mexicano-estadounidenses, 1865–1868. (*Iztapalapa/ México*, 18:43, enero/junio 1998, p. 279–304, bibl., facsim., maps)

Fascinating article begins with how struggles between Empire and the Republic affected the organization and resistance of textile workers in the Valley of Mexico. As the laborers created various mutual aid societies and complained about voucher payments and long working hours, employers resorted to lockouts as the struggle escalated into revolts.

1484 Tutino, John. The revolution in Mexican independence: insurgency and the renegotiation of property, production, and patriarchy in the Bajío, 1800–1855. (*HAHR*, 78:3, Aug. 1998, p. 367–418, tables)

Argues that popular participation in the independence insurgency led to an "enduring agrarian and social transformation." Uses case study of the hacienda Puerto de Nieto to demonstrate that agricultural losses affect everything in a region, including relations between husband and wife.

1485 Urbán Martínez, Guadalupe. La obra científica del doctor Leopoldo Río de la Loza. Edición y coordinación de Patricia Aceves Pastrana. México: Univ. Autónoma Metropolitana, Unidad Xochimilco, 2000. 277 p.: bibl. (Biblioteca historia de la farmacia; 1)

Provides useful and provocative material for historians of medicine and science, epidemiology, and ideas. Includes documents detailing contents of pharmacies. Recommended.

1486 Van Young, Eric. The other rebellion: popular violence, ideology, and the Mexican struggle for independence, 1810–1821. Stanford, Calif.: Stanford Univ. Press, 2001. 702 p.: bibl., index, 1 map.

Mammoth account of insurgency that helped make Mexico independent. In a beautifully written and formidably detailed work, author argues that insurgent countryside was resisting ethnic and cultural encroachment at least as much as growing threats to subsistence. Winner of the 2002 Bancroft Prize, volume likely to be discussed for decades. A must read.

1487 Veraza Urtuzuástegui, Jorge. Perfil del traidor: Santa Anna en la conciencia nacional (de la independencia al neoliberalismo); ensayo de análisis psicosocial sobre la cultura política mexicana. México: Editorial Itaca, 2000. 299 p.: bibl. (Santa Anna en la historiografía y en el sentido común; 1)

Author lays out many reasons why Santa Anna has been fetishized in Mexico as a corrupt traitor. Instead, he argues, Mexico should understand this early 19th-century leader in terms of the struggle to stave off US penetration, and invites comparison between "Su Alteza Generalíssima" and recent presidents of the PRI.

1488 Villaverde García, Elixio. Pioneiros na corrente do Golfo: a primeira emigración gallega a México, 1837–1936. Vigo, Spain: Edicións Xerais de Galicia, 2001. 537 p.: bibl., ill., maps. (Universitaria)

Very well researched and documented book on the unfamiliar topic of Galician emigration to Mexico. Includes interviews and a good bibliography. Fills a gap on the topic of Galician emigration to America. [J.M. Pérez]

1489 Vincent, Theodore G. The legacy of Vicente Guerrero: Mexico's first Black Indian president. Gainesville: Univ. Press of Florida, 2001. 336 p.: bibl., ill., index, maps.

Long-overdue look at Vicente Guerrero and his legacy, in terms of both his family and Mexican history. Devotes a chapter to his grandson Vicente Riva Palacio, the editor of *México a través de los siglos.*

1490 Wasserman, Mark. Everyday life and politics in nineteenth century Mexico: men, women, and war. Albuquerque: Univ. of New Mexico Press, 2000. 248 p.: bibl., ill., index, maps. (Diálogos)

Synthetic study of the period based almost exclusively on English-language sources. Focuses on how political and economic issues affected both men and women in their daily lives. Good summary for classroom use.

Zaragoza, José. Historia de la deuda externa de México, 1823–1861. See *HLAS 59:1636.*

REVOLUTION AND
POST-REVOLUTION

1491 Aboites Aguilar, Luis. José Fuentes Mares y la historiografía del norte de México: una aproximación desde Chihuahua, 1950–1957. (*Hist. Mex./México,* 48:3, enero/ marzo 2000, p. 477–507, bibl.)

Analysis of selected writings of Fuentes Mares as they relate to the idea of northern Mexico's uniqueness.

1492 Aboites Aguilar, Luis and Alba Dolores Morales Cosme. Amecameca, 1922: ensayo sobre centralización política y estado nacional en México. (*Hist. Mex./ México,* 49:1, julio/sept. 1999, p. 55–93, bibl., map, tables)

Explores effect of centralization on the local use of natural resources. As the federal government asserted its authority in the aftermath of the Revolution, this municipality lost control of waters, lands, and subsurface resources.

1493 Aguirre Cristiani, María Gabriela. Acciones y reajustes del clero católico en México, 1920–1924: una respuesta a la Constitución de 1917. (*Iztapalapa/México,* 18:43, enero/junio 1998, p. 119–138, bibl., facsim., table)

Explores Church's attempts to reorganize in the aftermath of the Revolution and to elaborate a plan of social and political activism in the face of threats from the constitution and the postrevolutionary state. Argues that this period of adjustment enabled the Church to confront the coming wave of anticlericalism.

1494 Aguirre Cristiani, María Gabriela. La injerencia de la Iglesia católica en la organización obrera mexicana, 1920–1924. (*Iztapalapa/México,* 18:44, julio/dic. 1998, p. 203–216, bibl.)

Examines growth of Catholic social action groups under relatively tolerant regime of Alvaro Obregón. Threatened with expansion of socialist ideas and by 1917 Constitution, the Catholic Church sought to present workers with an alternative means of organizing themselves: one based on the precepts of the Church.

1495 Alejos García, José. Ch'ol/Kaxlán: identidades étnicas y conflicto agrario en el norte de Chiapas, 1914–1940. México: Instituto de Investigaciones Filológicas, Centro de Estudios Mayas, UNAM, 1999. 340 p.: bibl., index, map.

Focusing on a mountainous region in northern Chiapas, examines ethnic conflicts and struggle over the land between the Ch'ol-speaking Maya of the area and the Kaxlán, or "outsiders," which include foreign investors and local ladinos. Opened up to plantation-style agriculture and extraction of resources in late Porfiriato, the region's landholding patterns underwent little change until 1930s land reform.

1496 Anaya, Héctor. Los parricidas del 68: la protesta juvenil. México: Plaza y Valdés, 1998. 494 p.

A journalist-novelist chronicles student movement of 1968 in which he participated. Bulk of the work is a collection of announcements and pronouncements in chronological order made by different groups and institutions representing both sides of the struggle.

1497 Anderson, Mark Cronlund. Pancho Villa's revolution by headlines. Norman: Univ. of Oklahoma Press, 2000. 301 p.: bibl., ill., index.

Examines how Pancho Villa attempted to influence the media's depiction of him, especially his efforts to avoid standard US racial stereotypes of Mexicans. Also gives considerable attention to similar efforts by Victoriano Huerta and Venustiano Carranza. Author sees Villa as a "canny propagandist" (p. 11) who manipulated US press and State Dept. See also item **1498.**

1498 Anderson, Mark Cronlund. "What's to be done with 'em?": images of Mexican cultural backwardness, racial limitations, and moral decrepitude in the United States press, 1913–1915. (*Mex. Stud.,* 14:1, Winter 1998, p. 23–70)

After examining reporting on Mexican Revolution in six newspapers and 11 national magazines, author concludes that US press was fascinated by the Revolution but based its reporting on stereotypical images of Mexico and Mexicans. Press depicted Mexicans as backward, savage, and lacking in morals— a result of their supposed racial limitations. See also item **1497.**

1499 Avances historiográficos en el estudio de Venustiano Carranza. Saltillo, Mexico: Fondo Editorial Coahuilense; Instituto Estatal de Documentación, 1996. 117 p.: bibl., ill.

Collection of seven papers from colloquium held in 1995. Topics relating to Carranza include the Porfirian background, Carranza's character as shaped by his Coahuilan experiences, Carranza's relations with President Wilson, and his term as governor of Coahuila.

1500 Avila Espinosa, Felipe Arturo. Organizaciones, influencias y luchas de los trabajadores durante el régimen maderista. (*Estud. Hist. Mod. Contemp. Méx.*, 18, 1998, p. 121–170, bibl.)

Detailed summary of worker activism and government response during early phase of the Revolution. Maderista years represented a golden age for organized labor.

1501 Beatty, Edward N. The impact of foreign trade on the Mexican economy: terms of trade and the rise of industry, 1880–1923. (*J. Lat. Am. Stud.*, 32:2, May 2000, p. 399–433)

Details Porfirian attempts to balance export growth with domestic agricultural development. Argues that the two processes were complementary and that a strong foundation was laid for Mexico's post-1940 industrial boom.

1502 Behrens, Benedikt. El movimiento inquilinario de Veracruz, México, 1922–1927: una rebelión de mujeres. (*JILAS/Bundoora*, 6:1, July 2000, p. 57–92, bibl., map, table)

Explores central role played by women in a militant movement for rent control and improved living conditions. Women were at the forefront of a spontaneous movement that included rent boycotts and daily street demonstrations, and that underscored their separation from formal political movements and structures. Most women saw their activism as an extension of their roles as mothers and heads of family.

1503 Benjamin, Thomas. La Revolución: Mexico's great revolution as memory, myth & history. Austin: Univ. of Texas Press, 2000. 237 p.: bibl., ill., index.

Excellent examination of how differing interpretations of the Revolution of 1910 came together to form the "Revolutionary Tradition" as it was remembered, imagined, and invented. Discusses how memory, myth, and history were combined to produce the concept of "La Revolución," then explores how it was represented in annual festivals, in the Monument to the Revolution, and in official histories.

1504 Bliss, Katherine Elaine. "Guided by an imperious, moral need": prostitutes, motherhood, and nationalism in revolutionary Mexico. (*in* Reconstructing criminality in Latin America. Edited by Carlos A. Aguirre and Robert Buffington. Wilmington, Del.: Scholarly Resources, 2000, p. 167–194)

Examines response of prostitutes in Mexico City to social reform policies that threatened their livelihood. Although unsuccessful in utilizing rhetoric of motherhood and the Revolution to halt government efforts to regulate their lives and restrict their activities, the city's prostitutes gained political experience through collective mobilization. For comment by historian on entire book, see item **932**. See also item **1506**.

1505 Bliss, Katherine Elaine. Paternity tests: fatherhood on trial in Mexico's revolution of the family. (*J. Fam. Hist.*, 24:3, July 1999, p. 330–350)

Interesting study uses legal records and letters to local authorities to explore how revolutionary-era social reformism affected notions of the proper role and conduct of fathers. Through court cases and letter-writing campaigns, fathers, mothers, and public officials in Mexico City debated this issue.

1506 Bliss, Katherine Elaine. The science of redemption: syphilis, sexual promiscuity, and reformism in revolutionary Mexico City. (*HAHR*, 79:1, Feb. 1999, p. 1–40, facsims.)

Examines efforts of reformers and social service agencies to address problem of sexually transmitted disease in the aftermath of the Revolution. Through their analyses of the problem of prostitution and prescriptions for reform, social workers revealed gender and class biases that were reminiscent of an earlier era. See also item **1504**.

1507 *Boletín del Fideicomiso Archivos Plutarco Elías Calles y Fernando Torreblanca.* No. 29, sept./dic. 1998. José María

Maytorena: trayectoria y gobierno. México: Fideicomiso Archivos Plutarco Elías Calles y Fernando Torreblanca.

Narrative traces rise and fall of key Sonoran leader from anti-Porfirian to *reyista* to *maderista* to *villista*. Governor in the crucial period of 1911–15, Maytorena spent a lengthy exile in the US (1916–38) before being rehabilitated as a revolutionary in 1943.

1508 *Boletín del Fideicomiso Archivos Plutarco Elías Calles y Fernando Torreblanca.* No. 30, enero/abril 1999. En el gabinete de Venustiano Carranza. México: Fideicomiso Archivos Plutarco Elías Calles y Fernando Torreblanca.

Examines Calles' brief and largely uneventful tenure (May 1919—Jan. 1920) as Secretario de Industria, Comercio y Trabajo in Carranza administration. Well illustrated with accompanying documents.

1509 *Boletín del Fideicomiso Archivos Plutarco Elías Calles y Fernando Torreblanca.* No. 33, enero/abril 2000. Tomás Garrido Canabal: *la prenda del callismo.* México: Fideicomiso Archivos Plutarco Elías Calles y Fernando Torreblanca.

Narrative of political career of two-time governor of Tabasco, whose anticlericalism and education programs sparked considerable controversy. Garrido served briefly as secretary of agriculture under Cárdenas, who soon dismissed him because of his close ties to Calles.

1510 *Boletín del Fideicomiso Archivos Plutarco Elías Calles y Fernando Torreblanca.* No. 34, mayo/agosto 2000. La muerte de Carranza: dudas y certezas. México: Fideicomiso Archivos Plutarco Elías Calles y Fernando Torreblanca.

Examination of flight and assassination of Carranza, with extensive illustrations and accompanying documents.

1511 *Boletín del Fideicomiso Archivos Plutarco Elías Calles y Fernando Torreblanca.* No. 35, sept./dic. 2000. Obregón y el centenario de la consumación de la independencia. México: Fideicomiso Archivos Plutarco Elías Calles y Fernando Torreblanca.

Examines how Obregón administration sponsored 1921 centennial of Mexico's achievement of independence as a way of improving Mexico's international image and promoting national unity. Obregón tried to make event as inclusive and conciliatory as possible while still trying to differentiate it from 1910 centennial celebration.

1512 *Boletín del Fideicomiso Archivos Plutarco Elías Calles y Fernando Torreblanca.* No. 36, 2001. De convenios y deudas en la Revolución mexicana. México: Fideicomiso Archivos Plutarco Elías Calles y Fernando Torreblanca.

Brief treatment of negotiations to refinance Mexico's debt immediately after the Revolution. Accompanied by documents from Calles-Torreblanca Archive.

1513 Bolívar Meza, Rosendo. Una interpretación de la Revolución mexicana a través de la teoría de las élites. (*Iztapalapa/México,* 18:43, enero/junio 1998, p. 103–118, bibl., facsim.)

Uses ideas of Vilfredo Pareto, Gaetano Mosca, and Robert Michels to present the Revolution as a struggle among elite groups that transformed rather than simply replaced older elites.

1514 Bortz, Jeffrey. The Revolution, the labour regime and conditions of work in the cotton textile industry in Mexico, 1910–1927. (*J. Lat. Am. Stud.,* 32:3, Oct. 2000, p. 671–703)

Discusses changes in working conditions and work culture. Contends that the Revolution provided an opening for workers to challenge authority and demand better conditions. Through their activism, workers succeeded in changing labor relations within the mills.

Brading, D.A. Edmundo O'Gorman y David Hume. See item **4631.**

1515 Brewster, Keith. Gabriel Barrios Cabrera: the anti-agrarian friend of the campesino. (*Bull. Lat. Am. Res.,* 17:3, Sept. 1998, p. 263–283, bibl.)

Discusses social and economic policies of a Puebla cacique during 1920s. Although often seen as an enemy of the agrarian cause, Barrios Cabrera's actions and his ability to retain popular support reflected a keen understanding of local needs and regional characteristics.

1516 Brewster, Keith. Militarism and ethnicity in the Sierra de Puebla, Mexico. (*Americas/Washington,* 56:2, Oct. 1999, p. 253–275)

Uses material from the Archivo de la Defensa Nacional and interviews to examine how, during immediate post-Revolutionary period, mestizo political elites in the Sierra de Puebla put their need for soldiers before their misgivings about arming the indigenous population. Indigenous population provided military service in exchange for fighting under their own leaders and limited service outside their region.

1517 Bruhn, Kathleen. Antonio Gramsci and the *palabra veradera:* the political discourse of Mexico's guerrilla forces. (*J. Interam. Stud. World Aff.*, 41:2, Summer 1999, p. 29–55)

Using political theories of Italian Marxist Gramsci, compares and contrasts propaganda efforts of the Ejército Zapatista de Liberación Nacional (EZLN) and the Ejército Popular Revolucionario (EPR). Concludes that EZLN has been much more effective in conveying its message to mainstream society by utilizing national symbols and avoiding more radical terminology.

1518 Butler, Matthew. The "liberal" *cristero:* Ladislao Molina and the *Cristero Rebellion* in Michoacán, 1927–1929. (*J. Lat. Am. Stud.*, 31:3, Oct. 1999, p. 645–671)

Explores participation of a Patzcuaro landowner in the revolt, and argues that Molina's actions stemmed from his own interests rather than from any religious conviction. Demonstrates that motives of *cristeros* were varied and complex.

1519 Cárdenas García, Nicolás. Empresas y trabajadores en la gran minería mexicana, 1900–1929: la Revolución y el nuevo sistema de relaciones laborales. México: Instituto Nacional de Estudios Históricos de la Revolución Mexicana, 1998. 362 p.: bibl., ill.

Excellent examination of dual impact of foreign investment and new technology on mining industry's labor system. The core of skilled, full-time workers that developed was not especially ideological or revolutionary, but did demand a fair share of the wealth they were producing and the right to resolve their problems through their own organizations. Approximately one-third of the work is devoted to the post-1910 period. See also related work by same author (*HLAS 58:1412*).

1520 Castellanos, José Alfredo. Empeño por una expectativa agraria: experiencia ejidal en el municipio de Acolman, 1915–1940. México: Instituto Nacional de Estudios Históricos de la Revolución Mexicana; Chapingo, Mexico: Univ. Autónoma Chapingo, 1998. 347 p.: bibl., ill., maps.

Extensively researched, well-organized, and highly detailed microhistory of agrarian struggle and agrarian reform in the municipality of Acolman in the state of Mexico. Traces bureaucratization and growing role of federal government in the agrarian reform process. A radical transformation of the agrarian structure was not completed until the Cárdenas years. See also *HLAS 56:1539.*

1521 Castillo Peraza, Carlos. De la fuerza a la maña: la lenta apertura del poder legislativo mexicano a la oposición política entre los años 1943 y 1958. (*Diálogo Debate Cult. Polít.*, 1:1, abril/junio 1997, p. 29–40, ill.)

Reveals crucial role of Partido Acción Nacional (PAN) in attempting to strengthen congressional power and challenge presidentialism.

1522 Chassen de López, Francie R. Maderismo or Mixtec empire?: class and ethnicity in the Mexican Revolution, Costa Chica of Oaxaca, 1911. (*Americas/ Washington*, 55:1, July 1998, p. 91–127)

Good discussion of conflict between mestizo ranchers and indigenous population of Costa Chica region over nature of the Revolution in Oaxaca. In the name of Maderismo, the mestizo ranchers suppressed efforts by indigenous population to create a true grassroots agrarian revolution.

1523 Cincuenta años de investigación histórica en México. Coordinación de Gisela von Wobeser. México: UNAM; Univ. de Guanajuato, 1998. 347 p.: bibl. (Serie Historia moderna y contemporánea; 29)

Proceedings from 1996 congress in Guanajuato covering directions in Mexican historiography over last 50 years. Covers wide range of topics, with regional history a major subject of interest.

1524 Colectivo Neosaurios (Mexico). La rebelión de la historia. (*Chiapas/ México*, 9, 2000, p. 7–33)

Analysis of EZLN communiqués and

their presentation of Mexico's past. Discusses Zapatista use of "Indian" cyclical view of history and modern, lineal, and "materialist" version of Mexico's history.

1525 Congreso de Historia Regional, 11th, Culiacán, Mexico, 1996. Memoria. Coordinación de Mario Alberto Lamas Lizárraga. Culiacán, Mexico: Instituto de Investigaciones Económicas y Sociales, Univ. Autónoma de Sinaloa, 1997. 380 p.: bibl.

Collection of papers on wide-ranging topics (a Sinaloan poet to agricultural modernization). Approximately one-third of the papers deal with post-1910 themes.

1526 Davis, Charles L. Mass support for regional economic integration: the case of NAFTA and the Mexican public. (*Mex. Stud.*, 14:1, Winter 1998, p. 105–130)

Examination of public reaction to various forms of trade liberalization that developed in 1990s based on public opinion surveys taken in 1991 and 1993. Both surveys showed a high level of public support for NAFTA, although approval rate declined between 1991–93.

1527 Dawson, Alexander S. From models for the nation to model citizens: *indigenismo* and the *revindication* of the Mexican Indian, 1920–40. (*J. Lat. Am. Stud.*, 30:2, May 1998, p. 279–308)

Challenges view that post-Revolution-era indigenismo involved an exclusively negative view of indigenous cultures. Indigenist thought also embraced a positive view of Mexico's native peoples and held that indigenous peoples had the capacity, values, and characteristics needed to aid in Mexico's transformation.

1528 Ensenada: nuevas aportaciones para su historia. Mexicali, Mexico: Univ. Autónoma de Baja California, 1999. 704 p.: bibl., ill., maps.

Collection of essays by 13 authors provides a somewhat uneven history of the city of Ensenada and—to a lesser extent—Baja California. About half of the work deals with the 20th century, but only through 1940. See also *HLAS 48:2111*.

1529 Fernández, Claudia and **Andrew Paxman.** El tigre Emilio Azcárraga y su imperio Televisa. México: Grijalbo, 2000. 542 p.: bibl., ill., index. (Raya en el agua)

Unauthorized biography of important business figure closely allied with the PRI. Authors try to find a middle ground between earlier works which tended to be either overly critical essays or "official" views of Azcárraga. Although motivated primarily by a drive for profit and growth, Azcárraga and Televisa did bring some benefits to Mexico, including resistance to further cultural inroads by the US.

1530 Ferrer Rodríguez, Eulalio. Páginas del exilio. México: Aguilar, 1999. 460 p.

Memoirs of a Spanish refugee who arrived in Mexico in 1940 and made a successful career in business, running one of the top advertising agencies in Mexico.

1531 Ferreyra, Aleida and **Renata Segua.** Examining the military in the local sphere: Colombia and Mexico. (*Lat. Am. Perspect.*, 27:2, March 2000, p. 18–35)

Compares and contrasts Mexican and Colombian militaries regarding their role in the democratization process. Concludes that in both countries the military has contributed to development of democracy at the national level, but has hindered its development at the local level.

1532 Fowler-Salamini, Heather. De-centering the 1920s: "socialismo a la tamaulipeca." (*Mex. Stud.*, 14:2, Summer 1998, p. 287–327)

Argues for a "de-centered" perspective on 1920s political developments which takes into account that the national state was not sole focus of economic and political power. Using formation of the Partido Socialista Fronterizo in the state of Tamaulipas under leadership of Emilio Portes Gil as basis, author describes a regional socialist movement that provided a popular alternative to the authoritarian centralism pursued by Obregón and Calles.

1533 García Ugarte, Marta Eugenia. Génesis del porvenir: sociedad y política en Querétaro, 1913–1940. Prólogo de D.A. Brading. México: Instituto de Investigaciones Sociales/UNAM; Gobierno del Estado de Querétaro; Fondo de Cultura Económica, 1997. 516 p.: bibl., maps. (Sección de obras de historia)

Excellent regional study describes diversity of interests, especially agrarian, driving or blocking the Revolution. The old center-periphery struggle involved not only the state government against the central government, but also local governments against the state government. In Querétaro it was not rural mobilization that led to revolution but rather the fall of the old regime that led to rural mobilization.

1534 Garza Guajardo, Juan Ramón. Municipio de General Escobedo, N.L.: história de sus ayuntamientos, 1868–1997. México: Ediciones Topo Grande, 1997. 126 p.: bibl., ill.

Brief history of the municipality of General Escobedo, Nuevo León, since its establishment in early 1868. Most of the coverage is devoted to the 20th century.

1535 Gill, Anthony. The politics of regulating religion in Mexico: the 1992 constitutional reforms in historical context. (*J. Church State*, 41:4, Autumn 1999, p. 761–794)

Excellent examination of background leading to 1992 major constitutional reforms in Church-state relations, and of the reforms themselves. Although reforms led to significant gains for the Catholic Church, author concludes that the Church is still dependent in many ways on the government and that general pattern of Church-state relations has not changed despite the reforms.

1536 Gilly, Adolfo; Lázaro Cárdenas; and Cuauhtémoc Cárdenas Solórzano. Tres imágenes del general. México: Taurus, 1997. 113 p.: bibl.

The three images of the general (Lázaro Cárdenas) consist of a sketch of the general's life and ideas by Gilly; a "farewell message" written by the general himself just before his death in 1970; and a brief remembrance by his son, Cuauhtémoc Cárdenas.

1537 Ginzberg, Eitan. Abriendo nuevos surcos: ideología, política y labor social de Lázaro Cárdenas en Michoacán, 1928–1932. (*Hist. Mex./México*, 48:3, enero/marzo 1999, p. 567–633, bibl., tables)

Detailed examination of how Cárdenas' political and social thought evolved during his governorship in Michoacán, setting the stage for his successful reforms as president.

1538 Ginzberg, Eitan. Formación de la infraestructura política para una reforma agraria radical: Adalberto Tejeda y la cuestión municipal en Veracruz, 1928–1932. (*Hist. Mex./México*, 49:4, abril/junio 2000, p. 673–727, bibl., tables)

Explores Tejeda's efforts to solidify control over local governments to advance his program of land reform. See also item **1539.**

1539 Ginzberg, Eitan. State agrarianism versus democratic agrarianism: Adalberto Tejeda's experiment in Veracruz. (*J. Lat. Am. Stud.*, 30:2, May 1998, p. 341–372, tables)

Cogent exploration of Tejeda's plan for decentralized land reform in Veracruz. His approach promised a more egalitarian future, but it was rejected in favor of a centralized program that effectively blocked any meaningful transformation in Mexico. See also item **1538.**

1540 Gojman de Backal, Alicia. Semejanzas y diferencias en cuanto a las políticas migratorias de Estados Unidos y México con respecto a los extranjeros, 1900–1950. (*Rev. Humanid./Monterrey*, 8, primavera 2000, p. 9–27)

Brief summary of development of immigration policies in both countries. Examines ideas that inspired policies and demonstrates that Mexico's approach to immigrants was largely similar to that of the US.

1541 González-Montagut, Renée. Factors that contributed to expansion of cattle ranching in Veracruz, Mexico. (*Mex. Stud.*, 15:1, Winter 1999, p. 101–130)

Author—an ecologist—takes a dim view of expansion of cattle industry in Veracruz during 20th century, concluding that it promoted destruction of the rainforest and takeover of subsistence farmers' land. Based on secondary sources.

1542 González y González, Luis. Invitación a la microhistoria. México: Clío, 1997. 249 p.: bibl., ill. (some col.), index. (Obras completas de Luis González y González; 9)

Ninth volume in author's collected works brings together five essays dealing with microhistory, regional history, and ethnohistory.

1543 Griswold del Castillo, Richard. The Los Angeles "Zoot Suit Riots" revisited: Mexican and Latin American perspectives. (*Mex. Stud.*, 16:2, Summer 2000, p. 367–391)

Examines Mexican response to WWII "Zoot Suit" riots. Influenced by economic, financial, and diplomatic considerations, Mexican government basically left investigation of the matter in US government hands. Some public demonstrations and press criticism occurred in Mexico, but Mexican government maintained its policy of restraint.

1544 Guerra Manzo, Enrique. Poder regional y mediación política en el Bajío zamorano, 1936–1940. (*Hist. Mex./México*, 49:1, julio/sept. 1999, p. 95–135, bibl., map)

Explores relationship between central government and a regional agrarian leader. Juan Gutiérrez Flores succeeded in solidifying his power in this region of Michoacán through both formal links to the federal government and more informal exercise of local power.

1545 Guillén, Diana. Arreglos nupciales, iras santas y disputas regionales: apuntes para la microhistoria de Chiapas, 1911–1912. (*Secuencia/México*, 47, mayo/agosto 2000, p. 5–38, bibl., photos)

Uses matrimony of a Maderista governor and daughter of an elite family to explore broader social forces and points of division within Chiapas society.

1546 Gutiérrez Gómez, José Antonio. El impacto del movimiento armado en el Estado de México, 1910–1920. Toluca, Mexico: Instituto Mexiquense de Cultura, 1997. 135 p.: bibl., ill. (Documentos y testimonios)

Good insight into impact of the Revolution on daily lives of the people. Using a chronological approach, describes actions of the different armed groups contending for power in the key state of Mexico—porfiristas, maderistas, zapatistas, huertistas, and carrancistas—and the varied responses they provoked. Closing chapter is a collection of personal insights by those involved in the Revolution.

1547 Haber, Stephen H. Anything goes: Mexico's "new" cultural history. (*HAHR*, 79:2, May 1999, p. 309–330)

Part of a series of articles on the "new cultural history." Critiques foundations of cultural studies, particularly the use of evidence, arguing that this approach lacks rigor. See also items **1561, 1568, 1623,** and **1633.**

1548 Henderson, Peter V.N. In the absence of Don Porfirio: Francisco León de la Barra and the Mexican Revolution. Wilmington, Del.: Scholarly Resources, 2000. 338 p.: bibl., ill., index. (Latin American silhouettes)

Excellent revisionist view of the "Porfirian progressive" who presided over transition from old regime to the elected administration of Francisco Madero. Author sees moderate reform originating with de la Barra, but his historical reputation was permanently damaged by serving as minister of foreign relations under Victoriano Huerta.

1549 Henderson, Timothy J. The worm in the wheat: Rosalie Evans and agrarian struggle in the Puebla-Tlaxcala Valley of Mexico, 1906–1927. Durham, N.C.: Duke Univ. Press, 1998. 288 p.: bibl., index.

Excellent case study of Evans' efforts to defend physically and legally her hacienda in the face of agrarian reform, which eventually resulted in her murder. Author views agrarian reform as a program driven primarily by political concerns and carried out by a central government whose weakness reduced it to the role of one faction among a number of factions trying to influence the agrarian question.

1550 Herr, Robert Woodmansee and **Richard Herr.** An American family in the Mexican Revolution. Wilmington, Del.: SR Books, 1999. 263 p.: bibl., ill., index, map. (Latin American silhouettes)

Narrative of experiences of an American mining engineer and his family involved in silver mining activities near Guanajuato from early 1900s-1932. Based on combination of letters, diaries, and personal reflections. Good insight into important themes of the Revolution, especially role played by foreign economic activity in generating anti-American feeling.

1551 Historia general de Chihuahua. v. 5, pt. 1, Periodo contemporáneo: trabajo, territorio y sociedad en Chihuahua durante el siglo XX. Ciudad Juárez, Mexico: Univ. Autónoma de Ciudad Juárez; Gobierno del Estado de Chihuahua, 1998. 1 v.: bibl., ill., maps.

Collection of essays by eight authors

deals with various aspects of labor in 20th-century Chihuahua. Work is divided according to different sectors of the state economy.

1552 Jardón, Raúl. 1968: el fuego de la esperanza. México: Siglo Veintiuno Editores, 1998. 335 p.: bibl. (Historia inmediata)

Developed out of a series of radio programs in 1993, work chronicles student movement of 1968. Approximately half of work, based on interviews or correspondence, offers accounts by participants inside and outside the movement. Author is a self-described "leftist militant" (p. 9) who was a member of the Consejo Nacional de Huelga in 1968.

1553 Jayne, Catherine E. Oil, war, and Anglo-American relations: American and British reactions to Mexico's expropriation of foreign oil properties, 1937–1941. Foreword by Julian Nava. Westport, Conn.: Greenwood Press, 2001. 210 p.: bibl., ill., index. (Contributions in Latin American studies, 1054–6790; 19)

Examines divergence of US and British policies before and after the oil expropriation. Responses of both countries reflected broader security interests as well as longstanding rivalries between US and British economic interests in the region. British policy was hampered by ignorance of the Mexican situation, while US policy reflected inconsistencies due to personal struggles for influence among policymakers.

1554 José Valenzuela, Georgette Emilia. La campaña presidencial de 1923–1924 en México. México: Instituto Nacional de Estudios Históricos de la Revolución Mexicana, 1998. 314 p., 16 p. of plates: bibl., ill. (Becarios INEHRM; 3)

Good overview of 1924 presidential campaign and accompanying de la Huerta revolt. After examining role of Partido Nacional Cooperatista in background to the elections, author traces individual candidacies of Adolfo de la Huerta, Plutarco Elías Calles, and Angel Flores, a military figure and governor of Sinaloa who ultimately provided the only competition for Calles. See also item **1601.**

1555 Kapur, Vatsala. Women's contribution to the democratization of Mexican politics: an exploration of their formal participation in the National Action Party and the Party of the Democratic Revolution. (*Mex. Stud.,* 14:2, Summer 1998, p. 363–398)

Compares and contrasts the two principal opposition parties' attitudes toward women and the roles women play in the parties. Concludes that political participation by women has contributed to democratization process but that political equality for women is still not a reality.

1556 Katz, Friedrich. The life and times of Pancho Villa. Stanford, Calif.: Stanford Univ. Press, 1998. 985 p.: bibl., ill., index.

Highly anticipated study of the controversial revolutionary leader and his movement by one of the most respected scholars on the Revolution. Work is divided into four major parts, each representing a phase in Villa's career and in revolutionary development in general. Exhaustively researched, work will serve as starting point for study of Villa and *villismo* for several generations of scholars and students. See also item **1615.**

1557 Katz, Friedrich. Mexico, Gilberto Bosques and the refugees. (*Americas/Washington,* 57:1, July 2000, p. 1–12, bibl.)

Examines efforts by Bosques, Mexico's consul general in France, to aid refugees from Spanish Civil War, and later Jewish refugees, in moving to Mexico. Bosques had to deal with a lack of funds, transportation shortages, and a new, more conservative government in Mexico.

1558 Lawson, Chappell. Mexico's unfinished transition: democratization and authoritarian enclaves in Mexico. (*Mex. Stud.,* 16:2, Summer 2000, p. 267–287)

After examining factors in decline of the PRI, describes areas which have been bypassed or less affected by democratic transition. Finds that, while national elections are more democratic, local elections still pose major problems. The federal judiciary, federal bureaucracy, and mass media continue to be heavily influenced by authoritarian legacy of the PRI.

1559 Lerner, Victoria. Estados Unidos frente a las conspiraciones fraguadas en su territorio por exiliados de la época de la Revolución: el caso huertista frente al villista, 1914–1915. (*Estud. Hist. Mod. Contemp. Méx.,* 19, 1999, p. 85–114)

Suggests avenue of research on fate of

Mexican exile groups during Revolution. Future of groups, and outcome of their plots, depended largely on attitude of US government.

1560 Liga de Comunidades Agrarias y Sindicatos Campesinos del Estado de Tamaulipas: 70 aniversario, 1926–1996. Tamaulipas, Mexico: CNC, 1996. 77 p.

Brief history of Liga de Comunidades Agrarias y Sindicatos Campesinos del Estado de Tamaulipas, accompanied by documents from its first convention in 1926.

1561 Lomnitz-Adler, Claudio. Barbarians at the gate?: a few remarks on the politics of the "new cultural history of Mexico." (*HAHR*, 79:2, May 1999, p. 367–383)

Part of a series of articles on the "new cultural history." Predicts a short life for this approach, and highlights differences in approach between American historians of Mexico and their Mexican counterparts. See also items **1547, 1568, 1623,** and **1633.**

1562 López-Montiel, Angel Gustavo. The military, political power, and police relations in Mexico City. (*Lat. Am. Perspect.*, 27:2, March 2000, p. 79–94)

Analyzes increasing role of the military in Mexico City's police force, beginning in 1996 with appointment of Gen. Enrique Salgado Cordero as police chief. This "militarization" of police did lead to a drop in the crime rate, but corruption and human rights violations continued to be major problems.

1563 Lorey, David E. The U.S.-Mexican border in the twentieth century. Wilmington, Del.: Scholarly Resources, 1999. 195 p.: bibl., ill., index, map. (Latin American silhouettes)

Well-organized and highly readable study of the border as a frontier, an international boundary, and a region. Emphasis is on economic (boom and bust) cycles and social (bilingual and multicultural) developments. Covers from 1880s through 1990s.

1564 Lujambio, Alonso and Ignacio Marván Laborde. La formación de un sistema electoral "netamente mexicano": la reforma de los "diputados de partido," 1962–1963. (*Diálogo Debate Cult. Polít.*, 1:1, abril/junio 1997, p. 41–75, appendices, ill., tables)

Explores attempts of PRI to reform system of congressional representation so as to give appearance of fairness toward opposition parties. Although changes appeared to create a more open political system, they helped to preserve absolute decision-making power of the PRI.

1565 MacGregor, Josefina. México y España: de la representación diplomática oficial a los agentes confidenciales, 1910–1915. (*Hist. Mex./México*, 50:2, oct./dic. 2000, p. 309–330, bibl.)

Brief exploration of relations between Mexico and Spain, and of the fate of Spanish interests in Mexico. Mexican Revolution ended an era of great privilege for foreigners, especially Spaniards.

1566 Macías González, Víctor Manuel. El caso de una beldad asesina: la construcción narrativa, los concursos de belleza y el mito nacional posrevolucionario, 1921–1931. (*Hist. Graf./México*, 13, 1999, p. 113–154)

Examines trial of "Miss Mexico 1928" who was accused and acquitted of murdering her husband, a bigamous army general. Incident demonstrates cultural clash between traditional and "modern" values, as well as persistence of certain class and ethnic attitudes.

1567 Madero, Francisco I. Madero y los sinaloenses: 1909–1910. Selección, notas y estudio introductorio de Gilberto López Alanís. Culiacán Rosales, Mexico: Colegio de Bachilleres del Estado de Sinaloa, 1996. 153 p. (Col. Crónicas; 6)

Collection of correspondence from Madero to various figures in Sinaloa in connection with his anti-reelection activities in 1909–10. Responses to Madero are not included.

1568 Mallon, Florencia E. Time on the wheel: cycles of revisionism and the "new cultural history." (*HAHR*, 79:2, May 1999, p. 331–351)

Part of a series of articles on Mexico's "new cultural history." Presents an optimistic view of this historiographical trend and calls for a continuation of the debate on methodologies. See also items **1547, 1561, 1623,** and **1633.**

1569 Martínez Guzmán, Gabino and Juan Angel Chávez Ramírez. Durango: un volcán en erupción. Durango, Mexico: Gobierno del Estado de Durango, Secretaría de Educación, Cultura y Deporte; México: Fondo de Cultura Económica, 1998. 342 p.: bibl., ill., maps. (Sección de obras de historia)

Detailed examination of the Revolution in Durango. This state saw a high degree of revolutionary turnover between 1914–20, with the *villistas* losing out to the *carrancistas*, who in turn lost out to the *obregonistas*.

1570   **Matesanz, José Antonio.** Las raíces del exilio: México ante la Guerra Civil Española, 1936–1939. México: Colegio de México, Centro de Estudios Históricos: UNAM, Facultad de Filosofía y Letras, 1999. 490 p.: bibl., index.

Author—from a Spanish immigrant family—focuses on background of Mexico's decision to admit high numbers of Spanish Republican exiles. Chapters deal with Mexican press coverage of Spanish Civil War, shipment of arms from Mexico to Republican Spain, diplomatic activities, and context within which Cárdenas decided to admit Republican exiles.

1571   **Maurer, Noel.** Banks and entrepreneurs in Porfirian Mexico: inside exploitation or sound business strategy? (*J. Lat. Am. Stud.*, 31:2, May 1999, p. 331–361)

Examines practice of "insider lending" by Mexico's financial elite. Although it restricted access to capital, this practice did not hamper economic growth. See also item **1450**.

1572   **McGregor Campuzano, Javier.** Elecciones municipales: en la ciudad de México, diciembre de 1925. (*Anu. Espacios Urbanos*, 1997, p. 117–133, bibl.)

Discusses role of Confederación Regional de Obreros Mexicanos and Partido Laborista Mexicana in contentious local elections.

1573   **McGregor Campuzano, Javier.** Política, organización y movimiento: un balance historiográfico del PCM, 1919–1940. (*Iztapalapa/México*, 18:43, enero/junio 1998, p. 175–196, bibl., facsims.)

Historiographical survey of works on Mexico's Communist party. Demonstrates that a wealth of scholarship exists, although quality is uneven.

1574   **McLynn, Frank.** Villa and Zapata: a biography of the Mexican Revolution. London: Jonathan Cape, 2000. 459 p.: bibl., ill., index, maps.

Overview of early years of the Revolution focuses on major players beyond just Villa and Zapata. Author sees Revolution as largely a "conflict within an existing bourgeoisie" (p. 401). Intended for a general readership.

1575   **Méndez Sáinz, Eloy.** Ciudades y arquitecturas del noroeste mexicano. (*Reg. Soc./Hermosillo*, 12:20, julio/dic. 2000, p. 3–42, bibl.)

Study of developments in urban planning in Chihuahua, Baja California, Sinaloa, and Sonora from 1917–57. Attempts to show how revolutionary values were reflected in patterns of urban development and architecture.

1576   **Mexía Alvarado, Miguel.** Cajeme de ayer. 2. ed. Cajeme, Mexico: Centro de Estudios Históricos del Municipio de Cajeme Miguel Mexía Alvarado, 1997. 214 p.: ill., index.

Personal chronicle of municipality of Cajeme, Sonora, by local journalist. Extensively illustrated.

1577   **Mexico's cinema: a century of film and filmmakers.** Edited by Joanne Hershfield and David R. Maciel. Wilmington, Del.: Scholarly Resources, 1999. 313 p.: bibl., ill., indexes. (Latin American silhouettes)

Collection of essays traces Mexican film industry from its birth to 1990s. Essays examine role of film industry in helping to build a national identity, and situate Mexican cinema in context of its relationship to the government, other national institutions, Hollywood, and the expanding global economy.

1578   **Meyers, William K.** Seasons of rebellion: nature, organisation of cotton production and the dynamics of revolution in La Laguna, Mexico, 1910–1916. (*J. Lat. Am. Stud.*, 30:1, Feb. 1998, p. 63–94, map)

Argues that environmental factors played a crucial role in mobilization of a powerful popular movement in southwestern Coahuila. Climatic shifts and an unpredictable water supply disrupted La Laguna's cotton economy on eve of the Revolution, transforming a seasonal labor pool into revolutionary recruits. Subsequent rebel activity and unrest mirrored region's agricultural cycle.

1579 Mijangos Díaz, Eduardo Nomelí. La Revolución y el poder político en Michoacán, 1910–1920. Morelia, Mexico: Univ. Michoacana de San Nicolás de Hidalgo, Instituto de Investigaciones Históricas, 1997. 278 p., 1 folded leaf of plates: bibl., map. (Col. Historia nuestra; 15)

Excellent study of political forces operating in Michoacán in the first decade of the Revolution. Author sees political factions rather than true parties at work, and believes that the Revolution did not truly arrive in the state until Constitutionalist triumph in summer of 1914. Gives considerable attention to activities of Governor—and later President—Pascual Ortiz Rubio. For related work, see *HLAS 52:1335.*

1580 Misión de Luis I. Rodríguez en Francia: la protección de los refugiados españoles; julio a diciembre de 1940. Prólogo de Rafael Segovia y Fernando Serrano. México: Colegio de México; Secretaria de Relaciones Exteriores; Consejo Nacional de Ciencia y Tecnología, 2000. 604 p.: index.

Collection of correspondence and diplomatic documents relating to efforts by Mexico's ambassador to France to protect Spanish exiles in France and to facilitate their travel to Mexico.

1581 Mizrahi, Yemile. Dilemmas of the opposition in government: Chihuahua and Baja California. (*Mex. Stud.,* 14:1, Winter 1998, p. 151–189)

Examines growing political power of Partido Acción Nacional (PAN) in two northern states. To achieve power, PAN changed its political approach, becoming less confrontational in its attitude toward the PRI, turning more local in its outlook, and placing more emphasis on administrative efficiency and fiscal responsibility.

1582 Montalvo Ortega, Enrique and Iván Vallardo Fajardo. Yucatán: sociedad, economía, política y cultura. México: UNAM, 1997. 247 p.: appendix, bibl. (Biblioteca de las entidades federativas; 30)

Good survey of political and economic developments in Yucatán from late 19th century to mid-1990s. The state has continued under control of an evolving elite which has frustrated efforts at popular reform. Authors contend that Catholic right has become increasingly important, as a crumbling PRI and a cooperative PAN work together to block real reform.

1583 Monterrey 400: estudios históricos y sociales. Coordinación de Manuel Ceballos Ramírez. Monterrey, Mexico: Univ. Autónoma de Nuevo León, 1998. 320 p.: bibl. (Col. Estudios sociales)

Collection of essays published in connection with 400th anniversary of founding of Monterrey. Emphasizes city's industrial role.

1584 Morris, Stephen D. Exploring Mexican images of the United States. (*Mex. Stud.,* 16:1, Winter 2000, p. 105–139)

Using editorials and political caricatures published in newspapers in Mexico City, Guadalajara, and Monterrey, author examines Mexican perceptions of US. While recognizing that Mexico may be revising its view of its northern neighbor, author concludes that older perceptions of US as power-hungry, hypocritical, exploitative, and racist are still widespread.

1585 Múgica Velázquez, Francisco José. Estos mis apuntes. Prólogo, edición y notas de Anna Ribera Carbó. México: Consejo Nacional para la Cultura y las Artes, 1997. 195 p.: index. (Memorias mexicanas)

Uneven but interesting memoirs of controversial revolutionary figure. Narrative ends in Aug. 1934, before Múgica assumed position in cabinet of President Cárdenas.

1586 Murillo, María Victoria. Recovering political dynamics: teachers' unions and the decentralization of education in Argentina and Mexico. (*J. Interam. Stud. World Aff.,* 41:1, Spring 1999, p. 31–57)

Compares and contrasts responses of teachers' unions to decentralization of education in early 1990s as part of a general restructuring of the public sector. In both Mexico and Argentina, the leading teachers' union initially opposed decentralization. In Mexican case, union eventually dropped its opposition to decentralization in exchange for government concessions. In Argentina, union continued its resistance only to have Menem administration impose decentralization anyway.

1587 Niblo, Stephen R. Mexico in the 1940s: modernity, politics, and corruption. Wilmington, Del.: Scholarly Resources, 1999. 408 p.: bibl., ill., index. (Latin American silhouettes: studies in history and culture)

Focusing on political and economic issues, author examines how official government policy moved away from traditional revolutionary themes such as agrarian reform toward a "new vision of industrial and urban modernity" (p. 361). Long-term impact of this new approach was highly negative. For companion piece by same author, see *HLAS 58:1511.*

1588 Nieto, Rafael. Rafael Nieto: la patria y más allá; antología. Estudio introductorio, selección y notas de Tita Valencia. Recabación de textos por Alberto Enríquez Perea. México: Fondo de Cultura Económica, 1998. 395 p.: bibl., ill. (Vida y pensamiento de México)

Pt. 1 is good biography of Nieto, an important political and diplomatic figure who was successively a *carrancista*, an *obregonista*, and a *callista*. Pt. 2 is collection of Nieto's extensive writings grouped into categories such as "the foreign debt" and "political economy."

1589 Ochoa, Enrique C. Reappraising state intervention and social policy in Mexico: the case of milk in the Federal District during the twentieth century. (*Mex. Stud.,* 15:1, Winter 1999, p. 73–99)

Traces growing government involvement in supplying of milk to Mexico City. At first government intervened to ensure quality of the milk, but later became involved in its availability. Government's primary method of dealing with supply was to import powdered milk from US and reconstitute it in government-owned factories.

1590 Oñate Villarreal, Abdiel. La batalla por el banco central: las negociaciones de México con los banqueros internacionales, 1920–1925. (*Hist. Mex./México,* 49:4, abril/junio 2000, p. 631–672, bibl.)

Explores process by which postrevolutionary state attempted to assert its financial independence, eventually establishing a national bank. Efforts of Alberto Pani succeeded in forging a link between the state and Mexican financiers, thus helping Mexico

to assert its sovereignty vis-à-vis the international banking community.

1591 Ortiz Pinchetti, José Agustín. Reflexiones privadas, testimonios públicos. México: Océano, 1997. 389 p.: index. (Con una cierta mirada) (Tiempo de México)

Author—a lawyer, journalist, and political activist—provides personalized chronicle of Mexico's uneven movement toward democratization in recent decades. Most of work devoted to 1990s political developments.

1592 Palacios, Guillermo. Julio Cuadros Caldas: un agrarista colombiano en la Revolución mexicana. (*Hist. Mex./México,* 48:3, enero/marzo 2000, p. 431–476, bibl.)

Relates life and activism of a foreign intellectual who fought alongside the Zapatistas and worked for land reform during 1920s-30s. Argues for importance of this highly visible but ignored figure in history of Mexican land reform.

1593 Palacios, Guillermo. Postrevolutionary intellectuals, rural readings and the shaping of the "peasant problem" in Mexico: El Maestro Rural, 1932–1934. (*J. Lat. Am. Stud.,* 30:2, May 1998, p. 309–339)

Uses magazine published by the Secretaría de Educación Pública to explore debate over how to integrate Mexico's campesinos into postrevolutionary state.

1594 El Partido de la Revolución: institución y conflicto, 1928–1999. Coordinación de Miguel González Compeán y Leonardo Lomelí. Colaboración de Pedro Salmerón Sanginés. México: Fondo de Cultura Económica, 2000. 814 p.: bibl., index. (Sección de obras de política y derecho)

Good history of Mexico's official party (PNR-PRM-PRI) focuses on its internal dynamics. Traces party evolution through three distinct phases: Origins (1928–45), Consolidation (1946–64), and Efforts at Reform (1964–99). Finds that a key factor in party's lengthy hold on power was its ability to resolve conflicts within its own ranks.

1595 Patrick, Jeffrey L. Guarding the border during the Mexican Revolution: the memoir of Ward Schrantz, 22nd U.S. Infantry. (*Mil. Hist. West,* 29:2, Fall 1999, p. 121–145)

Account of daily life of an army private stationed at El Paso, Texas. Schrantz's experiences demonstrate lack of training, supplies, and personnel that hampered US efforts to patrol the border.

1596 Paz Salinas, María Emilia. Strategy, security, and spies: Mexico and the U.S. as allies in World War II. University Park: Pennsylvania State Univ. Press, 1997. 264 p.: bibl., ill., index, maps.

Author focuses on security dimension of Mexico-US relations with emphasis on defense concerns, role of raw materials, and intelligence/counterintelligence activities. Narrative goes through 1946 Mexican presidential election. Extensively researched in Mexican and US archives.

1597 Piccato, Pablo. Urbanistas, ambulantes, and mendigos: the dispute for urban space in Mexico City, 1890–1930. (*in* Reconstructing criminality in Latin America. Edited by Carlos A. Aguirre and Robert Buffington. Wilmington, Del.: Scholarly Resources, 2000, p. 113–148)

As Porfirian elites and revolutionary reformers sought to modernize the capital, their vision of the ideal city threatened the urban poor who maneuvered for survival. Through increasing regulation, lower-class behaviors were "criminalized." For comment by historian on entire book, see item **932.**

1598 Pilcher, Jeffrey M. Cantinflas and the chaos of Mexican modernity. Wilmington, Del.: Scholarly Resources, 2001. 247 p.: bibl., ill., index. (Latin American silhouettes)

Author uses "dual biography" (the real Mario Moreno vs. the cinematic Cantinflas) to examine broader issues of constructing national identity, defining modernization, and making the difficult transition from an agrarian to an industrial society.

1599 Plana, Manuel. La cuestión agraria en La Laguna durante la Revolución. (*Hist. Mex./México*, 50:1, julio/sept. 2000, p. 57–90, bibl., tables)

Discusses changes in region's land tenure during periods of *villista* and *carrancista* control. Under both leaders, number of tenant farmers grew, setting the stage for a new middle class of farmers.

1600 Planes políticos, proclamas, manifiestos y otros documentos de la independencia al México moderno, 1812–1940. In-troducción y recopilación de Román Iglesias González. México: UNAM, Instituto de Investigaciones Jurídicas, 1998. 1013 p. (Serie C—Estudios históricos; 74)

Collection of plans, pronouncements, manifestos, and edicts drawn primarily from multivolume work, *Planes en la nación mexicana* (see *HLAS 50:1178*), published by Mexican Senate in 1987. Approximately one-third of work is devoted to 1903–40 period. Good representative selection, but no introductions for individual entries.

1601 Plasencia de la Parra, Enrique. Personajes y escenarios de la rebelión delahuertista, 1923–1924. México: Instituto de Investigaciones Históricas, UNAM; M.A. Porrúa Grupo Editorial, 1998. 317 p.: bibl., ill., index, maps. (Serie de historia moderna y contemporánea; 30)

Analysis of de la Huerta rebellion on a regional basis (East, West, South and Central, and Southeast), with focus on principal leaders. The immobility of, and lack of cooperation among, the rebels permitted Obregón administration to take regions in stages. The North was not a center of concern due to earlier assassination of Villa. See also item **1554.**

1602 Portnoy Grumberg, Ana. Ante el Cerro de la Silla: la presencia judía en Monterrey. (*Rev. Humanid./Monterrey*, 9, otoño 2000, p. 57–81, bibl.)

Interesting local study of a Jewish community that began forming in 1920s. Uses archival sources only recently made available by the community itself to examine characteristics of Jewish immigrants and steps they took to create a tight-knit community in this northern city. See also item **1641.**

1603 Post, David. Student movements and user fees: trends in the effect of social background and family income on access to Mexican higher education, 1984–1996. (*Mex. Stud.*, 16:1, Winter 2000, p. 141–163)

Against background of 1999 student strike at UNAM over higher fees, examines 1984–96 period to determine which groups benefit most from free tuition and low fees. Conclusion is that free tuition and low fees actually benefited the more affluent rather than the poorer classes, and that this trend intensified during the period studied. Student strikers of 1999 were incorrect in linking free tuition and low fees to equality of educational opportunity.

1604 Purnell, Jennie. Popular movements and state formation in revolutionary Mexico: the agraristas and Cristeros of Michoacán. Durham, N.C.: Duke Univ. Press, 1999. 271 p.: bibl., index, maps.

Re-explores basis for Cristero Rebellion in Mexico in the 1920s, asserting that it was neither a conflict between Church and state, nor was it a conflict, as argued by Jean Meyer in his classic work (see *HLAS 38: 2708*), of peasants battling against an oppressive state, controlled and manipulated by local agrarian bosses. Instead, author focuses on a multiplicity of issues represented by a heterogeneous peasantry. [R. Camp]

1605 Ramírez Hurtado, Luciano. En defensa de la trinchera: participación de las élites en el movimiento estudiantil de 1912 en el Instituto Científico y Literario de San Luis Potosí. (*Sólo Hist.*, 10, oct./dic. 2000, p. 61–69, bibl., photos)

Examines how students, teachers, alumni, and local elites protested a decision by Madero government to close their professional school. Protests became a forum in which local elites stood their ground against revolutionary change.

1606 Ramos Díaz, Martín. La bonanza del chicle en la frontera caribe de México: indígenas y empresarios, 1918–1930. (*Rev. Mex. Caribe*, 4:7, 1999, p. 172–193, bibl.)

Shows how Quintana Roo's rubber boom brought together Yucatán entrepreneurs and Mayan inhabitants of the state, ending traditional isolation and combativeness of the Maya.

1607 Rebellion in Chiapas: an historical reader. Compilation, translations, and introductory material by John Womack, Jr. New York: New Press; W.W. Norton, 1999. 372 p.: bibl., maps.

Introductory essay treats background and history of the Zapatista rebellion of 1994. Most of the work (approximately 300 pages) is a diverse collection of documents ranging from a selection by Bartolomé de las Casas to the Fifth Declaration from the Lacandón Jungle (1998).

1608 Los refugiados españoles y la cultura mexicana: actas de las segundas jornadas celebradas en El Colegio de México en noviembre de 1996. México: El Colegio de México, 1999. 516 p.: bibl., index.

Collection of essays on variety of topics concerning relationship between Mexico and Spain. For commentary on *Las primeras jornadas,* see item **4647.**

1609 Reguer, Consuelo. Dios y mi derecho. v. 1–4. México: Editorial Jus, 1997. 4 v.

Multivolume work on Cristero Rebellion and its aftermath from a pro-Church viewpoint. Vol. 1 deals with background to the conflict (1923–26); vol. 2 describes rebellion itself (1927–29); vol. 3 discusses settlement of conflict (1929–31); and vol. 4 covers "second uprising" (1932–37).

1610 Rendón Corona, Armando; Jorge González Rodarte; and Angel Bravo Flores. Los conflictos laborales en la industria petrolera. v. 2, Los conflictos laborales en la industria petrolera y la expropiación, 1933–1938. México: Univ. Autónoma Metropolitana, Unidad Iztapalapa, División de Ciencias Sociales y Humanidades, 1998. 1 v.: bibl. (Serie Iztapalapa, texto y contexto; 27)

Traces labor conflicts in oil industry from 1933–38 through four stages. Begins with local disputes that transform into regional conflicts with national repercussions ending in 1938 expropriation. Vast majority of disputes involved labor-management disagreements; only a small number (13 percent) involved interunion conflicts as various unions were combined into one industrial union. For commentary on vol. 1, see *HLAS 59:1583.*

1611 Reyes, Alfonso and Silvio Arturo Zavala. Fronteras conquistadas: correspondencia Alfonso Reyes-Silvio Zavala, 1937–1958. Compilación, introducción y notas de Alberto Enríquez Perea. México: Colegio de México, 1998. 341 p.: bibl., ill., index. (Col. Testimonios; 3)

Personal correspondence between two of Mexico's leading literary figures who were colleagues at El Colegio de México.

1612 Ruiz, Ramón Eduardo. On the rim of Mexico: encounters of the rich and poor. Boulder, Colo.: Westview Press, 1998. 258 p.: bibl., index, map.

Examines topical issues such as NAFTA, illegal immigration, drug trafficking, and maquiladoras within broader context of evolution and character of the border region stretching from Tijuana/San Diego to Matamoros/Brownsville.

1613 Ruiz Abreu, Carlos. Fuentes para el estudio de la Revolución en Tabasco. México: Instituto Nacional de Estudios Históricos de la Revolución Mexicana, 1997. 285 p.: bibl., ill., indexes. (Fuentes para el estudio de la Revolución Mexicana)

Annotated bibliography of letters and telegrams relating to Revolution in Tabasco drawn from the Fondos Francisco I. Madero and Período Revolucionario of the Archivo General de la Nación. Focus is on struggle for power among revolutionary leaders; period covered is 1911–20.

1614 Rural revolt in Mexico: U.S. intervention and the domain of subaltern politics. Edited by Daniel Nugent. Foreword by William C. Roseberry. 2nd ed., expanded ed. Durham, N.C.: Duke Univ. Press, 1998. 384 p.: bibl., index. (American encounters/global interactions)

Retitled and slightly expanded edition of work first published in 1988 (see *HLAS 52:1326*).

1615 Salmerón Sanginés, Pedro. Pensar el villismo. (*Estud. Hist. Mod. Contemp. Méx.*, 20, 2000, p. 101–128)

Explores historiographical trends in treatment of Villa from his own time to recent biography by Friedrich Katz (see item **1556**).

1616 Samaniego López, Marco Antonio. Formación y consolidación de las organizaciones obreras en Baja California, 1920–1930. (*Mex. Stud.*, 14:2, Summer 1998, p. 329–362)

Examines early development of labor unions in area marked by heavy US investment and presence of significant number of Chinese laborers. At first, unions tended to be more radical and to affiliate with non-government Confederación General de Trabajadores. However, most union leaders later softened their attitudes and affiliated with government-sponsored Confederación Regional Obrera Mexicana.

1617 Sanahuja, José Antonio. Trade, politics, and democratization: the 1997 global agreement between the European Union and Mexico. (*J. Interam. Stud. World Aff.*, 42:2, Summer 2000, p. 35–62)

Examines 1975 and 1991 "framework agreements" between Mexico and European Economic Community as background to more important 1997 agreement which actually led to a comprehensive program for phasing out tariffs. Mexico had hoped for trade liberalization without any political concessions but did agree to inclusion in 1997 agreement of a provision on democracy and human rights.

Savarino Roggero, Franco. Pueblos y nacionalismo, del régimen oligárquico a la sociedad de masas en Yucatán, 1894–1925. See *HLAS 59:4861*.

1618 Schedler, Andreas. Common sense without common ground: the concept of democratic transition in Mexican politics. (*Mex. Stud.*, 16:2, Summer 2000, p. 325–345)

Author believes that end of electoral authoritarianism arrived before elections of July 2000, but also contends that it is difficult to draw a line between authoritarian past and democratic present. The concept of democratic transition has become "common sense," but there is no common ground on exactly what the concept involves. However, suggests that, even though there is no general agreement on definition of "transition," the term is still useful in political discourse.

1619 Scherlen, Renee G. Lessons to build on: the 1994 Mexican presidential election. (*J. Interam. Stud. World Aff.*, 40:1, Spring 1998, p. 19–38)

Examines 1994 presidential election won by PRI's Ernesto Zedillo to determine how far democratization process has gone and what general lessons can be drawn from election results. While there was little overt fraud in the election, the lack of equal access to the media and absence of financial accountability favored Zedillo and the PRI.

1620 Sefchovich, Sara. La suerte de la consorte: las esposas de los gobernantes de México; historia de un olvido y relato de un fracaso. México: Océano, 1999. 470 p.: bibl., ill., index. (Primero vivo) (Tiempo de México)

Interesting series of portraits of wives of Mexico's rulers goes beyond biography to provide insight into changing situation of women in Mexican society and culture. Covers period 1520s-1990s, but most of work is devoted to 20th century.

1621 Sherman, John W. Reassessing Cardenismo: the Mexican right and the failure of a revolutionary regime, 1934–1940. (*Americas/Washington,* 54:3, Jan. 1998, p. 357–378)

Author adds to growing revisionism on Cárdenas, focusing on grassroots opposition to many of his reforms. Although state co-opted army and Church hierarchy, a number of conservative groups remained that opposed Cárdenas by appealing to nationalistic and family values.

1622 El siglo de la Revolución Mexicana. v. 1–2. México: Instituto Nacional de Estudios Históricos de la Revolución Mexicana, Secretaría de Gobernación, 2000. 2 v.: bibl.

Papers presented at 2000 colloquium at Instituto Nacional de Estudios Históricos de la Revolución Mexicana. Colloquium featured 90 leading academicians from Mexico, Europe, and US. Covers a wide range of topics, from agrarian problem to the Revolution on film.

1623 Socolow, Susan Migden. Putting the "cult" in culture. (*HAHR,* 79:2, May 1999, p. 355–365)

Part of series of articles on Mexico's "new cultural history." Criticizes sameness and postmodern jargon used by today's cultural historians. See also items **1547, 1561, 1568,** and **1633.**

1624 Solorzano Ramos, Armando. Fiebre dorada o fiebre amarilla?: la Fundación Rockefeller en México, 1911–1924. Guadalajara, Mexico: Univ. de Guadalajara, 1997. 300 p.: bibl., ill.

While acknowledging that Mexico benefited from Rockefeller Foundation's campaign against yellow fever in 1920s, contends that Foundation's campaign aimed to promote US government and investor (including Rockefeller oil) interests. Also suggests that Foundation attempted to legitimize Mexican government and impose a North American model of medical care.

1625 Stern, Alexandra Minna. Buildings, boundaries, and blood: medicalization and nation-building on the U.S.-Mexico border, 1910–1930. (*HAHR,* 79:1, Feb. 1999, p. 41–81, facsims., photos)

Discusses effects of US-imposed quarantine that subjected Mexicans to medical examinations and sanitation measures. As US officials attempted to stop diseases from crossing the border, perceptions of cultural difference between the two countries grew stronger.

1626 Suárez y López Guazo, Lara. La influencia de la Sociedad Eugénica Mexicana en la educación y en la medicina social. (*Asclepio/Madrid,* 51:2, 1999, p. 51–84)

Explores activities of Sociedad Eugénica Mexicana, founded in 1931. Society's members debated ideas about reproductive health and education against backdrop of Mexico's indigenist movement.

1627 Taylor Hansen, Lawrence Douglas. ¿Aventurero o defensor de los principios magonistas?: el papel de Jack Mosby en la revuelta de 1911 en Baja California. (*Reg. Soc./Hermosillo,* 12:20, julio/dic. 2000, p. 111–141, bibl.)

Examines rebel career of an American who participated in campaigns of Partido Liberal Mexicano (PLM) and who became a leader in PLM ranks. Mosby, like other foreign PLM supporters, was not simply a soldier of fortune; he embraced Magonismo's struggle for change.

1628 Taylor Hansen, Lawrence Douglas. The battle of Ciudad Juárez: death knell of the Porfirian regime in Mexico. (*N.M. Hist. Rev.,* 74:2, April 1999, p. 179–207)

Examines May 1911 Battle of Ciudad Juárez and related historiography. While recognizing importance of the battle to rebel victory in northern Mexico, emphasizes its significance in improving relations between rebels and US.

1629 Taylor Hansen, Lawrence Douglas. El papel de los Comités Pro-Estado en la creación del estado de Baja California. (*Reg. Soc./Hermosillo,* 11:17, enero/junio 1999, p. 75–111, bibl.)

Traces process by which one of Mexico's youngest states acquired statehood. Steps to integrate Baja California into Mexico began in earnest under Cárdenas and were advanced during WWII as local economy grew and population increased. While advocating statehood, local groups sought to preserve a degree of regional autonomy.

1630 Thacker, Strom C. NAFTA coalitions and the political viability of neoliberalism in Mexico. (*J. Interam. Stud. World Aff.*, 41:2, Summer 1999, p. 57–89)
Discusses process of building the coalition—composed mainly of government technocrats and major businessmen—that developed and lobbied for implementation of NAFTA. Also examines connection between NAFTA and 1994 peso crisis.

1631 Vaca, Agustín. Los silencios de la historia: las cristeras. Zapopan, Mexico: Colegio de Jalisco, 1998. 315 p.: bibl., index.
Using blend of interviews, documents, and literary images, author examines important role that women played in Cristero Rebellion. The rebellion gave women a chance to move beyond the activities of their daily life and function in the public arena; however, once the rebellion concluded, they returned to their original roles in society.

1632 Vanderbush, Walt. Assessing democracy in Puebla. (*J. Interam. Stud. World Aff.*, 41:2, Summer 1999, p. 1–27)
Analyzes democratization process at municipal level, focusing on city of Puebla where Partido Acción Nacional (PAN) gained control of local government in 1995. The PAN had to deal with internal divisions, harassment by PRI-controlled state government, and traditional lack of finances. Unable to raise living standards, PAN emphasized its anticorruption efforts.

1633 Vaughan, Mary Kay. Cultural approaches to peasant politics in the Mexican Revolution. (*HAHR*, 79:2, May 1999, p. 269–305)
Part of series of articles on the "new cultural history." Presents a detailed survey of representative works and analysis of their approaches. Argues that the "new cultural history" provides useful framework for understanding peasant-state relations in after-math of the Revolution. See also items **1547, 1561, 1568,** and **1623.**

1634 Veltmeyer, Henry. The dynamics of social change and Mexico's EZLN. (*Lat. Am. Perspect.*, 27:5, Sept. 2000, p. 88–110)
Author sees EZLN as important force in overall democratization process in Mexico. Zapatistas represent a new type of rebellion seeking political space rather than general transformation of society or conquest of state power. EZLN became rallying point throughout Mexico for groups which did not support government's technocratic, neoliberal agenda.

1635 Villarreal Ramos, Enrique. La autonomía claustral: el caso de la Universidad Nacional de México, 1929–1944. (*Rev. Mex. Cienc. Polít. Soc.*, 44:177/178, sept. 1999/abril 2000, p. 159–220, bibl.)
Theoretical discussion of one model of autonomy embraced by UNAM over 20-year period. University's stress on universal and humanistic values was criticized by revolutionary leaders as being divorced from "real world" needs of Mexico.

1636 Ward, Evan. Two rivers, two nations, one history: the transformation of the Colorado River Delta since 1940. (*Front. Norte*, 11:22, julio/dic. 1999, p. 113–140)
Exploration of Mexican and American approaches to developing a section of the border zone. Shows that current environmental problems are best understood in a historical context that includes consideration of different cultural presences in the area.

1637 Weiner, Richard. Battle for survival: Porfirian views of the international marketplace. (*J. Lat. Am. Stud.*, 32:3, Oct. 2000, p. 645–670)
Explores ideas held by *científicos* and other elites about promises and pitfalls of foreign involvement in Mexican economy during the Porfiriato. Challenges traditional view of Porfirian elites as enthusiastic proponents of laissez-faire. Instead, suggests that they feared a loss of sovereignty and were thus "ambivalent internationalists."

1638 **Weldon, Jeffrey A.** El crecimiento de los poderes metaconstitucionales de Cárdenas y Avila Camacho: su desempeño legislativo, 1934–1946. (*Diálogo Debate Cult. Polít.*, 1:1, abril/junio 1997, p. 11–28, bibl., ill., tables)

Analyzes reorganization of official structure of the Partido de la Revolución Mexicana under Cárdenas and Avila Camacho, and argues that reorganization facilitated concentration of presidential control over Mexican Congress.

1639 **Yankelevich, Pablo.** En la retaguardia de la Revolución mexicana: propaganda y propagandistas mexicanos en América Latina, 1914–1920. (*Bol. Am. / Barcelona*, 49, 1999, p. 245–278, bibl.)

Interesting look at Carranza's careful efforts to cultivate a positive image of the Revolution, particularly among nations of the Southern Cone. Carranza's agents successfully presented Mexico's Revolution as progressive and exemplary.

1640 **Yankelevich, Pablo.** Los magonistas en *La Protesta*: lecturas rioplatenses del anarquismo en México, 1906–1929.

(*Estud. Hist. Mod. Contemp. Méx.*, 19, 1999, p. 53–83)

Details coverage by an Argentine anarchist paper of the Partido Liberal Mexicano movement in Mexico.

1641 **Zárate Miguel, Guadalupe.** Integración económica e ideológica de los judíos en México, 1920–1930. (*Rev. Humanid. /Monterrey*, 9, otoño 2000, p. 83–102, bibl., tables)

Uses records of Jewish Chamber of Commerce to show how Mexican Jews successfully adapted to changing economic policies in postrevolutionary Mexico. Jewish entrepreneurs benefited from government support of production of Mexican-made consumer goods. See also item **1602.**

1642 **Zeferino Diego Ferreira: the life story of a Villista.** Edited by Laura Cummings. (*J. Southwest*, 41:1, Spring 1999, p. 1–51)

Series of interviews woven into first-person narrative by the editor. Emphasis is on Ferreira's service in Villa's División del Norte, but there is also coverage of his lengthy stay as a worker in California and on an ejido in Baja California.

CENTRAL AMERICA

DARÍO A. EURAQUE, *Associate Professor of History, Trinity College*
STEPHEN WEBRE, *Professor of History, Louisiana Tech University*

AS THE NEW CENTURY BEGINS, historical scholarship on Central America shows continued signs of growth and innovation. Trends described in previous essays persist, and there are signs of new trends emerging. Of particular note are studies that focus on women's experiences and also on broader issues of gender, among them works by Oyuela (item **1661**), Putnam (item **1765**), and Rodríguez Sáenz (item **1664**).

There has also been a reinvigoration of ethnohistory, embracing not only the frequently studied indigenous peoples of Guatemala, as seen in new works by Alda Mejías (item **1703**), Grandin (item **1738**), and Watanabe (item **1785**), but also groups less often addressed, reflected in studies by Lara Pinto for Honduras (item **1657**), Gould for Nicaragua (item **1737**), and Edelman (item **1723**), Soto Quirós (item **1775**), and Solórzano Fonseca (item **1666**) for Costa Rica. In addition, there is an indication of renewal in the history of ideas, to judge by innovative studies on the independence era by Bonilla Bonilla (item **1649**), Sierra Fonseca (item **1665**), and

Taracena (item **1667**), and on the Guatemalan intellectual engagement with the problem of the native "other" by Casaus Arzú (item **1711**).

For the colonial period, articles by Few and García are evidence of a growing interest in gender issues (items **1677** and **1679,** respectively). There has also been a striking increase in the attention paid to the African experience under Spanish rule, including contributions on Guatemala by Herrera and Lokken (items **1682** and **1686**), on Panama by Mena García (item **1690**), and on Costa Rica by Aguilar Bulgarelli and Alfaro Aguilar (item **1669**), Cáceres Gómez (item **1672**), and Lobo and Meléndez Obando (item **1685**). More traditional questions, such as the composition and behavior of regional elites in the 18th century, also continue to attract sound scholarship, as is evidenced by the appearance of major, long-awaited monographs on Guatemala by Santos Pérez (item **1696**) and on Honduras by Taracena (item **1699**).

Political history is in vogue again for the national period, now enriched by a new focus on the politics of nation and state formation at the local level, especially before the rise of agro-export economies in the 1860s–70s. Pioneering contributions include works by Alda Mejías and Avendaño Rojas on Guatemala and Nicaragua (items **1702** and **1707,** respectively) and Téllez Argüello also on Nicaragua (item **1779**). Some new work in this area continues to emphasize the social and economic context, such as Lauria-Santiago's revisionist history of peasant and community politics in 19th-century El Salvador (item **1748**). Another traditional field, diplomatic history, is giving way in Central America as elsewhere to the "new international history," characterized by ambitious multi-archival studies of foreign economic and political activity in the region, such as those by Quesada Monge on the British (item **1766**) and Schoonover on the French and the Germans (items **1772** and **1773**), all of which focus on the 19th century. Representative of the same tendency for the 20th century is Streeter's new book on US-Guatemalan relations after 1954 (item **1776**).

Among younger scholars, particularly in Costa Rica, the turn towards cultural history has led to an interest in previously underexplored topics, especially crime and its implications for communal solidarity in the late 19th and early 20th centuries, as seen in works by Alvarez Jiménez (item **1704**) and Gil Zúñiga (item **1731**). Also a new fusion of environmental and social history has emerged in studies of the banana industry by Marquardt and Soluri (items **1755** and **1774,** respectively).

Finally, historians of Central America are making greater use of the Internet to advance historical production, distribution, and the organization and networking of scholars. For example, colleagues interested in following the progress of the NEH-funded international project on "African American Identities in Central America," led by Gudmundson, Cáceres Gómez, and Meléndez Obando, can do so by visiting its attractive web site (item **1643**). The Internet has also played a significant role in the growing success of the biennial Central American historical congresses, held regularly since 1992. Approximately 115 papers from the V Congreso Centroamericano de Historia, held at the Universidad de El Salvador in July 2000, are available on the web at *http://www.ues.edu.sv/congreso/* (item **1651**). Ponencias from the VI Congreso, held at the Universidad de Panama in July 2002, are not available online; however, the official web page with a detailed program of the conference can still be accessed at *http://es.geocities.com/vicongcahist/*, and the VII Congreso, scheduled to take place in July 2004 in Tegucigalpa, has its official web page at *http://es.geocities.com/historiacolonial/7ccah.html.*

GENERAL

1643 African Americans and national identities in Central America. Compiled by Rina Cáceres, Mauricio Meléndez, and Lowell Gudmundson. South Hadley, Mass.: Mount Holyoke College, 2001. <http://www.mtholyoke.edu/acad/latam/africania.html>

Bilingual online home of National Endowment for the Humanities-funded collaborative research project features texts, images, news, and events related to history of African presence in Central America.

1644 Apuntes de historia económica de Nicaragua siglos XVI-XIX. Selección, notas y comentarios de Hamlet Danilo García. Managua: Editorial Universitaria "Juan Gutenberg": Univ. Evangélica Nicaragüense "Martin Luther King," 1998. 95 p.: bibl. (Cuaderno de trabajo)

Outline, notes, excerpts, and statistics for use by Nicaraguan students who lack access to more specialized literature. Extensive bibliography.

1645 Arellano, Jorge Eduardo. Brevísima historia de la educación en Nicaragua: de la colonia a los años '70 del siglo XX. Managua: Instituto Nicaragüense de Cultura Hispánica, 1997. 133 p.: bibl., ill. (Ediciones INCH; 8)

Short book outlines general history of phenomenon often marginalized in modern Central American historiography. Written by prolific historian of Nicaragua, value resides in survey of issues rather than in documentary base, innovative hypotheses, or theoretical approaches.

1646 Barrios y Barrios, Catalina. Estudio histórico del periodismo guatemalteco: período colonial y siglo XIX. Guatemala: Ediciones Don Quijote, 1997. 388 p.: bibl.

More of a detailed inventory than a history, careful compilation provides wealth of information on newspapers and other periodicals published in Guatemala during 18th-19th centuries.

1647 Blanco Odio, Alfredo. Los médicos en Costa Rica y su influencia en el desarrollo económico y social. San José: Imprenta y Litografía Nuevo Mundo, 1997. 534 p.: bibl.

Broad overview of origins and development of medical profession in Costa Rica, from colony to present. Features extensive listings of known practitioners, with some effort, as title suggests, to link medical history to social and economic history.

1648 Bolaños, Margarita. La colonia y la resistencia indígena en la configuración económica y cultural de las sociedades costarricense y guatemalteca del siglo XIX. (*in* Congreso Científico sobre Pueblos Indígenas de Costa Rica y sus Fronteras, *1st, San José, 1998.* Memorias. San José: EUNED, 1998, p. 153–172, bibl.)

Essay in comparative history, similar to other examples of the genre in that it focuses on extreme cases of Costa Rica and Guatemala, but unique in that it seeks to explain differences in the indigenous experience from the perspective of colonial history, *before* coffee instead of *after* coffee.

1649 Bonilla Bonilla, Adolfo. Ideas económicas en la Centroamérica ilustrada, 1793–1838. San Salvador: FLACSO Programa El Salvador, 1999. 370 p.: bibl., map.

Critical intervention in elite intellectual history for early Central America. Looks closely at writings of key thinkers of late colonial and early national periods, focusing especially on economic thought. Addressed in book are Antonio Goicoechea, José Aycinena, José María Peinado, José Cecilio del Valle, and Antonio García Redondo.

1650 Buitrago Matus, Nicolás. León: la sombra de Pedrarias. v. 1–2. Managua: Fundación Ortiz Guardian, 1998. 2 v.: ill.

Episodic history of Nicaragua's former capital, from founding in 1524 to coming of railroad in 1882. No references, but lengthy extracts from primary documents.

1651 Congreso Centroamericano de Historia, *5th, San Salvador, 2000.* Ponencias. San Salvador: Univ. de El Salvador, 2000. <http://www.ues.edu.sv/congreso/>

Online archive of approximately 115 papers presented at V Congreso Centroamericano de Historia, held at Univ. de El Salvador in July 2000. Easy access to extensive body of current research in wide variety of historical subfields.

1652 Documentos para la historia de Honduras. v. 1. Tegucigalpa: Honduras, Imágen y Palabra, 1999. 1 v.: bibl., ill., maps (some col.).

First of three projected volumes. Title is misleading, as collection reproduces not documents, but previously published essays and articles on Honduran history by 20th-century historians, mostly Honduran nationals. Vol. 1 covers beginning and end of colonial period, and future volumes will cover up to modern times.

1653 Esta tierra es nuestra: compendio de fuentes históricas sobre denuncias, medidas y remedidas, composiciones, titulaciones, usurpaciones, desmembraciones, litigios, transacciones y remates de tierra (años 1555–1952): área Mam de Quetzaltenango. v. 1, Municipios de Cabricán, Cajolá, Concepción Chiquirichapa, Huitán y San Martín Sacatepéquez. v. 2, Municipios de Ostuncalco, Palestina de los Altos, San Carlos Sija, San Miguel Sigüilá y Sibilia. Quetzaltenango, Guatemala: Centro de Capacitación e Investigación Campesina, 1997. 2 v.: bibl., ill., index, maps.

First of three volumes of land-related documents from Mam-speaking region in western Guatemalan highlands. Critical to specialists in Guatemalan colonial and postcolonial history. Important introductory essays by Gustavo Palma Murga and Carlos Guzmán-Böckler.

1654 Euraque, Darío A. Estado, poder, nacionalidad y raza en la historia de Honduras: ensayos. Obispado de Choluteca, Honduras: Ediciones Subirana, 1996. 106 p.: bibl. (Col. José Trinidad Reyes; 1)

Five essays on range of topics, from fiscal resources of the Honduran state from 1790s-1970s to final piece on official "construction of mestizaje" in Honduras between 1870s-1930s. Introductory chapter situates essays in context of "new historiography," which author outlines succinctly.

1655 Gargallo, Francesca. El pueblo garífuna: caribes y cimarrones hoy. (*Cuad. Am./México*, 13:76, julio/agosto 1999, p. 109–149)

Broad overview of Black Carib, or Garífuna, people, their history, and their place in contemporary Central American society.

1656 Juarros, Domingo. Compendio de la historia de la Ciudad de Guatemala. Recopilación de Ricardo Toledo Palomo. Guatemala: Academia de Geografía e Historia de Guatemala, 2000. 668 p.: bibl., ill., maps. (Biblioteca Goathemala; v. 33)

Classic work, first published in early 19th century, offers much more than historical data on Guatemala City or Guatemala. Welcome new edition includes preliminary study of Juarros and historical context of his *Compendio*.

1657 Lara Pinto, Gloria. Las poblaciones indígenas de Honduras: panorama histórico y tendencias modernas. (*Paradigma/Tegucigalpa*, 8:9, 1999, p. 11–42, tables)

Rare effort at demographic history for Honduras; essay summarizes much of the available secondary literature on indigenous peoples from colonial period to 1990s. Rich in tables and appendices.

1658 Luján Muñoz, Jorge. Breve historia contemporánea de Guatemala. México: Fondo de Cultura Económica, 1998. 523 p.: bibl. (Col. popular; 552)

Despite title, book opens with 16th century, and fully dedicates 100 pages to colonial period. Covers general history of Guatemala until early 1990s, and features excellent bibliography and useful 30-page chronology. Written by one of Guatemala's most prominent historians.

1659 Oyuela, Irma Leticia de. De la corona a la libertad: documentos comentados para la historia de Honduras, 1778–1870. Obispado de Choluteca, Honduras: Ediciones Subirana: Centro de Publicaciones, 2000. 341 p.: bibl., ill. (Col. Manuel Subirana; 11)

Published documents for 19th-century Honduras are rare. Oyuela collects 35 documents extracted largely from judicial archives in Tegucigalpa, ranging from criminal records to wills of extremely important elites, introducing each with erudite commentary.

1660 Oyuela, Irma Leticia de. De santos y pecadores: un aporte para la historia de las mentalidades, 1546–1910. Tegucigalpa: Editorial Guaymuras, 1999. 294 p.: bibl. (Col. Lámpara)

Short but important book by one of Honduras' most prolific historians in recent decades. Here, as elsewhere, Oyuela explores how individual stories of Hondurans over the centuries can be used to study the country's *mentalité*. Focus is on profane and sacred transgressors of hegemonic codes of behavior.

1661 Oyuela, Irma Leticia de. Mujer, familia y sociedad: una aproximación histórica. 2. ed. Tegucigalpa: Editorial Guaymuras, 2001. 352 p.: bibl. (Col. Códices)

Expanded edition of 1993 publication. General history of women in Honduras from colonial period to emergence of feminist organizations in 1990s. Based largely on secondary materials, but only study of its kind currently available.

1662 La patria del criollo, tres décadas después. Recopilación de Oscar Guillermo Peláez Almengor. Guatemala: Editorial Universitaria, Univ. de San Carlos de Guatemala, 2000. 336 p.: bibl., ill. (Col. Estudios y ensayos)

Essential for any consideration of 20th-century Guatemalan historiography. Collection of essays marks 30th anniversary of appearance of *La patria del criollo*, by Severo Martínez Peláez. Although not prolific, Martínez Peláez (1925–98) was in his day arguably Guatemala's most influential historian, and *Patria*, his most influential work (see *HLAS 34:1918*). Contributors include Aura Marina Arriola, José Enrique Asturias Rudeke, Julio Castellanos Cambranes, Edeliberto Cifuentes Medina, Carlos Figueroa Ibarra, Enrique Gordillo Castillo, Iván Molina Jiménez, Oscar Guillermo Peláez Almengor, Rafael Piedrasanta Arandi, Julio César Pinto Soria, Marco Augusto Quiroa, Edgar Ruano Najarro, Eduardo Antonio Velásquez Carrera, and Ralph Lee Woodward, Jr.

1663 Pérez Brignoli, Héctor. Estimaciones de la población indígena de América Central: del siglo XVI al siglo XX. (*in* De los mayas a la planificación familiar: demografía del istmo. Recopilación de Luis Rosero Bixby *et al.* San José: Editorial de la Univ. de Costa Rica, 1997, p. 25–35, maps, tables)

Handy synthesis of current state of estimates of indigenous population levels in Central America from contact to present.

1664 Rodríguez Sáenz, Eugenia. Civilizing domestic life in the central valley of Costa Rica, 1750–1850. (*in* Hidden histories of gender and the state in Latin America. Edited by Elizabeth Dore and Maxine Molyneux. Durham, N.C.: Duke Univ. Press, 2000, p. 85–107)

Pioneer in the study of gender in modern Central American historiography questions three main myths about marriage in Costa Rica during period: that domestic violence was unknown; that wives were passive victims of male violence; and that marriage "was a practice exclusive of popular sectors." For review of entire book, see item **889.**

1665 Sierra Fonseca, Rolando. La filosofía de la historia de José Cecilio del Valle. Obispado de Choluteca, Honduras: Ediciones Subirana, 1998. 111 p.: bibl. (Col. José Trinidad Reyes; 4)

Essay on theory and methods of history found in writings of Honduras-born José Cecilio del Valle (1777–1834), perhaps Central America's most important intellectual during transition between 18th and 19th centuries. For philosophy specialist's comment, see item **4661.**

1666 Solórzano Fonseca, Juan Carlos. Indígenas y neohispanos en las áreas fronterizas de Costa Rica, 1800–1860. (*Anu. Estud. Centroam.*, 25:2, 1999, p. 73–102)

Contribution to sparse historiography on indigenous peoples in Costa Rica is example of interesting results from use of new documentation. Focus is on Guatuso Indians in the north, and peoples of Talamanca coast in Caribbean south. At independence these regions remained under indigenous control, but the situation changed with penetration by outside settlers and other interlopers.

1667 Taracena, Luis Pedro. Uso de las palabras "patria" y "patriota" en *El Editor Constitucional* y *El Amigo de la Patria*, Guatemala, 1820–1821. (*Paraninfo/Tegucigalpa*, 8:16, dic. 1999, p. 1–43)

Thoughtful consideration of meaning and use of two fundamental political concepts during independence period, as reflected in writings of José Cecilio del Valle (see item **1665**) and Pedro Molina, two of the era's most important engaged intellectuals.

1668 Textos clásicos para la historia de Centroamérica. Recopilación de Jesús María García Añoveros. Madrid: Fundación Histórica Tavera, 2001. 1 computer optical disc. (Col. Clásicos Tavera, Serie I, 57)

Convenient digital reissue of hard-to-find standard sources on Central America, including León Fernández's 10-volume *Colección de documentos para la historia de Costa Rica* (see *HLAS 36:2169*) and monumental works by Hubert Howe Bancroft, Francisco Antonio de Fuentes y Guzmán, José Milla, Fray Francisco Vázquez, Fray Francisco Ximénez, and others. High-quality imaging, but editions reproduced are not always the most optimal available and search capability is limited.

COLONIAL

1669 Aguilar Bulgarelli, Oscar R. and Irene Alfaro Aguilar. La esclavitud negra en Costa Rica: origen de la oligarquía económica y política nacional. San José: Progreso Editorial, 1997. 503 p.: bibl., ill.

Based on notarial and other appropriate records, important study argues African slavery was more significant and widespread in colonial Costa Rica than traditionally thought. Colony's economic and political elite were built on wealth produced by slave labor.

1670 Arrea Siermann, Floria. Relaciones entre Misquitos y otros grupos étnicos de la Costa Atlántica centroamericana, del siglo XVII al siglo XVIII. (*in* Congreso Científico sobre Pueblos Indígenas de Costa Rica y sus Fronteras, *1st, San José, 1998.* Memorias. San José: EUNED, 1998, p. 217–225, bibl.)

Based on familiar printed sources, argues that, as consequence of prolonged relations with outsiders, by the 18th century Miskitos had become a mestizo people, with different settlements reflecting the influence of other indigenous groups, including Africans, Spaniards, and English.

1671 Barrios E., Lina E. La alcaldía indígena en Guatemala, época colonial, 1500–1821. Guatemala: Univ. Rafael Landívar, Instituto de Investigaciones Económicas y Sociales, 1996. 188 p.: bibl., ill. (Serie socio-cultural)

Welcome study of urbanism in colonial Guatemala, with emphasis on persistence of indigenous elites and governance in indigenous communities.

1672 Cáceres Gómez, Rina. El trabajo esclavo en Costa Rica. (*Rev. Hist. / Heredia,* 39, enero/junio 1999, p. 27–49, graph, table)

Synthetic overview of history of African slavery in colonial Costa Rica, based largely on secondary sources. Attempts to situate local experience in global historical context.

1673 Castillero Calvo, Alfredo. "La ciudad imaginada": contexto ideológico-emblemático y funcionalidad; ensayo de interpretación de la ciudad colonial. (*Rev. Indias,* 59:215, enero/abril 1999, p. 143–169)

Extended meditation on historical method and colonial urbanism, with focus on Panama City. Reconsiders historical precedents for city plan, and argues against socioracial heterogeneity of residential patterns, as proposed by María del Carmen Mena García in item **1689.**

1674 Chaverri, María de los Angeles. Elementos de lo político administrativo en la Alcaldía Mayor de Tegucigalpa durante la década de los cuarenta del siglo XVIII. (*Yaxkin/Tegucigalpa,* 17, 1998, p. 61–83, bibl., graphs, maps, tables)

Institutional history of Tegucigalpa mining district, with focus on period of Alcalde Mayor Don Baltazar Ortiz de Letona (1739–43), author of frequently cited *Relación geográfica.* Some effort to relate evolution of territorial boundaries and administrative forms to broader questions of social and economic history.

1675 Extractos de escrituras públicas: Archivo General de Centroamérica. v. 1, Años 1567 a 1648. v. 2, Años 1543 a 1659. v. 3, Años 1538 a 1657. Guatemala: J.J. Falla: Distribuido por Museo Popol Vuh de la Univ. Francisco Marroquín, 1994–2001. 3 v.: indexes, maps.

Fruit of lifetime's labor in Guatemala's colonial archives. Painstaking summaries of notarial acts provide rich source for social and economic history of period from 1538–1659. Organized alphabetically by notary, and, particularly welcome, thoroughly indexed by volume.

1676 Fernández Hernández, Bernabé. El gobierno del Intendente Anguiano en Honduras, 1796–1812. Sevilla, Spain: Univ. de Sevilla, Secretariado de Publicaciones, 1997. 231 p.: bibl., ill., maps. (Serie Historia y geografía; núm. 28)

Detailed study of Honduras during governorship of energetic Bourbon bureaucrat, Don Ramón de Anguiano (1743–1819?), whose ambitious efforts to remedy province's economic, political, and military problems achieved little because of late colonial crisis.

1677 Few, Martha. "No es la palabra de Dios": acusaciones de enfermedad y las políticas culturales de poder en la Guatemala colonial, 1650–1720. (*Mesoamérica/Antigua*, 20:38, dic. 1999, p. 33–54)

Innovative application of recent advances in cultural history, especially with regard to gender, power, and the body, to Inquisition and criminal records from late 17th-century Guatemala. Role as healers and midwives endowed women of all social and racial backgrounds with power and influence, but also made them vulnerable to accusations of witchcraft.

1678 Gallup-Díaz, Ignacio. "Haven't we come to kill the Spaniards?": the Tule upheaval in eastern Panama, 1727–1728. (*Colon. Lat. Am. Rev.*, 10:2, Dec. 2001, p. 251–271)

Reconsideration of frontier conflict in early 18th-century Darién, based on complete manuscript record, suggests difference in indigenous and Spanish understandings not only of specific episode, but also of relationship between indigenous peoples and Spanish authority in general.

1679 García, Claudia. Género, etnia y poder en la Costa de Mosquitos, siglos XVII y XVIII. (*Mesoamérica/Antigua*, 21:40, dic. 2000, p. 95–116, graphs, ill., map, photo)

Gender, and procreative role of women in particular, seen as key to understanding evolving power relationships in ethnically diverse world of Mosquito Coast of Honduras and Nicaragua in 17th-18th centuries. Rejects simplistic view of women as inevitably subordinate due to role in human reproduction. Degree of female control over sexual and reproductive options varied by ethnic group and over time.

1680 García, Claudia. Interacción étnica y diplomacia de fronteras en el reino miskitu a fines del siglo XVIII. (*Anu. Estud. Am.*, 56:1, enero/junio 1999, p. 95–121)

Earlier version, more detailed but less rigorously presented, of ideas discussed in item **1679**. Failure of Spanish attempt to colonize Mosquito Coast in late 18th century attributed, among other things, to fear among Miskitu elite males that stronger presence of Roman Catholic Church would lead to suppression of polygamy.

1681 Hernández Méndez, Rodolfo Esteban. Acercamiento histórico a las Bulas de la Santa Cruzada en el Reino de Guatemala. (*Estudios/Guatemala*, agosto 1998, p. 52–81, tables)

Detailed introduction to the Bula de la Santa Cruzada, as administered in Guatemala. Technically a sale of indulgences to finance war against infidels, bula was in reality a tax which accounted for a significant share of crown revenue.

1682 Herrera, Robinson A. "Por que no sabemos firmar": black slaves in early Guatemala. (*Americas/Washington*, 57:2, Oct. 2000, p. 247–267)

Well-documented overview of African experience in 16th-century Santiago de Guatemala. Although numerically a small component of early colonial society, slaves and free persons of color played important roles in city's economic and social life.

1683 Ibarra Rojas, Eugenia. Las epidemias del Viejo Mundo entre los indígenas de Costa Rica antes de la conquista española: ¿mito o realidad?, 1502–1561. (*Mesoamérica/Antigua*, 19:36, dic. 1998, p. 593–618, map, tables)

Despite lack of direct documentary evidence, author argues, on basis of what is known of Old World epidemics in neighboring Nicaragua and Panama, indigenous trade patterns, and movements of Spanish expeditions, that any of several European diseases (small pox, measles, influenza, typhus, plague) may have struck population of Costa Rica's central valley prior to belated Spanish conquest, which began in 1560s.

1684 Ibarra Rojas, Eugenia. Patrones de intercambio en el Golfo de Uraba, 1533. (*in* Congreso Científico sobre Pueblos Indígenas de Costa Rica y sus Fronteras, 1st, *San*

José, 1998. Memorias. San José: EUNED, 1998, p. 193–207, bibl.)

Analysis of published 1533 document suggests ways in which study of indigenous trading activity along Caribbean coast of Nicaragua, Costa Rica, and Panama can contribute to understanding of preconquest political structure, as well as role of exchange in establishing Spanish power in region.

1685 Lobo, Tatiana and Mauricio Meléndez Obando. Negros y blancos: todo mezclado. San José: Editorial de la Univ. de Costa Rica, 1997. 214 p.: bibl., ill.

Major work. Archives-based episodes of African experience in colonial Costa Rica are followed by exhaustively researched genealogies indicating slave ancestry of many of republic's contemporary elite families. Method and conclusions offer provocative challenge to those of Samuel Stone in *La dinastía de los conquistadores: la crisis del poder en la Costa Rica contemporánea* (1975). See also Stone's *The Heritage of the Conquistadors* (*HLAS 53:5116*).

1686 Lokken, Paul. Undoing racial hierarchy: mulattos and militia service in colonial Guatemala. (*SECOLAS Ann.*, 31, Nov. 1999, p. 25–36)

Argues that, in 18th-century Guatemala, persons of African descent used prominent role in militia service to leverage a gradual end to *laboría* tribute obligations. Racial hierarchy was realigned, but not subverted, and Crown's willingness to compromise assured black and mulatto loyalty, while widening social gap between these groups and tribute-paying Indians.

1687 Martínez Castillo, Mario Felipe. El cacicazgo de Camasca. (*Hist. Crít./Tegucigalpa*, 1, sept. 1998, p. 5–14)

Brief case study of indigenous elites in colonial Honduras. Founded by Mexican auxiliaries in wake of conquest, Camasca's noble families remained prominent in local affairs at least until late 19th century.

1688 Matthew, Laura. El náhuatl y la identidad mexicana el la Guatemala colonial. (*Mesoamérica/Antigua*, 21:40, dic. 2000, p. 41–68, facsims., ill.)

Study of colonial Guatemala's *mexicanos*, descendants of Mexican Indians who arrived in 16th century as auxiliary conquest troops, settled in Ciudad Vieja area and sub-

urbs of Santiago, and maintained privileged separation from neighboring Maya communities. Emphasis on politics of language choice, implicit in preference first for Náhuatl, then later willing acceptance of Spanish.

1689 Mena García, María del Carmen. Panamá en el siglo XVIII: trazado urbano, materiales y técnica constructiva. (*Rev. Indias*, 57:210, mayo/agosto 1997, p. 369–398, maps, tables)

Brief study of urbanism in late colonial Panamá, with emphasis on building materials and techniques.

1690 Mena García, María del Carmen. Religión, etnia y sociedad: cofradías de negros en el Panamá colonial. (*Anu. Estud. Am.*, 57:1, enero/junio 2000, p. 137–169, graphs, tables)

Black and mulatto lay brotherhoods in 18th-century Panama seen, despite some evidence of diverse membership, as sites for ethnic cohesion, mutual assistance, and mediation, both with supernatural and with other social groups.

1691 Olien, Michael D. General, Governor, and Admiral: three Miskito lines of succession. (*Ethnohistory/Columbus*, 45:2, Spring 1998, p. 277–318, bibl., maps, table)

Well-written article deals informatively with the British-created system of government among the Miskitos during the 18th-19th centuries. [R. Haskett/S. Wood]

1692 Potthast-Jutkeit, Barbara. Centroamérica y el contrabando por la Costa de Mosquitos en el siglo XVIII. (*Mesoamérica/Antigua*, 19:36, dic. 1998, p. 499–516, facsim.)

Explores contraband commercial activity on the Mosquito Coast and especially at the 18th-century English settlement at Black River, Honduras. Views contraband trade as less a foreign intrusion on Spanish sovereignty and more a vital link between Central America and global markets, as well as a basis for appreciating cultural and geographical continuities between isthmus and Caribbean.

1693 Quirós Vargas, Claudia. La sociedad dominante y la economía cacaotera de Rivas, factores determinantes para el surgimiento de la "Hacienda de Campo" en el Pacífico Norte costarricense: primera mitad del siglo XVIII. (*Anu. Estud. Centroam.*, 25:2, 1999, p. 49–71, maps, tables)

Emergence in 18th century of large landed estates devoted to stock-raising in Costa Rica's Guanacaste region is attributed to the expansion of economic activities by leading families of Granada, Nicaragua, and particularly to foundation of town of Rivas.

Randall, Stephen J.; Graeme Stewart Mount; and David Bright. The Caribbean Basin: an international history. See item **2093**.

Sanchiz Ochoa, Pilar. El trabajo de la mujer en América. See item **1055**.

1694 Santos Pérez, José Manuel. Los comerciantes de Guatemala y la economía de Centroamérica en la primera mitad del siglo XVIII. (*Anu. Estud. Am.*, 56:2, julio/dic. 1999, p. 463–484, graph, tables)

Examination of Guatemalan merchant activity in period before late-18th-century indigo boom describes economy as more diversified and prosperous than previously thought. Despite shrinking contacts with Spain, resourceful merchants found outlets for a variety of colonial products, especially in overland trade with Mexico.

1695 Santos Pérez, José Manuel. Las élites de Santiago de Guatemala y el cabildo colonial, 1700–1770. (*Rev. Hist./Heredia*, 38, julio/dic. 1998, p. 87–111, graphs, tables)

Prosopographical study of Guatemalan cabildo in 18th century concludes majority of municipal councilmen were merchants born outside colony. Origins, activities, and marital alliances determined factional allegiances, as well as positions adopted in colonial policy disputes.

1696 Santos Pérez, José Manuel. Elites, poder local y régimen colonial: el cabildo y los regidores de Santiago de Guatemala, 1700–1787. Cádiz, Spain: Servicio de Publicaciones de la Univ. de Cádiz; South Woodstock, Vt.: Plumsock Mesoamerican Studies; Miami, Fla.: Centro de Investigaciones Regionales de Mesoamérica, 1999. 416 p.: bibl., ill. (some col.).

Major work. Revised version of author's 1996 Univ. de Salamanca doctoral dissertation unites in single volume results of Santos' extensive research on 18th-century Guatemala's powerful families, their strategies for survival and advancement, and their

political and economic activities. Significant advance in cabildo historiography and in study of Bourbon era in Central America.

1697 Santos Pérez, José Manuel. La práctica del autogobierno en Centroamérica: conflictos entre la Audiencia de Guatemala y el Cabildo de Santiago en el siglo XVIII. (*Mesoamérica/Antigua*, 21:40, dic. 2000, p. 69–94, photo)

Conflicts in 18th-century Guatemala between Audiencia and Cabildo reinterpreted in context of evolving historiography of colonial bureaucracy. Quarrels over taxation, Indian labor, and precedence at public events had deep historical roots, but were aggravated by Bourbon reforms. Author argues disputes had origins more complex than simple Creole-peninsular rivalry and should not be seen as preparing way for independence.

1698 Solórzano Fonseca, Juan Carlos. Indígenas insumisos, frailes y soldados: Talamanca y Guatuso, 1660–1821. (*Anu. Estud. Centroam.*, 23:1/2, 1997, p. 143–197, maps, tables)

Heavily documented account of efforts by Franciscans and colonial authorities to expand Spanish territorial control on northern and southern frontiers of Costa Rica, beginning in late 17th century. Effectiveness of campaign limited by stiff indigenous resistance, especially Talamanca uprisings of 1709 and 1761.

1699 Taracena, Luis Pedro. Ilusión minera y poder político: la Alcaldía mayor de Tegucigalpa, siglo XVIII. Tegucigalpa: Editorial Guaymuras, 1998. 357 p.: bibl., ill., maps. (Col. Códices)

Major work. Sophisticated, well-documented study emphasizes role of silver mining in emergence of regional identity in southeastern Honduras. Examines evolution of social formations and political institutions, as well as background to controversies of late colonial and early national periods.

1700 Werner, Patrick S. Epoca temprana de León Viejo: una historia de la primera capital de Nicaragua. Managua?: Asdi: Instituto Nicaragüense de Cultura, 2000? 177 p.: bibl., ill., maps.

Not, as title suggests, history of 16th-century León, but of establishment of Spanish law and institutions in early Nicaragua. Author, a US-born attorney and long resident in Nicaragua, excels at analysis of legal documents, which constitute principal source. Sheds light on some well-known but little-studied episodes, such as Contreras revolt and assassination of Bishop Antonio de Valdivieso.

1701 Zapatero, Juan Manuel. El Fuerte San Fernando y las fortificaciones de Omoa. Tegucigalpa: IHAH, 1997. 317 p.: bibl., facsims., ill., maps, plans.

Publication of 1972 consultant's report on restoration of Honduras' 18th-century Caribbean fortress includes detailed history of works at Omoa and description of physical remains. Based on archival research and extensive on-site reconnaissance.

NATIONAL

1702 Alda Mejías, Sonia. El debate entre liberales y conservadores en Centroamérica: distintos medios para un objetivo común, la construcción de una república de ciudadanos, 1821–1900. (*Espac. Tiempo Forma Ser. V Hist. Contemp.*, 13, 2000, p. 271–311)

Major contribution to 19th-century Central American historiography from one of few specialists in the field working in Europe. Based largely on comprehensive reading of important secondary materials and some published documents, argues that liberals and conservatives developed three models of republican governance while fighting to establish a common citizenship.

1703 Alda Mejías, Sonia. La participación indígena en la construcción de la República de Guatemala, s. XIX. Madrid: UAM Ediciones, 2000. 285 p.: bibl. (Col. Estudios; 69)

Innovative work of historical sociology looks closely at local politics in 19th-century Guatemala, and relates projects and goals of indigenous communities to first phase of liberal reforms. Based mostly on secondary materials, but with some significant research in Guatemala's Archivo General de Centroamérica.

1704 Alvarez Jiménez, Francisco Javier. Homicidios en San José, 1880–1921. (*Rev. Hist./Heredia*, 33, enero/junio 1996, p. 103–140, graph)

Reflecting new efforts in Costa Rica to extend old social history to topics beyond workers, peasants, and resistance to exploitation, study focuses on 69 San José homicide cases, categorizing them by motive, with "conflicts of passion" recognized as primary in 17 instances. In most cases, killers and victims knew each other.

1705 Argueta, Mario. La primera generación liberal: fallas y aciertos, 1829–1842. Tegucigalpa: Banco Central de Honduras, 1999. 135 p.: bibl.

One of Honduras' most prominent historians draws on existing historiography to summarize achievements and mistakes made by country's first generation of liberals.

1706 Asturias Montenegro, Gonzalo. Miguel Angel Asturias: más que una biografía. v. 1. Guatemala: Editorial Artemis y Edinter, 1999. 1 v.: bibl., ill. (Ensayos literarios)

First of three projected volumes focuses on childhood, youth, and young adulthood of famed Guatemalan author, 1967 Nobel laureate in Literature.

1707 Avendaño Rojas, Xiomara. El pactismo: el mecanismo de ascenso de los notables, 1858–1893. (*Rev. Hist./Managua*, 7, primer semestre 1996, p. 26–41, bibl., photos, tables)

Enriches emerging historiography regarding politics in 19th-century Central America. Pioneering work that builds on doctoral dissertation (El Colegio de México, 1995). Focuses on Nicaragua, especially Granada, characterizing "unequal citizenship" that empowered elites (*notables*) to form pacts, electing themselves above majority of people constitutionally excluded from participation by property and income requirements.

1708 Bosch, Brian J. The Salvadoran officer corps and the final offensive of 1981. Jefferson, N.C.: McFarland & Co., 1999. 153 p.: bibl., ill., map.

Based on interviews and documentary sources, detailed examination of Salvadoran military leadership in face of FMLN "final offensive." Offers more positive assessment of military capacity of officers and troops than is usually seen.

1709 Canelas Díaz, Antonio. La Ceiba, sus raíces y su historia, 1810–1940. La Ceiba, Honduras: Tip. Renacimiento, 1999. 259 p.: bibl., ill., ports.

First comprehensive history of La Ceiba, most important town on Caribbean coast of Honduras, from frontier settlement and smugglers' nest to later importance as banana port. Long before United Fruit Co. made the city its corporate seat, La Ceiba was a vital community inhabited by Garífunas and migrants from Yoro and Olancho depts. Based on oral histories collected for decades by author, the descendant of prominent local residents.

1710 Cardenal, Ernesto. Vida perdida. Barcelona: Seix Barral, 1999. 459 p.: ill. (Los tres mundos. Memorias)

First part of autobiography of one of most important cultural figures of 20th-century Central America. Born in Nicaragua in 1925, Cardenal became Trappist monk in US in 1950s. Returning to Nicaragua in 1960s, he became involved in politics, while writing some of modern Central America's most important poetry. Cardenal served as minister of culture in Sandinista government of 1980s.

1711 Casaús Arzú, Marta Elena. Los proyectos de integración social del indio y el imaginario nacional de las elites intelectuales guatemaltecas, siglos XIX y XX. (*Rev. Indias*, 59:217, sept./dic. 1999, p. 775–813)

Essay offers hope for revival of Central American intellectual history. Reviewing arguments offered by nonindigenous intellectuals in Guatemala about Indians' role in national imagination, author sorts intellectuals into two general categories—those who argued for inclusion, and those who argued against exclusion from postindependence nation.

1712 Casaús Arzú, Marta Elena. La recomposición del bloque en el poder y el retorno de las élites familiares centroamericanas, 1979–1996. (*Estud. Int./Guatemala*, 9:17, enero/junio 1998, p. 83–112)

Interesting effort in comparative political history. Focusing on elite families with long roots in colonial past, argues that empowerment of more traditional political parties and especially their right-wing sectors in most of Central America by mid-1990s represented efforts by old elite colonial families to restore themselves to power after revolutionary threat of late 1970s.

1713 Centeno García, Santos. Historia del movimiento negro hondureño. Tegucigalpa: Editorial Guaymuras, 1997. 155 p.: ill.

Though brief, offers a first attempt to record the history of black organizing efforts in 20th-century Honduras, written by an important leader of the movement. Largely ethnographic and episodic, broadly registers the key moments and processes of "black history" in modern Honduras.

1714 Charlip, Julie A. "So that land takes on value": coffee and land in Carazo, Nicaragua. (*Lat. Am. Perspect.*, 26:1, Jan. 1999, p. 92–105, bibl.)

Innovative essay challenges existing work on implications of coffee production for landholding peasants. Based on research in the Registro de Propiedad, work questions the accepted view that the coffee economy "led to the systematic expropriation of land from the peasantry." Argues instead that, in Carazo, Nicaragua's first coffee-producing region, small landholders became active participants in coffee production and in marketing of land. For review of similar study on El Salvador, see item **1748.**

1715 Cobo del Arco, Teresa. Políticas de género durante el liberalismo: Nicaragua, 1893–1909. Managua: Colectivo Gaviota, 2000. 263 p.: bibl., ill.

Innovative monograph addresses neglected issue of state and gender with focus on policies of Gen. José Santos Zelaya, president of Nicaragua, 1893–1909. Based primarily on official newspapers and annual *Memorias* from Ministries of Interior and Development, so reveals little of women's reactions to policies. Nonetheless, an important contribution.

1716 Corrales, José R. El Banco Anglo Costarricense y el desarrollo económico de Costa Rica, 1863–1914. San José: Editorial de la Univ. de Costa Rica, 2000. 115 p.: ill.

Study of first stable private bank in Costa Rica, based on access to internal documents. More than traditional institutional history, links bank's history to general history and historiography of national development. Major contribution.

1717 Crisanto Meléndez, Armando and **Uayujuru Savaranga.** Adeija sisira gererun aguburigu garinagu = El enojo de las sonajas: palabras del ancestro. Tegucigalpa: Graficentro Editores, 1997. 91 p.: bibl., ill., ports. (Fondo de información garífuna; no. 12) (Bicentenario garífuna)

In 1997, much was written and published, especially in newspapers, about arrival in Honduras of Garífuna and their subsequent history. Essay is unique because it registers historiographical perspective of important Garífuna intellectuals, actively engaged in politics of ethnic movements in Honduras during last three decades.

1718 Crónicas y relatos para la historia de Puerto Limón. Recopilación de Fernando González Vásquez y Elías Zeledón Cartín. San José: Ministerio de Cultura, Juventud y Deportes, Centro de Investigación y Conservación del Patrimonio Cultural, 1999. 381 p.: ill., maps.

Collected documents on early history of Costa Rica's Caribbean port, with emphasis on construction of railroad and establishment of banana industry. Features rich collection of photographs dating from 1880s-1920s.

1719 Cruz Sequeira, Arturo J. Nicaragua's conservative republic, 1858–93. New York: Palgrave, 2002. 196 p.: bibl., index. (St. Antony's series)

Well-documented study by scholar with Conservative Party connections seeks to rehabilitate largely ignored conservative regimes that preceded liberal era of José Santos Zelaya (1893–1909). Argues conservatives laid foundation in Nicaragua for political order, economic development, and national sovereignty, usually attributed to Zelaya, and did so in atmosphere of "fiscal discipline and... high personal character."

1720 Deportivo Femenino Costa Rica F.C.: primer equipo de fútbol femenino del mundo, 1949–1999—reseña histórica. Investigación, levantado y diagrammación de Elías Zeledón Cartín. San José: Ministerio de Cultura, Juventud y Deportes, Editorial de la Dirección de Publicaciones, 1999. 225 p.: ill.

Unusual chronological and narrative history of first women to play organized soccer in Costa Rica and possibly in Central America. Wonderful photographs. Lacks analysis and theoretical insight, but merits consideration for opening historiographical field.

1721 Doctor Paul Vinelli. Recopilación de Oscar Acosta y Vicente Machado Valle. Tegucigalpa: Evensa, 1997. 210 p.: ill. (some col.). (Biografías ilustradas)

A must for modern Honduran economic history. Book's importance lies less in its documentary base and historical vision than in its topic: one of first IMF-trained economists to influence economic policy in Central America. Arriving in Honduras from US in late 1940s, Vinelli remained to become Honduras' central player in financial capitalism in post-WWII period.

1722 Ebel, Roland H. Misunderstood caudillo: Miguel Ydígoras Fuentes and the failure of democracy in Guatemala. Lanham, Md.: Tulane Studies in Political Science and Univ. Press of America, 1998. 343 p.: bibl., ill., index, 1 map.

Biography genre in Central America remains vital, but rarely well documented or coherently argued. Ebel breaks new ground, locating biography of Guatemalan president (1958–63) in historiographical context enriched by contributions from Piero Gleijeses, Paul Dosal, and Stephen Streeter. Based on available Guatemalan and US sources, and interviews with Ydígoras himself.

1723 Edelman, Marc. Un genocidio en Centroamérica: hule, esclavos, nacionalismo y la destrucción de los indígenas guatusos-malecus. (*Mesoamérica/Antigua,* 19:36, dic. 1998, p. 539–591, graph, map, photos)

Overdue systematic historical attention to smaller, less well-known indigenous groups in Central America. Explores how Guatusos-Malecus of southern Nicaragua fell prey in 19th century to rubber trappers, slavers, and missionaries. Equally interesting, uses history to address Costa Rican view of Nicaraguans as "barbarian other" long before the first Somoza.

1724 Elvir, Rafael Angel. La Villa de Triunfo de la Cruz, llamada Tela desde 1829. San Pedro Sula, Honduras: Centro Editorial, 2000. 249 p.: bibl., ill., maps.

Triunfo de la Cruz, or Tela, as it has been called since early 19th century, an important coastal city on Honduras' Caribbean coast, has for decades been corporate headquarters of United Fruit Co. and home to important local banana growers. Much-awaited short volume by son of banana grower sheds light on issues relevant to coastal past and banana companies.

1725 Enríquez Solano, Francisco José. Entre la tradición y la modernidad: la diversión pública en las localidades rurales de San José, 1880–1930. (*Rev. Cienc. Soc./San José*, 43:89, 2000, p. 69–83, bibl.)

Truly innovative essay treats popular culture not in urban context, but in rural areas. Equally interesting, explores relationships between urban and rural, especially how film and soccer were slowly transferred to rural areas and how these processes affected older traditions, such as Sunday *paseos* and *veladas*.

1726 Euraque, Darío A. The Arab-Jewish economic presence in San Pedro Sula, the industrial capital of Honduras: formative years, 1880s-1930s. (*in* Arab and Jewish immigrants in Latin America: images and realities. Edited by Ignacio Klich and Jeffrey Lesser. London; Portland, Ore.: F. Cass, 1998, p. 94–124, tables)

Extensively documented exploratory essay situates Honduran case in larger context of Arab and Jewish immigration to Latin America, but emphasizes uniqueness of San Pedro Sula in degree to which Palestinian Christians, in particular, came to dominate commerce and industry.

1727 Euraque, Darío A. Federico Lunardi, mayanización e identidad nacional. (*Paraninfo/Tegucigalpa*, 8:16, dic. 1999, p. 159–172)

Calls for more study of Italian amateur archeologist who served as papal nuncio to Honduras in 1940s, controversial both for exporting antiquities and for thesis of Maya origin of Honduras' indigenous culture. Cites benefit to cultural and intellectual history of probing why Honduran intellectuals persisted in accepting Lunardi's thesis despite substantial contradictory scientific evidence.

1728 Fischer, Thomas. Antes de la separación de Panamá: la Guerra de los Mil Días, el contexto internacional y el Canal. (*Anu. Colomb. Hist. Soc. Cult.*, 25, 1998, p. 73–108, photos)

Unlike much existing historiography, this study of Colombia's 1899 civil war, which led to Panama's independence and US construction of isthmian canal, focuses on international context, especially 1898 US-

Spain struggle over Cuba, rise of Pan-Americanism, and European indifference to region. Challenges view of US diplomatic action as deliberate plan to "take" Panama and its canal route.

1729 Fumero Vargas, Patricia. Entre el estado y la Iglesia: el teatro en San José a finales del siglo XIX. (*Jahrb. Gesch. Staat Wirtsch. Ges. Lat.am.*, 33, 1996, p. 239–265, tables)

Fresh perspective on established topic. Church-state issues in Central America, from conflict to accommodation, have received less scholarly attention than in rest of Latin America. Fumero helps address need by looking at government and Church pronouncements on nature of theater, its esthetics, and relevance to society.

1730 Garrard-Burnett, Virginia. Indians are drunks and drunks are Indians: alcohol and *indigenismo* in Guatemala, 1890–1940. (*Bull. Lat. Am. Res.*, 19:3, July 2000, p. 341–356, bibl., tables)

Perceptive essay explores how alcohol use was articulated in range of discourses on indigenismo offered by Guatemalan intellectuals during crucial period in country's history. By 1930s-40s, relationship between underdevelopment and "backwardness" of Indian majority involved assumptions about Indian alcoholism and even crime. New twist on old topic.

1731 Gil Zúñiga, José Daniel. Morigerando las costumbres, canalizando las disputas: a propósito de los conflictos en los pueblos heredianos, 1885–1915. (*Rev. Hist./Heredia*, 35, enero/junio 1997, p. 45–69, graphs)

Discusses infrequently addressed topic of provincial crime, focusing on Heredia region of Costa Rica during consolidation of coffee boom. Based on analysis of 87 homicide cases in local judicial archives, challenges perceived image of Heredia as tranquil, bucolic provincial town.

1732 Gobat, Michel. "Contra el espíritu burgués": la élite nicaragüense ante la amenaza de la modernidad, 1918–1929. (*Rev. Hist./Managua*, 13, primer semestre 1999, p. 17–34, bibl., ill., photos)

Study of Nicaraguan elite reactions to processes of modernization in Latin America, including urbanization, industrialization, popular mobilization, and expansion of national state. Argues that, for elite's most "cosmopolitan" sector, generation of antimodernist identity turned largely on perceived implications of US intervention between 1910–33.

1733 Gólcher, Erika. Imperios y ferias mundiales: la época liberal. (*Anu. Estud. Centroam.*, 24:1/2, 1998, p. 75–95, bibl.)

Examines official national identities as exported abroad by looking at Costa Rican official presentations at international fairs organized by the industrial powers in late 19th century. Based largely on reports published in official Costa Rican press.

1734 Gómez Miralles, Manuel. Costa Rica, América Central, 1922. 2. ed. San José: Ministerio de Cultura, Juventud y Deportes, Editorial de la Dirección de Publicaciones, 1997. 206 p.: chiefly ill.

Reprint of album containing 200 photographs of turn-of-the-century Costa Rica. Reproduction not best quality, but collection is important, not only for range of items illustrated—from haciendas to huts to churches—but also because Gómez Miralles was one of Costa Rica's most prolific photographers of period.

1735 González Ortega, Alfonso. Vida cotidiana en la Costa Rica del siglo XIX: un estudio psicogenético. San José: Editorial de la Univ. de Costa Rica, 1997. 321 p.: bibl.

Major contribution to Costa Rican women's history. Extensively documented study approaches sexuality and familial relations by focusing on everyday practices, especially individual subjectivities, including women's power.

1736 Gould, Jeffrey L. Orgullo amargo: el desarrollo del movimiento obrero nicaragüense, 1912–1950. Managua: Instituto de Historia de Nicaragua y Centroamérica, Univ. Centroamericana, 1997. 194 p.: bibl., ill., maps.

Major contribution to historiography of labor in Nicaragua and Central America by one of the most prominent historians writing on Nicaragua. Grounded in Nicaraguan archival sources, US diplomatic documents, and painstaking oral history, it is also amply illustrated with unusual photographs.

1737 Gould, Jeffrey L. To die in this way: Nicaraguan Indians and the myth of mestizaje, 1880–1965. Durham, N.C.: Duke Univ. Press, 1998. 305 p.: bibl., ill., index, map. (Latin America otherwise)

Well-researched work demonstrates how social history of Nicaraguan indigenous peoples contributes to our understanding of nation formation and elite discourse about race and ethnicity in 20th-century Nicaragua. Mestizaje is shown as a myth of national homogeneity. Draws on wealth of regional archives and oral history.

1738 Grandin, Greg. The blood of Guatemala: a history of race and nation. Durham, N.C.: Duke Univ. Press, 2000. 343 p.: bibl., facsims., index, maps, photos, tables. (Latin America otherwise)

Major contribution to historical scholarship on 19th- and 20th-century Guatemala. Focuses on Mayan elites of Quetzaltenango and their ability to maintain power over subaltern Maya, while advancing an alternative version of connection between race and nation during country's transition to coffee economy. Provocative and amply documented.

1739 Grant, Stephen H. Postales salvadoreñas del ayer = Early Salvadoran postcards: 1900–1950. Investigación histórica de Gustavo Herodier and Carlos Cañas-Dinarte. El Salvador: Fundación María Escalón de Nuñez: Banco Cuscatlán, 1999. 327 p.: bibl., ill. (some col.), indexes, maps.

Extraordinary collection of postcard images of urban and rural El Salvador, with detailed commentary, including printing dates, name of photographer or illustrator, etc. Collector is US citizen, expert on postcard collection worldwide, and, since 1996, resident of El Salvador. Historians will find images and illustrations relevant for historical analysis.

1740 Harpelle, Ronald N. Radicalism and accommodation: Garveyism in a United Fruit Company enclave. (*JILAS/Bundoora*, 6:1, July 2000, p. 1–28, bibl.)

Part of larger study of West Indian immigration to Costa Rica. Focus is on influence of Jamaican political activist Marcus Garvey, founder of Universal Negro Improvement Association (UNIA) in US, whose influence in Costa Rica was substantial among West Indians. This account covers into 1930s, a period largely neglected by existing historiography.

1741 Hawley, Susan. Protestantism and indigenous mobilisation: the Moravian Church among the Miskitu Indians of Nicaragua. (*J. Lat. Am. Stud.*, 29:1, Feb. 1997, p. 111–129)

Based largely on ethnographic work, study reflects growing interest in religious institutions and political mobilization in Central America. Argues that Moravianism became "cultural marker of Miskitu ethnicity" as result of changes in Moravian church in 1960s-70s, mainly because of impact of state policy, socioeconomic shifts, and internal conflicts within Miskitu society. For sociologist's comment, see *HLAS 57:4718*.

1742 Herrera C., Miguel Angel. Bongos, bogas, vapores y marinos: historia de los "marineros" en el Río San Juan, 1849–1855. Managua?: ANE; NORAD; CNE, 1999. 287 p.: bibl., ill., maps.

Innovative social history of Nicaragua at height of that country's popularity as transit point for US adventurers bound for California gold fields. Particularly interesting are sections on transport technology, labor, and cultural world of San Juan River boatmen.

1743 Historia y violencia en Nicaragua. Revisión y correción de Anastasio Lovo. Managua: UNESCO: NOS-OTROS, 1997. 402 p.: bibl., ill.

Eclectic collection of essays of varying quality, a few of which do seriously engage historical context of violence in Nicaragua. Particularly interesting are essays by Germán Romero Vargas and Francis Kinloch Tijerino.

1744 Identity and struggle at the margins of the nation-state: the laboring peoples of Central America and the Hispanic Caribbean. Edited by Aviva Chomsky and Aldo A. Lauria-Santiago. Durham, N.C.: Duke Univ. Press, 1998. 404 p.: bibl., index.

Major contribution to modern Central American labor historiography. Mostly historians trained and working in US, authors include Lauria-Santiago, Jeffrey Gould, Julie Charlip, Chomsky, Cindy Forster, and Darío A. Euraque, as well as Patricia Alvarenga, a Costa Rican who has published on El Salva-

dor. Introduction is by Lauria-Santiago and Chomsky, and senior scholars Lowell Gudmundson and Francisco Scarano contribute concluding essay.

1745 Inakeliginia. Así lo vi y así me lo contaron: datos sobre la verdad de la Revolución Kuna de 1925. Según la versión del Saila Dummad Inakeliginia y de kunas que tomaron las armas. Recopilación, sintetización y traducción de Aiban Wagua. Portada e ilustraciones internas de Ologuaidi. Kuna Yala, Panama: Congreso General de la Cultura Kuna, 1997. 152 p., 4 leaves of plates: ill. (some col.).

Rare testimony by a Kuna about 1920s Kuna indigenous rebellion in Panama. Like many such texts, lacks explicit connection to historiographical trends, but merits reading as basis for broader histories of indigenous past, using documents generated by indigenous peoples themselves.

1746 Krennerich, Michael. Esbozo de la historia electoral nicaragüense, 1950–1990. (*Rev. Hist./Managua*, 7, primer semestre 1996, p. 42–67, bibl., photos, tables)

Succinct panoramic view of history of elections in 20th-century Nicaragua, divided into broad periods: "Elections Somoza Style" and "Elections during the Sandinista Era." Narrative enriched by appendix with tables of results, mainly from presidential elections between 1912–90. For political scientist's comment, see *HLAS 59:3400*.

1747 Langlois, Robert. Becoming a Contra: the dilemma of peasants during the revolution in Nicaragua. (*Int. J./Toronto*, 52:4, Autumn 1997, p. 695–713)

Study of Nicaraguans who participated in armed opposition to Sandinistas in 1980s, based on interviews with 43 Contras. Argues that "middle-class peasants" were basis of movement. Rather than contrasting his work with others on Contras, Langlois instead questions Eric Wolf's views about peasants from 1960s.

1748 Lauria-Santiago, Aldo A. An agrarian republic: commercial agriculture and the politics of peasant communities in El Salvador, 1823–1914. Pittsburgh, Pa.: Univ. of Pittsburgh Press, 1999. 326 p.: bibl., index, maps. (Pitt Latin American series)

Product of years of research in difficult

archives, mostly in El Salvador, major monograph argues against existing historiography, showing that, as coffee economy grew in 19th century, Salvadoran peasantry did not simply lose lands to expanding haciendas. Peasant response to commercial agriculture was not limited to resistance, but included creative efforts often overlooked in other studies. For review of similar study on Nicaragua, see item **1714.**

1749 Lecturas de historia de Honduras: antología. Recopilación de Oscar Zelaya Garay. Tegucigalpa: Univ. Pedagógica Nacional Francisco Morazán, Depto. de Ciencias Sociales, 1998. 437 p.: bibl.

Collection of previously published works by Ramón Oquelí, Héctor Pérez Brignoli, Kenneth V. Finney, Mario Posas, and others. Not as comprehensive as Sosa's recent effort (item **1652**), but helps to fill need for compilations of best studies by Honduran and foreign historians.

1750 Lee Chung de Lee, Patricia Alma. Los Lee Chong: cinco generaciones de Panamá: en memoria de mis padres Víctor Ernesto Lee Chen y Alma Dorothy Chung de Lee. Panamá: P.A. Lee Chung de Lee, 1999. 160 p.: ill.

Mostly biographical sketches and genealogy. Welcome addition to historiography of Chinese immigration to Central America, a field less developed than those of larger immigrant communities in Mexico and Peru.

1751 León Sáenz, Jorge. Evolución del comercio exterior y del transporte marítimo de Costa Rica, 1821–1900. San José: Editorial de la Univ. de Costa Rica, 1997. 384 p.: bibl., ill. (some col.), indexes, maps. (Col. Historia de Costa Rica)

Major contribution to 19th-century economic history in Costa Rica and potential model for studies elsewhere in Central America. Amply documented and illustrated with maps, tables, graphs, and images from period. In addition to good endnotes, offers annotated bibliography on general and archival sources.

1752 López Bernal, Carlos Gregorio. Inventando tradiciones y héroes nacionales: El Salvador, 1858–1930. (*Rev. Hist. Am. / México,* 127, julio/dic. 2000, p. 117–151, bibl.)

Draws on work of Eric Hobsbawm and Benedict Anderson to explore how Salvadoran elites in late 19th century sought to particularize national identity separate from failed Central American union. Once in power, liberals promoted heroic cults dedicated to Francisco Morazán and Gerardo Barrios. Later, artisans and workers used these invented traditions in their own efforts at collective mobilization.

1753 Machuca, Alexis. José Reina Valenzuela: figura y obra de un hondureño distinguido. Tegucigalpa: Editorial Universitaria, Univ. Nacional Autónoma de Honduras, 2000. 1 v.: bibl., ill. (Col. Biografías)

Great service to Honduran historiography. First volume of first serious biography of one of 20th century's most prolific and important historians of Honduras. Reina Valenzuela, who died in 1995, published numerous books, including biographies of major Honduran historians.

1754 Madrigal Mendieta, Ligia. La evolución de las ideas: el caso de los protestantes en Nicaragua, 1856–1925. Managua: UNAN: CIEETS, 1999. 263 p.: bibl. (Historia de las mentalidades)

Welcome effort to study phenomenon of Protestantism in precontemporary times, with analysis grounded in famed French historiographical school dedicated to studying *mentalités.*

1755 Marquardt, Steve. "Green havoc": Panama disease, environmental change, and labor process in the Central American banana industry. (*Am. Hist. Rev.,* 106:1, Feb. 2001, p. 49–80)

Innovative merger of labor and environmental history to produce more nuanced understanding of United Fruit Co. activities in Central America. Argues social historians have underestimated significance of Panama disease. Recognition of ecological constraints within which banana industry functioned admits more complex view of its impact on labor, landscape, and national economies.

1756 Martínez B., Juan Ramón. Honduras, las fuerzas del desacuerdo: un ensayo histórico sobre las relaciones entre la Iglesia y el Estado, 1525–1972. Tegucigalpa: Editorial Universitaria, Univ. Nacional Autónoma de Honduras, 1998. 413 p.: bibl. (Col. Realidad nacional)

Offers most up-to-date history of relations between state and Catholic Church in Honduras between colonial period and early 1970s, when militarized state outwardly repressed segments of Church linked to liberation theology. Based primarily on published sources.

1757 McNairn, Rosemarie M. Baiting the British bull: a fiesta, trials, and a petition in Belize. (*Americas/Washington,* 55:2, Oct. 1998, p. 240–274)

Native response to 1860s attempt by magistrate to repress Maya ritual involving bull baiting is seen as revealing limits to British authority in 19th-century Belize, as well as the complexity of local politics and ethnic and class relations.

1758 Meding, Holger M. Panama: Staat und Nation im Wandel, 1903–1941. Köln, Germany: Böhlau, 2002. 464 p.: bibl., 4 maps. (Lateinamerikanische Forschungen; 30)

Meticulously researched and very well written, Meding's seminal work, with its uniquely European perspective, is based primarily on original documents from previously unused Panamanian archives, as well as English, French, German, and US archival sources. Traces Panama's political development, after it ceded its sovereignty with the Canal Treaty of 1903, through three formative political periods, during which the Panamanians continued to give the US a mandate for intervention. The Panama Canal policies of the US played a decisive role in Panama's demographic, social, and economic development, and in the definition of its geographic borders. Extensive bibliography, chronological table, and list of presidents and cabinets. [C. Converse]

1759 Memoria: política, cultura y sociedad en Centroamérica, siglos XVIII-XX. Recopilación de Margarita Vannini and Frances Kinloch. Managua: Instituto de Historia de Nicaragua y Centroamérica, 1998. 281 p.: bibl., ill., 1 map.

Published contributions from conference hosted by Instituto de Historia de Nicaragua y Centroamérica in mid-1990s. Authors, some of best young historians working on Nicaragua, Costa Rica, Guatemala, and El Salvador, address ethnic identity, local political power and culture, and even literary history. Particularly strong on 19th century.

1760 Mendoza, Breny. Sintiéndose mujer, pensándose feminista: la construcción del movimiento feminista en Honduras. Tegucigalpa: Editorial Guaymuras: Centro de Estudios de la Mujer Honduras, 1996. 259 p.: bibl., ill. (Col. Códices)

First contemporary history of upsurge of feminist organization in Honduras in 1980s. Largely based on ethnographic observation.

1761 Mujeres que cambiaron nuestra historia. Panamá: UNICEF: Embajada de Canadá: Instituto de la Mujer, Univ. de Panamá, 1996. 176 p.: bibl., ill.

Short but important book for general audience about women who led suffrage movement in Panama between 1920–46. Valuable bibliography, notes, and photographs.

1762 Nájera M., Carlos E. Fichas de finca: acuñaciones particulares de moneda en Guatemala, que se utilizaron como instrumento de explotación. Guatemala: Editorial Cultura, 1998. 50 p.: bibl., ill. (Col. Obra varia; 21)

Little book discusses "minting" of coins by private landowners in Guatemala in 19th century. Scholars have long been aware of circulation of foreign coins in this period to deal with lack of national currencies, but regional minting of coins has rarely been studied. Contains illustrations of such coins.

Nolin Hanlon, Catherine L. and **W. George Lovell.** Huida, exilio, repatriación y retorno escenarios de los refugiados guatemaltecos, 1981–1997. See *HLAS* 59:2452.

1763 Noriega, Manuel Antonio and **Peter Eisner.** America's prisoner: the memoirs of Manuel Noriega. New York: Random House, 1997. 293 p.: bibl., index.

Like memoirs by other Central American dictators, especially Anastasio Somoza, this one makes for important reading when checked against contemporary historiography. Made more valuable with introduction by Eisner, a reporter who covered 1989 US invasion of Panama for *Newsday.*

1764 Otras voces del 48. Heredia, Costa Rica: EUNA, 1998. 98 p.: ill.

First-person accounts of Costa Rica's 1948 civil war offer fresh perspectives by women, children, and other noncombatants.

1765 Putnam, Lara Elizabeth. Ideología racial, práctica social y estado liberal en Costa Rica. (*Rev. Hist./Heredia*, 39, enero/junio 1999, p. 139–186)

Innovative use of gender to rethink race relations and ethnic identities in Costa Rica. In model for similar studies needed elsewhere, Putnam systematically engages connections between gender and race, not only as they pertain to West Indian and Hispanic-Indian populations, but also to how West Indian men related to West Indian women in context of adaptation and struggle.

1766 Quesada Monge, Rodrigo. Recuerdos del imperio: los ingleses en América Central, 1821–1915. Heredia, Costa Rica: EUNA, 1998. 459 p.: bibl., ill., maps.

Study of British financial and commercial impact in 19th-century Central America. Proposes periodization of isthmian economic history based on degree and mechanisms of insertion into world market. Concludes with case studies of Guatemalan export development, Costa Rican railroads, and Honduran external debt.

Randall, Stephen J.; Graeme Stewart Mount; and David Bright. The Caribbean Basin: an international history. See item **2093.**

1767 Reina Idiáquez, Jorge Arturo. Historia de la UNAH en su época autónoma. Tegucigalpa: Univ. Nacional Autónoma de Honduras, 1999–2000. 2 v.

Most recent and up-to-date institutional history of Univ. Nacional Autónoma de Honduras, from establishment in 1840s to the 1980s, written by former rector. History of country's most important institution of higher learning offers much data.

1768 Ríos Esparíz, Angel María. Costa Rica y la Guerra Civil Española. San José: Editorial Porvenir: Embajada de España, Centro Cultural Español-ICI, 1997. 186 p.: bibl., ill., maps.

Unique book looks beyond local views of Costa Rica in 1930s to explore local concerns in context of government reactions to Spanish Civil War. A Spaniard who resided in Costa Rica for many years, author touches also on how Spaniards living in country reacted to events and politics in Europe.

1769 Salazar Mora, Jorge Mario. Crisis liberal y estado reformista: análisis político-electoral, 1914–1949. San José: Edi

torial de la Univ. de Costa Rica, 1995. 323 p.: bibl., ill. (Col. Historia de Costa Rica)

Important institutional political history emphasizes various mechanisms of state legitimacy in Costa Rica, including elections, party systems, and state social policies. Weak on relation between political history and society and economy, but strong in chosen approach and period covered.

1770 Sandino y los U.S. Marines: reportes de los agregados militares y comandantes marines en acción. Recopilación de R.R. Isaguirre and A. Martínez R. Tegucigalpa: Omni Editores, 2000. 490 p.: port. (Col. Informantes de la historia)

Collection of intelligence and military reports submitted by US Marines in Nicaragua between 1924–33, provides rare access for Spanish-only readers to documentation extracted from archives in Washington, D.C. Introduction situating documents in Sandino historiography would make book even more valuable.

1771 Sandoval García, Carlos. Notas sobre la formación histórica del "otro" nicaragüense en la nacionalidad costarricense. (*Rev. Hist./Heredia*, 40, julio/dic. 1999, p. 107–125)

Drawing on secondary literature and publications by intellectuals and journalists, essay analyzes Costa Rican representations of Nicaragua and Nicaraguan migrants and exiles, focusing on the period from the mid-19th century to the mid-20th century.

1772 Schoonover, Thomas David. The French in Central America: culture and commerce, 1820–1930. Wilmington, Del.: Scholarly Resources, 2000. 244 p.: bibl., ill., index. (Latin American silhouettes)

Major contribution by distinguished historian describes external influences on 19th- and 20th-century Central America. Based on archival research in Central America, US, and Europe. Welcome complement to Schoonover's monograph on German influence in the region (see item **1773**).

1773 Schoonover, Thomas David. Germany in Central America: competitive imperialism, 1821–1929. Tuscaloosa: The Univ. of Alabama Press, 1998. 317 p.: bibl., ill., index, maps.

Impressive multi-archival exercise in "new international history" analyzes German presence in 19th- and early 20th-century Central America within framework of great power competition for influence in region. For review of author's work on French influences in Central America, see item **1772.**

1774 Soluri, John. People, plants, and pathogens: the eco-social dynamics of export banana production in Honduras, 1875–1950. (*HAHR*, 80:3, Aug. 2000, p. 463–501, maps)

Historical studies of banana trade typically focus on foreign companies, workers, and US diplomatic interventions. This work shifts the focus, looking at *poquiteros* (small-scale banana growers), the diseases that affect bananas, and, equally important, the changing relationships among actors, contrasting these dynamics with those involving foreign companies and Honduran national state.

1775 Soto Quirós, Ronald. "Desaparecidos de la Nación": los indígenas en la construcción de la identidad nacional costarricense, 1851–1942. (*Rev. Cienc. Soc./San José*, 82, dic. 1998, p. 31–53, photo)

Because of comparatively small numbers, even within Central American context, Costa Rica's indigenous peoples are seldom subjects of historical inquiry. Article does not dispute this, but instead shows how even an absent "other" allowed elites to imagine a particular version of Costa Rican national identity. Grounded in broader international discussion on nationalism and identities.

1776 Streeter, Stephen M. Managing the counterrevolution: the United States and Guatemala, 1954–1961. Athens: Ohio Univ. Center for International Studies, 2000. 384 p.: bibl., index. (Research in international studies. Latin America series; 34)

Looking beyond 1954 CIA-sponsored coup, work examines US relationship with Guatemalan regimes of Carlos Castillo Armas (1954–57) and Miguel Ydígoras Fuentes (1958–63). Argues that Washington's policies responded more to perceived threat to US interests by Third World nationalism than to fear of Soviet expansionism. Important study.

1777 Sullivan-González, Douglass. Piety, power, and politics: religion and nation formation in Guatemala, 1821–1871. Pittsburgh, Pa.: Univ. of Pittsburgh Press, 1998. 182 p.: bibl., index. (Pitt Latin American series)

Catholicism among indigenous and mixed-race peoples seen as central element in popular identity, especially relevant during long dictatorship of Gen. Rafael Carrera. Offers an innovative approach to studying nation formation, while also providing new evidence from Church archives closed for decades.

1778 Szok, Peter. "La Patria es el Recuerdo": Hispanophile nationalism in early twentieth-century Panama, 1903–1941. (*J. Caribb. Hist.*, 31:1/2, 1997, p. 149–184, bibl.)

Rather than more familiar post-1968 anti-imperialist populism, focuses on conservative nationalism developed by Panamanian intellectuals in response to rapid modernization and immigration linked to construction of Panama Canal. Argues that elites reacted to changes not "by inviting the masses into history," but by generating a "sense of identity that was narrow and essentially restrictive." For a related study with a Nicaraguan comparison, see *HLAS 58:1740*.

1779 Téllez Argüello, Dora María. Muera la gobierna!: colonización en Matagalpa y Jinotega, 1820–1890. Managua: Univ. de las Regiones Autómas de la Costa Caribe Nicaragüense (URACCAN), 1999. 316 p.: bibl., ill., maps.

Innovative regional history examines indigenous resistance in face of state expansion during critical initial period of nation-building in 19th-century Nicaragua, time period not often covered with archival sources. Good bibliography and useful regional maps.

1780 Tischler Visquerra, Sergio. Guatemala 1944: crisis y revolución: ocaso y quiebre de una forma estatal. Guatemala City: Univ. de San Carlos de Guatemala, Escuela de Historia, Instituto de Investigaciones Históricas, Antropológicas y Arqueológicas; Puebla, Mexico: Benemérita Univ. Autónoma de Puebla, Instituto de Ciencias Sociales y Humanidades, 1998. 316 p.: bibl.

Good exercise in historical and political sociology, based only on secondary sources. Appraises brief but critical period in Guatemalan history, paralleling efforts by Costa Rican scholars to reinterpret implications of events of 1940s for late 20th century.

1781 Ulloa Hidalgo, Herberth. El Ferrocarril Costarricense al Pacífico: construcción e incidencias, 1897–1932. San José: Editorial Costa Rica, 1997. 228 p.: bibl., ill., maps.

Well-researched work looks at "other" railroad systems in Costa Rica. Presents a factual narrative of origins and early development of Pacific line, but lacks analytical perspective on relationship between railroad and national cultural history found in work by Murillo Chaverri (see *HLAS 58:1733*).

1782 Vázquez, Norma; Cristina Ibáñez; and Clara Murguialday. Mujeres—montaña: vivencias de guerrilleras y colaboradoras del FMLN. Madrid: Horas y Horas, 1996. 286 p.: bibl. (Cuadernos inacabados; 22)

Well-structured sociological analysis, based on extensive interviews, of impact of Salvadoran civil war of 1980s on "sexuality and maternity practices" of women involved in conflict on side of FMLN guerrillas.

1783 Vernooy, Ronnie. Looking for work: a Nicaraguan Atlantic coastal labour history. (*Rev. Eur. Estud. Latinoam. Caribe,* 58, June 1995, p. 23–44, bibl.)

Avoiding traditional view of history of Nicaragua's Atlantic Coast as series of foreign interventions, their impact on local populations, and reactions from Managua, this conceptually and methodologically innovative study draws instead on oral history of laborers in region during 20th century, narrat-

ing life of Santiago Rivas (b. 1929), lumber worker in many locales.

1784 Villegas Hoffmeister, Guillermo. La guerra de Figueres: crónica de ocho años. San José: Editorial Univ. Estatal a Distancia, 1998. 713 p.: ill., index.

Ambitious narrative history of Costa Rica's political crisis of 1940s, culminating in 1948 civil war. An experienced journalist with contacts on both sides, author includes photographs and extracts from documents, and states his desire "que lo malo de entonces, no se repita y lo bueno que se heredó, sea permanentemente mejorado."

1785 Watanabe, John M. Culturing identities, the state, and national consciousness in late nineteenth-century western Guatemala. (*Bull. Lat. Am. Res.,* 19:3, July 2000, p. 321–340, bibl.)

Innovative contribution to significant historiography on state formation in 19th-century Central America. Based on archival sources, offers subtle, detailed analysis of "everyday forms of state formation" in interaction between regional governors and Indians in rural Huehuetenango, Guatemala, emphasizing "procedural culture," defined as "associations, understandings, and conventional behavior that emerge from recurring social interactions across local and translocal boundaries."

THE CARIBBEAN, THE GUIANAS AND THE SPANISH BORDERLANDS

EDWARD L. COX, *Associate Professor of History, Rice University, Houston*
ANNE PÉROTIN-DUMON, *Professor of History, Universidad Jesuita Alberto Hurtado*
JOHN D. GARRIGUS, *Professor of History, Jacksonville University*
JOSÉ M. HERNÁNDEZ, *Professor Emeritus of History, Georgetown University*
ROSEMARIJN HOEFTE, *Head, Department of Caribbean Studies, Royal Institute of Southeast Asian and Caribbean Studies, The Netherlands*
TERESITA MARTÍNEZ-VERGNE, *Professor of History, Macalester College*
FÉLIX V. MATOS-RODRÍGUEZ, *Director, Center for Puerto Rican Studies, Hunter College*

THE BRITISH CARIBBEAN
SCHOLARLY INTEREST IN THE BRITISH CARIBBEAN during the past biennium remained strong. A decline in the number of truly excellent monographs published

has been compensated for by the emergence of edited volumes and highly original and important articles in major scholarly journals. Taken together, they reveal a renewed interest in familiar territory and recognition of the need to navigate previously uncharted waters.

Slavery and plantation studies continue to dominate the scholarly literature. The richness and scope of the collection of essays in Craton's *Empire, Enslavement, and Freedom* open the way for others to analyze more fruitfully the identities and ideologies of different hegemonic groups in the region over time and place (item **1942**). Drawing heavily on wills, inventories, and contemporary accounts, Welch provides useful glimpses of slaveholding patterns and slave life, showing planter assumptions and the recreation of slave communities in the urban context (item **1908**). Handler offers a fresh perspective on the nuanced nature of marronage on Barbados over time (item **1827**), while Beckles focuses on the attitudes of the slave elite towards slave insurrections (item **1848**).

Military history has been the subject of several highly significant studies. In an important break with the past, though, the authors beautifully combine social history with the traditional institutional history. Buckley's path-breaking works on the British army in the Caribbean show the social and political implications of war and the military presence in the region (items **1852** and **1931**). Concentrating on World War I, Howe examines health factors affecting soldiers (item **2066**), and how the selection process exposed the prevalence of diseases in West Indian societies, leading to renewed efforts by colonial authorities to improve health conditions in the colonies (item **2067**). Combined with the useful article by Simmonds on health factors affecting Jamaican slaves (item **1903**), we see an emerging emphasis on health and epidemiology in British Caribbean history. Healy reminds us of how racial considerations by British officials and military leaders adversely affected the Caribbean Regiment's ability to see military action in World War II (item **2062**).

In a continuation of a trend noted in previous *HLAS* volumes, women's history and gender studies continue to attract scholars. Shepherd examines the important role indentured Indian women played in Jamaica's economy (item **2016**), while Reddock's work on Trinidad points to considerable overlap in the private and public realms as planters supported and reinforced the notion of male dominance (item **1994**). Through an examination of plantation inventories, Mathurin-Mair notes the centrality of slave women's contributions to the Jamaican economy (item **1890**). Hutton's fascinatingly important study of women in Jamaica's Morant Bay Rebellion reminds us of the active participation of women in efforts to enhance their political and social well being (item **1961**). Finally, Saunders brings contemporary women to the forefront by presenting an excellent portrait gallery of Bahamian women who were leaders in their chosen fields (item **2102**).

While previous volumes have shown a predisposition of scholars to concentrate on the African and Indian dimensions of British Caribbean history, the current biennium has witnessed a felicitous shift highlighting other minorities. Johnson and Watson have edited a volume of highly original essays that reintroduces the white minority into the mainstream of scholarly discourse by showing the ways in which it maintained its elite position by uniting its ethnic and social groups whenever its dominance was challenged (item **2027**). The behavior of different groups of whites is the subject that Akenson engages quite skillfully when, debunking the myth of the "nice" slaveholder, he shows that in the Caribbean the Irish were equally as harsh as masters as the English and Scottish (item **1819**). Look Lai's excellent collection of important documents relating to the Chinese presence in the Caribbean promises to enhance considerably research and writing on this significant group (item **1936**). [EC]

THE FRENCH AND DANISH CARIBBEAN AND FRENCH GUIANA

What has been often remarked of French Caribbean and Guyanese culture is also true of its historical research: isolation and fragmentation translate into a great diversity of approaches combining various intellectual traditions.

In the publications annotated for *HLAS 60*, three trends are noticeable: the bulk of the research concentrates on the 19th century (as elsewhere in the Caribbean) with Haiti coming at the forefront; an Atlantic and comparative framework is gaining ground; and the liveliness of local historical research in historical and genealogical societies is bringing together the public and academics.

Among the increasingly abundant scholarship on the 19th-century Caribbean, Sheller's recent publications stand out for their breadth and creativity: "The Army of Sufferers" and *Democracy after Slavery* analyze a 19th-century political culture of resistance built by peasants and their idea of a democracy (items **2012** and **2013**, respectively). "The 'Haitian Fear'" reveals connections with Jamaican blacks (item **2014**). "Sword-Bearing Citizens" is a seminal reflection on the militarized and masculine ethos inherited by the Haitian nation from its veterans of the wars of independence (item **2015**).

While the importance of approaching the French-speaking Caribbean and Guyana within a broader framework has long been advocated, the benefit of such a perspective is now apparent in works mentioned below on labor-migrations, the church's missionary task, and peasants' political culture. *La ville aux Îles* by Pérotin-Dumon resurrects a multifaceted colonial Caribbean port-city that had been downplayed by the "plantation society" approach (item **1809**). This urban focus situates the Caribbean port-city within the range of similar settlements in the Americas and explains its role in the world of Atlantic trade, culture, and miscegenation. The same comprehensive treatment is applied to the beginnings of French, English, and Dutch settlements in the Caribbean from 1550–1650 (items **1836** and **1837**). Accounts of experimental research in tropical agronomy (items **1840** and **1897**) and state-sponsored scientific missions (items **1885** and **1906**) also reveal this interconnected world in which Caribbean colonies figured prominently. Two important compilations edited by Geggus and by Geggus and Gaspar demonstrate that the impact of the French and Haitian revolutions is best understood comparatively (items **1879** and **1905**, respectively). The works are particularly valuable for their inclusion of the Spanish Caribbean, Louisiana, and Florida.

Increasing interest in the formation of Creole identity across racial lines in Saint-Domingue can be seen in Ghachem (item **1875**) and Garrigus (item **1868**). Perhaps the most important work in this line of research is King's *Blue Coat or Powdered Wig* (item **1881**). Using thousands of notarized contracts, King advances the important hypothesis that prerevolutionary Saint-Domingue had a free colored "military leadership" class, with its own social networks separate from white colonists and the colony's wealthy free colored planters.

Almost alone in the field among English-language scholars, Geggus continues to enlarge our understanding of the slave population of prerevolutionary Saint-Domingue, describing slave life on different kinds of plantations (items **1871** and **1872**), and situating the French slave trade to this colony within the larger Atlantic context (item **1796**). Geggus has also written one of the most useful surveys of historiography on the Haitian Revolution (item **1874**).

Libraries will want to acquire several recent publications of use to researchers. Quite a few come from the region: 17th-century original narrative *De Wilde* (Martinique) (item **1826**), a new critical edition of Father Breton's *Dictionnaire Caraïbe-français* (Guadeloupe) (item **1789**), and Carstens' superb description of *St. Thomas in Early Danish Times* (Virgin Islands) (item **1856**). The CTHS Éditions, the official publisher for the federation of French historical societies, now includes the French Caribbean (item **1816**). Dion and Tizon-Germe produced a *Répertoire numérique* immensely helpful for research in notarial archives housed at the French National Repository of Overseas Archives (item **1859**). Among local publishers committed to history, CARET stands out for producing books that are models of both critical editions and works of art (items **1967** and **2059**).

Departmental archives are important promoters of historical research and publications as shown by the 2001 exhibition organized by the Archives of Martinique (item **1793**). To commemorate the Montagne-Pelée's volcanic eruption (1902), an Internet site created jointly by genealogical and historical societies with the departmental archive is digitizing privately and publicly held testimonies about this traumatic experience. A genealogical association with a historical bent which attracts an enlightened and ethnically diverse public, Généalogie et Histoire de la Caraïbe, issues a publication under the name of the organization. The articles are challenging our acceptance that slaves' descendants cannot know their ancestors, by producing genealogies that reveal intricate patterns of white and nonwhite branches and elaborate strategies of social integration in racist societies (item **1813**). This is a promising development and quite unique in the Caribbean. More information about the association and some full-text issues of their publication are available at their website: *http://www.ghcaraibe.org/*.

The themes of migration and ethnicity run throughout Caribbean history. Recent scholarship has been focused on minorities and "intermediary groups." Topics include occupations and demography, and also collective identity, meaningful experience, and political discourse.

Plummer's *Between Privilege and Opprobrium* provides an insightful view of Jewish trade communities, from colonial (Portuguese Jews from Bordeaux) to modern times (German and Palestinian Jews) (item **1810**). Garrigus locates the struggle for integration by Jews in Saint Domingue into the political agenda of a prerevolutionary French world—the formation of a nation's body of citizens (item **1867**). The social contours and culture of the free-colored group in Saint Domingue are being increasingly documented (items **1850** and **1881**). Garrigus' latest research on the group draws on a gender perspective to tie together convincingly the redrawing of the "color line" by white Creoles, free-coloreds' political struggle for civil rights, and the colony's politics at the end of the ancien régime (items **1868** and **1869**). Lafleur, who pioneered research on Protestant and Jewish minorities, documents the place of Lebanese and Syrians in the 20th-century economies of Guadeloupe and Martinique, using oral testimonies to trace their evolving sense of identity (item **1969**). A comprehensive study of 19th-century indentured labor migrations to the French Caribbean by Northrup substantially revises previous interpretations, which treated indentured labor as another form of bondage (item **1984**). White colonists—always a demographic minority—are receiving more attention: immigrants from the southwest of France (the single most important group), and the diaspora caused by the Revolution (items **1824** and **1891**, respectively). Diplomatic, political, economic, and religious history are not particularly "trendy" in general. Yet they fare surprisingly well here.

In recent years, historians have reassessed Haiti's 19th- and 20th-century history of dependence and dictatorship. *Un siècle de relations financières* by Blancpain shows the debt contracted toward the former metropolis in exchange for Haiti's independence was only marginal economically but decisive in fostering foreign intervention (item **1925**). New light is shed on the period of US occupation by *Haïti et les États-Unis 1915–1934*, which looks at presidential politics (item **2038**) and *Taking Haiti* in which Renda captures the experience of soldiers in the occupation force (item **2095**). Papers from the US naval mission open up unusual vistas on Duvalierism (item **2109**), a political phenomenon that receives its best treatment to date in Etzer's *Le pouvoir politique* (item **2044**).

More facets of 19th-century politics and political culture in Guadeloupe and Martinique are being explored: France's reformist agenda and the stubborn resistance enlightened officials met from the oligarchy (items **1967** and **2020**); the steady ascent of "men of color" into the islands' political institutions and politics from the 1840s onwards (items **1955** and **1966**); women's political hopes and actions in the years surrounding 1848 (item **1985**); and emotional and personalistic mechanisms of allegiance toward local *caciques* like Légitimus, Guadeloupe's first black representative in the French parliament (item **1956**).

The commemoration of 1848 spurred methodical research on French abolitionism, beginning with its emergence with Abbé Grégoire and Sonthonax during the French Revolution (item **1886**). With *French Anti-Slavery*, Jennings has written the definitive study on abolitionist societies (and the Creole lobbies that relentlessly opposed them) (item **1966**). Schmidt has edited an authoritative collection of writings by French abolitionists: *Abolitionnistes de l'esclavage* (item **2002**). Creative research is emerging on the views whites held in the 19th century about colonial society and environment, and their various blends of racist ideology, particularly that of Corre (item **1939;** see also items **1965** and **2051**).

The final century of the sugar industry and its aftermath are particularly well documented in the case of Guadeloupe. Schnakenbourg's most recent studies depict an inexorable worsening from one world financial crisis to the next in spite of major technological advances and new heights of sugar production (items **2006, 2007,** and **2008**). Research revealing the diligent and creative strategies employed by small peasants and the French government in the 20th century also emphasizes the impossible challenge of integrating a small island's economy into a powerful European one (items **1937** and **2036**).

As shown in Delisle's *Histoire religieuse* (item **1948**), church history increasingly focuses on a second missionary age beginning in 1848 with the creation of dioceses, and the controversial tasks of catechizing and educating "new citizens" as well as indentured workers (item **1947**). There is also valuable research on early female missionary work in Guyana (items **1930** and **1946**). [JG and APD]

THE DUTCH CARIBBEAN

The hot topic in Dutch Caribbean studies is the history and current status of the relations between the Netherlands and its former colonies in the "West." The most important work on this subject is the three-volume study *Knellende koninkrijksbanden* by Gert Oostindie and Inge Klinkers on Dutch decolonization policy in the Caribbean between 1940–2000, published in 2001 (see *HLAS 59:3461*). A much shortened version was published in English under the title *Decolonising the Caribbean: Dutch Policies in a Comparative Perspective* (to be reviewed in *HLAS 61*), which also compares Dutch policies with those of France, the United Kingdom, and the US. Other significant publications on this topic are by journalist John

Jansen van Galen, *Het Suriname-syndroom: de PvdA tussen Den Haag en Para-maribo* [*The Suriname-syndrome: Dutch Labor Party between The Hague and Paramaribo*] (see *HLAS 59:3466*) and by journalist and former Labor MP Wouter Gortzak, *Nederland-Suriname: de herkansing* (to be reviewed in *HLAS 61*).

In these books, the disappointment about the evolution of relations with and the present socioeconomic situation in independent Suriname and the autono-mous islands of the Netherlands Antilles and Aruba is evident. This disillusion-ment with developments in postindependence Suriname also shines through in the articles on the country's economy, politics, and foreign relations in the volume *Twentieth-Century Suriname: Continuities and Discontinuities in a New World Society* (2001). Specifically on the Dutch-Antillean relationship are the insights by Lammert de Jong, an experienced Dutch civil servant (item **2071**). A considerable number of articles in the popular and scholarly press also focus on the current prob-lems (drug trafficking, corruption, poverty) in Dutch-Caribbean relations and the question whether the islands should become independent or provinces of the Netherlands.

An important step in confronting the past was the 2002 unveiling of a monu-ment commemorating slavery and the subsequent opening of an institute on the Dutch history of slavery, both in Amsterdam. These events generated a flood of publications for and against the monument and the institute and what they repre-sent. *Facing up to the Past* (2001) collects different perspectives on the commemo-ration of slavery from Africa, the Americas, and Europe. Rose Mary Allen, Coen Heijes, and Valdemar Marcha edited a volume on representation, image, and iden-tity of Curaçaoans 140 years after the abolition of slavery titled *Emancipatie & Acceptatie: Curaçao en Curaçaoënaars: Beeldvorming en identiteit honderdveertig jaar na de slavernij* (2003).

A closely related topic is Surinamese political and cultural nationalism that flourished in the post-World War II period. Edwin Marshall's dissertation discusses the origins and institutional and ideological development of Creole nationalism in Suriname (item **2080**). Unfortunately, it does not significantly add to extant histori-ography as the well-written publication by Peter Meel, *Tussen autonomie en on-afhankelijkheid: Nederlands-Surinaamse betrekkingen 1954–1961* [*Between Au-tonomy and Independence: Dutch-Surinamese Relations, 1954–1961*] (see *HLAS 59:3467*), and Jansen van Galen, *Hetenachtsdroom* (2000) cover the same ground. An important addition to Suriname's cultural history, however, is Michiel van Kempen's two-volume dissertation on the history of Surinamese literature, *Een geschiedenis van de Surinaamse literatuur* [*A History of Surinamese Literature*] (item **1803**).

Finally, a survey of Dutch Caribbean history wouldn't be complete without references to slavery and marronage. Frank Dragtenstein's dissertation is a straight-forward chronological account of the earliest history of the Surinamese Maroons from the end of British rule in 1670 to the first peace treaty with the Matawai in 1768 (item **1860**). Interesting also is Hilde Neus-van der Putten's reconstruction of the life of slave mistress Susanna du Plessis in 18th-century Suriname, who lives on in oral tradition as one of the most cruel persons in the history of the colony, *Susanna du Plessis: portret van een slavenmeesteres* (item **1834**). [RH]

PUERTO RICO

Not unpredictably, an avalanche of writings focusing on 1898 is now available to fill the bookshelves of amateur and professional historians. As a corollary, Puerto Rico's relationship with the US continues to be examined using traditional sources and methods, and perhaps more aptly, applying the tools provided by subaltern and postcolonial studies. Women and gender have been well-represented topics in the past two years, much more so than the now conventional African slaves and class oppression.

The centenary of the US invasion of Puerto Rico became the occasion for numerous international conferences, special forums, political speeches, guest lectures at schools and community centers, and the like. Many of the proceedings were published, although not all are of the highest quality. Truly exceptional are the efforts of the *Revista de Indias* and the *Hispanic American Historical Review,* both of which gathered some of the leading historians to comment on several aspects of this historic moment. In volume 57 of the *Revista,* Castro, Cubano, García, Luque, and Picó examined the writings of local elites, Creole, and US officers to construct their particular understandings of the situations they faced (items **1935, 1944, 1957, 1989,** and **2078**). Cubano Iguina and Scarano published more politically oriented essays in volume 78 of the *HAHR* (items **1945** and **2103**). Worth mentioning as well are more extended views of 1898, such as Rivera Pérez's look at Catholic organizations as sites of resistance to Americanization (item **2097**), Bernabé's analysis of local party politics (item **2037**), and Rosario Natal's description of the situation of the indigent at the turn of the century (item **2000**).

As a logical extension to reexamining the events surrounding 1898, the working out of the political relationship between the island and the US has deserved the attention of a group of promising social scientists and humanists. Negrón Muntaner and Grosfoguel gathered some excellent essays under the title *Puerto Rican Jam: Rethinking Colonialism and Nationalism* (item **2092**). It is truly cutting-edge scholarship and writing, and will no doubt be controversial if only for its proposal to abandon the old colonialist/nationalist discursive dichotomy. Likewise, in *Popular Expression and National Identity in Puerto Rico,* Guerra introduces cultural studies material (folkloric tales) to examine how Puerto Ricans have constructed an identity in the face of colonialism and racial and class oppression (item **2060**). Cabán also makes use of theoretical literature on postcolonialism and globalization to explore the efforts of the imperial and colonial states to Americanize the Puerto Rican people, in *Constructing a Colonial People* (item **2042**).

Somewhat surprising is the profusion of writings on women—almost all of which carefully insert themselves in Latin American and Caribbean historiography; employ the theoretical constructs of postcolonial, postmodern, and subaltern studies; make use of the latest methodological tools in the field; and are accessible to a more general reading public. A variety of themes are covered: prostitution (item **1954**), representation (items **1800** and **2040**), and daily life (items **1978**). Two books (items **1800** and **1811**) embrace numerous topics that defy classification or that cross over neat categories, as do some of the items listed above.

In a class by themselves are two volumes entitled *Hispanofilia,* one of which is the catalog to an exhibit, while the other is a collection of discrete studies on Puerto Rican art, politics, and culture in the first half of the 20th century (items **2063** and **2064**). Both are exquisitely presented and finely written, and the editors, Vivoni Farage and Alvarez Curbelo, as well as the authors, deserve the highest praise—a fitting way to go beyond 1898–1998 and to start the new century. [TMV]

CUBA, DOMINICAN REPUBLIC, AND THE SPANISH BORDERLANDS

As might be expected, the centennial of the Spanish American War generated a flood of publications, not only on the conflict itself, but on the sequence of events that led to its outbreak: the Cuban wars of independence and related developments.

Nearly half of the books and articles reviewed in this section, most of them the result of Cuban and Spanish scholarship, are devoted to the subject, and some are truly notable, either for their high level of erudition, their innovative and challenging approaches, or the professionalism of their arguments.

Among the works noteworthy for the depth and breadth of their research, one of the most impressive is Maza's exhaustive study of the role and attitude of the Cuban Catholic Church during the 1895–98 struggle against Spain and the first occupation of Cuba by the US, a topic that until the present had received scant or only cursory attention (item **1980**). Equally deserving of mention is Casanovas' book *Bread or Bullets!*, in which he argues, based on a vast array of documents, that urban labor was not totally absent in the process of uncoupling Cuba and Spain (item **1933**).

Profoundly interesting as these books are, however, they do not spark the same intellectual excitement as Hoganson's thesis, which posits that gender beliefs actually embroiled the US in the conflict with Spain (item **1959**), and provides the boldest of the writings annotated below. Not as provocative, but just as groundbreaking and original are the assumptions of *Nacionalismo y revolución en Cuba* (item **2017**) and Loyola's speculative treatment of what happened in Cuba after 1898 (item **2077**). The first of these pieces deviates so much from Cubans' most cherished myths and traditions that the author hid his name under a pseudonym. The second is more cautiously written, but after reading it for the second time one realizes that it is nearly as much a debunker as the first.

Of course, this sort of work is rarely blessed with epithets such as "balanced" and "objective" until after a century has passed. This is precisely the amount of time that has elapsed between the publication of *Herida profunda* (item **1986**) and the murderous civilian reconcentration program that Capt. Gen. Valeriano Weyler forced upon the Cubans in 1896–97, which is its subject. Cubans have never been able to deal with this event with equanimity—understandably so—until Pérez Guzmán wrote his small volume. Perhaps another century will have to pass for someone to improve upon even his measure of fairness and impartiality.

Significant studies were also published on topics other than the events of 1898, such as Barcia Zequeira's great book on the group of Spanish financiers who were the power behind the throne in late-colonial Cuba (item **1922**), and Lugo-Ortiz's inquiry into the transformation of biographies of Cuban greats into hagiographies by prorevolutionary historians (item **1974**). At the same level is Ameringer's account of the eight years of democratic government that Cuba experienced before the 1952 military coup by Fulgencio Batista (item **2029**). It is a solid introduction to the period that can be trusted as a firm basis for future investigations.

Finally, there is one general observation to be made about the materials received for review in this reporting period: quality has continued to run in inverse proportion to quantity. For example, the publications on the Spanish borderlands have been few, as usual, but their level of scholarship has continued unabated. The superabundance of writings on the Cuban Revolution, on the other hand, has followed the pattern of previous years. Ideology, political preconceptions, and at times sheer propagandism have remained as its most distinguishing features. And, unfortunately, there is no relief in sight. [JMH]

GENERAL

1786 Abrams, Ovid. Metegee: the history and culture of Guyana. Queens Village, N.Y.: Ashanti Books, 1997. 456 p.: bibl., ill., index, map.

Somewhat unbalanced work. While some mention is made of other ethnic groups in early period, this general study highlights African presence and contributions to Guyana's history and development. Includes interesting material on folk culture as well as a fruitful discussion and evaluation of recent political developments and social concerns. [ELC]

1787 Afroz, Sultana. The manifestation of *Tawhid:* the Muslim heritage of the Maroons in Jamaica. (*Caribb. Q./Mona,* 45:1, March 1999, p. 27–40)

Contesting the notion that "there was lack of any general philosophy of freedom" among the Maroons, argues that Islamic concept of freedom constituted the basis of Maroon struggle against slavocracy. Islam was truly the unifying force for the heterogeneous ethnic groups of Maroon communities in their fight against the oppressor, *Bucra.* [ELC]

1788 Alvarez Santana, Fermín. San Pedro de Macorís: su historia y desarrollo. Santo Domingo?: Comisión Presidencial de Apoyo Desarrollo Provincial, 2000. 443 p.: bibl. (Col. Provincias; 10)

Winner of provincial history award for eastern region, volume avoids conventional political-institutional framework and organizes detailed information in various social, cultural, and economic categories such as health, immigration, education, the Scouts movement, recreational activities. Rightly identifies sugar boom as turning point in San Pedro's development beginning in late 19th century. Format is more or less the same for all the publications in the Colección Provincias series. [TMV]

1789 Breton, Raymond. Dictionnaire caraïbe-français. Paris: IRD-Karthala, 1999. 1 v.

Dictionary compiled by missionary who lived with Caribs provides unique source detailing their language, beliefs and values, social and economic organization, and rites and customs in 17th century. Critical edition draws comparisons between Caribs' language and contemporary languages in the region, as well as with those spoken today in the Guianas and Central America. [APD]

1790 Butel, Paul. Histoire des Antilles françaises: XVIIe-XXe siècle. Paris: Perrin, 2002. 423 p., 8 p. de pl., index. (Pour l'histoire)

Comprehensive treatment of social and economic history of Saint-Domingue/Haiti, Martinique, and Guadeloupe by senior historian. Although focus is on first colony and 18th century, also synthesizes and discusses extensively recent research by scholars writing in French. [APD]

1791 *Les Cahiers du patrimoine.* No. 17/18, 2000. Esclavage: de l'antiquité à la révolution de 1789. Fort-de-France: Conseil général de la Martinique.

Overview for general audience by professional historians. Locates French Caribbean slavery within world history beginning before the Atlantic slave trade. [APD]

1792 Dayfoot, Arthur Charles. A history of Protestant churches in the West Indies. Gainesville: Univ. Press of Florida, 1998. 1 v.: bibl., index.

To explain Christianity's peculiar shape in English-speaking Caribbean, traces development of churches from monopolistic Spanish state-church through Protestant "planters' church" and missions to Africans before and after emancipation. East Indian and other 19th- and 20th-century migrations provided additional religious pluralism. Covers material against backdrop of social, cultural, and ecclesiastical influences. [ELC]

Doel, H.W. van den and **Pieter C. Emmer.** De dekolnonisatie van Nederland [The decolonization of the Netherlands]. See *HLAS 59:4420.*

1793 L'église martiniquaise et la piété populaire, XVIIe-XX siècles. Sous la direction de Dominique Taffin. Fort-de-France: Archives Départementales, 2001. 124 p.

Catalog of exhibit held at Archives Départementales de Martinique, Feb.-May 2001. Studies by Abénon, Chauleau, Delisle, and Taffin, along with introductions to exhibit's sections, provide comprehensive treatment of popular belief and religious practice in the Catholic diocese created in

1851, and of the singularity of French Creole Catholicism. [APD]

1794 Enciclopedia dominicana. v. 1–8. 6. ed. Santo Domingo: Enciclopedia Dominicana, 2000. 8 v.: bibl., ill. (some col.), indexes.

Vols. 1–7 follow traditional format of encyclopedias—alphabetical annotations, with an index at end of each volume. Articles are not signed, although credits are given in Vol. 1 by area of expertise; many entries end with a list of bibliographical references. Content is of uneven quality, perhaps because some important researchers are notably absent. Tone is typically nationalistic and content is uncontroversial. Photos and illustrations, some in color, enrich the text, although quality of reproduction is sometimes disappointing. Vol. 8 is a collection of poems, organized chronologically, according to European and Hispanic-American paradigms, beginning in 19th century. [TMV]

1795 Esquea, Rosa Francia. La Vega: en una panorámica retrospectiva y actual. Santo Domingo?: Comisión Presidencial de Apoyo Desarrollo Provincial, 2000. 209 p.: bibl. (Col. Provincias; 16)

Awarded second place in a national competition on provincial history, book highlights local customs and notable events, such as athletic accomplishments of town dwellers, carnival festivities, trajectory of the two presidents who hailed from La Vega, and local population's particular ways of speaking. Format follows that of other Colección Provincias publications. [TMV]

1796 Geggus, David Patrick. The French slave trade: an overview. (*William Mary Q.*, 58:1, Jan. 2001, p. 119–138, tables)

Uses recently published Du Bois Institute slave database to summarize state of knowledge about the French slave trade and to offer hypotheses about strong imprint of Ewe-Fon people on Haitian culture. Confirms the extraordinary importance and commercial efficiency of Cap Français as a slave port, and describes factors affecting ethnic distribution of Africans among Saint-Domingue's three colonial regions. [JDG]

1797 Gobardhan-Rambocus, Lila. Onderwijs als sleutel tot maatschappelijke vooruitgang: een taal- en onderwijsgeschiedenis van Suriname, 1651–1975 [Education as a

key to social progress: a history of language and education in Suriname, 1651–1975]. Zutphen, The Netherlands: Walburg Pers, 2001. 553 p.: ill.

Dissertation focuses on developments in the Suriname educational system from postemancipation period to independence. According to author, development in Suriname society has led to social equality among social and ethnic groups. Presents new and important historical information, but is less strong in its analysis of consequences of Dutch educational and language policies in its Caribbean colony. Includes a short summary in English. [RH]

1798 González Vales, Luis E. La puertorriqueñidad: una visión histórica. (*Bol. Acad. Puertorriq. Hist.*, 18:54, 1 de julio 1997, p. 155–180)

Chronological reader of key historic documents reveals developing sense of Puerto Rican national spirit. By the 18th century a mature Creole Puerto Rican spirit is clearly identifiable in literary and historical records, according to the author. [FMR]

1799 Hernández Hernández, Wilhelm. Manatí: quinientos años de historia, 1508–1998. Manatí, P.R.: Biblioteca Francisco Alvarez Marrero, Gobierno Municipal de Manatí, 1999. 783 p.: bibl., ill.

Extensive traditional account of history of municipality of Manatí, from precolumbian times to present. Extensive bibliography. [FMR]

1800 Historia y género: vidas y relatos de las mujeres en el Caribe. Compilación de Mario R. Cancel. Mayagüez, P.R.: Asociación Puertorriqueña de Historiadores; San Juan: Postdata, 1997. 126 p.: bibl. (Serie Hermes; 3)

Insightful essays, mostly on Puerto Rico, by both well-known and relative newcomers to the field of women's studies. Introduction by Blanca Silvestrini puts in perspective the importance of this publication in establishing gender analysis as a legitimate research tool. [TMV]

1801 Identités caraïbes. Sous la direction de Pierre Guillaume. Paris: Éditions du CTHS, 2001. 2 v.

Papers focus on colonists' relationship with environment. Cherubini documents a century of French Canadian integration in

Kourou, Sinnamary, and Iracoubo, French Guiana. Rogers reevaluates Alexandre Le Brassey's (*intendant* of Saint-Domingue 1780–82) policy to develop Cap Français. Boye analyzes Itier's memoir on French Guiana's resources and development; Jolivet insightfully explores the changing representations of the past in the colony's collective memory. [APD]

1802 Jarvis Luis, Rafael. La Romana: origen y fundación. Santo Domingo?: Comisión Presidencial de Apoyo Desarrollo Provincial, 1999. 143 p.: bibl., ill. (Col. Provincias; 2)

Part of official effort to advance local history, monograph documents episodes in La Romana's evolution, such as establishment of the town council, development of the port area, construction of public buildings and private residences, etc. Format is similar to others in the Colección Provincias series. [TMV]

1803 Kempen, Michiel van. Een geschiedenis van de Surinaamse literatuur [A history of Surinamese literature]. Breda, Netherlands: De Geus, 2003. 2 v. (1396 p.): bibl., ill., indexes.

Excellent overview of Surinamese oral and written literature from the earliest known expressions through 2000. Vol. 1 (1596–1957) focuses on oral literature among different ethnic groups and written literature during the colonial period. Author relates the literature to social, economic, political, and cultural developments in the country. Vol. 2 surveys Surinamese written literature from 1957–2000. Author first discusses the nationalist generation between 1957–75. He then describes how the period immediately after independence was a less vibrant period, mainly due to the military regime, but literary life blossomed again after 1987. Sranan Tongo and Sarnami both gained importance as literary languages. [RH]

1804 Lizardi Pollock, Jorge L. Palimpsestos y heterotopias: el espacio y sus prácticas en el Viejo San Juan. (*Rev. Mex. Caribe*, 4:8, 1999, p. 90–127, bibl., ill., photos)

Reviews historiography of walled city of San Juan. Proposes new areas of research such as symbiosis with extramural section of the city and incorporation of contested spaces—in areas such as health, sexuality,

forced labor, and sociability, for example—into study of city's history. [FMR]

1805 Mam-Lam-Fouck, Serge. Les créoles: une communauté en voie de marginalisation dans la société guyanaise? (*Pagara/Cayenne*, 1, 1996, p. 147–160, bibl., table)

Discusses French Guiana's Creole population, which is still the most numerous and influential group today. Argues that crisis of plantations, rise of frontier economy, and immigration pushed Creoles into civil service and initiated their decline after 1870. [APD]

1806 Mam-Lam-Fouck, Serge. Historiography of the French Antilles and French Guiana. Part B: French Guyana. (*in* General history of the Caribbean. v. 6, Methodology and historiography of the Caribbean. Edited by B.W. Higman. London: UNESCO Publishers, 1999, p. 656–664)

Describes emergence of a professional and critical historiography on French Guiana in second half of 20th century, following a long period in which historical works were produced by either colonial boosters or popular writers stressing assimilation with France. [JDG]

1807 Parisis, Denise and **Henri Parisis.** Une ascendance de libres et d'affranchis qui remonte aux débuts de la Guadeloupe. (*Généal. hist. Caraïbe*, 133, jan. 2001, p. 3052–3058, 3135–3136)

Patient and successful research tracing a free-colored family to 17th century yields valuable reflection on use of birth registers to understand how color line was drawn in slave societies. See also item **1813**. [APD]

1808 Pérotin-Dumon, Anne. Historiography of the French Antilles and French Guiana. Part A: Martinique and Guadeloupe. (*in* General history of the Caribbean. v. 6, Methodology and historiography of the Caribbean. Edited by B.W. Higman. London: UNESCO Publishers, 1999, p. 631–664)

Survey of primary and secondary sources on this region from travelers of the late-16th century to 20th century. Impressive intellectual evolution and volume of French Caribbean historical studies. Especially valuable for its attention to issues of Creole identity formation and nonacademic historical traditions such as genealogy. [JDG]

1809 Pérotin-Dumon, Anne. La ville aux Iles, la ville dans l'île: Basse-Terre et Pointe-à-Pitre, Guadeloupe, 1650–1820. Paris: Karthala, 2000. 990 p.: bibl., ill. (some col.), maps (some col.).

Intellectual tour-de-force integrates Caribbean history into the historiography of Europe, Latin America, and North America by arguing for the pivotal role of the city in this region best known for plantation slavery. A revised version of author's 1996 *thèse d'État*, volume exceeds standard of erudition and exhaustive archival research associated with French academic tradition through author's mastery of scholarship in English, French, and Spanish on urban and New World colonial history. By reproducing over 100 written and visual primary sources including hand-drawn maps and little-known paintings, Pérotin-Dumon has created a work that deserves to be read by all historians of New World colonization as well as by those who study later periods of French imperialism. [JDG]

1810 Plummer, Brenda Gayle. Between privilege and opprobrium: the Arabs and Jews in Haiti. (*in* Arab and Jewish immigrants in Latin America: images and realities. Edited by Ignacio Klich and Jeffrey Lesser. London; Portland, Ore.: F. Cass, 1998, p. 80–93)

Insightful and well-documented study compares two merchant communities' experiences in Haiti. Earliest Jews arrived as correspondents to powerful Portuguese Jewish merchants in Bordeaux. They suffered genocide and early Republic's ban on white foreigners. In second half of 19th century German Jews migrated to Haiti as part of the growing trade with Germany. The period of greatest prosperity for this group (1891–1915) coincided with immigration of Jews from Palestine and Christians from Lebanon, both groups called "Syrians." Lebanese penetrated export and retail trade. [APD]

1811 Puerto Rican women's history: new perspectives. Edited by Félix V. Matos Rodríguez and Linda C. Delgado. Armonk, N.Y.: M.E. Sharpe, 1998. 262 p.: bibl., index. (Perspectives on Latin America and the Caribbean)

Historical writings on women's studies cover conventional topics (the suffrage movement, early industrial employment, political activity) and more cutting-edge themes (prostitution, urban slavery, migration). Important contribution. [TMV]

1812 Ramdin, Ron. Arising from bondage: a history of the Indo-Caribbean people. New York: New York Univ. Press, 2000. 387 p.: bibl.

Presents a history of Indian indentured immigrants in colonial British, Dutch, French, and Spanish Caribbean territories. Examines postindenture East Indian cultural integration within Guyana, Trinidad, Jamaica, Suriname, Grenada, Cuba, Martinique, and Guadeloupe. Explores the affirmation of distinctive East Indian Caribbean identities within Guyana, Trinidad, Suriname, and Guadeloupe. Both the text and an extensive bibliography support the author's contention that "Indo-Caribbean history and culture must be retrieved from the margins and placed at the center as an integral part of discourse on Caribbean historiography." [J. Higbee]

Ramirez Morillo, Belarminio. La sociedad dominicana: origen, evolución y perspectiva. See *HLAS 59:5059*.

1813 Rossignol, Bernadette and **Philippe Rossignol.** Les Cramesnil de Laleu, Clairice et Fifine. (*Généal. hist. Caraïbe*, 120, nov. 1999, p. 2680–2687)

In series of articles included in journal *Généalogie et histoire de la Caraïbe*, authors relate important examples of method developed over the years for tracing ancestry of former slaves and free-coloreds. These researchers and this serial are at the forefront of enlightened genealogical research on former slave societies. Other titles are: "Les Desfontaines ou Défontaine (Guadeloupe): Présence ou absence des mentions de couleur sur les registres" (No. 134, Feb. 2001, p. 3082–93); "La famille Hérisson Petit de Pointe-à-Pitre ou le mystère de Patronymes des Libres" (No. 136, April 2001, p. 3142–45); "Une famille de libres de Saint-Esprit (Martinique)" (No. 140, Sept. 2001, p. 3270–74); "Recherches généalogiques sur les Esclaves avant 1848" (No. 141, Oct. 2001, p. 3290–93); and "Une recherche d'ascendance au Gosier" (No. 141, Oct. 2001, p. 3291–92). See also item **1807**. [APD]

Schnepel, Ellen M. The language question in Guadeloupe: from the early chroniclers to the post-war generation. See *HLAS 59:911.*

1814 Sherlock, Philip Manderson and **Hazel Bennett.** The story of the Jamaican people. Kingston: I. Randle Publishers; Princeton, N.J.: M. Wiener Publishers, 1998. 434 p.: bibl., ill., maps.

Although essential material is hardly new, this engaging book, written with emphasis on and sensitivity for Afro-Jamaicans who constitute predominant sector of island's population, provides fresh perspective on Jamaica's history. Shows appreciation for contributions of Marcus Garvey and the Rastafarians, for example, in shaping present-day politics and culture in Jamaica. [ELC]

1815 Stéhlé, Guy. Petit historique des grands recensements antillo-guyanais et en particulier de la Guadeloupe. (*Bull. Soc. hist. Guadeloupe,* 115, 1998, p. 3–59, bibl., tables)

Useful compilation of regulations concerning official economic and demographic statistics of the French Caribbean since 17th century, with units of measure used. [APD]

1816 Le sucre de l'Antiquité à son destin antillais. Sous la direction de Danielle Bégot et Jean-Claude Hocquet. Paris: Éditions du CTHS, 2001. 408 p.

Some 20 papers provide fresh data from 17th-19th centuries in Martinique and French Guiana on sugar and other crops vital to local life and on impact of colonial agriculture and trade on France in 18th century. [APD]

1817 Les villes françaises du Nouveau Monde: des premiers fondateurs aux ingénieurs du roi, XVIe-XVIIIe siècles. Sous la direction de Laurent Vidal et Emilie d'Orgeix. Paris: Somogy; La Rochelle, France: Flash; Rochefort, France: Centre international de la mer; Aix-en-Provence, France: Centre des archives d'outre-mer, Archives nationales, 1999. 191 p.: bibl., ill. (some col.), indexes, maps (some col.).

Primarily concerned with ancien régime urban planning and map collections, this elegant survey is to be commended for its comparative focus. [APD]

1818 Wagenheim, Olga Jiménez de. Puerto Rico: an interpretive history from pre-Columbian times to 1900. Princeton, N.J.:

Markus Wiener Publishers, 1997. 291 p.: bibl., index.

History from below highlights contributions of indigenous peoples, women, Africans, and working class from earliest years of Christian era to US occupation. Follows traditional chronological and thematic organization. [TMV]

EARLY COLONIAL

1819 Akenson, Donald Harman. If the Irish ran the world: Montserrat, 1630–1730. Montreal; Buffalo, N.Y.: McGill-Queen's Univ. Press, 1997. 273 p.: bibl., index, maps. (The Joanne Goodman lectures of the University of Western Ontario; 1997)

Using Montserrat as case study of "Irish" imperialism, author seeks to ascertain if Irish would have been more humane than British as imperialists. Concludes that as colonists they were just as insensitive as English and Scottish, despite long history of oppression in Ireland. Points to need for examining ethnic strife within white ruling classes in Caribbean. [ELC]

1820 Arbell, Mordechai. Jewish settlements in the French colonies in the Caribbean (Martinique, Guadeloupe, Haiti, Cayenne) and the "Black Code." (*in* Jews and the expansion of Europe to the West, 1450–1800. New York: Berghahn Books, 2001, p. 287–313)

Useful overview of Jewish populations in the French Caribbean by former Israeli ambassador to Haiti. Covers from 16th century into the revolutionary period. Based on primary and secondary sources, as well as oral history and archeological evidence collected by the author. [JDG]

Benjamin, Anna. Fort Nassau and the Van Wallenburg thesis: a re-evaluation of the evidence. See *HLAS 59:599.*

Bolland, O. Nigel. Struggles for freedom: essays on slavery, colonialism, and culture in the Caribbean and Central America. See *HLAS 59:4954.*

Breton, Raymond. Dictionnaire caraïbe-français. See item **1789.**

1821 Burnard, Trevor. E Pluribus Plures: African ethnicities in seventeenth and eighteenth century Jamaica. (*Jam. Hist. Rev.,* 21, 2001, p. 8–22, tables)

Thorough examination of data on geographical and ethnic heterogeneity of slaves brought to Jamaica from Africa during this period, author confirms our assumptions regarding the syncretic nature of Jamaican slave culture even as slaves sought to regroup with others of their specific nation. [ELC]

1822 Camus, Michel Christian. Le Général de Poincy, premier capitaliste sucrier des Antilles. (*Rev. fr. hist. Outre-mer*, 84: 317, 1997, p. 119–125)

Examines career and activities of first governor-general of French Caribbean, rightly emphasizing his involvement in sugar production and maritime trade. [APD]

1823 Camus, Michel Christian. L'Ile de la Tortue au cœur de la flibuste caraïbe. Préface de Pierre Pluchon. Paris: L'Harmattan, 1997. 153 p.: bibl., map. (Col. Horizons Amériques latines)

Brings useful corrective to Oexquemelin's narrative (1686) which depicted Tortuga Island as center of piracy. From 1725 on, its importance was due to location in front of rich sugar mainland of northern Saint-Domingue. For more recent article on the same topic, see item **1825**. [APD]

1824 Cauna, Jacques. L'eldorado des Aquitains: Gascons, Basques et Béarnais aux Iles d'Amérique, XVIIe-XVIIIe siècles. Biarritz, France: Atlantica, 1998. 541 p.: bibl., index.

Drawing on extensive knowledge of French Caribbean colonists from the southwest of France, Cauna vividly portrays individual destinies within a stratified and interconnected Creole and migrant society, and documents existence of a colored elite with white relatives in Bordeaux and Toulouse regions. Wealth of quantitative data on geographical origins and destinations, and on occupations. [APD]

1825 Chopin, Jacques; Bernadette Rossignol; and Philippe Rossignol. Aux débuts de la Tortue et de l'île de Saint-Domingue: chapelain ou boucanier? (*Généal. hist. Caraïbe*, 129, sept. 2000, p. 2494–2497)

Family correspondence brings fresh data to study of on buccaneers' lives in legendary Tortuga Island at end of 17th century. See also item **1823**. [APD]

1826 De Wilde, ou les sauvages insulaires d'Amérique 1694. Fort-de-France?: Conseil général; Musée départemental d'archéologie et de préhistoire de la Martinique, 2002. 135 p.: ill.

Unpublished narrative by merchant from Northern Europe who visited the Lesser Antilles brings new data on Caribs. Valuable addition to 17th-century French-language narratives on the topic. [APD]

1827 Handler, Jerome S. Escaping slavery in a Caribbean plantation society: marronage in Barbados, 1650s-1830s. (*NWIG*, 71:3/4, 1997, p. 183–225, bibl., map, table)

Concludes that most 17th-century Barbados Maroons who absconded to island's caves and wooded gullies were African-born. By late 18th century, marronage included Creole slaves, some of whom were colored, who found haven in urban centers. Other Maroons sought refuge in neighboring islands where they remained either permanently or temporarily. [ELC]

1828 Hrodej, Philippe. Saint-Domingue en 1690: les observations du Père Plumier, botaniste provençal. (*Rev. fr. hist. Outre-mer*, 84:317, 1997, p. 93–117)

Welcome addition to growing field of environmental history. Edition of famous naturalist's report on his second trip to the Caribbean. Article also documents economic crisis in French colonies where freebooting and tobacco were prohibited by the king. [APD]

1829 Klein, Herbert S. The slave experience in the Caribbean: a comparative view. (*in* Slaves with or without sugar: registers of the international seminar, Funchal, 17th to 21st June 1996. Funchal, Portugal: Atlanti[c] History Study Center, Regional Tourist and Culture Office, 1996, p. 143–181)

Summary essay narrates basic findings regarding African slavery in Caribbean, with explanations of how systems differed. Suggests variations evident in differing social and economic outcomes for slaves before and after emancipation. Concludes that US "stands at a more extreme position from the rest of the American republics that used African slave labor." [ELC]

1830 Lavoie, Yolande; Carolyne E. Fick; and Francine M. Mayer. A particular study of slavery in the Caribbean island of Saint

Barthélemy: 1648–1846. (*Caribb. Stud.*, 28:2, July/Dec. 1995, p. 369–403, bibl., tables)

Saint Barthélemy's slaves were employed mostly on small farms. Slaves' low mortality and high reproductive rates lessened dependence on slave imports. Masters often worked alongside their slaves. Yet slaves often experienced "overwork and undernourishment" because of generalized poverty of island rather than any deliberately abusive policies of masters. [ELC]

1831 López y Sebastián, Lorenzo E. and **Justo L. del Río Moreno.** La ganadería vacuna en la isla Espanõla, 1508–1587. (*Rev. Complut. Hist. Am.*, 25, 1999, p. 11–49, bibl., graphs, tables)

Careful synopsis of cattle industry in the Dominican Republic in early colonial period. Although not successfully compared to mainland, provides interesting framework for study of the overlap between state and private enterprise. [TMV]

1832 Moscoso, Francisco. Juicio al gobernador: episodios coloniales de Puerto Rico, 1550. Hato Rey, P.R.: Univ. de Puerto Rico, Decanato de Estudios Graduados e Investigación; Publicaciones Puertorriqueñas Editores, 1998. 183 p.: bibl.

Analyzes role of *juicio de residencias* in political and economic life of 16th-century Puerto Rico. Based on these trials, author documents several aspects of 16th-century life such as commercial activity, city council rulings, land tenure, Inquisition trials, gambling, and persecution of Moors, among others. Includes very good historiographical chapter on 16th-century Puerto Rican history. [FMR]

1833 Moscoso, Francisco. Lucha agraria en Puerto Rico, 1542–1545. San Juan: Ediciones Puerto; Instituto de Cultura Puertorriqueña, 1996. 246 p.: bibl., map.

Narrative account of early collective demand for land, based on rich primary documentation. Author carefully places research within larger context of Puerto Rican and Latin American agrarian historiography. [TMV]

Navarro Rivera, Pablo. Control político y protesta estudiantil en la Universidad de Puerto Rico, 1903–1952. See item **2085.**

1834 Neus-van der Putten, Hilde. Susanna du Plessis: portret van een slavenmeesteres. Amsterdam: KIT Publishers, 2003. 181 p.: ill.

Challenges the traditional view that Susanna du Plessis was a particularly cruel slave mistress in 18th-century Suriname. Author studies archives and contemporary written sources to reconstruct Du Plessis' life amidst the dominant male, white planters. She questions why a woman remains in the popular imagery as an example of a cruel slave mistress, in light of the absence of memories of cruel slave masters. [RH]

1835 Pané, Ramón. An account of the antiquities of the Indians: chronicles of the New World encounter. Introductory study, notes, and appendixes by José Juan Arrom. Translated by Susan C. Griswold. Foreword by Neil L. Whitehead. Durham, N.C.: Duke Univ. Press, 1999. 72 p.: appendices, bibl. (Latin America in translation/en traducción/en tradução)

New critical edition and study of only surviving direct source of information on myths and ceremonies of first inhabitants of the Antilles. This first book written on American soil in a European language in 1498 is eyewitness account of Taino culture by friar who lived for two years among native inhabitants of Hispañola. He records initial encounters between Spaniards and indigenous, and observations about ceremonies, creation stories, language, and customs of Taino world. Griswold's clear translation makes this important primary source available in English for the first time. Three appendices of excerpts from Columbus' log and letters, a letter by Peter Martyr, and two chapters from Las Casas' *Apologética historia de las Indias* enable readers to consult passages by three of Pané's contemporaries who also refer to the Taino. Arrom's introductory study provides invaluable context, notes for the primary text, and review of essential bibliography. Translation maintains flavor of the period without artificial anachronisms. This significant and long-awaited contribution to colonial studies is highly recommended for scholars and students alike. [M. Ahern]

1836 Pérotin-Dumon, Anne. Los europeos del Norte en las Antillas Menores: el proceso de asentamiento en las márgenes de las Américas. (in Historia general de América Latina. v. 2, El primer contacto y la formación de nuevas sociedades. Paris: Ediciones UNESCO/Editorial Trotta, 2000, p. 237–252)

Useful overview of settlement of the Caribbean in 16th-17th centuries focuses on formation of "the most multicultural and polyglot region of the Hemisphere." Though Spain saw Lesser Antilles as "useless" islands, the English, French, and Dutch turned them into centers of Atlantic commerce and culture, and the birthplace of the Caribbean plantation system. See also item **1837**. [JDG]

1837 Pérotin-Dumon, Anne. French, English and Dutch in the Lesser Antilles: from privateering to planting, c. 1550-c. 1650. (in General history of the Caribbean. v. 2, New societies: the Caribbean in the long sixteenth century. New York: Macmillan; London: UNESCO Publishers, 1999, p. 114–158, facsims.)

Survey article based on mix of primary and secondary sources. Evokes early social and cultural history as well as war and trade. Argues convincingly that this was the key period for establishing future patterns and not merely the prelude to the age of sugar plantations. See also item **1836**. [JDG]

1838 Petitjean Roget, Jacques and **Eugène Bruneau-Latouche.** Personnes et familles à la Martinique au XVIIe siècle d'après les recensements et terriers nominatifs. v. 1, Documents. v. 2, Dictionnaire. Paris: Editions Desormeaux, 2000. 2 v.: ill.

Newly expanded edition of useful research tool for family and social history of early French Caribbean, first published in 1983 (see *HLAS 48:2410*). [APD]

1839 Peyronnin, Philippe. Contours d'une pastorale ultramarine: les missionaires jésuites dans les sociétés d'habitations des Antilles et Guyane françaises aux XVIIe et XVIIIe siècles. (*Bull. Soc. hist. Guadeloupe*, 126, 2000, p. 25–80)

Overview of Jesuit missionary activity in French colonial Caribbean and Guyana contains list of published narratives and untapped sources including Jesuit missionaries' reports and correspondence. [APD]

1840 Regourd, François. Maîtriser la nature, un enjeu colonial: botanique et agronomie en Guyane et aux Antilles, XVIIe-

XVIIIe siècles. (*Rev. fr. hist. Outre-mer*, 86:322/323, 1999, p. 39–63, bibl.)

Examines development of colonial agronomy in French Caribbean. Discusses state-sponsored missions of scientists and networks of correspondents to collect plants, establishment of botanical gardens, and agricultural experiments by colonists whose papers were discussed in the *sociétés d'agriculture*. See also item **1897**. [APD]

1841 Rodríguez Morel, Genaro. Cartas del cabildo de la ciudad de Santo Domingo en el siglo XVI. Santo Domingo: Centro de Altos Estudios Humanísticos y del Idioma Español, 1999. 501 p.: bibl., indexes.

Transcription of over 100 letters from the cabildo (town council) of Santo Domingo to the Crown from 1530 to end of 16th century, introduced by a short essay. Readers will get a sense of the concerns of town councillors (fiscal matters, commerce, depopulation) and of the conflict created by overlapping jurisdictions (the judicial branch, the Church). Unfortunately, author does not comment on how Santo Domingo fit into the larger bureaucratic structure of the nascent Spanish empire. [TMV]

1842 Rossignol, Bernadette. Quelques éléments sur les caractéristiques du peuplement normand aux Antilles françaises au cours du XVIIe siècle. (in Congrès des Sociétés historiques et archéologiques de Normandie, 36th, France, 2001. Les Normands et l'Outre-mer: actes. Caen, France: Annales de Normandie; Fédération des sociétés historiques et archéologiques de Normandie, 2001, p. 213–223)

Well-informed overview of what is known about earlier (17th-century) French migrations to the Caribbean, and where to locate relevant information. [APD]

1843 Shaklee, Ronald V. Historical hurricane impacts on the Bahamas: pt. 1, 1500–1749; pt. 2, 1750–1799. (*Bahamas J. Sci.*, 5:1, Oct. 1997, p. 7–9, bibl. [and] 5:2, Feb. 1998, p. 16–20, bibl., photo)

Bemoaning deficiency in coverage of hurricanes affecting Bahamas before 1871, author's research brings to consciousness of scholarly community and Bahamians the impact of large number of hurricanes on islands even during pre-European settlement era. While filling scholarly void, articles lack adequate coverage of human dimension of these catastrophes. [ELC]

1844 Szászdi León-Borja, István. Noticias de la carrera salmantina del primer Obispo de la Isla de San Juan Bautista. (*Bol. Acad. Puertorriq. Hist.,* 18:54, 1 de julio 1997, p. 181–203, appendix, bibl.)

Describes early years in Salamanca of Bishop Alonso Manso, Puerto Rico's first bishop. Stresses importance of understanding Manso as a crucial reformer of 15th-century Spanish Church. [FMR]

1845 Théodat, Jean-Marie. De la Bidassoa à l'Artibonite: une autre frontière franco-espagnole? (Saint-Domingue/Santo Domingo.) (*Cah. Am. lat.,* 28/29, 1998, p. 163–185, bibl., maps, photos)

Argues that political border drawn in 17th century between French and Spanish colonies of Hispaniola contradicted their environmental complementarity. [APD]

LATE COLONIAL AND FRENCH REVOLUTIONARY PERIOD

Arbell, Mordechai. Jewish settlements in the French colonies in the Caribbean (Martinique, Guadeloupe, Haiti, Cayenne) and the "Black Code." See item **1820.**

1846 Archives départemantales de Guadeloupe. Le fleuret et l'archet: Le Chevalier de Saint-George, 1739?-1799; créole dans le siècle des Lumières. Basse-Terre?: Conseil général de la Guadeloupe, 2001. 1 v.

Catalog of a small archival exposition about this Guadeloupe-born free man of color who became one of Europe's most talented violinists, swordsmen, and composers. Valuable for reproductions of numerous archival documents and 18th-century images, especially those depicting Saint-Georges' career in England and France. See also item **1893.** [JDG]

1847 Beahrs, Andrew. "Ours alone must needs be Christians": the production of enslaved souls on the Codrington estates. (*Plant. Soc. Am.,* 4:2/3, Fall 1997, p. 279–310, facsims., map, table)

Contends that actions of missionaries at Codrington "gradually reflected the new racial, slaveholding ideology" in which "black skin was not a covering only, signaling the nature of the person it encompassed,

but was itself a source of symbolic degradation." Missionaries completely misinterpreted planters and slaves in attempt to impose new social order. For ethnologist's comment, see *HLAS 57:796.* [ELC]

1848 Beckles, Hilary. Creolisation in action: the slave labour elite and antislavery in Barbados. (*Caribb. Q./Mona,* 44:1/2, March/June 1998, p. 108–128, tables)

Using Newton Plantation on Barbados as case study, author makes urgent call for closer examination of growth, social origins, and maturity of Creole slave labor elites throughout the Caribbean in order to better understand elites' ambivalent attitudes toward slave insurrections. [ELC]

1849 Bénot, Yves. La Guyane sous la Révolution française, ou, L'impasse de la révolution pacifique. Kourou, French Guiana: Ibis rouge éditions, 1997. 222 p.: bibl., index, map.

Opinionated account of 1789 Revolution in French Guiana based on administrative correspondence. Especially interesting on abolition of slavery, which provided soldiers and field workers to the colony, and on deportation to Cayenne of political and Church opponents of the French Revolution. [APD]

1850 Blood, Elizabeth A. "Barbares européens": colonial oppression and liberal discourse in Barbault-Royer's *Craon et les trois opprimés* (1791). (*Hist. Reflect./Waterloo,* 26:3, 2000, p. 447–469)

Sophisticated interpretation of a largely ignored philosophical novel published in revolutionary Paris by a free man of color from Saint-Domingue. Barbault-Royer saw extension of citizenship to French Caribbean people of color as beginning of a process bringing liberty and justice to peoples around the globe. [JDG]

Bolland, O. Nigel. Struggles for freedom: essays on slavery, colonialism, and culture in the Caribbean and Central America. See *HLAS 59:4954.*

1851 Bourrachot, Lucile. Les Levelu de Clairfontaine: d'Aiguillon à la Guadeloupe. (*Rev. Agen,* 2000)

Shows close links between legitimate and illegitimate, and white and mulatto members of a bourgeois family spanning southwest France and Guadeloupe. [APD]

1852 Buckley, Roger Norman. The British Army in the West Indies: society and the military in the revolutionary age. Gainesville: Univ. Press of Florida, 1998. 441 p.: bibl., ill., index.

Excellent work examines how British army affected and was affected by Caribbean's political, economic, and social landscape. Concentrates mostly on Jamaican and Windward and Leeward command. Shows recruitment for garrisons, civil-military conflicts, and impact of environment on army life. Argues that army became "one of the great innovators, organizers, and disseminators of new medical knowledge." [ELC]

1853 Bulletin de la Société d'histoire de la Guadeloupe. No. 116–118, 1998. Basse-Terre: Archives départementales.

Special issue focuses on slavery and runaways in French Caribbean. Articles include: Vincent di Ruggiero, "Le Marronnage en Guadeloupe à la veille de la Révolution Française de 1789;" Christian Bouchet, "L'utilisation de l'histoire de l'esclavage antique en France lors de la seconde abolition;" and Jocelyne Jacquot, "Historiographie du marronnage à la Martinique: de l'objet de polémique au sujet d'étude." [APD]

Burnard, Trevor. E Pluribus Plures: African ethnicities in seventeenth and eighteenth century Jamaica. See item **1821.**

1854 Calleja Leal, Guillermo and **Hugo O'Donnell y Duque de Estrada.** 1762, La Habana Inglesa: la toma de La Habana por los ingleses. Madrid: Agencia Española de Cooperación Internacional, Ediciones de Cultura Hispánica, 1999. 262 p.: bibl., ill. (some col.), maps (some col.).

Balanced and scholarly study based on extensive primary and secondary sources. Required reading for those interested in the British intervention in Cuba. See also item **1895.** [JMH]

Camus, Michel Christian. L'Île de la Tortue au cœur de la flibuste caraïbe. See item **1823.**

1855 Cardoso, Ciro Flamarion Santana. La Guyane française, 1715–1817: aspects économiques et sociaux: contribution à l'étude des sociétés esclavagistes d'Amérique.

Petit-Bourg, Guadeloupe: Ibis rouge éditions, 1999. 424 p.: ill., map.

Long-awaited publication of a PhD thesis written in 1970s on the economic and social history of French Guiana. [APD]

1856 Carstens, Johan Lorentz. J. L. Carstens' St. Thomas in early Danish times: a general description of all the Danish, American or West Indian Islands. English edition and translation by Arnold R. Highfield. St. Croix: Virgin Islands Humanities Council, 1997. 148 p.: bibl. (Sources in Danish West Indian and U.S. Virgin Islands history)

Splendid critical edition of geographical description by 18th-century wealthy planter and member of the Danish merchant company. Brief, precise, and candid observations cover a wide range of topics: race and gender relationships, natural resources, colonial administration, trade, agriculture, local shipping, urban life, etc. Introduction provides excellent survey of island's history under Danish rule. [APD]

1857 Cauna, Jacques. Haïti: l'éternelle révolution. Port-au-Prince: Henri Deschamps, 1997. 363 p., 38 leaves of plates: bibl., ill.

Overview of Haitian Revolution by French scholar who argues for its important impact on the French Empire. Based on secondary sources, including author's considerable publications in this field. Detailed bibliography and chronology. [JDG]

1858 Colson, Audrey Butt. "God's Folk": the evangelization of Amerindians in western Guiana and the Enthusiastic Movement of 1756. (Antropológica/Caracas, 86, 1994/96, p. 3–110, maps, photo)

Contextualization of two mid-18th-century reports of intruders in the Dutch colony of Essequibo, which, though investigated at the time, remained unexplained until now. Concludes that the reference to "God's Folk" refers to an "enthusiastic movement" of a religious nature, stemming from the Guianan mission of the Catalan Capuchins. [S. Ramírez]

1859 Dion, Isabelle and **Anne-Cécile Tizon-Germe.** Dépôt des papiers publics des colonies (DPPC): Notariat; répertoire numérique. Aix-en-Provence, France: Centre des Archives d'Outre-mer, 2001. 814 p.: bibl.

Superb research tool on public notaries

(close to 12,000 documents) in French overseas territories, including the French Caribbean. Covers mid-18th to early 19th centuries. [APD]

1860 Dragtenstein, Frank. "De ondraaglijke stoutheid der weglopers": marronage en koloniaal beleid in Suriname, 1667–1768 ["The unbearable audacity of the runaways": marronage and colonial policy in Suriname, 1667–1768]. Utrecht, The Netherlands: Univ. Utrecht, Culturele Antropologie, 2002. 309 p.: bibl., ill., maps, tables. (Bronnen voor de Studie van Suriname; 22)

Dissertation is first systematic account of earliest history of Suriname Maroons, particularly the Saramakas, Matawai, and Ndjuka. In this chronologically organized study, author describes origin and evolution of marronage in Suriname, and Dutch colonial policy from end of British rule in 1670 to first peace treaty with the Matawai in 1768. Based on archival research in Amsterdam, The Hague, and Middelburg. Includes five-page summary in English. [RH]

1861 Dubois, Laurent. Les esclaves de la République: l'histoire oubliée de la première émancipation, 1789–1794. Paris: Calmann-Lévy, 1998. 1 v.

Discusses free-coloreds' and slaves' unrest and mobilization in French Caribbean in years preceding 1794 abolition. Argues that there was a sharp distinction between slave and free-colored leaders. [APD]

1862 Dubois, Laurent. "The Price of Liberty": Victor Hugues and the administration of freedom in Guadeloupe, 1794–1798. (*William Mary Q.*, 56:2, April 1999, p. 363–392)

Examines well-known Jacobin official's administration in Guadeloupe during second part of French Revolution. Emphasizes instrumentalization of abolition of slavery to goals of military defense and plantation labor. See also item **1899**. [APD]

1863 Duffy, Michael. The French Revolution and British attitudes to the West Indian colonies. (*in* Turbulent time: the French Revolution and the Greater Caribbean. Bloomington: Indiana Univ. Press, 1997, p. 78–101)

Notes that the chaos created in the French colonies by the Revolution temporarily opened up opportunities for British impe-

rial expansion. However, diversionary impact on British officials led to changed attitudes in which they doubted efficacy of long-established policies. Author credits Revolution with halting western expansion of British Empire and promoting its growth in the East. [ELC]

1864 Fick, Carolyn E. Dilemmas of emancipation: from the Saint-Domingue insurrections of 1791 to the emerging Haitian state. (*Hist. Workshop*, 46, 1998, p. 1–15)

Brief essay on revolutionary goals of Saint-Domingue's slaves and problem of plantation agriculture in independent Haiti, based largely on author's important 1990 book on the Haitian Revolution. See *HLAS 54:1903*. See also item **1865**. [JDG]

1865 Fick, Carolyn E. Emancipation in Haiti: from plantation labour to peasant proprietorship. (*Slavery Abolit.*, 21:2, Aug. 2000, p. 11–40)

Emphasizing "history from below," author looks at enfranchised slaves' expectations and gains from abolition of slavery, their flight from the plantations when new rulers sought to impose discipline, and the lots received by veterans of the Revolution. See also item **1864**. [APD]

1866 García Muñiz, Humberto and **José Lee Borges.** U.S. consular activism in the Caribbean, 1783–1903: with special reference to St. Kitts-Nevis' sugar depression, labor turmoil and its proposed acquisition by the United States. (*Rev. Mex. Caribe*, 3:5, 1998, p. 32–79, appendices, bibl., table)

Careful examination of US diplomatic involvement in European colonies and ex-colonies of Caribbean. Emphasizes consuls' part in US annexationist policies. Some addressed sugar depression and labor turmoil on Saint Kitts and Nevis, and advocated annexing islands. Concludes with discussion of Joseph Chamberlain's colonial policies and Britain's growing retrenchment from Caribbean. [ELC]

1867 Garrigus, John D. New Christians/"new whites": Sephardic Jews, free people of color and citizenship in French Saint-Domingue, 1760–1789. (*in* Jews and the expansion of Europe to the West, 1450–1800. New York: Berghahn Books, 2001, p. 314–332)

Innovative research on improving civil

status for Jews and free-coloreds, as "new definitions of French citizenship" were elaborated based on property, loyalty, and civic utility rather than on being a Catholic. Documents importance of Jewish merchants' capital and expertise in opening southern agricultural frontier. Examines colonial politics around civil status of both groups. [APD]

1868 Garrigus, John D. Redrawing the colour line: gender and the social construction of race in pre-revolutionary Haiti. (*J. Caribb. Hist.*, 30:1/2, 1996, p. 28–50)

Shows how gender was instrumentalized in fight for reformulating racial categories. By portraying free-colored men as effeminized—meaning irrational—and women of color with ties to whites as social danger, whites sought to exclude free-coloreds from public community. Men of color responded by asserting their civic virtue and presenting themselves as citizen-soldiers, drawing on the political rhetoric emerging in France. See also item **1869**. [APD]

1869 Garrigus, John D. "Sons of the same father": gender, race, and citizenship in French Saint-Domingue, 1760–1792. (*in* Visions and revisions of eighteenth-century France. University Park: Pennsylvania State Univ. Press, 1997, p. 137–153)

Complements previous research (see item **1868**) regarding use of gender categories by white Creoles opposing social and economic ascent of free mulattoes and other nonenslaved people. "Feminized stereotypes [reinforced] the rejection of people of color who in wealth, education, distance from slavery, even physical appearance were indistinguishable from white." Traces rise of racist obsession after 1763. [APD]

1870 Garrigus, John D. White Jacobins/Black Jacobins: bringing the Haitian and French Revolutions together in the classroom. (*Fr. Hist. Stud.*, 23:2, Spring 2000, p. 259–275)

Shows that teaching on the two revolutions together is intellectually consistent, and suggests relevant reading. [APD]

1871 Geggus, David Patrick. Indigo and slavery in Saint-Domingue. (*Plant. Soc. Am.*, 5:2/3, Fall 1998, p. 189–204)

The most important scholar of prerevolutionary Haiti uses his database of slave plantation records to describe working condi-

tions, demography, and African ethnic groups associated with this important export crop, often neglected by historians in favor of sugar and coffee. Useful addition to Geggus' growing corpus of articles on French Caribbean slavery. [JDG]

1872 Geggus, David Patrick. Slave society in the sugar plantation zones of Saint Domingue and the revolution of 1791–93. (*Slavery Abolit.*, 20:2, Aug. 1999, p. 31–46, map, tables)

Sophisticated comparison of slave life on sugar estates in Saint-Domingue's three provinces, in 1770s, 1780s, and 1790s. Geggus describes important regional variations in plantation size, slave fertility, and slave ethnic identity, but does not discern any relationship between these local characteristics and history of the Haitian Revolution. [JDG]

1873 Geggus, David Patrick. Slavery, war, and revolution in the Greater Caribbean. (*in* Turbulent time: the French Revolution and the Greater Caribbean. Bloomington: Indiana Univ. Press, 1997, p. 1–50, table)

Wide-ranging article by one of foremost historians of revolutionary period presents excellent overview of impact of French and Haitian Revolutions on Caribbean region. Suggests difficulty exists in showing direct causal relationship between various uprisings and expressions of servile discontent. Extremely valuable analysis and critique of existing historiography. [ELC]

1874 Geggus, David Patrick. 30 years of Haitian Revolution historiography. (*Rev. Mex. Caribe*, 3:5, 1998, p. 178–197)

Searching and nuanced review of evolving scholarly approaches to and interpretations of this field by scholars writing in English and French. Although author's own work is an important component in several of the historiographical subfields he describes, his account is well-balanced. [JDG]

1875 Ghachem, Malick W. Montesquieu in the Caribbean: the colonial Enlightenment between Code Noir and Code Civil. (*Hist. Reflect./Waterloo*, 25:2, 1999, p. 183–210)

Describes complex intellectual relationship between Montesquieu and the legal and political culture of 18th-century Saint-Domingue. Traces formation of a Creole identity among French colonial jurists and writers like Émilien Petit, Michel René Hilliard-d'Auberteuil, and Moreau de Saint-Méry. [JDG]

1876 Greene, Jack P. Liberty, slavery, and the transformation of British identity in the eighteenth-century West Indies. (*Slavery Abolit.*, 21:1, April 2000, p. 1–31)

Examines how Englishmen who boasted of their free society were themselves transformed in Americas. Asserts that increasingly colonists demonstrated that chattel slavery had creolized settler identities as free-born Britons, and raised powerful question of how people so dependent on parent state for protection against their enslaved population could maintain credible claims to their own freedom. [ELC]

1877 Hackmann, William Kent. William Beckford: the Jamaican connection. (*J. Caribb. Hist.*, 32:1/2, 1998, p. 23–45, bibl.)

Interesting article focuses on important member of established planter family who also served in British parliament. Examines Beckford's family connections between England and Caribbean, his wealth, his leadership in Jamaican Assembly, and his experience as volunteer in military expedition from 1739–44. [ELC]

1878 Hamoir, Eric. Lettres de Geoffrion de Saint-Cyr: une traversée de l'Atlantique et la Guyane en 1773. (*Pagara/Cayenne*, 1, 1996, p. 83–96, bibl.)

Letters from young member of colonial administration shed light on French Guyana's small society and life in the colony at end of the ancien régime. [APD]

Handler, Jerome S. Escaping slavery in a Caribbean plantation society: marronage in Barbados, 1650s-1830s. See item **1827.**

1879 The impact of the Haitian Revolution in the Atlantic world. Edited by David Patrick Geggus. Columbia: Univ. of South Carolina, 2001. 261 p.: maps. (The Carolina lowcountry and the Atlantic world)

Geggus has convened fine group of scholars to bring new research and fresh insights to bear on the multifarious echoes and ambiguous repercussions of the Haitian Revolution on the Western world—direct and indirect, inspiring or menacing, in the Caribbean area and beyond. Work deals with all strata of Creole society, refugees abroad, con-

temporary journalism and literature, historiography. Well-written overview and epilogue by editor. [APD]

1880 L'insurrection des esclaves de Saint-Domingue, 22–23 août 1791: actes de la table ronde internationale de Port-au-Prince, 8 au 10 décembre 1997. Sous la direction de Laënnec Hurbon. Paris: Karthala, 2000. 271 p. (Col. Monde caribéen)

Proceedings of 1997 conference held in Port-au-Prince. Useful compendium on French revolutionary politics and ideology of the "colonial question." Also discusses Haitian Revolution and in particular the voodoo ceremony where conspirators allegedly plotted the 1791 insurrection. [APD]

1881 King, Stewart R. Blue coat or powdered wig: free people of color in pre-revolutionary Saint Domingue. Athens: Univ. of Georgia Press, 2001. 328 p.: bibl., maps.

Good introduction in English to mechanisms of upward social mobility in late 18th-century colonial Haiti. Notarial records allow reconstruction of two types of possibilities offered to free-coloreds: recent entrepreneurial urban artisans acquired small land tracts and counted on free-coloreds' networks; older rural landowners relied on connections with white relatives. [APD]

Klein, Herbert S. The slave experience in the Caribbean: a comparative view. See item **1829.**

1882 Knight, Franklin W. The Haitian Revolution. (*Am. Hist. Rev.*, 105:1, Feb. 2000, p. 103–115)

Welcome essay on the momentous process. Drawing on extensive literature in English, article brings particular insights from social history. [APD]

1883 Lafleur, Gérard. La protestantisme aux Antilles françaises, seconde moitié du XVIIIe-XIXe siècle. (*Bull. Soc. hist. Guadeloupe*, 114, 1997, p. 11–86)

Important addition to author's previous works on subject. Stresses late ancien régime royal policy of tolerance toward Protestants that made English-speaking entrepot of Saint Martin their main center for a century. Mentions brief revival of Protestantism in Capesterre when Guadeloupe became English (1810–15). [APD]

1884 Lamur, Humphrey E. O impacto das Guerras dos Quilombolas na política populacional durante a escravidão no Suriname. (*Afro-Asia/Salvador*, 25/26, 2001, p. 61–93, map, tables)

Discussion of Dutch population policy in the late 18th century designed to raise the rate of natural increase and lower the mortality rate of the slave population in Suriname. Concludes that this policy was not successful as the measures did not result in an actual rise in fertility nor did they lower the death rates. Originally published in English in *The Journal of Caribbean History*, Vol. 23, no. 1, 1989. [RH]

Lavoie, Yolande; Carolyne E. Fick; and **Francine M. Mayer.** A particular study of slavery in the Caribbean island of Saint Barthélemy: 1648–1846. See item **1830.**

1885 Leblond, Jean-Baptiste. Voyage aux Antilles: d'île en île, de la Martinique à Trinidad, 1767–1773. v. 1. 2. ed. Paris: Karthala, 2000. 1 v.: bibl., ill., map. (Relire)

Rich travel account from southern Lesser Antilles at the time of their economic development. A medical doctor, product of the pre-Romantic and Enlightenment eras, makes sharp observations on wide range of subjects: tropical diseases, contraband, class and color prejudice in colonial society, measures of temperature and air humidity, and the like. Expresses admiration of dramatic landscapes and storms. Documents Caribs shortly before their deportation to Central America. See also item **1906.** [APD]

1886 Léger-Félicité Sonthonax: la première abolition de l'esclavage; la Révolution française et la Révolution de Saint-Domingue. Textes réunis et présentés par Marcel Dorigny. Saint-Denis, France: Société française d'histoire d'outre-mer; Paris: Association pour l'étude de la colonisation européenne, 1997. 173 p.: bibl. (Bibliothèque d'histoire d'outre-mer. Nouvelle série. Etudes; 16)

Discusses life, ideas, and policy of Jacobin official who abolished slavery in Saint-Domingue/Haiti in 1793. Contributions by Blanchet, Laurent, and Stein are particularly useful for understanding Sonthonax's revolutionary project and the obstacles he faced during his second mission to Saint-Domingue. [APD]

1887 López Cantos, Angel. Miguel Enríquez. San Juan: Ediciones Puerto; Escuela de Estudios Hispanoamericanos, CSIC, 1998. 411 p.: bibl.

Biographical sketch of mulatto corsair and entrepreneur Miguel Enríquez, who was one of the richest and most influential men in the Caribbean during 18th century as documented in this detailed work. [FMR]

1888 López Cantos, Angel. La mujer puertorriqueña y el trabajo, siglo XVIII. (*Anu. Estud. Am.*, 57:1, enero/junio 2000, p. 195–222)

Using limited sources, author attempts to describe nature of working women's activities in 18th-century Puerto Rico. Article is divided between work done at home and work done outside the home. [FMR]

1889 López Cantos, Angel. Los puertorriqueños: mentalidad y actitudes, siglo XVIII. San Juan: Ediciones Puerto; Editorial de la Univ. de Puerto Rico, 2000. 375 p.: bibl.

Comprehensive account of many dimensions of 18th-century Puerto Rican life. Includes analysis of demographics, religious life, definitions of time, love and sexuality, gender constructions, leisure, and death rituals and practices. [FMR]

1890 Mathurin-Mair, Lucille. Women field workers in Jamaica during slavery. (*in* Women plantation workers: international experiences. Oxford, England; New York: Berg, 1998, p. 17–27)

Rejecting stereotype of female laborers as peripheral to dominant economic sectors, author shows that women slaves were engaged in limited though important spheres. They spent more of their working years in fields than men, and often subverted labor system. By preventing their children from becoming plantation laborers at emancipation, they also frustrated planter interests. [ELC]

1891 Meadows, R. Darrell. Engineering exile: social networks and the French Atlantic community, 1789–1809. (*Fr. Hist. Stud.*, 23:1, Winter 2000, p. 67–102)

Uses impressive primary research to sketch the diaspora created by the French and Haitian Revolutions. Meadows suggests that refugees' destinations were not chosen haphazardly. Referring to these destinations to suggest outline of a French Atlantic community, he challenges various theories of French identity. Article describes primarily the travels of upper-class individuals, but acknowledges that poor whites, free people of color, and former slaves may have used the same networks. [JDG]

Mentor, Gaétan. Histoire d'un crime politique: le géneral Etienne Victor Mentor. See item **1982**.

1892 Morgan, Peter. The 32nd Regiment in the Bahamas, 1797–1799. (*J. Bahamas Hist. Soc.*, 21, Oct. 1999, p. 23–29, photo)

Reconstructs regiment's travels and experiences on journey to Saint-Domingue, its stay in Bahamas, and public health issues faced by regiment and local inhabitants, especially from yellow fever. Many members opted to remain at end of deployment because of their favorable impression and fond memories of life in Bahamas. [ELC]

1893 Noël, Eric. Saint-Georges: un chevalier de sang-mêlé dans la société des Lumières. (*Bull. Cent. hist. atl.*, 8, 1998, p. 131–154)

Original research throws useful light on Guadeloupe's famous free-colored musician. Focuses particularly on his less-known political support of Saint-Domingue's free-coloreds and his service in the French and later Haitian revolutionary army. See also item **1846**. [APD]

1894 Oquendo, Eli. Historia de una familia: los de Torres, de Adjuntas, siglos XVIII al XX. (*Horizontes*, 41:81, oct. 1999, p. 17–61, bibl., tables)

Chronological depiction of De Torres family history starting with migration of several family members from Ponce to Utuado/Adjuntas in mid-18th century. Part of author's family history. [FMR]

1895 Parcero Torre, Celia María. La pérdida de La Habana y las reformas borbónicas en Cuba, 1760–1773. Valladolid, Spain: Junta de Castilla y León, Consejería de Educación y Cultura, 1998. 291 p.: bibl. (Estudios de historia)

Well-researched doctoral dissertation focuses on military aspects of loss of Havana to the British in 1761. See also item **1854**. [JMH]

1896 Pouliquen, Monique. Jean-Baptiste Mathieu Thibault de Chanvalon et "l'affaire du Kourou." (*Généal. hist. Caraïbe*, 144, jan. 2002, p. 3372–3379)

Uses new sources to present nuanced views on official blamed for disastrous 18th-century expedition that killed hundreds of settlers in French Guiana. [APD]

Regourd, François. Maîtriser la nature, un enjeu colonial: botanique et agronomie en Guyane et aux Antilles, XVIIe-XVIIIe siècles. See item **1840**.

1897 Regourd, François. La Société royale d'agriculture de Paris face à l'espace colonial, 1761–1793. (*Bull. Cent. hist. atl.*, 8, 1998, p. 155–194, appendix)

Discusses elites' awareness of colonial potential for French economy in 1780s as reflected in papers on colonial agriculture and resources published by most influential branch of the Société royale d'agriculture. Good discussion of Society's role in sponsoring and disseminating policy of agricultural development, its membership, correspondents in the colonies and their research, brutal interruption of scientific activity caused by revolutionary politics centered on slavery, and Society's survival thereafter. See also item **1840**. [APD]

1898 Revue française d'histoire d'Outre-mer. Vol. 87, No. 328/329, 2000. Grégoire et la cause des Noirs: combats et projets, 1789–1831. Paris: Société française d'histoire d'Outre-mer.

Documents courageous opposition to slavery and racial inequality demonstrated by prominent member of French revolutionary Church. Particularly interesting on Christian roots of Grégoire's abolitionism. [APD]

1899 Rossignol, Bernadette and Philippe Rossignol. La famille de Victor Hugues à Marseille, à Saint-Domingue et en Guyane. (*Généal. hist. Caraïbe*, 134, fév. 2001, p. 3096–3102)

Genealogical research reveals family origins and socioeconomic network of well-known colonial Jacobin portrayed in *El siglo de las luces*. Points to inaccuracies in historiography since early 19th century. See also item **1862**. [APD]

1900 Ryden, David B. "One of the fertilest pleasentest spotts": an analysis of the slave economy in Jamaica's St. Andrew Parish, 1753. (*Slavery Abolit.*, 21:1, April 2000, p. 32–55, graphs, map, tables)

Using detailed agricultural census of Jamaican parish, concludes that census gives clear view of wide range of agricultural pursuits carried out by free and enslaved Jamaicans at mid-century, and of slave organization for plantation agriculture. Contends "there was profit in kindness for those planters who made food more readily available to their slaves." [ELC]

Shaklee, Ronald V. Historical hurricane impacts on the Bahamas: pt. 1, 1500–1749; pt. 2, 1750–1799. See item **1843.**

1901 Shepherd, Verene. Questioning Creole: domestic producers in Jamaica's plantation economy. (*Caribb. Q./Mona,* 44:1/2, March/June 1998, p. 93–107)

Engaging Edward Kamau Brathwaite's narrowly defined concept of "Creole economy" (see *HLAS 35:1132*), author uses Jamaica's livestock farmers to show that planters' commitment to use of imported animals was oriented towards Spanish Caribbean and thus livestock production never achieved potential for local self-sufficiency. When resources permitted, some pen-keepers became absentees and remained uncommitted to Creole ideals. See also item **1902.** [ELC]

1902 Shepherd, Verene. Slavery without sugar in Caribbean plantation societies: examples from Jamaica. (*in* Slaves with or without sugar: registers of the international seminar, Funchal, 17th to 21st June 1996. Funchal, Portugal: Atlanti[c] History Study Center, Regional Tourist and Culture Office, 1996, p. 207–225)

Contends that emergence of livestock pens "created an alternative occupation for a significant number of slaves whose social and economic experiences deviated from those of their counterparts on the sugar estates." Based on findings from economically diverse agricultural settings on Jamaica. Calls for closer study of contrasting land-use types within same territory in slavery and in freedom. See also item **1901.** [ELC]

1903 Simmonds, Lorna E. The health care of Jamaican urban slaves, 1780–1838. (*Jam. Hist. Rev.*, 21, 2001, p. 31–37)

In analysis of hospitals, asylums, and nature of medical care in urban setting, author contends "it would be reasonable to conclude that urban slaves were probably better off" than their rural counterparts whose treatment occurred in the plantation "hot-house." [ELC]

1904 Sturtz, Linda E. The 1780 hurricane donation: "insult offered instead of relief." (*Jam. Hist. Rev.*, 21, 2001, p. 38–46)

Despite hurricane's baneful effects on all segments of Jamaica's population, relief commissioners remained generally lukewarm to plight of poor while favoring "wealthiest and most powerful residents" in administering disaster relief. Thus, assistance provided social stability by propping up prehurricane hierarchy. Petitions for relief by poor to Assembly indicate "alternative moral economy." [ELC]

1905 A turbulent time: the French Revolution and the Greater Caribbean. Edited by David Barry Gaspar and David Patrick Geggus. Bloomington: Indiana Univ. Press, 1997. 262 p.: bibl., index, maps. (Blacks in the diaspora)

Specialists on Caribbean slave rebellions examine "the pervasive and multilayered impact of the revolutions in the region." Named contributors provided essays, and collection includes works on Louisiana and Spanish Florida; all are very worthwhile. Common causes for rebellions emphasized by editors are continuous wars and economic upheaval of plantation economy that resulted. [APD]

1906 Les voyages de Jean Baptiste Leblond, médecin et naturaliste du Roi, 1767–1802: Antilles Amérique espagnole, Guyane. Sous la direction de Monique Pouliquen. Paris: Éditions du CTHS, 2000. 1 v.: bibl., index.

Complements Leblond's main narrative (see item **1885**), includes five additional texts by this scientific author. Carefully edited, with good introduction on Leblond's life and works. [APD]

1907 Wanquet, Claude. La France et la première abolition de l'esclavage, 1794–1802: le cas des colonies orientales, Ile de France (Maurice) et la Réunion. Paris: Karthala, 1998. 724 p.: bibl., ill., index, maps. (Col. Hommes et sociétés)

Carefully researched account brings much needed comparative dimension to understanding of the abolition of slavery. Moves from France and the Revolution of 1848 to distant colonies in the Indian Ocean where emancipation was implemented. [APD]

1908 Welch, Pedro L.V. The slave family in the urban context: views from Bridgetown, Barbados, 1780–1816. (*J. Caribb. Hist.,* 29:1, 1995, p. 11–24, tables)

Concludes that slave family in Bridgetown was mostly matrifocal, with occupational structure stressing ownership of female slaves. Slave ownership in Bridgetown also tended to be small scale, with women used in "feminine occupations" such as clothes washing and sewing. Thus slave women were pivotal in defining patterns of socialization that shaped slave-slave and slave-master/mistress relationships. [ELC]

1909 Widmer Sennhauser, Rudolf. El Higüey en el siglo XVIII: los inicios de la industria maderera en Santo Domingo, 1780–1800. (*Estud. Soc./Santo Domingo,* 34:123, enero/marzo 2001, p. 63–78, bibl.)

Cattle and tobacco promoted end of communal land in the Cibao and the Dominican-Haitian border, resulting in dislocation of peasants toward eastern part of the island, where the switch to mahogany lumbering facilitated absorption of this surplus labor under a variety of arrangements. [TMV]

SPANISH BORDERLANDS

1910 Dalleo, Peter T. Bahamian pioneers in the Florida Keys. (*J. Bahamas Hist. Soc.,* 21, Oct. 1999, p. 31–39, appendices, photo, tables)

In useful review essay, author argues that fruitful examination of Loyalist contributions to development of Bahamas also must contend with repatriation of Bahamians and their contribution to development of Florida Keys. Advocates comparative study of commercial nature of Bahamas and Keys that would point to similarities and dissimilari-ties between port cities and their respective rural island chains. See also item **1916.** [ELC]

1911 Elliott, Jack D. City and empire: the Spanish origins of Natchez. (*J. Miss. Hist.,* 59:4, Winter 1997, p. 271–321, appendix, map)

Traces founding of city of Natchez and its role as a major threshold in the social evolution that eventually resulted in birth of the state of Mississippi. Well written and documented. [JMH]

1912 Ewen, Charles Robin and **John H. Hann.** Hernando de Soto among the Apalachee: the archaeology of the first winter encampment. Gainesville: Univ. Press of Florida, 1998. 238 p.: bibl., ill., indexes, maps. (Ripley P. Bullen series) (A Florida heritage publication)

Eminently readable book, especially important because of the significance of the site reported and scholarly information provided. [JMH]

1913 Hanger, Kimberly S. "Desiring total tranquility" and not getting it: conflict involving free black women in Spanish New Orleans. (*Americas/Washington,* 54:4, April 1998, p. 541–556)

Offers glimpse of discrimination, desires, and frustrations experienced by free black women in Spanish New Orleans society. Worth reading. [JMH]

1914 Landers, Jane G. Female conflict and its resolution in eighteenth-century St. Augustine. (*Americas/Washington,* 54:4, April 1998, p. 557–574)

Author's knowledge of Spanish legal system is somewhat superficial; however, description of Spanish forms of control and conflict resolution is still interesting. [JMH]

1915 Milanich, Jerald T. Florida's Indians from ancient times to the present. Gainesville: Univ. Press of Florida, 1998. 194 p.: bibl., ill. (some col.), maps. (Native peoples, cultures, and places of the southeastern United States)

Study of Apalachee who once lived in Florida, and their neighbors. Of interest for both archeologists and the general reading public. [JMH]

A turbulent time: the French Revolution and the Greater Caribbean. See item **1905.**

1916 Whidden, Astrid. Key West's Conchs, 1763–1912: outlaws or outcasts? (*J. Bahamas Hist. Soc.,* 19, Oct. 1997, p. 30–43, photos)

Stresses important contributions Bahamian immigrants (wreckers especially) have made to Key West's economic and cultural development. Predominant initially in sponging and salt-raking, they also brought with them their religion, architectural styles, and other items of material culture. Recently, though, these Conchs have been increasingly marginalized as mainland US culture came to dominate the small town. See also item **1910.** [ELC]

1917 Worth, John E. The Timucuan chiefdoms of Spanish Florida. v. 1, Assimilation. v. 2, Resistance and destruction. Gainesville: Univ. Press of Florida, 1998. 2 v.: bibl., ill., index, maps. (The Ripley P. Bullen series)

These two volumes are the culmination of nearly a decade of original research and incorporate the most current archeological and historical investigations, especially many previously unknown or little-used Spanish documentary sources. Sheds new light on nature and function of Florida's mission system. [JMH]

19TH CENTURY

1918 Abénon, Lucien-René. L'activité du port de Saint-Pierre, Martinique à la fin du XIXe siècle. Paris: L'Harmattan, 1996. 155 p.: bibl., ill., indexes, map. (Col. Lettres des Caraïbes)

Covers activity in Martinique's leading port until 1902 Montagne Pelée eruption caused its abrupt downfall. Discusses long-term importance of coastal trade, sharp fluctuations in volume of shipping, and increasing importance of foreign trade from 1892–1902. [APD]

1919 Adélaïde-Merlande, Jacques. Les origines du mouvement ouvrier en Martinique: 1870–1900. Paris: Karthala, 2000. 236 p.: bibl. (Col. Monde caribéen)

Written in 1958, Adélaïde's MA thesis was the first research on the rise of the workers' movement and its bloody confrontations with police in Martinique as sugar industry went into deep crisis. [APD]

1920 El asesinato político en Puerto Rico. Recopilación de Ivonne Acosta Lespier. San Juan: Editora Lea, 1998. 123 p.: bibl., ill. (Cuadernos del 98/Ateneo Puertorriqueño; 9)

Includes six essays by historians and journalists on famous cases of political murder in 19th- and 20th-century Puerto Rico. [FMR]

1921 Baldrich, Juan José. From the origins of industrial capitalism in Puerto Rico to its subordination to the U.S. tobacco trust: Rucabado and Company, 1865–1901. (*Rev. Mex. Caribe,* 3:5, 1998, p. 80–106, bibl., graphs, tables)

Detailed description of ventures of tobacco merchants Rucabado and Company into manufacturing the leaf beginning in last third of 19th century, and their incorporation as junior partner in the US tobacco trust upon US invasion. Less an analysis of capitalism in a colonial context than a business history of the company. [TMV]

1922 Barcia Zequeira, María del Carmen. Elites y grupos de presión: Cuba, 1868–1898. La Habana: Editorial de Ciencias Sociales, 1998. 204 p.: bibl., ill. (Historia)

Important book clarifies how a group of Spanish financiers exploited colonial Cuba, and reveals their decisive influence on Spanish/Cuban relations. [JMH]

1923 Barcia Zequeira, María del Carmen. La historia profunda: la sociedad civil del 98. (*Temas/Habana,* 12/13, 1998, p. 27–33)

Traces changes that civil society underwent in Cuba during crucial 1878–98 period. Original and well-researched study. [JMH]

1924 Barcia Zequeira, María del Carmen. El 98 en La Habana: sociedad y vida cotidiana. (*Rev. Indias,* 58:212, enero/abril 1998, p. 85–99)

Fascinating and humorous study of everyday life in Havana before and after the blockade of the city by the US fleet in 1898. [JMH]

1925 Blancpain, François. Un siècle de relations financières entre Haïti et la France, 1825–1922. Préface de Jacques Cauna. Paris: L'Harmattan, 2001. 212 p.: bibl., index.

Well-researched book examines diplomatic and financial history of Haiti's national debt toward France (Haiti's price for its independence). Shows that debt was less important in causing country's underdevelopment than were the continuous civil wars among elites; however, debt was decisive in fostering foreign intervention into national politics. [APD]

Bolland, O. Nigel. Struggles for freedom: essays on slavery, colonialism, and culture in the Caribbean and Central America. See *HLAS 59:4954.*

1926 Bonnet, René. Le docteur Louis-Daniel Beauperthuy, pionnier de la médecine tropicale. (*Bull. Soc. hist. Guadeloupe,* 112/113, 1997, p. 3–53)

Brief note on Creole physician from Guadeloupe who pioneered tropical medicine. See also item **1983.** [APD]

1927 Bonó, Pedro Francisco. El montero; Epistolario. Estudio preliminar y notas de Raymundo González. Santo Domingo: Ediciones de la Fundación Corripio, 2000. 365 p.: port. (Biblioteca de clásicos dominicanos; 31)

Republication of *El montero,* a novel by Dominican Republic's most notable and admired literary figure of 19th century, and of his letters to political notables (Eugenio María de Hostos, Gregorio Luperón, Ulises Heureaux, and the like). Some of the letters advocate with characteristic zeal the high ideals of integrity, fairness, and justice for which Bonó is known. González's commentary situates Bonó's writings both historiographically and historically. [TMV]

1928 Boutin, Raymond. Entrer dans la vie en Guadeloupe entre 1850 et 1946. (*Bull. Soc. hist. Guadeloupe,* 111, 1997, p. 5–50)

This article and related work (item **1929**) show richness of approach combining demographic data and anthropological insights to document social processes of birth and death and their varied meanings in Caribbean culture over a century. [APD]

1929 Boutin, Raymond. La mort envisagée: notaires, testateurs et testaments en Guadeloupe entre 1849 et 1946. (*Bull. Soc. hist. Guadeloupe,* 114, 1997, p. 5–50)

See item **1928.**

1930 Bruleaux, Anne-Marie. Une expérience de préparation à la libération des esclaves: la Mère Javouhey à Mana. (*Pagara/Cayenne,* 1, 1996, p. 97–119, bibl.)

First study on unique experiment conducted over almost two decades by Mother Javouhey, influential superior of 19th-century female missionary religious order. Former slaves, relocated on an isolated settlement on the banks of the Mana River, were to become free peasants and good Christians. See also item **1946.** [APD]

1931 Buckley, Roger Norman. The admission of slave testimony at British military courts in the West Indies, 1800–1809. (*in* Turbulent time: the French Revolution and the Greater Caribbean. Bloomington: Indiana Univ. Press, 1997, p. 226–250)

Argues that demands of wartime experience, particularly conflicts over status of slaves in civil life and military, occasioned rethinking of larger issue of slave testimony in military and civilian courts. Admissibility of their evidence, despite strong opposition by planters, probably marked the beginning of the end for slavery. [ELC]

Buckley, Roger Norman. The British Army in the West Indies: society and the military in the revolutionary age. See item **1852.**

Bulletin de la Société d'histoire de la Guadeloupe. See item **1853.**

1932 Cabrera, Gilberto R. Puerto Rico y su historia íntima, 1500–1996. v. 2, Siglos XIX y XX. San Juan: G.R. Cabrera, 1997. 1 v.

Not an "historia íntima" at all, work is a chronological account, based on printed sources, of the tenure of governors over last two centuries of Puerto Rican history. [TMV]

1933 Casanovas Codina, Joan. Bread, or bullets!: urban labor and Spanish colonialism in Cuba, 1850–1898. Pittsburgh: Univ. of Pittsburgh Press, 1998. 333 p.: bibl., ill., index, maps. (Pitt Latin American series)

Based on a vast array of resources, argues that urban labor was not totally absent in the process of uncoupling Cuba and Spain. For review of Spanish-language edition, see item **1934.** [JMH]

1934 Casanovas Codina, Joan. O pan, o plomo!: los trabajadores urbanos y el colonialismo español en Cuba, 1850–1898.

Prólogo de Nicolás Sánchez-Albornoz. 1. ed. en español. Madrid: Siglo XXI, 2000. 326 p.: bibl., ill.

Perhaps the first thoroughly documented history of organized labor in 19th-century Cuba. Based on research in libraries and archives in Cuba, Spain, US, and The Netherlands. A major contribution despite some debatable conclusions. For review of English-language edition, see item **1933**. [JMH]

1935 Castro Arroyo, María de los Angeles.
"¿A qué pelear si los de Madrid no quieren?": una versión criolla de la guerra del '98 en Puerto Rico. (*Rev. Indias*, 57:211, sept./dic. 1997, p. 657–694)

Creole military officer's diary suggests to author that outcome of Spanish-American War in Puerto Rico was due to superior US weaponry, despondency of Spanish high command, and futility of Puerto Rico's efforts for increased political participation and economic development under Spanish rule. [TMV]

**1936 The Chinese in the West Indies,
1806–1995: a documentary history.**
Compiled by Walton Look Lai. Kingston: The Press, Univ. of the West Indies, 1998. 338 p.: bibl., ill., maps.

Excellent, well-chosen set of documents blends official records from Colonial Office, Colonial Land and Emigration Commission reports, parliamentary papers, and family biographies based on personal interviews with elderly family members covering period to about 1990. Documents deal with virtually every aspect of migration of Chinese to West Indies and their subsequent experiences. Contains useful introductory essay by author. See also item **1943**. [ELC]

1937 Chivallon, Christine. Espace et identité à la Martinique: paysannerie des mornes et reconquête collective, 1840–1960. Paris: CNRS, 1998. 298 p.: bibl., ill. (some col.).

Fine research in notarial deeds and land and civil registries, combined with oral testimonies. Documents land acquisition and use in Basse-Pointe, Rivière-Pilote, and Morne-Vert following abolition of slavery. Argues that formation of a small peasantry was underway prior to 1848 as slaves worked as paid workers on the land they would acquire later with savings from selling fresh produce and poultry or from plying a trade. [APD]

**1938 The colonial Caribbean in transition:
essays on Post-Emancipation social
and cultural history.** Edited by Bridget Brereton and Kevin A. Yelvington. Kingston: Press Univ. of the West Indies; Gainesville: Univ. Press of Florida, 1999. 319 p.: bibl., ill., map.

Combining social history with cultural studies approach that stresses continuity and change, essays explain broad social and cultural developments in region between 1830s-1940s. Essays, mostly on Trinidad and Guyana, focus on social and ethnic groups, class, gender relations, and interconnectedness of these with region's traditions. [ELC]

1939 Corre, Armand. Nos créoles: étude politico-sociologique, 1890. Texte établi, présenté et annoté par Claude Thiébaut. Paris: Harmattan, 2001. 303 p.: bibl. (Autrement mêmes)

Pamphlet by French army physician who was posted for a few years in Guadeloupe. Critique of white Creole oligarchy. Illustrates diversity in the racist ideology of the 1890s, as analyzed in good introduction by Thiébaut. [APD]

1940 Cottias, Myriam. "L'oubli du passé" contre la "citoyenneté": troc et ressentiment à la Martinique, 1848–1946. (*in* 1946–1996: Cinquante ans de départementalisation outre-mer. Paris: Éditions L'Harmattan, 1997, p. 293–313)

Interprets periodic eruptions of protest in century following abolition of slavery as manifestations of people's resentment for being asked to erase the memory of bondage in exchange for having been granted citizenship. [APD]

1941 Coupeau, Steve. Ethnicidade e cidadania como elementos de negociação: comerciantes árabes no Haiti, 1860–1910. (*Estud. Afro-Asiát.*, 33, set. 1998, p. 99–116, bibl., table)

Focuses on Haiti's first Arab community (ca. 10,000 persons) which rose up in 1891, with US support, to counter commercial power of the German colony. Haitian opposition to local competitors caused their expulsion and diaspora to other islands in 1905. For ethnologist's comment, see *HLAS 59:855*. [APD]

1942 Craton, Michael. Empire, enslavement, and freedom in the Caribbean. Kingston: Ian Randle Publishers; Princeton, N.J.: Markus Wiener Publishers, 1997. 520 p.: bibl., ill., maps.

Useful collection of 20 wide-ranging essays published elsewhere, some in hard-to-access sources, by preeminent scholar of Caribbean. Though some of author's conclusions may be contested within the scholarly community, the volume reflects ways in which Caribbean historiography has been redefined, and reveals Craton's wonderful skills in synthesizing previous scholarship. [ELC]

1943 Crespo Villate, Mercedes. Huaren Zai Zhetangzhi Guo: Guba. [Chinese in the land of sugarcane: Cuba]. Translated by Liu Zhenli. Shanghai: Fudan Univ. Press, 1998. 175 p.: appendices, bibl., plates.

Important work on Cuban Chinese in their early period. Examines arrival of Chinese laborers in Cuba, their tragic condition, contacts between China and Cuba, assimilation of Chinese into the Cuban nation, contributions of the Chinese to independence and development of Cuba, etc. Translated into Chinese from Spanish, work is dedicated to 150th anniversary of arrival in Cuba of first group of Chinese immigrants. Author is wife of Cuban ambassador to China (1988–99). See also item **1936.** [Mao Xianglin]

1944 Cubano, Astrid. Criollos ante el 98: la cambiante imagen del dominio español durante su crisis y caída en Puerto Rico, 1889–1899. (*Rev. Indias,* 57:211, sept./dic. 1997, p. 637–655)

The image of a proud and heroic Spain served native Puerto Rican elite both for identifying with larger Hispanic nation across the Atlantic and for affirming their social preponderance on the island. At the same time, a second representation of Spain as the symbol of privilege facilitated ideological distancing of certain Creoles. In either case, adoption of turn-of-the-century racist discourse of progress opened the door for domination by US occupation forces. See also item **1989.** [TMV]

1945 Cubano, Astrid. Political culture and male mass-party formation in late-nineteenth-century Puerto Rico. (*HAHR,* 78:4, Nov. 1998, p. 631–662)

Grounded on, and skillfully borrowing from, theoretical literature on subalternality and postcoloniality, argues that political culture of the Spanish Liberal Party was embraced wholeheartedly by the Puerto Rican elite who, upon the US invasion, rightly assessed their chances for influencing the turn of events as extremely limited, and acquiesced to less than universal male suffrage. [TMV]

1946 Delisle, Philippe. Colonisation, christianisation et émancipation: les Soeurs de Saint-Joseph de Cluny à Mana, Guyane française, 1828–1846. (*Rev. fr. hist. Outre-mer,* 85:320, 1998, p. 7–32)

Building on Bruleaux's study (see item **1930**), traces fate of Javouhey's mission established on French Guiana frontier and politics behind it. Javouhey's political leverage with the French government enabled her to apply her reformist ideal (a mixture of liberalism and paternalism) until Creole elites succeeded in having the mission shut down. [APD]

1947 Delisle, Philippe. Un échec relatif: la mission des engagés indiens aux Antilles et à la Réunion, seconde moitié du XIXème siècle. (*Rev. fr. hist. Outre-mer,* 88:330/331, 2001, p. 189–203)

Welcome research on Catholic Church policy toward Hindu labor force arriving in French Caribbean and island of Réunion (1854–89). Language barrier (Tamil), Indians' resistance, and planters' reluctance conspired to thwart Church's efforts to eradicate Asiatic cults. As descendants began speaking Creole, they became Catholic in large numbers. Worthwhile comparisons with Mascarene Islands and Trinidad. [APD]

1948 Delisle, Philippe. Histoire religieuse des Antilles et de la Guyane françaises: des chrétientés sous les tropiques, 1815–1911. Paris: Karthala, 2000. 347 p.: bibl., ill., maps. (Mémoire d'églises)

Examination of 19th-century Catholic Church in French Antilles and French Guiana singles out female and male religious orders' contribution to development of primary education in 1860s. Also considers planters' opposition to clergy sent in 1848 whose enlightened views helped propagate republicanism among colored elites. [APD]

1949 Delpuech, Claude and **Alain Buffon.** Les billets de banque de la Caraïbe: collection Maurice Muszynski. Pointe-à-Pitre, Guadeloupe: Association des retraités de banque de la Guadeloupe; Prim, 1998. 57 p.

Catalog of exhibit organized in Guadeloupe. Bank notes in use in the Caribbean since early 19th century offer astonishing representations of places and people of the islands. Introductions by numismatist and economic historian. [APD]

1950 D'une abolition à l'autre: anthologie raisonnée de textes consacrés à la seconde abolition de l'esclavage dans les colonies françaises. Sous la direction de Myriam Cottias. Marseille, France: Agone, 1998. 1 v.

Some 200 well-chosen texts on 1848 abolition of slavery. Valuable introduction. [APD]

1951 L'esclavage à Basse-Terre et dans sa région en 1844, vu par le procureur Fourniols. Sous la direction de Gérard Lafleur. Préface de Ghislaine Bouchet. Basse-Terre?: Société d'histoire de la Guadeloupe; Bibliothèque d'histoire antillaise, 2000. 1 v.: index.

Creole judge Fourniols prepared his inspection and wrote his report with care. Provides wealth of observations and data on slaves' diverse occupations and conditions of life in Guadeloupe's capital city and rural surroundings. Introduction provides valuable data on legal framework and terminology. [APD]

1952 Espacios en disputa: México y la independencia de Cuba. Estudio introductorio y compilación documental de Salvador E. Morales Pérez. México?: Centro de Investigación Científica Ing. Jorge L. Tamayo; Secretaría de Relaciones Exteriores, 1998. 523 p.: bibl., index. (Archivo histórico diplomático mexicano)

Required reading for anyone wishing to assess attitude of the Porfirio Díaz government toward 1895–98 Cuban war of independence. Includes literal transcriptions of many important documents. [JMH]

1953 Ferrer, Ada. Insurgent Cuba: race, nation, and revolution, 1868–1898. Chapel Hill: Univ. of North Carolina Press, 1999. 273 p.: bibl., ill.

Enlightening and well-researched discussion of Cuban insurgents' approach to the problem of race and their reconceptualization of race and nationality while they fought against Spain. [JMH]

1954 Findlay, Eileen. Decency and democracy: the politics of prostitution in Ponce, Puerto Rico, 1890–1900. (*Fem. Stud.*, 23:3, Fall 1997, p. 471–499)

Clever argument draws parallels between advances of political democracy and repression of notions of gender and class equality. The regulation of prostitution, author contends, served the interests of the Partido Liberal Autonomista de Puerto Rico by bringing together feminists and urban male workers in a not entirely coherent, yet binding, discourse of decency and morality. The Ponce campaign to control "scandalous women" went hand-in-hand with political schemes to shape the "great Puerto Rican family." [TMV]

1955 Francius-Figuières, Valérie. Les notables et la vie politique à Pointe-à-Pitre sous le Second Empire. (*Bull. Soc. hist. Guadeloupe*, 124/125, 2000, p. 3–19)

Charts ascent of colored elite in municipal politics of Pointe-à-Pitre. Although always a numerical minority who suffered purges following downfall of Second Republic, they soon controlled the municipal council with agreement of white notables. [APD]

Franco, Franklin J. Sobre racismo y anti-haitianismo y otros ensayos. See *HLAS* 59:5003.

1956 Fricoteaux, Benoît. Le Rapport Couderc, révélateur de la société guadeloupénne du début du XIXe siècle. (*Bull. Soc. hist. Guadeloupe*, 112/113, 1997, p. 19–53)

Report of parliamentary commission which initiated corruption charges against Légitimus, the first black MP and a socialist, throws interesting light on political culture in colonial microcosm of early 19th century. Perceptive analysis of highly emotional and personalistic mechanisms of political allegiance which combined with an acceptance of France's authority and political institutions. [APD]

1957 García, Gervasio Luis. El otro es uno: Puerto Rico en la mirada norteamericana de 1898. (*Rev. Indias*, 57:211, sept./dic. 1997, p. 729–759)

Argues that Puerto Rican elite paved the way for US domination prior to, and independently of, the war of 1898. Examines US brand of expansionism (an empire without colonies); the plurality of voices of the powerful; the "real" Puerto Rican context (the "class war" that took place before the military war of 1898); and the "similarity in difference" (between dominator and subaltern), which resulted in the "other" being "oneself"—hence article's title. Excellent essay fueled by postmodernist agenda: imbued in textual analysis and focused on postcolonial policies. [TMV]

García Muñíz, Humberto. Interregional transfer of biological technology in the Caribbean: the impact of Barbados' John R. Bovell's cane research on the Puerto Rican sugar industry, 1888–1920s. See item **2056.**

García Muñíz, Humberto and José Lee Borges. U.S. consular activism in the Caribbean, 1783–1903: with special reference to St. Kitts-Nevis' sugar depression, labor turmoil and its proposed acquisition by the United States. See item **1866.**

1958 Girollet, Anne. Victor Schoelcher, abolitionniste et républicain: approche juridique et politique de l'œuvre d'un fondateur de la République. Paris: Karthala, 2000. 409 p.: bibl., index. (Col. Hommes et sociétés)

Jurist examines legal foundations of Schoelcher's political views on French Caribbean as argued in his political speeches. Schoelcher advocated islands' full integration into French institutions and laws. See also items **2009** and **2010.** [APD]

Guerra Vilaboy, Sergio. Colombia y la independencia de Cuba. See item **2512.**

1959 Hoganson, Kristin L. Fighting for American manhood: how gender politics provoked the Spanish-American and Philippine-American Wars. New Haven, Conn.: Yale Univ. Press, 1998. 305 p.: bibl., ill. (Yale historical publications)

After insisting on causal significance of gender beliefs, author admits there is room for doubt in her argument. Still, an interesting and provocative book. [JMH]

1960 Howard, Philip A. Changing history: Afro-Cuban cabildos and societies of color in the nineteenth century. Baton

Rouge: Louisiana State Univ. Press, 1998. 227 p.: bibl., maps.

By using a different historical approach, shows that Afro-Cubans behaved much like other immigrants. A solid piece of research. [JMH]

1961 Hutton, Clinton. Women in the Morant Bay Rebellion. (*Jam. J.*, 26:2, Dec. 1997, p. 10–13, ill.)

Argues that although British government and colonial authorities did not recognize them politically, women played important role in Morant Bay Rebellion and in other efforts by black Jamaicans for political empowerment. Shows that although women participants apparently lacked major organizational and leadership roles in the rebellion, they were punished by flogging, sexual violence, and execution. [ELC]

1962 Iglesias García, Fe. El costo demográfico de la Guerra de Independencia. (*Debates Am.*, 4, julio/dic. 1997, p. 67–76, tables)

Scholarly attempt to refine available data on Cuban population losses owing to the wars of independence. No one dealing with the subject should pass it over. [JMH]

1963 Iglesias García, Fe. Las finanzas de Cuba en el ocaso colonial. (*Rev. Indias*, 58:212, enero/abril 1998, p. 215–235, tables)

Trustworthy account of deterioration of Cuba's economy as a result of the 1895–98 War of Independence. [JMH]

1964 El informe del Cónsul Carden sobre el impacto de la ocupación americana de Puerto Rico, en 1898, sobre el comercio. (*Bol. Acad. Puertorriq. Hist.*, 18:54, 1 de julio 1997, p. 205–210)

1898 report by US Consul Lionel Carden in Puerto Rico on economic effects of the Spanish-American War on the island. Mentions that commercial activity was at a standstill given uncertainty of island's immediate political future. [FMR]

1965 Jennings, Lawrence C. Associative socialism and slave emancipation in French Guiana, 1839–1848. (*Rev. fr. hist. Outre-mer*, 88:330/331, 2001, p. 167–188)

Important new research on development scheme promoted by planters in French Guiana in decade preceding abolition of slavery. Under fashionable name of "association," slaves would ostensibly receive vast tracts of uninhabited state lands, but its true goal was to guarantee to planters a coerced labor force. It is revealing of the time that French parliament objected to planters' conservatism and lack of ethical concern. [APD]

1966 Jennings, Lawrence C. French antislavery: the movement for the abolition of slavery in France, 1802–1848. Cambridge, England; New York: Cambridge Univ. Press, 2000. 320 p.: bibl., ill., index.

Comprehensive treatment by specialist, based on wide array of sources. Documents role of various organizations in obtaining legal reform, particularly the increasing influence of the Société française pour l'abolition de l'esclavage (1834). Stresses two limits of the movement: planters' lobbies were successful at curbing 1845 reform of slavery and abolitionism penetrated few socialist milieux or popular circles. [APD]

1967 Les kalmanquious: des magistrats indésirables aux Antilles en temps d'abolition; réédition des libelles de Xavier Tanc et Adolphe Juston. Introduction, notes et commentaires de Jacqueline Picard. Gosier, Guadeloupe: Caret, 1998. 151 p.: bibl., ill. (Petite bibliothèque du curieux créole; 1)

Beautiful critical edition of 19th-century political texts against Creole privileges and racist order. Young judges Tanc and Juston were sent to Guadeloupe and Martinique respectively to implement 1829 reform which limited planters' powers in the judiciary. Tanc is particularly informative and cogent. [APD]

1968 Karch, Cecilia and **Henderson Carter.** The rise of the phoenix: the Barbados Mutual Life Assurance Society in Caribbean economy and society, 1840–1990. Kingston: Ian Randle Publishers, 1997. 396 p.: bibl., ill.

Shows that during 155-year history of oldest surviving insurance company, Mutual reflected values, mores, attitudes, and social relations of Caribbean society, with growth in number of policy holders mirroring societal changes. A leader in productive investment, Mutual loaned money to all segments of Caribbean society. Important contribution to enhanced understanding of region's economic and social history. [ELC]

1969 Lafleur, Gérard. Les Libanais et les Syriens de Guadeloupe. Préface de Jacques Adélaïde-Merlande; Le Phénicien, 1999. Paris: Karthala; 222 p.: bibl., ill., maps.

Welcome study on Lebanese and Syrians who came to Guadeloupe fleeing religious persecution after 1860. Traces immigrants' geographical origins, demographic contours and occupations once in Guadeloupe, their integration into and contributions to local society. Shows their precarious political status until 1945 due to international context. [APD]

Lafleur, Gérard. La protestantisme aux Antilles françaises, seconde moitié du XVIIIe-XIXe siècle. See item **1883**.

1970 Lamaute, Emmanuel. Le vieux Portau-Prince. Port-au-Prince: Imprimerie de la Compagnie lithographique d'Haïti, s.d. 1 v.

Welcome reprint (facsimile) of 1939 brochure issued to celebrate 250th anniversary of Haiti's capital city. [APD]

Lavoie, Yolande; Carolyne E. Fick; and **Francine M. Mayer.** A particular study of slavery in the Caribbean island of Saint Barthélemy: 1648–1846. See item **1830**.

1971 Le Villain, Yvon. Gerville-Réache: la vérité. Pointe-à-Pitre, Guadeloupe: Ibis rouge éditions, s.d. 5 v.

Collection focuses on Guadeloupe's most influential politician in second half of 19th century. Vols. 1–3 retrace public and private life and works, thus providing a vivid picture of local politics. Vol. 4 deals with family origins and genealogy. Vol. 5 reproduces pieces written for *L'Éclair* (1892–1904). Includes index of names for Guadeloupe's elected bodies. [APD]

1972 Lépine, Edouard de. Dix semaines qui ébranlèrent la Martinique: 25 mars-4 juin 1848. Paris: Servédit; Maisonneuve et Larose, 1999. 230 p.: bibl.

Discarding exceptionalist interpretations, author places abolition process in Martinique within broader context of French colonial policy and the struggles for emancipation led by slaves themselves in all Caribbean societies. [APD]

1973 Loyola Vega, Oscar. Visión cubana de un conflicto finisecular. (*Hist. Contemp.*, 19, 1999, p. 17–38)

Shows clearly that the Cuban historical reconstruction of the pre-independence period (1868–98) developed almost at the same time that the events took place, and that in many cases was dictated by exigencies of the moment. Insightful and challenging. [JMH]

1974 Lugo-Ortiz, Agnes. Identidades imaginadas: biografía y nacionalidad en el horizonte de la guerra, Cuba 1860–1898. San Juan: Editorial de la Univ. de Puerto Rico, 1999. 281 p.: bibl.

Although basically a work of literary criticism, offers many insights into way in which the biographies of some Cuban greats have been written. [JMH]

1975 Manigat, Leslie François. La révolution de 1843: essai d'analyse historique d'une conjoncture de crise. Nouv. éd. Port-au-Prince: Centre Humanisme démocratique en action, 1997. 48 p.: bibl. (Les cahiers du CHUDAC; v. 1, no. 5–6)

Examines liberal revolution that ended long presidency of Boyer; drew together the middle class and masses; and revealed strength of black rural leadership (the "révolution des Piquets"). Brilliant interpretation of Haiti's political history and sociology. See also item 2012. [APD]

1976 Marie-Sainte, Daniel-Edouard. Les annales criminelles de la Guadeloupe de 1829 à 1848: cours d'assises et cour criminelle. (*Bull. Soc. hist. Guadeloupe,* 123, 2000, p. 3–74)

Intelligent use of press makes up for loss of judicial records to fire. Study documents working of justice in slave society following 1829 reform. Court cases capture many facets of social relations, economic activity, and colonial culture. [APD]

1977 Marqués, Jaime Oliver. Cortes constituyentes de 1869 y la abolición de la esclavitud en Puerto Rico. (*Milenio/Bayamón,* 1:1, enero/junio 1997, p. 7–35)

Analyzes political and economic context of reforms proposed in 1869 by Puerto Rican delegates in the Spanish parliament regarding abolition of slavery and indemnification of slave owners. Gives particular attention to forces that opposed abolition in favor of more gradual solutions. [FMR]

Mathurin-Mair, Lucille. Women field workers in Jamaica during slavery. See item **1890.**

1978 Matos Rodríguez, Félix V. Women and urban change in San Juan, Puerto Rico, 1820–1868. Gainesville: Univ. Press of Florida, 1999. 180 p.: bibl.

Vividly describes lives of working class women in San Juan and their interactions with elite women through Junta de Damas, a charitable organization. Argues that San Juan became a predominantly white and male city during 19th century, in the context of growth and decline of sugar industry, massive immigration, revival of slavery and other coerced labor mechanisms, political repression, and impetus for reform. Author's pointed discussions and broad coverage of key historical issues open a much needed conversation between Latin American, Caribbean, and Puerto Rican historiography. [TMV]

1979 Mauvois, Georges. Un complot d'esclaves: Martinique, 1831. Grenoble, France: Pluriels de Psyché, 1998. 153 p.: bibl., ill. (Col. Afrique, Antilles hier et aujourd'hui)

Based on court evidence, offers new interpretation of the fact that serious plot involved three *castes* in bustling Saint-Pierre: stresses that white liberals shared news of France's political revolution of 1830 with free-coloreds and domestic slaves. [APD]

1980 Maza Miquel, Manuel. Entre la ideología y la compasión: guerra y paz en Cuba, 1895–1903; testimonios de los archivos vaticanos. Santo Domingo: Instituto Pedro Francisco Bonó, 1997. 559 p.: bibl., ill.

Author is foremost authority on the subject; no one has studied its various ramifications as he has. [JMH]

1981 Méndez Rodenas, Adriana. Gender and nationalism in colonial Cuba: the travels of Santa Cruz y Montalvo, condesa de Merlin. Nashville, Tenn.: Vanderbilt Univ. Press, 1998. 317 p.: bibl., ill.

Argues that travel books and historical memoirs of 19th-century Cuban aristocrat Mercedes Santa Cruz, although written in French, cannot be excluded from national canon of Cuban literature nor from broader account of Spanish-American Romanticism. Scholarly book in which author rightfully contends that the *comtesse* is the first Cuban woman to assume seriously the task of the historian. [JMH]

1982 Mentor, Gaétan. Histoire d'un crime politique: le géneral Etienne Victor Mentor. Port-au-Prince: Le Natal, 1999. 174 p.: bibl., ill.

Focuses on a singular figure among first generation of Haitian black politicians. Mentor emerged from revolutionary army organized by French commissary Sonthonax to fight mulattoes' uprising. A staunch supporter of France's authority, Mentor later sided with Emperor Dessalines, which cost him his life. [APD]

1983 Mortagne, Anne. Le docteur Louis-Daniel Beauperthuy, pionnier de la médicine tropicale: précurseur de Carlos Finlay, de Louis Pasteur et de Robert Koch, 1807–1871. Paris: Éditions Hervas, 1998. 1 v.

Beauperthuy's research on yellow fever exemplifies contribution of Creole physicians to tropical medicine in 18th century. See also item **1926.** [APD]

1984 Northrup, David. Indentured Indians in the French Antilles = Les immigrants indiens engagés aux Antilles françaises. (*Rev. fr. hist. Outre-mer*, 87:326/327, 2000, p. 245–271)

Comprehensive study of recruitment and indenture of 68,000 Indians from French Pondichéry and Karikal, and British Calcutta. Describes their demographic profile (75 percent male), transportation, hiring and working conditions, and life once in the Caribbean. Recommended for comparative focus and careful examination of evidence. Based on immigrants' reactions and decisions, work argues convincingly against previous historiography which categorized indenture as a form of slavery, stressing instead workers' own choices and decisions. [APD]

Núñez Polanco, Diómedes. Anexionismo y resistencia: relaciones domínico-norteamericanas en tiempos de Grant, Báez y Luperón. See *HLAS 59:4472.*

Oquendo, Eli. Historia de una familia: los de Torres, de Adjuntas, siglos XVIII al XX. See item **1894.**

1985 Pago, Gilbert. Les femmes et la liquidation du système esclavagiste à la Martinique, 1848–1852. Fort-de-France?: Ibis rouge éditions, 1998. 1 v.

Insightful study uses official records to uncover black and colored female participation in demonstrations that precipitated abolition of slavery in Martinique; women's insistent requests to retain gardens and become landowners; and, although lacking the franchise, the beginning of their politicization. [APD]

1986 Pérez Guzmán, Francisco. Herida profunda. La Habana: Ediciones Unión, Unión de Escritores y Artistas de Cuba, 1998. 259 p.: bibl., ill. (Col. Clío)

A rather balanced (for a Cuban historian) monograph on the civilian reconcentration program of Capitan-General Weyler for the pacification of Cuba in 1896–98. [JMH]

1987 Phillips-Lewis, Kathleen. The poor and the powerful: the cocoa contracts crisis in Trinidad, 1884–1890. (*J. Caribb. Hist.*, 32:1/2, 1998, p. 1–22)

Contends that cocoa contracts, initially seen as symbiotic arrangement between capital and labor to benefit all parties, constituted system of domination. Contracts were entered into and reformulated by planters to control land and labor. Frequent abuses and conflicts nearly put a halt to the system, threatening island's prosperity at a time when cocoa accounted for most of its wealth. [ELC]

1988 Picó, Fernando. Los chivos expiatorios: los *tórtolos* en Puerto Rico, 1898–1899. (*Rev. Mex. Caribe*, 3:6, 1998, p. 100–115, bibl.)

Discusses how West Indian migrants, lumped together as *tórtolos* in reference to those coming from Tórtola, served as a foil for Puerto Rican repudiation of the unruly behavior by US military personnel between 1898–99. [FMR]

1989 Picó, Fernando. Las construcciones de lo Español entre los militares norteamericanos en Puerto Rico, 1898–99. (*Rev. Indias*, 57:211, sept./dic. 1997, p. 624–635)

Analyzing writings of three US military officers, shows that both negative and positive representations of Puerto Ricans were grounded in antithetical notions of

Spaniards. Puerto Ricans were construed either as politically inferior to their more advanced former Spanish masters, or as subjected to backward metropolitan policies. In addition, racist attitudes conveyed advantages of downplaying African or mixed ancestry. The Hispanic origins of Puerto Rico's national identity, then, were first conceived by the US invaders and not by 1930s nationalists. See also item **1944**. [TMV]

Picó, Fernando. La revolución puertorriqueña de 1898: la necesidad de un nuevo paradigma para entender el 98 puertorriqueño. See item **2090**.

1990 Placer Cervera, Gustavo. Las campañas militares y el Tratado de París. (*Bol. Acad. Puertorriq. Hist.*, 18:54, 1 de julio 1997, p. 135–154)

Chronological account of major battles of the 1898 Spanish-American War starting with US naval blockade of Spanish ships in April and leading up to the signing of the Treaty of Paris in Oct. 1898. [FMR]

1991 Política, identidad y pensamiento social en la República Dominicana, siglos XIX y XX. Recopilación de Raymundo González et al. Madrid: Doce Calles; Santo Domingo?: Academia de Ciencias Dominicana, 1999. 300 p.: bibl. (Col. Antilla)

Original essays by expert scholars explore sources of Dominican national identity and significant moments of historical development. Especially significant are the contributions of González, Cassá, Baud, and San Miguel. González, the country's resident *bonocista*, delights in showing the markedly moral ground from which Bonó and Hostos, two progressive thinkers, launched their blueprints for social progress. Cassá brilliantly revisits the persistent Dominican dilemma: whether to include "the (ignorant) people" as partners in government or to limit the task of state-building to the contributions of an (educated) minority. Baud boldy asserts that the anti-Haitianism that the Dominican elite erected as the foundation of nationalism was not necessarily shared by the popular classes, and in fact was refuted as Dominicans and Haitians interacted on a daily basis. San Miguel skillfully "narrates" the imagined community through an analysis of historical memory in the essays and

short stories of Juan Bosch, which San Miguel considers "a modernizing national project." The best and most complete coverage of these topics yet in print, the volume's intellectual reach probably will not be surpassed for many years to come. [TMV]

1992 Pulido Ledesma, José A. La deuda colonial y el Tratado de París. La Habana: Editorial de Ciencias sociales, 1999. 142 p.: bibl.

Lucid study shows how much Spain benefited from its Cuban colony. [JMH]

1993 Quiroz, Alfonso W. Loyalist overkill: the socioeconomic costs of "repressing" the separatist insurrection in Cuba, 1868–1878. (*HAHR*, 78:2, May 1998, p. 261–305, tables)

Objective assessment by a Peruvian historian of a situation in colonial Cuba that neither Cubans nor Spaniards have approached with equanimity. [JMH]

1994 Reddock, Rhoda. The indentureship experience: India women in Trinidad and Tobago, 1845–1917. (*in* Women plantation workers: international experiences. Oxford, England; New York: Berg, 1998, p. 29–48, photos, tables)

Demonstrates that supposedly private relationships between Indian men and women actually overlapped in public domains. Individual Indian women achieved relative autonomy despite constraints created by social relations in plantation society. Yet, planters imposed male dominance through reconstruction of state-supported patriarchal Indian family. See also item **2016**. [ELC]

1995 Remesal, Agustín El enigma del Maine: 1898; el suceso que provocó la guerra de Cuba; accidente o sabotaje? Barcelona: Plaza & Janés Editores, 1998. 259 p., 16 p. of plates: bibl., ill.

Sober account of Maine tragedy from a Spanish perspective. [JMH]

1996 Richardson, Bonham C. Economy and environment in the Caribbean: Barbados and the Windwards in the late 1800s. Foreword by David Lowenthal. Kingston: The Press, Univ. of the West Indies; Gainesville: Univ. Press of Florida, 1997. 294 p.: bibl., ill., index, maps.

Historical geography examines four

dissimilar British Caribbean islands at a time when severe economic depression, plunging sugar prices, and two catastrophes adversely affected them. Shows how major changes in land-use patterns were effected following these catastrophes. Concludes that working class discontent over land use eventually precipitated British government's decision to implement change. For comment by economist, see *HLAS 59:1841.* [ELC]

1997 Rodríguez González, Agustín Ramón. Operaciones de la Guerra de 1898: una revisión crítica. Madrid: Actas Editorial, 1998. 213 p., 40 p. of plates: bibl., ill., maps. (Col. El Estado de la cuestión; 2)
Balanced reassessment of Spanish military operations in the Spanish-American War that challenges many traditionally accepted opinions. Based on published sources and Spanish archival materials. [JMH]

1998 Roldán de Montaud, Inés. España y Cuba: cien años de relaciones financieras. (*Stud. Hist. Hist. Contemp.,* 15, 1997, p. 35–69, graph, tables)
Important contribution to the study of a usually neglected subject. [JMH]

1999 Romero Valiente, Juan Manuel. La inmigración española en la República Dominicana en el tránsito de los siglos XIX-XX. (*Estud. Soc./Santo Domingo,* 34:123, enero/marzo 2001, p. 45–61, bibl., tables)
Descriptive account of Spanish migration to Dominican Republic from 1880–1930. Although a million Spaniards migrated to the Americas, Dominican Republic received only 3,000. In last third of 19th century, mostly Andalusians went to Puerto Plata. In early decades of 20th century, Asturians and Galicians settled in Santo Domingo and San Pedro de Macorís. [TMV]

2000 Rosario Natal, Carmelo. Los pobres del 98 puertorriqueño: lo que le pasó a la gente. San Juan: Producciones Históricas, 1998. 159 p.: bibl., ill.
Claiming to add perspective of the indigent to our understanding of events preceding and following US invasion, work describes official measures to assist poor during preparations for 1898 war. Explains open-arm welcome to American invaders partly as a function of extreme situation of popular classes. Primary sources quoted and transcribed provide rich social history of the time. [TMV]

2001 Saunders, Gail. William Wylly and his slaves at Clifton Plantation. (*J. Bahamas Hist. Soc.,* 20, Oct. 1998, p. 27–31, facsims., photo)
In examination of relationship between Wylly and his slaves, author concludes that "perhaps Wylly's benevolence has been exaggerated." Despite his public stance favoring amelioration and his efforts promoting Christianity and encouraging slaves to maintain "stable unions" with a single spouse, Wylly's economic interests often took precedence over these ideals. [ELC]

2002 Schmidt, Nelly. Abolitionnistes de l'esclavage et réformateurs des colonies, 1820–1851: analyse et documents. Paris: Karthala, 2000. 1196 p.: bibl., ill., index. (Hommes et sociétés)
Authoritative study of 19th-century French abolitionism, its dynamic and specificity. Documents various strategies to oppose the slave trade, obtain free-coloreds' franchise, and reform colonial slave society. Enriched by 266 original documents (pamphlets, speeches, press articles, private and administrative correspondence, legislation). [APD]

2003 Schmidt, Nelly. 1848 dans les colonies françaises des Caraïbes: ambitions républicaines et ordre colonial. (*Rev. fr. hist. Outre-mer,* 85:320, 1998, p. 33–69, table)
Assessment of ambitious assimilationist policies launched after abolition of slavery (1848) in education, access to land, and rural labor force. Emphasizes restrictive measures adopted in all three spheres, and argues that they caused widespread political alienation among new citizens. [APD]

2004 Schmidt-Nowara, Christopher. The end of slavery and the end of empire: slave emancipation in Cuba and Puerto Rico. (*Slavery Abolit.,* 21:2, Aug. 2000, p. 188–207)
Compares historiographical accounts of the end of slavery in Cuba and Puerto Rico. Stresses importance of linking end of slavery with ruptures in legitimacy of the colonial order, and explores political effects of end of slavery on both islands. [FMR]

2005 Schmidt-Nowara, Christopher. National economy and Atlantic slavery: protectionism and resistance to abolitionism in Spain and the Antilles, 1854–1874. (*HAHR*, 78:4, Nov. 1998, p. 603–629)

Underscores centrality of slavery and protectionism to Spanish colonialism during second half of 19th century. [JMH]

2006 Schnakenbourg, Christian. La compagnie sucrière de la Pointe-à-Pitre— E. Souques & Cie: histoire de l'usine Darboussier de 1867 à 1907. Paris: Harmattan, 1997. 303 p.: bibl., ill., maps.

With this work and titles indicated below, author has written important series of monographs describing growth of Guadeloupe's largest sugar factories as they adapted to free labor force and industrialization, and their decline when confronted with a world crisis. In-depth research shows major differences in company structure, ownership, strategy regarding sugarcane supply, labor, financing, and technological modernization. Cautious management allowed Blanchet to make profits until the Great Depression, first doubling sugar output in 1880s and then squeezing labor to cut costs in half in 1900s. The aggressive policy of the influential Souques family—which owned Beauport and acquired Darboussier—in purchasing cane from plantations, hiring labor, contracting loans, and establishing partnership with French manufacturers was successful until 1884, when both its companies were trapped in debt; they eventually collapsed during 1894–1900. Author stresses that French banks, by draining cash flow, prevented the Souques from making sufficient local investments. Author's other relevant works are included in *Bulletin de la Société d'histoire de la Guadeloupe*: "Histoire de Beauport au temps des Souques—1836–1901: recherche sur les causes de la chute des usiniers créoles en Guadeloupe au début du XXe siècle" (No. 115, 1998); and "La Compagnie Marseillaise de sucrière coloniale: histoire de l'usine Blanchet de 1860 à 1993" (No. 120, 1999). See also item **2007.** [APD]

2007 Schnakenbourg, Christian. La création des usines en Guadeloupe, 1843–1884: recherches sur la modernisation d'industrie sucrière antillaise après l'abolition de l'esclavage. (*Bull. Soc. hist. Guadeloupe*, 124/125, 2000, p. 21–115)

Superbly researched study by senior historian on momentous shift from sugar plantations to factories, which led to Guadeloupe's historic record of monoculture by 1880 (87 percent of exports, 60 percent land and labor force). Overall survey establishes chronology for technological innovations, creation of *centrales*, and concentration of sugar-producing estates. Discusses credit and legal framework. Stresses that innovation was a gradual process in which merchants and engineers from France were prominent. See also item **2006.** [APD]

2008 Schnakenbourg, Christian. Les déportés indochinois en Guadeloupe sous le Second Empire. (*Rev. fr. hist. Outremer*, 88:330/331, 2001, p. 205–208)

Discusses the 268 educated and politically organized men, deported from Indochina where they opposed French colonization, who came to Guadeloupe as indentured workers. See also item **2049.** [APD]

2009 Schoelcher, Victor. Des colonies françaises: abolition immédiate de l'esclavage. Préface par Lucien Abénon. Paris: Editions du C.T.H.S., 1998. 443 p.: bibl. (Format; 28)

Present work, and that reviewed in item **1958,** are reissues of classics of French abolitionist literature. All have good introductions by specialists. [APD]

2010 Schoelcher, Victor and S. Linstant Pradine. Contre le préjugé de couleur [par Victor Schoelcher]. Le legs de l'abbé Grégoire [par S. Linstant Pradine]. Introduction par Anne Girollet. Paris: Éditions du CTHS, 2001. 415 p.

See item **2009.**

2011 Senior, C.H. Asiatic cholera in Jamaica: 1850–1855. (*Jam. J.*, 26:2, Dec. 1997, p. 25–42, facsim., map, photos)

Points to deteriorating public health system plagued by inadequate financial resources as aiding the spread of cholera epidemic that claimed more than 13,000 lives. Failure to deal with a situation that affected the impoverished masses remained the norm during "the decade of neglect" following outbreaks. [ELC]

2012 Sheller, Mimi. The army of sufferers: peasant democracy in the early Republic of Haiti. (*NWIG*, 74:1/2, 2000, p. 33–55, bibl.)

Breaks new ground on Haitian political history. British consular dispatches throw new light on peasants' actions and ideas in the *Révolution des Piquets* (1843–44). Disproves view that descendants of slaves would have lacked skills to foster a democratic culture. "Living on in a popular vision of national liberty, civic fraternity and racial equality," they backed liberals in the fight against President Boyer's authoritarian rule. Sheller argues that only the government's inability to control the army, which it needed against the blockade imposed by Western powers, caused peasants' defeat. See also item **1975**. [APD]

2013 Sheller, Mimi. Democracy after slavery: black publics and peasant radicalism in Haiti and Jamaica. Gainesville: Univ. Press of Florida, 2000. 270 p.: bibl., ill., maps.

Important contribution to Haiti's often neglected 19th-century history. Based on archival and literary evidence from Haiti and Jamaica, argues that peasants in both countries developed similar "repertoires of resistance" in attempts to achieve greater democratic rights after emancipation. Also reveals previously unknown connections between 19th-century opposition groups in the two societies. [APD]

2014 Sheller, Mimi. The "Haitian fear": racial projects and competing reactions to the First Black Republic. (*in* Global color line: racial and ethnic inequality and struggle from a global perspective. Greenwich, Conn.: JAI Press, 1999, p. 285–303)

Describes how both disgust and admiration for Haiti helped create self-consciously "white" and "black" communities in 19th-century Atlantic world. Article is most important for exploring how early 19th-century black Jamaicans' sympathy for Haiti and desire for increased trade helped create "an emerging Afro-Caribbean identity." [JDG]

2015 Sheller, Mimi. Sword-bearing citizens: militarism and manhood in nineteenth-century Haiti. (*Plant. Soc. Am.*, 4:2/3, Fall 1997, p. 233–278, ill.)

Innovative reading of the symbolic construction of the Haitian nation in gender terms. Argues that "a militarized and masculine model of citizenship" still plagues Haiti today. Tracing rhetoric in official documents, newspapers, and political writings, author shows how a revolutionary republican tradition of armed egalitarianism was transposed into the heroic figure of rebel slave and black general. Highlights two postindependence mechanisms of female exclusion: rights to land based on participation in armed defense, and political network of Freemasonry. [APD]

2016 Shepherd, Verene. Indian migrant women and plantation labour in nineteenth- and twentieth-century Jamaica: gender perspectives. (*in* Women plantation workers: international experiences. Oxford, England; New York: Berg, 1998, p. 89–106, tables)

While admitting that female plantation workers used resistance modes similar to those of their male counterparts, author contends that landholders' preference for male laborers and their irrational belief in inefficiency of female workers led to gender-specific immigration policy that privileged males. Relegated to low-paying jobs, Indian women remained at bottom of socioeconomic ladder into early 20th century. See also item **1994**. [ELC]

Shepherd, Verene. Slavery without sugar in Caribbean plantation societies: examples from Jamaica. See item **1902**.

Simmonds, Lorna E. The health care of Jamaican urban slaves, 1780–1838. See item **1903**.

2017 Sorel, Julián B. Nacionalismo y revolución en Cuba, 1823–1998. Prólogo de Carlos Alberto Montaner. Madrid: Fundación Liberal José Martí, 1998. 187 p.

Sharp attack on revolution as a means of achieving Cuban greatness. Although written under a pseudonym, work deserves to be read for its well-reasoned arguments and documentation. [JMH]

2018 Stéhlé, Guy. Les monnaies utilisées dans les colonies françaises au XIXe siècle et leur équivalence en France de 1837–1840. (*Généal. hist. Caraïbe*, 131, nov. 2000, p. 3012–3016)

Annotated list of currency used in French colonial empire (Antilles, Bourbon, and Senegal) on eve of 1848 abolition, with rates of conversion in francs. [APD]

2019 Themistocleous, Rosalyn. L.D. Powles, Stipendiary Magistrate. (*J. Bahamas Hist. Soc.*, 19, Oct. 1997, p. 19–29, photos)

Case study of official who played a crucial role in regulating freedom in postemancipation Bahamas demonstrates the misconception, biases, and challenges that characterized tenure of important government officials. Excellent study of transition from slavery to freedom. [ELC]

2020 Thésée, Françoise. Le général Donzelot à la Martinique: vers la fin de l'Ancien Régime colonial, 1818–1826. Paris: Editions Karthala, 1997. 246 p., 8 p. of plates: bibl., ill.

Focuses on first appointed governor in Martinique following revolutionary wars. Shows how competent French officials were ultimately defeated in their efforts to curb white Creoles' exorbitant privileges, pushing disappointed free-coloreds and urban slaves to stage major upheavals in 1820s. [APD]

2021 Thibault-Bourrel, Agnès. L'église catholique en Guadeloupe après l'abolition de l'esclavage: une société sous tutelle cléricale?, 1848–1879. (*Bull. Soc. hist. Guadeloupe*, 112/113, 1997, p. 55–109)

Confirms previous studies on conservative evolution of Catholic Church in postslavery society, after ministering to enfranchised former slaves and supporting universal suffrage during the Second Republic. Church came to emphasize formal religious practices and monopoly on primary schools during Second Empire. Relevant comparison with Réunion. [APD]

2022 Tinker, Keith. The socio-economic and political impact of Barbadian migration to The Bahamas. (*J. Bahamas Hist. Soc.*, 21, Oct. 1999, p. 4–11, facsim., photo)

Barbadian migrants to Bahamas in late 19th-early 20th centuries served society well and filled important void as policemen, educators, medical practitioners, artisans, and casual workers. Eventually they also became involved politically and helped transform Bahamian society. Author has interviewed some migrants and also consulted traditional written sources. [ELC]

2023 Torres Oliver, Luis J. La masonería en el Puerto Rico de 1898. (*Bol. Acad. Puertorriq. Hist.*, 18:54, 1 de julio 1997, p. 109–133, bibl., facsims., graphs, photos)

Brief history of masons in Puerto Rico focuses on 19th-century developments. Includes list of Puerto Rican notables who were masons. [FMR]

2024 Vila Miranda, Carlos. España y la Armada en las guerras de Cuba. Gijón, Spain: Fundación Alvargonzález, 1998. 319 p.: bibl., ill., index, maps.

Account of Cuban wars of independence is worth reading because of military background of author, an admiral in the Spanish navy. His assessment of the Santiago naval battle is especially interesting. [JMH]

2025 Weck, Lucie. Histoire de la psychiatrie en Guadeloupe. (*Rev. Soc. fr. hist. hôp.*, 96:4, 1999, p. 25–29)

New research on a new subject: the development of psychiatric treatment in specialized hospitals in Guadeloupe from 1850–1950. [APD]

2026 Welch, Pedro L.V. From laissez-faire to disinterested benevolence: the social and economic context of mental health care in Barbados, 1870–1920. (*J. Caribb. Hist.*, 32:1/2, 1998, p. 121–144, bibl., tables)

Author locates mental health practice within socioeconomic factors that shaped access to health care system. Concludes that in postemancipation Barbados, unemployment and underemployment contributed to workers' dependency on state-funded health care system, and workers were thus "offered a psychiatric care that locked them further into a healh care system that, for all its apparent benevolence, was a creature of its Eurocentric past." [ELC]

2027 The white minority in the Caribbean. Edited by Howard Johnson and Karl S. Watson. Kingston: Ian Randle Publishers; Oxford, England: J. Currey Publishers; Princeton, N.J.: M. Wiener Publishers, 1998. 180 p.: bibl.

Seeking to reposition scholarly trend on nonwhite majority in Caribbean, excellent collection of essays reminds us of enduring legacy of whites despite their diminished political and economic power. Authors conclude that white minority was "significantly differentiated along class, gender, and ethnic lines, as well as by Creole or European origins and identity." [ELC]

2028 Wilmot, Swithin R. The politics of Samuel Clarke: black Creole politician in free Jamaica, 1851–1865. (*Caribb. Q./Mona*, 44:1/2, March/June 1998, p. 129–144, table)

Chronicles political activities of Clarke, a fearless spokesman for the black settler class, over 15-year crucial transitional period in island's political evolution. At Morant Bay planters eventually silenced Clarke and other such blacks whom they regarded as "loud mouthed demagogues." Excellent work. [ELC]

20TH CENTURY

2029 Ameringer, Charles D. The Cuban democratic experience: the auténtico years, 1944–1952. Gainesville: Univ. Press of Florida, 2000. 229 p.: bibl., index.

Certainly not the last word on this turbulent period of Cuba's history, but a solid and respectable approach to the problems of interpretation it poses. Scholarly and free from bias and political prejudice. [JMH]

El asesinato político en Puerto Rico. See item **1920.**

2030 Ashie-Nikoi, Edwina. Cohobblopot: Africanisms in Barbadian culture through the lens of Crop-Over. (*J. Caribb. Hist.*, 32:1/2, 1998, p. 82–120, bibl.)

Bemoaning historical intolerance of, if not opposition to, African culture in this British Caribbean colony, author sees introduction of Crop-Over festival after independence as both a countermovement to the Black Power movement and a belated reaffirmation of potency of African cultural retentions in Barbados. [ELC]

2031 Baggio, Kátia Gerab. O Partido Nacionalista de Porto Rico: debates e questões da historiografia. (*Varia Hist.*, 17, março 1997, p. 132–152, bibl.)

Excellent summary of historiographical debates surrounding figure of Pedro Albizu Campos and the Partido Nacionalista. Reviews position of most important authors regarding political-ideological stance of the party, the reasons for its defeat, alliances

with workers' movements, relations with other parties, role in the process of commonwealth status, choice of armed struggle, relationship with Catholicism and the Church, and so on. [TMV]

2032 Baptiste, Fitzroy Andre. Developments in African history and the African diaspora at The University of the West Indies (the UWI), 1968–1998: a personal odyssey. (*Caribb. Q./Mona*, 46:2, June 2000, p. 1–15)

Recalling his difficulties as outspoken crusader on behalf of African studies in curriculum of Univ. of the West Indies, author blames reactionary political directorates for roadblocks and noncooperation. Considers Cave Hill campus as being best positioned to advance cause of African studies within University's system. [ELC]

2033 Baralt, Guillermo A. Desde el mirador de Próspero: la vida de Luis A. Ferré. v. 1, 1904–1968. San Juan: Fundación El Nuevo Día, 1996. 1 v.: bibl., ill., map., ports.

Frankly adulatory commissioned biography of Luis Alberto Ferré, Puerto Rico's industrialist par excellence and untiring proponent of statehood. Places events in his life in contexts of time and place, thus providing a history of 20th-century Puerto Rico's politics and economy. Richly illustrated and handsomely presented. [TMV]

2034 Barbotin, Maurice. Marie-Galante en Guadeloupe, sa vie créole et son guide historique. Paris: Harmattan, 2001. 359 p.: ill., maps.

Rich evocation of Creole culture and way of life—from tools to beliefs. Especially detailed on artisanal fishing as practiced up to 1950s. Author's years as Marie-Galante's parish priest made him island's best anthropologist. [APD]

2035 Barros, Juanita de. "To milk or not to milk?": regulation of the milk industry in colonial Georgetown. (*J. Caribb. Hist.*, 31:1/2, 1997, p. 185–208, bibl.)

Argues that Indo-Guyanese attempted to earn living by hawking milk on Georgetown streets to growing migrant and emancipated population. But they struggled with authorities who were informed by racist and sanitarian discourse. These conflicts mirror larger ones between officials and other economic entities seeking space, as epitomized in 1924 riots. [ELC]

2036 Beccaria, Pierre. La réforme foncière en Guadeloupe, 1950–1994 ou l'expansion et le repli des domaines sucriers depuis la départementalisation sans mécanisation adaptée pour les minifondistes attributaires. (*Bull. Soc. hist. Guadeloupe*, 111, 1997, p. 51–103)

Comprehensive treatment of four decades of agrarian policy. Shows that land reform and technological modernization briefly succeeded in reversing a century of decline in sugar production. Emphasizes problems caused by Guadeloupe's integration into European Community in 1970s-80s: sugar industry finally collapsed, to be replaced by banana exports and fresh produce for local consumption. [APD]

2037 Bernabé, Rafael. Respuestas al colonialismo en la política puertorriqueña: 1899–1929. Río Piedras, P.R.: Ediciones Huracán; Decanato de Estudios Graduados e Investigación, Univ. de Puerto Rico, 1996. 320 p.: bibl.

Author intends to modify established view of Puerto Rican politics in first decades of 20th century, first proposed by Angel Quintero Rivera, as a "triangular struggle" between seigneurial landowners, modern sugar capitalists, and a recent proletariat. He asserts that the Partido Unión included in its ranks more than traditional sugar growers and that its more radical leaders were far from revolutionary. [TMV]

2038 Blancpain, François. Haïti et les Etats-Unis: 1915–1934; histoire d'une occupation. Préface de Frédéric Mauro. Paris: L'Harmattan, 1999. 381 p.: bibl.

Directs attention to a pivotal epoch in Haitian history. Provides wealth of information on specific incidents, although author may overestimate President Borno's success at curbing US economic and educational policy in defense of Haitian interests. See also item **2039**. [APD]

2039 Blancpain, François. Louis Borno, président d'Haïti. Port-au-Prince?: Editions Regain, 1998? 322 p.: bibl., ill.

Private papers kept by descendants illuminate neglected figure of Louis Borno, Haiti's president during US occupation. A distinguished lawyer, Borno began his politi-

cal career in reformist circles. See also item **2038**. [APD]

Blancpain, François. Un siècle de relations financières entre Haïti et la France, 1825–1922. See item **1925**.

Boutin, Raymond. Entrer dans la vie en Guadeloupe entre 1850 et 1946. See item **1928**.

Boutin, Raymond. La mort envisagée: notaires, testateurs et testaments en Guadeloupe entre 1849 et 1946. See item **1929**.

2040 Briggs, Laura. Puerto Rican reproduction and the mainland imaginary: the problem of *overpopulation* in the 1930s. (*Rev. Rev. Interam.*, 27:1/4, 1997, p. 79–92)

Brief, provocative reflection on origins of discourse of pathological sexuality and overpopulation regarding groups of color in US. Argues that ideological constructs that serve to this day to marginalize by class, gender, and race have their roots in the Puerto Rico of the 1930s and even earlier. [TMV]

2041 Cabán, Pedro A. El Consejo Ejecutivo y la "norteamericanización" de Puerto Rico. (*Temas/Habana*, 12/13, 1998, p. 82–95)

Author demonstrates role of the Executive Council, established by Foraker Act in 1900, in Americanization of Puerto Rican population. Focuses particularly on roles of local Departments of Education and the Interior, and of Attorney General's Office, in this process of Americanization, or colonizing mission as defined by author. For related book by the same author, see item **2042**. [FMR]

2042 Cabán, Pedro A. Constructing a colonial people: Puerto Rico and the United States, 1898–1932. Boulder, Colo.: Westview Press, 1999. 282 p.: bibl.

Comprehensive study of conditions in early-20th century Puerto Rico and of attempts to Americanize island's inhabitants. Based on a critical reading of relevant secondary literature, examines US colonial policy in context of reconfiguration of capitalism and construction of a national identity during Progressive Era. Author's insights point to advantages of applying to Puerto Rico the theoretical constructs made available by the literature on postcolonialism and globalization. See also item **2041**. [TMV]

2043 Cassá, Roberto. Los orígenes de Movimiento 14 de Junio. Santo Domingo: Editoria Universitaria, 1999. 370 p.: bibl. (La izquierda dominicana; 1) (Publicaciones de la Universidad Autónoma de Santo Domingo; v. 1, 925. Col. Historia y sociedad; 93)

Serious work about rise and fall of the Dominican left, which had been brought to life by Trujillo's dictatorship. [JMH]

Castro Arroyo, María de los Angeles. "¿A qué pelear si los de Madrid no quieren?": una versión criolla de la guerra del '98 en Puerto Rico. See item **1935**.

2044 Charles, Etzer. Le pouvoir politique en Haïti de 1957 à nos jours. Préface de Jean Ziegler. Paris: ACCT; Editions Karthala, 1994. 440 p.: bibl. (Col. Hommes et sociétés)

Best study in French on Duvalier dictatorship (1957–86) and difficult road toward democracy following its downfall. Presents anatomy of a populist and manipulative political system functioning behind a constitutional facade, and describes its methods of governance from propaganda to repression with militias and army as favorite instruments. [APD]

The Chinese in the West Indies, 1806–1995: a documentary history. See item **1936**.

Chivallon, Christine. Espace et identité à la Martinique: paysannerie des mornes et reconquête collective, 1840–1960. See item **1937**.

2045 Chomsky, Aviva. The aftermath of repression: race and nation in Cuba after 1912. (JILAS/Bundoora, 4:2, Dec. 1998, p. 1–40)

Traces reconceptualizations of notions of race and their relationship to ideas about citizenship and nation after the revolt of the Colored Independents (Partido Independiente de Color) in 1912 was crushed by the Cuban government. A scholarly study of a very complex situation. [JMH]

2046 Chomsky, Aviva. "Barbados or Canada?": race, immigration, and nation in early-twentieth-century Cuba. (HAHR, 80:3, Aug. 2000, p. 415–462)

Provocative study of Cuban anti-immigrant racism, although author fails to notice that West Indian immigrants always did their best to avoid repatriation from Cuba. [JMH]

The colonial Caribbean in transition: essays on Post-Emancipation social and cultural history. See item **1938**.

Cottias, Myriam. "L'oubli du passé" contre la "citoyenneté": troc et ressentiment à la Martinique, 1848–1946. See item **1940**.

Cubano, Astrid. Criollos ante el 98: la cambiante imagen del dominio español durante su crisis y caída en Puerto Rico, 1889–1899. See item **1944**.

2047 Deere, Carmen Diana. Here come the Yankees!: the rise and decline of United States colonies in Cuba, 1898–1930. (HAHR, 78:4, Nov. 1998, p. 729–765, map, tables)

Shows that North American movement to annex Cuba continued up through WWI, fueled by growing migration of US citizens to the island. A seminal article. [JMH]

2048 Désinor, Carlo A. Un siècle au quotidien. v. 1, Le pari impossible. Port-au-Prince: Edition du centenaire, 1998. 1 v.

History of Haiti's oldest and most important newspaper, Le Nouvelliste, founded in 1898, as told by its editor-in-chief. [APD]

2049 Donet-Vincent, Danielle. Les bagnes des Indochinois en Guyane, 1931–1963. (Rev. fr. hist. Outre-mer, 88:330/331, 2001, p. 209–221)

Rich documentation describes opening of second penal colony for political prisoners on the frontier region of Maroni amidst mounting campaign to close Devil's Island. Facility received 500 Indochinese opponents of French colonization. See also item **2008**. [APD]

2050 Dubois, Laurent. Haunting Delgrès. (Radic. Hist. Rev., 78, Fall 2000, p. 166–177)

Discusses recent dedication of various memorials in Guadeloupe and France to its leader Louis Delgrès, a high-ranking black officer in French revolutionary army who led the uprising against reestablishment of slavery in Guadeloupe in 1802. [APD]

2051 Dumont, Jacques. La Guadeloupe pittoresque de Léon Le Boucher: naissance de l'excursion. (Bull. Soc. hist. Guadeloupe, 112/113, 1997, p. 9–17)

Examines Le Boucher's collection of narratives of excursions undertaken by white Creoles and civil servants during late 19th century into Guadeloupe's volcanic mountains. Dumont shows that Le Boucher's anthology, prepared for 1937 colonial exhibition in Paris, reflects new mystique of reaching summits and conquering the hostile wilderness. [APD]

2052 Fombrun, Odette Roy. Ma vie en trois temps. Port-au-Prince?: Imprimerie Henri Deschamps, 1998. 380 p.

Member of enlightened and public-oriented mulatto middle class and one of the two women called to draft the 1987 Constitution recalls years of opposition to Duvalier regime and life in Port-au-Prince. [APD]

2053 Forte, Janette. Karikuri: the evolving relationship of the Karinya people of Guyana to gold mining. (*NWIG*, 73:1/2, 1999, p. 59–82, bibl., map)

Focusing on interplay between Karinya of Guyana's North West District and the intensifying gold mining activities in their homeland, asserts that core group of Karinya work alongside multinationals, Brazilian entrepreneurs, individual porkknockers, and local operations of varied size. As they lost their autonomy, an unequal relationship with outside world bordering on marginalization evolved. For ethnologist's comment, see *HLAS 59:865*. [ELC]

Franco, Franklin J. Sobre racismo y anti-haitianismo y otros ensayos. See *HLAS 59:5003*.

2054 Fraser, Cary. The *new frontier* of empire in the Caribbean: the transfer of power in British Guiana, 1961–1964. (*Int. Hist. Rev./Burnaby*, 22:3, Sept. 2000, p. 583–610)

Argues that British Imperial disengagement from Guyana at independence was managed by Anglo-American coalition. British created conditions for US control and constantly negotiated the country's relationship with US to ensure maintenance of mutual strategic partnership in the region. Hence, Guyana was emblematic of the "imperialism of decolonization." [ELC]

Fuente, Alejandro de la and **Laurence Glasco.** Are blacks "getting out of control?": racial attitudes, revolution, and political transition in Cuba. See *HLAS 59:5004*.

García, Gervasio Luis. El otro es uno: Puerto Rico en la mirada norteamericana de 1898. See item **1957.**

2055 García Muñiz, Humberto. Geopolítica y geohistoria en el discurso de Eric Williams sobre integración caribeña. (*Tierra Firme/Caracas*, 16:63, julio/sept. 1998, p. 411–421, bibl.)

Describes Williams' conception of geopolitics as formulated relating to the Caribbean. His conception attacked colonial divisions in area and US hegemonic ambition. Because his ideas were formulated and disseminated at beginning of nationalist period in Caribbean history, they encouraged study of Caribbean by academics. See also item **2073.** [ELC]

2056 García Muñiz, Humberto. Interregional transfer of biological technology in the Caribbean: the impact of Barbados' John R. Bovell's cane research on the Puerto Rican sugar industry, 1888–1920s. (*Rev. Mex. Caribe*, 2:3, 1997, p. 6–40, bibl., graph, map, tables)

Focuses on transfer of biological technology, mostly in sugar industry, within the Caribbean during early 20th century. Argues that Puerto Rico survived a crop disease because of Bovell's research which was imported from Barbados. [FMR]

2057 García-Pérez, Gladys Marel. Insurrection & revolution: armed struggle in Cuba, 1952–1959. Translated by Juan Ortega. Boulder, Colo.: Lynne Rienner Publishers, 1998. 151 p.: bibl., map. (Studies in Cuban history)

Maintains that rebellion against Batista was basically a reaction to local grievances that affected a wide cross-section of the social strata. Castro's revolution succeeded because of its ability to address these local issues. Work is history at a grassroots level based on archival research, oral sources, and a review of the provincial press. [JMH]

2058 *Généalogie et histoire de la Caraïbe*. No. 148, 2002, p. 3493–3523. Le Pecq, France: Généalogie de la Caraïbe.

Special issue on volcanic eruption of Montagne Pelée (1902) which destroyed Saint-Pierre, Martinique. A dozen letters, narratives, and testimonies are published for the first time, conveying fully the panic and trauma. Innovative joint effort to rescue historical documentation by private individuals, genealogical associations, and public archives. A website is available at *www.stpierre1902.org.* [APD]

2059 La Guadeloupe en zigzag: journal du gendarme à cheval Georges Bonnemaison, 1900–1903. Sous la direction de René Martin et Jacqueline Picard. Basse-Terre?: CARET; Le Gozier, 2001. 268 p.: photos.

Exemplary critical edition of memoirs by French policeman on his years in Guadeloupe, with original photos. Conveys curiosity of newcomer and his gradual familiarization with Creole culture, landscape, social mores, and economy. [APD]

2060 Guerra, Lillian. Popular expression and national identity in Puerto Rico: the struggle for self, community, and nation. Gainesville: Univ. Press of Florida, 1998. 332 p.: bibl.

Historical analysis of 20th-century appropriations of the *jíbaro* (peasant) myth and other popular-class constructions of identity for purpose of understanding how national culture is expressed and lived by groups who may have only historical memory to produce contradictory representations of their past. Convincingly shows that to this day "folkloric" sources tell stories of resistance to colonialism, of adaptation, and of refusal to collaborate in class oppression. [TMV]

2061 Haïti à la une: une anthologie de la presse haïtienne de 1724 à 1934. v. 6, 1931–1934. Port-au-Prince: Imprimeur II, 1997. 1 v.

Welcome addition to Desquiron's multivolume study of Haitian press. In years following US occupation, two themes dominated: growing tension with the Dominican Republic and cultural renaissance. For annotation of Vol. 1, see *HLAS 56:1827.* For annotation of Vols. 2–4, see *HLAS 58:1790.* [APD]

2062 Healy, Michael S. Colour, climate, and combat: the Caribbean Regiment in the Second World War. (*Int. Hist. Rev./ Burnaby,* 22:1, March 2000, p. 65–85, table)

Created through political necessity, Caribbean Regiment did not see military action because of racism within British military establishment. "Administrative difficulties" stemming from regiment members' desire for pay and promotion opportunities equal to those of their white counterparts reflected Britain's determination to discriminate against black colonial soldiers. Individuals enlisting separately were promoted along with whites. [ELC]

2063 Hispanofilia: arquitectura y vida en Puerto Rico, 1900–1950 = Hispanophilia: architecture and life in Puerto Rico, 1900–1950. Recopilación de Enrique Vivoni Farage y Silvia Curbelo Alvarez. San Juan: Editorial de la Univ. de Puerto Rico, 1998. 366 p.: bibl., ill. (Serie Dédalo arquitectura y vida; 2)

Handsomely illustrated collection of essays by well-known scholars, in both English and Spanish, on Spanish revivalism in architecture, language, music, art, dance, politics, and assorted cultural objects. Cutting-edge and provocative. See also item **2064.** [TMV]

2064 Hispanofilia: el revival español en la arquitectura y la vida en Puerto Rico, 1898–1950 = Hispanophilia: the Spanish revival in architecture and life in Puerto Rico, 1898–1950. San Juan: Archivo de Arquitectura y Construcción de la Univ. de Puerto Rico, Escuela de Arquitectura, 1997? 56 p.: ill. (some col.).

Catalog to art exhibition on Spanish revivalism in architecture which curator Enrique Vivoni Farage suggests captures cultural development of the Puerto Rican people during first 50 years of 20th century. This book is totally different from other *Hispanofilia* title (item **2063**): it is an accessible, illustrated narration of the changes in Puerto Rico's cultural life that resulted from the island's political and economic transformation after 1898. [TMV]

2065 Howard, David. Coloring the nation: race and ethnicity in the Dominican Republic. Oxford, England: Signal Books; Boulder, Colo.: L. Rienner Publishers, 2001. 227 p.: bibl., map.

Welcome addition to recent corpus on Dominican race issues and national identity. Based on about 300 interviews with Dominicans from a variety of class, racial, educational, and experiential backgrounds, author argues that racism and anti-Haitianism pervade Dominican society, in the island and abroad. Informed by latest research on race, ethnicity, and class, proposes multiculturalism as a popular democratic ideology that simply makes sense. The marginality of gender in his analysis reflects lack of awareness of patriarchy as an oppressive force in island society. [TMV]

2066 Howe, Glenford D. Military-civilian intercourse, prostitution and venereal disease among black West Indian soldiers during World War I. (*J. Caribb. Hist.*, 31:1/2, 1997, p. 88–102, bibl.)

Article beckons military historians to examine social aspects of war experience rather than narrowly limiting their discourse to guns, bombs, and military maneuvers. Shows how soldiers of British West Indies regiment expressed sexuality in overseas environments, and reveals health consequences of these relations especially with prostitutes. Considers social and political consequences of interracial relationships experienced by returned soldiers. See also item **2067**. [ELC]

2067 Howe, Glenford D. Military selection and civilian health: recruiting West Indians for World War I. (*Caribb. Q./Mona*, 44:3/4, Sept./Dec. 1998, p. 35–49, table)

Examines processes involved in selection of recruits, impact of recruitment on popular consciousness, and official policy regarding local health problems. Shows that a study of war can shed light on health conditions, diseases, and medical practices within the civilian population during particular historical periods. [ELC]

2068 Jeannopoulos, Peter C. Port-au-Prince en images = Images of Port-au-Prince. New York: Next Step Technologies, 2000. 102 p.: bibl., chiefly ill. (some col.).

Valuable source for urban history and history of postcard industry in Haiti. [APD]

2069 Jennings, Eric T. Monuments to Frenchness?: the memory of the Great War and the politics of Guadeloupe's identity, 1914–1945. (*Fr. Hist. Stud.*, 21:4, Fall 1998, p. 561–592)

Looks at WWI veterans' memorials erected in interwar period. Shows variety of styles and inspiration of monuments (purchased from metropolitan artists or local sculptors), and multiple meanings. Notes assertion of "Frenchness" with a subtle play between "religious and secular symbolisms." [APD]

2070 Johnson, Robert David. Anti-imperialism and the Good Neighbour Policy: Ernest Gruening and Puerto Rican

affairs, 1934–1939. (*J. Lat. Am. Stud.*, 29:1, Feb. 1997, p. 89–110)

Author places reformist experiment in Puerto Rico formulated by Ernest Gruening, Director of the Division of Territories and Islands Possessions, in context of Roosevelt's Good Neighbor Policy along with economic internationalism and political non-interventionism. By late 1930s Gruening's anti-imperialist schemes were replaced by more pressing issues of national defense, but failure of the plan stands as an example of difficulty of effecting change from above. For international relations specialist's comment, see *HLAS 59:4448*. [TMV]

2071 Jong, Lammert de. De werkvloer van het Koninkrijk: over de samenwerking van Nederland met de Nederlandse Antillen en Aruba [The shop floor of the kingdom: On cooperation between the Netherlands, the Netherlands Antilles and Aruba]. Amsterdam: Rozenberg, 2002. 267 p.: bibl.

Critical, well-written analysis of the relationship between the Netherlands and its Caribbean possessions in the 1980s and 1990s by Dutch civil servant. He identifies a number of major problems in this relationship, including the structural inequality between the partners, financial and economic difficulties, constitutional and administrative dilemmas, and shifting Dutch policy. Includes a reaction by the author's Antillean counterpart. [RH]

2072 Julia, Lucie. Gerty Archimède: fleur et perle de Guadeloupe. Pointe-a-Pitre, Guadeloupe: Editions Jasor, 1996. 117 p.: bibl., ill.

Lively account of Archimède's political career. A lawyer and leftist opponent to Vichy regime, and from a political family (black on maternal, white on paternal side), she was first female to represent Guadeloupe in French parliament (1946). [APD]

Karch, Cecilia and **Henderson Carter.** The rise of the phoenix: the Barbados Mutual Life Assurance Society in Caribbean economy and society, 1840–1990. See item **1968**.

Kiely, Ray. The politics of labour and development in Trinidad. See *HLAS 59:5021*.

2073 Knight, Franklin W. Eric Williams' inward hunger: the Caribbean as a microcosm of world history. (*Caribb. Q./Mona*, 45:1, March 1999, p. 78–94)

Interesting overview and analysis of ideas and writings of one of Caribbean's foremost thinkers and politicians who became first Prime Minister of Trinidad and Tobago. Author sees him as a humanist and socialist who constantly struggled, with changed emphases at times, against colonialism. See also item **2055**. [ELC]

Lafleur, Gérard. Les Libanais et les Syriens de Guadeloupe. See item **1969**.

2074 Lamei Xiongying: Zhongguoren Yanlide Qie Gewala [The Condor of Latin America: Che Guevara in the eyes of Chinese]. Edited by Bing'an Pang. Beijing: World Affairs Press, 2000. 269 p.: plates.

Collection of articles by 20 authors from diplomatic, press, and academic circles who had dealings with this figure in one way or another. Writers look at Guevara from different angles based on their own experience. Editor is former vice president of Xinhua News Agency of People's Republic of China. [Mao Xianglin]

2075 Lluch Vélez, Amalia. Luis Muñoz Marín: poesía, periodismo y revolución, 1915–1930. Santurce, P.R.: Univ. del Sagrado Corazón; San Juan?: Fundación Luis Muñoz Marín, 1999. 382 p.: bibl.

Biographical account of early writings—poems, short stories, and newspaper articles—of Luis Muñoz Marín. Through these writings author describes literary and political battles of Muñoz Marín between 1915–30. Also documents Muñoz Marín's involvement in movement against dictator Gómez in Venezuela. [FMR]

2076 López Rojas, Luis Alfredo. Luis Muñoz Marín y las estrategias del poder, 1936–1946. San Juan: Isla Negra Editores, 1998. 141 p.: bibl., ill. (Col. Visiones y cegueras)

Using Foucault's theoretical conceptualizations, analyzes power dynamics operating behind Muñoz Marín's rise to political prominence. Author claims that Muñoz Marín not only succeeded in reforming government in late 1930s, but also managed to create new utopian and totalizing power and knowledge structures that made the state a much more visible and palpable force in everyday life. [FMR]

2077 Loyola Vega, Oscar. La alternativa histórica de un '98 no consumado. (*Temas/Habana*, 12/13, 1998, p. 19–26, tables)

Brilliant reassessment of respective roles of autonomism and independentism at end of the colonial period, and of the political arrangement that prevailed in Cuba after 1902. [JMH]

2078 Luque, María Dolores. Los conflictos de la modernidad: la elite política en Puerto Rico, 1898–1904. (*Rev. Indias*, 57:211, sept./dic. 1997, p. 695–727)

The modernizing project carried out under US sponsorship in early 20th century had been developed previously by Puerto Rico's Creole elite. Not everyone benefited, however, as evidenced by economic ruin of coffee areas, migration of thousands of agricultural workers, and numerous labor strikes. Consequently a discourse of resistance developed around defense of the Spanish language, the Catholic religion, and Hispanic customs. [TMV]

2079 Lynch, Grayston L. Decision for disaster: betrayal at the Bay of Pigs. Washington: Brassey's, 1998. 187 p.: bibl., ill.

Account of Bay of Pigs fiasco by an American agent on the spot, who takes to task the pro-Kennedy chroniclers on the matter of how and why the invasion failed. [JMH]

2080 Marshall, Edwin Kenneth. Ontstaan en ontwikkeling van het Surinaams nationalisme: natievorming als opgave [Origin and development of Surinamese nationalism: the challenge of nation building]. Delft, Netherlands: Eburon, 2003. 336 p.: appendix, bibl., ill.

Dissertation examines the origins and institutional and ideological development of Creole nationalism in Suriname in the period between WWII and independence. Author explores the reactions to this movement and asks how it contributed to the country's independence and the process of nation building. He argues that the nationalists in Suriname focused on independence from the Netherlands and paid little attention to the aspect of nation building, as they had no plans, ideas, or concepts for the postindependence era. As a result, the nationalists lacked goals after independence was achieved in 1975. The next-to-last chapter compares the nationalist movement in Suriname with nationalism in the Anglophone Caribbean, particularly Jamaica, Trinidad, and Guyana. Includes brief summaries in English and Sranantongo. [RH]

2081 McCormick, Gordon H. Che Guevara: the legacy of a revolutionary man. *(World Policy J.,* 14:4, Winter 1997/98, p. 63–79)

Debatable but still sober view of Guevara's legacy, which sets work apart from the generally hagiographic literature on the controversial guerrilla. [JMH]

Meel, Peter. Tussen autonomie en onafhankelijkheid: Nederlands-Surinaamse betrekkingen 1954–1961 [Between autonomy and independence: Dutch-Surinamese relations, 1954–1961]. See *HLAS 59:3467.*

2082 Méphon, Harry P. Le premier sélectionné olympique guadeloupéen: Maurice Carlton. *(Bull. Soc. hist. Guadeloupe,* 124/125, 2000, p. 12–19)

Documents origins of Guadeloupe's contemporary track and field prowess through black athletes of period 1890s–1930s. Discusses emblematic figure of Carlton, a runner who won a 4th place at Berlin Olympic Games (1936). [APD]

2083 Milia, Monique. Del Caribe al Hexágono: la emigración martiniquesa en los años cincuenta/sesenta. *(Estud. Ibero-Am. /Porto Alegre,* 26:1, julho 2000, p. 53–65, bibl.)

Good introduction in Spanish on state-managed emigration from the Caribbean to France after 1950. [APD]

2084 Monteith, Kathleen E.A. Competitive advantages through colonialism: Barclays Bank (DCO) and the West Indian sugar depression, 1926–1939. *(J. Caribb. Hist.,* 31:1/2, 1997, p. 119–148, bibl., graphs, tables)

Barclays Bank's West Indian operations were adversely affected by sugar depression, as evidenced by decline in regional branches' profits and West Indian section's contributions to bank. Its recovery by 1933 stemmed from support bank received from British government through favorable loan guarantees and extension of imperial preferential tariff on colonial goods entering Britain. [ELC]

2085 Navarro Rivera, Pablo. Control político y protesta estudiantil en la Universidad de Puerto Rico, 1903–1952.

(Rev. Cienc. Soc. /Río Piedras, 8, enero 2000, p. 143–169, bibl., photos)

Analyzes reasons for the numerous political battles waged at Univ. de Puerto Rico during first half of 20th century. Most student protests of the period reacted against political intervention and government control imposed on the university. Also discusses colonial origins and mission of the institution. [FMR]

2086 Nicolas, Armand. Histoire de la Martinique. v. 3, De 1939 à 1971. Paris: L'Harmattan, 1998. 1 v.

Vol. 3 of general history written for a wide audience. Centers on Vichy authoritarian rule during WWII and the *loi de départementalisation* (1946) which raised great expectations but brought disappointing results, fostering endemic social protest and periodic violent riots in the ensuing decades. For annotation of vols. 1 and 2, see *HLAS 58:1811.* [APD]

Oquendo, Eli. Historia de una familia: los de Torres, de Adjuntas, siglos XVIII al XX. See item **1894.**

2087 El Palacio Nacional de la Républica Dominicana: 50 años de su historia y arquitectura. Textos de José Chez Checo, Emilio José Brea García y Denise Morales. Fotografías artísticas de Julio González. Santo Domingo: Secretaría Administrativa de la Presidencia, 1997. 445 p.: bibl., ill. (some col.).

Of interest to architects, this handsome volume documents construction of the 50-year-old Palacio Nacional. Several authors comment on interior and exterior design, most prominent features, and residents and visitors. [TMV]

2088 Paz Sánchez, Manuel de. Zona rebelde: la diplomacia española ante la revolución cubana, 1957–1960. Tenerife, Spain: Centro de la Cultura Popular Canaria, 1997. 401 p.: bibl., ill. (Taller de Historia; 22)

Recounts history of anti-Batista revolution based chiefly on dispatches of the Spanish ambassador to Cuba. Helps to clarify Franco's policy toward Castro's Cuba and gives some insight into predicament of the Church and evolution of US policy. [JMH]

2089 Pérez Guerra, Rafael. Historia de los taínos modernos: la verdad del arte lítico "Los Paredones" de La Caleta, Republica Dominicana, Ramón María Mosquea (Benyi). Santo Domingo: Taller, Juan Valle-nila, 1999. 270 p.: ports.

Study of Taino in 20th century, during what seems to be a period of cultural revival. [R. Haskett/S. Wood]

Picó, Fernando. Las construcciones de lo Español entre los militares norteamericanos en Puerto Rico, 1898–99. See item **1989.**

2090 Picó, Fernando. La revolución puerto-rriqueña de 1898: la necesidad de un nuevo paradigma para entender el 98 puertor-riqueño. (*Hist. Soc./Río Piedras*, 10, 1998, p. 7–22)

Advocates construction of new paradigms against which to place events in Puerto Rico following 1898 US invasion. Despite Spain's grant of autonomy to island in 1897, there was much resistance to Spanish rule from different socioeconomic sectors. With arrival of US troops, absence of Spanish state opened the floodgates of internal discontent. [TMV]

Política, identidad y pensamiento social en la República Dominicana, siglos XIX y XX. See item **1991.**

2091 Price, Richard. The convict and the colonel. Boston, Mass.: Beacon Press, 1998. 284 p.: bibl., ill. (some col.), maps.

Historically minded anthropologist writes the life story of Médard Aribot, a former Devil's Island convict who became a well-known sculptor back in his fishing community. In Médard's works, Price reads the circuitous paths taken as reflecting the legacy of slavery and colonial oppression. [APD]

2092 Puerto Rican jam: rethinking colonial-ism and nationalism. Edited by Frances Negrón-Muntaner and Ramón Gros-foguel. Minneapolis: Univ. of Minnesota Press, 1997. 303 p.: bibl., index.

Provocative collection of essays fueled by postmodern agenda. In incisive introduction, editors challenge usefulness of colonial/national dichotomy dominating political debate on the island, proposing instead the useful concept of ethno-nation—the nation without a state. Objective of the volume, then, is to generate new discursive strategies—perhaps around race, class, gender configuration—that can revitalize political alternatives. [TMV]

2093 Randall, Stephen J.; Graeme Stewart Mount; and David Bright. The Caribbean Basin: an international history. London; New York: Routledge, 1998. 220 p.: bibl., ill., index, maps. (The new international history series)

Useful study charts Caribbean basin's (including Central America and Caribbean coast of northern South America) transition from colonialism to independence during course of 20th century. Authors beautifully weave narrative of major European powers' involvement into larger fabric of region's political, social, and economic history. [ELC]

2094 Ranely Verge-Depre, Colette. Quinze années de conteneurisation de trafics maritimes aux Antilles françaises: éléments d'un bilan. (*Cah. Outre-Mer*, 50:198, avril/juin 1997, p. 151–170, bibl., graphs, ill., maps, photos, table)

Describes introduction of container shipping in the banana trade, which placed Guadeloupe and Martinique ports in the third rank among all French ports. [APD]

Reddock, Rhoda. The indentureship experience: India women in Trinidad and Tobago, 1845–1917. See item **1994.**

2095 Renda, Mary A. Taking Haiti: military occupation and the culture of U.S. imperialism, 1915–1940. Chapel Hill: Univ. of North Carolina Press, 2001. 414 p.: bibl., ill., map.

Theoretically informed cultural history of long US occupation of Haiti is based on impressive oral history research as well as analysis of soldiers' journals and published accounts of the occupation. Despite her research in Haiti and commitment to understanding Haitian perspectives on this period, Renda's greatest contribution is her analysis of experience of US soldiers in the occupation force. Students of Haitian/US cultural relations will find work reinforces interpretations of Plummer, *Haiti and the United States: the Psychological Moment* (1992); and Dash, *Haiti and the United States* (see *HLAS 58:1782*). [JDG]

2096 Reynal, Bertrand de. Les dessins de Jeanne: le regard d'une femme béké sur la vie de l'habitation à la Martinique dans les années 20. Le Gros Morne, Guadeloupe: Éditions Traces, 2001. 1 v.

More than 100 drawings, sketches, and

watercolors by women from Creole upper class bring unique testimony on life in Martinique in 1920s. Outstanding esthetics and editing. [APD]

2097 Rivera Pérez, Jaime Moisés. La Asociación de Católicos de Ponce, 1899–1915: una reacción al proceso de americanización. (*Hist. Soc./Río Piedras*, 10, 1998, p. 49–70, ill.)

Uses Asociación de Católicos de Ponce to peek into resistance to Americanization following 1898. This organization reacted to the American presence by celebrating Hispanic religious traditions such as cults of the Virgin and certain saints. Suggests there may be a link between this movement—more manifest in Ponce, the cradle of liberalism—and Pedro Albizu Campos' intense nationalism and Catholicism in 1930s. [TMV]

2098 Rodríguez Beruff, Jorge. La pugna entre dos grandes sistemas: la guerra en el discurso político de Luis Muñoz Marín hasta Pearl Harbor. (*Tiempo Espacio/Caracas*, 15:29/30, 1998, p. 193–229)

Analyzes Luis Muñoz Marín's political positions vis-à-vis US participation in WWII in light of his internal political calculations. Argues that Muñoz Marín linked his support for the war effort and island's militarization to future maneuvering room for his local political and social policies. [FMR]

Romero Valiente, Juan Manuel. La inmigración española en la República Dominicana en el tránsito de los siglos XIX-XX. See item **1999.**

Rosario Natal, Carmelo. Los pobres del 98 puertorriqueño: lo que le pasó a la gente. See item **2000.**

2099 Santamaría García, Antonio. Un problema, múltiples intereses y dos enfoques historiográficos: la crisis de 1920–1921 en Cuba. (*Rev. Mex. Caribe*, 4:8, 1999, p. 158–191, bibl., graphs, tables)

Well-researched critique of the oversimplified approach of Cuban historians to 1920–21 crisis and its impact on banking. [JMH]

2100 Santiago-Valles, Kelvin A. "Higher womanhood" among the "lower races": Julia McNair Henry in Puerto Rico and the "burdens" of 1898. (*Radic. Hist. Rev.*, 73, Winter 1999, p. 47–73, photos)

Provocative reading of writings of Julia McNair Henry, a turn-of-the-century social activist and wife of Puerto Rico's second military governor. Author places her among imperial travelers who surveyed land and people with the authority conferred on them by their race and country of origin. As such, she feminized and infantilized the "natives," and consequently, the author, suggests, engaged in an apparently contradictory splintering of her own gender. [TMV]

2101 Saunders, Gail. The changing face of Nassau: the impact of tourism on Bahamian society in the 1920s and 1930s. (*NWIG*, 71:1/2, 1997, p. 21–42)

To boost numbers of tourists, Bahamian authorities improved Nassau's infrastructure, including construction of business houses, hotels, and cinemas. Greater wealth among Nassau's small mercantile elite contrasted sharply with poverty of black majority, who experienced social problems like increasing crime and vagrancy. A reminder of tourism's adverse impact on indigenous Bahamian culture. [ELC]

2102 Saunders, Gail. Profiles of several outstanding Bahamian women. (*J. Bahamas Hist. Soc.*, 19, Oct. 1997, p. 44–52, photos)

Seeking to fill historiographical gap that has kept women largely invisible, author provides useful biographical data on four Bahamian women who excelled in their fields and made important local contributions. Their careers, mostly in 20th century, ranged from publishing, education, politics, and women's rights struggle to social work and art. [ELC]

2103 Scarano, Francisco A. Liberal pacts and hierarchies of rule: approaching the imperial transition in Cuba and Puerto Rico. (*HAHR*, 78:4, Nov. 1998, p. 583–601)

Following examination of common understandings of 1898 transition, presents novel, speculative proposition regarding changing terms of negotiation between imperial rulers and local elites. [TMV]

Schnakenbourg, Christian. La compagnie sucrière de la Pointe-à-Pitre—E. Souques & Cie: histoire de l'usine Darboussier de 1867 à 1907. See item **2006.**

Shepherd, Verene. Indian migrant women and plantation labour in nineteenth- and twentieth-century Jamaica: gender perspectives. See item **2016.**

2104 Simposio Internacional de Historiadores en torno al 1898, *San Juan, 1996.* 1898: enfoques y perspectivas. Recopilación de Luis E. González Vales. San Juan: Academia Puertorriqueña de la Historia, 1997. 463 p.: bibl.

Essays by well-known Puerto Rican historians, selected graduate students, and invited North American, Spanish, Cuban, and Filipino scholars cover diverse themes surrounding US occupation of Spanish overseas colonies: historiography, military history, history of ideas, diplomatic history, and post-1898 developments. [TMV]

Sorel, Julián B. Nacionalismo y revolución en Cuba, 1823–1998. See item **2017.**

2105 A spirit of dominance: cricket and nationalism in the West Indies; essays in honour of Viv Richards on the 21st anniversary of his test début. Edited by Hilary Beckles. Kingston: Canoe Press, 1998. 186 p.: bibl., ill.

Essays are revised texts of a public lecture series organized by Centre for Cricket Research at Univ. of the West Indies, Cave Hill. Taken together, essays show role of cricket in shaping West Indian consciousness and enhancing nationalism. Extremely useful for cricket enthusiasts and students of West Indian society. [ELC]

2106 Tabares del Real, José A. La política exterior del Presidente Grau: 1944–1948. (*Rev. Bimest. Cuba.,* 84:9, julio/dic. 1998, p. 156–172)

Article is noteworthy for recognizing that at least during certain periods, prerevolutionary Cuba was not as true a lackey of Yankee imperialism as Castro has said. [JMH]

Tinker, Keith. The socio-economic and political impact of Barbadian migration to The Bahamas. See item **2022.**

2107 Toledo, Josefina. Reinaldo Trilla Martínez, caballero de amorosa dignidad, luchador incansable. Prólogo de Rafael Cancel Miranda. San Juan: Centro Cultural Ramón Aboy Miranda, Casa Aboy, 1998. 110 p.: bibl., ill.

Short biography of pro-independence supporter and nationalist Reinaldo Trilla Martínez, who was also an avid supporter and militant of the Cuban Revolution. Includes letters, documents, and other sources. [FMR]

2108 Torreira Crespo, Ramón and **José Buajasán Marrawi.** Operación Peter Pan: un caso de guerra psicológica contra Cuba. La Habana: Editorial Política, 2000. 443 p.: bibl.

During this operation over 14,000 unaccompanied children were taken to US in early days of the Castro revolution. Since one author is a former officer of the Cuban state security forces and book's sources were supplied largely by that agency, it measures up to a Cuban government report and should be judged as such. [JMH]

Weck, Lucie. Histoire de la psychiatrie en Guadeloupe. See item **2025.**

Welch, Pedro L.V. From laissez-faire to disinterested benevolence: the social and economic context of mental health care in Barbados, 1870–1920. See item **2026.**

The white minority in the Caribbean. See item **2027.**

2109 Williamson, Charles T. The U.S. naval mission to Haiti, 1959–1963. Annapolis, Md.: Naval Institute Press, 1999. 394 p.: bibl., ill., index, map.

Drawing on rich documentation, former member of US naval mission sent at request of Haitian government to train military officers tells the story. Unusual window on Duvalier's domestic and international policy, particularly on the 1963 crisis which saw Duvalier expel the US mission and army officers stage an unsuccessful coup. For comment by international relations specialist, see *HLAS 59:4498.* [APD]

SPANISH SOUTH AMERICA
General

MICHAEL T. HAMERLY, *Special Project Librarian, John Carter Brown Library, Brown University*

2110 Al final del camino. Recopilación de Luis Millones y Moisés Lemlii. Lima: Fondo Editorial SIDEA, 1996. 201 p.: bibl., ill., tables.

Addresses how death has been viewed and dealt with in the Andes from prehispanic through recent times. A major contribution to an important topic neglected by Andeanists. Authors include anthropologists, archeologists, historians, and psychiatrists. Chapters by Ricardo Morales Gamarra, Clara López Beltrán, and Teresa Gisbert are especially interesting. [MTH]

2111 Argentina-Chile: 100 años de encuentros presidenciales; una historia fotográfica. Buenos Aires: Editorial Centro de Estudios Unión para la Nueva Mayoría, 1999. 183 p.

A photographic account of a century of meetings between the presidents of Argentina and Chile (1899–1999), accompanied by brief essays by historians, diplomats, lawyers, and politicians regarding the significance thereof. [MTH]

2112 Cuesta Domingo, Mariano. Pervivencia de modelos de exploración territorial tras la independencia de América del Sur. (*Arch. Ibero-Am.*, 57:225/226, 1997, p. 471–514, appendix, bibl., ill., maps)

A solid study of Franciscan explorations of southern Chile, northern Argentina, and especially eastern Peru during 19th century. Highlights remarkable geographic discoveries and considerable cartographic achievements, exemplified through well-reported illustrations of the Minor Friars in the Upper Amazon basin. [MTH]

2113 Hampe Martínez, Teodoro. De la pasión por los libros: Gabriel René Moreno y Mariano Felipe Paz Soldán; seis cartas. (*Rev. Chil. Hist. Geogr.*, 163, 1997, p. 7–33, appendix, bibl.)

An appreciation of pioneering labors of the Bolivian Moreno (1836–1908) and Peruvian Paz Soldán (1821–86), and examination of the correspondence between the two. Although Moreno's *Biblioteca boliviana* (1879) and Paz Soldán's *Biblioteca peruana* (1879) continue to be indispensable for research on colonial, independence, and early national periods of both countries. [MTH]

2114 Quiroz, Alfonso W. Back to basics: migration, labor, markets, and the state in colonial and postcolonial Andes. (*LARR*, 33:3, 1998, p. 248–256)

Review of recent monographic contributions in English to history of Ecuador, Peru, and Bolivia during colonial and early national periods, specifically of: 1) Andrien's *The Kingdom of Quito* (*HLAS 58:2188*); 2) Cornbit's *Power and Violence in the Colonial City* (*HLAS 56:2475*); 3) Hünefeldt's *Paying the Price of Freedom* (*HLAS 56:2786*); 4) Jacobsen's *Mirages of Transition: Ethnicity, Markets, and Migration in the Andes* (*HLAS 54:2744*); 5) Powers' *Andean Journeys* (*HLAS 56:2363*); and 6) Zulawski's *They Eat from Their Labor* (*HLAS 56:2487*). One of Quiroz's points cannot be overemphasized: the best studies of Andean historiography are rooted in regional realities (not imported theories or "mechanical adaptations" of exogenous paradigms) and those that avoid "the pitfalls of postmodern exaggerations." [MTH]

2115 Stacey de Valdivieso, Marcia. La polémica sangre de los Riofrío: la Casa de Riofrío en Segovia, Ecuador, Perú, Chile. Quito: M. Stacey Ch., 1997. 686 p.: appendix, ill., index.

A genealogical and biographical study of the Riofríos in Spain, Peru, Chile, and particularly Ecuador. Includes appendices on related members of the Borrero, Eguiguiren, Lequerica, Sánchez de Orellana, and Suárez families. Extensively researched. Rich in detail but desperately in need of onomastic index. A major contribution to the family history of Spanish South America. Part of the elusive series "S.A.G." (111 according to the title page; 112 according to a sticker on the front cover). [MTH]

Tabanera, Nuria; Joan del Alcázar; and Gonzalo Cáceres. Las primeras democratizaciones en América Latina: Argentina y Chile, 1880–1930. See item **951.**

Colonial Period

LANCE R. GRAHN, *Dean, College of Letters and Science and Professor, University of Wisconsin, Stevens-Point*
MICHAEL T. HAMERLY, *Special Project Librarian, John Carter Brown Library, Brown University*
S. ELIZABETH PENRY, *Assistant Professor of History, Fordham University*
SUSAN M. SOCOLOW, *Professor of History, Emory University*

GENERAL

JUDGING BY THE "GENERAL WORKS" on Spanish South America that have come to our attention during the last quinquennium, the production of specialized study after specialized study and of microhistory after microhistory continues unabated. Even the general works of overarching importance herewithin noted are themselves anthologies of specialized studies and/or microhistories, namely *Al final del camino*, which focuses on death or rather how the living have dealt with death in the Andean world (item **2110**), and *Saberes andinos*, which consists of seven essays on the inadequately known history of science and technology in Ecuador, Peru, and Bolivia (item **2122**). [MTH]

VENEZUELA AND NUEVA GRANADA

Guided still by the work of masters of their craft, some who continue to build an impressive legacy such as Tovar Pinzón (item **2163**) and Del Rey Fajardo, S.J. (item **2135**), and others like Colmenares, whose books remain a historiographical touchstone (items **2147** and **2148**), this biennial collection of current scholarship demonstrates noteworthy maturity and insight. Several publications tackle the complexity of interlocking power relationships that move beyond essential, but foundational, institutional histories to concentrate instead on their contested character. Ferrigni's important study of the late-colonial Venezuelan economy casts change as a broadly based rejection of colonial priorities (item **2126**). Assessments of *cabildo* influence and aspirations, such as those of Meza (item **2134**) and Guerrero Rincón (item **2153**) appropriately exhibit more concern for the mix of economic, social, and political conflict funneled through this crucial local body than for the council's governmental mechanics. Similarly, Uribe places legal education in late-colonial New Granada as a focal point in the battle between the state and its rivals for dominant sociopolitical influence (item **2164**). Foz y Foz also takes education as an analytical framework but uses it to examine the quest for gendered self-expression within the dialectic of faith and reason (item **2150**). Similarly, Troconis de Veracoechea complements solid but more traditional studies of the well-known

Venezuelan conspiracy of 1797 (see, for example, item **2132**) with her emphasis on Juaquina Sánchez de España, wife of the infamous rebel José María de España. Ramírez and Rodríguez shift the focus of conflict to the confrontation between the moralism of the patriarchal state and alleged sinfulness of quotidian life among the popular sectors (items **2136** and **2158** respectively), while still emphasizing the dynamic and multilayered nature of sociopolitical contestations.

Four other works merit special mention. Three books beautifully exhibit the power of artifacts and illustrations to both enliven a text and to substantiate an argument as text themselves: Vivas Pineda's *La aventura naval de la Compañía Guipuzcoana de Caracas* (item **2141**), Amodio's *El camino de los Españoles (HLAS 59:713)*, and Morales Folguera's *Tunja* (item **2157**). And Solórzano's *Se hizo señas* (item **2138**) presents an intriguing analysis of the societal construction and interpretation of time in 18th-century Caracas. [LRG]

QUITO

An exceptionally significant number of books and articles on the future of Ecuador appeared in the second half of the 1990s. The most important books are: 1) Büschges' *Familie, Ehre und Macht: Konzept und soziale Wirklichkeit des Adels in der Stadt Quito (Ecuador) während der späten Kolonialzeit, 1765–1822* (Stuttgart, 1996); fortunately, Büschges has been making his work available to those who do not read German in an ongoing series of revisionist, multifaceted articles in Spanish on the titled nobility of Quito during the late colonial and independence periods (represented in *HLAS 60* by items **2169, 2170, 2171**); 2) Jamieson's *Domestic Architecture and Power*, the first major study of the historical archeology of the country (item **2189**); 3) a set of documents on *oidor* Martínez de Arizala's important but forgotten *visita* of 1735–36 to Cuenca with a pithy introductory study by Paniagua Pérez, Ramos Gómez, and Ruigómez Gómez (item **2208**); and 4) Poloni-Simard's doctoral dissertation, *La mosaïque indienne*, a truly pioneering and revealing history of *indigenes* and mestizos in urban and rural Azuay and Cañar from the Spanish conquest through the late 1700s (item **2210**).

As for the articles, only a few salient points can be made in order to accommodate as many as possible of the growing number of worthwhile publications. Well-researched and written studies are being produced on a variety of topics that heretofore had received inadequate attention: the essays on domestic violence (item **2168**); the Caja Real de Quito during the first half of the colonial period (item **2172**); and nunneries (items **2207**), for example. New, novel studies have also appeared on places, periods, personages, and themes that have already been well worked. Exceptionally significant are: Aburto Cotrina and Newson's articles on the late and early colonial history of the Oriente (items **2165** and **2203**); Lane's piece on slavery in Quito and Popayán (item **2196**); León Borja de Szászdi's monograph on early Guayaquil (item **2198**); the five studies by Ramos Gómez and others on the *oidor* Martínez de Arizala and his *visita* (items **2215, 2216, 2217, 2218**, and **2219**); and Simard's splendid study of the demography and morphology of Santa Ana de los Ríos de Cuenca (item **2209**). [N.B. Jacques Poloni, Jacques Poloni-Simard, Jacques P.-Simard, and Jacques P. Simard are one and the same person.] The third and final point is that there has been a delay in receipt of recent issues of *Procesos* and other significant serials due to a serious arrearage at the Library of Congress. Once again, therefore, we will play catch up in *HLAS 62*.

Clearly what has long since been true for Peru now also holds for Ecuador. The quantity and quality of literature, especially, but hardly exclusively on the colonial period, has become nearly overwhelming. What is now needed is a one-volume history of the former Audiencia of Quito that pulls the new and recent work into a comprehensive whole. [MTH]

PERU

Two outstanding works considered here are the prize-winning *Colonial Habits* by Burns (item **2229**), and the seminal study by Mills, *Idolatry and its Enemies* (item **2263**). Burns' book (along with her 1998 *HAHR* article, item **2230**) makes two important and distinct contributions: first, it puts colonial nuns squarely in the center of Cuzqueña economic life; and second, it reveals the role of the convent in gendered dimensions of power. Mills' work moves beyond the simplistic dichotomous image of Andean religiosity as either resistance or complete conversion and instead focuses on "lived" religion. (For a similar perspective on the Charcas region, see Abercrombie's fine work on extirpation and idolatry (*HLAS 59:1040*).)

Many other praiseworthy studies also take religion as their focus. Hampe Martínez's article reviews much of this literature published in the 1990s (item **2249**). Castañeda Delgado's *La Inquisición de Lima* will surely serve as a standard reference on the Inquisition for years to come (item **2262**), and Muñoz Delaunoy's article complements this institutional history with a finely detailed case study of an Inquisition trial (item **2265**). The body of work by Van Deusen contributes to a deeper understanding of the institution of *recogimiento* and shows that it frequently served other purposes than religious functions (items **2286** and **2287**). Still in the vein of religion, but linking it more precisely to power, Ramírez makes a fine case illustrating how *curacas* used religion to maintain legitimacy in their communities (item **2276**).

Another noteworthy and ongoing trend is the interest in literacy and related issues of book and newspaper circulation, and readership. Clément's book-length study on the *Mercurio Peruano* is encyclopedic (item **2238**), while Peralta seeks to locate a change in reading habits that would underpin the independence movements (item **2273**). González Sánchez (items **2246** and **2247**) and Hampe Martínez (item **2250**) provide detailed information on books available to and held by colonials.

Rebellion continues to attract scholarly attention. O'Phelan, the dean of Andean rebellion studies, has produced a fine analysis of the transition from *curacas* to *alcaldes* (item **2269**). One of the major strengths of O'Phelan's work is that she considers regional rebellion as a whole rather than anachronistically separating "Bolivian" events from "Peruvian" ones. Sala i Vila investigates a similar issue as O'Phelan's latest work, the transition in authority in indigenous communities (see *HLAS 58:2335*). Much like O'Phelan, Sala i Vila sees the 1780 rebellions as pivotal events leading the Spanish state to force a change from hereditary *caciques* to elected *alcaldes*. Turning to an earlier period of rebellion, Jeremy Mumford's judicious review of Onqoy studies and the materials on which those studies are based, provides a much needed perspective (item **770**). A number of important primary sources have recently been published, among them are Anello Oliva's *Historia del reino y provincias del Perú* (item **2227**), Cantos de Andrade's *El señorío de Pachacamac* (item **2233**), Lanuza y Sotelo's *Viaje ilustrado a los reinos del Peru* (item **2257**), and the recently discovered third part of Cieza de León's monumental history of Peru (item **2237**). The late-18th- and early-19th centuries, the "middle period" integrated within the framework of this reference book, though not treated as a separate period, has produced major studies. In the rush to trace the transition to independence and nation-state formation, the 17th century has been left relatively un-studied, in spite of its clear centrality to the formation of Creole consciousness, the "crystallization" of colonial indigenous social formations in the wake of massive popular movements, indigenous religiosities, and the like. An important exception is Peru's version of Mexico's Gruzinski, the prolific and inventive Glave, whose *De Rosa y espinas* presents a vital addition to the study of baroque culture in the vein of history of mentalidades (item **2244**). [SEP]

CHARCAS

As Bolivian historian and former director of the Archivo y Biblioteca Nacional de Bolivia, Barnadas has pointed out, Bolivia was never officially referred to as Alto Peru during its colonial period. Instead, it was the Audiencia of Charcas. In keeping with the other headings for this section, it is appropriate to consider this area by its named government, Charcas. The most significant trend in the works under consideration here is the decisive shift from political economy to works in social and cultural history. In particular, younger scholars in Bolivia are turning to considerations of gender. Notable here is the support for publication provided by the Subsecretaria de Asuntos de Género of the national government. Three books reviewed in *HLAS 60* were produced as part of their series "Protagonistas de la Historia": *De indias a doñas* (item **2308**), *Mujeres en rebelión* (item **2294**), and *María Sisa y María Sosa* (item **2309**). Although these small books are clearly aimed at a broad audience in Bolivia, they are sufficiently scholarly to be of use to historians. Like *De indias a doñas*, Pentimalli, Albornoz, and Luján's *Mirar por su honra: matrimonio y divorcio en Cochamba, 1750–1825* draws from the still largely untapped riches of the municipal archives of Cochabamba (item **2310**). The other notable work that treats gender is Beltrán's long-awaited book based on her dissertation research, *Alianzas familiars: elite, género y negocios en La Paz* (item **2305**).

A very welcome trend is the continuing publication of primary sources. I have noted in the annotations for this chapter those works with documentary appendices. Two articles on Polo de Ondegardo with transcriptions are particularly important for early colonial scholars: "El encomendero Polo de Ondegardo" (item **2316**) and "Trabajadores forzados en el Cusco" (item **2300**). A work that will interest historians of popular culture, literacy, and issues related to independence is the slim volume *El pasquín en la independencia del Alto Perú* by Torrico Panozo, which brings together all the known protest broadsides issued in major towns (item **2315**). The single most important primary source to appear for many years is Alvarez's massive *De las costumbres y conversion de los indios del Perú*, a document that only recently came to light but is already being eagerly mined by scholars (item **2293**). The multivolume *Historia de Tarija*, the colonial portion of which was edited by Julien, makes accessible documents from American and European archives (item **2302**). Also significant among the published primary documents is the Spanish translation of du Biscay Acarete's travel diary (item **2291**). Finally, two outstanding books that treat both colonial and republican history should be noted, Abercrombie's *Pathways of Memory and Power* (item **655**) and the second edition of Larson's important work on the agrarian economy of Cochabamba (item **2303**). [SEP]

CHILE

Colonialists in Chile have been more productive than recent *Handbook* listings give us to understand. The late Jara, together with Mellafe, for example, gave us a major source group, *Portocolos de los escribanos de Santiago: primeros fragmentos, 1559 y 1564–1566* (Santiago de Chile: Dirección de Bibliotecas, Archivos y Museos, Centro de Investigaciones Diego Barros Arana, 1996; 2 v.; [Fuentes para el estudio de la Colonia; 3]), before his death and on his own a pithy summary and commentary upon several of his own contributions, *Nuestro hacer de la historia: de guerra y sociedad en Chile a El costo del imperio español, 1700–1810* (Santiago: Ediciones del Depto. de Estudios Humanísticos, Facultad de Ciencias Físicas y Matemáticas, Univ. de Chile, 1996).

Although there has been no lack of interest in 19th- and 20th-century Chile by North American scholars, no one in the US or Canada appears to be doing anything of significance on the colonial period. The late Della Flusche (1936–99) had been the only North American scholar publishing anything of importance on colonial Chile for some time. See, for example, her posthumously published, pioneering analysis of the records of the Juzgado de Bienes de Difuntos (item **2329**).

European scholars, on the other hand, have been somewhat more active as exemplified by the multiple contributions of Boccara (items **2322, 2323,** and **2324**). Even more important has been the impact of French scholarship and training on Chilean historians. Much of the work in question is either too new for coverage herewithin or came to our attention too late for inclusion this time around and therefore will have to wait until *HLAS 62*. In the meantime, see the two articles by Valenzuela annotated below (items **2340** and **2341**). [MTH]

RIO DE LA PLATA

While much of the historiography of colonial Buenos Aires is still centered on rural issues (items **2371, 2377, 2378, 2379, 2400, 2401**), a new generation of social history of regions other than Buenos Aires is beginning to appear (items **2354, 2391, 2398, 2399, 2402, 2411**). The new work coming from historians trained in Spain is also striking (items **2349, 2354, 2417,** and **2424**). While the interest in land continues, the Church in general, and the Jesuits and their aftermath in particular, is a growing field. There is also a developing ethnohistorical literature, and interestingly two books on the mission experience in the Chaco (items **2418** and **2424**). While the 18th century continues to produce the majority of the colonial literature, there is also new interest in the intellectual currents entering the region during first decade of the 19th century with the introduction of newspapers. [SMS]

GENERAL

2116 Andrien, Kenneth J. The *Noticias secretas de América* and the construction of a governing ideology for the Spanish American empire. (*Colon. Lat. Am. Rev.*, 7:2, Dec. 1998, p. 175–192, bibl.)

As Andrien convincingly argues, Juan's and Ulloa's *Noticias secretas* was predicated on an ideological bias: that government had gone astray in the colonies and that it had to be reformed. Especially important is Andrien's recovery of some of the colonial roots on which the Spanish reformers' discourse was based, including that of the Franciscan

mestizo Brother Calixto de San José Túpak Inka. [MTH]

2117 Areta Marigó, Gema. El barroco y sus máscaras: vida y sucesos de la monja alférez. (*Anu. Estud. Am.*, 56:1, enero/junio 1999, p. 241–252)

Fascinating article about that convoluted *personaje* Catalina de Erauso, whose autobiography recently appeared in English (see *HLAS 58:2122*). Incredible as it may seem, Catalina's story did not end with her disclosure in 1625. Five years later she returned to the New World, this time to Mexico where she spent her remaining years as

Antonio, a muleteer. See also item **2118**. [MTH]

2118 Castro Morales, Belén. Catalina de Erauso, la monja amazona. (*Rev. Crít. Lit. Latinoam.*, 26:52, 2000, p. 227–242) See item **2117** and *HLAS 58:2122*. [MTH]

2119 Klein, Herbert S. The American finances of the Spanish empire: royal income and expenditures in colonial Mexico, Peru, and Bolivia, 1680–1809. Albuquerque: Univ. of New Mexico Press, 1998. 221 p.: appendix, bibl., ill., index, maps.

Exceptionally important work adds appreciably to knowledge of royal fiscal and economic developments (in general) in New Spain and the Perus during late 17th, 18th, and early 19th centuries. Difficult to understand textually and tabularly at times, however. Also, the 65-page appendix, "Income-Producing Taxes by Type of Activity," is virtually useless as it lacks definitions of terminology and is inconsistent in use of abbreviations, which are nowhere spelled out. [MTH]

Loza, Carmen Beatriz. Du bon usage des *quipus* face à l' administration coloniale espagnole, 1550–1600. See item **749**.

2120 Lucena Salmoral, Manuel. El carimbo de los indios esclavos. (*Estud. Hist. Soc. Econ. Am.*, 14, enero/junio 1997, p. 125–133)

Reviews practice of facial branding of Indian slaves in Spanish America—a hideous custom even by standards of early modern period—with particular reference to Chile where the practice continued at least through middle colonial period, if not longer. [MTH]

Martín Rubio, María del Carmen. El mundo andino como paradigma de perseverancia en su ancestral cultura. See item **756**.

2121 Nocetti, Oscar R. and **Lucio B. Mir.** La disputa por la tierra: Tucumán, Río de la Plata y Chile, 1531–1822. Buenos Aires: Editorial Sudamericana, 1997. 331 p.: bibl., maps.

History of jurisdictional conflicts among the three major administrative units of southern Spanish America. [SMS]

2122 Saberes andinos: ciencia y tecnología en Bolivia, Ecuador y Perú. Recopilación de Marcos Cueto. Lima: Instituto de Estudios Peruanos, 1995. 213 p.: bibl., ill. (Serie Estudios históricos; 19)

Anthology of seven, largely original, mostly novel essays on various aspects of history of science and technology in the central Andean countries during colonial and national periods by Marcos Cueto, Suzanne Austin Alchon, Eduardo Estrella, Kendall W. Brown, Jorge Cañizares, Leonicio López-Ocón Cabrera, and Manuel Contreras. Especially interesting are the contribution by Cañizares on the ideology and thought of Hipólito Unanue, and Cueto's "Guía para la historia de la ciencia: archivos y bibliotecas en Lima." [MTH]

Saito, Akira. La conquista de la historia: la extirpación de la idolatría y la transformación de la conciencia histórica en los Andes. See item **808**.

VENEZUELA

2123 Academia Nacional de la Historia (Venezuela). Indice sobre esclavos y esclavitud: Sección Civiles-Esclavos. Recopilación y estudio preliminar por Carmen Torres Pantin. Coordinación de Marianela Ponce de Behrens. Caracas: Academia Nacional de la Historia, Depto. de Investigaciones Históricas, 1997. 445 p.: bibl., indexes. (Biblioteca de la Academia Nacional de la Historia. Serie Archivos y catálogos; 11)

Valuable research tool presents catalog of the Sección Civiles-Esclavos of the Archivo del Registro del Distrito Federal and some additional *expedientes* from the Cajas Negras now housed at the Academia Nacional de la Historia. Work also includes a bibliographic history of the documents covered in the catalog, and onomastic, geographical, and topical indexes. [LRG]

2124 Amodio, Emanuele. La tan apetecible profesión de médico: de Campins a Vargas; la constitución de la élite médica en Caracas, 1750–1850. (*Tierra Firme/Caracas*, 16:62, abril/junio 1998, p. 293–319, bibl.)

Overview of professionalization of the late colonial medical community in Caracas. This Enlightenment project began with successful efforts of Lorenzo Campins y Ballester in 1777 to establish both a medicine chair at the Univ. Pontificia de Caracas and a provincial *protomedicato*. The professionalizing impetus waned during independence era, but was revived in 1820s largely at urging of the physician and later prominent politician José María Vargas. [LRG]

Amodio, Emanuele; Rodrigo Navarete Sánchez; and Ana Cristina Rodríguez Yilo. El camino de los españoles: aproximaciones históricas y arqueológicas al Camino Real Caracas-La Guaira en la época colonial. See *HLAS 59:713.*

Bastidas Valecillos, Luis. Una mirada etnohistórica a las tierras indígenas de Mérida: época colonial. See item **675.**

2125 Celis Parra, Bernardo. Mérida ciudad de águilas. v. 1–2. Mérida, Venezuela: B. Celis Parra, 1997. 2 v.: bibl., ill. (some col.).

Encyclopedic history of Mérida celebrates city's past and its place in Venezuelan history. Vol. 1 concentrates on sociocultural history from precolumbian times through the independence era. Vol. 2 contains a worthwhile economic overview and a series of biographical sketches. [LRG]

Cuñarro Conde, Edith Mabel. El origen del liberalismo en Venezuela: el Acta del Cabildo Extraordinario realizado en la ciudad de Caracas, el 19 de abril de 1810. See item **4686.**

2126 Ferrigni Varela, Yoston. La crisis del régimen económico colonial en Venezuela, 1770–1830. v. 1. Transición económica y conflicto de intereses, 1770–1810. v. 2, Producción y comercio en época de guerra, 1810–1830. Caracas: Banco Central de Venezuela, 1999. 2 v.: bibl., ill., indexes. (Col. V centenario del encuentro entre dos mundos, 1492–1992, 1498–1998; 8)

Important study of late colonial-early national economic change that builds upon the earlier work of Germán Carrera Damas (see *HLAS 40:3348*) and the Equipo Sociohistórico del Centro de Estudio del Desarrollo (CENDES), Univ. Central de Venezuela. Argues that not only did Venezuela's agroexport economy crystallize in this period but that such development signaled a more important societal rejection of colonial patterns and policies. Contains valuable tables of agricultural production and commodity prices. [LRG]

2127 García de Cuevas, Gines. Fuentes documentales para el estudio de la conspiración de Juan Picornell, Manuel Gual y José María España, existentes en el Archivo

de la Academia Nacional de la Historia. (*Bol. Acad. Nac. Hist./Caracas,* 82:319, julio/sept. 1997, p. 23–79, appendix)

Useful bibliographic catalog of documentary sources that complements collection of essays (see item **2132**) on this famous 1797 conspiracy. [LRG]

2128 Hernández González, Manuel. Los canarios en la Venezuela colonial, 1670–1810. Tenerife, Spain: Centro de la Cultura Popular Canaria, 1999. 443 p.: bibl., map. (Taller de Historia; 25)

Survey of Canary Islanders who immigrated to colonial Venezuela, organized by Venezuelan region, provides yet another important resource for study of transatlantic migrations within Spanish Empire. Especially offers useful background for studies such as author's biography of the illustrious 18th-century figure Juan Perdomo Bethencourt (see item **2129**) and complementary works such as that of José Eliseo López's study of emigration (see item **2130**). [LRG]

2129 Hernández González, Manuel. Ciencia e Ilustración en Canarias y Venezuela: Juan Antonio Perdomo Bethencourt. Icod de los Vinos, Spain: Ayuntamiento de Icod de los Vinos; Tenerife, Spain: Centro de la Cultura Popular Canaria, 1997. 93 p.: bibl., ill.

Brief biography of noted physician is based on primary sources in Venezuela, Spain, the Canary Islands, and the US. Responsible for introducing smallpox vaccine into Venezuela in 1766 and instrumental in promoting French Enlightenment thought throughout the colony, Perdomo also illustrated connections between his Canary Islands homeland and Venezuela, and the cultural battle between forces of modernization (represented by growing influence of Enlightenment secularism and idealism) and tradition (represented especially by the Inquisition). See also item **2128**. [LRG]

2130 López, José Eliseo. La emigración desde la España penínsular a Venezuela en los siglos XVI, XVII y XVIII. v. 1–2. Caracas: Consejo de Desarrollo Científico y Humanístico; Biblioteca de Autores y Temas Mirandinos, 1999. 2 v.: bibl., ill., maps. (Biblioteca de autores y temas mirandinos; 68. Col. Francisco de Paula Alamo; 8–9)

Detailed annual catalog of immigrants from Spain to Venezuela supports generalization that the 16th century was a period of conquest, the 17th a time of evangelization and governance, and the 18th a century of evolving colonial maturity. Documentary sources and demographic statistics provide rich resources for social historians. See also item **2128.** [LRG]

2131 Mago de Chópite, Lila. La población de Caracas, 1754–1820: estructura y características. (*Anu. Estud. Am.*, 54:2, julio/dic. 1997, p. 511–541, graphs, tables)

Valuable examination of the parochial censuses of Caracas from 1772–1815 displays shifting short-term demographic patterns by neighborhood and ethnic-social group within an overall 40-year pattern of general stability. [LRG]

2132 Manuel Gual y José María España: valoración múltiple de la conspiración de La Guaira de 1797. Recopilación de Alí Enrique López Bohórquez. Caracas: Comisión Presidencial del Bicentenario de la Conspiración de Gual y España, 1997. 783 p.: bibl.

Extensive collection of previously published essays and excerpts covering pro-independence 1797 conspiracy led by Juan Bautista Picornell (1759–1825), Manuel Gual (1749–1800), José María España (1761–99), and Manuel Cortés de Campomanes (1777–1826). See also items **2127** and **2139.** [LRG]

2133 Méndez Salcedo, Ildefonso. La Real Compañía Guipuzcoana de Caracas: una relación biblio-hemerográfica comentada. Caracas: Fundación Polar, 1997. 83 p.: indexes.

Useful annotated bibliography organized by reference works, published primary sources, general histories, monographs, and articles and essays. Citations also include pieces in which Caracas Company is featured but not necessarily the central focus. Indexes by author or editor, titles, and topics enhance work's utility. [LRG]

2134 Meza, Robinzon and **Héctor Molina.** La lucha por el poder en Venezuela durante el siglo XVIII: conflictos y acuerdos del Cabildo de Caracas con las autoridades coloniales. Mérida, Venezuela: Fundación para el Desarrollo Cultural del Municipio Tovar; Grupo de Investigación sobre Historiografía de Venezuela, 1997. 137 p.: bibl.

Drawing mainly on archival sources, author clearly argues that developments within the Caracas cabildo illustrated the

battle for predominance between metropolitan policies and policymakers on one hand and colonial interests and economic evolution on the other. The 1810 rupture represented culminating victory of local elite interests over royal institutions, pretensions, representatives, and reforms. [LRG]

Ocampo López, Javier. Colombia en sus ideas. See item **4703.**

Parada Soto, Ana Isabel. Pueblos de Indios de la provincia de Mérida: su evolución, 1558–1657. See item **779.**

2135 Rey Fajardo, José del. Una utopía sofocada: reducciones jesuíticas en la Orinoquia. Caracas: Univ. Católica del Táchira; Univ. Católica Andrés Bello, 1998. 115 p.: ill. (some col.), maps (some col.).

Brief but informative and handsomely illustrated overview of 150-year history of Jesuit missions in eastern Venezuela by one of the country's leading Catholic scholars. Volume highlights issues treated in more detail in his *Introducción a la topohistoria misional jesuítica llanera y orinoquense* (*Paramillo*, 11/12, 1992/93, p. 92–227), and *Misiones jesuíticas en la Orinoquía* (see *HLAS 42:2753*), among other works. [LRG]

2136 Rodríguez, José Angel. Babilonia de pecados—: norma y transgresión en Venezuela, siglo XVIII. Caracas: Alfadil Ediciones; Univ. Central de Venezuela, Facultad de Humanidades y Educación; Comisión de Estudios de Postgrado, 1998. 219 p.: bibl. (Col. Trópicos; 60)

Plainly situated within an *annales* framework of analysis and based largely on data from archival sources in Spain and Venezuela, revised doctoral thesis aims to restore concept of human sinfulness, and so the reality of praxis, to the picture of late colonial Venezuelan society. Governmental and ecclesiastical efforts to curb sexual and other moral transgressions did reflect attempts to enforce social inequalities, but they also illustrated the falsity of an idealized society. [LRG]

2137 Rojas, Reinaldo. Parentesco y poder en Barquisimeto, provincia de Venezuela, 1530–1830. (*Rev. Hist. Am./México*, 120, julio/dic. 1995, p. 67–84, bibl., table)

Genealogical examination of elites of Barquisimeto who maintained and solidified their economic, political, and social power through family intermarriages. Parallels Vásquez's work (item **2140**). [LRG]

2138 Solórzano, Katty. Se hizo seña: medición y percepción del tiempo en el siglo XVIII caraqueño. Caracas: Planeta, 1998. 254 p.: bibl. (Premio de historia)

Prize-winning book examines structure and understanding of time in 18th-century Caracas. Arguing that time is a unique sociocultural construct of interlocking measurements, rhythms, perceptions, and symbols, author studies *caraqueño* time as determined by celestial movements, economic patterns, human aging and concomitant belief in eternity, and predominance of Catholic thought and influence. Examines ways in which human personality and psychological needs put all of this together in a social interpretation of temporal realities and past experiences. [LRG]

2139 Troconis de Veracoechea, Ermila. Doña Joaquina Sanchez de España. (*Bol. Acad. Nac. Hist./Caracas*, 82:319, julio/sept. 1997, p. 3–21, bibl.)

Biographical approach to famous Gual and España 1797 rebellion highlights latter's best ally, his wife Joaquina Sánchez de España, and the personally tragic impact of the conspiracy on all of the leaders' wives. See also items **2127** and **2132**. [LRG]

2140 Vásquez de Ferrer, Belín. Matrimonio, estatuto social y poder en la familia maracaibera de fines del antiguo régimen. (*Opción/Maracaibo*, 13:22, abril 1997, p. 5–26, bibl., table)

Using the Baralt-Sánchez family as a case study, article applies genealogical and prosopographical methodologies to an examination of rise of new elite families in late colonial Maracaibo. Matrimonial alliances were central to acquisition and maintenance of social status and power and to linkage of immigrant commercial interests and local Creole nobility. See also parallel study by Rojas, item **2137**. [LRG]

2141 Vivas Pineda, Gerardo. La aventura naval de la Compañía Guipuzcoana de Caracas. Caracas: Fundación Polar, 1998. 418 p.: bibl., col. ill.

Beautifully illustrated volume that more importantly provides a valuable maritime history of the Caracas Company. Sur-

veys cargos and commerce, ship crews, ship design and selection, ports, and maritime organization of the company. Concludes that company's maritime character reflected its self-sufficiency and its capacity for illegal activities. [LRG]

NUEVA GRANADA

2142 Aguilera Peña, Mario. La rebelión de los comuneros. Bogotá: Panamericana Editorial, 1998. 90 p.: appendix, bibl., ill.

Succinct overview of the Comunero Rebellion of 1781 and the role of social rebellion in making possible political revolution 30 years later. [LRG]

2143 Bohórquez M., Carmen L. El resguardo en la Nueva Granada: proteccionismo o despojo? Bogotá: Editorial Nueva América, 1997. 229 p.: appendices, bibl., ill., maps. (Antropología; 7)

Solid study of indigenous alienation and dependency with a Marxist bent by a French-trained historian. Rather than safeguarding indigenous communities, the institution of the *resguardo* effectively fragmented and dissolved them. An individualistic means-of-production structure was imposed, thereby facilitating Spanish domination as signaled by the central position of the Church therein. Includes a useful set of appendices. [LRG]

2144 Cabildos de la ciudad de San Juan de Pasto, 1561–1569. Recopilación de Emiliano Díaz del Castillo Zarama. Bogotá: Academia Colombiana de Historia, 1999. 378 p.: col. ill., indexes. (Biblioteca de historia nacional; 154)

Edited transcriptions of Libros de Cabildo de Pasto complements Díaz del Castillo's earlier transcriptions of the 1573–79 minutes of Pasto town council meetings (see *HLAS 58:2161*). Like the set of 1570s records, these documents from 1560s illustrate full range of municipal affairs. Appendices listing office holders and three indexes facilitate the use of this research tool. [LRG]

2145 Cartagena de Indias y su historia. Recopilación de Haroldo Calvo Stevenson y Adolfo Meisel Roca. Bogotá: Univ. Jorge Tadeo Lozano, Sección del Caribe; Banco de la República, 1998. 285 p.: bibl.

Published proceedings of 1997 conference on historiography of Cartagena de Indias from the 16th-20th centuries and documentary sources for subsequent research. This collection, which represents contributions of some of Colombia's best known historians, includes an engaging roundtable critique of the work of Eduardo Lemaitre and a useful annotated bibliography of 16th- and 17th-century Cartagena history. [LRG]

Casado Arboniés, Manuel. La primera contaduría ecuatoriana: la Caja Real de Quito en el siglo XVI. See item **2172.**

Casas Aguilar, Justo. Evangelio y colonización: una aproximación a la historia del Putumayo desde la época prehispánica a la colonización agropecuaria. See item **2494.**

2146 Castillo Mathieu, Nicolás del. Los gobernadores de Cartagena de Indias, 1504–1810. Prólogo de Rodolfo Segovia. Bogotá: Academia Colombiana de Historia, 1998. 191 p.: bibl., maps (some col.). (Biblioteca de historia nacional; 152)

Valuable reference tool dominated by encyclopedic descriptions of Cartagena governors. Also includes two edited documents related to the French expedition against the city in 1697 led by the Baron de Pointis. [LRG]

Chenu, Jeanne. De la médecine à la politique: Espejo et les Lumières en Nouvelle-Grenade. See item **2176.**

2147 Colmenares, Germán. Cali, terratenientes, mineros, y comerciantes, siglo XVIII. 4. ed. Bogotá: TM Editores, 1997. 187 p.: bibl., maps. (Biblioteca Germán Colmenares; 3)

Part of a series of re-editions of Colmenares' books, this work is latest publication of a now classic text by one of Colombia's very best historians (see *HLAS 40:3131*). Representing cutting-edge methodology and an impressive mastery of documentary sources, Colmenares models the best of socioeconomic and regional history in this examination of economic and societal development of Cali and its hinterlands. [LRG]

2148 Colmenares, Germán. La Provincia de Tunja en el Nuevo Reino de Granada: ensayo de historia social, 1539–1800. 3. ed. Bogotá?: Univ. del Valle; Banco de la República; Colciencias; TM Editores, 1997. 217 p.: bibl., ill. (Obra completa/ Germán Colmenares; 5)

Part of a series of republications of Colmenares' books, this work is latest edition of a classic text by one of Colombia's very best historians (see *HLAS 34:1148*). Rather than focusing on history of the city of Tunja per se, work examines reconstruction of indigenous society through colonial institutions of domination, notably the *resguardo*. Study remains a foundational text for the colonial history of New Granada. [LRG]

2149 Domínguez Ortega, Montserrat. Análisis metodológico de dos juicios de residencia en Nueva Granada: D. José Solís y Folch de Cardona y D. Pedro Messía de la Cerda, 1753–1773. (*Rev. Complut. Hist. Am.*, 25, 1999, p. 139–165)

Informative discussion of often conflictive process that characterized compilation of formal end-of-tenure reviews of viceroys José Solís Folch de Cardona (1753–61) and Pedro Messía de la Cerda (1761–73). While text of the reviews says much about emphases of viceregal rule and the Bourbon project in New Granada, the activities that produced those critiques highlight the mechanics of colonial administration and its imperial oversight. [LRG]

2150 Foz y Foz, Pilar. Mujer y educación en Colombia, siglos XVI-XIX: aportaciones del Colegio de la Enseñanza, 1783–1990. Bogotá: Academia Colombiana de Historia, 1997. 349 p., 8 p. of plates: bibl., ill. (some col.), index, maps. (Biblioteca de historia nacional; 148)

Despite title, this detailed and carefully documented book concentrates on second half of 18th century. Focusing on developments over 10- or 20-year periods during late Bourbon era, and using Clemencia de Caycedo (1710–79) as an exemplar, author demonstrates interlocking influences of faith and reason, of spirituality and learning, that provided an expanding, albeit still relatively limited, avenue for gendered self-expression and personal potential. [LRG]

2151 Garrido, Margarita. Entre el honor y la obediencia: prácticas de desacato en la Nueva Granada colonial. (*Hist. Soc./ Medellín*, 5, dic. 1998, p. 4–35, bibl., table)

Uses four of 103 cases of contempt or public disrespect of local officials found in Audiencia records to inquire into dynamic forces behind local political disrespect. Such factors include sociopolitical inequality, differing interpretations of rule of law and responsible citizenship, and competing perceptions of honor. [LRG]

2152 Guerra Curvelo, Weilder. La ranchería de las perlas del Cabo de la Vela, 1538–1550. (*Huellas/Barranquilla*, 49/50, abril/agosto 1997, p. 33–51, bibl., ill.)

Informative overview of the social and economic construction of the pearl industry in the Guajira peninsula. [LRG]

2153 Guerrero Rincón, Amado Antonio. El poder político local y la conformación de las élites regionales en la sociedad colonial: el caso de la gobernación de Girón en los siglos XVII y XVIII. (*Hist. Soc./Medellín*, 3, dic. 1996, p. 59–82, tables)

Careful and substantive study of cabildo of Girón highlights key role of local administration in both regional and colonial political developments as well as means by which local elites consolidated their dominance. [LRG]

2154 Gutiérrez de Pineda, Virginia and **Roberto Pineda Giraldo.** Miscegenación y cultura en la Colombia colonial, 1750–1810. v. 1–2. Bogotá: Ediciones Uniandes, 1999. 2 v.: appendices, bibl.

Encyclopedic treatment of miscegenation bolstered by illustrative censuses and documentary sources in the appendices. Vol. 1 concentrates on indigenous peoples and mestizos; Vol. 2 on Africans and mulattoes. Vol. 1 is arranged geographically as well as topically, covering both provinces and urban centers as well as issues such as the cultural and religious place of mestizos and indigenous peoples, economic patterns, and elements of identity. Vol. 2 presents topical overviews of mulatto and African life such as patterns of daily life, family structures, manumission, social mobility, and employment. [LRG]

2155 Gutiérrez Ramos, Jairo. El mayorazgo de Bogotá y el marquesado de San Jorge: riqueza, linaje, poder y honor en Santa Fé; 1538–1824. Bogotá: Instituto Colombiano de Cultura Hispánica, 1998. 154 p.: bibl., ill. (Ediciones de Cultura hispánica)

Prosopographical study of an elite Bogotá lineage whose wealth and status began with a 1538 encomienda granted to Antón de Olalla (one of Gonzalo Jiménez de Quesada's

soldiers) and culminated with the naming of Jorge Miguel Lozano de Peralta as the first *marqués* of San Jorge de Santafé de Bogotá in 1772. Solidly grounded and nicely illustrative examination of evolution, maintenance, and display of socially elite status in Spanish America. [LRG]

Jaramillo E., Luis Gonzalo. Guerra y canibalismo en el Valle del Río Cauca en la época de la conquista española. See item **731.**

Lane, Kris E. Captivity and redemption: aspects of slave life in early colonial Quito and Popayán. See item **2196.**

2156 McFarlane, Anthony. The state and the economy in late colonial and early republican Colombia. (*Ibero-Am. Arch.*, 23:1/2, 1997, p. 61–89, tables)

Study based on secondary sources demonstrates basic continuity in economic goals and policies in period 1770–1830. Colombian governments both before and after independence targeted economic growth through enlarging export markets and selective intervention in the domestic economy. The external efforts largely failed and so the republican governments of the 1830s-40s focused more on promoting domestic production. [LRG]

2157 Morales Folguera, José Miguel. Tunja: Atenas del Renacimiento en el Nuevo Reino de Granada. Prólogo de Antonio Bonet Correa. Málaga, Spain: Servicio de Publicaciones, Univ. de Málaga, 1998? 347 p.: bibl., ill., map.

Nicely illustrated study of artistic patrimony of Tunja by a noted art historian celebrates urban architecture of the city and the paintings housed within those buildings. His iconographic interpretation supports Juan de Castellano's 16th-century characterization of Tunja as an "American Athens." [LRG]

Múnera, Alfonso. El Caribe colombiano en la república andina: identidad y autonomía política en el siglo XIX. See item **2523.**

Peralta Barrera, Napoleón. El país de los muzos. See item **782.**

Quesada Vanegas, Gustavo Adolfo and **Patricia Illera Pacheco.** Filosofía del descubrimiento y la conquista en Colombia. See item **4704.**

2158 Ramírez, María Himelda. El género y el desorden en Santafé Colonial, 1750–1810. (*En Otras Palabras*, 5, junio 1998/enero 1999, p. 26–41, bibl., photos, tables)

Archival-based demonstration of how local political authorities viewed women, and immigrant poor women in particular, as threats to the social order of their urban ideal in Bogotá. For example, women involved in the manufacture and sale of chicha menaced the rule of law, public health, political authority, and moral behavior. [LRG]

2159 Restrepo Zea, Estela. La formación de la memoria: el Archivo de la Compañía de Jesús, 1767. (*Anu. Colomb. Hist. Soc. Cult.*, 24, 1997, p. 79–100, facsims.)

Overview of regulations within the Society of Jesus for keeping records, and consequent kinds of documents to be found in Jesuit archives at time of 1767 expulsion. [LRG]

2160 Rey Fajardo, José del. Las mentalidades en el nuevo reino: la Universidad Javeriana. v. 2, La biblioteca en 1767. Bogotá: Pontificia Univ. Javeriana; San Cristóbal, Colombia: Univ. Católica del Táchira, 1998. 1 v.: indexes.

Published before introductory first volume that will provide the context, this volume presents 1767 inventory of Javeriana's library collection which was completed as part of the Jesuit expulsion of that year. This important university catalog contains entries for more than 2,300 authors and over 3,100 titles, organized into 14 broad categories such as "Holy Fathers," "Theology," "Philosophy," and "History." Useful indices by title and author enhance catalog's usefulness. [LRG]

Roldán, Mary. Violencia, colonización y la geografía de la diferencia cultural en Colombia. See item **2536**.

2161 Romero Jaramillo, Dolcey. Esclavitud en la provincia de Santa Marta, 1791–1851. Santa Marta, Colombia: Fondo de Publicaciones de Autores Magdalenses, Instituto de Cultura y Turismo del Magdalena, 1997. 206 p.: bibl., ill., map.

Developed as part of an initiative to promote regional history of northern New Granada, this valuable study of slavery in a lesser-known province amplifies an understanding of commerce and labor dominated by the patterns in and around Cartagena de Indias. Beginning with the concession of Bourbon free trade in slaves to Santa Marta in 1791 until abolition of slavery in 1851, African labor failed to pull the colony out of relative poverty or exceed 10 percent of the provincial population. But the slave trade did more actively integrate Santa Marta into the Caribbean economy. [LRG]

2162 Santos Molano, Enrique. Antonio Nariño, filósofo revolucionario. Bogotá: Planeta, 1999. 595 p.: bibl. (Col. Biografías)

Careful biography of Antonio Nariño (1765–1823) driven by significant inclusion of documentary text, which places him squarely in the Enlightenment context of late colonial New Granada and numbers him among the revolutionary elite. Work emphasizes development and articulation of his political philosophy which clearly reflects his historical context. [LRG]

2163 Tovar Pinzón, Hermes. La estación del miedo o la desolación dispersa: el Caribe colombiano en el siglo XVI. Bogotá: Editorial Ariel, 1997. 256 p.: bibl., maps. (Ariel historia)

This important study of the Caribbean provinces of 16th-century New Granada by a premier Colombian historian, while not new in its emphasis on the conquest, dislocation, and resistance of indigenous peoples, is nonetheless impressive in its clarity and pointedness of argumentation, rich documentary foundations, and social analysis. Especially useful for understanding regional development of the encomienda out of the practice of ransom and reassertion of the importance, particularly economic, of coastal regions of Colombia in early history of the Spanish Empire. [LRG]

Tovar Pinzón, Hermes; Luis Enrique Rodríguez Baquero; and **Marta Herrera Angel.** Territorio, población y trabajo indígena: Provincia de Pamplona, siglo XVI. See item **824**.

2164 Uribe, Víctor M. Disputas entre estado y sociedad sobre la educación de los abogados a finales de la etapa colonial en la Nueva Granada. (*Hist. Soc./Medellín*, 3, dic. 1996, p. 33–57)

Solidly based study of political developments in late viceregal period as reflected in conflicts over the university training of lawyers. In both 1770s and 1790s, the state sought to assert some control over legal training, first to counter the influence of the Church and later to repress activism of young attorneys and law students. Efforts at secularizing legal education, however, largely stalled in tumultuous environment of late 18th century. [LRG]

Vanegas Munõz, Sayed Guillermo. Cuña del mismo palo: participación política de la élite muisca en las instituciones del Nuevo Reino de Granada, siglos XVII y XVIII. See item **829.**

Zambrano, Marta. Trabajo precioso, trabajadores despreciables: prácticas conflictivas y consenso epistémico en el discurso colonial. See item **835.**

QUITO

2165 Aburto Cotrina, Carlos Oswaldo. Régimen político y economía en un espacio fronterizo colonial: Mayas durante la segunda mitad del siglo XVIII. (*Histórica/Lima,* 20:1, julio 1996, p. 1–28, bibl., maps)

Drawing on research in Peru's Archivo Histórico de Límites, the author sketches a much more dynamic and fluid picture of what happened in the Governorship of Mayans after the expulsion of the Jesuits than had been depicted. Has much of interest to say on the less than successful efforts of Franciscans from Popayán to pick up the pieces and on the labor and proposals of Francisco Requena, the head of the Spanish Boundary Commission. Also examines commercial developments. Whets the appetite for more. [MTH]

2166 Aguila, Yves. Estrategias del discurso científico criollo: Espejo y Alzate. (*Jahrb. Gesch. Staat Wirtsch. Ges. Lat.am.,* 34, 1997, p. 245–257)

A comparative study of the scientific discourses of the "Ecuadorian" Eugenio Espejo (1747–95) and the "Mexican" Antonio Josef de Alzate (1737–99). See also items **2170, 2176, 2197,** and **2214.** [MTH]

2167 Altuna, Elena María. Ciencia, aventura y pública: La Condamine y los componentes de su relato de viaje al Ecuador. (*Colon. Lat. Am. Rev.,* 8:2, Dec. 1999, p. 207–224, bibl.)

An exercise in discourse analysis that reminds us that the travel literature of yesteryear, just like that of today, was/is being produced for a defined group of readers with certain expectations; therefore, accounts such as that of La Condamine have to be read as contrived, not spontaneous, exposition. Altuna, however, used a modern Spanish version instead of the final French version of La Condamine's *Relation abrégée d'un voyage fait dans l'intérieur de l'Amérique Méridionale* (1773), or at least a facsimile reprint thereof, thus negating at least in part the purpose of her analysis. [MTH]

Aráuz, Maritza. Pueblos de indios en la costa ecuatoriana: Jipijapa y Montecristi en la segunda mitad del siglo XVIII. See item **663.**

Arosemena, Guillermo. La historia empresarial del Ecuador. See *HLAS 59:1943.*

2168 Borchart de Moreno, Christiana Renate. Violencia cotidiana y de género en Quito a fines del siglo XVIII. (*Memoria/ Quito,* 7, 1999, p. 1–31, bibl.)

Pioneering study of domestic violence in Quito and its hinterland during second half of 18th century. Well researched, written, and analyzed. Exceptionally important contribution to limited literature on history of women in Ecuador during the colonial period. [MTH]

2169 Büschges, Christian. Entre el antiguo régimen y la modernidad: la nobleza quiteña y la Revolución de Quito, 1809–1812. (*CLAHR,* 8:2, Spring 1999, p. 133–151, map)

Well-informed review of the composition, political machinations, and failures of juntas of 1809 and 1810–12. Author places juntas in their social and ideological contexts and makes sense of both. He maintains that the nobility of Quito were neither patriots nor traitors, but conservatives and traditionalists who sought to enhance their position in local and regional society by attempting to achieve self-government dominated by themselves and their families, clients, and retainers, while they remained loyal subjects of the crown. Ultimately they were forced into declaring independence from the mother country. See also items **2170** and **2171.** [MTH]

2170 Büschges, Christian. Eugenio Espejo, la Ilustración y las élites. (*Jahrb. Gesch. Staat Wirtsch. Ges. Lat.am.*, 34, 1997, p. 259–275)

Argues convincingly that egalitarianism of the most radical of Quito's late-colonial period *pensadores* alienated majority of the titled nobility and other high-ranking members of local society. That someone like the Marqués de Villa Orellana, who was the official *consiliario* of the Univ. de Santo Tomás, was offended by Espejo is easy enough to understand. On the other hand, the reasons why the Marqués de Selva Alegre patronized and to some extent protected the mestizo medic remain to be elucidated. See also items **2166, 2169, 2171, 2176, 2197,** and **2214.** [MTH]

2171 Büschges, Christian. Linaje, patrimonio y prestigio: la nobleza titulada de la ciudad de Quito en el siglo XVIII. (*Anu. Estud. Am.*, 56:1, enero/junio 1999, p. 123–145)

Analyzes economic base, social status, lineage, and interrelationships of the 10 titled families of Quito during late-colonial period. One of Büschges' most significant points is that power base and influence of the nobility was regional (i.e., rooted in and limited to north-central highlands), not "national." This article, together with items **2169** and **2170,** are exceptionally important contributions to the social and economic historiography of the late-colonial and independence periods. [MTH]

2172 Casado Arboniés, Manuel. La primera contaduría ecuatoriana: la Caja Real de Quito en el siglo XVI. (*Memoria/Quito*, 6, 1998, p. 231–261)

Reports preliminary results of the Univ. de Alcalá project to reconstruct, publish, and analyze 16th- and 17th-century *cartas cuentas* of the royal treasuries of colonial Colombia and Ecuador. Insofar as the Caja Real de Quito is concerned, the Alcalá team has found utilizable fiscal data in the Archivo General de Indias and in Ecuador's Archivo Nacional de Historia for almost all of the 1500s and for most of the second, third, and fourth quarters of the 1600s. [MTH]

2173 Cazorla, Jorge Isaac. Fundación de la villa de San Miguel de Ibarra, siglo XVII: versión del acta de fundación, 1606 de la escritura paleográfica—letra procesal encadenada. Quito: Casa de la Cultura Ecuatoriana Benjamín Carrión, Fondo Editorial, 1997. 61 p.

Popular account of foundation of San Miguel de Ibarra in 1606 and a modernized version of Jorge A. Garcés' "paleographic translation" thereof with related period sources. Cazorla is a conservative Catholic with all the concomitant biases thereof. [MTH]

2174 Chaves, María Eugenia. Honor y libertad: discursos y recursos en la estrategia de libertad de una mujer esclava; Guayaquil a fines del periodo colonial. Göteborg, Sweden: Depto. de Historia e Instituto Iberoamericano de la Univ. de Gotemburgo, 2001. 311 p.: bibl. (Avhandlingar från Historiska institutionen i Göteborg; 26)

The author's doctoral dissertation, and her most detailed and sophisticated study to date, of female slavery in Guayaquil during late-colonial period. A major revision and expansion of her licentiate thesis (see item **2175**). English summary includes "Slave Women's Strategies for Freedom and the Late Spanish Colonial State," originally published in *Hidden Histories of Gender and State in Latin America* (see item **889**). Illuminates private life as well as public world of slaves. [MTH]

2175 Chaves, María Eugenia. María Chiquinquirá Díaz: una esclava del siglo XVIII; acerca de las identidades de amo y esclavo en el puerto colonial de Guayaquil. Guayaquil, Ecuador: Archivo Histórico del Guayas, 1998. 139 p.: bibl., ill. (Col. Guayaquil y el río; 7)

Multifaceted, sophisticated study of slavery in the port city during 18th century based on archival materials. Originally presented as author's licentiate thesis at the Pontificia Univ. Católica de Quito. Analyzes case of a slave of a local priest who sought freedom for herself and her daughter. Seeks to recreate both her private and her public world. See also item **2174.** [MTH]

2176 Chenu, Jeanne. De la médecine à la politique: Espejo et les Lumières en Nouvelle-Grenade. (*Jahrb. Gesch. Staat Wirtsch. Ges. Lat.am.*, 34, 1997, p. 213–228)

Restates that which is well known: that Espejo was current with the medical thinking of the times and that he advocated a much more active role for the state in matters of public health. See also items **2166, 2170, 2197,** and **2214.** [MTH]

2177 Costales, Piedad Peñaherrera de and **Alfredo Costales Samaniego.** La exploración de los Machutacas en el río Corino o Pastaza. Quito: Ediciones Abya-Yala, 1997. 50 p.: bibl., ill. (Tierra incognita; 25)

Publishes "in photocopy" and in transcript Pedro Fernández de Cevallos' account of his 1775 excursion into Canelos via the Río Pastaza. Also includes a poorly edited account of a mid-19th century exploration of the Pastaza. Zeballos (d. 1810), as he signed himself, was the paternal grandfather of the historian Pedro Fermín Cevallos. In-terestingly enough, in the introduction Costales and his late spouse do an ideological about-face from their usual stance: they side with the elite against the people, herewithin derogatively referred to as "la plebe." [MTH]

2178 Cuatro textos coloniales de quichua de la "Provincia de Quito." Estudio introductorio de Fernando Garcés. Quito?: Proyecto de Educación Bilingüe Intercultural, 1999. 266 p.: bibl.

Critical edition of four colonial-period grammars and vocabularies of "Ecuadorian" Quichua: 1) *Breve instrucción, o, arte para entender la lengua común de los indios según se habla en la Provincia de Quito* (Lima, 1753), attributed by some scholars to Tomás Nieto Polo del Aguila; 2) Juan de Velasco's 1787 *Vocabulario de la lengua indica,* finally published in 1964 (Quito: Instituto Ecuatoriano de Antropología y Geografía; Biblioteca Ecuatoriana Aurelio Espinosa Pólit); 3) the anonymous, undated but apparently 18th-century *Breve instruccion, o, Arte para entender la lengua comun de los indios,* originally published by Otakur J. Janota as *Španelská mluvnice jazyka peruán šého* in Prague in 1908; and 4) the anonymous, undated but 17th- or 18th-century, recently recovered *Arte de la lengua jeneral del Cusco llamada Quichua* published by Sabine Dedenbach-Salazar Sáenz as *Gramática colonial del quichua del Ecuador* (Bonn: Bonner Amerikanische Studien; St. Andrews, Scotland: Institute of Amerindian Studies, Univ. of St. Andrews, 1993). The "introductory study" constitutes a detailed, in-depth, but not always adequately grounded, analysis of

historic Quichua. Raises issues of the extent to which the grammars and vocabularies in question were based on earlier treatises of "Peruvian" Quechua. Maintains, for example, that Juan de Velasco's 1787 "Vocabulario B" is based on the anonymous 1586 *Arte y vocabulario en el Perú llamada Quichua, y en la lengua española,* incorrectly cited by Fernando Garcés as *Vocabulario y phrases de la lengua general de los indios del Perú llamada Quichua.* Includes a "reconstruction" of Velasco's lost "Vocabulario A" and a concordance of the four vocabularies. See also item **2186.** [MTH]

2179 Di Capua, Costanza. La luna y el Islam, la serpiente y el Inca: la semántica de la Inmaculada en España y su mensaje ulterior en la "Virgen de Quito." (*Memoria/Quito,* 7, 1999, p. 95–119, bibl., ill.)

Suggests that the "Virgen de Quito" was deliberately employed, if not conceived, by the Franciscans as a symbol of the triumph of Christianity and civilization over Andean paganism and barbarism, the defeated serpent being *amaru* and therefore Atahualpa. This could well have been the case. The Augustinians in the Perus also employed the Virgin of Copacabana as symbolic of the triumph of Christianity over indigenous beliefs and traditions. Therefore the Virgin Mary was not a postconquest manifestation of *mamapacha* in the northern Andes in all cases. [MTH]

2180 Estupiñán Viteri, Tamara. Diccionario básico del comercio colonial quiteño. Prólogo de Susana Cordero de Espinosa. Quito: Ediciones del Banco Central del Ecuador, 1997. 345 p. (Col. Fuentes documentales; 1)

A dictionary of some of the commercial terminology of the colonial period. Helpful, but a number of basic terms such as *balsa* and *carga* (nominally equivalent to 81 *libras,* at least in the case of cacao) do not appear. Not specific to Ecuador, or even to Andean region at large, inasmuch as Estupiñán Viteri apparently took her definitions at random from 1780 and later editions of the *Diccionario* of the Real Academia Española. [MTH]

2181 Estupiñán Viteri, Tamara. El mercado interno en la Audiencia de Quito. Quito: Ediciones del Banco Central del Ecuador, 1997. 224 p.: bibl., ill., map. (Biblioteca de historia económica; 7)

Reports results of Banco Central's potentially promising research project on commerce of Quito and north-central highlands during colonial period. Based on notarial records of financial transactions in the Archivo Histórico of the Banco and in the Archivo Nacional de Historia. Unfortunately, resultant time series are seriously flawed methodologically and analysis suffers from exceptional ignorance and ill-founded preconceptions notwithstanding author's professional training, thereby nullifying majority of her findings. [MTH]

2182 Fernández Rasines, Paloma. Cuerpos nombrados por la esclavitud: discontinuidades en la categorización racial y sexual en la Real Audiencia de Quito. (*Memoria/Quito*, 6, 1998, p. 177–192, bibl.)

Interesting essay makes an important point: that meaning and usage of "racial" and "sexual" terms in a society are not static but vary from time to time as well as from "class" to "class." Unfortunately, study is couched in not altogether intelligible qualitative discourse. [MTH]

2183 La fundación de Guayaquil: un tema controversial. Guayaquil, Ecuador: Archivo Histórico del Guayas, Banco Central del Ecuador, 1997. 138 p.: bibl. (Col. Guayaquil y el río; 1)

Anthology of articles and excerpts from books on the disputed foundation of Guayaquil. Includes the final conclusions of the late Julio Estrada Ycaza, previously divulged only locally. Estrada accepts Miguel Aspiazu's thesis that Santiago de Guayaquil was originally founded as Santiago de Quito on Aug. 15, 1534. Unfortunately, this potentially valuable compendium is marred by careless editing. [MTH]

2184 Garay Arellano, Ezio. Varios escritos históricos de Guayaquil y su provincia. Guayaquil: Archivo Histórico del Guayas, 1999. 289 p.: bibl., index. (Col. Guayaquil y el río; 10)

Anthology of previously published articles on indigenous peoples, mestizos, and blacks in heretofore unpublished enumerations of former Provincia de Guayaquil during colonial period. Garay works mostly from primary sources. Although he does not

always know how to analyze data, one may have confidence in his findings, dished up quasi-raw and therefore all the more valuable. Furthermore, Garay demonstrates that considerable data awaits the historian of the coast in the Archivo Histórico Arquidiocesano de la Curia de la Ciudad de Cuenca through his publication here of several late-colonial period *padrones* of the *poblaciones* of Santa Clara de Daule, Santa Rita de Babahoyo, and Santa Ana de Samborondón. [MTH]

2185 Guayaquil y el río: una relación secular. v. 1, 1555–1765. v. 2, 1767–1844. v. 3, 1844–1871. v. 4, 1876–1955. Guayaquil, Ecuador: Archivo Histórico del Guayas, 1997–98. 4 v.: bibl. (Col. Guayaquil y el río ; 3–6)

The most comprehensive anthology of coeval accounts of the port city yet compiled. Spans 1550s-1940s. Each volume opens with a set of "Notas Históricas" by Gómez Iturralde. Less useful that it could be, however, because editors are amateurs and autodidacts, well-meaning but inadequately grounded in editorial standards and procedures. [MTH]

2186 Hartmann, Roswith. Fuentes quechuas de la época colonial con referencia al Ecuador. (*Jahrb. Gesch. Staat Wirtsch. Ges. Lat.am.*, 34, 1997, p. 53–72)

Reviews handful of known grammars and vocabularies of Quichua or "Ecuadorian Quechua" from colonial period. Argues that recently published *Gramática colonial del quichua del Ecuador* (Bonn: Bonner Amerikanisische Studien; St. Andrews, Scotland: Institute of Amerindian Studies, Univ. of St. Andrews, 1993) dates from second quarter of 18th century at the earliest, not from 17th century as Dedenbach-Salazar Sáenz suggests. See also item **2178**. [MTH]

2187 Herzog, Tamar. Reglas jurídicas e integración social: el comercio; Quito, primera mitad del siglo XVIII. (*in* Congreso del Instituto Internacional de Historia del Derecho Indiano, *11th, Buenos Aires, 1995*. Actas y estudios. Buenos Aires: Instituto de Investigaciones de Historia del Derecho Indiano, 1997, v. 4, p. 379–396)

Data-rich analysis of how merchants interacted with one another in Quito during the first half of 18th century. The law was one thing, but family and business norms were quite another and usually preferred. Based on notarial records. [MTH]

2188 Hidalgo Nutri, Fernando. Reconstrucción de los antiguos paisajes forestales de la sierra norte del Ecuador. (*Memoria/Quito*, 6, 1998, p. 1–38, bibl.)

Pioneering attempt to reconstruct type and extent of forestation in highlands of provinces of Carchi, Imbabura, and Pichincha before and following Spanish conquest. Based on travelers' accounts, other published sources, and archival materials. [MTH]

2189 Jamieson, Ross William. Domestic architecture and power: the historical archaeology of colonial Ecuador. New York: Kluwer Academic/Plenum Publishers, 2000. 244 p.: bibl., ill., index. (Contributions to global historical archaeology)

Studies domestic architecture of Cuenca and its suburbs during the colonial period. This exciting and important book combines archival research and spade work "to examine the role of domestic architecture and domestic material culture"—significant aspects of daily life heretofore neglected in Andean studies—in one of the more traditional towns in South America. Neglects some details, including, for example, an inventory and map of all remaining colonial structures in and around the city, which are de rigor for this kind of work. But it must be remembered that this is a pathbreaking study as well as a first book. [MTH]

Jaramillo Cisneros, Hernán. El trabajo textil de Peguche. See *HLAS 59:1136*.

2190 Jibaja Rubio, Leopoldo. El ayer de un pueblo de la sierra, 1543–1950. Quito: Producciones Gráficas, 1999. 499 p.: bibl. (Col. Pueblos y gente de Carchi y Nariño; 1)

Detailed history of El Angel in the north highland province of Carachi from prehispanic times through recent present. Appears to be factually sound; especially strong on developments and events of 19th-20th centuries. About one-fourth is given over to "Genealogías de algunas familias de El Angel" (p. 387–480). Illustrations are poorly reproduced, however. [MTH]

2191 Jurado Noboa, Fernando. Las Peñas: historia de una identidad casi perdida, 1497–1997. Quito: Ediciones del Banco del Progreso, 1997. 320 p.: bibl., ill.

Not a historical study per se of the only traditional neighborhood left in Guayaquil (although it does contain some data on surviving late-19th—early-20th century houses in, and vicissitudes suffered by, the Barrio de las Peñas). Rather, work focuses on families and individuals who have lived there, some of them quite important in the history of Ecuador and almost of all them fascinating. Based on oral history as well as archival sources. [MTH]

2192 Jurado Noboa, Fernando. Quito secreto: historia documentada y desconocida sobre el orígen y el desarrollo de esta ciudad andina. Quito: Grupo Cinco, 1998. 308 p.: bibl., ill., maps. (Col. Amigos de la Genealogía; 135. Nuestra piel social; 10)

Another of Jurado Noboa's potboilers, this time on various aspects of history of Quito and of famous and infamous *quiteños* from the Incas through early 20th century. Rich in juicy tidbits served semicrude, with interesting but badly reproduced illustrations. Generally reliable on genealogy and biography, Jurado Noboa is not altogether sound on history however, inasmuch as he tends to accept all sources as equally reliable and valid. [MTH]

2193 Kennedy Troya, Alexandra. Circuitos artísticos interregionales: de Quito a Chile, siglos XVIII y XIX. (*Historia/Santiago*, 31, 1998, p. 87–111, facsim., photos)

Cogent review of production of paintings and sculptures in Quito for the Chilean market, and of Ecuadorian artists in Chile in 1700s-1800s. Ecuador was a principal purveyor of art to Chile during second half of colonial and early national periods. One of the more interesting questions explored is importance of art as an export. [MTH]

2194 Landázuri N., Cristóbal. Caciques coloniales y poderes locales: sierra norte del Ecuador. (*Memoria/Quito*, 7, 1999, p. 209–228, bibl.)

Case study of the changing role and declining importance of *kurakas* in the northern highlands. Proposes a chronology of developments vis-à-vis the exogenous state and the endogenous community. Well researched but not as detailed as one would like. Nonetheless, a significant contribution to the limited body of scholarly acceptable literature on history of ethnic lords in the Audiencia of Quito. [MTH]

2195 Lane, Kris E. Buccaneers and coastal defense in late-seventeenth-century Quito: the case of Barbacoas. (*CLAHR*, 6:2, Spring 1997, p. 143–173, maps)

Mostly novel essay on impact of pirate raids up and down the Pacific Coast of what are now southern Colombia (then part of the Audiencia of Quito), Ecuador, and northern Peru during 1680s-90s. Fortunately, some residents of the port cities affected were able to profit from the situation, especially as Quito was unable to succor anyone. [MTH]

2196 Lane, Kris E. Captivity and redemption: aspects of slave life in early colonial Quito and Popayán. (*Americas/Washington*, 57:2, Oct. 2000, p. 225–246)

Original, pioneering study details and illuminates multiple aspects of black slavery in city of Quito and district of Popayán during late 16th-early 17th centuries. Culled from earliest extant notary records in the Archivo Nacional de Historia in Quito. [MTH]

Lane, Kris E. Taming the master: *brujería*, slavery, and the *encomienda* in Barbacoas at the turn of the eighteenth century. See item **740.**

2197 Lavallé, Bernard. Para volver a Espejo. (*Jahrb. Gesch. Staat Wirtsch. Ges. Lat.am.*, 34, 1997, p. 209–211)

Pithy review of the state of historiography on Espejo as of 1995. Suggests that what are now needed are studies comparing his writings with those of his counterparts in Spanish America, and more studies of economic, social, and political developments and events in Quito during second half of 18th century, so as to be able to better appreciate and properly place the *pensador* and precursor in his time and space. See also items **2166, 2170, 2176,** and **2214.** [MTH]

2198 León Borja de Szászdi, Dora. La incautación de las salinas de Guayaquil por la Corona. (*in* Congreso del Instituto Internacional de Historia del Derecho Indiano, *11th, Buenos Aires, 1995. Actas y estudios.* Buenos Aires: Instituto de Investigaciones de

Historia del Derecho Indiano, 1997, v. 4, p. 397–418)

Original study of salt trade during second half of 16th century. Especially concerned with *salinas* of Puná and their quasi-monopolistic exploitation by Toribio de Castro. Significant contribution to economic history of Guayaquil and its district. [MTH]

2199 León Galarza, Natalia. La primera alianza: el matrimonio criollo; honor y violencia conyugal, Cuenca, 1750–1800. Quito: FLACSO, Sede Ecuador, 1997. 189 p.: bibl.

A pioneering MA thesis in history on concepts of women's honor, the "proper" role of women, marriage patterns, and spouse abuse among "whites" in Cuenca and its district during late-colonial period. Based on considerable research in ecclesiastical and other archives. An exceptionally important contribution to the history of women in Ecuador and the social history of Cuenca and the southern highlands. [MTH]

2200 Minguet, Charles. Alexandre de Humboldt et les amis d'Espejo à travers le journal inédit de son séjour en Equateur, en 1802. (*Jahrb. Gesch. Staat Wirtsch. Ges. Lat.am.*, 34, 1997, p. 277–284)

Focuses on importance as a historical source of the recently published journal of Humboldt's lengthy stay in the future Ecuador in 1802. Skeletal but important article demonstrates how much remains to be recovered on the late colonial and independence periods from such heretofore overlooked materials. [MTH]

2201 Morelli, Federica. Las reformas en Quito: la redistribución del poder y la consolidación de la jurisdicción municipal, 1765–1809. (*Jahrb. Gesch. Staat Wirtsch. Ges. Lat.am.*, 34, 1997, p. 183–207)

Argues that President Ramón García de León y Pizarro favored the local aristocracy over fiscal reform. Pizarro strengthened power of the local elite by delegating judicial authority within the former Corregimiento de Quito (abolished in 1781) to the *alcaldes* and their agents, the *jueces pedáneos.* In the process, the nobles of Quito gained even greater control over the countryside and indigenous labor. Morelli's findings suggest promising venues for further research on local developments, especially as they relate to the then-forthcoming movements for independence. [MTH]

2202 **Morgan, Ronald J.** "Just like Rosa": history and metaphor in the life of a seventeenth-century Peruvian saint. (*Biography/Honolulu*, 21:3, Summer 1998, p. 275–310)

Analysis of the Jesuit Jacinto Morán de Butrón's early 18th-century *La Azucena de Quito* (originally published in abridgement: Lima: J. de Contreras, 1702). Among other important findings is the deliberate comparison of the Lily of Quito to Rose of Lima by Mariana de Jesús' principal hagiographer. [MTH]

2203 **Newsom, Linda A.** Between Orellana and Acuña: a lost century in the history of the North-West Amazon. (*Bull. Inst. fr. étud. andin.*, 25:2, 1996, p. 203–231)

Reexamines the history of the Quijos region, following the uprising of 1578, utilizing new data from the Archivo General de Indias and the Jesuit archives in Rome on the several all-but-forgotten Spanish expeditions into the Coca, Aguarico, and Napo valleys between 1580–1636. Demonstrates that the Alonso de Miranda expeditions (1618–22) had an especially devastating impact on the populations of the Omaguas and the other ethnic groups because the *entradas* "disrupted existing social relations, enhanced intertribal warfare, and resulted in large numbers being enslaved or killed in conflict." [MTH]

2204 **Núñez Sánchez, Jorge.** La defensa del país de Quito. Quito: Ministerio de Defensa Nacional, Centro de Estudios Históricos del Ejército, 1999. 217 p.: appendix, ill. (some col.), map. (Biblioteca del ejército ecuatoriano; 16)

Of the several works reviewed in *HLAS* by this author, a professionally trained historian, this book on the defense of the Audiencia is the most important and best written. Mostly given over to a wholly original study of the organization, field actions (especially in the putting down of various rebellions of "Indians"), and "sociopolitical" structure of the militia of Quito as reorganized and augmented under the Bourbons. One of Núñez Sánchez's more interesting points is that events of Aug. 10, 1809, constituted a coup d'état; the local militia had developed

an esprit de corps of its own, notwithstanding its domination by the local elite. Includes a substantial appendix of documents on the state of the militia in 1788–90. [MTH]

2205 **Núñez Sánchez, Jorge.** Guayaquil: una ciudad colonial del trópico. Guayaquil, Ecuador: Archivo Histórico del Guayas, 1997. 174 p.: bibl. (Col. Guayaquil y el río; 2)

A curious work on various aspects of economic and social history of the port city during 18th-early 19th centuries. Reflects considerable research in the Archivo General de Indias but fails to take into account historical studies of other scholars on Guayaquil, studies of which, curiously enough, Núñez is fully aware. Therefore not nearly as complete or comprehensive an account as it could and should have been. Also, work lacks an introduction, conclusion, table of contents, and index. See also item **2206.** [MTH]

2206 **Núñez Sánchez, Jorge.** Historias del país de Quito: historia. Quito: Eskeletra Editorial, 1999. 263 p.: bibl. (Historia)

A potpourri of mostly novel articles on sundry aspects of, and various persons prominent in, the Audiencia of Quito. Written in a popular vein albeit footnoted and clearly based on original research in Spanish and Ecuadorian archives. Like author's work annotated in item **2205,** book lacks a table of contents and index, but at least has an introduction. While less substantial than they should be, the curious structure of both works becomes intelligible when one realizes that both originated as a series of newspaper articles. [MTH]

2207 **Paniagua Pérez, Jesús.** Las décadas iniciales del Monasterio de Santa Clara de Quito: reflejo de su medio, 1596–1640. (*Arch. Ibero-Am.*, 58:229, enero/abril 1998, p. 127–144)

A solid review of the origins of the Monasterio de Santa Clara de Quito. Delineates the foundation of the convent in 1596; examines finances of the convent during its first half-century; and discourses on nuns' life, their retainers, and their charges. Based on research in Archivo General de Indias (Seville), work is one of a series of studies by the author on history of cloistered orders of women in Ecuador. See also the review of his essay "Los inicios del monacato femenino en Quito: Mariana de Jesús" (*HLAS 58: 986*). [MTH]

2208 Paniagua Pérez, Jesús; Luis Javier Ramos Gómez; and Carmen Ruigómez Gómez. El proyecto reformista del oidor Pedro Martínez de Arizala, 1732–1748: consecuencia de su visita al Corregimiento de Cuenca. Cuenca, Ecuador: Instituto de Investigaciones de la Univ. de Cuenca, 1997. 319 p.: bibl.

This two-part study is a major contribution to the political economic history of the Corregimiento of Cuenca and to administrative history of the Audiencia of Quito and the Consejo de Indias under the early Bourbons. Pt. 1 is a terse analysis of the organization and undertaking of the *visita* of 1735–36 to Santa Ana de los Ríos de Cuenca and its *alfoz*—the first undertaken to any part of the Audiencia since 1685—and of the *visita's* antecedents and consequences. Pt. 2 transcribes the 82 primary sources, the originals of which are in the Archivo General de Indias, on which this and related studies are based (see items **2216** and **2219**). Almost impossible to obtain, these sources fortunately have been republished as *Documentos sobre la visita a Cuenca, Ecuador, del oidor Pedro Martínez de Arizala y su proyecto de reforma, 1726–1748* (Madrid: Fundación Histórica Tavera, 2000). [MTH]

Peralta A., Luz. La serie "Documentos de Jaén, Maynas y Chachapoyas 1776–1887" del Archivo Arzobispal de Lima. See item **2272.**

2209 Poloni-Simard, Jacques. Formación, desarrollo y configuración socio-étnica de una ciudad colonial: Cuenca, siglos XVI-XVIII. (*Anu. Estud. Am.*, 54:2, julio/dic. 1997, p. 413–445, maps, tables)

Splendid study of growth of Santa Ana de los Ríos de Cuenca and its population from city's foundation (in 1557) through late 18th century. Exceptionally rich economic and social data. Especially interesting is analysis of continuity and change in the ethnic makeup of the city by parishes and *barrios*. [MTH]

2210 Poloni-Simard, Jacques. La mosaique indienne: mobilité, stratification sociale et métissage dans le corregimiento de Cuenca, Equateur, du XVIe au XVIIIe siècle. Paris: Editions de l'Ecole des hautes etudes

en sciences sociales, 2000. 514 p.: bibl., ill., index, maps. (Civilisations et sociétés; 99)

Author's doctoral dissertation is a well written, solidly interpreted, extraordinarily detailed, exceptionally well researched, thoroughly documented study of indigenes and mestizos in what are now the provinces of Cañar and Azuay from 1533–1780. This work's importance for the historiography of the city and district of Cuenca cannot be overemphasized, inasmuch as it delineates and elucidates demographic, economic, and social events and developments for the first time, for the most part in the southern Ecuadorian Andes, during the time period studied. For ethnohistorian's comment, see item **788**. [MTH]

2211 Poloni-Simard, Jacques. Testamentos indígenas e indicadores de transformación de la sociedad indígena colonial: Cuenca, siglo XVII. (*in* Saberes y memorias en los Andes: in memoriam Thierry Saignes. Paris: Institut des hautes études de l'Amérique latine; Lima: Institut français d'études andines, 1997, p. 279–299, bibl., tables)

An exceptionally interesting article. Poloni-Simard analyzes a total of 171 last wills and testaments of indigenes in the Corregimiento of Cuenca from the 1600s to examine ways and means by which Andeans took advantage of economic changes to maintain, and in some cases improve, their socioeconomic situations. Demonstrates that middle colonial period was dynamic and flexible insofar as continuity and change in native society was concerned. See also *HLAS 57:1044.* [MTH]

2212 Ponce Leiva, Pilar. El poder del discurso o el discurso del poder: el criollismo quiteño en el siglo XVII. (*Procesos/Quito*, 10, 1997, p. 3–20, bibl.)

Thought-provoking analysis of writings of 17th-century *quiteños* and clerics Gaspar de Villarroel (who went on to become bishop of Santiago de Chile and archbishop of La Plata), Francisco Rodríguez Fernández, and Diego Rodríguez Docampo, regarding nature of New World society, rights and aspirations of *criollos*, role of the Church and Christianity, and the differences between Europeans and Andeans. A major contribution to the history of mentalities and philosophy of history of regional and local elite. See also item **2318.** [MTH]

2213 Ponce Leiva, Pilar. El poder informal: mujeres de Quito en el siglo XVII. (*Rev. Complut. Hist. Am.*, 23, 1997, p. 97–111, bibl.)

Novel essay on spouses of 17th-century members of the Cabildo de Quito as informal power brokers. They were linch-pins in marriage alliances and were some-times wealthier than their husbands. That is to say, some Spanish women were sought as spouses as much, if not more, for their dowries as for their relatives. However, the degree of influence that elite *quiteñas* exer-cised within their own and between allied families, and the extent to which they man-aged their own financial affairs, are only broached in this tantalizing piece. Hopefully these subjects are more fully answered in author's *Cartezas ante la incertidumbre: élite y Cabildo de Quito en el siglo XVII* (Quito: Ediciones Abya-Yala, 1998). [MTH]

2214 Potelet, Jeanine. Eugenio Espejo: la défense des indiens. (*Jahrb. Gesch. Staat Wirtsch. Ges. Lat.am.*, 34, 1997, p. 229–243)

Reexamines Espejo's denunciation of abuses committed against Andeans and his defense of their abilities in *pensador's Defensa de los curas de Riobamba* (1786). Con-cludes that Espejo believed education to have been the key to "the Indian problem." See also items **2166, 2170, 2176,** and **2197.** [MTH]

2215 Ramos Gómez, Luis Javier. Dos pare-ceres sobre el salario de los mitayos de Quito en 1735: el informe a la Audiencia de Martínez de Arizala, Visitador de Cuenca, y el parecer del fiscal Luján. (*Histórica/Lima*, 20:2, dic. 1996, p. 271–283, bibl.)

A well-researched article on the diver-gent views of two members of the Audiencia regarding the salary to be paid and treatment accorded *mitayos*. Luján, who was also the *protector de naturales*, argued in favor of the status quo and therefore against Martínez de Arizala's proposed reforms. [MTH]

2216 Ramos Gómez, Luis Javier. El escrito del visitador Martínez de Arizala a la Audiencia de Quito sobre la situación de los indígenas de Cuenca. (*in* Entre Puebla de Los Ángeles y Sevilla: estudios americanistas en homenaje al Dr. José Antonio Calderón Qui-jano. Recopilación de María Justina Sarabia

Viejo *et al.* Sevilla, Spain: Escuela de Estu-dios Hispano-Americanos de Sevilla: Univ. de Sevilla, 1997, p. 333–351)

Analyzes *oidor's* report of Sept. 21, 1735, on condition of indigenous peoples of city and district of Cuenca and his propos-als for alleviation of the abuses to which they were subject. See also items **2208** and **2219.** [MTH]

2217 Ramos Gómez, Luis Javier. La situación del indio de obraje en la ciudad de Quito según la visita realizada en 1743 por el Presidente José de Araujo. (*Rev. Esp. Antropol. Am.*, 28, 1998, p. 151–168, bibl.)

Able analysis of treatment of indige-nous labor in textile workshops of Quito in 1743 according to results of inspection un-dertaken by the president of the Audiencia. See also item **794.** [MTH]

2218 Ramos Gómez, Luis Javier and **Carmen Ruigómez Gómez.** La entrada en religión—1739—de Pedro Martínez de Arizala, oidor de la Audiencia de Quito, y sus consecuencias. (*Rev. Complut. Hist. Am.*, 22, 1996, p. 209–237, bibl.)

An exceptionally important article on an exceptionally important individual. Martínez de Arizala (d. 1755) was not only a judge of the Audiencia but was charged with inspection of the entire Presidency, the in-vestigation of President Araujo y Río, of the office of the presidency itself, and if that were not enough, an audit of the Caja Real de Quito, all at the same time. Martínez de Arizala's attempt to renounce his secular responsibilities for religious life was only partially successful. He still had to dis-charge some of his preexisting responsi-bilities. [MTH]

2219 Ramos Gómez, Luis Javier and **Carmen Ruigómez Gómez.** Una pro-puesta a la corona para extender la mita y el tributo a negros, mestizos y mulatos: Ecua-dor, 1735–1748. (*Rev. Complut. Hist. Am.*, 25, 1999, p. 99–110)

Although free blacks, mestizos, and mulattoes were legally subject to tribute and the *mita* since 1570s and early 1600s, respec-tively, very little tribute was ever collected from more than a few nonindigenous in Au-diencia of Quito and they never seem to have been conscripted for labor. Neither consideration stopped Martínez de Arizala from proposing that the *castas* be included in the tribute and *mita* rolls, but after review at Audiencia and Consejo de Indias levels, his reforms were shelved. See also items **2208** and **2216**. [MTH]

2220 Rappaport, Joanne and **Tom Cummins**. Between images and writing: the ritual of the king's *quillca*. (*Colon. Lat. Am. Rev.*, 7:1, June 1998, p. 7–32, bibl., ill.)

Putatively concerned with ethnic groups, especially Pastos, in northern highlands of Audiencia of Quito, a poorly written and ideologically tendentious article that obfuscates rather than elucidates Andean interpretations of community land records not just as textual but also as iconographic accounts. But see also Cummins' and Rappaport's "The Reconfiguration of Civic and Sacred Space: Architecture, Image, and Writing in the Colonial Northern Andes" (*Lat. Am. Lit. Rev.*, 26:52, July/Dec. 1998, p. 174–200) in which they employ as example the Muisca. A much better written and much more understandable piece. [MTH]

2221 Sevilla Larrea, Carmen. "...Y encaminé mi ánima en carrera de salvación": vida y muerte en la colonia temprana. (*Memoria/Quito*, 7, 1999, p. 121–134, bibl.)

A working paper on the mentality of Spanish inhabitants of San Francisco de Quito during second half of 16th century, especially insofar as burial beliefs and practices are concerned. Clearly written and well focused, but so tantalizingly brief as to leave the reader's appetite more whetted than satisfied. [MTH]

2222 Stolley, Karen. "Llegando a la primera mujer": Catalina de Jesús Herrera y la invención de una genealogía femenina en el Quito del siglo XVIII. (*Colon. Lat. Am. Rev.*, 9:2, Dec. 2000, p. 167–185, bibl.)

Analysis of "autobiography" of Catalina de Jesús María Herrera's *Secretos entre el alma y Dios* (1758–60), posthumously published nearly two centuries later by Alfonso A. Jerves as *Autobiografía de la Vble. Madre Sor Catalina de Jesús Ma. Herrera: religiosa de Coro del Monasterio de Santa Catalina de Quito* (1950, reprinted 1954). Born in Guayaquil in 1717, Sor Catalina de Jesús died in cloister sometime in 1790s. (The year of her death has been given variously as 1792, 1795, and 1796.) Useful introduction to the *mentalité* and cloistered life of Dominican nuns in Ecuador during the late colonial period. But Stolley's concluding paragraphs are overblown, being based on excessive importance she assigns to the slapdash entry on Herrera in Rodolfo Pérez Pimentel's not always reliable *Diccionario biográfico del Ecuador* (Guayaquil, Ecuador: Litografía e Imp. de la Univ. de Guayaquil, 1987). [MTH]

2223 Townsend, Camilla. "Half my body free, the other half enslaved": the politics of the slaves of Guayaquil at the end of the colonial era. (*Colon. Lat. Am. Rev.*, 7:1, June 1998, p. 105–128, bibl.)

Able analysis of political beliefs and active role assumed by some slaves in the port city in order to obtain their freedom during late colonial and independence periods. Townsend utilizes the case of Angela Batallas to exemplify and illuminate her points. Batallas even approached Simón Bolívar to intervene on behalf of her liberation. [MTH]

2224 Townsend, Camilla. Story without words: women and the creation of a mestizo people in Guayaquil, 1820–1835. (*Lat. Am. Perspect.*, 24:4, July 1997, p. 50–68, bibl.)

A somewhat disappointing essay. Townsend constructs a vivid, more or less valid albeit overly impressionistic, portrait of lower-class women in the port city during late colonial and independence periods, skillfully teased and woven together from a wide variety of sources. But she confuses becoming *guayaquileño* with becoming mestizo. Neither ethnic nor class differences disappeared in the urbanization process, although it was relatively easy for the indigenous to pass as mestizos in the port city or elsewhere on the coast. The real problem, however, is that Townsend nowhere addresses the issue of what it was/is to become mestizo. [MTH]

2225 Truhan, Deborah L. and **Jesús Paniagua Pérez**. Los portugueses en América: la ciudad de Cuenca del Perú, 1580–1640. (*Rev. Ciênc. Hist.*, 12, 1997, p. 201–220, map, tables)

Solid study of presence and activities of the Portuguese in Cuenca during the union of the two crowns. Based on intensive and extensive archival research, especially on the last wills and testaments of 22 Portuguese individuals who testified during the 61 years in question. An important contribution to the economic and social history of the city during the early colonial period. [MTH]

PERU

Abercrombie, Thomas Alan. Pathways of memory and power: ethnography and history among an Andean people. See item **655.**

2226 Aldana Rivera, Susana. No por la honra sino por el interés: piratas y comerciantes a fines del siglo XVII. (*Bol. Inst. Riva-Agüero,* 24, 1997, p. 15–44, bibl.)
Examines Lima merchants' reactions to pirate threats. [SEP]

2227 Anello Oliva, Giovanni. Historia del reino y provincias del Perú y vidas de los varones insignes de la Compañía de Jesús. Edición, prólogo y notas de Carlos M. Gálvez Peña. Lima: Pontificia Univ. Católica del Perú, Fondo Editorial, 1998. 387 p.: bibl., ill., indexes. (Col. Clásicos peruanos)
An Italian-born Jesuit, Anello Oliva came to Peru in 1597 and completed this history in 1630. A third of his manuscript treats the preconquest history of the Inca. The manuscript is from the British Museum Library (Additional Ms. # 25327). [SEP]

2228 Arrelucea Barrantes, Maribel. De curanderos y bandoleros: opciones del cimarronaje en la costa central; siglo XVIII. (*Rev. Arch. Gen. Nac./Lima,* 17, mayo 1998, p. 151–174, bibl., map, tables)
Drawing material from the Archivo General de la Nación in Lima, examines lives of two runaway slaves. One joined a *palenque*; the other became a healer in an indigenous community. [SEP]

Ayala Loayza, Juan Luis. Etnohistoria de Huancané. See item **672.**

2229 Burns, Kathryn. Colonial habits: convents and the spiritual economy of Cuzco, Peru. Durham, N.C.: Duke Univ. Press, 1999. 307 p.: bibl., ill., index, map.
Prize-winning, well-written study of the Convent of Santa Clara in Cuzco. Shows that nuns' economic dealings (especially loans) made them key actors in the colonial

city. See also item **2230,** reprinted here as a crucial chapter. [SEP]

2230 Burns, Kathryn. Gender and the politics of mestizaje: the Convent of Santa Clara in Cuzco, Peru. (*HAHR,* 78:1, Feb. 1998, p. 5–43, appendix)
Fascinating, prize-winning study of how the convent acculturated mestiza daughters in order to consolidate their encomendero fathers' wealth and position in Creole society in the first generations following conquest. See also item **2229.** [SEP]

2231 Cáceres, Eduardo. No hay tal lugar: utopía, ucronía e historia. (*in* Encuentro Internacional de Peruanistas, *1st, Lima, 1996.* Estado de los estudios histórico-sociales sobre el Perú a fines del siglo XX. Lima: UNESCO; Univ. de Lima; Fondo de Cultura Económica, 1998, v. 1, p. 285–295)
An analysis of Alberto Flores Galindo's *Buscando un inca* (see *HLAS 50:2212*), with comparison to Manuel Burga's similarly themed book, *El nacimiento de una utopía* (see *HLAS 52:586*). For the author, the key difference in the two works was Flores Galindo's recognition of a plurality of utopias, "que no había un proyecto, un contenido único, uniforme, sino un abanico de practicas." [SEP]

Cahill, David Patrick. After the fall: constructing Incan identity in late colonial Cuzco. See item **685.**

2232 Cahill, David Patrick. From rebellion to independence in the Andes: soundings from southern Peru, 1750–1830. Amsterdam: Aksant, 2002. 215 p.: bibl., index. (CEDLA Latin America studies; 89)
Collection of nine essays on social basis of politics in a time of transition. Articles were individually published between 1984–98, but places and dates of original publication are not given. First four essays cover social structures and social change. The next chapter considers methodological and theoretical problems, while the next three essays discuss insurrection and insurgency. The last contribution addresses the levels of mortality and material destruction attendant upon the Túpac Amaru rebellion. All essays are based on archival research in Cuzco and Seville. [R. Hoefte]

2233 Cantos de Andrade, Rodrígo. El
señorío de Pachacamac: el informe
de Rodrigo Cantos de Andrade de 1573. Recopilación de María Rostworoski de Diez
Canseco. Apuntes biográficos de Rodrigo
Cantos de Andrada por Carlos Gálvez Peña.
Versión paleográfica del documento por
Laura Gutiérrez Arbulú. Lima: Instituto de
Estudios Peruanos; Banco Central de Reserva
del Perú, Fondo Editorial, 1999. 238 p.: bibl.,
map. (Serie Fuentes e investigaciones para la
historia del Perú; 12)

Cantos de Andrade was a Toledan *visitador*; this work contains that report as well
as an investigation of accusations made
against local encomenderos by "their Indians" that they had not been properly evangelizing them. Document is from the
Archivo Nacional de Santiago de Chile.
Wonderful detail; testimony from indigenous witnesses born prior to the Spanish
invasion. [SEP]

2234 Carcelén Reluz, Carlos. Las doctrinas
de Chaclla-Huarochirí en los siglos
XVI y XVII. (*Rev. Andin.*, 16:1, primer semestre 1998, p. 99–118, bibl.)

Based on series of cases, convincingly
argues that most complaints against parish
priests made by indigenous Andeans were
based on priests' religious conduct (i.e., refusal to administer sacraments) rather than
economic abuse. Concludes that by mid-17th
century the teachings of Catholicism had
been internalized so that, no matter what
their origins, grievances were expressed in
the language of faith. [SEP]

2235 Caro López, Ceferino. Las minas del
Perú, concubinas de los ambiciosos:
la crítica moralizadora de la conquista de
América. (*Anu. Estud. Am.*, 55:2, julio/dic.
1998, p. 441–458)

Golden Age Spanish literature cri-
tiqued the conquest through two stock characters: the noble savage and the cynical *indiano*. The *indiano* (rich returned Spaniards)
revealed the negative impact on Spain of the
wealth coming from America. [SEP]

Chang-Rodríguez, Raquel. Hidden messages:
representation and resistance in Andean colonial drama. See item **3358.**

2236 Charney, Paul. A sense of belonging:
colonial Indian *cofradías* and ethnicity in the Valley of Lima, Peru.

(*Americas/Washington*, 54:3, Jan. 1998,
p. 379–407, tables)

Builds on thesis of Olinda Celestino
and Albert Meyers (see *HLAS 44:1579* and
HLAS 46:1604), which holds that *cofradías*
had an ethnogenic function. Much valuable
information here, but little analysis. [SEP]

2237 Cieza de León, Pedro de. The discovery and conquest of Peru: chronicles of
the New World encounter. Edited and translated by Alexandra Parma Cook and Noble
David Cook. Durham, N.C.: Duke Univ.
Press, 1998. 501 p.: bibl., ill., index, maps.
(Latin America in translation/en traduc-
ción/em tradução)

First English translation of Pt. 3 of the
history written by "the prince of Peruvian
chroniclers." The complete manuscript was
discovered in the Vatican library in the
1970s. Highly detailed, important account
of the conquest. Excellent introduction and
translation by Noble David Cook and
Alexandra Parma Cook. For review of Spanish edition, see *HLAS 50:610.* [SEP]

2238 Clément, Jean-Pierre. El Mercurio Pe-
ruano, 1790–1795. v. 1, Estudio. v. 2,
Antología. Frankfurt: Vervuert; Madrid:
Iberoamericana, 1997–98. 2 v.: bibl., indexes.
(Textos y estudios coloniales y de la indepen-
dencia; 2–3)

Detailed study of the mental world
(*mentalité*) of Creole *limeños* through analysis of the newspaper *El Mercurio Peruano*,
the first modern newspaper of the viceroyalty. Fascinating, accessible account considers how the newspaper circulated, who the
readers were, the types of articles, and specific use of language during the era (*nación,
patria*). [SEP]

2239 Cosamalón Aguilar, Jesús A. Indios
detrás de la muralla: matrimonios indígenas y convivencia inter-racial en Santa
Ana; Lima, 1795–1820. Lima: Pontificia
Univ. Católica del Perú, 1999. 273 p. (some
folded): bibl., ill., col. maps.

Through creative use of matrimonial
records, analyzes indigenous-black relations.
The records, housed in the Archivo Arzobispal de Lima, indicate that those to be married
were required to provide witnesses to attest
to their single state. Through the witnesses,
identified by race, occupation, and their relationship to the affianced, author is able to

trace informal networks of affiliation, demonstrating that colonial society was much more integrated than is contemporary Lima. A well-documented, well-written study. [SEP]

2240 Domínguez Faura, Nicanor. Crónica personal sobre los archivos de Huancavelica. *(Rev. Arch. Gen. Nac./Lima, 17, mayo 1998, p. 25–35)*

Description of the contents of the Archivo de la Municipalidad Provincial and the Archivo de la Sub-prefectura of Huancavelica. Includes addresses, phone numbers. [SEP]

2241 Duhart Mendiboure, Carmen G. Vida cotidiana y órdenes religiosas en el siglo XVIII: el caso de los agustinos en el Virreinato del Peru. *(Anu. Hist. Iglesia Chile, 16, 1998, p. 21–38)*

Quantitative and qualitative study of Augustinians in what are now Peru and Chile during second half of 18th century. Especially concerned with day-to-day life led by the friars within the walls of their monasteries. Refreshing, nonhagiographic, and remarkably free from jargon. [MTH]

2242 Escobedo Mansilla, Ronald. Las comunidades indígenas y la economía colonial peruana. Bilbao, Spain: Servicio Editorial, Univ. del País Vasco, 1997. 231 p.: bibl.

Focused on early colonial period. Little attempt to link indigenous and Creole economic activities. No treatment of mita, or mining industry; only two pages on labor in *obrajes*. More concerned with land issues. [SEP]

Espinoza Soriano, Waldemar. Trabajadores forzados en el Cusco, La Paz, y Potosí en 1550: una información inédita de Juan Polo de Ondegardo. See item **2300.**

2243 Gareis, Iris. La enfermedad de los dioses: las epidemias del siglo XVI en el virreinato del Perú. *(Bulletin/Geneva, 61, 1997, p. 83–90, bibl.)*

Taking evidence from Jesuit accounts, argues that Andeans understood diseases as a punishment from their gods, thus revealing the strength of those gods. Although not noted by the author, great similarity to European interpretation of disease. [SEP]

Gates Chávez, Carlos. La historia inédita de los chachapoyas: descendientes de los constructores de la fortaleza de Kuélap. See item **712.**

2244 Glave Testino, Luis Miguel. De Rosa y espinas: economía, sociedad y mentalidades andinas, siglo XVII. Lima: Instituto de Estudios Peruanos; Banco Central de Reserva del Perú, Fondo Editorial, 1998. 387 p.: bibl. (Serie Estudios históricos; 24)

Important work on 17th-century cultural crises of colonial ancien régime. Surveys baroque *mentalités*, masterfully tracing shifts in indigenous social forms, rise of Creole consciousness. Sensitive to matters of gender as well as political and intellectual history. [SEP]

2245 Gonzales, Donato Amado. Establecimiento y consolidación de la hacienda en el Valle de Chinchaypucyo, 1600–1700. *(Rev. Andin., 16:1, primer semestre 1998, p. 67–98, bibl., maps, tables)*

Examines privatization of land and creation of haciendas near Cuzco, done either through grants to *conquistadores* or sales from either *caciques* and their communities or the state. Concludes that this was not a response to markets but rather a desire for *señorial* status on the part of Spaniards and Inca descendents. [SEP]

2246 González Sánchez, Carlos Alberto. Consideraciones sobre el comercio de libros en Lima a principios del siglo XVII. *(Anu. Estud. Am., 54:2, julio/dic. 1997, p. 665–692, appendix, tables)*

Inventories and analysis of two Spanish book merchants. Appendix lists volumes. See also items **2247** and **2250**. [SEP]

2247 González Sánchez, Carlos Alberto. La cultura del libro en el Virreinato del Perú en tiempos de Felipe II. *(Colon. Lat. Am. Rev., 9:1, June 2000, p. 63–80, bibl.)*

Broad overview of subject based on individual library holdings as revealed in wills and testaments held in the Archivo General de Indias. See also items **2246** and **2250**. [SEP]

2248 Graubart, Karen B. El tejer y las identidades de género en el Perú en los inicios de la Colonia. *(Bol. Inst. Riva-Agüero, 24, 1997, p. 145–165)*

Shows that colonial division of labor

in weaving by gender was a projection of gender roles as understood by Spaniards (men in commercial weaving, women for home use). With anecdotal archeological evidence (textbook interpretations of Moche pottery depicting weaving), Graubart makes a case that contemporary scholars continue to project these roles into the preconquest era. Interesting and well written. [SEP]

Hampe Martínez, Teodoro. La Colección Brüning de documentos para la etnohistoria del Perú: inventario de sus fondos. See item **721**.

2249 Hampe Martínez, Teodoro. Cristianización y religiosidad en el Perú colonial: un estudio sobre la bibliografía de los años 1990. (*Anthropol. Dep. Cienc. Soc.*, 15:15, 1997, p. 338–354, bibl.)

A very useful review of Spanish- and English-language literature divided into five broad categories: early efforts at evangelization, 17th-century saints (St. Rose of Lima, St. Martín de Porres), the Holy Office of the Inquisition, extirpation, and manifestations of religiosity. [SEP]

2250 Hampe Martínez, Teodoro. Fuentes y perspectivas para la historia del libro en el Virreinato del Perú, siglos XVI-XVIII. (*Bol. Acad. Nac. Hist./Caracas*, 83:320, oct./dic. 1997, p. 37–54, appendix)

Very useful appendix lists information on 40 private libraries (15 each from the 16th and 17th centuries, 10 from 18th; but other than Garcilaso de la Vega, only one from an indigenous person) and citations indicating where additional information can be found. See also items **2246** and **2247**. [SEP]

2251 Hampe Martínez, Teodoro. José Durand, bibliófilo: su colección de libros y papeles en la Universidad de Notre Dame. (*in* Encuentro Internacional de Peruanistas, *1st, Lima, 1996.* Estado de los estudios histórico-sociales sobre el Perú a fines del siglo XX. Lima: UNESCO; Univ. de Lima; Fondo de Cultura Económica, 1998, v. 1, p. 383–396, appendix)

Durand, a noted scholar of Garcilaso de la Vega, bequeathed his recreation of Garcilaso's library to the Univ. of Notre Dame. Description of Durand's career and list of books now housed in the Hesburgh Library. [SEP]

2252 Hampe Martínez, Teodoro. El patrimonio de la Inquisición: los bienes y rentas del Santo Oficio limeño en el siglo XVII. (*Bol. Inst. Riva-Agüero*, 24, 1997, p. 227–244, bibl.)

Brief article contextualizing documents, now housed in the Archivo Nacional de Chile, related to financial dealings of the Lima inquisition. See also items **2253, 2261,** and **2262**. [SEP]

2253 Hampe Martínez, Teodoro. Santo Oficio e historia colonial: aproximaciones al tribunal e la Inquisición de Lima, 1570–1820. Lima: Ediciones del Congreso del Perú, 1998. 212 p.: bibl.

A collection of previously published (some twice) essays by one of Peru's most prolific authors. Three items first covered in *HLAS 56:2411*. Still, an important contribution. See also items **2252, 2261,** and **2262**. [SEP]

2254 Hampe Martínez, Teodoro. El servicio de Chasquis: organización y funcionamiento de los correos indígenas en el Perú colonial. (*in* Congreso del Instituto Internacional de Historia del Derecho Indiano, *11th, Buenos Aires, 1995.* Actas y estudios. Buenos Aires: Instituto de Investigaciones de Historia del Derecho Indiano, 1997, v. 2, p. 189–203)

Cogent review of manuscript as well as published sources on utilization of indigenous runners as postal carriers during the colonial period. Also includes some data on the Carvajal, the Spanish family that held the office of "Correo Mayor" (equivalent to postmaster general) from 1599 through the mid-1750s, if not longer. [MTH]

2255 Heras, Julián. Principales archivos y bibliotecas de la Orden Franciscana en el Perú actual. (*Arch. Ibero-Am.*, 57:225/226, 1997, p. 79–105, bibl.)

Surveys Archivo de San Francisco de Lima, Archivo Provincial de los Descalzos de Lima, Archivo Conventual de los Descalzos (Lima), Archivo del Convento de Ocopa and Archivo de San Francisco de Cajamarca; also Biblioteca de San Fransisco de Lima, Biblioteca de los Descalzos de Lima, Biblioteca de Ocopa, and Biblioteca de la Recoleta de Arequipa. [SEP]

Huertas Vallejos, Lorenzo. Conformación del espacio social en Huamanga, siglos XV y XVI. See item **727.**

Hyland, Sabine. The imprisonment of Blas Valera: heresy and Inca history in colonial Peru. See item **728.**

2256 Juan Pablo Viscardo y Guzmán, 1748– 1798: el hombre y su tiempo. v. 1–3. Lima: Fondo Editorial del Congreso del Perú; Consorcio de Universidades, 1999. 3 v.: bibl., ill. (some col.), map.

Three-volume collection of essays from a conference held in Lima to celebrate 200th anniversary of the birth of author of the famous "Carta a los Españoles Americanos." Excellent introduction by David Brading. Essays deal with sources of Vizcardo y Guzmán's ideas, their impact on the Creole movement, and the idea of the nation. [SEP]

2257 Lanuza y Sotelo, Eugenio. Viaje ilustrado a los reinos del Perú en el siglo XVIII. Recopilación de Antonio Garrido Aranda y Patricio Hidalgo Nuchera. Lima: Pontificia Univ. Católica del Perú, Fondo Editorial, 1998. 254 p.: col. ill., indexes. (Col. Clásicos peruanos)

In 1730s Lanuza y Sotelo was a secretary to Alonso López de Casas, the newly appointed Comisario General of the Franciscans in Peru. The diary follows López de Casas' travels from Spain to Peru and in the Viceroyalty. The document is Manuscript #68 from the Biblioteca Provincial de Córdoba with a very fine introduction by Antonio Garrido Arranda and Patricia Hidalgo Nuchera. [SEP]

2258 Latasa Vassallo, Pilar. Administración virreinal en el Perú: gobierno del marqués de Montesclaros, 1607–1615. Madrid: Editorial Centro de Estudios Ramón Areces, 1997. 709 p.: bibl., ill., map.

Juan de Mendoza y Luna became Viceroy of Peru at age 36 after having held the same office in Mexico. This lengthy, encyclopedic study, from author's dissertation, is based on extensive research in American and European archives. Mendoza, a product of his time, "era un hombre autoritario que trató de reforzar al máximo las prerrogativas que las leyes de Indias le daban." [SEP]

2259 Lohmann Villena, Guillermo. Las minas de Huancavelica en los siglos XVI y XVII. 2. ed. Lima: Pontificia Univ. Católica del Perú, Fondo Editorial, 1999. 511 p.: bibl., ill., indexes.

A reprint of 1948 edition (see *HLAS 15:1569*), a classic on mining from the dean of Peruvian historians. A chronological, institutional study with emphasis on careers of viceroys and their impact on mercury mining. See also items **2266** and **2271.** [SEP]

2260 MacCormack, Sabine. History and law in sixteenth-century Peru: the impact of European scholarly traditions. (*in* Cultures of scholarship. Ann Arbor: Univ. of Michigan Press, 1997, p. 277–310, bibl.)

Sophisticated argument that European scholarly traditions not only influenced how Spaniards understood the Inca Empire (i.e., with frequent analogies to Rome), but also, by end of 16th century, how Andeans understood their own past. Thus, Andeans could anachronistically attribute the Spanish resettlement policy to the Inca Tupac-Yupanqui, whose claim to sovereignty was expressed in Christian terminology. See also item **2284.** [SEP]

2261 Millar Carvacho, René. El Archivo del Santo Oficio de Lima y la documentación inquisitorial existente en Chile. (*Rev. Inquis.*, 6, 1997, p. 101–116)

A description of Lima Inquisition documents held in Chile: over 500 bound volumes that were part of original archive of the Santo Oficio de Lima, plus documents from Spanish archives copied by José Toribio Medina in late 19th century. See also items **2252, 2253,** and **2262.** [SEP]

2262 Millar Carvacho, René. La Inquisición de Lima. v. 3, 1697–1820. Madrid: Deimos, 1998. 1 v.: bibl., indexes.

Third of three volumes on the Inquisition. Work began as a 1981 doctoral thesis at the Univ. de Sevilla. Shows that the Holy Office concentrated much of its efforts on bigamy and witchcraft. Suffered a "decline in prestige" from the mid-18th century on. Well researched; very fine fundamental study on the topic. For comment on Vol. 1, see *HLAS 54:2364.* For comment on Vol. 2, see *HLAS 58:2283.* See also items **2252, 2253,** and **2261.** [SEP]

Millones, Luis. Logros y azares de la cristianización colonial: el obispado de Huamanga. See item **764.**

2263 Mills, Kenneth. Idolatry and its enemies: colonial Andean religion and extirpation, 1640–1750. Princeton, N.J.: Princeton Univ. Press, 1997. 337 p.: bibl., ill., index, map.

The key work on extirpation of idolatry for the Andes. Subtle treatment of "lived" religion of native Andeans which avoids the pitfalls of both resistance and accommodation studies. [SEP]

2264 Montero, A. and C. Diéguez. Datos para la paleontología chilena: la paleontología en la expedición Heuland a Chile y Perú, 1795–1800. (*Asclepio/Madrid*, 50:1, 1998, p. 69–78, bibl., map, photos)

Brief description of items in the collection of the Museo Nacional de Ciencias Naturales de Madrid from the first paleontological expedition to the region. [SEP]

Mumford, Jeremy. The Taki Onqoy and the Andean nation: sources and interpretations. See item **770.**

2265 Muñoz Delaunoy, Ignacio. Solicitación *in loco confessionis:* un estudio de caso, 1650–1666. (*Historia/Santiago*, 32, 1999, p. 177–264)

Fascinating case of a Lima Jesuit prosecuted by Inquisition for soliciting women for sexual favors during confession. Emphasis is on inquisitional process. Argues that, rather than repressing society, the Inquisition was in line with society's mores. Lengthy trial copied by Medina from the Archivo General de Simancas in Spain. [SEP]

2266 Navarro Abrines, María del Carmen. El gobierno de Carlos de Beranger en Huancavelica, 1764–1767. (*Jahrb. Gesch. Staat Wirtsch. Ges. Lat.am.*, 34, 1997, p. 105–126)

Argues that peninsular Spaniard Beranger, by seeking support of miners' guild rather than following a policy of confrontation as his predecessor did, was able to implement some limited reforms which increased mercury production. See also items **2259** and **2271.** [SEP]

2267 Noack, Karoline. El cacicazgo de Huamán dentro de la jurisdicción de Trujillo, siglo XVII: desarrollo de su estruc-

tura y principios de organización. (*Bol. Inst. Riva-Agüero*, 24, 1997, p. 343–367)

Compares the 1566–67 visita of Gregorio González de Cuenca and a *retasa* from 1688 to claim that internal sociopolitical structures of the *repartimientos* of Chimo and Chicama remained closer to precolumbian forms than to those in the *repartimiento* of Guañape. The great ethnographic detail in *visitas* and *retasas* could be put to more interesting uses. [SEP]

2268 Nowack, Kerstin and Catherine Julien. La campaña de Toledo contra los señores naturales andinos: el destierro de los Incas de Vilcabamba y Cuzco. (*Hist. Cult./Lima*, 23, 1999, p. 15–81, appendices, bibl., tables)

Very helpful introduction to previously unpublished documents in the AGI, portions of which are included in appendices. Interesting in light of Toledo's successful efforts to undermine legal rights of Inca nobility. Documents indicate nature of prosecutions from Vilcabamba and Toledo's efforts to link Cuzco nobility to their cause. [SEP]

Olivari Ortega, Jorge. Pachacutec y los lavaderos de oro de Chuquibamba. See item **774.**

2269 O'Phelan Godoy, Scarlett. Kurakas sin sucesiones: del cacique al alcalde de indios; Perú y Bolivia, 1750–1835. Cuzco, Peru: Centro de Estudios Regionales Andinos Bartolomé de Las Casas, 1997. 100 p.: bibl., col. ill. (Archivos de historia andina; 25)

Argues that two separate factors led to discrediting of *caciques* and their replacement by *alcaldes* at end of 18th century: 1) *caciques* were the prime movers in the Great Rebellion and therefore discredited themselves in Spanish eyes; 2) intruder *caciques* pushed the hated *reparto* system and earned the wrath of indigenous communities. [SEP]

2270 Parrón Salas, Carmen. Perú y la transición del comercio político al comercio libre, 1740–1778. (*Anu. Estud. Am.*, 54:2, julio/dic. 1997, p. 447–473, graphs, table)

Argues that during mid-18th century, foreign trade shifted to the Southern Cone, leading to an acceleration of the "mercantile dynamic" in Peru as Lima merchants were forced to compete with one another. [SEP]

2271 Pearce, Adrian J. Huancavelica 1700–1759: administrative reform of the mercury industry in early Bourbon Peru. (*HAHR*, 79:4, Nov. 1999, p. 669–702, graphs, tables)

Argues that while active Bourbon administration in early decades led to successful mercury mining, Huancavelica's decline at mid-century was also the product of Bourbon reforms which were then directed toward wider imperial aims. See also items **2259** and **2266**. [SEP]

2272 Peralta A., Luz. La serie "Documentos de Jaén, Maynas y Chachapoyas 1776–1887" del Archivo Arzobispal de Lima. (*Rev. Arch. Gen. Nac./Lima*, 15, mayo 1997, p. 199–210)

Useful checklist of the 85 documents and *expedientes* in what appears to be the only *legajo* in the Archivo Arzobispal de Lima that registers activities of the Catholic Church in the Upper Amazon basin during late colonial, independence, and early national periods. An important record group regardless of whether one considers the areas in question to have been Ecuadorian or Peruvian. N.B. The *Catálogos* of the Archivo Arzobispal de Lima are now available on CD-ROM through the Fundación Histórica Tavera and the Agencia Española de Cooperación Internacional. [MTH]

2273 Peralta Ruiz, Víctor. La revolución silenciada: hábitos de lectura y pedagogía política en el Perú, 1790–1814. (*Anu. Estud. Am.*, 54:1, enero/junio 1997, p. 107–134, table)

Succinct argument that during late colonial period reading habits changed from religious to political topics. Three separate events fueled this change: 1) circulation of newly established newspapers in 1790s; 2) the 1808 Napoleonic invasion of Spain; and 3) the decrees of the Cortes of Cádiz freeing the press. [SEP]

2274 Pérez-Mallaína Bueno, Pablo Emilio. La fabricación de un mito: el terremoto de 1687 y la ruina de los cultivos de trigo en el Perú. (*Anu. Estud. Am.*, 57:1, enero/junio 2000, p. 69–88)

Sophisticated argument for "constructed memory." Newly discovered documents from the AGI demonstrate that 1687 earthquake did not impact the coastal wheat industry. Rather, later interelite fights over locally produced versus foreign wheat led supporters of foreign wheat to make this charge. [SEP]

2275 Quiroz, Francisco. Tendencias hacia la manufactura en la industria urbana limeña colonial. (*in* Encuentro Internacional de Peruanistas, 1st, Lima, 1996. Estado de los estudios histórico-sociales sobre el Perú a fines del siglo XX. Lima: UNESCO; Univ. de Lima; Fondo de Cultura Económica, 1998, v. 1, p. 493–499, bibl.)

Argues that attempts to set up small-scale manufacturing were thwarted by Bourbon reform-era idea that Spain should produce and America consume. [SEP]

2276 Ramírez, Susan E. La legitimidad de los curacas en los Andes durante los siglos XVI y XVII. (*Bol. Inst. Riva-Agüero*, 24, 1997, p. 467–492, bibl.)

Examines religious basis of power, and argues that *curacas* were intermediaries not only between the Spanish and their own subjects, but also between the living and the dead. This religious function allowed traditional *caciques* to maintain power over their communities during the 16th-17th centuries. [SEP]

2277 Rice, Prudence M. Wine and brandy production in colonial Peru: a historical and archaeological investigation. (*J. Interdiscip. Hist.*, 27:3, Winter 1997, p. 455–480, graphs, maps, tables)

Drawing from archeological and documentary evidence, quantifies production for the Moquegua Valley. Argues that Moquegua Valley was capable of producing enormous quantities of both wine and brandy, plus foodstuffs. [SEP]

2278 Sánchez, Ana. "El talismán del diablo": la Inquisición frente al consumo de coca; Lima, siglo XVII. (*Rev. Inquis.*, 6, 1997, p. 139–162, bibl.)

Overview of coca use emphasizes social repercussions. Coca, regarded as addictive and intoxicating, was seen as used only in indigenous idolatrous practices and mestizo witchcraft, and therefore became a target of the Inquisition. [SEP]

2279 Seminario Ojeda, Miguel Arturo. Itinerario de la visita pastoral del Obispo Martínez Compañón, 1782–1785. (*Rev. Arch. Gen. Nac./Lima*, 15, mayo 1997, p. 209–220)

Quite literally a detailed account of Bishop Martínez Compañon's *visita*. [SEP]

2280 Solano, Francisco de. Los resultados científicos de la real expedición hispanofrancesa al virreinato de Perú, 1749–1823. (*Hist. Mex./México*, 46:4, abril/junio 1997, p. 723–743)

Brief study of the nearly 3,000 published pages resulting from the 11-year expedition of Jorge Juan and Antonio de Ulloa. [SEP]

Someda, Hidefuji. El imperio de los Incas: imagen del Tahuantinsuyu creada por los cronistas. See item **815.**

2281 Stavig, Ward. "Continuing the bleeding of these pueblos will shortly make them cadavers": the Potosí mita, cultural identity, and communal survival in colonial Peru. (*Americas/Washington*, 56:4, April 2000, p. 529–562)

Intriguing thesis argues that mita system provided a structure that allowed indigenous communities in the Cuzco region to maintain identity and solidarity. Offers much detail on how the mita worked. [SEP]

Stavig, Ward. The world of Túpac Amaru: conflict, community, and identity in colonial Peru. See item **816.**

2282 Tardieu, Jean-Pierre. El negro en el Cuzco: los caminos de la alienación en la segunda mitad del siglo XVII. Lima: Pontificia Univ. Católica del Perú; Banco Central de Reserva del Perú, 1998. 196 p.: bibl., ill., maps. (Publicación del Instituto Riva-Agüero; 170)

Based on 1655–82 Libros de la Escribanía de Lorenzo Messa Andueza from the Archivo Departamental de Cuzco. Accessible introduction to little-studied topic of Africans in the Peruvian highlands. [SEP]

2283 Tarragó, Rafael Emilio. Dual identities?: the Andean gentry in Peru and Alto Peru, 1533–1826. (*in* Seminar on the Acquisition of Latin American Library Materials, *44th, Vanderbilt University, 1999.* Documenting movements, identity, and popular culture in Latin America. Austin: SALALM Secretariat, Benson Latin American Collection, The General Libraries, Univ. of Texas at Austin, 2000, p. 270–289, bibl.)

An annotated guide to published sources and studies on the *kurakas* of Lower

and Upper Peru during colonial and independence periods. Limited to materials in English and Spanish. [MTH]

Torchia-Estrada, Juan Carlos. Los estudios de filosofía (Artes) en el siglo XVI: México y Perú. See item **4620.**

2284 La tradición clásica en el Perú virreinal. Recopilación de Teodoro Hampe Martínez. Lima: Sociedad Peruana de Estudios Clásicos; Fondo Editorial Univ. Nacional Mayor de San Marcos, 1999. 344 p.: bibl., ill.

A collection of essays by various authors looks at the "influence of the Greek-Latin tradition in the cultural activity of the Viceroyalty: its arts, letters, philosophy, jurisprudence, historiography." Articles focus on individuals such as Garcilaso de la Vega. See also item **2260.** [SEP]

2285 Van Deusen, Nancy E. The "alienated body": slaves and *castas* in the Hospital de San Bartolomé in Lima, 1680–1700. (*Americas/Washington*, 56:1, July 1999, p. 1–30, tables)

Tables provide much detail on specific illnesses. [SEP]

2286 Van Deusen, Nancy E. Defining the sacred and the worldly: *beatas* and *recogidas* in late-seventeenth-century Lima. (*CLAHR*, 6:4, Fall 1997, p. 441–477, tables)

Examines a *casa de recogimiento* (a home for "repentant" women), demonstrating that the women, who came from all sectors of society, were enclosed for a variety of reasons. While some came for spiritual motives, others were awaiting divorce or had been abandoned or abused by their husbands. Author uses this case to show that "the colonial Catholic world" was not always neatly divided into purely sacred and worldly spaces. See also item **2287.** [SEP]

2287 Van Deusen, Nancy E. Determining the boundaries of virtue: the discourse of *recogimiento* among women in seventeenth-century Lima. (*J. Fam. Hist.*, 22:4, Oct. 1997, p. 373–389)

Sophisticated analysis of *recogimiento* as both a virtue and an institutional practice to illustrate gendered and ethnically defined notions of honor. See also item **2286.** [SEP]

2288 Villanueva C., Carlos Alfonso. Religiosidad y patronazgo: la fundación de la Recolección Concepcionistas Descalzas de San José de Lima. (*Rev. Arch. Gen. Nac./Lima*, 17, mayo 1998, p. 37–90)

Detailed empirical account of convent foundation based on Calancha and author's exceptional access to primary documents in convent. [SEP]

CHARCAS

2289 Abercrombie, Thomas Alan. Q'aqchas and the plebe in "rebellion": carnival vs. lent in 18th century Potosí. (*J. Lat. Am. Anthropol.*, 2:1, Fall 1996, p. 62–111)

Detailed account of supposed 1751 rebellion of q'aqcha mineral thieves' union. Describes confraternal-guild organization leadership and threat posed to Creoles by mixed peoples. Proposes theory of racial thinking among Creoles. See also Tandeter's analysis of q'aqchas in *HLAS 54:2451* and *56:2486*. For review of entire journal, see *HLAS 57:743*. [SEP]

2290 Abercrombie, Thomas Alan. Tributes to bad conscience: charity, restitution, and inheritance in *cacique* and *encomendero* testaments of sixteenth-century Charcas. (*in* Dead giveaways: indigenous testaments of colonial Mesoamerica and the Andes. Edited by Susan Kellogg and Matthew Restall. Salt Lake City: Univ. of Utah Press, 1998, p. 249–289, table)

Compares *encomendero* and *cacique* wills from 16th-century Charcas. Finds both equally concerned with contradictory goals of perpetuating social personhood (through inheritance) and saving eternal souls (through charitable donations). Published with testaments; useful as teaching tool. For review of entire work, see item **467**. [SEP]

2291 Acarete, du Biscay. Viaje al cerro rico de Potosí, 1657–1660. La Paz: Editorial Los Amigos del Libro, 1998. 115 p.: bibl., ill., maps. (Sendas abiertas. Franceses en Bolivia)

One of the earliest accounts by a French traveler. Translation of diary of trip from Buenos Aires to Potosí, with descriptions of both cities. Especially detailed description of mining operations and organization of labor in Potosí. Part of a series on French travelers in Bolivia. [SEP]

Adrián, Mónica. El espacio sagrado y el ejercicio del poder: las doctrinas de Chayanta durante la segunda mitad del siglo XVIII. See item **657**.

2292 Alegría Uria, Patricia. Otro representante de la marginalidad criolla: el cronista Arzáns. (*Estud. Boliv.*, 4, sept. 1997, p. 77–92, bibl., photo)

Textual analysis of Arzáns' history of 17th-century war of *vicuñas* and *vascongadas*, drawing on Benveniste and Mabel Moraña. Argues that Arzáns projects into fictitious 17th-century *vicuña* Creole leader the Creole baroque patriotism of his own, 18th-century day. See also item **2297**. [SEP]

2293 Alvarez, Bartolomé. De las costumbres y conversión de los indios del Perú: memorial a Felipe II, 1588. Recopilación de María del Carmen Martín Rubio, Juan J.R. Villarías Robles, y Fermín del Pino Díaz. Madrid: Ediciones Polifemo, 1998. 462 p.: bibl., ill. (Crónicas y memorias)

Written to convince Felipe II that the Inquisition should be introduced against indigenous people, this extraordinary memorial came to light only in 1991. Alvarez was a parish priest in what is now the dept. of Oruro. Annotated transcription, plus studies by Xavier Albó, Fermín del Pino Díaz, and others. Wonderful detail on religious practices and ideas. A major new source for colonialists. See also item **2307**. [SEP]

2294 Arze, Silvia; Magdalena Cajías de la Vega; and Ximena Medinaceli. Mujeres en rebelión: la presencia femenina en las rebeliones de Charcas del siglo XVIII. La Paz: Ministerio de Desarrollo Humano, 1997. 158 p.: bibl., ill.

Brief overview of late colonial rebellions that took place in what is now Bolivia is drawn primarily from secondary sources. Shows that female leaders in rebellions were involved primarily because of family ties. [SEP]

2295 Barragán Romano, Rossana. Españoles patricios y españoles europeos: conflictos intra-élites e identidades en la ciudad de La Paz en vísperas de la Independencia, 1770–1809. (*Estud. Boliv.*, 1, 1995, p. 121–182, bibl., graphs, tables)

Carefully researched article by one of Bolivia's finest young scholars. Calls into question categories of "criollo" and "mestizo" to argue that place of birth was not the decisive variable in determining political position, but rather the degree to which the person was involved in local society. [SEP]

2296 Corvera, Pedro. Archivo del Colegio Franciscano de Tarija. Madrid: Fundación Histórica Tavera: Instituto Italo-Latinoamericano, 1998. 111 p.: indexes. (Documentos Tavera; 6)

Publishes the 1916 semi-catalog, semi-inventory of the Franciscan Archives in Tarija, a major repository for the study of the activities of the Franciscans in Bolivia and Argentina from the early 17th century through the present. This repository remains much as it was, hence the utility of this document, in and of itself a historical source. Fleshed out and updated by Father Gerardo Maldini, the current director of the Archivo, who has also added onomastic indexes. [MTH]

2297 Crespo R., Alberto. La guerra entre vicuñas y vascongados: Potosí, 1622–1625. 4. ed. Sucre, Bolivia: Univ. Andina Simón Bolívar, 1997. 171 p.: bibl.

A classic work (fourth printing) on civil wars between Creoles and their allies (vicuñas) and recent Basque immigrants in Potosí. See also item **2292.** [SEP]

2298 Díaz Rementería, Carlos J. Panorama institucional de la mita potosina. (in Congreso del Instituto Internacional de Historia del Derecho Indiano, 11th, Buenos Aires, 1995. Actas y estudios. Buenos Aires: Instituto de Investigaciones de Historia del Derecho Indiano, 1997, v. 4, p. 469–490)

Careful institutional political study of 16th-century creation of capitanía general of mita of Potosí and later transformations through end of mita. Illustrates substitution of Spaniards for indigenous caciques and reduction of indigenous authority to capitanes chicos of pueblos rather than Incaic provinces. [SEP]

2299 Doucet, Gastón Gabriel. Entre la historia y la fábula: los hermanos Don Francisco y Don Manuel Uriondo, proceres tarijeños. (Anuario/Sucre, 1998, p. 163–208, bibl.)

An attempt to reconstruct history of independence-era heroes from Tarija. Lengthy treatment of genealogies. [SEP]

2300 Espinoza Soriano, Waldemar. Trabajadores forzados en el Cusco, La Paz, y Potosí en 1550: una información inédita de Juan Polo de Ondegardo. (Rev. Arch. Gen. Nac./Lima, 16, dic. 1997, p. 79–137, bibl., tables)

Succinct treatment of 1550 controversy over legality of forced labor (mita) in Potosí mining. Published with transcription of part of encomendero response to Gascan prohibition with close analysis of indigenous testimony. Detail for Cuzco and La Paz districts (not La Plata). Full citation of document in Archivo General de Indias (AGI) not provided (Document is Pieza 5 of AGI Justicia 667, 7 piezas, 226 fs.). See also item **2316.** [SEP]

Freyer, Bärbel. Los chiquitanos: descripción de un pueblo de las tierras bajas orientales de Bolivia según fuentes jesuíticas del siglo XVIII. See item **709.**

Gavira Márquez, María Concepción. La minería del cobre en el Alto Perú: las minas de Corocoro, 1750–1870. See item **2653.**

2301 Gordillo, José M. La región de Cochabamba desde una perspectiva ilustrada: el programa del intendente Francisco de Viedma a fines del siglo XVIII. (Decursos/Cochabamba, 2:4, junio 1997, p. 59–72, bibl.)

Study based on de Viedma's published report to royal authorities. Elaborate plans to grow the regional economy had limited success. The program increased tribute revenue but ironically impoverished the regional economy by decreasing monies available for other projects. [SEP]

2302 Historia de Tarija: corpus documental. v. 5–6. Tarija, Bolivia: Prefectura del Depto. de Tarija; Univ. Autónoma Juan Misael Saracho, 1997. 2 v.: indices.

Indispensable source for studies of the Bolivian frontier. Vol. 5, edited by Erick Langer, covers the Republican era; Vol. 6, edited by Catherine Julien, contains 16th-century documents including 1540 encomienda grant from Pizarro to Francisco de Retamoso. Documents are from Archivo y Biblioteca Nacionales de Bolivia, Archivo General de Indias (Seville), Biblioteca Nacional in Buenos Aires, as well as Tarija area archives. For comment on vols. 1–4, see *HLAS 52:2195*. [SEP]

2303 Larson, Brooke. Cochabamba, 1550–1900: colonialism and agrarian transformation in Bolivia. New foreword by William Roseberry. Expanded ed. Durham, N.C.: Duke Univ. Press, 1998. 422 p.: bibl., index, maps.

Revised and expanded second ed. of seminal work on rural political economy. A new chapter reviews recent Andean literature with emphasis on popular culture, and points to new areas of research. For comment on first ed., see *HLAS 52:2196*. [SEP]

Lecoq, Patrice. Algunos apuntes sobre la importancia de las caravanas de camélidos en el desarrollo de la ciudad de Potosí, comienzo del período colonial. See item **743.**

2304 Lleó, Estanislao Just. El carisma ignaciano de la misión en Charcas, 1572–1767. (*Casa Lib.*, 1:1, 1997, p. 110–137, bibl.)

Brief and uncritical history of Jesuits in Charcas, written to commemorate 500th anniversary of birth of Order's founder. Useful for citations from Potosí and Spanish archives. [SEP]

2305 López Beltrán, Clara. Alianzas familiares: élite, género y negocios en La Paz, s. XVII. Lima: Instituto de Estudios Peruanos, 1998. 289 p.: appendices, bibl., ill., maps, tables. (Serie Estudios históricos; 23)

Revised version of author's Columbia Univ. dissertation. Well researched. Some little jewels in appendices include a 1663 promise of marriage contract for a seven year old Paceña. [SEP]

2306 Luque Alcaide, Elisa. Política eclesiástica de Carlos III en América: instancias de reforma en Charcas. (*in* Encuentro-Debate América Latina ayer y hoy = Trobada-Debat Amèrica Llatina ahir i avui, 6th, Barcelona, Spain, 1997. Lo que duele es el olvido: recuperando la memoria de América Latina = El que dol és l'oblit: recuperant la memòria d'Amèrica Llatina. Barcelona, Spain: Univ. de Barcelona, 1998, p. 141–151)

Examination of Holy Synod held in Charcas in 1773 seeks to move beyond Church-state conflict. Takes priests at their word that evangelizing mission was upper-

most in their minds, and that reform was motivated by fear that their parishoners were sliding into idolatry and "ancient superstition." Ignores fights over priestly stipends and numbers of indigenous in Church service which precipitated the Synod. [SEP]

2307 Martín Rubio, María del Carmen. Costumbres de los indios del Perú: un temprano antecedente de la política de extirpación de idolatrías en el virreinato peruano. (*Bol. Inst. Riva-Agüero*, 24, 1997, p. 295–307)

Brief study by one of the editors of Bartolomé Alvarez's work (see item **2293**) puts the memorial in context of other early colonial accounts of extirpation. [SEP]

Medinaceli, Ximena. Nombres disidentes: mujeres aymaras en Sacaca, siglo XVII. See item **762.**

2308 Medinaceli, Ximena and Pilar Mendieta Parada. De indias a doñas: mujeres de la élite indígena en Cochabamba, siglos XVI-XVII. La Paz: Ministerio de Desarrollo Humano, Secretaría de Asuntos Etnicos, de Género y Generacionales, Subsecretaría de Asuntos de Género, Coordinadora de Historia, 1997. 112 p.: bibl., ill. (Serie Protagonistas de la historia)

Tapping into the riches of the Archivo Histórico Municipal de Cochabamba, this little book tells the story of three women. One, a noblewoman of Cuzco, born about 1520, married a Portuguese merchant and moved to Cochabamba; the other two were members of the regional elite. Uses these stories to discuss construction of mestizaje. [SEP]

Medinaceli, Ximena and Silvia Arze. Los mallkus de Charkas: redes de poder en el norte de Potosí, siglos XVI y XVII. See item **763.**

2309 Mendieta Parada, Pilar and Eugenia Bridikhina. María Sisa y María Sosa: la vida de dos empleadas domésticas en la ciudad de La Paz, siglo XVII. La Paz: Ministerio de Desarrollo Humano, Secretaría de Asuntos Etnicos, de Género y Generacionales, Subsecretaría de Asuntos de Género, 1997. 70 p.: bibl., ill. (Serie Protagonistas de la historia)

The 1684 *padrón* of La Paz listed domestic servants by household. Beginning with this source and drawing on secondary sources, book traces lives of an indigenous woman and a black woman. The name "Sisa" was used in a generic fashion by Spaniards to denote domestics. [SEP]

O'Phelan Godoy, Scarlett. Kurakas sin sucesiones: del cacique al alcalde de indios; Perú y Bolivia, 1750–1835. See item **2269.**

2310 Pentimalli, Michela; Pedro Albornoz; and Paula Luján. Mirar por su honra: matrimonio y divorcio en Cochabamba, 1750–1825. (*Anuario/Sucre*, 1997, p. 151–163)

Treating a handful of 18th-century divorce cases and marriage oppositions found in archives of Cochabamba, authors cogently rehearse theorization of honor, gender, marriage, and power. Solid promise of future mining in rich documentary and theoretical veins. [SEP]

2311 Radding Murrieta, Cynthia. Voces chiquitanas: entre la encomienda y la misión en el oriente de Bolivia, siglo XVIII. (*Anuario/Sucre*, 1997, p. 123–137)

Interesting case study of *indios ladinos* who successfully sued their encomendero for their freedom by arguing that they were free vassals of the king, who of their own free will had contracted their labor to the previous holder of the encomienda. [SEP]

2312 Robins, Nicholas A. Genocidio y exterminio cultural en la rebelión del Alto Perú, 1780–1782. (*Anuario/Sucre*, 1998, p. 103–138)

While asserting that rebels were not "prepolitical," analysis reduces rebels to leaderless mobs intent primarily on mass murder of Spaniards and Creoles. Problematic use of "genocide" as an analytic category. [SEP]

Robins, Nicholas A. El mesianismo y la semiótica indígena en el Alto Perú: la gran rebelión de 1780–1781. See item **796.**

2313 Serrano Bravo, Carlos. Religión, religiosidad e iglesia en las actividades productivas potosinas. (*Anuario/Sucre*, 1997, p. 19–48, bibl.)

A general overview and top-down treatment of religion in Potosí taken mostly from secondary sources. [SEP]

2314 Serrano Bravo, Carlos and **Ana Forenza A.** Peculiaridades de la minería potosina en el siglo XVI. (*Anuario/Sucre*, 1998, p. 41–62)

Very detailed information drawn from Minas section of the Archivo Nacional de Bolivia in Sucre using the comprehensive catalog compiled by the section's late director, Don Gunnar Mendoza. While article lacks a clear thesis, it is still extremely useful to gain an overview of the available wealth of materials on mining. [SEP]

Tarragó, Rafael Emilio. Dual identities?: the Andean gentry in Peru and Alto Peru, 1533–1826. See item **2283.**

2315 Torrico Panozo, Vitaliano. El pasquín en la independencia del Alto Perú. Puebla, Mexico: Benemérita Univ. Autónoma de Puebla; México: Plaza y Valdés, 1997. 185 p.: bibl.

Brief study and complete chronological list of pasquins (broadsides or posters) written in what is now Bolivia from roughly 1548–1809. Although most have been published previously, this is the first study that makes them accessible in one volume. Argues that the pasquins as a form of mass media created a sense of nationalism. [SEP]

2316 Villarías Robles, Juan J.R. and **Itala de Mamán.** El encomendero Polo de Ondegardo y los mitimaes del valle de Cochabamba: los interrogatorios contra los indios de Paria y Tapacarí. (*Anu. Estud. Am.*, 55:2, julio/dic. 1998, p. 631–651, appendix)

Welcome advance on future compilation of Polo writings, work provides transcriptions of two *interrogatorios* (correcting errors in earlier publications) and insightful commentary. Fundamental source on *mitimaes*. See also item **2300.** [SEP]

2317 Zamora R., Gaby and **Teresa Miranda C.** Catálogo del archivo histórico. (*Casa Lib.*, 1:1, 1997, p. 145–186)

Catalog from the Casa de la Libertad in Sucre. The earliest documents were mostly transcribed or photocopied from other locations. Documents from 1535 (foundation of Lima) to 1823. Earliest Charcas document is a *cofradía* foundation from 1541. [SEP]

CHILE

2318 Acevedo, Alba María. Epistolario de Fray Gaspar de Villarroel, Obispo de Santiago de Chile, 1637–1651. (*Rev. Hist. Am. Argent.*, 19:37, 1997, p. 31–84)

Detailed analysis of 15 letters that Villarroel (1587–1665) wrote to the Crown and the governor of Santiago de Chile during his intensive visits to his extensive diocese. These epistles constitute significant sources on the state of the Church and the clergy in Chile and Cuyo (part of postindependent Argentina), and on social and economic conditions during mid-17th century, especially after the devastating earthquake of 1647. See also item **2212**. [MTH]

2319 Araya Espinoza, Alejandra. Cuerpos aprisionados y gestos cautivos: el problema de la identidad femenina en una sociedad tradicional, Chile 1700–1850. (*Nomadías/Santiago*, 1, junio 1999, p. 71–84)

Exploratory essay raises more questions than it answers. Utilizes criminal records to elucidate the question of feminine identities, primarily as defined and perceived by men, during late colonial, independence, and early national periods. [MTH]

2320 Barrios Valdés, Marciano. La primera evangelización en Chile. (*in* Confronto de culturas: conquista, resistência, transformação. Rio de Janeiro: Expressão e Cultura; São Paulo: Edusp, 1997, p. 161–172)

Provocative outline of the history of the colonial period from the point of view of an unabashed Catholic historian. Important because work encapsulates much of the ideology of traditional Chilean historiography and nationalism. Emphasizes importance of Araucanian frontier and of *mestizaje* in the formation of Chile and *lo chileno*. Stresses the importance of popular faith and religious practices as well as the role and mandates of the institutional Church. [MTH]

2321 Bauer, Ralph. Imperial history, captivity, and creole identity in Francisco Núñez de Pineda y Bacuñán's *Cautiverio feliz*. (*Colon. Lat. Am. Rev.*, 7:1, June 1998, p. 59–82, bibl.)

A sophisticated analysis of Pineda's account of his six-month captivity among the Reche/Mapuche in 1629. Examines historiographic and literary value of the *Cautiverio feliz* (1672) and endeavors to recreate and explicate Pineda's *mentalité*. [MTH]

Boccara, Guillaume. Análisis de un proceso de etnogénesis: el caso de los Reche-Mapuche de Chile en la época colonial. See item **682**.

2322 Boccara, Guillaume. Etnogénesis mapuche: resistencia y restructuración entre los indígenas del centro-sur de Chile, siglos XVI-XVIII. (*HAHR*, 79:3, Aug. 1999, p. 425–461, facsims., map)

Focuses on transformation of the Reche of early colonial Chile into the Mapuche of the late colonial and national periods. In the process, offers new information on and insights into preconquest society and polity and the substantial changes both underwent during the course of the colonial period. See also items **2323** and **2324**. [MTH]

2323 Boccara, Guillaume. Guerre et ethnogenèse mapuche dans le Chili colonial: l'invention du soi. Avant-propos de Nathan Wachtel. Paris: L'Harmattan, 1998. 391 p.: bibl., ill, maps. (Recherches Amériques latines)

A major ethnohistory of the Reche/Mapuche during the colonial period, and author's doctoral dissertation. Based on considerable archival research and rereading of traditional sources. Examines impact of war with their would-be conquerors/pacifiers, and effect of adoption of the horse, wheat, iron, and other Old World innovations on the political and economic structures of what became by end of the 18th century "une nouvelle et puissante ethnie, les Mapuche ou 'gens de la terre.'" See also items **2322** and **2324**. [MTH]

2324 Boccara, Guillaume. El poder creador: tipos de poder y estrategias de sujeción en la frontera sur de Chile en la época colonial. (*Anu. Estud. Am.*, 56:1, enero/junio 1999, p. 65–94)

The novelty of this piece lies not in the dichotomization of the "pacification" of the Reche/Mapuche into two periods: that lof failed conquest and incorporation (1550–1641), and that of cultural assimilation and coexistence (1641–1810). Nor is it found in the emphasis on the importance of the Jesuits in implementing the second model (see *HLAS 58:2403*). Rather, it lies in Boccara's recognition of the pivotal role played by civilian authorities, especially Capitan General Ambrosio O'Higgins in the "homogenization" of the misnamed "Araucanians" and therefore the ethnogenesis of the modern Mapuche. See also items **2322** and **2323**. [MTH]

2325 Cáceres Múñoz, Juan C. Familia, matrimonio y poder en Chile central: los Maturana, 1660–1800. (*Contrib. Cient. Tecnol. Cienc. Soc. Humanid.*, 26:118, julio 1998, p. 81–95, tables)

A case study of the rise and perpetuation of the Maturana family of Colchagua, members of a regional elite. An exceptionally important contribution to the as yet little studied history of elite families in Chile and the means by which they achieved and perpetuated their status and power. See also item **2328**. [MTH]

2326 Carrasco Notario, Guillermo. La esclavitud negra en la Provincia Agustina de Chile. (*Anu. Hist. Iglesia Chile*, 17, 1999, p. 9–24)

Examines treatment accorded to black slaves by the Augustinians during colonial and independence periods, and role played by the "white robes" in the gradual emancipation of slaves. Somewhat apologetic but brimming with new archival data. [MTH]

2327 Cavieres Figueroa, Eduardo. Faltando a la fe y burlando a la ley: bígamos y adulteros en el Chile tradicional. (*Contrib. Cient. Tecnol. Cienc. Soc. Humanid.*, 26:118, julio 1998, p. 137–151)

A minor study of limited interest that barely penetrates the surface of the topics broached. It does demonstrate, however, that the heretofore mostly neglected court records of the late 1700s-early 1800s are a potentially rich source of data for the reconstruction of multiple aspects of the social history of the late colonial, independence, and early national periods. See also items **2330** and **2338**. [MTH]

2328 Cavieres Figueroa, Eduardo. Transformaciones económicas y sobrevivencia familiar: elites en la transición hacia un capitalismo periférico; Chile, 1780–1840. (*in* Formas familiares, procesos históricos y cambio social en América Latina. Recopilación de Ricardo Cicerchia. Quito: Ediciones Abya-Yala, 1998, p. 97–111)

Summarizes conclusions of an important work: the author's *El comercio chileno en la economía colonial* (1996). Argues that insofar as elites of Chile were concerned, the only changes independence brought was their ascension to power at the national level and incorporation of the country into the European sphere as a source of agricultural and primary materials. Internally, however, little or nothing changed insofar as social and economic structures were concerned. See also item **2325**. [MTH]

Cerda-Hegerl, Patricia. Fronteras del sur: la región del Bío Bío y la Araucanía chilena, 1604–1883. See item **2706**.

Chile, 1541–2000: una interpretación de su historia política. See item **2707**.

Delrio, Walter Mario. Sobre los elementos de la política mapuche durante la segunda mitad del siglo XVIII. See item **696**.

Duhart Mendiboure, Carmen G. Vida cotidiana y órdenes religiosas en el siglo XVIII: el caso de los agustinos en el Virreinato del Peru. See item **2241**.

2329 Flusche, Della M. The tribunal of posthumous estates in colonial Chile, 1540–1769. Pts. 1–3. (*CLAHR*, 9:1, Winter 2000, p. 1–66; 9:2, Spring 2000, p. 243–298; 9:3, Summer 2000, p. 379–428)

Minute analysis of financial records of the Juzgado de Bienes de Difuntos. The kind of pathbreaking, cumbersome, yet eminently readable and well-worked study that could be undertaken only by a seasoned scholar. A major contribution to the economic and social history of the 16th, 17th, and 18th centuries. [MTH]

Gascón, Margarita. La articulación de Buenos Aires a la frontera sur del Imperio español, 1640–1740. See item **2381**.

2330 Goicovic Donoso, Igor. El amor a la fuerza o la fuerza del amor: el rapto en la sociedad chilena tradicional. (*Contrib. Cient. Tecnol. Cienc. Soc. Humanid.*, 26:118, julio 1998, p. 97–135)

A fascinating, pioneering study of abduction culminating in consensual sexual intercourse as a means by which lovers, mostly young, endeavored to circumvent ecclesiastical, civil, and societal norms governing relationships between the sexes and families.

Based on court records of the 18th-19th centuries. See also items **2327** and **2338**. [MTH]

2331 Hidalgo Lehuedé, Jorge. La rebelión de los Amarus y Cataris, 1781, en el norte de Chile. (*in* Confronto de culturas: conquista, resistência, transformação. Rio de Janeiro: Expressão e Cultura; São Paulo: Edusp, 1997, p. 309-328, bibl.)

A brief but novel examination of the little known participation of indigenous communities in Arica, Tacna, Tarapacá, and Atacama in the Túpac Amaru and Túpac Katari rebellions. For more detailed coverage, see author's 1986 Univ. of London doctoral dissertation "Indian Society in Arica, Tarapacá and Atacama, 1750-1793, and Its Response to the Rebellion of Túpac Amaru." [MTH]

Juliano, María Dolores. Los mapuches, la más larga resistencia. See item **735.**

Kennedy Troya, Alexandra. Circuitos artísticos interregionales: de Quito a Chile, siglos XVIII y XIX. See item **2193.**

2332 Lorenzo, Santiago. El corregidor chileno en el siglo XVIII. (*Historia/Santiago*, 32, 1999, p. 131-139)

Exemplifies through archival detail the extent to which the otherwise unremunerated 1700s *corregidores* engaged in monopolistic trade to the detriment of the merchants not in partnership with the *corregidores*. Also looks at the execution of justice. [MTH]

Lucena Salmoral, Manuel. El carimbo de los indios esclavos. See item **2120.**

2333 Luque Azcona, Emilio José. Fray Antonio Rendón: un mercedario en el Chile del quinientos. (*Temas Am.*, 14, 1998, p. 8-14, table)

A useful recapitulation of life and career of an early colonial period Mercedarian friar. Rendón had a long and distinguished career, mostly in Chile and Peru. [MTH]

Montero, A. and **C. Diéguez.** Datos para la paleontología chilena: la paleontología en la expedición Heuland a Chile y Perú, 1795-1800. See item **2264.**

2334 Nauman, Ann Keith. The career of Doña Inés de Suárez: the first European woman in Chile. Lewiston, N.Y.: Edwin

Mellen Press, 2000. 181 p.: bibl., ill. (some col.), index, map. (Latin American studies; 7)

Retells conquest and settlement of Chile by Pedro de Valdivia and in passing says something, but far less than title imples, about Valdivia's mistress Inés Suárez (ca. 1507-80), the first European woman in Santiago and as fierce a warrior as any conquistador when she had to be. Based entirely on published materials. Anachronistic in approach and apologetic in tone. [MTH]

2335 Nicoletti, María Andrea. La configuración del espacio misionero: misiones coloniales en la Patagonia Norte. (*Rev. Complut. Hist. Am.*, 24, 1998, p. 87-112)

Solid, objective study of Jesuit and Franciscan missions in Northern Patagonia. Emphasizes their importance as outposts of the Crown and the colony as well as of the Church. [MTH]

Nocetti, Oscar R. and **Lucio B. Mir.** La disputa por la tierra: Tucumán, Río de la Plata y Chile, 1531-1822. See item **2121.**

2336 Odone, María Carolina. El Valle de Chada: la construcción colonial de un espacio indígena de Chile central. (*Historia/Santiago*, 30, 1997, p. 189-209, bibl., map)

A careful, well-documented analysis of continuities and changes in indigenous and European land-use patterns in the Chada Valley. See also item **2342.** [MTH]

2337 Salinas Araneda, Carlos René. La política regalista en las vistas fiscales de la Audiencia de Chile de fines del siglos XVIII. (*in* Congreso del Instituto Internacional de Historia del Derecho Indiano, *11th, Buenos Aires, 1995.* Actas y estudios. Buenos Aires: Instituto de Investigaciones de Historia del Derecho Indiano, 1997, v. 2, p. 345-364)

Institutional study of attempts by attorneys general of the Audiencia of Santiago de Chile to promote Crown policies and to short-circuit ecclesiastical immunity during last quarter of the 1700s. [MTH]

2338 Salinas Meza, René and **Igor Goicovic Donoso.** Amor, violencia y pasión en el Chile tradicional, 1700-1850. (*Anu. Colomb. Hist. Soc. Cult.*, 24, 1997, p. 237-268)

Sophisticated review of romantic love, violence, and passion in traditional Chile during 18th and first half of 19th centuries. Well written and researched for the most part. Breaks much new ground. Unfortunately, marred by major typographical errors. See also items **2327** and **2330**. [MTH]

2339 Soto Lira, Rosa. Matrimonio y sexualidad de las mujeres negras en la Colonia. (*Nomadías/Santiago*, 1, junio 1999, p. 61–70, table)

Outlines and exemplifies marriages between slaves and the different types of sexual relationships into which female slaves entered, especially during second half of the colonial period. Draws on published materials and archival sources. [MTH]

2340 Valenzuela Márquez, Jaime. De las liturgias del poder al poder de las liturgias: para una antropología política de Chile colonial. (*Historia/Santiago*, 32, 1999, p. 575–615)

This piece on utilization of local celebrations of major events in the lives of Spanish monarchs "in a peripherical province such as Chile" as a means of legitimating royal and imperial power holds appeal for those enamored of Michel Foucault. For most of the rest of us it makes for difficult reading. This work and that annotated in item **2341** are based on author's 1998 École des Hautes Études en Sciences Sociales doctoral dissertation: *Liturgies et imaginaire du pouvoir: fêtes, cérémonies publiques et légitimation politique à Santiago du Chili, 1609–1709*. [MTH]

2341 Valenzuela Márquez, Jaime. Rituales y "fetiches" políticos en Chile colonial: entre el sello de la Audiencia y el pendón del Cabildo. (*Anu. Estud. Am.*, 56:2, julio/dic. 1999, p. 413–440)

Examines symbolic importance of the royal seal as held by the Audiencia and of the royal standard as held by the Cabildo. Includes description and analysis of the official reception accorded the royal seal in 1609 upon establishment of the Audiencia. See also item **2340**. [MTH]

2342 Vega, Alejandra. Asentamiento y territorialidad indígena en el Partido del Maule en el siglo XVI. (*Historia/Santiago*, 32, 1999, p. 685–708, bibl., map)

Examines indigenous patterns of occupation and utilization of land following the Spanish conquest. Based on careful analysis

and judicious reading of extant, necessarily Spanish and therefore nonindigenous, sources. See also item **2336**. [MTH]

2343 Whipple Morán, Pablo. Encomienda e indios de estancia durante la segunda mitad del siglo XVII: Melipilla, 1660–1681. (*Historia/Santiago*, 31, 1998, p. 349–382)

Good case study of transformation of encomienda indigenous peoples into estate laborers on the Estancia of Nuestra Señora de Copacabana during the 1660s-70s. Probably attributes too much credit to *encomendero* owner Juan de Ureta and not enough to coeval circumstances, however. [MTH]

2344 Zaldívar, Trinidad; María José Vial; and Francisca Rengifo. Los vascos en Chile, 1680–1820. Santiago: Editorial los Andes, 1998. 269 p.: bibl., ill.

Detailed account of Basques in Chile during second half of colonial period. Based on extensive archival research. A major contribution to multiple aspects of the history of the colony, given the multiple roles played by this major ethnic group. Unfortunately, not indexed. [MTH]

RIO DE LA PLATA

2345 Academia Nacional de la Historia (Argentina). Nueva historia de la nación argentina. v. 1, La Argentina aborigen; La conquista española. v. 2, La Argentina en los siglos XVII y XVIII (pt. 1). Buenos Aires: Planeta, 1999. 2 v.: bibl., ill., maps.

Vol. 1 features several essays on indigenous peoples of each region of present-day Argentina, and detailed information on Spanish settlements in each part of the country. Vol. 2 concentrates on social, political, and Church history. Both volumes are well illustrated with excellent and clear maps. [SMS]

2346 Acevedo, Edberto Oscar. Controversias virreinales rioplatenses. Buenos Aires: Ediciones Ciudad Argentina, 1997. 181 p.: bibl., index.

Each chapter of this brief book is devoted to a different political controversy, usually a jurisdictional problem between different agents of royal government. A worthwhile read for those interested in the everyday political machinations of the Viceroyalty. [SMS]

2347 Aguerre Core, Fernando. La Visita General de la Diócesis del Paraguay realizada por el Ilmo. D. Manuel Antonio de la Torre, 1758–1760. (*Rev. Complut. Hist. Am.*, 25, 1999, p. 111–138, appendices)

Based on a two-year *visita general* of the diocese of Paraguay, provides information on population of the region, administrative organization, lifestyle, and resources in towns and missions throughout the region. [SMS]

2348 Alemán, Bernardo E. La Estancia San Antonio de la Compañía de Jesús y su desalojo por invasión de los Guaycurúes. (*Rev. Junta Prov. Estud. Hist. Santa Fe*, 62, 1998/99, p. 9–28, bibl., graph, maps)

In tracing history of this Santa Fe estancia, Alemán provides a vivid account of a region increasingly subjected to attacks first by the Calchaquí and later by various Guaycurúan tribes. He documents how indigenous under attack along the Tucumán and Salta frontiers found Santa Fe a more vulnerable place to raid. [SMS]

2349 Arazola Corvera, María Jesús. Hombres, barcos y comercio de la ruta Cádiz-Buenos Aires, 1737–1757. Sevilla, Spain: Diputación de Sevilla, 1998. 468 p.: bibl. (Serie Nuestra América; 5)

Detailed study of shipping between Cádiz and Buenos Aires during early Bourbon period finds extensive use of *registros sueltos* throughout the period. Arazola presents information on the merchants, sailors, and ships that kept Spanish trade with Río de la Plata open, and sees this period as key to Basque domination of *porteño* commerce. [SMS]

2350 Arcondo, Aníbal B. La población de Córdoba según el Empadronamiento de 1778. Córdoba, Argentina: Instituto de Economía, Facultad de Ciencias Económicas, Univ. Nacional de Córdoba, 1998. 40 p.: diskette, graphs, tables. (Serie de estudios; 27)

Published as a working paper, Arcondo presents synopsis of 1778 census data tabulated by sex, age, civil state, and place of residence, with the original data included on a diskette. [SMS]

Areces, Nidia R. Paraguayos, portugueses y Mbayás en Concepción, 1773–1840. See item **664.**

2351 Arias Divito, Juan Carlos. Consumo de tabaco y Real Hacienda en Córdoba, 1779–1812. (*in* Congreso Argentino de Americanistas, 2nd, Buenos Aires, 1997. Buenos Aires: Sociedad Argentina de Americanistas, 1998, t. 2, p. 15–34, tables)

Article concentrates on consumer taste, tobacco quality, supply and demand, scarcity, and sale of fraudulent products in the Córdoba region. La Dirección-General de la Real Renta de Tabacos faced a constant scarcity of those products held in highest regard by the local consumer. See also item **2352.** [SMS]

2352 Arias Divito, Juan Carlos. Organización de la Administración de Tabacos y Naipes de Mendoza, 1778–1812. (*Nuestra Hist./Buenos Aires*, 26:47/48, julio 1999, p. 91–108)

Study of the Administración de Tabacos y Naipes in Mendoza, San Juan, and San Luis is based primarily on Francisco de Paula Sanz' *visita*. Another piece of this scholar's ongoing research on tobacco in the Río de la Plata, article concentrates on organizational and administrative issues. See also item **2351.** [SMS]

Arteaga, Juan José. Las consecuencias del Tratado de Madrid en la desarticulación de la frontera demográfica de la Banda Oriental, 1750–1761. See item **3142.**

Avellaneda, Mercedes. Orígenes de la alianza jesuita-guaraní y su consolidación en el siglo XVII. See item **670.**

2353 Barriera, Darío. Derechos, ganados, pleitos, tierras: acceso a la propiedad de las tierras y practicas sociales en una sociedad de frontera; Santa Fe, 1620–1640. (*Varia Hist.*, 19, nov. 1998, p. 5–37, appendices, table)

Author uses one legal suit between the Jesuits and the heirs of Diego Ramírez to discuss both the weakness of land titles and the strength of personal networks along the Santa Fe frontier. [SMS]

2354 Bascary, Ana María. Familia y vida cotidiana: Tucumán a fines de la colonia. Tucumán, Argentina: Facultad de Filosofía y Letras, Univ. Nacional de Tucumán, 1999. 373 p.: bibl., ill.

Based on census materials and archival sources, solid study encompasses the physical and demographic setting, a discussion of family structure for different social groups, as well as information on work, dress, sickness, religious devotion, and festivals. [SMS]

2355 Bianchi, Diana. Asistencialismo en el Montevideo colonial: el caso de los gallegos en el Hospital de Caridad. *(Anu. Cent. Estud. Gallegos,* 1999, p. 115–137, tables)

After a brief discussion of the Hospital de Caridad in Montevideo, author concentrates on demographic characteristics of the men and women from Galicia (approximately 10 percent of all patients) interned there between 1787–1806. [SMS]

2356 Boixadós, Roxana. Transmisión de bienes en familias de elite: los mayorazgos en La Rioja colonial. *(ANDES Antropol. Hist.,* 10, 1999, p. 51–78, bibl.)

Analyzes property inheritance in three of the seven *mayorazgos* founded in the Rioja region of northwestern Argentina. Author suggests that the largest portions of inheritable goods were not included in the *mayorazgos,* and that the desire to perpetuate one's name, especially if only female children were the legal heirs, was a factor in the creation of these entails. [SMS]

2357 Calvo, Luis María. Construcciones para el comercio, la producción y el alquiler en Santa Fe colonial. *(Rev. Junta Prov. Estud. Hist. Santa Fe,* 62, 1998/99, p. 29–96, photos, tables)

Survey of urban properties used as shops, warehouses, gaming houses, mills, bakeries, and rental property in 17th- and 18th-century Santa Fe, listing architectural features when known. Although somewhat dry, article gives an idea of the economic activity of the city. [SMS]

Calvo, Luis María. Familia y ámbito doméstico en Santa Fe la Vieja: la casa de Hernando Arias Montiel. See item **56.**

2358 Celton, Dora Estela. La venta de esclavos en Córdoba, Argentina: entre 1750 y 1850. *(Cuad. Hist. Ser. Poblac.,* 2, dic. 2000, p. 5–20, bibl., graph, tables)

In this study of slave sales based on notarial records, Celton looks at overall trends, gender, age, and color over a 100-year period. She finds that Córdoba served as a center for slave distribution to Chile and Alto Perú during colonial period, but that numbers of sales and slave prices declined precipitously after 1812. [SMS]

2359 Cooney, Jerry W. Dubious loyalty: the Paraguayan struggle for the Paraná frontier, 1767–1777. *(Americas/Washington,* 55:4, April 1999, p. 561–578, map)

Interesting article documents Curuguatí uprising and suggests that inhabitants of northeastern Paraguay were more than willing to engage in contraband and political collaboration with the Portuguese. Challenges a historiography that accepted the sentiments of the Asunción cabildo as those of Paraguayan *vecinos* and considered Paraguayans' universal hostility to the Portuguese as essential to their national identity. [SMS]

2360 Cooney, Jerry W. Un rey inca para el Paraguay: Guarambaré en 1809. *(Desmemoria/Buenos Aires,* 6:23/24, julio/dic. 1999, p. 118–125, map)

Brief article shows that in 1809 rumors of the coronation of Tupac-Amaru as the new Inca king spread through the Villeta region of Paraguay and were taken seriously by the Asunción authorities. [SMS]

2361 Crespi, Liliana. Contrabando de esclavos en el puerto de Buenos Aires, durante el siglo XVII: complicidad de los funcionarios reales. *(Desmemoria/Buenos Aires,* 7:26, segundo cuatrimestre 2000, p. 115–133, ill., tables)

Documents contraband slave trade into Buenos Aires from 1587–1640. Although theoretically prohibited from engaging in trade, Portuguese merchants introduced thousands of slaves in return for Alto Peruvian silver during terms of office of nine different governors. Author finds that Union of the Crowns had an enormous influence on region's economy. [SMS]

2362 Dalla Corte, Gabriela. La red social frente a la crisis del orden colonial: compensación judicial y vínculos de parentesco entre Buenos Aires y Cataluña. *(CLAHR,* 9:3, Summer 2000, p. 347–377, graphs)

Interesting article concentrates on Catalan-born merchant Jaime Alsina i Verjés. Although Alsina arrived in Buenos Aires in 1780s, commercial and personal fortune of the Alsina family and failure of commercial/

kinship networks after 1810 are the focus of this study. See also item **2363**. [SMS]

2363 Dalla Corte, Gabriela. Vida i mort d'una aventura al Riu de la Plata: Jaime Alsina i Verjés, 1770–1836. Barcelona: Publicacions de l'Abadia de Montserrat, 2000. 323 p.: bibl., ill., maps. (Biblioteca Serra d'or; 241)

Biography of Jaime Alsina i Verjés, a moderately successful merchant who was part of the late Catalan immigration to the Río de la Plata. A Spanish translation of this Catalan work would probably win a larger audience. See also item **2362**. [SMS]

2364 Di Stefano, Roberto. De la cristianidad colonial a la iglesia nacional: perspectivas de investigación en historia religiosa de los siglos XVIII y XIX. (*ANDES Antropol. Hist.*, 11, 2000, p. 83–113, bibl.)

Think piece in which Di Stefano lays out his vision of the colonial Church, suggestions for future research, and overview of Church's transition in Argentina from colonial to national institution. Underscores the complexity of the Church and its importance in the local economy. See also item **2366**. [SMS]

2365 Di Stefano, Roberto. Magistri clericorum: estudio eclesiásticos e identidades sacerdotales en Buenos Aires a fines de la época colonial. (*Anu. IEHS*, 12, 1997, p. 177–195)

Interesting article centers on post-Jesuit clerical education and clerical politics. Author sees split between more traditional Seminario Conciliar and Enlightenment-influenced Reales Estudios, both of which trained priests in last decades of viceregal Buenos Aires. See also item **2366**. [SMS]

2366 Di Stefano, Roberto. Poder episcopal y poder capitular en lucha: el conflicto entre el Obispo Malvar y Pinto y el Cabildo Eclesiástico de Buenos Aires por la cuestión de la liturgia. (*Mem. Am.*, 8, 1999, p. 67–82, bibl.)

Another fine article by an outstanding historian. Here Di Stefano discusses a dispute between Bishop Malvar y Pinto and the ecclesiastical cabildo over liturgy as an example of both the increasing independence of this cabildo and internal conflicts in the late colonial Church. See also items **2364** and **2365**. [SMS]

Díaz, Sandra Liliana. Lo diario y lo extraordinario en el entorno material del guarani de las misiones. See item **697**.

2367 Duarte de Vargas, Alberto. Cartografía colonial asuncena. Asunción: Academia Paraguaya de la Historia; Municipalidad de Asunción, 2001. 43 p., 4 folded leaves of plates: bibl., ill., maps (some col.).

Comparison of four maps of colonial Asunción (César, 1785; Azara, 1786; César, 1786; Azara, 1793) drawn up in last decades of 18th century. [SMS]

2368 Endrek, Emiliano. La ciudad de La Rioja en 1767. (*in* Congreso Nacional de Historia Argentina, *Buenos Aires, 1995*. Buenos Aires: Comisión Post Congreso Nacional de Historia Argentina, 1997, t. 1, p. 101–112, tables)

Description and analysis of 1767 census of La Rioja discovered by author. The 15-page document was drawn up to enable circulation of the Santa Cruzada Bull, and consisted of a household listing of the entire urban population of 2,008 inhabitants. [SMS]

2369 Farberman, Judith. Trabajar con fuentes parcas en regiones marginales: reflexiones metodológicas acerca del estudio de las poblaciones indígenas rurales en el noroeste argentino; siglos XVIII y XIX. (*Rev. Hist. Am./México*, 127, julio/dic. 2000, p. 35–62)

A reflection on the theoretical and methodological difficulties of researching topics for which archival resources are scarce, with examples from Farberman's work on Santiago del Estero. A must read for graduate students before going into the field. [SMS]

2370 Fogelman, Patricia A. Una cofradía mariana urbana y otra rural en Buenos Aires a fines del período colonial. (*ANDES Antropol. Hist.*, 11, 2000, p. 179–207, bibl.)

Comparison of the Cofradía de Nuestra Señora de los Dolores y Animas in Buenos Aires with more modest Cofradía del Rosario in Luján concentrates on organization, religious devotion, and finances. As expected, there is more information on the wealthier *porteño* brotherhood. [SMS]

2371 Fradkin, Raúl O. La campaña de Buenos Aires: los arrendatarios a mediados del siglo XVIII. (*CLAHR*, 7:3, Summer 1998, p. 265–291, tables)

In this study of *arrendatarios* of rural land based on 1744 census of the *campaña* and archival documents, Fradkin finds that renting agricultural land and, to a lesser degree, estancias was widespread. Among those offering land for rent were the Jesuits, who used the system to make their large properties profitable. Small migrant farmers who cultivated rental land used family labor to exploit the property in the hope of eventually owning some land themselves. [SMS]

2372 Fraschina, Alicia. "Comian de la mesa del Señor": el espíritu de pobreza en el monasterio de las monjas capuchinas de Buenos Aires, 1749–1810. (*Arch. Ibero-Am.*, 60:235, enero/abril 2000, p. 69–86, bibl.)

Examines practice of poverty among Capuchine nuns within the Church in general and specifically in Buenos Aires. Although author finds Capuchine dedication to "santa pobreza" to have been an important motivating factor in the nuns' life, she also points out that a socioeconomic hierarchy existed within the convent that belied the much-desired ideal. See also items **2373** and **2374**. [SMS]

2373 Fraschina, Alicia. Los conventos de monjas en el Buenos Aires del siglo XVIII: requisitos para el ingreso. (*in* Congreso Argentino de Americanistas, 2nd, *Buenos Aires, 1997*. Buenos Aires: Sociedad Argentina de Americanistas, 1998, t. 2, p. 91–115)

General discussion of requirements for entering into either of the two convents in colonial Buenos Aires, with vague pretensions to understanding relationship between religious and secular "spaces." See also items **2372** and **2374**. [SMS]

2374 Fraschina, Alicia. La dote canónica en el Buenos Aires tardocolonial: monasterios Santa Catalina de Sena y Nuestra Señora del Pilar, 1745–1810. (*CLAHR*, 9:1, Winter 2000, p. 67–102, table)

Examines use of the dowry granted to women entering one of Buenos Aires' two convents. Fraschina is interested in degree of freedom enjoyed by the individual nun, her family, and the convent in structuring the dowry and using it to further personal or in-

stitutional ends. See also items **2372** and **2373**. [SMS]

2375 Galafassi, Guido P. La producción agraria del Río de la Plata colonial y las relaciones con el mercado urbano: una recorrida por el debate actual. (*Bol. Am./Barcelona*, 50, 2000, p. 61–82, bibl.)

Overview of seemingly endless discussion on nature of Buenos Aires *campo* in late colonial period should prove helpful to those seeking encapsulated version of major historians and positions involved in debates about ranching, agriculture, workforce, standard of living, and commercialization of agrarian products. See also items **2377, 2378,** and **2379**. [SMS]

2376 Galmarini, Hugo R. Los negocios del poder: reforma y crisis del estado, 1776–1826. Buenos Aires: Corregidor, 2000. 334 p.: bibl.

Interesting book highlights major economic changes from late Bourbon period through the revolution and 1820 reform period. Uses material about two extraordinary businessmen, the colonial merchant Tomás Antonio Romero and independence-period entrepreneur Braulio Costa, to illustrate shifting economic scene. [SMS]

2377 Garavaglia, Juan Carlos. Pastores y labradores de Buenos Aires: una historia agraria de la campaña bonaerense 1700–1830. Buenos Aires: Ediciones de la Flor, 1999. 385 p.: bibl., ill., maps. (Aquí mismo y hace tiempo)

Summarizes most of Garavaglia's work on rural Buenos Aires, bringing together work on population, social organization, ranching and farming production, technology, markets, and labor relations. See also items **2375, 2378,** and **2379**. [SMS]

2378 Garavaglia, Juan Carlos. Un siglo de estancias en la campaña de Buenos Aires: 1751 a 1853. (*HAHR*, 79:4, Nov. 1999, p. 703–734, graphs, map, tables)

Another study of Buenos Aires rural sector, this one based on 636 estate inventories from six regions over a 99-year period. Finds an increase in large animal stock over the period. For 19th-20th century historian's comment, see item **2865**. See also items **2375, 2377,** and **2379**. [SMS]

2379 Garavaglia, Juan Carlos and **Jorge Daniel Gelman.** Mucha tierra y poca gente: un nuevo balance historiográfico de la historia rural platense, 1750–1850. (*Hist. Agrar.*, 15, enero/junio 1998, p. 29–50, bibl., maps)

Update of previous article (see *HLAS 58:2446*) incorporates findings and bibliography of last 10 years including new material on demography, agrarian production, and labor force, as well as markets, rural justice, and patterns of sociability. See also items **2375, 2377,** and **2378.** [SMS]

2380 Garcés, Carlos Alberto. Brujas y adivinos en Tucumán, siglos XVII y XVIII. Prefacio de Mary Gibson. San Salvador de Jujuy, Argentina: Univ. Nacional de Jujuy, 1997. 179 p.

Based on documents from Tucumán archives, Garcés has chosen seven illustrative cases in which women were tried for witchcraft. See also item **2390.** [SMS]

2381 Gascón, Margarita. La articulación de Buenos Aires a la frontera sur del Imperio español, 1640–1740. (*Anu. IEHS*, 13, 1998, p. 193–213)

Interesting article sees Santiago de Chile, Mendoza, Córdoba, and Buenos Aires as four peripheral colonies that profited from their proximity to the frontier. Author examines how each of these cities was affected by the flow of material and persons needed to maintain control of the frontier; the economic and political consequences of collecting "forced contributions" to maintain the troops; and the use of a military career for rapid social advancement. [SMS]

2382 Gelman, Jorge Daniel. Campesinos y estancieros. Buenos Aires?: Editorial Los Libros del Riel, 1998. 333 p.: bibl., maps.

In this detailed study of Colonia region of the Banda Oriental, a well-watered region producing both meat and grain, Gelman emphasizes both production and population. He is careful to compare this region to other areas and to give equal emphasis to both estancias and small farming. [SMS]

2383 Gonzalez, Rubén. Fray Benjamín de Santo Domingo o Benjamín Gordon O.P., 1703–1762: un dominico rioplatense inglés del siglo XVIII. (*Nuestra Hist./Buenos Aires*, 26:47/48, julio 1999, p. 77–90)

Biography of Benjamín Gordon, an Englishman who was a respected Dominican cleric in both Córdoba and Buenos Aires at a time when only the Jesuits had permission to bring non-Spanish priests to America. Author suggests that Gordon never used his last name so as not to call attention to his English roots, and was well respected as a *sabio* in the region. [SMS]

González Coll, María Mercedes. Conquista, evangelización y relaciones interétnicas: una visión etnohistórica del problema. See item **714.**

2384 Gorla, Carlos María. La gestión de Domingo de Reynoso y Roldán como intendente de Buenos Aires. (*in* 500 años de Hispanoamérica: congreso internacional, 1492–1992. Mendoza, Argentina: Univ. Nacional de Cuyo, Facultad de Filosofía y Letras, 1996, t. 2, p. 319–343, bibl.)

Detailed description of futile attempts of Domingo de Reynoso, named *intendente* of Buenos Aires when office was revived in 1803, to carry out the terms of his much weakened office. [SMS]

2385 Gorla, Carlos María. El itinerario de la expedición de Manuel de Pinazo al Río Colorado, 1770. Viedma, Argentina: Fundvall, 1997. 92 p.: bibl., maps. (Col. Revisiones históricas patagónicas; 2)

Day-by-day recounting of Pinazo expedition to Río Colorado, undertaken in an attempt to prevent Tehuelche attacks along the frontier, includes reproductions of several early-19th-century maps. [SMS]

2386 Guzmán, Florencia. Formas familiares en la ciudad de Catamarca: el caso de los indios mestizos y castas, 1770–1812. (*in* Formas familiares, procesos históricos y cambio social en América Latina. Recopilación de Ricardo Cicerchia. Quito: Ediciones Abya-Yala, 1998, p. 39–58, bibl., graphs, tables)

Based on analysis of marriage records of the city of Catamarca during viceregal period, Guzmán finds that indigenous, zambos, and rural people were most likely to marry outside their racial group. [SMS]

Hall, Thomas D. The Río de la Plata and the Greater Southwest: a view from world-system theory. See item **1373.**

Hernández, Juan Luis. Tumultos y motines: la conflictividad social en los pueblos guaranís da la región misionera, 1768–1799. See item **724.**

2387 Jiménez, Juan Francisco. Encomenderos arruinados, incas fugitivos, beliches y corsarios holandeses: los orígenes de la expedición en búsqueda de los Césares de Jerónimo Luis de Cabrera, 1620–1621. (*Anu. IEHS*, 13, 1998, p. 173–192, bibl.)

Although its organizers used a growing Dutch threat and the promise to found a settlement in the Magellan Straits to justify their expedition to the Crown, author sees Cabrera expedition that made its way from Córdoba to Neuquén as driven by a need to find a new source of indigenous labor. Jiménez also argues that the Spaniards, in their search for the Césares, confused the Incas with the Hilliches. [SMS]

Juliano, María Dolores. Los mapuches, la más larga resistencia. See item **735.**

2388 Libros registros-cedularios del Tucumán y Paraguay, 1573–1716: catálogo. Dirección de Víctor Tau Anzoátegui. Buenos Aires: Instituto de Investigaciones de Historia del Derecho, 2000. 414 p.

Catalog of all royal *cédulas* in Archivo General de Indias in Seville pertaining to the *gobernaciones* of Tucumán and Paraguay. Latest in ongoing series of catalogs published for various types of *cédulas* issued for the entire region. [SMS]

2389 Lobos, Héctor Ramón and **Eduardo G.S. Gould.** El trasiego humano del viejo al nuevo mundo: la inmigración a Córdoba del Tucumán durante los siglos XVI y XVII. Buenos Aires: Academia Nacional de la Historia, 1998. 634 p.: bibl., ill. (Biblioteca de historia argentina y americana; 25)

Massive study of 16th- and 17th-century immigration to Córdoba examines origin, occupation, social background, sex, and age of those who arrived, as well as the rhythms of the migration itself. Authors identify 1,218 immigrants coming chiefly from Spain and then Portugal. Includes lengthy list of all immigrants identified by the historians as coming to Córdoba from anywhere outside the Spanish colonies. [SMS]

2390 López Campeny, Sara M.L.; M. Lorena Cohen; and **Silvana V. Urquiza.** De mujeres, indios y demonios: la hechicería en San Miguel de Tucumán, siglos XVI y XVII. (*Desmemoria/Buenos Aires*, 23/24, julio/dic. 1999, p. 99–117, bibl., ill.)

An attempt at analyzing a series of witchcraft accusations (*hechicería*) brought against indigenous, mestizo, and poor white women who were charged with trying to bewitch several important local people. Authors see these accusations as a way of establishing social and religious control. See also item **2380.** [SMS]

2391 Lorandi, Ana María. Las residencias frustradas: el juez Domingo de Irazusta contra el cabildo de Salta. (*ANDES Antropol. Hist.*, 11, 2000, p. 51–80, bibl.)

Thick on theory and discussion of historical anthropological perspectives, article finally gets down to analysis of one topic: the *residencia* of Esteban de Urízar (d. 1724), perpetual governor of Salta. Lasting over 10 years, this *residencia* produced a political imbroglio involving the *residencia* judge, various factions in the cabildo, the several governors, the Audiencia of Charcas, and the Lima *fiscal*. [SMS]

2392 Maeder, Ernesto J.A. Administración y destino de las temporalidades de los jesuitas en Corrientes. (*Folia Hist. Nordeste*, 13, 1997, p. 117–141, map, tables)

Discusses Jesuit holdings in Corrientes (churches, ranches, slaves, a brick oven, *chacras*) and income derived from the sale of this property by the *temporalidades* after the Jesuit expulsion. Part of an ongoing study of the aftermath of Jesuit expulsion in the Missiones area that underscores administrative and economic consequences. [SMS]

Mandrini, Raúl J. Las fronteras y la sociedad indígena en el ámbito pampeano. See item **754.**

2393 Mandrini, Raúl J. El viaje de la fragata San Antonio en 1745–1746: reflexiones sobre los procesos políticos operados entre los indígenas pampeano-patagónicos. (*Rev. Esp. Antropol. Am.*, 30, 2000, p. 235–263, bibl.)

Within framework of increased 18th-century interest in Patagonia, Mandrini discusses voyage of the San Antonio, concentrating on an indigenous tomb described in an accompanying priest's journal and what this tomb tells us about its builders. [SMS]

2394 Mariluz Urquijo, José María La Colonia del Sacramento en la vida porteña. (*in* Congreso Argentino de Americanistas, *2nd, Buenos Aires, 1997*. Buenos Aires: Sociedad Argentina de Americanistas, 1998, t. 2, p. 173–194)

An interesting overview of the relationship between Buenos Aires and the Portuguese-controlled entrepot of Colonia during the 18th century. Mariluz considers Colonia as a supplier of immigrant labor, Portuguese furniture, and naval stores for the larger port city. [SMS]

2395 Martínez de Sánchez, Ana María. La Hermandad de la Caridad en Córdoba, epoca colonial. (*in* Congreso Argentino de Americanistas, *2nd, Buenos Aires, 1997*. Buenos Aires: Sociedad Argentina de Americanistas, 1998, t. 2, p. 225–256)

Rather traditional history of Hermandad de la Caridad concentrates on its origin, regulations, officers, fundraising, and social action. In Córdoba the Hermandad seems to have been more effective in providing burial for the poor than in aiding orphans or sick women. [SMS]

2396 Martínez Martín, Carmen. Datos estadísticos de población sobre las misiones del Paraguay durante la demarcación del Tratado de Límites de 1750. (*Rev. Complut. Hist. Am.*, 24, 1998, p. 249–261, facsim., tables)

Attempts to trace indigenous population before and after the Treaty of 1750 which redrew the boundary between Spain and Portugal to the detriment of the Jesuit missions. Author tries to figure out where Jesuits relocated populations on the Portuguese side of the new line of demarcation. [SMS]

2397 Martini, Mónica P. Francisco Antonio Cabello y Mesa: un publicista ilustrado de dos mundos, 1786–1824. Buenos Aires: Instituto de Investigaciones sobre Identidad Cultural, Univ. del Salvador, 1998. 465 p.: bibl., ill., index.

Lengthy study of author and editor of *Telégrafo Mercantil* (1801–02). Focuses on life, philosophy, and writings of this Spanish-born literary figure. See also item **2414.** [SMS]

2398 Mata de López, Sara. La conformación de las elites a fines de la colonia: comerciantes y hacendados en la sociedad de Salta, Argentina. (*CLAHR*, 9:2, Spring 2000, p. 164–208, facsim., map, tables)

Against a background of economic growth and immigration of peninsula merchants, Mata de López investigates extent to which traditional families were able to preserve their economic and political power. Finds that because much of the new commercial prosperity was based on mule trade, landowners continued to be an important and self-contained sector of the region's most important families. See also items **2399, 2402,** and **2409.** [SMS]

2399 Mata de López, Sara. Población y producción a fines de la colonia: el caso de Salta en el noroeste argentino en la segunda mitad del siglo XVIII. (*ANDES Antropol. Hist.*, 9, 1998, p. 143–169, graphs, map, tables)

In a solid study of economic and demographic changes in Salta during the second half of 18th century, author examines changes produced in the local economy by growing trade (both legal and illegal) through Buenos Aires and the Pacific coast, as well as increased silver production. See also item **2398.** [SMS]

2400 Mayo, Carlos A. Estructura agraria, revolución de independencia y caudillismo en el Río de la Plata, 1750–1820: algunas reflexiones preliminares. (*Anu. IEHS*, 12, 1997, p. 69–77, bibl.)

Preliminary thoughts of an outstanding historian about why rural population of the two sides of the Río Uruguay exhibited such different political behaviors following 1810. Author seeks answers in nature of each region's landholding patterns and owners' ability to generate political power. An interesting article in what we hope will be Mayo's future research. [SMS]

2401 Mayo, Carlos A. Patricio de Belén: nada menos que un capataz. (*HAHR*, 77:4, Nov. 1997, p. 597–617)

Mayo continues to be the historian who excels in introducing a human dimension into discussions of the nature of colonial Buenos Aires rural society. Here he discusses the life of a slave employed as a foreman on the Estancia de las Vacas, providing a picture of the duties and responsibilities of this position as well as information on diet, social life, and daily activities of the ranch workforce. [SMS]

2402 Miller Astrada, Luisa. Salta hispánica: estudio socio-económico; desde el siglo XVI hasta la primera década del siglo XIX. Buenos Aires: Ediciones Ciudad Argentina, 1997. 399 p.: bibl., index. (Monografías históricas)

Rather ambitious overview of Salta attempts to provide more than 200 years of information on demography, social groups, land ownership, production, and administration. See also items **2398** and **2409.** [SMS]

Montes, Aníbal. El Gran Alzamiento Diaguita, 1630–1643. See item **767.**

2403 Morales, Martín María. Los comienzos de las Reducciones de la Provincia del Paraguay en relación con el derecho indiano y el Instituto de la Compañía de Jesús: evolución y conflictos. (*Arch. Hist. Soc. Iesu*, 67:133, Ian./Iun. 1998, p. 3–130)

Lengthy article on Paraguayan Indian towns created by the Jesuits in early years of their evangelization in the Americas. Morales concentrates on jurisdictional conflicts with the government and other religious orders that the Jesuits had to overcome. [SMS]

2404 Moreno, Carlos. Las cosas de la ciudad y la campaña. Buenos Aires: Icomos Comité Argentino, 1997. 241 p.: bibl., ill. (Españoles y criollos; 2)

A mixture of architectural and social history, book concentrates on plazas and municipal and religious buildings. Text is lavishly illustrated throughout, with drawings, maps, and floor plans. [SMS]

2405 Moreno, José Luis. El delgado hilo de la vida: los niños expósitos de Buenos Aires, 1779–1823. (*Rev. Indias*, 60:220, sept./dic. 2000, p. 663–685)

Interesting article on the Buenos Aires orphanage, tracing internal politics, finances, and child mortality from creation of the institution until it was turned over to the Damas de Beneficencia. Moreno finds that an aver-

age of 56 percent of all children turned over to the Casa de Expósitos died. [SMS]

2406 Moreno, José Luis and **Marisa M. Díaz.** Unidades domésticas, familias, mujeres y trabajo en Buenos Aires a mediados del siglo XVIII. (*Entrepasados/Buenos Aires*, 8:16, 1999, p. 25–42, ill., tables)

Demographic analysis of household size and its relationship to social class and race, based on 1744 census of Buenos Aires. Authors find that number of one-person households was surprisingly large for a traditional society. They also stress that women had a larger role in the workforce and as heads of household than previously thought. [SMS]

Nicoletti, María Andrea. La configuración del espacio misionero: misiones coloniales en la Patagonia Norte. See item **2335.**

Nocetti, Oscar R. and **Lucio B. Mir.** La disputa por la tierra: Tucumán, Río de la Plata y Chile, 1531–1822. See item **2121.**

2407 Paura, Vilma. El problema de la pobreza en Buenos Aires, 1778–1820. (*Estud. Soc./Santa Fe*, 9:17, segundo semestre 1999, p. 49–68)

Discussion of poverty somewhat marred by "social construction" jargon. Argues that 1810 marked an important change in definition of poverty, making a distinction between "the true poor" and "the shiftless and criminal." One result of this dichotomy was the decline of the traditional idea of public responsibility for the poor. [SMS]

2408 Perri, Gladys. El trabajo libre en la sociedad rural colonial: el caso de la Chacarita de los Colegiales, 1798–1806. (*Quinto Sol/Santa Rosa*, 2:2, 1998, p. 83–109, bibl., tables)

An interesting analysis of working patterns of the free rural population of Buenos Aires, based on *bandos* and records of the Colegiales farm. [SMS]

2409 Persistencias y cambios: Salta y el noroeste argentino, 1770–1840. Recopilación de Sara Mata de López. Rosario, Argentina: Prohistoria, 1999. 239 p.: bibl., ill., maps. (Col. Universos históricos)

A series of essays on social and economic history of Salta that cover marriage, mestizaje, rural investment, inheritance, and revolutionary changes. See also items **2398** and **2402**. [SMS]

2410 Prieto, María del Rosario and **Roberto G. Herrera.** Naos, clima y glaciares en el Estrecho de Magallanes durante el siglo XVI. (*Anu. Estud. Am.*, 55:2, julio/dic. 1998, p. 413–439, graphs, maps, tables)

Another contribution to climate history of southern realms of South America. Using navigational diaries and contemporary reports, authors examine rainfall, storms, temperature, wind, and weather to determine years of greatest glacial formation. [SMS]

2411 Punta, Ana Inés. Córdoba borbónica: persistencias coloniales en tiempo de reformas, 1750–1800. Córdoba, Argentina: Univ. Nacional de Córdoba, 1997. 336 p.: bibl., ill.

Social and economic study of Córdoba city has strong chapters on mule trade, commerce, public finance, daily life, and social control. [SMS]

2412 Quarleri, Lía. Alianzas y conflictos en La Rioja colonial: el colegio de los jesuitas, el cabildo, los encomenderos y el pueblo indígena de Malligasta. (*ANDES Antropol. Hist.*, 10, 1999, p. 79–111, bibl., map, tables)

Interesting study of lengthy litigation over water rights between Jesuits on the one hand, and La Rioja's cabildo and indigenous communities on the other. Shows how in regions of scarce resources, Jesuit control of the most productive land and much needed water could produce a deep animosity on the part of the local elite toward these relative latecomers. See also item **2413**. [SMS]

2413 Quarleri, Lía. Los jesuitas en La Rioja colonial: los mecanismos de adquisición de tierras; integración y conflicto, 1624–1767. (*Mem. Am.*, 8, 1999, p. 101–139, bibl., maps, tables)

In this skillful analysis of strategies used by the Jesuits to accumulate rural property in La Rioja from early 17th century to mid-18th century expulsion, Quarleri examines ambivalent reaction of the local elite in the face of increasing Jesuit encroachment. See also item **2412**. [SMS]

2414 Quintian, Juan Ignacio. El nacimiento del periodismo en el Río de la Plata a través del Telégrafo Mercantil. (*Rev. Arch. Reg. Cusco*, 15, junio 2000, p. 75–100, bibl., table)

Interesting article attempts to put the first newspaper published in Buenos Aires into context before discussing principal ideological currents that influenced this short-lived publication. Author finds a "dangerous innocence" in some of the early rioplatense intellectuals who believed they could easily achieve progress and prosperity. See also item **2397**. [SMS]

2415 Roberts, Carlos. Las invasiones inglesas del Río de la Plata, 1806–1807. Buenos Aires: Emecé Editores, 2000. 599 p.: bibl., ill., maps. (Memoria argentina)

Detailed political and military history of the two British invasions of Buenos Aires based on British and Argentine sources. [SMS]

2416 Rodriguez Otheguy, Victor A. and **Nelson Dellepiane.** Cabalgando en la frontera: historia de los blandengues orientales. Montevideo: Imprenta del Ejército, 1997. 223 p.: bibl., ill. (some col.).

History of the military company charged with defending the Montevideo frontier from indigenous and Portuguese incursion follows the Blandengues de Artigas from their formation to their role in the Artigas revolution. [SMS]

2417 Rubio Durán, Francisco A. Punas, valles y quebradas: tierra y trabajo en el Tucumán colonial, siglo XVII. Sevilla, Spain: Diputación Provincial de Sevilla, 1999. 567 p.: bibl., ill. (Nuestra América; 7)

Detailed study of several types of highland properties including haciendas, estancias, *chacras*, and *solares* transferred from indigenous to Spanish ownership during 17th century. Among these properties were those granted as *mercedes* after the two Calchaquí wars. [SMS]

2418 Saeger, James Schofield. The Chaco Mission Frontier: the Guaycuruan experience. Tucson: Univ. of Arizona Press, 2000. 266 p.: bibl., ill., index, map.

Excellent study of largest indigenous group of the Chaco traces their contact with the Spanish from mid-16th to 19th century.

Saeger is careful to present both indigenous and Spanish points of view, while respecting complex intra-Guaycuruan relations. Considers effect of missions on the indigenous society, the economy, politics, warfare, and religion. [SMS]

2419 Salinas de Brignardello, María Laura. Evolución de las encomiendas indígenas en el Paraguay, 1754–1780. (*in* Encuentro de Geohistoria Regional, *16th, Resistencia, Argentina, 1996. Reglamento y exposiciones.* Resistencia, Argentina: Instituto de Investigaciones Geohistóricas; Conicet, 1997, p. 511–523, bibl., tables)

Article on encomiendas in Paraguay stresses that this institution was still in force in 18th century, long after it had disappeared from most of Spanish America. Finds several new encomiendas of both *originarios* and *mitayos* created between 1754–80, and an increase in number of indigenous subjected to forced labor. [SMS]

Santamaría, Daniel J. Población y economía interna de las poblaciones aborígenes del Chaco en el siglo XVIII. See item **811.**

2420 Socolow, Susan Migden. Women of the Buenos Aires frontier, 1740–1810: or the Gaucho turned upside down. (*in* Contested ground: comparative frontiers on the northern and southern edges of the Spanish Empire. Edited by Donna J. Guy and Thomas E. Sheridan. Tucson: Univ. of Arizona Press, 1998, p. 67–82, graphs, tables)

Careful analysis of 1774 census returns demonstrates that white and mestizo women were present in significant numbers and played major roles as wives and mothers in rural districts, especially Areco and Magdalena, of Buenos Aires prov., during late-colonial period. Shatters the shibboleth of the pampas peopled almost entirely by males. [MTH]

2421 Tejerina, Marcela Viviana. El gobierno español y las reducciones jesuitas al sur de Buenos Aires: el caso del fracaso de "Nuestra Señora de la Concepción de los Pampas," 1751–1753. (*Rev. Hist. Am./ México,* 121, 1996, p. 131–142, bibl.)

Interesting article on history of last Jesuit mission founded in the Pampas. Argues that the mission south of the Salado River failed within 10 years because of great diversity of indigenous tribes in the region and lack of support provided by the Spanish government. [SMS]

2422 Troisi Melean, Jorge C. Una residencia, dos sistemas: el hospicio jesuita de Catamarca bajo administración religiosa y laica, 1743–1769. (*ANDES Antropol. Hist.,* 9, 1998, p. 115–142, graphs, tables)

Study of the Jesuit *hospicio* and school of Catamarca from its founding in 1743 to Jesuit expulsion in 1767, based on Jesuit accounts and *visitas* as well as *temporalidades* documents. Although Jesuits were latecomers to the region, they established four haciendas that produced wine, raisins, corn, cotton, and wheat to support the *hospicio.* Author sees this economic history as a model of how the Jesuits operated during the early years of installing themselves in a region. [SMS]

2423 El Tucumán colonial y Charcas. v. 1–2. Buenos Aires: Univ. de Buenos Aires, Facultad de Filosofía y Letras, 1997. 2 v.: bibl., ill., maps. (Serie Libros)

Edited collection of several papers touching on indigenous society before and after the conquest, ethnic identities, uprisings, Spanish encomiendas, and elite society, all produced by students of Lorandi, the primer ethnohistorian of the Argentina Andes. [SMS]

2424 Vitar Mukdsi, María Beatriz. Guerra y misiones en la frontera chaqueña del Tucumán, 1700–1767. Madrid: Consejo Superior de Investigaciones Científicas, 1997. 372 p.: bibl., ill. (Col. Biblioteca de historia de América; 17)

Solid study of Chaco frontier of Tucumán, a region that presented the Spanish with challenges throughout the colonial period. Examines early attempts to create encomiendas in the region, followed by 18th-century warfare and missionizing. [SMS]

Wilde, Guillermo. La actitud guaraní ante la expulsión de los jesuitas: ritualidad, reciprocidad y espacio social. See item **834.**

2425 Wilde, Guillermo. ¿Segregación o asimilación?: la política indiana en América meridional a fines del período colonial. (*Rev. Indias*, 59:217, sept./dic. 1999, p. 619–644)

Argues that end of Jesuit mission control of indigenous populations represented a shift from a policy of segregation to one of assimilation as theoretically espoused by the Bourbon Crown. [SMS]

19th and 20th Centuries
Venezuela

PETER S. LINDER, *Associate Professor of History, New Mexico Highlands University*

AMID VENEZUELA'S CURRENT POLITICAL TURMOIL, the historiography of the 19th and 20th centuries continues to evolve and develop. Indeed, current political controversies have led some historians of modern Venezuela to question long-held beliefs and assumptions about the history of the 20th century. In addition, studies in economic, social, and cultural history continue to illuminate new aspects of the nation's past. Finally, regional and local history are becoming more sophisticated and professional, providing a more nuanced understanding of a history traditionally written overwhelmingly from the viewpoint of Caracas.

The independence period remains a source of fascination for many. Simón Bolívar continues to inspire historical investigation, and the search continues for new directions to explore in relation to his life. Noteworthy recent examples are Alfonzo Vaz's analysis of the Liberator's religious beliefs (item 2427) and Beltrán Salmón's discussion of Bolívar's communication skills (item 2431). Also of interest is a compilation of letters exchanged between Bolívar and Manuela Sáenz, including many never before published in Venezuela (item 2570).

As the bicentennial of the revolt of 1810 nears, other independence-era figures have become the subject of increasingly intense historical scrutiny. Castellanos examines the role played by José Antonio Sucre in the diplomacy of the post-independence era (item 2442), while Sant Roz focuses on Sucre's assassination and its implications for liberal politics in Colombia (item 2477). Francisco de Miranda also has received considerable recent attention. A number of biographies and studies explore the career of this controversial figure. Racine has written an engaging study of Miranda's career and impact on the struggle for independence (item 2468), while Bencomo Barrios focuses on his military career (item 2432).

Venezuelan foreign policy remains an area emphasized by historians. Picón offers a useful, brief history of Venezuelan diplomacy from the First Republic until the mid-1980s (item 2462). Hernández explicates the links between political liberalism and Venezuela's international relations through a study of the life of Juan Viso, a 19th-century lawyer and diplomat (item 2451). Sanz examines Venezuelan public opinion concerning the Spanish Republic before and during the Spanish Civil War of the 1930s (item 2478). Finally, Quintero Torres reassesses US-Venezuelan relations during the Pérez Jiménez regime (item 2467).

Unsurprisingly given the current political climate, 20th-century political history has received considerable recent attention. Many works represent a reevaluation of—or challenge to—long-standing tenets of Venezuelan historiography. Herrera and Alva explore the complexities of politics in the immediate aftermath of the death of Juan Vicente Gómez (item **2452**). Battaglini argues, contrary to existing beliefs, that the government of Isías Medina Angarita represented a democratizing trend in Venezuelan politics, and that the 1945 coup that brought *Acción Demo-crática* to power lacked legitimacy (item **2430**). A missive written by Manuel Pérez Guerrero to Rómulo Betancourt sheds a critical light on the *AD* trienio of 1945–48 (item **2461**).

Several publications have responded to the trend of reevaluating common historical interpretations. For example, Caldera explores the Pact of Puntofijo and the enduring political accommodation it made possible (item **2439**). Catalá details the crimes and abuses of the dictatorship of Marcos Pérez Jiménez, and argues that only ignorance of that period would enable an unfavorable comparison of the governments of the 1960s–90s with the military dictatorships of earlier eras (items **2428** and **2444**).

Recent studies in social and cultural history represent significant advances in those fields. Two consequential works focus on African slavery and its aftermath. Pollak-Eltz analyzes the development and subsequent collapse of the institution, and calls for further research (item **2464**); Rodríguez Arrieta has produced a significant and detailed regional study of the processes of manumission and abolition in the province of Maracaibo, based on in-depth archival research (item **2474**). Regarding cultural history, Prieto Soto describes the influences instrumental in the development of Zulian popular culture (item **2465**), while Franceschi González explores the use of the pantheon of the War of Independence in order to promote a national culture and identity (item **2448**).

Economic history continues to develop as well. Lucas discusses the role of the state in the process of industrialization (item **2455**); Alcibíades R. provides a fascinating analysis of the links between the cigarette industry, advertising, and publishing (item **2426**). Two recent studies explore the history of monetary policy in Venezuela: Stohr investigates the role of monetary policy—especially the use of paper money—in the downfall of the First Republic (item **2479**), while Cordeiro analyzes Venezuela's recent economic woes and advocates a new national monetary policy (item **2446**). Two commendable studies explore the intersection between economic and environmental history. Zerpa Mirabal analyzes the economic, political, and ecological aspects of the trade in egret feathers in turn-of-the-century Venezuela (item **2481**). The other study, although not reviewed here, is worthy of brief mention: Kozloff's 2002 doctoral dissertation from St. Hugh's College, Oxford, "Maracaibo Black Gold: Venezuelan Oil and Environment During the Juan Vicente Gómez Period, 1908–1935," which explores the environmental impact of early petroleum development in Zulia and Lake Maracaibo.

As noted in *HLAS 58*, regional and local studies continue to reflect growing professionalization. In addition to the works already discussed, several others are noteworthy. Botello has written a useful—though still primarily descriptive—history of an important community in the Llanos (item **2433**). Castillo de López discusses the negative impact of Eleázar López Contreras' nationalization of the port of La Guaira on that community (item **2443**). Urdaneta's study examines resistance to the regime of Juan Vicente Gómez in the state of Zulia (item **2480**).

Thus, the quality and professionalization of Venezuelan historiography continues to improve. Political studies and works focusing on the heroes of independence remain a staple, but significant works have also appeared in economic, social, and cultural history. The proliferation of thoughtful and analytical regional studies continues.

2426 Alcibíades R., Mirla. Publicidad, comercialización y proyecto editorial de la empresa de cigarrillos "El Cojo," 1873–1892. Caracas: Fundación Centro de Estudios Latinoamericanos Rómulo Gallegos, 1997. 89 p.: bibl. (Col. Cuadernos)

Interesting study of the vagaries of a Venezuelan manufacturing concern, El Cojo Cigarette Company. Explores the links between the cigarette manufacturer and *El Cojo Ilustrado,* one of the most important Venezuelan periodical publications of the late 19th century. Useful contribution to the history of business and advertising in Venezuela.

2427 Alfonzo Vaz, Alfonso de Jesús. Bolívar católico. Caracas: Fundación Hermano Nectario María para la Investigación Histórico-Geográfica de Venezuela, 1999. 145 p.: bibl., ill. (Colección Simón Bolívar; t. 10)

Argues that despite Bolívar's attack on the political and ideological status quo, he was in fact a devout Catholic. Contains excerpts from Bolívar's correspondence and other documents to advance this thesis.

2428 Los archivos del terror: 1948–1958, la década trágica: presos, torturados, exiliados, muertos. Recopilación de José Agustín Catalá. Mérida, Venezuela: Gobernación del Estado Mérida: IDAC: El Centauro, 1998. 480, 23 p.: bibl., ill.

Presents a collection of biographies of the victims of the terror during the regime established by the military conspirators that toppled the Gallegos government in 1948.

2429 Azpúrua E., Miguel. El último general: vida y obra revolucionaria del Dr. Gustavo Machado M. Lara, Venezuela: Tipografía y Litografía Horizonte, 1999. 361 p.: bibl., ill.

Biography of 20th-century radical Gustavo Machado, detailing his evolution as a political and social activist. Provides useful insights into Machado's career and the evolution of 20th-century politics. Lacks documentation.

2430 Battaglini, Oscar. El medinismo: modernización, crisis política y golpe de estado. Caracas: Monte Avila Editores Latinoamericana: Dirección de Cultura, Univ. Central de Venezuela, 1997. 283 p.: bibl. (Estudios. Serie Historia)

Argues persuasively that Venezuelan democracy dates back to 1936, and that the 1945 coup represented the interruption of democracy, rather than its triumph. Also asserts that the government of Acción Democrática was of questionable legitimacy, and portrays the government of Medina Angarita as bourgeois, reformist, and modernizing.

2431 Beltrán Salmón, Luis Ramiro. El gran comunicador Simón Bolívar. La Paz: Plural Editores, 1998. 259 p.: bibl., ill. (Serie Historia)

Bolivian book discusses Bolívar's activities as a "great communicator." Argues that, in addition to many other areas of greatness, Bolívar was a genius in communicating and promoting his ideas and plans.

2432 Bencomo Barrios, Héctor. Miranda y el arte militar. Prólogo por Tomás Polanco Alcántara. Los Teques, Venezuela: Biblioteca de Autores y Temas Mirandinos, 2000. 176 p.: bibl., maps. (Biblioteca de autores y temas mirandinos; 72) (Biblioteca de autores y temas mirandinos; Colección Ambrosio Plaza; no. 9) (Homenaje del Gobierno del Estado Miranda; 2)

Investigates military aspects of Francisco de Miranda's career. Bencomo Barrios, a general in the Venezuelan army and a corresponding member of the Academia Nacional de la Historia, details Miranda's work as a military agent in Cuba and the US, and notes that Miranda was self-taught as a military commander and administrator. Written to commemorate the 250th anniversary of Miranda's birth.

2433 Botello, Oldman. Guasdualito, navegación por su historia. Venezuela: Publicaciones de la Alcaldía del Municipio Páez: Ateneo Popular de Guasdualito, 1998. 138 p.: bibl., ill.

A traditional narrative and anecdotal study of an important community in the Llanos, extending from prior to first contact until the 20th century.

2434 Bravo, Manuel J. Militarismo y política en Venezuela, 1945–1958. Prólogo de Omar Galíndez Colmenares. Caracas: Fondo Editorial de la Univ. Pedagógica Experimental Libertador, 1999. 300 p.: bibl.

Revisionist study asserts a fundamental continuity between the coup that brought Acción Democrática to power in 1945 and the one that displaced them three years later. Holds Rómulo Betancourt responsible for the military uprising of 1948. Attacks the notion of Venezuelan exceptionalism by putting the 1948 coup in the context of post-WWII US-Latin American relations.

2435 Briceño-Iragorry, Mario. Mérida, la hermética. Compilación, introducción y notas, Rafael Angel Rivas Dugarte. Mérida, Venezuela: Gobernación del Estado Mérida, Instituto de Acción Cultural, Comisión Presidencial para el Centenario del Nacimiento de Mario Briceño-Iragorry, 1997. 451 p.: bibl., ill., index.

New edition of a work originally written by Briceño-Iragorry and reissued in 1997. Provides a straightforward, chronological and topical study of the history of Estado Mérida.

2436 Briceño-Iragorry, Mario *et al.* Defensa y enseñanza de la historia patria en Venezuela. 2. ed. aum. Caracas: Fondo Editorial 60 Años de la Contraloría General de la República, 1998. 271 p.

Collection of essays details the teaching of history in Venezuela, and recounts the evolution of Venezuelan historiography. Argues that the professionalization of Venezuelan historians is continuing.

2437 Caballero, Manuel. Contra el golpe, la dictadura militar y la guerra civil. Caracas: Ediciones Centauro, 1998. 173 p.

A compilation of columns and essays dealing with recent Venezuelan political history, particularly the upheavals of the 1990s. Work is critical of the regime of Hugo Chávez.

2438 Caballero, Manuel. Las crisis de la Venezuela contemporánea: 1903–1992. Caracas: Monte Avila Editores Latino-americana: Contraloría General de la República de Venezuela, 1998. 176 p.: bibl. (Estudios. Serie Historia)

Examines the many political crises in 20th-century Venezuelan history. Compares recent political upheavals unfavorably with earlier coups, rebellions, and other crises.

2439 Caldera, Rafael. Los causahabientes de Carabobo a Puntofijo. Caracas: Editorial Panapo de Venezuela, 1999. 203 p.: bibl.

Written as a response to rhetorical attacks by the Chávez administration upon the Pact of Puntofijo. Presents a historical defense of the politics of 1958–99. Argues that, despite widespread public ignorance of the terms of the pact, it did provide for political stability.

2440 Carrera Damas, Germán. Una nación llamada Venezuela. Prólogo de Elio Gomez Grillo. 5. ed. Caracas: Monte Avila Editores Latinoamericana, 1997. 219 p.: bibl. (Colección documentos)

First published in 1980, a series of transcribed conferences provides a broad overview of sociohistorical and political development of Venezuela, from independence to the present. Advocates development of a new model of participatory democracy to overcome the nation's ongoing economic and social problems.

2441 Carrera Damas, Germán *et al.* Comprensión de nuestra democracia: 40 años de historia venezolana. Caracas: Fondo Editorial 60 Años, Contraloría General de la República, 1998. 276 p.: bibl.

Collection of essays reflects author's preoccupation with the trajectory of Venezuelan democracy.

2442 Castellanos, Rafael Ramón. La dimensión internacional del Gran Mariscal de Ayacucho: Sucre diplomático y creador del derecho internacional humanitario. Caracas: Alcaldía del Municipio Pampán, 1998. 532 p.: bibl., ill. (some col.), index.

Hagiographic study explores the international dimension of Sucre's career. Portrays him as a pioneer in the development of international relations. Based on secondary sources and published documents.

2443 Castillo de López, Haydeé. La nacionalización del Puerto de La Guaira. Los Teques, Venezuela; Caracas: Fondo Editorial A.L.E.M., 1998. 184 p.: bibl., ill. (Colección Doxa y episteme)

Discusses the López Contreras administration's decision to nationalize the port of La Guaira. Argues that the nationalization of the port had profoundly negative consequences for the community and its inhabitants.

2444 Catalá, José Agustín. Pérez Jiménez: el dictador que en 40 años olvidó sus crímenes. Caracas: El Centauro, 1997. 183 p.: ill. (Memorial de testigo; no. 1)

Attempts to inform Venezuelans born since 1958 of the crimes and human rights violations committed under the military dictatorship of 1948–58. Motivated by recent political developments; argues that support for the Chávez government is explicable only through the ignorance of recent generations about the dictatorship that ended in 1958.

Celis Parra, Bernardo. Mérida ciudad de águilas. See item **2125.**

2445 Consalvi, Simón Alberto. El perfil y la sombra: ensayos. Los Palos Grandes, Venezuela: Tierra de Gracia Editores, 1997. 236 p.: ill. (Colección Viaje al amanecer)

A collection of biographical essays by the well-known Venezuelan diplomat, profiling such prominent figures as Juan Vicente Gómez, Ramón J. Velásquez, Pedro Emilio Coll, and Rómulo Gallegos.

2446 Cordeiro, José Luis. La segunda muerte de Bolívar— y el renacer de Venezuela. Caracas: CEDICE, 1998. 185 p.: bibl., ill.

Examines history of Venezuelan monetary policy. Argues for the development of a new monetary policy to end Venezuela's economic woes and return to economic and social stability. Also criticizes the economic activities of the Venezuelan state, and argues that new monetary policy should be part of a broader agenda involving spending cuts and fiscal restraint.

2447 Díaz Rangel, Eleazar. Días de enero: cómo fue derrocado Pérez Jiménez. Caracas: Monte Avila Editores Latinoamericana, 1998. 296 p.: bibl., ill. (Colección 300. aniversario; 5)

Attempts to resolve contradictions and clarify uncertainties surrounding the overthrow of Marcos Pérez Jiménez in Jan. 1958. Makes extensive use of oral history, including more than 80 interviews. Challenges the revisionist thesis that the dictatorship was a more efficient and orderly government than those that have followed (from 1959–98).

Ferrigni Varela, Yoston. La crisis del régimen económico colonial en Venezuela, 1770–1830. See item **2126.**

2448 Franceschi González, Napoleón. El culto a los héroes y la formación de la nación venezolana: una visión del problema a partir del estudio del discurso historiográfico venezolano del período, 1830–1883. Caracas: s.n., 1999. 325 p.: bibl.

Examines historiography of Venezuelan independence, focusing on 1830–83 era. Argues that the "cult of the heroes" was a key element in the development and consolidation of the nation-state. Based on newspaper and library research.

2449 García Díaz, Luis. Cumaná: historia increíble. Caracas: Editorial Kinesis, 2000. 263 p.: bibl., ill.

A traditional local study written by a journalist and native of Carúpano, focusing on the history of Cumaná from colonization to the 1990s. Although not characterized by analysis, offers an interesting narrative treatment of the city's history.

2450 El glorioso ayer: Maracaibo 1870–1935. Recopilación de Julio Portillo. 2. ed. Venezuela: s.n., 1998. 209 p.: bibl., chiefly ill.

Presents a fascinating collection of photographs from Maracaibo, compiled by Portillo. Includes pictures depicting various aspects of social, economic, political, and cultural life of that important western city.

2451 Hernández, Adriana. Jurisprudencia, liberalismo y diplomacia: la vida pública de Julián Viso (1822–1900). Asistente de investigación, Henry Suárez. Caracas: Ministerio de Relaciones Exteriores: Instituto de Altos Estudios Diplomáticos "Pedro Gual", 1999. 278 p.: bibl., index. (Serie Ensayos de investigación; 1)

Explores the Venezuelan diplomatic corps in the 19th century by analyzing the career of lawyer and diplomat Julián Viso.

Viso participated in many key diplomatic disputes of the era, particularly in the delineation of the border with Colombia. Argues that Venezuelan diplomacy in the 19th century reflected the prevailing liberal ideology.

2452 Herrera, Bernardino and **Rosa María Alva.** ORVE: el diseño del país: el discurso político en la Venezuela de 1936. Caracas: Fondo Editorial de la Facultad de Humanidades y Educación, UCV: Tierra Firme Revista de Historia y Ciencias Sociales Historiadores, 1998. 226 p.: bibl., ill. (Colección Estudios)

Analyzes formation of ORVE (Organización Venezolana) and its role in the political changes that occurred upon death of Juan Vicente Gómez. Argues that ORVE was a key political actor during the brief but significant political opening during the presidency of Eleázar López Contreras. Seeks to convey a nuanced and complex view of the transition after the death of Gómez.

2453 Imágenes de la Venezuela del siglo XX: fotografías del Archivo Histórico de Miraflores. Caracas: Fundación Galería de Arte Nacional, 1998. 59 p.: ill.

Interesting and evocative collection of photographs relating to presidential administrations and activities. Offers a useful introduction to the collections of the Archivo Histórico de Miraflores.

2454 Linder, Peter S. "An immoral speculation:" Indian forced labor on the haciendas of Venezuela's Sur Del Lago Zuliano, 1880–1936. (*Americas/Washington*, 56:2, Oct. 1999, p. 191–220)

Pioneering article uses regional archival materials to study exploitative labor relationships in Sur del Lago, Zulia, where *hacendados* routinely enslaved Guajiro indigenous peoples through a system of debt servitude. Notwithstanding Guajiro resistance, local officials supported the practice which collapsed only in the 1930s when the central government under Gómez imposed control over the regional economy. [J. Rausch]

2455 Lucas, Gerardo. La industrialización pionera en Venezuela: 1820–1936. Caracas: Univ. Católica Andrés Bello, 1998. 187 p.: bibl.

Valuable discussion of evolution of Venezuelan industry prior to WWII. Orga-

nized topically, discusses development of various industries over time, and argues that 1936 represented a turning point for Venezuelan industry, in which the state established a more direct role in the process of industrialization.

2456 Méndez Echenique, Argenis. Historia de Apure. San Fernando de Apure, Venezuela: Fondo Editorial Otomaquia, 1998. 294 p.: bibl., maps. (Biblioteca de historia apureña; 1)

Presents a general history of Estado Apure, traditional in approach and relying on printed documents, hemerographic sources, and secondary materials.

2457 Mieres, Antonio. Mario Briceño-Iragorry, o, La historia como disciplina moral. Caracas: Fondo Editorial Tropykos, 1997. 189 p.: bibl.

Analyzes the philosophy of history of the discipline of history of iconic Venezuelan historian Briceño-Iragorry. Notes the evolution of his historical outlook from support to opposition, to militaristic dictatorship. Argues that Briceño conceived of the study of history as a moral discipline, and that this belief underlay his nationalism and anti-imperialism.

Molina, Luis E. De los trapiches decimonónicos a los centrales protoindustriales: aproximación histórico-arqueológica a los establecimientos cañeros de la segunda mitad del siglo XIX y primera del XX en Venezuela. See item **766.**

2458 Moya, Pedro O. De Cristóbal a Hugo: gobernantes de Venezuela. Caracas: Ediciones CO-BO, 1999. 176 p.: bibl., ill. (Colección Biblioteca Escolar CO-BO)

Presents a chronology of people who have held executive power at the national level in Venezuela, no matter how briefly or ephemerally. Useful basic reference for the history of national politics.

2459 Murguey Gutiérrez, José. Construcción, ocaso y desaparición de los ferrocarriles en Venezuela. Mérida, Venezuela: Univ. de los Andes, Consejo de Publicaciones, Vicerrectorado Académico, Facultad de Humanidades y Educación, 1997. 594 p.: bibl., ill. (Colección Ciencias sociales. Serie Historia)

Important study of the railroad industry in Venezuela argues that railroads developed in Venezuela as a result of external economic processes, and collapsed as a result of internal government policies, particularly the promotion of highway construction to compete with rail lines.

2460 Ojeda Olaechea, Alonso. Dos nombres, una vida de acción y pasión—. Caracas: Monte Avila Editores Latinoamericana, 1999. 467 p.: bibl., ill. (Colección Documentos)

Personal account of a member of the Venezuelan Communist Party, detailing his experiences and observations from 1937 until the 1980s. Attempts to justify the efforts of the Communist Party to seize power, including the armed struggle against the elected governments of the 1960s. Includes a number of relevant documents, particularly speeches made by Ojeda Olaechea in the Congress during the 1970s-80s.

2461 Pérez Guerrero, Manuel. Manuel Pérez-Guerrero: el 18 de octubre, el 24 de noviembre, 1945/1948: un documento que (no) hizo historia, pero es historia. Prólogo de Simón Alberto Consalvi. Caracas: Fundación Rómulo Betancourt, 1998. 103 p.: bibl. (Colección Tiempo vigente; 11)

Reprints a long letter that Pérez Guerrero sent to Rómulo Betancourt in the wake of the 1948 coup that toppled the first Acción Democrática government. Provides an insider's perspective of many of the problematic aspects of the Betancourt regime during the 1945–48 *trienio*.

2462 Picón, Delia. Historia de la diplomacia venezolana: 1811–1985. Caracas: Univ. Católica Andrés Bello, 1999. 331 p.: bibl., index.

Written by the daughter of Mariano Picón Salas, provides a comprehensive history of Venezuelan diplomacy. Roughly chronological in organization, by presidential administration. Also contains additional chapters on oil and border issues. Based on published primary and secondary sources, but a useful overview nonetheless.

2463 Picón Febres, Gabriel. Datos para la historia de la Diócesis de Mérida. 2a ed. Mérida, Venezuela: Instituto de Acción Cultural, Consejo de Desarrollo Científico, Humanístico y Tecnológico, 1998. 183 p. (Solar de clásicos merideños)

Published originally in 1916 by a doctor, politician, and diplomat from Estado Mérida. Presents a narrative history of the diocese of Mérida from the 18th century until 1830. Also reproduces a number of relevant documents.

2464 Pollak-Eltz, Angelina. La esclavitud en Venezuela: un estudio histórico-cultural. Caracas: Univ. Católica Andrés Bello, 2000. 158 p.: bibl.

A useful brief survey intended as a spur to research in slavery and Afro-Venezuelan culture in Venezuela; represents the distillation of more than 40 years of work in the field. Argues that formal abolition was the culmination of a process initiated perhaps a century earlier. Topics of discussion include slavery's classical and medieval roots, its role in Venezuelan development, and its eventual collapse.

2465 Prieto Soto, Jesús. Mestizaje y cultura costanera. v. 1. Maracaibo, Venezuela: s.n., 1999. 1 v.: bibl., ill.

Interesting descriptive work explores origins and development of music and dance in the western state of Zulia. Particularly interesting in terms of the recognition of various contributors to Zulian popular culture. Based primarily on secondary sources.

2466 Quintero Montiel, Inés Mercedes and Floreal Contreras. Antonio José de Sucre: dos ensayos sobre el personaje y su tiempo. Mérida, Venezuela: Univ. de los Andes, Facultades de Humanidades y Educación, 1998. 98 p.: bibl.

A compilation of two essays focusing on the Battle of Ayacucho and the role of Antonio José de Sucre. The first essay, by Quintero, is particularly interesting. She explores the implications of the battle in Spain and the Americas, arguing that news of the battle's outcome was especially devastating to Spanish public opinion.

2467 Quintero Torres, José Gilberto. Venezuela-U.S.A.: estrategia y seguridad en lo regional y en lo bilateral, 1952–1958. Caracas: Fondo Editorial Nacional, 2000. 239 p.: bibl.

Revised doctoral dissertation of Adm. Quintero Torres, presents a study of the military and strategic relationship between Venezuela and the US during the regime of Marcos Pérez Jiménez. Argues that Venezuela maintained significant autonomy in terms of weapons procurement and training, and occasionally disagreed with US policymakers.

2468 Racine, Karen. Francisco de Miranda, a transatlantic life in the Age of Revolution. Wilmington, Del.: Scholarly Resources, 2003. 336 p.: bibl., ill., index, maps. (Latin American silhouettes)

Readable and lively biography of the Venezuelan patriot and figure of the early phases of the struggle for Spanish American independence. Seeks to transcend traditional biographies of Miranda by putting him into broad international context. Argues that his key role was as a popularizer and inspiration, rather than as leader of the struggle.

2469 Ramírez Rojas, Kléber. Historia documental del 4 de febrero. Caracas: U.C.V.: Asamblea Legislativa del Edo. Miranda, 1998. 360 p.

Useful collection of documents relating to the attempted military coup of Feb. 4, 1992. Displays definite sympathy to aims of attempted coup, asserting that it represented an effort to break with the "estado gomecista" dominated by mainstream political parties.

2470 Rangel, Domingo Alberto. Venezuela en 3 siglos. Caracas: Catalá/El Centauro: Vadell Hermanos, 1998. 248 p.

While denouncing Venezuela's current political and economic situation, Rangel turns speculatively to the future. This nationalist work focuses mainly on market solutions for the nation's problems. Decries regionalism, arguing that only strong centralization will preserve the nation.

2471 Rivas Dugarte, Rafael Angel. Andrés Eloy Blanco: cronología mayor y bibliografía. 2a. ed. Caracas: Ediciones de la Comisión Presidencial y la Comisión Estadal del Estado Sucre, 1997. 93 p.: bibl., ill.

Second edition of the biography of Eloy Blanco, a noted poet of Cumaná, in the state of Sucre. Reflects on the role of intellectuals in political movements of the early 20th century.

2472 Rivas Rivas, José. Ocurió en Miraflores. Maracay, Venezuela: Playco Editores, 1999. 181 p.: bibl., ill. (some col.).

Fascinating work compiles photographs and brief accounts of presidential tenure and events taking place in and around the palace. Visually pleasing.

2473 Rodríguez, José Angel. Venezuela en la mirada alemana: paisajes reales e imaginarios en Louis Glöckler, Carl Geldner y Elisabeth Gross, 1850–1896. Caracas: Comisión de Estudios de Postgrado, Fondo Editorial de Humanidades y Educación, Facultad de Humanidades y Educación, Univ. Central de Venezuela; Fundación Edmundo y Hilde Schnoegass, 2000. 190 p.: bibl., col. ill., 1 map.

Explores experience of Venezuela's 19th-century German community through analysis of memoirs of three German residents in Venezuela. Argues that the vision of Venezuela they provided sheds light on topics generally ignored by Venezuelan observers, as well as by historians.

2474 Rodríguez Arrieta, Marisol. La ley sobre aprendizaje de manumisos en la provincia de Maracaibo y sus efectos en el proceso de manumisión, 1840–1848. (*Tierra Firme/Caracas,* 17:67, julio/sept. 1999, p. 403–413, bibl.)

Significant regional study focuses on the decline and abolition of slavery in Maracaibo. Argues that the processes of manumission and abolition were slower than in central Venezuela, due to factors such as distance from Caracas and limited resources and power of provincial and local authorities. Based on research in Zulian archives.

2475 Sáez Mérida, Simón. La cara oculta de Rómulo Betancourt: el proyecto invasor de Venezuela por tropas norteamericanas. Caracas: Fondo Editorial Almargen, 1997. 433 p.: bibl., ill., maps.

An extreme example of recent challenges to the orthodoxy of history in the post-1958 era, this work is extremely critical of Betancourt, as well as broadly critical of the historiographical mainstream for being excessively adulatory of Acción Democrática and post-Pérez Jiménez governments. Accuses Betancourt of purposeful fabrication and manipulation of his image, along with hypocrisy for criticizing Juan Vicente Gómez for soliciting US assistance in blocking the return of ousted president Cipriano Castro, then planning for possible US military intervention in 1963.

2476 Saher, José Manuel. Chema: testimonio de una vida revolucionaria. Coro, Venezuela: Ediciones Calicanto, 1997. 265 p.: ill.

Memoir of—and documents relating to—a young militant. Born in Coro to prominent parents, Chema Saher became first a militant for Acción Democrática, then part of the breakaway MIR, and finally a guerrilla in the Sierra de Coro. Provides interesting insights into the political conflicts of the 1960s.

2477 Sant Roz, José. El Jackson granadino, José María Obando: recuento político-religioso del asesinato de Sucre. Mérida, Venezuela: Kariña Editores, 2000. 470, 14 p.: bibl., index.

One of a group of books produced to commemorate the bicentennial of the birth of Sucre. Focuses on the life and career of Obando, explicitly comparing him to American president and politico-military icon Andrew Jackson. Argues that, like Jackson, Obando was a leader with extraordinary rapport among the lower classes. Also argues that the assassination of Sucre was portrayed in Colombia as a patriotic, almost sacrificial act by liberals, including Obando.

2478 Sanz, Víctor. Venezuela ante la República española, 1931–1939. Recopilación de José Agustín Catalá. Caracas: Centauro Ediciones, 1997. 474 p.: bibl.

Discusses public and press opinion in Venezuela regarding the Spanish Republic and its Civil War. Argues that the citizens and press of Venezuela had limited interest in the events in Spain. Also notes that official policy shifted over time, but tended to favor Franco and the Nationalist regime.

Saturno Canelón, Jesús. Barberos y sucesores: medio milenio de odontología en Iberoamérica. See item **943.**

2479 Stohr, Tomás. El papel moneda en la primera república. Caracas: Banco Central de Venezuela, 1999. 179 p.: bibl., ill. (Colección Banca central y sociedad)

Examines monetary policy, specifically the use of paper money, during the First Republic. Study relies on money itself as the most important primary source. Argues that the issuance of paper money contributed to—but did not cause—the collapse of the First Republican government. Narrowly focused.

2480 Urdaneta, Yeris. Gómez y gomecismo en el Zulia, 1928–1937. Maracaibo, Venezuela: Sinamaica, 2000. 207 p.: bibl., ill. (Biblioteca de historia e identidad)

Analyzes development of opposition to the Gómez regime in the state of Zulia, mainly in the city of Maracaibo. Distinguishes between opposition to the dictator himself and opposition to the regime he established and nurtured—a regime which outlived him, according to the author. Pays particular attention to the career of Valmore Rodríguez as an opponent of the regime.

2481 Zerpa Mirabal, Alfonso J. Explotación y comercio de plumas de garza en Venezuela: fines del siglo XIX-principios del siglo XX. Caracas: Ediciones del Congreso de la República, 1998. 205 p.: bibl., ill.

Study treats egret feathers as an economic commodity subject to boom and bust cycles. Analyzes causes of initial boom, decline, and ultimate collapse. Argues that, while some positive aspects to trade in feathers existed, the overall impact of the trade was negative, and resources generated were largely wasted. Based on newspapers and published government documents. Useful as a study of an ill-understood aspect of the Venezuelan economy, as an example of the growing power and intrusiveness of the national state, and as a case study in environmental history.

2482 Zerpa Rojas, José Acacio. Las fuerzas armadas y la democratización nacional, 1945–1948. Mérida, Venezuela: Univ. de los Andes, Consejo de Publicaciones; Sucre: Alcaldía del Municipio Sucre, 1998. 120 p.: bibl., ill. (Colección Ciencias sociales. Serie Historia)

Brief study of the Venezuelan military's role in the movement that brought Acción Democrática and Rómulo Betancourt to power in 1945, and the motives and reasons for the 1948 coup that ended the elected government of Rmulo Gallegos. Blames the "demagogy and sectarianism" of AD for provoking the military coup that toppled him.

Colombia and Ecuador

JANE M. RAUSCH, *Professor of History, University of Massachusetts-Amherst*

THE RELENTLESS VIOLENCE that has plagued Colombia over the last decade has not deterred Colombian and foreign scholars from publishing a wealth of innovative books and articles dealing with all aspects of Colombian history. While the output from Ecuador continues to be somewhat spotty, there are, nevertheless, two fine contributions worthy of special note.

The papers presented at the 10th and 11th Congresos de Historia de Colombia held in Tunja (1995) and Medellín (1997) reveal that professional graduate history programs at Colombian universities are producing masters theses that, as well as examining such tried and true topics as "mentalidades," education, and regional and frontier history, are tapping previously ignored notarial archives and other local sources to delve into gender and race-related issues (items **2496** and **2530**). In addition, the Universidad Nacional in Bogotá inaugurated its PhD program in March 1997 with a symposium featuring five noted scholars (item **2531**). Incorporating fresh material, editor Tirado Mejía has expanded the *Nueva Historia de Colombia* with three new volumes covering political history since 1986; economy and regions; and ecology and culture (item **2527**).

Looking at various subfields, one finds works utilizing innovative approaches in almost every category. For example, among the seven books dealing with the independence era, there is Rodríguez G.'s careful analysis of 320 wills written by Bogotanos between 1800–31 in which she investigates changing attitudes about death at the beginning of the century (item **2534**). Among economic studies, Ramírez Bacca's doctoral thesis examines administrative organization and labor systems between 1882–1907 on a farm in Líbano, Tolima, to illuminate entrepreneurial strategies that promoted coffee-growing by the end of the 19th century (item **2533**).

Under the rubric of social history, three works deal with women's issues (items **2517, 2521,** and **2547**), and Ospina's biography of her mother, Bertha Hernández de Ospina, the wife of President Mariano Ospina, offers unusual insight into the life of an influential 20th-century woman (item **2529**). An important work on Manuel Quintín Lame shows how his ideals continue to inspire Indians to defend their territories, culture, and autonomy with weapons and the law (item **2500**). There are four fine books on Medellín that range from histories of the city (items **2492** and **2501**) to an investigation of child labor in its factories during the first three decades of the 20th century (item **2507**). In this category, we may also put six immigration studies that address a topic too-long neglected by Colombian historians. One of these examines the impact of Syrians and especially Lebanese on the Chocó (item **2510**); another looks at the influence of these same groups on the Atlantic Coast (item **2502**); while a third by Silva Téllez shows how Italian influence left its mark on Colombian culture despite the fact that in 1985 there were only 13,000 people of Italian heritage living in the country (item **2539**). Finally, there are four studies of frontier regions including a collection of informative essays that provide a regional history of the Chocó (item **2497**), Aguilar's study of efforts to evangelize and colonize the Putumayo (item **2494**), and Franco's well-researched history of Orocué, the first serious monograph about a key town in Casanare (item **2504**).

For the first time in many years, works on the Violencia do not dominate entries under political history although Alape has published the second volume of his biography of Manuel Marulanda, the principal leader of the FARC (item **2484**). There are three studies dealing with Rojas Pinilla, including one by his daughter, Rojas de Moreno, who seeks to redeem her father's career and presidency (item **2535**). More innovative in approach, however, are a prize-winning monograph by Aguilera Peña about the artisan insurgencies of 1893 and 1894 (item **2483**), and Green's essay that reviews the evolution of "left-Liberal" national identity in the 19th–20th centuries (item **2511**).

Regretfully, many of the Ecuadorian entries continue to rehash familiar themes by dealing with 19th-century figures Pedro Fermín Cevallos and Eloy Alfaro or the 1922 general strike. However, there are two studies that break new ground. First, complementing similar studies on Colombia, Lois J. Roberts has produced an excellent monograph on the influence of the Lebanese (including Syrians and Palestinians) in Ecuador (item **2569**). The second truly innovative work is *Tales of Two Cities* in which Townsend compares the social history of Guayaquil with that of Baltimore in the 1820s–30s. By employing an "economic culture" paradigm, she explains how differing attitudes toward race and class affected local ways of doing business and allowed the North American city to attain greater prosperity (item **2573**).

COLOMBIA

2483 Aguilera Peña, Mario. Insurgencia urbana en Bogotá: motín, conspiración y guerra civil, 1893–1895. Bogota?: Instituto Colombiano de Cultura, 1997. 475 p.: bibl. ill., map. (Premios nacionales de cultura, 1996)

Prize-winning study of artisan movement. Uses archival documents to suggest that 1893 riot and 1894 conspiracy in Bogotá were the most important 19th-century urban protests, and that they previously have been overlooked as the first serious challenge to Regeneration policies.

2484 Alape, Arturo. Manuel Marulanda "Tirofijo": Colombia, 40 años de lucha guerrillera. Tafalla, Spain: Txalaparta, 2000. 308 p.: bibl.

Second installment of two-vol. biography of Marulanda, principal leader of the FARC guerrilla movement. Beginning in 1964, it charts Marulanda's formation of an insurgent force with characteristics of a small army, the FARC's development in the next decade, and concludes with signing of peace agreement between Marulanda and President Betancur in 1984. For review of first installment, see *HLAS 52:2340* and *HLAS 56:2688.*

2485 Alarcón Meneses, Luis. Las elecciones en el estado soberano del Magdalena, 1857–1872: entre la participación y el fraude. (*Hist. Soc./Medellín*, 3, dic. 1996, p. 117–139, maps, tables)

Well-researched MA thesis describes election procedures in the coastal state of Magdalena, where both Liberals and Conservatives mobilized significant portions of the population and manipulated the ballot outcome. Concludes that since electoral fraud was openly practiced, successful candidates lost legitimacy—a situation that encouraged three local revolts between 1864–79.

2486 Alvarez de Huertas, Rubby Amelia. Entre el gorro frigio y la mitra. Tunja, Colombia: Academia Boyacense de Historia, 1998. 301 p.: bibl., ill. (Biblioteca de la Academia Boyacense de Historia. Serie Obras fundamentales; 22)

Analyzes conflict in New Granada between defenders of traditional and modern mentalities, or more specifically, looks at the conflict between Church and state as seen through ideas, attitudes, opinions, and expressions of influential sectors of society in second half of 19th century.

2487 Appelbaum, Nancy P. Whitening the region: Caucano mediation and "Antioqueño colonization" in nineteenth-century Colombia. (*HAHR*, 79:4, Nov. 1999, p. 631–667, maps)

Innovative regional study highlights role of 19th-century *caucanos* in creation of Caldas, a region sometimes known as Greater Antioquia, to show that so-called *antioqueño* colonization was not an exclusively *antioqueño* endeavor. Also demonstrates the pervasiveness of regional and racial differentiational discourse that associates *antioqueños* with whiteness and native-born *caucanos* with blackness.

2488 Archila, Mauricio. El Frente Nacional: una historia de enemistad social. (*Anu. Colomb. Hist. Soc. Cult.*, 24, 1997, p. 189–215, tables)

Overview of bipartisan Frente Nacional (1958–74). Argues that because of elites' political compromise, government opponents were forced to become more radical social activists. Result was emergence of class conflict and loss of civil society.

2489 Ayala Diago, César Augusto. Fiesta y golpe de estado en Colombia. (*Anu. Colomb. Hist. Soc. Cult.*, 25, 1998, p. 274–308, photo)

Interesting investigation shows how supporters of Rojas Pinilla converted popular enthusiasm sparked by his seizure of power on June 13, 1953, into a civic holiday "marked by religious characteristics with a decided aroma of conservative revenge and reconstruction," despite the nearly universal rejection of the Gómez dictatorship.

2490 Barón Ortega, Julio. El conservatismo colombiano, su historia y sus hombres. v. 1–2. Tunja, Colombia: Editorial Talleres Gráficos, 1999. 2 v.: bibl., ill.

Brief biographies of key Partido Conservador members from late-18th century to 1930. Vol. 1 includes revolutionary heroes, presidents, and archbishops. Vol. 2 lists significant women, presidential candidates, regional leaders, and army officers. Despite prosaic entries, a useful reference work for gauging party influence throughout national period.

2491 Bejarano, Jesús Antonio. Guía de perplejos: una mirada a la historiografía colombiana. (*Anu. Colomb. Hist. Soc. Cult.*, 24, 1997, p. 283–329)

Impassioned essay blames decline of economic history in the last decade on popularity of the new paradigm stressing historical mentalities. Argues that the *dependista* model still can contribute to our historical understanding through its ability to explain, quantify, and raise points for debate.

2492 Botero Gómez, Fabio. Cien años de la vida de Medellín, 1890–1990. 2. ed. Medellín, Colombia: Editorial Univ. de Antioquia; Municipio de Medellín, 1998. 623 p.: ill. (some col.), indexes. (Memoria de ciudad. Ciencias sociales)

Draws on variety of sources to present an affectionate economic, social, cultural, and political portrait of development of Medellín from a uniquely Colombian city in 1890 to an internationalized metropolis in 1990. Many illustrations, including caricatures of prominent Medellín figures. Footnotes, but no bibliography. See also item **2493.**

2493 Botero Herrera, Fernando. Medellín 1890–1950: historia urbana y juego de intereses. Medellín, Colombia: Editorial Univ. de Antioquia, 1996. 360 p.: bibl., ill., index, maps. (Col. Clío)

Well-written and researched monograph surveys development of Medellín as a "pioneer" in import-substitution industrialization and a model of development characterized by predominance of private over public interest. Includes history of development of popular and worker barrios at turn of century. Profusely illustrated. See also item **2492.**

Cartagena de Indias y su historia. See item **2145.**

2494 Casas Aguilar, Justo. Evangelio y colonización: una aproximación a la historia del Putumayo desde la época prehispánica a la colonización agropecuaria. Bogotá: ECOE Ediciones, 1999. 259 p.: bibl., ill., maps. (Col. Interés general. Area Historia)

Thoughtful, well-written history of efforts to missionize and colonize the Amazon part of Putumayo from the arrival of the Spaniards to 1933. Other topics included are precolumbian societies, the impact of rubber boom, and border conflicts with Peru. Excellent maps. Ideal primer for anyone interested in this Colombian region.

2495 Cátedra Anual de Historia Ernesto Restrepo Tirado, 3rd, Bogotá, 1998. Colombia en la negociación de conflictos armados, 1900–1998. Bogotá: Museo Nacional de Colombia, 1999. 222 p.: bibl.

Nine thoughtful papers detail Colombian participation in international treaty negotiations spanning 1903 Wisconsin and Nerlandia Agreements to 1980s Contadora Initiative for Peace in Central America. Excellent insight into Colombia's role in hemispheric affairs.

2496 Congreso de Historia de Colombia, 9th, Tunja, Colombia, 1995. Actas. v. 1, Colombia y América Latina después del fin de la historia. v. 2, Regiones, ciudades, empresarios y trabajadores en la historia de Colombia. v. 3, Cultura y mentalidades en la historia de Colombia. v. 4, Iglesia, movimientos y partidos: política y violencia en la historia de Colombia. Colombia: Univ. Pedagógica y Tecnológica de Colombia; Archivo General de la Nación; Asociación Colombiana de Historiadores, 1996. 4 v.: bibl. (Col. Memorias de historia)

Selection of papers includes works by scholars from US, Canada, Puerto Rico, Panama, Brazil, Ecuador, France, Spain, and Venezuela. Over 200 papers were presented in 15 thematic symposiums. Editors chose a representative selection and organized them into four volumes. While most essays focus on Colombia, many deal with other Latin American regions. Quality varies considerably, but taken together they underscore the remarkable blossoming of professional historical work taking place in and about Colombia during 1990s.

2497 Construcción territorial en el Chocó. v. 1, Historias regionales. v. 2, Historias locales. Bogotá: Programa de Historia Local y Regional del Instituto Colombiano de Antropología ICAN-PNR, 1999. 2 v.: bibl., ill., maps.

Informative essays written by team of experts from the Instituto Colombiano de Antropología provide regional history of Chocó and the evolution of its individual municipalities from 18th century to present. Includes chapters on *baldíos* (public lands) and formation of the collective identity of Afro-Colombian inhabitants.

2498 Dávila, Carlos. Estado de los estudios sobre la historia empresarial de Colombia. (*in* Empresa e historia en América Latina: un balance historiográfico. Bogotá:

Colciencias; TM editores, 1996, p. 87–136, bibl.)

Updates review of 314 works on business history originally published in 1991 (*Historia empresarial de Colombia: estudios, problemas y perspectivas.* Bogotá: Univ. de los Andes). Includes extensive bibliography. Emphasizes regional history and period from end of 19th century to 1930s. Argues for testing of more significant theoretical hypotheses. Indispensable tool for economic historians.

2499 Díaz Granados, José Luis. Viajeros extranjeros por Colombia. Bogotá: Presidencia de la República, 1997. 513 p.: bibl. (Biblioteca familiar de la Presidencia de la República; 25)

Selections from 35 representative traveler accounts arranged chronologically from Baron von Humboldt to Paul Theroux. Selected excerpts encapsulate "the most picturesque and the most profound aspects of a given time," as well as what is "most Colombian about Colombia as seen through the eyes of foreigners." A fascinating collection for exploring an important genre of documentary sources.

2500 Fajardo Sánchez, Luis Alfonso; Juan Carlos Gamboa Martínez; and Orlando Villanueva Martínez. Manuel Quintín Lame y los guerreros de Juan Tama: multiculturalismo, magia y resistencia. Epílogo de Juan Ibeas. Madrid: Nossa y Jara Editores, 1999. 244 p.: appendices, bibl., ill., map. (Madre tierra; 16)

Chronicles the efforts of the sons of Juan Tama, another celebrated Paez cacique, to show how ideals of Lame have continued to inspire indigenous peoples to defend their territories, culture, and autonomy with weapons and the law. Includes indigenous demands presented at the 1991 Asamblea Nacional Constituyente.

2501 Farnsworth-Alvear, Ann. Dulcinea in the factory: myths, morals, men and women in Colombia's industrial experiment, 1905–1960. Durham, N.C.: Duke Univ. Press, 2000. 303 p.: bibl., ill., index, maps. (Comparative and international working-class history)

History of the Medellín textile industry focuses on changes in workplace organization that accompanied the gradual masculinization of the mill. Disputes idea that shift was based solely on economic factors and shows how gender and class relations, as social practices, converged to shape industrial development.

2502 Fawcett, Louise and Eduardo Posada-Carbo. Arabs and Jews in the development of the Colombian Caribbean 1850–1950. (*in* Arab and Jewish immigrants in Latin America: images and realities. Edited by Ignacio Klich and Jeffrey Lesser. London; Portland, Ore.: F. Cass, 1998, p. 57–79)

Contrasts experiences of Sephardic Jews, Syro-Lebanese, and Levantine and European Jews who immigrated to northern coast of Colombia between 1850–1950. Concludes that although their numbers were quite small, these communities prospered. Especially in Barranquilla, their contributions in commerce and the professions were substantial, and some individuals even joined the political elite.

Ferreyra, Aleida and Renata Segua. Examining the military in the local sphere: Colombia and Mexico. See item **1531.**

2503 Fischer, Thomas. Desarrollo hacia afuera y guerras civiles en Colombia, 1850–1910. (*Ibero-Am. Arch.,* 23:1/2, 1997, p. 91–120)

Suggests that 19th-century underdevelopment was due not just to geographical obstacles and world market conditions as previously argued by Safford and Ocampo, but more importantly to continual civil wars which in turn reflected inability of Colombian elites to coordinate their interests and create favorable conditions for productive investment.

2504 Franco, Roberto. Historia de Orocué. Prólogo de Getulio Vargas Barón. Bogotá: Kelt Colombia/Ecopetrol, 1997. 269 p.: bibl., ill., maps.

One of the first serious monographs about a key town in Casanare. Uses national and local archival sources as well as oral interviews to trace history from precolumbian times to the Violencia. Includes footnotes and bibliography.

2505 Friedman, Max Paul. Specter of a Nazi threat: United States-Colombian relations, 1939–1945. (*Americas/Washington,* 56:4, April 2000, p. 563–589)

Based on careful review of US State Dept. papers, essay shows how American efforts to eliminate the Nazi threat in Colombia resulted in expropriation of Colombian-based German companies, internment within Colombia of 98 Germans, and deportation and detention of several hundred Colombian-Germans (including some German Jews) at Camp Kennedy in Texas.

2506 García Estrada, Rodrigo. Extranjeros en Medellín. (*Bol. Cult. Bibliogr.,* 34:44, 1997, p. 102–120, photos)

Beautifully illustrated essay reviews impact of foreigners in Antioquia from early 19th century to the present. Discusses their role in mining, commerce, music, and banking. Concludes that although immigrants were never more than one percent of the population, their presence had "a direct relationship with economic and social modernization processes."

2507 García Londoño, Carlos Edward. Niños trabajadores y vida cotidiana en Medellín, 1900–1930. Medellín, Colombia: Editorial Univ. de Antioquia, 1999. 122 p.: bibl., ill., index. (Clío)

Careful analysis of archival materials related to child labor in Medellín during first three decades of 20th century. Discusses social atmosphere in Medellín, daily life of boy and girl workers, and changing attitudes about child labor during this era. Insightful and well-written.

2508 Gómez L., Augusto J. La guerra de exterminio contra los grupos indígenas: cazadores-recolectores de los llanos orientales, siglos XIX y XX. (*Anu. Colomb. Hist. Soc. Cult.,* 25, 1998, p. 351–376, bibl.)

Drawing on travelers' accounts and archival materials, Gómez, a leading Colombian historian-anthropologist, surveys race relations in the Llanos to demonstrate that a calculated effort by white settlers to exterminate the indigenous peoples has existed over several centuries.

2509 González, Fernán E. Para leer la política: ensayos de historia política colombiana. v. 1–2. Bogotá: Cinep, 1997. 2 v.: bibl.

Collection of articles written by political scientist Fernán González over period of 25 years designed to illuminate 14 key issues in Colombian history ranging from "El proyecto político de Bolívar: mito y realidad" to "Clientelismo y administración pública." Good introduction to a wide variety of topics.

2510 González Escobar, Luis Fernando.
Sirio-libaneses en el Chocó, cien años de presencia económica y cultural. (*Bol. Cult. Bibliogr.*, 34:44, 1997, p. 73–101, photos)

Reveals how small numbers of Syrians and especially Lebanese made a substantial impact in the development of Chocó between 1850–1950 through their involvement in commerce and agriculture. Shows how second generation intermarried with afro-chocoanos to produce a "region amply multiethnic and culturally pluralistic."

2511 Green, W. John. Left liberalism and race in the evolution of Colombian popular national identity. (*Americas/Washington*, 57:1, July 2000, p. 95–124, bibl.)

Reviews evolution of left-liberal national identity in 19th-20th centuries, showing how racial considerations have contributed to its development. Argues that under Gaitán, "país nacional" referred to a mestizo nation, while "país político" referred to the oligarchy. Concludes that *colombianidad* is tied to race in "arbitrary, confusing and deceptive ways," especially with regard to the largely ignored Afro-Colombians.

2512 Guerra Vilaboy, Sergio. Colombia y la independencia de Cuba. (*Tierra Firme/Caracas*, 17:68, oct./dic. 1999, p. 649–659)

Cuban scholar underlines major role played by a sector of Colombian society in aborted Cuban independence movments of the 1820s, as well as Colombian support of the Cuban insurrections of 1868 and 1898. Argues that US opposition was primary reason for failure of all these efforts.

2513 Gutiérrez Jaramillo, Camilo. José Hilario López: un hombre de su siglo. Bogotá: C. Gutiérrez Jaramillo, 1997. 341 p.: bibl.

Uses primary and secondary sources for well-written biography of López (1798–1869)—general, legislator, and president of New Granada (1849–53). Concludes that although he was reviled at his death for his anticlericalism, López nevertheless led Colombia out of its colonial past and helped create

a new generation that became the Olimpo Radical.

2514 Helg, Aline. The limits of equality: free people of colour and slaves during the first independence of Cartagena, Colombia, 1810–15. (*Slavery Abolit.*, 20:2, Aug. 1999, p. 1–30)

Careful examination of archival material reveals that free blacks and mulattoes did not demand elimination of slavery in 1811 when Cartagena declared independence, because they identified more with whites than slaves and to them independence meant equality and decency. Helpful comparisons with similar situations in Venezuela, Cuba, and Haiti. Important contribution to study of race in Colombia.

2515 König, Hans-Joachim. Los años 20 y 30 en Colombia: ¿época de transición o cambios estructurales? (*Ibero-Am. Arch.*, 23:1/2, 1997, p. 121–155)

Argues that economic changes made before 1929, which left coffee under Colombian control and created a national market infrastructure, produced the necessary conditions for 1930s reform programs and that, even if the structural transformation was incomplete, the era nevertheless was a period of enormous transition.

2516 Loaiza Cano, Gilberto. Acerca de la vida privada de un hombre público del siglo XIX: el caso de Manuel Ancízar. (*Anu. Colomb. Hist. Soc. Cult.*, 26, 1999, p. 59–82)

Interesting essay reviews private life of Manuel Ancízar to show how it interacted with and supported his public activities. Includes much information about his wife Agripina Samper Agudelo, and provides insight into lives of mid-19th-century elite women.

2517 Luna, Lola G. La feminidad y el sufragismo colombiano durante el período 1944–1948. (*Anu. Colomb. Hist. Soc. Cult.*, 26, 1999, p. 193–212)

Investigates feminist movement's effort to achieve suffrage between 1944–48, underlining conflict between Conservatives who believed that voting would destroy the traditional role of women, and Liberals who regarded suffrage as an expansion of women's rights. Work is part of book published in Barcelona covering female participation in Colombian politics from 1930–91.

2518 Martínez, Frédéric. Apogeo y decadencia del ideal de la inmigración europea en Colombia, siglo XIX. (*Bol. Cult. Bibliogr.*, 34:44, 1997, p. 3–46, bibl., ill., maps, photos)

French scholar analyzes why Colombia was unable to attract European immigrants in 19th century despite vigorous efforts by both Liberal and Conservative regimes. The "nearly absolute failure" of these attempts contrasted sharply with ongoing debate among the political elite over need for immigration.

2519 Martínez Carreño, Aída. La Guerra de los Mil Días: testimonios de sus protagonistas. Bogotá: Planeta, 1999. 232 p.: bibl., ill., index. (La línea del horizonte)

Uses diaries, letters, memoirs, and private papers of Gen. Próspero Pinzón to provide expanded view of War of the Thousand Days. Shows impact of the conflict on civilian populations by acknowledging women, campesinos, and priests who played a role. Concludes that "the worst option for achieving peace is war."

McFarlane, Anthony. The state and the economy in late colonial and early republican Colombia. See item **2156.**

2520 Mejía Pavony, Germán. Los itinerarios de la transformación urbana: Bogotá, 1820–1910. (*Anu. Colomb. Hist. Soc. Cult.*, 24, 1997, p. 101–137, maps, tables)

Uses primary documents to challenge prevailing view of Bogotá as an isolated, backward capital. Demonstrates its transformation from a "colonial city" to a "bourgeois city" between 1820–1910. Emphasizes that while the perimeter of the city remained the same, its population increased five-fold.

2521 Melo G., Blanca Judith. Primero muertas que deshonradas: Antioquia, 1890–1936. (*Hist. Soc./Medellín*, 6, dic. 1999, p. 109–125)

UNC-Medellín MA thesis analyzes 165 *expedientes* (legal investigations) conducted between 1890–1937. Most concern crimes of rape and violence committed by men against women. Concludes that because the mentality of the age embraced a feminine ideal that tended to blame the victim, the violence that women endured caused them to lose their status as virgins and honorable women, their innocence notwithstanding.

2522 Montenegro González, Augusto. La enseñanza de la historia en Colombia entre 1902 y 1945: de la armonía entre investigación y docencia de la historia al auge de la renovación pedagógica. (*Bol. Hist. Antig.*, 85:800, enero/marzo 1998, p. 129–165)

Useful synopsis of factors that influenced teaching of national and world history in secondary school and universities. Emphasizes influence of Henao/Arrubla text, the German Pedagogical Mission of 1924, and reforms introduced during regime of López.

2523 Múnera, Alfonso. El Caribe colombiano en la república andina: identidad y autonomía política en el siglo XIX. (*Bol. Cult. Bibliogr.*, 33:41, 1996, p. 29–49, ill., maps, photos)

Path-breaking essay debunks myths established by José Manuel Restrepo in *Historia de la revolución de Colombia* (Paris: Librería Americana, 1827) that on eve of independence New Granada was a unified political entity; that the split between Andean and Caribbean elites prevented a unified independent nation; and that independence was won by the Creoles alone since indigenous peoples, blacks, and mestizos played a passive role.

2524 Navarrete, María Cristina. Inmigrantes de la India oriental en el Valle del Río Cauca. Bogotá?: Gobernación del Valle del Cauca, Gerencia Cultural, 1996. 205 p.: bibl., ill., maps. (Col. de autores vallecaucanos)

Uses materials from Archivo General and Ministerio de Gobierno to investigate the fate of a group of Muslims who left India in early 20th century, and after remaining in Panama for some time, established themselves as sugar laborers and merchants in towns along the Cauca River in the 1920s. Fascinating contribution to understudied Colombian immigration history.

2525 Niño Murcia, Carlos. Los ferrocarriles en Colombia: genealogía de un fracaso. (*Ciudad Territ. Estud. Territ.*, 30:117/118, otoño/invierno 1998, p. 721–738, bibl., maps, photos)

Critical analysis of Colombian railroad construction argues that regional interest, dysfunctional government policy, and union greed prevented creation of a national system of rail transport. Calls for reorganization of the few lines that once again might become operational and for historical preservation of the railway stations.

2526 Noguera R., Carlos Ernesto. La higiene como política: barrios obreros y dispositivo higiénico; Bogotá y Medellín a comienzos del siglo XX. (*Anu. Colomb. Hist. Soc. Cult.*, 25, 1998, p. 188–215, tables)

Compares efforts by governments in Bogotá and Medellín to construct workers' barrios which would be small educational cities: centers for living, hygiene, recreation, and culture. Regards this process, which was quite rapid between 1920–30, as part of a "scientific" political-medical strategy to improve the lives of the workers.

2527 Nueva historia de Colombia. v. VII, Historia política desde 1986. v. VIII, Economía y regiones. v. IX, Ecología y cultura. Bogotá: Planeta, 1998. 3 v.: bibl.

Editor Tirado Mejía updates *Nueva historia de Colombia* with three new volumes covering political history from 1986–94, economy and regions, and ecology and culture, adding 36 newly written chapters to the 87 already published in earlier volumes. The continued high quality of individual contributions ably meets the project's goal of "safeguarding the indispensable unity of the encyclopedic work" so that it can be consulted by younger generations of Colombians "without hiding the most critical aspects of national reality, but also indicating the positive advances and progressive factors in Colombia during the most recent years." With the three new volumes, this series remains indispensable for research libraries and scholars studying 20th-century Colombia.

2528 Obregón, Diana. De "árbol maldito" a "enfermedad curable": los médicos y la construcción de la lepra en Colombia, 1884–1939. (*in* Salud, cultura y sociedad en América Latina. Lima: Instituto de Estudios Peruanos; Washington: Organización Panamericana de la Salud, 1996, p. 159–178)

Stimulating history of leprosy demonstrates how 19th- and 20th-century Colombian doctors used fear of the disease to enhance their position as a professional group vis-à-vis the state and the Catholic Church. Argues that their changing views of treat-

ment came more from internal social and political needs than from scientific discoveries.

Ocampo López, Javier. Colombia en sus ideas. See item **4703.**

2529 Ospina, María Clara. Doña Bertha. Bogotá: Espasa, 1998. 344 p.: bibl., ill. (Biografías Espasa)

Hernández de Ospina (1907–93), while staunchly supporting her husband President Mariano Ospina, was a political actor in her own right. She lobbied for improvements in the civil status of women, including the right to vote, granted in 1954. She published newspaper columns and designed orchid gardens now open to tourists. This biography, written by her daughter, offers unique insight into the life of an influential 20th-century woman.

2530 Patiño Millán, Beatriz. Balance del Décimo Congreso de Historia de Colombia, Medellín, 1997. (*Hist. Soc. /Medellín*, 4, dic. 1997, p. 17–31)

Insightful synopsis of 151 papers presented at 10th Congreso de Historia de Colombia held in Medellín (1997). Major themes deal with culture and "mentalidades," history of education, and regional and frontier history. While praising quality of the research, Patiño suggests need for more investigations on religion, comparative studies, and works of synthesis.

2531 Pensar el pasado. Bogotá: Univ. Nacional de Colombia, Depto. de Historia; Archivo General de la Nación, 1997. 192 p.: bibl.

Papers on diverse aspects of Colombian history presented by five scholars at inauguration of the Univ. Nacional's PhD program in history in March 1997. Includes essays by Tovar Pinzón, Medina Pineda, Archila Neira, Tovar Zambrano, and the Polish historian Jerzy Topolski.

2532 Pérez Silva, Vicente. Anécdotas de la historia colombiana. Bogotá: Planeta, 2000. 269 p.: bibl. (Memoria de la historia)

Collection of anecdotes from different historical eras taken directly from primary sources. Includes interesting details about 26 historical figures as well as anecdotes dealing with the clergy, courts, and army. Colorful stories humanize these well-known figures and are authenticated with appropriate footnotes.

2533 Ramírez Bacca, Renzo. Formación de una hacienda cafetera: mecanismos de organización empresarial y relaciones administrativo-laborales; el caso de La Aurora, Líbano, Colombia, 1882–1907. (*Cuad. Desarro. Rural,* 42, p. 83–115, bibl., photos, tables)

Doctoral thesis analyzes forms of administrative organization and labor systems employed between 1882–1907 at La Aurora, a coffee-growing farm in Líbano, Tolima. Describes foundation of a coffee-growing enterprise in barren fields as well as entrepreneurial strategies that permitted expansion of coffee-growing by end of 19th century.

2534 Rodríguez G., Ana Luz. Testadores y finados: miembros activos de la sociedad independentista; actitudes y representaciones en torno a la muerte a comienzos del siglo XIX. (*Anu. Colomb. Hist. Soc. Cult.,* 25, 1998, p. 35–72, graphs, tables)

Analysis of 320 wills written by *bogotanos* between 1800–31 investigates changing attitudes about death at beginning of 19th century. Data include breakdown by individuals' residence, economic situation, reasons for making wills, civil state, literacy, and types of burial requested. Carefully done study about a little-known aspect of social history.

2535 Rojas de Moreno, María Eugenia. Rojas Pinilla, mi padre. Bogotá: M.E. Rojas de Moreno, 2000. 500 p.: bibl., ill. (some col.).

Spirited defense of Gen. Rojas Pinilla's career and presidency (1953–57) by his daughter María Eugenia who was a key player in 1950s political events and in founding of ANAPO, the party that supported Rojas after the flawed election of 1970, which many believe deprived him of victory.

2536 Roldán, Mary. Violencia, colonización y la geografía de la diferencia cultural en Colombia. (*Anál. Polít./Bogotá,* 35, sept./dic. 1998, p. 3–25)

Shows development of violence in the Urabá section of Antioquia from colonial times to present as the result, not necessarily of party conflict, but rather of a frontier region's lack of access to national resources

due to misgovernment on the part of the Medellín authorities.

2537 Sánchez G., Gonzalo *et al.* Grandes potencias, el 9 de abril y la violencia. Bogotá: Planeta, 2000. 362 p.: bibl., ill. (La línea del horizonte)

Five historians outline US, British, and French interpretations of events surrounding the April 9, 1948, murder of Gaitán. They argue that the US saw the events as a threat to hemispheric security; Great Britain as a threat to its economic relations with the developing world. France was concerned about social agents intervening in Latin American violence.

2538 Serpa Erazo, Jorge. Rojas Pinilla: una historia del siglo XX. Bogotá: Planeta, 1999. 557 p. (Biografía)

Objective, well-written biography argues that Rojas Pinilla has been unfairly treated by historians, and that while he may have seized power on June 13, 1953, his administration was no more "dictatorial" than those of three immediate past presidents. Lacks bibliography and index, but incorporates written sources and personal reminiscences which provide much insight into 20th-century events.

2539 Silva Téllez, Armando. Cultura italiana en Colombia: reflexión sobre etnias y mestizajes culturales. Bogotá: TM Editores; Instituto Italiano di Cultura, 1999. 101 p., 16 p. of plates: bibl., ill.

Suggests that while there were only 13,000 people of Italian heritage living in Colombia in 1985, Italian influence has made its mark on Colombian culture since 19th century in geography, film, architecture, fine arts and letters, the penal code, the Catholic Church, sciences, education, and business.

2540 Sowell, David. Miguel Perdomo Neira: healing, culture, and power in the nineteenth-century Andes. (*Anu. Colomb. Hist. Soc. Cult.,* 24, 1997, p. 167–188)

Discusses clash of traditional versus scientific medical practices in Colombia and Ecuador by focusing on career of Perdomo Neira (1833–74), a *curandero* branded a charlatan by trained physicians. Shows that Perdomo's case reflects development of medical pluralism and the clash of Catholic traditional beliefs with scientific rationalism introduced from Western Europe.

2541 Toro Sánchez, Edgar. El liderazgo de Rafael Uribe Uribe y la modernización de la nación y el estado. Bogotá: Teleobjetivo Editores, 2000. 228 p.: bibl., ill., maps.

Sociologist examines Uribe's leadership in Colombia's drive for modernization. Emphasizes his role in development of coffee as an export crop and in diplomatic relations with the US. Based on extensive use of archival materials. Includes comprehensive bibliography of writings on and about Uribe Uribe.

2542 Urrego, Miguel Ángel. Sexualidad, matrimonio y familia en Bogotá, 1880–1930. Bogotá: Ariel; Fundación Univ. Central-DIUC, 1997. 367 p.: bibl., ill. (Ariel historia)

Analyzes changing cultural concepts of marriage and the family in Bogotá from 1880–1930, a period of great national transformation. Outlines national context, and looks at impact of modernizing public services, industrialization, and Church and state policies on notions of intimacy at all social levels. Serious investigation combines historical and social science methodology.

2543 Valderrama Andrade, Carlos. Miguel Antonio Caro y la Regeneración: apuntes y documentos para la comprensión de una época. Bogotá: Instituto Caro y Cuervo, 1997. 823 p.: bibl., ill., index. (Publicaciones del Instituto Caro y Cuervo; 96)

Uses documents from Caro's archive to investigate his relationships with "all and each one" of the men involved with the Regeneración from 1860–1909. Includes profiles of each of the delegates chosen by the nine existing states to the Constitutional Convention of 1885. Extensive and authoritative.

2544 Vargas de Castañeda, Rósula. La vida cotidiana del Altiplano Cundiboyacense en la segunda mitad del siglo XIX, Tunja-Bogotá. Tunja, Colombia: Academia Boyacense de Historia, 1998. 256 p.: bibl., ill., map. (Biblioteca de la Academia Boyacense de Historia. Serie Obras fundamentales; 21)

Meticulously researched social history of collective mentalities and daily life in the last half of 19th century when English and French influences were being absorbed especially into upper class lives. Covers all aspects of material culture including houses, clothing, family customs, religious life, fiestas, diversions, and ways of dealing with sickness and death.

2545 Vásquez Carrizoza, Alfredo. José María Samper: su vida de escritor y la Regeneración dirigida por Rafael Núñez en 1886. (*Bol. Hist. Antig.*, 86:807, oct./dic. 1999, p. 1037–1062, port.)

Brief review of Samper's career emphasizing injustice of his imprisonment by Santiago Pérez in 1875 and Samper's subsequent support of Rafael Núñez. Provides insight into nature of politics during Liberal Era of 1849–84.

2546 Villegas Botero, Luis Javier. Las vías de legitimación de un poder: la administración presidida por Pedro Justo Berrío en el Estado Soberano de Antioquia, 1864–1873. Bogotá: Tercer Mundo Editores, 1996. 169 p.: bibl., maps. (Premios nacionales de cultura, 1995)

Prize-winning MA thesis reviews Berrío's administration in Antioquia. Argues that while Radical governments in other states failed, Berrío succeeded because he combined traditional Catholic values with liberal objectives of labor, democracy, and efficiency. Rather than rejecting the clergy, he used them to achieve his goals without sacrificing the supremacy of civil power.

2547 Vos Obeso, Rafaela. La religiosidad en la vida de las mujeres barranquilleras. (*Bol. Cult. Bibliogr.*, 33:42, 1996, p. 47–64, photos)

Well-illustrated and fascinating study of Marianism in early 20th-century Barranquilla. Shows how priests and church rituals regulated the lives of women, and argues that 1920s material development had little impact on their religious rigidity.

2548 Zalamea, Alberto. Gaitán: autobiografía de un pueblo. Bogotá: Zalamea Fajardo Editores, 1999. 472 p.: bibl., index.

Sympathetic examination regards Gaitán's life as a reflection of 20th-century development of Colombian people. Access to official Gaitán archive is most evident in the verbatim reproduction of previously unavailable correspondence between Gaitán, his wife Amparo, and labor leaders from the 1930s-40s.

2549 Zapata, Ramón. Libros que leyó el libertador Simón Bolívar. Bogotá: Instituto Caro y Cuervo, 1997. 174 p.: bibl., ill.

Zapata, who died in 1977, elaborated in 1970s this analysis of books that Bolívar read to show how ideas expressed by various writers may have influenced his career. Divided into books by French, English, Italian, Greek, and Spanish authors, bibliography is correlated with primary documents by or about Bolívar indicating their significance.

ECUADOR

Arosemena, Guillermo. La historia empresarial del Ecuador. See *HLAS 59:1943.*

2550 Becker, Marc. Comunas and indigenous protest in Cayambe, Ecuador. (*Americas/Washington,* 55:4, April 1999, p. 531–559, graphs, maps, table)

Discusses impact of 1937 Ley de Comunas which extended legal recognition to indigenous communities. Explains why some communities embraced the law while others rejected it. Concludes that the law was really an attempt to deepen indigenous dependence on the dominant culture, and that those indigenous leaders who resisted it recognized the law for what it was.

Borrero Vintimilla, Antonio. Filosofía, política y pensamiento del presidente Antonio Borrero y Cortázar, 1875–1876: aspectos de la política del Ecuador del siglo XIX. See item **4706.**

2551 Bouisson, Emmanuelle. La abolición de la esclavitud en la Provincia de Imbabura, 1821–1854. (*Memoria/Quito,* 6, 1998, p. 193–208, bibl., tables)

Delineates gradual abolition of slavery in the Chota Valley, the second largest slave-holding area in Ecuador, during the independence and early national periods. An exceptionally interesting and important contribution to the social history of the independence and early national periods inasmuch as the postcolonial fate of blacks in the northern highlands has been slighted. [M.T. Hamerly]

2552 Cevallos, Pedro Fermín. Epistolario de Cevallos a Mera. Ambato, Ecuador: Editorial Pio XII, 1996. 626 p.: ill.

Collection of 300 letters written by Cevallos to Juan León Mera between June 9, 1854, and Aug. 6, 1890. Offers insight into personality of a major 19th-century historian as well as social history of the republic. Unfortunately, lack of subject index makes access to information difficult.

2553 Clark, A. Kim. Racial ideologies and the quest for national development: debating the agrarian problem in Ecuador, 1930–1950. (*J. Lat. Am. Stud.,* 30:2, May 1998, p. 373–393)

Anthropologist reviews debate over improving agrarian production during an economic crisis. Concludes that racial ideologies were fundamental to the conceptualization of the problem, and that the widely held image of indigenous peoples as "passive" made unfeasible proposals of a peasant path of agricultural development formulated by peasant leaders and social activists.

2554 Clark, A. Kim. The redemptive work: railway and nation in Ecuador, 1895–1930. Wilmington, Del.: SR Books, 1998. 244 p.: bibl., index, maps. (Latin American silhouettes)

Tackles a little-explored time period and theme: transport in Ecuador's liberal period. In the building of the Guayaquil-Quito railway, transport was the principal goal of the highland landowning elite, whereas the agro-export coastal elite saw it as a vehicle for expanding its labor market. Nevertheless, the elites succeeded in achieving an unstable consensus, and this work tells a lively story of the problems and successes of nation building from multiple perspectives. For economist's comment, see *HLAS 59:1947.* [L. Seligmann]

2555 Cordero Aroca, Alberto P. Don Vicente Rocafuerte: diputado por la Provincia de Guayaquil a las Cortes Ordinarias de Madrid. (*Rev. Inst. Hist. Marít.,* 13:23, julio 1998, p. 109–145, bibl., facsims.)

Uses archival materials to review efforts of Rocafuerte and José Joaquin de Olmedo on behalf of Guayaquil while they were in Spain from 1813–20. Discusses brief existence of the Cortes de Cádiz (1813–14). Includes facsimilies of two documents. Lacks footnotes.

2556 Cubitt, David. Economy and politics in independent Guayaquil: Francisco Roca's "El Amigo del País," 1822. (*Rev. Hist. Am./México*, 121, 1996, p. 84–129, tables)

Introduction and text of pamphlet published in 1822 by Francisco María Claudio Roca, a key figure in coastal Ecuador's independence. Describing the pamphlet as "an illuminating source," Cubitt provides biographical background on Roca, discusses his political theory, and sets his pamphlet within the context of the debates over Guayaquil's future given the ambitions of Peru and Colombia.

2557 Destéfani, Laurio H. Argentina y Ecuador, 1815–1822. (*Invest. Ens.*, 46, 1996, p. 15–43, appendix, maps)

An unusual account of William Brown's naval campaign against royalist Ecuador. [T. Whigham]

2558 Díaz Cueva, Miguel and **Fernando Jurado Noboa.** Alfaro y su tiempo. Quito: Fundación Cultural del Ecuador, 1999. 315 p.: ill. (Col. SAG; 118) (Serie Alfarada; 6)

Iconography consisting of over 100 photos and brief biographies of Eloy Alfaro, his family, associates, opponents, and his horrific murder on Jan. 28, 1912. Unique contribution to Alfaro studies.

2559 Esvertit Cobes, Natàlia. Estado y Amazonía en el Ecuador del siglo XIX: los fracasos de una propuesta de articulación del área amazónica al estado nacional—la "Vía Proaño." (*in* Raíces de la memoria: América Latina, ayer y hoy, quinto encuentro debate = Amèrica Llatina, ahir i avui, cinquena trobada debat. Barcelona: Univ. de Barcelona, 1996, p. 483–500, bibl., map)

Examines failure of Liberal plan to build road connecting the highlands with the Amazon to show "contradictions in the Ecuadorian state in the treatment of questions related with the Amazon." Concludes that this debacle reveals "failure of political will" on the part of the state which led to more aggressive Peruvian development of the Amazon.

2560 Esvertit Cobes, Natàlia. Las políticas del liberalismo ecuatoriano sobre el oriente: articulación y control del territorio a través de la legislación, 1895–1925. (*in* Encuentro-Debate América Latina ayer y hoy =

Trobada-Debat Amèrica Llatina ahir i avui, 6th, Barcelona, 1997. Lo que duele es el olvido: recuperando la memoria de América Latina = El que dol és l'oblit: recuperant la memòria d'Amèrica Llatina. Barcelona: Univ. de Barcelona, 1998, p. 257–269)

Overview of Liberal policies toward the eastern frontier. Suggests that various attempts to incorporate this area made it a fundamental part of Ecuadorian nationalism. Efforts failed due to inadequate financial resources, ignorance of the region, and the state's inability to establish its presence vis-à-vis the pressures of Colombian and Peruvian rubber collectors. For comment on similar article based on same dissertation, see *HLAS 58:2617.*

2561 Gándara Enríquez, Marcos. El Ecuador del año 1941 y el Protocolo de Río: antecedentes, hechos subsiguientes; Arroyo y su tiempo. Quito: Centro de Estudios Históricos del Ejército, 2000. 930 p.: bibl., index. (Biblioteca del Ejército Ecuatoriano; 17)

Ecuadorian general refutes accusations made by former president Carlos Arroyo del Río in *Por la pendiente del sacrificio* (Guayaquil: Banco Central del Ecuador, 1996) by vehemently defending the army's actions during the Peruvian invasion of 1941 and subsequent Rio Protocol. Includes bibliography and extensive documentation.

Gonzales Posada, Luis. Los antipatriotas: Perú-Ecuador, historia de un conflicto. See item **2594.**

2562 González Leal, Miguel Angel. Insurgencia popular, oligarquía regional y estado en el Ecuador liberal, 1895–1925: la huelga general de Guayaquil, 1922. (*Anu. Estud. Am.*, 54:1, enero/junio 1997, p. 159–184)

Revisionist view of 1922 general strike based on a Spanish doctoral dissertation analyzes involvement of popular sectors, the oligarchy (i.e., agroexporters and importers), and the government to demonstrate that the strike, which marked the end of the Liberal regime, was not simply the work of one labor union.

Guayaquil y el río: una relación secular. See item **2185.**

Jaramillo Cisneros, Hernán. El trabajo textil de Peguche. See *HLAS 59:1136.*

Jibaja Rubio, Leopoldo. El ayer de un pueblo de la sierra, 1543–1950. See item **2190.**

Jurado Noboa, Fernando. Las Peñas: historia de una identidad casi perdida, 1497–1997. See item **2191.**

Jurado Noboa, Fernando. Quito secreto: historia documentada y desconocida sobre el orígen y el desarrollo de esta ciudad andina. See item **2192.**

2563 Latorre, Octavio. El hombre en las Islas Encantadas: la historia humana de Galápagos. Quito: s.n., 1999. 446 p.: bibl., ill. (some col.), maps (some col.).

History of human occupation of the Galápagos Islands based on 20 years of investigation in Quito and Guayaquil archives, periodicals, and other primary and secondary sources. Clearly supports ongoing efforts to save islands from exploitation and preserve them for future generations.

2564 Latorre, Octavio. Los primeros pobladores de las Islas Galápagos. (*Rev. Inst. Hist. Marít.*, 13:23, julio 1998, p. 39–51, facsims., photo, map)

History of permanent settlement from 1832–79. [B. Meggers]

2565 Milk Ch., Richard L. Movimiento obrero ecuatoriano: el desafío de la integración. Quito: Ediciones Abya-Yala, 1997. 208 p.: bibl.

Spanish translation of 1977 Indiana Univ. PhD dissertation provides overview of labor union movement from 1895–1977. Postscript by Dr. Chiriboga Zambrano carries narrative up to 1997. Essential introductory study for labor historians.

Morillo Batlle, Jaime. Economía monetaria del Ecuador. See *HLAS 59:1967.*

2566 Ogaz Arce, Leonardo. ¡Todo el poder a Velasco!: la insurreción del 28 de mayo de 1944. Quito: Ediciones Abya-Yala, 1998. 280 p.: bibl.

Chilean scholar analyzes the May 28, 1944, overthrow of Ecuadorian government, regarding it as a frustrated revolutionary process which destroyed the old regime but was incapable of creating an alternative. Shows how Velasco Ibarra, in the service of the dominant classes, disarmed the popular sectors and assumed control.

2567 Pérez, Galo René. Sin temores ni llantos: vida de Manuelita Sáenz. Quito: Ediciones del Banco Central del Ecuador, 1997. 441 p.: bibl., ill. (Col. histórica; 26)

Prize-winning Ecuadorian writer and journalist presents thoughtful, well-researched biography of Sáenz, regarding her as "one of the admirable women of the Spanish American independence period." Although there is nothing particularly new here about her life and achievements, the work is a solid introduction to a complex and much mythologized historical figure.

2568 Rajo Serventich, Alfredo. Alfaro y la iniciativa hispanoamericanista de 1896. (*in* Latinoamérica entre el Mediterráneo y el Báltico. México: Instituto Panamericano de Geografía e Historia, Fondo de Cultura Económica, 2000, p. 109–123, bibl.)

Mexican scholar investigates efforts of Alfaro, "an exponent of radical Latin American liberalism," to encourage Latin American unity in the face of renewed US aggression in 1890s. These efforts culminated in the Congreso Internacional Americano in 1896. Well-researched article explores little-known aspect of Alfaro's career.

2569 Roberts, Lois J. The Lebanese immigrants in Ecuador: a history of emerging leadership. Boulder, Colo.: Westview Press, 1999. 242 p.: appendices, bibl., index.

Examines historical roots of both Lebanese (including Syrians and Palestinians) and Ecuadorians, and offers a systematic treatment of Lebanese in 20th-century Ecuador as they gained political and economic power and struggled for social acceptance. Solidly researched contribution to global diasporas and Latin American immigrant history.

2570 Sáenz, Manuela. Las más hermosas cartas de amor entre Manuela y Simón, acompañadas de los diarios de Quito y Paita, así como de otros documentos. Caracas: Ediciones Piedra, Papel y Tijera, 1998. 200 p.: ill.

A collection of love letters exchanged by Bolívar and Sáenz, many of which have never before been published in Venezuela. Also includes excerpts from Sáenz's diaries. The editors posit that a "conspiracy or understanding" has sought to limit the public's understanding of the importance of Manuela Sáenz in the process of independence. Provides interesting insights into the personal lives and character of these two main figures, as well as into the dynamics of the liberation movement. [P. Linder]

2571 Sinardet, Emmanuelle. Charles Wiener, viajero frances, y el Guayaquil de los años 1880–1883. (*Rev. Inst. Hist. Marít.*, 14:26, p. 85–116, bibl., ill.)

Wiener was a French archeologist, anthropologist, and professor who spent 13 months in Guayaquil between 1880–82. Essay reviews his most important observations about the city, concluding that his account is a unique and valuable social document that offers a realistic view of the port.

2572 Sinardet, Emmanuelle. L'éducation équatorienne et la Révolution Julienne, juillet 1925-août 1931: rupture ou continuité? (*Bull. Inst. fr. étud. andin.*, 28:1, 1999, p. 123–157, bibl.)

Examines educational policies of the legal texts, ordinances, and 1929 Constitu-tion which emerged after the 1925 July Revolution. Concludes that in spite of official speeches, this regime did not make school democratization a priority. In fact, in education, the July Revolution represents continuity rather than discontinuity with the past.

Sowell, David. Miguel Perdomo Neira: healing, culture, and power in the nineteenth-century Andes. See item **2540.**

2573 Townsend, Camilla. Tales of two cities: race and economic culture in early republican North and South America; Guayaquil, Ecuador, and Baltimore, Maryland. Austin: Univ. of Texas Press, 2000. 320 p.: bibl., ill., index, map.

Intriguing social history of Guayaquil and Baltimore in the 1820s and 1830s. Extensive archival research compares economic ideas and behavior of elites, "middling sectors," and very poor of each city. Employs "economic culture" paradigm to explain how differing attitudes toward race and class affected local ways of doing business and allowed North Americans to attain greater prosperity.

Velasco Ibarra, José María. José María Velasco Ibarra: una antología de sus textos. See item **4707.**

Peru

STEVEN J. HIRSCH, *Associate Professor of History, University of Pittsburgh at Greensburg*

THE HISTORIOGRAPHY ON REPUBLICAN PERU for this reporting period is characterized by an increasing methodological sophistication and an expanding topical reach. The declining influence of conventional structural and class paradigms, as noted by reviewers Nils Jacobsen and Daniel Masterson in *HLAS 56* and *58* respectively, has had a salutary effect on the scholarly literature. Deterministic and unproblematic renderings of social, economic, and political history have yielded to a more complicated and profound understanding. Historical contingency has supplanted historical inevitability. This shift in historical perspective, as Jacobsen observed in *HLAS 56*, is mainly attributable to the growing influence of the new political/cultural history with its emphasis on agency, identity construction, discursive practices, and the processes of representation and meaning formation. Combining innovative approaches drawn from discourse and gender analyses, subaltern and cultural studies, and the literature on hegemony, this new fusion of political and cultural history continues to inspire investigations into neglected fields of inquiry in Peruvian history. The politics of state formation; the development of civil society; and the constructions of class, race, ethnicity, gender, and popular culture are among the understudied topics currently receiving scholarly attention.

Although the literature on women and gender in republican Peru lags behind other Latin American historiographies, significant advances are being made. The volume edited by Zegarra and published by the research center CENDOC-MUJER provides valuable essays on several important 19th century topics: the development of liberal legal codes and women's civil rights, women's cultural representations, and disease and mortality rates for men and women (item **2611**). The collection includes an outstanding essay by Mannarelli that links socioeconomic changes in early 20th century Lima to new public definitions of masculinity and femininity as well as discourses on female sexuality. Mannarelli amplifies her analysis of gender identities and roles in a seminal study that scrutinizes the influences of public health authorities, the medical profession, and feminist discourse in Lima between 1900–30 (item **2603**). This study demonstrates the value of examining the interconnections between gendered private and public discourses and the formation of gender regimes. More multilevel analyses that historicize gender arrangements in terms of larger socioeconomic processes and state policies are needed for both the 19th and 20th centuries. In addition, the construction of human sexuality during the republican period, which remains largely unexamined, warrants further investigation.

Another overlooked subject area that is beginning to garner scholarly attention is the social history of disease. In the first major historical study of epidemics in 20th-century Peru, Cueto significantly advances our knowledge of popular perceptions of disease and disease control policies (item **2586**). He persuasively argues that authoritarian public health campaigns strengthened state power and often ignored or trampled on the sensibilities of ethnic and underclass groups most affected by disease. Cueto's study is particularly noteworthy due to its multidimensional approach. By integrating social history, public policy, and cultural processes, with an analysis of disease characteristics, he provides a paradigm for future studies.

Sophisticated works on urban history continue to appear. Joffré presents new methods of conceptualizing urban change in his award-winning study of Lima in the second half of the 19th century (item **2597**). Utilizing Angel Rama's notion of the city as text and the category of space, Joffré sheds light on how government authorities and the urban elite appropriated and redefined Lima's public space following the War of the Pacific. His analysis significantly adds to our understanding of how elite conceptions of modernity and uses of public space shaped municipal reforms aimed at restricting the movements of the urban poor. Lima's macro and micro public spaces (cafes, salons, streets, barrios) are the focus of Aguila Peralta's study of informal political relations during "la república de notables" (1895–1919) (item **2574**). Aguila Peralta elucidates the quotidian ritualization of paternalism and clientelism. However, her conclusion that reciprocal and vertical relations pervaded Lima society and muted counter-hegemonic ideas and practices ignores the well-documented sociocultural and political resistance of urban workers for this period.

The literature on 19th century Peruvian social and political history, as Masterson observed in *HLAS 58*, continues to expand and mature. Nevertheless, much work still remains to be done on nation-building processes associated with the formation of civil society and the constitution of a political citizenry. During this biennium, two exemplary articles grapple with these themes. Forment's excellent study of elite civic associations and elite modes of sociability in Lima, Cuzco, and Arequipa (1845–75), is both methodologically sophisticated and revisionist (item **2591**). Drawing on Habermasian and Foucauldian concepts of civic associations and democracy, he argues that Peru's social and cultural elite developed a "democratic culture" predicated on "civic Catholicism," which stressed the need for an orderly, moral, and independent civil society. This vision of public life, he concludes, served as a counterpoint to the liberal and authoritarian visions emanating from the state and the market. Mücke's important article offers a rare analysis of the totality of the electoral process (campaigns, electoral communications and mobilizations, voting, legal verification of results) during the protracted presidential election of 1871–72 (item **2609**). In a significant reinterpretation of 19th-century electoral history, he suggests that electoral campaigns contributed to the development of a national identity and consciousness. Mücke's work underscores the need for additional studies on 19th–20th century Peruvian electoral history.

Of the few works on the historical construction of ethnic, racial, and national identities to appear during this biennium, Méndez-Gastelumendi's study stands out for its impressive primary documentation and probing analysis (item **2605**). Her article explores the ways in which 19th-century national politics contributed to the invention and appropriation of politically defined ethnic identities. In particular, she shows how indigenous peasants in Huanta province, Ayacucho, assumed an Iquichano ethnic identity, originally derived from Spanish monarchist rebellions (1826–28), in order to leverage post-1830 national caudillos for assistance. Further research on identity construction and peasant politics during the republican period is clearly needed.

Regional history continues to attract scholarly attention. In addition to Ayacucho, valuable publications on Cerro de Pasco, Arequipa, Cuzco, and Amazonas were reviewed for this *HLAS* volume. Among these works, the study by anthropologist Nugent on the nature of hegemony and subaltern agency in the Chachapoyas region (1885–1930) is particularly noteworthy (item **2616**). Thoroughly researched, Nugent's book analyzes the formation and competition between an aristocratic and a subaltern political culture on the geographic periphery of the central state. By illustrating the ways that subaltern groups appropriated state discourses on nationhood, popular sovereignty, and modernity to advance their own political liberation, this regional study bolsters the case for state-making "from below."

Following a longstanding trend, relatively little scholarly work on either economic or business history appeared during this reporting period. However, the magisterial, synthetic essay on Peruvian business history by Miller deserves mention (item **2606**). Highly informative, Miller's essay discusses the availability of primary sources and provides a trenchant analysis of the thematic and regional imbalances in the extant literature. He strongly suggests that future analyses focus on provincial, medium-sized firms oriented toward the internal market. This essay is invaluable for researchers of economic and business history during the republican era.

Urban labor history continues to receive scant attention from scholars. No major publications on unions, labor relations, or working-class politics were reviewed with the single exception of the work by sociologist Parodi, which was originally published in Spanish in 1986. Parodi's case study of metallurgical union workers in Callao during the 1970s and early 1980s underscores the protean character of working-class identity and political behavior (item **2618**). In stark contrast to the majority of Peruvian labor historiography, Parodi depicts workers with multiple and overlapping identities (ethnic, generational, regional, family, union, political). That he finds putative leftist workers to be less ideologically driven and more concerned with self-improvement a uniquely 1980s phenomenon underscores the need for further research on 20th-century labor history.

In *HLAS 56*, Jacobsen astutely noted that photographs and paintings are becoming increasingly important sources for understanding Peruvian history. Two collections of rare archival photos reviewed for this volume reaffirm the validity of this observation. Herrera Cornejo's corpus of photos taken by Courret and Dubreuil families' studio in Lima (1863–1934) offers revealing portraits of urban social types and captures urban life and material culture (item **2595**). The social history of Peru's Chinese immigrants and their descendants is portrayed in a beautiful photo album assembled by Peruvian historian Derpich. This commemorative edition, published by Peru's Congreso Nacional, highlights the Chinese community's economic and cultural contributions to the nation over a 150-year period (item **2588**).

Immigration studies and works on Peru's ethnic minorities are emerging in increasing numbers. Much of this historical scholarship focuses on previously understudied groups (Eastern Europeans, Jews, Africans). To a large extent the Editorial Fund of Peru's Congreso Nacional is responsible for these publications. In addition, the Fund has promoted a series on the history of mass cultural production and consumption, with individual studies on the Peruvian theater, television industry, and press. These works tend to be undertheorized and reflect the fledgling state of the field.

With the resolution of Peru's boundary disputes with Ecuador and Chile, it is likely that the spate of monographs on diplomatic history will abate. Perhaps now professional and amateur historians can turn their attention to overlooked areas. There remains an urgent need for historical studies on religion, popular culture, crime, and the environment for the republican period. The recent opening of the Soviet archives may allow for new perspectives on the history of the Peruvian left. Given the recent phoenix-like resurgence of the APRA, it may be a propitious moment to research the understudied post-World War II party history.

Lastly, I would be remiss if I failed to mention the premature death of Pedro Planas, a dedicated Peruvian scholar and prolific writer on a broad range of historical topics. His study on decentralization reviewed in this volume reflects the passion he devoted to his subjects and his commitment to social, economic, and political justice in Peru (item **2623**).

2574 Aguila Peralta, Alicia del. Callejones y mansiones: espacios de opinión pública y redes sociales y políticas en la Lima del 1900. Lima: Pontificia Univ. Católica del Perú, Fondo Editorial, 1997. 249 p., 1 folded leaf of plates: bibl., ill.

Paternalism, clientelism, and *compadrazgo* produced formal and informal relations of reciprocity and verticality in Lima society and insured political stability under Civilista rule (1895–1919). To this conventional interpretation, the author adds that ritualized paternalism in the form of public ceremonies and festivals also reinforced elite control. Based on primary research.

Apel, Karin. De la hacienda a la comunidad: la sierra de Piura, 1934–1990. See *HLAS 59:1153.*

2575 Arequipa del '50: documentos y testimonios. Recopilación de Eusebio Quiroz Paz Soldán, Julio José Fuentes Fuentes, and Roberto Ruelas Vera. Arequipa, Peru: Editorial UNSA, 2000. 293 p.: ill.

Valuable commemorative volume of June 1950 popular uprising in Arequipa sparked by Odría's rejection of Democratic League's presidential candidates. Presents contemporary newspaper accounts, testimonials by main protagonists, and graphic materials without explanation. Focuses on life and martyrdom of Arturo Villegas Romero, a local journalist. Compiles important documents reflecting anti-Odria middle-class perspective.

2576 Ayala Calderón, Kristhian and **Enrique León Huamán.** El periodismo cultural y el de espectáculos: trayectoria en la prensa escrita, Lima siglos XIX y XX. Lima: Univ. de San Martín de Porres, Escuela Profesional de Ciencias de la Comunicación, 2000. 218 p.: bibl., ill. (Serie Prensa / Instituto de investigaciones)

Informative historical synthesis of cultural journalism in 19th- and 20th-century Lima. Stresses 20th-century development of a "cultural industry" linked to mass dailies and magazines (e.g., *Variedades, Mundial, Cultura Peruana, El Comercio*) that disseminate cultural and educational information. Special attention is given to post-WWII "spectacle" publications covering music, television, and theater, and the advent of "fanzines" (inexpensive cultural leaflets) in the 1980s and 1990s.

Ayala Loayza, Juan Luis. Etnohistoria de Huancané. See item **672.**

2577 Balta, Aída. Historia general del teatro en el Perú. Jesús María, Lima: Escuela de Ciencias de la Comunicación, Univ. de San Martín de Porres, 2001. 335, 4 p.: bibl., ill. (Serie Comunicación y sociedad / Instituto de investigaciones)

Ambitious synoptic study of Peruvian theater from precolumbian era until the 1990s. Concentrates on 20th-century theater in Lima and Arequipa. Discusses cross-fertilization of indigenous and European influences and the impact of romanticism, modernism, vanguardism, and politics on Peruvian theater. Includes biographical vignettes of Peruvian playwrights. Useful for 20th-century social and cultural historians.

2578 Banco Central de Reserva del Perú. El Banco Central: su historia y la economía peruana, 1821–1992. v. 2. Lima: Banco Central de Reserva del Perú, 2000. 1 v.: bibl., ill.

Vol. 2 in luxurious multivolume official history of Peru's Central Reserve Bank (BCRP). Covers period from 1960–65. Offers detailed examination of BCRP's tense negotiations with the military (1962–63) and Belaúnde (1963–68) governments over mone-

tary and fiscal policies, agrarian reform, and national economic development. Draws on unpublished bank documents and includes excerpts from internal bank reports. Contains highly useful economic statistics. Important source for specialists in Peruvian poliical economy, finance, and banking. For review of vol. 3, see item **2579.**

2579 Banco Central de Reserva del Perú. El Banco Central: su historia y la economía peruana, 1821–1992. v. 3. Lima: Banco Central de Reserva del Perú, 2001. 1 v.: bibl., ill.

Vol. 3 examines BCRP history for the period 1966–69. Topics include turmoil within the BCRP directorate, Peru's acute fiscal and monetary instability, and conflicts with Gen. Velasco's revolutionary government (1968–75) over regulation of banking sector and national capital. Stresses failure of Belaúnde and Velasco governments to adopt sound fiscal and economic policies to insure economic stability and growth. Rich in statistical data and color illustrations. Important source. For review of vol. 2, see item **2578.**

2580 Bonfiglio, Giovanni. La presencia europea en el Perú. Lima: Fondo Editorial del Congreso del Perú, 2001. 381 p.: bibl., ill.

Significant survey of European immigration to Peru from 1821–1950 by noted sociologist and immigration historian. Analyzes European and Peruvian contexts, immigrant strategies and settlement patterns, and Peru's immigration policies. Finds English, German, and Italian immigrants were predominantly males of relative means who retained their original culture while integrating into Peruvian society. Includes useful statistical data and valuable discussion of literature and documentary base. Also presents exploratory case studies of uneven quality. Handsome publication.

2581 Busto Duthurburu, José Antonio del. Breve historia de los negros del Perú. Lima: Fondo Editorial del Congreso del Perú, 2001. 126 p.: bibl., ill. (some col.).

Afro-Peruvian history for the 19th-20th centuries receives scant coverage in this slender volume. Briefly mentions abolition of slavery, race mixture, racism, and political and economic themes. Emphasizes contributions by Afro-Peruvians to music, the arts, sports, and national cuisine. Useful for generalists and students of Afro-Peruvian history and culture.

2582 Chambers, Sarah C. Crime and citizenship: judicial practice in Arequipa, Peru, during the transition from colony to republic. (*in* Reconstructing criminality in Latin America. Edited by Carlos A. Aguirre and Robert Buffington. Wilmington, Del.: Scholarly Resources, 2000, p. 19–39)

Between 1780–1854, civilian authorities in Arequipa increasingly utilized criminal courts and new law enforcement agencies to maintain social control. Plebeians resisted legal and social regulation by invoking colonial honor codes, early republican norms of respectability, and liberal principles. Well-researched, insightful article based on criminal cases stored in the Archivo Regional de Arequipa.

2583 Chiaramonti, Gabriela. La ley y las costumbres: apuntes sobre los registros civiles y los libres parroquiales en el Perú de la segunda mitad del siglo XIX, 1857–1879. (*Rev. Complut. Hist. Am.*, 26, 2000, p. 199–232)

Thoroughly researched article on tensions arising from liberal state's extension of civil power under Manuel Pardo (1872–76) and Mariano Ignacio Prado (1877–79). Stresses that provincial ecclesiastical and civil authorities resisted demands by new Dept. of Statistics for access to civil registers and parochial books. Draws heavily on correspondence between Manuel Atanasio Fuentes, dept. director, and provincial clergy and subprefects.

2584 Coloquio de Historia de Lima, *6th, Lima, 1999.* Historia de Lima y otros temas. Recopilación de Miguel Maticorena Estrada. Lima: Fondo Editorial, Univ. Nacional Mayor de San Marcos, 1999. 111 p.: bibl.

Presents précis of conference papers by faculty, students, and researchers. Topics on precolumbian and colonial Peru predominate. Briefly cites new research on urban reforms, press, lodgings, and police in Lima during the 19th-20th centuries. Prologue provides *in memoriam* profiles and bibliographies of three notable historians: Ella Dunbar Temple, Félix Denegri Luna, and Aurelio Miró Quesada Sosa.

2585 Contreras, Carlos and **Marcos Cueto.** Historia del Perú contemporáneo: desde las luchas por la independencia hasta el presente. 2. ed. Lima: Pontificia Univ. Católica del Perú: Univ. del Pacífico, Centro de Investigación: Instituto de Estudios Peruanos, 2000. 386 p.: bibl., ill., index, maps.

Updated historical synthesis of republican Peru by accomplished, young Peruvian historians. This new university textbook integrates social and culture processes and focuses on political reform projects. Best chapters cover 19th-century state formation. Includes select bibliography, statistical tables, valuable photos and illustrations, and excerpts from primary documents. Useful for generalists.

2586 Cueto, Marcos. El regreso de las epidémias: salud y sociedad en el Perú del siglo XX. Lima: Instituto de Estudios Peruanos, 1997. 256 p.: bibl., ill. (Serie Estudios históricos, 1019–4533; 22)

First major scholarly work on epidemics in 20th-century Peru. Examines five cases: bubonic plague in Lima and north coast (1902–30), yellow fever in north coast (1919–22), typhus and smallpox in Dept. of Puno (1930), malaria in provinces (c. 1930–70), and cholera in central and north coast (1991). Based on exhaustive primary research, author analyzes ecological, social, cultural, and political dimensions of epidemics. Particular attention is given to popular perceptions and reactions to disease and public health policies. Concludes that epidemics disproportionately affected serranos and poor, reinforcing negative stereotypes, and resulting in authoritarian public health interventions. An important study.

2587 Dager Alva, Joseph. La historiografía peruana de la segunda mitad del siglo XIX: una presentación inicial a través de la obra de José Toribio Polo. (*Rev. Complut. Hist. Am.*, 26, 2000, p. 135–179, bibl.)

Thoughtful, suggestive article on Peru's "transitional historians" who bridged unscientific early 19th-century historians (e.g. Manuel de Mendiburu) and late 19th-century historicists (e.g. Riva-Agüero). Argues that transitional historians like Toribio Polo were profoundly influenced by Spencerian ideas. Concludes that positivism had relatively little influence on 19th-century Peruvian historiography.

Delgado-Guembes, César and **Wilo Rodríguez Gutiérrez.** Los viajes del presidente, 1822–1998. See *HLAS 59:3677.*

2588 Derpich, Wilma. El otro lado azul: 150 años de inmigración china al Perú. Lima: Fondo Editorial del Congreso del Perú, 1999. 166 p.: bibl., ill. (some col.).

Handsome commemorative photo album by authority on social history of Chinese coolies, immigrants, and their descendants in Peru. Draws on an array of archival sources to illustrate and describe Chinese living and working conditions, associational life, community-government relations, and anti-Chinese racism. Centerpeice is chapter on Chinese entrepreneurs accompanied by portraits and biographical sketches. Invaluable source for understanding the integration and influence of first two generations of Chinese in Peru.

2589 Drinot de Echave, Paulo. After the Nueva Historia: recent trends in Peruvian historiography. (*Rev. Eur. Estud. Latinoam. Caribe,* 68, April 2000, p. 65–76)

Perceptive, well-written article by a young Peruvian historian. Provides a judicious assessment of the historiography of Nueva Historia (1970s-80s), emphasizing class analysis and historical agency. Points out that recent publications on republican period continued to stress agency while highlighting categories of difference (race, gender, ethnicity, nationality). Notes "professionalization of history in Peru." Excellent bibliography.

Fernández Valdés, Juan José. Chile-Perú: historia de sus relaciones diplomáticas entre 1819 y 1879. See item **2714.**

2590 Fisher, John Robert. The Royalist regime in the Viceroyalty of Peru, 1820–1824. (*J. Lat. Am. Stud.,* 32:1, Feb. 2000, p. 55–84)

Valuable, rare article on royalist policies in Peru in the final years of Spanish rule. Author, a leading authority on late colonial Peru, scrutinizes the crisis of royal authority precipitated by San Martín's invasion in 1820, and assesses the impact of Cuzco's conversion into a viceregal capital (1822–24). Includes a review of historiography and an excellent discussion of 1810–20 historical context. Based on Spanish and Peruvian archival materials.

2591 Forment, Carlos A. La sociedad civil en el Perú del siglo XIX: democrática o disciplinaria. (*in* Ciudadanía política y formación de las naciones: perspectivas históricas de América Latina. Coordinación de Hilda Sabato. México: Colegio de México, 1999, p. 203–230)

Informed by the ideas of Jürgen Habermas and Michel Foucault, author reassesses the development and influence of civil society on democratization of public life from 1830–79. Offers a novel interpretation that Peru's sociocultural elite, via civic associations, advanced "civic catholicism" as an alternative to liberal and authoritarian visions of public life. Concludes that this elite significantly democratized public life between 1846–1879, especially in social and communication terms, by promoting a vibrant, morally coherent, independent civil society.

2592 Gameros Castillo, Wilfredo. Semblanzas biográficas y episodios de la independencia. Jesús María, Lima: Editorial SM, 2000. 322, 3 p.: bibl., ill. (some col.).

Seeks to highlight contributions of lesser-known Peruvian and foreign military commanders to Peru's independence. Profiles 26 patriotic heroes, including a martyred black soldier and a mestizo guerrilla fighter. Study briefly examines obscure battles and the liberation of provincial capitals. Informative, if conventional military history based on primary sources. Includes color portraits of military leaders.

2593 Gonzales, Osmar. El gobierno de Guillermo E. Billinghurst, 1912–1914: anuncio del populismo peruano. (*Mapocho/Santiago,* 48, segundo semestre 2000, p. 195–214)

Examines Billinghurst's nationalist discourse, strategies to co-opt subalterns, and attempts to reconcile the interests of capital and labor. Portrays Billinghurst as a progenitor of both democratic and authoritarian populist politics. Not a balanced appraisal. Based mainly on secondary sources.

2594 Gonzales Posada, Luis. Los antipatriotas: Perú-Ecuador, historia de un conflicto. Lima: Decisión Gráfica, 1999. 211, 13 p.: bibl., col. maps.

Interview with former Minister of Foreign Relations in Garcia government (1985–90). Openly biased, author argues that Ecuador's "false claims" to Peruvian territory in the 19th century initiated the border conflict. Merits attention due to critical Aprista perspective on Fujimori's purging of the diplomatic corps, secret negotiations with Ecuador, and agreement to cede Peruvian territory (Tiwinza) in the 1998 peace treaty.

Hampe Martínez, Teodoro. La Colección Brüning de documentos para la etnohistoria del Perú: inventario de sus fondos. See item **721.**

Heras, Julián. Principales archivos y bibliotecas de la Orden Franciscana en el Perú actual. See item **2255.**

2595 Herrera Cornejo, H. Andrés. La Lima de Eugenio Courret, 1863–1934. Lima: Gráfica Novecientos Seis, 1999. 244 p.: bibl., ill., index.

Valuable promotional study by the conservator of the photographic Archive of Eugenio Courret. Presents a concise history of the Courret and Dubreuil families, who owned a photography studio in Lima from 1863–1934. A selection of over 200 rare portraits, ethnographic images, and photos of urban life and architecture in Lima and Callao accompany the brief text.

2596 Historia de la minería en el Perú. Directed by José Antonio del Busto Duthurburu. Lima: Milpo, 1999. 445 p.: bibl., col. ill.

Beautiful, highly useful company study of 2,000 years of mining activity in Peru. Includes 13 chapters by prominent historians and specialists, five of which consider the 19th and 20th century. Chapters by Dager Alva on mining in the early republic and by Guera Martinère on mining between 1950–98, are particularly informative. Study addresses mining production, technology, finance, and legislation; labor and work conditions; and processes of nationalization and denationalization. Contains numerous photos of mines and miners, statistical tables and graphs, maps, and color plates of metal objects. Important source for generalists and specialists.

2597 Joffré, Gabriel Ramón. La muralla y los callejones: intervención urbana y proyecto político en Lima durante la segunda mitad del siglo XIX. Lima: SIDEA: Prom Perú, 1999. 239 p.: bibl., ill., maps.

Winner of María Rostworowski Award for young scholars, this revised MA thesis analyzes the understudied phenomena of Lima's physical and demographic change, modernization, and use of public and private space during the 19th century. Inspired by Angel Rama's La ciudad letrada (see HLAS 50:3069), focuses on the modernizing projects of political authorities and urban intellectuals in the wake of the War of the Pacific. Lima's revival is linked to urban reforms regulating hygiene, housing, and access to public space. Contains an excellent bibliography and maps of Lima (1613, 1859, 1872, 1904). Indispensable source for specialists in Latin America urban history.

2598 Krüggeler, Thomas. Indians, workers, and the arrival of "modernity": Cuzco, Peru, 1895–1924. (Americas/Washington, 56:2, Oct. 1999, p. 161–189)

Important, suggestive article on the interplay of ethnicity and class in early 20th-century Cuzco. Focuses on relationship between early labor movement led by the Artisan Society of Cuzco and the student and indigenista movements. Argues that social-climbing mestizo artisans, influenced by a positivist modern self-image, were disinclined to identify with indigenous peoples and to ally with pro-indigenista students or working-class radicals in the late 1920s. Well-researched but lacks statistical evidence.

2599 Leibner, Gerardo. El mito del socialismo indígena: fuentes y contextos peruanos de Mariátegui. Lima: Pontificia Univ. Católica del Perú, Fondo Editorial, 1999. 261 p.: bibl.

Based on dissertation research, this important study demonstrates that anarcho-syndicalist intellectuals originally formulated the myth of indigenous socialism. Argues convincingly that the influence of anarcho-syndicalism, indigenista intellectuals, and Indian-campesino struggles in the 1920s led Mariátegui to adopt the myth for his own national political and cultural project. Includes a stimulating discussion of indigenista writings and discourse. For philosophy specialist's comment, see item **4717.**

2600 Leyva Arroyo, Carlos Alberto. De vuelta al barrio: historia de la vida de Felipe Pinglo Alva. Lima: Biblioteca Nacional del Perú, 1999. 225 p.: bibl., ill., music. (Avances de investigación / II. Convocatoria Nacional "José María Arguedas")

Valuable biography of the legendary Limeño composer who popularized vals criolla. Uses oral histories and secondary sources to portray Pinglo as an innovator who incorporated new musical forms and social themes. Links Pinglo's artistry to sociocultural context of Lima in 1910s-20s. Contains excellent bibliography, catalog of songs, music sheets, and lyrics.

2601 Lima, paseos por la ciudad y su historia. Dirección de Rocío Flórez. Recopilación de Mónica Ricketts. 2a ed. corr. y aum. Lima: Adobe Editores, 1999. 580 p.: ill. (some col.), maps (some col.). (Guías Adobe)

Lavish traveler's guide to Lima's history (prehispanic-1990s) and culture. Essays by scholars offer succinct, cursory examinations of diverse 19th and 20th century topics. Chapters include Lima and Independence, Guano Boom, Diversions and Spectacles, and Foreign Immigrants. Gives short shrift to 1930-90 period and indigenous migrations and presence in Lima. Valuable source for rare historic photos, maps, and illustrations.

2602 Macera, Pablo and **Santiago Forns.** Nueva crónica del Perú, siglo XX. Lima: Fondo Editorial del Congreso del Perú, 2000. 591 p.: bibl., ill.

Guamán Poma's trenchant chronicle of colonial society provides the model for this ethnographic compendium of 20th-century Peru. Replete with 191 illustrations, offers cursory, often humorous and insightful commentaries on a wide range of topics: popular culture, cities, racism, natural disasters, bureaucracy, pornography, and important historical figures. Useful for nonspecialists.

Mamani Coaquira, Leoncio F. El pueblo aimara y los conflictos con el poder: caso de la zona aimara norte de Puno, 1915–1925. See item **753.**

2603 Mannarelli, María Emma. Limpias y modernas: género, higiene y cultura en la Lima del novecientos. Lima: Ediciones Flora Tristán, 1999. 361 p.: bibl., ill.

Important, sophisticated study of gender identities and relations, and public and private representations of the female body and women's sexuality in Lima for period 1900–30. Deftly analyzes discourses of the medical profession, female hygienists, and feminist writers on such topics as marriage, reproduction, domesticity, hygiene, and public health administration. Argues that medical and feminist discourses expanded the state's role in private health matters, often reinforcing traditional values like female domesticity and marriage.

2604 McEvoy, Carmen. La experiencia republicana: política peruana, 1871–1878. (in Ciudadanía política y formación de las naciones: perspectivas históricas de América Latina. Coordinación de Hilda Sabato. México: Colegio de Mexico, 1999, p. 253–269)

Presents arguments and evidence derived from author's monograph La utopía republicana (see HLAS 58:2676). Highlights Peru's "ambivalent republican legacy" and the inherent tensions in Manuel Pardo's (1872–76) republican discourse and public policies. Overstates causal link between Pardo's republican ideology and the emergence of "a class struggle" (plebeians v. decentes) by 1878.

2605 Méndez-Gastelumendi, Cecilia. The power of naming, or the construction of ethnic and national identities in Peru: myth, history and the Iquichanos. (Past Present, 171:1, May 2001, p. 127–160)

Important, sophisticated essay on the origins and uses of Iquichano ethnic identity. Draws on author's extensive archival and ethnographic research on indigenous peasants of Huanta province in Dept. of Ayacucho, who backed monarchist rebellions (1826–28). Concludes that early republican conflicts between national caudillos were instrumental in forging Iquichano identity. Suggests that Iquichano was less a cultural and more a political identity, appropriated and used by Huanta villagers for their own ends. Includes a stimulating, insightful discussion of the Urchuraccay Massacre (1983) involving Iquichano peasants.

2606 Miller, Rory. Business history in Peru. (in Business history in Latin America: the experience of seven countries. Edited by Carlos Dávila and Rory Miller. Liverpool, England: Liverpool Univ. Press, 1999, p. 128–157, bibl., graphs)

Highly significant essay by leading authority on Peruvian business history. Provides critical review of the scholarly literature and assesses state of the field. Observes preponderance of studies on pre-1950 foreign and export-oriented firms in Lima and coastal region. Recommends research on post-1950 manufacturing concerns, medium-sized firms oriented toward internal economy, and businesses in provincial cities. Includes valuable discussion of available primary sources and excellent bibliography.

2607 Montoya Rivas, Gustavo. La independencia del Perú y el fantasma de la revolución, 1821–1822. (*Social. Particip.*, 89, dic. 2000, p. 91–123, bibl.)

Draws mainly on contemporary newspapers and published documents on Peru's independence to highlight the variable political impulses of plebeians in Lima during the "*gobierno Protectoral.*" Presents a suggestive examination of public debates over political liberty and forms of government and plebeian involvement in civic bodies, urban militia, liberation army, and royalist opposition.

2608 Mostajo, Francisco. Mostajo y la historia de Arequipa. Recopilación de Héctor Ballón Lozada. Arequipa, Peru: Univ. Nacional de San Agustín, Centro de Ediciones UNSA, 2000. 431 p.: bibl., col. ill.

Valuable collection of newspaper articles and essays by Mostajo, a prominent Arequipeño liberal intellectual. Written between 1896–1950, the texts present his views on Arequipa's colonial and early republican history, and his ideas on decentralization, indigenismo, university reform, and the National Democratic League. Includes an interpretive essay by a local sociologist and admirer who emphasizes Mostajo's contribution to debunking the myth of Arequipa as a city of social, racial, and political harmony.

2609 Mücke, Ulrich. Elections and political participation in nineteenth-century Peru: the 1871–72 presidential campaign. (*J. Lat. Am. Stud.*, 33:2, May 2001, p. 311–346)

Major contribution to neglected area of 19th-century electoral history. Focuses on the lengthy, urban-centered residential campaign of 1871–72. Argues electoral process promoted autonomous popular mobilization and electoral communication helped forge a national consciousness. Interpretation relies on problematic distinction between clientelist structures and relations. Offers valuable review of scholarly studies on 19th-century Peruvian elections. Based on dissertation research.

2610 Mücke, Ulrich. Das Indianerbild des peruanischen Liberalismus im 19. Jahrhundert. Hamburg: LIT, 1998. 128 p.: bibl. (Hamburger Ibero-Amerika Studien; 11)

Argues that the topic of national identity and the role of the indigenous population of Peru was not ignored prior to the War of the Pacific (1879–83) but was already subject to debate by liberal, social, and political leaders during the mid-19th century. Concentrating exclusively on contemporary writings of authors who did not question the idea of a republican liberal state, examines these debates, which, using the Inca Empire as a link to antiquity, expressed the writers' desires to modernize the large indigenous population to fit the image of the citizenry of a liberal state. Well-written contribution to Peruvian intellectual history. [C. Converse]

2611 Mujeres y género en la historia del Perú. Recopilación de Margarita Zegarra F. Lima: CENDOC-Mujer, 1999. 487 p.: bibl.

Significant collection of papers presented at 1996 conference. Thirteen of 27 essays correspond to republican period, concentrating on 1830–1930. Topics include women and health, feminist writers, marriage and divorce laws, images of women in literature and theater, and discourses on female sexuality. Few essays employ nuanced gender analysis. Volume is first synthetic, if unsystematic treatment of women and gender in Peruvian history.

2612 Muñoz Cabrejo, Fanni. The new order: diversions and modernization in turn-of-the-century Lima. (*in* Latin American popular culture. Edited by William H. Beezley and Linda A. Curcio-Nagy. Wilmington, Del.: Scholarly Resources, 2000, p. 155–168, bibl.)

Analyzes civilizing project of Lima's liberal elite during the late 19th century. Demonstrates elite suppression of popular forms of entertainment (i.e., gambling, cockfights) and promotion of European sports (cycling, tennis, soccer) and theater deemed more compatible with modernization. Focuses on regulation of public space and public morality. Useful article on understudied topic.

2613 Murra, John V. Nispa ninchis/decimos diciendo: conversaciones con John Murra. Recopilación de Victoria Castro, Carlos Aldunate y Jorge Hidalgo. Lima: IEP-Instituto de Estudios Peruanos: IAR-Institute of Andean Research, 2000. 253 p.: bibl., ill., ports (some col.). (Serie Fuentes e investigaciones para la historia del Perú, 1019–4487; 13)

Transcription of interviews with John Murra, renowned Andeanist and ethnohistorian. Relates illuminating details about his personal, intellectual, and professional development. Offers significant observations on important Peruvian intellectuals and scholars (i.e., José Maria Arguedas, Luis Valcárel, Franklin Pease, Oscar Nuñez del Prado) and the increasing influence of anthropology on history. Useful to intellectual and ethnohistorians.

2614 Neira Samanez, Hugo. Hacia la tercera mitad: Perú XVI-XX: ensayos de relectura herética. Lima: SIDEA, 1996. 754 p.: bibl.

Extraordinary tome of polemical essays by French-trained Peruvian social scientist. Presents trenchant critique of Peruvian historiography and thought-provoking discussion of major 19th- and 20th-century topics: independence, caudillismo, *huachafería*, indigenous problem, state formation, Shining Path, neopopulism, and postmodernism in Peru. Stresses recent emergence of autonomous social subjects and a national community. Sparsely footnoted. Highly recommended for specialists on republican Peru.

2615 Novak Talavera, Fabián. Las conversaciones entre Perú y Chile para la ejecución del Tratado de 1929. San Miguel, Peru: Pontificia Univ. Católica del Perú, Instituto de Estudios Internacionales, Fondo Editorial, 2000. 223 p.: bibl., 1 map.

In Nov. 1999, Peru and Chile resolved their differences over the 1929 Treaty of Lima, settling their longstanding border dispute. Discusses previous diplomatic efforts to end the conflict and provides a detailed account of the successful 1998–99 negotiations. Author acted as legal advisor to Peru's

delegation. Includes important prologue by Peru's chief negotiator, treaty documents, and a helpful bibliography. Useful for specialists.

2616 Nugent, David. Modernity at the edge of empire: state, individual, and nation in the northern Peruvian Andes, 1885–1935. Stanford, Calif.: Stanford Univ. Press, 1997. 404 p.: bibl., index, maps.

Important, if controversial ethnographic study of state-making "from below." Describes in rich detail the formation of two competing political cultures (white aristocratic ruling clans v. subaltern) in Chachapoyas region. Emphasizes subaltern discursive appropriation of concepts of popular sovereignty, nation, and modernity as basis for political emancipation in early 1930s. Identification of middle class groups as subaltern and uncritical view of APRA marinterpretation. Based on archival sources, newspaper accounts, and interviews with local APRA millitants. For ethnologist's comment, see *HLAS 59:1174.*

Nugent, David. The morality of modernity and the travails of tradition: nationhood and the subaltern in northern Peru. See *HLAS 59:1175.*

2617 Ortíz Sotelo, Jorge. El almirante Miguel Grau (1834–1879): una aproximación biográfica. Piura, Peru: Caja Municipal de Ahorro y Crédito de Piura, Asociación de Historia Marítima y Naval Iberoamericana, 1999. 296 p.: bibl., ill.

Revised and expanded version of author's 1995 biography entitled *El almirante Miguel Grau.* Uses previously untapped naval, maritime, and Ministry of Foreign Relations sources to reconstruct Grau's family life in Piura, employment history, and naval service. Includes an excellent bibliography and discussion of documentary base. Essential reference for scholars and students of 19th-century naval and maritime history.

Palacios Rodríguez, Raúl. Redes de poder en el Perú y América, 1890–1930. See item **926.**

2618 Parodi Solari, Jorge. To be a worker: identity and politics in Peru. Chapel Hill: Univ. of North Carolina Press, 2000. 177 p.: bibl., index. (Latin America in translation/en traducción/em tradução)

Important, insightful case study of

Callao metallurgical workers and the rise and fall of Left party-directed class struggle (*clasismo*) unionism between 1970-early 1980s. Based on worker interviews in 1984, finds *clasismo* promoted worker solidarity but stifled internal union democracy and proved an ineffective strategy for the depressed 1980s economy. Highlights multiple identities (regional, ethnic, age) and variable character of workers' social and political consciousness. Debunks essentialist revolutionary image but views pragmatic, self-improvement oriented workers as unique to 1980s owing to insufficient historical perspective. Originally published in 1986 as *Ser obrero es algo relativo* (see *HLAS 51:4827*).

2619 Peralta Ruiz, Víctor. El mito del ciudadano armado: la "Semana Magna" y las elecciones de 1844 en Lima. (*in* Ciudadanía política y formación de las naciones: perspectivas históricas de América Latina. Coordinación de Hilda Sabato. México: El Colegio de México, 1999, p. 231–251)

Highly original interpretation of the 1844 presidential election and the civil uprising that preceded it. Stresses that Gen. Ramón Castilla's election victory over liberal rival Domingo Elías marked a defeat for an alternative vision of power based on an armed citizenry led by a liberal corporate elite. Employs contemporary newspaper accounts and memoirs. Important article.

2620 Pérez Arauco, César. Cerro de Pasco: historia del "Pueblo Mártir" de Perú. v. 1, Siglos XVI, XVII, XVIII y XIX. Pasco, Peru: Instituto Nacional de Cultura, 1996. 1 v.: bibl.

Provincial monograph drawn from extensive published writings by local scholar. Provides strictly empirical analysis of 19th-century events, women, social classes, church, and mining industry in Cerro de Pasco. Offers portraits of famous persons and valuable discussion of local military history. Based on municipal records, private collections, and national military archives.

2621 Pérez Arauco, César. Cerro de Pasco: historia del "Pueblo Mártir" de Perú. v. 2, 1901–1913. Pasco, Peru: Instituto Nacional de Cultura, 1997. 1 v.: bibl.

Second vol. of local scholar's comprehensive regional study. Chapters correspond to years under examination and highlight

main events. Mainly descriptive, book provides wealth of data on mining industry, US-owned Cerro de Pasco Copper Corp., living and working conditions of miners, and labor conflicts. Contains significant information on popular culture, education, and housing.

2622 Pérez Arauco, César. Cerro de Pasco: historia del "Pueblo Mártir" de Perú. v. 3, 1914–1920. Pasco, Peru: Instituto Nacional de Cultura, 1997. 1 v.: bibl.

Vol. 3 in synthetic regional history by local scholar. Focuses on land conflicts between peasants, hacendados, and Cerro de Pasco Copper Corp., Rumimaqui uprising, miners' struggles, and unionization. Offers valuable portraits of local writers and discusses impact of development of radio and telegraph communications.

2623 Planas Silva, Pedro. La descentralización en el Perú republicano, 1821–1998. Lima: Municipalidad Metropolitana de Lima, 1998. 588 p.: bibl.

Well-researched, monumental study of the intellectual, legal, and political history of decentralization in republican Peru. The late author, an acclaimed journalist and proponent of decentralization, highlights Manuel Pardo's (1873–80) decentralist project and the fiscal and administrative decentralization of the late 19th and early 20th century. Argues that authoritarianism and centralism in the 20th century, and "hypercentralism" in the 1990s, are to blame for Peru's persistent social inequalities and uneven development. Though biased, work is essential for scholars of constitutional projects, congressional debates, intellectual formulations, and quantitative data on decentralization.

2624 Un plebiscito imposible...: Tacna y Arica, 1925–1926. Lima: Ediciones Análisis, 1999. 179 p.: bibl.

In June 1926, the US-led Plebiscite Commission for Tacna and Arica ruled that a plebiscite to determine the disposition of the disputed provinces between Peru and Chile could not be held. This important scholarly study seeks to explain this failure. Draws on the voluminous, heretofore untapped report of the Plebiscite Commission; official US, Peruvian, and Chilean papers; and Peru Foreign Ministry documents. The author, a leading Peruvian diplomatic historian, adduces ample evidence to indict Chile for undermining the commission and for preventing a "fair and just" election.

Ranque, Axel. La genèse de la première organisation prochinoise au Pérou, 1963–1964: idéologie et acteurs de la IVème Conférence Nationale du Parti Communiste Péruvien, Janvier 1964. See *HLAS 59:3705*.

2625 Reyes Flores, Alejandro. Libertos en el Perú 1750–1854. (*Hist. Cult./Lima*, 24, 2001, p. 41–54, bibl., tables)

Free blacks outnumbered slaves in Peru from the late 18th century until abolition in 1854. Article explores how slaves attained freedom prior to abolition. Well-documented analysis stresses the high frequency of grants of liberty (*libertad de gracia*) by slave-owners to very young, old, and domestic slaves. Concludes that most free blacks in Piura, Lima, Cañete, and Camaná-Arequipa lacked any material wealth. Contains useful statistical data.

2626 Riviale, Pascal. Los viajeros franceses en busca del Perú antiguo, 1821–1914. Lima: IFEA: Fondo Editorial de la Pontificia Univ. Católica del Perú, 2000. 456 p.: bibl., index.

Ponderous, exhaustive study of the origins of French collections of Peruvian antiquities. Animated by positivism and Social Darwinism, French archeologists, museums, and scientific societies excavated sites and aggressively collected precolumbian artifacts in Peru during the 19th century. Provides a plethora of data and maps on France's vast archeological enterprise. Neglects economic and cultural impact of French activities.

2627 Rodríguez González, Agustín Ramón. La Armada Española, la campaña del Pacífico, 1862–1871: España frente a Chile y Perú. Madrid: Agualarga, 1999. 141 p.: bibl., ill., map.

Conventional military history of Spanish naval confrontations with Peru and Chile in the 1860s. A biased account, based almost exclusively on Spanish primary sources, argues that Peru provoked the conflict and Spain achieved an unqualified victory restoring honor to its navy. Richly illustrated with drawings and photos of warships, commanders, and crews.

2628 Sakuda, Alejandro. El futuro era el Perú: cien años o más de immigración japonesa. Lima: ESICOS, 1999. 600 p.: bibl., ill.

Ambitious, generally well-researched study by journalist of Japanese descent. Explores social, economic, cultural, and political contributions of Japanese-Peruvians since the late 19th century. Offers extensive coverage and documents of US internment of Japanese-Peruvians during WWII. Sympathetic treatment of Fujimori's presidency. Includes many graphic materials on hacienda workers, business leaders, and Fujimori.

2629 Salomón Herrada, César. Historia de inmigrantes y el problema de la inmigración italiana en el Perú, 1855–1890. Lima: Optimice, 1999. 295 p.

Informative, empirical study of mid-19th century Italian immigration to Lima, Callao, and the jungle region of Chanchamayo in the dept. of Junin. Contrasts the failure of the Italian colony in Chanchamayo (1853–75), sponsored by several Peruvian governments, with the success of Italian entrepreneurs in Lima and Callao. Includes reprinted government documents and newspaper clippings, and lists Italian-owned businesses.

2630 Segal Freilich, Ariel. Jews of the Amazon: self-exile in earthly paradise. Philadelphia, Penn.: Jewish Publication Society, 1999. 341 p.: bibl., ill., index, maps.

Interesting, if problematic study of the descendants of indigenous women and Jewish prospectors who settled in the city of Iquitos amid the rubber boom of the late 19th and early 20th centuries. Author explores his own Jewish identity while addressing complex issues of religious and ethnic identity construction and community formation among "Jewish mestizos."

Sheahan, John. Searching for a better society: the Peruvian economy from 1950. See *HLAS 59:2073*.

2631 Simposio Internacional Amauta y su Epoca, Lima, 1997. Actas. Lima: Librería Editorial "MINERVA", 1998. 615 p.: bibl., ill.

In this collection of conference papers (Lima, 1997), Peruvian and international scholars assess the impact of *Amauta* (1926–30), Mariátegui's influential review on culture and politics in Peru and Latin America. Contains important works on the nationality debate (Roland Forges) and on female discourse (Sara Beatriz Guardia) in Amauta. Also includes important essays on indigenism, literature, religion, and intellectual life under Leguía.

2632 Taylor, Lewis. The origins of APRA in Cajamarca, 1928–1935. (*Bull. Lat. Am. Res.,* 19:4, Oct. 2000, p. 437–459)

Examines understudied phenomenon of APRA's political preeminence in the dept. of Cajamarca in the early 1930s. Attributes APRA's popularity to Haya's charisma, anti-imperialist discourse, sociocultural organizations, and support from middle class and new labor groups. Contributes valuable discussion on the role of women and gender. Leaves aside question of political alternatives to APRA. Based on interviews with old Apristas and archival sources.

2633 Vásquez Gonzales, José María. Huamanga: una historia para meditar: aproximación a la historia regional. Huan-

cayo, Peru: Diseño Gráfico, 2000. 194 p.: bibl., ill.

Written for nonspecialists by local academic. Study traces the history of Huamanga from precolumbian era through the 19th century. Offers biographical sketches of famous 19th-century Ayacuchano military leaders, politicians, and artisans.

2634 Vivas Sabroso, Fernando. En vivo y en directo: una historia de la televisión peruana. Lima: Univ. de Lima, Fondo de Desarrollo Editorial, 2001. 482 p.: bibl., ill., index. (Colección Documentos)

Broad overview of locally produced Peruvian television from 1958–2000. Traces evolution of popular genres (telenovelas, comedy, talk-shows, news) but eschews systematic analysis of program content related to ethnicity, class, gender, and race. Provides useful data on television pioneers (Delgado Parker family), government regulation, and Fujimori's conflict with Baruch Ivcher and channel 2.

Bolivia

ERICK D. LANGER, *Professor of History, Georgetown University*

BOLIVIAN HISTORIOGRAPHY ADVANCED tremendously since *HLAS 58,* with a much more equal distribution of work between the 19th and 20th centuries. In the past few years, the emphasis on the construction of the nation-state has clearly benefited 19th-century Bolivian history, largely ignored until now except for traditional political history and the history of indigenous groups. Another marked characteristic is that most research, other than biographies, has been published in article rather than book form. Part of the reason for this trend has been the publication of three volumes of essays, one on the 19th century (item **2697**) and two on the 20th century (*Bolivia en el siglo XX*—item **2640** and *Visiones de fin de siglo*—item **2702**). These collections of essays will be important references for years to come. In addition, the Bolivian National Archives has published many articles in its annual *Anuario,* several of which are annotated in this chapter, constituting an additional outlet for historical research.

Historians have made advances in the study of 19th-century mining, politics, the eastern frontiers, indigenous peoples, and economics. Nineteenth-century mining has received the most attention with works by Platt, who has examined mining technology from an anthropological perspective (items **2680, 2681,** and **2683**); Bravo Quezada, who studied Chilean investments in Caracoles (items **2641** and **2642**); and others who turned to the study of mining complexes (items **2653,**

2665, and **2689**). The "Indian problem" as intellectual history has been the subject of Larson (item **2668**) as well as Mariaca Iturri (item **2669**) and Irurozqui (item **2664**). Calderón Jemio has begun to publish parts of his excellent dissertation on the indigenous communities in the Altiplano in the 19th century (item **2646**). Mendieta Parada published a masterful essay on the reasons for the 1899 Indian rebellion (item **2672**). Platt summarized his influential arguments about indigenous communities, making clear how they relate to the present (item **2682**). And Martínez shows how the elites tried to integrate the Indians into the nation by "civilizing" them through education at the beginning of the 20th century (item **2671**).

Irurozqui continued to publish extensively on 19th-century political history, including an attempt to show why democracy failed in Bolivia during that period (items **2662** and **2663**) and, with Peralta Ruiz, examined caudillo rule as a relatively constructive political system (item **2676**). Pérez also added to the analysis of caudillo rule under Belzu and its economic basis (item **2678**). Richard likewise tackled Belzu, but examined his failed attempt to marshal the support of the Catholic Church (item **2686**). The 19th-century history of the eastern regions is beginning to fall under the study of a solid group of historians. In addition to the above-cited Pérez article that deals with cinchona bark on the eastern frontier, García Jordán has published two essays on the mission experience, one on the Guarayos in central Bolivia and the other on the overall institutional and legislative context of the missions (items **2651** and **2652**, respectively). General essays by geographer Roux (item **2693**) and Langer (item **2667**) round out the works on the eastern frontiers.

Economic history appears to be making a splash, with essays on the railroads (item **2654**), and arguments about the validity of Mitre, Platt, and Langer's theses about the effects of adulterated coinage in 19th-century development (items **2658** and **2684**). Soux shows that colonial trade patterns persisted in the La Paz area (item **2701**). Arze Cuadros analyzes the economic aspects of the power struggle between Sucre and La Paz (item **2637**).

The 20th century continues to attract primarily the attention of political historians. The most important form of political history for this period is biography and here, the book form reigns supreme. These biographies range from that of a Cochabamba peasant leader (item **2687**) and a Movimiento Nacional Revolucionario (MNR) leader, Carlos Montenegro (item **2636**), to those of former presidents Enrique Herzog (item **2649**), Hernán Siles Zuazo (item **2647**), Víctor Paz Estenssoro (item **2639**), and Lydia Gueiler (item **2648**). An important book on the assassination of leftist President Juan José Torres receives treatment (item **2698**), and Che Guevara is never forgotten, with the publication of a lengthy interview of Rodolfo Saldaña, one of the urban organizers for Che's guerrilla band (item **2695**). Most useful is a very complete bibliographical essay on the Guevara oeuvre by Soria Galvarro (item **2700**). Gordillo provides a detailed historical treatment of the Cochabamba peasant movement after the 1952 Revolution, which also takes into account gender relations (item **2655**).

Mine labor received some attention, but less than previously, perhaps because of its lessening importance in Bolivia's economy. Ibáñez Rojo adds to the theoretical literature, providing reasons for militancy of the mine labor (item **2660**), whereas Rodríguez Ostria focuses on labor's destruction over the past two decades (item **2690**). Cajías provides a fine summary of miners' political activities from the 1960s to 1971 (see *HLAS 58:2713*). An important addition is Chilean historians

Pinto Vallejos and Valdivia's explanation of why Chileans flooded the labor market on the Bolivian Pacific coast prior to the War of the Pacific and their reasons for maintaining their Chilean identities (item **2679**).

The history of Bolivian women finally receives some attention. In addition to Gueiler's biography (item **2648**), María Luisa Sánchez Bustamante de Urioste, another important MNR leader, merits a biography (item **2659**) as part of a series of woman artists and politicians' biographies written by members of the Coordinadora de Historia and issued by the Secretaría de Asuntos Étnicos, de Género y Generacionales. Gotkowitz shows the ambivalence towards women and also *cholas* in turn-of-the-century Cochabamba (item **2656**), a topic that Romero Pittari also broaches among the literary set (item **2691**).

2635 Abecia Baldivieso, Valentín. Historia del Parlamento. v. 1–3. 2. ed. La Paz: Congreso Nacional, 1999. 3 v.: bibl., ill. (some col.).

Very useful summary of parliamentary debates from 1826 to the end of the 20th century, organized by year. Researchers can then go to the original *Redactores* to check the full debate.

2636 Abecia López, Valentín. Montenegro: homenaje del Honorable Senado Nacional, a los 44 años de su muerte. La Paz: Honorable Senado Nacional, 1997. 485 p.: bibl., ill.

Major biography of one of the most important nationalist ideologues of the Movimiento Nacional Revolucionario, Carlos Montenegro. Shows his importance not only as a man of political ideas, but also as a diplomat. Unfortunately, lacks footnotes.

2637 Arze Cuadros, Eduardo. El papel de la economía en la evolución del conflicto regional en Bolivia: el caso de Sucre y la Paz, 1800–1898. (*Rev. Interam. Planif.*, 30:117/118, enero/junio 1998, p. 133–150, tables)

Summarizes and compares the economic situations of Sucre and La Paz in two time periods: 1800–25 and 1885–98. Shows that La Paz was already economically ascendant at independence, a trend that even the late-19th-century silver boom did not change. Based exclusively on secondary or printed materials.

2638 Asbun-Karmy, Luis Alberto. La migración árabe y su descendencia en Bolivia. Santa Cruz, Bolivia: Impr. Landívar, 2000. 498 leaves: ill., maps.

A great source for research on the *turcos* of Bolivia. Primarily genealogical information—organized by family names. Does not include information on activities of this immigrant community or how it has contributed to the Bolivian economy.

2639 Bedregal Gutiérrez, Guillermo. Víctor Paz Estenssoro, el político: una semblanza crítica. México: Fondo de Cultura Económica, 1999. 713 p.: bibl., ill., index. (Tierra firme)

Heavily documented and favorable biography of the most important political figure of 20th-century Bolivia, written by one of his most important collaborators. Useful especially for the primary documents incorporated into the text.

2640 Bolivia en el siglo XX: la formación de la Bolivia contemporánea. Recopilación de Fernando Campero Prudencio. La Paz: Harvard Club de Bolivia, 1999. 634 p.: bibl., ill. (some col.), index.

Systematic attempt to understand the past century of Bolivian history. Well-known experts address issues such as mining, education, demography, mentalities, and daily life. Includes many photographs and a timeline.

2641 Bravo Quezada, Carmen Gloria. La dinámica de la especulación bursátil: la formación de sociedades anónimas y el mineral de Caracoles, 1870–1878. (*Anuario/Sucre*, 2000, p. 229–247, tables)

The mining boom in the Caracoles district of Atacama dept. was financed in large part by Chilean capital. Contrasts the primitive extraction methods in Caracoles with the sophisticated financial instruments of the Santiago stock market, but shows that these were also highly speculative, leading to a quick collapse before the War of the Pacific.

2642 Bravo Quezada, Carmen Gloria. La flor del desierto: el mineral de Caracoles y su impacto en la economía chilena. Santiago, Chile: Dirección de Bibliotecas, Archivos y Museos: Ediciones LOM: Centro de Investigaciones Diego Barros Arana, 2000. 150 p.: bibl., ill., maps. (Col. Sociedad y cultura; 23)

Excellent short history of the Caracoles silver boom in the 1870s. The Caracoles silver mines led to a rush of Chileans into the Bolivian litoral region, often with Chilean financing. Describes the poor conditions of the Atacama desert mining camps, primitive mining methods, and speculative financing of mining companies. The silver boom brought a large Chilean population with financial interests in the region to Caracoles, leading to Bolivia's subsequent loss of access to the sea in the War of the Pacific.

2643 Bresson, André. Bolivia, siete años de exploraciones, viajes y vivencias: Sudamérica, una visión francesa del litoral boliviano y de la Guerra del Pacífico. La Paz: Embajada de Francia en Bolivia: Alianza Francesa: Colegio Franco-Boliviano Alcide d'Orbigny: Instituto Francés de Estudios Andinos: Instituto Francés de Investigación Científica para el Desarrollo en Cooperación, 1997. 202 p.: bibl., ill., maps.

Reprint and Spanish translation of the classic Bolivian travel account during the time of the War of the Pacific. Bresson was an engineer who was contracted by the Bolivian government to find a rail route to the Pacific coast. Great primary source both for the international politics of the period and for descriptions of the Bolivian coast.

2644 Cáceres Bilbao, Pío. Bolivia: el Senado Nacional (album): bosquejo histórico parlamentario, 1825–1925. 2da. ed. La Paz: Biblioteca del H. Congreso Nacional, 2000. 414 p.: bibl., col. ill.

A useful guide of summaries of legislative sessions for the first century of Bolivia, though the ones from 1852–80 are missing. Short biographies of the important legislators for this period round out this second edition.

2645 Cajías, Lupe. Historia del tabaco y de su industrialización en Bolivia. La Paz: Compañia Industrial de Tabacos, 1999. 198 p.: bibl., ill. (chiefly col.).

A great deal of research on the cultivation, commerce, and consumption of tobacco since colonial times marks this industry-sponsored book. The author looks on the use of tobacco favorably and thus does not examine the health risks or efforts to diminish tobacco use. This book will probably be the standard on this topic for some time to come.

2646 Calderon Jemio, Raul Javier. Años de ambigüedad: propuestas y límites de la política y legislación de tierras durante la consolidación republicana—Umasuyu y Paria, 1825–1839. (*Estud. Boliv.*, 4, sept. 1997, p. 93–124)

Valuable study of the early 19th-century legal responses of Aymara communities to hacienda owners. Shows that the ambiguity of Andres de Santa Cruz's legislation aided the communities and provided an image of dynamism for the Santa Cruz administration.

Contreras C., Manuel E. *et al.* El desarrollo humano en el siglo XX boliviano: una perspectiva histórica. See *HLAS 59:5203.*

2647 Crespo, Alfonso. Hernán Siles Zuazo: el hombre de abril. La Paz?: Plural Editores, 1997. 545 p.: bibl., ill.

A lengthy biography of one of the most important political actors in 20th-century Bolivia and one of the supreme leaders of the Movimiento Nacional Revolucionario (MNR). Biography does not engage in controversies, such as political repression during the first Siles administration (1956–60), or the economic fiasco of his second one (1982–85).

2648 Crespo, Alfonso. Lydia: una mujer en la historia. La Paz: Plural Editores, 1999. 265 p.: ill.

Competent biography of Latin America's first female president that tries to burnish her image. Details her militancy in the MNR and especially her unfortunate interim presidential period (1979–80), prior to the "cocaine coup" of her cousin, Gen. Luis García Meza.

2649 Crespo, Alfonso and Mario Lara. Enrique Hertzog: el hidalgo presidente. Lima: Didi de Arteta, 1997. 236 p.: ill.

An attempt to restore the reputation of one of the last oligarchic presidents, whose illness and subsequent resignation in 1949 inexorably led to the Bolivian Revolution of 1952. In this version, the actions of Herzog and his allies are considered to be positive and the actions of the MNR revolutionaries are viewed as nefarious. Nevertheless, work offers an interesting counterpoint to standard histories.

2650 Durán de Lazo de la Vega, Florencia. Efectos de la migración judía en Bolivia, 1936–1955. (*in* Visiones de fin de siglo: Bolivia y América Latina en el siglo XX. Recopilación de Dora Cajías *et al.* La Paz: IFEA: Coordinadora de Historia: Embajada de España, 2001, p. 563–582)

A nice introduction to this topic, with plenty of data on Jewish migration. Shows how Jews were important in changing retail operations and building a textile industry. Also discusses the exploitation of Jews by Bolivians and growing anti-Semitism. For review of entire work, see item **2702.**

2651 García Jordán, Pilar. ¿De bárbaros a ciudadanos?: Tutela, control de mano de obra y secularización en las misiones de Guarayos, Amazonía norboliviana, 1871–1948. (*in* Fronteras, colonización y mano de obra indígena, Amazonia andina, siglo XIX-XX: la construcción del espacio socioeconómico amazónico en Ecuador, Perú y Bolivia, 1792–1948. Recopilación de Pilar García Jordán. Lima: Pontificia Univ. Católica del Perú, Fondo Editorial; Barcelona: Univ. de Barcelona, 1998, p. 23–124)

A useful history of the Franciscan missions among the Guarayos, based on printed sources. Shows the various phases of mission purpose, from the capturing of indigenous labor to liberal and anticlerical onslaught against the missions by the early 20th century. Lacks use of general mission bibliography of Bolivia and thus contextualization.

2652 García Jordán, Pilar. "De la colonización depende el porvenir de la república": una historia de la colonización en Bolivia, 1825–1935. (*Anuario/Sucre*, 2000, p. 53–106)

A very good administrative and legislative history of the frontiers, taking into account the failure to attract immigration, the religious missions, and the various economic and political factors that led to different colonization schemes throughout the eastern lowlands of Bolivia.

2653 Gavira Márquez, María Concepción. La minería del cobre en el Alto Perú: las minas de Corocoro, 1750–1870. (*Anuario/Sucre*, 2000, p. 107–141, tables)

Uses case study of Bolivia's largest copper mine to analyze the copper mining industry in Bolivia. Deals mainly with copper production, mine owners, and the town of Corocoro.

2654 Gómez Zubieta, Luis Reynaldo. Políticas de transporte ferroviario en Bolivia 1860–1940. (*in* Visiones de fin de siglo: Bolivia y América Latina en el siglo XX. Recopilación de Dora Cajías *et al.* La Paz: IFEA: Coordinadora de Historia: Embajada de España, 2001, p. 363–387)

An excellent overview of all the railroad projects in Bolivia. Legislative debates, financing, and cost are discussed, including the Mollendo railway in Peru. For review of entire work, see item **2702.**

2655 Gordillo, José M. Campesinos revolucionarios en Bolivia: identidad, territorio y sexualidad en el Valle Alto de Cochabamba, 1952–1964. La Paz: Promec: Univ. de la Cordillera: Plural Editores: CEP, 2000. 281 p.: bibl., indexes, maps.

Based on both archival and oral testimonies, this book is the best and most detailed work on the struggles of the Cochabamba peasants after the 1952 Bolivian Revolution. The dense narrative shows the complex alliances of the struggles, including the early revolutionary fervor, the divisions between Ucureña and Quillacollo, and the virtual civil war between these groups in the early 1960s.

2656 Gotkowitz, Laura. "¡No hay hombres!": género, nación y las heroinas de la Coronilla de Cochabamba 1885–1926. (*in* Siglo XIX, Bolivia y América Latina. Recopilación de Rossana Barragán; Dora Cajías; and Seemin Qayum. La Paz: Muela del Diablo Editores, 1997, p. 701–711)

Analyzes the monument put up in 1925 in honor of the mestizas who defended Cochabamba during the independence wars. Shows the ambivalence with which the male-dominated polity viewed the role of women and also that of *cholas* during that period. For review of entire work, see item **2697.**

2657 Hollweg, Mario Gabriel. Alemanes en el oriente boliviano: su aporte al desarrollo de Bolivia. v. 2, 1918–1945. Santa Cruz de la Sierra, Bolivia: s.n., 1997. 1 v.: bibl., ill., index, maps, photos.

As with vol. 1 (see *HLAS 58:2722*),

this is an indispensable and quite exhaustive guide to Germans and their descendants in the Santa Cruz region. A fine complement to any history of Bolivia in the 20th century.

2658 Huber Abendroth, Hans. Comercio, manufactura y hacienda pública en Bolivia entre 1825 y 1870. (*in* Siglo XIX, Bolivia y América Latina. Recopilación de Rossana Barragán; Dora Cajías; and Seemin Qayum. La Paz: Muela del Diablo Editores, 1997, p. 329–371)

Argues that protectionist measures for the textile industry failed in 19th-century Bolivia because of contraband and the lack of an effective exchange barrier in terms of an adulterated coinage. Analyzes protectionists and free traders and shows that community Indians provided more than half of all national income through tribute and indirect taxes. For review of entire work, see item **2697**.

2659 Huber Abendroth, Hans. Pequeña biografía de María Luisa Sánchez Bustamante de Urioste (Malú): una feminista sui géneris. La Paz: Ministerio de Desarrollo Humano, Secretaría de Asuntos Etnicos, de Género y Generacionales, Subsecretaría de Asuntos de Género, 1997. 55 p.: bibl., ill. (Serie "Protagonistas de la historia")

Short popular biography of one of the most important female political leaders from La Paz. Shows her political development from the Ateneo Feminino in the 1920s to an activist in the Movimiento Nacional Revolucionario (MNR). Part of a series on women leaders from the Coordinadora de Historia.

2660 Ibáñez Rojo, Enrique. La política desde el socavón: el movimiento obrero en la historia de Bolivia, 1940–1970. Madrid: Entinema, 1999. 94 p.: bibl. (Serie Con-textos de ciencias sociales; 5)

This pamphlet-sized book argues that the solidarity and revolutionary political ideology of the Bolivian mine workers was due to the relative backwardness of Bolivia. Reformism never improved conditions of the workers. It meant that the unions' revolutionary ideology was appropriate, since the only way to improve conditions permanently was to overthrow the capitalist state.

2661 Inch C., Marcela. Bibliotecas privadas y libros en venta en Potosí y su entorno, 1767–1822. (*Paramillo/San Cristóbal,* 19, 2000, p. 5–241, appendix, bibl., tables)

Excellent encyclopedic analysis of libraries extant in Potosí at the end of the colonial period. Describes not just types of books (religious and law books were most important), but also book costs and the owners of the libraries. Appendix lists all the books found.

2662 Irurozqui, Marta. "A bala, piedra y palo": la construcción de la ciudadanía política en Bolivia, 1826–1952. Seville, Spain: Diputación de Sevilla, 2000. 451 p.: bibl. (Nuestra América no. 8)

First lengthy study of electoral politics in 19th-century Bolivia. Examines the role of political ideology and analyzes the behaviors around national elections, concentrating on the 1880–1920 period. Shows how artisans were partially incorporated and how parties used the accusations of fraud. Does not incorporate indigenous peoples. Focuses on the idea of democracy in 19th-century Bolivia, which is not the best way to frame the data.

2663 Irurozqui, Marta. La conquista de la ciudadanía: artesanos y clientelismo político en Bolivia, 1880–1925. (*Tiempos Am./Castellón,* 3/4, 1999, p. 99–117)

A somewhat confusing but well-documented essay, showing how the artisans of La Paz gained or failed to gain rights of citizenship in turn-of-the-century Bolivia.

2664 Irurozqui, Marta. Las paradojas de la tributación: ciudadanía y política estatal indígena en Bolivia, 1825–1900. (*Rev. Indias,* 59:217, sept./dic. 1999, p. 705–740)

Argues that indigenous peoples were not granted full citizenship rights in Bolivia because most were illiterate and because of the paternalistic relationship between the Bolivian state and the Indian communities— after all, the state treasury depended on Indian tribute until late in the 19th century. This legal limbo prevented the full incorporation of indigenous peoples into the nation.

2665 Jiménez Chávez, Iván Ramiro. Comerciantes, habilitadores e inmigrantes en la formación del capital minero de Corocoro, 1830–1870. (*in* Siglo XIX, Bolivia y América Latina. Recopilación de Rossana Barragán; Dora Cajías; and Seemin Qayum. La Paz: Muela del Diablo Editores, 1997, p. 437–460)

Examines the early history of the copper mines of Corocoro, mined primarily by small miners. Purchasers of the mineral ended up owning the mines, but the entrance of commercial capital did not stop the decline of the mines in the 1850s, when copper prices declined precipitously. For review of entire work, see item **2697**.

2666 Jordán, Florencia Durán and **Ana María Seoane Flores.** El complejo mundo de la mujer durante la Guerra del Chaco. La Paz: Ministerio de Desarrollo Humano, 1997. 220 p.: bibl., ill. (Serie "Protagonistas de la historia")

Looks at the impact of the Chaco War on middle-class women in La Paz. Not a very complete picture, but interesting nonetheless. [J. Horowitz]

2667 Langer, Erick D. The Eastern Andean frontier (Bolivia and Argentina) and Latin American frontiers: comparative contexts, 19th and 20th centuries. (*Americas/ Washington*, 59:1, July 2002, p. 33–63, map)

Provides a conceptual and periodic framework for the analysis of Latin American frontiers, based on the case of the eastern Andes. Argues that indigenous groups had the upper hand militarily during most of the 19th century. Economic and political integration were also much greater than previously thought, though by the late 19th century, stronger states were able to invade and defeat autonomous indigenous groups.

2668 Larson, Brooke. Indios redimidos, cholos barbarizados: imaginando la modernidad neocolonial boliviana, 1900– 1910. (*in* Visiones de fin de siglo: Bolivia y América Latina en el siglo XX. Recopilación de Dora Cajías et al. La Paz: IFEA: Coordinadora de Historia: Embajada de España, 2001, p. 27–48)

Excellent summary of intellectual history of the "Indian problem." Shows how indigenistas used their ethnographic knowledge to "lead the Indian to civilization" and also denigrate the mestizo, who earlier had served as intermediary between Indian and Creole. For review of entire work, see item **2702**.

2669 Mariaca Iturri, Guillermo. "Otros serán los que gocen de los frutos del árbol de la libertad": nación y narración en la Bolivia del siglo XIX. (*Silabario/Córdoba*, 4:4, junio 2001, p. 27–44, bibl.)

A brief analysis of the works of Nataniel Aguirre, Gabriel René Moreno, the diary of the Tambor Vargas, and the work of

El Aldeano to show that 19th-century elites could not imagine a multi-ethnic country, but instead insisted on "civilizing" the natives. The author, a literary critic, criticizes historians for being too literal in their use of sources.

2670 Martinez, Françoise. Una obra liberal impostergable: hace 90 años, la primera escuela normal. (*Anuario/Sucre*, 1999, p. 169–196)

Important essay shows how liberal ideology created pressure for establishing a school that would professionalize the teaching profession. The first teaching college was started in Sucre and employed largely foreign professors, among them the Belgian Georges Rouma.

2671 Martinez, Françoise. La peur blanche: un moteur de la politique éducative libérale en Bolivie, 1899–1920. (*Bull. Inst. fr. étud. andin.*, 27:2, 1998, p. 265–283, bibl.)

Asserts that the educational policies for Indians of liberal Bolivian governments were directed at incorporating them into the body politic by de-Indianizing them. The author claims that the liberal elites feared Indian uprisings after their experience in the Federalist War (1898–99) and for this reason chose these policies. The frontier missions likewise were now to be educational institutions for the "savages" under their care. However, government rhetoric asserted that this was to "emancipate" the Indian.

2672 Mendieta Parada, Pilar. Iglesia, mundo rural y política: Jacinto Escobar párroco de Mohoza y su participación en la masacre de 1899. (*Estud. Boliv.*, 8, 1999, p. 121–168, bibl.)

Excellent study of Bolivian rural society at the end of the 19th and beginning of the 20th centuries. Shows how the massacre of a liberal squadron by Aymaras during the Federalist War revealed the power struggles between the Catholic Church, town mestizos, community Indians, and local authorities.

2673 Mesa, José de; Teresa Gisbert; and **Carlos D. Mesa Gisbert.** Historia de Bolivia. Con 307 dibujos de J. de Mesa y T. Gisbert. 2. ed. corr. y actualizada. La Paz: Editorial Gisbert, 1998. 803 p.: bibl., ill., maps.

Magisterial effort at rewriting Bolivian

history from prehistory to the present day mainly for students. Useful charts and illustrations. However, for better synthesis and higher analysis, see H. Klein, *Bolivia* (*HLAS 56:2841*).

2674 Osterweil, Marc J. The economic and social condition of Jewish and Arab immigrants in Bolivia, 1890–1980. (*in* Arab and Jewish immigrants in Latin America: images and realities. Edited by Ignacio Klich and Jeffrey Lesser. London; Portland, Ore.: F. Cass, 1998, p. 146–166)

A good and quick comparative summary, arguing that the Arab migrants assimilated quickly, whereas most of the Jewish migrants remained only long enough to move elsewhere. The small Jewish population and the much larger Arab one both occupy the same elite socioeconomic niche.

2675 Paredes, Manuel Rigoberto. Relaciones históricas de Bolivia. v. 1. La Paz: Ediciones ISLA, 1997. 1 v.: bibl., ill. (Obras completas; 1)

Vol. 1 in a projected five-vol. series, this book brings together Paredes' historical works, first published in the early 20th century. Well-written, traditional, narrative political history, ranging from an analysis of the colonial regimes to various facets of the independence struggles (a vision firmly planted in the leadership) and René Gabriel Moreno. Valuable biography of Paredes by Ramiro Condarco Morales rounds out the book.

2676 Peralta Ruiz, Víctor and Marta Irurozqui. Por la concordia, la fusión y el unitarismo: estado y caudillismo en Bolivia, 1825–1880. Madrid: Consejo Superior de Investigaciones Científicas, 2000. 277 p.: bibl. (Col. Tierra nueva e cielo nuevo; 41)

Revises our understanding of caudillismo in Bolivia, arguing that it was different than as depicted by Alcides Arguedas (Bolivian intellectual, 1879–1946). Through this top-down institutional history, Peralta asserts that caudillos contributed to Bolivian state formation and were agents of modernization. In pt. 2, Peralta takes an intellectual history approach to argue that Indians were denied citizenship, but that they participated in politics through rebellions. This latter point is a bit simplistic.

2677 Pereira Fiorilo, Juan. Historia secreta de la Guerra del Chaco: Bolivia frente al Paraguay y Argentina. v. 1–2. La Paz: Creactiva Gráfica & Impr., 1999? 2 v.: bibl.

A documentary history of the conduct of the Chaco War, based in large part on the secret legislative sessions of the Bolivian parliament. Indicts Argentina and Chile for favoring Paraguay in the conflict. Shows how woefully unprepared Bolivia was and asserts that its motives were not as aggressive as those of Paraguay.

2678 Perez, Carlos. Caudillos, comerciantes y el estado nacional en la Bolivia decimonovena. (*Anuario/Sucre, 1999, p. 331–350*)

Demonstrates how caudillismo and commerce, especially that of the cinchona bark, intersected in the 19th century. President José Ballivián gave the cinchona bark monopoly to the Argentine merchant house of Tezanos Pinto and halted trade with Peru that harmed La Paz merchants. They and small producers helped Isidoro Belzu overthrow the Ballivián administration in hopes that free trade would be reinstituted.

2679 Pinto Vallejos, Julio and Verónica Valdivia Ortiz de Zárate. Peones chilenos en tierras bolivianas: la presencia laboral en Antofagasta, 1840–1879. (*in* Siglo XIX, Bolivia y América Latina. Recopilación de Rossana Barragán; Dora Cajías; and Seemin Qayum. La Paz: Muela del Diablo Editores, 1997, p. 179–201)

Excellent essay shows how the Bolivian coast became populated mostly by Chilean workers. Bolivian community Indians had no incentive to move to the dry coast, whereas Chile's central valley was a region of labor expulsion. Chilean investments in guano and later nitrates also brought workers from that country. Labor problems and Bolivian government repression fed a sense of Chilean worker identity. For review of entire work, see item **2697**.

2680 Platt, Tristan. La alquimia de la modernidad: los fondos de cobre de Alonso Barba y la independencia de la metalurgía boliviana, 1780–1880. (*Anuario/Sucre, 1999, p. 37–104*)

Turns the history of technology on its head by showing that 16th-century advances in the refining of silver came from Bolivia and were adapted in the late-19th century as a modern technique. These techniques also were adopted in Europe and the US.

2681 Platt, Tristan. Historias unidas, memorias escindidas: las empresas mineras de los hermanos Ortiz y la construcción de las elites nacionales; Salta y Potosí, 1800–1880. (*ANDES Antropol. Hist.*, 7, 1995/96, p. 137–220, graphs, ill., tables)

Brilliant essay on the definition of nationality in the 19th century, using the history of the Ortiz family of miners, landowners, and merchants in what is now Bolivia and Argentina. Until the mid-19th century, the Ortiz family combined mining and trade in both Salta and Potosí and considered themselves "españoles americanos." By the late 19th century each branch of the family went its own way, with family members defining themselves as Argentines or Bolivians.

2682 Platt, Tristan. La persistencia de los ayllus en el norte de Potosí: de la invasión europea a la República de Bolivia. La Paz: Fundación Diálogo: Centro de Información para el Desarrollo, 1999. 53 p.: bibl., ill., maps. (Col. Textos breves/Fundación Diálogo)

A short history of the Andean indigenous communities of northern Potosí. Shows how the communities have been able to survive not only 19th-century dictators, but also the 1953 agrarian reform and attempts by the left in the 1980s-90s to convert communities into peasant unions.

2683 Platt, Tristan. Producción, tecnología y trabajo en la Rivera de Potosí durante la República temprana. (*in* Siglo XIX, Bolivia y América Latina. Recopilación de Rossana Barragán; Dora Cajías; and Seemin Qayum. La Paz: Muela del Diablo Editores, 1997, p. 395–435)

Analyzes production of the Ortiz brothers in Potosí, arguing that new, locally made technology and a strict work organization brought about a mining boomlet at the end of the 1830s. Mineral "theft" by Indians working in Potosí helped end this period. For review of entire work, see item **2697.**

2684 Prado Robles, Gustavo A. Efectos económicos de la adulteración monetaria en Bolivia, 1830–1870. (*in* Siglo XIX, Bolivia y América Latina. Recopilación de Rossana Barragán; Dora Cajías; and Seemin Qayum. La Paz: Muela del Diablo Editores, 1997, p. 299–325)

In a strict economic analysis of the effects of adulterated coinage, asserts that the adulteration had neither the effect of protecting industries within the region of circulation of this coinage, nor did it bring about economic prosperity in southern Peru and northern Argentina. Rather, the 1872 law that permitted the free export of silver made possible a silver mining boom. For review of entire work, see item **2697.**

2685 Qayum, Seemin; María Luisa Soux; and Rossana Barragán Romano. De terratenientes a amas de casa: mujeres de la élite de La Paz en la primera mitad del siglo XX. La Paz: Ministerio de Desarrollo Humano, Secretaría de Asuntos Etnicos, de Género y Generacionales, Subsecretaría de Asuntos de Género, 1997. 100 p.: bibl., ill. (Serie "Protagonistas de la historia")

Brief social history of elite women in La Paz. Many illustrations, aimed at a popular audience. Through interviews and other sources, shows the daily lives of women in a variety of roles, including hacienda owners. Part of a series on women leaders from the Coordinadora de Historia.

2686 Richard, Frédéric. Política, religión y modernidad en Bolivia en la época de Belzu. (*in* Siglo XIX, Bolivia y América Latina. Recopilación de Rossana Barragán; Dora Cajías; and Seemin Qayum. La Paz: Muela del Diablo Editores, 1997, p. 619–634)

Using the concepts of F.X. Guerra, shows that although Belzu tried to use religion as a means of political control, his project did not work. Modernity was already established as popular sovereignty, and religion had no place in creating political legitimacy. For review of entire work, see item **2697.**

2687 Rivas Antezana, Sinforoso. Los hombres de la revolución: memoria de un líder campesino. Recopilación e introducción de José M. Gordillo. La Paz: Plural Editores: CERES, 2000. 155 p.: bibl., ill.

Valuable autobiography of principal Cochabamba peasant leader from the 1953 agrarian reform through 1964. Shows the complexity of the reform process and demonstrates how peasants used their political power after the reform. Many photographs supplement the volume.

2688 Rodríguez Ostria, Gustavo. Energía eléctrica y desarrollo regional: ELFEC en la historia de Cochabamba, 1908–1996. Cochabamba, Bolivia: ELFEC, 1997. 91 p.: bibl., ill. (some col.).

Well-illustrated industry-sponsored history of the Cochabamba electric company by prominent historian. Traces use of electricity and the electric cars in Cochabamba, tying it to the flux of the regional economy. Electric company goes from private in early 20th century, to state-owned in the 1930s, and privatized again in the 1990s.

2689 Rodríguez Ostria, Gustavo. Guadaloupe: una mina-hacienda en Bolivia, 1825–1906. (*Anuario/Sucre*, 2001, p. 93–109)

Explores the combination of capitalist (the silver mines) and "precapitalist" enterprises by studying the agricultural haciendas that Guadaloupe Company had attached as a means to provide a secure labor force to the mines. Argues that this combination was unprofitable but perhaps more typical of silver mining than the Huanchaca mine.

2690 Rodríguez Ostria, Gustavo. Los mineros de Bolivia en una perspectiva histórica. (*Convergencia/Toluca*, 8:24, enero/ abril 2001, p. 271–297, bibl.)

A quick overview of mining labor history in Bolivia, with about half the article dedicated to the last 20 years. Shows how neoliberal policies destroyed miners' unions from 1985 onward.

2691 Romero Pittari, Salvador. Las claudinas: libros y sensibilidades a principios de siglo en Bolivia. La Paz: N. Lorenzo E., Caraspa S. Editores, 1998. 134 p.: bibl., ill. (Sociología. Serie Investigaciones sociales)

Essays explore Bolivian sensibilities through literature at the beginning of the 20th century. Most significant are the chapters on the *cholas*, in which Romero shows how writers tried to understand the "cholification" of Bolivia, and the sexual and class dangers that the sexually attractive *chola* women represented for the upper classes.

2692 Rossells, Beatriz. Las frustraciones de la oligarquía del sur: cultura y identidad en Chuquisaca de XIX. (*in* Siglo XIX, Bolivia y América Latina. Recopilación de Rossana Barragán; Dora Cajías; and Seemin

Qayum. La Paz: Muela del Diablo Editores, 1997, p. 265–277)

The 19th-century cultural production of Sucre was limited because the southern oligarchy remained very small and literacy was low. Although the oligarchy created cultural institutions such as the National Archives, libraries, and museums, there were no organized efforts to maintain these institutions and open them up to members of the lower orders. For review of entire work, see item **2697.**

2693 Roux, Jean-Claude. La Bolivie orientale: confins inexplorés, battues aux Indiens et économie de pillage, 1825–1992. Paris: Harmattan, 2000. 317 p.: bibl., maps. (Recherche Amériques latines)

Useful summary of eastern Bolivian history from independence to the end of the 20th century, written by a geographer with sensitivity to spatial and demographic changes. Based almost exclusively on published sources.

2694 Salazar Mostajo, Carlos. 1809: el complejo de Esaú. La Paz: Muela del Diablo Editores, 1998. 100 p.: bibl., ill.

One of many refutations by an author from La Paz against *La mesa coja* by Mendoza Pizarro (see *HLAS 58:2735*). It purports to show that the La Paz Junta Tuitiva of 1809 was indeed the first proclamation of independence.

2695 Saldaña, Rodolfo. Fertile ground: Che Guevara and Bolivia: a firsthand account. Edited by Mary-Alice Waters. New York: Pathfinder, 2001. 86 p., 8 p. of plates: bibl., ill., index, 1 map.

A brief volume that provides limited additional information on the Che Guevara fiasco. Based on an interview of Rodolfo Saldaña, one of the Communist Party members who helped Guevara, it shows that Saldaña remained a true believer until his death. Includes some new information about the decision to select the Ñancahuazú area and the relations between the guerrillas and leftist organizations.

2696 Sánchez Guzmán, Luis Fernando. Boquerón 1932. La Paz: Editorial Dirección de Comunicación Social del Ejército, 1998. 510 p.: bibl., ill., maps.

Most complete account of one of the most important battles of the Chaco War.

Combines photographs, interviews, maps, and biographies from both sides to create a detailed and well-written description.

2697 El siglo XIX, Bolivia y América Latina. Recopilación de Rossana Romano Barragán; Dora Cajías; and Seemin Qayum. La Paz: Muela del Diablo Editores, 1997. 750 p.: bibl., ill. (Historias)

Results of 1994 conference, the book includes many of the most important Bolivianist historians on three continents. Includes essays on the "regional question," independence, oligarchies, economies, social dynamics, and national projects, incorporating some essays on Chile and Peru. Great starting place for those studying 19th-century Andes. A number of individual papers are reviewed separately in this section.

2698 Sivak, Martín. El asesinato de Juan José Torres: Banzer y el Mercosur de la Muerte. Buenos Aires: Ediciones del Pensamiento Nacional, 1998. 251 p.: bibl., ill.

Well-documented journalistic account, showing how Operation Condor worked. Indicts Hugo Banzer for his masterminding the plot in 1976 to assassinate Torres, the leftist president who Banzer replaced. For political scientist's comment, see *HLAS 57:3534*.

2699 Soria Galvarro Rosales, Jorge. La tímida "historia diplomática" de Bolivia. Santa Cruz, Bolivia: Imprenta Sirena, 2000. 560 p.: ill., maps.

Uses case studies organized by country to demonstrate the ineffectiveness of Bolivian diplomacy. Helpful general summary because of its detailed nature. Lack of citations hampers scholarly use.

2700 Soria Galvarro T., Carlos. Che Guevara: las fuentes bolivianas y su tratamiento biográfico. (*in* Visiones de fin de siglo: Bolivia y América Latina en el siglo XX. Recopilación de Dora Cajías *et al.* La Paz: IFEA: Coordinadora de Historia: Embajada de España, 2001, p. 249–270)

Extremely useful bibliographical essay that cuts through the thicket of Che Guevara literature, categorizing the large production, including a 100-plus bibliography of publications about the fallen guerrilla leader. For review of entire work, see item **2702.**

2701 Soux, María Luisa. La persistencia de los circuitos coloniales: el comercio en torno a La Paz a mediados del siglo XIX. (*in* Integración surandina: cinco siglos después. Arica, Chile: Corporación Norte Grande Taller de Estudios Andinos; Antofagasta, Chile: Univ. Católica del Norte de Antofagasta; Cuzco, Peru: Centro de Estudios Regionales Andinos Bartolomé de Las Casas, 1996, p. 363–379, bibl., tables)

Analyzes commerce of the city of La Paz from the export books of 1853. Colonial commercial circuits remained important; only in the 1870s did trade patterns change to an export-oriented economy.

2702 Visiones de fin de siglo: Bolivia y América Latina en el siglo XX. Recopilación de Dora Cajías *et al.* La Paz: IFEA: Coordinadora de Historia: Embajada de España, 2001. 813 p.: bibl., ill., maps. (Travaux de l'Institut français d'études andines; 134) (Historias)

An excellent compendium of works by established and new historians on 20th-century history, interspersed with speeches by notable Bolivians. Includes essays on many other countries in Latin America as well. For reviews of individual chapters, see items **2650, 2654, 2668,** and **2700.**

Chile

WILLIAM F. SATER, *Professor Emeritus of History, California State University, Long Beach*

INTEREST IN ALLENDE, his government, its overthrow, and the Pinochet years has revived. Some of the recent books are simply memoirs; others are apologies either for Allende or Pinochet; and most because of their narrow focus, are not worth reading. But a few authors, like Garretón Merino and Rojas Sánchez, provide useful chronologies (items **2717** and **2745**). Merino Castro is worthwhile because he explains the role of the navy, which he commanded, in the 1973 coup (item **2731**). Also of great interest is the Rettig report, which dispassionately provides the names of those who perished between 1973 and the late 1980s (item **2733**). Wright's study employs oral history to offer an objective accounting of the exiles (item **2716**). Gazmuri Riveros, Arancibia Clavel, and Góngora Escobedo's magisterial two-volume biography of Frei provides a penetrating glimpse into the life and government of the Christian Democratic leader (item **2719**). All encompassing in vision and marvelous in detail, this is a superb work.

Military and naval history have made a comeback. In the best of the essays, the Hungarian, Ferenc Fisher, describes German attempts to supplant Britain as chief supplier for Chile's fleet (item **2715**). Bravo Valdivieso very ably analyzes the 1931 naval mutiny, its roots in the past, and its somewhat anticlimatic resolution (item **2705**). On the military side, Sater and Herwig indicate that Emile Körner's vaunted reforms provided at best ephemeral changes (see *HLAS 58:2787*), while Valdés Urrutia clarified some of the events surrounding what has become known as the "Pig's Feet Plot," a conspiracy that occurred during the second presidency of Carlos Ibáñez (item **2754**).

Economic history, as always, has been an area that has produced rich rewards. Worthy of special mention is Soto Cárdenas' masterful study of British involvement in the nitrate industry (item **2751**). Pozo's pioneering work has opened up a new area of investigation: the development of Chile's wine industry, which many of us know has produced rich results (item **2740**). The work on the Cristaleros, which focuses on the history of a single factory, provides an excellent vision of labor relations from the perspective of the shop floor (item **2744**). On the other side of the spectrum Mazzei de Grazia (item **2730**) and Lorenzo (item **2728**) explain the economic elites and their own conflicts. Pinto Vallejos' edited volume is essential for understanding the development of mining (item **2710**). His article (item **2737**), as well as those of Grez and Sanhueza (items **2720** and **2748**), demonstrate that Chilean workers supported a variety of political parties, sometimes not always those of the extreme left, to achieve their goals.

As in the US, the amount of material describing the roles of women has increased. Yeager has shown that nuns provided the example and encouragement for well-born Chilean women to become involved in secular contemporary issues (item **2760**). As Veneros Ruiz-Tagle demonstrates, securing the right to vote only provided a limited gain (item **2735**); women still had to confront more entrenched biases including, as Zárate Campos notes, health problems unique to women (item **2761**) before they could achieve meaningful advances.

Social history does not seem to have attracted as much interest this biennium. Thanks to Romero's splendid study, however, we know a great deal more about Chile's urban poor and the various attempts, generally futile, to improve their lot (item **2746**). Some historians have turned their attention from immigrants to the indigenous, exploring the relations between the Moneda and the Mapuche (item **2736**) as well as other aspects of indigenous life in Chilean society (item **2706**). Material has appeared dealing with the role of the Roman Catholic Church. As Sol Serrano demonstrated, however, the Moneda emerged triumphant in the Church-state struggle (item **2749**).

Studies on political topics have increased. The often denigrated and often overlooked political right attracted the attention of scholars. Etchepare offered a more extended view of the right's participation in Chile's political life (item **2711**). For a study of the left, Loyola and Rojas edited a series of extremely perceptive and objective essays on Chile's Communist Party, often explaining the relations between Santiago and Moscow (item **2739**). Couyoumdjian's examination of *La Hora* provides a rare opportunity to trace the impact of a newspaper on political life (item **2708**).

Diplomatic history also seems to be enjoying a revival. Fernández Váldes describes the often contentious relations between Santiago and Lima up to the War of the Pacific (item **2714**), while Rinke shows how Chile hoped to use its close post-World War I ties to Germany to offset US influence (item **2743**). It would be extremely valuable if Rinke followed up with a study focusing on the years after 1884, when Germany first gained an important foothold in Chile's economy and military. Fermandois Huerta (item **2712**) ably concentrates on Chile's relations with Washington immediately after World War II, noting that the Moneda did not profit from its decision to repress Chile's Communist Party.

Abbagliati Boils, Enzo. Desencuentros en la encrucijada: perspectivas sobre las relaciones económicas entre Chile y EE.UU., 1958–1961. See *HLAS 59:4573.*

Araya Espinoza, Alejandra. Cuerpos aprisionados y gestos cautivos: el problema de la identidad femenina en una sociedad tradicional, Chile 1700–1850. See item **2319.**

2703 Artaza Barrios, Pablo. La formación de la pareja y sus conflictos: Chile en el siglo XIX. (*Nomadías/Santiago*, 1, junio 1999, p. 145–161, table)

Chileans who married in 19th century did so for economic or social reasons; romance, alas, came in a distant third. Interesting, but with such a small statistical sample, drawn from essentially primary sources, that the data have very limited application.

2704 Boccara, Guillaume and **Ingrid Seguel-Boccara.** Políticas indígenas en Chile, siglos XIX y XX, de la asimilación al pluralismo: el caso mapuche. (*Rev. Indias*, 59:217, sept./dic. 1999, p. 741–774)

Chilean governments initially tried to assimilate the Mapuche. The Unidad Popular regime, however, saw and treated them as a specific ethnic group, while Pinochet returned to the policy of assimilation. Now the government promotes indigenous identity within a more pluralistic society. Although relying on secondary works, provides interesting overview.

2705 Bravo Valdivieso, Germán. La sublevación de la Escuadra y el período revolucionario 1924–1932. Viña del Mar, Chile: Ediciones Altazor, 2000. 213 p.: bibl., ill.

Traces origins of 1931 naval mutiny back to navy's earlier involvement in politics, particularly during the Ibañez period. Indicates that Communists used post-1929 economic downturn to launch the failed movement. Well researched, but lack of footnotes makes it hard to discover and use sources.

2706 Cerda-Hegerl, Patricia. Fronteras del sur: la región del Bío Bío y la Araucanía chilena, 1604–1883. Berlin: Instituto Latinoamericano de la Univ. Libre de Berlín; Temuco, Chile: Univ. de la Frontera, 199-. 185 p.: bibl., maps.

Using mainly primary sources, author provides good overview of the conquest of Chile's south. While comparing pacification of Araucania with US experience in the West, shows how the Spanish and Chileans created a Hispanoamerican culture which developed the local economy before integrating it into the nation.

2707 Chile, 1541–2000: una interpretación de su historia política. Coordinación de Alvaro Góngora Escobedo. Santiago: Santillana, 2000. 375 p.: bibl.

Four historians, each specializing in a different time period, cover Chile's history from colonial period to post-Pinochet era. Good overview, but flawed by absence of footnotes.

2708 Couyoumdjian, Juan Ricardo. *La Hora*, 1935–1951: desarrollo institucional de un diario político. (*Historia/Santiago*, 31, 1998, p. 5–56, tables)

As the voice of the Partido Radical, *La Hora* should have prospered: by using it to publish official notices, the Radical governments guaranteed the newspaper a steady source of income. Personnel problems, however, forced the newspaper to fold. Interesting study uses archival materials to discuss a heretofore neglected topic.

2709 Cruz de Amenábar, Isabel. Diosas atribuladas: alegorias cívicas, caricatura y política en Chile durante el siglo XIX. (*Historia/Santiago*, 30, 1997, p. 127–171, ill.)

Unlike France, the image of Chile as a woman did not occur until the late 19th century, and then as a result of the popular penny press. These images quickly became part of popular culture, inculcating a sense of national pride. Interesting article, but limited because of its sources.

2710 Episodios de historia minera: estudios de historia social y económica de la minería chilena, siglos XVIII-XIX. Recopilación de Julio Pinto Vallejos. Santiago, Chile: Editorial Univ. de Santiago, 1997. 289 p.: bibl., ill. (Col. Ciencias sociales. Historia)

Excellent collection of essays describes various aspects of mining in 19th-century Chile. Editor's introductory bibliographical article is a must read for economic scholars. Venegas' work on creation of a proletariat in Atacama is fascinating, as is Pereira's biography of José Vallejo. Essential for economic historians.

2711 Etchepare Jensen, Jaime. La derecha chilena, principales vertientes ideológicas, partidismo y evolución electoral. (*Rev. Hist./Concepción*, 7, 1997, p. 93–109)

Using a variety of primary sources, provides an overview of the right in Chile, discussing its various manifestations, its electoral successes and failures, and its role in the nation's politics. Excellent for those unfamiliar with Chilean politics.

2712 Fermandois Huerta, Joaquín. Guerra Fría y economía política internacional: el cobre en Chile, 1945–1952. (*Ciclos Hist. Econ. Soc.*, 8:16, segundo semestre 1998, p. 143–162)

Relying on diplomatic sources, shows that Chilean hostility toward Communism, more than US pressure, led González Videla to outlaw the Partido Comunista. Once it was done, however, Washington did not, as it had promised, purchase Chile's raw materials so that it could industrialize. Excellent study of an often debated topic.

2713 Fernández Fernández, David. Cristianos por el socialismo en Chile, 1971–1973: aproximación histórica a través del testimonio oral. (*Stud. Zamorensia*, 4, 1997, p. 187–202, bibl.)

Using mainly interviews, author explains Christian Socialism. Parish priests, not the hierarchy, supported Unidad Popular because they regarded poverty as the result of social injustice. They helped the poor because it was their Christian duty and they hoped to ensure that the Chilean Church did not become marginalized as it had in Cuba.

2714 Fernández Valdés, Juan José. Chile-Perú: historia de sus relaciones diplomáticas entre 1819 y 1879. Santiago?: Editorial Cal & Canto, 1997. 515 p.: bibl., ill.

Straightforward study, based almost exclusively on archival materials, recounts Chile's often difficult relations with Peru. Diplomatic historians will profit from this excellent portrayal of a conflicted 60-year relationship. Extensive use of archival materials makes this work a must.

2715 Fisher, Ferenc. El model militar prusiano y las fuerzas armadas de Chile, 1885–1945. Pécs, Hungary: Pécs Univ. Press, 1999. 1 v.

Some of the essays included argue that the Germans dramatically improved the Chilean army. Berlin, however, could not break the British hold on Santiago's navy. Because author relied almost exclusively on German archives, military historians should use these works with some caution. Useful view of a neglected perspective.

2716 Flight from Chile: voices of exile. Compiled by Thomas C. Wright and Rody Oñate. Translations by Irene Hodgson. Albuquerque: Univ. of New Mexico Press, 1998. 239 p.: bibl., index, map.

Traces experiences of various Chileans, explaining how they reacted to the coup d'état (1973) and what they did after the military seized power. Some continued to resist, and those who did often suffered terrible torture when captured. Others fled; a few remained in exile while many returned. Excellent example of oral history.

2717 Garretón Merino, Manuel Antonio; Roberto Garretón Merino; and Carmen Garretón Merino. Por la fuerza sin la razón: análisis y textos de los bandos de la dictadura militar. Santiago, Chile: LOM Ediciones, 1998. 100 p.: bibl. (Col. Septiembre)

Analyzes military junta's first pronouncements as it sought to legitimize the overthrow of the Allende government. The military used national security as justification not merely for the right to rebel, but also for retaining power. Work tends to become tautological but does include military government's initial decrees.

2718 Gazmuri Riveros, Cristián. Eduardo Frei Montalva: niñez y adolescencia. (*Historia/Santiago*, 31, 1998, p. 57–86)

Although from an economically strapped family, Frei won scholarships to various parochial schools where, after a slow start, he excelled. By the time he was ready to enter university, he was a serious youth with intellectual aspirations. Using numerous interviews, Gazmuri provides interesting insights into the future president's early life. See also item **2719.**

2719 Gazmuri Riveros, Cristián; Patricia Arancibia Clavel; and Alvaro Góngora Escobedo. Eduardo Frei Montalva y su época. Santiago, Chile: Aguilar, 2000. 2 v.: bibl., index.

Superb biography based on wide selection of primary material including numerous interviews, as well as on secondary works. Frei's life is charted from his modest beginnings and intellectual development to his political life. Relates with candor Frei's life, growth, government, and dealings with the junta. Essential work of enduring quality. See also item **2718.**

2720 Grez Toso, Sergio. El liberalismo popular: características y rol en la constitución del movimiento popular en el Chile decimonónico. (*Rev. Chil. Hist. Geogr.*, 163, 1997, p. 201–232)

Based on secondary materials, shows that working class, particularly artisans, participated in politics prior to 1860 when these elements became involved with the Partido Liberal. Realizing that they could influence neither the Liberals nor the Radicals, the workers, without relying on Marxist or Anarchist thought, formed their own party.

2721 Harris Bucher, Gilberto. La inmigración extranjera en Chile a revisión: también proletarios, aventureros, desertores y deudores. (*Anu. Estud. Am.*, 54:2, julio/dic. 1997, p. 543–566)

Citing examples of deserters from British and American navy or merchant marine, demonstrates that these men, as well as many German colonists, not only did not contribute to Chile's development but became a burden on society. While employing primary sources, revisionist study lacks cohesion and elegance.

2722 Harris Bucher, Gilberto. Notas sobre mentalidad empresarial de los comerciantes-industriales en Chile, 1840–1879. (*Rev. Hist./Concepción*, 7, 1997, p. 149–159)

Arguing that it would reduce imports, employ people, and make the nation self sufficient, various individuals applied for and received concessions to create protected industries. These entrepreneurs, according to various primary sources, still depended upon foreign capital, technology, or labor to establish themselves. Nonetheless they did help modernize Chile. See also item **2723.**

2723 Harris Bucher, Gilberto. Privilegios exclusivos y mentalidad empresarial en la temprana industrialización chilena, 1840–1879. (*Mapocho/Santiago*, 44, segundo semestre 1998, p. 105–122)

Thanks to government's granting of monopolies, which generally lasted for a fixed period, Chilean industrialists had the means to create various local manufacturing concerns. After 1870, these privileges increasingly focused on the mining sector. Uses archival material to show early development of Chilean industries. See also item **2722.**

2724 Hickman, John. News from the end of the Earth: a portrait of Chile. New York: St. Martin's Press, 1998. 250 p.: bibl., ill., index, maps.

Quick study of historical events in Chile written by former British diplomat. Although based on secondary works, provides some interesting perspectives on the fall of Allende, the Pinochet period, the Falklands War, and the Aylwin regime.

2725 Historia contemporánea de Chile. v. 1, Estado, legitimidad, ciudadanía [de] Gabriel Salazar Vergara, Arturo Mancilla y Carlos Durán. v. 2, Actores, identidad y movimiento [de] Julio Pinto, Azún Candina y Robinson Lira. Santiago: LOM Ediciones, 1999. 2 v.: bibl. (Historia)

Throughout the 19th and much of 20th centuries, Chile achieved political stability at the cost of minimizing, if not eradicating, civil liberties. The system accepted the middle and even lower classes, but only as long as elites would tolerate them. Well researched, densely written, and offering thought-provoking insights, but presupposes that reader is well versed in Chilean history.

2726 Lausic Glasinovic, Sergio. Migraciones del archipiélago de la isla grande de Chiloé hacia la Patagonia (Chile-Argentina) y participación en el sindicalismo obrero. (*Rev. Hist./Concepción*, 7, 1997, p. 203–214)

Beginning in the period 1900–1910, various *chilotes* migrated to the Magallanes region, attracted by its pastoral economy and meat packing industry. Later, politically aware foreigners arrived. These people created a union movement to protect the workers' rights. Relies on archives and press to show creation and evolution of a labor movement.

2727 Lorenzo, Santiago. La élite de Valparaíso: sus puntos de vista acera de la organización del estado y de la economía, 1830–1850. (*Rev. Hist./Concepción*, 7, 1997, p. 171–176)

Elites of Santiago and Valparaíso disagreed on the path to Chilean economic development. The port's leaders regarded the capital's citizens as favoring the status quo. Conversely, the *porteños* advocated limited government, free trade, and, paradoxically, protectionism to create local industries. Interesting thesis, based mainly on the newspaper *El Mercurio de Valparaíso*.

2728 Mazzei de Grazia, Leonardo. Antiguos y nuevos empresarios en la region de Concepción en el siglo XIX. (*Rev. Hist./Concepción*, 7, 1997, p. 177–187)

The agrarian elites of Concepción, without entrepreneurial spirit and laboring under geographical disadvantages, allowed the business interests of the capital, Valparaíso, and other countries to win control of the provincial economy. Thus Concepción became integrated into the national economy but at great cost to the region's local landowners and bourgeoisie. See also item **2730**.

2729 Mazzei de Grazia, Leonardo. Los británicos y el carbón en Chile. (*Atenea/Concepción*, 475, 1997, p. 137–167)

British merchants did not dominate Chile's coal industry; however, Englishmen did lend money to develop these mines as well as introduce technology and provide skills essential to coal's development. Employs a mix of sources to discuss an often neglected topic.

2730 Mazzei de Grazia, Leonardo. Terratenientes de Concepción en el proceso de modernización de la economía regional en el siglo XIX. (*Historia/Santiago*, 31, 1998, p. 179–215, tables)

Citing example of Urrutia and Urreola families, shows that traditional landholding elite lost their position of ascendancy to those individuals, some foreign, who made their fortunes selling flour and coal and participating in commerce. Due to intermarriage, old elites became more isolated. Excellent work based on archival sources. See also item **2728**.

2731 Merino Castro, José Toribio. Bitácora de un almirante: memorias. Barcelona; Santiago, Chile: A. Bello, 1998. 537 p.: bibl., ill.

Actually three books in one: an autobiography, an analysis of postcoup Chile, and—the most important—Merino's account of events leading to the overthrow of Allende. Although skewed, his reporting on the navy's reasons for rebelling and its participation in the uprising nonetheless helps historians.

2732 Nazer Ahumada, Ricardo. Las finanzas municipales chilenas: 1833–1887. (*Historia/Santiago*, 32, 1999, p. 265–314, appendix, graph, tables)

The 1833 Constitution authorized creation of Chile's municipalities. Unfortunately, the cities, lacking financial resources to provide needed services, had to borrow large sums. The 1891 law not only reorganized the structure of local government; it provided the governments with new sources of income. Contains interesting data.

2733 Nunca más en Chile: síntesis corregida y actualizada del informe Rettig. 2. ed. Santiago: LOM Ediciones; Comisión Chilena de Derechos Humanos; Fundación Ideas, 1999. 231 p. (Col. Septiembre)

Corrected and updated version of the Rettig report not only provides lists of those killed on both sides of the struggle, but breaks these down by region, year, political affiliation, and responsibility. Essential for anyone studying Chile from the early 1970s-late 1980s.

Ortega, Luis. Historia empresarial en Chile, 1850–1945: el estado de la literatura. See *HLAS 59:2041.*

2734   Pacheco Silva, Arnoldo. El fenómeno de migración del campo a la ciudad: Concepción, 1850–1880. (*Rev. Hist./Concepción*, 7, 1997, p. 189–202)

Development of the coal industry, milling, and growth of export trade in Talcahuano led people to move from the countryside into Concepción. Uses mainly archival material to show that these young men, contrary to what Gabriel Salazar had alleged (see *HLAS 50:2306*), managed to prosper by becoming skilled workers.

2735   Perfiles revelados: historias de mujeres en Chile, siglos XVIII-XX. Recopilación de Diana Veneros Ruiz-Tagle. Santiago: Editorial Univ. de Santiago, 1997. 242 p.: bibl. (Col. Ciencia sociales. Historia)

Of particular merit in this work on women's history are the introductory articles which examine evolving image of women and their attempt to win political equality. The other essays focus on more limited topics—violence, prostitution, and work—in various provincial cities. Welcome addition to a growing field of study. See also item **2757.**

2736   Pinto Rodríguez, Jorge. Del antiindigenismo al proindigenismo en Chile en el siglo XIX. (*in* Del discurso colonial al proindigenismo: ensayos de historia latinoamericana. Temuco, Chile: Ediciones Univ. de la Frontera, 1996, p. 83–116, bibl.)

The government justified displacement of the Mapuche on the grounds that it was asserting its sovereign rights and that the Indians were inferior. Uses primary materials to show that pro-indigenous sentiment would not appear until the late 19th century when the Mapuche simply had tired of the Chilean government.

2737   Pinto Vallejos, Julio. ¿Cuestión social o cuestión política?: la lenta politización de la sociedad popular tarapaqueña hacia el fin de siglo, 1889–1900. (*Historia/Santiago*, 30, 1997, p. 211–261)

Northern workers did not support the Partido Democrático or anarchism. Rather,

they favored the Partido Radical and Partido Liberal-Democrático, which eventually became vehicles for their demands. A well-researched, innovative, and insightful article.

2738   Pinto Vallejos, Julio. Socialismo y salitre: Recabarren, Tarapacá y la formación del Partido Obrero Socialista. (*Historia/Santiago*, 32, 1999, p. 315–366)

Luis Emilio Recabarren had to experience the northern *salitreras* to see that socialism provided the only means to resolve the "cuestión social." Working as an editor, he managed to mobilize politically the miners, creating the Partido Obrero Socialista whose message he would bring to the rest of Chile.

Pinto Vallejos, Julio and Verónica Valdivia Ortiz de Zárate. Peones chilenos en tierras bolivianas: la presencia laboral en Antofagasta, 1840–1879. See item **2679.**

Un plebiscito imposible...: Tacna y Arica, 1925–1926. See item **2624.**

2739   Por un rojo amanecer: hacia una historia de los comunistas chilenos. Compilación de Manuel Loyola T. y Jorge Rojas Flores. Santiago?: s.n., 2000. 277 p.: bibl., ill.

Essays focus on different aspects of the Partido Comunista de Chile. Rojas Flores provides a superb short history of this party with a long tradition. Others survey specific time periods including the post-Pinochet era. Incorporating materials gleaned from ex-Soviet archives, these works are excellent sources for political historians.

2740   Pozo, José del. Historia del vino chileno: desde 1850 hasta hoy. Santiago: Editorial Universitaria, 1998. 315 p.: bibl., ill., indexes. (Col. Imagen de Chile)

Innovative and well-researched work chronicles formation, growth, and modernization of Chile's wine industry. Thanks to foreign capital and expertise, Chile produced wines which, unlike the native Chilean vintage, were more subtle and hence more popular abroad. Delightful monograph should appeal to wine lovers as well as historians.

2741   Pozo, José del. El régimen de trabajo en las grandes viñas de la región central de Chile: *trateros* y obreros de bodega en el siglo XX. (*Can. J. Lat. Am. Caribb. Stud.*, 22:43, 1997, p. 21–45)

Allende did not expropriate the vineyards in part because they were too important to the economy. After 1973, *inquilinos* lost their traditional perks when the vineyard owners mechanized and used all of their land to produce more grapes. Ably relies on primary and secondary sources to discuss a neglected topic.

2742 Ravest Mora, Manuel. Ocupación militar de la Araucanía, 1861–1883. Santiago, Chile: Impresos Bernatz, 1997. 147 p.: bibl., maps.

Short, competent history of Chile's slow, painful, and often costly campaign to push south to the Araucanian frontier. Eventually the government concluded that it had to either eradicate or subjugate the indigenous peoples if it hoped to develop the south. Renegade whites proved almost as dangerous as the indigenous population.

2743 Rinke, Stefan H. Las relaciones germano-chilenas, 1918–1933. (*Historia/Santiago*, 31, 1998, p. 217–308, tables)

Although limited by the Versailles Treaty, a lack of capital, and global adoption of the Haber-Bayer nitrate manufacturing process, by 1930 Berlin had rebuilt its economic and military ties to Chile. The Great Depression and currency controls then reduced Germany's involvement. Using German archives, author shows how Berlin and Santiago saw each other as allies in a plan to resist US incursions.

Rodríguez González, Agustín Ramón. La Armada Española, la campaña del Pacífico, 1862–1871: España frente a Chile y Perú. See item **2627**.

2744 Rojas Flores, Jorge; Cinthia Rodríguez Toledo; and Moisés Fernández Torres. Cristaleros: recuerdos de un siglo; los trabajadores de Cristalerías de Chile. Padre Hurtado, Chile: Sindicato No. 2 de Cristalerías de Chile; Programa de Economía del Trabajo, 1998. 189 p.: bibl., ill.

Integrating interviews and archival material, traces development of Chile's first bottle factory. Provides insights into the workers and their various struggles to achieve union recognition. Particularly useful for explaining how the company functioned during the Allende period when it became part of the public sector.

2745 Rojas Sánchez, Gonzalo. Chile escoge la libertad: la presidencia de Augusto Pinochet Ugarte. v. 1, 11.9.1973—11.3. 1981. Santiago: Zig Zag, 1998. 1 v. (Col. Temas de hoy)

A pro-Pinochet study that nonetheless presents a straightforward, detailed history of Chile from the coup to 1990. Work's most attractive quality is its use of primary sources which it ties to specific legislative acts. An alternative but not an antidote to the pro-Allende literature.

2746 Romero, Luis Alberto. ¿Qué hacer con los pobres?: elite y sectores populares en Santiago de Chile, 1840–1895. Buenos Aires: Editorial Sudamericana, 1997. 211 p.: bibl. (Col. Historia y cultura)

Superb study explains how migration of peasants into Santiago led to creation of new social classes as well as new social problems. Some of Santiago's *intendentes* attempted to deal with the problems, but these proved overwhelming. Drawing on a wealth of primary materials, author provides a magisterial social history.

2747 Sagredo B., Rafael. Chile, 1823–1831: el desafío de la administración y organización de la hacienda pública. (*Historia/Santiago*, 30, 1997, p. 287–312)

Revisionist article employing mainly primary material convincingly argues that Diego José Benavente, not Manuel Rengifo Cárdenas, deserves the credit for reviving Chile's postindependence economy. Benavente had excellent ideas—including protecting local industry and using the *estanco*—which the 1820s political upheaval prevented from coming to fruition.

2748 Sanhueza Tohá, Jaime. La Confederación General de Trabajadores y el anarquismo chileno de los años 30. (*Historia/Santiago*, 30, 1997, p. 313–382, appendix)

Anarchism's popularity was confined to certain geographic areas—mainly Chile's south—and to certain occupations, primarily the building trades. Ibáñez's repression plus the rise of legal unions limited growth of anarchist influence. Still, enough survived to contribute to change, although eventually leftist unions supplanted it. Well researched and worth studying.

2749 **Serrano, Sol.** La conflictiva definición de lo público en un estado católico: el caso chileno, 1810–1885. (*Anos 90*, 10, dez. 1998, p. 76–88)

While permitting some degree of latitude to the individual, the Roman Catholic Church occupied the public space. Over the years, the state forced the Church to yield, insisting on religious pluralism which made the government the most powerful force in Chile.

2750 **Soto, Oscar.** El último día de Salvador Allende: crónica del asalto al Palacio de la Moneda, contada por sus protagonistas. Prólogo de José Antonio Martín Pallín. Presentación de Hortensia Bussi de Allende. Madrid: El País/Aguilar, 1998. 281 p.: ill.

A participant observer to the assault on the Moneda, author offers a portrait of the last day of the Unidad Popular government. Highly opinionated, author provides one perspective on the coup and the fate of Allende's most adamant supporters. Contains some useful documents, but no sources other than author's memory.

2751 **Soto Cárdenas, Alejandro.** Influencia británica en el salitre: origen, naturaleza y decadencia. Santiago, Chile: Editorial Univ. de Santiago, 1998. 675 p.: bibl. (Col. Ciencias sociales. Historia)

Uses primary sources to demonstrate that while British initially controlled the *salitreras*, a clash over production levels led Ibáñez to limit English involvement. Although British ownership of mines declined, the English still maintained heavy investments in Compañía de Salitres de Chile (COSACH) as well as in the successor, Corporación de Ventas de Salitre y Yodo de Chile (COVENSA). Excellent work which economic historians will value.

2752 **Turra Diaz, Omar.** Inmigración colonizadora y modernización agrícola: Chile en el siglo XIX. (*Rev. Hist./Concepción*, 7, 1997, p. 159–170)

The Chilean government funded projects to attract European immigrants, thereby hoping to improve the country by replacing Spanish colonial mentalities and customs with progressive European ideas. It was also hoped that these immigrants would cultivate the south, thereby modernizing the economy and assuring Chile's participation in the North Atlantic economy. Uses mainly secondary materials in an interesting, but not innovative essay.

2753 **Urriola Pérez, Ivonne.** Espacio, oficio y delitos femeninos: el sector popular de Santiago, 1900–1925. (*Historia/Santiago*, 32, 1999, p. 443–483, map, tables)

Records of criminal courts reveal that many poor women worked at home doing washing or piece work, or as live-in domestic servants, seamstresses, or prostitutes in brothels. Superb but depressing insight into these women's often desperate lives as they struggled to survive in the capital's *conventillos*.

2754 **Valdés Urrutia, Mario.** Chile ruido de sables en 1948: la conspiración en contra del Presidente Gabriel González Videla. (*Rev. Hist./Concepción*, 7, 1997, p. 111–137)

Hostility toward González Videla as well as low salaries and rampant inflation, and not Perón and Argentine meddling, forced the officers and noncommissioned officers to back the putsch which the Moneda managed to quash before conspirators could act. Uses primary sources to clarify an interesting episode in Chilean history.

2755 **Valdivia Ortiz de Zárate, Verónica.** Yo, el León de Tarapacá: Arturo Alessandri Palma, 1915–1932. (*Historia/Santiago*, 32, 1999, p. 485–551)

Alessandri could not fulfill his 1920 campaign promises. Much as he wanted reforms, he had to maintain order first. After 1930, he did begin to use the state to foment development. Based mainly on primary sources, a good insight into a leading Chilean politician.

Valenzuela, J. Samuel. Building aspects of democracy before democracy: electoral practices in nineteenth century Chile. See *HLAS 59:5285.*

2756 **Vargas Cariola, Juan Eduardo.** Aspectos de la vida privada de la clase alta de Valparaíso: la casa, la familia y el hogar entre 1830 y 1880. (*Historia/Santiago*, 32, 1999, p. 617–684)

Delightful study of lives of the *porteño* elites, explaining relations between families and spouses. Use of a host of primary materials provides insight into the lifestyle of the most important figures in Valparaíso, noting how they began to imitate the opulent of Santiago.

2757 Veneros Ruiz-Tagle, Diana. Sufragismo y roles femeninos: de las paradojas de "la mujer moderna," 1946–1952. (*Nomadías/Santiago*, 1, junio 1999, p. 239–263)

Winning the right to vote did not alter the role of women as wives and mothers, in part because feminists based their campaign on traditional values. Unfortunately, the movement failed to achieve more because of exhaustion, because the state itself had changed, and because of severe class differences among the women. See also item **2735.**

2758 Viera-Gallo, José Antonio. 11 de septiembre: testimonio, recuerdos y una reflexión actual. Santiago: Ediciones ChileAmérica CESOC, 1998. 155 p.

Interesting diary of a middle-rung functionary in the Ministerio de Justicia is valuable for describing the 1973 coup and the subsequent days. Author concludes with an interesting essay discussing inevitability of the fall of Allende.

2759 Vos Eyzaguirre, Bárbara de. El surgimiento del paradigma industrializador en Chile, 1875–1900. Santiago: Dirección de Bibliotecas, Archivos y Museos, Centro de Investigaciones Diego Barrios Arana,

1999. 109 p.: bibl., ill. (Col. Ensayos y estudios; 1)

Relying heavily on primary sources, argues that various organizations like Sociedad de Fomento de Fabril (SOFOFA), and journals such as *La Industria Chilena*, saw industrialization not simply as a means of diversifying the economy but of introducing social and political changes as well. Not until late 1930s did the largely landowning legislators provide needed support.

2760 Yeager, Gertrude Matyoka. Female apostolates and modernization in mid-nineteenth century Chile. (*Americas/Washington*, 55:3, Jan. 1999, p. 425–458, tables)

Women became more active in Chile as religious orders generally took over administration of various health care and social institutions. The nuns encouraged other women, generally from the upper class, to become involved in these institutions thus marking the emergence of affluent women into Chilean life. Excellent for bibliographical leads.

2761 Zárate Campos, María Soledad. Proteger a las madres: origen de un debate público, 1870–1920. (*Nomadías/Santiago*, 1, junio 1999, p. 163–182)

A desire to protect the lives of newborns inevitably made Chileans and their government focus on caring for the mother as well. This well-researched article traces growth of this movement to make obstetrics a medical speciality and prenatal care plus breast-feeding a matter of national concern.

Argentina, Paraguay, and Uruguay

JOEL HOROWITZ, *Professor of History, Saint Bonaventure University*
THOMAS WHIGHAM, *Professor of History, University of Georgia*

ARGENTINA
ARGENTINE HISTORIOGRAPHY HAS MOVED IN EXCITING DIRECTIONS over the last several years, yielding some high-quality, well-researched analyses of traditional topics and branching out into new areas of study. Though the field of 19th-century Argentine history as a whole remains spotty, often the works being produced are exceptional and will reward the careful reader.

Studies of the *gaucho*—once a mainstay among Argentine historians—have in recent times given way to more comprehensive, sophisticated, and specialized examinations of rural life in the 19th century. Among the better works to trod this particular ground are those of Gelman (item **2875**), Johnson (item **2907**), and especially Amaral (item **2766**). On a related subject—the figure of the rural boss or *caudillo*—Goldman and Salvatore have produced an excellent compilation that summarizes and explicates much of the current literature (item **2812**).

One aspect of the field that bears watching is the historical analysis of folklore and song. In this arena, De la Fuente has paved the way with a groundbreaking, suggestive piece on folkloric characterizations of two of the most infamous Riojano *caudillos*, Facundo Quiroga and "el Chaco" Peñaloza (item **2833**).

Biography has returned to favor among Argentine scholars after several years of seeming decline. Traditionally, a plethora of thin hagiographies on José de San Martin and Juan Manuel de Rosas are published, and the current biennium is no exception. Yet new biographies on such unusual figures as Juan José Paso (item **3033**) and even Evaristo López (item **2988**) are worthy of mention. Perhaps Duarte has provided the most interesting biographical treatment of all—a solid, sympathetic, and wholly convincing examination of the final years of Ricardo López Jordan (item **2845**).

Among the most impressive of the works reviewed in this chapter are those which focus on early Argentine nationalism, and specifically, on how the peoples of La Plata defined themselves, participated in the construction of new states, ran elections, and organized a political order that in some sense reflected public opinion. The works of Lettieri (item **2918**) and Sábato (item **3010**) stand out as fine examples of this encouraging trend.

Any discussion of Argentine nationalism must necessarily address the historical role of foreign intervention. Thus, diplomatic studies have long held a key place in Argentine historiography. They are especially well-represented in this chapter by an impressive six-volume account by Cisneros and Escude that deals with more than the English invasions of the early 1800s and their effect on porteño trade (item **2997**). The authors show that diplomacy went beyond the goals and perspectives of the capital city, and involved rival governments and strategies to form an Argentine nationhood based on provincial interests.

Following a path blazed years ago by Braudel and other historians of the *Annales* chool, Argentine scholars have made several useful forays into the nature of private life (family, social life and customs, fashion, etc.). These works, which include the edited compilation of Devoto and Madero (item **2895**) and the analytically rich study of Cicerchia (item **2818**), show great promise. They may serve as catalysts in launching new approaches to historical research.

Demography remains an important focus of Argentine scholarship, most likely due to the large number of immigrants in the country. Two works stand out among many this biennium: Vázquez Rial's study of the convoluted politics of migration (item **3046**), and Baily's long-awaited comparison of Italian immigrants in Buenos Aires and New York City (item **2781**).

Several of the more important recent studies defy categorization, save that they illustrate the myriad ways in which Argentines have confronted and adapted to modern life. For instance, Bordi de Ragucci's history of drinking water in Buenos Aires is one of the most creative historical studies to appear of late (item **2793**), as is Ragini's account of telegraphy during the Sarmiento presidency (item **2994**). Zaragoza Rovira has written what is likely the definitive work on early Argentine anarchism (item **3058**), and Fernández has produced a wonderfully evocative, carefully researched study of magic and magicians in Argentina that is a pleasure to read (item **2851**). [TW]

As is the case throughout the society, the ability to publish works on the history of Argentina since the 1880s has been strongly affected by the recent economic crisis. By 2002, due to the dire economic situation, journal publication has been severely limited and book publication has decreased dramatically. Despite the economic problems, the quality of work remains extremely high, though many Argentines are publishing outside their country. Were it not for the barriers presented by the economic catastrophe, this era could easily be a golden age of Argentine history. Numerous first rate historians are joined by many more who write competent works. It is difficult to believe, however, that the high quality can be sustained over time, given the economic implosion.

The last few years have seen a surge in the writing of political history due to the return to democracy in the 1980s. New works of political history have been transformed by their integration with social and intellectual history. Political failures had helped open the way to the horrific military regime that came to power in 1976, and historians tried to understand what lay behind that failure and to find elements of the political traditions worth saving. Certainly the return to interest in politics in other regions of the world has also had an impact. The maturity of this movement can be seen in Sábato's award winning book on Buenos Aires of the 1870s–80s (item **3010**) and the work of Alonso on the first decade of the Radical Party (item **2764**). Both destroy past stereotypes and reveal a political world vastly more complex and nuanced than previous studies indicated. Many recent historical studies emphasize that the political world is integrated in a real way with other parts of the society. For example, Zanatta's important examination of the Catholic Church's ideological project in the years 1943–46, and its relationship with the military, helps explain many aspects of the military regime which then controlled Argentina (item **3057**). Halperín Donghi, in a contribution to his edited series of primary sources with extensive introductions, provides an insightful picture of the Radical years (item **2893**).

Complementing these scholarly works are those intended for popular audiences. Although frequently lacking the necessary apparatus, such as footnotes and sources, to check assertions, the works do contribute to the base of knowledge and can be entertaining. One good example is Seoane's biography of José Ber Gelbard (item **3024**), which tells us a great deal about the man, one of the most intriguing and mysterious figures of modern Argentina. Academic historians have also produced popular works. Particularly noteworthy are the popular short biographies of Carlos Pellegrini by Gallo (item **2859**) and Marcelo T. de Alvear by Cattaruzza (item **2811**).

A sign of the increasing competency among historians is the growing number of works written in and about the provinces. While problems with the circulation of some of these works exist, the new focus represents an important shift away from the Buenos Aires-centered works produced in the capital. For too long, the historiography has reflected events in the capital and has failed to show the very different life of the provinces, especially those away from the pampas. An example of the kind of history which, if it continues, should eventually transform that vision are the numerous works being done on Neuquén (e.g., items **2775, 2834,** and **2949**). Equally important and interesting work is also been done elsewhere throughout the provinces.

Not surprisingly, work is also being done on the city of Buenos Aires. Two important books look at the nature of the city and its physical and intellectual world (items **2800** and **2887**). Important studies at the level of the barrio have also been published (items **2983** and **3005**).

As in past years, much has been written about immigration. This continuation reflects both the growing interest in so-called hyphenated identity, as well as the considerable influence of international scholarly trends. A superb book, Moya's work on Spanish immigration to Buenos Aires, has set new standards for immigration studies in several ways (item **2945**). Its focus on the conditions and regional differences in the sending country is a crucial nuance, as is his ability to examine social mobility and adjustments to the receiving society. Also important is Moya's continual movement from the micro level of several individuals or small groups to the macro level of generalization. This study of the so-called invisible immigrants has restored them to the place in history that they deserve. In addition, many competent smaller scale works have been published. As usual, many popular works on immigration, some written to commemorate communities and/or ethnic organizations, have appeared. Although frequently filiopietistic, the best of them make important contributions to overall knowledge.

Recent attempts to identify both nations that aided Germany economically during World War II and the locations of perpetrators of the horrors who fled have had an impact on Argentine scholarship. Motivated by promises to open government archives as well as the creation of a commission to study Argentina's role as a haven for war criminals and Axis money, scholars have begun to publish a series of studies on the topic, and more will undoubtedly appear in future years. While research findings to date have not produced sensational revelations, they have dispelled some of the myths produced by politicians, propaganda, and Hollywood. Solid studies debate the existence of sizeable in-flows of money from German-occupied Europe (items **2986** and **2991**), and continue to uncover information about how those seeking to avoid the Allies at the war's conclusion came to Argentina (items **2836, 2882,** and **2913**). Nevertheless, much more remains to be discovered.

The writing on the rural economy of the Pampas has apparently slowed, and no overview exists to pull together the many small-scale studies of land tenure and settlement. One important publication on this topic is Hora's study of the creation of the *estanciero* class in Buenos Aires province (item **2896**). It is not so much an economic study, but rather a social, intellectual, and political examination of the rise and fall of a dominant class.

Numerous publications continue to appear that address the traumas of the 1960s–70s. Much of the work has been in the form of participant memoirs or popular histories, and many are important sources. Together, they begin to fill in the gaps of our knowledge, especially helping to establish the mentalité of the period (e.g., items **2611, 2770,** and **2814**).

Labor history continues as an important research area. Several works stand out and epitomize some dominant trends as labor history moves beyond merely an examination of trade unions. Suriano provides an excellent history of the cultural world created by anarchists in the period between 1880–1914 (item **3030**). Lobato's innovative, important community study discusses the meat-packing industrial town of Berisso (item **2921**). Iñigo Carrera impressively examines a 1936 general strike in Buenos Aires and attempts to draw larger conclusions (item **2900**). McGuire's important book focuses on the relationship between Peronist unions and politics, especially in the 1960s–80s (item **2937**). In addition, James' new work, while not readily classified as labor history, is of note (item **2905**). It is both a life history of a union and political activist from Berisso and a meditation on the use of sources.

Intellectual history has undergone a great deal of change in recent years as the lines between it and other subfields of history have become increasingly blurred. On this topic, two authors in particular stand out this biennium. Saítta contributes an excellent study of the best selling newspaper of the 1920s, *Crítica*, which had a major political and cultural impact (item **3012**). She also produced a biography of the novelist Roberto Arlt, placing him in the changing society in which he wrote (item **3011**). Plotkin delivers two studies on the development of psychoanalysis in Argentina and how it became a part of everyday life (items **2975** and **2976**). The importance of the latter lies in what they show about the nature of Argentine society.

One curious phenomenon is the almost simultaneous publication of three multivolume histories of Argentina. The one written by Luna, the popular historian, is similar in orientation to his other writings (item **2923**). The other two are massive collective histories that demonstrate well the progress that has been made in recent decades in studying Argentina's past. Both include contributions from some of the country's best historians. The volumes compiled by the Academia Nacional de la Historia, while up-to-date, are much more traditional in their approach (item **2957**). The third set, published by Sudamericana and coordinated by Suriano, is much more attuned to the latest trends in history in the topics it covers (items **2952, 2953, 2954, 2955**, and **2956**).

Overall the quality of historical production remains very high. It is difficult to be sanguine about the future, not only because of the economic problems facing the publishing industry, but more importantly, because of the problems facing the writers of history. [JH]

PARAGUAY

In recent years, Paraguayan historiography has made some significant advances. For the late Bourbon and early national periods, for instance, considerable attention has been given to the rarely studied northern frontier, especially in articles by Areces on ranching (item **3060**) and indigenous-white relations (item **3061**), and by Cooney on the *yerba* industry (item **3074**).

The Francia era (1814–40) has received comparatively less emphasis than in years past, though an excellent essay by Cooney on the Afro-Paraguayans should not be missed (item **3073**), nor should Vázquez's perceptive biography of Vicente Antonio Matiauda (item **3089**).

Brezzo has produced a useful and extensively detailed account of Argentine-Paraguayan relations in the 1850s (item **2799**). Sadly, it stands almost alone among new works on the Carlos Antonio López era (1844–62).

Not surprisingly, given its overall importance in Paraguayan historiography, the Triple Alliance War of 1864–70 has engendered more scholarly investigations than other 19th-century themes. Brezzo, for example, contributes a useful account of life in Asunción under Allied occupation (item **3064**), while Moby Ribeiro da Silva dissects social gatherings and dances in the same urban environment, concluding that more was happening than met the average observer's eye (item **3086**).

Several memoirs of participants in the Great War—always a favorite among scholars and casual readers alike—have been published recently, including the accounts of three members of the Argentine Army's medical corps (item **2804**) and a new and much-welcomed Spanish translation of Burton's *Letters from the Battlefields of Paraguay, Cartas desde los campos de batalla del Paraguay* (item **3065**). The most attractive new work on this crucial period comes from the late Argentine photohistorian Cuarterolo, who has assembled an array of images from the conflict, many never previously seen, and has provided erudite commentary both on the technical aspects of early photography and on the complexities of the war itself (item **3087**).

The period between the end of the Paraguayan War (1870) and the beginning of the Chaco War with Bolivia (1932) has failed to receive consistent attention from historians, though exceptions exist, even in the latest biennium. Heyn has produced a multivolume account of the Salesian Order's work in Paraguay (items **3067, 3068, 3069, 3070, 3071,** and **3072**); and Baratti and Candolfi's eye-catching biography of the Swiss naturalist Moises Bertoni gives the pursuit of scientific knowledge in Paraguay its proper historical due (item **3063**). [TW]

The writing on the history of Paraguay since 1880 remains scarce and traditional. Political partisans continue to write history from the point of view of their party, and the Chaco War continues as a topic of examination. Pieces on the Stroessner period have finally begun to emerge, giving hope that a widening of subjects will occur. Two works argue that Stroessner's use of culture and ideology were important in maintaining his hold on society (items **3078** and **3081**). Lastly, Fogel offers an interesting look at the effect of ecological degradation on the inhabitants of the region of Ñeembucú (item **3075**). [JH]

URUGUAY

Though progress in 19th-century Paraguayan historiography has been steady if somewhat limited in recent years, in Uruguay the situation has been less fruitful. Predictably, several standard accounts of the life of Artigas have appeared, but only the short works of González Rissotto (item **2886**) and Vázquez Franco (item **3119**) display even a glimmer of innovation.

Pelfort's study on Afro-Uruguayans (item **3110**) is a useful contribution. Yet the real triumph to come out of Uruguay of late is Barán's history of medicine, which offers many shrewd insights and interpretations (item **3096**). [TW]

Scholarly writing on Uruguay since 1880, which in recent decades has been excellent, is much less in evidence this biennium. In all probability, this decline reflects the economic problems that beset the country. Balbis has produced an important series of data on land prices and rents (item **3094**). Some works look at how history is used in politics and how the military dictatorship of the 1970s changed the writing of history (items **3115** and **3121**).

Immigration, the 1930s, and the problems of the 1960s–70s dominate much of the other writing. One work that any scholar working on independent Uruguay should find extremely useful is an updated historical chronology covering events from 1830–1985 (item **3102**). [JH]

ARGENTINA

Abreu, Marcelo de Paiva. Foreign debt policies in South America, 1925–1945. See *HLAS 59:1349.*

2762 Agnese, Graciela. Historia de una enfermedad y espacio rural: la fiebre hemorrágica argentina. (*Res Gesta,* 36, 1997, p. 115–130)

Studies the political and medical responses to the eruption of a new disease, *fiebre hemorrágica argentina,* in a rural segment of Buenos Aires prov. Shows how the scientific response was limited by politics. Covers the period 1943–90. [JH]

2763 Alberdi, Juan Bautista. Alberdi, periodista en Chile. Recopilación de Carolina Barros. Buenos Aires: Verlap, 1997. 473 p.: bibl., ill., 1 map.

Fascinating collection of 172 rarely seen articles and editorials by Argentine philosopher Alberdi, written for several Valparaíso and Santiago newspapers between 1844–53. [TW]

2764 Alonso, Paula. Between revolution and the ballot box: the origins of the Argentine Radical Party in the 1890s. Cambridge, England: New York: Cambridge Univ. Press, 2000. 242 p.: bibl., index. (Cambridge Latin American studies; 82)

An excellent example of the political history being written by Argentine historians. Clearly written, theoretically well grounded, and deeply researched in primary sources, presents a revisionist version of the formation of the Radical Party and its early years under Alem. Argues convincingly that the party was extremely different than in later years under Yrigoyen. Sees the party as essentially backward-looking. Places the Radicals carefully within the political traditions of the decade of the 1890s and makes clear that elections were much more closely contested than has previously been thought. [JH]

2765 Alonso, Paula. La reciente historia política de la Argentina del ochenta al centenario. (*Anu. IEHS*, 13, 1998, p. 393–418, bibl.)

Useful bibliographic piece traces the contributions of modern scholars to the study of Argentine politics between the 1880s and 1910. Notes the development of several key themes: elections, the press and political publicity, and political biography. [TW]

2766 Amaral, Samuel. The rise of capitalism on the pampas: the estancias of Buenos Aires, 1785–1870. Cambridge; New York: Cambridge Univ. Press, 1998. 359 p.: bibl., ill., index, maps. (Cambridge Latin American studies; 83)

A brilliant and highly detailed analysis of the Argentine estancia in its formative period. Focuses on internal structure and conditions of production within this all-important institution. Argues that estancia owners routinely sought profits over rents and avidly linked their efforts with those of outside entrepreneurs in marketing their product. [TW]

2767 Amézola, Gonzalo de. Levingston y Lanusse, o, El arte de lo imposible: militares y políticos de la Argentina a fines de 1970 y principios de 1971. La Plata, Argentina: Editorial de la U.N.L.P.: Ediciones Al Margen, 2000. 149 p.: bibl. (Colección universitaria. Historia)

Examines in great detail the maneuvering of politicians and military officers during this conflictive period. Based on periodicals and memoirs. [JH]

2768 Andrews, George Reid. The Afro-Argentine officers of Buenos Aires province, 1800–1860. (*in* Recruiting, drafting, and enlisting: two sides of the raising of military forces. Edited with introductions by Peter Karsten. New York: Garland Pub., 1998, p. 85–100, tables)

Well-designed and imaginative study demonstrates that officers of African descent served in appreciable numbers in the Bonaerense army (particularly in the seven black line battalions). Some attained the rank of colonel, though no higher, due to the social stigma of racism. [TW]

2769 Andújar, Andrea. Combates y experiencias: las luchas obreras en Villa Constitución, 1974–1975. (*Taller/Buenos Aires*, 3:6, abril 1998, p. 93–146)

Based on oral histories, union publications, and daily newspapers, presents a sympathetic picture of the attempt by metalworkers to maintain a left-wing and independent union organization in the factory city located between Rosario and Buenos Aires. Complements the work of María Cecilia Cangiano. For historian's comment on Cangiano's work, see item **2970**. [JH]

2770 Anzorena, Oscar R. Tiempo de violencia y utopía: de Golpe de Onganía (1966) al Golpe de Videla (1976). Ed. ampliada. Argentina: Ediciones del Pensamiento Nacional, 1998. 355 p.: bibl., ill., 1 map.

Intended to illuminate a forgotten past, provides a political history of the period from 1966 until March 1976. Although mostly favorable to the left-wing guerrillas, it is at times highly critical of their actions. [JH]

2771 Archivo General de la Nación (Argentina). Departamento Documentos Escritos. Colección Mario César Gras (1577–1883): catálogo sumario. Descripción por Liliana Crespi. Índices por Aldo Botto. Buenos Aires: Archivo General de la Nación, Documentos Escritos, 1997. 129 p.: ill. (Col. Referencia. Serie Descriptores; 10)

Descriptive catalog of a collection of 690 documents, mostly originals, that previously belonged to Santafecino historian Gras. Covers a variety of topics and historical periods. Especially strong in Rosas-era materials. [TW]

2772 Area, Lelia. Juana Manso y el periodismo femenino en la Argentina del siglo XIX. (*ALFA/Rosario*, 1:1, 1997, p. 35–55, bibl.)

Interesting and well-written effort—only partly successful—to rescue Manso (1818–75) from undeserved obscurity. In fact, she was one of the first feminists in Argentine letters. [TW]

2773 Argeri, María Elba. "La peor plaga que pudo haber traído la locomotora": prostitución y control estatal en un territorio nacional norpatagónico: Río Negro, 1880–1920. (*Anu. Estud. Am.*, 56:1, enero/junio 1999, p. 217–235)

Examines the government's attempt to control prostitution in Río Negro. Uses archival sources and reflects French historiography. [JH]

2774 Ascolani, Adrián. Hacia la formación de un mercado de trabajo rural *nacional:* las migraciones laborales en la region cerealera, 1890–1930. (*Res Gesta*, 36, 1997, p. 5–25)

Primarily using newspapers as a source, generally traces the creation of a rural labor force for grain. At first, the labor force was composed mainly of immigrants, but later included a heavier participation of internal migrants. [JH]

2775 Asquini, Norberto G.; H. Walter Cazenave; and Jorge R. Etchenique. Conflictos sociales en La Pampa, 1910–1921. Santa Rosa, Argentina: Fondo Editorial Pampeano, 1999. 162 p.: bibl., ill.

Presents studies of four conflicts. Two chapters look at the events in 1910 in Machachín that have become, in myth, the birthplace of the demands that later *colonos* made for improvements in conditions on the pampas. It appears, however, that reality is quite different from myth. Also looks at agricultural unemployment and tensions between 1914–17; the great agricultural strike of 1919; and the 1921 confrontation between workers and police in Jacinto Arauz. [JH]

2776 Atán, Adriana. Cuatro historias de anarquistas: testimonios orales de militantes del anarcosindicalismo argentino. 1. ed. en la Argentina. Argentina: A. Atán, 2000. 209 p.: ill.

Interviews with four anarchists who had been active in the labor movement: Jesús Gil, Enrique Palmeiro, José Grunfeld, and Domingo Trama. [JH]

2777 Avenel, Jean-David. L'affaire du Rio de la Plata, 1838–1852. Paris: Economica, 1998. 152 p., 12 p. of plates: bibl., ill., index, maps. (Col. Campagnes & stratégies. Les grandes batailles; 26)

Though not on par with the 1929 John Frank Cady study, *Foreign Intervention in the Rio de la Plata, 1835–50*, this new analysis of the Anglo-French interventions in the Plata provides some interesting details from the French perspecitve. Suffers from weak use of English-language sources. [TW]

2778 Ayrolo, Valentina. El matrimonio como inversión: el caso de los Mendeville-Sánchez. (*Anu. Estud. Am.*, 56:1, enero/junio 1999, p. 147–171)

Curious and attractive study of the 1820 nuptials between the former French consul and Mariquita Sánchez, a key dame of criollo Buenos Aires and later a major figure in Argentine education. Sees their marriage as a social and material investment of great consequence for both parties. [TW]

2779 Azaretto, Roberto A. Federico Pinedo: político y economista. Buenos Aires: Emecé Editores, 1998. 299 p.: bibl., ill.

A political biography of the socialist who became a conservative, and a three-time economic minister. Written without footnotes by a man involved in conservative politics. Most attention focused on the 1930–43 period. Attempts to defend the conservative past. [JH]

2780 Baer, James A. Buenos Aires: housing reform and the decline of the liberal state in Argentina. (*in* Cities of hope: people, protests, and progress in urbanizing Latin America, 1870–1930. Edited by Ronn Pineo and James A. Baer. Boulder, Colo.: Westview Press, 1998, p. 129–152, map, tables)

Offers an overview of the housing crisis in Buenos Aires in the period before 1930 and reviews efforts to alleviate it. For historian's comment on entire book, see item 856. [JH]

2781 Baily, Samuel L. Immigrants in the lands of promise: Italians in Buenos Aires and New York City, 1870–1914. Ithaca, N.Y.: Cornell Univ. Press, 1999. 308 p.: bibl., ill., index, maps. (Cornell studies in comparative history)

Studies of Italian immigrants to Buenos Aires are surprisingly rare—especially given their overwhelming impact on the city's cultural and economic life. Baily's focused and readable study is thus an important contribution, doubly so, since it makes broad and specific comparisons with the Italian immigrant experience in New York City (and parenthetically with San Francisco, São Paulo, and Toronto). He shows that Italians of all economic and social levels generally fared better in Buenos Aires, where adjustment and assimilation was a comparatively easy task at the turn of the century. [TW]

2782 Barbero, María Inés. El proceso de industrialización en la Argentina: viejas y nuevas controversias. (*Anu. IEHS*, 13, 1998, p. 131–144, bibl.)

Historiographical essay examines major interpretations of why Argentina's industrialization process was not more successful. Discusses and contrasts explanations from the 1940s-present. [JH]

2783 Barbero, María Inés and **Mariela Ceva.** El catolicismo social como estrategia empresarial: el caso de Algodonera Flandria, 1924–1955. (*Anu. IEHS*, 12, 1997, p. 269–289)

A case study of a textile factory near Luján whose owner was a believer in social Catholicism. Looks at how the owner applied his beliefs and his relative success in maintaining control of his factory. [JH]

2784 Baschetti, Roberto. Peronismo y fuerzas armadas. v. 4, 1973–1976. v. 5, 1976–1998. Buenos Aires: Biblioteca Nacional, 1998. 2 v. (Bibliográficas, 38–39)

Continuation of the series of useful but unannotated bibliographies covering the relationship between peronismo and the army between 1973–98. Extremely useful for researchers. [JH]

2785 Bellotta, Araceli. Aurelia Vélez, la amante de Sarmiento: una biografía amorosa. Buenos Aires: Planeta, 1997. 239 p.: bibl., ill.

Sentimental account of the love affair between the married Sarmiento and the daughter of Dalmacio Vélez Sarsfield. Author's research reveals in Sarmiento a tender and attentive suitor, very different from the dour politician usually seen in accounts of the period. [TW]

2786 Bernand, Carmen. Histoire de Buenos Aires. Paris: Fayard, 1997. 432 p.: bibl., indexes. (Histoire des grandes villes du monde)

Part of a "Great Cities of the World" series, this interesting study is as much a medley of *porteño* themes as a straightforward history of Buenos Aires. Though it lacks the insight of Scobie's classic work (see *HLAS 37:9908*), this examination still merits attention, especially the sections on Perón and the modern age. [TW]

2787 Bilbao, Manuel. Vindicación y memorias de don Antonino Reyes. Buenos Aires: El Elefante Blanco, 1998. 273 p.

A classic work, originally published in 1883 as part biography, part apologia for Reyes, the officer who served as base commander at the notorious Santos Lugares prison during the late Rosas period. Bilbao uses all his polemical skills to present Reyes as a basically good man caught up in violent times who was forced to carry out political executions (most notably those of Uladislao Gutiérrez and the pregnant Camila O'Gorman). [TW]

2788 Bjerg, María Mónica. Educación y etnicidad en una perspectiva comparada: los inmigrantes daneses en la Pradera y en la Pampa, 1860–1930. (*Estud. Migr. Latinoam.*, 12:36, agosto 1997, p. 251–280)

Compares Danish immigration in Iowa and the Pampas of Buenos Aires between the 1860s and the Great Depression. Notes the continuity of certain cultural institutions in both places, especially the Lutheran Church. [TW]

2789 Blengino, Vanni. Il vallo della Patagonia: i nuovi conquistatori; militari, scienziati, sacerdoti, scrittori. Introduzione di Ruggiero Romano. Reggio Emilia, Italy:

Diabasis, 1998. 172 p.: ill., index, map. (L'albero del cadirà; 4)

Imaginatively presents late-19th century Argentine "conquest of the desert" as a quest to make Argentine culture whole, excluding the indigenous population of the pampas, in part by constructing a "Chinese wall" three meters deep across the country. The wall was the dream of Ministro de Guerra y Marina Adolfo Alsina (1874–77), who died before he could implement his plan. Blengino artfully links the subsequent expansionist project to the civilizing dreams of Argentine warriors, priests, scientists, and writers. Notes that extermination campaign carried out later by Julio Roca (1879) surpassed the objective of the wall and emptied the region between Buenos Aires and the Río Negro for settlement by more European types. Helpful photos and map. An excellent, well-documented essay in cultural history. [V. Peloso]

2790 Bohdziewicz, Jorge C. and Elena Bonura. Bernardo de Irigoyen y su notable informe sobre el comercio mendocino en 1848. (*Rev. Junta Estud. Hist. Mendoza*, 1, 1997, p. 133–150)

An interesting treatment of trade relations between Chile and the Argentine province of Mendoza during the late Rosas period, as encapsulated in a critical report by Irigoyen. [TW]

2791 Bonaudo, Marta and Elida Sonzogni. Empresarios y poder político en el espacio santafesino, 1860–1890: Carlos Casado y su estrategia de acumulación. (*Hist. Graf./ México*, 11, 1998, p. 39–64, map)

Studies entrepreneur, Carlos Casado, by reviewing his activities and strategies. Demonstrates the political implications of the success of this businessman. [JH]

2792 Bonaudo, Marta and Elida Sonzogni. To populate and to discipline: labor market construction in the province of Santa Fe, Argentina, 1850–1890. (*Lat. Am. Perspect.*, 26:1, Jan. 1999, p. 65–91, bibl.)

Discusses the emergence of a capitalist labor market in the cereal-producing areas of Santa Fe province. Argues that tensions between private landowners and the state facilitated the development of more modern conditions for immigrant laborers. [TW]

2793 Bordi de Ragucci, Olga N. El agua privada en Buenos Aires 1856–1892: negocio y fracaso. Buenos Aires: Vinciguerra, 1997. 347 p.: bibl. (El libro argentino)

Fascinating, detailed account of the politics of drinking water in 19th-century Buenos Aires. Contends that, in assigning a concession to a private British water company in 1888, municipal and federal authorities initially lost the chance to establish control over community health standards. [TW]

2794 Bosch, Beatriz. En la Confederación Argentina, 1854–1861. Buenos Aires: EUDEBA, 1998. 324 p.: bibl., index. (Temas historia)

A classic biographer of Urquiza here provides a well-researched general study of the Confederation period. The historian of ideas will particularly appreciate the sophisticated treatment of Aliberdi, Facundo Zuviria, Juan María Gutiérrez, and Martín Zapata. [TW]

2795 Bosch, Beatriz. Salvador María del Carril, vice-presidente de la Confederación Argentina: 1854–1860. (*Invest. Ens.*, 47, 1997, p. 163–186)

Short biography fills an important gap in the historiography of the Confederation period. [TW]

2796 Boulgourdjian, Nélida Elena. Los armenios en Buenos Aires: la reconstrucción de la identidad, 1900–1950. Buenos Aires: Edición del Centro Armenio, 1997. 206 p.: bibl., ill.

Examines creation and development of the Armenian community in the city of Buenos Aires. Looks principally at why the Armenians came to Buenos Aires and how institutions were created in the city. Based largely on primary sources. [JH]

2797 Bragoni, Beatriz. Los hijos de la revolución: familia, negocios y poder en Mendoza en el siglo XIX. Buenos Aires: Taurus, 1999. 372 p.: bibl., ill.

Rigorously documented study of how one family—the Gonzalez Troncosos—rose from modest beginnings to become one of the great elite families of Cuyo. [TW]

2798 Brailovsky, Antonio Elio and Dina Foguelman. Epidemias y medio ambiente. (*in* Jornadas de Historia de la Ciudad de Buenos Aires, 7th, Buenos Aires?, 1990. Texto y discurso. Buenos Aires: Gobierno de la Ciudad de Buenos Aires, Secretaría de Cultura, Subsecretaría de Desarrollo Cultura, Instituto Histórico de la Ciudad de Buenos Aires, 1997, t. 1, p. 297–309)

Brief but interesting study of sanitary conditions in the city of Buenos Aires from the colonial period onward. Argues that ideological and polemical responses to environmental problems have always outweighed practical solutions. [TW]

2799 Brezzo, Liliana María. La Argentina y el Paraguay: 1852–1860. Argentina: Corregidor, 1997. 238 p.: bibl.

Finely detailed diplomatic history, focusing on shifting relations between Paraguay and Argentina before the War of 1864–70. Especially solid on the mediation efforts of Francisco Solano López during the Buenos Aires-Paraná confrontation of 1859. [TW]

Buenos Aires, Argentina (prov.). Governor. Mensajes de los gobernadores de la Provincia de Buenos Aires a la Honorable Asamblea Legislativa: 1881–1905. See HLAS 59:2154.

2800 Buenos Aires 1910: el imaginario para una gran capital. Recopilación de Margarita Gutman and Thomas Reese. Buenos Aires: Eudeba, 1999. 404 p.: bibl., ill. (some col.). (Col. CEA; 22)

A fascinating book that collects papers delivered at a conference on imagining Buenos Aires in 1910, part of a series of such conferences on American cities. Chapters deal with living in the city, foreign influences, beliefs about the future of the city, and discussion of its physical aspects. [JH]

2801 Bushnell, David. The Indian policy of Jujuy province, 1835–1853. (Americas/Washington, 55:4, April 1999, p. 579–600, map)

Innovative, well-researched article on Indian legislation during the Rosas period. Points out the continuity of links between Jujuy, Bolivia, and the rest of the Andean world throughout the time period under discussion. Article is also available in Spanish in Revista de Historia del Derecho, Vol. 25, 1997, p. 59–84. [TW]

2802 Cagiao Vila, Pilar et al. La Galicia austral: la inmigración gallega en la Argentina. Recopilación de Xosé Núñez Seixas. Prólogo de Antonio Pérez-Prado. Buenos Aires: Editorial Biblos, 2001. 320 p.: bibl., ill. (Col. La Argentina plural)

Compilation edited by a well-known Gallego historian from the Univ. de Santiago de Compostela. Essays by prominent Gallego historians cover various aspects of Gallego life in Argentina including adaption to a new environment, political and economic activities, as well as cultural activities. [J.M. Pérez]

2803 Caimari, Lila M. Whose criminals are these?: Church, state, and patronatos and the rehabilitation of female convicts, Buenos Aires, 1890–1940. (Americas/Washington, 54:2, Oct. 1997, p. 184–208, graphs, table)

A well-written and insightful article explains the apparent anomaly of a government known for secularizing tendencies and a positivistic belief in scientific penalology, turning its women's prison over to a religious order. Illuminates aspects of the political elite's view of women and criminals. Also describes prison conditions. [JH]

2804 Canard, Benjamín; Joaquín Cascallar; and Miguel Gallegos. Cartas sobre la Guerra del Paraguay. Buenos Aires: Academia Nacional de la Historia, 1999. 198 p.: bibl., ill.

An impressive compilation of war correspondence written by Canard, Cascallar, and Gallegos, all three members of the Argentine army's medical corps during the Triple Alliance War. Only a portion of these letters have previously been published. [TW]

2805 Canclini, Arnoldo. Juicios en las Malvinas. (Todo es Hist., 372, julio 1998, p. 32–37, map)

Describes two unusual legal cases involving British authorities in the Falkland Islands. The first concerned a massacre of British missionaries by Fuegian Indians in 1859. No punitive action was ever attempted. The second case, which occurred in 1867, concerned salvage rights over a beached British vessel. Documentation for both cases comes from the Public Records Office. [TW]

2806 **Canclini, Arnoldo.** Piedra Buena: su tierra y su tiempo. Buenos Aires: Emecé Editores, 1998. 452 p.: bibl., ill., 1 map. (Escritores argentinos)

Useful biography of Luis Piedra Buena (1833–83), a perennial figure in Patagonia, where he acted as landowner, sea captain, government official, and defender of Argentine territorial interests in the southern region. [TW]

2807 **Canclini, Arnoldo.** William H. Smyley, un personaje de los mares australes. (*Invest. Ens.*, 47, 1997, p. 307–329)

Details the career of New England trader Smyley, who acted as a US "commercial agent" in Patagonia and the Falklands in the 1850s. Frequently accused of piracy, Smyley was an ambiguous figure who influenced the southern trade for nearly four decades. [TW]

2808 **Cañedo-Argüelles Fábrega, Teresa.** La comunidad de Itatí, un marco para el debate cultural y la afirmación identitaria en el Paraná. (*Rev. Complut. Hist. Am.*, 25, 1999, p. 195–217, table)

Suggestive study of a Franciscan mission town that resisted the appeal of Bourbon liberalism and continued to define freedom and happiness in communitarian terms even in the 1800s. [TW]

2809 **Capobianco, Carina** and **Eduardo Matuc.** No teníamos otra voz: una aproximación a la militancia peronista de base en Rosario; la resistencia peronista, 1955–1958. (*Cuad. CIESAL*, 3:4, 1998, p. 89–109)

Through a series of oral interviews and well aware of the problems of memory, the authors sketch a picture of the nature of the Peronist resistance in Rosario. Rather than focusing on details, highlights feelings and goals of the resistance. [JH]

2810 **Carrizo, Idrael Eligio.** Las luchas peronistas: una aproximación crítica a los orígenes del peronismo y la inserción del menemismo en el gran movimiento nacional justicialista. La Rioja, Argentina: Editorial Canguro, 1999. 270 p.

The author is a railroader who became a union leader and then a Peronist politician in La Rioja. Discusses his union and political trajectory, which includes a break with Menem and the dominant forces in La Rioja

(Menem's home province). Interesting local view of politics. [JH]

Cattarulla, Camilla. El viaje del emigrante: un proyecto individual entre utopías y dudas. See item **3253.**

2811 **Cattaruzza, Alejandro.** Marcelo T. de Alvear: el compromiso y la distancia. Buenos Aires: Fondo de Cultura Económica, 1997. 111 p.: bibl., ill. (some col.). (Los nombres del poder)

A short popular biography focusing on Alvear's political life. Extremely well done. Contains numerous photos. [JH]

2812 **Caudillismos rioplatenses: nuevas miradas a un viejo problema.** Recopilación de Noemí Goldman and Ricardo Salvatore. Buenos Aires: Eudeba, Facultad de Filosofía y Letras, Univ. de Buenos Aires, 1998. 351 p.: bibl. (Temas. Historia)

First-rate compilation of 12 essays on Argentine and Uruguayan caudillismo, with one essay on Artigas, six on the Rosas period, and five on other topics. The most noteworthy essay is Salvatore's "Expresiones federales: formas políticas del federalismo rosista," which details mid-century political culture and the meaning of "el ser federal." [TW]

2813 **Cena, Juan Carlos.** El guardapalabras: memorias de un ferroviario. Buenos Aires?: Editorial La Rosa Blindada, 1998. 637 p.: ill. (Col. de ensayos Emilio Jáuregui; 2)

An informative autobiography of a militant Peronist railroader who was active in union affairs from the 1950s through the early 1990s. Offers a different perspective. [JH]

2814 **Chaves, Gonzalo Leonidas** and **Jorge Omar Lewinger.** Los del 73: memoria montonera. La Plata, Argentina: Editorial de la Campana, 1998. 252 p.: ill. (Col. Campana de palo)

A series of fragments of memoirs by two militants of the Organización Montoneros, alternating pieces between the two writers. While the work lacks coherence, it does contribute to documenting the events of the period and, more importantly, the mentalité of the participants. [JH]

2815 Chaves, Liliana. Tradiciones y rupturas de la élite política cordobesa, 1870–1880: la clave conservadora de la modernización política. Córdoba, Argentina: Ferreyra Editor, 1997. 229 p.: bibl.

Well-crafted study of elite politics in Córdoba, bolstered by solid use of archival and periodical materials. Paints a picture of a malleable elite that is able to reinvent itself repeatedly and always come out on top. [TW]

2816 Chávez, Fermín. De don Juan Bautista a don Juan Manuel. Buenos Aires: Instituto Nacional de Investigaciones Históricas Juan Manuel de Rosas, 1997. 127 p.: ill. (Col. Estrella federal; 15)

Peronist historian offers essays on different aspects of the Rosas period, and on the influence of Giambattista Vico in Argentina. [TW]

2817 Chiappero, Rubén Osvaldo. Urbanismo hispanoamericano: el plano de Santa Fé de 1811. (*Invest. Geogr./Alicante,* 20, julio/dic. 1998, p. 181–192, bibl., maps)

Brief description of the urban layout of the town of Santa Fe in 1811, based on a little-known map in the Servicio Cartográfico del Ejército de España. For geography specialist's comment, see *HLAS 59:2729.* [TW]

2818 Cicerchia, Ricardo. Historia de la vida privada en la Argentina. Buenos Aires: Troquel, 1998. 281 p.: bibl., ill., maps.

Though framed by an unconvincing, jargon-laden argument, this study of Argentine private life in the 1800s nonetheless reads well, for it contains innumerable details on consumer habits, the family, fashion, social customs, etc. It is, in sum, a veritable encyclopedia for the social historian. [TW]

2819 Cieza, Fernanda. El triunfo de La Esperanza: los trabajadores del Ingenio y la crónica de su heroica lucha. Buenos Aires: Editorial Agora, 2000. 62 p.: ill. (Cuadernos de Editorial Agora; 8)

Examines in a favorable light the seizure of the Ingenio La Esperanza in Jujuy two times in 1999. Presents the view of the Corriente Clasista y Combativa. Useful and interesting. [JH]

2820 Ciollaro, Noemí. Pájaros sin luz: testimonios de mujeres de desaparecidos. Buenos Aires: Editorial Planeta Argentina, 2000. 345 p. (Espejo de la Argentina)

Presents oral histories of the wives of disappeared men. The moving accounts concentrate on the period after the disappearances and how the women attempted to go on with their lives. [JH]

2821 La conformación de las identidades políticas en la Argentina del siglo XX. Recopilación de María Estela Spinelli *et al.* Córdoba, Argentina: Univ. Nacional de Córdoba; Buenos Aires: Univ. Nacional del Centro de la Provincia de Buenos Aires; Mar del Plata, Argentina: Univ. Nacional de Mar del Plata, 2000. 373 p.: bibl.

Part of an ongoing exploration of political history in the provinces. Compiles well-done articles with a coherent focus on political identity. Almost all focus on the provinces of Córdoba and Buenos Aires. Papers are a product of a conference held at the Univ. Nacional de Córdoba (1998). [JH]

2822 Congreso de Historia de los Pueblos de la Provincia de Buenos Aires, 4th, Mar del Plata, Argentina, 1993. Cuarto Congreso. v. 1. Buenos Aires: Archivo Histórico de la Provincia de Buenos Aires "Dr. Ricardo Levene"; Buenos Aires: Ediciones Theoría, 1997. 1 v.: bibl.

Presents 11 studies on different aspects of the provincial history of Buenos Aires. Best of the lot is an intriguing account by Carlos María Birocco of a slave's metamorphosis into a freedman and finally into an *hacendado* (rancher) of some consequence in 18th-century Luján. [TW]

2823 Congreso Internacional de Historia y Genealogía Gallega, 1st, Buenos Aires, 1999. Ponencias. Buenos Aires: Instituto Argentino Gallego de Ciencias Históricas y Genealógicas, 1999. 251 p.: bibl., ill.

Presents proceedings of the First International Congress of Galician History and Genealogy, held in Buenos Aires, in 1999. An additional work that reflects a renewed interest in Galicians in Latin America. [J.M. Pérez]

2824 Corbière, Emilio J. Los archivos secretos del PC argentino: la internacional comunista en la Argentina, 1919–1943. (*Todo es Hist.,* 372, julio 1998, p. 8–23, photos)

Presents some idea of the nature of the documents collected in Moscow about and from the Argentine Communist Party. The documents have been microfilmed and are now available in the Biblioteca del Congreso de la Nación in Buenos Aires. [JH]

2825 Coria López, Luis Alberto and **Lidia Fortín de Iñones.** El *boom* vitivinícola mendocino, 1883–1912, y la acción del Estado. (*Rev. Junta Estud. Hist. Mendoza*, 1, 1997, p. 151–160)

Explains the 100-fold increase in the value of Mendocino wine production between 1883–1912. The expansion resulted from the introduction of improved varietals, new production techniques, improved transportation, and increased availability of labor. The Argentine government aided greatly with protective tariffs, easy credit, and promotion of irrigation. [TW]

2826 Cox, Guillermo E. Viaje en las rejiones septentrionales de la Patagonia, 1862–1863. Buenos Aires: Elefante Blanco, 1999. 293 p.: 1 map.

Fascinating travel account of Patagonia, originally published in Santiago de Chile in 1863. Offers particularly evocative descriptions of the Nahuel Huepi lake region. Recommended. [TW]

2827 Cresto, Juan José. Presupuestos militares durante las presidencias de Sarmiento y Avellaneda. (*An. Inst. Hist. Mil. Argent.*, 1997, p. 105–120, bibl., table)

Discusses the politics behind Argentine military budgets of the late 1860s-70s. Mentions that both Sarmiento and Avellaneda wished to reduce the military portion of the national budget and were pulled inexorably in the opposite direction. [TW]

2828 La cuestión social en Argentina, 1870–1943. Recopilación de Juan Suriano. Buenos Aires: Editorial La Colmena, 2000. 334 p.: bibl.

Presents articles on the social question, including a thoughtful introductory piece by Suriano on the definition of the social question in Argentina. Considers the notion in regard to such topics as workers, anarchists, criminology, state-worker relations, women, and Native Americans. [JH]

2829 Cúneo, Dardo. Bolivar en Buenos Aires. (*Desmemoria/Buenos Aires*, 5:19/20, sept./dic. 1998, p. 43–53, facsims., ill.)

Short but insightful article describes porteño reactions to the Bolivarian revolution in the north of the continent. Not surprisingly, the local federal party supported the Liberator's politics, while the unitarians opposed it. [TW]

2830 D'Alessandro de Brandi, Hilda. La inmigración bóer en Patagonia. (*Todo es Hist.*, 366, enero 1998, p. 81–93, bibl., map, photos)

Interesting account of Afrikaner migration to Chubút in the wake of the Boer War. Granted land around Comodoro Rivadavia, the immigrants developed orchards and pastoral enterprises in a marginal setting. One of these immigrants discovered the oil for which the region is known today. [TW]

2831 Darío Salas, Rubén. La categoría Sistema Representativo y su re-presentación y recepción en el discurso político de las minorías reflexivas rioplatenses, 1816–1827. (*Anu. Estud. Am.*, 55:2, julio/dic. 1998, p. 531–563)

A detailed and sophisticated examination of the semantics of representative government in the early national period. Analyzes early periodicals and the *Actas* of the various congresses of the day. Recommended. [TW]

2832 Darío Salas, Rubén. Lenguaje, estado y poder en el Río de la Plata: el discurso de las minorías reflexivas y su representación del fenómeno político-institucional rioplatense, 1816–1827. Prólogo de Reinhold Blaurock. Buenos Aires: Instituto de Investigaciones de Historia del Derecho, 1998. 641 p.: bibl.

Exceptionally well-focused and insightful study of Platine republicanism. Focuses on how the republicanism reflected Enlightenment ideology and frontier necessity. Deftly notes the subtle changes in revolutionary and monarchist rhetoric and legal usage. Study reads well when set alongside the works of José Carlos Chiaramonte and Jorge Myers. [TW]

2833 De la Fuente, Ariel. Facundo and Chacho in songs and stories: oral culture and the representations of caudillos in the nineteenth-century Argentine interior. (*HAHR*, 80:3, Aug. 2000, p. 503–535)

First-rate study of folkloric accounts of Argentine caudillos. Stresses the utility of oral culture in establishing images that ultimately entered the broader national consciousness. [TW]

2834 Debattista, Susana; Carla Gabriela Bertello; and Carlos Gabriel Rafart. El bandolerismo rural en la última frontera: Neuquén, 1890–1920. (*Estud. Soc./Santa Fe,* 8:14, primer semestre 1998, p. 129–147)

Within the context of theoretical studies, examines the nature of banditry during a period of loose governmental control. Based mostly on archival sources. [JH]

2835 DeSantis, Daniel. Testimonio y memoria: la lucha obrera en Propulsora Siderúrgica, 1974–1975. (*Taller/Buenos Aires,* 2:5, nov. 1997, p. 122–149)

An interesting autobiographical, historical study of labor unrest in a metallurgical plant in the La Plata industrial belt. Presents the type of material which is unavailable from other sources. The author was a member of the Comisión Interna and an important activist in the Partido Revolucionario de los Trabajadores. [JH]

Destéfani, Laurio H. Argentina y Ecuador, 1815–1822. See item **2557**.

2836 Devoto, Fernando J. Inmigrantes, refugiados y criminales en la "vía italiana" hacia la Argentina en la segunda posguerra. (*Ciclos Hist. Econ. Soc.,* 10:19, 2000, p. 151–176)

Sketches the attitudes and policies of the Argentine government towards emigration from Italy. Covers Italians and non-Italians during the period directly following WWII. [JH]

2837 Devoto, Fernando J. *et al.* Estudios de historiografía argentina. Buenos Aires: Editorial Biblos, 1999. 1 v.: bibl.

Four essays that examine different aspects of the Nueva Escuela Histórica and the professionalization of the writing of history in Argentina. [JH]

2838 Devoto, Fernando J.; Marcela Ferrari; and Julio Melón. The peaceful transformation?: changes and continuities in Argentinian political practices, 1910–22. (*in* Political culture, social movements and democratic transitions in South America in the XXth century. Edited by Fernando J. Devoto and Torcuato S. Di Tella. Milano: Fondazione Giangiacomo Feltrinelli, 1997, p. 167–191)

A thoughtful and well-done rethinking of certain aspects of the political process, as Argentine politics changed under the impact of the Ley Sáenz Peña. Looks at why the law was passed as well as some of the changes that the law brought about regarding political conditions in the country. Stresses both continuity and change. [JH]

2839 Diana, Marta. Mujeres guerrilleras: la militancia de los setenta en el testimonio de sus protagonistas femeninas. Buenos Aires: Planeta, 1996. 445 p. (Espejo de la Argentina)

Driven by the death of a high school classmate, the author conducted a series of interviews with female activists of the 1960s-70s. (Some interviews were also conducted with men.) The interviews are interesting and revealing about the general mood of many youths in the 1970s and help make clearer the role of women in guerrilla organizations. Most of the interviews were conducted with former ERP activists, though some attention is paid to the Peronist left. [JH]

2840 Los días de Mayo. v. 1–2. San Isidro, Argentina: Academia de Ciencias y Artes de San Isidro, 1998. 2 v.: bibl., ill., indexes.

Two-volume compilation of 36 essays describes Argentine social life and customs at the time of independence. Includes some unusual studies of tobacco marketing, silversmiths, theater, and children's games. [TW]

Díaz Rementería, Carlos J. Supervivencia y disolución de la comunidad de bienes indígena en la Argentina del siglo XIX. See item **698**.

2841 Dios de Martina, Angeles de. Vascos en el Chaco: historias de vida. Buenos Aires: Editorial Dunken, 1999. 135 p.: appendices, bibl., photos.

Presents a series of short life histories of Basque emigrants to the Province of Chaco. Based primarily on interviews with the immigrants themselves or their descendants. [JH]

2842 Documentos diplomáticos sobre historia argentina. v. 1–3. Mendoza, Argentina: C.E.I.H.C., 1994–1999. 3 v.: bibl., indexes. (Col. Historia argentina; 1)

Impressive compilation of diplomatic

notes and records taken from the Public Records Office (London), the Archivo del Ministerio de Asuntos Exteriores (Madrid), and the Archive du Ministère des affaires étrangères (Paris). Extremely useful for specialists. [TW]

2843 Domínguez Soler, Susana T.P. de. Urquiza: bibliografía. Con la colaboración de José Teófilo Goyret et al. Buenos Aires: Instituto Urquiza de Estudios Históricos, 1999. 492 p.

A bibliography of printed sources on Urquiza. Should prove very useful. [JH]

2844 Dorn, Glenn J. "Bruce Plan" and Marshall Plan: the United States's disguised intervention against Peronism in Argentina, 1947–1950. (*Int. Hist. Rev./Burnaby*, 21:2, June 1999, p. 331–351)

Shows how the US used economic pressure to influence Peronist economic policy. According to the author, the US was successful in bringing about change in Argentina's economic policies. [JH]

2845 Duarte, María Amalia. Prisión, exilio y muerte de Ricardo López Jordán. Buenos Aires: Academia Nacional de la Historia, 1998. 251 p.: bibl., ill. (some col.). (Biblioteca de historia argentina y americana; t. 26)

Broad, well-researched study of a key Entrerriano caudillo—a culmination of the author's long-term work on Gen. López Jordán. Highly recommended for students of the transitional era of the mid-1800s, when Argentina traded its *caudillaje* for conservative oligarches. [TW]

2846 Eberle, Adriana Susana. Reflexiones culturales y cuestionamientos geopolíticos en torno a la colonización galesa en la Patagonia durante la presidencia del General Mitre. (*in* Congreso Nacional de Historia Argentina, *Buenos Aires, 1995.* Congreso Nacional de Historia Argentina: celebrado en la Ciudad de Buenos Aires del 23 al 25 de noviembre de 1995 bajo la advocación de los 150 años de la Batalla de la Vuelta de Obligado/entidades convocantes, Archivo General de la Nación et al. Buenos Aires: Comisión Post Congreso Nacional de Historia Argentina, 1997, t. 1, p. 501–514, bibl.)

Suggests that the 1863 effort by the Mitre government to encourage Welsh immigration to Patagonia was progressive and po-

litically astute. Those who squelched the project in the Senate, however, feared both the spread of Protestantism as well as British influence in an area critical to the long-term development of Argentina. [TW]

2847 Etchenique, Jorge. Pampa libre: anarquistas en la Pampa argentina. Santa Rosa, Argentina?: Univ. Nacional de Quilmes: Ediciones Amerindia, 2000. 242 p.: bibl., ill., maps. (Colección Documentos)

Looks at anarchism on the pampas, focusing on La Pampa but also in neighboring areas, from 1915–30. Much is seen through the lens of the anarchist paper *Pampa Libre*. [JH]

2848 Eujanian, Alejandro Claudio. Historia de revistas argentinas, 1900/1950: la conquista del público. Buenos Aires: Asociación Argentina de Editores de Revistas, 1999. 181 p.: bibl.

Offers an overview of the history of magazines published in Argentina, with general information on circulation and distribution. Contains more detailed looks at some literary magazines (such as *Nosotros, Martín Fierro, Claridad* and *Sur*) as well as more general magazines, especially *Caras y Caretas, El Hogar, Para Ti,* and *Billiken*. [JH]

2849 Eujanian, Alejandro Claudio. Polémicas por la historia: el surgimiento de la crítica en la historiografía argentina, 1864–1882. (*Entrepasados/Buenos Aires*, 8:16, 1999, p. 9–24, ill.)

Brief description of the historiographical polemic between Bartolomé Mitre and Vicente Fidel López. [TW]

2850 Favaro, Orietta and Graciela Iuorno. Libaneses y sirios: actividad comercial y participación en el espacio neuquino. (*Entrepasados/Buenos Aires*, 9:17, 1999, p. 27–48, bibl., ill.)

Makes the connection between commercial and political activities among the Sirio-Lebanese community in Neuquén's early political history. Particular attention is paid to the Sapaq family. [JH]

2851 Fernández, Mauro A. Historia de la magia y el ilusionismo en la Argentina: desde sus orígenes hasta el siglo XIX inclusive. Prólogo histórico de Teodoro Klein. Prólogo mágico de Ricardo "Fantasio" Roucau. Buenos Aires: Producciones Gráficas,

Servicio Editorial, 1996. 429 p.: bibl., ill., indexes.

Lovingly crafted look at magic and magicians in Argentina, from obscure origins in the 1700s through the end of the 19th century. The author, vice-president of the Argentine Magicians' Association, has carefully combed archives, newspapers, and private collections to put together a highly readable and suggestive account. [TW]

2852 Ferreira de Cassone, Florencia. Claridad y el internacionalismo americano. Buenos Aires: Editorial Claridad; Editorial Heliasta, 1998. 309 p.: bibl. (Biblioteca de historia)

Presents a study of the magazine *Claridad*, an independent organ of the left with ties to the Socialist Party, which was published between 1926–41. Focuses on Latin American issues, while at the same time revealing a great deal about the nature of the magazine. For philosophy specialist's review, see item **4802**. [JH]

2853 Ferrero, Roberto A. Progresividad y barbarie de los caudillos provinciales. (*Desmemoria/Buenos Aires*, 6:21/22, enero/junio 1999, p. 8–32, ill.)

Polemical look at the familiar civilization versus barbarism debate in the Plata. Accuses the urban liberals of being more barbarous than their rural opponents. Offers a standard revisionist interpretation. [TW]

2854 Flores, María Alejandra. La integración social de los inmigrantes: los llamados turcos en la ciudad de Córdoba, 1890–1930. Córdoba, Argentina: Centro de Estudios Históricos, 1996. 132 p.: bibl.

Examines social integration of Middle Eastern immigrants to the city of Córdoba, especially residential and marriage patterns. Differentiates between the various groups that comprise these immigrant communities. Based on primary documentation and interviews. [JH]

2855 Forte, Riccardo. La crisis argentina de 1890: estado liberal, política fiscal y presupuesto público. (*Relaciones/Zamora*, 17:67/68, verano/otoño 1996, p. 127–171, bibl., graphs, tables)

Erudite study of Argentine budgetary policy under the Conservatives. Well worth reading, as it covers far more than just the financial crisis of 1890. Argues that the 1890 crisis ushered in a return to preliberal approaches to fiscal organization. [TW]

2856 Fotheringham, Ignacio Hamilton. La vida de un soldado: reminiscencias de las fronteras. Presentación y arreglo de la edición de Isidoro J. Ruiz Moreno. Buenos Aires: Ediciones Ciudad Argentina, 1998. 684 p.: ill. (Col. Testimonios nacionales)

An attractive reissue of a 1909 memoir of Argentine military life. Fotheringham (1842–1925) participated in the Paraguayan War and several Indian campaigns and civil conflicts, and eventually earned the rank of general. He is equally remembered as one of the founders of Río Cuarto and several communities in the Chaco and Patagonia regions. His memoir still sparkles with spontaneity and thoroughness. [TW]

2857 Fradkin, Raúl O. Entre la ley y la práctica: la costumbre en la campaña bonaerense de la primera mitad del siglo XIX. (*Anu. IEHS*, 12, 1997, p. 141–156)

Suggestive analysis of rural customs and social control in Buenos Aires prov. during the early 1800s. Based in part on the theoretical works of Marc Bloc and E.P. Thompson. [TW]

2858 Frid de Silberstein, Carina. Surcos tempranos, pioneros tardíos: agricultores italianos y producción cerealera en el sur de la provincia de Santa Fe, 1900–1930. (*Estud. Migr. Latinoam.*, 13:38, abril 1998, p. 109–136, maps, table)

Looks at the strategies employed by Marchegiani immigrants to overcome their late arrival in the cereal zone. Shows some of the complexities of rural economies. [JH]

2859 Gallo, Ezequiel. Carlos Pellegrini: orden y reforma. Buenos Aires: Fondo de Cultura Económica, 1997. 111 p.: bibl., ill. (some col.). (Los nombres del poder)

Directed at a popular audience and with numerous photos, offers an excellent biography of Pellegrini, president of Argentina from 1890–92. [JH]

2860 Garavaglia, Juan Carlos. De "mingas" y "convites": la reciprocidad campesina entre los paisanos rioplatenses. (*Anu. IEHS*, 12, 1997, p. 131–139)

A brief but suggestive analysis of traditional relations of reciprocity among Argentine peasants and gauchos whereby the rural poor shared supplies of beef, wine, bread, tobacco, etc. [TW]

2861 Garavaglia, Juan Carlos. Escenas de la vida política en la campaña: San Antonio de Areco en una crisis del rosismo. *(Estud. Soc./Santa Fe,* 8:15, segundo semestre 1998, p. 9–30)

Readable account of the twists and turns of political culture in the Bonaerense countryside, 1839–40. Demonstrates how one tiny pueblo can represent a cultural and symbolic microcosm of the challenges facing the country as a whole. [TW]

2862 Garavaglia, Juan Carlos. Intensidad de uso de la tierra y tasas de ocupación ganadera en la pradera pampeana, 1816–1852. *(Quinto Sol/Santa Rosa,* 2:2, 1998, p. 5–23, bibl., maps, tables)

Another of Garavaglia's finely wrought microhistories of the Argentine pampa, focusing on labor and land usage in Buenos Aires province before the fall of Rosas. Based on extensive archival research. [TW]

2863 Garavaglia, Juan Carlos. Paz, orden y trabajo en la campaña: la justicia rural y los juzgados de paz en Buenos Aires, 1830–1852. *(Desarro. Econ.,* 37:146, julio/ sept. 1997, p. 241–260, bibl., graphs, map, tables)

Fascinating, well-documented analysis of the rural Juzgado de Paz during the Rosas years. Drawing material from six different districts within the Bonaerense countryside, perceives a clear differentiation between the north—where the Juzgado acted effectively as an agent of social discipline, and the south— where stability came much later. [TW]

2864 Garavaglia, Juan Carlos. Pobres y ricos: cuatro *historias edificantes* sobre el conflicto social en la campaña bonaerense, 1820–1840. *(Entrepasados/Buenos Aires,* 8:15, 1998, p. 19–40, ill., tables)

Four *historietas* of class conflict in the early Argentine countryside, all focusing on poor people seeking a measure of justice and honor from the elites. Though too abbreviated, these cases represent the best of social history research available for Argentina. [TW]

2865 Garavaglia, Juan Carlos. Un siglo de estancias en la campaña de Buenos Aires: 1751 a 1853. *(HAHR,* 79:4, Nov. 1999, p. 703–734, graphs, map, tables)

An impressive general analysis of Bonaerense ranching from before the Viceroyalty until just after the fall of Rosas. Based on the inventories of 328 ranches, the study suggests a much slower transformation to a capitalist model than hitherto suspected. For colonial historian's comment, see item 2378. [TW]

2866 García, Ignacio. El 2 de mayo de 1898 en el Teatro Victoria de Buenos Aires. *(JILAS/Bundoora,* 3:2, Dec. 1997, p. 33–53)

Well-written, deft account of the predictable reactions of the Spanish community in Buenos Aires to the US invasion of Cuba in 1898. Excellent case study. [TW]

2867 García, Pedro Andrés. Un funcionario en busca del Estado: Pedro Andrés García y la cuestión agraria bonaerense, 1810–1822. Presentación y selección de documentos de Jorge Gelman. Buenos Aires: Univ. Nacional de Quilmes, 1997. 193 p.: bibl. (La ideología argentina)

An intriguing and useful compilation of writings by García, a key functionary in early 19th-century Buenos Aires, and one of the few to devote himself extensively to the agrarian question. Recommended. [TW]

2868 García Basalo, J. Carlos. Presidio militar en la isla de los Estados. *(Todo es Hist.,* 366, enero 1998, p. 28–44, maps, photos)

Fascinating account of the establishment and administration of a military presidio on a remote island off Tierra del Fuego in the 1890s. Poor conditions and a terrible climate led to high mortality among prisoners. Includes a brief description of a prison rebellion just before closure in the early 1900s. Well documented. [TW]

2869 García Belsunce, César A. Feliciano Pueyrredon. *(Invest. Ens.,* 47, 1997, p. 187–216, appendix)

Brief account traces the life of a minor cleric and bibliophile who worked to rid the Bonaerense countryside of smallpox at the beginning of the 1800s. Includes a partial inventory of his library. [TW]

2870 García de Flöel, Maricel. La oposición española a la revolución por la independencia en el Río de la Plata entre 1810 y 1820: parámetros políticos y jurídicos para la suerte de los españoles europeos. Hamburg, Germany: Lit, 1997? 229 p.: bibl., index, maps. (Hamburger Ibero-Amerika Studien; Bd. 12)

Heavily annotated study traces the fate of peninsular populations in the Rio de la Plata during the revolutionary era. Argues convincingly that without Crown patronage, these populations could never have competed with local Creoles. [TW]

García Heras, Raúl. La Argentina y el Club de París: comercio y pagos multilaterales con la Europa Occidental, 1955–1958. See *HLAS* 59:2176.

2871 García Heras, Raúl. La historiografía de empresas en la Argentina: estado de conocimiento. (*in* Empresa e historia en América Latina: un balance historiográfico. Bogotá: Colciencias; TM editores, 1996, p. 1–33, bibl.)

A solid analysis of the state of the study of companies in Argentina. Includes some suggestions for future work. [JH]

2872 Gavirati, Marcelo. La desviación del río Fenix: ¿una *travesura* del Perito Moreno o proyecto colonizador galés? (*Todo es Hist.*, 366, enero 1998, p. 8–26, bibl., maps, photos)

Interesting account of the 1887 exploration of the Andean sections of Chubút and Santa Cruz by various Welsh settlers, including Llwyd Ap Iwan. The abortive plans to divert the waters of the Fenix River into the Deseado are given careful attention. For geography specialist's comment, see *HLAS* 59:2749. [TW]

2873 Gay, Luis. El Partido Laborista en la Argentina. Recopilación de Juan Carlos Torre. Buenos Aires: Editorial Biblos: Fundación Simon Rodríguez, 1999. 216 p.: bibl. (Cuadernos Simón Rodríguez; no. 39)

First of four parts is a history of the Partido Laborista, which was key to electing Perón in 1946. This section was written by party president, labor leader Luis Gay. Pt. 2 presents the constitution of the party. Pt. 3 is an interview with Luis Gay from Dec. 1970, by Leandro Gutiérrez and Luis Alberto Romero. The last segment is a reprint of a classic article from *Todo es Historia*—Juan Carlos Torre's "La Caída de Luis Gay." [JH]

2874 Gayol, Sandra. Las alteridades de la modernidad: Buenos Aires, 1880–1910. (*Allpanchis/Cuzco*, 30:52, segundo semestre 1998, p. 9–38)

Interesting think piece examines the interplay between the "modern" and the "anti-modern" in late 19th-century Argentina. Gives specific attention to the process whereby "personal" honor was subsumed by the "national" honor. [TW]

2875 Gelman, Jorge Daniel. El fracaso de los sistemas coactivos de trabajo rural en Buenos Aires bajo el rosismo, algunas explicaciones preliminares. (*Rev. Indias*, 59:215, enero/abril 1999, p. 123–141, graph, table)

Succinct investigation into the failure of the Bonaerense ranching system to generate sufficient free labor for its needs and its subsequent reliance on forced labor in the 1800s. [TW]

2876 Ghigliani, Pablo. Las experiencias antiburocráticas de los obreros gráficos: la huelga de 1966 y el peronismo combativo. (*Taller/Buenos Aires*, 3:6, abril 1998, p. 65–92)

Studies the print workers strike of 1966 and investigates the subsequent coming to power in the union of the antibureaucratic Peronist Raymundo Ongaro. [JH]

2877 Giacobone, Carlos Alberto and **Edit Rosalía Gallo.** Radicalismo bonaerense: la ingeniería política de Hipólito Yrigoyen, 1891–1931. Buenos Aires: Corregidor, 1999. 446 p.: bibl.

Detailed traditional political history with little interpretive material but strongly pro-Radical. Focuses on the outward mechanisms of politics in Buenos Aires province. Also includes some material on national-level politics. [JH]

2878 Giménez, Luis Jorge. La provincia de Buenos Aires y el problema del costo del Ferrocarril del Sud (F.C.S.), 1861–1865. (*FACES/Mar del Plata*, 3:4, oct. 1997, p. 9–19, appendix, bibl.)

Brief article addresses the conflicts between the city and province of Buenos Aires arising from the high cost of railroad construction. Relies heavily on author's doctoral thesis on the Mariano Saavedra government (1862–66). [TW]

2879 Goldman, Noemí and **Nora Souto.** De los usos de los conceptos de "nación" y la formación del espacio político en el Río de la Plata, 1810–1827. (*Secuencia/México*, 37, enero/abril 1997, p. 35–56, bibl., maps)

Short but suggestive piece on the meaning of "nation" for political elites in early independent Argentina. Notes how differing concepts of "nation" undergirded the later struggle between federalists and unitarians. [TW]

2880 Gómez, Alejandro. Un siglo—, una vida: de la soberanía a la dependencia. Prólogo de Oscar Troncoso. Buenos Aires: Editores de América Latina, 2001. 457 p.: bibl., ill.

Political memories of the Radical militant who served as Arturo Frondizi's vice president. Concentrates on his troubled and controversial tenure as vice president but includes information as far back as the 1920s. [JH]

2881 Goñi, Uki. Judas: la verdadera historia de Alfredo Astiz, el infiltrado. 2. ed. Buenos·Aires: Editorial Sudamericana, 1996. 219 p.

A journalist recounts the founding of the Mothers of the Plaza de Mayo, the infiltration of the organization by the naval officer Alfredo Astiz, and the subsequent murder of a number of the founding members. Based on a series of interviews. [JH]

2882 Goñi, Uki. Perón y los alemanes: la verdad sobre el espionaje nazi y los fugitivos del Reich. Buenos Aires: Editorial Sudamericana, 1998. 317 p., 8 p. of plates: bibl., ill., index.

Examines ties between Nazi Germany and Perón based on extensive archival work and interviews. Sees much more substantial and closer ties than other recent serious works have found. [JH]

2883 Goñi Demarchi, Carlos Alberto; José Nicolás Scala; and Germán W. Berraondo. A un año de la revolución de mayo: "resumen de acontecimientos en las Colonias españolas de América en 1810–1811"; Foreign Office, Londres, 12 de mayo de 1811. (*Nuestra Hist./Buenos Aires*, 26:47/48, julio 1999, p. 109–115)

Analysis of an 1811 Foreign Office report indicates continued British support for Spain's New World pretensions, despite the many contacts already established with patriot regimes in Buenos Aires and elsewhere in Latin America. [TW]

2884 González Leandri, Ricardo. Asociacionismo y representación de intereses médicos en Buenos Aires, 1852–1880. (*Asclepio/Madrid*, 50:2, 1998, p. 187–203)

Examines the early attempts of porteño doctors to organize into professional associations that were independent of the elite-oriented medical school. [TW]

2885 González Leandri, Ricardo. La higiene antes de los médicos higienistas: Buenos Aires; 1850–1870; las epidemias. (*Desmemoria/Buenos Aires*, 5:18, mayo/agosto 1998, p. 41–56, facsim., photos)

Well-written account discusses how the onslaughts of epidemic disease (especially yellow fever) helped reinforce the professionalization of medicine in mid-19th century Buenos Aires. Based in part on careful readings of the *Revista Médico-Quirúrgico*. [TW]

2886 González Rissotto, Luis Rodolfo. Artigas: la formación de la liga de los pueblos libres y las limitaciones que supuso la aplicación del liberalismo económico. (*in* Encuentro de Geohistoria Regional, *16th, Resistencia, Argentina, 1996. Reglamento y exposiciones. Resistencia, Argentina: Instituto de Investigaciones Geohistóricas; Conicet, 1997, p. 227–242, bibl.*)

Insightful study ties the federalism of Artigas as seen in the Litoral provinces and the Banda Oriental to the economic liberalism of the age. Contrasts views in both locations with the more conservative order of the Argentine interior. [TW]

2887 Gorelik, Adrián. La grilla y el parque: espacio público y cultura urbana en Buenos Aires, 1887–1936. Buenos Aires: Univ. Nacional de Quilmes, 1998. 455 p.: bibl., ill., maps. (La ideología argentina)

A tour-de-force that combines intellectual and cultural history with urban planning. Argues successfully that the government played a crucial role in shaping the physical nature of Buenos Aires. Discusses the many plans for Buenos Aires, their impacts, and relates what people thought about the city. In an insightful way, compares developments in Buenos Aires with developments in cities elsewhere. [JH]

Gorla, Carlos María. La frontera de Patagones en el período 1820–1840. See item **716.**

2888 Gorostiaga Saldías, Leonor. Adolfo Saldías: leal servidor de la República. Buenos Aires: Corregidor, 1999. 381 p.: bibl., ill.

Sympathetic biography written by Saldías' granddaughter using his personal archive as well as material from the AGN. Emphasizes political and intellectual realms with the subtitle demonstrating author's belief. [JH]

2889 Graham-Yooll, Andrew. Rosas visto por los ingleses. Buenos Aires: Editorial de Belgrano, 1997. 179 p.

Former editor of the *Buenos Aires Herald* here offers a useful compilation of correspondence and records of British diplomatic personnel resident in Buenos Aires during the Rosas dictatorship. Scholars will wish to consult the English-language originals in the Public Records Office in London and in the *Times* of London. [TW]

2890 Grandes entrevistas de la historia argentina, 1879–1988. Selección y prólogo de Sylvia Saítta y Luis Alberto Romero. Buenos Aires: Aguilar, 1998. 406 p.: bibl.

An excellent compilation of interviews conducted over the years with such important Argentine luminaries as Julio Roca, Lucio Mansilla, José Ingenieros, Hipólito Yrigoyen, Eva Duarte, Juan Perón, Jorge Luis Borges, and Julio Cortázar. [TW]

2891 Grunfeld, José. Memorias de un anarquista. Buenos Aires: Nuevohacer: Grupo Editor Latinoamericano, 2000. 369 p. (Colección Temas)

Autobiography of an anarchist born in 1907 in Moisés Ville. A largely self-taught intellectual, active in the union movement, Grunfeld went to Spain during the Civil War and subsequently opposed Perón during and after his rise to power. Story continues until 1962. Interesting reading. [JH]

2892 Gutiérrez Viñuales, Rodrigo. Presencia de España en la Argentina: dibujo, caricatura y humorismo, 1870–1930. (*Cuad. Arte/Granada,* 28, 1997, p. 113–124, facsims.)

Brief article describes Spanish influences on Argentine caricature art at the turn of the century. The presence of European illustrated magazines, such as *La Ilustración Artística,* provided inspiration for Argentine cartoonists, but the main influences came

from Spanish immigrants in Buenos Aires, who continued the artistic work they started in Europe. [TW]

2893 Halperín Donghi, Tulio. El espejo de la historia: problemas argentinos y perspectivas hispanoamericanas. 2. ed. Buenos Aires: Editorial Sudamericana, 1998. 347 p.: bibl. (Colección Historia y cultura)

Reprint includes two additional important essays on the impact of the repression carried out by the military regime that took power in 1976. One compares the impact of repression on cultural institutions in Chile and Argentina. Concludes that there was a greater rupture in Argentina, leading to a discussion of the lack of continuity during much of the existence of the Univ. de Buenos Aires. The other examines how visions of the past in novels and movies have been altered by the most recent dictatorship. For review of 1st ed., see *HLAS 52:2704.* [JH]

2894 Harris, Jonathan. Bernardino Rivadavia and Benthamite "discipleship." (*LARR,* 33:1, 1998, p. 129–149, bibl., photo)

Argues that the influences of utilitarian philosopher Jeremy Bentham on Bernardino Rivadavia were somewhat less crucial than is usually suggested, and that the latter was certainly not a disciple of the former. For philosophy specialist's comment, see item **4808.** [TW]

2895 Historia de la vida privada en la Argentina. v. 1, País antiguo, de la colonia a 1870. v. 2, La Argentina plural: 1870–1930. v. 3, La Argentina entre multitudes y soledades: de los años treinta a la actualidad. Madrid; Buenos Aires: Taurus, 1999. 3 v.: bibl., ill.

Although somewhat mistitled as some of the chapters seem unconnected with theme, on the whole compilation is well done, even if many obvious subjects are not discussed. Two chapters cover domestic architecture; two chapters review the formation of the model middle-class family; one looks at childhood at the turn of the last century; and one addresses cafes, operas, and circuses. Also includes chapters on Mar del Plata, the creation of a social life in the pampa gringa, television and football, and private life in places where the disappeared were held, especially the Escuela de Mécanica de la Armada. Highly recommended. [JH]

2896 Hora, Roy. The landowners of the Argentine Pampas: a social and political history, 1860–1945. Oxford: Clarendon Press; New York: Oxford Univ. Press, 2001. 264 p.: bibl., index. (Oxford historical monographs)

A well-written, clear presentation of the emergence of the estancieros as a separate, powerful, and influential class, and their subsequent decline. Focuses on the great landowners of the pampas, particularly those of the province of Buenos Aires. An important book that should help to move the image of estancieros beyond stereotypes. [JH]

2897 Horowitz, Joel. Bosses and clients: municipal employment in the Buenos Aires of the Radicals, 1916–30. (*J. Lat. Am. Stud.*, 31:3, Oct. 1999, p. 617–644)

Deft analysis of municipal employment statistics calls into question David Rock's clientelistic model of the Yrigoyen regime. Shows that spoils systems existed before and after Yrigoyen and that all major political factions shared in the patronage. Concludes that Yrigoyen's popularity cannot be reduced to machine politics alone. [TW]

2898 Höttcke, Jochen August. Argentinien zwischen Deutschland und den USA, 1939–45: Prolog zu Peron? Vorgelegt von Jochen August Höttcke. Berlin: Dissertation.de, 2000. 297 p.: bibl. (Premium)

Using Argentine, German, and US archives, examines Argentine foreign policy with a distinctly German point of view. Questioning the ferocity of US antagonism toward Argentine neutrality, looks at the role and motives of German and US influences and activities. Concludes that, while German foreign policy influence held for a limited time, and Argentina—whether under civilian or military governments—followed its own interests, the basic conflict rested on Argentina's refusal to submit to US hegemony. Ironically, the overstated and exaggerated US response and interventionist tactics, which increased after the military coup of 1943, contributed to the rise of Perón. [C. Converse]

2899 Hunt, Patricio Julio. Historia de los subtes de Buenos Aires. Buenos Aires: Mompracem Editores, 1998. 173 p.: bibl., ill.

A useful history of the Buenos Aires subways, concentrating on the technology. [JH]

2900 Iñigo Carrera, Nicolás. La estrategia de la clase obrera, 1936. Buenos Aires: La Rosa Blindada: PIMSA, 2000. 318 p.: bibl., ill., maps. (Col. de ensayos Emilio Jáuregui)

Argues that a self-conscious working class with ties to the left existed in the mid-1930s and attempts to prove that point by describing in detail a violent general strike in Buenos Aires in Jan. 1936. The discussion of the strike is very impressive but whether it proves the theoretical argument is debatable. [JH]

2901 La inmigración española en la Argentina. Recopilación de Alejandro E. Fernández y José C. Moya. Buenos Aires: Editorial Biblos, 1999. 271 p.: bibl., ill., maps. (Col. La Argentina plural; 2)

An excellent series of articles on different aspects of Spanish immigration in Argentina. The work is divided into three sections: one looks at demographic aspects; the second at economic and social integration into the host society; and the third segment examines political participation and how the immigrants' presence in Argentina reshapes their identities. The final section is particularly interesting. [JH]

2902 Instrucciones diplomáticas argentinas. v. 1, Años 1820–1874. Córdoba, Argentina: Centro de Estudios Históricos, 1997. 1 v.: bibl. (Serie documental; 7)

Documentary collection of Argentine government instructions to diplomatic agents in Ecuador, Chile, Peru, Brazil, Bolivia, Colombia, Paraguay, Uruguay, Britain, and various European states, from 1820–74. Originals held in the Archivo del Ministerio de Relaciones Exteriores y Culto and in the AGN. Of minor interest to diplomatic historians. [TW]

2903 Iriani, Marcelino. Presencia vasca en el primer enclave industrial rioplatense, 1840–1870. (*Entorno Urbano*, 2:4, julio/dic. 1996, p. 25–54, bibl., maps, photo, tables)

Demonstrates that a substantial proportion of Basque immigrants to Argentina did not move to the countryside but in fact remained in the city of Buenos Aires (especially the Barracas district). [TW]

2904 Iriani, Marcelino. Trabajadores vascos en el recuerdo popular rioplatense. (*Rev. Indias*, 57:210, mayo/agosto 1997, p. 399–419, tables)

Readable and suggestive study of the development of Basque stereotypes in 19th-century Argentina. Based partly on censal records. [TW]

2905 James, Daniel. Doña María's story: life history, memory, and political identity. Durham, N.C.: Duke Univ. Press, 2000. 316 p.: bibl., ill., index. (Latin America otherwise)

An important book that combines the life history of María Roldán, a working class Peronist activist from the industrial suburb of Berisso, with discussions of how one reads oral histories and other types of sources, the role of the historian, and other historiographical notions. Roldán's stories allow the reader to see an important vision of working-class life. [JH]

2906 Jauretche, Ernesto. No dejés que te la cuenten: violencia y política en los 70. Buenos Aires: Ediciones del Pensamiento Nacional, 1997. 310 p.: bibl.

Compiled by a former Montonero, combines short summaries of occurrences during the period with interviews of people who belonged to the Peronist leftist youth movement. [JH]

2907 Johnson, Lyman L. The frontier as an arena of social and economic change: wealth distribution in nineteenth-century Buenos Aires province. (*in* Contested ground: comparative frontiers on the northern and southern edges of the Spanish Empire. Edited by Donna J. Guy and Thomas E. Sheridan. Tucson: Univ. of Arizona Press, 1998, p. 167–181)

Suggestive investigation of wealth distribution in rural Buenos Aires during the Rosas era. Notes that the same policies that promoted inequality by redistributing wealth away from the masses into the hands of the ranching elite also led to increased average wealth throughout the province. [TW]

2908 Juan B. Justo. Recopilación de Javier Franzé. Madrid: Ediciones de Cultura Hispánica, 1998. 229 p.: bibl. (Antología del pensamiento político, social y económico de América Latina; 18)

Useful anthology of essays by Justo

(1865–1928), the principal figure of the early Argentine socialist movement and translator of *Das Kapital*. [TW]

2909 La Junta de Historia y Numismática Américana y el movimiento historiográfico en la Argentina: 1893–1938. v. 2. Buenos Aires: Academia Nacional de la Historia, 1996. 1 v.: bibl., ill. (some col.), index.

A continuation of commemorative volumes for the Academia Nacional de la Historia. Includes 26 chapters by different authors; divided into three sections. The first part discusses the writing of history in the interior of the country. The second examines the relationship between historiography and other disciplines such as law, sociology, folklore, etc. The third looks at the impact of historiography on society, including historical instruction at all three levels of schooling, historical novels, and movies. For review of vol. 1, see *HLAS 58:2936*. [JH]

2910 Jurkowicz de Eichbaum, Marta E. Cuando las mujeres hacen memoria: testimonios de historia oral de la inmigración judía en la Argentina. Prólogo de Hebe Clementi. Buenos Aires: Grupo Editor Latinoamericano, 1999. 198 p.: bibl., ill. (Col. Temas)

Presents short segments of oral histories arranged by themes and given by older Jewish women. Emphasizes the process of immigration, though includes other themes as well. Interesting, but the segments could be longer. [JH]

2911 Kindgard, Adriana M. Los sectores conservadores de Jujuy ante el fenómeno peronista, 1943–1948: a propósito de la dimensión estructural en el análisis de los procesos políticos. (*Estud. Soc./Santa Fe*, 9:16, primer semestre 1999, p. 77–94)

Contributes to our understanding of how traditional provincial political forces reacted to Perón's rise. Shows how the traditional conservative forces that were tightly tied to the sugar industry opposed Perón during his rise to power because of his social policies. Dissident radicals provided key political mobilization for Perón. [JH]

2912 Klich, Ignacio. Arab-Jewish coexistence in the first half of 1900s' Argentina: overcoming self-imposed amnesia. (*in* Arab and Jewish immigrants in Latin America: images and realities. Edited by Ignacio

Klich and Jeffrey Lesser. London; Portland, Ore.: F. Cass, 1998, p. 1–37)

Demonstrates that Arab-Jewish relations in Argentina before the founding of the state of Israel were very good. Finds that this was particularly true for those who shared the Arab language and culture. [JH]

2913 Klich, Ignacio. La contratación de nazis y colaboracionistas por la Fuerza Aérea Argentina. (*Ciclos Hist. Econ. Soc.*, 10:19, 2000, p. 177–216)

Reviews old stories of Argentina importing Nazi collaborators to build airplanes. Then analyzes what information can be obtained from the available documentation. [JH]

2914 Labaké, Juan Gabriel. El presidente que sí fue. Buenos Aires: Corregidor, 1997. 190 p.: ill.

An attack on Miguel Bonasso's *El presidente que no fue* (see *HLAS 58:2829*), written by a Peronist politician active in the 1970s. Aims to defend the positions of Perón and attack those of the Montoneros and the Peronist left in general. Also includes some attacks on López Rega. Includes information on the author's political history. [JH]

2915 Lázzaro, Silvia B. Estado y arrendamientos rurales en los años '50. (*Ciclos Hist. Econ. Soc.*, 12, 1997, p. 145–177, table)

Examines state regulation of tenant farming during the period of the decline of the institution. [JH]

2916 Lépori de Pithod, María Estela. Selección de informes franceses sobre Argentina, 1897–1930. Mendoza, Argentina: Univ. Nacional de Cuyo, Facultad de Filosofía y Letras, 1998. 409 p.

A selection of 186 French diplomatic dispatches translated into Spanish, almost all from 1916–30. Those selected concentrate on the internal affairs of Argentina, but seem less interesting than their British and US counterparts. Nonetheless, a useful set of documents. [JH]

2917 Lettieri, Alberto Rodolfo. Una experiencia republicana en Buenos Aires, 1852–1861. (*Desarro. Econ.*, 39:154, julio/sept. 1999, p. 285–307, bibl.)

Well-focused study of porteño politics from the fall of Rosas to Pavón. Argues that

the system then operating in Buenos Aires, though usually seen as an "aristocratic republic," in fact enjoyed some popular legitimacy because it broadly reflected public opinion. [TW]

2918 Lettieri, Alberto Rodolfo. La república de la opinión: política y opinión pública en Buenos Aires entre 1852 y 1862. Buenos Aires: Editorial Biblos, 1998. 166 p.: bibl., ill.

Fascinating, well-researched study of political change in Buenos Aires during the 1850s. Shows how returned liberals, ex-rosistas, and socioeconomic elites came together to construct a more modern regime in the province, and how public opinion shaped and legitimized that regime. [TW]

2919 Lewis, Colin M. Explaining economic decline: a review of recent debates in the economic and social history literature on the Argentine. (*Rev. Eur. Estud. Latinoam. Caribe*, 64, June 1998, p. 49–68, tables)

Examines in broad terms when the slowdown in growth occurred. Then discusses in a clear and fair fashion different arguments on why the Argentine economy failed to continue to grow at a rapid pace. [JH]

2920 Lewis, Paul H. Guerrillas and generals: the "Dirty War" in Argentina. Westport, Conn.: Praeger, 2002. 263 p.: bibl., index.

Attempts to present an even-handed account of the violence from the mid-1960s to the trials after the fall of the military. While appalled by the violence of the military, the author is more favorable to the armed services than many other commentators. [JH]

2921 Lobato, Mirta Zaida. La vida en las fábricas: trabajo, protesta y política en una comunidad obrera, Berisso, 1904–1970. Buenos Aires: Prometeo Libros, 2001. 333 p.: bibl., ill. (Col. Entrepasados libros)

A detailed, excellent study of work, protest, and politics in the meat-packing town of Berisso. A unique study for Argentina in its depth and span. Uses a wide range of sources, including numerous interviews. [JH]

2922 Luna, Félix. La emancipación argentina y americana. Buenos Aires: Planeta, 1998. 158 p.: bibl., ill. (some col.). (Momentos clave de la historia integral de la argentina; 1)

Well-written, well-illustrated summary treatment of the independence struggles in Latin America, with particular attention given to the Argentine case. [TW]

2923 Luna, Félix. Historia integral de la Argentina. v. 8, Los años de prosperidad. v. 9, Conservadores y peronistas. v. 10, El largo camino a la democracia. Buenos Aires: 1997. 3 v.: bibl.

A popular multivolume history that concentrates on politics with some attention to social and intellectual history but ignores economics. Attempts to place Argentina in a changing world. Illustrated with photographs. Presents a solidly pro-Radical view, especially of the Yrigoyenist variety. For review of vol. 1, see *HLAS 58:2460.* For review of vol. 2, see *HLAS 58:2461.* For review of vol. 6, see *HLAS 58:2958.* [JH]

2924 Luna, Félix. Segunda fila: personajes olvidados que también hicieron historia. Buenos Aires: Planeta, 1999. 318 p.

Departing from his usual focus on the "great men" of Argentine history, Luna here sheds light on some lesser-known figures of the 18th-19th centuries, including a clerical librarian, a spy, an English prostitute, a Spanish militiaman, a French geographer, an assassin turned schoolteacher turned beggar, and the "uncrowned Indian king of Paraguay." Readable and amusing. [TW]

2925 Lvovich, Daniel. La imagen del enemigo y sus transformaciones en *La Nueva República,* 1928–1931. (*Entrepasados/Buenos Aires,* 9:17, 1999, p. 49–71, bibl., ill.)

Finds three separate stages in the underlying ideology of this far-right periodical. Illustrates how the rapidly changing political situation helped shape the ideology. [JH]

2926 Machón, Jorge Francisco. El coronel Vicente Antonio Matiauda: Teniente de Gobernador de los pueblos misioneros. (*in* Encuentro de Geohistoria Regional, *16th, Resistencia, Argentina, 1996.* Reglamento y exposiciones. Resistencia, Argentina: Instituto de Investigaciones Geohistóricas; Conicet, 1997, p. 287–304)

Paraguayan dictator José Gaspar de Francia tried to stay neutral in the on-again, off-again struggle between Buenos Aires and Artigas, but was sorely tested when his southern-most *subdelegado,* Matiauda, defected to the latter's forces in 1814. As this impressively researched study points out, however, Artigas got poor recompense, for within months of his appointing Matiauda commandante of Yapeyú, the Paraguayan officer switched allegiances again, this time defecting to the porteños. [TW]

2927 Machón, Jorge Francisco. José Artigas: gobernador de Misiones. Misiones, Argentina: J.F. Machón, 1998. 105 p.: bibl., ill., maps.

A worthy though brief addition to the huge corpus of materials on Artigas, specifically dealing with his short-term governorship of the Misiones region (1811–12). [TW]

2928 Macor, Darío and Eduardo Iglesias. El peronismo antes del peronismo: memoria e historia en los orígenes del peronismo santafesino. Santa Fe, Argentina: Univ. Nacional del Litoral, Centro de Publicaciones, 1997. 295 p. (Sociedad y cultura)

Pt. 1 of two includes two short essays on the city of Santa Fe. The first looks at the nationalist movement, especially the impact of Jordán Bruno Genta and his intervention in the university. The second examines in detail the events of Oct. 1945. Pt. 2 offers 17 short oral histories of people who played a role in the advent of Peronism in Santa Fe province, with an introduction. [JH]

2929 Malamud, Carlos. Partidos políticos y elecciones en la Argentina: la Liga del Sur santafesina, 1908–1916. Madrid: Univ. Nacional de Educación a Distancia, 1997. 331 p.: bibl. (Aula abierta; 107)

A detailed history of the brief life of the Liga del Sur, which is seen both as a party representing regional interests of the southern part of Santa Fe province, but also as a modern political party. The Liga served as a launching pad for the national career of Lisandro de la Torre. Part of the new political history emerging from Argentina. [JH]

Mandrini, Raúl J. Las fronteras y la sociedad indígena en el ámbito pampeano. See item **754.**

2930 Marco, Miguel Angel de. Bartolomé Mitre: biografía. Buenos Aires: Planeta, 1998. 498 p.: bibl., ill. (Historia argentina)

Readable, well-documented biography of the Argentine publicist, historian, and statesman. Considers Mitre to have been one of the "great men" of Argentine history, and treats him with an appropriate reverence rather than with a critical eye. Good illustrations. [TW]

2931 Mariel Erostarbe, Juan A. El epistolario íntimo de Sarmiento. San Juan, Argentina: Editorial Fundación, Univ. Nacional de San Juan, 1997. 260 p.: bibl., ill.

An unusual selection of 37 Sarmiento letters, chosen specifically for their intimate character. Recipients include "Don Yo's" daughter and mistress. Of interest mainly to the Sarmiento specialist. [TW]

2932 Martí, Gerardo Marcelo. El colapso del sistema de emisión, depósitos y descuentos en la Argentina: el caso del Banco de la Provincia de Buenos Aires, 1887–1891. (Trimest. Econ., 65:258, abril/junio 1998, p. 175–212, bibl., graphs, tables)

Analyzes the impact of Argentina's 1890–91 financial crisis on the most important domestic bank in Buenos Aires. The withdrawal of foreign deposits, the overextension of credit, and the lack of adequate reserves eventually brought about the bank's collapse. [TW]

2933 Martí, Gerardo Marcelo. El sistema bancario en vísperas de la crisis de 1890: una revisión crítica de su incidencia en la política económica de Juárez Celman, 1887–1889. (Ciclos Hist. Econ. Soc., 9:17, 1999, p. 47–82, bibl.)

Incisive study of the state of Argentine banking just prior to the 1890 crisis. Argues that official and quasi-official banks played no role in spurring the development of regional economies. [TW]

2934 Martín de Codoni, Elvira. Sarmiento y el médico Rivera en el ocaso de Aldao. (Rev. Junta Estud. Hist. Mendoza, 2, 1998, p. 179–197, bibl.)

Historiographical treatment of Miguel Rivera Rondon's Mi viaje al pie de los Andes, written in the mid-1840s, at the same time Sarmiento penned his Biografía de Aldao, both of which describe the waning years of the priest-caudillo of Cuyo. [TW]

2935 Martínez, Tomás Eloy. Las memorias del general. Buenos Aires: Planeta, 1996. 218 p. (Espejo de la Argentina)

Contains an unedited version of Martínez's famous interviews with Perón as well as fragments of other information gathered for a biography of him. Also includes several short pieces dealing with the 1970s. One sees clearly the documentary basis for Martínez's fictional work, La novela de Perón (see HLAS 50:3458). [JH]

2936 Mazzei, Daniel Horacio. Primera Plana: modernización y golpismo en los sesenta. (Real. Econ. /Buenos Aires, 16 de mayo/30 de junio 1997, p. 72–99, bibl., ill., tables)

Continues the author's studies of how the important news magazine, Primera Plana, attempted to manipulate public opinion (see HLAS 58:2972). While style is discussed, the focus here is on how the magazine helped set the stage for the overthrow of Illia. [JH]

2937 McGuire, James William. Peronism without Perón: unions, parties, and democracy in Argentina. Stanford, Calif.: Stanford Univ. Press, 1997. 388 p.: bibl., index.

Focuses on the failure of the institutionalization of democracy in Argentina by examining the weak party structure of the Peronists. Shows that during two periods (1962–66 and 1984–88), when attempts at party building seemed promising, they were undermined in large part by elements of the labor movement. Presents a detailed discussion of the labor movement, documented and excellent, especially regarding the first period. [JH]

2938 Mead, Karen. Gendering the obstacles to progress in positivist Argentina, 1880–1920. (HAHR, 77:4, Nov. 1997, p. 645–675)

Presents the views on women of three key positivistic writers, José María Ramos Mejía, Carlos Octavio Bunge, and José Ingenieros. Although these thinkers were considered advocates of women's rights, finds that all were ambivalent about the place of women in modern society. [JH]

2939 Meli, Rosa. Ocupación militar del Chaco, 1852–1919. (*Nuestra Hist. / Buenos Aires*, 26:47/48, julio 1999, p. 3–76, table)

Extensive summary of Indian campaigns in the Argentine Chaco, and the military men who participated in them during the late 19th and early 20th centuries. Based partly on archival documentation. [TW]

2940 Miller, Jonathan M. Courts and the creation of a "spirit of moderation": judicial protection of revolutionaries in Argentina, 1863–1929. (*Hastings Int. Comp. Law Rev.*, 20:2, Winter 1997, p. 231–329)

Focusing on the 19th century, argues that the Supreme Court developed much more independence in arbitrating conflicts between economic and political elites than is usually thought. The court never expands its role beyond that point. Written by a professor of law at a US university. [JH]

2941 Miranda, Omar A. De ganaderos a fruticultores: transición social e innovación institucional en el Alto Valle del Río Negro, 1900–1940. (*Ciclos Hist. Econ. Soc.*, 12, 1997, p. 179–202, graphs, tables)

Examines the rapid change in the nature of land-use in the Alto Valle from grazing to grazing on alfalfa raised with irrigation to the growing of fruit. Focuses particularly on the institutions that made the rapid change possible. [JH]

2942 Mittelbach, Federico. San Martín, organizador militar. Buenos Aires: Ediciones Dunken, 1998. 215 p.: bibl., folded ill.

A useful contribution to the many studies of San Martín, this one concentrating on his talents as a military planner in the early phases of the independence wars and in the Andes campaign. [TW]

2943 Molinari, Irene Delfina. Desde la otra orilla: las trabajadoras marplatenses—formas y condiciones del trabajo femenino en una sociedad en transformación. (*Mora/Buenos Aires*, 3, agosto 1997, p. 95–112, tables)

Examines the changing nature of female employment in Mar del Plata as the city's economic structure changed, becoming a center of summer tourism for the middle and working classes as well as a textile and fish processing center. Concentrates on the 1940–70 period. [JH]

2944 Montenegro, Liliana. Las Provincias Unidas y el Brasil ante la cuestión de la Banda Oriental, a la luz de *El Centinela: 1822–1823*. (*Rev. Junta Prov. Estud. Hist. Santa Fe*, 61, 1996/97, p. 83–124, bibl.)

Examines the stance of a key Buenos Aires newspaper regarding the competition with Brazil in the Banda Oriental, 1822–23. [TW]

2945 Moya, Jose C. Cousins and strangers: Spanish immigrants in Buenos Aires, 1850–1930. Berkeley: Univ. of California Press, 1998. 567 p.: bibl., ill., index, maps.

Excellent work revolutionizes the study of immigration. Manages to look at both societies, Spain and Argentina, beyond the macro level. Recognizes the importance of the different regions of Spain. Also focuses on how immigrants lived in Buenos Aires. Discussion is crucial for social history as well. Based on prodigious research using a vast range of sources. [JH]

2946 Múgica, María Luisa. Cuerpos fabricados en reglamentos: obligaciones y prohibiciones para las prostitutas del Rosario en los umbrales del siglo. (*Estud. Soc. /Santa Fe*, 7:12, primer semestre 1997, p. 83–96)

Describes how prostitution was legally controlled and channeled at the turn of the century in Rosario. [JH]

Murillo, María Victoria. Recovering political dynamics: teachers' unions and the decentralization of education in Argentina and Mexico. See item **1586.**

2947 Nario, Hugo. Los picapedreros. Tandil, Argentina: Ediciones del Manantial, 1997. 285 p.: bibl., ill. (Tandil, historia abierta; 2)

Solid local history describes the social and work worlds of the stone cutters of Tandil, as well as their history of unionization, with emphasis on the latter. Based on interviews and existing local documents. [JH]

2948 Nascimbene, Mario Carlos. Italianos hacia América: los flujos emigratorios regionales y provinciales peninsulares con destino al Nuevo Mundo, 1876–1978. Buenos Aires: Museo Roca, Centro de Estudios sobre Inmigración: Secretaría de Cultura, Ministerio de Cultura y Educación de la República Argentina, 1994. 127 p.: bibl., maps.

Based on official Italian data, presents detailed charts, tables and maps giving regional and provincial data on Italian emigration to Argentina, Brazil and the US. Some information is given on Uruguay. No interpretation but a wonderful place to find data. [JH]

2949 Neuquén: la construcción de un orden estatal. Recopilación de Orietta Favaro. Argentina: Centro de Estudios Históricos de Estado, Política y Cultura, 1999. 294 p.: bibl., ill.

Solid chapters investigate the unusual political history of Neuquén since it became a province. Looks at both the Sapag family—the dominant political force—and the unusual local economy based on the export of energy. [JH]

2950 Nicolau, Juan Carlos. Comerciantes y banqueros en Buenos Aires, 1810–1825. (*Invest. Ens.*, 47, 1997, p. 433–449)

Short but useful account of trading and banking in unitarian Buenos Aires. Based in part on documentation from the Baring Brothers in London. [TW]

2951 Nicolau, Juan Carlos. Pedro Andrés García, 1758–1833: el colonizador, caballero español en la pampa. Córdoba, Argentina: Centro de Estudios Históricos, 1998. 126 p.: bibl. (Cuaderno, no. 25)

Brief, readable biography of García, the Spanish-born author of the *Diario de un viaje a Salinas Grandes en los campos del sud de Buenos Aires* (originally published by Pedro de Angelis in 1836; for review of 1974 edition, see *HLAS 38:3185*) and other works of exploration and colonization along the indigenous frontiers of Buenos Aires. Based partly on documents held in the Museo Mitre and Archivo General de la Nación. [TW]

2952 Nueva historia argentina. v. 5, El progreso, la modernización y sus límites, 1880–1916. Buenos Aires: Editorial Sudamericana, 2000. 1 v.: bibl., ill. (some col.), maps (some col.).

Based on recent historiography—examines the economy, the economy of the north, the settlement of Patagonia, politics including separate chapters on the Radical Party and the Socialist Party, workers, anarchists, intellectual history, urbanization,

daily life, immigration, and disease a social problem. [JH]

2953 Nueva historia argentina. v. 6, Democracia, conflicto social y renovación de ideas, 1916–1930. Buenos Aires: Editorial Sudamericana, 2000. 1 v.: bibl., ill. (some col.), maps (some col.).

Looks at, in separate chapters, politics, the economy, the labor movement, the role of entrepreneurs in the economy, the social question in the countryside, the shape of cities, and intellectual history. Writers are part of the latest currents in the historiography. [JH]

2954 Nueva historia argentina. v. 7, Crisis económica, avance del estado e incertidumbre política, 1930–1943. Buenos Aires: Editorial Sudamericana, 2000. 1 v.: bibl., ill. (some col.), maps (some col.).

Based on recent studies of the 1930s, discusses politics, the economy, urban workers, the labor movement, disease, and intellectual history from various angles. Illustrated with well-selected photographs. [JH]

2955 Nueva historia argentina. v. 8, Los años peronistas, 1943–1955. Buenos Aires: Editorial Sudamericana, 2001. 1 v.: bibl., ill. (some col.), maps (some col.).

Like the others in the series, this volume presents up-to-date, well-done chapters by important historians. Begins with a long, important introduction by Torre and includes chapters on the armed services, the economy, politics, the democratization of welfare, Evita, unions, entrepreneurs, the Church, intellectuals, and foreign policy. [JH]

2956 Nueva historia argentina. v. 11, Atlas histórico de la Argentina. Buenos Aires: Editorial Sudamericana, 2001. 1 v.: bibl., ill. (some col.), maps (some col.).

More than just a compendium of historical maps. An important source for political, economic, and population data. An extremely useful work when looking for a quick reference. [JH]

2957 Nueva historia de la nación argentina. v. 5. Buenos Aires: Planeta, 2001. 1 v.: bibl., ill., maps.

A series of well-written chapters discuss the creation of the modern Argentine nation from 1810–1914. Looks at political thought, the nature of government, foreign relations, the Church, justice, and the economy. While up-to-date, work is traditional in approach. [JH]

2958 Olds, Harry Grant. Fotografías, 1900–1943. Idea y selección de fotografías de Luis Priamo. Textos de Fernando Rocchi *et al*. Buenos Aires: Fundación Antorchas, 1998. 107 p.: bibl., chiefly ill. (some col.).

After informative introductions, presents photographs mostly of Buenos Aires with a few of the provinces by an early North American commercial photographer. Many are interesting street scenes from Buenos Aires, taken in the early years of the 20th century. [JH]

2959 Ornstein, Leopoldo R. Entretelones de la Revolución del 4 de junio de 1943. (*Desmemoria/Buenos Aires*, 7:26, segundo cuatrimestre 2000, p. 45–62, photos)

Publishes previously unknown comments written by an important participant, Col. Leopoldo R. Ornstein, on the events of June 1943. Decidedly anti-Perón. [JH]

2960 Oven, Wilfred von. Ein "Nazi" in Argentinien. 2. Aufl. Duisburg, Germany: VAWS, 1999. 224 p.: ill.

An autobiography by an admittedly incorrigible ideological Nazi, who had served as Goebbels' personal secretary, immigrated to Argentina in 1952, and worked primarily with the right-wing German-language press in Buenos Aires. A journalist, Oven met notorious Nazis as well as Argentine and German officials during the postwar decades. His observations, along with innuendoes and rumors, provide a rare but curiously slanted insight into the German-Argentine community. [C. Converse]

2961 Oyhanarte, María. Los Oyhanarte: gente con historia. Buenos Aires: Fundación Editorial de Belgrano, 1998. 295 p.: bibl., ill.

Presents the history of late-19th and 20th-century Argentina as seen through the experiences of a prominent Radical family. [TW]

2962 Panella, Claudio. La gran huelga de los trabajadores textiles de Berisso, 1960–1961. La Plata, Argentina: C. Panella, 1997. 110 p.: bibl., ill.

A brief discussion of a nine-month strike at the Patent Knitting Company is followed by documents concerning the stoppage as well as short interviews with some of the participants in the strike. [JH]

2963 Parada, Alejandro E. El mundo del libro y de la lectura durante la época de Rivadavia: una aproximación a través de los avisos de *La Gaceta Mercantil*, 1823–1828. Buenos Aires: Univ. de Buenos Aires, Facultad de Filosofía y Letras, Instituto de Investigaciones Bibliotecológicas, 1998. 174 p.: appendices, bibl., index, tables. (Cuadernos de bibliotecología, no. 17)

Fascinating analysis of the reading public's tastes in the city of Buenos Aires during the 1820s. Detailed lists note 727 different book titles available and another 44 minor publications. [TW]

2964 Paredes, Rogelio C. El aristócrata y la inmigración: la inmigración italiana a la Argentina segun el *Diario de viaje a Europa* de Estanislao Zeballos, 1903–1904. (*Estud. Migr. Latinoam.*, 12:36, agosto 1997, p. 305–324)

A well-known Argentine intellectual and politician made a trip to Italy in 1903–04. While there, he reflected on Italian immigration. Paredes uses this discourse as an opportunity to examine the private thoughts of a key public figure. [JH]

2965 Pasolini, Ricardo O. Entre la evasión y el humanismo—lecturas, lectores y cultura de los sectores populares: La Biblioteca Juan B. Justo de Tandil, 1928–1945. (*Anu. IEHS*, 12, 1997, p. 373–401, appendix, graphs, tables)

Shows that members of the Socialist library in Tandil between 1928–45 read mostly fiction. Also discovers that the second most popular author of the time was right-wing anti-Semite Hugo Wast. [JH]

2966 Pasquali, Patricia. San Martín: la fuerza de la misión y la soledad de la gloria: biografía. Buenos Aires: Planeta, 1999. 460 p.: bibl., ill. (Historia argentina)

A well-written, sophisticated biography, based in part on archival documentation. Impressive for both the scholar and the casual reader. [TW]

2967 **Pasquaré, Andrea.** Las imágenes de la frontera sur argentina en la construcción del estado nacional. (*in* Reunión del Proyecto, *2nd, Salamanca, Spain, 1996.* Espacio en la cultura latinoamericana: diccionario analítico. Warsaw: Uniw. Warszawski, Centro de Estudios Latinoamericanos, 1997, p. 253–270, bibl.)

Argues persuasively that the occupation of Patagonia and the construction of the modern state were naturally reinforcing phenomena in the minds of most Argentines. [TW]

2968 **La patria en el riel: un siglo de lucha de los trabajadores ferroviarios.** Recopilación de Eduardo Lucita. Buenos Aires: Del Pensamiento Nacional, 1999. 251 p.: bibl., ill.

Presents four studies of key struggles by railroad workers. The chapters covering the movements of 1950–51, 1961, and 1990–92 were written by railroad workers (Héctor Laerte Franchi, Antonio Di Santo, and Eduardo Lucita). The fourth examination is a reprint of the now almost-classic study of the 1912 strike by Juan Suriano. [JH]

Paura, Vilma. El problema de la pobreza en Buenos Aires, 1778–1820. See item **2407.**

2969 **Los periodistas desaparecidos: las voces que necesitaba silenciar la dictadura.** Introducción de Juan Carlos Camaño. Prólogo de Osvaldo Bayer. Buenos Aires: Grupo Editorial Norma, 1998. 256 p.: ill.

Reprint of a 1986 work compiled by press workers about reporters who disappeared during the last military government. Provides brief histories and memories about the reporters. [JH]

2970 **Peronism and Argentina.** Edited by James P. Brennan. Wilmington, Del.: SR Books, 1998. 233 p.: bibl., index. (Latin American silhouettes)

An excellent collection intended to present the entire sweep of Peronism. Focuses on the intellectual debates about Peronism. Contains two important historiographical articles by Cristián Buchrucker and Mariano Plotkin. Especially noteworthy are Brennan's piece on business support for Perón and María Cecilia Cangiano's chapter on steel workers in Villa Constitución during the first years of the Menem presidency. [JH]

2971 **Perren, Jorge Enrique.** Puerto Belgrano y la revolución libertadora. Buenos Aires: Solaris, 1997. 515 p.

Memoir and history of the events surrounding the Revolución Libertadora in Puerto Belgrano, written by the port's commander. Provides detailed information on the plotting of the event as well as its execution. Carries story of the author's involvement in naval affairs through the first segment of the Frondizi government. [JH]

2972 **Philp, Marta.** En nombre de Córdoba: sabattinistas y peronistas: estrategias políticas en la construcción del estado. Córdoba, Argentina: Ferreyra Editor, 1998. 174 p.: bibl.

A thesis written for FLACSO (Mexico) which compares the growth of the provincial government of Córdoba during the years in which Amadeo Sabattini was governor with the growth during the time of Perón. Points out the similarities. [JH]

2973 **Pírez, Pedro.** La ciudad de Buenos Aires: una cuestión federal. (*Hist. Mex./México,* 46:4, abril/junio 1997, p. 193–212, bibl., tables)

Well-written examination of the 1880 federalization of Buenos Aires suggests that conflicts between the Argentine central government and that of the province of Buenos Aires made possible the design of local administrations that were clearly subordinate to national level decision-making processes. [TW]

2974 **Pisarello Virasoro, Roberto Gustavo** and **Emilia Edda Menotti.** Los Virasoro en la organización nacional. Prólogo de Carlos María R. Vargas Gómez. Buenos Aires: Ediciones Depalma, 1997. 472 p.: bibl., ill. (some col.), maps.

Well-crafted history of the Virasoro family, focusing on political and military affairs of the Confederation period. Particularly useful on Corrientes and the provinces of Cuyo. [TW]

2975 **Plotkin, Mariano Ben.** Freud in the Pampas: the emergence and development of a psychoanalytic culture in Argentina. Stanford, Calif.: Stanford Univ. Press, 2001. 314 p.: bibl., index.

Important contribution explains how and why psychoanalysis became such a major part of Argentine daily culture, thereby illuminating the general cultural evolution, especially during the 1960s and early 1970s. This well-written work combines scientific, intellectual, cultural, and political history. [JH]

2976 Plotkin, Mariano Ben. Tell me your dreams: psychoanalysis and popular culture in Buenos Aires, 1930–1950. (*Americas/Washington*, 55:4, April 1999, p. 601–629)

Psychoanalysis became part of the porteño popular discourse in the 1960s and Plotkin studies how it entered the popular consciousness. Demonstrates that, unlike in many other countries, in Argentina the discipline did not enter mainstream culture through literature. Shows the presence of psychoanalysis in three popular magazines. Well done. [JH]

2977 Podgorny, Irina. De la santidad laica del científico Florentino Ameghino y el espectáculo de la ciencia en la Argentina moderna. (*Entrepasados/Buenos Aires*, 6:13, 1997, p. 37–61, ill.)

Shows how and why a myth was created about the naturalist Ameghino in the years immediately following his death. Demonstrates how the making of the myth emerged from political divisions, nationalism, and visions of the definition and scope of science. [JH]

2978 Podgorny, Irina. Desde la tierra donde los monstruos aún no tienen nombre: el ordenamiento de la naturaleza a través de los museos y de la ciencia en la Confederación Argentina. (*Quipu/México*, 12:2, mayo/agosto 1999, p. 167–186)

Well-researched account of Argentine efforts to publicize the country's natural wonders to the outside world, using science museums and international exhibitions to legitimate an image of a modern, progressive Confederation. [TW]

2979 Poggi, Rinaldo Alberto. Alvaro Barros en la frontera sur: contribución al estudio de un argentino olvidado. Buenos Aires: Fundación Nuestra Historia, 1997. 157 p.: bibl., ill., maps. (Monografías; 2)

Well-written and informative biography of the military man who brought a measure of peace to the Bonaerense frontier in the 1860s by dealing openly and fairly with Calfucurá and other indigenous leaders. [TW]

2980 Política, médicos y enfermedades: lecturas de la historia de la salud en la Argentina. Recopilación de Mirta Zaida Lobato. Textos de Adriana Alvarez *et al.* Buenos Aires: Editorial Biblos, 1996. 246 p.: bibl., ill.

Important articles on the history of health in Argentina with a focus on Buenos Aires. Topics include the professionalization of the delivery of health care; epidemics in 19th century Rosario; and the medical discourses of Ramos Mejía, the Anarchists, and the Socialists. Also offers articles on the debate over the dropping birth rate and the use of contraceptives; the connection between law and medicine at the end of the 19th century; and whether the government's attempts to deal with social welfare problems in the 1940s were a radical change. [JH]

2981 Pozzi, Pablo A. and **Alejandro Schneider.** Los setentistas, izquierda y clase obrera, 1969–1976. Buenos Aires: Editorial Universitaria de Buenos Aires-EUDEBA, 2000. 458 p.: bibl. (Mundo contemporáneo)

Authors feel that the role of Marxists and unions have been neglected in studies of the 1960s and 1970s. They hope to change this. Much is based on a series of interviews with militants. Eight of the interviews are presented here. [JH]

2982 La primacía de la política: Lanusse, Perón y la Nueva Izquierda en tiempos del GAN. Recopilación de Alfredo Pucciarelli. Buenos Aires: Eudeba, 1999. 393 p.: bibl. (Estudios de sociología)

Offers an interesting collection of essays examining the turmoil surrounding the return of Juan Perón and the Peronists to power. Several chapters deal with the politics of the period, while others look at cultural aspects. [JH]

2983 Privitellio, Luciano de. Un caso de periodismo barrial: la imagen del barrio y el vecino en Boedo, 1936–1943. (*in* Jornadas de Historia de la Ciudad de Buenos Aires, 7th, *Buenos Aires?, 1990*. Texto y discurso. Buenos Aires: Gobierno de la Ciudad de Buenos Aires, Secretaría de Cultura, Subsecretaría de Desarrollo Cultura, Instituto Histórico de la Ciudad de Buenos Aires, 1997, t. 1, p. 383–401)

Examines the nature of a barrio in Buenos Aires through a study of a barrio newspaper. Well done. [JH]

2984 Quattrocchi-Woisson, Diana. Relaciones con la Argentina de funcionarios de Vichy y de colaboradores franceses y belgas, 1940–1960. (*Estud. Migr. Latinoam.*, 14:43, dic. 1999, p. 211–239)

A preliminary study of the movement to Argentina of Belgian and French collaborators with the Nazis after WWII. Shows the extent of the movement and helps illuminate the attitude of the Peronist government. [JH]

2985 Quijada, Mónica. La *ciudadanización* del "indio bárbaro": políticas oficiales y oficiosas hacia la población indígena de la pampa y la Patagonia, 1870–1920. (*Rev. Indias*, 59:217, sept./dic. 1999, p. 675–704)

Looks at policies toward the indigenous peoples of the pampas and Patagonia after the "conquest of the desert." Shows that attempts were made to include the indigenous peoples as citizens, but the policies largely failed. [JH]

2986 Quijada, Mónica and Víctor Peralta Ruiz. El triángulo Madrid-Berlín-Buenos Aires y el tránsito de bienes vinculados al Tercer Reich desde España a la Argentina. (*Ciclos Hist. Econ. Soc.*, 10:19, 2000, p. 129–149)

Looks at the three-sided relationship during WWII between Madrid, Berlin, and Buenos Aires. Argues that information on the transference of German assets to Buenos Aires through Madrid cannot be found. [JH]

2987 Quintar, Juan. Los trabajadores en los orígenes del Movimiento Popular Neuquino. (*Entrepasados/Buenos Aires*, 7:14, 1998, p. 21–43)

Looks at this provincial party in Neuquén which maintained itself as both independent and Peronist simultaneously. The working class was deeply Peronist but resentment against Buenos Aires existed and workers made gains under the provincial party. Partially based on judicial documents. [JH]

2988 Ramírez Braschi, Dardo. Evaristo López, un gobernador federal: Corrientes en tiempos de la Guerra de la Triple Alianza. Corrientes, Argentina: D. Ramírez Braschi, 1997. 116 p.: bibl.

Painstaking reconstruction of Co-

rrentino political life during the Paraguayan War, focusing on the career of López, a minor figure in the Federal movement of Urquiza and Nicanor Cáceres. Based on archival sources. [TW]

2989 Ramírez Braschi, Dardo. La guerra de la Triple Alianza a través de los periódicos correntinos, 1865–1870. Estudio preliminar de Benjamín Vargas Peña. Corrientes, Argentina: Amerindia Ediciones, 2000. 295 p.: bibl.

Thoroughly researched account of Correntino journalism during the Paraguayan War, a conflict that saw local newspapermen both support and oppose the Argentine national government. [TW]

2990 Rapalo, María Ester. Los empresarios y la reacción conservadora en la Argentina: las publicaciones de la Asociación del Trabajo, 1919–1922. (*Anu. IEHS*, 12, 1997, p. 425–441)

Analyzes the publications of the right-wing employer association created to try to enforce labor peace. Looks particularly at *La Concordia*, which was intended to influence the workers themselves. [JH]

2991 Rapoport, Mario and Andrés Musacchio. El Banco Central de la República Argentina y el "oro nazi": certezas y interrogantes sobre un mito histórico. (*Ciclos Hist. Econ. Soc.*, 10:19, 2000, p. 77–101)

Examines existing sources on the movement of gold into the Argentine Banco Central during WWII and finds no evidence of a significant amount of gold entering the country from Germany. In particular, looks at movement of gold from neutral states such as Switzerland and Portugal, which might have been used to launder the gold. Thoughtful and careful. [JH]

2992 Ratto, Silvia. La estructura de poder en las tribus amigas de la provincia de Buenos Aires, 1830–1850. (*Quinto Sol/Santa Rosa*, 1:1, 1997, p. 75–102, bibl.)

Rosas' policy of supplying cattle to friendly indigenous peoples on the Bonaerense frontier changed power relations with those groups. Through the distribution of rations, certain caciques gained power over others. These same policies, while helpful in maintaining peace, made indigenous groups highly dependent on the government. Well documented. [TW]

2993 Reber, Vera Blinn. Misery, pain and death: tuberculosis in nineteenth century Buenos Aires. (*Americas/Washington,* 56:4, April 2000, p. 497–528)

Award-winning account of early Argentine reactions to tuberculosis, focusing on both hygenic campaigns and porteño social attitudes. [TW]

2994 Reggini, Horacio C. Sarmiento y las telecomunicaciones: la obsesión del hilo. Buenos Aires: Ediciones Galápago, 1997. 243 p.: bibl., ill., index.

First-class study of early telegraphy in Argentina, focusing on Sarmiento's efforts to promote modern communications in his country (and his fascination with gadgetry as a means of building a civilized order). Recommended. [TW]

2995 Rein, Mónica Esti. Politics and education in Argentina, 1946–1962. Translated by Martha Grenzeback. Armonk, N.Y.: M.E. Sharpe, 1998. 225 p.: bibl., index. (Latin American realities)

Studies the impact of politics on education during the Peronist era and its direct aftermath. Looking at all three levels of education, uses the educational system to draw conclusions about the political system. Does not attempt to analyze the impact of educational policy on the students. Particularly useful for the Peronist era. [JH]

2996 Rein, Raanan. Peronismo, populismo y política: Argentina, 1943–1955. Traducción de Eliezer Nowodworski. Buenos Aires: Editorial de Belgrano, 1998. 282 p.: bibl., index.

A series of loosely connected and interesting essays on Peronist Argentina. One chapter discusses the concept of populism in relation to peronismo, arguing for the importance of secondary figures to mediate between Perón and his followers. Topics of other chapters include foreign policy (relying heavily on the Braumaglia papers), as well as primary school policies and efforts to use sports to attract political support. [JH]

2997 Las relaciones exteriores de la Argentina embrionaria. v. 1–6. Argentina: Centro de Estudios de Política Exterior: Consejo Argentino para las Relaciones Internacionales; Buenos Aires: Nuevohacer, Grupo Editor Latinoamericano: Distribuidor exclusivo, Galerna, 1998. 6 v.: bibl., ill., maps.

(Historia general de las relaciones exteriores de la República Argentina) (Col. Estudios internacionales)

An impressive six-volume study of Argentine diplomacy focusing on the confused period of national definition in the 1800s. Unlike many treatments that allude to an inexorable "Argentina-in-the-making," this study stresses the weak and conditional character of the new nation-state. Rejects the oft-told tale of massive Argentine territorial loss, noting instead that the Plata was a "constellation of mini-states," each with its own interests and politics, some of which gravitated toward Buenos Aires (others did not). There was little inevitable about the process—as the various foreign interventions and the Paraguayan War clearly demonstrated. Backed by a large array of archival and secondary sources, this study is perhaps the most innovative work on Argentine foreign relations to appear in some time. [TW]

2998 Retrato de un siglo: una visión integral de Santiago del Estero desde 1898 en el centenario del diario *El Liberal.* Bajo la dirección de Julio César Castiglione. Con la colaboración de Elsa Castillo de Giménez. Santiago del Estero, Argentina: Editorial El Liberal, 1998. 465 p.: bibl., ill. (some col.), maps (some col.).

Written to commemorate the centenary of the newspaper *El Liberal,* presents a solid history of the last 100 years of Santiago del Estero. Covers politics, economics, and demographics. Useful. [JH]

2999 Richard Jorba, Rodolfo A. Poder, economía y espacio en Mendoza, 1850–1900: del comercio ganadero a la agroindustria vitivinícola. Mendoza, Argentina: Univ. Nacional de Cuyo, Facultad de Filosofía y Letras, 1998. 347 p.: bibl., ill., maps.

Sophisticated analysis of economic development in Mendoza in the second half of the 1800s. Shows in clear detail how ranching elites were eclipsed by wine production. [TW]

3000 Rivas, Ricardo Alberto. Abreu e Lima, Páez y la élite argentina. (*Cuad. CISH,* 3:4, segundo semestre 1998, p. 119–140)

Interesting examination of Argentine elite politics in the 1860s, as reflected in a letter of Venezuelan caudillo José Antonio Páez. [TW]

3001 Rocchi, Fernando. Consumir es un placer: la industria y la expansión de la demanda en Buenos Aires a la vuelta del siglo pasado. (*Desarro. Econ.*, 37:148, enero/marzo 1998, p. 533–558, table)

An interesting look at how the growing consumer society of turn-of-the century Buenos Aires shaped the process of industrialization. An important first step in examining the nature of consumption in Argentina. [JH]

3002 Rocchi, Fernando. El imperio del pragmatismo: intereses, ideas e imágenes en la política industrial del orden conservador. (*Anu. IEHS*, 13, 1998, p. 99–130, table)

After a solid discussion of the existing literature on early industrialization in which most authors insist that tariffs were low and the government did little to encourage industrialization, Rocchi shows that a significant portion of the political elite were supportive of high tariffs and worked to implement those ideas. [JH]

3003 Rock, David. Argentina under Mitre: porteño liberalism in the 1860s. (*Americas/Washington*, 56:1, July 1999, p. 31–63)

Well-crafted account of the liberal order established by Mitre in the 1860s includes interesting details on policy failures and contradictions, especially in the western provinces. Oddly lacking in coverage of the Paraguayan War. Based partly on Foreign Office documentation. [TW]

3004 Rodríguez Molas, Ricardo E. Presencia de África negra en la Argentina: etnias, religión y esclavitud. (*Desmemoria/Buenos Aires*, 6:21/22, enero/junio 1999, p. 33–70, appendices, ill.)

Some summary thoughts on the history and culture of Afro-Argentines. Includes as appendices several archival documents on the marketing of slaves and the organization of African philanthropic societies. [TW]

3005 Romero, Luis Alberto. Católicos en movimiento: activismo en una parroquia de Buenos Aires, 1935–1946. (*Estud. Soc./Santa Fe*, 8:14, primer semestre 1998, p. 89–104)

Part of a revived interest in the history of Catholicism merged with the author's well-known work on Buenos Aires neighborhoods. Looks at the growth of activism in a new parish in Buenos Aires in the context of the Catholic revival of the 1930s. Based primarily on a parochial newspaper. [JH]

3006 Rosal, Miguel A. La exportación de cueros, lana y tasajo a través del puerto de Buenos Aires entre 1835 y 1854. (*Anu. Estud. Am.*, 55:2, julio/dic. 1998, p. 565–588, graphs, tables)

Well-researched piece confirms the general interpretation that Buenos Aires province dominated the hide, wool, and dried beef trade during the Rosas period. [TW]

3007 Rosas, Manuelita. Manuelita Rosas y Antonino Reyes: el olvidado epistolario, 1889–1897. Buenos Aires: Archivo General de la Nación, 1998. 117 p.: ill. (Col. Edición de fuentes; 1)

A collection of 63 letters, 59 of which were written by Manuelita Rosas from her long London exile. Once the hostess of Palermo, and a woman to be feared during her father's dictatorship, by the 1890s she was reduced to recounting medical complaints and details of housekeeping. [TW]

3008 Ruiz Jiménez, Laura. El debate económico en la prensa argentina durante la gran depresión: detractores y nostálgicos del libre comercio. (*Anu. IEHS*, 15, 2000, p. 267–286)

By examining newspapers with the largest circulation, argues that the abandonment of the idea of free trade came about much more slowly than is usually thought. [JH]

3009 Ruiz Moreno, Isidoro J. Alianza contra Rosas: Paz-Ferré-Rivera-López. Buenos Aires: Academia Nacional de la Historia, 1999. 240 p.: bibl.

Sophisticated examination of various unitarian, liberal, and regional interests and how they constructed an anti-Rosas alliance in the early 1840s. [TW]

3010 Sábato, Hilda. La política en las calles: entre el voto y la movilización: Buenos Aires, 1862–1880. Buenos Aires: Editorial Sudamericana, 1998. 290 p.: bibl., ill. (Col. Historia y cultura)

Ambitious, well-written analysis studies the political culture of Buenos Aires in the 1860s-70s, arguing that politics was a much more disputed field than previously thought. Looks at electioneering, voting, and political mobilization. Also examines the nature of civic culture, including the politics of demonstrations. Makes deft use of contemporary newspapers. Excellent work. Also available in English as *The Many and the Few: Political Participation in Republican Buenos Aires* (2001). [JH/TW]

3011 Saítta, Sylvia. El escritor en el bosque de ladrillos: una biografía de Roberto Arlt. Buenos Aires: Editorial Sudamericana, 2000. 325 p.: bibl.

A well-written and thoughtful biography of Arlt that places him in the period in which he lived and wrote. Sees him as a key participant in a changing intellectual environment in which authors began to address mass audiences. Contains a list of all of his writings, including those printed in newspapers. [JH]

3012 Saítta, Sylvia. Recueros de tinta: el diario *Crítica* en la década de 1920. Buenos Aires: Editorial Sudamericana, 1998. 316 p.: bibl. (Col. Historia y cultura)

An excellent intellectual history of the influential and sensational afternoon paper, *Crítica*. Covers the period from 1913–32, with particular attention paid to the Radical years. Looks at the topics that the paper covered, how its approach changed over time, and the impact of the paper on society. Well grounded in the period and contextualized by theoretical works. [JH]

3013 Salduna, Horacio. La muerte romántica del general Ramírez. Buenos Aires: Corregidor, 1998. 223 p.: bibl., ill.

Attempts to shed light on the death of Gen. Francisco Ramírez—the "Supreme Entrerriano"—who perished trying to save the paramour who had accompanied him while on campaign. Also includes a broad discussion of Ramírez's place in Platine historiography. [TW]

3014 Salvatore, Ricardo Donato. Los crímenes de los paisanos: una aproximación estadística. (*Anu. IEHS*, 12, 1997, p. 91–100)

Examines the official statistics on crime in the Bonaerense countryside from 1831–51. Suggests that violent crimes against persons were far less prevalent than has hitherto been suggested. [TW]

3015 Santiago Sanz, Luis. El caso Baltimore: una contribución al esclarecimiento de la actitud argentina. Buenos Aires: Instituto de Publicaciones Navales de Centro Naval, 1998. 239 p.: bibl., ill. (1280 título de las Ediciones del Instituto de Publicaciones Navales. Vigésimo sexto libro de la Col. Historia)

An attractive diplomatic study of Argentine reactions to the 1891 Baltimore incident between the US and Chile. Notes that Argentina was prepared to aid the Americans against the Santiago government, if necessary in alliance with Peru. [TW]

3016 Santos Martínez, Pedro. El conflicto político sanjuanino de noviembre de 1852: notas para su estudio. (*Invest. Ens.*, 47, 1997, p. 99–115)

Detailed account of political infighting in the wake of Caseros. Examines how such conflicts permitted a readjustment of interests among San Juan, Parana, and Buenos Aires. [TW]

3017 Sarmiento, Domingo Faustino. Campaña en el Ejército Grande aliado de Sud América. Edición, prólogo y notas de Tulio Halperín Donghi. Buenos Aires: Univ. Nacional de Quilmes, 1997. 306 p. (La ideología argentina)

A new edition of a classic work, this one introduced by Halperín-Donghi, who places the *Campaña* within a general context of 1850s Platine politics. [TW]

3018 Sarmiento, Domingo Faustino. Correspondencia de Sarmiento: enero-mayo 1862. Argentina: Edición de la Asociación de Amigos del Museo Histórico Sarmiento, 1997. 294 p.

A collection of transcribed letters to and from Sarmiento during the first few months of 1862. Between the time of Pavón and his nomination by President Mitre as minister to the US, Sarmiento served as governor of San Juan. In addition to his provincial duties, Sarmiento maintained an avid correspondence with politicians and scholars, which explains the broad number of subjects covered by these documents. [TW]

3019 Scarzanella, Eugenia. El ocio peronista: vacaciones y "turismo popular" en Argentina, 1943–1955. (*Entrepasados/ Buenos Aires,* 7:14, 1998, p. 65–84)

Studies how the Peronist government of the 1940s-50s helped shape the working class's use of free time. In doing so, the government changed how many Argentines lived and established a pattern for later years. A well-done work that sets the stage for further study. [JH]

3020 Schaller, Enrique Cesar. La legislación sobre derechos aduaneros de la provincia de Corrientes, 1810–1855. (*Folia Hist. Nordeste,* 13, 1997, p. 143–195)

Cogent examination of *correntino* trade policies from independence to the nationalization of the customs house in 1855. Based on thorough archival research. [TW]

3021 Schvarzer, Jorge. Nuevas perspectivas sobre el origen del desarrollo industrial argentino, 1880–1930. (*Anu. IEHS,* 13, 1998, p. 77–97, bibl.)

A thought-provoking essay looks at the classic question of why growth slowed in Argentina after 50 years of rapid economic expansion. [JH]

3022 Schwarzstein, Dora. Actores sociales y política inmigratoria en la Argentina: la llegada de los republicanos españoles. (*Estud. Migr. Latinoam.,* 12:37, dic. 1997, p. 423–445)

Teases a great deal from a single event—the permission to land given to 60 Spanish Republican intellectuals who arrived on a single ship. The permission was obtained through the intervention of the owner of the newspaper *Crítica,* Natalio Botana. Analyzes Botana's role as well as some of the cleavages that the Spanish Civil War produced in Argentine society. [JH]

3023 Segreti, Carlos S.A. Un caos de intrigas: estrategia británica, maquinaciones lusitanas, desconcierto español y acción revolucionaria en el Río de la Plata, 1808–1812. Buenos Aires: Academia Nacional de la Historia, 1997. 372 p.: bibl., indexes. (Biblioteca de historia argentina y americana; t. 24)

Aptly titled study discusses the confusing events surrounding Argentine independence. Segreti is especially skilled at explaining the maneuverings of those factions that favored a pro-Portuguese monarchy under Princess Carlota Joaquina. [TW]

3024 Seoane, María. El burgués maldito. 2. ed. Buenos Aires: Planeta, 1998. 467 p.: bibl., ill., index. (Espejo de la Argentina)

A well-done, popular biography of one of the most interesting figures in modern Argentina, José Ber Gelbard. A Polish-born Jew, Gelbard became a businessman, and was the force behind the Confederación General Económica in Argentina as well as economic minister for Perón upon his return in the 1970s. Simultaneously, he helped to bankroll the Communist Party and maintained close ties to the Israelis. The work lacks footnotes, making its assertions impossible to verify. [JH]

3025 Serie Archivo Alvear. v. 1, La crisis de 1930. v. 2, La abstención del radicalismo, 1931–1934. Buenos Aires: Instituto Torcuato Di Tella, 1997–99. 2 v.

Compiles the political correspondence of Marcelo T. De Alvear. Alvear received many more letters than he wrote and he wrote very little, but the letters he received, principally from a wide range of Radical party figures, are vital for political history. Vol. 1 covers March 9, 1929-Aug. 31, 1931, and vol. 2 covers Aug. 3, 1931-Feb. 4, 1934. The senders or recipients are identified where possible, constituting the only editorial comments. Also includes useful political chronologies abstracted from the press. [JH]

3026 Servetto, Alicia. El derrumbe temprano de la democracia en Córdoba: Obregón Cano y el golpe policial, 1973–1974. (*Estud. Soc./Santa Fe,* 9:17, segundo semestre 1999, p. 91–109)

Examines the political context in which the Peronist governor identified with the left wing of the movement was overthrown by the police with the approval of Perón. [JH]

3027 Sierra e Iglesias, Jobino Pedro. Un tiempo que se fue: vida y obra de los hermanos Leach en el Departamento San Pedro, Provincia de Jujuy, Argentina. San Pedro de Jujuy, Argentina: Municipalidad de San Pedro de Jujuy: Univ. Nacional de Jujuy: Provincia de Jujuy, 1998. 511 p.: bibl., ill., maps. (Col. Arte-ciencia. Serie Jujuy en el pasado)

Details the role of a key Anglo-Argentine family in the development of the Jujeño sugar industry. Although text is spotty, work does include excellent photographs. Especially good on coverage of the settlement of the Upper Bermejo during the late 1800s. [TW]

3028 Sobre maestros y escuelas: una mirada a la educación desde la historia, Neuquén, 1884–1957. Bajo la dirección de Mirta Teobaldo. Con la codirección de Amelia Beatriz García. Rosario, Argentina: Arca Sur Editorial, 2000. 320 p.: bibl., ill.

Diverse essays on education in Neuquén. Does not attempt to be comprehensive. Worthwhile for those interested in schooling in Argentina. [JH]

3029 Stewart, Iain A.D. Living with dictator Rosas: Argentina through Scottish eyes. (*J. Lat. Am. Stud.,* 29:1, Feb. 1997, p. 23–44)

Offers a perceptive analysis of the Rosas era as seen through the eyes of Robert and George Gibson, pioneering sheepbreeders and merchants who were well-situated to interpret the politics of Argentina in the 1830s. [TW]

3030 Suriano, Juan. Anarquistas: cultura y política libertaria en Buenos Aires, 1890–1910. Buenos Aires: Manantial, 2001. 361 p.: bibl. (Cuadernos argentinos)

An excellent look at the ideological and cultural world created by anarchists in Buenos Aires. Based solidly in the sources and well aware of previous work on the topic. [JH]

3031 Suriano, Juan. Las prácticas políticas del anarquismo argentino. (*Rev. Indias,* 57:210, mayo/agosto 1997, p. 421–450)

An intellectual history of Argentine anarchist ideas about politics prior to the opening of the political system. Looks at ideas about abstention from voting, revolutionary general strikes, and direct action. Argues that the Ley Sáenz Peña helped to marginalize anarchism. For philosophy specialist's comment, see item **4833**. [JH]

3032 Taboada, María Stella and **Héctor Angel Lobo.** Los dueños de la zafra: vida y trabajos en un ingenio azucarero. Tucumán, Argentina: CERPACU, 1996. 135 p.: bibl., ill. (Col. Patrimonio. Serie La memoria oral; 2)

Taboada conducted an oral history with Lobo, who was a sugar worker and union leader in Tucumán directly before and after 1943. Provides interesting information on living and working conditions in the province. [JH]

3033 Tanzi, Héctor José. Juan José Paso, el político. Buenos Aires: Ciudad Argentina, 1998. 376 p.: bibl., ill.

Readable, well-documented biography of Paso (1758–1833), a minor porteño statesman and diplomat whose period of influence saw the coming of independence and the rise and fall of the early unitarian regimes. [TW]

3034 Tcach, César. La experiencia Nores Martínez: entre la Córdoba de las campanas y la ciudad obrera. (*Estud. Soc./Santa Fe,* 9:17, segundo semestre 1999, p. 69–89)

Political history with an unusual approach. Examines the attempt by a member of the traditional Catholic elite to rule Córdoba during the presidency of Guido. Shows how this effort was impossible given the rapidly changing nature of the society. [JH]

3035 Terragno, Rodolfo H. Maitland & San Martín. Buenos Aires: Univ. Nacional de Quilmes, 1998. 261 p.: bibl., index. (Documentos)

A curious and somewhat speculative look at possible collusion between San Martín and British agents during the struggle for control of Chile and Peru. Fascinating, but difficult to interpret, despite solid use of archival documentation. [TW]

3036 Tica, Patricia Ana. La inseguridad en la campaña santafesina en tiempos de la confederación, 1852–1861. (*Res Gesta,* 36, 1997, p. 51–93, graphs, map, tables)

In-depth study of rustling and social disorder in Santa Fe province during the Urquiza years. Based on contemporary newspapers and archival documentation. [TW]

3037 Tolcachier, Fabiana Sabina. The historiography of Jewish immigration to Argentina: problems and perspectives. (*in* Arab and Jewish immigrants in Latin America: images and realities. Edited by Ignacio Klich and Jeffrey Lesser. London; Portland, Ore.: F. Cass, 1998, p. 204–226)

A thoughtful presentation of the historiography of the Jewish presence in Argentina. A good place to begin an investigation. [JH]

3038 Torres, Elpidio. El cordobazo organizado: la historia sin mitos. Buenos Aires: Catálogos, 1999. 254 p.: bibl., ill.

The long-time head of the Córdoba branch of the mechanics union (SMATA) argues for his own key role in creating the Cordabazo. [JH]

3039 Tripaldi, Nicolás María. Las primeras bibliotecas socialistas de la Ciudad de Buenos Aires 1894–1899. (*Rev. Univ./La Plata,* 31, 1996/97, p. 79–87, bibl.)

A short but interesting look at the three libraries operated by socialist organizations in Buenos Aires during the 1890s. The libraries were small and irregularly run but nonetheless lively places where then-current economic theory was avidly discussed and political tracts penned. [TW]

3040 El trotskismo obrero e internacionalista en la Argentina. v. 3, Palabra obrera, el PRT y la Revolución Cubana. Buenos Aires: Editorial Antídoto, 1999. 1 v.

The third installment of the official history of the Trotskyist faction led by Nahuel Moreno. Volume covers the spreading impact of the Cuban Revolution. This volume is less tightly focused on the activities of the Argentine Trotskyists. For review of vol. 1, see *HLAS 56:3140.* For review of vol. 2, see *HLAS 58:3063.* [JH]

3041 Ulanovsky, Carlos. Paren las rotativas: una historia de grandes diarios, revistas y periodistas argentinos. Con la colaboración de Ana Laura Pérez and Fernando Cáceres. Asistencia periodística de Ricardo Dios Zaid and Ligia López. Buenos Aires: Espasa, 1997. 524 p.: bibl., ill., index.

A popular history of the press—newspapers and magazines—in Argentina. Heavy focus on Buenos Aires and the last three decades. [JH]

3042 Urquiza, Fernando Carlos. La reforma eclesiástica de Rivadavia: viejos datos y una nueva interpretación. (*Anu. IEHS,* 13, 1998, p. 237–246)

Analyzes tensions within the Bonaerense church just prior to the regalist reforms of the 1820s. Concludes that secular clergy benefitted from reforms while regular clergy did not. [TW]

3043 Uzal, Francisco Hipólito. La conciencia nacional y el enfrentamiento de Obligado. (*in* Congreso Nacional de Historia Argentina, *Buenos Aires, 1995.* Congreso Nacional de Historia Argentina: celebrado en la Ciudad de Buenos Aires del 23 al 25 de noviembre de 1995 bajo la advocación de los 150 años de la Batalla de la Vuelta de Obligado/entidades convocantes, Archivo General de la Nación *et al.* Buenos Aires: Comisión Post Congreso Nacional de Historia Argentina, 1997, t. 1, p. 297–310)

Jejune speculation on Argentine "national" reactions to the Anglo-French intervention of the 1840s. [TW]

3044 Vagliente, Pablo. Fiesta en todos lados: el carnaval en su marco regional; Córdoba y sus pueblos, 1890–1912. (*Estud. Soc./Santa Fe,* 10:18, primer semestre 2000, p. 103–122)

Examines carnival in the province of Córdoba as it developed in regional centers. Ties the festivities to the increasing trend of families leaving the city for more remote areas during the summer. [JH]

3045 Vale, Brian. A war betwixt Englishmen: Brazil against Argentina on the River Plate, 1825–1830. London; New York: I.B. Tauris, 2000. 275 p., 8 p. of plates: bibl., ill., index, maps.

Self-explanatory title effectively introduces this broad, well-crafted account of the Cisplatine conflict on the high seas. With the focus more on the naval war than land engagements, the English dimension may be slightly exaggerated. Even so, this work is a solid contribution backed by an array of archival documents from the PRO and elsewhere. [TW]

3046 Vázquez Rial, Horacio. La formación del país de los argentinos. Buenos Aires: J. Vergara Editor, 1999. 402 p.: bibl., maps.

A perceptive analysis of the politics of Argentine demography from the colonial period through the early 1900s. Succeeds at debunking the *leyenda negra* of the earliest commentators (Funes *et al.*) and the *leyenda rosa* of the subsequent nationalist writers. Well worth reading. [TW]

3047 Velcamp, Theresa Alfaro. The historiography of Arab immigration to Argentina: the intersection of the imaginary and the real country. (*in* Arab and Jewish immigrants in Latin America: images and realities. Edited by Ignacio Klich and Jeffrey Lesser. London; Portland, Ore.: F. Cass, 1998, p. 227–248)

Presents a general overview of Arab immigration to Argentina and a review of what has been written on the topic. Attempts to evaluate the perception of Arabs in the country over time and discusses the significance of the findings. [JH]

3048 Vera de Flachs, María Cristina. Finanzas, saberes y vida cotidiana en el Colegio Monserrat: del antiguo al nuevo régimen. Córdoba, Argentina: Univ. Nacional de Córdoba, 1999. 274 p.: bibl., ill.

Finely researched, well-executed study of the Colegio Nacional de Monserrat, for many years the key institution of higher education in colonial Argentina. Portrays the school first as a center of civilization on an isolated frontier, then as a bastion of tradition (even reaction), and finally as a site for partisan rivalry in the 19th century. [TW]

3049 Vida y muerte de la república verdadera, 1910–1930. Recopilación de Tulio Halperín Donghi. Buenos Aires: Editorial Planeta Argentina: Ariel, 1999. 671 p.: bibl. (Biblioteca del pensamiento argentino; 4) (Ariel historia)

Part of a series collecting documents that attempt to lay bare the ideological underpinnings of the period studied. The almost 400 pages of primary sources are from a wide variety of places and are quite revealing. A penetrating 251-page discussion of the period introduces the sources. A crucial work for understanding the *república verdadera* period. [JH]

3050 Vidal, Gardenia. El Partido Demócrata y sus tensiones internas: diferentes perspectivas sobre ciudadanía y participación; Córdoba 1922–1925. (*Cuad. Hist. Ser. Econ. Soc.*, 3, 2000, p. 169–206)

Looks at the problems within the Conservative Party and how this tension brought out crucial ideological differences. [JH]

3051 Villa de Caride, Sandra. Orígenes del cooperativismo agrario en el sur de la Provincia de Santa Fe: el caso de la cooperativa de Alvarez. (*Res Gesta*, 36, 1997, p. 95–113)

A short history of a cooperative founded in Alvarez, Santa Fe prov., during the upheaval in the humid pampas in the years directly following WWI. [JH]

3052 Villanueva, Guillermo H. La complicada vida de Pablo Villanueva entre federales y unitarios de Mendoza. (*Rev. Junta Estud. Hist. Mendoza*, 2, 1998, p. 31–54, bibl.)

One family's experience in navigating the complicated political waters of Mendoza during the unitario-federal struggles of the early 1800s. [TW]

3053 Villar, Daniel and Juan Francisco Jiménez. *Aindiados*, indígenas y política en la frontera bonaerense, 1827–1830. (*Quinto Sol/Santa Rosa*, 1:1, 1997, p. 103–146, bibl.)

Curious study of Chilean veterans who opted to live with the indigenous peoples of the Pampas after the wars of independence. Several of these "renegades" became important middlemen between indigenous and white communities. [TW]

3054 Villar, Daniel; Juan Francisco Jiménez; and Silvia Ratto. Relaciones inter-étnicas en el sur bonaerense, 1810–1830. Presentación de Raúl J. Mandrini. Bahía Blanca, Argentina: Depto. de Humanidades, Univ. Nacional del Sur; Buenos Aires: Instituto de Estudios Histórico-Sociales, Univ. Nacional del Centro de la Provincia de Buenos Aires, 1998. 287 p.: bibl.

Presents three useful studies on indigenous-white relations on the bonaerense frontier, together with a curious record-book (from Aug.-Dec. 1830) of the frontier post at Bahia Blanca. [TW]

3055 Viñas, David. De Sarmiento a Dios: viajeros argentinos a USA. Buenos Aires: Editorial Sudamericana, 1998. 357 p.

Compelling, fascinating analysis of Argentine travelers to the US. Discusses their reactions to their travels and the implications of their American experiences for Argentine culture. Figures covered include Alberdi, Sarmiento, Eduarda Mansilla, Paul Groussac, Eduardo Wilde, Carlos Pellegrini, José Ingenieros, Victoria Ocampo, and Alberto Vanasco. [TW]

3056 Yankelevich, Pablo. Miradas australes: propaganda, cabildeo y proyección de la Revolución Mexicana en el Río de la Plata,

1910–1930. México: Instituto Nacional de Estudios Históricos de la Revolución Mexicana: Secretaría de Relaciones Exteriores, 1997. 418 p.: bibl., ill., index.

Based on extensive use of archives in Mexico and Argentina, as well as newspapers and other periodicals, studies the impact of the Mexican Revolution on Argentine diplomacy and the Argentine intellectual world. Pays particular attention to Mexican attempts to shape that reaction. Extremely thorough and detailed. [JH]

3057 Zanatta, Loris. Perón y el mito de la nación católica: Iglesia y Ejército en los orígenes del peronismo, 1943–1946. Traducción de Luciana Daelli. Buenos Aires: Editorial Sudamericana, 1999. 452 p.: bibl. (Col. Historia y cultura)

A more detailed continuation of *HLAS 58:3074.* Largely intellectual history of the Catholic Church's role in creating the atmosphere that made the rise of Perón possible. Shows how the Church reacted to the complex world at war and what it wanted to see in Argentina. A very important work. [JH]

3058 Zaragoza Rovira, Gonzalo. Anarquismo argentino, 1876–1902. Madrid: De la Torre, 1996. 539 p.: bibl. (Col. Nuestro mundo; 47. Serie Historia)

The product of 25 years of research in archives and obscure journals and newspapers, this in-depth study of Argentine anarchism is a must-read for any scholar of Latin American labor history. Touches *in extenso* on anarcho-syndicalist theory, popular poetry, theater, and bourgeois reactions to anarchist activities. [TW]

3059 Zimmermann, Eduardo A. La prensa y la oposición política en la Argentina de comienzos de siglo: el caso de *La Nación* y el Partido Republicano. (*Estud. Soc./Santa Fe,* 8:15, segundo semestre 1998, p. 45–70, tables)

Well-written, focused study of Argentine journalism, and the political activities of *La Nación* in the twilight of Bartolomé Mitre's editorship. [TW]

PARAGUAY

3060 Areces, Nidia R. La expansión criolla en la frontera norte del Paraguay: estancieros y chacreros en Concepción, 1773–

1840. (*Rev. Eur. Estud. Latinoam. Caribe,* 62, June 1997, p. 54–69, bibl., map)

Deft examination of the growth of the cattle frontier in Paraguay during the late 18th century. Inexplicably omits reference to the critical works of Renee Ferrer de Arrellaga. [TW]

3061 Areces, Nidia R. Los Mbayás en la frontera norte paraguaya: guerra e intercambio en Concepción, 1773–1840. (*Anos 90,* 9, julho 1998, p. 56–82)

Carefully crafted account of indigenous-white relations along Paraguay's northern frontier with Brazil. Roughly comparable to John Hoyt Williams' earlier works on the "deadly selva." [TW]

3062 Ashwell, Washington. Concepción, 1947: cincuenta años después. Asunción: W. Ashwell, 1998. 529 p.: bibl.

A detailed account of the convoluted political and military events of 1946–47 with primary attention paid to the activities of the political parties. Written by a militant in the Colorado Party who participated in the events as a young man. [JH]

3063 Baratti, Danilo and Patrizia Candolfi. Vida y obra del sabio Bertoni: Moisés Santiago Bertoni, 1857–1929: un naturalista suizo en Paraguay. Asunción: Helvetas, 1999. 334 p.: bibl., ill., maps (some col.).

A tight, well-crafted biography of the Italian-Swiss naturalist who pioneered the study of Paraguayan linguistics, botany, biology, and anthropology at the beginning of the 1900s. Includes an extensive selection of his letters and some excellent illustrations. [TW]

Brezzo, Liliana María. La Argentina y el Paraguay: 1852–1860. See item **2799.**

3064 Brezzo, Liliana María. Civiles y militares durante la ocupación de Asunción: imágenes del espacio urbano, 1869. (*Res Gesta,* 37, 1998/99, p. 23–53)

A broad vignette of Asunción under Allied military occupation at the end of the Paraguayan War. Demonstrates that, although his army had already been destroyed, Solano López could nonetheless continue to command a measure of support in urban areas. [TW]

3065 Burton, Richard Francis, Sir. Cartas desde los campos de batalla del Paraguay. Traducción de Rosa María Torlaschi. Buenos Aires: Librería "El Foro," 1998. 584 p.: bibl., ill., map (folded).

New translation of a classic work on the Paraguayan War, originally written in 1870 by the famous British explorer (and then-consul at Santos). Continues to be a crucial tool for anyone interested in the conflict. [TW]

3066 Casabianca, Ange-François. Una guerra desconocida: la campaña del Chaco Boreal, 1932–1935. v. 1–7. Asunción: Lector, 1999–2000. 7 v.: bibl., maps.

A massive translation of a 7-vol. doctoral dissertation by a Frenchman, written at the Univ. de Paris III (1995). Claims to be more objective than past works on the Chaco War. The first two volumes discuss the lead-up to the war. The remaining five volumes cover the war itself. [JH]

3067 Colección del centenario salesiano: salesianos, 100 años en Paraguay. v. 1, San Juan Bosco y el Paraguay. Asunción: Sociedad Salesiana del Paraguay, Editorial Don Bosco, 1996. 1 v.: bibl., ill.

Spotty account of Juan Bosco (1815–88), Italian founder of the Salesian Order. Notes that Bosco's plans to open Paraguay to new missionary efforts were realized only after his death. [TW]

3068 Colección del centenario salesiano: salesianos, 100 años en Paraguay. v. 3, Monseñor Juan Sinforiano Bogarín y los salesianos. Asunción: Sociedad Salesiana del Paraguay, Editorial Don Bosco, 1996. 1 v.: bibl., ill.

Presents a short biographical sketch of Bogarín—modern Paraguay's most important cleric—who for 54 years (1895–1949) served as bishop, then archbishop, of Asunción. [TW]

3069 Colección del centenario salesiano: salesianos, 100 años en Paraguay. v. 4, La venida de los salesianos al Paraguay. Asunción: Sociedad Salesiana del Paraguay, Editorial Don Bosco, 1996. 1 v.: bibl., ill.

Brief, informative essay on the experience of the Salesian Order in Paraguay. Though small in numbers, the order had a great impact in the country throughout the 20th century. [TW]

3070 Colección del centenario salesiano: salesianos, 100 años en Paraguay. v. 5, Salesianos y comunidades de la Inspectoría Paraguaya en su primer centenario, 1896–1996: con la lista general de ingreso al trabajo, por año, y la nómina, por order alfabético. Asunción: Sociedad Salesiana del Paraguay, Editorial Don Bosco, 1996. 1 v.: bibl., ill.

Presents a listing of every Salesian brother to have worked in Paraguay since 1896. [TW]

3071 Colección del centenario salesiano: salesianos, 100 años en Paraguay. v. 7, Orígenes de la misión salesiana del Chaco paraguayo, 1917–1948: memorias de Monseñor Emilio Sosa Gaona, S.D.B. Asunción: Sociedad Salesiana del Paraguay, Editorial Don Bosco, 1996. 1 v.: bibl., ill.

Interesting yet somewhat spotty memoir of Salesian missionary efforts among the Lengua Indians of the Gran Chaco just prior to the outbreak of war between Bolivia and Paraguay. [TW]

3072 Colección del centenario salesiano: salesianos, 100 años en Paraguay. v. 8, Reseña histórica de las misiones salesianas del Chaco paraguayo. Asunción: Sociedad Salesiana del Paraguay, Editorial Don Bosco, 1996. 1 v.: bibl., ill.

Intelligent summary treatment of Salesian missionary efforts in the Paraguayan Chaco. Includes a useful documentary section as well as some unusual photographs. [TW]

3073 Cooney, Jerry W. El afroparaguayo. (*in* Presencia africana en Sudamérica. Coordinación de Luz María Martínez Montiel. México: Consejo Nacional para la Cultura y las Artes, 1995, p. 449–527, bibl., maps, tables)

Building on his earlier work on abolition (see *HLAS 38:3900*), Cooney here covers the broad trajectory of blacks in Paraguay from earliest colonial times to the 1960s. Worthwhile. [TW]

3074 Cooney, Jerry W. North to the yerbales: the exploitation of the Paraguayan frontier, 1776–1810. (*in* Contested ground: comparative frontiers on the northern and southern edges of the Spanish Empire. Edited by Donna J. Guy and Thomas E. Sheridan. Tucson: Univ. of Arizona Press, 1998, p. 135–149, table)

Insightful look at the settlement of northern Paraguay, conflicts with the Portuguese and indigenous peoples, and the development of the yerba mate industry in the late 1700s and early 1800s. [TW]

3075 Fogel, Ramón B. La ecorregión de Ñeembucú: infortunio, dignidad y sabiduría de sus antiguos pobladores. Asunción: Centro de Estudios Rurales Interdisciplinarios; Pilar, Paraguay: Univ. Nacional de Pilar, 2000. 206 p.: bibl., ill. (some col.), maps.

Work on human ecology and nature in Paraguay contains two key segments. Pt. 1 offers a serious look at the impact of ecological degradation in the region on local inhabitants. Pt. 2 provides a rapid overview of the history of the region. [JH]

3076 Frutos, Juan Manuel. Luchador y doctrinario. Asunción: Editorial Medusa, 1997. 569 p.: bibl., ill.

A miscellany of essays and other writings by Frutos (1879–1960), a key figure in Paraguay's Asociación Nacional Republicana (Partido Colorado) for nearly 60 years (and provisional president of the country in 1948). [TW]

3077 Ganser, Cristian. Historia documental de San Bernardino. Prólogo de Carlos Villagra Marsal. Asunción: Editora Litocolor, 1997. 214 p.: bibl., ill.

Unusual regional history of San Bernardino, once a German agricultural colony along the shores of Lake Ypacaraí, and now the wealthiest resort town in Paraguay. [TW]

3078 González Delvalle, Alcibíades. Contra el olvido: la vida cotidiana en los tiempos de Stroessner. Asunción: Intercontinental Editora, 1998. 195 p.: bibl., ill.

Motivated by a desire to point out to Paraguayans the danger of a return to strong political leadership, the author has written an indictment of the Stroessner regime. Attempts to demonstrate the nature of the regime by showing, in addition to using repression, how the regime manipulated Paraguayan culture to strengthen its control. [JH]

3079 Jara Goiris, Fabio Aníbal. Descubriendo la frontera: historia, sociedad y política en Pedro Juan Caballero. Ponta Grossa, Brazil: Industria Pontagrossente de Artes Gráficas, 1999? 363 p.: bibl., ill., maps.

Spotty but nonetheless attractive study of the Amambay region of northeastern Paraguay. Includes some fascinating details on the early yerba mate industry. [TW]

3080 Kegler, Rolando. 1900–2000 Hohenau: cien años en las Altas Praderas. Posadas, Argentina: Dirección Nacional del Derecho del Autor, 2000. 258 p.: bibl., ill. (some col.), maps.

Written on the 100th anniversary of the founding of Hohenau, a town on the Paraná river, by German Brazilians. Provides a traditional outline of the history of the town. [JH]

3081 Lambert, Peter. Ideology and opportunism in the regime of Alfredo Stroessner, 1954–1989. (*in* Ideologues and ideologies in Latin America. Edited by Will Fowler. Westport, Conn.: Greenwood Press, 1997, p. 124–138)

Argues that while Stroessner did not have a strongly held personal ideology, he used ideology to keep his hold on the society. For political scientist's comment, see *HLAS 59:3948.* [JH]

3082 Llano, Mariano. Eligio Ayala: el milagro paraguayo. 2. ed. Asunción: Editora Ricor Grafic, 1998. 158 p.: ill.

Popular political biography sketches the story of Eligio Ayala, Paraguayan president during the mid-1920s. Lacks footnotes. [JH]

3083 Llano, Mariano. Victor Rojas: el hombre de hierro. Asunción: Editora Ricor Grafic, 1998. 236 p.: ill.

Spotty biographical treatment of Rojas, a liberal politician who served as Paraguay's War Minister during the 1932–35 Chaco conflict. [TW]

3084 Potthast-Jutkeit, Barbara. Hogares dirigidos por mujeres e hijos naturales: familia y estructuras domésticas en el Paraguay del siglo XIX. (*in* Formas familiares, procesos históricos y cambio social en América Latina. Recopilación de Ricardo Cicerchia. Quito: Ediciones Abya-Yala, 1998, p. 131–147)

Shrewd, insightful study of female-headed households in 19th-century Paraguay, especially useful for understanding the social and demographic impact of the Triple Alliance War. [TW]

3085 Rodríguez Alcalá de González Oddone, Beatriz. La misión José de Abreu. (in Congreso das Academias da História Ibero-Americanas, 4th, Lisbon and Porto, Portugal, 1994. Lisboa: Academia Portuguesa da História, 1996, p. 581–599, bibl.)

After the Paraguayans defeated Manuel Belgrano's army in 1811, they sealed their separation from Buenos Aires without becoming independent themselves. At this juncture, Portuguese Brazil dispatched José de Abreu as an emissary to Asunción, where he attempted unsuccessfully to entice the Paraguayans into an alliance. This well-written piece describes his efforts in detail. The author ascribes to Governor Bernardo de Velasco a far greater willingness to cooperate with the Portuguese than John Hoyt Williams and others have previously argued. [TW]

3086 Silva, Alberto Moby Ribeiro da. Bailes e festas públicas em Asunción no pós-guerra da Tríplice Aliança: mulher e resistência popular no Paraguai. (Estud. Ibero-Am./Porto Alegre, 25:1, junho 1999, p. 39–80)

Fascinating, multifaceted analysis of postwar Asunción, where Paraguayan women turned social gatherings into shows of passive resistance to Brazilian occupation. A well-documented chapter from the author's doctoral dissertation. [TW]

3087 Soldados de la memoria: imágenes y hombres de la Guerra del Paraguay. Recopilación de Miguel Angel Cuarterolo. Buenos Aires: Planeta, 2000. 165 p.: bibl., ill. (some col.), 1 map.

Attractive and well-researched account of photography during the Triple Alliance War. Profusely illustrated with images of the period, many of which are available here for the first time. Highly recommended. [TW]

3088 Vargas Peña, Benjamín. Los orígenes de la diplomacia en el Paraguay. Asunción: Estudio Gráfico, 1996. 155 p.

An unusual précis on the diplomacy of early national period Paraguay. Argues, al-though not very convincingly, that Dr. Francia sought to deliver his newly independent country into the hands of the Infanta Carlota of Portugal. [TW]

3089 Vázquez, José Antonio. Matiauda, capitán y vértice de mayo: la Revolución de los Patricios. Edición de Ana Sofía Piñeiro. Asunción: El Gráfico, 1998? 173 p.: ill.

Published posthumously, this attractive biography details the ideas and career of Manuel Matiauda, Paraguayan militia commander and patriot leader. Explains that, initially, Matiauda was an ally of Dr. Francia, but he later became a bitter enemy. [TW]

3090 Whigham, Thomas. The Paraguayan War. v. 1, Causes and early conduct. Lincoln: Univ. of Nebraska Press, 2002. 1 v.: bibl., ill., maps. (Studies in war, society, and the military)

A well-written tour de force based on research in archives in the four participating countries, as well as in the US and Britain. Narrative in approach, the author argues that politics lay behind the war. The background and causes presented are highly detailed, making sense of the tangled events in the four countries. This is followed by a description of the first year of the war. Whigham, even in his discussion of the war, keeps a sharp eye on the role of politics. This work is extremely important, not just for those interested in the war itself, but also for those wanting information on political developments in the entire region. [TW]

3091 Zenequelli, Lilia. Crónica de una guerra: la Triple Alianza, 1865–1870. Buenos Aires: Ediciones Dunken, 1997. 294 p.: bibl., ill.

Presents a derivative history of the Paraguayan conflict of the 1860s. [TW]

URUGUAY

3092 Aldrighi, Clara. Luigi Fabbri en Uruguay, 1929–1935. (Estud. Migr. Latinoam., 12:37, dic. 1997, p. 389–422)

Looks at the exile of Fabbri, an important Italian anarchist in Montevideo. Much of the focus is on the politics of Italian anti-Fascist exiles, but does have interesting material on Fabbri's relationship with anarchists in Uruguay and Argentina. Based on detailed personal archives. [JH]

3093   **Ardao, Arturo.** La tricolor revolución de enero: recuerdos personales y documentos olvidados. Montevideo: Biblioteca de Marcha: FCU, 1996. 232 p.: bibl., ill.

Offers both a history and a memoir of the preparations for and the revolt against the dictatorial government of Terra in Jan. 1935. The author, a participant in the revolt, mixes his personal observations with supporting documentation, including articles reprinted from the magazine *Cuadernos de Marcha* from April-Dec. 1995. [JH]

3094   **Balbis, Jorge.** La evolución del precio de la tierra en Uruguay, 1914–1924. (*Quantum/Montevideo*, 2:5, otoño/invierno 1995, p. 114–141, graphs, tables)

Fills an important gap in historical statistics for the rural economy. Presents land prices and rents for 1914–24, bridging the gap between the statistics gathered by Barrán and Nahum for 1852–1913 and by Reig and Vigorito between 1925–70. [JH]

3095   **Barrán, José Pedro.** Biología, medicina y eugenesia en Uruguay. (*Asclepio/Madrid*, 51:2, 1999, p. 11–50)

Fascinating account of the reception of science in early 20th-century Uruguay. Shows how Positivist doctors highlighted eugenics as the scientific breakthrough of the times. [TW]

3096   **Barrán, José Pedro.** Medicina y sociedad en el Uruguay del novecientos. v. 1–3. Montevideo: Ediciones de la Banda Oriental, 1992–95. 3 v.: bibl

Engrossing three-volume account of medicine, public hygiene, and social conceptualizations of health in 19th- and early 20th-century Uruguay. Not a mere political or administrative study, this highly detailed analysis highlights the power of traditionalism, changing notions of intimacy, and the reception of *lo moderno*. Highly recommended. [TW]

3097   **Beretta Curi, Alcides.** El imperio de la voluntad: una aproximación al rol de la inmigración europea y al espíritu de empresa en el Uruguay de la temprana industrialización, 1875–1930. Con la colaboración de Ana García Etcheverry. Montevideo: Editorial Fin de Siglo, 1996. 331 p.: bibl., ill. (Colección Raíces)

Detailed, sophisticated work examines the role of immigrants in the industrializa-

tion of Uruguay. The focus is on the creation of markets. [JH]

3098   **Blixen, Samuel.** Seregni: la mañana siguiente. Montevideo: Ediciones de Brecha, 1997. 255 p.: bibl., ill., index.

A biography primarily based on roughly 60 hours of interviews with Líber Seregni. Concentrates on politics and the era after the formation of the Frente Amplio. [JH]

3099   **Bresciano, Juan Andrés.** El Centro Gallego de Montevideo bajo la presidencia de Constantino Sánchez Mosquera. (*Anu. Cent. Estud. Gallegos*, 1999, p. 141–172)

Details the vigorous actions by Montevideo's Centro Gallego in promoting Spanish nationalism and loyalty to Primo de Rivera in the 1920s. Unlike those immigrants from Spain who favored socialism and republicanism, the individuals associated with this group took a strong rightest stand. [TW]

Caudillismos rioplatenses: nuevas miradas a un viejo problema. See item 2812.

3100   **Chumbita, Hugo.** El bandido Artigas. (*Todo es Hist.*, 356, marzo 1997, p. 8–27, ill., maps, photos)

Interesting study of Artigas' early years places the Oriental chieftain within a broad tradition of banditry in the Platine region. Claims that Artigas approximated Eric Hobsbawm's notion of the "social bandit." [TW]

3101   **Cores, Hugo.** El 68 uruguayo: los antecedentes, los hechos, los debates. Montevideo: Ediciones de la Banda Oriental, 1997. 179 p.: bibl.

An examination of the events of 1968 in Uruguay, written by a union activist of the time, with particular attention given to the actions and activities of the different factions of the left. Also presents the necessary background to place the events in context. [JH]

3102   **Faraone, Roque; Blanca París; and Juan Oddone.** Cronología comparada de la historia del Uruguay, 1830–1985. Montevideo: Univ. de la República, 1997. 395 p.: bibl., ill., index, maps. (Colección del rectorado; 3)

A wonderful tool for anyone working

on the history of Uruguay. Presents annual information from 1830–1985 in three categories: political and administrative; technical, economic and society; and culture. Each column includes information on events in Uruguay as well as throughout the rest of the world. The layout is easy to follow. The information for 1830–1945 first appeared in 1966 and 1968. The second and new segment, 1946–85, follows the same model and provides even more data. [JH]

3103 Mercader, Antonio. El año del León: Herrera, las bases norteamericanas y el "complot nazi" en el Uruguay de 1940. Montevideo: Aguilar, 1999. 293 p.: bibl., ill., maps.

A detailed study, based on a wide range of archives—especially in the US, of events in the year 1940 in Uruguay. Specifically addresses the ties between an alleged Nazi plot to take over Uruguay and a US attempt to build a base there. Highly favorable toward Luis Alberto de Herrera. [JH]

3104 Montaño, Oscar D. Umkhonto: la lanza negra: historia del aporte negroafricano en la formación del Uruguay. Montevideo: Rosebud Ediciones, 1997. 252 p.: bibl., ill.

Interesting but spotty investigation of Afro-Uruguayans during the Artigas period. Offers speculations on the slave trade, manumission, participation in military campaigns, and Candomblé. Of particular interest is a short section on those Black Uruguayans who accompanied Artigas into his Paraguayan exile in 1820. Includes useful archival materials. [TW]

3105 Mujeres uruguayas: el lado femenino de nuestra historia. Textos de Ana Inés Larre Borges et al. Montevideo: Fundación Banco de Boston: Extra Alfaguara, 1997. 267 p.: bibl., ill.

Useful work sketches the lives of 11 interesting and important Uruguayan women. [JH]

3106 Nahum, Benjamín. Informes diplomáticos de los representantes de Francia en el Uruguay. v. 1, 1896–1910. Montevideo: Univ. de la República, Depto. de Publicaciones, 1996. 327 p.

Complete compilation of official cor-respondence from French diplomatic agents at Montevideo, 1896–1910. Excellent sources on the history of trade, immigration, and the early Batlle period. For annotation of vol. 2, see item **3107**. [TW]

3107 Nahum, Benjamín. Informes diplomáticos de los representantes de Francia en el Uruguay. v. 2, 1911–1914. Montevideo: Univ. de la República, Depto. de Publicaciones, 1998. 1 v.

Texts of French diplomatic dispatches. Of particular interest, as it shows the French reaction to the changes in the scope of government during the onset of the second Batlle administration. Part of a larger series. For annotation of vol. 1, see item **3106**. [JH]

3108 Oddone, Juan Antonio. Serafino Mazzolini: un misionario del fascismo en Uruguay, 1933–1937. (*Estud. Migr. Latinoam.*, 12:37, dic. 1997, p. 375–387)

Short article studies the impact of an Italian diplomat on attitudes towards Fascism in Uruguay. Deals more with official attitudes than mass mobilizations. [JH]

3109 Partes e informes referentes a la toma de la ciudad de Florida por el ejercito del General Venancio Flores el 5 de agosto de 1864. (*Bol. Bibl. Artiguista*, 24:94, nov. 1996/ feb. 1997, p. 38–45)

Official recounting of a Colorado victory over the Blanco armies during the *Cruzada Libertadora* of 1864. Useful documentation. [TW]

3110 Pelfort, Jorge. Abolición de la esclavitud en el Uruguay: 150 años. Montevideo: Ediciones de la Plaza, 1996. 145 p.: ill. (Colección Testimonios)

Solid, well-researched account of Afro-Uruguayan history, focused on—but not limited to—the abolition question. [TW]

3111 Pino Menck, Alberto del. El Segundo Escuadrón Ligero, 1865–1869: artilleros orientales en la Guerra del Paraguay. (*Bol. Hist. Ejérc.*, 69:298/300, 1998, p. 33–102, bibl., facsims., ill., photos, tables)

Offers a detailed look at Uruguayan artillerymen during the Paraguayan War. Includes unusual illustrations. [TW]

3112 Porrini, Rodolfo; Oribe Cures; and **Nelly da Cunha.** Desde abajo: sectores populares en los años treinta. Montevideo:

Ediciones de la Banda Oriental, 1998. 190 p.: bibl., 1 ill.

Three essays written by three different authors, looking at the popular sector during the 1930s. The first studies the health and material existence of factory workers; the second examines *vendedores ambulantes;* while the third analyzes the conditions of the rural poor. [JH]

3113 Rela, Walter. Uruguay: cronología histórica anotada. v. 2–6. Montevideo: ALFAR, 1998–2000. 5 v.: bibl., indexes.

Presents an attractive array of historical information on 19th-century Uruguay. Especially useful for the beginning or casual student. [TW]

3114 Ribeiro, Ana. Los tiempos de Artigas. v. 1–6. Montevideo: El País, 1999. 6 v.: bibl., ill. (some col.), maps (some col.).

The profuse illustrations are the chief attraction of this 6-vol. account of the Oriental caudillo. [TW]

3115 Rilla, José Pedro. Cambiar la historia: historia política y elite política en el Uruguay contemporáneo. (*Rev. Urug. Cienc. Polít.,* 11, 1999, p. 107–127)

Essay discusses the changing uses of history in the politics of Uruguay. Reflects on what is history and how it is used in politics. [JH]

3116 Rosenthal, Anton. Dangerous streets: trolleys, labor conflict, and the reorganization of public space in Montevideo, Uruguay. (*in* Cities of hope: people, protests, and progress in urbanizing Latin America, 1870–1930. Edited by Ronn Pineo and James A. Baer. Boulder, Colo.: Westview Press, 1998, p. 30–52, map, photos)

An imaginative look at how electric street cars changed patterns of living, entertainment, and protest in Montevideo. For historian's comment on entire book, see item **856.** [JH]

3117 Ruiz Moreno, Isidoro J. Anexión de la Mesopotamia a Uruguay: un fraude histórico. (*Invest. Ens.,* 47, 1997, p. 217–266)

Debunks the misconception—popularized by Saldías and others—that Entre Rios, Corrientes, and the Misiones were the periodic object of annexationist plots hatched in unitarian-dominated Montevideo.

A fine job of reconstructing and then rejecting an old historiographical claim. [TW]

3118 Suárez, Matías E. Logias unitarias contra Rosas en la Banda Oriental, 1834–1836. (*Nuestra Hist./Buenos Aires,* 24:45/46, marzo 1997, p. 72–104, bibl., facsims., tables)

Unusual piece addresses the political activities of unitarian exiles in Montevideo during the mid-1830s. Led by Valentín Alsina, one small group of these displaced men formed a critically important Masonic lodge that organized resistance against the Rosas regime from across the river. Based on archival documentation—some originally written in secret code. [TW]

3119 Vázquez Franco, Guillermo. Artigas, la escuela y el ejército en los orígenes del estado uruguayo. (*Desmemoria/Buenos Aires,* 5:18, mayo/agosto 1998, p. 165–179, facsims., photo)

Innovative look at how the image of Artigas—as opposed to his historical reality—was used by the Uruguayan state to propagate its version of nationalism during the last decades of the 19th century. [TW]

3120 Zubillaga, Carlos. Religiosidad e inmigración española en Uruguay. (*Anu. IEHS,* 12, 1997, p. 197–222)

Thoughtful and highly original study of popular religiosity among Spanish (mainly Basque) immigrants to Uruguay from the mid-19th through the mid-20th centuries. Excellent use of documents taken from ecclesiastical archives. [TW]

3121 Zubillaga, Carlos. Renovación historiográfica en el Uruguay de la dictadura y la reinstitucionalización democrática, 1973–1995. (*Rev. Indias,* 57:210, mayo/agosto 1997, p. 511–537)

Looks at how the attempts by the practitioners of the Nueva Historia to revitalize the study of history were altered by the onset of the dictatorship. Suggests that this shift occurred in part because the dictatorship forced many historians out of official institutions. The return of democracy once again altered trends in the study of history. Examines major texts. [JH]

BRAZIL

DAIN BORGES, *Associate Professor of History, University of Chicago*
DAVID MCCREERY, *Professor of History, Georgia State University*
JOAN E. MEZNAR, *Associate Professor of History, Eastern Connecticut State University*

COLONIAL PERIOD

THE 500TH ANNIVERSARY OF Cabral's South American landfall has reinvigorated work on the Portuguese voyages of exploration and the early years of European presence in Brazil. New work on Pedro Álvares Cabral, for example, situates his life and accomplishments in the broader context of the European Renaissance (items **3168** and **3172**). The first decades of the 16th century also provide the parameters for several anthologies of primary source material, including letters from sailors and early descriptions of the new land (items **3136** and **3158**). International conferences on themes related to the Portuguese voyages generated several volumes illustrating some of the best recent scholarship on the colonial experience. Examples of transatlantic scholarly collaborations include a volume of papers presented at a conference in Lisbon on slavery in colonial Brazil (item **3148**), a volume on the Dutch presence in 17th-century Brazil based on papers from a conference held in Recife, Brazil (item **3222**), and a volume of essays on European views of colonial Brazil produced in France (item **3155**).

Recent publications demonstrate promising signs of innovation and vigor, particularly on the part of a productive group of Brazilian scholars anchored in the graduate programs of the Universidade de São Paulo (USP), the Universidade de Campinas (Unicamp), and the Universidade Federal Fluminense (UFF). Social history still dominates, shining a light on the "hidden" actors in Brazil's historical drama. Now joining works on women, slaves, free poor and people of color, are studies of freed women, gypsies, and abandoned children. Of particular note is the outstanding work by Júnia Ferreira Furtado in reconstructing the life and family of Chica da Silva, presenting her as a model of what many freed women in Minas Gerais hoped to accomplish for themselves and for their children in the heady days of the gold rush (item **3170**). Also significant is Sheila de Castro Faria's research on the financial savvy of freed African women who accumulated the funds necessary to purchase their freedom and, once free, carefully managed their income and assets to the point of drawing up prenuptial contracts with future husbands (item **3166**). Carlos de Almeida Prado Bacellar's work on Sorocaba gives good insight into the lives of rural women and abandoned children (item **3143**). Recent research on *degredados*, those sentenced to banishment in Brazil from Portugal, adds to our awareness of the role of outcasts in shaping colonial society (items **3134, 3201,** and **3202**).

Longstanding interest in the variety and complexity of the African experience in Brazil has prompted more scholars to look across the Atlantic for insight into Afro-Brazilian culture (items **3133, 3181, 3183,** and **3210**). Luiz Geraldo Silva argues for the importance of considering local politics in the African regions from which slaves were brought to better understand slave rebellion in Brazil (item **3215**). Linda Heywood highlights the role of Luso-African Catholic traditions in shaping Afro-Brazilian popular culture (item **3129**). And Mariza de Carvalho Soares examines the terminology used to describe Africans as a way of discerning the changing role of the Portuguese in Africa and in Brazil (item **3217**). On the other hand, Elizabeth

Kiddy (item **3178**) and Carlos A.M. Lima (item **3182**) demonstrate that Africans united for political and cultural purposes once in Brazil. Rethinking the role of black confraternities seems appropriate: while they provided space for African culture, they also helped slaves and free blacks to navigate the often treacherous political conditions of Portuguese Brazil.

Regional histories continue to provide a focus for scholars of colonial Brazil. Some outstanding recent work deals with Minas Gerais in the 18th century. Of particular note is Kathleen Higgins' rich portrayal (heeding Joan Scott's call to use gender as a tool of analysis) of the social and economic transformations generated by the gold boom and bust (item **3177**). Anita Novinsky's preliminary work on New Christians in Minas Gerais illustrates the value of using global themes to better understand local communities (item **3195**). In Ilana Blaj's attempt to debunk the myth of the exceptional *paulistas,* she approaches regional history from a different angle, linking the region more tightly to a national political and economic tradition (items **3146** and **3147**). And the work by (and critique of) João Fragoso and Manolo Florentino notes the ascendancy of Rio de Janeiro as the premier south Atlantic port of the late 18th century and its significance for the "late colonial" Brazilian economy and for the Portuguese empire (items **3169** and **3186**).

Scholarship on colonial Brazil also continues to be enriched by the shift toward cultural history. Adriana Romeiro, drawing on the work of Natalie Davis and Carlo Ginzburg, recalls the life of Pedro de Rates Henequim to illuminate essential connections between religion and politics in the 18th-century Luso-Brazilian world (item **3209**). Others look to popular *festas* both as the breeding ground for political discontent (item **3214**) and as space for developing new ideas about citizenship and nation (items **3140, 3148, 3221,** and **3304**).

Finally, the field of environmental history appears to be budding. José Augusto Pádua, for example, points to early environmentalist concerns among a Brazilian-born elite in the late 18th century, tying environmentalism to the Enlightenment and the birth of the modern era (item **3199**). Robin Anderson, on the other hand, describes the seriously flawed 18th-century policy for settling the Amazon as a precursor to ecological disaster in that region in the late 20th century (item **3137**). And Shawn Miller blames royal monopoly for the wasteful destruction of Brazil's timber resources (item **3189**). These early steps, pioneer efforts in a new research field, hold promise for a richer appreciation of the social, economic, political, and cultural transformations that accompanied the transformation of the Brazilian landscape. [JM]

NATIONAL PERIOD

Cultural history studies reviewed here indicate that this subfield is now an established research area within Brazilian historiography. Histories starting from the personal, the private, or the marginal are now enriching and challenging our understanding of social and political institutions. The most ambitious recent achievement is the *Historia da vida privada no Brasil,* under the general editorship of Novais, a four-volume collection of essays on private life, stretching from the colonial period to the present (see *HLAS 58:3177* and items **3277, 3278,** and **3279**). It is also notable that monographs on sexuality and honor by Green (item **3275**) and Caulfield (item **3254**), or an article on military recruits by Beattie (item **3238**), can greatly illuminate traditional assumptions about the relationship between power and politics. In comparison with works informed by cultural history, such as Barman's definitive political biography of Dom Pedro II (item **3237**) and Schwarcz's work that studies imperial rituals in Rio de Janeiro (item **3331**), there is a steep drop in quality to the more conventional elite biographies and memoirs that have flooded Brazilian bookstores, such as Sandroni on Austregésilo de Athayde (item **3326**), or Montello on Kubitschek (item **3302**).

Still, recent solid publications that examine the history of cultural representations are rather scarce, though Cunha shows how treatment in a mental hospital reinforced gender stereotypes (item **3258**), Rodrigues analyzes Rio funerals (item **3324**), and Mesquita surveys efforts to "Europeanize" Manaus in the late 19th century (item **3301**). Many works study press coverage: *Folhas do tempo* looks at Belo Horizonte's popular culture (item **3273**); Schpun discusses women in the 1920s (item **3328**); Paula examines photos of the 1932 rebellion (item **3312**); Figueiredo reviews 1950s advertising (item **3268**); and Aquino discusses 1970s censorship (item **3233**). *São Paulo em revista* offers a bibliographic guide to periodicals (item **3327**), and Levine reveals Naylor's documentary photojournalism (item **3291**).

More conventional intellectual and literary history flourished in articles about a single author, such as Mota's collection (item **3130**), or Amory on Da Cunha (item **3232**). Some broader monographs include Paim on liberalism (item **3311**) and Langer on imaginary cities (item **3131**). Work on historians and historiography, other than Arruda and Tengarrinha (item **3123**), has dwindled. Matory uproots "African purity" in Brazilian anthropology by arguing that what is known in conventional scholarship as traditional Yoruba culture was in fact selected and compiled, or even invented, by Afro-Brazilian returnees in Lagos (item **3299**).

Beyond the familiar topic of travelers and naturalists (item **3128**), areas beginning to receive attention in Brazil include the history of ethnography and archeology (item **3266**) and historical archeology, not only of urban areas (items **3294** and **3337**), but on the frontier as well (items **3314** and **3329**). Langfur debunks myths of the peaceful subjugation of the Bororo early in the 20th century (item **3286**) and Lima looks at the *sertão* in the construction of a national identity in the Old Republic (item **3292**).

Slavery continues to be a dominant theme in the historiography of 19th-century Brazil, as it was a dominant theme for Brazilians who lived under the Empire. Several recent studies, including Bergad (item **3240**), Carvalho (item **3252**), Florentino (item **3272**), and Lima (item **3293**), examine slave life and slave demography, while Vasconcellos focuses on the role of kinship in helping slaves to form communities and develop strategies of resistance (item **3343**). When considering such resistance, historians such as Brown (item **3247**), Carvalho (item **3252**), Florence (item **3271**), Reis (item **3318**), and Zubaran (item **3350**) have emphasized "everyday" forms of resistance, as well as state and employer reactions, while Azevedo compares how abolitionists in the US and Brazil reacted to slave violence (item **3235**). Welcome are treatments of slavery outside the usual Rio de Janeiro-São Paulo axis, for example, Carvalho on Recife (item **3252**), Lima on Rio Grande do Sul (item **3293**), Bergad on Minas Gerais (item **3240**), and Westphalen on Paraná (item **3348**), as well as those of slavery in less well studied activities such as transport (item **3251**) and small scale, nonexport agriculture (item **3236**). Studies by McCann (item **3300**) and Bivar Marquese (item **3298**) look at slave management techniques, and Reis provides an excellent survey of the recent historiography of Brazilian slavery (item **3319**).

Butler (item **3248**) and Loner (item **3295**) show how ex-slaves attempted to adapt and survive after abolition, while other historians, including Neder (item **3306**), Peraro (item **3315**), Schueler (item **3330**), and especially Moura (item **3305**),

Silva (item **3332**), and Wissenbach (item **3349**) address similar questions for the working classes and free poor. The unlucky ones found their activities criminalized and themselves coerced by forced labor schemes (items **3333** and **3334**), but immigrants more than freedmen were the concern of Rio's police force (item **3246**). Moura's beautiful *Vida cotidiana* collects primary sources for a broad look at life in 19th-century São Paulo (item **3345**).

Recent medical history of Brazil has tended to focus on social control and especially state public health measures (items **3231, 3262, 3263, 3323,** and **3338**). The photographs in *O Rio de Janeiro do bota-abaixo* document many of the changes made to the city (item **3296**). Crocitti on housing projects (item **3257**) and Salla on São Paulo prisons (item **3325**) address overlapping issues of social control.

Some medical history provides a different perspective. A major study is Peard's *Race, Place and Medicine,* arguing that not all Brazilian doctors accepted European climate and race prejudices (item **3313**). Some, instead, struggled to construct a useful medicine for a modern tropical nation. Several pieces highlight conflicts between popular medicine and efforts to professionalize and regulate the field (items **3203, 3267,** and **3269**). Elder surveys the historiography of 19th century medicine (item **3262**), and in a related area, Figueirôa shows that natural science in Brazil was not just the province of visiting foreigners (item **3270**).

Particularly important for political history are the two superb new studies of Pedro II and his involvement in forming and maintaining the Empire (items **3237** and **3331**). Shifting the focus from the Corte to the *sertão*, Beiber argues that political violence in the interior was not endemic but rather the result of Imperial consolidation (item **3242**). Several items examine press discourse (items **3244, 3255, 3303,** and **3335**), while others explore the meanings and mechanisms of citizenship in the early Empire (items **3274, 3306,** and **3336**). Dolhnikoff provides a useful synthesis of the ideas of one of the founders of the Empire, José Bonifácio (item **3261**). Studies by Beattie (item **3238**) and Kraay (items **3281** and **3282**) advance our understanding of civil-military relations, and Amaral de Toral shows how photographs from the Paraguayan War affected the civilian population and politics (item **3340**).

Post-1922 political history maintains its focus on familiar topics of the Vargas era (items **3316** and **3317**). The 30th anniversary of 1968 inspired histories, memoirs, and ghastly albums about prisons, torture, and authoritarian politics: *Tiradentes* (item **3339**), Couto (item **3256**), and Capitani (item **3250**). More illuminating were detailed chronicles of state politics such as Dantas on Sergipe (item **3259**) and Buzar on Maranhão in the earlier period of 1945–64 (item **3249**). A preference for studying the left continues to skew what we know about politics. Coronéis and the technocrats have vanished, but Hecker offers a meticulous history of the microscopic Partido Socialista Brasileiro (item **3276**), and we learn more about anarchists from Valente (item **3342**) and Bertucci (item **3241**). Deutsch on *Las derechas* fills gaps (item **870**), but we are grateful for even a pedestrian Integralista memoir like that of Nogueira (item **3307**).

Brazil, like the US, was a creation of immigrants, both forced and voluntary, and immigration continues to attract attention in Brazilian historiography. The Portuguese, for example, early in the Empire concentrated in Rio de Janeiro (items **3308** and **3320**), to the occasional concern of the state (item **3321**); other Europeans favored rural areas (item **3253**) where they commonly fell afoul of existing power structures (item **3285**). Lesser shows that local prejudices hampered the efforts of Chinese, Japanese, and "Turcos" to settle in Brazil (item **3290**). Repatriated migrants are studied in Portugal (item **3245**) and Italy (item **3283**).

Several items detail the 19th-century economy outside the main export sectors, including the excellent new books by Barickman on Bahia (item **3236**) and Bell on Rio Grande do Sul (item **3239**), and Bichao's study of commercial and industrial entrepreneurship in Minas Gerais (item **3243**). Coffee, of course, continues to draw attention: Padua, for example, demonstrates domestic capital accumulation in southern Minas Gerais (item **3310**) and Nozoe documents the transition from small- to large-scale production in one area of São Paulo (item **3196**). Studies of 20th-century economic history include Leite's historical geography of land grabs (item **3289**); Abreu on international trade and finance, 1930–45 (item **3230**); Alberti's collection on insurance markets (item **3264**); and Vogt on tobacco farming (item **3347**). [DB and DM]

GENERAL

3122 Alves Filho, Ivan. Brasil, 500 anos em documentos. Rio de Janeiro: MAUAD, 1999. 653 p.: bibl.

Useful collection of documents, carefully introduced and annotated. Beginning with Pero Vaz de Caminha's letter to the king, volume highlights documents related to colonial rebellions and to issues involving 20th-century workers. Examples include transcription of first manifesto of Brazilian women (1823); text of Brazil's first constitution (1824) and of 1850 land law; and documents on first Brazilian Black Congress (1850) and on resignation of Jânio Quadros. Excellent bibliography. [JM]

3123 Arruda, José Jobson de Andrade and **José Manuel Tengarrinha.** Historiografia luso-brasileira contemporânea. Bauru, Brazil: Editora da Univ. do Sagrado Coração; Brasília: Embaixada de Portugal, Instituto Camões, 1999. 189 p.: bibl. (Col. História)

Not an integrated analysis, but rather separate sections on Brazil and Portugal, with useful overviews of major trends and works in historiography, especially since 1970. Discussions avoid controversy. Brazilian section emphasizes recent emergence of fragmentary, cultural histories as alternative to totalizing, analytical historiography. [DB]

3124 Bernecker, Walther L.; Horst Pietschmann; and **Rüdiger Zoller.** Eine kleine Geschichte Brasiliens. Frankfurt: Suhrkamp, 1999. 250 p. (Edition Suhrkamp; 2150)

Well-written general overview of Brazilian history by three German scholars. [F. Obermeier]

3125 Biblioteca Nacional (Brazil). Brasiliana da Biblioteca Nacional: guia das fontes sobre o Brasil. Organização de Paulo Roberto Dias Pereira. Rio de Janeiro: Editora Nova Fronteira; Ministério da Cultura, Fundação Biblioteca Nacional, 2001. 637 p.: bibl., ill. (some col.), maps (some col.).

Published on occasion of the 190-year anniversary of the Biblioteca National, work is more accurately described as a useful and well-illustrated presentation of the various Brazil-related documents held by the Biblioteca, rather than as a bibliography or user's guide. [F. Obermeier]

3126 O Brasil dos brasilianistas: um guia dos estudos sobre o Brasil nos Estados Unidos, 1945–2000. Organização de Rubens Antônio Barbosa, Marshall C. Eakin e Paulo Roberto de Almeida. São Paulo: Paz e Terra, 2002. 512 p.: bibl.

Provides an overview of publications on Brazil by North American scholars. A must-read for all Brazilianists and Latin American scholars with an interest in Brazil. English-language version, *Envisioning Brazil: A Guide to the Study of Brazil in the United States, 1945–2002*, also available. [K. Muller]

3127 Guia de fontes para a história franco-brasileira: Brasil Colônia, Vice-Reino e Reino Unido. Apresentação de Francisco Corrêa Weffort. Estudo introdutório Vasco Mariz. Recife, Brazil: L. Dantas Silva, 2002. 303 p.

User's guide for unpublished material related to Brazil in selected French archives, provided by the Resgate de Documentação Histórica project. Work focuses principally on state archives; a few others are included. [F. Obermeier]

3128 Halfeld, Henrique Guilherme Fernando and Johann Jakob von Tschudi.
A província brasileira de Minas Gerais. Traduzido de Myriam Avila. Ensaio crítico, notas e revisão da tradução de Roberto Borges Martins. Belo Horizonte, Brazil: Fundação João Pinheiro, Centro de Estudos Históricos e Culturais, 1998. 176 p.: bibl., ill., map. (Col. Mineiriana. Série Clássicos)

Good critical introduction and translation of Swiss naturalist and immigration envoy Tschudi's geological and social description of Minas localities circa 1860 that were published in *Petermann's Geographischen Mitteilungen* (1862) along with 1855 Halfeld-Wagner map. Chapters concerning Tschudi's voyage through Minas Gerais published in *Reisen durch Südamerika* (1866–69) apparently remain untranslated, although chapters on Rio and São Paulo have long been available (see *HLAS 19:4078*). [DM]

3129 Heywood, Linda M. The Angolan/Afro-Brazilian cultural connections. (*Slavery Abolit.*, 20:1, April 1999, p. 9–23)

Calls for serious study of African as well as Portuguese roots of a Brazilian popular culture deeply rooted in folk Catholicism. Some black confraternities in Brazil, for example, appear to have been based on and influenced by Catholic confraternities first established by the Portuguese in Africa. See also items **3178, 3182,** and **3214.** [JM]

3130 Introdução ao Brasil: um banquete no trópico. Organização de Lourenço Dantas Mota. São Paulo: Editora SENAC São Paulo, 1999. 419 p.: bibl.

Succinct critical introductions by top scholars to 19 key texts about Brazilian society. Mostly a predictable selection of mainstream classics, half of them published between 1930–60; however, covers some less-studied works such as Visconde de Mauá's autobiographical memorandum to his creditors (see *HLAS 8:3510* and *HLAS 9:3445*), Victor Nunes Leal's *Coronelismo* (*HLAS 14:1611* and *HLAS 41:7554*), and Florestan Fernandes' *Revolução burguesa* (*HLAS 39:9302*). [DB]

3131 Langer, Johnni. As cidades imaginárias do Brasil: ensaio. Curitiba, Brazil: Governo do Estado do Paraná, Secretaria de Estado da Cultura; Document Company-Xerox do Brasil, 1997. 213 p.: bibl., ill. (some col.).

Clever study about theme of imaginary cities in Brazilian interior. First half surveys colonial search for "fantastic cities" of gold and popular folklore of "enchanted cities," following cues of Holanda (see *HLAS 32:2829a*). Second half is an original contribution, tracing reciprocal influences between literary fiction and archeological expeditions to find ruined "lost cities" in 19th and 20th centuries. [DB]

A paisagem carioca. See item **410.**

Roland, Ana Maria. Fronteiras da palavra, fronteiras da história: contribuição à crítica da cultura do ensaísmo latino-americano através da leitura de Euclides da Cunha e Octavio Paz. See item **4762.**

Ruiz-Peinado Alonso, José Luis. Insurrecciones negras. See item **939.**

COLONIAL

3132 Abreu, João Capistrano de. O descobrimento do Brasil. São Paulo: Martins Fontes, 1999. 210 p. (Temas brasileiros)

Besides title piece (the thesis written by Abreu in 1883 when competing for a professorship of Brazilian history), volume also includes "O Descobrimento do Brasil pelos Portugueses," first published on May 3, 1900, in *Jornal do Comércio*; and "O Descobrimento do Brasil: povoamento do solo; evolução social," from *Livro do Centenário—1500–1900*, commemorating 400th anniversary of Cabral's landing in Brazil. Volume begins with biographical essay on Abreu written by Hélio Vianna in 1953 that highlights significance of Abreu's work on Brazilian history. [JM]

3133 Aguilar, Marcos Magalhães de. A coartação: uma singularidade mineira no sistema de alforria colonial? (*Rev. SBPH*, 18, 2000, p. 77–91, tables)

Fascinating description of the written contracts (*papéis de corte*) that delineated payments slaves had to make to gain manumission. These documents became part of the *carta de alforria* granted to slaves only after the master had received full payment. Author sees *coartação* as more typical of credit-based societies, thus explaining why, in Brazil, Minas Gerais appears to be the region where it was most in evidence. [JM]

Almeida, Rita Heloísa de. O diretório dos índios: um projeto de "civilização" no Brasil do século XVIII. See item **661.**

3134 Amado, Janaína. Crimes domésticos: criminalidade e degredo feminino. (*Textos Hist.*, 6:1/2, 1998, p. 143–168, tables)
Part of a larger project, article focuses on the 125 Portuguese women sentenced by secular courts to exile between 1737–1800. Of the 125, 33 were exiled within Portugal, while 89 were banished to Brazil and three to Africa. Almost half had their sentences commuted. Interesting analysis of gender, crime, and punishment. [JM]

3135 Amado, Janaína. Mythic origins: Caramuru and the founding of Brazil. (*HAHR*, 80:4, Nov. 2000, p. 783–811)
Excellent analysis of trajectory of the story of Caramuru and Paraguaçu from late 16th-20th centuries, discussing its use in constructing a particular vision of "Brazilness." [JM]

3136 Amado, Janaína and Luiz Carlos Figueiredo. Brasil 1500: quarenta documentos. São Paulo: Imprensa Oficial SP; Brasília: Editora UnB, 2001. 550 p.: bibl., ill. (some col.), col. maps.
Collection of documents from Portuguese archives (letters from sailors, diary entries, early histories of reign of D. Manuel) deals with first years of Portuguese contact with Brazil. Thirty-two of the 40 documents were written between 1500–05. Most are transcribed in their entirety and all are superbly introduced and annotated by the editors. Sections on *trajetória do documento* provide detailed background to each document. [JM]

3137 Anderson, Robin Leslie. Colonization as exploitation in the Amazon rain forest, 1758–1911. Gainesville: Univ. Press of Florida, 1999. 197 p.: bibl., index.
Examines problems of colonizing the Amazon, from expulsion of the Jesuits to collapse of rubber boom in 1911. Demonstrates that late-20th-century attempts to settle the Amazon repeated many of the mistakes committed in earlier centuries. [JM]

3138 Animai-vos, povo bahiense!: a Conspiração dos Alfaiates. Organização de Carlos Vasconcelos Domingues, Cícero Bathomarco Lemos, e Edyala Yglesias. Salvador, Brazil: Governo do Estado da Bahia, Secretaria da Cultura e Turismo, 1999. 258 p.: bibl., ill. (some col.).
Beautifully produced and illustrated volume commemorating bicentennial of Tailors' Conspiracy. Includes essays on role of women as witnesses in the legal proceedings, music of the period, military, press, race, and contraband. This retrospective on late 18th-century Bahian society also celebrates memory of the conspiracy with 20th-century artifacts: artwork, the text of a play, *cordel* literature, and even a screenplay. [JM]

3139 Araujo, Jorge de Souza. Perfil do leitor colonial. Ilhéus, Brazil: Editus, Editora da UESC, 1999. 502 p.: bibl.
Based on estate inventories that include private libraries, author describes what the small, literate elite read in colonial Brazil. Especially useful in that it covers entire colonial period and not simply 18th century. [JM]

3140 Araújo, Rita de Cássia B. de. Cruzes, plumas e batuques: festas públicas e colonização na América portuguesa. (*Ciênc. Tróp.*, 28:2, julho/dez. 2000, p. 161–181)
Describes ways in which religious as well as secular *festas* meshed Portuguese, indigenous, and African traditions from earliest days of colonization. Sees greatest contribution of these *festas* in promoting an *imaginário social comum* that was peculiarly Brazilian. See also item **3224.** [JM]

3141 Arruda, José Jobson de Andrade.
Decadência ou crise do império luso-brasileiro: o novo padrão de colonização do século XVIII. (*Rev. USP/São Paulo*, 46, julho/agôsto 2000, p. 66–78, graphs, table)
Provides overview of argument that there was no decadence in 18th-century Luso-Brazilian empire. Rather, early industrialization allowed for development of a new relationship between the metropolis and the colony. The crisis of growth in Portugal and independence of Brazil reified the myth of decadence. Article is also available in English as "Decadence or Crisis in the Luso-Brazilian

Empire: A New Model of Colonization in the Eighteenth Century" in *HAHR*, Vol. 80, No. 4, Nov. 2000, p. 865–878. [JM]

3142 Arteaga, Juan José. Las consecuencias del Tratado de Madrid en la desarticulación de la frontera demográfica de la Banda Oriental, 1750–1761. Prólogo de Marta Canessa de Sanguinetti. Montevideo: Ministerio de Educación y Cultura, Archivo General de la Nación, Centro de Difusión del Libro, 1999. 397 p.: bibl., ill., maps. (Col. Ensayos históricos; 2)

Carefully documented account of human cost of dismantling Jesuit missions following 1750 Treaty of Madrid. Argues that the tremendous suffering of the 30,000 Guarani who lived in the missions' territory illustrates one of the worst atrocities perpetrated in colonial America. Author is particularly concerned with significance of Treaty of Madrid for Uruguayan history, first in evolution of the border between Portuguese and Spanish America, and later for defining the border between Uruguay and Brazil. [JM]

3143 Bacellar, Carlos de Almeida Prado. Viver e sobreviver em uma vila colonial: Sorocaba, séculos XVIII e XIX. São Paulo: Annablume; FAPESP, 2001. 274 p.: bibl., ill. (Selo universidade; 152. História)

Based on exhaustive archival research and analysis of local nominative censuses, demonstrates how colonial economy shaped society in Sorocaba. Although region produced little for export, it thrived by supplying cattle to mining, sugar, and coffee regions. Provides fascinating information on role of women and children, especially those children abandoned by their mothers and raised by others. [JM]

3144 Belluzzo, Ana Maria de Moraes. O Brasil dos viajantes. v. 1, Imaginário do novo mundo. 2. ed. São Paulo: Metalivros; Rio de Janeiro: Editora Objetiva, 1999. 192 p.: bibl., ill. (some col.), indexes, col. maps.

Second ed. of important overview of iconographic traditions in travelers' books for 15th through 19th-century Brazil. Originally based on material shown in a 1994 exhibition in the Museu de Arte de São Paulo Assis Chateaubriand, book contains a vast selection of the material in very good reproductions. [F. Obermeier]

Bergad, Laird W. Slavery and the demographic and economic history of Minas Gerais, 1720–1888. See item **3240.**

3145 Bicalho, Maria Fernanda. Centro e periferia: pacto e negociação política na administração do Brasil colonial. (*Leituras/Lisboa,* 6, primavera 2000, p. 17–39, bibl., maps)

Drawing on work of C.R. Boxer and other scholars in Portugal and Brazil, author addresses important role of *câmaras municipais* throughout Portugal's far-flung empire in perpetuating notion of a pact between monarch and subjects that resulted in strong loyalty to the king. The possibility of negotiating favorably with the king helped to keep empire united. In Brazil the colonial *câmaras* also served as a model for municipal government in the independent empire. [JM]

3146 Blaj, Ilana. Agricultores e comerciantes em São Paulo nos inícios do século XVIII: o processo de sedimentação da elite paulista. (*Rev. Bras. Hist./São Paulo,* 18:36, 1998, p. 281–296)

Argues that in late 17th-early 18th centuries, a São Paulo elite crystallized, based on wealth generated by supplying foodstuffs to gold mining region. These elite families quickly became important in local politics. After 1730, with arrival of more Portuguese merchants, clashes between already established landowning/merchant class and the newcomers intensified. Does not, therefore, see São Paulo as unique but rather as very much a part of slaveholding/landholding pattern prevalent in colonial Brazil. [JM]

3147 Blaj, Ilana. Mentalidade e sociedade: revisitando a historiografia sobre São Paulo colonial. (*Rev. Hist./São Paulo,* 142/143, primeiro e segundo semestres 2000, p. 239–259, bibl.)

Argues against image of colonial *paulistas* as independent, brave *bandeirantes,* somehow different from other inhabitants of Brazil. Shows this image of the exceptional *paulista* to be a construct of the Instituto Histórico e Geográfico de São Paulo in 1950s-60s for the purpose of explaining region's leading role in the Old Republic. Author, instead, demonstrates that *paulistas* were very much a part of the Brazil dominated by slaveholders and large property owners. [JM]

3148 Brasil: colonização e escravidão. Organização de Maria Beatriz Nizza da Silva. Rio de Janeiro: Editora Nova Fronteira, 1999. 417 p.: bibl., ill.

Essays by Portuguese, Brazilian, and North American scholars first presented at 1996 colloquium on "Colonization and Slavery" held at the Fundação Calouste Gulbenkian in Lisbon. Contributors (including Laura de Mello e Souza, Valentim Alexandre, Mary Karasch, Alida Metcalf, Muriel Nazzari, A.J.R. Russell-Wood, and Donald Ramos) address topics dealing with enslavement of indigenous peoples, slavery and culture, slave resistance, the Church and slavery, and abolition. [JM]

3149 O Brasil e os holandeses, 1630–1654. Organização de Paulo Herkenhoff. Rio de Janeiro: Sextante Artes, 1999. 271 p.: bibl., ill. (chiefly col.), maps.

Originally published on the occasion of an exhibition held at the Banco Real in São Paulo and three other Brazilian galleries. Provides a beautiful illustrated overview of the Dutch in colonial Brazil. [F. Obermeier]

Caazapá: las reducciones franciscanas y los Guaraní del Paraguay. See item **55.**

3150 Caldeira, Jorge. A nação mercantilista: ensaio sobre o Brasil. São Paulo: Editora 34, 1999. 415 p.: bibl., index.

Argues that a strong internal market, generated by demand for goods following 18th-century gold strikes, characterized colonial Brazil. Considers Portugal's taxation policy, adopted by 19th-century Brazilian elites, to be greatest hindrance to long-term economic development. Thus concludes that Brazil's lag in development was based on internal factors. [JM]

3151 Caneca, Joaquim do Amor Divino. Frei Joaquim do Amor Divino Caneca. Organização e introdução de Evaldo Cabral de Mello. São Paulo: Editora 34, 2001. 643 p.: bibl., ill. (Col. Formadores do Brasil)

Important collection of Frei Caneca's political work (including sermons, newspaper articles, his war diary) documenting his decision to embrace radical republicanism following disenchantment with Pedro I's au-

thoritarian acts. Also includes 1824 *processo* that resulted in his execution. Introduction by Mello discusses radical option of many *pernambucanos* for an independence movement that was republican, separatist, and nativist. [JM]

3152 Castelnau-L'Estoile, Charlotte de. Les ouvriers d'une vigne stérile: les jésuits et la conversion des Indiens au Brésil, 1580–1620. Paris: Centre culturel Gulbenkian, 2000. 557 p.

The beginning of the Spanish rule of Portugal in 1580 coincided with a visitation to Brazil's Jesuit province by the Jesuit Cristovão de Gouvea. Focusing primarily on internal organization of missionary work, study provides important examination of this rather neglected phase. [F. Obermeier]

3153 Chahon, Sérgio. Liturgia e espaço doméstico no Rio de Janeiro colonial e arredores. (*Anais/São Paulo*, 18, 1998, p. 227–231)

Examines requests of individuals to endow their home oratories with sacramental privileges for baptisms, weddings, masses, and holy day celebrations. Speculates on reasons some preferred to practice rites of faith at home. Also addresses efforts by Church hierarchy to restrict certain rites to the Church alone. [JM]

3154 Coelho, Geraldo Mártires. A pátria do Anticristo: a expulsão dos jesuítas do Maranhão e Grão-Pará e o messianismo milenarista do Padre Vieira. (*Luso-Braz. Rev.*, 37:1, Summer 2000, p. 17–32, bibl.)

Sees Antônio Vieira's "Sermão da Epifania" as more than a political chastisement of colonists in Brazil. Since Vieira believed that the Jesuit missionaries' conversion efforts were preparing the way for the Fifth Kingdom prophesied in Scriptures, expulsion of the Jesuits from northern Brazil meant the momentary triumph of the Anti-Christ. [JM]

3155 Colloque de l'Institut de recherches sur les civilisations de l'Occident moderne, *20th, Paris, 1997*. Naissance du Brésil moderne: 1500–1808. Sous la direction de Katia de Queiros Mattoso, Idelette Muzart-Fonseca dos Santos et Denis Rolland. Paris: Presses de l'Univ. de Paris-Sorbonne, 1998. 350 p.: bibl., ill. (Civilisations, 22)

Outstanding collection of essays on

European views of colonial Brazil. Roughly half of contributors address French presence in Brazil or Brazilian indigenous people who traveled to France in 16th century. [JM]

3156 Costa, Maria de Fátima Gomes.
História de um país inexistente: o Pantanal entre os séculos XVI e XVIII. São Paulo: Estação Liberdade; Livraria Kosmos Editora, 1999. 277 p.: bibl., ill. (some col.), maps (some col.).

Describes how Pantanal region and its inhabitants came to be known by Europeans. Focusing on geography and cartography, author traces transformation of Pantanal from a place of legend to a region inhabited also by individuals of European descent. Beautifully illustrated with map plates. [JM]

3157 Delson, Roberta Marx. Military engineering and the "colonial" project for Brazil: agency and dominance. (*Leituras/Lisboa*, 6, primavera 2000, p. 73–96, bibl., ill.)

Urges rethinking of notion of "colonial dominance" for interior regions of Brazil in 18th century. Finds much social leveling in backlands of Brazil where society was marked as much by mixture of blood and culture as by sheer dominance (the Portuguese, in fact, encouraged intermarriage). Yet author cautions that society was certainly not democratic. [JM]

3158 O descobrimento do Brasil nos textos de 1500 a 1571. Organização de José Manuel Garcia. Lisbon: Fundação Calouste Gulbenkian, Serviço de Bibliotecas e Apoio à Leitura, 2000. 87 p.: bibl., col. ill., col. maps.

Collection of annotated documents includes material from period immediately preceding Cabral's voyage to Brazil (the instructions he received from Vasco da Gama), eyewitness accounts from sailors in Cabral's fleet, letters written in 1501 after return to Lisbon (five of which were written by Italians), documents written between 1502–19 reflecting on discovery of Brazil, and selections from early chroniclers who wrote about Brazil between 1525–71. Includes thorough introduction to each document and good bibliography. [JM]

3159 Dias, Ondemar F. O índio no recôncavo da Guanabara. (*Rev. Inst. Hist. Geogr. Bras.*, 159:399, abril/junho 1998, p. 399–461, bibl., tables)

Documents indigenous-European rela-

tions from first encounter to census of 1851 (which does not include any indigenous peoples) based on research in local archives. Purpose is to counter traditional perspective that ignores impact of indigenous culture on modern Brazilian society. [B. Meggers]

3160 Domingues, Ângela. Quando os índios eram vassalos: colonização e relações de poder no norte do Brasil na segunda metade do século XVIII. Apresentação de Joaquim Romero Magalhães. Lisboa: Comissão Nacional Comemorações dos Descobrimentos Portugueses, 2000. 388 p.: bibl. (Col. Outras margens)

Analyzes Portuguese indigenous policy in territory of Grão Pará during time of Pombaline reforms. Finds many similarities with Spanish policy in Amazon basin, as monarchs of both Spain and Portugal sought to transform indigenous peoples into subjects of the Crown despite objections of churchmen and white settlers. [JM]

3161 Duque Estrada, Luís Gonzaga. Revoluções brasileiras: resumos históricos. Organização de Francisco Foot e Vera Lins. São Paulo: FAPESP; Editora Giordano; Fundação Editora UNESP, 1998. 211 p.: bibl. (Memória brasileira; 9)

New edition of anarchist text first published in 1898. The 18 chapters begin with Palmares and end with proclamation of the Republic. Author looks to examples from the past of those who strived to achieve a society governed more justly. Underlying the stories of the *mascates, cabanos, farrapos, praieiros,* and others is a critique of those who enrich themselves at expense of Brazilian people. [JM]

3162 Dutch Brazil. Rio de Janeiro?: Editora Index, 2001. 3 v.: bibl., ill. (some col.).

Presents rather unknown material about the Dutch in colonial Brazil (1624–54). Vols. 2 and 3 relate to European works based on Dutch iconographic material from Brazil: Vol. 2 considers elements of Dutch Brazil derived from Eckhout's Indian portraits now in Copenhagen and other drawings and tapestries by him. Vol. 3 discusses a contemporary allegory of the continents by Jan van Kessel. See also items **3163** and **3164.** [F. Obermeier]

3163 Dutch Brazil. v. 1, Frans Post: The British Museum drawings. v. 2, Niedenthal Collection "Animaux et insectes." v. 3, Cuthbert Pudsey: Journal of a resident in Brazil. Petrópolis, Brazil: Editora Index, 2000. 3 v.: bibl., col. ill., facsims. (some col.), ports.

Collection contains iconographic material about the Dutch in colonial Brazil (1624–54); the British Museum drawings by Frans Post, drawings on natural history from the Niedenthal collection and a manuscript source; and Pudsey's "Journal of a resident in Brazil." See also items **3162** and **3164**. [F. Obermeier]

3164 Dutch Brazil. v. 1, The Niedenthal collection. v. 2, Animaux et oiseaux. v. 3, The "Naturalien-Buch" by Jacob Wilhelm Griebe. Rio de Janeiro: Editora Index, 1998. 3 v.: bibl., ill.

Similar to other collections with the same title and different content (see items **3162** and **3163**), the collection contains obscure materials about the Dutch and their interest in natural history in colonial Brazil (1624–54). [F. Obermeier]

3165 Die Entdeckung der Welt—die Welt der Entdeckungen: österreichische Forscher, Sammler, Abenteurer [The discovery of the World, the world of discovery: Austrian investigators, collectors, adventurers]. Herausgegeben von Wilfried Seipel. Redaktion von Christian Höhl und Marianne Hergovich. Vienna: Kunsthistorisches Museum; Milano, Italy: Skira editore, 2001. 437 p.: ill. (mostly col.).

Catalog of exhibition shown from Oct. 2001-Jan. 2002 in the Wiener Künstlerhaus on Austrian contribution to discovery. Even if Latin America hasn't been the focus of Austrian expeditions, some scientific expeditions such as Natterer's voyage to Brazil are worth re-evaluation for important but little-known material collected by the explorer. [F. Obermeier]

3166 Faria, Sheila Siqueira de Castro. Mulheres forras: riqueza e estigma social. (*Tempo/Rio de Janeiro*, 5:9, julho 2000, p. 65–92, table)

Using estate inventories and prenuptial contracts of freed black women in São João del Rei, author finds that *pretas forras* were excellent administrators of their material goods. Suggests that freed women, especially Africans, often were fairly well-to-do, making money through trade and possibly

prostitution. Their ability to earn enough to purchase freedom also may indicate that they could replenish their resources once freed. Nonetheless, despite their financial success, social prejudice against black women has all but erased them from the historical record. [JM]

Figueirôa, Silvia Fernanda de Mendonça. Mundialização da ciência e respostas locais: sobre a institucionalização das ciências naturais no Brasil, de fins do século XVIII à transição ao século XX. See item **3270.**

3167 Figueirôa, Silvia Fernanda de Mendonça and **Clarete da Silva.** Enlightened mineralogists: mining knowledge in colonial Brazil, 1750–1825. (*Osiris/Chicago*, 15, 2000, p. 174–189, facsims.)

Based on lives of two Brazilian mineralogists of late colonial period, authors conclude that Portuguese Enlightenment science, even in Brazil, worked in favor of the metropolitan government by linking the colony more tightly to the mother country. [JM]

Florentino, Manolo Garcia and **José Roberto Góes.** A paz das senzalas: famílias escravas e tráfico atlântico, Rio de Janeiro, c. 1790-c. 1850. See item **3272.**

3168 Fonseca, Luís Adão da. De Vasco a Cabral: oriente e ocidente nas navegações oceânicas. Revisão técnica de Maria Helena Ribeiro da Cunha. Bauru, Brazil: EDUSC; Brasília: Embaixada de Portugal, Instituto Camões, 2001. 248 p.: bibl., ill. (some col.), maps (some col.). (Col. História)

Biographer of Vasco da Gama and Pedro Alvares Cabral provides valuable new work focusing on formative period of modern seafaring. Work shifts focus from the men to the age, and to the manner in which the lives of da Gama and Cabral can serve as entry points to studying the spirit of that age. Highlights international context and consequences of first and second Portuguese expeditions to India. [JM]

3169 Fragoso, João Luís Ribeiro. Algumas notas sobre a noção de colonial tardio no Rio de Janeiro: um ensaio sobre a economia colonial. (*LOCUS Rev. Hist.*, 6:1, 2000, p. 9–36, bibl., tables)

Describes Rio de Janeiro in late colonial times as a society marked by the presence of merchants engaged in both internal commerce and trade across the South Atlantic. In early 19th century, by then dominating Atlantic slave trade, Rio de Janeiro had without question surpassed Salvador and Recife in economic importance. Late colonial Brazil thus was characterized by rising ascendancy of Rio de Janeiro's port, a thriving mercantile center looking inward (to commerce with Minas Gerais in particular) and outward across the Atlantic. [JM]

3170 Furtado, Júnia Ferreira. Família e relações de gênero no Tejuco: o caso de Chica da Silva. (*Varia Hist.*, 24, jan. 2001, p. 33–74, bibl.)

Excellent debunking of popular image of Chica da Silva, based on meticulous archival work using baptismal records, episcopal visit records, and confraternity records. Finds that Chica lived in a stable relationship with João Fernandes de Oliveira from 1755 until his return to Lisbon in 1770. Their 13 children were all formally recognized by their father; were named after relatives of both João Fernandes and Chica; and were educated in the best schools in the region. Chica and her children, as befitted their social status, were involved in all the confraternities of Tejuco. This story succeeds in demonstrating the hopes and accomplishments of at least one freed woman in Minas Gerais. [JM]

3171 Furtado, Júnia Ferreira. Homens de negócio: a interiorização da metrópole e do comércio nas Minas setecentistas. São Paulo: Editora Hucitec, 1999. 289 p.: bibl. (Estudos históricos; 38)

Based largely on correspondence of Francisco Pinheiro (a wealthy Portuguese merchant) with his commercial agents in Minas Gerais between 1712–44. Demonstrates how webs of commerce contributed to solidify not only economic ties but also cultural connections between colony and mother country. [JM]

3172 Galvani, Walter. Nau capitânia: Pedro Alvares Cabral; como e com quem começamos. Rio de Janeiro: Editora Record, 1999. 320 p.: bibl., ill. (some col.), index, col. maps.

Researched in Brazil, Portugal, Spain, France, and Italy, this engagingly written biography of Cabral is told primarily in Cabral's own voice, giving reader sense of being with him through his childhood, his voyages, and, ultimately, his disappointments in the Portuguese court. Author grounds Cabral (and Portugal more generally) firmly in the Renaissance, demonstrating how the captain was shaped and influenced by the age in which he lived. [JM]

3173 González de Canales y López Obrero, Fernando. Iconografía española en la defensa hispana de Brasil, 1624–1640. (*Rev. Hist. Nav.*, 18:69, 2000, p. 7–36, bibl., ill.)

Describes and analyzes significance of 16 Spanish paintings that depict Spain's efforts to keep Brazil from falling to the Dutch between 1624 Flemish attack on Bahia and restoration of a Portuguese king in 1640. [JM]

3174 Gouvêa, Maria de Fátima Silva. Redes de poder na América Portuguesa: o caso dos homens bons do Rio de Janeiro, 1790–1822. (*Rev. Bras. Hist./São Paulo*, 18:36, 1998, p. 297–330)

Good summary of recent work on significance of Rio de Janeiro in late-18th through early-19th-century Luso-Brazilian empire. Demonstrates that after 1815, wealthy merchants gained access to important public offices and strongly supported the monarchy. Proposes a more careful study of lists describing those men who could hold office in Rio de Janeiro. Eight such lists, compiled between 1794–1822, are now housed in the Arquivo Nacional and the Arquivo Geral da Cidade do Rio de Janeiro. [JM]

3175 Guia de fontes para a história do Brasil holandês: acervos de manuscritos em arquivos holandeses. Organização de Marcos Galindo e Lodewijk Hulsman. Apresentação de Francisco Weffort. Estudo introdutório e organização editorial de Leonardo Dantas Silva. Brasília: Projeto Resgate; Recife, Brazil: Fundação Joaquim Nabuco, Editora Massangana, Instituto de Cultura, 2001. 376 p.: bibl. (Série Obras de consulta; 22)

Excellent guide to Dutch archives housing materials pertaining to colonial Brazil. Includes basic information on access to the archives: location, hours of operation, research facilities. Also includes research reports of José Hygino Duarte Pereira (from 1885–86) and José Antônio Gonsalves de Mello (from 1957–58). [JM]

3176 Hermann, Jacqueline. Sebastianismo e sedição: os rebeldes do Rodeador na "Cidade do Paraíso Terrestre", Pernambuco, 1817–1820. (*Tempo/Rio de Janeiro*, 6:11, julho 2001, p. 131–142)

Based on 1820 *devassa* (housed in the Arquivo Nacional in Rio de Janeiro) of the rebellion at Serra do Rodeador, author links search for an earthly paradise and return of King Sebastian to both old Portuguese traditions and more recent 1817 revolution in Pernambuco. [JM]

3177 Higgins, Kathleen J. "Licentious liberty" in a Brazilian gold-mining region: slavery, gender, and social control in eighteenth-century Sabará, Minas Gerais. University Park: Pennsylvania State Univ. Press, 1999. 236 p.: bibl., ill., index, maps.

Outstanding study of changing fortunes of slaves in a mining economy gives particular attention to how women and children fared, in times of both growing wealth and scarcity of free females, and declining wealth and increased presence of white women. Under Higgins' careful scrutiny, Minas Gerais gold rush provides backdrop for examining complexities of human relations in a colonial society. [JM]

3178 Kiddy, Elizabeth W. *Congados, calunga, candombe:* Our Lady of the Rosary in Minas Gerais, Brazil. (*Luso-Braz. Rev.*, 37:1, Summer 2000, p. 47–61, bibl.)

Examines *congados* as a medium in which Portuguese and African traditions mixed. Argues that slave participation in confraternities should not be seen as either accommodation or resistance to slavery; instead, it is best understood as a conscious move from social marginality to incorporation, and ultimately from slavery to freedom. Traces devotion to Our Lady of the Rosary to Africa and association with African cosmologies. See also items **3129, 3182,** and **3214.** [JM]

3179 Kühn, Fábio. A fronteira em movimento: relações luso-castelhanas na segunda metade do século XVIII. (*Estud. Ibero-Am./Porto Alegre*, 25:2, dez. 1999, p. 91–112, bibl., tables)

A contribution to Brazilian borderland studies. Author uses parish records to gauge presence of Portuguese and Spanish individuals in southern Brazil's "moving frontier,"

claimed by both Portugal and Spain. Highlights significant cooperation between the two groups. Animosities grew, however, during Seven Years' War when Portugal supported England and Spain sided with France. [JM]

3180 Leite, Edgard. Resistências à "língua geral" no Brasil e Maranhão, século XVIII. (*Rev. Inst. Hist. Geogr. Bras.*, 160:403, abril/junho 1999, p. 399–423)

Examines Jesuit-created indigenous language as a cultural space hovering between colonizer and colonized. By 18th century Portuguese-speaking colonists were complaining that they had to learn the *língua geral* in order to communicate with indigenous peoples who would not learn Portuguese. Author sees Pombal's attempts to enforce royal authority as tied to attacks on the *língua geral* and on the Jesuits who created and propagated the new hybrid language. [JM]

3181 Libby, Douglas Cole and Clotilde Andrade Paiva. Manumission practices in a late eighteenth-century Brazilian slave parish: São José d'El Rey in 1795. (*Slavery Abolit.*, 21:1, April 2000, p. 96–127, map, tables)

Excellent quantitative analysis of material contained in recently uncovered "Rol dos Confessados da Freguezia de São José" (Minas Gerais). Demonstrates strength of the local economy (seen in the balanced sex ratio), the fairly egalitarian distribution of slaves (the overwhelming majority of slaveowners held fewer than 20 slaves), the diversity of the slave population, and the intricacies of manumission (a number of slaves were purchasing their freedom in installments). [JM]

3182 Lima, Carlos A.M. *Em certa corporação:* politizando convivências em irmandades negras no Brasil escravista, 1700–1850. (*Hist. Quest. Debates*, 16:30, jan./junho 1999, p. 11–38, bibl.)

Interesting interpretation of why certain racial and ethnic groups joined specific Catholic confraternities. Joining these groups is seen not so much as reconnecting to an African ethnic past, but rather as establishing political links in the New World through membership in Crown-sanctioned organizations that represented members in day-to-day political matters. Restricting membership solidified a sense of belonging for those who were admitted. See also items **3129, 3178,** and **3214.** [JM]

3183 Lima, Carlos A.M. Escravos artesãos: preço e família, Rio de Janeiro, 1789–1839. (*Estud. Econ./São Paulo,* 30:3, julho/set. 2000, p. 447–484, bibl., graphs, tables)

Based on 296 estate inventories that include references to 3,268 slaves (of whom 1,132 were artisans), author uses price of slaves to elucidate how much artisan slaves might be expected to earn for their masters. Concludes that investing in artisan slaves was a more speculative venture than was buying field hands. Draws on work of Robert Fogel, Stanley Engerman, and Eugene Genovese, using discussions of slavery throughout the Americas to analyze a very specific segment of Brazilian slave population. Finds that the more specialized slaves were least likely to become part of a family unit. [JM]

3184 Lima, Carlos A.M. Sobre migrações para a América Portuguesa: o caso do Rio de Janeiro, com especial referência aos açorianos, 1786–1844. (*Estud. Ibero-Am./Porto Alegre,* 26:2, dez. 2000, p. 91–120, bibl., table)

Using baptismal records from parish of São José, author examines family strategies of a significant number of immigrants from mainland Portugal and the Azores to Rio de Janeiro in late 18th-early 19th centuries. Many saw Brazil as a land of opportunity, especially for women who were able to rise socially through marriage. [JM]

3185 López Gómez, Pedro and **María del Mar García Miraz.** Fuentes archivísticas para la historia del Brasil en España, siglos XV-XVII. (*Rev. Indias,* 60:218, enero/abril 2000, p. 135–179, tables)

Excellent short guide of sources for colonial Brazilian history located in Spain. Describes archives and materials related to Brazil in Archivo General de Simancas, Archivo General de las Índias, Archivos de las Reales Chancillerías de Valladolid y Granada, Archivo del Reino de Valencia (Jesuits' collection), Archivo del Reino de Galicia, Archivos Militares, and Archivos de la Casa de Alba y de los Duques de Medinaceli. [JM]

Maestri Filho, Mário José. Jesuítas e Tupinambas: a catequese impossível. See item **751.**

Maldi, Denise. De confederados a bárbaros: a representação da territorialidade e da fronteira indígenas nos século XVIII e XIX. See item **752.**

3186 Mariutti, Eduardo Barros; Luiz Paulo Ferreira Noguerói; and **Mário Danieli Neto.** Mercado interno colonial e grau de autonomia: críticas às propostas de João Luís Fragoso e Manolo Florentino. (*Estud. Econ./São Paulo,* 31:2, 2001, p. 369–393, bibl., graphs, tables)

A critique of the revisionism of Fragoso and Florentino, article stresses that Rio de Janeiro was a special case (the most important South Atlantic port and headquarters of the Portuguese monarchy in early 19th century) and cannot be used to make generalizations for all of Brazil. Also argues that Fragoso's and Florentino's numbers do not actually indicate that Brazil's colonial economy was spared from European economic fluctuations between 1790–1830; and that Fragoso and Florentino essentially agree with the traditional view that slavery perpetuated hierarchical social relations and the exclusion of many, a situation that continues to characterize Brazilian society today. [JM]

3187 Mariz, Vasco and **Lucien Provençal.** Villegagnon e a França Antártica: uma reavaliação. Rio de Janeiro: Biblioteca do Exército Editora; Editora Nova Fronteira, 2000. 211 p.: bibl., ill., map. (Publicação/Biblioteca do Exército Editora; 707. Col. General Benício; 370)

Biography of Villegaignon focuses on his years in Brazil. Downplaying descriptions of him by Protestants such as Jean de Léry, author presents a very favorable picture of this protagonist. [JM]

3188 Mata, Sérgio da. *Religionswissenschaften* e crítica da historiografia da Minas colonial. (*Rev. Hist./São Paulo,* 136, primeiro semestre 1997, p. 41–57, bibl.)

Argues that there was extreme intolerance toward African religious practices in colonial Minas Gerais. Urges a more careful consideration of connections between faith and religious practice, and faith and politics. Good bibliography. [JM]

3189 Miller, Shawn W. Fruitless trees: Portuguese conservation and Brazil's colonial timber. Stanford, Calif.: Stanford Univ. Press, 2000. 325 p.: bibl., ill., map.

Argues that Portuguese crown's monopoly on timber contributed to devastation of valuable forests. Extends argument on evils of monopoly to most of Brazil's colonial economy: monopoly contributed to waste and benefited no one in the long run. Provides fascinating view of wealth and variety of timber in Brazil's Atlantic forest. [JM]

3190 Miller, Shawn W. Merchant shipbuilding in late-colonial Brazil: the evidence for a substantial private industry. (*CLAHR*, 9:1, Winter 2000, p. 103–135, ill., map, tables)

Marshals evidence suggesting that private shipbuilding was a fairly significant component of Brazil's colonial economy. Although opening of Brazilian ports to foreign trade in 1808 demonstrated that Brazilian products could not compete with manufactures from Northern Europe, Brazil's abundant supply of excellent timber made it competitive in shipbuilding. In fact, Brazil may have supplied as much as half of Portugal's merchant fleet in the 50 years preceding independence. [JM]

3191 Monteiro, John Manuel. The heathen castes of sixteenth-century Portuguese America: unity, diversity, and the invention of the Brazilian Indians. (*HAHR*, 80:4, Nov. 2000, p. 697–719)

Analyzes Gabriel Soares de Sousa's 16th-century description of different groups of Brazilian indigenous peoples. Also looks at how his work was used in 19th century, particularly by Francisco Adolfo de Varnhagen in creating Brazilian myth of the "disappearing" Indian. [JM]

3192 Monteiro, John Manuel. Sal, justiça social e autoridade régia: São Paulo no início do século XVIII. (*Tempo/Rio de Janeiro*, 4:8, dez. 1999, p. 23–40)

Based on accounts of 1710 attack on salt storage sites in Santos, author explores world of miscegenation, power, and violence in 18th-century São Paulo as landowners sought to preserve control over their captive indigenous peoples and to survive in face of mounting prices fueled by gold rush in Minas Gerais. [JM]

3193 Monteiro, Rodrigo Bentes. A Rochela do Brasil: São Paulo e a aclamação de Amador Bueno como espelho da realeza portuguesa. (*Rev. Hist./São Paulo*, 141, segundo semestre 1999, p. 21–44, bibl.)

Examines attempt to crown Amador Bueno king in São Paulo following reception of news in 1640 of restoration of a Portuguese dynasty. Explains attempt as linked to concerns that Portugal was too favorable to the Jesuits (who had been expelled from São Paulo in 1640) and not concerned enough with *paulistas'* need for indigenous labor (the Braganças supported use of African labor instead). [JM]

Morel, Marco. A política nas ruas: os espaços públicos na cidade imperial do Rio de Janeiro. See item **3304.**

3194 Nazzari, Muriel. Vanishing Indians: the social construction of race in colonial São Paulo. (*Americas/Washington*, 57:4, April 2001, p. 497–524, tables)

Using 13 manuscript censuses for Santana, a rural neighborhood of São Paulo, article demonstrates that the six racial categories used in 18th century (*branco, carijó, bastardo, mulato, pardo*, and *negro*) were reduced to three in the 19th (*branco, pardo*, and *negro*). Concludes that as Indians and *bastardos* became *pardos*, distinctions between whites and "others" became more glaring, to the advantage of the white population. Provides a good reminder that one must not assume that the category *pardo* in 19th century refers only to those of mixed African and European descent. [JM]

3195 Novinsky, Anita. Ser marrano em Minas colonial. (*Rev. Bras. Hist./São Paulo*, 20:40, 2001, p. 161–176)

Although Minas Gerais was third (after Bahia and Rio de Janeiro) in number of Judaizers tried by the Inquisition, a full 42 percent of those burned at the stake were from Minas Gerais. Author stresses importance of understanding local New Christian communities throughout Brazil and their particular traits, while not losing sight of what contributed to the continued separation of *marranos* from the larger society. [JM]

3196 Nozoe, Nelson Hideiki and José Flávio Motta. Os produtores eventuais de café: nota sobre os primórdios da cafeicultura paulista; Bananal, 1799–1829. (*LOCUS Rev. Hist.*, 5:1, 1999, p. 51–84, bibl., tables)

Study of Bananal region of São Paulo finds that by late 18th century, small farmers were producing coffee for market, but their involvement with the crop was unstable and most had abandoned it by late 1820s. Process of accumulation of land and labor tended over time to concentrate production of the crop in a few hands. [DM]

3197 Oliveira, Mário Mendonça de. A engenharia militar de batina. (*Def. Nac. / Rio de Janeiro*, 85:784, maio/agôsto 1999, p. 33–45, bibl., ill.)

Describes significant contributions of clerics to military science in 17th-18th centuries. Many who became military engineers had studied in Jesuit schools, and many of the original designs for fortifications along the Brazilian coast appear to have been drawn by Jesuit fathers. [JM]

3198 Osório, Helena. Comerciantes do Rio Grande de São Pedro: formação, recrutamento e negócios de um grupo mercantil da América Portuguesa. (*Rev. Bras. Hist. /São Paulo*, 20:39, 2000, p. 99–134, tables)

Analysis of a merchant community examines emergence of trade networks in Rio Grande do Sul in 18th century. Author is particularly interested in comparisons with Rio de Janeiro merchants of the same period. Finds that many of the southern merchants had links to Colônia do Sacramento, Angola, Rio de Janeiro, and Bahia. Most were from Portugal (Minho in particular), and were careful to maintain family ties across the Atlantic. [JM]

3199 Pádua, José Augusto. "Aniquilando as naturais produções": crítica iluminista, crise colonial e as origens do ambientalismo político no Brasil, 1786–1810. (*Dados/ Rio de Janeiro*, 42:3, 1999, p. 497–538, bibl.)

Builds on Richard Groves' findings that environmentalism began in European colonies. While Groves found that colonial administrators raised environmental concerns, Pádua claims that native-born members of Brazilian elite became concerned with degradation of natural environment between late 18th-late 19th centuries. Thus environmentalism should not be seen as a critique of modernity but as a product of the very forces that shaped the modern world: the growing

sense of interconnectedness, the Enlightenment, and tensions between colonies and mother countries. [JM]

A paisagem carioca. See item **410.**

3200 Pedreira, Jorge Miguel Viana. From growth to collapse: Portugal, Brazil, and the breakdown of the old colonial system, 1760–1830. (*HAHR*, 80:4, Nov. 2000, p. 839–864, graphs, table)

Disputes thesis put forward by Fernando Novais that 1808 opening of Brazil's ports was culmination of long period of crisis in colonial system. Argues instead that what had favored Portuguese economic growth in late 18th century (international wars that increased value and production of Brazilian cotton and sugar) worked against it under Napoleon's continental system, leading to an abrupt crisis and to Brazil's independence. [JM]

3201 Pieroni, Geraldo. Os degredados na colonização do Brasil. (*in* 1500/2000 trajetórias. Belo Horizonte, Brazil: Centro Universitário Newton Paiva Curso de História, 1999, p. 55–68)

Focusing on 16th-century materials in Lisbon's Arquivo Nacional da Torre do Tombo, provides good overview of banishment to Brazil, including legislation governing the practice and Inquisition records of those sentenced to exile. [JM]

3202 Pieroni, Geraldo. Vadios e ciganos, heréticos e bruxas: os degredados no Brasil-colônia. Rio de Janeiro: Ministério da Cultura, Fundação Biblioteca Nacional, Depto. Nacional do Livro; Bertrand Brasil, 2000. 136 p.: bibl.

Following introduction that discusses role of those banished from Portugal to colonizing Brazil, author examines legislation that governed banishment as well as life of some of the exiles. [JM]

3203 Pimenta, Tânia Salgado. Barbeiros-sangradores e curandeiros no Brasil, 1808–28. (*Hist. Ciênc. Saúde Manguinhos*, 5:2, julho/out. 1998, p. 349–373, bibl., graphs)

Growing emphasis on academic medicine in first half of 19th century led doctors and the state to denigrate and then persecute practitioners of popular medicine. *Sangradores* and *curandeiros* typically were ex-slaves or free blacks, who found a clientele for their herbs and indigenous/African remedies chiefly among the poor who could not afford doctors. [DM]

3204 Pires, Maria do Carmo. Glossário jurídico: a justiça eclesiástica no Brasil setecentista. (*Estud. Hist./Franca*, 7:1, 2000, p. 215–223, bibl.)

Useful brief glossary of terms used in ecclesiastical tribunals in colonial Brazil. [JM]

3205 Pompa, Cristina. As muitas línguas da conversão: missionários, Tupi e "Tapuia" no Brasil colonial. (*Tempo/Rio de Janeiro*, 6:11, julho 2001, p. 27–44)

Examines complexities of cultural transfers between indigenous peoples and Europeans by describing how evangelization of the more hostile Tapuya was carried out with experience gained from earlier interaction with friendlier Tupi, thus demonstrating ways in which colonial encounters transformed Catholic endeavors. [JM]

3206 Os primeiros 14 documentos relativos à Armada de Pedro Álvares Cabral = The first 14 documents about Pedro Álvares Cabral's Armada. Edição de Joaquim Antero Romero Magalhães e Susana Münch Miranda. Lisboa: Comissão Nacional para as Comemorações dos Descobrimentos Portugueses: Instituto dos Arquivos Nacionais/Torre do Tombo, 1999. 130 p.: bibl. (Col. Outras margens)

Anthology of first documents about the discovery of Brazil contains the Vaz de Caminha letter and lesser-known documents. [F. Obermeier]

3207 Raynal, abbé. O estabelecimento dos portugueses no Brasil. Prefácio de Berenice Cavalcante. Rio de Janeiro: Ministério da Justiça, Arquivo Nacional; Brasília: Editora UnB, 1998. 160 p.: bibl. (Publicações históricas; 93)

Re-edition of section of Abbé Raynal's 1770 work dealing with Brazil. Interesting for insight provided into thinking of Enlightenment figure who influenced conspirators of Vila Rica in 1789 and Salvador in 1798. [JM]

Reis, João José. Identidade e diversidade étnicas nas irmandades negras no tempo da escravidão. See item **3318.**

Reis, João José. Slaves as agents of history: a note on the new historiography of slavery in Brazil. See item **3319.**

3208 Reis Filho, Nestor Goulart. Imagens de vilas e cidades do Brasil colonial. Colaboração de Beatriz Piccolotto Siqueira Bueno e Paulo Júlio Valentino Bruna. São Paulo: Editora da Univ. de São Paulo; Imprensa Oficial do Estado, 2000. 411 p.: chiefly col. ill., col. maps. (USPIANA—Brasil 500 anos)

Outstanding edition of maps and views of Brazil's colonial cities contains very good reproductions. Material is of great value for research on colonial urban history. Particularly rich is material from 17th-century Dutch colonies of Recife and Pernambuco, created mainly for military purposes. [F. Obermeier]

3209 Romeiro, Adriana. Um visionário na corte de D. João V: revolta e milenarismo nas Minas Gerais. Belo Horizonte, Brazil: Editora UFMG, 2001. 286 p.: bibl. (Humanitas; 57)

Inspired by Natalie Davis and Carlo Ginsburg, author illuminates 18th-century complexities and tensions within Portuguese empire by following life of Pedro de Rates Henequim. Henequim conspired to convince Infante D. Manuel (younger brother of D. João V) to come to Brazil to inaugurate the millennial kingdom of peace prophesied in the Hebrew Scriptures. Henequim was eventually accused of heresy for, among other things, claiming that Brazil was the location of the earthly paradise as well as the place from which God created the world. [JM]

3210 Russell-Wood, A.J.R. Ambivalent authorities: the African and Afro-Brazilian contribution to local governance in colonial Brazil. (*Americas/Washington*, 57:1, July 2000, p. 13–36)

Despite very clear laws banning individuals of African descent from certain offices and social positions, author demonstrates that Brazilians with African blood could, at times and based on merit, receive such appointments and honors. The largest contribution of Africans and Afro-Brazilians to local governance, however, was in preserving order as bush captains and members of militias. [JM]

3211 Russell-Wood, A.J.R. Holy and unholy alliances: clerical participation in the flow of bullion from Brazil to Portugal during the reign of Dom João V, 1706–1750. (*HAHR*, 80:4, Nov. 2000, p. 815–837)

Uses ships' manifests of gold, silver, and jewels sent from Brazil to Portugal in first half of 18th century (recorded in 756 bound volumes housed in Lisbon's Casa da Moeda) to illuminate circulation of wealth among religious orders throughout the Portuguese empire. [JM]

3212 Schultz, Kirsten. Royal authority, empire and the critique of colonialism: political discourse in Rio de Janeiro, 1808–1821. (*Luso-Braz. Rev.*, 37:2, Winter 2000, p. 7–31)

Describes ways in which different visions of constitutionalism in Portugal and Brazil paved the way for Brazilian independence based on a monarchical tradition that incorporated a new view of monarchy's legitimacy. [JM]

3213 Silva, Flávio Marcus da. Agricultura e pecuária em Minas Gerais no século XVIII: uma abordagem política. (*Hist. Perspect.*/*Uberlândia*, 20/12, 1999, p. 9–31)

Arguing against notion that Portuguese government solely emphasized Brazilian export production, author points to documentation illustrating concern that scarcity and high price of food would cause riots and other criminal disturbances. To avoid this outcome, the state intervened to promote local production of food. [JM]

3214 Silva, Luiz Geraldo. Da festa à sedição: sociabilidades, etnia e controle social na América portuguesa, 1776–1814. (*Hist. Quest. Debates*, 16:30, jan./junho 1999, p. 83–110, bibl.)

Describes variety of lay and religious organizations in Recife and Olinda to which slaves and free blacks belonged. These organizations included all sorts of offices; at the very top was the Rei do Congo, elected in the annual meeting of the confraternity of Nossa Senhora do Rosário dos Pretos. Increasingly, this black hierarchy was used to keep ordinary blacks under control. During the Enlightenment, author argues, new forms of social control were introduced that curbed African practices, angering blacks in Brazil and leading to revolt. See also items **3129**, **3178**, and **3182**. [JM]

3215 Silva, Luiz Geraldo. "Sementes da sedição": etnia, revolta escrava e controle social na América Portuguesa, 1808–1817. (*Afro-Asia*/*Salvador*, 25/26, 2001, p. 9–60)

By addressing question of why slaves in Bahia seemed so much more rebellious during early 19th century than slaves in Pernambuco, author provides complex analysis of social control and slavery in Brazil. More of the Pernambuco slaves, he argues, had come from Angola where local strife had subsided, while slaves in Bahia tended to be from the Gulf of Benin where local conflict continued. Conditions within Brazil also contributed to the difference: blacks in Pernambuco, for example, had become more integrated into local society since 17th-century War of Restoration against the Dutch. [JM]

3216 Soares, Carlos Eugênio Líbano. O triângulo da desordem no Rio de Janeiro de D. João VI: escravos, senhores e policiais. (*An. Mus. Hist. Nac.*, 31, 1999, p. 69–80, bibl.)

Demonstrates ways in which police force created after arrival of Portuguese court in Brazil was used by both slaves and masters to promote their own interests. Thus, in early 19th century, state and private interests were not always united in matters involving control of slaves. [JM]

3217 Soares, Mariza de Carvalho. Descobrindo a Guiné no Brasil colonial. (*Rev. Inst. Hist. Geogr. Bras.*, 161:407, abril/junho 2000, p. 71–94, table)

Examines slow shift in terminology describing African slaves from more generic *gentios de Guiné* to *escravos da nação*, as expressed purpose of slave traffic changed from a supposed emphasis on religious conversion to use of Africans for agricultural labor in Brazil. As number of imported slaves grew, there was greater differentiation among those from different regions of Africa. Uses baptismal records from 18th-century Rio de Janeiro to support more firmly this shift seen in other sources. [JM]

3218 Souza, Antonio de. Do recôncavo aos Guararapes, ou, História resumida das guerras holandesas ao norte do Brasil. Rio de Janeiro: Biblioteca do Exército Editora, 1998. 209 p.: bibl., ill., maps. (Publicação/Biblioteca do Exército Editora; 665. Col. General Benício; 337)

Written to commemorate 300th anniversary of second Battle of Guararapes, volume provides detailed accounts of the two battles of Guararapes. Last section, titled "Brazilian Heroes," is comprised of short biographies of officers who led their soldiers against the Dutch. [JM]

3219 Souza, Iara Lis Carvalho. Pátria coroada: o Brasil como corpo político autônomo, 1780–1831. São Paulo: Editora UNESP Fundação, 1999. 396 p.: bibl., ill. (some col.). (Col. Prismas)

Examines emergence of a Brazilian nation through public festivities surrounding figure of the monarch, first as they took place in Portugal and then as they were transferred along with the Portuguese court to Brazil. Special attention is given to Pedro I—from his acclamation in 1822, to his abdication in 1831, to erection of a statue in his honor in 1862 on the site of execution of Tiradentes. Demonstrates how public debates surrounding person of the king helped to shape the new nation. [JM]

3220 Souza, Laura de Mello e and Maria Fernanda Bicalho. 1680–1720, o império deste mundo. Coordenação de Laura de Mello e Souza e Lilia Moritz Schwarcz. São Paulo: Companhia das Letras, 2000. 121 p.: bibl., ill., maps. (Virando séculos; 4)

Between 1680–1720, hope for a "divine kingdom" was replaced by a new enthusiasm for the "kingdom of this world." Decade of 1690s marked not only the death of Father Antônio Vieira and his prophetic vision of Portugal's role in the "fifth kingdom" of millennial peace, but also destruction of Palmares and discovery of gold. Although material wealth proved as fleeting as celestial peace, author argues that end of 17th century was the last time Portuguese elites embraced messianic views. [JM]

3221 Stella, Roseli Santaella. O domínio espanhol no Brasil durante a monarquia dos Felipes, 1580–1640. Prefácio de Luiz Felipe de Seixas Corrêa. São Paulo: UNIBERO, Centro Universitário Ibero-Americano; CenaUn Editora, 2000. 374 p.: bibl., ill., index.

Based on material housed in the Archivo General de Simancas, argues that European efforts to administer Brazil increased after 1580 when colony was governed from Madrid. This Spanish influence had permanent effects as seen in importance of

Spanish legal code (the *ordenações filipinas*) and of Spanish missionaries long after restoration of the Portuguese crown in 1640. Also available in Spanish as *Brasil durante el gobierno español, 1580–1640* (2000). [JM]

3222 Tempo dos flamengos e outros tempos: Brasil século XVII. Organização de Manuel Correia de Oliveira Andrade, Eliane Moury Fernandes, e Sandra Melo Cavalcanti. Brasília: Conselho Nacional de Desenvolvimento Científico e Tecnológico; Recife, Brazil: Fundação Joaquim Nabuco, Editora Massangana, 1999. 351 p.: bibl., ill., maps. (Série Descobrimentos; 12)

Proceedings of 1998 conference at Fundação Joaquim Nabuco in Recife celebrating quincentenary of arrival of Dutch in Brazil. This is second of four such conferences, each named after title of an important book on Brazilian history and culture written by a *pernambucano*. Includes papers on Maurício de Nassau, religion (Calvinist and Roman Catholic) in 17th-century northeast Brazil, and role of different ethnic groups in Dutch Brazil. [JM]

3223 A terra de Vera Cruz: viagens descrições e mapas do século XVIII; exposição integrada nas comemorações do V Centenário da Descoberta do Brasil. Coordenação de Jorge Costa. Texto de João Carlos Garcia e André Ferrand de Almeida. Porto, Portugal: Biblioteca Pública Municipal do Porto, 2000. 102 p.: bibl., maps (chiefly col.).

Catalog of exhibition of 18th-century manuscript maps and travel accounts housed in the Biblioteca Pública Municipal do Porto. Much of the exhibit came from private collection of the Viscondes de Balsemão (the first of whom was governor of Mato Grosso and Cuiabá between 1767–72, then Minister of State during reign of D. Maria I), which became part of the Porto library after 1833. [JM]

3224 Tinhorão, José Ramos. As festas no Brasil colonial. São Paulo: Editora 34, 2000. 173 p.: bibl., ill.

Descriptions, accompanied by illustrations (often drawings by travelers who had visited Brazil), of ways in which Africans transformed Portuguese civic and religious festivities in the colony. See also item **3140.** [JM]

3225 Torres Londoño, Fernando. A outra família: concubinato, igreja e escândalo na colônia. São Paulo: História Social,

USP; Edições Loyola, 1999. 214 p.: bibl. (Série Teses; 10)

Traces development of out-of-wedlock unions from simply a practical way of forming families in early colonial Brazil to a "scandalous sin" that could lead to public excommunication by 18th century. According to author, accusations and confessions that accompanied ecclesiastical *devassas* helped to crystallize acceptance of common values and rejection of concubinage for Brazilian Christians. [JM]

3226 Varela Marcos, Jesús. Castilla descubrió el Brasil en 1500. Valladolid, Spain: Instituto Interuniversitario de Estudios de Iberoamérica y Portugal; Madrid: Editorial Deimos, 2001. 156 p.: bibl., ill., maps (some col.).

Discusses expedition of Vicente Yáñez Pinzón to northern coast of Brazil in Jan. 1500. Highlights close ties (rather than competition) between Portugal and Spain during years immediately before and after Columbus' first voyage to America. [JM]

3227 Visões do Rio de Janeiro colonial: antologia de textos, 1531–1800. Organização de Jean Marcel Carvalho França. Rio de Janeiro: EdUERJ; J. Olympio Editora, 1999. 261 p.: bibl.

Useful anthology collecting 35 unusual and hard-to-find sources written by travelers (Portuguese, French, Saxon, Dutch, Spanish, English, and German) who visited Rio de Janeiro during colonial period. These important texts helped to construct a "European vision" of Brazil. Editor provides excellent background information for each selection. Accounts describe land and its indigenous inhabitants, as well as the Portuguese and their descendants in Rio de Janeiro. As a whole, volume also gives good insight into geopolitics of the period as readers consider what brought these foreigners to Rio de Janeiro. [JM]

3228 Wehling, Arno and **Maria José Wehling.** A justiça colonial: fundamentos e formas. (*Rev. SBPH*, 17, 1999, p. 3–16)

Good overview of Portuguese system of justice, both civil and religious, as adapted to Brazil. [JM]

3229 Wehling, Arno and **Maria José Wehling.** Racionalismo ilustrado e prática jurídica colonial: o direito das

sucessões no Brasil, 1750–1808. (*Rev. Inst. Hist. Geogr. Bras.*, 159:401, out./dez. 1998, p. 1607–1623)

Examines reforms instituted in Portugal under Pombal administration that changed laws of inheritance in order, authors believe, to limit wealth being willed to the Church in Brazil through individual *terças*. With fall of Pombal, the legislation was reversed. Article describes challenges as well as accommodations to new legislation. [JM]

NATIONAL

3230 Abreu, Marcelo de Paiva. O Brasil e a economia mundial, 1930–1945. Traduzido de Eduardo Loyo e Mário Mesquita. Rio de Janeiro: Civilização Brasileira, 1999. 398 p.: bibl.

Important study of international trade and financial relations attributes decline of British influence to short-sighted defense of bondholders' interests, rise of US influence, and strategic sacrifice of financial claims in order to achieve both short-term security goals and long-term trade and investment goals. Author disputes conventional wisdom on fiscal policy of early 1930s, impact of German trade (it displaced British, not US, trade), nature of tariff policy, and impact of indirect and direct protection on industrial development. Based on British, Brazilian, and US diplomatic archives. [DB]

3231 Adamo, Sam. The sick and the dead: epidemic and contagious disease in Rio de Janeiro, Brazil. (*in* Cities of hope: people, protests, and progress in urbanizing Latin America, 1870–1930. Edited by Ronn Pineo and James A. Baer. Boulder, Colo.: Westview Press, 1998, p. 218–239, graphs, table)

Argues that disease control and public health measures in Rio were intended primarily to protect elites and improve city's image, not to alleviate the suffering of predominantly black and mulatto poor. For historian's comment on entire book, see item **856.** [DM]

3232 Amory, Frederic. Euclides da Cunha and Brazilian positivism. (*Luso-Braz. Rev.*, 36:1, Summer 1999, p. 87–94, bibl.)

Auguste Comte and French positivism had less influence than Charles Darwin and Herbert Spencer's evolutionism upon Da

Cunha's *Rebellion in the Backlands* (1902). [DB]

Anderson, Robin Leslie. Colonization as exploitation in the Amazon rain forest, 1758–1911. See item **3137.**

3233 Aquino, Maria Aparecida de. Censura, imprensa, estado autoritário, 1968–1978: o exercício cotidiano da dominação e da resistência, *O Estado de São Paulo* e *Movimento.* Bauru, Brazil: EDUSC, 1999. 269 p.: bibl., ill. (Col. História)

Compares censors' cuts of mainstream newspaper *O Estado de São Paulo* and alternative *Movimento,* from 1968–78, both to assess range of press coverage and editorial opinion, and to outline military government's ideology and propaganda policy. Originally presented as MA thesis, based on periodicals' archives, amply illustrated with photos of correspondence and censored pages. [DB]

3234 Araújo, Ubiratan Castro de. 1846: um ano na rota Bahia-Lagos; negócios, negociantes e outros parceiros. (*Afro-Asia/Salvador,* 21/22, 1998/99, p. 83–110, bibl., tables)

Observations of the French consul at Bahia form the basis for discussion of the late slave trade in Brazil. Article provides useful description of mechanics of the trade and highlights participation by local officials. [DM]

3235 Azevedo, Celia Maria Marinho de. Raza e historia: Africa, Haití, y la rebelión de los esclavos en el imaginario abolicionista. (*Allpanchis/Cuzco,* 30:52, segundo semestre 1998, p. 165–182)

Comparison of attitudes of abolitionists in Brazil and US toward Africa and toward violent slave resistance shows that those in US were more supportive of rebellion because of country's revolutionary past, because their approach was rooted in religious-based morality, and because they operated from outside a slave system. [DM]

3236 Barickman, B.J. A Bahian counterpoint: sugar, tobacco, cassava, and slavery in the Recôncavo, 1780–1860. Stanford, Calif.: Stanford Univ. Press, 1998. 276 p.: bibl., ill., index, maps.

Innovative study of 19th-century nonsugar economies of the Recôncavo. Many small commercial producers of cassava and tobacco employed slaves, together with family members and *agregados,* and they worked their own land, although "ownership" was often clouded by competing claims. [DM]

3237 Barman, Roderick J. Citizen emperor: Pedro II and the making of Brazil, 1825–1891. Stanford, Calif.: Stanford Univ. Press, 1999. 548 p.: bibl., ill., index, maps.

The long-awaited, probably definitive, biography of Pedro II focuses on how the Emperor's personality and interactions with political elites helped form the new nation. Over time Pedro lost touch with the changes occurring in Brazil, and his interventions came to be seen as counterproductive, contributing to overthrow of the Empire. See also item **3331.** [DM]

3238 Beattie, Peter M. Conscription versus penal servitude: army reform's influence on the Brazilian state's management of social control, 1870–1930. (*J. Soc. Hist.,* 32:4, Summer 1999, p. 847–878, bibl., tables)

Documents the transition in thinking about the army, which came to be considered an instrument for social reform rather than a punitive institution, with a parallel shift from forced conscription to a lottery draft system. The army resented its role as a dumping ground for petty criminals and sought to professionalize as well as to be released from policing functions. [DM]

3239 Bell, Stephen. Campanha gaúcha: a Brazilian ranching system, 1850–1920. Stanford, Calif.: Stanford Univ. Press, 1998. 292 p.: bibl., ill., index, maps.

Historical geographer documents development of Rio Grande do Sul as a "subsidiary economy" linked to export sector indirectly through *charque* production. Small profits, a scarcely functioning legal system, and political violence limited investment in modernization until after turn of the century. [DM]

3240 Bergad, Laird W. Slavery and the demographic and economic history of Minas Gerais, 1720–1888. New York: Cambridge Univ. Press, 1999. 298 p.: bibl., index, maps. (Cambridge Latin American studies)

While chiefly an analysis of slave demographics and prices based on some 10,000 inventories, this also provides general introduction to economic history of Minas Gerais. Contests much-debated thesis of self-sustained growth during 19th century. See also item **3243**. [DM]

3241 Bertucci, Liane Maria. Saúde: arma revolucionária; São Paulo, 1891/1925. Campinas, Brazil: Centro de Memória, Unicamp, 1997. 232 p.: bibl. (Col. Tempo & memória; 3)

MA thesis quotes amply from anarchist and labor press to make sensible point that radicals did not simply resist São Paulo state government's public health interventions. They actively called for measures to redress epidemics, alcoholism, syphilis, and tuberculosis that they saw were also symptoms of a sick society. [DB]

3242 Bieber, Judy. Power, patronage, and political violence: state building on a Brazilian frontier, 1822–1889. Lincoln: Univ. of Nebraska Press, 1999. 253 p.: bibl., ill., index, map.

Uses example of northern Minas Gerais to argue that party politics in the interior during Empire had ideological content and were not simply personalist or family feuds. Comparison of several municipalities shows differing political adaptations to economic changes and to the central state. Finds that political violence did not precede consolidation; rather, it was a result. [DM]

3243 Birchal, Sérgio de Oliveira. Entrepreneurship in nineteenth-century Brazil: the formation of a business environment. New York: St. Martin's Press, 1999. 233 p.: bibl., index.

Industrialization in 19th-century Minas Gerais did not follow the pattern of first industrializing countries: there were no "self-made man" stereotypes; most entrepreneurs came from local elites; businesses were typically family enterprises and remained heavily influenced by nonmarket factors such as politics and kinship concerns. See also item **3240**. [DM]

3244 Blanco, Silvana Mota Barbosa. Um povo para a república: discursos republicanos na imprensa paulista do século XIX. (*Cad. Hist. Soc.*, 4, out. 1996, p. 41–56)

If under a republic the "people" were sovereign, who or what was this *povo* and how was its presence to be manifested in the postimperial state? The *paulista* press took for itself the role of voice and tutor of the people, arguing that popular rule was not necessarily violent but that the common man had to be educated to participate effectively in politics. [DM]

3245 Os "brasileiros" da emigração: seminário no Museu Bernardino Machado, Câmara Municipal de Vila Nova de Famalicão, 22 e 23 de setembro de 1998. Coordenação de Jorge Fernandes Alves. Vila Nova da Famalicão, Portugal: A Câmara, 1999. 249 p.: bibl., ports. (Colecção Cadernos / Museu Bernardino Machado)

Short papers from a symposium of Portuguese scholars on aspects of Luso-Brazilian migrations, especially emigrants who returned from Brazil to Portugal. Topics include remittances, political exiles, and anti-Portuguese prejudice. [DB]

3246 Bretas, Marcos Luiz. Ordem na cidade: o exercício cotidiano da autoridade policial no Rio de Janeiro, 1907–1930. Traduzido de Alberto Lopes. Rio de Janeiro: Rocco, 1997. 221 p.: bibl., ill., map.

Study of daily routine of police forces, based on official reports and sample of police station log books. Argues that while sources are insufficient to establish trends in crime, they demonstrate that police lacked accountability and professionalization. As in São Paulo, police in early 20th-century Rio attributed crime mostly to foreign-born males. [DB]

3247 Brown, Alexandra K. "A black mark on our legislation": slavery, punishment, and the politics of death in nineteenth-century Brazil. (*Luso-Braz. Rev.*, 37:2, Winter 2000, p. 95–121)

Examination of policing and judicial systems early in the Empire shows that, in a slave society, liberty had to cede to order, and property rights to social control. Slave offenders were not candidates for "rehabilitation" and could be controlled only by force, although this went against Brazil's efforts to construct a "civilized" national image. [DM]

3248 Butler, Kim D. Freedoms given, freedoms won: Afro-Brazilians in postabolition, São Paulo and Salvador. New Brunswick, N.J.: Rutgers Univ. Press, 1998. 285 p.: bibl., ill., index, map.

Brazilian elites found they could not easily impose their will on postabolitionist freed persons, whereas those freed persons found that "full freedom" would require continuing struggle and negotiations. Generally the ex-slaves found more opportunities in São Paulo than in Salvador where police repression forced them to carry on their activities in such underground associations as, for example, in *candomblé* groups. [DM]

3249 Buzar, Benedito. O vitorinismo: lutas políticas no Maranhão de 1945 a 1965. São Luís, Brazil: Lithograf-Indústria Gráfica e Editora, 1998. 527 p.: bibl., ill., index.

Useful reconstruction of state politics in Maranhão, mid-20th century, based on newspapers. Chronicle of entangled political alliances and parties, centered around bossism of Victorino Freire, stays at level of heated interactions among politicians and army officers, omitting analysis of local electoral machines. Mild partisanship for José Sarney, presented as reformer. [DB]

3250 Capitani, Avelino Bioen. A rebelião dos marinheiros. Porto Alegre, Brazil: Artes e Ofícios, 1997. 191 p.

Memoir by a leader of sailors in the enlisted men's movement that precipitated 1964 officers' coup. Some discussion of 1963–64 crisis, but focuses on his experiences of political imprisonment and torture, exile, and MR-8 rural and urban guerrillas. [DB]

3251 Carvalho, Marcus J.M. de. Os caminhos do Rio: negros canoeiros no Recife na primeira metade do século XIX. (*Afro-Asia/Salvador*, 19/20, 1997, p. 75–93, facsim., graphs)

Short but interesting discussion of river traffic and the slave and free *canoeiros* of mid-19th-century Recife. See also item 3252. [DM]

3252 Carvalho, Marcus J.M. de. Liberdade: rotinas e rupturas do escravismo no Recife, 1822–1850. Recife, Brazil: Editora Universitária UFPE, 1998. 353 p.: bibl., ill.

Well-researched overview of slavery in Recife during first half of 19th century. Pt. 1 looks at spatial distribution of population and slavery in the city; Pt. 2 examines the international slave trade and importance of the trade and traders in Recife; and Pt. 3 focuses on slave resistance, both open rebellions and "everyday" forms of resistance. See also item 3251. [DM]

3253 Cattarulla, Camilla. El viaje del emigrante: un proyecto individual entre utopías y dudas. (*Estud. Ibero-Am./Porto Alegre*, 25:2, dez. 1999, p. 113–130)

Author examines autobiographies of emigrants from Italy to Brazil and Argentina to see why they left Europe and what they imagined about the New World. Though most were peasants, those who immigrated to Argentina generally stayed in the cities, while those who went to Brazil were more likely to end up in rural areas. What from afar looks like a mass phenomenon up close is seen to be the result of countless individual decisions. [DM]

3254 Caulfield, Sueann. In defense of honor: sexual morality, modernity, and nation in early-twentieth century Brazil. Durham, N.C.: Duke Univ. Press, 1999. 311 p.: bibl., ill., index.

Analyzes Rio de Janeiro seduction cases, 1900–30, to argue that female honor was less a traditional holdover than a continually reinvented modern practice. Enlightened medical debunking of objective physical virginity exams paradoxically forced women to resort to claims of social or racial respectability. Builds on work by Martha de Abreu Esteves (see *HLAS 54:3282*). [DB]

3255 Costa, Francisca Deusa Sena da. Imprensa operária em Manaus: tendências e discurso, 1890–1920. (*Rev. APG*, 5:10, 1997, p. 133–152)

Surprisingly active workers' press in turn-of-century Manaus provides insights into workers' lives and activities. Reformist socialists struggled to increase worker participation in politics by promoting party organization, literacy, and the image of manual labor, while anarchists opposed involvement with the system. [DM]

3256 Couto, Ronaldo Costa. Memória viva do regime militar: Brasil, 1964–1985. Rio de Janeiro: Editora Record, 1999. 391 p.: bibl., index.

Compilation of 26 interviews conducted from 1994–97. A broad cross-section of surviving political elite (military and civilian, supporters and opposition) were questioned about their memory of Brazilian authoritarian regimes of 1964–85 and transition to democracy. [DB]

3257 **Crocitti, John J.** Social policy as a guide to economic consciousness: *villas operárias* in Río de Janeiro, 1890–1910. (*Luso-Braz. Rev.*, 34:1, Summer 1997, p. 1–15)

Efforts to develop affordable working-class housing in turn-of-century Rio de Janeiro generally failed, in part because little federal funding was available to help those displaced by urban reforms and the program offered scant profit for private capital. Government plans reveal both an emphasis on housing reform as social control and the discomfort of elites with new urban working class. [DM]

3258 **Cunha, Maria Clementina Pereira.** De historiadoras, brasileiras e escandinavas: loucuras, folias e relações de gêneros no Brasil; século XIX e início do XX. (*Tempo/ Rio de Janeiro*, 3:5, julho 1998, p. 181–215)

Treatment of the mentally ill at Hospício do Juquery near São Paulo, while intended to be modern and "scientific," in fact defined any deviation from gender, race, or class stereotypes as "mental illness" and sought to return patients to their "normal" state. For women, "deviance" included improper manifestations of intelligence or independence. [DM]

3259 **Dantas, José Ibarê Costa.** A tutela militar em Sergipe, 1964/1984: partidos e eleições num estado autoritário. Rio de Janeiro: Tempo Brasileiro, 1997. 363 p.: bibl., ill.

Chronicle of state-level politics in Sergipe under "military tutelage" integrates narrative of destruction and reconstitution of party system with account of repression of leftists. Rich detail on elections, military commands, growth of bureaucracy, and brutal repression is solidly documented in newspapers, government reports, and interviews. [DB]

3260 **Deutsche am Amazonas Forscher oder Abenteurer?: Expeditionen in Brasilien 1800 bis 1914 [Germans in the Amazon region, explorers or adventurers?: expeditions to Brazil, 1800–1914].** Redaktion von Anita Hermannstädter. Berlin: Staatliche Museen zu Berlin, Preussischer Kulturbesitz, Ethnologisches Museum; Münster, Germany: Lit, 2002. 139 p.: bibl., ill. (some col.), map. (Veröffentlichungen des Ethnologischen Museums Berlin; n.F., 71. Fachreferat Amerikanische Ethnologie; 9)

Exhibition catalog from Ethnologischen Museums Berlin, part of the Staatliche Museen Preussischer Kulturbesitz in Berlin, on German contribution to knowledge about Amazonia and its indigenous people from 1800–1914. Includes contributions not only of the well-known ethnologists Karl von den Steinen, Theodor Koch-Grünberg, and Wilhelm Kissenberth, but also of lesser known travelers and collectors. [F. Obermeier]

Dias, Ondemar F. O índio no recôncavo da Guanabara. See item **3159**.

3261 **Dolhnikoff, Miriam.** O projeto nacional de José Bonifácio. (*Novos Estud. CEBRAP*, 46, nov. 1996, p. 121–141)

Analysis of Bonifácio's writings reveals a broad national project to modernize Brazil, including an effective constitutional monarchy, homogenization—not "whitening"—of the population, education, and land reform. But his efforts were stymied by indifference of Brazil's elites and by his own lack of confidence in possibilities of the country's common people. [DM]

Duque Estrada, Luís Gonzaga. Revoluções brasileiras: resumos históricos. See item **3161**.

3262 **Edler, Flavio Coelho.** A medicina brasileira no século XIX: un balanço historiográfico. (*Asclepio/Madrid*, 50:2, 1998, p. 169–186, bibl.)

Useful survey of historiography of medicine and public health in 19th-century Brazil, including information on both pioneering and more recent studies. See also item **3267**. [DM]

3263 **El-Kareh, Almir Chaiban.** Estado e assistência pública: as epidemias dos anos 1850 na cidade do Rio de Janeiro. (*Anais/São Paulo*, 18, 1998, p. 255–260)

Disease epidemics in 1850s paralyzed Rio de Janeiro as never before, prompting the state to respond by expanding its role in public health: funding a hospital system, providing relief for the poor, clearing out and fumigating crowded housing, and moving noxious industries. [DM]

3264 Entre a solidariedade e o risco: história do seguro privado no Brasil. Coordenação de Verena Alberti. Rio de Janeiro: Fundação Escola Nacional de Seguros; Fundação Getulio Vargas Editora, 1998. 316 p.: bibl., ill.

Five neatly coordinated articles outline history of private insurance market, 1860–1998. Discusses laws and regulations, monopoly of reinsurance by Instituto de Resseguros do Brasil (1939–95), dramatic growth of insurance market in 1960s-70s, and major firms. Periodization emphasizes regulation 1930–50; deregulation 1985–99. [DB]

3265 Estrela, Raimundo. Pau-de-Colher, um pequeno Canudos: conotações políticas e ideológicas. Salvador, Brazil: Assembléia Legislativa do Estado da Bahia, 1997. 278 p.: bibl., ill., index.

Uneven compilation of documents and essays on repression of messianic uprising at Pau-de-Colher, Bahia, in 1938. Author was horrified by his experiences as army physician during campaign that killed 400; he considers the uprising a tragic episode of irrational fanaticism inspired by figure of Padre Cícero. [DB]

3266 Ferreira, Lúcio M. Vestígios de civilização: o Instituto Histórico e Geográfico Brasileiro e a construção da arqueologia imperial, 1838–1870. (*Rev. Hist. Reg.*, 4:1, verão 1999, p. 9–36, bibl.)

A history of the development of archeology in 19th-century Brazil, based largely on the Instituto's *Revista*. Archeology was mixed with early ethnography, and the two together were part of nationalist efforts to construct a usable past. [DM]

3267 Ferreira, Luiz Otávio. Os periódicos médicos e a invenção de uma agenda sanitária para o Brasil, 1827–43. (*Hist. Ciênc. Saúde Manguinhos*, 6:2, julho/out. 1999, p. 331–351, bibl., table)

Medical journals played important role in professionalizing and institutionalizing medicine in 19th-century Brazil. The editors made a conscious effort to speak to elites in order to expand acceptance of modern medicine and to combat activities of folk practitioners. See also item **3262.** [DM]

3268 Figueiredo, Anna Cristina Camargo Moraes. "Liberdade é uma calça velha, azul e desbotada": publicidade, cultura de consumo e comportamento político no Brasil, 1954–1964. São Paulo: Editora Hucitec; História Social, USP, 1998. 169 p.: bibl., ill. (Série Teses; 3)

MA thesis from USP (1996) surveys magazine advertisements to trace themes directed toward, and presumably acceptable to, emerging urban middle class mentality: extension of progress to rural nation, commensurability of work and leisure as dimensions of commodified time; privileging of self and private life; liberty as consumer choice. Claims that these themes are consistent with political mentalities and ultimately with conservative ideology. [DB]

3269 Figueiredo, Betânia Gonçalves. Barbeiros e cirurgiões: atuação dos práticos ao longo do século XIX. (*Hist. Ciênc. Saúde Manguinhos*, 6:2, julho/out. 1999, p. 277–292, bibl.)

Using Minas Gerais as an example, author shows a growing split in the 19th century between academically trained "surgeons" and "barbers," whose medical interventions were more closely linked to popular medicine. Both came under increasing pressure from the more highly schooled "doctors," but continued to practice, drawing customers chiefly from among the poor. [DM]

3270 Figueirôa, Silvia Fernanda de Mendonça. Mundialização da ciência e respostas locais: sobre a institucionalização das ciências naturais no Brasil, de fins do século XVIII à transição ao século XX. (*Asclepio/Madrid*, 50:2, 1998, p. 107–123, bibl.)

Historiographical essay on 19th-century development of natural sciences in Brazil makes it clear that considerable scientific research took place, and not just by visiting foreigners. At least from late 18th century, the state subsidized research directly and through support of private institutions, as part of modernization schemes. [DM]

3271 Florence, Afonso Bandeira. Resistência escrava em São Paulo: a luta dos escravos da fábrica de ferro São João de Ipanema, 1828–1842. (*Afro-Asia/Salvador*, 18, 1996, p. 7–32)

Slaves working in an iron mill in São Paulo state repeatedly petitioned the president complaining about working conditions, food, clothing, etc. But by late 1820s the slaves were abandoning such negotiations to engage in sabotage, flight, and more direct forms of resistance, often in alliance with free blacks and *quilombolas*. [DM]

3272 Florentino, Manolo Garcia and **José Roberto Góes.** A paz das senzalas: famílias escravas e tráfico atlântico, Rio de Janeiro, c. 1790-c. 1850. Rio de Janeiro: Civilização Brasileira, 1997. 250 p.: bibl., ill. (some col.).

Historical demographic study of slave life in Rio de Janeiro based chiefly on wills. Much of the "peace of the *senzalas*" rested on relatively strong slave families and kinship alliances that helped the captives to resist and survive their situations. The masters were not powerful enough to rule only by force, and they needed the ingenuity of the slaves, forcing compromises. [DM]

3273 Folhas do tempo: imprensa e cotidiano em Belo Horizonte, 1895–1926. Belo Horizonte, Brazil: Univ. Federal de Minas Gerais; Associação Mineira de Imprensa; Prefeitura Municipal de Belo Horizonte, 1997. 240 p.: bibl., ill.

Collaborative project examines the early "artisan" period of newspaper publishing in Belo Horizonte. Essays discuss the organization and layout of these newspapers and how they changed. Also shows how papers treated "culture" in general, specifically the cinema, crime, and sports. Interesting effort with applications beyond Belo Horizonte. [DM]

3274 Goodwin Junior, James William. Império do Brasil: nesta nação nem todo mundo é cidadão! (*Cad. Filos. Ciênc. Hum.*, 5:9, out. 1997, p. 26–35, bibl.)

Uses the content and enforcement of municipal *posturas* to examine construction of "citizenship" at the local level (Juiz de Fora). *Posturas* were meant to define who was and was not a member of the community, and to impose patterns of behavior characteristic of good citizens upon unruly lower orders. [DM]

3275 Green, James Naylor. Beyond carnival: male homosexuality in twentieth-century Brazil. Chicago, Ill.: Univ. of Chicago Press, 1999. 408 p.: bibl., ill., index, maps. (Worlds of desire)

Pioneering study chronicles evolution of social roles and identities in metropolitan cities of Rio de Janeiro and São Paulo, as male homosexual communities recognized themselves and emerged from clandestinity into militancy. Scrupulously documented in medical and social science literature, gay press, and interviews. [DB]

3276 Hecker, Alexandre. Socialismo sociável: história da esquerda democrática em São Paulo, 1945–1965. São Paulo: Editora Unesp Fundação, 1998. 389 p.: bibl. (Prismas)

Detailed study, based on interviews and party newspaper, of ideologies and actions of São Paulo wing of tiny Partido Socialista Brasileiro (PSB). The PSB backed Jânio Quadros as reform mayor of São Paulo in 1953, but not as presidential candidate in 1960. The PSB was an antipopulist and anti-Stalinist precursor of the Partido dos Trabalhadores (PT) and the noncommunist "democratic left." [DB]

3277 História da vida privada no Brasil. v. 2, Império, a corte e a modernidade nacional. Organização de Luiz Felipe de Alencastro. São Paulo: Companhia das Letras, 1998. 1 v.: bibl., ill. (some col.), indexes, maps.

Indispensable collection of essays by leading scholars on aspects of private life during the Empire. Topics include urban daily life, funeral customs, migration, family patterns, seigneurialism, and regional differences. Unified by theme that slavery conditioned the lives of both free and enslaved Brazilians. For review of vol. 1, see *HLAS* 58:3177. For review of vols. 3–4, see items **3278** and **3279.** [DB]

3278 História da vida privada no Brasil. v. 3, República—da Belle Epoque à era do rádio. Organização de Nicolau Sevcenko. São Paulo: Companhia das Letras, 1998. 1 v.: bibl., ill. (some col.), indexes, maps.

Superb collection of richly illustrated articles by top scholars on topics relating to private life during the First Republic, 1889–1930: Afro-Brazilians after slave emancipation; urban and rural housing and city planning; types of immigrant communities; themes of social satire and humor; and women's domestic lives. Particularly original are Nelson Schapochnik on family photographs and other collected images, and Nicolau Sevcenko's book-length chapter, "A capital irradiante," on changes in mentalities during the technological modernization of Rio de Janeiro, 1880–1940, very similar to his study of São Paulo (see *HLAS 56:3359*). For review of vol. 1, see *HLAS 58:3177*. For review of vols. 2 and 4, see items **3277** and **3279**. [DB]

3279 História da vida privada no Brasil.
v. 4, Contrastes da intimidade contemporânea. Organização de Lilia Moritz Schwarcz. São Paulo: Companhia das Letras, 1998. 1 v.: bibl., ill. (some col.), indexes, maps.

Final volume of outstanding series on private life covers 1930–90s. Essays by leading social scientists and historians range widely from central topics: assimilation of immigrants; religious pluralism; racial consciousness; urban violence; the middle class under dictatorship; television and media; and daily life on rural frontiers. Text is complemented by striking illustrations, underlining argument that Brazilian domestic privacy is now pervaded by public media images. Unified by themes of inequality of the conditions of private life in era of "late capitalism" and collapse of state's disciplining project for lives of the poor. For review of vol. 1, see *HLAS 58:3177*. For review of vols. 2–3, see items **3277** and **3278**. [DB]

3280 Italiani in Rio Grande: testimonianze di storia umana e civile. Organizzazione di Abrelino Vicente Vazatta. Presentazione e appendice di Candido Tecchio. Introduzione di Mário Gardelin. Venice, Italy?: Istituto Veneto per i Rapporti con l'America Latina, 1997. 202 p.: bibl.

Testimonials and histories by Italo-Brazilians date from 1925, some 50 years after beginning of Italian immigration to Brazil. Informative introductory essay by Gardelin offers interesting population data by area, and valuable notes include genealogy of Empress Teresa Cristina and relate other links between Brazil and Italy. Essays are varied recollections on Italy and the Republic of Piratiny; the spiritual life of Italian colony of Rio Grande do Sul, heavily dominated by priests of the era; and Italian contribution to development of Rio Grande do Sul industry

and work of Italian women in the region. Of varying usefulness to the historian. [V. Peloso]

3281 Kraay, Hendrik. Reconsidering recruitment in imperial Brazil. (*Americas/ Washington,* 55:1, July 1998, p. 1–33, graphs)

In 19th-century Brazil, "recruitment" meant forced recruitment into the military and often involved complicated, if sometimes implicit, negotiations among the state, local elites, and the free poor. An 1874 draft lottery did not end impressment, particularly of those defined by the locally powerful as "vagrants" or "criminals," or of those who were without patronage protection. [DM]

3282 Kraay, Hendrik. Slavery, citizenship and military service in Brazil's mobilization for the Paraguayan War. (*Slavery Abolit.,* 18:3, Dec. 1997, p. 228–256, graph, tables)

Slaves were not enlisted to fight in Brazilian army during the Paraguayan War, and only about 7,000 freedmen joined. Enlistment depended entirely on wishes of the master and never challenged property rights. There is little evidence that the war changed the army's attitude toward slavery or slaves. [DM]

3283 La Cava, Gloria. Italians in Brazil: the post-World War II experience. New York: P. Lang, 1999. 174 p.: bibl., ill., maps. (Studies in modern European history; 30)

Examines high rate of post-WWII (1952–70) Italian repatriation from Brazil. Argues that Italian emigrants reacted against low wages, social insecurity, and scant opportunities relative to Italy and other countries accepting immigrants at the time. Documents include interviews with migrants. [DB]

3284 Lacerda Paiva, Cláudio. Carlos Lacerda e os anos sessenta. v. 1, Oposição. Rio de Janeiro: Editora Nova Fronteira, 1998. 1 v.

Interviews, speeches, and writings of Carlos Lacerda from 1960s, compiled by his nephew. Slightly augmented version of author's previous work (see *HLAS 52: 3037*). [DB]

3285 Lamb, Roberto Edgar. Uma jornada civilizadora: imigração, conflito social e segurança pública na província do Paraná,

1867 a 1882. Curitiba, Brazil: Aos Quatro Ventos, 1997. 114 p.: bibl.

European immigrants who came to agricultural colonies in Paraná had expectations different from those of local elites. Elites wanted labor and expected to maintain social relations that reinforced their own power, while immigrants sought land and freedom to construct a popular culture that satisfied their needs. Resulting conflicts caused elites to rethink the "superiority" of immigrant labor. [DM]

3286 Langfur, Hal. Myths of pacification: Brazilian frontier settlement and the subjugation of the Bororo Indians. (*J. Soc. Hist.*, 32:4, Summer 1999, p. 879–905, map)

Challenges standard myth of peaceful pacification of the Bororo of Mato Grosso in early 20th century. Only a small minority accepted settlement, and these did so more as a result of planter and squatter violence or to gain access to material goods, rather than out of love for Rondon or the Salesians. [DM]

3287 Langsdorff, Georg Heinrich von. Os diários de Langsdorff. v. 1–3. Campinas, Brazil: Associação Internacional de Estudos Langsdorff; Rio de Janeiro: Casa de Oswaldo Cruz; Editora Fiocruz, 1997–98. 3 v.: bibl., ill. (some col.), indexes.

Presents translation, with notes and color reproductions, of the drawings and 1820s travel diaries from the German-born naturalist and scientist who visited Brazil in the early 1800s and was a Russian diplomat from 1813–19. Beautifully done. [DM]

3288 Leandro, José Agosto. Devastação e tráfico de madeira no litoral do Paraná provincial. (*Rev. Hist. Reg.*, 4:2, inverno 1999, p. 93–106, bibl.)

Little attention has been given to history of coastal Paraná or to the largely illegal forest industries developed there during 19th century. Lacking land surveys, local officials were unable to discover extent of the lumber trade or control it. Elites saw the industry as a refuge for vagrants and a drain on agricultural labor. [DM]

3289 Leite, José Ferrari. A ocupação do Pontal do Paranapanema. São Paulo: Editora Hucitec; Fundação Unesp, 1998. 202 p.: bibl., ill., maps. (Geografia, teoria e realidade; 43)

Geographical study, well illustrated

with maps, of deforestation and privatization of a western São Paulo frontier. Emphasizes questionable legality of land titles and chronicles political disputes over forest reserves, 1930–64. Little analysis, but useful presentation of stages in process of private appropriation, documented in court cases and newspaper reports. [DB]

3290 Lesser, Jeffrey H. Negotiating national identity: immigrants, minorities, and the struggle for ethnicity in Brazil. Durham, N.C.: Duke Univ. Press, 1999. 281 p.: bibl., ill., index.

Surveys Chinese, Japanese, and Middle Eastern immigration to Brazil in the century after 1850, and the debates surrounding this phenomenon. Their arrival blurred traditional "black-white" dichotomy and posed a challenge to construction of national identity in 20th-century Brazil, producing what author labels "predominant but unacknowledged" hyphenated identities. [DM]

3291 Levine, Robert M. The Brazilian photographs of Genevieve Naylor, 1940–1943. Durham, N.C.: Duke Univ. Press, 1998. 155 p.: bibl., ill.

Excellent collection of American photojournalist's urban and rural images, notably of Minas Gerais towns and São Francisco River region. [DB]

3292 Lima, Nísia Trindade. Missões civilizatórias da República e interpretação do Brasil. (*Hist. Ciênc. Saúde Manguinhos*, 5, julho 1998, suplemento, p. 163–193, bibl., ill., table)

Dualism of coast-interior/civilization-barbarism made the *sertão* a key element in construction of national identity under the Old Republic. Romanticism cohabitated uneasily with positivism in a mission to civilize the interior while at the same time recognizing the essential national character of the mixed blood "pre-citizens" of the *sertão*. [DM]

3293 Lima, Solimar Oliveira. Triste pampa: resistência e punição de escravos em fontes judiciárias no Rio Grande do Sul, 1818–1833. Porto Alegre, Brazil: EDIPUCRS; Instituto Estadual do Livro, 1997. 208 p.: bibl., ill. (Col. Ensaios)

Myths notwithstanding, court records show that daily physical violence accompanied slavery in early 19th-century Rio

Grande do Sul, and that the captives were marked by malnutrition, disease, and effects of harsh punishments. Owners depended on violence to control their slaves, and slaves resisted violently to survive. [DM]

3294 Lima, Tânia Andrade. Chá e simpatia: uma estratégia de gênero no Rio de Janeiro oitocentista. (*An. Mus. Paul.*, 5, 1997, p. 93–129, bibl., photos)

Historical archeology of sherds of English china together with literary evidence illuminate the social differences between middle class and elite in 19th-century Brazil. "Tea" as an event was a site for female-controlled social negotiations, but social space for women remained extremely limited until end of the century. [DM]

3295 Loner, Beatriz Ana. Negros: organização e luta em Pelotas. (*Hist. Rev./ Pelotas*, 5, dez. 1999, p. 7–27, bibl., tables)

Ex-slaves of Pelotas created artisan, religious, political, and social organizations before and after 1889 to help deal with their changing situation and to struggle against a marginalization provoked by preferences given to European immigrants. Most organizations disappeared in 1920s-30s for reasons that are unclear. [DM]

3296 Malta, Augusto. O Rio de Janeiro do bota-abaixo. Textos de Marques Rebelo e Antônio Bulhões. Rio de Janeiro: Salamandra, 1997. 124 p.

An amplification of earlier book *Rio 1900* (1976), this collection of photographs shows work and effects of "hygenic" reconstruction of turn-of-century Rio de Janeiro. See also item **3306**. [DM]

3297 Marcílio, Maria Luiza. A demografia histórica brasileira nesse final de milênio. (*Rev. Bras. Estud. Popul.*, 14:1/2, 1997, p. 125–143, bibl.)

Outlines the development of historical demography in Brazil. Includes extensive bibliography. [DM]

3298 Marquese, Rafael de Bivar. A administração do trabalho escravo nos manuais de fazendeiro do Brasil Império, 1830–1847. (*Rev. Hist./São Paulo*, 137, segundo semestre 1997, p. 95–111, bibl.)

Study of mid-century planters' manuals written with the purpose of promoting rational, scientific administration of slave labor. Such treatment would better preserve slaves after the international traffic ended and reduce the likelihood of violent resistance. [DM]

3299 Matory, J. Lorand. The English professors of Brazil: on the diasporic roots of the Yoruba nation. (*Comp. Stud. Soc. Hist.*, 41:1, 1999, p. 72–103)

Based on fieldwork and histories of returnees, argues that Brazilians in return migration to Lagos selected and defined Yoruba culture. Yoruba culture is less a primordial African tradition "retained" in the Americas than a modern transatlantic synthesis. [DB]

3300 McCann, Bryan Daniel. The whip and the watch: overseers in the Paraíba Valley, Brazil. (*Slavery Abolit.*, 18:2, Aug. 1997, p. 30–47)

Overseers on coffee plantations typically were single immigrants or free mulattoes without local connections who relied on physical coercion to maintain discipline; most were hated by the slaves and disdained and distrusted by owners. McCann outlines overseer's duties; notes his tendency to rely on the whip; and shows how owners used overseers to disavow responsibility for violence. [DM]

3301 Mesquita, Otoni Moreira de. Manaus: história e arquitetura, 1852–1910. Manaus, Brazil: Editora da Univ. do Amazonas, 1997. 461 p.: bibl., ill., photos.

Survey of changes in architecture and public works in 19th-century Manaus argues that importation of European styles, accoutrements, and immigrants into the middle of the Amazon basin was part of Brazil's efforts to "modernize" and appear "civilized." Includes photographs and drawings. [DM]

3302 Montello, Josué. O Juscelino Kubitschek de minhas recordações. Rio de Janeiro: Editora Nova Fronteira, 1999. 261 p.: index.

Surprisingly dull memoir by author who was Kubitschek's presidential aide and lifelong friend. More than half of book concerns years of political eclipse and exile after presidency. [DB]

3303 Morel, Marco. Animais, monstros e disformidades: a "zoologia política" no processo de construção do império do

Brasil. (*Estud. Hist./Rio de Janeiro*, 13:24, 1999, p. 251–265, bibl.)

Early political combat under the Empire utilized animals as public representations of opponents. Essay looks at the animals and monsters identified with different political groups to see what attributes they were meant to represent. More broadly, animals were thought not to exhibit rationality or restraint and to lack the soul necessary for rational politics. [DM]

3304 Morel, Marco. A política nas ruas: os espaços públicos na cidade imperial do Rio de Janeiro. (*Estud. Ibero-Am./Porto Alegre*, 24:1, junho 1998, p. 59–73)

Interesting discussion of changes in public spaces in Rio de Janeiro from 1820–40, as the ancien régime gave way to popular sovereignty. Sees streets and squares as places of intensified political participation where individuals from different social classes came together and contributed to shape ideas about nationality and citizenry. [JM]

3305 Moura, Denise Aparecida Soares de. Saindo das sombras: homens livres no declínio do escravismo. São Paulo: FAPESP; Campinas, Brazil: Centro de Memória-UNICAMP, 1998. 312 p.: bibl., ill. (Col. Campiniana; 17)

Based chiefly on wills and criminal cases, looks at condition of free poor in coffee areas of São Paulo during half century before the end of slavery. Topics include slave owning, work arrangements, effects of 1850 Lei de Terras, migration, vagrancy and recruiting, participation in politics, and popular amusements. Useful treatment of a neglected group. [DM]

3306 Neder, Gizlene. Cidade, identidade e exclusão social. (*Tempo/Rio de Janeiro*, 2:3, junho 1997, p. 106–133, maps, tables)

The end of slavery broke down the established order and prompted physical restructuring of Rio de Janeiro to separate poor and black from elite and middle class, as well as stepped-up policing and harassment of real or imagined criminals and *capoeiras*. All of these actions were part of a project of "conservative modernization." See also item **3296.** [DM]

3307 Nogueira, Rubem. O homem e o muro: memórias políticas e outras. São Paulo: Edições GRD, 1997. 415 p.: bibl., ill.

Memoirs of this politician and jurist are interesting primarily for his account of Ação Integralista Brasileira party in Bahia during 1930s and of his leadership in its post-1945 avatars such as Partido de Representação Popular. [DB]

Nozoe, Nelson Hideiki and **José Flávio Motta.** Os produtores eventuais de café: nota sobre os primórdios da cafeicultura paulista; Bananal, 1799–1829. See item **3196.**

3308 Nunes, Rosana Barbosa. Portuguese migration to Rio de Janeiro, 1822–1850. (*Americas/Washington*, 57:1, July 2000, p. 37–61, tables)

General examination of Portuguese migration to Rio de Janeiro in first half of 19th century. Most immigrants were young men who came to work in commerce, for which few in local population were thought to be prepared. Others arrived illegally, chiefly in ships' crews. Few women migrated, and few of the emigrants returned to Portugal. [DM]

3309 Oliveira, Mônica Ribeiro de. Os espaços do crédito e as estratégias sócio-familiares em uma sociedade em transformação: cafeicultura mineira no século XIX. (*LOCUS Rev. Hist.*, 5:2, 1999, p. 23–44, tables)

In 19th-century Minas Gerais coffee production was financed largely through the transfer of merchant capital to the new crop, most commonly through links of family, marriage, and kinship. There were few formal mortgages, but analysis of active-passive debts shows process of endogenous capital formation. [DM]

3310 Pádua, José Augusto. "Cultura esgotadora": agricultura e destruição ambiental nas últimas décadas do Brasil Império. (*Estud. Soc. Agric.*, 11, out. 1998, p. 134–163, bibl.)

While most late-19th century discussions of coffee's problems focused on labor and credit, a minority of intellectuals and planters also gave attention to questions of improved techniques and to causes of environmental damage, increasingly evident in areas such as Paraíba Valley. But planters remained unable to think beyond slaves and exploitation of virgin forests. [DM]

3311 Paim, Antônio. História do liberalismo brasileiro. São Paulo: Editora Mandarim; Brasília: Instituto Tancredo Neves, 1998. 305 p.: bibl. (Col. Biblioteca liberal)

Valuable survey of liberal intellectual tradition by senior historian. Through 1930, focus is on constitutional ideas. After 1930, focus is on liberalism's response to social problems and authoritarian ideas. Good chapter on post-1980 variants of liberal ideas and influence of neoconservativism, but studiously avoids discussing influence from or dialogue with Marxism. [DB]

A paisagem carioca. See item 410.

3312 Paula, Jeziel de. 1932: imagens construindo a história. Campinas, Brazil: Editora da UNICAMP, Centro de Memória—UNICAMP; Piracicaba, Brazil: Editora UNIMEP, 1998. 310 p.: bibl., ill. (some col.). (Tempo & memória; 7)

Published MA thesis on São Paulo revolt of 1932 analyzes use of photographs as propaganda during the revolt. Proposes that critical examination of photos as documents can debunk legends about the war. Ample illustrations, but mediocre reproductions obscure the details. [DB]

3313 Peard, Julyan G. Race, place, and medicine: the idea of the tropics in nineteenth century Brazilian medicine. Durham, N.C.: Duke Univ. Press, 1999. 315 p.: bibl., index.

Examines how members of Salvador medical establishment attempted to adapt Western medicine and innovate new approaches to deal with health conditions in 19th-century tropics. They rejected European racist stereotypes and fatalistic assumptions, and instead sought to develop a national tropical medicine that would enable a healthy and civilized life in the tropics. [DM]

3314 Peixoto, José Luis S. and Pedro Ignácio Schmitz. A missão Nossa Senhora do Bom Conselho Pantanal, Mato Grosso do Sul. (*Pesqui. Hist.*, 30, 1998, p. 133–155, bibl., ill., map, photo)

Historical archeology of a mission site

(founded 1851) in Mato Grosso do Sul reveals a variety of ceramics, glass, and metal artifacts, as well as remains of an indigenous population that survived only about 10 years before collapsing. See also item **3329.** [DM]

3315 Peraro, Maria Adenir. O princípio da fronteira e a fronteira de princípios: filhos ilegítimos em Cuiabá no séc. XIX. (*Rev. Bras. Hist./São Paulo*, 19:38, 1999, p. 55–80, graph, tables)

Conditions in 19th-century Cuiabá, where men frequently were drafted for frontier defense or remained absent in river commerce for long periods, made female-headed households and illegitimate births common, even among prominent families. Unwanted children rarely were left on *roda*, but instead were raised within extended family networks. [DM]

3316 Prestes, Anita Leocádia. Luiz Carlos Prestes e a Aliança Nacional Libertadora: os caminhos da luta antifascista no Brasil, 1934/35. Petrópolis, Brazil: Editora Vozes, 1997. 149 p.: bibl., ill.

One in a series of studies of political career of Prestes by his daughter, this volume demonstrates antifascist and mass-oriented ideology in manifestos and correspondence of Prestes' Aliança Nacional Libertadora. Argues against putschist image of 1935 Communist coup as presented by Waack (see *HLAS 56:3371*), but does not directly address Waack's evidence from Russian COMINTERN documents. [DB]

3317 Prestes, Anita Leocádia. Tenentismo pós-30: continuidade ou ruptura?. São Paulo: Paz e Terra, 1999. 98 p.: bibl., ill.

Thin booklet in series of studies by Prestes' daughter argues that after Prestes broke with *tenentes* in 1930, they lost their liberal ideas and became a petit-bourgeois fragment co-opted by oligarchies' authoritarianism represented by Getúlio Vargas. Refers to selected archival documents only when they confirm this argument. For deeper examination of question, see Peter Flynn, "The Revolutionary Legion and the Brazilian Revolution of 1930" (St. Antony's Papers, 22, 1970, p. 63–105). [DB]

Raça, ciência e sociedade. See *HLAS 59:5365*.

3318 Reis, João José. Identidade e diversidade étnicas nas irmandades negras no tempo da escravidão. (*Tempo/Rio de Janeiro*, 2:3, junho 1997, p. 7–33, tables)

Slaves in Salvador, Bahia, organized themselves into *irmandades* based on *nações*—"ethnicities" created in large part by the slave trade itself. Such groups served to release tensions and gave the slaves an opportunity for relative autonomy, as well as providing training grounds and vehicles for organized resistance. [DM]

3319 Reis, João José. Slaves as agents of history: a note on the new historiography of slavery in Brazil. (*Ciênc. Cult.*, 51:5/6, Sept./Dec. 1999, p. 437–445)

Excellent short examination of recent historiography of Brazilian slavery emphasizes social history. Includes useful notes. [DM]

Ribeiro, Darcy. O povo brasileiro: a formação e o sentido do Brasil. See item **4761.**

3320 Ribeiro, Gladys Sabina. Imigração portuguesa, política e cotidiano no Rio de Janeiro do início do século XIX. (*Estud. Ibero-Am./Porto Alegre*, 26:1, julho 2000, p. 93–106, tables)

Post-1808 Rio de Janeiro witnessed large influx of poor, white Portuguese immigrants, helping to counter perceived "Africanization" of the city. Although these young male immigrants sometimes found themselves in competition for work with *escravos de ganho* and free blacks, racial prejudice tended to segment the labor market. See also item **3321.** [DM]

3321 Ribeiro, Gladys Sabina. Inimigos mascarados com o título de cidadãos: a vigilância e o controle sobre os portugueses no Rio de Janeiro do Primeiro Reinado. (*Acervo/Rio de Janeiro*, 10:2, julho/dez. 1997, p. 71–96, facsims.)

After Independence a growing concern arose among the populace and government in Rio de Janeiro about possible subversive threat from the "Portuguese." In fact, "Portuguese" was increasingly an ideological construct applied to real or imagined political opposition. Article examines laws and other government efforts to control this perceived menace up to 1834. See also item **3320.** [DM]

3322 Rio Branco, José Maria da Silva Paranhos Júnior, Barão do. Efemérides brasileiras. Organização de Rodolfo Garcia. Brasília: Senado Federal, 1999. 734 p.: indexes. (Col. Brasil 500 anos)

Reprint of Rio Branco's work, first published in *Jornal do Brasil* beginning in 1891, in the form of short descriptions of historical events that occurred on particular days. Organized as a calendar, work provides insight into what Rio Branco and other literate Brazilians of his day considered noteworthy historical events. As Rio Branco served as Ministro das Relações Exteriores under four presidents, it is not surprising that his *efemérides* dealt overwhelmingly with political events. [JM]

3323 Rodrigues, Cláudia. A cidade e a morte: a febre amarela e seu impacto sobre os costumes funebres no Rio de Janeiro, 1849–50. (*Hist. Ciênc. Saúde Manguinhos*, 6:1, março/junho 1999, p. 53–80, bibl., facsims.)

Deaths resulting from 1849–50 yellow fever epidemic in Rio de Janeiro changed popular customs surrounding death and provided final evidence needed by doctors to convince the government to "medicalize" death and regulate funeral procedures. See also item **3324.** [DM]

3324 Rodrigues, Cláudia. Lugares dos mortos na cidade dos vivos: tradições e transformações fúnebres no Rio de Janeiro. Rio de Janeiro: Prefeitura da Cidade do Rio de Janeiro, Secretaria Municipal de Cultura, Depto. Geral de Documentação e Informação Cultural, Divisão de Editoração, 1997. 275 p.: bibl., ill., maps. (Col. Biblioteca carioca; 43. Série Publicação científica)

MA thesis based on solid archival research charts trends of death and funeral practices in Rio de Janeiro, 1812–85, following lines of Reis' work on Bahia (see *HLAS 54:3410*). Burial in churches gave way to interment in cemeteries after 1850s epidemics; street processions declined and sacraments at home were emphasized; burial in shroud of brotherhoods also declined. Suggests greater separation of living and dead, privatization, and perhaps secularization. See also item **3323.** [DB]

3325 Salla, Fernando. As prisões em São Paulo: 1822–1940. São Paulo: Annablume; FAPESP, 1999. 371 p.: bibl., ill.

Detailed historical sociology relating social relations and ideology to changes in São Paulo prison system. Based on official reports, criminological literature, and prison records, particularly those of state penitentiary built in 1920 which author uses to document daily life of prisoners. Sees harsh treatment and desire to confine and conceal convicts as a constant; associates abolition and founding of republic with some 1890s changes in practices; but finds that biggest change came in 1920, based on belief that modern science could engineer regeneration of convicts. Useful contribution to fast-growing field of works such as Ricardo Salvatore's "Penitentiaries, Visions of Class, and Export Economies: Brazil and Argentina Compared" in *The Birth of the Penitentiary in Latin America* (1996). [DB]

3326 Sandroni, Cícero and **Laura Constância A. de A. Sandroni.** Austregésilo de Athayde: o século de um liberal. Rio de Janeiro: Agir, 1998. 810 p.: bibl., ill., index.

Biography of journalist-publisher, drafter of UN Declaration of Human Rights, and president of Academy of Brazilian Literature. Emphasizes encounters with public figures. Written by daughter and son-in-law, not footnoted, but includes ample quotations from correspondence and published work. [DB]

3327 São Paulo em revista: catálogo de publicações da imprensa cultural e de variedades paulistana, 1870–1930. Organização de Heloisa de Faria Cruz. São Paulo: CEDIC PUC-SP; Arquivo do Estado, 1997. 280 p.: ill. (some col.), indexes. (Memória, documentação e pesquisa; 4)

Guide to holdings of magazines and periodicals other than newspapers in libraries and archives of São Paulo from 1870–1930. Provides descriptions of coverage, history, illustrations, and advertisers. Includes periodicals specializing in humor, political satire, sports, carnival, theater and entertainment, and children's entertainment. [DB]

3328 Schpun, Mônica Raisa. Les années folles à São Paulo: hommes et femmes au temps de l'explosion urbaine, 1920–1929. Préface de Michelle Perrot. Paris: L'Harmattan, 1997. 265 p.: bibl., ill. (Col. Recherches et documents-Amériques latines)

Survey of ideas expressed in novels and women's periodicals for 1920s São Paulo elite regarding men's and women's roles in marriage, public space and professions in the city, and sports and beauty. Although work frames modernity as arena for tensions between new immigrant rich and older coffee elite, it conveys much less conflict than previous works by Besse (see *HLAS 57:5219*) and Sevcenko (see *HLAS 56:3359*). [DB]

3329 Schuch, Maria Eunice Jardim. Missões capuchinhas entre os Guaná sul-mato-grossenses. (*Pesqui. Hist.*, 30, 1998, p. 89–131, bibl., map)

Capuchin-controlled missions in Mato Grosso, set up in response to government's 1845 regulations of indigenous relations, were more interested in preparing indigenous population for participation in the work force than in converting them to Christianity. Schuch puts events in Mato Grosso in larger context of the national Church and the interests of the Papacy. Item **3314** deals with one of these missions. [DM]

3330 Schueler, Alessandra F. Martinez de. Crianças e escolas na passagem do Império para a República. (*Rev. Bras. Hist. / São Paulo*, 19:37, 1999, p. 59–84)

A modern Brazil needed to remove poor children from streets, eliminate crime, and prepare its children for work. The state responded after mid-19th-century by expanding the network of public schools and forcibly enrolling "vagrant" children, apprenticing them to trades, or sending them to work in the arsenals. [DM]

3331 Schwarcz, Lilia Moritz. As barbas do imperador: D. Pedro II, um monarca nos trópicos. São Paulo: Companhia das Letras, 1998. 623 p.: bibl., ill. (some col.), index.

Thorough study of the construction of the Empire as a political-social entity, a process that made use of buildings and monuments, rituals, festivals, medals and emblems, and particularly of the person and activities of the Emperor. The goal was creation of a New World monarchy out of the fusion of European, African, and indigenous elements, one that these diverse groups could recognize and that would hold Brazil together. See also item **3237**. [DM]

Sérgio Buarque de Holanda e o Brasil. See item **4763**.

3332 Silva, Adhemar Lourenço da. Etnia e classe no mutualismo do Rio Grande do Sul, 1854–1889. (*Estud. Ibero-Am./Porto Alegre*, 25:2, dez. 1999, p. 147–174, graph, tables)

In second half of 19th century various mutual aid organizations were organized in Rio Grande do Sul, some along class lines and others by race or cultural background. Most provided death benefits and some helped ill members and their families, but sociability may have been the most important function for many members. [DM]

Skidmore, Thomas E. Onde estava a "Malinche" brasileira?: mitos de origem nacional no Brasil e no México. See item **4764**.

3333 Soares, Carlos Eugênio Líbano. Da presiganga ao dique: os capoeiras no Arsenal de Marinha. (*Estud. Afro-Asiát.*, 33, set. 1998, p. 151–181, bibl.)

Of broader scope than title suggests, article discusses makeup of labor force and working conditions in 19th-century naval yards on Ilha das Cobras. Arrested *capoeiras* labored alongside sailor-convicts, slaves, *escravos de ganho*, forced recruits, and free workers, allowing the groups to learn about each other and share information. See also item **3334**. [DM]

3334 Soares, Carlos Eugênio Líbano. A negregada instituição: os capoeiras na Corte Imperial, 1850–1890. Rio de Janeiro: Access Editora, 1999? 362 p.: bibl., ill., maps.

Detailed study of *capoeira* in turn-of-century Rio de Janeiro. Gangs played important roles in political street violence; they included whites and immigrants as well as blacks; and were associated with specific areas of the city and certain occupations. Although *capoeira* was not technically criminalized until 1890s, police harassed the groups from early in the Empire until the temporary repression of the activity under the Republic. See also item **3333**. [DM]

3335 Souza, Christiane Laidler de. Nação e nacionalismo na imprensa do Rio de Janeiro de 1808 a 1850. Rio de Janeiro: Instituto Universitário de Pesquisas do Rio de Ja-

neiro, Univ. Candido Mendes, 1999. 49 p.: bibl., table. (Série Estudos; 102)

Given that reading in 19th-century Brazil was often a social activity, nationalist discourse in the press had a wider audience and impact than might be imagined. Over time a liberal race/class-inclusive rhetoric that valorized the *homem nacional* tended to give way to support for European immigration to "civilize" Brazil. Cultural prejudice undercut legal equality. [DM]

Souza, Francisco Martins de. Raízes teóricas do corporativismo brasileiro. See item **4765**.

3336 Souza, Iara Lis Carvalho. A adesão das câmaras e a figura do Imperador. (*Rev. Bras. Hist./São Paulo*, 18:36, 1998, p. 367–394)

A long tradition of correspondence and debate made the *câmaras* the logical vehicle for local elites to express their adhesion to the Empire. The *câmaras' atas* denounced a colonial past and recognized a new social contract that promised loyalty to Pedro in return for preservation of a hierarchical system that kept slaves and lower orders under control. [DM]

3337 Symanski, Luís Cláudio Pereira. Espaço privado e vida material em Porto Alegre no século XIX. Porto Alegre, Brazil: EDIPUCRS, 1998. 276 p.: bibl., ill. (Col. Arqueologia; 5)

Combination of archival documentation and the results of historical archeology in a private home (now a museum) documents the transition of a residential area from semirural to urban and shows changing consumption patterns. [DM]

3338 Telarolli Júnior, Rodolpho. Assistência sanitária e condições de saúde na zona rural paulista na Primeira República. (*Rev. Bras. Estud. Popul.*, 14:1/2, 1997, p. 3–17, bibl., tables)

Early in 20th century public health efforts by government of São Paulo state emphasized epidemic infections; when these eased in 1920s, attention shifted to endemic diseases. But the state gave almost no attention to individual health problems such as tuberculosis, already by 1890s the greatest killer of the poor. [DM]

3339 Tiradentes, um presídio da ditadura: memórias de presos políticos. Organização de Alipio Freire, Izaías Almada, e José

Adolfo de Granville Ponce. São Paulo: Scipione Cultural, 1997. 518 p.: bibl., ill.

Documentary collection on life of political prisoners in Tiradentes prison in São Paulo, from 1969–74. Includes 32 interviews or statements, photographs and artwork, and an anthology of historical and social essays interpreting repression. Statements are by men and women; however, student and middle-class prisoners, particularly those who later became university professors, are overrepresented. [DB]

3340 Toral, André Amaral de. Entre retratos e cadáveres: a fotografia na Guerra do Paraguai. (*Rev. Bras. Hist./São Paulo,* 19:38, 1999, p. 283–312, bibl., ill., photos)

Brief history of the development of photography in Brazil prefaces examination of the work of photographers during Paraguayan War. Their photographs made the war more real for the population at home and undermined government efforts to control information and manipulate public sentiment. [DM]

3341 Turazzi, Maria Inez. "Missão fotográfica": documentação e memória das obras públicas no século XIX. (*Cad. Antropol. Imagem,* 8:1, 1999, p. 37–63, bibl., photos)

Use of photographs as instrument of observation, documentation, and memory helped professionalize and improve the status of engineers in 19th-century Brazil. Photographs of public works were an important element in forming a popular consciousness and memory of the modernization of Brazil. [DM]

3342 Valente, Silza Maria Pazello. A presença rebelde na cidade sorriso: contribuição ao estudo do anarquismo em Curitiba, 1890–1920. Londrina, Brazil: Editora UEL, 1997. 199 p.: bibl., ill.

Rudimentary sketch of Colônia Cecília, 1890–94, a short-lived Italian anarchist utopian commune in rural Paraná, and of early anarchist movement and press in Curitiba, 1894–1917. Based on anarchist newspapers and interviews with descendants of commune members who disbanded after croup epidemic. [DB]

3343 Vasconcellos, Marcia Cristina de. Que Deus os abençõe: batismo de escravos em Angra dos Reis, Rio de Janeiro, no século

XIX. (*Hist. Perspect./Uberlândia,* 16/17, 1997, p. 7–28, map, tables)

Examination of 19th-century baptisms in a non-export-producing rural area of Rio de Janeiro shows a slave population dependent on local reproduction and formed into a community by extensive kinship and fictive kinship links. With marriage came status but most births were illegitimate, and fellow slaves were favored as godparents. [DM]

3344 Vasquez, Pedro Karp. Fotógrafos alemães no Brasil do século XIX = Deutsche Fotografen des 19. Jahrhunderts in Brasilien. São Paulo: Metalivros, 2000. 203 p.: bibl., facsims., ill.

Publication in German and Portuguese about German photographers' importance in 19th-century Brazil, with reproduced examples of their work and biographic information. [F. Obermeier]

3345 Vida cotidiana em São Paulo no século XIX: memórias, depoimentos, evocações. Organização de Carlos Eugênio Marcondes de Moura. Cotia, Brazil: Ateliê Editorial; São Paulo: Imprensa Oficial SP, Secretaria de Estado da Cultura; Editora UNESP Fundação, 1999. 407 p.: bibl., ill. (some col.), index, col. maps.

This beautifully produced collection, which includes many color plates, brings together various writings on 19th-century everyday life, including chronicles of last years of the Capitania, the remembrances of D. Maria Paes de Barros (94 years of age when she wrote in 1940s), diary of a visit by Princess Isabel, two theater pieces, and descriptions and visual representations of the city. [DM]

3346 Villela, André. Brazil in mid-empire: the Council of State and the banking question, 1850–1870. (*Estud. Econ./São Paulo,* 30:4, out./dez. 2000, p. 629–651, bibl., tables)

Records of the activities of the Seção de Fazenda of the Conselho de Estado for 1850–70 show that, although there were technical and ideological differences and debates among the members, partisan politics played no role in the Seção's decisions. [DM]

3347 Vogt, Olgário Paulo. A produção de fumo em Santa Cruz do Sul, RS, 1849–1993. Santa Cruz do Sul, Brazil: EDUNISC, 1997. 283 p.: bibl., ill., maps.

Economic and social history of stages of production in world's current leading tobacco-export district. Region settled by immigrant colonists producing tobacco as artisan cash crop shifted to industrialized production for national cigarette market around 1917, and to contract-farming system selling to international market around 1970. Main complaint of small farmers is failure of Associação dos Fumicultores do Brasil (AFUBRA) in negotiating with multinational tobacco companies that hold near-monopoly. Well documented with statistics, reports, and interviews; richly detailed on some issues but thin on others. [DB]

3348 Westphalen, Cecília Maria. Afinal, existiu ou não, regime escravo no Paraná? (*Rev. SBPH*, 13, 1997, p. 25–63, bibl., graphs, map, tables)

Slavery was widespread in Paraná, at different times amounting to as much as 20 percent of the population. A wealth of quantitative information is presented here to support this conclusion. [DM]

3349 Wissenbach, Maria Cristina Cortez. Sonhos africanos, vivências ladinas: escravos e forros em São Paulo, 1850–1880.

São Paulo: Editora Hucitec; História Social, USP, 1998. 287 p.: bibl., ill. (Série Teses; 4)

Criminal records help detail the daily life of slaves, freed blacks, and poor whites in São Paulo during second half of 19th century. Small-scale ownership of slaves in rural areas declined as some were sold to coffee frontiers and others escaped to the city. The free black community was relatively small, disorganized, and disadvantaged by the whitening ideology advanced by *paulista* planters. [DM]

3350 Zubaran, Maria Angélica. Escravos e a justiça: as ações de liberdade no Rio Grande do Sul, 1865–1888. (*Rev. Catarin. Hist.*, 4, 1996, p. 87–103, graphs)

As slave system collapsed, the law and the courts became increasingly important sites for struggles over meaning of slavery and freedom. Slaves sought to free themselves through forced self-purchase, by exploiting 1831 slave trade law, or by claiming past residence in free countries, while after 1884 *contratados* sued to avoid further service. [DM]

LITERATURE

SPANISH AMERICA
Colonial Period

JENNIFER L. EICH, *Associate Professor of Modern Languages and Literatures, Loyola Marymount University*

RECENT CURRENTS OF CRITICAL THEORY that carried scholars into new fields of literary inquiry and stimulated their interest in re-examining canonical texts also have prompted the publication of new editions of works written in the colonial era. These bibliographic and historical efforts have continued, producing attractive editions and thought-provoking studies of traditional works (items **3366, 3372, 3379, 3400,** and **3405**). In addition, updated versions of literary histories are appearing, especially in regard to national literatures (item **3407**). These relatively new theories also have prompted scholars to put together anthologies of traditional and/or marginalized works, which generally focus on a specific genre (e.g., drama, epistolary, sermons, essay, and poetry) (items **3355, 3380, 3383, 3401, 3402, 3403, 3404,** and **3412**). Moreover, the numbers of high-quality literary studies of newly discovered or recuperated colonial and 19th-century texts have continued to increase in the years covered by *HLAS 60* (items **3360, 3386, 3398, 3409,** and **3410**).

Scholars continue to look at transcultural connections and European influences in the Americas (items **3358, 3374, 3375, 3378,** and **3391**) in texts that chronicle the European/American encounter during different historical periods as well as autochthonous literary and visual representations (items **3378, 3382,** and **3395**). They also continue to recuperate forgotten and/or lost texts. Thus, recent studies focus on analyzing and including authors, such as women or indigenous writers, whose works were either previously marginalized or assigned a secondary status (items **3373, 3374, 3381,** and **3399**). Interestingly, new subareas of this subject are beginning to appear that are promising both in content and theoretical grounds, such as cartography, and queer theory (item **3390**). The re-evaluation of canonic works and authors is fruitful as well: Sor Juanistas continue to produce new editions and studies of her works and influence (items **3384, 3385, 3393,** and **3408**). Studies of previously ignored or unpublished works by other colonial nuns and female religious and inquisitional documents are also proving fertile ground (items **3365, 3369, 3370, 3376, 3383, 3392, 3411,** and **3413**). Finally, scholars now demonstrate great interest in fashioning new theories to account for or explain textual, visual, and verbal expressions by indigenous, American subaltern/colonized, and marginalized subjects (items **3353, 3359, 3363,** and **3397**). However, more traditional studies of colonial culture and texts have been widened in scope and intriguingly informed by new theories and ideas of cultural formation and many authors suggest the need for continued research (items **3354, 3357, 3361, 3366,**

3367, 3368, 3391, and **3396**). Indeed, this direction is wonderfully exemplified by scholars studying narratives chronicling colonial era explorations on the northern frontiers of Mexico and in South America. These works, often authored by less well-studied religious and secular chroniclers, offer new possibilities for cultural studies and theoretical formation (items **3351, 3352, 3354, 3371,** and **3388**).

Conferences honoring scholars for their professional contributions and scholarly work have led to publications that either continue these scholars' approaches or take a new theoretical and critical look at canonic and newly recuperated texts by canonic authors (items **3359, 3362, 3377,** and **3389**). Other conferences have addressed questions of how to use and teach these newly discovered and published documents. All of them have brought together national and international scholars who are interested in including authors and representative works written during the colonial era (item **3387**). A new and exciting interdisciplinary approach reflects a need to examine literary and historical texts from a cultural, rather than purely disciplinary, perspective. Many of these conferences, symposia, and meetings have issued publications of their proceedings or individual studies that remark on the topics discussed. A common thread has been examinations of how to combine previously separate areas of study, such as the Spanish, English, and French-speaking sections of the American continents, or how to insure inclusion of areas such as Central America (items **3364** and **3406**).

As technology has advanced, the range of resources available to students, scholars, and general readers has increased, including the ever growing number of electronic journals and websites. Archives and libraries alike now selectively digitize and mount on their websites excerpts and entire texts from their collections, thereby granting document-level access to those with access to the internet (items **3406** and **3415**). In general, creators wish to offer access to written, visual, and cultural texts and objects. Nevertheless high maintenance costs and frequent software upgrades or conversions continue to frustrate institutions and users lacking the necessary funds or skills to implement needed changes. Online resources may vanish as suddenly as they appeared for want of funding, technological expertise, or staff time.

Finally, and perhaps most intriguing, has been the explosion in contemporary literature that treats colonial Latin American topics and events. This literature includes both translated texts and historical novels, many giving life once again to canonic and marginalized historical figures who participated in events that shaped the colonial era in large and small ways. Four examples show the breadth of this interest: the Peruvian Álvaro Vargas Llosa's *La mestiza de Pizarro: una mestiza entre dos mundos* (2003), the Spanish Ángeles de Irisarri, *América: La aventura de cuatro mujeres en el Nuevo Mundo* (2002), the Chicana Alicia Gaspar de Alba's *Sor Juana's Second Dream: A Novel* (1999), and the scholarly collection of essays on representations of the colonial era encounter between Europe and the Americas in Iberian and Iberian American literature and film (item **3394**).

INDIVIDUAL STUDIES

3351 Ahern, Maureen. "Dichosas muertes:" Jesuit martyrdom on the northern frontier of La Florida. (*Roman. Philol.,* 53:1, 1999, p. 1–21, bibl., ill.)
Pioneering discussion of literary and cultural consequences of the martyrdom of eight Spanish Jesuits in 1571 in Virginia. Looks at impact on subsequent Spanish narratives and cultural discourses recounting evangelization of New Spain, specifically how Pérez de Ribas' *Historia* retelling of the massacre constitutes a baroque reverse world image which this time ends, not disastrously, but triumphantly. In a special issue of the

journal titled "Documenting the Colonial Experience, with Special Regard to Spanish in the American Southwest," edited by Barbara De Marco and Jerry R. Craddock.

3352 Ahern, Maureen. Visual and verbal sites: the construction of Jesuit martyrdom in northwest New Spain in Andrés Pérez de Ribas' *Historia de los Triumphos |de nuestra Santa Fee* (1645). (*Colon. Lat. Am. Rev.*, 8:1, June 1999, p. 7–33, bibl., ill.)

Pioneering, intriguing, and well-written study examines strategies from baroque retablos, hagiographies, and biblical imagery used in Pérez de Ribas' narrative to recount evangelization of indigenous peoples. Also focuses on how martyrdom became a "foundational element in the social construction of the northern frontier." Of interest to scholars and students in various disciplines.

3353 Bolaños, Alvaro Félix. Indígenas, fracasos y frontera cultural en Pascual de Andagoya—Nuevo Reino de Granada, siglo XVI. (*in* Formación de la cultura virreinal. Recopilación de Karl Kohut and Sonia V. Rose. Madrid: Iberoamericana; Frankfurt: Vervuert, 2000, p. 299–317)

Excellent and well-written analysis of an epistolary relation, chronicle, and other documents by de Andagoya, a participant in conquest, occupation, and sacking of large sections of Caribbean, Nicaragua, Panama, and Colombia. Also compares his work with now canonic texts of the period written by his contemporaries or rivals. For review of entire work, see item **3367.**

3354 Bolaños, Alvaro Félix. The requirements of a memoir: Ulrich Schmidel's account of the conquest of the River Plate, 1536–54. (*Colon. Lat. Am. Rev.*, 11:2, Dec. 2002, p. 231–250, bibl.)

Thought-provoking and documented study examines "notion of exceptionality" previously granted to Schmidel and his text, then offers new interpretation reflecting on how conquistadors-turned-chroniclers, exposed to legal instruction and culture of power through public acts, composed works omitting or glossing over violence and conflictive nature of occupation and colonization of American territories.

3355 Burkhart, Louise M. Before Guadalupe: the Virgin Mary in early colonial Nahuatl literature. Albany, N.Y.: Institute for Mesoamerican Studies, Univ. at Albany: Distributed by Univ. of Texas Press, 2001. 165 p.: bibl., ill., index. (IMS monograph; 13)

Intriguing historical, literary historical, and cultural introduction to representative compilation of texts in Nahuatl with English translations. Study examines how Marian devotion was preached before 1648 through "art and iconography" and demonstrates how these related to European corpus of written texts such as sermons. Valuable for scholars and students of different disciplines.

3356 Buxó, José Pascual. El resplandor intelectual de las imágenes: estudios de emblemática y literatura novohispana. Prefacio de Octavio Castro López. México: UNAM, 2002. 298 p.: bibl., ill. (Estudios de cultura iberoamericana colonial)

Volume collects meticulous and thoughtful essays, previously published elsewhere, that focus on history and use of hieroglyphics, emblems, and symbols found in New Spain cultural works, primarily poetic texts. Of interest to scholars and graduate students.

3357 Camacho, Jorge Luis. Meta-historia y ficción en la *Brevísima relación de la destrucción de las Indias,* de fray Bartolomé de las Casas. (*Hispanófila/Chapel Hill,* 45:2, enero 2002, p. 37–47, bibl.)

Based on Hayden White's theories on the relation between literary theory and history, author studies how work was structured as a literary and ideological dialogue in order to persuade the reader and deconstruct the rhetoric of violence characteristic of earlier chronicles, specifically Cortez's work, and historical accounts of the conquest.

3358 Chang-Rodríguez, Raquel. Hidden messages: representation and resistance in Andean colonial drama. Lewisburg, Pa.: Bucknell Univ., Press, 1999. 145 p.: bibl., ill., index.

Significant study uses theoretically and multiculturally informed approach to examine four colonial-era dramatic works, written in Quechua and Spanish, that represent and reveal resistance to religious, civil, and cultural European imperialism. Ably discusses and documents these critical contributions to Spanish American colonial literature and culture. For graduate students and scholars. [S. Penry]

3359 Chang-Rodríguez, Raquel. Iconos inestables: el caso de la Coya Chuquillanto en *Primer Nueva Corónica y Buen Gobierno*, 1615. (*in* Convegno internazionale "Huaman Poma y Blas Valera: tradición andina e historia colonial," *Istituto italo-latino americano*, Rome, 1999. Actas del coloquio internacional. Recopilación de Francesca Cantù. Rome: A. Pellicani, 2001, p. 293–312, bibl., ill.)

Valuable, nicely written, and well-documented study of depictions of Andean indigenous women in historical-literary texts, primarily in Guaman Poma's work. Raises thought-provoking questions in regard to colonial authors' sources for their visual, literary, and historical representation of these women. Valuable to scholars of different disciplines and undergraduate and graduate students.

3360 Chang-Rodríguez, Raquel. Las mujeres españolas en el *Primer nueva corónica y buen gobierno:* intersecciones genéricas y culturales. (*in* Hombre y los Andes: homenaje a Franklin Pease G.Y. Recopilación de Javier Flores Espinoza and Rafael Varón Gabai. Lima: Pontificia Univ. Católica del Perú, Instituto Francés de Estudios Andinos, 2002, t. 1, p. 345–358, bibl., ill.)

Well-documented and stimulating thematic study of depiction and role of Spanish women, narrative function of their presence, and the intertextual nature of dialogue, between overall narrative and individual depictions and accounts, created by their inclusion in the indigenous chronicler's masterpiece. Of interest to graduate students, scholars, and general readers.

3361 Colonialism past and present: reading and writing about colonial Latin America today. Edited by Alvaro Félix Bolaños and Gustavo Verdesio. Albany, N.Y.: State Univ. of New York Press, 2002. 300 p.: bibl., ill., index. (SUNY series in Latin American and Iberian thought and culture)

Intriguing, informative, and nicely selected group of theoretically focused yet content-based essays focusing on colonial topics and cultural interests. Authors study texts and writers traditionally assigned to the colonial periphery for ideological, social,

and geographical reasons in order to highlight the participation and legacies of the subaltern in contemporary Latin America. Highly recommended.

3362 De palabras, imágenes y símbolos: homenaje a José Pascual Buxó. Coordinación y recopilación de Enrique Ballón Aguirre and Oscar Rivera Rodas. Con la colaboración de Dalia Hernández Reyes and Dalmacio Rodríguez Hernández. México: UNAM: Instituto de Investigaciones Bibliográficas, 2002. 716 p.: bibl., ill., 1 port.

Widely varied and useful collection of 35 essays by junior and senior scholars that reflect Buxó's poetic activities, scholarly reflections, and life-long critical interests. Divided into four topics: New Spain poetic endeavors and thematics, Sor Juana's works, viceregal literary culture, and contemporary Spanish American poetry. Useful for students and scholars.

3363 De tlacuilos y escribanos: estudios sobre documentos indígenas coloniales del centro de México. Coordinación de Xavier Noguez and Stephanie Wood. Zamora, Mexico: El Colegio de Michoacán; Zinacantepec, Mexico: El Colegio Mexiquense, 1998. 221 p.: bibl., ill. (Colección Memorias)

Interesting and valuable collection of essays originating from 47th Congreso Internacional de Américas meeting in New Orleans. Includes literary, linguistic, and cultural studies of different documents from Central Mexico and is informed by theoretical, interdisciplinary, literary, and ethnic studies approaches. Essays focus on representations, thematics, and stylistics of colonial codices. For ethnohistorian's comment, see item **466.**

3364 El discurso colonial: construcción de una diferencia americana. Recopilación de Catherine Poupeney-Hart and Albino Chacón Gutiérrez. Heredia, Costa Rica: Editorial Univ. Nacional, 2002. 357 p.: bibl.

Originally presented at conference cosponsored by Univ. Nacional in Costa Rica and Univ. of Montreal in 1999, essays look at emergence of criolla conscience, construction of identities of marginalized groups, and regional imaginary and colonial discourse. High quality, well-researched articles constitute an innovative focus on colonial Central America.

3365 Eich, Jennifer L. The body as a conventual space of resistance. (*in* Mapping colonial Spanish America: places and commonplaces of identity, culture, and experience. Edited by Santa Arias and Mariselle Meléndez. Lewisburg, Pa.: Bucknell Univ. Press; London: Associated Univ. Presses, 2002, p. 202–220, bibl.)

Using descriptions of illness and suffering intercalated in spiritual narratives written in by or about colonial nuns and female lay religious, study examines transformative nature of women's use of their physical body and intellect as loci for self-affirmation, self-presentation as religious and cultural exemplars, and resistance to patriarchal and social expectations. For comment on entire book, see item **3374.**

3366 Esta, de nuestra América pupila: estudios de poesía colonial. Recopilación de Georgina Sabat de Rivers. Houston, Tex.: Society for Renaissance & Baroque Hispanic Poetry, 1999. 341 p.: bibl., ill.

First-rate collection of essays in Spanish and English by junior and senior Hispanists from Spain, Spanish America, and the US. Divided into four groups: cultural context, lyric and satiric poetry, epic poetry, and dramatic poetry. Studies treat canonical and rediscovered works, as well as reconsidering some texts and authors. Highly recommended for students, scholars, and general readers with some background in the topic.

3367 La formación de la cultura virreinal. v. 1, La etapa inicial. Madrid: Iberoamericana; Frankfurt: Vervuert, 2000. 1 v.: bibl., index. (Textos y estudios coloniales y de la Independencia; v. 6)

Excellent collection of articles by junior and senior scholars from Europe and the Americas. Studies treat some canonic, but mostly new texts from different genres using various critical, cultural, philosophical, and traditional close-reading approaches that educate, illuminate, and stimulate discussion about viceregal culture. Highly recommended for scholars of different disciplines and graduate students.

3368 García Rodríguez, Adriana. Vasco Núñez de Balboa y la geopsiquis de una nación. (*Rev. Iberoam.*, 67:196, julio/sept. 2001, p. 461–473, bibl.)

Using colonial-era chronicles and historical figures to inform her concept of a "geopsiquis," author focuses on formation and conception of national identity "como forma de un discurso de orígenes" wherein the division between "native and conqueror" blurs before the new "americano" to explain origins of Panamanian literature.

3369 Ibsen, Kristine. Theatrical devices and the liberating power of laughter in Ursula Suárez's *Relacion autobiografica.* (*Hispanófila*/Chapel Hill, 45:2, enero 2002, p. 49–62, bibl.)

Well-written, interesting theoretical study of how this nun author outwardly embraced while cleverly altering traditional gravity inherent in hagiographical and autobiographical models of spiritual textuality through her incorporation of humor and theatrical presentation of anecdotal incidents as a narrative and psychological tool of enlightenment and autonomy.

3370 Ibsen, Kristine. Women's spiritual autobiography in colonial Spanish America. Gainesville: Univ. Press of Florida, 1999. 202 p.: bibl., index.

First rate, well-written, and well-documented analyses of representative group of personal narratives composed by colonial-era nuns and female lay religious. Theoretically informed studies look at self-representation, discursive strategies, visionary/mystic authority, and hagiographic literary traditions as transformed by these women. Highly recommended for students, scholars of different disciplines, and general readers. For historian's comment, see item **1172.**

3371 Invernizzi, Lucía. La conquista de Chile en textos de los siglos XVI y XVII: "Los trabajos de la guerra" y "Los trabajos del hambre." (*in* Estudios coloniales. Coordinación de Julio Retamal-Avila. Santiago de Chile: RIL editores; Editorial Americana, Univ. Andrés Bello, 2000, p. 7–27)

Literary study of how the trope of "difficulties" caused by war and hunger figure as narrative strategies in primarily historical, although also poetic, works chronicling colonial era of Chilean history. Of interest to graduate students and scholars in literature and history.

3372 Johnson, Julie Greer. Ercilla's construction and destruction of the city of Concepción: a crossroads of imperialist ideology and the poetic imagination. (*in* Mapping colonial Spanish America: places and commonplaces of identity, culture, and experience. Edited by Santa Arias and Mariselle Meléndez. Lewisburg, Pa.: Bucknell Univ. Press; London: Associated Univ. Presses, 2002, p. 237–250, bibl.)

Well-written and theoretically informed essay studies how Ercilla uses Golden Age notions of affluence, influence, and power to designate a space as an "ideological and theological symbol," specifically by studying how he uses space and time to compose the destruction of Concepción and creates meaning through "intertextual linkage to European culture." For comment on entire book, see item **3374.**

3373 León-Portilla, Ascensión H. de. El rescate de las literaturas mesoamericanas: ensayo documental y bibliográfico. (*Lit. Mex.*, 11:1, 2000, p. 11–30, bibl.)

Diachronic and valuable essay giving bibliographical and thematic description of historical, critical, and literary works and anthologies that focus on analysis of primary sources and translation of Mesoamerican literature and oral texts. Useful to students and scholars in several disciplines.

3374 Mapping colonial Spanish America: places and commonplaces of identity, culture, and experience. Edited by Santa Arias and Mariselle Meléndez. Lewisburg, Pa.: Bucknell Univ. Press; London: Associated Univ. Presses, 2002. 302 p.: bibl., ill., index. (The Bucknell studies in Latin America [sic] literature and theory)

Excellent collection of essays treating different colonial era works by junior and senior scholars. Contributors look at the author's use of space in texts through a variety of critical and theoretical lenses and focus on canonic works as well as texts and documents traditionally treated as secondary or marginalized from traditional literary studies. Well-documented, wide-ranging, and innovative contribution to colonial American studies.

3375 Marrero Fente, Raúl. Lengua, imitación y diálogo en la *Historia de la inuención de las Yndias* de Fernán Pérez de Oliva. (*Hispanófila/Chapel Hill*, 45:1, sept. 2001, p. 1–15, bibl.)

Proposes that Pérez de Oliva participates significantly in Renaissance historiography by writing in Spanish, entering into dialogue about new American territories, and contributing to European historiographical discourse. He essentially rewrites three earlier dramatic works and translates/rewrites Mártir de Anglería's magnum opus yet advances literary historiographical rhetoric in his use of authorial intervention. Useful for graduate students and scholars.

3376 McKnight, Kathryn Joy. The mystic of Tunja: the writings of Madre Castillo, 1671–1742. Amherst: Univ. of Massachusetts Press, 1997. 284 p.: bibl., ill., index.

Well-written and cogent rereading of Madre Castillo's writings. Provides excellent theoretical framework, knowledge of references to primary and secondary sources, and cultural context as framework for illuminating analyses. Highly recommended for scholars of different disciplines, students, and general readers.

3377 Mercado, Juan Carlos. En torno a Fray Marcos de Niza y la configuración del discurso histórico. (*in* Silva: studia philologica in honorem Isaías Lerner. Coordinación de Isabel Lozano-Renieblas y Juan Carlos Mercado. Madrid: Editorial Castalia, 2001, p. 457–470, bibl.)

Historical contextualization and descriptive study of Fray Marcos de Niza's use of myths and legends to establish personal credibility and the veracity of his expedition's success, specifically by constructing his narrative recounting the journey to the northern frontier of New Spain "a partir del mito de las Siete Ciudades."

3378 Monasterios P., Elizabeth. De ángeles y otros demonios: lógicas de confrontación en la colonialidad andina—la Audiencia de Charcas. (*Rev. Can. Estud. Hisp.*, 26:1/2, otoño/invierno 2001/02, p. 41–62, bibl.)

Critical look at act and conditions of production of specific artistic styles of colonial period in order to postulate that cultural forms, represented here in visual works traditionally seen as representative of "Andean baroque" and defined as mestizas, hybrid, or transcultural, actually constituted a product of a "logic of confrontation" manifesting "una mecánica cultural de doble registro."

3379 Nicolopulos, James. The poetics of empire in the Indies: prophecy and imitation in "La araucana" and "Os lusíadas." University Park: Pennsylvania State Univ. Press, 2000. 332 p.: bibl., index. (Penn State studies in Romance literatures)

Sophisticated and erudite study comparing "La Araucana" and "Os lusíadas" that examines dialogic relationships between them and their connection to classical and Spanish canonical authors in order to show different and varied textual influences that created a "poetics of empire" in Ercilla's work. Highly recommended for scholars and graduate students.

3380 Orjuela, Héctor H. Primicias del ensayo en Colombia: el discurso ensayístico colonial. Bogotá: Editora Guadalupe?, 2002. 146 p.: bibl., index. (Colección Héctor H. Orjuela)

Traditional, chronological, and somewhat impressionistic literary history and review of essays by authors associated with New Granada. Addresses omission of colonial writers' efforts and texts prior to Independence period in prior anthologies of Colombian essays. Of interest to literary scholars and advanced graduate students.

3381 La otra Nueva España: la palabra marginada en la Colonia. Coordinación de Mariana Masera. Barcelona: Azul Editorial, 2002. 270 p.: bibl.

Collection of comparative essays focusing on marginalized texts and subjects, primarily from New Spain, that study material and narratives from different genres and disciplines (music, poetry, medicine, religious texts, and inquisitional documents). Opens up new areas of inquiry and offers access to primary and secondary documents. Of interest to scholars and students.

3382 Padrón, Ricardo. Charting empire, charting difference: Gómara's *Historia general de las Indias* and Spanish maritime cartography. (*Colon. Lat. Am. Rev.*, 11:1, June 2002, p. 47–69, bibl.)

Intriguing and valuable study of "territorial imagination" manifested in López de Gómara's work that explores how the work reveals a "prose cartography" of the Americas, one permitting readers to appreciate "this spatial and geographical imagination within a broader poetics of culture." For stu-

dents and scholars of different disciplines and general readers.

3383 La palabra amordazada: literatura censurada por la Inquisición. Selección y comentarios de Margarita Peña. México: Facultad de Filosofía y Letras, UNAM, 2000. 129 p.: bibl. (Col. Paideia)

Interesting collection of texts written by authors living in New Spain, Guatemala, and the Philippine Islands during the colonial period and early 19th century. Censored by the Holy Office, they are primarily poetic and treat both secular and religious themes. Each item has brief historical introduction to the work's political, literary, thematic, and/or cultural context.

3384 Pérez Amador Adam, Alberto. Sor Juana revisitada o las trampas de la bibliografía. (*Iberoamericana/Madrid*, 2:5, marzo 2002, p. 169–173)

Well-documented review of bibliography and summary of changes resulting from discovery of documents, focusing on how these texts and current research have had literary and historical consequences for understanding cultural, sociopolitical, and religious influences on Sor Juana's life and works. Useful to students, scholars, teachers, and general readers.

3385 Poot Herrera, Sara. Los guardaditos de Sor Juana. México: Coordinación de Difusión Cultura, Dirección de Literatura, UNAM, 1999. 350 p.: bibl. (Textos de difusión cultural. Serie El Estudio)

Collection of 13 essays that establish important literary relationships between canonic texts and recently found letters written by or to Sor Juana as well as a dramatic work (*La segunda Celestina*) attributed to her. Of interest to graduate students and scholars.

3386 Poupeney-Hart, Catherine. Peregrinación por los mares del Norte, o la vindicación del criollo—Juan Francisco de la Bodega y Quadra, 1775. (*Colon. Lat. Am. Rev.*, 11:1, June 2002, p. 109–122, bibl.)

Sociohistorical contextualization and literary study of discourse, language, and narrative practices used in 1775 navigation diary kept by Peruvian naval officer, a work that critic posits also reveals author as representative of Creole criticism of European expansionism during the Enlightenment. Of interest to graduate students and scholars.

3387 Producción simbólica en la América colonial: interrelación de la literatura y las artes. Recopilación de José Pascual Buxó. Con la colaboración de Dalia Hernández Reyes and Dalmacio Rodríguez Hernández. México: UNAM, 2001. 600 p.: ill. (Estudios de cultura literaria novohispana; 15)

Outstanding and wide-ranging collection of essays first presented at IV International Symposium hosted by *Seminario de Cultura Literaria Novohispana* in Mexico. Essays by well-established scholars treat academic and popular works by canonic and newly discovered authors. Focusing on poetry, theater and art pieces, histories, conventual prose, and inquisitional documents, studies employ different theoretical approaches, all illuminating and provocative.

3388 Rabasa, José. Writing violence on the northern frontier: the historiography of sixteenth century New Mexico and Florida and the legacy of conquest. Durham, N.C.: Duke Univ. Press, 2000. 359 p.: bibl., ill. (some col.), index. (Latin America otherwise)

Six provocative and challenging essays that treat violence as depicted in 16th-century New Spain northern frontier narratives, and question inherent geocultural constructions in colonial visual and verbal representations, colonization theories, and colonialist programs. Drawing and building on postcolonial theory and subaltern studies, suggests rethinking area studies and disciplinary boundaries.

3389 Rivarola, José Luis. Apuntes léxicos sobre la *Historia del descubrimiento y conquista del Perú* de Agustín de Zárate. (*in* Silva: studia philologica in honorem Isaías Lerner. Coordinación de Isabel Lozano-Renieblas and Juan Carlos Mercado. Madrid: Editorial Castalia, 2001, p. 569–583, bibl.)

Well-documented study of Zárate's chronicle provides a valuable background to the variety of lexical elements that reveal the influence and presence of a diversity of European and American languages and texts, focusing on linguistic uses of *indigenismos*. Of interest to literary and linguistic scholars and students.

3390 Roa-de-la-Carrera, Christián. El nuevo mundo como problema de conocimiento: Américo Vespucio y el discurso

geográfico del siglo XVI. (*Hisp. Rev./Philadelphia*, 70:4, Autumn 2002, p. 557–580, bibl.)

Intriguing examination of monolithic nature of postcolonial discourse about 16th century representations of the Americas. Examines practices of writing and reading determined by cultural context. Emphasizes corrections and revisions of earlier geographical discourses and anthologized travel accounts that reflect a period in which cosmographical knowledge was a dynamic construct.

3391 Rodrigo, Enrique. Carrió de la Vandera y Dufresny: el uso de interlocutores ficcionales en dos libros de viaje. (*Hisp. J.*, 21:1, Spring 2001, p. 141–150, bibl.)

Study examining specific and general parallels between two 18th-century works as well as possible influence of the French work on *El lazarillo*, principally focusing on their use of fictional interlocutors who use the artifice of a travel book to reveal the author's worldview.

3392 Schlau, Stacey. Spanish American women's use of the word: colonial through contemporary narratives. Tucson: Univ. of Arizona Press, 2001. 221 p.: bibl., index.

Collection of cogent, well-documented, and theoretically attentive essays that study evocative group of colonial and contemporary Spanish-American women's writings. First essay treats autobiographical narratives of two newly discovered colonial nun authors, second focuses on inquisitional cases to study gendering of crime and punishment in New Spain. Accessible to students, scholars, and general readers.

3393 Solares-Larrave, Francisco José. El discurso es un acero: las metáforas escriturales en la Respuesta a Sor Filotea de la Cruz. (*Lit. Mex.*, 13:1, 2002, p. 27–54, bibl.)

Sound and theoretically aware discussion of how Spanish American literary works are characterized from beginning by contestatory, "in certain way vindicating," rhetoric. Specifically examines how Sor Juana's use of scriptural metaphors and religious references reveals a macro discourse that is secular and religious, Americanist, and critical of Spanish imperialist designs yet politically orthodox.

3394 A twice-told tale: reinventing the encounter in Iberian/Iberian American literature and film. Edited by Santiago Juan-Navarro and Theodore Robert Young. Newark, Del.: Univ. of Delaware Press; London: Associated Univ. Press, 2001. 301 p.: bibl., index.

Interdisciplinary collection of essays by mostly junior scholars treat mélange of colonial era topics such as American/European encounter, mestizaje and transculturation, reinvention of the past, parody and the carnivalization of history as they appear in contemporary Spanish American literary and cinematic works. For graduate students and scholars from different disciplines.

3395 Vaccarella, Eric. Estrangeros, uellacos, santos y rreys: la representación de los negros en la obra de Felipe Guamán Poma de Ayala. (*Rev. Iberoam.*, 67:198, enero/marzo 2002, p. 13–26, bibl.)

Response to categorization of Poma de Ayala as a racist by examining his textual and visual representations and history of Africans in Peruvian society. Shows that despite his pro-indigenous stance, the indigenous chronicler's position as part of a marginalized group, and his criticisms of the behavior of many Africans, he felt granting their freedom to be an act of "buen gobierno."

3396 Verdesio, Gustavo. El retorno del indio olvidado o los usos del pasado indígena en el imaginario uruguayo. (*Rev. Can. Estud. Hisp.*, 26:1/2, otoño/invierno 2001/02, p. 63–82, bibl.)

Addresses reasons for virtually nonexistent interest in, awareness of, and significant presence of indigenous cultural heritage in scholarly or artistic venues and general society in colonial and contemporary Uruguay. Offers well-documented study of sociocultural activities and scholarly and artistic works. Looks critically at different academic and nonacademic activities focusing on or assuming an indigenous past and/or present.

3397 Voight, Lisa. Captivity, exile, and interpretation in *La Florida del Inca*. (*Colon. Lat. Am. Rev.*, 11:2, Dec. 2002, p. 251–273, bibl.)

Persuasive study of *La Florida* . . . that establishes how the mestizo writer used his sociocultural and racial complexity to present himself as a "new voice" and to construct a strategy of self-legitimation. Specifically author reinscribes the traditional captivity narrative and transforms it into an empowering vehicle "from a marginal and bicultural perspective of a mestizo."

3398 Ward, Thomas. Expanding ethnicity in sixteenth-century Anahuac: ideologies of ethnicty and gender in the nation-building process. (*MLN/Baltimore*, 116:2, March 2001, p. 419–452, bibl.)

Interesting and well-documented reading of chronicles and works from early period of Spanish-American nation formation. Using theoretical studies of ethnicity and referring to gender and political elements affecting cultural constructs of authority, illustrates how indigenous, mestizo, Spanish, and criollo writers manifested these elements in self and cultural definitions. For ethnohistorian's comment, see item **646.**

3399 Women in the Inquisition: Spain and the New World. Edited by Mary E. Giles. Baltimore, Md.: Johns Hopkins Univ. Press, 1999. 402 p.: bibl., index.

Excellent collection brings together scholars from history, literature, and religious studies whose essays focus on Hispanic women native to or inhabiting Hispanic countries and their experiences with the Holy Office. Well-rounded introduction to subject. Highly recommended for students, scholars, and general readers.

3400 Yorba-Gray, Galen B. *La Christiada* in its colonial context. (*Hispania/University*, 85:1, March 2002, p. 1–11, bibl.)

Solid study of how fray Diego de Hojeda's epic poem manifests universal, through religious orthodoxy, and imperial Spanish beliefs and practices while also reflecting the beginnings of Latin American self-identification. Using Bakhtinian definition of text as a materialization of dominant ideological realism, author considers how poem reveals, and extratextual sources provide, ideological and cultural background for Hojeda's monumental work.

TEXTS, EDITIONS, ANTHOLOGIES

3401 Antología general del teatro peruano. v. 1, Teatro quechua. Lima: Banco Continental: Pontificia Univ. Católica del Perú, 2000. 1 v.: bibl., ill. (some col.).

Includes a very general and impressionistic historical introduction to theater and evolution of indigenous Peruvian theater followed by brief biography and bibliography of the Quechua authors whose rediscovered and edited works, translated into Spanish, appear in the anthology of dramatic works. Valuable to scholars, students, and libraries.

3402 Antología general del teatro peruano. v. 2, Teatro colonial, siglos XVI-XVII. Lima: Banco Continental: Pontificia Univ. Católica del Perú, 2000. 1 v.: bibl., ill. (some col.).

Modernized collection of dramatic texts from colonial era includes a brief literary historical, biographical, and bibliographical introduction to a work by Juan de Espinosa Medrano, one by the Spanish fray Diego de Ocaña, whose time in Peru was "decisiva para la composición de sus obras," and the Peruvian Valentín Antonio de Céspedes, who moved to Spain and did not return. Valuable to scholars, students, and libraries.

3403 Antología general del teatro peruano. v. 3, Teatro colonial, siglo XVIII. Lima: Banco Continental: Pontificia Univ. Católica del Perú, 2000. 1 v.: bibl., ill. (some col.).

Anthology includes four plays and two entremeses by anonymous authors from 18th century. Volume also includes brief biographical and bibliographical introductions. Authors include Pedro de Peralta Barnuevo, Jerónimo de Monfort y Vera, Sor Josefa de Azaña y Llamo, Fray Francisco del Castillo. Valuable to scholars, students, and libraries.

3404 Barnadas, Josep María. Del barroco literario en Charcas: doce cartas de Alonso Ortiz de Abreu a su esposa, o, las trampas del amor y del honor, 1633–1648. Sucre, Bolivia: Historia Boliviana, 2000. 62 p.: bibl., index.

Fascinating collection of 12 transatlantic colonial era epistles exchanged by a husband and wife who apparently did not succeed in reuniting in Charcas, Bolivia, where he remained. Primary epistolary documents of literary, historical, and sociological interest to students, scholars of different disciplines, and general readers.

Bonó, Pedro Francisco. El montero; Epistolario. See item **1927.**

3405 Carvajal y Robles, Rodrigo de. Poema heróico del asalto y conquista de Antequera: Lima, 1627. Recopilación, introduc-

ción y notas de Bautista Martínez Iniesta. Málaga, Spain: Servicio de Publicaciones de la Univ. de Málaga, 2000. 331 p.: bibl. (Autores recuperados; 4)

Modernized edition of this epic, the author includes an extensive introduction to life and bibliography of this transplanted Spaniard as well as a generic, thematic, and theoretical study of the work. Splendid contribution. Valuable to students and specialists in the field.

3406 Early Americas digital archive. Ralph Bauer, general editor. College Park, Md.: Maryland Institute for Technology in the Humanities, 2003. <http://www.mith2.umd.edu/eada/index.jsp>

The Maryland Institute for Technology in the Humanities has launched a collection of electronic texts—poems, prose, histories, diaries, journals, and letters—written in or about the Americas from 1492 to approximately 1820. English and Spanish texts from the Early Americas digital archive (EADA) are available.

3407 Historia de las literaturas del Ecuador. v. 1, Períodos, 1534–1594; 1594–1700. v. 2, Períodos, 1700–1767; 1767–1830. Quito: Univ. Andina Simón Bolívar, Sede Ecuador: Corporación Editora Nacional, 2000–2001. 2 v.: bibl., ill.

General historical, sociocultural, and economic introduction to colonial period as well as Ecuadorian literature of the period. Latter includes a general discussion of literary currents and themes as well as secular and religious generic productions. Followed by much lengthier introductions to life and works of specific authors along with an analysis of their poetic, narrative, dramatic, and essayistic works.

3408 Juana Inés de la Cruz, Sor. Sonetos. Edición preparada por Luis Iñigo-Madrigal. Madrid: Biblioteca Nueva, 2001. 100 p. (Col. Nuestros poetas; 4)

Compilation of Sor Juana's sonnets in chronological order with regard to their initial publication and prefaced by very brief description of her life and works. Includes index of first lines and appendices with two sonnets written to Sor Juana. For students and general readers.

3409 Llamosas, Lorenzo de las. Obra completa y apéndice. Introducción, texto y notas por César A. Debarbieri. Peru: s.n., 2000. 533, 170 p.: bibl., ill.

Anthology of only known works, published between 1689–1705, by almost unknown Peruvian author. Includes theater pieces (3 in verse, 3 in prose), a panegyric in verse, and poem dedicated to Sor Juana Inés de la Cruz originally published in vol. 3 of her works. Introduction offers biography, literary context, thematic description, and brief analyses of works. Highly specialized.

3410 Manzano, Juan Francisco. Juan Francisco Manzano, esclavo poeta en la isla de Cuba. Recopilación de Abdeslam Azougarh. Valencia, Spain: Ediciones Episteme, 2000. 389 p.: bibl. (Colección Humanitas)

Excellent edition of works, including his autobiography, poetry, and a dramatic piece. Also includes excellent but brief introduction with extensive notes including references to early criticism, which began in the introduction to second part of his autobiography, of the almost forgotten and recently rediscovered Cuban writer and his work.

3411 María de San José, Madre. A wild country out in the garden: the spiritual journals of a colonial Mexican nun. Selected, edited, and translated by Kathleen A. Myers and Amanda Powell. Bloomington: Indiana Univ. Press, 1999. 386 p.: bibl., ill., index, maps.

First part contains reconstruction of secular, religious, and spiritual life of Sor María de San Joseph, a 17th-century Augustinian nun from Puebla, whose writing career produced 10 volumes from which edited selections are taken. Second part contains studies of her life and text and the genre/tradition of autobiographical visionary writings. For additional review, see item **1294**.

3412 Menéndez de Avilés, Pedro. Cartas sobre la Florida, 1555–1574. Edición, traducción y notas de Juan Carlos Mercado. Frankfurt: Vervuert; Madrid: Iberoamericana, 2002. 293 p.: bibl., ill., maps. (Textos y estudios coloniales y de la independencia; vol. 7)

First annotated edition of epistles by the Capt. Gen. of the Armada of the Indies in which he narrates the expedition, assault on the French forts and massacre of their inhabitants as well as foundation of St. Augustine, the first Spanish-American city in Florida. Editor's introduction briefly examines cultural context, literary sources, and thematics.

3413 Sampson Vera Tudela, Elisa. Colonial angels: narratives of gender and spirituality in Mexico, 1580–1750. Austin: Univ. of Texas Press, 2000. 202 p.: bibl., index.

Informative and interesting essays. Second half of book is collection of primary documents included in appendices. Valuable to students and scholars of different disciplines and of interest to general readers.

3414 Torre Villar, Ernesto de la. El deceso de Felipe II: sus repercusiones en Nueva España. (*Humanitas/Monterrey*, 26, 1999, p. 471–495)

Surveys the artistic expressions of sorrow on the death of Philip II and offers an extensive sampler of the poems written for the occasion. Of interest to literary historians. [A. Lavrin]

3415 Vistas: visual culture in Spanish America, 1520–1820. Project directors, Dana Leibsohn and Barbara E. Mundy. Northampton, Mass.: Smith College, Dept. of Art, 2003. <http://www.smith.edu/vistas/>

Collection of primary sources, textual and image, and essays on colonial history and culture. Items include paintings, sculptures, architectural monuments, and Spanish American everyday objects used between 1520–1820.

20th Century Prose Fiction
Mexico

JOSÉ MANUEL GARCÍA-GARCÍA, *Associate Professor of Spanish, New Mexico State University*

HABLARÉ EN ESTA OCASIÓN de dos tendencias que me parecen importantes en la literatura mexicana contemporánea. La primera es relacionada con la literatura posmoderna, la segunda con la literatura de la nostalgia de la izquierda. La primera tendencia se refiere a la experimentación, la segunda a la documentación memoriosa. Veamos cada una de ellas.

La literatura posmoderna comparte con la literatura de Vanguardia de principios del siglo veinte, la necesidad (la angustia) por la experimentación. Es una tendencia que se inicia en la década de los sesenta, cuando ocurre el llamado "boom" latinoamericano (pienso en Cortázar y Benedetti) y se establece definitivamente en el periodo del post-boom de la década de los setenta (con escritores como Eduardo Galeano (Uruguay), Roque Dalton (El Salvador), Augusto Monterroso (Guatemala-México), Guillermo Cabrera Infante (Cuba) para nombrar a los más conocidos).

En los años 70 y 80, se publican en México obras experimentales de géneros indefinidos (yo les llamaré aquí *libros híbridos*, los autores son: Elena Poniatowska, Carlos Monsiváis, Guillermo Samperio, Hugo Hiriart, Martha Cerda, José Fuentes Mares, Guillermo Samperio, Jaime Moreno Villarreal, Laura Ezquivel, Gabriel Zaid, y otros. Son libros cuyas características más destacadas son una autoconciencia explícita del autor de su experimento literario, una actitud crítica y humorismo textual. Hay un sobre-uso de diversos géneros y subgéneros en su composición: poesía, ensayo, narración, diálogo dramático, epístola, autobiografía, artículo periodístico, y se utilizan los recursos de los transgéneros (conocimientos y modelos de discursos sociológicos, filosóficos, históricos, etcétera). Estas obras también emplean recursos como el collage o los modelos multimediático (fotografía, pintura, comic, diseños especiales). En cuanto a los temas, éstos pueden ser de intertextualidades literarias y/o socioculturales. No pocos autores de estos libros híbridos (no hablo aquí de "géneros" o de "textos" híbridos, sino de libros), usan los recursos del fragmento, el aforismo y la escritura breve (microcuento, poemínimo, microcrónica, etcétera). Algunas de estas características ya han sido investigadas por Francisca Noguerol Jiménez (en "Híbridos genéricos: la desintegración del libro en la literatura hispanoamericana del siglo XX." *Del 98 al 98: literatura e historia literaria en el siglo XX hispánico,* 1999); ella bautiza a estos producción experimental literaria como "híbridos genéricos."

Para mí se trata de una forma de experimentación que pone en primer plano el libro, como objeto de consumo. Los *libros híbridos* no son novelas o poemarios o reuniones de cuentos, son todo eso y más. Van más allá del concepto del género se trata de poner en primer plano el libro-objeto. Los libros híbridos de Elena Poniatowska y de Carlos Monsiváis nos ofrecen crónicas urbanas, ejercicios de collage testimonial y reflexivo, puestas en práctica de un periodismo cultural y literario. Los libros híbridos de Gabriel Zaid, Julio Torri, Jaime Moreno Villarreal y Hugo Hiriart, nos dan reflexiones ensayísticas nacidos de las ciencias sociales, de la filosofía y de la historia. Y los libros híbridos de Martha Cerda, Guillermo Samperio, Emiliano González, Alberto Chimal, José de la Colina, y Pedro Ángel Palou, son buenos ejemplos en el uso de subgéneros lírico-narrativos.

Otra de las corrientes temáticas de la literatura mexicana contemporánea es la de la nostalgia de la izquierda. Los rojillos de los años sociales de los 60, ahora andan frisando en los años biológicos de los 50, y ya le dio el síndrome de Jano; la inteligencia roja tiene ahora un par de ojos puestos al futuro, y otro par de ojos que vigilan el pasado. Anda entre el anhelo y la nostalgia. Es una condición poco estable, pero inevitable: ver el pasado ayuda a reflexionar, a saber quienes fueron o creyeron ser, y en qué momento esa identidad quedó hecha añicos en algún camino. Antes, los jóvenes aquellos decían o repetían la frase conocida: "un fantasma recorre Europa, el fantasma del Comunismo"; ahora otro fantasma recorre a la vieja izquierda; el fantasma de la nostalgia. La producción de literatura de la nostalgia política, viene de investigadores como Julio Moguel, o de viejos militantes como Adolfo Gilly y José Woldenberg, y el conocido autor José Agustín (especialmente en su libro *Tragicomedia mexicana 2: la vida en México 1970 a 1988*, Editorial Planeta, 1992). Las evaluaciones del pasado se combinan con ensayos sobre la cultural del 1968 (masacres, guerrillerismos, movimientos populares, etcétera), hasta los escritos reflexivos en torno al fenómeno zapatista de Chiapas que tienen sus obvias raíces en aquellas guerrillas pretéritas.

La experimentación literaria y la literatura de la militancia: dos temas que parecen dominar el mural móvil de la producción literaria contemporánea mexicana.

PROSE FICTION

3416 Arreola, Juan José and **Orso Arreola.** El último juglar: memorias de Juan José Arreola. México: Editorial Diana, 1998. 422 p.: bibl., ill.

Orso, recupera la detallada biografía de su padre. Tenemos otro álbum familiar que va de 1937 a 1968: hay fotos, fotocopias de manuscritos, recuerdos de amistades, de escritores, de proyectos literarios, de talleres y de revistas. Es el mundo fascinante de un hombre de teatro, un cuentista perfeccionista, un mentor de generaciones de virtuosos de la literatura mexicana. Es un libro para conocer el contexto íntimo (personal) en que fueron creadas las obras de Arreola.

3417 Una ciudad mejor que ésta: antología de nuevos narradores mexicanos. Compilación de David Miklos. México: Tusquets Editores, 1999. 236 p. (Col. Andanzas)

Es una antología de buena calidad, y no podía ser de otra forma; están las jóvenes promesas que ya van madurando en los premios, las publicaciones y las destrezas narrativas. Algunos mencionables: el ensayista Mario Bellatin, el ácido Guillermo Fadanelli, y el ganador de premios y ahora embajador cultural Jorge Volpi (antiguo miembro diri-

gente del clan cultural llamado "El Crack" y ahora ahijado del noble Carlos Fuentes). Me gustó particularmente el cuento "Lo que natura no da," precisamente de Volpi. Se trata de un joven mexicano que va a estudiar a España, y se encuentra en la academia a un profesor soberbio y aburrido y a su contraparte, la bella esposa del profesor soberbio y aburrido. Por supuesto, el joven mexicano, acelera hormonas y amor, y se lanza a la caza de la bella Felicidad. Al final, sabremos que todo fue un juego manipulado por el profesor que quería darles una lección didáctica del amor clásico imposible.

3418 Cluff, Russell M. Panorama crítico-bibliográfico del cuento mexicano, 1950–1995. Tlaxcala, Mexico: Univ. Autónoma de Tlaxcala; Provo, Utah: Brigham Young Univ., 1997. 379 p.: bibl. (Serie Destino arbitrario; 15)

Es el tipo de libro que sirve en las bibliotecas como referencia abierta para los estudiosos apresurados. La bibliografía como inventariado para un estudiante graduado (o un profesor sin fichas bibliográficas) que busca tener un mapa de los nombres de los cuentistas mexicanos y de sus obras. Cluff divide su libro en dos partes; la primera, demasiado corta, es para dar un panorama autoritario (en el buen sentido académico del término) de los que escriben y valen en la cuentística mexicana. Hace una división facilista por décadas que sin embargo, sirve para tener una buena idea de lo que se produce en México. La segunda parte es una extensa exposición de subdivisiones bibliográficas ad infinitum que son para especialistas. Son el tipo de libros que han nacido en una mentalidad pre-internet.

3419 Colina, José de la. Tren de historias. México: Editorial Aldus, 1998. 139 p. (Col. La torre inclinada)

Perogrullo: el atractivo del cuento breve es que se lee muy rápido. Y bueno, de la Colina hace memorable el género. El cuento titulado "La función hace al órgano," dice: "De tanto practicar el cunnilingus le quedó una lengua cunniforme." Otro título, "Una bella": "Desnuda, su tontería quedaba considerablemente mitigada." Otro más, "La culta dama," dice: "Le pregunté a la culta dama si conocía el cuento de Augusto Monterroso titulado "El dinosaurio."—¡Ah, es una delicia!—me respondió—ya estoy leyéndolo." Como es sabido, el cuento "El dinosaurio" tiene siete palabras.

3420 Domínguez Michael, Christopher. Servidumbre y grandeza de la vida literaria. México: Joaquín Mortiz, 1998. 329 p.: bibl. (Contrapuntos)

Domínguez Michael hace un recuento de los daños, o mejor, de las mortificaciones que todo crítico literario sufre a manos de las diversas tribus lectoriles. El crítico es el no comprendido, el de la labor tortuosa, el nunca satisfecho. Y es al mismo tiempo, el que cumple la función social de ser el filtro darwiniano por el que las obras literarias pasan sus más duras pruebas.

3421 Gilly, Adolfo. Pasiones cardinales. México: Cal y Arena, 2001. 113 p.

Este libro pertenece a la genealogía de las memorias de la izquierda mexicana. Gilly, luchador de peso completo de las arenas marxistas de los años setenta, nos trae nostalgias razonadas, recuerdos intelectuales de sus amigos de viaje: Ernest Mandel, Michel Pablo y otros figurones de la mitificable inteligencia marxista ahora camino al olvido. Gilly logra, sin embargo, nuestras simpatías por ese pasado tan inmejorable y tan vivido.

3422 Ibargüengoitia, Jorge. Ideas en venta. 1. ed. en Obras de Jorge Ibargüengoitia. México: J. Mortiz, 1997. 362 p. (Obras de Jorge Ibargüengoitia)

Rescatar de las hemerotecas del olvido la obra de Ibargüengoitia es (por lo menos) una meta heróica, y la editorial Joaquín Mortiz la ha realizado. Este libro contiene más de 100 artículos que son verdaderos ejercicios de *new journalism* o periodismo cultural. Ibargüengoitia escribe aclarándose y aclarando para nosotros sus mundos: el de la literatura, el de sus lectores, el de México y sus problemas cotidianos. Las soluciones swiftianas de Ibargüengoitia nos invitan a la resistencia moral ante cualquier barbajanada institucional. No es exagerado decir que del centenar de artículos del libro, el 80 por ciento se disfrutan, se aceptan y nos convencen de ver el mundo a través de la ironía serena, del sarcasmo suave (que nos parece el filo de una navaja que el degollado ni siente). Ibargüengoitia sigue siendo contemporáneo de nuestro México actual.

3423 Ibargüengoitia, Jorge. ¿Olvida usted su equipaje? México: Joaquín Mortiz, 1997. 241 p. (Obras de Jorge Ibargüengoitia)

Es parte de la gran cantidad de artículos que Ibargüengoitia publicó en *Excélsior* entre 1968 y 1976. Es una continuación de libros como *Autopsias rápidas* (ver *HLAS 52:3485*), *Instrucciones para vivir en México* (1990), *La casa de usted y otros viajes* (1991), *Ideas en venta* (1997) (ver ítem **3422**), y *Misterios de la vida diaria* (1997). Hay artículos sabrosos e ilustrativos, como el de la experiencia de viaje a Egipto y Alejandría.

3424 Martínez Chimal, Mauricio Alberto. Gente del mundo. México: CONACULTA, 1998. 106 p. (Fondo editorial tierra adentro; 174)

Chimal crea un narrador que recorre etnias fantásticas, grupos humanos fantásticos. Como los Mibule que "son llamados, también, la Gente Raíz. El mote proviene de su costumbre de elegir un sitio para vivir, sentarse en él y no volver jamás a levantarse." Nos recuerda aquel librito de Borges de la zoología fantástica, aunque el estilo de Chimal sería como esos cigarros llamados "ultra-light"; fácil de leer, difícil de recordar (en sus detalles).

3425 Morales Baranda, Francisco. Maliahtzin Ichpantenco = María Ichpantenco. (*Estud. Cult. Náhuatl*, 27, 1997, p. 445–451)

Transcription of a Náhuatl text, presented with a Spanish translation on the facing page, recounts a woman's life and stories of her family during and after the Mexican Revolution. Part of a new feature of *ECN* introduced in this issue, which presents examples of the "new word" of indigenous literature. [R. Haskett/S. Wood]

3426 Novo, Salvador. La estatua de sal. Prólogo de Carlos Monsiváis. 1. ed. en Memorias mexicanas. México: Consejo Nacional para la Cultura y las Artes, 1998. 141 p.: col. ill. (Memorias mexicanas)

Este libro es doblemente interesante: Monsiváis opina acerca de los recuerdos íntimos de su maestro Novo; y Novo es conocido públicamente en sus reflexiones de identidad homosexual. Mosiváis y Novo hablan del tema que sigue siendo tabú en México (y que por lo menos garantiza un buen número de lectores en los Estudios Queer en las universidades de los EU) y de paso nos enteramos de toda una época de intolerancia antigay y pánico existencial del homosexual en México.

3427 Palou, Pedro Angel. El último campeonato mundial. México: Editorial Aldus, 1997. 209 p.: ill. (Col. La torre inclinada)

Es el proyecto de Guillermo Samperio (*Lenin en el fútbol*) llevado a su extremo posmoderno. Es un híbrido literario donde escritores y filósofos juegan su fútbol en el Campo del Surrealismo más disparatado. Es (llamemos este texto así) una novela donde entra de todo: música, fotografía, dibujo, microrrelato, tablas estadísticas, índices apócrifos, de todo. Es la novela que todo profesor de literatura buscaba para decir: "Vean, esto es posmodernidad." Y Palou (ex-miembro del grupo "Crack," estudiante de literatura en escuelas norteamericanas, profesor de literatura en la Univ. de las Américas en Puebla) lo sabe; él es parte de esa tribu académica que busca el Holy Grail, el prototipo de la novela posmo. Y para qué ir tan lejos si el buscador puede ser el creador (es como si un arqueólogo se pusiera a hacer sus propias pirámides para descubrirlas luego).

3428 Paz, Octavio. La casa de la presencia: poesía e historia. 2. ed. Galaxia Gutenberg, Círculo de Lectores. Barcelona: Galaxia Gutenberg: Círculo de Lectores, 1999. 827 p.: bibl. (Opera mundi) (Obras completas; 1)

En este tomo se reúnen los textos clásicos de Paz acerca del ejercicio poético y de la tradición de la poesía. Están: Los hijos del limo, Los signos en rotación, El ocaso de la vanguardia y otros textos igual de conocidos, comentados y architicados. Es un Octavio en su mero mole, zapatero a sus zapatos; habla y sabe bien de qué y cómo habla y opina y diserta siempre en su obsesivo discurso estructuralista de binarios opuestos: blanco, negro, esto y aquello, sí y no y así ad infinitum.

3429 Poniatowska, Elena. Me lo dijo Elena Poniatowska: su vida, obra y pasiones. Contadas por ella misma; Entrevistado por Esteban Ascencio. México: Ediciones del Milenio, 1997. 95, [3] p.: ill.

Si Elena Poniatowska juega a ser ingenua (o lo es, en su literatura testimonial), en una entrevista confirma su estilo naif-juguetón. Ascencio hace un buen trabajo reconstruyendo esa ingenuidad expuesta, abierta para todos: leemos que Elenita es descendiente de un príncipe Poniatowski, nos enteramos de los estudios de Elena, sus amistades (Benítez, Monsi, la gente de Nexos), sus aventuras políticas (Tlatelolco 68) y sus diversas opiniones de la mujer y su papel en la historia mexicana. Es una lectura fácil, sabrosa, chísmica (el neologismo quiso decir: hay un tono coloquial o de franco anecdotario tribial). Hay buenas fotos, por ejemplo, la de Monsiváis, Elena, García Márquez y Camín con el Presidente Salinas de Gortari—¡santo dios, todos tan escandalosos a la hora de la denuncia!—o aquella donde están Elena y Camín en la celebración del cumpleaños de Monsiváis, éste abrazado a una mata de mariguana (buen puntacho escandalizador). En fin, el libro tiene la intención de ser un álbum familiar abierto al público lector las 24 escandalosas horas.

3430 Samperio, Guillermo. Cuaderno imaginario. México: Editorial Diana, 1990. 174 p.: ill.

Es un libro híbrido donde se incluye el relato corto, el aforismo, el dibujo, el poema breve, la viñeta. Los relatos son de corte fantástico. Samperio también utiliza el humor y el fraseo que produce un sentimiento de extrañamiento en el lector.

3431 Villarreal, José Javier. Los fantasmas de la pasión. México: Editorial Aldus, 1997. 237 p.: bibl. (Col. Las horas situadas)

A pesar del título telenovelesco, el libro es una colección de ensayos sabrosos y académicos, impresionistas e inteligentes. Villarreal es lo que conocemos como un autor enjundioso; sabe de lo que escribe y lo hace bien. Demuestra que se ha leído la literatura clásica y la nacional. Me recuerda a esos estudiantes graduados que saben conceptos, biografías y referencias por triplicado, y que dejan al profesor en turno perplejo ante el momento epifínico de su ignorancia. No sé si Villarreal escribió este texto para convencer a los convencidos de la buena literatura que han generado personalidades como Julio Torri, Alí Chumacero o José Emilio Pacheco; o bien, es un diálogo continuado con sus viejos maestros de literatura. Ambas

ideas son válidas. Y si usted no ha leído a sus clásicos, es tiempo de hacerlo para aproximarse intertextualmente a los escritores mexicanos.

LITERARY CRITICISM AND HISTORY

Reyes, Alfonso and **Silvio Arturo Zavala.** Fronteras conquistadas: correspondencia Alfonso Reyes-Silvio Zavala, 1937–1958. See item **1611.**

Roland, Ana Maria. Fronteiras da palavra, fronteiras da história: contribuição à crítica da cultura do ensaísmo latino-americano através da leitura de Euclides da Cunha e Octavio Paz. See item **4762.**

Skidmore, Thomas E. Onde estava a "Malinche" brasileira?: mitos de origem nacional no Brasil e no México. See item **4764.**

Central America

WILFRIDO H. CORRAL, *California State University, Sacramento*

AS MAY BE EVIDENT from the works reviewed in this chapter, Central American literature has not completely absorbed the impact of entering a new century. Nor is there any sign that globalization has replaced regional politics as the obligatory referent for authors and their interpreters. This condition is further complicated by an increasing gap between Central American authors who have settled outside of the region and those who have stayed. That disparity frequently separates those who best depict life in the region and those who best commercialize abroad the stories of compatriots who suffered and survived the violence of the last century. The deaths of Augusto Monterroso (in Feb. 2003), the most canonical of Central American writers, as well as that of the very committed Mario Monteforte Toledo, leave great conceptual voids in the literary world of the region.

In *HLAS 58*, I pointed out the paucity of Central American women authors. That situation has not been resolved, and the problem does not lie only with the books available for review or with the inherent quality of texts by Central American women, but with editorial decisions. In this regard it is a pleasure to point out that Honduras' Editorial Iberoamericana and the Universidad Pedagógica Nacional Francisco Morazán have embarked on publishing ventures in all genres. Foremost among these projects are Oscar Acosta's editions of the complete short stories of various Honduran authors, most of which should be available for review in *HLAS* 62. Without a doubt, Argueta's *Siglo de o(g)ro: bio-novela circular* (item **3433**) and Helen Umaña's *Panorama crítico del cuento hondureño (1881–1999)* (item **3465**) are the memorable items in this collection, but the resilience of Central American prose will soon produce another round of valuable prose.

PROSE FICTION

3432 Amaya-Amador, Ramón. Cuentos completos. Recopilación de Oscar Acosta. Tegucigalpa: Editorial Iberoamericana: Editorial Guaymuras, 1997. 436 p. (Col. Fragua)

Compiles 32 fairly conventional stories—in terms of mixing literature and history, anecdote and local color—by Amaya-Amador (1916–66), who died in the Czech Republic. Only "El cuento de un cuentista" and "Hombres de cerro y pino" show an opening to novel narrative techniques and a departure from themes of social commitment. Perhaps this is to be expected considering the era and social context in which these stories were written. Among the rest of the stories "El santo limosnero," "Ñeco" and "Quiero pan" stand out.

3433 Argueta, Manlio. Siglo de o(g)ro: bio-novela circular. San Salvador: Consejo Nacional para la Cultura y el Arte, Dirección de Publicaciones e Impresos, 1997. 356 p. (Col. Ficciones; 5)

Divided into 111 sections, this "novel" by one of the best Salvadoran novelists of the last century is a nostalgic *bildungsroman* centered on the life of Alfonso Trece Duque from the age of three to 12. Combines memories of a matriarchal rural life, with much folklore, as in the story of Siguanaba who punishes gay men. Alfonso wants to be a poet (several sections describe his readings), opposes violence, and survives with the help of women like Crista and Herminia. The novel covers a wide period of time, including the wars that sent many Salvadorans to the US. The inclusion of historical events and characters leads one to conclude that circumstances have not really changed in the country.

3434 Arroyo, Justo. Héroes a medio tiempo. Panamá: Univ. Tecnológica de Panamá, 1998. 123 p.

Eleven stories in which literature of the fantastic and experimental techniques morph into one another to produce fairly compact narratives. Arroyo tends to portray types (the functional drunks in "Los sueños de Sepúlveda" and the title story, the nasty waiter, the clumsy man, etc.) rather than particular individuals. Humor is not absent from stories like "¿Por qué, Vivian?," which is the best of the collection.

3435 Bencastro, Mario. Arbol de la vida: historias de la guerra civil. Houston, Tex.: Arte Público Press, 1997. 111 p.

The realistic tenor of these stories is merely apparent, since the use of journalistic discourse produces the magical realism that still sells in the US. Every one of the 11 stories and one *nouvelle* ("Había una vez un río") has the Central American conflicts of the 1980s as its underlying theme; questioning the cathartic value and predictability of this type of prose does not diminish the real events on which it is based. The only story hopeful about the future is "Árbol de la vida." The stories date from 1979–96, and Bencastro adds an explanatory Epilogue which proves to be unnecessary once one has read the opening story.

3436 Cantú Aragón, Angel. La hora cero en tiempos de guerra: testimonio de un combatiente de la guerrilla guatemalteca. Guatemala: Editorial Artemis & Edinter, 1997. 234 p.

This is testimonial literature at its best, at least because of its synthetic values. Based on first-hand knowledge—Cantú Aragón was a member of the URNG and FRA guerrilla groups—these stories recount the daily lives of the hundreds of Guatemalans who made the 1996 peace accord possible. Objectivity about the larger social and political picture is not Cantú Aragón's goal, and some of the reported conversations between the guerrillas and the common folk (always "compañeros"—no other form of address seemed available) seem naïve, as do the harangues. Yet, the author's words may not be far from the truth.

3437 Carrera, Mario Alberto. El contar de los contares. Guatemala: Editorial Artemis-Edinter, 1997. 88 p. (Ayer y hoy; 31)

The seven stories collected here purport to show a 20-year development in literary prose writing. Other than the first story, "Casi Hopalong Cassidy, casi Roy Rogers . . .," these stories are weak, sentimental, frequently sexist, and ultimately uninspiring. The author is actually a slightly better interpreter of literature than a short story writer.

3438 Corleto, Manuel. Con cada gota de sangre de la herida. Panamá: Univ. Tecnológica de Panamá, 1997. 197 p. (UTP; 1)

Performance and Brechtian distance, as in the theater, are rampant in this Guatemalan novelist's portrayal of institutions like the army, the family, and the church. The novel's two symmetrical parts take place in the Guatemala of the dictator Ubico (1931–44), and is, on the surface, a generational saga, which departs from the experiences of two young boys. But if the first chapter is extremely promising, the novel loses steam when love is brought in as the remedy for dysfunction (Gabriel, the protagonist, is dying). The better moments take place when the inhabitants of "Gerona," a sort of Guatemalan Macondo, appear to be living in a state similar to the world created by the Uruguayan Juan Carlos Onetti.

3439 Cuevas Molina, Rafael. Vibrante corazón arrebolado: novela. San José: EUNED, 1998. 105 p.: ill. (Col. Vieja y nueva narrativa costarricense; no. 35)

A short novel in three parts that narrates the story of a Guatemalan who remembers his life in great strokes. After meeting an Argentine woman (Leonidia), with whom he travels to an Eastern European country (probably Romania), both come back to where the story started: Guatemala. The novel fails when the author tries to give a mythical vision of Central America and connect it (skipping across chronological time) to his protagonist's life during the last 30 years of Guatemalan history. This weakness is exacerbated by the narrator's constant mention of the phrase "mythic time," when an allusion would have done the trick.

3440 Díaz de Ortega, Rubenia. Cuentos y relatos. Tegucigalpa: Alin Editora, 1998. 118 p.: ill.

Presents 15 very brief stories in which any possible sophistication is undermined by the author's evident belief system. There is no examination of life's greater issues, and stories like "El anillo," set in Brussels, cannot escape the author's combination of pathetic, effective, and intentional fallacies.

3441 Endara, Ernesto. Pantalones largos. Panamá: Impresiones Generales, 1998. 256 p.

Presumably autobiographical, this is the second of five novels in which the author plans to lay out his life. Divided into two parts, the first consisting of 16 chapters and the second of 19, sports seem to be the activities which best define the narrator's goals in life. Rites of male adolescent initiation, such as masturbation and listening to music (mainly nauseating boleros) and pontificating about it do not add much, since the narrator never wonders whether these occupations help him see life differently later on. If the author's intention was to make the voyage the centerpiece of his novel, he must have also considered whether the trip would be worth sharing with his readers: It is not. Adding a glossary of local terms—which seems to be a self-imposed requirement for many of the writers reviewed for this volume—actually detracts from the story, since many of the terms are not exclusive to Panamanian usage.

3442 Escalante Lobo, Melba. Plomo. San José: M. Escalante Lobo, 1999. 128 p.

Purportedly a fictionalization of acts of commitment to the Nicaraguan revolution against Somoza, the 17 brief chapters of this testimonial novel become increasingly predictable. Pablo, the protagonist, is idealistic (he quits high school to fight against Somoza), pure, devoted to the women in his life (from his mother to his lovers), brave, and a cliché. What is perhaps new is the manner in which the author builds a case for the solidarity this commitment engendered throughout Central America, but the reproduction of anti-Yankee slogans is foreseeable, as is the attendant victimology.

3443 Escobar, María del Carmen. En la floresta no había flores: novela. Guatemala: Editorial Palo de Hormigo, 1999. 220 p.

This novel represents a pattern: with

some well-known exceptions, many Central American woman authors born around the time of WWII hinge their writings on sentimentality. While this may have its own values, it is disappointing when so many practice that particular literary worldview, especially since the Central American women whose writings have had a good reception outside the continent have generally strayed from conformity. Escobar does not. Her novel maintains almost literally that life is not a bed of roses. Her protagonist's "vice" is the cinema, her "big secret" is to find out if men and women can have sex, and her dream is to learn a musical instrument. These, and similar desires, are a counterpoint to the religious instruction the protagonist's mother urges on her daughters. The novel is mainly a conversation between the protagonist and her mother, and one that not many readers will want to share.

3444 Escoto, Julio. Todos los cuentos. Tegucigalpa: Centro Editorial, 1999. 236 p.: ill.

Actually an anthology of the stories and a short novel that this Honduran wrote between 1969–94, this volume compiles the work of an author who has not had the exposure he deserves. There is tremendous thematic variety here, and obvious evidence of craft. "El castillo," the last story in the third section, is a masterful composition, broad in its allegory. Humor finds a comfortable home in "Cuestión de amor en la perversa banda de los monjes orales," and "La banda de las mujeres pérfidas" is a subtle, modern picaresque exercise. The theme of madness appears in various stories, as does the inescapable Latin American theme of violence ("Aurelina no existe, ni está triste," "Resistir. No resistir. La resistencia. ¿Por qué la resistencia?" and others). Different from other authors, there is no glossary here, and there are some stories for which it is necessary.

3445 Espinoza Corrales, Luis. Es grandioso soñar! San José: Editorial Guayacán, 1999? 366 p.

If sentimentality is a detectable pattern among some women writers in Central America, its counterpart among male authors is the mainly autobiographical tale of a voyage abroad. There is also a subcategory: the trip to the former Soviet Union for fur-

ther professional training, especially among "committed" youth, and the inevitable love affair with a local woman and other foreigners. Espinoza Corrales is faithful to the pattern. His protagonist, Dany, is going to the Soviet Union to study astronomy. Once there, he realizes that some stars are better or larger than others, and, expectedly, concludes that a cold paradise is no place for a hot-blooded Central American. Naturally, he returns to his country, not as an astronomer but as a doctor. The sentimentality expressed here is attached to his idealism, and it rings true, since the critique of the Soviet system is as thorough as the critique of his fellow Central Americans.

3446 Flores, José. Sombras de selva. Guatemala: Editorial Estudiantil Fénix, 1997. 221 p.

Another testimonial fictionalization that is more revealing of hubris than of catharsis. It is as if some of the Guatemalans who stayed in their country during the repression, or returned after some exile, were so impacted that writing their experiences is the only means of achieving closure. The difference is that Flores wants to show how "subversive" movements also had sympathizers in the armed forces, and above all wants to denounce the truly guilty.

3447 Gaitán, Héctor. Cuentos de muertos y cementerios. Guatemala: Editorial Artemis-Edinter, 1997. 78 p. (Ayer y hoy; 33)

Ten stories whose palimpsest is the Guatemalan oral tradition, centered on ghost stories. The twist is that Gaitán transposes those foundational fictions onto "real" events that affect today's "common" Guatemalan, and that is where the stories become weak, lest one believe in maintaining such traditions as an important literary heritage that reveals the "soul" of the average citizen. La Siguanaba (see item **3433**) who appears in "La mujer del cementerio," and "Los esposos de Silvano" may be the best character in these stories. But the fact remains that Asturias did much more with those traditions, and versions of them are not uncommon in other parts of Spanish America, thereby raising questions about the Guatemalan uniqueness the author attributes to them.

3448 González, Mariher. Los sueños de Elena Quiroga. Guatemala: Editorial Artemis & Edinter, 1997. 202 p.

The 10 chapters of this competent novel take readers to Spain (mainly Galicia and Madrid) and some Latin America countries (mainly Colombia and the Dominican Republic). Although the trials and tribulations of a bourgeois woman may not be attractive, or now nowadays, their persistence in Central American prose may be revealing of the greater problems González hints at: Elena, the protagonist, can only comment on her boredom, and Don Servando Quiroga makes all important decisions, leaving her to dream and question her immediate reality, without realizing she may be living a nightmare. Every one of the locales visited in the novel has the sea in common, and González uses sea imagery to depict mood. The dialogs appear stilted, and the quite mild references to sexual experience and real political events seem artificial when the novel is considered as a whole.

3449 González, Otto Raúl. Gente educada. Guatemala: Editorial Cultura, 1997. 124 p. (Col. Narrativa guatemalteca siglo XX; 22. Serie Augusto Monterroso)

This is the 22nd volume in the "Augusto Monterroso" series devoted to Guatemalan narrative, and it is fitting that it be devoted to González's short stories (fragments or epigrams in most cases). González has lived in exile in Mexico since the early 1950s, and although these texts, written in the 1980s, do make reference to political events, their subtlety relies on the irony and humor at which Monterroso is still the master in Spanish American letters. "La blasfemia" is an ingenious exercise in constructing palindromes, and many of the other 60 texts have plots that would be considered sexist in a US milieu. Two stories related to García Márquez's Nobel Prize are priceless, and "Celestina 96" finds Calixto and Melibea in a subway. But the generally literary world in which González moves saves the day, since he is talking about the human condition after all.

3450 Guatemala, cuentos escogidos. Selección y prólogo de Arturo Arias. 2. ed. San José: EDUCA, 1998. 216 p. (Col. Séptimo día)

An overview of the 20th-century Guatemalan short story, this anthology has an excellent prologue by Arias, and the selection tries to do justice to canonical authors like Arévalo Martínez, Asturias, Cardoza y Aragón, Monteforte Toledo, and Monterroso. Among the younger authors Llano [sic], and Payeras stand out, and it is comforting to see women like Rodas and Hernández (both of whose stories have popular music as incipit) included. However, Rodrigo Rey Rosas (perhaps the only Guatemalan prose writer who has the potential of the late Monterroso) is missing. His inclusion would have provided a more accurate view of Guatemalan narrative.

3451 Honduras, cuentos escogidos. Selección y prólogo por Roberto Sosa. 2. ed. San José: EDUCA, 1998. 204 p.: bibl. (Colección Séptimo día)

The youngest authors included in this anthology were born in the 1950s, and their thematic preferences reflect the de-politicized interests that now generally define Spanish American narrative. Medina García's (b.1948) "Los irredentos" deals with foreign military and religious presences in Honduras, but most of the 18 authors included here tow the realist line, with some magical realism thrown in for good measure. Authors like Turcios, Martínez Galindo, Juárez Fiallos, and Castillo are represented by two stories. Sosa's prologue is unnecessarily profligate.

3452 Lindo, Ricardo. Arca de los olvidos: antología narrativa. Presentación de Márgara de Simán. San Salvador: Dirección de Publicaciones e Impresos, Consejo Nacional para la Cultura y el Arte, 1998. 208 p. (Biblioteca básica de literatura salvadoreña, 30)

Selections from three of Lindo's books, including short stories, novels, and some unpublished tales. Many of the stories are humorous, very distinct from the committed writing of his contemporaries. (Lindo was born in 1947 and has been publishing since 1970.) Along with the humor, Lindo gives attention to the times of the Spanish conquest, the search for indigenous roots, the Judeo-Christian tradition, and Salvadoran folklore. The most representative stories are those drawn from *XXX cuentos* (which should be read as "thirty stories") and *Lo que dice el río Lempa*.

3453 Menen Desleal, Alvaro. La ilustre familia androide. Alvaro Menen Desleal. Presentación por Luis Melgar Brizuela. 2. ed. San Salvador: Dirección de Publicaciones e Impresos, Consejo Nacional para la Cultura y el Arte, 1997. 109 p. (Biblioteca básica de literatura salvadoreña, 19)

This is a welcome second edition of a collection of science fiction short stories originally published in 1972 in Argentina. Menen Desleal, still El Salvador's greatest living prose writer, is not interested in speculations about the future here (and by this date the stories included seem technologically naive), but instead explores the parallels between the 20th century and other eras, ancient and future. The most outstanding story is "Una cuerda de nylon y oro." "Venera2, Venera," the longest story, is memorable for the characters' names, which are presented typographically as symbols (Mr. /////, Mrs. Ooooo, Mr. *****, and the like); these peculiarities ultimately do not interfere with the author's gift for dialog.

3454 Nicaragua: cuentos escogidos. Selección y prólogo de Julio Valle-Castillo. 2. ed. San José: EDUCA, 1998. 208 p. (Colección Séptimo día)

This collection begins with Rubén Darío and ends with Sergio Ramírez, which is a good indication of the Nicaraguan short story canon, though perhaps indicates a need to revise the scope of the canon to include new authors (Irma Prego, Gioconda Belli, and others not included, but who are mentioned in the editor's prologue). It seems a questionable decision to include in this work authors whose prominence is due to their poetry (Ernesto Cardenal), or literary criticism (Mejía Sánchez). Authors like Aburto and Chávez Alfaro are underrepresented, and Ramírez has certainly progressed in his practice, which is not represented by the selection of his work in this volume.

3455 Panamá, cuentos escogidos. Selección y prólogo de Franz García de Paredes. 2. ed. San José: EDUCA, 1998. 204 p.: bibl. (Col. Séptimo día)

A welcome volume since very few Panamanian short story writers, with the exception of Rogelio Sinán, are known outside their country. Unfortunately, this work, like others in the collection (and for that matter, like other anthologies published in the US), includes only one story per author. The better stories are those by Sinán (represented by his classic and sophisticated "La boina roja"), Endara (whose novel *Pantalones largos* is reviewed in this volume, see item **3441**), Pittí and Jaramillo Levy (who picks up where Sinán left off). Includes only one female writer, Britton, whose story is markedly conventional in style and theme. Also this anthology gives no sign that the US presence in Panama has had a thematic impact on the literature of that country.

3456 Pinto, Julieta. Detrás del espejo. San José: EUNA, 2000. 80 p.

The 19 very brief stories collected here have dreams and mirrors as a running thread, which fits neatly with Pinto's efforts to weave together history and poetry. The former is harder to find in this work, since an air of sentimentality and nostalgia for an indefinable past tends to blur any direct historical references. Pinto is nevertheless successful in her endeavor, and "La voz del río," "Desdemona," "Sueño compartido," "Miradas," and "La casa de las hortensias" are proof of her talent.

3457 Ramírez, Sergio. Cuentos completos. México: Alfaguara, 1997. 340 p.

Since this volume became available, the ever-prolific Ramírez has published at least one new collection of stories. Yet, this tome, which includes two short novels (*Suprema ley* and *Vallejo*) and the fragment collection "De tropeles y tropelías" (published earlier as a separate volume) will become, as occurs with much Central American writing, the volume by which readers will have access to Ramírez. "Charles Atlas también muere" and "El centerfield," from his earlier collections of stories, and "Catalina y Catalina," among the most recently written of the stories in this volume, are most representative of Ramírez's work. The volume includes a much too brief prologue by Mario Benedetti, great interpreter and practitioner of the genre.

3458 Ríos, Herman. Sueños de amor en un país desafortunado. Managua: Centro Nicaragüense de Escritores, 1997. 227 p.

Ríos' second novel is a run through 80 years of the history of his native Nicaragua from the perspective (physical, but above all mental) of Irineo Torremolino, a physician. Prodded by the death of a close friend, Torremolino crisscrosses Nicaragua, and each of the ten chapters offers the reader a glimpse of an historical moment in the country (slavery in rubber plantations, work in the mines, civil wars, etc.). The eleventh and final chapter is an overly sentimentalized projection about Torremolino's descendants. Overall, Ríos' novel does not offer a new thematic or stylistic approach.

3459 Salarrué. "La lumbra" y otros textos. Recopilación de Antonio Fernández Ferrer. Madrid: Agencia Española de Cooperación Internacional: Ediciones de Cultura Hispánica, 1998. 358 p.: bibl., ill. (Biblioteca literaria iberoamericana y filipina, 9)

An excellent selection of short novels and short stories by El Salvador's greatest writer, edited by one of the most learned Spanish Latin Americanists. Although we now have the three volumes of Salarrué's complete prose, edited by Ricardo Roque Baldovinos (see *HLAS 58:3543*), Fernández Ferrer's work has the advantage of being more accessible, and his excellent prologue provides a fuller context in which to understand this most understudied author. Extremely useful glossary.

LITERARY CRITICISM AND HISTORY

3460 Arias, Arturo. La identidad de la palabra: narrativa guatemalteca del siglo veinte. Guatemala: Artemis & Edinter, 1998. 254 p.: bibl.

A good collection of essays by one of the better-known younger Guatemalan writers settled in the US. Arias discusses canonical and younger Guatemalan authors (Liano and Méndez Vides) in seven essays, and devotes another chapter to his own fictional work, adding an interview between him and Carlos Illescas (a member of the famous 1940 Guatemalan generation) as an appendix. This book is marred by errata, and vanity press physical quality, but its author's insights on Asturias, Monteforte Toledo, Cardoza y Aragón, and Monterroso are competent. Yet, this book's overall effect is undermined in every chapter by its author's patent need to please a "committed constituency" in the US and to seem up-to-date, without ever questioning his arguments, the use of almost

exclusively non-Guatemalan sources, or, for example, the wisdom of defining a symbol by resorting to a fashionable sociologist.

3461 Chase, Alfonso. Los herederos de la promesa: ensayos sobre literatura costarricense. San José: Editorial Costa Rica, 1997. 292 p.: ill.

The prolific Chase, whose fiction, essays, and anthologies have been reviewed in previous volumes of *HLAS*, has now gathered some of his prologues and other essays on Costa Rican novelists and critics. Although he starts with an article on Darío and Costa Rica, his focus is on his fellow Costa Ricans, and some of the best essays are on women writers like Lyra, Oreamuno, and Odio. This collection includes a wonderful essay on the unjustly forgotten literary critic Roberto Brenes Mesén, a forerunner to critics like Henríquez Ureña, and an unfortunately brief note on the cultural critic Joaquín García Monge. Chase, mainly a prose writer, is also an excellent poetry critic, and his work makes clear that there is a need to have practitioners criticize their own work.

3462 Cross, Neville and **María Elsa Vogl.** A cuatro manos. Managua: Graffitti Ediciones, 1998. 122 p.

In eight chapters not free of errata, Cross and Vogl expound on law, politics, sociology, anthropology, philosophy, and even theology. These texts originally appeared in newspaper columns, and the authors have not changed that format. This collection is indicative of the widespread publication of "light" prose throughout the continent.

3463 Liano, Dante. Visión crítica de la literatura guatemalteca. Quezaltenango, Guatemala: Editorial Universitaria, Univ. de San Carlos de Guatemala, 1997. 326 p.: bibl. (Col. Monografías; vol. no. 5)

Excellent, sensible overview of Guatemalan literature since prehispanic times. In 19 chapters, Liano, a fiction writer and essayist, treats movements, schools, authors, and general tendencies, always emphasizing and determining each work's literary value. His preference for sociological analysis and context is never hindered by pamphleteering or encumbered by trendy obfuscations. The best chapters are on the indigenous *Rabinal Achí*, Guatemalan *modernismo*, Asturias, Monterroso, Arce, narrative centered on violence, and Rigoberta Menchú, on whose work he is an expert. Moreover, these chapters are easily threaded with the others. His passion for his country's literature is obvious, and tempered by his tolerance for others' views, as is evident in the last chapter devoted to poetry.

3464 Oscar Acosta, poeta de Honduras: juicios, testimonios y valoraciones. Tegucigalpa: Editorial Guaymuras, 1996. 316 p.: bibl., ill.

Acosta, who has edited at least eight of the other complete short story collections by Honduran authors reviewed for this volume, is undoubtedly the most energetic advocate of his country's literature. He is a poet (this volume includes an early [1958] appraisal by Gregory Rabassa), short story writer, and essayist himself, as well as an anthologist, journalist, and diplomat. This work rightly pays homage to each of those endeavors, conveying Acosta's wonderful capacity to undertake each of his responsibilities with aplomb.

3465 Umaña, Helen. Panorama crítico del cuento hondureño: 1881–1999. Ciudad de Guatemala: Editorial Letra Negra; Tegucigalpa: Editorial Iberoamericana, 1999. 521 p.: bibl. (Ensayo centroamericano; 1)

By far the most serious and thorough critical study of this period, Umaña's study is an in-depth analysis of the Honduran short story from the romanticism of the 1860s to what she terms the *Postvanguardia* that be-

gins with the Generation of 1984. Each of the five sections into which she has divided her study examines scores of authors, and although some analyses don't take up more than a page, her interpretations are on target. Her research in periodicals is simply outstanding, accurate, and above all pertinent. When she does stop for a longer analysis her conclusions are convincing, and generally contextualized within the great corpus she has compiled.

3466 Volver a imaginarlas: retratos de escritoras centroamericanas. Recopilación de Janet N. Gold. Tegucigalpa: Editorial Guaymuras, 1998. 356 p.: bibl. (Col. Lámpara)

Gold, author of an excellent literary biography of Clementina Suárez, has once again contributed greatly to the field of Central American literature by compiling this group of portraits, memoirs, and personal reflections. The 16 contributions are even in quality and frequently revealing of woman authors whose works are unfortunately unknown outside of the continent. Wisely, Gold has opted for concentrating on less commercial authors (mainly poets), and although Aguilar Umaña's biographical note on Spínola may seem out of proportion when compared to the other authors whose works are analyzed, Gold has done a wonderful job in allowing readers to make generational and thematic connections among all the authors examined.

Hispanic Caribbean

UVA DE ARAGÓN, *Associate Director, Cuban Research Institute, Florida International University*
JUAN FLORES, *Professor of Puerto Rican and Cultural Studies, Hunter College*

CUBA AND THE DOMINICAN REPUBLIC

EN LOS ÚLTIMOS AÑOS, se distingue en la narrativa cubana un renovado interés por el género del cuento, como lo demuestran las antologías *Aire de luz* (ítem 3467), *Cuentos de La Habana Vieja* (ítem **3485**), *Poco antes del 2000* (ítem **3515**), *Nuevos narradores cubanos* (ítem **3509**), *El ojo de la noche: nuevas cuentistas cubanas* (ítem **3510**), e incluso el tomo en inglés *Cuba: Short Stories* from the series *A Traveler's Literary Companion* (ítem **3484**). Se puede observar asimismo a autoras consagradas, como son los casos de Amelia del Castillo y Mirta Yáñez, que en estos momentos sacan a la luz un compendio de sus cuentos, publicados a través de los años, bajo los títulos, respectivamente, *De trampas y fantasías* (ítem **3478**) y *Narraciones desordenadas e incompletas* (ítem **3532**). Otros autores, ya conocidos por sus narraciones breves, incursionan por vez primera en el género de la novela, como Ena Lucía Portela con *El pájaro: pincel y tinta china* (ítem **3518**) y Abilio Estévez con *Tuyo es el reino* (ítem **3489**).

En el género de la novela publican nuevas obras, autores ya consagrados como Eliseo Alberto, Antonio Benítez Rojo, Daína Chaviano, Jesús Díaz, Mayra Montero, Matías Montes Huidobro, Leonardo Padura Fuentes, y Zoe Valdés. Surgen otras voces nuevas de gran interés como las de Andrés Jorge y Pedro Juan Gutiérrez.

En cuanto a la temática, la literatura cubana se mantiene muy apegada a la realidad, sin poder escapar las circunstancias políticas, que a veces se incorporan en la obra de forma imaginativa y oblicua, y en otras más directa y crudamente. El erotismo, los elementos de religiones afrocubanas, la dura realidad de la isla, la nostalgia del exilio, y la angustia existencial ante un futuro incierto son motivos constantes en diversos autores. Pocos logran no escribir sobre Cuba. Una de esas excepciones es la magnífica novela de Mayra Montero, *El capitán de los dormidos* (ítem **3505**).

Los cubanos siguen publicando en diversas partes del mundo, de La Habana a Miami, de Madrid a Ciudad México, de Cincinnati a Barcelona, lo cual muestra que no ha decaído el interés universal por la producción literaria en la isla caribeña.

Si bien el afán de integrar la literatura escrita en la isla y la de la diáspora, largamente escindida, data de hace varios años, y se puede comprobar aquí con las antologías que incluyen a escritores residentes en la isla y fuera de ella, así como con la publicación en Cuba de novelas de escritores en el exterior (i.e., *Las historias prohibidas de Marta Veneranda* de Sonia Rivera-Valdés, ítem **3522**), hay otro fenómeno de interés. Escritores en la isla intentan incluir el fenómeno de la diáspora en sus obras. Tal es el caso de Leonardo Padura Fuentes en *La novela de mi vida* (ítem **3511**), mientras que autores largamente ausentes de Cuba se esfuerzan por reproducir la vida allá, como en algunos de los cuentos de Amelia del Castillo, ya mencionados aquí. Aunque el intento de entender al otro es digno de elogio desde un punto de vista humano y político, en el plano literario aún no ha cuajado.

Los estilos varían desde la prosa poética al realismo sucio, desde la difícil prosa sencilla y directa, en apariencia fácil, hasta los juegos barrocos en el lenguaje y la misma estructura.

La narrativa dominicana sigue igualmente aferrada a la problemática nacional. El fantasma de Trujillo continúa apareciendo en un gran número de obras. Se observan elementos de realismo mágico, recreación de viejas leyendas y mitos, y una inexplicable nostalgia por un pasado que sin embargo se denuncia lleno de espanto. [UA]

PUERTO RICO

Dramatic political events at the turn of the millennium have made their mark on Puerto Rican literature. The commemoration of the centenary of the North American occupation of the island in 1898 occasioned an array of publications, including the reissuing of earlier literary works and some original writings on the theme of modern colonial history (item **3499**) and a re-examining of the nation's past (items **3483, 3493,** and **3502**). Other influential events of those turbulent years were the release of long-held political prisoners and, most dramatically, the opposition to US military presence on the island of Vieques. The latter struggle occasioned a range of literary works (e.g., item **3525**), as well as poetry and abundant nonfiction commentary on citizenship, the environment, and military occupation.

During the late 1990s and early 2000s, literature from women writers and the Puerto Rican diaspora in the US continued to play a major role in Puerto Rican cultural expression. The ongoing work of internationally prominent women authors such as Rosario Ferré, Ana Lydia Vega, and Magali García Ramis has been amplified by the writings of Mayra Santos-Febres, Mayra Montero, and others, with continued attention to themes of gender and family relations. Fictional and poetic writing by Puerto Ricans in the US has continued, and is receiving increased attention from the general readership—including the reading public in Puerto Rico. Most well-known among these is Esmeralda Santiago, whose stories and novels sell widely in both languages and are available throughout the island, while works by writers such as Judith Ortíz Cofer, Abraham Rodriguez, and others are also becoming more familiar to readers in Puerto Rico.

Despite striking continuities with literature of earlier decades, present-day writing also indicates the emergence of a new literary generation. The recent passing of some major writers from the generation of the 1950s such as José Luis González, Pedro Juan Soto, Clemente Soto Vélez, and René Marqués, mark the end of an era in the country's literary activity. Yet even the thematics and stylistic tendencies of the highly visible "generation of the 70s" appear to be giving way to new developments. While writers of that period such as Rosario Ferré, Edgardo Rodríguez Juliá, and Luis Rafael Sánchez continue to publish important new works, contemporary younger writers place stronger emphasis on the subjects of race and sexuality, and tend to question long-held assumptions about national culture and identity. Some of these new tendencies are evident in the writings of Santos-Febres as well as in her anthology *Mal(h)ab(l)ar* (item **3500**).

While local events and controversies generate and nourish these new perspectives, literary and cultural expressions of the diaspora are also strong influences. As is particularly noteworthy among the cultural expression of Puerto Rican youth, current poetic creativity demonstrates the influences of rap rhyming, slam poetry, and open-mic performance prevalent among African-American, Latino, and Asian-American youth in the US. Further evidence of the literary presence of the diaspora is the appearance of works such as Piri Thomas' *Down These Mean Streets* (new edition published in 1997); Judith Ortíz Cofer's *Line of the Sun* (1989; Spanish original: *Línea del sol*, 1986); and Abraham Rodriguez's *Spidertown* (1993), also available in Spanish translation (1999) and available to readers on the island.

Important works on literary and cultural criticism are also directed at these new orientations. Notable during recent years are Arcadio Díaz Quiñones' essays in *El arte de bregar* (see *HLAS 58:3600*), Juan Flores' *From Bomba to Hip-Hop: Puerto Rican Culture and Latino Identity* (see *HLAS 58:3601*), and Jorge Duany's *The Puerto Rican Nation on the Move* (2002), all of which point toward the centrality of transnational interactions as crucial to understanding contemporary Puerto Rican culture. Among nonfiction works, the theme of literature in its relation to popular music is of central interest, as in the works by Angel Quintero Rivera, *Salsa, sabor y control!: sociología de la música "tropical"* (1998); Frances Aparicio, *Listening to Salsa: Gender, Latin Popular Music, and Puerto Rican Cultures* (see *HLAS 58:3597*); and Juan Otero Garabís, *Nación y ritmo, descargadas desde el Caribe* (2000). [JF]

PROSE FICTION

3467 Aire de luz: cuentos cubanos del siglo XX. Repertorio y estudio preliminar de Alberto Garrandés. La Habana: Editorial Letras Cubanas, 1999. 620 p.

Como en toda antología, ni son todos los que están, ni están todos los que son. Aunque el estudio preliminar está libre de la retórica ideológica que tanto ha teñido los trabajos académicos cubanos, la falta de siquiera una frase que mencione la escisión de la cultura cubana a partir de 1959 y el caudal de obras escritas fuera de la isla, no es superado por la inclusión de un narrador que vive en EE.UU. y dos o tres más que murieron en el exilio. En el caso de algunos de los clásicos del género, como Alfonso Hernández-Catá y Enrique Labrador Ruiz, se han incluido cuentos frecuentemente antologados, en vez de buscar nuevas selecciones. Se echa de menos también siquiera un párrafo bibliográfico de cada autor que permitiera a los lectores ubicar los cuentos escogidos dentro del contexto de la obra de cada autor.

3468 Alberto, Eliseo. Caracol Beach. Madrid: Alfaguara, 1998. 365 p.

En palabras del autor, se trata de una novela "sobre el miedo, la locura, la inocencia, el perdón y la muerte." Según el jurado que le otorgó el Premio Alfaguara 1998, está escrita "con un lenguaje audaz, siempre sorprendente, un destino en el que el azar rompe a cada momento la lisura de lo cotidiano." Sin duda una metáfora de este fin de siglo, "Caracol Beach," quizás como el tiempo en que inscribe, sufre de esa precisión que se convierte en ambigüedad, de ese cosmopolitismo que se linda en la deshumanización, de ese realismo que hace dudar de la verosimilitud de la fantasía, de ese posmodernismo que deja al lector como si hubiera llegado a una playa donde el sol le nublara la visión. Para el comentario sobre la traducción al inglés de esta obra, ver ítem **4273.**

3469 Alonso, Nancy. Tirar la primera piedra. La Habana: Editorial Letras Cubanas, 1997. 79 p. (Cemí. Cuento)

En la abundante narrativa sobre las dificultades de la vida cotidiana en Cuba, sobresalen estas siete narraciones escritas con sobriedad de recursos, precisión de lenguaje y sensibilidad. El libro pone al desnudo las contradicciones éticas y humanas que viven a diario los cubanos.

3470 Aponte Alsina, Marta. La casa de la loca. Cayey, Puerto Rico: Sopa de Letras Editores, 1999. 143 p.

Collection of stories gives life to eccentric characters, often referring to famous artists such as Alejandro Tapia, Luis Palés Matos, and Ramón Frade. The author, a prize-winning novelist (*El cuarto rey mago*, 1996), utilizes techniques and themes of magical realism to introduce the reader to some of the fantastic aspects of Puerto Rican society, and more generally, contemporary reality.

3471 Arenal, Humberto. Caribal. La Habana: Editorial Letras Cubanas, 1997. 121 p. (Cemí. Novela)

Historia con poco vuelo de imaginación en que un aspirante a Caruso asedia a una joven viuda que sólo aspira a cantar boleros. La seducción termina en crimen. El asesino se excita con la perspectiva de engullirse las carnes de su víctima mucho más que los lectores podrán hacerlo con una narración de estilo descuidado, que no alcanza el clímax dramático que aún una trama tan manida podría ofrecer.

3472 Bacardí Moreau, Emilio. Filigrana. Santiago, Cuba: Editorial Oriente, 1999. 344 p.

Novela romántica y costumbrista que se desarrolla en el Santiago de Cuba de 1800, escrita en las primeras décadas del siglo XX, por uno de los cronistas más amenos de la ciudad oriental. La obra, aunque publicada en España, nunca había visto la luz en Cuba, donde el hallazgo de un manuscrito con correcciones del puño y letra del autor han hecho posible esa edición, un revelador espejo de la Cuba colonial.

3473 Bähr, Aida. Espejismos. La Habana: Ediciones Unión, 1998. 97 p. (La rueda dentada) (Cuento)

Amores, desilusiones, muerte, erotismo, cansancio, una gama de emociones, y vivencias cotidianas recogidas desde la voz de sujetos femeninos, en ocho breves cuentos que denotan el dominio del género que tiene la autora.

3474 Benítez Rojo, Antonio. El mar de las lentejas. Prologado por Angel G. Loureiro. Barcelona: Editorial Casiopea, 1999. 238 p. (Col. Ceiba)

Novela de aventuras, amores e insólitos personajes que se desarrolla en África, España y el Nuevo Mundo durante el imperio de Felipe II. Con infinita y sabia comprensión del Caribe, y con prosa tersa y exacta, el autor nos entrega una metáfora sobre una realidad que perdura en el actual siglo XXI.

3475 Bosch, Juan. Antología personal. Edición al cuidado de Avelino Stanley. San Juan: Editorial de la Univ. de Puerto Rico, 1998. 476 p.: bibl.

Selección de cuentos, fragmentos de novelas y leyendas, así como ensayos y conferencias de una de las figuras predominantes en la literatura dominicana del siglo XX. Son de especial interés los dos trabajos de teoría sobre el cuento, género ampliamente cultivado en la tierra del autor.

3476 Bragado Bretaña, Reinaldo. La noche vigilada. Tempe, Ariz.: Bilingual Press, 1999. 137 p.

Novela testimonial sobre la vida política, social y cultural de La Habana y Miami. El exceso de explicaciones y datos resta en ocasiones vuelo poético a esta historia de miedos, amores, muerte y nuevos comienzos, que queda salvada por el tono menor que utiliza el autor para fabular sobre una realidad dramática de por sí.

3477 Canetti, Yanitzia. Al otro lado. Barcelona: Seix Barral, 1997. 253 p.

Una joven escritora muestra sus indudables pero aún incipientes cualidades de narradora en una novela de deseo, rebeldía y trasgresión en una isla del Caribe, fácilmente identificable como la Cuba natal de la autora.

3478 Castillo, Amelia del. De trampas y fantasías. Miami, Fla.: Ediciones Universal, 2001. 142 p. (Col. Caniquí)

La autora, que ocupa un merecido lugar en la poesía cubana contemporánea, reúne por vez primera 26 relatos, escritos a través de los años. La buena prosa, la fórmula de Edgar Allan Poe de cuentos cerrados y finales sorprendentes y la variación de temas, mantienen el interés del lector.

3479 Cazorla, Roberto. Ceiba Mocha: cuentos y relatos cubanos. Prólogo de Isabel Martínez Pita. Madrid: Editorial Betania, 1997. 200 p.: ill. (Col. Narrativa)

Estampas de la infancia del autor en el pueblo matancero de Ceiba Mocha que reproducen la devoción filial por la madre, el miedo y desprecio al padre borrachín e infiel, la sensibilidad del poeta en ciernes y el ambiente rural de la Cuba de los años 40.

3480 Chaviano, Daína. Casa de juegos. Barcelona: Planeta, 1999. 192 p. (Autores españoles e iberoamericanos)

El erotismo, lo sobrenatural, el ambiente de una Cuba que oscila entre las limitaciones a la libertad y la voluptuosidad más atrevida, y una prosa exacta y apretada, son los elementos con que la autora crea esta *Casa de juegos.*

3481 Chaviano, Daína. El hombre, la hembra y el hambre. Barcelona: Planeta, 1998. 312 p. (Autores españoles e iberoamericanos)

Novela que se inscribe en la actual tendencia narrativa se regodearse en la miseria, el sexo y el hambre de los cubanos, pero en este caso, con dominio del género y el lenguaje y sin intenciones de malabarismos literarios. Una historia humana, con cierto vuelo de la imaginación, y la chata realidad cotidiana de la Cuba de los 90 como trasfondo.

3482 Collado, Lipe. Después del viento: novela. Santo Domingo: Editora Collado, 1997. 366 p.

Historia que mezcla el realismo crudo y lo mágico para contar la historia del diario vivir de un barrio, microcosmo simbólico del país. Hay nostalgia de pasado y frustración por lo que no fue, afincado todo en personajes y tradiciones emblemáticas de la cultura dominicana.

3483 Córdova Landrón, Arturo. Ilusión y aventura de Aquiles Zurita. San Juan: Editorial LEA, Librería Editorial Ateneo, Ateneo Puertorriqueño 1998. 484 p.: ill. (Cuadernos del 98; 1)

Historical novel originally written in 1951, published under the auspices of the Ateneo Puertorriqueño as part of the series "Cuadernos del 98" on the occasion of the centenary of the US invasion of Puerto Rico in 1898. The plot revolves around a love story, but seeks to dramatize historical events on the island during the first half of the 20th century, especially the destructive impact of US domination on both land-owners and peasants. Two prologues, one by well-known folklorist Marcelino Canino Salgado, provide a helpful introduction to the author and his work.

3484 Cuba: short stories. Edited and with a preface by Ann Louise Bardach. Berkeley, Calif.: Whereabouts Press, 2002. 234 p.: maps. (A traveler's literary companion)

Al igual que un creciente número de antologías cubanas recientes, esta colección de cuentos del siglo XX incluye autores de la isla y el destierro. Contiene narraciones de algunos de los clásicos del género de la primera mitad del siglo, como Alfonso Hernández-Catá y Lino Novas Calvo, al igual que de jóvenes escritores como Antonio José Ponte y Ana Menéndez. Los relatos están unidos por el hilo conductor de contener descripciones del paisaje, tanto físico como interior, de Cuba y los cubanos. Aunque inevitablemente siempre se pierde algo en las traducciones, es un buen recurso para los lectores en inglés que desean acercarse a la literatura de la isla.

3485 Cuentos de La Habana Vieja. Madrid: Olalla Ediciones, 1997. 174 p.: ill. (Serie Literatura)

El volumen recoge textos de desigual calidad de cinco jóvenes periodistas. Más que cuentos, se trata de viñetas, reflexiones y estampas. Es interesante señalar que a pesar de la juventud de los autores, estas páginas están impregnadas de nostalgia. Los ángeles, los fantasmas, las estrellas se colocan en pugna con la realidad chata que los rodea. A pesar de algunos pasajes de innegable valor, los textos no están a la altura de las fotografías de uno de los autores—Tomás Barceló—que adornan el libro.

3486 Díaz, Jesús. Dime algo sobre Cuba. Madrid: Espasa, 1998. 261 p. (Espasa narrativa)

Más que decir algo sobre Cuba, el autor sitúa su novela en un Miami y un exilio que desconoce. La prosa es buena, pero a la literatura que falsea la realidad (que no es lo mismo que inventarla) siempre se le ven las costuras.

3487 Díaz Llanillo, Esther. Cuentos antes y después del sueño. La Habana: Editorial Letras Cubanas, 1999. 97 p. (Cemí. Cuento)

Más de una veintena de narraciones cortas, muchas de corte fantástico y que se acogen a la estructura clásica del cuento que predicara Edgar Allan Poe. Sin embargo, no siempre la autora alcanza el clima de terror o asombro que se espera de este género de cuentos.

3488 Estévez, Abilio. El horizonte y otros regresos. Barcelona: Tusquets Editores, 1998. 208 p. (Col. Andanzas; 348)

Colección de narraciones cortas creadas a lo largo de una década—de mediados de los 80 hasta 1996—y pobladas de protagonistas muy disímiles, pero unidos por la búsqueda de un horizonte, que, más que una línea imaginaria, supone un infinito, un escape de anhelos incumplidos y el acoso del miedo.

3489 Estévez, Abilio. Tuyo es el reino. Barcelona: Tusquets Editores, 1997. 346 p. (Col. Andanzas; 317)

Primera novela de un escritor que ya ha dado muestras de su talento en los géneros de teatro, poesía y cuento. La Isla, una pequeña comunidad cerca de La Habana, donde una familia vive en un viejo caserón en Más Allá, en espera de un acontecimiento que logre sacarlos de la inercia, es sin duda una metáfora de la Cuba actual. Contrario a otros autores del momento, Estévez escribe un texto transgresor, no porque desnude la realidad, sino la reinventa, en este himno de fe en el poder de las palabras.

3490 Fernández Fe, Gerardo. La falacia. La Habana: Ediciones Unión, 1999. 113 p.

Novela corta que mezcla la angustia existencial con los recuerdos de una infancia habanera no tan lejana para el joven protagonista ni para el joven autor. La obra es un buen ejemplo de algunos de los senderos por los que transita la actual narrativa cubana.

3491 Fernández Pintado, Mylene. Anhedonia. La Habana: Ediciones Unión, 1999. 79 p.

Este manojo de cuentos, que mereció el Premio David en 1998, tiene como tema central la vida de jóvenes cubanos en distintas latitudes, incluso la de la ilusión. Hay un manejo hábil de personajes y situaciones así como un dominio del idioma y de las estructuras narrativas, pero falta profundidad, aunque, quizás, de eso se trate precisamente, de una generación que logra invertir el orden de los valores, tornar en frívolo lo trascendente y aferrarse a lo más mínimo como salvación.

3492 Fernández Spencer, Antonio. Un pueblo sin memoria y otros cuentos. Santo Domingo: Ediciones El Pez Rojo, 1997. 85 p. (Col. El pez rojo)

Manojo de cuentos publicados póstumamente del ensayista y poeta, merecedor del Premio Nacional de Literatura de 1995. Tanto a través de la recreación de mitos clásicos como en las narraciones en que se utiliza el realismo mágico, característica de la literatura latinoamericana de gran parte de este siglo, se destaca el rechazo a la guerra y a la violencia, y la defensa del bien. A pesar de que el autor se acerca a menudo a ese didactismo que puede fácilmente cancelar los méritos de las obras literarias, el volumen se redime por la clásica sencillez de la prosa, y por un hilo conductor que propone que cuanto aconteció en el pasado se repetirá hoy y mañana, pues el hombre es un actor atrapado en un drama tan antiguo como la humanidad.

3493 Ferré, Rosario. La extraña muerte del capitancito Candelario. Barcelona: Plaza & Janés Editores, 1999. 93 p. (Relatos; 24)

Originally a story appearing in the author's well-known *Maldito amor* (1986), winnner of the literary prize of the Frankfurt Book Fair. Ferré is one of the most famous contemporary Puerto Rican writers, having gained international recognition for both her poetry and her many books of prose fiction and nonfiction. In this story, considered by many a gem of contemporary Puerto Rican writing, Ferré offers her subtle, deeply ironic critique of the country's historical reality as forged by its dominant, Hispanophile elite and by the ubiquitous presence of North American empire.

3494 Gutiérrez, Pedro Juan. Trilogía sucia de La Habana. Barcelona: Anagrama, 1998. 359 p. (Narrativas hispánicas; 251)

Un libro duro, escrito a punta de bis-

turí, a golpe de ron, música y sexo, a medio camino entre la exuberancia tropical y la negra realidad de un habanero descreído. Una crónica de tiempos contradictorios y desoladores, no exenta de humor y de irreverencia, donde la visión del desencanto se torna en esperpento y el escape erótico en el vórtice de la rabia contenida.

3495 Habanera fué. Barcelona: Muchnik Editores, 1998. 123 p.: ill.

Tres cuentos de tres hermanos de la familia Abreu (Nicolás, José y Juan) en homenaje a su madre, atropellada por un auto en Miami. Los sentimientos de dolor, ternura, rebeldía y venganza hallan cauce en una prosa igualmente tersa en los tres autores, que buscan retar el olvido en estos relatos conmovedores, donde se mezcla la fantasía, el recuerdo y el arte de saber narrar.

3496 Holguín Veras, Miguel A. Juro que sabré vengarme—: novela histórica. Santo Domingo: Editora de Colores, 1998. 163 p.: ill. (Literatura dominicana)

Novela histórica basada en el secuestro de una joven de la ciudad de Monte Cristi, Ozema Petit, hecho de violencia considerado por el autor como el comienzo de la era dictatorial de Trujillo. El uso y abuso del poder, la impunidad, la compra de conciencias prefiguran los horrores que sufriría durante las próximas décadas el pueblo dominicano, y que han dado lugar a una abundante novelística sobre el tirano y sus víctimas.

3497 Jorge, Andrés. Te devolverán las mareas. México: Planeta, 1998. 285 p. (Autores latinoamericanos)

El autor explora la compleja sexualidad de cuatro mujeres con sensibilidades de épocas y mundos diferentes. La actitud ante los hombres, la búsqueda de la libertad, la creatividad y el mismo don visionario de Safo, Izuno Shikibu, Virginia Wolf y Ofelia Ibarra cobran un sentido de continuidad en esta historia, que incita al amor y a la muerte. La prosa es límpida y la complejidad aumenta a través de las páginas y del fatalismo que parece signar a los personajes.

3498 Jorge, Andrés. Voyeurs. Mexico: Alfaguara, 2002. 290 p.

El autor alterna los hilos narrativos de dos historias en apariencia inconexas: la del balsero cubano Ulises que es rescatado por un vapor donde sus pasajeros se reúnen por las noches a fabular historias, y la de un pintor en trámites de divorcio que espía a su vecina. Las aventuras de Ulises, salpicadas de frases y realidades de la actualidad cubana, están escritas en un estilo que remeda el de Cervantes en el Quijote, lo cual produce al lector una sensación de zozobra, como si el presente hubiera transgredido el tiempo pasado. El Pintor, sin embargo, vive en un tiempo postmoderno. Al final, todo se entreteje—planos narrativos, tiempo, y lenguaje—y la única certeza es que todos somos, de una forma u otra, voyeurs clandestinos y gozosos.

3499 López Nieves, Luis. La verdadera muerte de Juan Ponce de León. Hato Rey, Puerto Rico: Editorial Cordillera, 2000. 120 p.

A collection of five interrelated stories, all referring to 16th-century Puerto Rico. In a manner present in the author's best-known novel, *Seva: historia de la primera invasión norteamericana de la Isla de Puerto Rico, occurida en mayo de 1898* (1984), recognized historical events and figures are subjected to imaginative inquiry and presented in terms of what could or might have happened. Here again, as with the imaginary resistance to American occupation presented in *Seva*, López Nieves teases the country's historical imagination to awaken a sense of alternative political and cultural possibilities generally omitted from official historiography.

3500 Mal(h)ab(l)ar: antología de nueva literatura puertorriqueña. Recopilación de Mayra Santos Febres. Puerto Rico: Fundación Puertorriqueña de las Humanidades: Yagunzo Press International, 1997. 244 p.

Anthology of recent generation of Puerto Rican writers introduces poets and fiction writers who have emerged since the later 1980s. Prologue offers a lucid and thoughtful explanation of this generational demarcation, pointing to a new tone and new thematic concerns among younger writers. Some of the writers included are Noel Luna, Rafael Acevedo, Juan López Bauzá, as well as the prize-winning editor herself. This collection offers the best available representation of present-day Puerto Rican authors writing in Spanish.

3501 Marcallé Abréu, Roberto. Las siempre insólitas cartas del destino: detalles inéditos de una venganza: novela. Santo Domingo: Cocolo Editorial, 1999. 396 p.

El autor utiliza la técnica de la novela policial para enfrentar al lector no sólo a la violencia y el crimen, sino a toda una atmósfera de sospecha y miedo. A través de personajes bien trazados, ofrece un perfil de la psicología del pueblo dominicano. Más allá de la tragedia nacional, la larga carrera de las vidas de los protagonistas hacia la nada, la monotonía que invade las conversaciones entre amigos, los ademanes casi rituales del amor y el odio, expresan la angustia existencial del hombre moderno.

3502 Martínez-Maldonado, Manuel. Isla verde: el Chevy azul. Madrid: Editorial Verbum, 1999. 194 p.: port. (Narrativa)

A novel set in Puerto Rico during the 1950s. Author captures much of the social and cultural sensibility of the island during those dramatic years. Considered by prominent writer Edgardo Rodríguez Juliá to be a "stupendous novel" with a sensitive combination of picaresque and sentimental qualities, *Isla verde* is the first book-length work of fiction by Martínez-Maldonado, a medical specialist better known for his poetry and critical commentary.

3503 Mattos Cintrón, Wilfredo. El colapso: novela. San Juan: Ediciones La Sierra, 2000. 241 p.

A novel comprised of two intertwined stories, one relating the collapse of Soviet hegemony in Eastern Europe and the other about the demise of a philosophy professor affiliated with a communist party. The author, a well-known political commentator in Puerto Rico, clearly intends to reflect on what he perceives as the inappropriateness of outdated ideological stances in the island's complex political situation.

3504 Minaya, Ligia. Palabras de mujer. Santo Domingo: s.n., 1997. 212 p.

Viñetas a través de las cuales la autora expresa sus puntos de vista sobre temas eternos—amor, sexo, la naturaleza humana, desigualdades sociales, Dios—en el contexto de la vida moderna. A pesar del estilo desenfadado, abundan los clichés. Un airecillo de superioridad en la voz de la autora contradice algunos de sus propios postulados.

3505 Montero, Mayra. El capitán de los dormidos. Barcelona: Tusquets Editores, 2002. 215 p. (Col. Andanzas; 472)

Cada novela de esta autora parece superar la anterior. Sus narraciones se desarrollan siempre en el Caribe, y esta novela tiene como escenario las islas de Vieques y Santa Cruz. Con una prosa de perfección geométrica, Montero parte de un re-encuentro y una conversación entre dos hombres, para desarrollar una trama de intriga, amor y muerte, rica en las sutilezas que sólo puede plasmar en obra literaria quien conoce a fondo los misterios de la naturaleza humana.

3506 Montero, Mayra. Como un mensajero tuyo. Barcelona: Tusquets Editores, 1998. 261 p. (Col. Andanzas; 331)

La misteriosa desaparición de Enrico Caruso, tras la explosión de una bomba en el Teatro Nacional de La Habana en 1920, momentos antes de que el famoso tenor fuera a presentarse en escena, sirven de trasfondo a esta novela de impecable estructura y lenguaje preciso y precioso. El manejo del tiempo, el trazo de los personajes, la mezcla de investigación e imaginación, contribuyen también a que la novela se destaque entre la abundante novelística cubana contemporánea.

3507 Montes-Huidobro, Matías. Concierto para sordos. Tempe, Ariz.: Bilingual Press, 2001. 129 p.

La temática histórico-política parece inagotable en los autores del destierro. En este caso el devenir de la isla se convierte en una especie de pesadilla esperpéntica, macabra danza de la muerte, en la cual el pasado indígena y el colonial sirven de contrapunto a la actualidad.

3508 Novás Calvo, Lino. Pedro blanco, el negro. Prólogo de Alberto Garrandés. Dibujo de Eduardo Roca (Choco). La Habana: Editorial Letras Cubanas, 1997. 299 p.: bibl., ill.

Reedición de la famosa novela sobre la trata de esclavos a Cuba publicada originalmente por su autor en Madrid en 1933, donde le ganó merecidos reconocimientos. Este volumen incluye un prólogo de Garrandés que

sitúa la obra en el contexto de la identidad literaria hispanoamericana.

3509 Nuevos narradores cubanos. Edición a cargo de Michi Strausfeld. Madrid: Ediciones Siruela, 2000. 341 p. (Libros del tiempo; 126)

Esta antología de cuentos de 25 autores nacidos a partir de 1959, año del triunfo de la Revolución, es un intento más de mostrar que la literatura cubana es una, y cobijar en el mismo volumen a escritores residentes en la isla y en el extranjero. Resalta que la antóloga hace una diferencia entre los de la "diáspora" y los del "exilio," término el último de mayor carga política. Las narraciones ofrecen variedad de estilos y temas y son una muestra más de la importancia del género del cuento en la actual literatura cubana.

3510 El ojo de la noche: nuevas cuentistas cubanas. Compilación, prólogo y notas de Amir Valle. La Habana: Editorial Letras Cubanas, 1999. 222 p.

Un buen muestrario de la vigencia del género cuentístico y de la fuerza de la escritura femenina. Se trata de relatos de jóvenes narradoras que empiezan a darse a conocer después de 1984. La temática y los estilos son distintos pero hay un aliento transgresor común que da unidad al volumen.

3511 Padura Fuentes, Leonardo. La novela de mi vida. Barcelona: Tusquets Editores, 2002. 345 p. (Col. Andanzas; 470)

Sin duda la más ambiciosa del autor, esta novela se desarrolla en tres tiempos. Un hilo narrativo en primera persona intenta reproducir la voz del poeta José María Heredia durante el siglo XIX. Otro plano describe la trayectoria de un descendiente del bardo en la Cuba de los años 30, quien confía a sus compañeros masones el destino del manuscrito. Un joven profesor que regresa a Cuba en busca de las misteriosas memorias de Heredia es el personaje central del tercer argumento, que tiene lugar en la actualidad. Las traiciones que sufre el escritor decimonónico parecen duplicarse en la Cuba actual, pero al final el autor acaba por no atreverse a dibujar el reflejo en el espejo, y el traidor resulta ser el que se ha marchado al dudar de sus compatriotas, todos inocentes. Aunque la estructura y el manejo del tiempo son excelentes, Padura tampoco logra que la voz del poeta decimonónico adquiera verosimilitud. Algunos pasajes, como los dedicados al poeta Eugenio Florit, hieren por su crueldad y falta de veracidad histórica.

3512 Padura Fuentes, Leonardo. Paisaje de otoño. Barcelona: Tusquets Editores, 1998. 260 p. (Col. Andanzas; 345)

Ultima novela de una tetralogía que comenzó el autor en 1990 con *Pasado perfecto*, en estas páginas el teniente investigador Mario Conde vuelve a sus menesteres cuando unos pescadores descubren en una playa habanera el cadáver de Miguel Forcade Mier. El autor utiliza los recursos del género negro en una trama de corrupciones y ambiciones frustradas que pasa por la requisa de bienes a la burguesía por la Revolución, el exilio de Miami, y la espera de un huracán y del fin del mundo.

3513 Pérez Lozano, Sandra. Crónicas de un sueño. Madrid: Grupo Santillana, 1998. 324 p. (Extra Alfaguara)

La historia de una joven cubana, narrada en forma de diario, y a través de cartas, fechadas en La Habana y en Madrid. El lenguaje es sencillo y directo, la trama casi inexistente, y el exceso de información (o desinformación) que se le ofrece al lector nubla lo que hubiera podido ser una visión juvenil de la vida para acercarse peligrosamente al campo de la propaganda y de la tontería.

3514 Piñera, Virgilio. Cuentos completos. Madrid: Alfaguara, 1999. 603 p.

Aunque Piñera (1912–79) es más conocido por su teatro de la crueldad, su cuentística merece una publicación completa. Antón Arrufat, en el prólogo, describe con justicia a Piñera como a un escritor que siempre vivió marginado. Ha sido después de su muerte que ha recibido mayor reconocimiento, aunque no aún la fama que merecería por la alta calidad de su obra literaria, que puede contarse entre las más importantes de la literatura cubana de este siglo. Ojalá esta edición contribuya a una difusión más amplia de su obra.

3515 Poco antes del 2000: jóvenes cuentistas cubanos en las puertas del nuevo siglo. Selección y presentación de Alberto Garrandés. La Habana: Editorial Letras Cubanas, 1997. 159 p.

Toda antología de cuentos responde, naturalmente, a ciertos criterios de selección. Garrandés incluye entre sus parámetros a autores que se hayan dado a conocer en la década de los 90, que expresen en sus relatos una mirada globalizadora del mundo actual y que respondan al espectro heterogéneo de modos y actitudes en que los jóvenes narradores cubanos se relacionan con el lenguaje. Sorprende, pues, la ausencia absolutamente total de mujeres. La exclusión pone en dudas que la visión del autor sobre la realidad mundial pueda considerarse moderna y globalizadora.

3516 Ponte, Antonio José. Cuentos de todas partes del imperio. Ilustrado con dibujos de Ramón Alejandro. France: Deleatur, 2000. 77 p.: ill. (Col. Baralanube)

Este libro, bellamente ilustrado por el pintor Ramón Alejandro, está compuesto por cinco cuentos cortos de las andanzas de miembros de ese imperio de aire—aroma amargo del café, humo picante del tabaco, palabras y compases lanzadas al viento—que es Cuba para el autor. La cultura literaria del Ponte es obvia, pero no la utiliza de forma paródica como otros escritores de su generación. Con un estilo cuidado y una dosis exacta de lirismo y ternura, el autor parte de lo inmediato y cotidiano para fabular con imaginación, talento y oficio.

3517 Portela, Ena Lucía. Una extraña entre las piedras. La Habana: Editorial Letras Cubanas, 1999. 122 p. (Cemí. Cuento)

Personajes sutilmente exhibicionistas, actos de naturaleza simbólica, un sentido de lo ceremonial y un claro nexo entre el curso del pensamiento y el de acción, dan una peculiar densidad a esta media docena de narraciones cortas escritas por una de las autoras más interesantes de "Los novísimos."

3518 Portela, Ena Lucía. El Pájaro, pincel y tinta china. La Habana: Ediciones Unión, 1998. 217 p.

Esta primera novela de quien ya se ha destacado en el género del cuento se instala en una tendencia de la narrativa de los 90 que abre nuevos espacios semánticos a través de la intertextualidad, las parodias, las alusiones, y el humor. Un texto francamente transgresor.

3519 Prats Sariol, José. Mariel. México: Editorial Aldus, 1997. 491 p. (Col. La torre inclinada)

No se trata, como el título pudiera hacer pensar, de la historia del gran éxodo de cubanos por ese puerto norteño de Cuba, sino de la historia de una ciudad, sus barrios, cantinas, playas y personajes. Con tono irónico y muchas veces crítico, sirviéndose de diversos recursos narrativos, el autor ofrece el retrato de una sociedad que cambia para que todo siga igual. Entre el orden urbano y el desorden sensual de la naturaleza, los cubanos de Mariel se enfrentan con humorística irrealidad a una realidad muy seria.

3520 Prieto, Abel Enrique. El vuelo del gato. La Habana: Editorial Letras Cubanas, 1999. 315 p. (La novela)

Primera novela del Ministro de Cultura de Cuba, quien ya ha incursionado en el género del cuento. Sin ser una autobiografía, la novela narra la historia de su generación, aquellos jóvenes que en los años 70 estudiaban y escuchaban la música de los Beatles y de Janis Joplin. Aunque ser *hippy* en Cuba no estaba bien visto, eran fanáticos del rock y se sentían muy a la vanguardia, respetando sin embargo los límites que les permitían sobrevivir y hasta llegar a altas posiciones, como en el caso de Prieto. La novela se torna en momentos reflexiva, casi ensayística, con toques antropológicos. Está presente asimismo el tema de la santería, el espiritismo, la religión, todo mezclado en un ajiaco de creencias a la cubana.

3521 Prieto González, José Manuel. Livadia. Barcelona: Mondadori, 1999. 318 p. (Literatura Mondadori; 96)

Con una trama que mezcla el género de aventuras con el epistolar y la iniciación mística, la novela de este cubano residente en México, gira en torno a un contrabandista nómada que espera en Livadia, antigua residencia veraniega del zar Nicolás II, las cartas que le envía una mujer en Estambul. Se trata de una muestra de la vocación de universalidad, rara quizás, pero siempre presente en la narrativa de Cuba.

3522 Rivera-Valdés, Sonia. Las historias prohibidas de Marta Veneranda. La Habana: Fondo Editorial Casa de las Américas, 1997. 140 p.

Ocho narraciones cortas, todas en primera persona, con la frescura de las historias contadas verbalmente, confiadas a un interlocutor—Veneranda, personaje ficticio que investiga historias prohibidas. Los protagonistas son todos cubanos exiliados residentes en Nueva York y sus vidas, unidas por el recuerdo de la isla de su nacimiento, muestran los complejos laberintos de las pasiones humanas. La autora vive fuera de Cuba desde los años 60 y la edición de este libro es un ejemplo de autores exiliados publicados en Cuba en la última década, fenómeno impensado hace unos años. Para comentario sobre la traducción al íngles, ver ítem **4270.**

3523 Robreño, Eduardo. Del pasado que fue. La Habana: Ediciones Unión, Unión de Escritores y Artistas de Cuba, 1998. 98 p. (La rueda dentada) (Crónica)

Colección de estampas que recogen una serie de anécdotas, la mayoría de ellas durante el período colonial o republicano. A pesar del uso de frases de cajón desarrolladas en las últimas décadas para enjuiciar peyorativamente los tiempos prerevolucionarios, el libro muestra una cierta nostalgia por "el pasado que fue," una de las tendencias más singulares de la actual literatura cubana, que se resintió durante años de los estrechos límites del realismo socialista y las entusiastas loas revolucionarias.

3524 Rodríguez Juliá, Edgardo. Cortejos fúnebres: relatos. Río Piedras, Puerto Rico: Editorial Cultural, 1997. 186 p.

In this collection of stories by one of Puerto Rico's most prolific writers, some of the phobias and manias present in contemporary society are evoked in subtle and often bitterly ironic tones. With his usual insight, Rodríguez Juliá combines fiction, memoir, and social chronicle to probe some of the country's most glaring taboos and contradictions. The San Juan area beaches provide a memorable background to these sharp, controversial, and often autobiographical reflections on religion and sexuality, politics, and art.

3525 Rodríguez Torres, Carmelo. Vieques es más dulce que la sangre. Edited by Francisco M. Vázquez. Río Piedras, Puerto Rico: Editorial Cultural, 2000. 78 p.

A collection of stories occasioned by the recent attention to the long-standing confrontation over the future of the island of Vieques. A well-known political commentator and activist, the author utilizes techniques of modernist fiction, in particular that of Borges, to shed light on the social contradictions of present-day Puerto Rico. His political and biographical closeness to Vieques make the stories, significant reflections on this momentous period in the country's colonial history, relevant and credible.

3526 Sención, Viriato. Los ojos de la montaña: novela. Santo Domingo: Editora de Colores, 1997. 181 p.

Novela que recrea mitos y leyendas del sur de la República Dominicana. El hibridismo cultural y el mestizaje de ancestrales tradiciones con situaciones de conflicto, muestran un mundo cerrado, alejado de la cultura de la informática que ha revolucionado al mundo en la última década. El estilo conserva un cierto anacronismo a tono con la realidad que narra.

3527 Tejera, Nivaria. Espero la noche para sonärte, revolución. 1. ed. en español. Miami, Fla.: Ediciones Universal, 2002. 161 p. (Col. Caniquí)

A medio camino entre el testimonio y la ficción, la novela y el ensayo, este texto transgresor, tanto en la temática como en su estilo y lenguaje, es una denuncia despiadada del proceso revolucionario cubano, pero también un itinerario de la ilusión y el escepticismo, el entusiasmo y el miedo, el protagonismo y la marginalidad de quiénes son héroes, víctimas o ambas cosas, de un movimiento tan violento como la espiral de un tornado o la carrera suicida de un tren descarrilado.

3528 Valdés, Zoé. Traficantes de belleza. Barcelona: Planeta, 1998. 236 p. (Autores españoles e iberoamericanos)

Más de seis narraciones cortas, con el tono desenfadado, la carga política y la intertextualidad que caracterizan a la autora.

3529 Valdez, Diógenes. Retrato de dinosaurios en la era de Trujillo: novela. Santo Domingo: Edita-Libros, 1997. 305 p.

Novela de amor e intrigas, infidelidades y traiciones, donde personajes del pasado histórico inmediato se mezclan con los ficticios, con la dictadura de Trujillo como escenario. El personaje central es femenino, y su tensa batalla con la todopoderosa Primera Dama de la República Dominicana ofrece un ángulo interesante en

medio de una violencia perpetrada principalmente por los hombres, de la que no escapan, sin embargo, las mujeres.

3530 Valle Ojeda, Amir. Manuscritos del muerto. La Habana: Editorial Letras cubanas, 2000. 130 p.

Colección de cuentos de fuerte carga erótica, común en la narrativa cubana actual, pero con una dosis de lirismo que la distancia de la tendencia actual del "realismo sucio."

3531 Villaverde, Fernando. Las tetas europeas. Cincinnati, Ohio: Término Editorial, 1997. 239 p. (Col. Ficciones)

Tres relatos independientes pero entrelazados por el tema de la seducción femenina. El trasfondo varía: de la pantalla del cine europeo de postguerra, a una Habana en pleno furor revolucionario, a los paisajes de Nápoles, pero el tono es uno, de lúdico juego, de rítmica ondulación entre los cuerpos, y entre la realidad, verídica o imaginada, y los guiños literarios que nos hace el autor.

3532 Yáñez, Mirta. Narraciones desordenadas e incompletas. La Habana: Editorial Letras Cubanas, 1997. 160 p.

Recopilación de narraciones cortas, algunas publicadas en libros anteriores, otras inéditas, escritas por la autora a lo largo de 25 años. Hay variedad de temas, soltura de estilo, dominio del género del cuento y un punto de humor y agridulce ironía, siempre presente en la obra de esta importante figura de las letras cubanas.

LITERARY CRITICISM AND HISTORY

3533 Alvarez-Borland, Isabel. Cuban-American literature of exile: from person to persona. Charlottesville, Va.: Univ. Press of Virginia, 1998. 198 p.: bibl., index. (New World studies)

La autora enmarca el estudio de la literatura escrita por cubanos en el exilio a partir de 1959 en su contexto histórico. A pesar de las inevitables omisiones, y de un énfasis en los autores que escriben en inglés, el estudio aporta conocimientos sobre las obras de escritores que suelen quedar fuera de todos los cánones, puesto que no son reconocidos en su país de origen ni son parte de las corrientes dominantes en el país de adopción.

3534 *Anales literarios.* Vol. 3, No. 3, 2001. Narradores. Honolulu, Hawaii: Matías and Yara Montes Foundation.

El volumen contiene 14 trabajos de corte académico. Algunos, como los de Isabel Álvarez Borland y Julio Hernández-Miyares, ofrecen visiones panorámicas, mientras que los demás analizan una o varias obras de un solo autor. En general, hay rigor, sensibilidad en los enfoques, y una adecuada utilización de los marcos teóricos para interpretar los textos.

3535 Canales, Nemesio R. Antología de Nemesio R. Canales. Recopilación de Servando Montaña. 2. ed. Río Piedras, Puerto Rico: Editorial de la Univ. de Puerto Rico, 2000. 474 p.: ill.

A selection of the voluminous writings of Puerto Rico's most famous satirist of the early 20th century, Nemesio Canales (1878–1923). The editor, a scholarly specialist on the life and work of Canales, explains in his introduction that this compilation comprises a selection from his earlier, multivolume collection of the author's complete oeuvre (*Antología nueva de Canales*, 1974). In this helpful compilation, the reading public now has ready access to some of the biting satire and hilarious commentary which are among the classics of Puerto Rican literature.

3536 Domínguez, Carlos Espinosa. El peregrino en comarca ajena: panorama crítico de la literatura cubana del exilio. Boulder, Colo.: Society of Spanish and Spanish-American Studies, 2001. 384 p. (Cuban literary studies)

Un esfuerzo útil y meritorio de resumir la producción literaria—tanto en prosa como en poesía—de los cubanos en el exilio durante más de cuatro décadas. Aunque sufre de inevitables errores y omisiones, y los juicios críticos parten más de los gustos y prejuicios del autor que de un adecuado

marco teórico, se trata de un ensayo ameno y una excelente fuente bibliográfica.

3537 Garrandés, Alberto. Silencio y destino: anatomía de una novela lírica. La Habana: Editorial Letras Cubanas, 1996. 172 p.: bibl.

Análisis de los sentidos míticos y místicos de la novela lírica *Jardín* (1951) de Dulce María Loynaz, merecedora del Premio Cervantes. El crítico sitúa el texto como una aventura del conocimiento donde el espíritu dionisíaco y el apolíneo forman un armónico contrapunteo.

3538 Zatlin, Phyllis. The novels and plays of Eduardo Manet: an adventure in multiculturalism. University Park: Pennsylvania State Univ. Press, 2000. 243 p.: bibl., ill., index. (Penn State studies in Romance literatures)

Aunque más conocido por sus obras de teatro, Manet ha escrito un buen número de novelas, muchas de ellas traducidas a varios idiomas, que son analizadas en este tomo, al igual que el resto de su producción literaria. Su caso es un ejemplo de uno de los principales cuestionamientos que surge de la producción literaria de los cubanos en la actualidad. Manet nació y se crió en Cuba, y sus novelas contienen muchos temas cubanos, pero son escritas en francés, al igual que muchos de las jóvenes generaciones de cubano-americanos producen en inglés. ¿Pertenecen estas obras a la literatura cubana? ¿Define el idioma la identidad de un texto o por el contrario, pesa más el origen nacional del autor y la temática de su obra? En un mundo globalizador, donde se borran algunas fronteras pero prevalecen aún los nacionalismos, las respuestas definitivas las dará un solo juez: el tiempo.

Andean Countries

CÉSAR FERREIRA, *Associate Professor of Spanish, University of Oklahoma*
GILBERTO GÓMEZ-OCAMPO, *Associate Professor of Spanish, Wabash College*

COLOMBIA AND VENEZUELA

LA TENDENCIA MÁS DESTACADA en la literatura colombiana del pasado bienio quizá ha sido la marcada reducción de la actividad editorial en comparación con el resto de los años 90. Se destaca, en particular, la quiebra de la prestigiosa y antes muy activa editorial Tercer Mundo, que durante décadas ocupó un sitio destacado tanto en la literatura como en las ciencias sociales. Evidentemente, esa reducción ha limitado la aparición de títulos y autores nuevos a medida que algunas de las editoriales existentes con frecuencia se limitan a ofrecer títulos de reposición que garanticen un nivel mínimo de ventas. Por otro lado, las pequeñas editoriales de provincia, algunas veces con subsidios gubernamentales, continúan sorprendiendo por la calidad de sus ofertas, como en el caso de Manuel Moya, *Cuéntelos bien como yo le conté* (ítem **3559**). Julio Paredes, ganador de la Beca Colcultura 1992 y 1994, presenta una obra original en *Guía para extraviados* (ítem **3564**). La más reciente novela de Illán, *Maracas en la opera,* ganadora del Premio de la Cámara de Comercio de Medellín en 1996, se perfila como una de los textos más innovadores del período (ítem **3562**). El programa de coediciones del recién creado Ministerio de Cultura ha sido puesto en marcha exitosamente con la publicación de obras nuevas como la de Consuelo Triviño, *Prohibido salir a la calle* (ítem **3566**) o la reedición de obras hace tiempo agotadas en el mercado editorial, como los cuentos de Germán Espinosa, *Cuentos completos* (ítem **3561**).

Los autores venezolanos continuaron durante el bienio con la exploración de diferentes aperturas narrativas, que incluyen alusiones a lo paisajístico en la ficción hasta la búsqueda del absurdo en la existencia contemporánea, llegando a observarse el énfasis en la introspección en autores como Francisco Massiani, *Con agua en la piel* (ítem **3616**). La reposición de clásicos como la de Mariano Picón-Salas, *Registro de huéspedes* (ítem **3617**) es una afortunada selección editorial, como lo es, por otra parte, la publicación de la obra de talleristas jóvenes *Voces nuevas: 1995–1997* (ítem **3621**) que permite una visión de los intereses temáticos, técnicos y estilísticos de las más recientes generaciones. En una demostración de la diversidad de la narrativa venezolana actual, José Simón Escalona, en *Amargo de angostura* (ítem **3611**), evoca aspectos primordiales de terruños específicos aunque periféricos, mientras que hay también textos de naturaleza prioritariamente citadina que testimonian la incorporación de mujeres de origen extranjero, judío una, italiano otra, a la Caracas en expansión urbana de la primera época posgomecista, tales como los de Elisa Lerner, *Carriel para la fiesta* (ítem **3613**), y Marisa Vannini de Gerulewicz, *Arrivederci Caracas* (ítem **3620**). Finalmente, cabe llamar la atención sobre la muy útil compilación de ensayos de diversos autores venezolanos y extranjeros, sobre el perfil y características de la literatura venezolana en el contexto americano, reunida por Karl Kohut, *Literatura venezolana hoy: historia nacional y presente urbano* (ítem **3543**). [GG]

BOLIVIA, ECUADOR, PERU

En Bolivia, la producción novelística sigue contando con el protagonismo de Edmundo Paz Soldán, cuya prolífica obra sigue gozando de la acogida de un número cada vez mayor de lectores. A su importante obra cuentística se suman ahora las novelas *Río fugitivo,* finalista del premio Rómulo Gallegos, y *La materia del deseo* (ítems **3551** y **3552**). Destaquemos también *La casilla vacía* de Ramón Rocha Monroy (ítem **3554**), así como la novela de Tito Gutiérrez, *Magdalena en el paraíso,* ésta última un estupendo relato sobre la ecología y el narcotráfico (ítem **3547**). En el cuento, conviene revisar la antología editada por Juan González, *Memoria de lo que vendrá,* un magnífico muestrario sobre el relato breve boliviano que cuenta con muchos cultivadores de calidad (ítem **3548**). Susan Benner y Kathy Leonard también publicaron un útil volumen en inglés titulado *Fire from the Andes,* que da cuenta de la variada producción de cuentistas mujeres en Bolivia, Perú y Ecuador (ítem **3546**).

La novela en el Ecuador sigue produciendo interesantes obras de carácter histórico entre las que destacan *Y amarle pude* de Alicia Yánez Cossío (ítem **3579**) y *Las esclavas de Manuela* de Reinaldo Miño (ítem **3572**). Señalemos también la originalidad de *Acoso textual* de Raúl Vallejo Corral, novela que pone en entredicho el quehacer tradicional de la literatura al entrar en contacto con el mundo de la cibernética (ítem **3577**). En el cuento, conviene destacar el talento de Simón Espinosa Jalil en dos libros de cuentos aquí reseñados (ítems **3570** y **3571**), así como un libro de temática amorosa, *Huellas de amor eterno*, de Raúl Vallejo Corral (ítem **3578**).

En el Perú, la abundante producción novelística tuvo como protagonistas a Alfredo Bryce Echenique, autor de *El huerto de mi amada* (ítem **3586**), Jaime Bayly, Miguel Gutiérrez, Juan Morillo Ganoza y Mario Bellatin. Asimismo, Edgardo Rivera Martínez entregó un excelente volumen de novelas cortas titulado *Ciudad de fuego* (ítem **3598**).

En el cuento, conviene destacar la calidad demostrada por nuevos narradores como Carlos Schwalb y Jorge Ninapayta. A ellos se suma la publicación de una nueva antología de los relatos de Julio Ramón Ribeyro hecha en España por Angel Esteban (ítem **3597**). Por su parte, Mario Vargas Llosa añadió dos títulos más a su abundante producción ensayística: el primero de ellos un estudio sobre los orígenes artísticos del poeta nicaragüense Rubén Darío que data de sus años universitarios en la Universidad de San Marcos (ítem **3541**), y una recopilación de sus artículos periodísticos publicados durante la década de los 90 titulado *El lenguaje de la pasión* (ítem **3607**).

En el campo de la crítica, conviene destacar el valioso trabajo hecho por Giovanna Minardi sobre escritoras peruanas (ítem **3589**), así como un nuevo volumen sobre el cuento peruano a cargo de Ricardo González Vigil (ítem **3590**). Por su parte, Ricardo Silva-Santisteban y Cecilia Moreano reunieron toda la obra narrativa de César Vallejo con un útil estudio introductorio (ítem **3606**). Otra contribución importante de Silva-Santisteban fueron sus volúmenes sobre la obra de Abraham Valdelomar, sin duda la recopilación más completa hecha hasta el momento sobre este escritor (ítems **3604** y **3605**). [CF]

LITERARY CRITICISM AND HISTORY
Colombia

3539 Ospina, William. Las auroras de sangre: Juan de Castellanos y el descubrimiento poético de América. Bogotá: Ministerio de Cultura: Grupo Editorial Norma, 1999. 446 p.: bibl., index. (Col. Biografías y documentos)

A la vez biografía de Castellanos, revisión de la crítica existente y estudio literario del poema más extenso en español, la *Elegía de varones ilustres de Indias* (1589). Ospina propone convincentemente la originalidad de Castellanos y su papel en la creación de la identidad americana, con numerosos ejemplos que respaldan esos asertos. [GG]

3540 Saldívar, Dasso. García Márquez: el viaje a la semilla: la biografía. Madrid: Alfaguara, 1997. 611 p.: bibl., ill., index.

En una instancia de un género raramente practicado en Colombia, Saldívar ofrece una monumental biografía del famoso escritor. La obra se destaca por la minuciosa investigación en archivos y hemerotecas, y reconstruye en detalle la cadena de acontecimientos de la actividad periodística y literaria del biografiado, quien autorizó la obra y colaboró con Saldívar. [GG]

Peru

Hintze de Molinari, Gloria. Género e indigenismo. See item **4715**.

3541 Vargas Llosa, Mario. Bases para una interpretación de Rubén Darío: tesis universitaria, 1958. Recopilación y prólogo de Américo Mudarra Montoya. Lima: Univ. Nacional Mayor de San Marcos, Facultad de Letras y Ciencias Humanas, Instituto de Investigaciones Humanísticas, 2001. 169 p.: bibl., ill.

Tesis presentada en 1958 por el joven Vargas Llosa para optar por el grado de Bachiller en Humanidades en la Univ. de San Marcos. El novelista peruano indaga en la construcción de Darío como artista (su biografía, sus lecturas y su contexto), así como su complejo universo literario. En suma, los elementos que configurarían su vocación de escritor. [CF]

3542 Williams, Raymond L. Vargas Llosa: otra historia de un deicidio. Col. del Valle, Mexico: Taurus/UNAM, 2001. 304 p.: bibl.

Estudio que revisa toda la obra de Vargas Llosa. Se incluye un extenso capítulo biográfico sobre el escritor, seguido de lecturas críticas de toda su obra desde su libro de cuentos *Los jefes* (1959) hasta su novela *La fiesta del chivo* (ver *HLAS 58:3691*). [CF]

Venezuela

3543 Literatura venezolana hoy: historia nacional y presente urbano. Recopilación de Karl Kohut. Frankfurt: Vervuert; Madrid: Iberoamericana, 1999. 432 p.: bibl., index. (Publikationen des Zentralinstituts für Lateinamerika-Studien der Katholischen Universität Eichstätt, Serie A, Kongressakten; 20)

Muy útil compilación de ponencias leídas en el congreso de la Univ. Eichstätt de Alemania en 1996. La obra reúne algunas de las más importantes voces de la literatura venezolana: desde Garmendía y Britto García hasta jóvenes críticos y autores. Un tema común de ese simposio fue la elucidación de la identidad literaria de un país cuyos autores no figuraron en el boom. Incluye también capítulos sobre teatro y poesía. [GG]

PROSE FICTION
Bolivia

3544 Aliaga Flores, Fernando. Los Huanca. La Paz: Talleres de Imprenta "Ochoa," 1999. 102 p.

Novela que tiene como protagonista a Pedro Huanca, un niño lustrabotas. Su vida recrea el duro mundo urbano de Bolivia

donde la supervivencia es asunto de todos los días, producto de la economía informal y la indiferencia social. [CF]

3545 Costa, Edgar. En busca de una quimera. La Paz: s.n., 1999. 217 p.: ill.

Novela de adolescencia de una cuadrilla infantil ambientada en un barrio popular de La Paz. Julián, su joven protagonista, vive una historia de amor en un momento histórico de trascendencia en la vida nacional. [CF]

3546 Fire from the Andes: short fiction by women from Bolivia, Ecuador, and Peru. Edited and translated by Susan E. Benner and Kathy S. Leonard. Foreword by Marjorie Agosín. Albuquerque: Univ. of New Mexico Press, 1998. 189 p.: bibl., ill.

Excelente antología de escritoras de Bolivia, Ecuador y Perú. Las obras de algunas de estas escritoras (Alicia Yánez Cossío, Laura Riesco, Pilar Dughi M., entre otras) ocupan lugares protagónicos en la literatura de sus respectivos países. El volumen constituye un estupendo muestrario del talento narrativo existente. [CF]

3547 Gutiérrez, Tito. Magdalena en el paraíso. La Paz: Alfaguara, 2001. 288 p.

Novela sobre la coca y el narcotráfico con ribetes ecológicos que forma parte de una trilogía del autor. La misma está narrada por las voces de un periodista, un cura, un médico y un alcalde. Gutiérrez utiliza la imagen de una mariposa blanca cuya figura simboliza la utopía del paraíso. Pero un plan de manipulación genética y de fumigación de la coca terminará por desertizar el Chapare. En medio de estos sucesos está Magdalena, una mujer que atiende un bar y cuya belleza tiene obsesionados a los hombres del pueblo. Cuando el capitán de policía la hace detener acusándola de narcotráfico, su arresto desencadena el fin del paraíso. [CF]

3548 Memoria de lo que vendrá: selección sub-40 del cuento en Bolivia. Recopilación de Juan González. La Paz: Editorial Nuevo Milenio, 2000. 291 p.

Excelente antología del cuento boliviano cuyos autores bordean los 40 años de edad. Cada relato se presenta con palabras del autor antologado o con alguna opinión crítica sobre su trabajo. Una excelente muestra de toda una nueva generación de escritores, algunos de los cuales cuentan ya con una obra extensa. [CF]

3549 Montes, José Wolfango. Sagrada arrogancia. La Paz: Alfaguara, 1998. 441 p.

Novela epistolar en la que Ismael Quadros, un estudiante de Derecho, le cuenta a un interlocutor singular, Papa Noel, su intención de ascender socialmente enamorando a una aristócrata. La narración le sirve al protagonista para canalizar sus frustraciones y hacer un retrato de la conservadora sociedad en la que vive su frustrado idilio. [CF]

3550 Padilla, Feliciano. Calicanto. La Paz: Artes Gráficas Sagitario, 1999. 100 p.

Aunque publicados en Bolivia, el autor de estos relatos es oriundo de Abancay, en la sierra sur del Perú. Estos cuentos recrean anécdotas sobre su infancia en ese lugar. En ellos el mito indígena comparte un mismo espacio con la cultura occidental. Al mismo tiempo, la memoria individual y colectiva propia del imaginario indígena debe enfrentarse al inevitable avance tecnológico y sus inevitables consecuencias. [CF]

3551 Paz Soldán, Edmundo. La materia del deseo. Miami, Fla.: Alfaguara, 2001. 284 p.

Novela en que la observación sociológica y la confesión íntima se enlazan hábilmente en el relato. Destaca la sobriedad de la prosa y la verosimilitud de los diálogos, así como la identidad del protagonista, alimentada por el mundo académico, el rock y la política. Este nuevo libro de Paz Soldán confirma que es una de las voces más novedosas de la novela boliviana actual. [CF]

3552 Paz Soldán, Edmundo. Río fugitivo. La Paz: Alfaguara, 1998. 452 p.

Novela que exorciza la idea del artista adolescente. El narrador de la historia, Roby, es un joven del colegio Don Bosco que se dedica a escribir novelas policiales y pretende convertirse en escritor. Alrededor de él se mueven distintos personajes que pertenecen a su entorno familiar y colegial. Así, la obra enfrenta el tópico de las tradiciones y épocas de la novela de aprendizaje. [CF]

3553 Paz Soldán, Edmundo. Simulacros. Prólogo por Sergio Ramírez. La Paz: Santillana, 1999. 172 p. (Biblioteca boliviana Santillana; 2)

Selección de cuentos de la producción

inicial del narrador boliviano. Algunos temas recurrentes son los temores de la adolescencia, lo bello y horroroso de la imaginación y la fantasía y los amores truncos. El volumen incluye un prólogo del escritor nicaragüense Sergio Ramírez. [CF]

3554 Rocha Monroy, Ramón. La casilla vacía. La Paz: Alfaguara, 1998. 264 p.

Novela que enfrenta al lector a las contradicciones que se gestan en medio de una dictadura. Construida a partir de un sinnúmero de voces y situaciones, la obra discurre sobre la soledad de Manuel Paz, un periodista y militante de izquierda en la clandestinidad. Agobiado por la soledad y el aislamiento, el protagonista vive una lenta agonía por mantener la comunicación con sus seres queridos y sus compañeros políticos. Estamos ante una historia de amor que desemboca en los vaivenes del pensamiento crítico y la lucha ideológica. [CF]

Romero Pittari, Salvador. Las claudinas: libros y sensibilidades a principios de siglo en Bolivia. See item **2691.**

3555 Santa Cruz, Giovanna Rivero. Las bestias. Santa Cruz de la Sierra, Bolivia: s.n., 1997. 73 p.: ill.

Estupenda colección de relatos breves que ofrecen al lector cuentos sobre mundos paralelos, construidos en función de sus propios designios. En cada historia se edifican estructuras oníricas de erotismo, extravagancias, amores y miedos. [CF]

Colombia

3556 Alvarez Revuelta, Alejandro. Madre mía, América: novela. Bogotá: Taller Cinco, Centro de Diseño, 1997. 247 p.: ill.

Novela de ambiente histórico que busca recrear aspectos de la colonización de América, centrándose en la saga de una hipotética familia y un mítico gallo de pelea. Es un intento en general fallido de combinar ficción histórica con una mitología de lo familiar. Quizá lo más notable sea reexaminar el concepto de América como extensión de España en una obra que valida nociones premodernas como "raza" y "sangre." [GG]

3557 Anjel, José Guillermo. De dictadores, ángeles peatones y pecados renovados: un texto sin remordimientos: libro fabuloensayístico. Medellín, Colombia: Editorial Univ. Pontificia Bolivariana, 1997. 103 p. (Col. de ensayo latinoamericano)

Se trata de una innovadora obra que combina la fábula y el ensayo. Partiendo de una propuesta según la cual el ensayo debe estar precedido de una fábula, Anjel explora una multitud de sincretismos de la cultura latinoamericana en los que privilegia el papel de la imaginación como recurso adaptativo esencial, y concilia temáticas tan disímiles como los dictadores y los ángeles. [GG]

3558 Collazos, Oscar. Morir con papá. Bogotá: Seix Barral, 1997. 142 p. (Biblioteca breve)

Incursión en el relato criminal indicativa del creciente interés de los narradores colombianos en la temática de la violencia urbana. Se trata de un binomio de asesinos a sueldo, padre e hijo, generaciones distintas pero unificadas por la abyección del *sicariato*. Exitoso retrato de un mundo violento de alianzas efímeras y traiciones permanentes que se retroalimenta constantemente. [GG]

3559 Cuéntelos bien como yo le conté: cuentos emberá. Recopilación y traducción de Manuel Críspulo Moya Mecha. Ilustraciones de Adriana Sanín Escobar. Colombia: Editorial Univ. de Antioquia, 1998. 145 p.: ill. (some col.).

Importante colección de cuentos de la comunidad indígena emberá, del depto. del Chocó, en la costa del Pacífico. Se trata de un muy loable esfuerzo editorial para hacer conocer una rica tradición oral hasta ahora estudiada por unos pocos investigadores. La edición incluye un mapa regional y un útil diccionario de términos emberá. [GG]

3560 Escobar Giraldo, Octavio. De música ligera. Bogotá: Ministerio de Cultura, 1998. 131 p.

Recipiente del Premio Nacional de Cultura en la modalidad de cuento. Se trata de narraciones unidas por la evocación de ambientes y lugares a través de aires de música popular, desde el tango de Gardel hasta el disco de los años 70. En apariencia una celebración de lo efímero, los cuentos representan con éxito el tono de oralidad característico de la subcultura estudiantil bogotana. [GG]

3561 Espinosa, Germán. Cuentos completos. Bogotá: Ministerio de Cultura: Arango Editores, 1998. 474 p. (Narrativa colombiana)

Compilación que reúne la obra cuen-

tística completa del destacado novelista, desde *La noche de la trapa* (1965) hasta *El naipe negro* (1990). Una buena cantidad de los cuentos, en los que prima el interés en lo fantástico, permanecían inéditos. Una cuidadosa edición que permitirá la relectura de uno de los escritores más importantes del país. [GG]

3562 Illán Bacca, Ramón. Maracas en la opera. 2. ed. Planeta Colombiana Editorial Colombia: Planeta Colombiana Editorial, 1999. 172 p. (Espasa narrativa)

Cómica recreación de eventos de la historia del país a finales del siglo XIX a través de tres generaciones que entrelazan a Europa con América, la ópera y el bolero. Illán apela a un importante componente histórico yuxtapuesto a una desmesura de tipo garciamarquiana. La novela ha sido recibida con unanimidad como un logro de humor y de imaginación. [GG]

3563 Méndez Bernal, Rafael Mauricio. Grandes escándalos en la historia de Colombia. Bogotá: Ediciones Martínez Roca, 1998. 229 p.

A medio camino entre la historia y la recreación literaria, Méndez Bernal trata aquí de episodios de la vida nacional signados por la corrupción y el escándalo. Las viñetas, en general breves y con énfasis en lo anecdótico, tienen la virtud de conectar el pasado con el presente y apelan al gran público, en un momento de intensa fragmentación política y social. [GG]

3564 Paredes, Julio. Guía para extraviados. Bogotá: Colcultura: Grupo Editorial Norma, 1997. 202 p. (Col. La otra orilla)

Excelente colección de 10 depurados cuentos. Aunque cada uno está precedido de un epígrafe de un autor europeo o norteamericano, se trata de situaciones de misterio, ocurridas en lugares nacionales. El énfasis es en situaciones aparentemente anodinas, pero que reciben un tratamiento donde cosas en apariencia banales alcanzan la poesía de lo insólito. [GG]

3565 Sánchez Suárez, Benhur. Esta noche de noviembre: confesión de oficio. Bogotá: Sandíaz Ediciones, 1998. 53 p.

Breve "confesión de oficio" y biografía intelectual de Sánchez, miembro del grupo "Contracartel." El autor evoca su infancia en la ciudad de Pitalito, Huila, su iniciación literaria, y los éxitos y resistencias que su obra ha encontrado (Sánchez ganó los premios Esso y Planeta). En particular, detalla la suerte de la literatura de compromiso social en el cambiante mercado editorial colombiano. [GG]

3566 Triviño, Consuelo. Prohibido salir a la calle. Bogotá: Ministerio de Cultura: Planeta, 1998. 240 p.

Debut novelístico de Triviño, hasta ahora conocida por sus cuentos. Novela narrada desde el punto de vista de una niña que describe sucesos familiares de modo en apariencia ingenuo, pero que con éxito recrea aspectos de la interioridad familiar y la transición personal y colectiva en el contexto de los años 60. [GG]

Ecuador

3567 Aulestia, Carlos. La obscuridad: novela. Quito: Ediciones El Tábano, 2000. 167 p.

Novela de corte detectivesco en la que Marcos Luna, el protagonista, buscará las respuestas al suicidio de su amigo Ernesto Leiva. Destaca la agilidad y el suspenso que logra el autor en la narración. [CF]

3568 Bueno Ortiz, Rodolfo. Pasiones a la sombra del Kremlin. Quito: Editorial El Conejo, 1999. 399 p.

Novela que narra las vivencias de un grupo de jóvenes de distintos países que estudiaron en la Univ. Patricio Lumumba y analiza su choque cultural y su necesidad de adaptación a una realidad que desconocen por completo. El texto abre un abanico de temas: desde la corrupción política, la belleza del arte, el valor de la ciencia y las vicisitudes del amor. Un retrato singular de la sociedad soviética y su desencanto. [CF]

3569 Durán Barba, Rocío. El loco, o, todos enloquecimos. Quito: R. Durán Barba, 2000. 334 p.

Novela sobre el dictador latinoamericano. El eje del relato es la obsesión por el poder, encarnado en un personaje a quien apodan "El Loco," un político convertido en presidente vitalicio. Durán Barba logra una escritura libre y alucinada, de enorme efectividad narrativa, para narrar los absurdos a los que llega el protagonista. [CF]

3570 Espinosa Jalil, Simón. El autobús en el barranco. Quito: Casa de la Cultura Ecuatoriana Benjamín Carrión, 2000. 107 p.

Cuentos en los que predomina una temática de iniciación para sus jóvenes protagonistas. Tampoco está ausente la problemática de la diferencia de clase y la jerarquización social en el contexto ecuatoriano. Ejemplos excelentes al respecto son "El autobús en el barranco" y "Nuestro amor privado." [CF]

3571 Espinosa Jalil, Simón. El fenómeno del niño. Quito: La Posada de Borges, 2000. 176 p. (Serie Colibrí—Juvenil. Cuentos)

Segundo libro de relatos de este joven cuentista. Se incluyen seis textos, algunos de ellos de gran extensión, que examinan diversos matices conflictivos de la sociedad ecuatoriana. De singular calidad es el cuento que le da título al libro, donde temas como el poder, el dinero y la homosexualidad son tratados por un narrador maduro y con mucho oficio. [CF]

Fire from the Andes: short fiction by women from Bolivia, Ecuador, and Peru. See item 3546.

3572 Miño, Reinaldo. Las esclavas de Manuela. Quito: Casa de la Cultura Ecuatoriana "Benjamín Carrión," 1999. 87 p.

Novela histórica que tiene como protagonista a Manuela Sáenz, la mítica compañera del Libertador Simón Bolívar. En ella se narra la estrecha amistad que unió a Jonatás y Nathan, las esclavas negras de Manuela, con su ama. La obra ilustra cómo se instaló el racismo en América con la llegada de los europeos. [CF]

3573 Páez, Santiago. Los archivos de Hilarión: novela. Quito: Ediciones El Tábano, 1998. 209 p.

Novela negra en la que un aventurero persigue a un reportero de crónica roja desaparecido misteriosamente. En su búsqueda se relaciona con una mujer bella e incestuosa, escapa de una pandilla de asesinos alucinados y se enfrenta a una cofradía de ciegos enloquecidos. Dentro de una atmósfera fantástica y enigmática, la persecución lleva al protagonista al descubrimiento de una deidad que le revela la clave de su destino. [CF]

3574 Páez, Santiago. Shamanes y reyes: novela. Quito: Ediciones El Tábano, 1999. 112 p.

Novela de ciencia ficción. Páez crea una nave de nombre Cronopios en la que los últimos seres humanos viajan hacia un lugar desconocido de la galaxia. Pero Cronopios es también un mundo de reyes, shamanes y demonios, es decir, un campo de batalla en donde se enfrentan las más oscuras y antiguas fuerzas. El futuro de la humanidad dependerá del resultado de esta lucha. [CF]

3575 Samaniego, Alvaro. Crónicas de héroes y mártires. Quito: Editorial El Conejo, 1999. 99 p.

Crónicas basadas en personajes y hechos de la guerra que disputaron los ejércitos de Ecuador y Perú en enero y febrero de 1995. Destaca la humanidad y el realismo de los personajes evocados. [CF]

3576 Saravia, Patricio. Balada para Simón. Quito: Casa de la Cultura Ecuatoriana Benjamín Carrión, 1999. 126 p.

Conjunto de microcuentos, a manera de fragmentos y memorias, ambientados en la Amazonia ecuatoriana. El tono de los relatos es sin aspavientos, narrando lo trivial y cotidiano, dejando que el lector saque sus conclusiones sobre la anécdota narrada. [CF]

3577 Vallejo Corral, Raúl. Acoso textual. Quito: Editorial Planeta del Ecuador, 1999. 143 p. (Seix Barral Biblioteca Breve)

Novela experimental que se interroga acerca del valor de la palabra escrita enfrentada al mundo virtual de la internet. Las relaciones que se entretejen entre los personajes son quimeras pues estos no salen al mundo a corroborar sus ilusiones sino que esperan que su interlocutor aparezca en las pantallas de sus computadoras. El universo de la novela problematiza con originalidad las relaciones entre realidad y ficción. [CF]

3578 Vallejo Corral, Raúl. Huellas de amor eterno. Quito: Pontificia Univ. Católica del Ecuador/Editorial Planeta del Ecuador, 2000. 141 p.

Colección de cuentos de temática amorosa. Los relatos equilibran una buena dosis de vida cotidiana con rasgos de humor y cierta veta trágica. El autor logra engarzar, con eficacia narrativa, la reflexión personal, para así construir universos psicológicos que evocan las muchas contradicciones de la experiencia sentimental. [CF]

3579 Yánez Cossío, Alicia. Y amarle pude. Quito: Editorial Planeta del Ecuador, 2000. 123 p. (Seix Barral Biblioteca Breve)

Novela que recrea la vida de la poeta decimonónica ecuatoriana Dolores Veintimilla de Galindo. Atrapada en una sociedad conservadora y pacata, y en medio de un fondo histórico de luchas revolucionarias y cambios políticos, la escritora quiteña desafía "el establishment" y acaba suicidándose a los 28 años de edad. [CF]

Peru

3580 Aguila, Irma del. Tía, saca el pie del embrague y otros relatos. Lima: Editorial San Marcos, 2000. 128 p.

Lima es la protagonista de este conjunto de cuentos: una ciudad dura, que maltrata a sus habitantes y los lleva a situaciones extremas. Dentro de su supuesta modernidad, en ella abunda un racismo hondo que crea espacios sociales que se tornan en abismos. Destaca en el conjunto el buen perfil de personajes femeninos, así como el tema de la psicosis de la guerra. [CF]

3581 Anselmi Samanez, Rafael. El mirador de la ciudad. Lima: Arteidea Editores, 1999. 81 p.

Conjunto de relatos donde destaca la confrontación de lo cuzqueño y lo peruano con otras culturas y otras lenguas. El Cuzco tradicional es retratado desde locales nocturnos y rutas turísticas para problematizar la presencia foránea en la vieja ciudad incaica que se enfrenta así a las voces de una forzada modernidad. [CF]

3582 Bayly, Jaime. Los amigos que perdí. Lima: Alfaguara, 2000. 359 p.

Novela de corte epistolar en la que el protagonista dirige cinco cartas a cinco viejos amigos con los que rompió tiempo atrás. Dentro de una narración de tipo confesional e intimista, destaca la exploración psicológica de los personajes y la revelación final que éstos han sido convertidos en criaturas de ficción, motivo inicial de la ruptura con el protagonista. [CF]

3583 Bayly, Jaime. Yo amo a mi mami. Barcelona: Editorial Anagrama, 1999. 401 p. (Narrativas hispánicas; 261)

Novela de aprendizaje que narra la vida de Jimmy, un personaje de la clase alta limeña, donde, además de retratar la vida privilegiada de la burguesía peruana, se cuentan los sinsabores de un amor roto y desbordado. Destaca la agilidad narrativa y el marcado estilo oral de Bayly. [CF]

3584 Beleván, Harry. Una muerte sin medida. Lima: Alfaguara, 2000. 390 p.

Novela narrada desde la técnica del contrapunto. Félix Aguilar es embajador del Perú en La Paz. El otro Félix ("el compañero Chang") es un guerrillero. La primera historia es la sucesión de aventuras entre el embajador y toda mujer que se le pone enfrente; la segunda una meditada venganza y el plan para consumarla. Destaca la destreza para estructurar la novela, así como los diálogos que despliega Beleván. [CF]

3585 Bellatin, Mario. El jardín de la señora Murakami = Oto no-Murakami monogatari. Lima: Pontificia Univ. Católica del Perú, Fondo Editorial, 2001. 120 p. (Serie Ficciones: Narrativa)

Novela corta de aliento y sensibilidad oriental donde el estilo impersonal del autor vuelve a tener ese brillo afilado y frío que sorprende al lector. La historia de la anciana Izu es tal vez el mejor de los libros de este importante narrador peruano. [CF]

3586 Bryce Echenique, Alfredo. El huerto de mi amada. Barcelona: Planeta, 2002. 286 p. (Autores españoles e iberoamericanos)

Novela que recrea una historia de amor imposible entre un adolescente limeño, Carlitos Alegre, y la aristócrata Natalia de Larrea, una mujer divorciada de 33 años en la Lima de los años 50. Destaca el irónico retrato que Bryce hace de la clase alta limeña en medio de una narración oral, siempre expansiva y plena de humor. [CF]

3587 Calderón Fajardo, Carlos. La conquista de la plenitud: las aventuras de Santiago Feijó, marino. Lima: Univ. Nacional de Ingeniería, Facultad de Ingeniería Económica y Ciencias Sociales, 2001. 282 p.

Novela histórica en la que Santiago Feijó es un marino que se ve envuelto en la revolución de Vivanco contra Castilla en las postrimerías del siglo XIX. En medio de un viaje alrededor del mundo a bordo del Amazonas, su camino se cruza con el de Daniel de la Torre Ugarte, misterioso personaje con el que establece una tácita complicidad en la conspiración. Lejos de la pretenciosa utilización de un lenguaje de época, Calderón nos remite a los azarosos años del Perú republicano mediante una sutil recreación de las costumbres, el apasionamiento y la

desolación de un tiempo beligerante y conflictivo. [CF]

3588 Carreón, Marco. Dos tiempos y una utopía: crónicas del milenio andino. Lima: Mosca Azul Editores, 2000. 1 v.

Texto basado en una reflexión que hace un personaje sobre el Perú sometido a la intensidad política de los años 70 hasta la llegada del milenio. Su intención es lograr una confluencia panandina que permita encontrar una nueva identidad nacional. El relato apuesta a una visión integradora del espacio geográfico y cultural, así como a una sociedad pluriétnica como producto de la globalización. [CF]

3589 Cuentos: narradoras peruanas del siglo XX. Recopilación de Giovanna Minardi. Lima: Ediciones Flora Tristán/Santo Oficio, 2000. 292 p.: bibl.

Excelente y necesaria antología de narradoras peruanas. No obstante el título del volumen, la antologadora presenta a narradoras nacidas desde la segunda mitad del siglo XIX y todo el siglo XX. En un esclarecedor prólogo, Minardi entrega un muestrario de la escritura de cada una de las autoras incluidas. Este es un valioso libro de consulta para todo investigador de literatura peruana escrita por mujeres. [CF]

3590 El cuento peruano, 1990–2000. Selección, prólogo y notas de Ricardo González Vigil. Lima: Depto. de Relaciones Públicas de PetroPerú, 2001. 846 p.: bibl.

Con este tomo dedicado a la producción cuentística de la década de los 90 culmina la excelente muestra del género breve en el siglo XX a cargo de este importante crítico peruano. González Vigil reúne en esta entrega una amplia lista de cultivadores del género, así como una selección que ilustra las muchas tendencias que practican sus cultivadores: la etnoliteratura o tradición oral, el realismo, lo fantástico y la línea historicista. [CF]

Fire from the Andes: short fiction by women from Bolivia, Ecuador, and Peru. See item 3546.

3591 Gutiérrez, Miguel. El mundo sin Xóchitl. Lima: Fondo de Cultura Económica, 2001. 585 p.: col. ill.

Novela que aborda el tema del incesto. Se narra la historia de Wences, un hombre viejo que escribe sus memorias en las que confiesa el acontecimiento que marcó toda su vida: el amor a Xóchitl, su hermana, quien murió aún púber de una peste que asoló Piura, en el norte del Perú. Aunque el epicentro de la narración es la búsqueda del amor, la novela describe un universo más complejo: el seno de una familia terrateniente venida a menos que recuerda el decaimiento de un orden señorial. El universo memorioso de Wences recrea escenas en que la transgresión, la fantasía, el amor, el erotismo, el dolor forman el mismo cuerpo de una historia de un hombre no ajeno a sí mismo ni a sus circunstancias sociales. [CF]

3592 Manrique, Nelson. La piel y la pluma: escritos sobre literatura, etnicidad y racismo. Lima: CIDIAG/SUR Casa de Estudios del Socialismo, 1999. 134 p.: bibl.

Colección de ensayos que examina el problema del racismo en el Perú y sus consecuencias en el imaginario nacional. Además de rastrear el problema histórico que el tema conlleva en el ordenamiento de la sociedad peruana, el autor comenta aproximaciones al tema en la obra de Clorinda Matto de Turner, Mariátegui y Arguedas, entre otros. [CF]

3593 Morillo Ganoza, Juan. El río que te ha de llevar. Lima: Editorial San Marcos, 2000? 488 p.

Doce capítulos o "jornadas," como las denomina el autor, y un epílogo componen la historia de los Ponte, familia dueña de grandes extensiones de tierra en una comunidad andina a fines del siglo XIX. El relato brota de los labios de Zoila, una mujer ciega de memoria prodigiosa y último vestigio de los Ponte. Es ella quien, además de evocar la saga de su familia, narra importantes hechos históricos en el Perú decimonónico como la invasión chilena, las guerras civiles de los caudillos políticos y la rebelión indígena de Atusparia. [CF]

3594 Morillo Ganoza, Juan. Las trampas del diablo. Recopilación de Aníbal Jesús Paredes Galván. Beijing; Lima: Editorial San Marcos, 1999. 232 p. (Biblioteca de narrativa peruana contemporánea; 27)

Cuentos que recrean la atmósfera de un pequeño pueblo ubicado en la zona del Marañón. En algunos cuentos como "El Achacay" o "La esperanza," una audaz fabulación actualiza las virtudes de la narrativa popular tradicional; en otros como "Pedro y Pilanco" o "Los yuyos," una oportuna con-

cepción de la estructura permite la inserción de elementos de la fábula popular. [CF]

3595 Ninapayta de la Rosa, Jorge. Muñequita linda. Recopilación de Jaime Campodónico. Lima: Ed. del Autor, 2000. 162 p.

Libro que reúne 10 relatos de este nuevo escritor. El cuento que le da título al volumen obtuvo el "Premio Internacional Juan Rulfo" de París en 1998. El libro todo es una suerte de ópera bufa sobre la mediocridad existencial y de la fantasía como mecanismo de refugio. El estupendo cuento que da título al libro es un buen ejemplo de esa psicología. [CF]

Padilla, Feliciano. Calicanto. See item **3550.**

3596 Pérez Huarancca, Julián. Fuego y ocaso. Lima: Editorial San Marcos, 1998. 168 p. (Biblioteca de narrativa peruana contemporánea)

Novela que es una evocación de un supuesto ex-reportero, ahora convertido en un anciano, arraigado en su ostracismo de maestro primario quien, para escapar de la opresión del ambiente y de la temprana decrepitud moral, se dedica a novelar los reportajes que escribiera y que nunca llegaron a publicarse. [CF]

3597 Ribeyro, Julio Ramón. Cuentos: antología. Recopilación de Angel Esteban. Madrid: Espasa Calpe, 1998. 441 p.: bibl. (Col. Austral; 453. Narrativa)

Excelente antología de relatos de uno de los narradores peruanos más importantes del siglo XX. Además de una generosa selección de textos, el recopilador ofrece un valioso estudio preliminar para situar la obra de Ribeyro en el contexto de la literatura peruana y latinoamericana. [CF]

3598 Rivera Martínez, Edgardo. Ciudad de fuego y otras dos novelas cortas. Lima: Alfaguara, 2000. 127 p.

Libro que incluye tres novelas cortas cuyos escenarios son barrios de una Lima neblinosa, deteriorada y sin embargo bella. De los tres textos, destaca el segundo relato, "Un Viejo Señor en la Neblina," cuyo protagonista, Juan Clodoveo, es un sujeto misterioso, alto y callado que se pasa los días sentado en un precario techo, dejándose envolver en la neblina limeña y soñando con el vuelo fatal de Icaro. Rivera Martínez es dueño de una prosa finamente trabajada, logrando un perfecto equilibrio entre la ternura, el misterio y un sutil asombro. [CF]

3599 Rodríguez, Gustavo. La furia de Aquiles. Lima: Alfaguara, 2001. 335 p.

Novela de aprendizaje sobre la vida adolescente de Aquiles, un enclenque pero astuto muchacho provinciano que llega a Lima para estudiar en la universidad y "convertirse en hombre." Destaca una prosa ligera e hipnotizante que se alimenta del lenguaje de la calle, lleno de humor y juego de palabras. [CF]

3600 Rosas, Patrick. Un descapotable en invierno. Lima: Editorial San Marcos, 2000. 203 p.

Libro de relatos de seres obsesionados por el fracaso, la enfermedad, la transgresión sexual y la muerte. Destaca entre ellos la novela corta que da título al volumen y que cuenta la vida de un joven peruano en París que vive de gigoló. Su vida está hecha de encuentros y desencuentros amorosos con otros personajes marginales que rompen con el mito glamoroso de la capital francesa. [CF]

3601 Schwalb, Carlos. Dobleces. Lima: Editorial Nido de Cuervos, 2000. 172 p. (Col. "Punto final")

Excelente colección de relatos en los que se forjan universos narrativos nunca obvios ni transparentes; más bien, éstos están difuminados por los sucesivos velos o dobleces de la conciencia de sus personajes. Como tema recurrente destaca la constante exploración psicológica de los personajes y el análisis de los sentimientos en las relaciones de pareja (hombre y mujer, padre e hijo). [CF]

3602 Segovia Saavedra, Edwin. Eorindari, al sur del paraíso. Lima: Hude & Mihans Print, 1999. 241 p.

Novela ambientada en el sur de la Amazonia peruana, específicamente en el depto. de Madre de Dios. Destaca el buen perfil de sus personajes, su ambientación con ecos de lo real maravilloso, una temática donde entra en conflicto la noción de progreso del mundo occidental y el mundo mágico de la sierra y selva del Perú. [CF]

3603 Torres Rotondo, Carlos. Nuestros años salvajes. Lima: Alfaguara, 2001. 309 p.

Conjunto de cuatro novelas cortas, todas contenidas en una, escritas en cuatro personas gramaticales (yo, tú, él, nosotros)

para contar variaciones sobre un mismo tema: un grupo de amigos que vaga por la cadavérica Lima de fines del siglo XX. [CF]

3604 Valdelomar, Abraham. Obras completas. Recopilación de Ricardo Silva-Santisteban. Lima: Ediciones Copé: Depto. de Relaciones Públicas de PetroPerú, 2001. 4 v.: bibl., ill. (some col.).

Valioso conjunto de cuatro volúmenes que reúne no sólo todos los cuentos, los poemas, las piezas dramáticas y los ensayos, sino también una innumerable cantidad de artículos periodísticos y crónicas del autor. Además de un excelente ensayo introductorio de parte de Silva-Santisteban, se incluye una útil bibliografía y un valioso material gráfico que incluye reproducciones de manuscritos, autógrafos, portadas de primeras ediciones y algunas fotografías poco conocidas de Valdelomar. Se trata de la edición más completa hecha de la obra de Valdelomar hasta el momento. [CF]

3605 Valdelomar, Abraham. Valdelomar por él mismo: cartas, entrevistas, testimonios y documentos biográficos e iconográficos. v. 1–2. Lima: Fondo Editorial del Congreso del Perú, 2000. 2 v. (469 p.): ill. (some col.).

Volúmenes que recogen cartas, noticias, testimonios, fotografías, portadas de diarios y revistas que dan cuenta de la vida de Valdelomar, considerado el fundador del cuento moderno en el Perú. Los documentos aquí incluidos permiten reconstruir la cultura limeña de la época y las inquietudes más personales del autor. [CF]

3606 Vallejo, César. Narrativa completa. Presentación de Salomón Lerner Febres. Recopilación de Ricardo Silva-Santisteban y Cecilia Moreano. Lima: Pontificia Univ. Católica del Perú, 1999. 462 p.: bibl., ill.

Volumen que recopila toda la obra narrativa del célebre poeta peruano que incluye *Escalas* (edición original de 1923 y manuscrito de Claude Couffon); *Fabla salvaje; Hacia el reino de los sciris; Contra el secreto profesional; Sabiduría; El tungsteno; Paco Yunque; Ultimos cuentos* y una sección de documentos que ilustran su producción narrativa. [CF]

3607 Vargas Llosa, Mario. El lenguaje de la pasión. Madrid: Ediciones El País, 2001. 336 p.: bibl., index.

Volumen que reúne 46 ensayos publicados entre 1992–2000 en diversos diarios de habla hispana. Los textos versan sobre temas variados como la política, la cultura, sucesos de actualidad, crónicas de viaje, así como textos críticos sobre arte, literatura, pintura y música. El novelista se muestra una vez más como un ensayista de altísima calidad y un observador agudo de la escena contemporánea. [CF]

3608 Yauri Montero, Marcos E. No preguntes quién ha muerto: Atusparia y Cochachin en una fascinante novela histórica. 3. ed., corr. Lima: Editorial San Marcos, 1999. 388 p. (Biblioteca de narrativa peruana contemporánea; 16)

Novela que recrea las rebeliones populares de Atusparia y Ucchu Pedro del siglo XIX en el depto. de Ancash. Se incluye un interesante estudio preliminar de Ismael P. Márquez que subraya la importancia del hecho histórico y su repercusión en las letras peruanas. [CF]

Venezuela

3609 Bolívar Graterol, Víctor Hugo. Peripecias de los sueños. Villa de Cura, Venezuela: Ediciones del Cerro, 1997. 150 p.: col. ill.

Compilación de breves fragmentos narrativos caracterizados por el humor y una aguda percepción del absurdo cotidiano. Los objetos de reflexión van desde situaciones propias de la vida provinciana en los primeros textos hasta los azares de la cibernética al final. [GG]

3610 Echeto, Roberto. Cuentos líquidos. Caracas: Grupo Editorial Ballgrub, 1997. 159 p. (Joyas del patio; 3)

Primera colección de cuentos de este autor que afirma no estar interesado en la dimensión ética o moralizante de la literatura y se propone entretener. Echeto recupera el tono oral de las historias escuchadas a su barbero. En realidad, son cuentos con rasgos fantásticos que trascienden la oralidad y proponen una reconsideración profunda del entorno social en una época de desánimo. Las ilustraciones, del propio Echeto, evidencian la búsqueda de trascendencia. [GG]

3611 Escalona, José Simón. Amargo de angostura. Caracas: Editorial Panapo, 1999. 113 p.

Primera novela del conocido dramaturgo. A través de múltiples personajes Escalona presenta una evocación de Angostura (hoy Ciudad Bolívar). El mayor logro consiste en el rastreo de su ilustre historia y la construcción de una mitología propia. Un exitoso ejemplo de narrativa de interés regional. [GG]

3612 Ferrero, Mary. Desde Caracas: crónicas. Caracas: Fundarte/Alcaldía de Caracas, 1998. 112 p. (Col. Rescate)

Colección de breves crónicas unidas por la evocación nostálgica y admirativa de eventos y personajes de la vida cultural venezolana, escritos desde una perspectiva de *insider*. Util ejercicio de intrahistoria a pesar de la extrema brevedad de los artículos. [GG]

3613 Lerner, Elisa. Carriel para la fiesta. Caracas: Editorial Blanca Pantín, 1997. 136 p. (Col. Narrativa)

Compilación de crónicas marcadas por un sutil humor y una mirada perspicaz sobre las múltiples incongruencias de la vida citadina venezolana desde el inmediato posgomecismo y la infancia en un hogar judío de inmigrantes. De particular interés es el enfoque implícito en los efectos de la industria cultural en el mundo de las mujeres, desde Corín Tellado hasta Simone de Beauvoir, y desde las radionovelas hasta las cadenas periodísticas. [GG]

3614 Lizaire, Lydie. El beso de la rosa. Caracas: Librería Destino, 1998. 218 p.

Novela en la que la protagonista debe resolver cruciales asuntos de identidad: hija de un importante escritor inglés, ha crecido en los trópicos ignorante de su pasado hasta la vispera de su viaje a Harvard como becaria. Aunque reincidiendo en una retórica muy convencional, la novela plantea llamativos aspectos identitarios tales como género, nacionalidad y cultura. [GG]

3615 Marcano Salazar, Luis Manuel. El encanto de los angeles. Caracas: Nuevas Letras, 1999. 199 p.

Una historia de amor vagamente enmarcada en los sucesos post-1983 que en principio podría recoger las incidencias de la problemática juvenil de la Venezuela reciente. Marcano opta empero por un tono moralizante y condenatorio: el narrador reafirma los valores del matrimonio patriarcal, mientras que los jóvenes amantes ("carne condenada") son víctimas del SIDA. [GG]

3616 Massiani, Francisco. Con agua en la piel. Caracas: Monte Avila Editores Latinoamericana; Nueva Esparta, Venezuela: Fondo para el Desarrollo de Nueva Esparta, FONDENE, 1998. 195 p. (Continentes)

Más conocido por su novelística, Massiani reúne aquí 14 relatos escritos en diferentes épocas. Son cuentos de atmósfera decididamente cosmopolita y de extraordinaria calidad que versan sobre los conflictos en apariencia ínfimos de personajes comunes. A través de ellos Massiani explora elementos insólitos en la cotidianidad. [GG]

3617 Picón-Salas, Mariano. Registro de huéspedes. 1. ed. venezolana. Mérida, Venezuela: Ediciones Actual, Dirección General de Cultura y Extensión ULA, 1997. 150 p. (Col. "Va de ensayo") (Col. "Letras nuestras")

Primera y oportuna reedición de una obra de 1932. Se trata de seis novelas cortas que son esenciales para conocer la menos conocida faceta de narrador de Picón-Salas, y en general el período de entreguerras, aunque algunos relatos reconstruyen episodios del siglo XIX. [GG]

3618 Sambrano Urdaneta, Oscar. El arcángel: relatos. Caracas: Planeta, 1998. 128 p.

Primera edición de los relatos de Sambrano Urdaneta, más conocido como crítico literario, que habían circulado antes de modo restringido. Son cuentos de gran concisión y de estilo depurado que exploran situaciones insólitas del diario vivir. Se destaca en parti-

cular "El Hombre que Cuidaba su Propia Tumba." [GG]

3619 Urdaneta, Ramón. Adan y Eva se odiaban. Caracas?: Fundur Editores, 1998. 308 p.

Urdaneta apela a diversas cosmologías religiosas con el propósito no de una yuxtaposición gratuita o de seguir una moda. En una novela en la que domina una atmósfera de alucinación y humorismo, su objetivo es más profundo: mostrar la complementariedad de esas visiones, presentando una visión muy particular del mito adánico. [GG]

3620 Vannini de Gerulewicz, Marisa. Arrivederci Caracas. Caracas: Fundarte, Alcaldía de Caracas, 1997. 318 p. (Col. Delta; 26)

Colección de breves textos entre la crónica y la viñeta que evocan con ternura y nostalgia la inmigración desde Italia a la Caracas de medio siglo. Importante testimonio desde el punto de vista femenino de las costumbres familiares y de la etiología de las relaciones amorosas narrado de manera sencilla pero con gran efectividad. [GG]

3621 Voces nuevas 1995–1997. Caracas: Fundación CELARG, 1999. 299 p.

Excelente testimonio de la febril actividad de los talleres literarios. Aquí se recogen talleres de narrativa (dirigidos por Antonio López Ortega y Carlos Noguera) y de poesía (dirigido por Yoland Pantín). La mayoría de las piezas seleccionadas acusan un intenso interés en la autorreflexividad literaria y escenas urbanas. Lamentablemente, la edición no incluye ninguna información biobibliográfica sobre los 23 talleristas reunidos. [GG]

Chile

JOSÉ PROMIS, *Professor of Latin American Literature and Literary Criticism, University of Arizona*

LA NOTICIA SOBRESALIENTE DEL PERÍODO DE 1997 HASTA 2001 es la concesión en 1999 del prestigioso premio Cervantes al novelista Jorge Edwards. Su novela *El sueño de la historia* (ítem **3637**) es también uno de los mejores relatos publicados en el mismo período. Al año siguiente ocurre el deceso de Mauricio Wacquez (ítem **3665**), uno de los representantes de la generación que seguía inmediatamente a la de Jorge Edwards, Enrique Lafourcade (ítem **3646**) y José Donoso, con cuya sensibilidad histórica mantenía indudables relaciones de proximidad.

Desde 1997, la prosa chilena tiende a recuperar un lenguaje que exhibe las mejores características de la narración tradicional. Los experimentos formales de las décadas anteriores parecieran definitivamente olvidados en pro de restablecer un contacto más directo y personal con el lector. La crítica ha destacado el magnífico tono balzaciano de novelas como *La ley del gallinero* de Jorge Guzmán (ítem **3644**) o *Cuando éramos inmortales* de Arturo Fontaine (ítem **3640**). El lenguaje paródico y humorístico es también utilizado con el propósito de obtener la participación y la complicidad del lector cuando se trata de ofrecer interpretaciones escépticas, desencantadas o pesimistas de la situación histórica actual. Así ocurre en los cuentos de Jaime Collyer (ítem **3633**), o en las novelas de Luis López-Aliaga (ítem **3648**) o Javier Campos (ítem **3631**).

La prosa chilena del período ofrece tendencias fuertemente individualizadas a nivel de la representación artística. Como consecuencia del colapso del gobierno militar, muchos novelistas han dirigido su interés hacia el escrutinio del pasado para tratar de descubrir las raíces de una identidad quebrada o para recuperar una tradición interrumpida. Isabel Allende publica sucesivamente dos novelas: *Hija de la fortuna* (ítem **3622**) y *Retrato en sepia* (ítem **3623**) que rastrean los orígenes de la dinastía Del Valle, y Antonio Skármeta recrea la llegada de los inmigrantes croatas a Chile, fundadores de su familia, en las dos primeras novelas: *La boda del poeta* (ítem **3660**) y *La chica del trombón* (ítem **3661**) de una trilogía inconclusa a esta fecha. Dentro de esta misma tendencia destaca también la representación imaginaria de momentos críticos del desarrollo social chileno, como la citada novela de Arturo Fontaine, *La esfera media del aire* (ítem **3654**), *Muriendo por la dulce patria mía* (ítem **3632**) o *Uñas de muerto* (ítem **3663**). Esta última pretende contemplar el período de la dictadura desde el punto de vista de sus sostenedores. La figura del progenitor es utilizada con frecuencia como el responsable de la culpa, como ejemplifica la novela *El sueño de mi padre* (ítem **3643**), al punto que críticos como Rodrigo Cánovas han denominado "novela de los huérfanos" a esta variante narrativa.

El escrutinio del pasado también se proyecta más lejos. Edwards se interesa por la figura de Joaquín Toesca, constructor del Palacio de La Moneda (ítem **3637**); la mencionada novela de Jorge Guzmán y *La emperrada* (ítem **3628**) de Marta Blanco, indagan en los orígenes de la historia republicana de Chile centrándose en la figura de Diego Portales, considerado por algunos como el primer dictador de la historia chilena y por otros como el constructor de la república. Dentro de esta misma tendencia se manifiesta también el propósito de rescatar figuras femeninas postergadas por el discurso histórico tradicional. Junto a la excelente historia novelada *Déjame que te cuente*, publicada por Juanita Gallardo en 1997 (ver *HLAS 58: 3723*), ejemplos importantes son *Javiera Carrera, madre de la patria* (ítem **3664**) y la citada novela de Marta Blanco, cuyo último propósito es recuperar para la historia la figura de Constanza Nordenflycht, la trágica compañera de Diego Portales.

Junto al escrutinio del pasado la prosa chilena de ficción se interesa por la observación artística del presente. Sus representaciones aparecen teñidas de escepticismo e ironía hacia el sistema económico en uso. Muchas novelas destacan el motivo de *la culpa* (por irresponsabilidad y falta de compromiso) y crean el tipo literario del *Triunfador con pies de barro*. Los cuentos de Ernesto Ayala (ítem **3627**) y la novela de Oscar Bustamante (ítem **3630**) ofrecen excelentes ejemplos de lo anterior. El problema del poder político, económico y sexual en la sociedad contemporánea es representado en novelas como las de Fernando Jerez (ítem **3645**), Alejandra Rojas (ítem **3656**) y E. Subercaseaux (ítem **3662**). *Tengo miedo torero* (ítem **3647**) instala agresivamente a la figura del homosexual como un personaje protagónico de la sociedad y de la literatura actual.

Finalmente hay que mencionar la presencia adquirida por la *novela negra*, donde el crimen se interpreta como indicio de un estado social desequilibrado. *Los siete hijos de Simenón* (ítem **3636**) y *Cita en el Azul Profundo* (ítem **3624**) son sus ejemplos más destacados. En *Los detectives salvajes* de Roberto Bolaño (ítem **3629**), la búsqueda de la esencia de la poesía se produce bajo una forma policial y Marcela Serrano (ítem **3659**) utiliza este relato para representar la temática feminista. Esta misma forma narrativa sostiene las novelas de Luis Sepúlveda (ítem **3658**) y Sergio Gómez (ítem **3642**).

PROSE FICTION

3622 Allende, Isabel. Hija de la fortuna. 2. ed. Barcelona: Plaza & Janés, 1999. 428 p.: 1 map.

Narración de los orígenes de la dinastía Del Valle, una de las dos familias que participan en *La casa de los espíritus* (ver *HLAS 48:5565*). Eliza Sommers viaja de Valparaíso a California a mediados del siglo XIX buscando a su novio, quien quizás se haya transformado en Joaquín Murieta. Pero su encuentro con el médico chino Tao Chi'en cambiará su vida. Para comentario sobre la traducción al íngles de esta obra, ver ítem **4274**.

3623 Allende, Isabel. Retrato en sepia. Barcelona: Plaza & Janés Editores, 2000. 343 p.

Continuación cronológica de *Hija de la fortuna* (ver ítem **3622**), transcurre a fines del siglo XIX. Aurora del Valle, hija de Eliza Sommers, decide explorar el misterio de su pasado que su abuela, Paulina del Valle, le niega obstinadamente. Los episodios del desenlace constituyen el comienzo de la historia de *La casa de los espíritus* (ver *HLAS 48:5565*).

3624 Ampuero, Roberto. Cita en el azul profundo. Santiago, Chile: Planeta, 2001. 387 p.

Cuarta novela de la serie del detective Cayetano Brulé. Este viaja a Suecia, Cuba y México investigando un crimen que oculta a una organización internacional dedicada a desestabilizar la economía de los países en proceso de desarrollo para que no amenace los intereses de las grandes compañías transnacionales.

3625 Ampuero, Roberto. Nuestros años verde olivo. Santiago, Chile: Planeta, 1999. 407 p.

Novela con engañosa apariencia de autobiografía que relata la historia de una desilusión. Un joven parte a Cuba empujado por sus ideales sociales y por el amor de una muchacha cubana. Su experiencia le permitirá conocer las dos caras del sistema político impuesto en la isla y su entusiasmo inicial comenzará a erosionarse.

3626 Arenas, Desiderio. Lo que Bob Dylan se llevó. Santiago, Chile: Planeta, 2000. 198 p. (Biblioteca del sur)

Representación del conglomerado humano que se reunía en el barrio Bellavista de Santiago: artistas, intelectuales, burgueses ilustrados, durante los últimos años del régimen militar. Con un lenguaje marcado por la ironía y la desenvoltura, desnuda los apetitos escondidos de una sociedad reprimida y frustrada.

3627 Ayala, Ernesto. Trescientos metros. Santiago, Chile: Alfaguara, 2000. 238 p.

Diez relatos que proponen ángulos distintos para contemplar un misma actitud frente a la realidad: individuos que no asumen su responsabilidad en el momento decisivo, cuando todo exige una respuesta final. El temor al compromiso es uno de los motivos más reiterado en la narrativa chilena de los últimos años.

3628 Blanco, Marta. La emperrada. Santiago, Chile: Aguilar Chilena de Ediciones, 2001. 190 p. (Alfaguara)

La voz de Constanza Nordenflycht y las voces de los sirvientes que la rodeaban, recrean la confusión de la época posterior a la

Independencia de Chile y los altibajos de las relaciones de Portales y Constanza. Excelente novela donde se contempla el pasado desde los ojos de la mujer.

3629 Bolaño, Roberto. Los detectives salvajes. Barcelona: Editorial Anagrama, 1998. 609 p. (Narrativas hispánicas; 256)

Premio Rómulo Gallegos de Novela. Premio Herralde de Novela. Premio del Consejo Nacional del Libro y la Lectura (Chile). Comparada con *Rayuela* de Julio Cortázar, relata las circunstancias que rodean el viaje de Arturo Belano, alter-ego del autor, y Ulises Lima, en búsqueda de Cesárea Tinajero, la madre de la poesía mexicana.

3630 Bustamante, Oscar. Una mujer convencional. Providencia, Chile: Editorial Sudamericana, 2001. 151 p. (Narrativa)

Historia de un triunfador con pies de barro que tiene que pagar la culpa de su falta de compromiso y desdén por los valores del espíritu. El análisis que hace de sí mismo el narrador es un diagnóstico negativo de lo que se ha llamado la nueva sociedad chilena.

3631 Campos, Javier F. Los saltimbanquis. Santiago, Chile: RIL Editores, 1999. 186 p. (Serie El cruce; 1)

Diversos discursos narrativos crean la imagen carnavalesca de las aventuras de un circo pobre que recorre los escenarios rurales de Chile, y que se ve profundamente afectado por la situación política del régimen militar. Con la farsa se pretende impedir que el olvido se apodere de la memoria colectiva.

3632 Castillo Sandoval, Roberto. Muriendo por la dulce patria mía. Santiago, Chile: Planeta, 1998. 316 p. (Biblioteca del sur)

Utilizando un discurso que aparenta ser verdadero, el autor hace una excelente recreación imaginaria de la situación espiritual del país en la primera parte del siglo XX, cuyos rasgos se simbolizan en la personalidad del pugilista chileno Arturo Godoy, personaje central de esta historia.

3633 Collyer, Jaime. La bestia en casa. Santiago, Chile: Alfaguara, 1998. 225 p.

Cuentos de excelente factura literaria que ofrecen un sentido a la dirección con frecuencia incomprensible que adquieren los comportamientos individuales. El humor, la ironía y el sarcasmo típicos del estilo de Collyer se reflejan magníficamente en ellos.

3634 Contreras, Gonzalo. Los indicados. Providencia, Chile: Editorial Sudamericana Chilena, 2000. 201 p. (Biblioteca transversal/Dos)

Diez relatos que hurgan en los vericuetos más profundos de la existencia cotidiana para sacar a luz el perfil del individuo en la sociedad contemporánea. Los gestos domésticos son vistos como el cristal que refleja la naturaleza auténtica de los comportamientos diarios.

3635 Délano, Poli. Rompiendo las reglas: cuentos casi completos. México: Mondadori, 2001. 355 p.

La más reciente antología de uno de los escritores chilenos más influyentes sobre las nuevas generaciones de narradores. Trae una excelente introducción donde Nelson Osorio destaca los tres intereses que caracterizan la producción del autor: el motivo del amor y de la soledad, la periferia social y cultural, y la experiencia del exilio.

3636 Díaz Eterović, Ramón. Los siete hijos de Simenon. Santiago, Chile: LOM Ediciones, 2000. 293 p. (Narrativa)

Séptima novela de la serie del detective Heredia, quien tiene que resolver un asesinato que conduce a un crimen de proporciones ecológicas. No sólo la deducción, sino también el azar y la buena suerte colaboran para resolver el enigma, pero Heredia sabe que una batalla no es la guerra.

3637 Edwards, Jorge. El sueño de la historia. 2a. ed. Barcelona: Tusquets Editores, 2000. 412 p. (Colección Andanzas; 407)

Una voz se desdobla en narrador, historiador y cronista para investigar la vida del arquitecto Joaquín Toesca, autor del proyecto del Palacio de la Moneda, y demostrar que pasado y presente constituyen dos expresiones de una realidad social que conserva su identidad a través del tiempo. Una novela sobresaliente.

3638 Eltit, Diamela. Los trabajadores de la muerte. Santiago, Chile: Seix Barral: Biblioteca Breve, 1998. 205 p.

La historia de Edipo sirve como correlato mítico de la experiencia de un hombre que viaja desde Santiago hacia Concepción (lugar genésico, espacio de concebir) sin saber que su viaje es el cumplimiento de un destino, el encuentro con sus orígenes y el sentido de su vida.

3639 Fernández, Nona. El cielo. Santiago, Chile: Editorial Cuarto Propio, 2000. 177 p.

Siete relatos que escudriñan el carácter accidental de la personalidad humana y que revelan el engaño de la identidad que nos conduce a creer que somos los mismos de una vez y para siempre.

3640 Fontaine Talavera, Arturo. Cuando éramos inmortales. Santiago, Chile: Alfaguara, 1998. 393 p.

Un relato escrito a la manera realista tradicional que el autor recuperó con gran dominio técnico en su novela anterior, *Oír su voz* (1992). Un niño criado y educado en las instituciones pertenecientes a la clase conservadora chilena es testigo del derrumbe del orden social que la sostenía.

3641 Forch, Juan. Bar paraíso: los caminos del amor. Santiago, Chile: Editorial Cuarto Propio, 1999. 174 p. (Serie Narrativa)

Mediante el recurso de publicar un manuscrito de un viejo librero de Valparaíso, el autor presenta una serie de cuentos en torno al tema del amor, ambientados en los escenarios más típicos de la ciudad. Pero el espíritu del puerto se despliega principalmente a partir del comportamiento de los personajes.

3642 Gómez, Sergio. La mujer del policía. Santiago, Chile: Alfaguara, 2000. 199 p.

Historia policial que comienza "cuando los militares estaban volviendo a los cuarteles." Una mujer es asesinada en un pueblo del Sur. Las sospechas recaen sobre diferentes personajes. La investigación sólo conduce a demostrar el inexplicable carácter ambiguo de la verdad. Buen ejemplo de la llamada novela negra chilena.

3643 González, Sonia. El sueño de mi padre. Santiago, Chile: Planeta, 1998. 229 p.

Relato que representa bien dos motivos recurrentes de la narrativa chilena actual: la destrucción de la imagen de la casa como símbolo de protección y el enjuiciamiento de la figura del padre, a quien se lo considera culpable del descalabro de la historia política vivida en Chile a partir de 1973.

3644 Guzmán, Jorge. La ley del gallinero. Providencia, Chile: Editorial Sudamericana, 1999. 392 p. (Biblioteca transversal)

Entre las mejores novelas publicadas en Chile después de 1997. Un discurso que acertadamente la crítica ha denominado balzaciano recrea de manera magistral los ambientes, los espacios y los personajes que rodearon a la figura de Diego Portales, centro del relato, quien permanece como un enigma histórico: dictador o visionario.

3645 Jerez, Fernando. El himno nacional. Santiago, Chile: Editorial LOM, 2001. 246 p. (Narrativa)

Una excelente narración farsesca sobre el tema del poder maligno y omnímodo ambientada en Santiago durante 1985. Bajo un sistema totalitario, todos son víctimas y victimarios a la vez y las fronteras entre la bondad y la maldad se tornan difusas y contradictorias.

3646 Lafourcade, Enrique. Otro baile en París. Providencia, Chile: Alfaguara, 2000. 290 p.

Un abuelo recorre París buscando a su nieta Dominique, anécdota que permite recrear la atmósfera maravillosa del surrealismo. El narrador deja su huella de manera solapada en el discurso para recordarnos que entre el mundo de la niñez y el de la senectud sólo existe el espacio de la magia.

3647 Lemebel, Pedro. Tengo miedo torero. Santiago, Chile: Editorial Planeta Chilena, 2001. 217 p. (Biblioteca breve)

La novela más agresiva y polémica publicada hasta la fecha en Chile. La historia del homosexual llamado la Loca del Frente cuestiona la dualidad de los estereotipos sexuales y configura una personalidad sostenida sobre la identidad del principio femenino y masculino. Significativamente, los años más duros de la dictadura militar constituyen el escenario narrativo.

3648 López-Aliaga, Luis. El verano del ángel. Providencia, Chile: Dolmen Ediciones, 2000. 264 p. (Barba azul)

Relato que destruye paródicamente el mito romántico del triunfo de las virtudes sobre el poder del dinero, que Alberto Blest Gana impuso en su novela clásica *Martín Rivas* (1860). En este sentido es también un ejemplo de la crítica presente en muchas novelas chilenas actuales hacia la economía neoliberal.

3649 Manns, Patricio. Buenas noches los pastores. Santiago, Chile: Editorial Sudamericana, 2000. 350 p. (Narrativa)

Importante reedición de la novela que originalmente se publicó en 1973 y que fue retirada de la circulación inmediatamente después del mes de sept. de ese año. El autor ha introducido algunos cambios para actualizarla.

3650 Marks, Camilo. La dictadura del proletariado. Santiago, Chile: Alfaguara, 2001. 371 p.

Conjunto de cuatro relatos escritos por uno de los críticos literarios más conocidos del país. Todos tienen como referente a Chile durante y después del régimen militar y giran en torno al motivo de la realidad como creación de las palabras y de su carácter siempre desconocido y espejístico.

3651 Parra, Marco Antonio de la. Novelas enanas. Santiago, Chile: Alfaguara, 2000. 211 p.

Relatos característicos del estilo del autor. Sirven para mostrar los conflictos interiores de personajes que se mueven en un país transformado por un nuevo sistema político y económico que convierte a las actitudes humanas esenciales en comportamientos esquizofrénicos. El rutilante mundo neoliberal es exorcizado por la fuerza del lenguaje literario.

3652 Pascal, León. Delirium: cuentos con y sin droga. Santiago, Chile: LOM Ediciones, 2000. 224 p. (Narrativa)

Incluye 25 cuentos donde actúan seres marginales y periféricos, extraviados en las drogas, sexo y alcohol. Representan el lado oscuro de una superficie social brillante. Su lenguaje expresa bien el carácter descarnado y violento de muchos relatos chilenos actuales. Ejemplo de la literatura de la inconformidad y la cólera.

3653 Pualuan, Liliana. Sobre voces de islas. Providencia, Chile: RiL Editores, 2000. 145 p.

Intento de rescatar el mundo marginal de las provincias, escasamente atendido en la narrativa chilena. Incluye 21 relatos breves que presentan la existencia del sur del país.

como una realidad donde lo mágico y lo insólito alternan naturalmente con lo cotidiano y corriente.

3654 Río, Ana María del. La esfera media del aire. Santiago, Chile: Alfaguara, 1998. 333 p.

El norte de Chile y su historia son representados míticamente mediante una polifonía de voces que recrean episodios que tienen origen en 1526 y se extienden hasta el presente. Dos mellizas, Collasuri y Piricutie, recorren el tiempo demostrando que la historia es un episodio misterioso que se repite circularmente.

3655 Rivera Letelier, Hernán. Los trenes se van al purgatorio. Buenos Aires: Planeta, 2000. 191 p.

El fantasmal viaje del tren Longitudinal Norte despliega las historias de diversos personajes característicos de la pampa salitrera en el norte del Chile. Se crea una atmósfera a la vez costumbrista y alucinante del escenario que el autor ha representado desde su novela *La Reina Isabel cantaba rancheras* (ver *HLAS 56:3795*).

3656 Rojas, Alejandra. Stradivarius penitente. Madrid: Ollero y Ramos, 1999. 387 p.: bibl.

Dos individuos participan y se enfrentan en la búsqueda de un Stradivarius, conflicto que remite en último término a la oposición entre el poder y el deseo. El relato asume la forma de una novela de intriga tradicional, pero el discurso está siempre marcado por un tono humorístico e irónico.

3657 Sáez, Fernando. La novela de Amanda Romo. Santiago, Chile: Planeta, 1999. 188 p.

Un crítico literario se enfrenta al desafío de transformar a una exitosa narradora para el consumo de masas en una auténtica artista del lenguaje literario. La anécdota permite plantear el conflicto que se establece en la sociedad actual entre los intereses del mercado y la individualidad artística.

3658 Sepúlveda, Luis. Diario de un killer sentimental; seguido de Yacaré. Barcelona: Tusquets Editores, 1998. 140 p. (Col. Andanzas; 338)

Dos relatos breves de corte policiaco donde se rompe intencionalmente la estructura del género porque el personaje principal no cumple con uno de sus requisitos y que sirven para representar las preocupaciones ecológicas del autor.

3659 Serrano, Marcela. Nuestra Señora de la Soledad. Santiago, Chile: Alfaguara, 1999. 247 p.

El interés hacia los problemas de la mujer contemporánea se representa en un relato de estructura policial. Rosa Alvallay debe resolver el misterio del desaparecimiento de una escritora chilena. Tres hombres ofrecen tres posibles caminos para la solución: el marido, un escritor mexicano y un guerillero, ex-amante de la desaparecida.

3660 Skármeta, Antonio. La boda del poeta. Barcelona: Plaza & Janés Editores, 1999. 306 p.

Primer volumen de una trilogía sobre inmigrantes yugoslavos en Chile. La historia comienza con una tragedia en una isla del Adriático y termina con la llegada de un grupo de jóvenes croatas a Antofagasta. Todos los recursos narrativos característicos de la prosa skarmetiana están presentes en este relato.

3661 Skármeta, Antonio. La chica del trombón. Barcelona: Plaza & Janés Editores, 2001. 314 p.

Segundo volumen de la trilogía sobre inmigrantes yugoslavos en Chile. Esteban Coppeta, uno de ellos, se traslada de Antofagasta a Santiago acompañado de su nieta Magdalena; se instala en un caserón frente a la popular Plaza Brasil, escenario testigo de la mayor parte de la historia que avanza hasta los años del triunfo de Salvador Allende.

3662 Subercaseaux, Elizabeth. Una semana de octubre. México: Grijalbo, 1999. 163 p.

El diario de vida de una mujer que sufre de cáncer es leído por su esposo, circunstancia que hace surgir el problema de la realidad y la imaginación, de la vida y la literatura y, en último término, el enigma de lo femenino.

3663 Uribe-Etxeverría, Juan Pablo. Uñas de muerto. Providencia, Chile: Alfaguara, 1998. 444 p.

Primer premio del Concurso de Novela 1998 de la "Revista de Libros" de *El Mercurio*. Según el propio autor, se trata de un esfuerzo para recrear la época de Salvador Allende y Augusto Pinochet desde la mirada y la sensibilidad de una persona de ideología conservadora.

3664 Vidal, Virginia. Javiera Carrera: madre de la patria. 1. ed. en Editorial Sudamericana. Santiago, Chile: Editorial Sudamericana, 2000. 285 p.: bibl. (Narrativas históricas)

Biografía novelada de Javiera, hermana de los próceres de apellido Carrera, cuyo trágico destino marcó los inicios de la independencia chilena. Relato que ejemplifica los esfuerzos por rescatar a las figuras femeninas que la historia oficial del país ha dejado tradicionalmente en la penumbra.

3665 Wacquez, Mauricio. Epifanía de una sombra. Providencia, Chile: Editorial Sudamericana, 2000. 408 p. (Biblioteca transversal) (Trilogía de la oscuridad; 1)

Novela póstuma de Wacquez (1939–2000). Texto de gran profundidad narrativa qu presenta el conflicto de los jóvenes de los años 50, encarnado en un adolescente escindido entre el recuerdo de un pasado feliz y el proyecto quimérico del futuro, contemplado por una mirada social que controla ambas posibilidades.

River Plate Countries

MAGDALENA GARCÍA PINTO, *Associate Professor of Spanish and Director of Women's Studies, University of Missouri-Columbia*
CLAIRE MARTIN, *Professor of Spanish, California State University, Long Beach*
FLORA SCHIMINOVICH, *Professor of Spanish, Barnard College/Columbia University*

ARGENTINA

LA NARRATIVA ARGENTINA de los últimos años del siglo XX no produce un cambio fundamental con la literatura anterior aunque profundiza el sentido de ruptura y de crisis de la sociedad. En su conjunto, los escritores construyen una representación crítica de la realidad ideológica, política y cultural del país. El uso de la ciencia-ficción, la fantasía como crítica del presente, rasgos retóricos paródicos, irónicos y del absurdo contrastan con el ambiente previo de la persecución ideológica y del conformismo. Merecen destacarse los textos de Martínez, *Infierno grande* (ítem **3704**); Antognazzi, *Mare Nostrum* (ítem **3670**); Fernández Moreno, *Un amor de agua* (ítem **3688**); Bioy Casares, *De un mundo a otro* (ítem **3671**); Bizzio en *Planet* (ítem **3675**) y Jitrik, *Mares del sur* (ítem **3699**).

El pasado histórico surge como una presencia que propone interrogantes sobre las nuevas realidades para cuestionarlas, agudizando la toma de conciencia y las responsabilidades individuales y colectivas. La novela histórica adquiere una vigencia notoria por sus implicaciones políticas y la numerosa producción en este género sirve a veces como modelo de reflexión sobre acontecimientos tristemente recientes y familiares para la sociedad actual. En cierta manera, la ficción se vuelve depósito del memorial de un pueblo marcado por la incertidumbre y la amenaza de un fracaso rotundo y quizás permanente. Ante este escenario angustioso, la ficción adopta la forma documental y acude a estrategias antiguas—y por ende reconfortantes—para presentar un material histórico aún candente. Entre estos autores resaltan: Rosemberg, *Un hilo rojo* (ítem **3716**); Tello, *Los días de la eternidad* (ítem **3723**); Víctor Crespo, *Los estrategas* (ítem **3684**); Orgambide, *Memorias de un hombre de bien* (ítem **3711**); Viñals, *Padreoscuro* (ítem **3726**); Aguinis, *La matriz del infierno* (ítem **3667**); Fingueret, *Hija del silencio* (ítem **3689**); Guido, *El traidor* (ítem **3698**); Merkin, *Camila O'Gorman: la historia de un amor inoportuno* (ítem **3707**); y las novelas de Miguens, *Lupe* y *Ana y el Virrey* (ítems **3708** y **3709**).

Descreída de las grandes prédicas universalistas o de utopías salvadoras, la narrativa de este período refleja la crisis y el desencanto por medio de un reciclaje de formas tradicionales en las estrategias del discurso narrativo creando la ambigüedad entre la realidad y la ficción o los juegos de identidades y palabras que remiten al absurdo o lo irrelevante para expresar la desilusión y disolución de valores sociales. Se destacan los textos de Shúa, *La muerte como efecto secundario* (ítem **3720**); Chitarroni, *El carapálida* (ítem **3680**); Garcés, *Diciembre* (ítem **3693**) y Osorio, *A veinte años, Luz* (ítem **3712**) y Gorodisher, *Cómo triunfar en la vida* (ítem **3695**).

Dentro de la búsqueda realizada por la imaginación contemporánea de esos autores para lograr un estilo capaz de enfrentarse con su mundo, notamos una vertiente hacia el erotismo: la intensificación del placer y del dolor, del goce o padecimiento, abismo o plenitud, son contrarios que permiten la liberación. Se destacan las obras de Dujovne Ortiz, *Mireya* (ítem **3687**); Giardinelli y Gliemmo, compiladores de *La venus de papel* (ítem **3725**) y Andahazi, *Las piadosas* (ítem **3669**). Emparentada con la vertiente erótica, ya explorada, la narrativa se vuelca desde una perspectiva tanto feminista como postfeminista a las temáticas sobre la mujer. Se destacan: Borinsky, *Cine continuado* (ítem **3676**); Civale, *Perra Virtual* (ítem **3682**); Gorodischer, *Mala noche y parir hembra* (ítem **3696**); Kociancich, *Cuando leas estas cartas* (ítem **3700**).

La literatura ensayística del período sigue la tendencia de la metanarrativa anterior, que tiende a experimentar lo literario dentro de su mismo espacio y trata de afirmar la experiencia literaria. *El cuarteto de Buenos Aires* de Alvaro Abós (ítem **3666**), la colección de Soriano *Piratas, fantasmas y dinosaurios* (ítem **3721**) y *La trompeta de mimbre* de Aira (ítem **3668**) señalan esta inclinación de la prosa ensayística de la época.

PARAGUAY

Si bien más escasos, se destaca una colección de textos de Bareiro Saguier y una novela histórica sobre Don Pedro de Mendoza (ítems **3727** y **3728**). De gran importancia para la literatura paraguaya es la colección de cuentos y relatos en español y en guaraní compilados en dos tomos por Teresa Mendez-Faith, que permite una mirada histórica de la narrativa de este país (ítem **3729**).

URUGUAY

Los libros seleccionados para este período corresponden a los años 1997, 1998 y algunos de 1999. En ellos hay un balance entre cuento y novela, y en algunos casos reediciones o nuevas ediciones de autores ampliamente difundidos en la literatura del Uruguay. Courtoisie está presente con un volumen de cuentos y una novela (ítems **3733** y **3734**). Notamos una nueva y breve colección de cuentos de Porzecanski (ítem **3744**) y una edición nueva de los cuentos completos de Quiroga en dos tomos con un exelente prólogo del editor (ítem **3746**). De Giorgio marca este periodo con la publicación de relatos eróticos de alta calidad (ítem **3735**). Marcamos asimismo una nueva novela de Conteris (ítem **3732**).

PROSE FICTION
Argentina

3666 **Abós, Alvaro.** El cuarteto de Buenos Aires. Buenos Aires: Colihue, 1997. 158 p.: ill. (Puñaladas)

Libro de ensayos cuya finalidad es establecer correspondencias literarias y diálogos imaginarios entre figuras reconocidas del mundo literario universal. Los integrantes del "cuarteto" son Roberto Arlt, Jorge Luis Borges, Witold Gombrowicz y Juan Carlos Onetti. Junto a ellos circulan otros como Stephan Zweig, Pavese, Pessoa. Camus, Blanchot, Tolstoy, Hemingway, Kafka y Borges. El enfoque central de los ensayos es la literatura y los temas giran en torno a diarios, novelas perdidas e inconclusas, primeras lecturas y el papel de la crítica contemporánea. [FS]

3667 **Aguinis, Marcos.** La matriz del infierno. Buenos Aires: Editorial Sudamericana, 1997. 559 p.

La trama narrativa de esta novela desarrolla relaciones personales y momentos históricos que giran en torno al holocausto y expone la posición ambivalente de los judíos frente a la historia: ¿es mejor recordar u olvidar? La personalidad del joven protagonista de la obra ha sido modelada o deformada por sus instructores alemanes que lo convierten en un psicópata. Representa una crítica al antisemitismo no sólo argentino sino internacional y a las instituciones religiosas. Transforma la imagen idílica de la Argentina como el oasis de los judíos en un lugar donde prevalece el antisemitismo. [FS]

3668 **Aira, César.** La trompeta de mimbre. Rosario: Beatriz Viterbo Editora, 1998. 159 p. (Ficciones)

Los doce relatos ensayísticos: especulativos, teóricos y filosóficos, revelan la gran capacidad analítica del autor. Temas variados que giran en torno a viajes desmemoriados por las lecturas infantiles, el cine, la televisión, el teatro, la pintura, la identidad y los mecanismos de la creación artística. El autor da su visión personal y mezcla digresiones con intervenciones originales y propuestas de nuevas creaciones en un estilo claro y directo. [FS]

3669 Andahazi, Federico. Las piadosas. Buenos Aires: Editorial Sudamericana, 1998. 222 p.

Después del éxito controversial de su primera novela *El anatomista*, Andahazi publica esta novela en la que aparecen conocidos personajes del mundo literario como Lord Byron y Mary Shelley, entre otros. El asistente de Lord Byron es el resentido personaje que se convierte en el centro de una trama de acentos góticos. Las cartas y otros intercambios entre los personajes son de una extrema sensualidad y erotismo. La imaginación creativa bordea con lo perverso. Para comentario sobre la traducción al inglés de esta obra, ver ítem **4276.** [FS]

3670 Antognazzi, Carlos O. Mare nostrum: cuentos. Santa Fe, Argentina: Ediciones Tauro, 1997 115 p.

Colección de relatos que apuntan hacia una nueva narrativa argentina, original en el estilo y en la temática. El autor retoma la tradición de Borges y Cortázar en cuanto a estrategias del discurso narrativo e incorpora su propia visión de las posibilidades de la fantasía de niños, adolescentes y adultos. El resultado es siempre inesperado y reconfortante. Ciencia ficción, fantasía y realismo se mezclan con la emotividad, el dolor de la ausencia y una búsqueda desesperada de la aventura real o soñada. El autor ha recibido el Primer Premio Internacional "Felisberto Hernández." [FS]

3671 Bioy Casares, Adolfo. De un mundo a otro. Buenos Aires: Temas Grupo Editorial, 1998. 78 p. (Temas de literatura)

Novela de ciencia-ficción en la que dos personajes, un periodista y una astronauta parten en una nave espacial hacia otro planeta. Un accidente inesperado los lleva a otro mundo sideral habitado por pájaros con características humanas. La novela mantiene un clima de suspenso y refleja un mundo inquietante y desconocido. [FS]

3672 Bioy Casares, Adolfo. Una magia modesta. Buenos Aires: Temas Grupo Editorial, 1997. 152 p. (Colección Temas de literatura)

Colección de cuentos de carácter breve, casi bosquejos que siempre sorprenden y narraciones más extensas. En ambos casos, Bioy Casares revela una vez más la seguridad del narrador conciente de su destreza y aún maravillado por el poder de la palabra. En los cuentos más sintéticos es posible vislumbrar la estructuración quasi matemática del material narrativo. Es ésta una colección para saborear sorbo a sorbo. [CEM]

3673 Bioy Casares, Adolfo *et al.* Cuentos de fútbol argentino. Selección y prólogo, Roberto Fontanarrosa. Buenos Aires: Aguilar, Altea, Taurus, Alfaguara, 1997. 267 p. (Extra Alfaguara)

El fútbol argentino es telón y actor principal en esta colección de cuentos algo inusitada. Diversos autores como Bioy Casares, J.L. Borges, Marcelo Cohen, Rodrigo Fresán, Fontanarrosa, Liliana Heker y Luisa Valenzuela, entre otros, elaboran la metáfora deportiva para desentrañar el ser nacional y su circunstancia. [CEM]

3674 Bioy Casares, Adolfo *et al.* Cuentos de historia argentina. Selección y prólogo de Guillermo Saavedra. Buenos Aires: Alfaguara, 1998. 245 p. (Extra Alfaguara)

Colección de cuentos de substrato histórico nacional nacidos de las voces de los mejores narradores argentinos del siglo XX. Desde la independencia, pasando por la época de Rosas, hasta llegar a nuestros días, la historia nacional se reconstruye desde perspectivas tan diversas como esclarecedoras. Se establecen lazos significativos entre las narraciones que forman en su todo el cañamazo ficcional en dónde se halla, tímida y parcial, la verdad histórica. [CEM]

3675 Bizzio, Sergio. Planet. Buenos Aires: Editorial Sudamericana, 1998. 239 p. (Narrativas argentinas)

Novela de ciencia-ficción en la que dos actores argentinos de telenovela son raptados y transportados a otro planeta desconocido en el que los canales de televisión se disputan a la población más culta del universo. Los dos actores logran un gran éxito, son elevados a la categoría de dioses y abren así el interés hacia la literatura, la música y el arte argentinos. Todo cambia cuando los actores quiebran la armonía de "Planet" y son encarcelados. La perversidad de los habitantes de ese lugar, considerados hasta ese momento como los más cultos de la creación, se hace explícita. [FS]

3676 Borinsky, Alicia. Cine continuado. Buenos Aires: Ediciones Corregidor, 1997. 207 p.

Esta novela hecha a retazos ensarta en una galería de episodios las vidas sórdidas de varias mujeres, sus familias y sus amantes. El vocabulario estridente, el humor escatológico y la imaginería erótica hacen de esta narrativa una heredera directa de la nueva narrativa hispanoamericana en su variante femenina y feminista. La apariencia esconde todo un mundo de relaciones humanas equívocas. Las tramas se entrecruzan, prometen una resolución y terminan en la opacidad. [CEM]

3677 Brascó, Miguel. Quejido huacho. Buenos Aires: Tusquets Editores, 1999. 297 p. (Col. Andanzas)

Un ingeniero viaja a la provincia de Buenos Aires y se encuentra atrapado en una cadena de peripecias inauditas que reflejan el caos y la sinrazón del país. Entre la comicidad y el guiño irónico surge nítida la realidad Argentina. [CEM]

3678 Canclini, Arnoldo. El fueguino, Jemmy Button y los suyos. Buenos Aires: Sudamericana, 1998. 338 p.: bibl. (Narrativas históricas)

Novel on intercultural contact and conflict based on the lives of native inhabitants of Tierra del Fuego, who in 1830 were taken by Capt. Robert FitzRoy to England aboard the Beagle. Before returning to their native communities, they were "civilized" and converted to Christianity. [S. Ramírez]

3679 Castillo, Laura del. Mirar el limonero y morir; Una ciruela para Coco. Buenos Aires: Vinciguerra, 1998. 102 p. (La novela universal)

Mirar el limonero y morir fue publicada en Ecuador en 1958. *Una ciruela para Coco* obtuvo el premio de la revista *Life* y fue publicada en 1960 por Doubleday. Las dos novelas cortas representan una estremecedora búsqueda por la libertad y la razón existencial del individuo frente al sufrimiento ajeno. El vocabulario poético concretiza la angustia de la auténtica soledad humana. [CEM]

3680 Chitarroni, Luis. El carapálida. Buenos Aires: Tusquets Editores, 1997. 265 p. (Col. Andanzas)

La novela no trata de una simple descripción costumbrista de un grupo juvenil sino que el marco de una escuela argentina a comienzos de los años 70 le permite al autor dar una visión mucho más amplia de la sociedad. El relato permea una ironía sagaz e invita a ahondar en una realidad dominada por contrastes entre la falsedad y lo verdadero, la inocencia y la culpabilidad dentro de un clima inexplicable. [FS]

3681 Cichero, Daniel. El corsario del Plata: Hipólito Bouchard y su viaje alrededor del mundo. Buenos Aires: Editorial Sudamericana, 1999. 418 p.: 1 map. (Narrativas históricas)

La novela cuenta la historia del Capitán Hipólito Bouchard, un marino de origen francés que por circunstancias azarosas se convierte en corsario de las Provincias Unidas del Río de la Plata en la época de la independencia de España. Las aventuras de Bouchard tienen lugar en dos expediciones, la primera por el Pacífico, junto al almirante Brown y la segunda, mucho más ambiciosa, alrededor del mundo contra naves y colonias españolas (1817–19). La novedad de esta obra es que ofrece una visión poco conocida de la historia de los corsarios marinos en las Guerras de la Independencia. [FS]

3682 Civale, Cristina. Perra virtual. Buenos Aires: Seix Barral, 1998. 153 p.

Las protagonistas de estos cuentos lacerantes viven al borde de la desesperación y la autodestrucción. El lenguaje de la posmodernidad otorga a estos relatos un cariz doloroso y vacuo para llenar la angustia existencial de las mujeres que existen en la penumbra de un mundo diabólico y paralelo. [CEM]

3683 Covadlo, Lázaro. Agujeros negros. Barcelona: Ediciones Altera, 1997. 217 p.

El humor negro, la ironía y la compasión por las debilidades humanas se dan cita en esta colección de cuentos originales. Las pasiones más viles coexisten con la inocencia en personajes ordinarios que intentan salir del anonimato o de la mediocridad. El absurdo de las situaciones límite ponen en marcha inexorable el destino de los personajes. Cuentos bien ejecutados que deleitan y sorprenden. [CEM]

3684 Crespo, Osvaldo Víctor. Los estrategas. Córdoba, Argentina: Editorial de la Municipalidad de Córdoba, 1998. 161 p.

Segundo Premio Municipal de Literatura "Luis José de Tejeda" 1997. En el ámbito de un colegio de provincia y de su universidad, un grupo de profesores, alumnos y administradores mueven las piezas de un juego cruel e injusto que revela desapasionadamente la grandeza y la debilidad humanas. Crespo logra corporeizar en su novela las circunstancias existenciales que empujan al individuo a actuar o a omitir su actuación. [CEM]

3685 Cuentos de amor de autores argentinos. Selección de Marta Giménez Pastor; Prólogo de Jorge Cruz. Buenos Aires: Ameghino Editora, 1998. 206 p.

Relatos reunidos en torno al tema amoroso. Volumen bien equilibrado en el cual están representados los mejores cuentistas argentinos. Incluye relatos de Bioy Casares, Marco Denevi, Gudiño Kieffer, Martha Mercader, Manuel Mujica Láinez, Silvina Ocampo, Elvira Orphée y D.F. Sarmiento, entre otros muchos. [CEM]

3686 Denevi, Marco. Nuestra señora de la noche. Buenos Aires: Corregidor, 1997. 223 p.

Denevi despliega sus dotes de narrador innovador y arriesgado en esta breve y apasionante novela. La sexualidad y el espíritu del ser humano se confunden en una trama arraigada en la realidad pero sujeta a ella. Imaginativo y poético, el lenguaje de Denevi revela y escarba más allá de la superficie. [CEM]

3687 Dujovne Ortiz, Alicia. Mireya. Buenos Aires: Alfaguara, 1998. 239 p.

Inspirada en una fantasía de Julio Cortázar, la novela narra la vida de Mireya, una prostituta inmortalizada por el pintor Toulouse-Lautrec. Mireya viaja a Buenos Aires seducida por un galán porteño. En el burdel se hace testigo de acontecimientos importantes de la Argentina de principios del siglo XX y se convierte en fuente de inspiración del famoso Carlos Gardel. Los cuadros de vida rioplatense son recreados con humor e ironía. La novela es como un fresco brillante y pictórico y su estilo narrativo es rico y dinámico. Mireya regresa finalmente a su lugar natal para llevar a cabo una venganza. [FS]

3688 Fernández Moreno, Inés. Un amor de agua. Buenos Aires: Aguilar, Altea, Taurus, Alfaguara, 1997. 157 p.

Colección de relatos que oscilan entre lo analítico y lo fantástico. Los personajes son hombres y mujeres en búsqueda de un cambio de vida. Desesperados y angustiados se someten al modo surrealista de la conquista del deseo en el mundo cotidiano. Amor, erotismo y recetas de cocina, infidelidades y alucinaciones forman el tejido central de estos relatos no desprovistos de humor. [FS]

3689 Fingueret, Manuela. Hija del silencio. Buenos Aires: Planeta, 1999. 218 p.

En una mezcla de ficción y autobiografía literaria, la protagonista judía recrea el pasado de su madre y abuela en los campos de concentración en Terezín. La novela ofrece un contrapunto entre múltiples herencias: historias talmúdicas, la mujer como víctima de violaciones y el marco de la militancia peronista. El pasado y el presente se unen formando un círculo doloroso y conflictivo. La experiencia de lo vivido en la Argentina durante la dictadura militar gravita en la conciencia de las víctimas como un espectro amenazador. La tortura, el crimen y la locura son parte esencial de la obra en la que se incluyen textos de Martín Buber, poemas de Miroslav Kosek y Franta Bass y dibujos y poemas de los campos de concentración. [FS]

3690 Fogwill, Rodolfo Enrique. Cantos de marineros en la Pampa. Barcelona: Mondadori, 1998. 350 p. (Literatura Mondadori; 83)

Fogwill recoge en este tomo ocho cuentos y una novela, todos ellos escritos entre 1979–83. Los Pichiciegos, novela basada en los acontecimientos nefastos de la guerra de Las Malvinas, ofrece una versión delirante de este episodio nacional. El genio de Fogwill radica en su uso del lenguaje común destilado en su esencia y la locura sana de sus tramas entre cómicas, absurdas y tiernas. [CEM]

3691 Fontanarrosa. Una lección de vida. Buenos Aires: Ediciones de la Flor, 1998. 347 p.

Cuentos de gran lucidez humana. El lenguaje coloquial capta las facetas más íntimas de los personajes de estos relatos a veces humorísticos y otras graves. La manipulación del idioma de la calle adquiere, en esta colección, el papel protagónico. [CEM]

3692 Foster, David William. Buenos Aires: perspectives on the city and cultural production. Gainesville: Univ. Press of Florida, 1998. 232 p.: bibl., ill.

En esta obra ensayística, Foster analiza la integración de la ciudad de Buenos Aires en la producción cultural. En su estudio sobre el tango señala las divisiones entre hombres y mujeres y relaciona la producción teatral con aspectos de la vida social argentina. El realismo de Enrique Medina enfoca aspectos del paisaje urbano de sectores marginados y la fotografía de Sara Facio se abre a los espacios públicos. El libro es un compendio de historia, literatura, antropología y arquitectura. Una dimensión ecléctica y rica en formas de lenguaje y cultura popular revela el poder de los estudios culturales para analizar la vida urbana. [FS]

3693 Garcés, Gonzalo. Diciembre. Buenos Aires: Editorial Sudamericana, 1997. 169 p.

Exploración de la sensibilidad de los jóvenes de los noventa. Un viaje a París abre un mundo de experiencias y amistades donde todo tiene el signo de la aventura, incluyendo el amor. En esta primera novela, el autor revela y define su capacidad para destacar aspectos importantes de la vida de esos jóvenes en busca de una identidad dentro de su tiempo inestable. Novela escrita con precisión estilística y profundidad literaria. [FS]

3694 Giardinelli, Mempo. Cuentos Completos. Buenos Aires: Seix Barral, 1999. 392 p.

Colección de casi todos los cuentos escritos por Giardinelli. Incluye varios cuentos publicados únicamente en periódicos y revistas. Los cuentos pertenecen a las siguientes colecciones: *Vidas Ejemplares* (1982); *La Entrevista* (1986); *Antología Personal* (1987); *Carlitos Dancing Bar* (1992); *El castigo de Dios* (1993), y siete cuentos inéditos. [CEM]

3695 Gorodischer, Angélica. Cómo triunfar en la vida. Buenos Aires: Emecé Editores, 1998. 184 p. (Escritores argentinos)

Los cuentos de esta colección ponen una vez más de manifiesto la imaginación, el humor y la capacidad de la autora para construir mundos que van de lo cotidiano a lo misterioso, inexplicable o extraño. Los personajes femeninos de la colección asumen o simulan distintos roles: parecen tontas o sumisas pero son capaces de convertirse en expertas criminales o peligrosas delincuentes. Las actitudes y cambios en los personajes resultan por lo general inesperados. El estilo dinámico y poético evoca una tradición que va desde lo clásico a lo posmoderno. [FS]

3696 Gorodischer, Angélica. Mala noche y parir hembra: cuentos. Nueva ed. ampliada por las musas. Buenos Aires: Héctor Dinsmann, 1997. 163 p.

Colección de cuentos ya publicados en 1983 y reeditados con alteraciones. La imaginación febril y al mismo tiempo razonada de Gorodischer deleita en una docena de relatos escrupulosamente construidos en torno a personajes inusitados. Las mujeres de estos relatos alteran la realidad por medio de la inteligencia y de la fantasía, burlan y se burlan de sus destinos para elaborarse mundos más abiertos y libres en los cuales encarnan el papel protagónico que se merecen. [CEM]

3697 Gudiño Kieffer, Eduardo. Malas, malísimas: cinco damas perversas. Buenos Aires: Ameghino, 1998. 123 p.: ill. (Cuentos)

Entre la crónica y la ficción, las historias de cinco mujeres que vivieron en tiempos remotos le permiten al autor explorar ciertos aspectos de las personalidades de esos personajes y revelar intrigas y fantasías crueles que lindan en el sadismo. El estilo ingenioso e irreverente caracteriza estas historias que juegan con lo prohibido y la libertad sexual revelando vínculos entre la política y el sexo. [FS]

3698 Guido, Horacio J.M. El traidor: Telmo López y la patria que no pudo ser. Buenos Aires: Editorial Sudamericana, 1998. 301 p. (Narrativas históricas)

El autor logra en esta novela un fresco novedoso y sorprendente de la historia argentina desde la Revolución de Mayo hasta finales de la guerra contra el Paraguay. Telmo López era hijo del caudillo Estanislao López y en contra de los ideales de su padre se unió a los enemigos de la Argentina e hizo armas contra ese país en el ejército de Solano López. [FS]

3699 Jitrik, Noé. Mares del sur. Buenos Aires: Tusquets Editores, 1997. 267 p. (Col. Andanzas)

Esta novela desarrolla una intriga policial en el marco de la ciudad de Mar del Plata y el contexto de la dictadura militar de los años setenta. El crimen de un conocido empresario provoca una serie de situaciones delirantes e inesperadas. El estilo refleja la capacidad creativa, ensayística y teórica del autor. [FS]

3700 Kociancich, Vlady. Cuando leas esta carta. Buenos Aires: Seix Barral, 1998. 173 p. (Biblioteca breve)

Colección de cuentos de gran imaginación y originalidad. La autora utiliza el humor y la ironía para desconcertar y hacer reflexionar sobre la condición humana. Crea un mundo entre cotidiano e insólito por el cual deambulan personajes inolvidables. [CEM]

3701 López, Fernando. El enigma del ángel. Córdoba, Argentina: Narvaja Editor, 1998. 115 p. (Col. las fuerzas extrañas)

Novela que mezcla la ciencia ficción con el supenso de los relatos policiales. El personaje principal es ambiguo y a veces hasta inverosímil pero su versión apunta a otras realidades ocultas en las que el misterio se asocia con lo político. El cruce de lo fantástico con lo histórico social mantiene el suspenso y el interés del lector. [FS]

3702 Lorenzo Sanz, Ricardo. Ituzaingo-Ituzaingó. Buenos Aires: Vinciguerra, 1999. 175 p. (La novela universal)

Novela de sorprendente alcance estilístico en la que los personajes niños y más tarde ya adultos, circulan por un terreno entre lo mágico y lo real. Uso eficaz—humor, ternura, crítica, nostalgia—de los medios de difusión asociados con diferentes etapas históricas del país. [CEM]

3703 Marechal, Leopoldo. Obras completas. v. 1, La poesía; v. 3–4, Las novelas. Buenos Aires: Perfil Libros, 1998. 3 v.: bibl., ill. (La biblioteca)

La edición ha sido coordinada por María de los Angeles Marechal y está encabeza por un prólogo de Jorge Lafforgue. El tomo I recopila toda la poesía y lleva un prólogo de Pedro Luis Barcia. La parte I incluye los poemarios: *Los Aguiluchos, Días como flechas, Odas para el hombre y la mujer,*

Laberinto de amor, Poemas australes, El centauro, Sonetos a Sophia y otros poemas, Canto de San Martín, Heptamerón, El poema de robot, Poema de la física y Poema de Psiquis. La parte II incluye poemas dispersos y desconocidos. III contiene Adán Buenosayres y Claves de Adán Buenosayres. El tomo IV, prologado por Graciela Maturo y Dinko Cvitanovic, incluye las novelas El banquete de Severo Arcángel y Megafón o la Guerra. Para el comentario de vol. 2 de esta obra, ver ítem **4027.** [MGP]

3704 Martínez, Guillermo. Infierno grande. Buenos Aires: Destino, 2000. 174 p. (Col. Ancora y delfín)

Reedición de esta serie de 12 relatos que oscilan entre el humor y lo grotesco, lo policial y lo fantástico, lo absurdo y lo normal cotidiano, lo existencial y lo intrascendente. La escritura es fluida pero su lectura provoca la perturbación del lector, llevándolo hacia los límites de la realidad, a comprender el horror y la denuncia. La comicidad le confiere a estos cuentos salpicados de neorrealismo, un tono original y estimulante. [FS]

3705 Martínez, Guillermo. La mujer del maestro. Buenos Aires: Planeta, 1998. 159 p.

Relata la atracción de un joven escritor por la agradable y refinada mujer de su maestro Jordán. Los encuentros entre el protagonista y Cecilia son fugaces e intensos. Por esa relación se nos revelan aspectos importantes de la personalidad del maestro. El autor es hábil en construir atmósferas y en el manejo del tiempo. La trama de la novela refleja las preocupaciones ocasionadas por la práctica de la escritura y los conflictos que surgen por las relaciones amorosas. [FS]

3706 Masetto, Antonio dal. Hay unos tipos abajo. Buenos Aires: Planeta, 1998. 174 p.

Un periodista regresa a su casa y en la esquina un grupo misterioso de hombres vigilan o esperan. La novela reproduce el ambiente anormal del período de la dictadura militar. A la normalidad propuesta por las expectativas del campeonato mundial de fútbol se oponen la inquietud y el miedo impuestos por la represión. Novela de suspenso que transmite magistralmente el desasosiego y la inquietud de personajes inocentes que se sienten perseguidos por un clima contagioso de locura colectiva. [FS]

3707 Merkin, Marta. Camila O'Gorman: la historia de un amor inoportuno. Buenos Aires: Editorial Sudamericana, 1997. 230 p. (Narrativas históricas)

La película de María Luisa Bemberg contribuyó a diseminar la historia del romance clandestino de Camila y Ladislao en la época de Juan Manuel de Rosas. Merkin continúa la mitología con una novela que mantiene el interés de los lectores porque junto a las peripecias de la romántica y desafiante pareja se detallan acontecimientos históricos que revelan el afán de investigación de la autora. El estilo es dinámico y mezcla lo testimonial con rasgos poéticos y transmite vívidamente una época sangrienta con cuadros crueles y a veces desgarradores. [FS]

3708 Miguens, Silvia. Ana y el virrey. Buenos Aires: Planeta, 1998. 285 p.

En su segunda novela histórica, la autora trata de los amores de Ana Perichón de O'Gorman y Santiago de Liniers. El personaje femenino es rebelde y amante de la libertad. Su familia llegó a Buenos Aires cuando ésta era todavía una colonia española. La novela cuestiona la actitud de hombres y mujeres frente a la historia y los amores prohibidos de los personajes revelan su dolorosa impotencia ante la sociedad. [FS]

3709 Miguens, Silvia. Lupe. Buenos Aires: Tusquets Editores, 1997. 294 p. (Col. Andanzas)

La protagonista Lupe se casa con Mariano Moreno cuando ella era una adolescente. En Buenos Aires frecuenta tertulias junto a Mariquita Sánchez de Thompson y la famosa Perichona. Lupe se convierte en un personaje testigo de las Invasiones Inglesas, disiente de las posiciones políticas de su marido y cuando se separan porque él está en Inglaterra, ella trata de continuar la relación. La novela recrea el período fundacional de la Argentina e invoca el amor, la soledad, el miedo y la fortaleza de las mujeres de ese tiempo. [FS]

3710 Onetti, Jorge. Siempre se puede ganar nunca. Madrid: Alfaguara, 1998. 192 p.

Colección de cuentos publicados póstumamente. Onetti traza personajes complejos y sinuosos que viven a veces al margen de los acontecimientos o por el contrario, completamente sumergidos por éstos. El humor, la compasión, la crítica feroz y una visión humanista del pasado reciente constituyen la base de estos relatos cuidadosamente estructurados, de un lenguaje expresivo y rico en matices. [CEM]

3711 Orgambide, Pedro G. Memorias de un hombre de bien. Buenos Aires: El Francotirador Ediciones, 1998. 119 p.

Las memorias de un argentino nacido con el siglo 20 revelan la compleja trama que une la individualidad a la historia nacional. El protagonista—suerte de pícaro aristocrático—echa su mirada sagaz sobre el pasado turbio argentino y las fuerzas psicológicas, políticas y culturales que lo formaron. [CEM]

3712 Osorio, Elsa. A veinte años luz. 2a. ed. Barcelona: Alba Editorial, 1999. 509 p. (Literaria; 38)

Esta novela trata de una joven de 20 años que cree haber sido una de las niñas nacidas en cautiverio durante la época de la dictadura militar de los setenta. La novela desata una búsqueda desesperada y se ofrece un macrocosmos de la sociedad argentina bajo los efectos de la dictadura. El suspenso, lo inesperado y la revelación psicológica forman la trama de la novela en la que aparecen personajes diversos envueltos en historias de amor que los obligan a tomar conciencia de su condición. [FS]

3713 Peltzer, Federico. La puerta del limbo. Buenos Aires: Emecé Editores, 1997. 138 p.

Premio Fondo Nacional de las Artes, 1996. Narraciones de estilo sobrio e íntimo. Las diarias tragedias humanas se reflejan desde la visión de una voz narrativa discreta o inocente. Peltzer estructura con parsimonia y delicadeza el edificio de su ficción. [CEM]

3714 Posse, Abel. Los cuadernos de Praga. Buenos Aires: Editorial Atlántida, 1998. 318 p.

Escritor y diplomático, el autor de esta novela se propone esclarecer una etapa de la vida de Ernesto Che Guevara durante los primeros seis meses de 1966. Posse estuvo en Praga cinco años como embajador y allí y en Cuba buscó documentos y anécdotas para escribir esta obra que tiene carácter de novela histórica. Se nos revela a un Che Guevara vestido de burgués, con gafas y corbata de seda. Implica su rechazo de la ideología comunista a la vez que intenta afirmarla y difundirla. [FS]

3715   Rivera, Andrés. La lenta velocidad del coraje. Buenos Aires: Alfaguara, 1998. 203 p.

Colección de relatos de gran riqueza estilística. La psicología de los personajes orienta hacia una resolución en instancias sorprendente. La violencia parece ser el cañamazo sobre el cual se tejen las historias aparentemente banales, pero que revelan lo más absurdamente humano. Rivera demuestra una gran facilidad para encontrar el tono que corresponde mejor a cada relato. [CEM]

3716   Rosenberg, Sara. Un hilo rojo. Madrid: Espasa, 1998. 203 p. (Espasa narrativa)

Novela estructurada en forma de cintas grabadas. Diversos personajes situados en el centro y en la periferia de los hechos históricos recuerdan y graban la memoria colectiva sobre los acontecimientos que marcaron una nueva etapa de ignominia en la Argentina de los años setenta. Fluidez en la narración, sutilezas de la imaginación y reflexiones astutas hacen que esta novela se lea con placer y con amarga inquietud. [CEM]

3717   Rosenfeldt, Sergio. La voz amiga. Buenos Aires: Fundación Octubre: Ediciones de la Flor, 1998. 238 p. (Col. Narrativa)

Premio del Area de Literatura. Fundación Ocubre, 1997. Primera novela que reúne todos los atributos de la buena novelística. Rosenfeldt emplea el humor, la sensibilidad y un oído genuino al representar las voces dispares de un elenco de personajes que transitan en la ciudad y viven a través del hilo telefónico las vidas ajenas. [CEM]

3718   Santis, Pablo de. La traducción. Buenos Aires: Planeta, 1998. 183 p.

Novelas de corte policial que enmascara una historia de amor. Los signos de dos muertes en un hotel deben ser descifrados por los conferenciantes de un congreso de traductores. Humor y astucia intelectual permean la novela que se ubica en la frialdad de un puerto-ciudad del sur. [CEM]

3719   Sexshop: cuentos eróticos argentinos. Selección, prólogo y notas de Adriana Fernández, Mercedes Güiraldes y Eduardo

Hojman. Buenos Aires: Emecé Editores, 1998. 249 p. (Escritores argentinos)

Colección que aborda el tema del erotismo desde diferentes perspectivas y variantes. Representados en este tomo se encuentran los mejores narradores argentinos: Silvina Ocampo, Juan José Saer, Ana María Shúa, Rodolfo Fogwill, entre otros. [CEM]

3720   Shua, Ana María. La muerte como efecto secundario. Buenos Aires: Editorial Sudamericana, 1997 235 p.

Entre el realismo y la ciencia-ficción la novela denuncia la vuelta a la democracia ya que la sociedad parece encontrarse en la actualidad en una situación mucho peor que durante la dictadura militar. La novela relaciona el centro de hegemonía de los grupos militares con las ideologías del poder económico. Un tono deliberadamente morboso permea las páginas del libro que habla sobre el amor, la desesperanza y las relaciones entre padres e hijos. [FS]

3721   Soriano, Osvaldo. Piratas, fantasmas y dinosaurios. Barcelona; Bogotá: Grupo Editorial Norma, 1997. 269 p. (Col. La otra orilla)

Libro que recopila relatos ficcionales, notas y escritos diversos. Hay ensayos sobre Roberto Arlt, Graham Greene, Bioy Casares y Salman Rushdie, entre otros. Los cuentos de ficción se mezclan con homenajes, invocaciones e historias de fútbol. Representan fragmentos de la vida y creación del escritor. [FS]

3722   Taján, Alfredo. El pasajero. Barcelona: Ediciones Destino, 1997. 223 p. (Colección Ancora y delfín; v. 804)

Cuidada novela sobre los estragos de la pasión amorosa en un círculo de literatos e intelectuales argentinos. Taján logra un estilo híbrido en el que se asocian la autobiografía, el testimonio, el relato amoroso y la novela policial. Agil y humorística con un dejo de decepción y nostalgia, la trama se mueve recreando un trayecto existencial. Premio Café Gijón 1996. [CEM]

3723   Tello, Antonio. Los días de la eternidad. Barcelona: Muchnik Editores, 1997. 199 p. (Novela)

Narrativa que testimonia de modo innovador las atrocidades de la época de la represión política en Argentina. Las voces de los tres narradores se tejen para dar a la historia de un desaparecido un matiz aún más complejo y problematizado. La novela se erige en un homenaje al poder cicatrizante a lo menos balsámico—de la palabra escrita. [CEM]

3724 Valenzuela, Luisa. Antología personal. Buenos Aires: Ediciones Instituto Movilizador de Fondos Cooperativos, 1998. 126 p. (Desde la gente)

Colección de cuentos seleccionados por la autora que incluye textos de la mayor parte de sus libros publicados anteriormente en *El gato eficaz*, en *Aquí pasan cosas raras* y otras colecciones. Forman un muestrario de la capacidad lingüística e imaginativa de Valenzuela. Desde el fluir de la conciencia hasta la captación de la inmediatez de la paranoia ambiental o del realismo y amor a Buenos Aires relacionados con el tema del tango, los relatos aparecen en el orden cronológico de publicación previa. [FS]

3725 La Venus de papel: antología del cuento erótico argentino. Compilación de Mempo Giardinelli y Graciela Gliemmo. Buenos Aires: Planeta, 1998. 236 p.

Las veinticuatro narraciones de esta colección son diversas en la temática y el uso del lenguaje. Algunas bordean en lo fantástico, otras se desarrollan en lugares públicos o privados e incluyen lo auto-referencial. Los temas del amor y el erotismo se presentan en contextos que van desde lo político social hasta la fantasía que linda en lo pornográfico. Por lo general, lo sexual en los relatos se asocia con la libertad frente a contextos represivos. Incluye cuentos de autores reconocidos como Luisa Valenzuela, David Viñas, Angélica Gorodisher, Ricardo Piglia, Abelardo Castillo y Liliana Hecker, entre otros. [FS]

3726 Viñals, José. Padreoscuro. Barcelona: Montesinos, 1998. 248 p.

Novela estructurada como entrevista grabada por un interlocutor que se revela en la segunda parte como hijo del entrevistado. La búsqueda del padre da origen a la narrativa. La imagen paterna va adquiriendo cada vez más resonancia a medida que se va revelando pausadamente, con parsimonia al inicio para llegar a un paroxismo narrativo al final de la entrevista. La visión parcial de toda una vida, recuperada a través de la palabra del padre, cobra matices paradójicos cuando

el hijo entrevista al hermano que no conocía y que lleva en su sangre la misma violencia del padre. Lo sorprendente está en la explosión del lenguaje que se transforma con cada giro en la conversación del padre. [CEM]

Paraguay

3727 Bareiro Saguier, Rubén. Cuentos de las dos orillas. Asunción: Editorial Don Bosco, 1998. 237 p.

Precedido por un excelente prologo de Helio Vera sobre este escritor y crítico paraguayo, la colección incluye dos grupos de textos: "Ojo por diente" con 11 relatos y "El séptimo pétalo de viento" con 12. Los temas están desarrollados desde la experiencia personal de habitar dos mundos diversos, el Paraguay y varios países de Europa. [MGP]

3728 Cabañas, Esteban. Lo dulce y lo turbio: crimen y castigo de don Pedro de Mendoza. Buenos Aires: Editorial Sudamericana, 1998. 174 p.: ill., maps. (Narrativas históricas)

Esta novela obtuvo el Primer Premio del Club Centenario de Asunción. El relato de carácter histórico cuenta el arribo de don Pedro de Mendoza y sus soldados al Río de la Plata y los muchos acontecimientos que tuvieron lugar a raíz de la lucha por el poder de los colonizadores, de las enfermedades que plagaron la expedición, la relación del Almirante con Ayolas e Irala. Dice el maestro Roa Basto de esta novela que "renueva creativamente el género de la novela histórica en América Latina." [MGP]

3729 Narrativa paraguaya de ayer y de hoy. Compilación de Teresa Méndez-Faith. Con una cronología de autores y obras narrativas paraguayas de José Vicente Peiró. Asunción: Intercontinental Editora, 1999. 2 v. (847 p.): bibl., ill., indexes.

La distinguida investigadora paraguaya ha reunido en estos dos tomos más de 80 autores y más de 180 relatos en español y en guaraní—cuentos cortos y largos—textos completos que representan 45 narradores y 105 relatos en el tomo I (A-L) y 39 autores y 79 cuentos en el tomo II (M-Z). La compilación está organizada por orden alfabético de autores y por lo tanto no es una ordenación cronológica de escritores de la segunda mitad del siglo XX. [MGP]

Uruguay

3730 Benítez, Luis G. Tango del mudo: novela. Montevideo: Ediciones de la Plaza, 1997. 201 p. (Col. Ficciones)

Esta novela recibió el Premio Novela del "Concurso Internacional de Ficción sobre Gardel" (1996)—segundo año del premio que promueve este género. [MGP]

3731 Burel, Hugo. Los dados de Dios. Montevideo: Alfaguara, 1997. 373 p.

Escritor y periodista, ha publicado tres libros de cuentos y tres novelas. En 1995 el cuento "El elogio de la nieve" recibió el Premio Juan Rulfo de Radio Francia Internacional. Esta novela obtuvo el Premio Juan Rulfo 1995. El texto está estructurado en tres partes: I, Figuras de un paisaje; II, El arte de perseguir una sombra; III, La orilla de arena, que le permiten narrar desde tres puntos de vista una historia de amor entre una argentina y un artista uruguayo. [MGP]

3732 Conteris, Hiber. Round trip: viaje regresivo. Montevideo: Planeta, 1998. 236 p. (Biblioteca del sur)

Nueva novela del reconocido narrador uruguayo, tiene como escenario la Europa urbana de los años 70: Ginebra, París, Londres y otras en las que vive el protagonista, quien debe seguir los hilos de una historia misteriosa. [MGP]

3733 Courtoisie, Rafael. Agua imposible. Montevideo: Alfaguara: El Observador, 1998. 94 p. (Lecturas de verano; 6)

Precedido de un prologo del autor desde Roma, mirando el río Tíber, el volumen incluye 15 cuentos, entre ellos, uno que da el nombre a la colección y "La última noche de José Asunción Silva," de gran interés para los investigadores de la narrativa de Courtoise y del cuento contemporáneo. [MGP]

3734 Courtoisie, Rafael. Vida de perro. Montevideo: Alfaguara, 1997. 213 p.

Conocido como poeta, premiado por su obra que incluye el Premio Internacional de Poesía Plural (Mexico, 1991) por el poemario Textura, recibió también el Premio de la Crítica Bartolomé Hidalgo por su último libro de cuentos Cadáveres exquisitos, y en 1997 publica esta su primera novela. En la que explora la idea de vidas paralelas entre perro y ser humano, aun cuando anota que

los perros parecen haber estado en el planeta antes que los primeros humanos. [MGP]

3735 Di Giorgio, Marosa. Camino de las pedrerías: relatos eróticos. Montevideo: Planeta, 1997. 165 p. (Biblioteca del sur)

Reconocida por su importante obra poética recopilada en Papeles salvajes, dos tomos publicados entre 1989 y 1991, publicó Misales, textos eróticos en 1993. El que se anota es el libro más reciente de la autora. Estos relatos son textos cortos, numerados de 1 a 71, narrados en tercera persona, relatan una variedad de aventuras eróticas creadas mediante la combinación de figuras de a veces diseño fantástico y misterioso, a veces maravilloso, con elementos de violencia sexual. [MGP]

3736 Fernández Pagliano, Alvaro. El ojo en el espejo. Montevideo: Ediciones Trilce, 1997. 117 p.

Colección de siete cuentos homoeróticos que exploran temas del amor, la soledad, y celos, entre otros. Una novedad en las letras uruguayas. Este escritor tiene publicado un libro de poemas, Los enanitos sufren de vértigo (1993). [MGP]

3737 Gelbtrunk, Aída. Aire de familia. Montevideo: Editorial Fin de Siglo, 1998. 154 p. (Col. Deletras)

Una colección de cuentos sobre la experiencia judía en el barrio La Unión en el Uruguay por los años 50, desde una perspectiva femenina. [MGP]

3738 Lissardi, Ercole. Ultimas conversaciones con el fauno. Montevideo: Editorial Fin de Siglo, 1997. 139 p. (Col. Literotismo)

Texto erótico póstumo del tempranamente desaparecido y misterioso autor (1950–1993). La publicación de este texto es debido a un coleccionista de erótica bajo el nome de plume de Delia Fuentes. [MGP]

3739 Mario Benedetti: inventario cómplice. Recopilación de Carmen Alemany Bay, Remedios Mataix y José Carlos Rovira. Alicante, Spain: Univ. de Alicante, 1998. 618 p. (Col. América Latina; 3)

Un volúmen crítico dedicado a la

obra del prolífico maestro uruguayo, consiste de una introducción por los editores y cinco partes. La primera parte reúne trabajos sobre "Cuestiones generales" acerca de la obra. Contribuyen entre otros, J. Rufinelli, S. Matalía, Sylvia Lagos y Roberto Fernández Retamar. La segunda parte está dedicada a la obra poética del maestro, la tercera a la narrativa y la cuarta a la obra crítica, periodística y teatral. La quinta parte es un apéndice que incluye el "Discurso de investidura" al recibir el Doctor Honoris Causa de la Univ. de Alicante. Indispensable para el estudio de la obra de Benedetti. [MGP]

3740 Mella, Daniel. Derretimiento. Montevideo: Ediciones Trilce, 1998. 117 p.

El narrador relata en primera persona una experiencia electrificante de postración total en cama, dependiendo totalmente del cuidado de unos padres que se transforman de pacientes cuidadores en los verdugos de este pobre ser a merced de las crueldad más aterradora. Desde una memoria que acumula todos los detalles y nada olvida, lo único que funciona en su miserable humanidad, este joven recorre dolorosamente el camino de un paciente acicateado por el miedo físico y mental. [MGP]

3741 Mondragón, Juan Carlos. Siete partidas. Montevideo: Librería Linardi y Risso, 1998. 217 p.

Este volumen incluye seis cuentos y una novela breve que combinan la experiencia uruguaya de los protagonistas en narraciones que incorporan un género rioplatense, el fantástico. [MGP]

3742 Ortega, Ginette. Expreso al paraíso. Buenos Aires: Solaris; Montevideo: Blanes, 1996. 479 p.

Una novela que con gran detalle construye escenarios en donde los protagonistas viven su vida diaria en un centro urbano del Cono Sur, que puede ser Montevideo o Buenos Aires, en busca de un sentido que rebase el conformismo contemporáneo. [MGP]

3743 Paternain, Alejandro. El oro de las sierras. Montevideo: Alfaguara: El Observador, 1998. 79 p. (Lecturas de verano; 5)

El protagonista está conectado a Lucy Bristol, personaje central de *Las aventuras de Lucy Bristol* (1991), sobre los buscadores de oro de Minas de Gerais hacia el siglo XVIII. [MGP]

3744 Porzecanski, Teresa. Nupcias en familia y otros cuentos. Montevideo: Alfaguara: El Observador, 1998. 78 p. (Lecturas de verano; 8)

Con prólogo de la autora desde Montevideo, se abre el breve volumen con el cuento "Nupcias en familia" junto a 11 relatos que la reconocida narradora uruguaya ha seleccionado de su obra anterior. [MGP]

3745 Prego, Omar. El sueño del justo y otros cuentos. Montevideo: Alfaguara: El Observador, 1998. 92 p. (Lecturas de verano; 4)

Incluye 10 cuentos policiales, realistas y fantásticos de este conocido crítico literario narrador. [MGP]

3746 Quiroga, Horacio. Cuentos completos. v. 1–2. Buenos Aires: Seix Barral, 1997. 2 v.: bibl. (Biblioteca mayor)

Carlos Dámaso Martínez estuvo a cargo de esta nueva edición de Seix Barral que incluye un informativo estudio preliminar. Los cuentos se reúnen bajo los siguientes títulos en el tomo I: *Los arrecifes de coral* (1901), *El crimen del otro* (1904), *Los perseguidos* (1908), *Cuentos de amor de locura y de muerte* (1917), *Apéndice: Tres cuentos suprimidos en la Tercera y cuarta ediciones*, *Cuentos de la selva para los niños* (1918), *El salvaje* (1920), *Anaconda* (1921). En el tomo II se incluyen los siguientes títulos: *El desierto* (1924), *Los desterrados* (1926), *Más allá* (1935), Cuentos (67 en total) no recopilados en libros (1899–1935), Cartas de un cazador, cuentos para niños publicados en *Mundo argentino* (1922) y *Billiken* (1924). Incluye asimismo una nota sobre el criterio utilizado para la edición y una bibliografía crítica de Quiroga. [MGP]

3747 Rossello, Renzo. Trampa para angeles de barro. Montevideo: Editorial Graffiti, 1997. 156 p. (Col. de narrativa El Cuarto sello)

Esta novela obtuvo el Premio Dashiell Hammet 1992 de Novela Policial del Río de la Plata, es otra muestra de la renovación de este género que tiene antecedentes de calidad en el Río de la Plata. Recientemente se explora la realidad social sórdida de algunos sectores de la sociedad contemporánea. [MGP]

3748 **Silva Schultze, Marisa.** La limpieza es una mentira provisoria. Montevideo: Alfaguara, 1997. 138 p.

Primera novela de esta autora que ha obtenido el primer premio de narrativa 1996 de la Intendencia Municipal de Montevideo. Es la historia de una mujer que reflexiona sobre su vida mientras realiza la rutina diaria de la vida familiar. Una buena muestra de literatura femenina. [MGP]

LITERARY CRITICISM AND HISTORY

Argentina

Gil Q., Mauricio. El escepticismo de Borges o la filosofía como literatura fantástica. See item **4806**.

Mateos, Zulma. La filosofía en la obra de Jorge Luis Borges. See item **4815**.

Poetry

FRANCISCO CABANILLAS, *Associate Professor of Spanish, Bowling Green State University*
MIGUEL GOMES, *Associate Professor of Spanish, University of Connecticut*
ELIZABETH MONASTERIOS, *Associate Professor of Latin American Literature, University of Pittsburgh*
GUIDO PODESTÁ, *Associate Professor of Spanish, University of Wisconsin, Madison*
OSCAR RIVERA-RODAS, *Professor of Spanish, University of Tennessee, Knoxville*
OSCAR SARMIENTO, *Associate Professor of Spanish, State University of New York, Potsdam*
JACOBO SEFAMÍ, *Associate Professor of Spanish, University of California, Irvine*
LILIÁN URIBE, *Professor of Spanish, Central Connecticut State University*

GENERAL

ADEMÁS DE LA PRODUCCIÓN POÉTICA destacada en las anotaciones que siguen, una de las tendencias más estimulantes de este período ha sido el afán de fortalecer el diálogo entre la poesía de España y la de América Latina. Entre ellas, sobresale la nueva y ampliada edición de la antología de *Poesía modernista hispanoamericana y española*, preparada con indiscutible competencia por Iván A. Schulman y Evelyn Picón Garfield (ítem **3761**). Consuelo Triviño es la coordinadora del volumen *Norte y sur de la poesía iberoamericana: Argentina, Brasil, Colombia, Chile, España, México, Venezuela* (ítem **3757**) que, más allá de las discrepancias que pueda suscitar respecto al criterio de selección de autores y países, resulta un proyecto no exento de méritos no sólo por la difusión de ciertos poetas sino también como invitación al desarrollo de futuras antologías y aproximaciones que reúnan las manifestaciones poéticas de ambas márgenes del Atlántico.

También de carácter general es la *Muestra de poesía hispanoamericana actual: 34 nombres en 34 años, 1963–1997* (item **3880**), compilada por Alvaro Salvador, en la que es necesario reconocer la justa inclusión de poetas de innegable importancia en el marco de la actual poesía hispanoamericana, tales como Eduardo Chirinos (Perú), Rafael Courtoisie (Uruguay), Jorge Boccanera (Argentina), José Pérez Olivares (Cuba), y Teresa Calderón (Chile), entre otros.

El análisis de Jaime Concha (ítem **3963**) sobre poesía hispanoamericana desde 1920–50 ofrece una aproximación a los estudios en esta área no solamente idónea y competente sino sugerente y provocadora.

Uno de los acontecimientos más encomiables de este período fue el "Encuentro Internacional de Poetas" realizado en Chile en marzo de 2001 y que agrupó a reconocidos escritores del ámbito no sólo latinoamericano sino mundial como Nicanor Parra, Ledo Ivo, Adrienne Rich, Juan Gelman, Raúl Zurita, Amanda Berenguer, Hans Magnus Enzensberger, Gonzalo Rojas, Rita Dove, y Blanca Varela, entre otros. [LU]

MÉXICO

En el periodo que va de 1998 a 2001, quizá la noticia más importante fue la muerte de Jaime Sabines el 19 de marzo de 1999 (11 meses exactos después de la de Octavio Paz). Sabines (Tuxtla Gutiérrez, Chiapas, 1926) fue, quizá, el poeta más popular de México. Prueba de su popularidad es que cuando dio un recital en el Palacio de Bellas Artes no sólo abarrotó el enorme recinto sino que todavía quedó una multitud afuera, en la calle, escuchando su poesía a través de una pantalla grande. Luis Donaldo Colosio, el candidato asesinado a la presidencia, se sabía de memoria los poemas y, con él, mucha gente en México. Poemas como "Los amorosos" y "Algo sobre la muerte del mayor Sabines" van a quedar en el imaginario colectivo por generaciones. De Sabines siguen saliendo ediciones múltiples de su obra, muchas de ellas de lujo, además de grabaciones o versiones fílmicas de algunos poemas.

En este periodo han salido varias antologías con un enfoque particular. Destaca, por su originalidad, la dedicada a los poemas sobre el cine (ítem **3904**), donde uno puede leer textos sobre María Félix, Dolores del Río o sobre películas como *Casablanca, Un perro andaluz* o *Prospero's Books*. También es interesante la antología de poesía popular mexicana (ítem **3762**), que nos hace ver que el periodo preferido a nivel de difusión mayor es el del Modernismo. Curiosamente, se incluyen muy pocos escritores del siglo XX.

Continúan publicándose sistemáticamente nuevas ediciones de la poesía completa de escritores conocidos. Tal es el caso de Manuel Acuña (ítem **3766**), Rosario Castellanos (ítem **3798**), Marco Antonio Montes de Oca (ítem **3877**) y Tomás Segovia (ítem **3923**). También salió el volumen 13 de las *Obras completas* de Octavio Paz (ítem **3898**), que incluye los poemas y ensayos con que se inició como escritor (queda aún por salir el volumen 12, que incluirá su última poesía, incluyendo un libro póstumo). También se han publicado libros que recogen la obra poética de escritores más jóvenes que ya han llegado a consolidarse en el panorama de la literatura mexicana actual: Efraín Bartolomé (ítem **3778**) y Antonio Deltoro (ítem **3808**).

De los libros individuales reseñados de este periodo, predominan los poetas nacidos en las décadas de los 40 y 50: Cross (ítem **3802**), Gervitz (ítem **3829**), Ruiz Dueñas (ítem **3918**), Huerta (ítem **3842**), Bartolomé (ítem **3778**), Rivas (ítem **3912**), Bracho (ítem **3787**), Castañón (ítem **3797**), Vargas (ítem **3943**), Moscona (ítem **3879**), Piña Williams (ítem **3903**), Villarreal (ítem **3947**), y López Mills (ítem **3860**). Aunque es prácticamente imposible concebir una unidad en esta heterogeneidad de voces, esta generación constituye la médula de la poesía mexicana actual. Del neobarroco (Bracho, Piña Williams), a la poesía urbana (Huerta, Ramírez, Vázquez Martín), al cuestionamiento del lenguaje y el silencio, y el diálogo implícito o explícito entre mujeres (Cross, Gervitz, Moscona, Baranda, Lara), a los cantos de celebración (Deltoro, Vargas), a la poesía preocupada por la naturaleza (Ruiz Dueñas, Bartolomé), a las rememoraciones de la infancia o juventud (Deltoro, Rivas, Castañón), los poetas actuales de México recorren caminos que se bifurcan y, muchas veces, se vuelven a unir.

En términos críticos, siguen apareciendo libros sobre los poetas de Contemporáneos (Escalante, Stanton), Paz (Sosa) y Pacheco (Friis). También, salieron libros que reúnen entrevistas y/o estudios críticos sobre generaciones más recientes (Haladyna, Horno Delgado y Paredes).

Crisis o no, en México se siguen publicando un gran número de libros de poesía. Además de editoriales muy conocidas como Fondo de Cultura Económica (serie Letras Mexicanas), Editorial Era y la UNAM, en este periodo resalta la cantidad de poemarios producidos por Ediciones Sin Nombre. Otras editoriales que se han especializado en poesía son: El Tucán de Virginia, Editorial Aldus, UAM (a través de sus colecciones Margen de poesía de la revista *Casa del Tiempo*, y Molinos de Viento) y CONACULTA (en sus series Práctica Mortal, Los Cincuenta, y Fondo Editorial Tierra Adentro). [JS]

CENTROAMÉRICA

La revisión de este período revela hasta qué punto en Centroamérica las tradiciones poéticas heredadas de la vanguardia han dejado de constituir el único horizonte posible. Así lo indica la vigorosa consolidación de poetas jóvenes anticanónicos y el surgimiento de colectivos poéticos que, desentendiéndose del exteriorismo de los años 60, se proponen dar a conocer la poesía de las últimas dos décadas del siglo XX. Entre las poéticas más representativas de este giro operado en la poesía centroamericana destacan los costarricenses Luis Chávez, María Montero, Oswaldo Sauma, y José María Zonta; los guatemaltecos Humberto Ak'abal, Gerardo Guinea Diez, y Juan Sobalvarro, y la panameña Mireya Hernández.

Hay que observar que esta explosión anticanónica coexiste con la publicación de autores canónicos cuyos textos sin duda han de tener hondas repercusiones en la historia literaria latinoamericana. De particular importancia es la aparición de *Cartas desconocidas de Rubén Darío 1882–1916*, epistolario que reúne 250 cartas personales, en su mayoría desconocidas o inéditas (ítem **3806**). La compilación, cronología, y selección está a cargo de José Jirón Terán, Julio Valle Castillo, y Jorge Eduardo Arellana. También importante es la aparición de *Miguel Angel Asturias, raíz y destino: poesía inédita, 1917–1924* (volumen que divulga textos no canonizados del escritor guatemalteco) (ítem **3773**) y *El Nicán-Náuat*, de Pablo Antonio Cuadra (poemario que, inscrito en la tradición indigenista inaugurada por Ernesto Cardenal, se propone una re-escritura de la historia destinada a resarcir la indignidad en que han caído las culturas indígenas (ítem **3803**).

Entre las antologías que registra este período, vale la pena mencionar la provocadora *Poesía de fin de siglo Nicaragua-Costa Rica*, compilada por Adriano Corrales Arias, Marta Leonor González y Juan Sobalvarro (ítem **3759**). Destaca también la aparición de *Poesía turrialbeña, 1960–1999*, compilada por Erick Gil Salas, cuyo objetivo es mostrar el rol de los poetas turrialbeños en el cambio de piel de la poesía costarricense (ítem **3763**). [EM]

EL CARIBE

Según termina el siglo XX, la producción poética en el Caribe subraya una constancia: nada altera lo que ha venido pasando desde los ochenta. Por un lado, la producción cubana se mantiene dentro del espacio ya establecido por los llamados poetas "nuevos y novísimos." Por el otro, la producción dominicana y puertorriqueña, a la vez que engendra nuevas voces, se mantiene circunscrita a las poéticas establecidas. Parecería que, cautelosa, la poesía, siempre indagadora, se autocontiene en sus formas.

Entre lo establecido, cabe destacar de la producción cubana la publicación de unos poemas inéditos en prosa de Dulce María Loynaz (ítem **3861**), al igual que, por un lado, la antología poética de Cintio Vitier publicada en Venezuela (ítem **3950**), y, por el otro, la edición conmemorativa de los 30 años del poemario de Heberto Padilla (ítem **3895**) y la antología de Fina García Marruz (ítem **3824**). En cuanto a las voces más nuevas, habría que señalar el poemario filosófico-poético de Zoé Valdés (ítem **3940**); la propuesta entre la comunicación y el hermetismo de Carlos Augusto Alfonso Barroso (ítem **3770**); y la evocación esperanzadora de Roberto Friol (ítem **3822**).

En cuanto a la poesía dominicana establecida, cabe destacar la antología publicada en Argentina sobre la poesía afroantillana y social de Manuel del Cabral (ítem **3789**), al igual que la rearticulación de la llamada "poesía sorprendida" que hace uno de sus integrantes, Mariano Lebrón Saviñón (ítem **3854**), así como la propuesta de Manuel Rueda en torno a lo hatiano en el contexto dominicano (ítem **3917**). De las nuevas voces, cabe destacar la fuga hacia lo inasible de Basilio Belliard (ítem **3782**), el planteamiento de lo erótico de Adrián Javier (ítem **3847**), y el juego entre el amor y la nostalgia de Hugo Tolentino Dipp (ítem **3931**).

En la poesía puertorriqueña establecida, se recuperan unos poemas inéditos de Antonio Pérez Pierret, poeta modernista (ítem **3901**); una de las voces de la poesía de los setenta, Jan Martínez, publica una selección de su obra (ítem **3866**), y, desde la poesía de la diáspora nuevayorquina, Julio Marzán plantea un regreso al pasado sin nostalgia (ítem **3869**). Entre las voces más nuevas, está la reivindicación del amor lesbiano del poemario de Lilliana Ramos Collado (ítem **3910**), la respuesta al universo de la teoría posestructuralista que plantea Aurea María Sotomayor (ítem **3928**), y, la más nueva de estas voces, un poeta con mucho futuro, el diálogo entre el caos y la esperanza que plantea Elidio La Torre Lagares (ítem **3850**).

En cuanto a las antologías temáticas, cabe señalar las tres que publica Manuel de la Puebla: sobre ecología y poesía (ítem **3974**), sobre el perfil femenino en Puerto Rico (ítem **3976**) y sobre la madre en el mundo hispanoparlante (ítem **3983**). Hay que mencionar la antología de poetas cubanos marginados de Francisco J. Peñas Bermejo (ítem **3982**) y la que Fiume Gómez Sánchez publica sobre el concepto de patria entre dominicanos (ítem **3981**). [FC]

COLOMBIA Y VENEZUELA

En el período que aquí se cubre las transformaciones más notables de la poesía de Colombia y Venezuela se localizan no tanto en el dominio de lo artístico como en la crisis general del estado que afecta a lo que Pierre Bourdieu denomina "campo literario." Si ninguna renovación memorable se percibe en la orientación estética, con la continuidad de obras ya establecidas (las de Eugenio Montejo (ítem **3875**) o Juan Liscano (ítem **3857**)—recientemente fallecido, cuya poesía se divulga ahora en Colombia) o la recuperación justa de títulos importantes que la precariedad editorial de la región habían convertido en rarezas (*El cuerpo de ella* de Jotamario Arbeláez (ítem **3848**) o *Los poemas de la ofensa* de Jaime Jaramillo Escobar (ítem **3846**)), en lo que concierne al acceso de autores al mercado cultural o a cualquier espacio que les permita acumular capital y poder tangibles o simbólicos la situación se ha hecho visiblemente ardua, cuando no desesperanzadora. La larga guerra civil encubierta que aflige a Colombia desde hace varios decenios ha mantenido los medios de divulgación literaria en manos de las élites tradicionales, disminuyendo el número de lectores y dispersando en el exterior a los escritores cuya clase social no les permite permanecer en su país.

En Venezuela, de manera más dramática por el contraste con la bonanza petrolera de los 1960–70, la situación caótica de la economía, al reflejarse en la desorientación política de la mayoría de la población, con una demagogización circense e irrelista de la izquierda y una radicalización de los sectores más reaccionarios de la derecha, ha alterado la lógica del mundo literario de los años precedentes, inmovilizando el aparato editorial del estado, antes admirable: Monte Ávila, después de una época de revitalización prometedora en la que Rafael Arráiz Lucca logró agilizar tanto la producción como la distribución, a fines de los 1990 y principios de los 2000 se encuentra al borde de la bancarrota; Fundarte se muestra incapaz de recuperar su antigua vitalidad; la Biblioteca Ayacucho ha reducido drásticamente sus ediciones e, incluso, ha postergado la publicación de títulos de clásicos continentales para ceder lugar en sus colecciones a poetas mediocres vinculados a las esferas oficiales. No muy distinta es la situación de las publicaciones universitarias o académicas dedicadas a la investigación en el terreno de la poesía. Como consecuencia de todo lo anterior, los autores se han visto en la necesidad de recurrir a editoriales "independientes," de fines encomiables, pero, por limitaciones económicas que entorpecen la publicidad y la circulación, destinadas a minorías (mucho más que en otros tiempos) y condenadas al desconocimiento internacional. Pequeña Venecia, aún activa, sigue siendo, pese a los obstáculos, una empresa intelectual modelo, no sólo en su país, sino en toda Latinoamérica. [MG]

BOLIVIA Y ECUADOR

La producción bibliográfica de la poesía boliviana y ecuatoriana de este período podría ser vista, en términos generales, según tres tipos de publicaciones: en primer lugar, reediciones y ediciones póstumas de autores consagrados ya fallecidos que ofrecen la posibilidad de una relectura desde una perspectiva temporal contemporánea; en segundo lugar, nuevas publicaciones, re-impresiones o antologías personales de autores ya vigentes; y en tercer lugar, poemarios de autores nuevos y no conocidos hasta ahora.

En Bolivia, la publicación de un homenaje a Franz Tamayo (1879--1956) es un signo positivo de la vigencia de este poeta y pensador de indudable valor e importancia para la cultura y el pensamiento de la primera mitad del siglo XX en su país (ítem **3821**). Ese volumen reúne textos de poetas que, por otra parte, se destacaron con obra propia en la segunda mitad del mismo siglo. Esta publicación es un reconocimiento implícito de la autoridad y elevada calidad literaria del homenajeado. Tamayo, como poeta, es un caso singular por las cualidades de su poesía. A partir de su participación en la corriente modernista hispanoamericana, su expresión poética desarrolló un estilo muy personal en una decena de libros publicados entre 1898 y 1947. Poesía profundamente reflexiva no ha merecido aún un estudio apropiado a su dimensión, aunque, como este homenaje lo demuestra, ha sido inspiración y modelo para muchos poetas bolivianos del siglo XX.

Otro homenaje póstumo constituye la publicación del libro de romances del historiador y narrador Hernando Sanabria Fernández (1909–86), aunque este homenaje tiene carácter oficial pues el libro apareció en la colección del Fondo Editorial Municipal de la ciudad de Santa Cruz (ítem **3920**). Los textos recopilados en este volumen—más de un centenar de romances escritos en más de 40 años— demuestran la voluntad para el cultivo de una expresión poética ligada a la tradición e historia de su país.

Poetas con vigencia actual en la literatura boliviana se han dado a la tarea de seleccionar textos de su propia obra, como Borda Leaño (ítem **3785**), Wiethüchter (ítem **3951**), y Suárez Arauz (ítem **3764**). Este ejercicio de autolectura y autovaloración no deja de tener rasgos implícitos de autocrítica que pueden orientar mejor el estudio interesado en esas obras. Borda Leaño, además, reafirma su interés por el acontecer político y social de América Latina con su poemario inspirado en el guerrillero Che Guevara. Por su parte, el libro de Suárez Arauz sorprende por su alta y renovada calidad poética que se incorpora con distinción al repertorio de la poesía latinoamericana de la posmodernidad.

Entre la poesía boliviana escrita por autores nuevos, se destaca el poemario de Aquím Chávez, presentado por el poeta consagrado Pedro Shimose (ítem **3771**). También se distinguen las publicaciones de Mac Lean Estrada, y Villena Alvarado (ítems **3862** y **3949**). En su conjunto estos textos son heterogéneos y hay que esperar nuevas publicaciones de estos jóvenes antes de intentar señalar características que puedan definir el estilo y los temas de este grupo en formación.

En el Ecuador también despunta una publicación póstuma y de homenaje a Gonzalo Escudero (1903–71), uno de los poetas ecuatorianos más importantes del siglo XX (ítem **3816**). Esta publicación representa la obra completa pues, además de los ocho poemarios conocidos, incluye dos volúmenes inéditos. Poesía de elaboración rigurosa y de constante actitud reflexiva, la obra de Escudero es una de las más importantes no solo de su país, sino del proceso de la modernidad poética de Hispanoamérica, pues muestra una evolución constante a través de cincuenta años, desde su comienzos en el período vanguardista.

Poetas consagrados de este país también se han dado a la tarea de reeditar su obra en selecciones antológicas, con una intención clara de depurar textos ya publicados. Entre estos casos están Adoum, Estrella y Preciado. El primero conmemora cincuenta años de escritura con un volumen que selecciona textos de los siete poemarios publicados en las últimas cinco décadas. El segundo retomó un poemario publicado en 1989 para revisarlo, ampliarlo y presentarlo otra vez con un título diferente. El tercero, en un gesto similar, volvió a dos poemarios publicados en 1993 y 1996 para corregirlos y republicarlos en un volumen único, con el cual, además, desconoce la primera edición de los poemarios revisados. Estos tres poetas comparten afinidades por su preocupación por la realidad social y la historia ecuatoriana. Adoum (ítem **3767**) amplía su preocupación hacia las condiciones generales de las naciones latinoamericanas, mientras Estrella (ítem **3817**) se remonta hasta la historia colonial de su país, y Preciado (ítem **3907**) asume la denuncia y protesta por las condiciones de la población afroecuatoriana.

Dentro de la poesía joven de este país merece mención especial la obra de poetisas, bien representadas en esta oportunidad por Laso (ítem **3853**) y Gordon-Vailakis (ítem **3835**). La primera, ya conocida por dos poemarios previos, cultiva una expresión de sensualidad delicada y original. La segunda, que presenta su primera colección de textos poéticos, muestra una clara conciencia femenina desde la cual critica y rechaza los papeles tradicionales asignados por la sociedad a la mujer. Entre los jóvenes varones se destaca Báez, con una obra prolífica de calidad, definida por discursos poéticos organizados desde perspectivas que imponen unidad y homogeneidad. Sus libros no son colecciones de textos heterogéneos y dispersos, sino elaborados desde posiciones que unifican y globalizan aspectos temáticos, expresivos y de géneros literarios. [ORR]

PERU

Aunque es casi imposible elaborar un comentario general de la poesía peruana, es posible decir, antes que nada, que la poesía continúa siendo una actividad literaria importante dentro de la literatura peruana y su presencia es notable también fuera del país, como se pone en evidencia en los premios internacionales que algunos escritores han recibido en años recientes: Blanca Varela y Eduardo Chirinos (ítem 3973). En relación al mercado peruano, es posible decir que la economía no ha afectado seriamente la publicación de libros de poesía y hasta casi se podría sostener que una crisis más o menos sostenida ha tenido el efecto contrario. Sin embargo, pese a que la población general del Perú ha aumentado, como es de amplio conocimiento, las tiradas de las ediciones no necesariamente aumentan. Hay una gran variedad dentro de este campo—en términos de estilo, autores, filiaciones, etc.—de tal manera que han encontrado en éste cabida tanto escritores/as que saben su oficio y lo cultivan profesionalmente, como espontáneos/as a los/las que les ha bastado la inspiración, y otros/as que lo hacen de manera regular, acumulando incluso una producción considerable, pero que no han logrado por eso llegar a destacar por lo menos en los estudios de la crítica. Al mismo tiempo, diferentes casas editoriales han hecho posible la continua circulación de cuidadas, bien presentadas y confiables ediciones de poetas cuyos trabajos literarios han estado agotados por bastante tiempo, haciendo disponibles incluso ediciones completas o críticas. Tanto casas editoriales de reconocida trayectoria como otras, más bien pequeñas y poco conocidas, han realizado esfuerzos extraordinarios para mantener la vitalidad de este tipo de expresión literaria que no puede competir con las posibilidades económicas que favorecen, por ejemplo, narradores. En contados casos, instituciones financieras han hecho importantes contribuciones en el área editorial con elegantes y casi lujosas ediciones que, quizás debido a ello, son de difícil acceso y tienen una circulación bastante circunscrita, no obstante, son sumamente valiosas desde un punto de vista académico. En cuanto a la crítica literaria de poesía, ésta ha contribuido con interesantes estudios, sobre todo comparativos. También ha revisado la recepción de escritores consagrados y trabajos considerados canónicos. Puede decirse que actualmente es posible considerar como la poesía más interesante aquella que experimenta con tradiciones literarias y convenciones que no manifiestan ninguna ansiedad respecto a la continua presencia e influencia de escritores reconocidos y venerados. Se ha llegado a ese punto sin cuestionar arbitrariamente el trabajo de poetas destacados como los recientemente fallecidos Washington Delgado y Adolfo Westphalen. Todo lo contrario, la nueva poesía se está haciendo de un espacio propio sin descuidar las contribuciones de poetas que les antecedieron. Para bien de la literatura peruana, continua habiendo siempre una *nueva* poesía que se vincula y diferencia de sus predecesores por más respeto que les tenga. [GP]

CHILE

La poesía chilena confirma su valor literario por la diversidad de publicaciones del momento. Estas tanto ayudan a solidificar un corpus textual canónico como confirman el trabajo de décadas de varios autores y las múltiples y válidas opciones de escritura por las cuales los poetas más recientes han estado optando.

En términos de los poetas mayores del siglo XX, que determinaron la vitalidad del corpus poético chileno, en *Poesías completas* encontramos la publicación cuidadosa de todos los libros de poemas de Gabriela Mistral realizada por Jaime Quezada (ítem 3872); también el interés crítico de Nain Nómez vuelve a resaltar la compleja, díscola situación cultural de Pablo de Rokha en *Poesías inéditas* (ítem 3915). A lo anterior, se suma la importante publicación del tercer tomo de las *Obras completas* de Pablo Neruda que da cuenta de la obra póstuma del poeta en una cuidadosa edición de Hernán Loyola (ítem 3884).

Por otra parte, el libro *Obra selecta* reafirma la presencia decisiva de la poesía de Gonzalo Rojas que, en vez de amoldarse a una fórmula de mecanismos consabidos, ha revitalizado sus esfuerzos y desplegado un incesante retorno a la intensidad y exactitud de la visión poética durante los últimos años (ítem **3914**).

De los poetas que comienzan a publicar a partir de la segunda mitad del siglo XX, destacan los siguientes libros: *A peor vida* de Armando Uribe, por su contundente escritura epigramática que consolida una escéptica visión de la realidad cotidiana (ítem **3938**); *Vida probable* de Omar Lara, por ser una antología inteligente y sensible de sus mejores poemas (ítem **3852**); y *Suma alzada* de Manuel Silva Acevedo, por llevar a cabo una meticulosa selección de poemas en que el horror se aúna a una visión religiosa de corte trágico que confirma su contribución a la poesía chilena (ítem **3925**).

Destacan en el período los siguientes libros de poetas más recientes: Itaca de Tomás Harris, por su renovada exploración de un mundo pesadillesco que se fusiona a una visión desilusionada de corte posmoderno (ítem **3838**); la recopilación *Mandar al diablo al infierno* (ítem **3897**) de Sergio Parra por su descarnada visión de la experiencia de un sujeto al margen de la sociedad del éxito; el libro Carnal (ítem **3906**) de Nadia Prado por la complejidad y densidad retórica con que explora una fuerte subjetividad autocrítica; y el libro de Manuel Vicuña *Sin pieles ni cebos* por su precisión y capacidad de sugerencia plástica desprovista de ampulosidades (ítem **3946**).

Las recopilaciones de libros llevadas a cabo por sus propios autores dan cuenta de un trabajo progresivo y consistente con formulaciones autónomas y complementarias dentro del espectro de posibilidades de la poesía chilena contemporánea. En este caso debemos destacar a Oscar Hahn, con *Antología retroactiva* (ítem **3837**); Manuel Silva Acevedo con *Suma alzada* (ítem **3925**); Javier Campos con *El astronauta en llamas* (ítem **3791**) y Sergio Parra con *Mandar al diablo al infierno* (ítem **3897**). [OS]

ARGENTINA, URUGUAY Y PARAGUAY

No ha sido éste un período distinguido en la poesía paraguaya. La producción poética y de investigación es escasa y de poco valor.

El balance de la producción poética y editorial argentina es altamente positivo. Dentro de las recopilaciones y muestras generales, sobresale la antología *Siete poetas surrealistas* preparada por Javier Cofreces (ítem **3969**). Además de la reafirmación del protagonismo de Aldo Pellegrini en este grupo y la caracterización de las principales revistas o medios de difusión del mismo, el análisis de Cofreces es una sugerente aproximación a los vínculos y distancias entre el surrealismo argentino y el europeo. Aunque de criterio selectivo debatible, la muestra de Antonio Aliberti, *Poesía argentina de fin de siglo*, tiene esencialmente el mérito de ofrecer un espectro bastante amplio de la producción más reciente (ítem **3958**).

La actividad poética de voces de reconocida trayectoria como de otras de promisorios valores también ha sido muy apreciable. La obra completa o extensamente recopilada de varios poetas argentinos ya consagrados fue objeto de encomiables ediciones. De ellas, sobresalen *Elegía de Alondra*, de Baldomero Fernández Moreno (ítem **3819**), y las recopilaciones de la obra de Evaristo Carriego (ítem **3794**), Joaquín O. Giannuzzi (ítem **3831**), José Pedroni (ítem **3899**), César Fernández Moreno (ítem **3820**), Edgar Bayley (ítem **3780**), y Néstor Perlongher (ítem **3902**). La obra de Juan Gelman continúa siendo objeto de difusión, esta vez mediante la edición de una nueva *Antología poética* (ítem **3827**). Con prólogo de este poeta argentino aparecen también la antología *Poemas de batalla* de Francisco Urondo (ítem **3939**) y *Despedida de los ángeles* de Miguel Ángel Bustos (ítem **3788**). Gelman, que había sido distinguido con el Premio Nacional de Literatura en 1997, fue galardonado durante este periodo con el Premio Juan Rulfo (2000). También merece destacarse la edición antológica *Relámpagos de lo invisible* (ítem **3891**) de la recientemente fallecida Olga Orozco (1999) quien también había sido merecedora del Premio Juan Rulfo en 1998. El obra de Arturo Carrera (ítem **3792**) continúa reafirmando su importancia.

Dentro de la producción poética uruguaya caben destacar los volúmenes de Jorge Arbeleche (item **3772**), Víctor Cunha (ítem **3804**), y Rafael Gomensoro (ítem **3832**). [LU]

ANTHOLOGIES

3749 El aliento en las hojas: otras voces de la poesía boliviana. Recopilación de Eduardo Mitre. La Paz: Plural Editores, 1998. 226 p.: bibl. (Plural/poesía)

Antología de siete poetas bolivianos contemporáneos: Matilde Casazola (1943), Norah Zapata Prill (1943), Blanca Wiethüchter (1947), Humberto Quino Márquez (1950), Guillermo Bedregal García (1954–74), María Soledad Quiroga (1957) y Antonio Rojas (1963). La selección está precedida por siete artículos del compilador sobre la obra de cada uno de los poetas elegidos. Son artículos principalmente impresionistas y que no revelan un estudio profundo de los autores elegidos. Destacan por su calidad los textos de las poetas Casazola y Zapata Prill. El compilador afirma que este libro es continuación de otras dos antologías de poesía bolivianas también editadas y publicadas (1988 y 1994) por él mismo, con selecciones de poetas pertenecientes a periodos anteriores. Agrega que con la nueva antología espera "fundamentar una intuición: la continuidad de nuestra poesía como una crítica implícita al violento y fragmentado curso de la historia política del país." [ORR]

3750 Antología de la poesía joven chilena: poesía de fin de siglo. Selección, prólogo y notas de Francisco Véjar. Santiago, Chile: Editorial Universitaria, 1999. 156 p.: bibl., ill. (Literatura)

Selección de 28 poetas nacidos entre 1964–75. En esta antología hay valiosas contribuciones que indagan en el discurso de largo aliento, el poema evocativo con alusiones culturales claves, las fabulaciones borgianas, la torsión existencial de tono expresionista, o el desenfado punk. [OS]

3751 Charpentier, Jorge. La pasión inconclusa: antología. San José: Editorial Costa Rica, 1999. 228 p.: bibl.

Antologado por el propio autor, este volumen reúne la obra de un destacado representante de la segunda vanguardia poética costarricense, iniciada en la década de los cincuenta y cuyos integrantes (Eunice Odio, Mario Picado, Alfredo Sancho, Ana Antillón, Raúl Morales, Virginia Grütter, Carlos Rafael Duverrán) ya forman parte del canon nacional. El volumen antologa poemarios publicados entre 1955–97 y lo acompañan, a manera de prólogo, tres notas introductorias escritas por Alfonso Chase, Víctor Hugo Fernández, y Carlos Francisco Monge. Breves pero sugerentes, estas notas sitúan la poesía de Charpentier en el panorama nacional como el resultado de una tensión entre la "ética del solipsismo" que inicialmente asumieron los poetas de la segunda vanguardia, y una urgencia de comunicación que se hizo imperiosa conforme avanzaba el siglo, hasta encontrar su más lograda expresión en la poesía social de los 60. Los poemas antologados responden a estas apreciaciones y muestran los haceres de una poética íntima y solipsista que lucha por conquistar dimensión dialógica. Cuando mejor lo logra es en el último poemario, significativamente titulado *El abuelo en el espejo* (1997). [EM]

3752 Cíbola: cinco poetas del norte. México: UNAM, Coordinación de Humanidades, 1999. 181 p.: ill. (El ala del tigre)

Selecciones de Jorge Humberto Chávez (1959), Alfredo Espinosa (1954), Gabriela Borunda (1973), José Joaquín Cosío (1962), y Rogelio Treviño (1953), todos nacidos o residentes en Chihuahua. Salvo en el primer caso, esta poesía no delata el sitio donde se vive; todos incluyen poemas amorosos o de ausencia. En el último poeta sobresalen ciertos ecos de lo oriental. [JS]

3753 Fragmentos fantasmas: 1988–1996.
Recopilación de Cristián Marcelo. San José: Ministerio de Cultura, Juventud y Deportes, Dirección General de Cultura, Dirección de Publicaciones, 2000. 118 p.

En las décadas de los 80 y 90 la poesía costarricense se caracterizó por el surgimiento de innumerables grupos y talleres poéticos que desestabilizaron el canon nacional con la irrupción de voces nuevas, antihegemónicas e iconoclastas. El volumen que se reseña ofrece una muestra representativa de la producción poética de uno de esos grupos, denominado "R.I.P." (Requiescat in pace) y liderado por Francisco Sierra y Manuel Coto. Fundado en 1987 y disuelto en 1996, el grupo funcionó al margen del sistema literario nacional y publicó intensamente en revistas de América Latina y España. La modalidad poética que asumieron sus integrantes queda definida por el término "hiperbarroquismo," que en palabras del mismo Sierra apela a la imagen que se sabe imagen, fragmento de posibles historias. Cristián Marcelo antologa a los cinco integrantes del grupo (Francisco Sierra, Manuel Coto, Carlos Correa, Fernando Marcial, William Zúñiga) y deja constancia de los ángulos menos frecuentados de la poesía escrita en Costa Rica a fines del siglo XX. [EM]

3754 Laude madre. Trujillo, Peru: Agrupación de Escritoras Norteñas del Perú, 1997. 122 p.

Second publication by the Northern Peruvian Writers Association. All poems, narrations, and musical compositions presented here are intended to be an homage to the mother. Brings together poems written by more than 40 women poets and almost 10 narrators. Scores and lyrics for the two musical compositions are also included. As the editors point out, the volume was not intended as a collection written for literary critics. [GP]

3755 La mejor poesía gauchesca: antología rioplatense. Selección, prólogo y notas de Julio Imbert. Buenos Aires: Ameghino Editora, 1999. 394 p.

La selección, que incluye no sólo los nombres consagrados de la poesía gauchesca del siglo XIX (Hidalgo, Ascasubi, del Campo,

Hernández, Lussich, Obligado) sino también a otros autores más contemporáneos (Silva Valdés, Yamandú Rodríguez, Atahualpa Yupanki, León Benarós), está dirigida a un lector no especializado. Por este criterio, se incorporan sinopsis argumentales de algunas obras, reseñas biobibliográficas y un "glosario esencial" de términos. [LU]

3756 Memoria del sol: nueva poesía iqueña.
Selección, bibliografía y notas de Jesús Cabel. Lima: Editorial San Marcos, 1997. 127 p.: ill. (Col. Huarango; 1)

Described as the "definitive" anthology of poetry written by Ica writers; Ica is a dept. south of Lima. The prologue, by Cabel, is entitled "Praise of Valdelomar and/or Itinerary to Read the Poets of Ica." Includes an interesting essay about the predicaments confronting regional writers. Also contains bibliographic information for the writers included in the anthology. [GP]

3757 Norte y sur de la poesía iberoamericana: Argentina, Brasil, Chile, Colombia, España, México, Venezuela. Coordinación de Consuelo Triviño. Madrid: Editorial Verbum, 1997. 547 p. (Verbum poesía)

El objetivo primordial de esta antología es la difusión de poetas cuya obra se publica en la segunda mitad del siglo XX. La validez de establecer un diálogo intercontinental a través de la poesía hubiera merecido, sin embargo, un criterio de selección más claro y coherente. [LU]

3758 Panamá: poesía escogida. Selección y prólogo de Aristides Martínez Ortega. 2. ed. San José: EDUCA, 1998. 187 p. (Col. Séptimo día)

Hay que admitir la poca circulación de la poesía panameña y el poco conocimiento que en general de ella se tiene. La colección reseñada cumple entonces una doble función: dar a conocer la producción poética de Panamá fuera de sus fronteras nacionales, y contribuir a la historia literaria de ese país con una muestra que permite apreciar los distintos momentos constitutivos de su poesía. Martínez Ortega ya había publicado antes *La modalidad vanguardista en la poesía panameña* (1973) y *Las generaciones de poetas panameños* (1992), donde recurría al método generacional y a la perspectiva hispánica (que deja sin consideración el amplio caudal indígena que incide en esta poesía) para abordar el corpus poético panameño desde sus más tempranas manifestaciones, que en Panamá remiten al estilo neoclásico. En este libro la modalidad es la misma, pero el objetivo está dirigido a captar las preferencias poéticas de cada generación a partir de la tercera generación romántica, que en opinión de Martínez Ortega marca el momento en que la poesía panameña se regulariza y empieza a adquirir carácter de producción poética nacional. Con este principio ordenador, el lector encontrará una muestra que más que exhaustiva es el resultado apretado de una investigación. La muestra arranca con la tercera generación romántica (representada únicamente por Amelia Denis de Icaza) y concluye con la segunda generación vanguardista (representada por Manuel Orestes Nieto). El aporte de este trabajo se aprecia también en su capacidad para mostrar las dimensiones más concurridas de la poesía panameña: la experiencia de una geografía violentada y de una historia de despojos. [EM]

3759 Poesía de fin de siglo Nicaragua-Costa Rica. Recopilación de Adriano Corrales Arías; Marta Leonor González; y Juan Sobalvarro. San José: Ediciones Perro Azul; Revista Fronteras; Revista 400 Elefantes, 2001. 164 p. (Col. de poesía)

El proyecto de componer esta muestra de fin de siglo se lo debemos a los editores de dos prestigiosas revistas centroamericanas: *Fronteras* (Costa Rica) y *400 Elefantes* (Nicaragua). El volumen se propone divulgar el trabajo poético producido en estos países durante los 80 y 90. Los poetas seleccionados nacieron entre 1952–78 y no todos cuentan con obra publicada. Comparten, sin embargo, un atributo común: replantear la función del artista y de la poesía en las castigadas sociedades contemporáneas. El objetivo de los compiladores recae en la idea de que no todo se detuvo en la década de los 60, con el triunfo del exteriorismo (cuyo eje fue Cardenal) y los últimos gestos vanguardistas (liderados por Coronel Urtecho y Pablo Antonio Cuadra), sino que surgieron, en Nicaragua y Costa Rica, profundas renovaciones poéticas con capacidad de cambiarle el rumbo a la poesía centroamericana. Profundamente anti-canónica, esta muestra recoge el gesto postutópico de la década de los 80 y la vocación antihegemónica de los 90. Actos no asumidos desde una idea de ruptura (como el mo-

dernismo) o experimentalismo (como el vanguardismo), sino más bien como síntoma de una poesía que se hace con independencia de criterios políticos y estéticos hegemónicos. El tiempo dirá si estas apuestas construyen efectivamente nuevos horizontes poéticos o si naufragan en el mar de las buenas intenciones. Por lo que atañe al presente, sólo cabe celebrar iniciativas como ésta. [EM]

3760 Poesía joven: veinticinco años de un premio literario. Selección, nota introductoria y prólogo de Eduardo Langagne y Juan Domingo Argüelles. Guadalajara, Mexico: Secretaría de Cultura del Gobierno de Jalisco, 1999. 173 p.: bibl.

Antología de los ganadores del Premio Nacional de Poesía Joven de México, de 1975–99. Con sede en Guadalajara, la distinción ayuda a comprender el panorama de la poesía de los jóvenes (definidos como menores de 30 años de edad) y la revelación de voces que después adquirirán mayor prestigio. En la lista de ganadores, encontramos nombres como Vicente Quirarte, José Manuel Pintado, Kyra Galván, y entre los más recientes, Luigi Amara y Julio Trujillo. Lamentablemente, el volumen recoge pocos poemas por poeta, lo que impide una apreciación seria, y termina por ser un simple gesto conmemorativo. [JS]

3761 Poesía modernista hispanoamericana y española: antología. Edición de Iván A. Schulman y Evelyn Picón Garfield. 2a. ed. San Juan: Editorial de la Univ. de Puerto Rico, PR., 1999. 384 p.: bibl.

El Estudio Preliminar que antecede esta antología comienza con una sintética discusión de la unidad de la crisis en el mundo hispánico de finales del siglo XIX tal como la planteara Federico de Onís en su consagrada definición de modernismo. A partir de allí, los autores pasan revista de la evolución de los conceptos de modernismo y modernidad y, más que fijar los límites temporales del modernismo, esbozan los vínculos de éste con el desarrollo de la cultura, lo cual resulta en una propuesta más sugestiva. La selección antológica es representativa de las múltiples manifestaciones estilísticas del discurso modernista y se agregan, en esta segunda edición, tres poetas puertorriqueños: José de Jesús Domínguez (1843–98), José de Diego y Martínez (1866–1918), y

Luis Llorens Torres (1876–1944). Para el comentario de la primera edición, ver *HLAS 52: 3995*. [LU]

3762 Poesía popular mexicana. Selección y prólogo de Luis Miguel Aguilar. México: CONACULTA; Cal y Arena, 1999. 499 p.: bibl. (Los Imprescindibles)

Excelente antología que recoge la poesía culta (predominan los modernistas) que se ha hecho popular; es decir, en lugar de incluir canciones de Agustín Lara o José Alfredo Jiménez, o los corridos, albures y adivinanzas, Aguilar se dedica a seleccionar textos apropiados por el gusto popular (en general, aprendidos de memorias y declamados en escuelas y/o eventos sociales). No sólo incluye poetas mexicanos, sino también extranjeros que son declamados como si fueran mexicanos. Prólogo útil e interesante. [JS]

3763 Poesía turrialbeña, 1960–1999: antología. Recopilación de Erick Gil Salas. San José: Editorial Univ. Estatal a Distancia, 2000. 172 p.: ill.

En las últimas décadas la poesía costarricense viene experimentando la contundente búsqueda de un estilo y de una estética que se adapten a las realidades y exigencias del siglo XX. Turrialba y los poetas turrialbeños tuvieron (y todavía tienen) un rol protagónico en este cambio de piel de la poesía costarricense. La primera generación de poetas turrialbeños, conocida como Grupo de Turrialba, venció el cerco provincial y se hizo oír en San José, donde se puso a la vanguardia del movimiento poético e intelectual de los 60 e inauguró la poesía social. Es la generación de Jorge Debravo, Marco Aguilar, y Laureano Albán. La antología de Gil Salas reúne los mejores aportes de este grupo y también la producción de poetas turrialbeños posteriores, pertenecientes a la generación de los 70, 80, y 90, entre ellos Jorge Treval, Francisco Delgado, y Yenory Bonilla. [EM]

3764 Poeta Movima. Loén: amazonía, amnesis, América: selección de textos. Nicomedes Suárez Araúz. Santa Cruz, Bolivia: N. Suárez Araúz, 1997. 177 p.: ill.

Poesía sorprendente por su alta calidad y variedad, cuyo autor es un poeta original aunque lamentablemente poco divulgado. Nicomedes Suárez Araúz (1946), que también es catedrático universitario en los EE.UU., ha unido su experiencia de investigador del arte y de la literatura a su talento de poeta, con lo cual logra un discurso de rasgos sorprendentes, y que representa muy bien las tendencias de la poesía hispanoamericana de la posmodernidad. El libro, que lleva el sello del Fondo Editorial del Gobierno Municipal de Santa Cruz, Bolivia, es una antología con selecciones de cinco publicaciones anteriores de Suárez Araúz (*Cartas a la amnesia* (1974), *Los escribanos de Loén* (1974, 1982), *Caballo al anochecer* (1977), *El poema América* (1976), *Cinco poetas amazónicos* (1995)) y un volumen inédito (*Poemas y protemas*). La obra poética de Suárez Araúz sigue la escasa tradición de los textos y autores apócrifos, que ha sido recuperada por muy pocos y excelentes poetas hispanoamericanos de finales del siglo XX. Las dos primeras publicaciones de este poeta boliviano representan muy bien esa tendencia, surgida como una consecuencia de la invalidez del concepto de autor. Este rasgo, propio de las últimas décadas del siglo pasado y que ayudan a definir la posmodernidad en las letras latinoamericanas, resuelve, además, uno de los mayores tópicos de la literatura de este continente y que se refiere al enfrentamiento con la propia identidad latinoamericana. [ORR]

3765 Romancero nicaragüense. Selección e introducción de Roberto Aguilar Leal. Managua: Ediciones Distribuidora Cultural, 1998. 70 p.

El Romancero nicaragüense es probablemente uno de los textos menos conocidos de la literatura centroamericana. Recién en el siglo XIX viajeros europeos como Squier y Belly dieron noticia de la existencia de esta lírica popular que, en opinión de Pablo Antonio Cuadra, contiene los primeros trazos originales de la literatura nicaragüense. A principios del siglo XX, Anselmo Fletes Bolaños recopiló por primera vez estos cantares centroamericanos, refiriéndose a ellos con el nombre genérico de "cantares regionales." Posteriormente, fue el trabajo de Ernesto Mejía Sánchez el que formalizó el estudio y difusión de estas composiciones. En la década de los 40, Mejía Sánchez recopiló un corpus extenso de literatura popular que publicó en México con el título de *Romances y corridos nicaraguenses* (1946). El volumen que ahora presenta Aguilar es una muestra selectiva (ofrece únicamente una versión de entre las muchas que se tienen) de los romances y corridos recopilados por Mejía Sánchez, y de los cantares regionales que recopiló Fletes Bolaños. Es de esperar que esta publicación del Romancero nicaragüense despierte el interés de la crítica especializada y fortalezca la investigación de la tradición popular centroamericana. [EM]

BOOKS OF VERSE

3766 Acuña, Manuel. Obras: poesía y prosa. Edición, prólogo y notas de José Luis Martínez. México: Factoria Ediciones, 2000. 413 p.: bibl., ill. (La serpiente emplumada; 16)

Reconocido por su "Nocturno a Rosario," Acuña (México, 1849–73) es el poeta/suicida romántico que sigue declamándose a nivel popular. Esta edición (hecha originalmente en 1949) agrega nuevas pesquisas de Martínez, con lo que se asume que se consolida la versión definitiva de las obras completas de este escritor. [JS]

3767 Adoum, Jorge Enrique. Antología poética: 1949–1998. Madrid: Visor, 1998. 195 p. (Col. Visor de poesía; 404)

Este libro reúne una selección de la poesía publicada por su autor durante el pasado medio siglo. Esta antología de uno de los poetas ecuatorianos contemporáneos más importantes incluye textos de los siete libros publicados por Adoum—*Ecuador amargo* (1949), *Notas del hijo pródigo* (1953), *Relato del extranjero* (1955), *Los cuadernos de la tierra* (1952–62), *Yo me fui con tu nombre por la tierra* (1964), *Currículum mortis* (1968), *Prepoemas en postespañol* (1972)— aunque las selecciones en cada caso son excesivamente breves, con excepción de la serie de los *Cuadernos*, cuyo tema es la historia del Ecuador, particularmente en sus orígenes propios, y también hispánicos. Otra colección bien representada en la antología es la de 1968, cuyo texto refleja la condición social no sólo del Ecuador sino de las naciones latinoamericanas de los años 60. La poesía de Adoum, ciertamente, es un discurso que sabe expresar la condición incierta de las naciones latinoamericanas a causa de la condición política nacional e internacional. El libro incluye textos menos conocidos e inéditos como *El amor desenterrado* y otros poemas, *Cementerio personal* y *Textos dispersos*. [ORR]

3768 Ak'abal, Humberto. Gaviota y sueño: Venezia es un barco de piedra. Guatemala: Editorial Cultura, 2000. 30 p. (Colección Poesía guatemalteca. Serie Rafael Landívar; 24)

La obra de Humberto Ak'abal (Momostenango, Guatemala, 1952) es seguramente una de las expresiones más logradas de la poesía guatemalteca contemporánea. Sus libros, que gozan de una gran difusión nacional e internacional, cuentan ya con re-ediciones y han obtenido premios importantes, como el Quetzal de Oro (1993), el Premio Internacional de Poesía Blaise Cendrars (1997), y el Premio Continental Canto de América, UNESCO (1998). *Gaviota y sueño* es una breve colección de poemas escritos a raíz del encuentro con Venecia, ciudad que Ak'abal percibe como "irreal, encantada, mágica," y al mismo tiempo con capacidad para despertar "una nostalgia de cuchillo en el corazón." Se trata también del único libro que Ak'abal no escribió en lengua materna (Maya k'iché). [EM]

3769 Alfonso, Domingo. Vida que es angustia. La Habana: Ediciones Unión, 1998. 74 p. (Contemporáneos)

Dividido en dos secciones de diferente cronología (la primera escrita entre 1957–69; la segunda entre 1970–97), en este poemario lo cotidiano, por cuya presencia se destaca el poeta, coexiste con lo filosófico, que puede presentarse como la "Saga del tiempo," o la queja tácita que angustia. [FC]

3770 Alfonso Barroso, Carlos Augusto. Cabeza abajo. La Habana: Ediciones UNION, 1997. 91 p.

Ganador del premio "Julián del Casal" de 1997. Dividido en cinco partes, la poesía surge como el deseo de una comunicación que el propio lenguaje problematiza. Dramatizado el traspaso del mensaje, el hermetismo parece incidir en la soledad ("en la amalgama de recuerdos/no me acompaña nadie y sea eso la vida"). [FC]

3771 Aquim Chávez, Rosario. Detrás del Cristal. La Paz?: R. Aquim, 1997. 73 p.

Poemario primero de Aquim Chávez y que goza de una presentación del poeta boliviano consagrado Pedro Shimose. Aunque primero, este volumen no es, sin embargo, obra intelectual primeriza. Shimose informa que la autora, también boliviana, "ha tocado puerto en la poesía después de navegar por arduas corrientes de las teorías de la comunicación, la sociología y la filosofía. Algunos de sus trabajos ensayísticos versan, precisamente, sobre aspectos del pensamiento de Baudrillard, Derrida, Nietzsche, Deleuze, Guattari y Bataille." Estos datos permiten reconocer y entender la perspectiva de la autora en el contexto de las corrientes del pensamiento que han sido definidas como de la modernidad. Sus poemas son textos breves ordenados bajo cuatro temas generales: el amor, la ausencia, el olvido, y la tierra propia (como lugar de origen e identidad). Por encima de esos temas, sin embargo, los textos de esta poeta se caracterizan por una actitud contemplativa de espera, que no deja de ser esperanzada aunque bajo cierto asedio de la incertidumbre. Ciertamente, hay una oscilación entre la esperanza y la incertidumbre, lo que reflejaría la posición intelectual de la autora ubicada en un estado de transición entre la tradición y la modernidad. [ORR]

3772 Arbeleche, Jorge. El hilo de la lumbre. Prólogo y selección Gerardo Ciancio. Montevideo: Ediciones de la Plaza, 1998. 128 p.: bibl.

Este poemario es una clara muestra de "esa especie de moderno carpe diem" (Martha Canfield) que es la poesía del uruguayo Arbeleche por el rescate de la fugaz eternidad de las cosas que pueblan nuestro universo cotidiano a través de una escritura fundada y fundida con y en otras y un refinado lirismo. [LU]

3773 Asturias, Miguel Angel. Miguel Angel Asturias, raíz y destino: poesía inédita, 1917–1924. Guatemala: Editorial Artemis Edinter, 1999. 195 p.: bibl., ill. (Ensayos literarios)

Publicado en ocasión del centenario del nacimiento de Asturias (1899–1999), este volumen se propone la divulgación de textos no canonizados del escritor guatemalteco ganador del premio Nobel de Literatura 1967. Marco Vinicio Mejía brinda al lector la oportunidad de conocer de cerca al joven Asturias, fundamentalmente poeta, y anterior a su definitivo viaje a París, a mediados de 1924, cuando abandonó la poesía para optar de lleno por la narrativa. Este Asturias poeta es presentado como integrante de la generación de 1920, de la que surgieron las primeras vanguardias artístico-políticas guatemaltecas comprometidas con la utopía socialista que desde París emitía el Grupo Claridad (Anatole France y Henry Barbusse). Esta misma utopía era la que, por esos mismos años, compartían intelectuales latinoamericanos como Vasconcelos, Haya de la Torre, y Mariátegui. Inaugura el volumen un prólogo de Roberto Cabrera Padilla seguido por un extenso estudio crítico de Vinicio Mejía. En este estudio, se advierte que el descubrimiento de la poesía juvenil de Asturias más que a los científicos de la literatura busca a los buenos lectores. Se advierte también que esta producción poética no está a la altura de la obra posterior, pero que pese a ello merece ser apreciada como parte del proceso creativo asturiano. La última parte del libro contiene una muestra de poesía (en verso y en prosa) que permite apreciar el tránsito de un lenguaje de connotaciones románticas hacia uno de personalidad modernista y rasgos vanguardistas. Este proceso es particularmente evidente en el poema inédito *Los crepúsculos de la montaña* (escrito en el año 1917), que concluyó trágicamente con el terremoto del 25 de diciembre. Del horror de esa noche surgió uno de los mejores poemas del joven Asturias: "Noche sin Dios." [EM]

3774 Azcona Cranwell, Elizabeth. Antología poética. Buenos Aires: Fondo Nacional de las Artes, 1998. 144 p. (Poetas argentinos contemporáneos; 12)

La muestra aquí reunida abarca con justicia y representatividad la obra de esta poeta argentina (nacida en 1933) que comienza con *Capítulo sin presencia*. [LU]

3775 Báez, Marcelo. Hijas de fin de milenio: 1988–1996. Guayaquil, Ecuador: Manglar, 1997. 101 p.

Pocos libros de poesía gozan en la actualidad de una característica tan importante como es la unidad temática. El joven poeta ecuatoriano Báez (1969) ha invertido ocho años en reflexionar y escribir un centenar de textos dedicados al mar, a partir de experiencias vividas en lugares aledaños al archipiélago de las islas Galápagos. Este joven poeta, de indudable valor, reconoce, mediante dos epígrafes y una afirmación en el prólogo, la influencia de dos autores: Charles Darwin y Herman Melville. La contemplación del mar conduce a este autor a trascender sus propias percepciones y alcanzar dimensiones más amplias y profundas a partir de las imágenes del mar y del agua. El agua se convierte de ese modo en un símbolo de múltiples significaciones como origen mítico del mundo, o la existencia humana vista como una continua navegación, o comparable en su complejidad al lenguaje. No se trata de la recuperación del viejo tópico de Jorge Manrique (según el cual las aguas de la vida desembocan en el mar de la muerte), sino del testimonio de una experiencia personal y legítima. [ORR]

3776 Báez, Marcelo. Tan lejos, tan cerca. Quito: Editorial El Conejo, 1997? 158 p.

Los editores de este libro lo presentan como el ganador del "Segundo Premio, IV Bienal de Novela." Sin embargo, por una serie de valores implícitos en el discurso de los textos que lo configuran, puede ser leído como un libro de poesía. Su autor, el joven poeta ecuatoriano, no abandona su voz poética en el ejercicio de su escritura que en ciertos segmentos acude a la prosa y en otros al verso. Por otra parte, necesitado de una comunicación efectiva, el narrador poético instala permanentemente en la estructura de sus textos un receptor explícito. Así, estos textos devienen en cartas o locuciones de un interlocutor que monologa. Desde el punto de vista de los géneros literarios, Báez logra un acierto excepcional al unificarlos y borrar los límites prescritos para ellos por la retórica antigua y tradicional. Cada uno de los textos de este denso libro, por otra parte, es respuesta a un conjunto de enunciados transmitidos por diversos medios de comunicación masiva, desde canciones populares en inglés o castellano hasta citas de libros de varios autores. Báez articula de este modo una intertextualidad muy amplia y compleja que corresponde en su heterogeneidad a la instancia lingüística de la producción de su escritura. Este libro perfila muy bien los caracteres fundamentales de la literatura hispanoamericana de la posmodernidad. [ORR]

3777 Barrientos, Raúl. El balsero de Cucao. Santiago, Chile: Editorial Univ. de Santiago, 2000. 121 p. (Col. Humanidades. Poesía)

En el prólogo Grinor Rojo señala que:

"Barrientos es el último, y probablemente el más radical, de los surrealistas chilenos." Un poema completo hecho de fragmentos en que resalta la oscuridad onírica sin concesiones. [OS]

3778 Bartolomé, Efraín. Oficio: arder; obra poética, 1982–1997. México: UNAM, 1999. 546 p. (Poemas y ensayos)

Libro voluminoso que consolida a Bartolomé (Ocosingo, Chiapas, México, 1950) como uno de los poetas más importantes de su generación. El poeta se dio a conocer con *Ojo de jaguar* (1982), libro que no sólo canta a la naturaleza de la selva tropical chiapaneca, sino que además instaura una voz con convicción ecológica que hace cobrar conciencia del deterioro del medio ambiente. [JS]

3779 Basualto, Alejandra. Casa de citas. Santiago, Chile: LOM Ediciones, 2000. 85 p. (Col. Entre mares)

Usando el epígrafe como astucia intertextual, se confrontan diversos momentos conflictivos y de crecimiento de manera directa y sugerente. [OS]

3780 Bayley, Edgar. Obras. Presentación de Francisco Madariaga y prólogo de Rodolfo Alonso. Edición de Julia Saltzmann. Revisión y estudio preliminar de Daniel Freidemberg. Buenos Aires: Grijalbo Mondadori, 1999. 859 p.: bibl. (Clásicos Mondadori)

La cuidada edición de este volumen resulta un aporte invalorable para el estudio de Bayley (1919–90) pues completa las recopilaciones anteriores publicadas por Corregidor (1976) y el Centro Editor de América Latina (1983) con la incorporación de sus libros posteriores, poemas inéditos e inclusive ensayos y artículos sobre artes plásticas, teatro, y poesía. [LU]

3781 Bellessi, Diana. Sur. Buenos Aires: Libros de Tierra Firme, 1998. 123 p. (Col. de poesía Todos bailan)

Desde la publicación de "Destinos y propagaciones" (1970), la poesía de Bellessi (1946) parece ser una constante indagación por el sujeto y el espacio que lo rodea. En "Sur" se trata de un espacio poblado además por voces (Mistral, por ejemplo) de las que la poeta se nutre y por la que recupera una imagen del mundo a modo de toponimia poética. [LU]

3782 Belliard, Basilio. Diario del autó-
fago. Santo Domingo: Editora Búho,
1997. 53 p.

"No vivimos en el cuerpo / Vivimos
en lo que se va / En la nada del ahora." He
ahí una de las propuestas de este poemario:
ese ahora inasible que la poesía testimonia
como ausencia, una que condena al poeta a
desaparecer en las palabras que nunca le
pertenecen. [FC]

3783 Benedetti, Mario. Próximo prójimo:
1964–1965. Madrid: Visor, 1998. 53 p.
(Biblioteca Mario Benedetti; 5. Poesía) (Col.
Visor de poesía)

La reedición de este poemario de mediados de los años 60—recopilado también en
el volumen "Inventario I" (1980)—vuelve a
poner al alcance de los lectores la obra de
uno de los poetas más prolíficos, reconocidos, y estudiados del continente. [LU]

3784 Bignozzi, Juana. La ley tu ley. Notas
sobre Juana Bignozzi por Jorge Lafforgue. Prólogo por D.G. Helder. Buenos
Aires: Adriana Hidalgo editora, 2000. 278 p.
(La lengua. Obra reunida)

El libro reúne la obra anterior de Bignozzi, una de las fundadoras del grupo "El
Pan Duro," con excepción de sus dos primeros poemarios. La búsqueda y recreación de un espacio propio como casa o
patria y la preocupación por la fugacidad
del tiempo dan unidad a la obra poética
aquí presentada. [LU]

3785 Borda Leaño, Héctor. Las claves del
comandante: poesía. La Paz: Azul Editores, 1997. 73 p.: ill.

El contenido de este volumen es un
poema extenso, dividido en cinco partes, en
homenaje al Comandante guerrillero Che
Guevara, y cuya publicación se realiza para
conmemorar los 30 años de su asesinato. En
la presentación del poemario, su autor, el poeta Borda Leaño (1927) escribe: "a 30 años del
asesinato del Che y a 30 años de su 'derrota
militar,' el Comandante vive candente en el
corazón de las generaciones jóvenes, como
un verdadero símbolo de libertad e independencia." El texto es orientado y desarrolla su
discurso por la lectura de otro texto: el diario
de la campaña del Che en el territorio boliviano, particularmente en la región de Ñancahuazú, donde fue capturado y asesinado por
los militares bolivianos. El discurso del poeta

asume una función de crónica poética
cuya imaginación, a través de un lenguaje
adiestrado por las preocupaciones sociales,
trata de reconstruir el espacio, las acciones,
el pensamiento, y la emoción de la lucha
guerrillera en Bolivia y América Latina.
Este es un texto muy propio de la historia
política y social de la América Latina del
siglo XX. [ORR]

3786 Borda Leaño, Héctor. Poemas desban-
dados: antología mínima. La Paz:
Plural Editores, 1997. 189 p.

Importante publicación que reúne selecciones de siete poemarios de Borda Leaño,
uno de los poetas bolivianos contemporáneos
cuya vida y obra se han caracterizado por
la lucha social. Muy comprometido con la
historia del siglo XX latinoamericano, en el
que las revoluciones atrajeron a sus pueblos
como la solución más apropiada para elimi-
nar la injusticia y las desigualdades sociales,
Borda Leaño sufrió la cárcel y el exilio de los
regímenes militares dictatoriales porque su
voz poética se identificó con las clases trabajadoras de su país, especialmente los mineros
explotadores del estaño, expoliados irónica-
mente por las clases con poder económico y
político. Su poesía es sin duda una poesía social marcada por la historia de su país. En la
presentación de este libro, su autor escribe:
"La presente Antología ha sido escrita para
bolivianos, los temas son bolivianos, el
lenguajes es boliviano, la forma literaria
boliviana y la paciencia, la persistencia y
la humildad hasta la última letra del libro,
bolivianas." Sin embargo, y pese a la adver-
tencia del propio poeta, su obra trasciende
las fronteras nacionales pues muestra una
auténtica faceta de genuino humanismo
universal. [ORR]

3787 Bracho, Coral. La voluntad del ámbar.
México: Ediciones Era, 1998. 71 p. (Biblioteca Era)

Bracho (Ciudad de México, 1951) continúa explorando la sensualidad del lenguaje,
a través de versos sinuosos, derivativos que
acuden a imágenes inusitadas. En este volumen sorprenden (por su contraste con la
poética prevaleciente) un par de poemas
(véase, particularmente, "Los murmullos")
que insertan coloquialismos mexicanos e,
incluso, voces que hacen evocar a Rulfo. De
cualquier modo, prevalecen el ritmo y la
encantación del lenguaje. [JS]

3788 Bustos, Miguel Angel. Despedida de los ángeles. Buenos Aires: Libros de Tierra Firme, 1998. 142 p. (Col. de poesía Todos bailan; 260)

Nacido en 1932 y desaparecido en 1976, Bustos integró la llamada "generación del sesenta" junto con Gelman, Conti, Urondo, etc. Leopoldo Marechal definió su obra como "poesía celestial con verbo demoníaco." [LU]

3789 Cabral, Manuel del. Antología poética. Buenos Aires: Biblioteca Nacional, 1998. 203 p.

Se incluye de la producción poética entre 1930–65, nueve poemarios importantes que reflejan cabalmente la estética del poeta dominicano que tanto contribuyó, entre otros aportes, al desarrollo de la poesía afroantillana durante los años 30–40. Más allí de la temática afroantillana, se incluye también la poesía social. [FC]

3790 Cadenas, Rafael. Obra entera: poesía y prosa, 1958–1995. México: Fondo de Cultura Económica, 2000. 724 p.: bibl. (Tierra firme)

Primera compilación de la obra poética y ensayística (1958–95) de un autor que hasta ahora era paradójicamente semi-canónico en su país (Venezuela) y casi del todo desconocido en el exterior. Las huellas de José Antonio Ramos Sucre, Fernando Pessoa y la poesía oriental filtrada por autores anglonorteamericanos de la primera mitad del siglo XX son patentes en sus versos, con la variedad de registros que esas modulaciones permiten adivinar. La sabiduría visiblemente perseguida por sus hablantes poéticos con frecuencia encuentra ecos en sus textos de reflexión acerca de la literatura y el idioma. Nadie mejor que José Balza, presentador de este volumen, ha podido caracterizar en conjunto, con el tono, la precisión y la lucidez crítica adecuadas, la labor de Cadenas: "desde la intuición puberal hasta la luz adulta, desde la ceguera hasta el instinto." [MG]

3791 Campos, Javier F. El astronauta en llamas. Santiago, Chile: Lom Ediciones, 2000. 142 p. (Col. Entre mares)

Incluye previos libros del poeta y extiende su preocupación por escribir una poesía directa, a ratos descriptiva, inserta en los desarrollos tecnológicos contemporá-

neos, y cuyo núcleo metafórico es la figura del astronauta como sujeto en tránsito por un espacio en permanente expansión. [OS]

3792 Carrera, Arturo. El vespertillo de las Parcas. Buenos Aires: Tusquets Editores, 1997. 172 p. (Marginales. Nuevos textos sagrados)

Nueva entrega de una de las voces más singulares e importantes, junto con María Negroni, de la poesía contemporánea argentina. Desde su primera publicación, *Escrito con un nictógrafo* (1972), la obra de Carrera, vinculada a la estética del "neobarroso," según la denominación de Perlongher, pone a prueba los límites de la lengua a través de ejercicios lúdicos no excentos de rigor poético. [LU]

3793 Carrera, Calixto. Clangor: poemas navideños. San Juan: Instituto de Cultura Puertorriqueña, 1997. 127 p.

Conjunto de poemas que, según Francisco Lluch Mora en el prólogo, obedecen a dos estructuras técnicas y a dos maneras de "ver" y "entender" el mundo: "la ascética-religiosa y la hedonística." De ambiente religioso, este poemario celebra el "drama histórico de Belén y a las personas que viven la acción." [FC]

3794 Carriego, Evaristo. Obra completa de Evaristo Carriego. Prólogo y compaginación de Marcela Ciruzzi. Buenos Aires: Ediciones Corregidor, 1999. 333 p.: ill.

La obra de Carriego (1883–1912) aquí reunida resulta un importante aporte para situar a este inquietante y eficaz versificador dentro de la poesía hispanoamericana del siglo XX, explorar la recurrencia de sus temas y el lenguaje que lo caracteriza. [LU]

3795 Carvajal, Iván. Inventando a Lennon. Quito: Ediciones Libri Mundi E. Grosse-Luemern, 1997. 101 p. (Poesía)

Texto que puede desconcertar a la mayoría de sus lectores, porque si bien el título del poemario apunta un acto específico, el discurso se expande considerablemente y se dispersa al extremo de disolver todo motivo o tema central. De este modo, el motivo del título (John Lennon) apenas es aludido directamente a lo largo de las 101 páginas del volumen. Carvajal, uno de los poetas con más prestigio del Ecuador, en este volumen desarrolla una escritura al sesgo de su propio motivo y resulta oblicua, constantemente digresiva, tortuosa, perifrásica y finalmente laberíntica. Ciertamente, hay un afán por abrazar un amplio contexto—en cierto sentido sin límites—en el cual ubicaría al motivo aparente de su discurso ("inventar a Lennon"). Llama la atención que, pese a su dispersión de la figura central, el autor no deja de observar reflexivamente su propia figura, convirtiéndola en el centro de su discurso. Esa reflexividad se caracteriza por un tono de incertidumbre que en el nivel de su lenguaje se expresa por constantes interrogantes. [ORR]

3796 Casal, Selva. El infierno es una casa azul y otros poemas. Buenos Aires: Libros de Tierra Firme, 1999. 318 p. (Col. de poesía Todos bailan)

Desde 1958 con la publicación de "Arpa," la poesía de la uruguaya Selva Casal (1927) ha sido reconocida por su claridad y calidad estética. [LU]

3797 Castañón, Adolfo. Tránsito de Octavio Paz, 1914–1998: seguido de Recuerdos de Coyoacán. Prólogo de Soledad Alvarez. Santo Domingo: Comisión Permanente de la Feria del Libro, 1999. 83 p. (Ediciones Ferilibro; 15)

Castañón (Ciudad de México, 1952) es uno de los escritores más prolíficos del México actual. Aquí reúne dos poemas largos, dedicados o inspirados en Octavio Paz. El primero es una reflexión poética, hecha a partir de la muerte de Paz y el segundo se deriva de "Nocturno de San Ildefonso," en donde Paz hablaba de su juventud, además de otro poema de Alfonso Reyes. Castañón se apropia de sus maestros al insertar un examen de sí mismo. [JS]

3798 Castellanos, Rosario. Obras. v. 2, Poesía, teatro y ensayo. México: Fondo de Cultura Económica, 1998. 1 v.: ill. (Letras mexicanas)

Desde la recopilación Poesía no eres tú (1972), no se había publicado la poesía de Castellanos (Chiapas, México, 1925–74) en su forma conjunta. Esta edición agrega, además, teatro y ensayo, con lo que se complementa el primer volumen (narrativa) publicado con anterioridad. La poeta es célebre por sus versos claros y coloquiales que hacen obvia la injusta condición de la mujer. [JS]

3799 Castelpoggi, Atilio Jorge. Antología poética. Buenos Aires: Fondo Nacional de las Artes, 1998. 108 p. (Poetas argentinos contemporáneos; 15)

Desde Tierra sustantiva (1952), su primer poemario, este poeta de la llamada "generación del 50," recientemente fallecido (2001), ha centrado su poesía en un constante rescate de los referentes populares de su entorno, el barrio y Buenos Aires. [LU]

3800 Castro, Alejandra. Tatuaje giratorio. San José: Editorial Costa Rica, 1999. 104 p.

Este poemario obtuvo el Premio Joven-Creación 1997 que otorga la Editorial Costa Rica. Alejandra Castro (San José, 1974) se ha destacado ya como una de las voces femeninas más logradas de la última poesía costarricence. Cuenta hasta la fecha con dos premios literarios y sus textos empiezan a aparecer en muestras y antologías de la poesía latinoamericana. Isaac Felipe Azofeifa prologa Tatuaje giratorio, presentándolo como representativo de una poesía que, como la que hoy día se está escribiendo en Costa Rica, se ha independizado de escuelas literarias y direcciones estético-ideológicas para entregarse de lleno a la exploración del poema difícil, la imagen dislocada y el lenguaje despersonalizado. Tatuaje giratorio responde a este diagnóstico, pero hay que anotar que su excelencia radica en la conquista de una dinámica interna que, contrariamente al juicio de Azofeifa, no descuida los logros de la poesía anterior ni olvida sus enseñanzas. [EM]

3801 Chaves, Luis. Historias polaroid. San José: Ediciones Perro Azul, 2000. 73 p. (Col. de poesía)

Luis Chaves (Costa Rica, 1969) pertenece al grupo de poetas jóvenes que le están cambiando el rumbo a la poesía centroamericana contemporánea. Hasta el momento ha publicado tres libros, uno de ellos ganador del Premio Hispanoamericano de poesía Sor Juana Inés de la Cruz 1997 (Los animales que imaginamos). La poesía que encontramos en Historias polaroid se caracteriza por el tono irreverente y amargo con que el autor descifra la soledad del siglo XX y la poca eficacia de sus aciertos. Inquietantes preguntas sacuden al lector y lo obligan a repensar la función de la poesía: ¿en qué momento la rebeldía se convierte en estupidez?

¿Será que mojarse los pies en el mar basta para comprender las profundidades? Habrá que esperar más libros de Chavez para apreciar el desarrollo que ha de tener una poética que promete obra y continuidad. [EM]

3802 Cross, Elsa. Cantáridas. México: Ediciones Sin Nombre; Juan Pablos Editor, 1999. 32 p. (Col. poesía cuadernos de la salamandra)

24 poemas breves que se concentran en el diálogo entre la palabra y el silencio. Además de la evocación de Rimbaud, el título alude a los insectos que se comen todo, aun el lenguaje; además de que la palabra, cantáridas, hace eco del canto. Con esta poesía sensorial y depurada, Cross (Ciudad de México, 1946) apunta hacia la iluminación y el hallazgo espiritual como una de las claves de su obra. [JS]

3803 Cuadra, Pablo Antonio. El Nicán-Náuat. Prólogo de Conny Palacios. Managua: Academia Nicaragüense de la Lengua, 2000. 82 p.

En la tradición indigenista de Ernesto Cardenal, y orquestando los horizontes abiertos por la crítica postcolonial, Cuadra ofrece un poemario centrado en la figura del Gran Cacique de Nicaragua, Tlatoani. Como antes Cardenal, Cuadra intenta una re-escritura de la historia destinada a resarcir la indignidad en que han caído las culturas indígenas, revelar el hondo contenido filosófico de su pensamiento, y construir una identidad nicaraguense informada por la antigüedad náhuatl. En ningún momento, sin embargo, revela sus fuentes históricas ni cuestiona esa tendencia hispanista a percibir al antiguo náhuatl como guerrero, poeta, filósofo, y cristiano. [EM]

3804 Cunha, Victor. Cuaderno de Nueva York y otros poemas. Maldonado, Uruguay: Civiles Iletrados, 1998. 127 p.: ill. (Col. de náufragos; 3)

Nacido en Uruguay en 1951, esta nueva entrega de Cunha se suma a sus anteriores Poesía (1973), Título umbral contribución (1979), Ausencia del pájaro (1981), y Artificio con doncella (1986). Es la suya una poesía rica en referentes culturales que este nuevo poemario continúa. De este libro, el poema "Brooklyn bridge" es un buen ejemplo de una propuesta estética marcada por la distancia y objetividad que guarda el sujeto lírico respecto al mundo que recrea. [LU]

3805 Dalton, Roque. La ternura no basta: antología poética. Prólogo de Víctor Casaus. La Habana: Fondo Editorial Casa de las Américas ; Sevilla, Spain: Diputación de Sevilla, Area de Cultura, 1999. 478 p.: bibl. (Col. Literatura latinoamericana; 139)

Anteriormente publicada como Poesía escogida (1989), esta antología constituye una selección que el propio Dalton hizo de aquellos poemarios (10 en total) que, entre las décadas de los 60 y 70, escribió, corrigió o reorganizó en Cuba. Para el interesado en la poesía social, ésta mantiene su valía. [FC]

3806 Darío, Rubén. Cartas desconocidas de Rubén Darío, 1882–1916. Recopilación general de José Jirón Terán. Cronología de Julio Valle Castillo. Introducción, selección y notas de Jorge Eduardo Arellano. Managua: Academia Nicaragüense de la Lengua, 2000. 431 p.: bibl., ill.

La publicación de este epistolario es un acontecimiento para celebrar. Tres de los más reconocidos especialistas de la obra dariana han reunido sus esfuerzos para ofrecer al lector un volumen en el que han sido compiladas (por Jirón Terán), anotadas (por Arellano) y comentadas cronológicamente (por Valle-Castillo) 250 cartas personales, la mayoría desconocidas o inéditas. Voluntariamente quedaron al margen las piezas de intención literaria o ensayística. Para componer esta epistolografía personal el compilador revisó distintas fuentes, desde el trabajo pionero de Ventura García Calderón (que en 1920 compuso Epistolario de Rubén Darío, donde aparecieron 33 cartas), hasta los epistolarios preparados por Alberto Ghiraldo (tres en total, fechados en 1926, 1940, 1943). Pero además de este material ya conocido, Jirón Terán trabajó con un extenso corpus de documentación inédita que en 1946(?) Ghiraldo había entregado a la Biblioteca Nacional de Santiago y que desde entonces se había conservado en esa institución. Dicho corpus alcanza las 2,340 páginas, y de él sólo 45 cartas fueron dadas a conocer por Lom Ediciones (Epistolario selecto, 1999). Pero además de esta documentación, Arellano revisó también las 409 cartas darianas que se conservan en el Seminario-Archivo de la Univ. Complutense. De esta amplia documentación seleccionó las 250 cartas que se publican en este volumen y que corresponden a los años 1882–1916. Frases significativas extraídas del propio texto sirven de título a estas cartas, que

aparecen numeradas, anotadas, y cronolo-
giadas. Complementa el volumen una serie
de reproducciones facsimilares, fotografías,
índices (correlativo y por destinatario), y bibliografía. Un trabajo de expertos que sin
duda ha de tener importantes repercusiones
en los estudios darianos. [EM]

3807 Delmar, Meira. Pasa el viento: antología poética, 1942–1998. Prólogo de
Fernando Charry Lara. Bogotá: Instituto Caro
y Cuervo, 2000. 244 p. (La granada entre-
abierta; 88)

Esta selección de poemas de Delmar,
que abarca varios decenios podría constituir
un valioso instrumento para quienes con el
fin de replantear cuestiones de historiografía
literaria quieran constatar los numerosos
tiempos estéticos que convergen en lapsos
cronológicos muy precisos, como es el caso
del siglo XX colombiano. En efecto, tal como
en la obra de Aurelio Arturo o en la de León
de Greiff no resulta difícil advertir prolon-
gadas y tremendamente creadoras super-
vivencias de ideologemas o estilemas post-
modernistas, en *Pasa el viento* el simbolismo
y algunas preferencias imaginales parna-
sianas dan indicios de vitalidad mucho después de institucionalizadas varias generaciones de la vanguardia y la postvanguardia.
El respaldo que ofrecen Fernando Charry
Lara y Juan Gustavo Cobo Borda a este volumen con un prólogo y un epílogo respectivamente permite suponer que esas asincronías
se perciben como legítimas y representativas
de la lírica colombiana actual. [MG]

3808 Deltoro, Antonio. Poesía reunida,
1979–1997. México: UNAM, 1999.
287 p. (Poemas y ensayos)

Recopilación de los tres libros de poemas publicados a la fecha, Deltoro (Ciudad
de México, 1947) destaca por su elaboración
de lo cotidiano en términos de hallazgo celebratorio. En la misma línea de las odas elementales, de Neruda, aunque con un verso
largo y muy acompasado, Deltoro vuelve a la
infancia y evoca el asombro de descubrir la
maravilla de las cosas por primera vez. Contiene una entrevista al final que ayuda a des-
glosar las visiones del poeta. [JS]

3809 Deniz, Gerardo. Visitas guiadas: 36 poemas comentados por su autor. Mé-
xico: Gatupério, 2000. 156 p.

Libro útil y fascinante para aquellos
interesados en descubrir los repertorios lite-

rarios y culturales que conforman ciertos poemas de Deniz (pseudónimo de Juan Almela,
nacido en España, 1934; vive en México
desde 1942). Aunque su poesía está en contra
del uso convencional de lo "literario," este
antipoeta se jacta de su amplia cultura,
mostrando que sus poemas están plagados
de citas directas e indirectas. A eso se agrega
un tono sardónico y soez que hace uso frecuente de palabras burdas. [JS]

3810 Díaz Martínez, Manuel. Señales de
vida: 1968–1998. Prólogo de Luis Alberto de Cuenca. Madrid: Visor, 1998. 129 p.
(Col. Visor de poesía; 407)

Antología poética, ésta contiene cuatro poemarios publicados a partir de 1968, y,
además, incluye material inédito ("Paso a
nivel"). Considerado un poeta meditativo,
el devenir poético transita del intimismo a
un coloquialismo "entre irónico y sentimental." Voz lírica y reflexiva, la de este poeta
cubano busca una comprensión "del ser en
la vida." [FC]

3811 Domínguez, Delia. Huevos revueltos.
Santiago, Chile: Tacamó Ediciones,
2000. 81 p.

Incursiones reflexivas donde la geografía del sur de Chile asoma junto con
una mirada sorprendida por las paradojas
de la vida y de la muerte. [OS]

3812 Eguren, José María. Obras completas.
Edición, prólogo, notas, bibliografía y
dirección de Ricardo Silva-Santisteban. Estudio y catálogo de la obra plástica de Luis
Eduardo Wuffarden. Fotografías de Daniel
Giannoni. Lima?: Ediciones Centenario;
Banco de Crédito del Perú, 1997. 731 p.: bibl.,
ill. (some col.), index. (Biblioteca Clásicos
del Perú; 7)

Critical edition prepared by Silva-
Santisteban, who also wrote the prologue
and endnotes, and compiled the bibliography.
In addition to his poetry, this edition also
contains Eguren's articles, letters, and interviews, as well as his paintings, drawings,
photographs, and watercolors. Also includes
a study of Eguren's visual works by Wuffarden. [GP]

3813 Elvir Rivera, Raúl. Círculo de fuego.
Managua?: Anamá Ediciones Centroamericanas, 1999. 251 p.

Círculo de fuego fue publicado por
primera vez en 1971, y ya entonces era una
muestra significativa de la obra poética de

Elvir Rivera, poeta hondureño residido en Nicaragua, país donde falleció en 1998. El volumen que ahora se reseña incluye al anterior, pero es definitivamente un nuevo libro. Además de las composiciones de 1971, esta edición da a conocer gran parte de la obra poética de Elvir Rivera, incluida la obra inédita, entre la que destaca una composición titulada "Este me estar muriendo poco a poco," expresamente escrita para ser publicada después de la muerte del poeta. [EM]

Enciclopedia dominicana. See item **1794**.

3814   Errasti, Mariano. Viaje al otro Caribe. San Juan: Instituto de Cultura Puertorriqueña, Programa de Publicaciones y Grabaciones, 1998. 132 p.: ill.

Una visión franciscana de la pobreza, vista por un fraile vasco radicado en el Caribe (Cuba, Puerto Rico y República Dominicana) desde hace 40 años, nos convoca a solidarizarnos con los "hijos del suburbio." De estilo "alegre y espontáneo," la denuncia descansa en la fe de un devenir mejor. [FC]

3815   Escobar Varela, Angel. Cuando salí de La Habana. La Habana: Ediciones Unión, 1997. 92 p. (Contemporáneos)

Compuesto de poemas escritos en Cuba y Chile (adonde fue a vivir el poeta), este poemario, según Efraín Rodríguez Santana, está hecho de "esa multiplicidad de deseos encontrados y contrapuestos, de ese torbellino de sensaciones y angustias, de la vigilia y la pesadilla, de lo inconcluso y heredado." [FC]

3816   Escudero, Gonzalo. Obra poética. Prólogo de Iván Carvajal. Edición de Javier Vásconez. Quito: Acuario, 1998. 341 p.

Volumen muy valioso que recopila la poesía de uno de los poetas ecuatorianos más importantes del siglo XX, Gonzalo Escudero (1903–71). Incluye los ocho poemarios publicados por el autor—*Los poemas del arte* (1919), *Las parábolas olímpicas* (1922), *Hélices de huracán y de sol* (1933), *Altanoche* (1947), *Estatua de aire* (1951), *Materia de ángel* (1953), *Autorretrato* (1957), *Introducción a la muerte* (1960)—y dos publicaciones póstumas: la serie de textos "Réquiem por la luz" (1971) y el poema "Nocturno de Septiembre" (1971). La obra de Escudero es una de las más sobresalientes en la poesía hispanoamericana, pues la totalidad de su discurso poético es un aporte de elevada cali-

dad a la evolución de la lírica regional entre el periodo del vanguardismo hasta la poesía finisecular del siglo XX. Toda esta obra se destaca por su impecable manejo del lenguaje, y sobre todo por una reflexión constante, rigurosa y profunda que, lamentablemente, no ha sido todavía estudiada en los términos que merece. Este volumen lleva un prólogo de otro poeta ecuatoriano, Iván Carvajal. [ORR]

3817   Estrella, Ulises. Mirar de frente al sol. Quito: E.P. Centro de Impresión, 1997. 96 p.: ill.

Con esta publicación, el poeta ecuatoriano Estrella ofrece a sus lectores una nueva versión, corregida y aumentada, del poemario que en 1989 apareció con otro título aunque no muy diferente: *Cuando el sol se mira de frente*. Con la presente publicación, asimismo, el poeta vuelve sobre uno de sus temas favoritos: la meditación sobre la realidad ecuatoriana, particularmente la ciudad de Quito, en el contexto de su historia que se remonta no sólo a la fundación que se atribuyó la invasión española en 1534, sino a más de 10,000 años que señala la arqueología, información de la que el poeta no se aleja. Su reflexión sobre su ciudad o lugar de origen no deja de incorporarse a una contexto más amplio y que corresponde a la poesía hispanoamericana propia de las décadas finales del siglo XX, una poesía que ha tornado su atención y meditación sobre el origen y la identidad del ser hispanoamericano, dando un rasgo más para definir la poesía de la posmodernidad. Estrella mostró similares preocupaciones y actitud en publicaciones anteriores como *Peatón de Quito* (1992) y *Fábula del soplador y la bella* (1995). [ORR]

3818   Falconí Almeida, Patricio. Poemas que aprendí en tu cuerpo. Quito: FundaFuturo, 1997. 139 p.

El poeta ecuatoriano Patricio Falconí presenta ahora una colección de textos poéticos cuyo tema es la experiencia amorosa y sexual de la pareja. Estos textos, breves en su extensión, pueden ser considerados como testimonios de la experiencia erótica masculina expresada muy libremente, sin límites ni reparos respecto a las descripciones o afirmaciones con las que conforma su discurso. El cuerpo femenino es el centro de la cotidianidad del poeta, para quien, según el testimonio de varios textos, la actividad principal del ser humano es la relación sexual. El tono desenfadado y lúdico, unas veces irónico y otras veces burlón o crítico, acude siempre al enunciado breve, escrito indiferentemente en prosa o verso. La liberalidad del lenguaje de estos textos con frecuencia cae en la superficialidad e intrascendencia. Sin embargo, no se puede desconocer que en su desenfado sexual logra expresiones personales con cierta frescura. [ORR]

3819 Fernández Moreno, Baldomero. Elegía de Alondra: poemas inéditos. Selección y prólogo de Mario Benedetti. Buenos Aires: Seix Barral, 1998. 155 p.

La publicación de estos poemas inéditos no sólo ayuda a completar la obra de Fernández Moreno, ese "poeta de su pretérito" como lo llamó Ezequiel Martínez Estrada, reafirmando sus características—sencillez, tono coloquial, etc.—sino que ofrece también la peculiar proyección de un sujeto poético comprometido con sus pasiones, de diáfano intimismo. Benedetti señala certeramente la importancia de Fernández Moreno en las promociones poéticas argentinas subsiguientes como la del grupo de Boedo y la llamada "generación del sesenta" que esta publicación colabora a delimitar. [LU]

3820 Fernández Moreno, César. Obra poética. v. 1, Argentino hasta la muerte y otros libros. v. 2, Querencias y otros libros. Buenos Aires: Perfil Libros, 1999. 2 v.: bibl., ill. (La biblioteca)

Esta cuidada edición de la obra del escritor y crítico Fernández Moreno (1919–85) permite el seguimiento y evolución de una poesía vinculada en sus comienzos a la estética del neorromanticismo por sus preferencias temáticas y estilísticas dentro de cánones tradicionales. [LU]

3821 Franz Tamayo en la poesía boliviana: ofrendas líricas consagradas al pensador paceño. Recopilación y edición de Augusto Camacho Bernal. La Paz: s.n., 1998. 50 p.

Singular importancia tiene esta publicación de homenaje a uno de los mayores pensadores y poetas bolivianos de la primera mitad del siglo XX, Franz Tamayo (1879–1956), cuya obra lamentablemente no ha sido estudiada aún en la medida que merece, lo cual tampoco debe llamar la atención dada la complejidad de la misma. La compilación

reúne 25 textos en verso dedicados a Tamayo. Entre los autores de esos poemas destacan poetas importantes del siglo XX como Gregorio Reynolds, Juan Capriles, Antonio Avila Jiménez, Oscar Cerruto, Yolanda Bedregal, Alcira Cardona, Julio de la Vega, Mery Flores Saavedra y Gonzalo Vázquez Méndez. Los textos de estos poetas no sólo elogian explícitamente rasgos importantes y reconocidos de la obra y personalidad del homenajeado, como el rigor y la disciplina que caracterizó a su vida, su actuación pública de probidad y su pensamiento alimentado por fuentes clásicas; sino que muchos de los textos toman en préstamo de la obra de Tamayo aspectos de contenido (ideas, conceptos, temas) y aspectos de su estilo, en un esfuerzo por imitarlo admirativamente. La lectura de esta antología deja claro un hecho importante de la historia literaria de este país: que Franz Tamayo, sin proponérselo, ha creado una escuela de la que emergieron los mejores poetas bolivianos del siglo XX, un tema de estudio para futuros investigadores. [ORR]

3822 Friol, Roberto. Tramontana. La Habana: Ediciones Unión, 1997. 70 p. (La rueda dentada. Poesía)

Dos veces ganador del Premio Crítica (1988 y 1991), la poesía de Friol, como plantea en este poemario, surge de "los cimientos del ser." "Esperanzado en la resurrección," el poeta se afinca en la esperanza, una que tramita entre "océanos del ser y del estar." [FC]

3823 Gallardo y Guido, César. Por mi hasta lo que soy: antología breve. Callao, Peru: Ediciones Línea Eter, 1999. 52 p.

While the editors describe Gallardo y Guido as a prolific writer, this is actually only his third published work; to this day, most of his works remain unpublished. The brief prologue entitled "Poetic Essence" was written by Nello Marcos Sánchez Dextre. Gallardo y Guido approaches everyday events and characters in a narrative manner that does not challenge the reader or his/her capacity for understanding. [GP]

3824 García Marruz, Fina. Antología poética. Selección y prólogo de Jorge Luis Arcos. La Habana: Editorial Letras Cubanas, 1997. 220 p.: bibl.

Además de una muestra de textos ya publicados, se incluye material inédito de

"Verso amigo." Una de las grandes poetas católicas de la poesía cubana contemporánea, el trabajo de García Marruz está íntimamente ligado al de los origenistas que, como Lezama y Vitier, se valían de la religión para plantear lo nacional. [FC]

3825 Garrido Chalén, Carlos. Confesiones de un arbol. Lima?: Kapeluz Editores, 1997. 77 p.: col. ill.

Garrido Chalén published seven books of poetry between 1969–97. According to Antonio Cisneros, myth and reality are two of the components in Garrido Chalén's poetry, however, it also embraces metaphysical and ethnic concerns. The poems are accompanied by several photographs of abstract paintings by Pedro Caballero. The poet transforms himself into things and natural objects with a deep imagination. [GP]

3826 Gaztelu, Angel. Gradual de laudes. La Habana: Ediciones Unión, 1997. 126 p. (La rueda dentada. Poesía)

Uno de los integrantes importantes del grupo Orígenes, el padre Gaztelu publicó dos libros de poesía. Este, cuya publicación original data de 1955, está dividido en siete partes correspondientes a diferentes composiciones literarias (décimas, canciones, romances, sonetos, versos libres, poemas sacros, versiones latinas). Contiene una valiosa introducción de Lezama Lima. [FC]

3827 Gelman, Juan. Antología poética. Selección de Horacio Salas. Buenos Aires: Fondo Nacional de las Artes, 1998. 146 p. (Poetas argentinos contemporáneos; 16)

La obra del argentino Juan Gelman (1930) sigue difundiéndose a través de reediciones y recopilaciones antológicas como la preparada aquí por Horacio Salas. Esta selección incluye poemas desde *Gotán* (1962) hasta *Anunciaciones* (1988). [LU]

3828 Germán, Orlando. Ascensión a la noche. Lima: Lluvia Editores, 1997. 46 p.

Poetry book with two sections entitled "Vuelo o cumplimiento del vaticinio" and "Roads," totaling 15 poems. In these poems, the nostalgic and refreshing setting of peasant life in a rural environment is the background for the presentation of emotional experiences in a confessional mood. The poems also attempt to relive experiences and emotions, particularly those involving all five senses. [GP]

3829 Gervitz, Gloria. Migraciones. México: G. Gervitz, 2000. 189 p.

Bajo la palabra *Migraciones* es que Gervitz (Ciudad de México, 1943) ha ido comprendiendo su obra poética (las ediciones anteriores son de 1991 y 1996), corrigiendo y agregando nuevas secciones a cada nueva versión. El libro está construido a base de fragmentos que, leídos en forma secuencial, no hilan una historia completa; sin embargo, sí es posible seguir cierta pauta que se repite como motivo en el poema: los recuerdos de un pasado devastado, alusivo a mujeres judías que migran de Rusia a México. A las secciones "Fragmento de ventana," "Del libro de Yiskor," "Leteo," "Pythia," "Equinoccio," esta edición (de lujo) agrega "Treno." Para el comentario de la edición de 1991, ver *HLAS 56:3998*. [JS]

3830 Giannuzzi, Joaquín O. Antología poética. Buenos Aires: Fondo Nacional de las Artes, 1998. 127 p. (Poetas argentinos contemporáneos; 17)

Desde *Nuestros días mortales* (1958), la obra de Giannuzzi refleja las viscisitudes de un mundo de desencantos cuya única salvación depende de la justeza y justicia de la palabra poética. La selección aquí reunida es representativa de esa búsqueda de un poeta cuya ascendencia sobre las nuevas promociones argentinas es un desafío crítico aún pendiente. [LU]

3831 Giannuzzi, Joaquín O. Obra poética. Buenos Aires: Emecé Editores, 2000. 537 p.

Galardonado con el Premio Nacional de Poesía en 1981, la obra aquí reunida de Giannuzzi (1924) revela claramente su magisterio poético. Este volumen incluye los poemarios *Nuestros días mortales* (1958), *Contemporáneo del mundo* (1962), *Las condiciones de la época* (1967), *Señales de una causa personal* (1977), *Principios de incertidumbre* (1980), *Violín obligado* (1984), *Cabeza final* (1991), y *Apuestas en lo oscuro* (2000). [LU]

3832 Gomensoro Riverós, Rafael. Uno solo y dos. Montevideo: Ediciones de la Banda Oriental, 1997. 56 p.

Con Pórtico de Marosa de Giorgio se

abre esta nueva entrega del uruguayo Gomensoro (1946) que se suma a sus anteriores *Hemisferios de Silencio* (1981), *El Redentor* (1983), y *Las viejas estaciones* (1986). El tema del desdoblamiento como mutación, no como repetición (a través de la presencia de espejos, de elementos en apariencia simétricos—ojos, gemelos, equinoccios— o de imágenes emblemáticas del sujeto poético—figuras de piedra, estatuas, etc.) da unidad a este poemario que revela la inclaudicable responsabilidad estética de Gomensoro. [LU]

3833 González, Ronel. Desterrado de asombros. La Habana: Editorial Letras Cubanas, 1997. 73 p. (Cemí. Poesía)

De aliento filosófico, tras el sentido de las palabras que "milagrosamente sobreviven," el poeta busca nuevos caminos, se plantea nuevas estéticas que nos obliguen a meditar, melancólicamente, en "las derrotas del Hombre," esas que conducen a la "tempestad del Ser," donde nadie se detiene a gozar en "la consumación de la utopía." [FC]

3834 González Vigil, Ricardo. Génesis continuo: (árbol de poemas). Lima: J. Campodónico Editor, 1997. 47 p. (Col. del sol blanco)

Collection of poems by a member of the "generación de los 70." González Vigil is also a well-known literary critic, scholar, and journalist. This book, his fifth book of poetry, includes significant connections with Latin American poetry, as well as philosophical reflections. In some poems, he converses with major Latin American poets and cultural personalities. Presented as a celebration of the universe as a continuous creation. [GP]

3835 Gordon-Vailakis, Ivón. Colibríes en el exilio. Quito: Editorial El Conejo, 1997. 73 p.

Obra primera de una joven escritora ecuatoriana que es también profesora universitaria. La poesía de Gordon-Vailakis es poesía de la cotidianidad por la elección de motivos sencillos que, sin embargo, son percibidos desde una sensibilidad no exenta de frescura y sorpresa, y sobre todo a partir de una conciencia que se sabe ubicada en el cuerpo femenino, y que debe enfrentarse a un mundo condicionado por prescripciones tradicionales respecto a los géneros humanos

(papeles femeninos/papeles masculinos) que en los tiempos actuales, en general, se invalidan por ausencia de fundamento racional. El vocabulario elegido corresponde a una voz femenina en situaciones y actividades asignadas tradicionalmente a la mujer en la sociedad, a las que critica. El estilo de los textos no deja de mostrar sus orígenes en las experiencias y experimentos del vanguardismo hispanoamericano, cuyos recursos de una estructura breve, fragmentada, yuxtapuesta y dispersa se pueden observar todavía en este discurso poético. [ORR]

3836 Guinea Diez, Gerardo. Ser ante los ojos. Guatemala: Letra Negra, 2000. 82 p. (Poesía centroamericana; 2)

Ganador del Premio Nacional de Poesía César Brañas, este poemario es el segundo que publica Guinea Diez (Guatemala, 1955), más conocido por su obra narrativa. El poemario está construido en base a una sostenida indagación al ser, al "yo" congregado a orillas del fin de siglo y perceptible en la pupila de un niño que no alcanza a comprender "el cabreo del tiempo." Con extraordinaria originalidad, Guinea Diez articula una poética yoísta que evita el cerco de la individualidad. Su "yo" es un "yo congregado," extensivo a todos los otros "yos" y embarcado en la tarea de ayudar al caos a ordenar el universo. [EM]

3837 Hahn, Oscar. Antología retroactiva. Caracas: Monte Avila Editores Latinoamericana, 1998. 86 p. (Altazor)

Antología de poemas de cinco libros publicados por el autor entre 1977–95. Combinatoria delicada de la retórica de la poesía del siglo de oro con el rigor fantasmático de la literatura fantástica, el Apocalipsis bíblico, la modernidad de Apollinaire y la veracidad paradójica de la antipoesía de Nicanor Parra. [OS]

3838 Harris, Tomás. Itaca. Santiago, Chile: LOM Ediciones, 2001. 182 p. (Col. Entre mares. Poesía)

Poemas visionarios donde abundan las referencias literarias (Cioran, Poe), plásticas (Géricault, Dix) y cinematográficas (David Lynch). Una serie de pesadillas por las cuales navegan personajes que agonizan y especulan y pueden, tal vez, entrever una suerte de integración sensual y mística difusa con el caos, las obsesiones y la violencia en que se desenvuelve su ilusoria realidad. [OS]

3839 Häsler, Rodolfo. De la belleza del puro pensamiento. Barcelona: Los Libros de la Frontera, 1997. 76 p. (El Bardo; 46)

Ganador en 1993 del premio Oscar B. Cintas de Nueva York, este poemario se plantea como una ofrenda directa e indirecta a la cubanía recordada, inventada desde la distancia, desde el eco. En las dos primeras partes domina la tradición libresca; en las dos últimas, la popular. En ambas, la escritura es primero. [FC]

3840 Hernández, Mireya. El espacio prohibido de los pájaros. Panamá: Instituto Nacional de Cultura: Editorial Mariano Arosemena, 1998. 70 p. (Colección múltiple)

La poesía panameña se enriquece con este poemario de Mireya Hernández (Panamá 1942), que con audacia creativa sabe "meterse en la palabra" y llegar a los laberintos de un país "desdibujado," pero en el que todavía cabe "esperar que salga la primera estrella." Siendo mujer, Hernández no apela a la mujer, sino más bien a la garganta, a la locura, al miedo, "para ir hacia adentro." Asombra la calidad poética de este poemario que confirma la profunda renovación artística que se está dando en Centroamérica. [EM]

3841 Herrera Ysla, Nelson. Pájaros de pólvora. La Habana: Ediciones Unión, 1998. 95 p.: ill. (Contemporáneos)

A través de los ruidos del país, de la poesía y de los poetas, del amor, de los viajes al extranjero, de lo íntimo dicho con desdén, el poeta nos invita a espiar su cotidianidad hecha de virtudes y defectos que son también los del país, al que odia con amor. [FC]

3842 Huerta, David. La música de lo que pasa. México: Consejo Nacional para la Cultura y las Artes, 1997. 101 p. (Práctica mortal)

Huerta (Ciudad de México, 1949) es uno de los poetas mexicanos más versátiles, practicando todo tipo de registros poéticos, desde el poema corto, que evoca el haikú, hasta el versículo al estilo de Lezama Lima. En este volumen acude a un lenguaje claro, coloquial, para reflexionar poéticamente acerca de las materias de la cotidianidad (en su mayor parte urbana). [JS]

3843 Huezo Mixco, Miguel. Comarcas. Panamá: Univ. Tecnológica de Panamá, 1999. 99 p.

Este poemario obtuvo el Premio Centroamericano de Literatura "Rogelio Sinán" (1998–99) que otorga la Univ. Tecnológica de Panamá. Se trata sin duda de un importante aporte a la poesía salvadoreña contemporánea, sobre todo por el acierto de superar la retórica del compromiso con una poética que, desde el Caribe centroamericano, dialoga con su época y con el espíritu de la poesía griega. [EM]

3844 Ita Gómez, Jorge. Ansianhelante. Lima: Colegio Privado Nuestra Señora de la Merced, 1998. 79 p.

Ita Gómez's third book of poetry begins with an essay of literary criticism by Raúl Jurado Párraga. Gómez's poetry shows his concern with his self-consciousness as a poet as well as the need to elaborate foundational principles without forgetting how to be playful even in sentimental matters. The book has three sections, entitled "Razón de canto," "Ricardo Corazón de León," and "Tratados del Alma." [GP]

3845 James, Miguel. A las diosas del mar. Mérida, Venezuela: Ediciones MUCUGLIFO, Dirección de Literatura del CONAC, 1999. 98 p.

Aunque este poemario no altera en nada las direcciones estéticas que caracterizan la obra de James (trinitario residente en Venezuela y definitivamente asimilado a su vida literaria), confirma, eso sí, la coherencia de su proyecto creador, que reivindica el primitivismo y una ingenuidad cuyo equivalente pictórico sin duda sería lo que Franz Roh en el decenio de 1924 denominó *realismo mágico*. En esta ocasión, James desarrolla el tono infantil tan sólo marginal en sus poemarios previos, obteniendo resultados muy similares a los del *Primeiro Caderno do Aluno de Poesia* publicado por el brasileño Oswald de Andrade en 1927. [MG]

3846 Jaramillo Escobar, Jaime. Los poemas de la ofensa. 4. ed. Medellín, Colombia: Editorial Univ. de Antioquia, 2000. 156 p. (Col. de poesía)

Esta cuarta edición de uno de los conjuntos más representativos del nadaísmo ha sido, como advierte en un prólogo su autor, "retocada," aunque sin modificar en lo esencial los textos originales escritos hacia 1963. Jaramillo Escobar como pocos otros nadaístas hace patente las raíces vanguardistas de su retórica de la violencia, que sintetizan la imaginería apasionada del expresionismo con la disolución de la razón a la que aspiraron los surrealistas, ambas al servicio de una realidad social muy específica: "Es cierto que nos pesaba demasiado el corazón y, arrancándonoslo, lo echamos a un basurero/y cuando fracasó nuestro último intento de suicidio nos recluimos atemorizados/en nuestra cabaña de cinabrio" ("El viajero de veinte cabezas"). La sección sexta, "Aproximación a la muerte," revela afinidad estética con experiencias hispanoamericanas anteriores y posteriores como las del primer Gonzalo Rojas, Oscar Hahn y, últimamente, Carlos López Degregori. [MG]

3847 Javier, Adrián. Erótica de lo invisible. Santo Domingo: Editora Cole, 2000. 126 p.: ill.
Considerada una de las voces importantes de la Generación de los 80, la de este poemario, según Manuel García Cartagena, plantea lo erótico no tanto como referencia a una "praxis amatoria," sino como "la conciencia rítimica que ubica la lectura en el ámbito del placer." [FC]

3848 Jotamario. El cuerpo de ella: poema orgánico. Ilustraciones de Máximo Flórez. Bogotá: Alcaldía Mayor de Santafé de Bogotá, 1999. 113 p.: ill. (Un poema en el umbral)
Esta serie de poemas breves (legible también como composición extensa que adopta una forma fragmentada) data de principios del decenio de 1960, pero se recoge en libro por primera vez. El subtítulo, *Poema orgánico*, adelanta la configuración externa del texto, que cataloga las distintas partes de la anatomía de Dina Merlina, "mujer bella y bellaca," como advierte una dedicatoria. Aunque la imaginería ofrezca una apariencia de novedad por su violencia erótica, puede observarse igualmente el perfil tradicionalista de este tipo de lírica, erigida sobre la persistente cosificación del cuerpo femenino, usual en las culturas patriarcales más conservadoras: la carne de la modelo "fue un guante para mi alma," añade

un epílogo en prosa significativamente titulado "Postmortem." [MG]

3849 La Hoz, Luis. Oscuro y diamante: poemas escogidos. Lima: Fondo Editorial del Banco Central de Reserva del Perú, 1998. 149 p.
In the prologue, Antonio Cornejo-Polar praises La Hoz's use of metaphors, the intensity of his love poems, and the authenticity of his representations of life. The selection, made by La Hoz himself, includes poems previously published between 1984–93 in four different books as well as 12 previously unpublished poems. La Hoz is a writer who has found in poetry his real vocation. This selection offers an overall sample of his complete works. [GP]

3850 La Torre Lagares, Elidio. Cuerpos sin sombras. San Juan: Isla Negra, 1998. 77 p. (Col. Josemilio González)
Desde una subjetividad transitiva ("soy nadie y soy todo el mundo"), este joven poeta puertorriqueño de los noventa, que trabaja "por debajo de las palabras para tocarte/ y para que toques al otro," confronta el sin sentido de la realidad social con una mirada "prospectiva," al cabo de la cual supone la esperanza. [FC]

3851 Lara, Magali and **María Baranda.** Causas y azares. México: Editorial Aldus, 2000. 64 p.: col. ill. (Col. Los Poetas)
Con imágenes de Lara, versos de Baranda y, posiblemente, prosas de Lara, este pequeño volumen muestra que la colaboración y compenetración de los artistas y poetas (habría que agregar, además, las traducciones al inglés de Roberto Tejada) puede dar frutos muy interesantes. Énfasis en lo femenino, pero de una manera subrepticia y sutil. Los textos y las imágenes delatan heridas, ausencias y traslados. [JS]

3852 Lara, Omar. Vida probable: antología personal. Santiago: Ediciones Chile-América, CESOC 1999. 130 p.
Certera selección realizada por el propio autor de poemas escritos desde 1967–91. Poemas discretos y llenos de insinuaciones vitales y mortales que entretejen la historia con mayúscula a los avatares de un sujeto perplejo ante su propia experiencia incierta. [OS]

3853 Laso, Margarita. El trazo de las cobras. Quito: Abrapalabra Editores, 1997. 77 p.

Laso (1963) ratifica con la publicación de este poemario el prestigio que ganó desde la aparición de sus primeros poemarios, *Erosonera* (1991) y *Queden en la lengua mis deseos* (1994). Esta poeta ecuatoriana mantiene y renueva su lenguaje con rasgos propios. No sólo son los temas que permiten esa renovación, temas generalmente ligados a la experiencia de la sensualidad humana y desde una perspectiva femenina, con lo cual sigue una de las tendencias del pensamiento moderno de la literatura hispanoamericana iniciado a finales del siglo XIX; es también la imaginación de la poeta, que si bien contemplativa aún de los fenómenos de la naturaleza, describe a ésta a partir de percepciones originales. Del mismo modo, en el nivel del estilo y manejo del lenguaje se advierte evidentemente una búsqueda y experimentación de rasgos sintácticos. [ORR]

3854 Lebrón Saviñón, Mariano. Vuelta al ayer: poemas. Santo Domingo: Ediciones El Pez Rojo, 1997. 85 p.

Integrante del importante e histórico grupo literario conocido como "La poesía sorprendida," en este poemario se reitera esa poética: "la de hacer una poesía con el hombre universal." De tono lírico, el poeta cede a menudo ante la nostalgia: "vuelvo a ser ruiseñor nostálgico de auroras." El universalismo acentúa la dominicanidad. [FC]

3855 Leguía Olivera, Enriqueta. Poemario de amor: vivencias y recuerdos de una vida que pudo ser la de cualquiera. Lima: Editorial Horizonte, 1999. 115 p.

Leguía Olivera is a historical figure, the daughter of Augusto B. Leguía, who was president of Peru from 1919–30. Nevertheless, the cover and title page of the book include the following message: "Vivencias y recuerdos de una vide que pudo ser la de cualquiera." The narrative and almost testimonial elements are noticeable. [GP]

3856 Lima Quintana, Hamlet. Las memorias y Diario del regreso. Buenos Aires: Ediciones del Valle, 1999. 127 p.

La figura del Che Guevara motiva la cantata de este escritor, periodista y compositor argentino recientemente fallecido (21 de feb., 2002). Su primer poemario, *Mundo en el rostro*, había aparecido en 1954. [LU]

3857 Liscano, Juan. Sola evidencia: poemas, 1996–1998. Barcelona: Grupo Editorial Norma, 2000. 108 p. (Col. Poesía)

Este volumen, que recoge composiciones fechadas entre 1996 y 1998, ilustra con eficacia la etapa final de la poesía de Liscano. En esta se percibe de inmediato un despojamiento y una sencillez que contrastan con la monumentalidad o el tono arcano—siempre bien llevados—de otras épocas. Los temas usuales (el mito, el tiempo, la condición enigmática del hombre) se retoman, pero ahora con dejo nostálgico cuya expresividad a veces adopta la concisión del apotegma y de las pasiones contempladas a distancia. [MG]

3858 Loo Lynch, Esteban A. Una primavera en Cañete: poemas. Lima: Editorial Argos, 1997. 71 p.

In an introductory note, Loo Lynch tries to explain why he writes poetry and manifests his admiration of César Vallejo. The poems included here are by no means the result of intense experimentation, but the self-expression of memorable personal experiences is considerable. [GP]

3859 López, Marcos. Metálogos. Santiago, Chile: Bellavistinos Unidos, 1999. 40 p.

Poemas que representan a veces ácidamente y a veces humorísticamente las experiencias del sujeto. La factura epigramática, irónica, se anuda a una capacidad metafórica fluída. [OS]

3860 López Mills, Tedi. Horas. México: Trilce Ediciones, 2000. 71 p. (Tristán Lecoq)

Respaldada por la primera Beca Octavio Paz de poesía y, más tarde, por el Premio Caniem al Arte Editorial 2000, López Mills (Ciudad de México, 1959) muestra su talento poético en este volumen preocupado por el detalle y la minucia. Poesía que observa, cuestiona e investiga la realidad en busca de respuestas que satisfagan la curiosidad de la que no acepta respuestas convencionales. [JS]

3861 Loynaz, Dulce María. Melancolía de otoño: poesía. Pinar del Río, Cuba: Ediciones Hnos. Loynaz, 1997. 92 p. (Col. Laurel)

Inéditos hasta el momento, estos poemas en prosa, escritos durante la década de los 20, muestran la influencia del hinduismo en boga durante dicha época ("Uno no es uno, sino su amor"). [FC]

3862 Mac Lean Estrada, Juan Cristóbal. Paran los clamores. La Paz?: Plural Editores, 1997. 89 p.

El autor de este poemario es un joven valor que aparece en el panorama de la poesía boliviana contemporánea. Su poesía es un discurso que se caracteriza por la descripción novedosa y personal de la realidad. Esto se debe a la perspectiva personal desde la cual el joven poeta se enfrenta a la realidad. Su expresión, predominantemente metafórica e imaginativa, es un lenguaje que busca la novedad acorde con la manera diferente de mirar el mundo, el cual, para el autor, es un mundo de tecnología moderna que sin embargo no ha logrado velar la realidad natural. El poemario está dividido en cuatro secciones, cuyos títulos son: "Animal de silencio," "Tu mano dormida contra el alba," "Me está matando en todos los campos," y "Paran los clamores." A través de las diversas secciones se observa una misma actitud autobiográfica y anecdótica personal, pero llevada a un nivel de constante reflexión poética. [ORR]

3863 Mamani Laruta, Clemente. Jallalla warminaka. La Paz: Subsecretaría de Asuntos de Género, 1997. 81 p.: ill.

Colección de poemas de un autor aymara, que incluye versiones bilingües (castellano/aymara) de algunos de los textos; la mayoría de ellos están en castellano. La publicación ha sido patrocinada por el gobierno boliviano a través de la Subsecretaría de Asuntos de Género. De acuerdo a la "Presentación," dos son las razones que fundamentan la publicación del poemario: primero, el tema de la colección: "la mujer;" segundo, "la necesidad de abrir espacios que permitan la difusión de aquellas manifestaciones artísticas vinculadas a la narrativa y poesía aymara, en esta ocasión, y de otros idiomas que conforman nuestra riqueza como país multicultural y multilingüe."

En cuanto al tema, no todos los textos se refieren a la mujer; y los que sí lo enfocan obviamente lo hacen desde la percepción masculina del autor. El interés del volumen radica en la segunda razón, que es ratificada por otra explicación de los auspiciadores: prestar atención "a esa producción poética acallada por el desconocimiento y el silenciamiento al que ha conducido la discriminación étnica y de género." Parte del substrato imaginario de los textos principales de esta colección corresponde a los mitos y pensamiento simbólico de las culturas andinas. [ORR]

3864 Maradiaga, David. Música de animal lluvioso y otros poemas. San José: Ministerio de Cultura, Juventud y Deportes, Dirección General de Cultura, Dirección de Publicaciones, 1999. 141 p.: ill. (Col. de poesía. Imago)

En esta colección el poeta costarricense Guillermo Fernández reúne gran parte de la obra poética de Maradiaga (Nicaragua 1968—Costa Rica 1995) y de paso rinde homenaje al que fuera su compañero de ruta y un reconocido integrante de la joven poesía costarricense. La obra de Maradiaga consta de tres libros (*Música de animal lluvioso, Pasos en la madrugada,* y *Canción del extranjero*) y una extensa cantidad de poemas inéditos y dispersos que ni siquiera la labor recopiladora de Fernández ha conseguido reunir. El lector que se aventure en la lectura de estos poemas apreciará la dimensión post-utópica, irreverente, y madura con que Maradiaga dialogó con su tiempo. [EM]

3865 Mario Antonio. Misivas para los tiempos de paz. San Juan, Puerto Rico: Isla Negra, 1997. 75 p. (Col. Josemilio González)

Dieciséis poemas, en su mayoría extensos, desbordantes, integran este poemario en el que, ante cualquier otra pretensión, sobresale la del escritor, el poeta que trabaja sobre una multitud de imágenes, de metáforas articuladas para decir, como en un cuento, algo (sobre el amor, la soledad) que requiere esmero formal y estructural. [FC]

3866 Martínez, Jan. Jardín: obra escogida, 1977–1997. Santurce, Puerto Rico: Gráfica Metropolitana, 1997. 168 p.: ill.

"En la vela se devela la niñez del fuego." Reconocido como una de las voces líricas de la segunda mitad de los setenta, esta poesía se caracteriza por la economía verbal, la precisión, el tono existencial, la imantación hacia lo cotidiano en busca de lo universal. "Siempre apostaremos al amor." [FC]

3867 Martínez Sobrino, Mario. Cabellera de un relámpago. La Habana: Ediciones Unión, Unión de Escritores y Artistas de Cuba, 1998. 110 p.: ill. (Contemporáneos)
"Sólo por la poesía es posible interactuar en los desastres del cosmos caótico," plantea el poeta, miembro de la Generación del 50, en la introducción. Poemario éste en el que, "sin después ni antes," los límites de la realidad están en continua transformación ("Isla de las islas/siempre descubriéndose"). [FC]

3868 Martínez Torres, Renato. Estaciones. Santiago, Chile: LOM Ediciones, 1997. 74 p. (Col. Entre mares. Poesía)
Cautelosas meditaciones de un sujeto extraviado y reencontrado tras una ventana que se abre tanto al largo invierno de Iowa City como a los espejismos cotidianos de una memoria chilena. [OS]

3869 Marzán, Julio. Puerta de tierra. San Juan: Editorial de la Univ. de Puerto Rico, 1998. 67 p. (Col. Aquí y ahora; 40)
Dividido en tres partes que, en conjunto, reclaman el tiempo de la niñez, en este poemario la vuelta al pasado (el recuerdo) se da sin caer en la nostalgia. Entre Puerto Rico y Nueva York, el poeta de la diáspora articula los recuerdos como si fuera un álbum cuyas páginas mitigan la ruptura. [FC]

3870 Medina Méndez, Violeta. Juegos de humedad. Madrid: Ediciones Endymion, 2000? 81 p. (Poesía; 274)
En un lenguaje podado de exclamaciones, se auscultan diversos reflejos de una realidad personalizada, abierta a rumores o ecos de una otredad persistente. [OS]

3871 Miranda Casanova, Hernán. Anna Pink y otros poemas. Santiago, Chile: Ediciones Barbaria, 2000. 84 p.
Poemas que revelan la inmersión del sujeto en "el promiscuo universo humano" en su vertiente pesadillesca, amorosa y elegíaca. [OS]

3872 Mistral, Gabriela. Poesías completas. Estudios preliminar y referencias cronológicas de Jaime Quezada. Barcelona;

Santiago, Chile: Editorial Andrés Bello, 2001. 788 p.: bibl.
Imprescindible edición de todos los libros de Mistral con un estudio preliminar y cronología detallada de la vida de la poeta realizados por el poeta Jaime Quezada. [OS]

3873 Mitre, Eduardo. Camino de cualquier parte. Madrid: Visor, 1998. 117 p. (Col. Visor de poesía; 401)
La poesía del poeta boliviano Mitre (1943) se había caracterizado hasta ahora por ser de textos breves—oscilantes entre el juego y el experimento—siguiendo todavía las corrientes del vanguardismo hispanoamericano de los años de 1920. El presente volumen resulta ser novedoso en la obra de este autor, puesto que presenta un conjunto considerable de textos de mayor extensión que los contenidos en las colecciones abreviadas anteriores. Por eso, este libro puede ser considerado el volumen más importante del autor, obra de su madurez poética. Dividido en cuatro secciones ("Pasajes," "Parajes," "De Seca en Meca," y "Camino de cualquier parte"), los poemas, diversos y espontáneos en su motivación y sentido, tienen el rasgo común de haber sido generados por las circunstancias imprevistas y accidentales. El epígrafe de la primera sección ("I am what is around me," de Wallace Stevens) explica muy bien la instancia enunciativa que produjo estos textos: el recorrer pasajes, detenerse en parajes ajenos, añorar el lugar propio y llegar a la conclusión de que la vida del ser humano es un tránsito constante. Ciertamente, pese al carácter aparentemente circunstancial de estos textos, en su conjunto conforman la mejor colección publicada por su autor, cuyo tema es el contexto espacial del sujeto como parte de su individualidad, en términos de Stevens. [ORR]

3874 Molina, Mauricio Abominable libro de la nieve. San José: Ediciones Perro Azul, 1999. 60 p.
Este poemario obtuvo el Premio Hispanoamericano de Poesía Sor Juana Inés de la Cruz (1998), convocado por el Centro Cultural de la Embajada de México en Costa Rica. Su autor pertenece a las jóvenes generaciones costarricenses que desde la década de los 80 están replanteando el canon nacional ya sea desde propuestas antihegemónicas o desde una escritura post-utópica. Molina es

también uno de los poetas antologados en la recientemente publicada *Poesía de fin de siglo: Nicaragua-Costa Rica*, que reúne lo más representativo de la producción poética anti-canónica de las últimas dos décadas. En *Abominable libro de la nieve* el lector encontrará una poesía madura, certera en sus desafíos y definitivamente post-utópica. [EM]

3875 Montejo, Eugenio. Papiros amorosos. Madrid: Pre-Textos, 2002. 67 p. (Col. La Cruz del Sur; 562)

La trayectoria poética de Montejo es, sin duda, una de las más sólidas—si no la más memorable—de la segunda mitad del siglo XX venezolano. Este poemario, que reúne 50 piezas, de las cuales sólo 10 habían aparecido anteriormente, confirma al autor como figura central de la escena literaria hispanoamericana. La restricción temática que anuncia el título es engañosa: el erotismo constituye menos un fin que un medio para la expresión de una cosmología muy personal en la que cuerpo, naturaleza y cultura trazan dominios dependientes unos de otros, jamás excluyentes o guiados por la voluntad de poder. La fluidez y equivalencia de esos espacios se opone a las jerarquías patriarcales de la "mundialización," carentes de Eros, que el capitalismo tardío desea imponer como nueva *imago mundi*. [MG]

3876 Montero, María. La mano suicida. San José: Ediciones Perro Azul, 2000. 64 p. (Col. de poesía)

En la reciente poesía costarricense escrita por mujeres la obra de Montero (n. 1970) destaca por varias razones. Su primer poemario (*El juego conquistado*) obtuvo el Premio Joven Creación 1985, y en la década de los noventa sus textos poéticos empezaron a aparecer en antologías nacionales. En *La mano suicida* Montero sorprende al lector con una poesía femenina "suave pero de actitud feroz." La imagen de mujer que filtran sus poemas es francamente conmovedora, escapa a estereotipos feministas y resiste la interpretación fácil. Esta mujer "no tiene dirección: todos sus costados son profundos" y "escucha el amor sólo cuando viene en boca de los muertos." Inquietante y certera, la poética de Montero es sintomática de la profunda renovación por la que atraviesa la poesía costarricense contemporánea. [EM]

3877 Montes de Oca, Marco Antonio. Delante de la luz cantan los pájaros: poesía, 1953–2000. México: Fondo de Cultura Económica, 2000. 1181 p.: bibl., ill. (Letras mexicanas)

Enorme tomo que recopila la poesía completa (hasta la fecha) de Montes de Oca (Ciudad de México, 1932). Poeta prolífico (aquí agrega cinco libros inéditos) que deslumbra por su despliegue de metáforas, al principio contagiado por la energía febril del surrealismo. En las últimas entregas destaca el tono lúgubre, consciente ante la proximidad de la muerte. La amplitud y verbosidad de este volumen hacen pensar en los proyectos descomunales del barroco que desbordan todos los límites de sus propias poéticas. [JS]

3878 Montoya, Pablo. Viajeros. Medellín, Colombia: Editorial Univ. de Antioquia, 1999. 103 p. (Poesía)

Esta serie de poemas en prosa ilustra con eficacia tanto los límites como las ventajas de su género. Si por una parte la forma permite que se infiltren en la composición frases y pasajes enteros que en poco contribuyen a una tensión expresiva, por otra, lo prosaico esporádicamente enriquece al poema con las posibilidades dramáticas e imaginativas propias de la narrativa. Marco Polo, Magallanes, Cabeza de Vaca, Enrique el Navegante, Gulliver, los Argonautas, Moisés: lo histórico y lo mitológico conviven en esta galería de exploradores, desterrados y apátridas que monologan en un mundo donde las fronteras se borran, sea por los desplazamientos físicos, sea por las fuerzas del deseo. Notable para quienes estudien la producción poética de fines del siglo XX en Colombia es la aparente ausencia de los numerosos "desplazados" que la realidad nacional ha producido durante decenios: las migraciones, a veces clandestinas, siempre desesperadas, tanto a los EE.UU, a Venezuela, a distintos puntos de Europa, como a diversos márgenes de la sociedad. [MG]

3879 Moscona, Myriam. Negro marfil. México: Univ. Autónoma Metropolitana; Oak editorial, 2000. 87 p.: ill. (El Pez en el agua)

Inmerso en la tradición que se inicia con Rimaud y continúa con Mallarmé, Paz, y Haroldo de Campos, este libro explora las sinestesias y combinaciones de colores e imágenes. A la vez, Moscona (Ciudad de

México, 1955) busca el reverso del lenguaje entre los silencios que se desprenden de los blancos de la página. Las imágenes visuales (semejan paredes con inscripciones de un lenguaje cifrado, que se escribe al revés) dan una pauta de lectura que abre otra dimensión a la experiencia poética. [JS]

3880 Muestra de poesía hispanoamericana actual: 34 nombres en 34 años, 1963–1997. Recopilación de Alvaro Salvador. Granada, Spain: Diputación de Granada, 1998. 429 p. (Col. Maillot amarillo; 36)

Representativa selección de la mejor poesía del continente de la que sobresalen Marco Martos y Eduardo Chirinos (Perú), Rafael Courtoisie (Uruguay), José Pérez Olivares y Reina María Rodríguez (Cuba), José Luis Vega (Puerto Rico), Santiago Sylvester y Jorge Boccanera (Argentina), Raúl Zurita y Teresa Calderón (Chile), y Juan Gustavo Cobo Borda (Colombia). [LU]

3881 Muñoz Castillo, Arnaldo. Aroma de palabra entre mil mundos. Lima: A. Muñoz Castillo, 1997. 116 p.

The 29 poems included here constitute Muñoz Castillo's fourth book of poetry. His three earlier books were published in 1970, 1971, and 1994. This book has two prologues entitled, respectively, "Palabras frescas y antiguas," by Sandro Chiri Jaime, and "Palabras para 'Aroma de palabra entre mil mundos'," by Graciela Briceño. Includes five sections and an epilogue. Muñoz Castillo's own introspective meditations dominate the collection. [GP]

3882 Naranjo, Alexis. La piel del tiempo. Quito?: Corporación Cultural Eskeletra, 1998. 96 p. (Col. La última cena)

El poeta ecuatoriano Naranjo (1947) confirma con este nuevo poemario la calidad de un lenguaje poético sutil en su referencia a los objetos y situaciones de que trata. Anteriormente había publicado *Profanaciones* (1988), *Ontogonías* (1990), *El oro de las ruinas* (1994), e *Interegnum* (1996). En el presente poemario, su reflexión sobre las cosas y situaciones se realiza a través de una perspectiva consciente del transcurrir del tiempo, tema, y preocupación que sostienen cierta uniformidad de su discurso poético. La presencia del tiempo se manifiesta de diversas maneras: desde el simple transcurso de un momento a otro en un día, hasta la referencia

y representación simbólica de entidades temporales míticas y trascendentes. Contrariamente, la percepción del espacio surge como la de un objeto familiar y conocido que puede ser descrito sin connotaciones simbólicas y metafísicas, pero sobre todo sin la incertidumbre que implica hablar sobre el tiempo. [ORR]

3883 Negro, Héctor. Y voy cantando al andar: obra poética; selección 1957–1997. Buenos Aires: Corregidor, 1998. 222 p.

La selección aquí presentada es clara muestra de la coherencia y evolución de la poesía de este no siempre reconocido integrante de la llamada "generación del 60" en Argentina con quienes comparte, a través del lenguaje coloquial, el rescate de lo cotidiano y los temas urbanos. [LU]

3884 Neruda, Pablo. Obras completas. v. 3. De "Arte de pájaros" a "El mar y las campanas," 1966–1973. Barcelona: Galaxia Gutenberg; Círculo de Lectores, 2000. 1 v. (Opera mundi)

Incluye textos publicados entre 1923–73. Prólogo detallado y claramente informativo de Joaquín Marco. Cuidada edición y notas precisas de Hernán Loyola para cada libro incluído. [OS]

3885 Núñez, Guillermo. Antología del mar, 1964–1996. Selección de poemas por Ana Elba Irizarry de Olivero. San Juan: Editorial de la Univ. de Puerto Rico, 1999. 137 p.

Compuesta de siete poemarios, esta antología recoge el trabajo de un poeta autodidacta en cuya obra plantea el litoral de la isla, y no como plantea la tradición, la montaña, supone la "esencia ontológica." Sus grandes temas, según Irizarry de Olivero, son la patria, la libertad, el amor y la identidad. [FC]

3886 Núñez, Serafina. En las serenas márgenes: antología poética. Selección, presentación y notas biobibliográficas de Teresita Hernández de Cárdenas. La Habana: Editorial Letras Cubanas, 1998. 210 p.

Entre 1937–95 han salido a la luz pública ocho poemarios de la autora, una de las voces líricas de la poesía femenina cubana contemporánea, cuya poesía, según Fernández Retamar, tocada por la de Juan Ramón Jiménez, "arranca de la producción nerudiana." [FC]

3887 Ocampo Abásolo, Carolina. Oda a la utopía. Lima: Ediciones Capuli, 1998. 121 p.

Manuel J. Baquerizo's prologue, entitled "Poesía y Esperanza," refers to Ocampo's poetry as the interplay of existential meditations and reality checks. Most of the poems included in this compilation are short, with simple and direct language that is also expressive and intense. [GP]

3888 Oraá, Pedro de. Umbral. La Habana: Ediciones UNION, 1997. 110 p. (La rueda dentada. Poesía)

Miembro establecido de la generación del 50. Dividido en tres partes, en este poemario, de factura barroca, la poesía celebra el artificio ("la artimaña del papel coloreado"), el preciosismo de las cosas insignificantes, a la vez que hurga en el sentido profundo de la poesía ("vigilia / en el sueño"). [FC]

3889 Oré, Ricardo. Inscripciones en un campo de retamas. Lima: Ediciones Los Olivos, 1997. 69 p.

Published the same year as *El sombreado de la liebre* (see item **3890**), this collection contains 14 poems, one of which is also the book's title. Most of these long poems, with rich and elaborate language, are arranged with somewhat of a narrative. The spatial and biographical references are used to explore imaginative relationships. [GP]

3890 Oré, Ricardo. El sombreado de la liebre. Lima: Ediciones Los Olivos, 1997. 70 p.

The 32 poems collected here represent Oré's third book of poetry. There is a narrative component in most of the poems within the boundaries of an elaborate language intended to resemble the act of painting. Oré has also published narrations, essays, and plays. [GP]

3891 Orozco, Olga. Relámpagos de lo invisible: antología. Selección y prólogo de Horacio Zabaljáuregui. Buenos Aires: Fondo de Cultura Económica, 1998. 312 p.: ill. (Col. Tierra firme)

Muestra antológica de esta extraordinaria poeta argentina que recibiera el Premio de Literatura "Juan Rulfo" en 1998. El tiempo y la memoria van cifrando esta poesía donde la palabra es presagio y el poeta es vidente y alquimista que transforma lo real en imágenes de dimensión simbólica. [LU]

3892 Orta Ruiz, Jesús. Desde un mirador profundo. La Habana: Ediciones Unión; Letras Cubanas, 1997. 283 p. (Bolsilibros Unión) (Poesía)

Conocido como "el indio Naborí," y asociado con el uso de la décima, en esta "compilación selectiva" se ofrece una muestra de poemarios publicados entre 1955–95; incluye además, otro inédito. "Poesía íntima, vivencia y autobiográfica," ésta cambia, en su fase madura, "la pasión por la ternura." [FC]

3893 Pacheco, José Emilio. La arena errante: poemas, 1992–1998. México: Ediciones Era, 1999. 123 p. (Biblioteca Era)

Nueva entrega de Pacheco (Ciudad de México, 1939), quien se mantiene fiel a una voz concisa que se consolidó desde 1969. Pacheco es el poeta de la cotidianeidad que observa con agudeza y pesimismo la transitoriedad y las novedades del momento. En este volumen continúa con la conciencia crítica acerca de la muerte y el milagro de saberse vivos. [JS]

3894 Pacheco, José Emilio. Siglo pasado: desenlace; poemas, 1999–2000. México: Ediciones Era, 2000. 60 p. (Era 40) (Biblioteca Era)

No sólo el libro que culmina la poética de Pacheco (Ciudad de México, 1939), sino también un adiós al siglo XX y al segundo milenio. En su mayor parte, poemas concisos que esbozan en unos cuantos versos ironías acerca de la poesía, el paso del tiempo y reflexiones del momento. El tono habitual de Pacheco se reduce aquí a lo esencial, a veces a través de la exploración de una sola imagen o idea. [JS]

3895 Padilla, Heberto. Fuera del juego. Ed. conmemorativa, 1968–1998; 1. ed. conmemorativa. Miami: Ediciones Universal, 1998. 199 p.: bibl. (Col. Clásicos cubanos; 19)

Además del poemario que tanto escándalo causó en la Cuba de 1968 al ganar el Premio de Poesía Julián del Casal, esta edición contiene una amplia documentación (declaraciones, documentos, estudios) sobre lo que se conoció como el "caso Padilla." [FC]

3896 Pancorvo, José. Profeta el cielo. Lima: Alba Editores, 1997. 153 p.

This book of poems has seven sections with such titles as "Invasión de la eternidad," "Expedición espejo espíritu," "Post

Ierusalem, cantos sobre los milenios," "Sao Paulo mientras se estremece la tierra," and "Inmediación del Incarrey." The book includes many references to everyday life and historical events, and occasionally uses Latin expressions. With these references, Pancorvo attempts to explore existential matters. [GP]

3897 Parra, Sergio. Mandar al diablo al infierno. Santiago: LOM Ediciones, 1999? 116 p. (Col. Entre mares. Poesía)

Incluye *La manoseada* (1987), *Poemas de Paco Bazán* (1993), y *Mandar al diablo al infierno.* Al travestismo contestatario de voz quebrada de los primeros textos se integra la crudeza poética de un sujeto ágil, descreído, cuyo cuerpo revela, desde una marginalidad hipersensitiva, los dobleces de una sociedad consumida por un presente triunfalista. [OS]

3898 Paz, Octavio. Obras completas. v. 13, Miscelánea I. Primeros escritos. México: Fondo de Cultura Económica, 2000. 432 p. (Letras mexicanas)

Este volumen recoge los primeros poemas y ensayos de Paz. Por mucho tiempo, Paz desdeñó su poesía inicial; algunos textos fueron corregidos y otros nunca se volvieron a publicar. Al final de su vida, Paz decidió publicar los textos él mismo, antes que otros los editen sin su supervisión. El volumen es interesantísimo para todos los estudiosos de Paz: prefigura la obra posterior en casi todas sus dimensiones. [JS]

3899 Pedroni, José. Obra poética. Prólogo de Juan José Saer. Apéndice con textos de Leopoldo Lugones *et al.* 3. ed. Santa Fe, Argentina: Univ. Nacional del Litoral; Provincia de Santa Fe, 1999. 675 p.: bibl.

Bienvenida reedición de la obra de este santafesino a quien Lugones llamó "el hermano luminoso" con motivo de la publicación de *Gracia plena* (1925). Poesía de marcado lirismo y panteísmo que recuerda la de su coetáneo, el entrerriano Juan L. Ortiz. El lenguaje de Pedroni celebra la elementalidad del mundo, su comunión con la tierra y sus habitantes, con idéntica pureza. [LU]

3900 Pérez, Floridor. Obra completamente incompleta. Santiago, Chile: Univ. Nacional Andrés Bello; Editorial Planeta, 1997. 169 p.

Poemas que vinculan lo folclórico popular con lo culto y entre los cuales se encuentran textos que vinculan la relación amorosa y la violenta represión política del autoritarismo de manera espléndida. [OS]

3901 Pérez Pierret, Antonio. Antonio Pérez Pierret: obra poética. Edición de Antonio Colberg Pérez. San Juan: Editorial de la Univ. de Puerto Rico, 1998. 194 p.: bibl., 2 ill.

Una de las luminarias del modernismo puertorriqueño, la poesía de Pérez Pierret (1885–1937) es ampliada en esta nueva edición: se incluyen ahora unos 50 poemas inéditos que complementan las dos ampliaciones anteriores (1959 y 1968). Se incluye también el ensayo de Félix Franco Oppenheimer de 1959. [FC]

3902 Perlongher, Néstor Osvaldo. Poemas completos: 1980–1992. Edición y prólogo de Roberto Echavarren. Con una nota de Reynaldo Jiménez sobre Aguas aéreas y un epílogo de Tamara Kamenszain. 1. ed. en esta biblioteca. Buenos Aires: Seix Barral, 1997. 382 p.: bibl. (Biblioteca breve)

La obra de Perlongher (1949–92) ha suscitado, desde su primer poemario, *Austria/Hungría* (1980), la inquietud de la crítica por su audacia poética y radicalidad discursiva asociada con los códigos expresivos del neobarroco o "neobarroso," según terminología acuñada por el propio Perlongher. Sus poemas constituyen una "épica del deseo" (Modarelli) altamente sugestiva. La cuidada edición y estudios de Echavarren, Kamenszain, y Jiménez hacen de ésta una obra de consulta ineludible para los estudiosos no sólo de Perlongher sino de la poesía argentina contemporánea. [LU]

3903 Piña Williams, Víctor Hugo. Rimas rumias. México: Editorial Aldus, 1999. 64 p.: col. ill. (Col. Aldus. Los poetas)

Piña Williams (Ciudad de México, 1958) es el poeta de la paronomasia y la aliteración, siguiendo la tradición del neobarroco de las *Galaxias* de Haroldo de Campos o del argentino Néstor Perlongher. En este volumen practica una poesía lúdica que juega con los sentidos o sinsentidos del lenguaje, burlándose de las categorías fijas y estéticas. Véase "Neuralgia de la muerte," título que parodia el célebre *Nostalgia de la muerte,* de Villaurrutia. [JS]

3904 Los poetas van al cine. Selección y notas de Angel Miquel. México: Ediciones Sin Nombre; Juan Pablos Editor, 1997. 182 p.: bibl. (Pantalla de papel)

Antología muy original que recoge el diálogo entre la poesía y el cine. Organizado por secciones "En el cine" (descripción de la experiencia en la sala), "Estrellas," "Películas" y "Desde el cine" (reflexiones poéticas a partir del cine). La muestra incluye escritores mexicanos o poetas que residieron por un tiempo en ese país, abarcando el periodo de 1915–96 (fecha en que se conmemoran los 100 años del cine en México). [JS]

3905 Pollarolo, Giovanna. La ceremonia del adiós. Lima: PEISA, 1997. 103 p. (Alma matinal)

This is Pollarolo's third book of poems; two previous books were published in 1986 and 1991 (see *HLAS 54:4422*). The book has three different sections ("Noche oscura," "Vida nueva," and "Plegarias, conjuros y delirios") and appropriately ends with a poem entitled "Diálogo entre Elizabeth Taylor y su amigo y confidente Truman Capote." The poems deal with intense emotions through a language which seems to come from a believer in language more than in religion. Using a conversational tone, the poems espouse qualities of transparency. [GP]

3906 Prado, Nadia. Carnal. Santiago, Chile: Editorial Cuarto Propio, 1998. 92 p. (Serie Poesía)

Este libro explora, mediante un lenguaje poético, lúcido y descarnado, una experiencia radical de mujer que se interroga sobre su palabra y su crítica relación con la elusiva presencia del amante. [OS]

3907 Preciado, Antonio. De par en par. Guayaquil?, Ecuador: Casa de la Cultura Ecuatoriana Benjamín Carrión: Fondo Editorial C.C.E., 1998. 195 p.

Preciado (1941) es uno de los poetas más destacados de la poesía ecuatoriana contemporánea, y en este libro reúne los dos últimos poemarios ya publicados: *De ahora en adelante* (1993) y *Jututo* (1996). La reedición de ambas publicaciones obedece al deseo del autor de corregir los errores de las ediciones anteriores, las cuales obviamente quedan descalificadas por el propio poeta. Los eventuales estudiosos de esta poesía deben tener en cuenta este hecho. Los textos revisados y corregidos conservan el tono que este poeta afroecuatoriano ha mostrado desde sus inicios: protesta y crítica sociales por las condiciones adversas de las comunidades de negros del Ecuador. Es una poesía de preocupaciones sociales focalizadas sobre la realidad social e histórica de un grupo étnico específico. Sin embargo, la poesía de Preciado tiene siempre presente un contexto literario amplio: la mejor tradición de la lírica castellana de protesta: desde la crítica severa de Francisco de Quevedo hasta la protesta dolorosa de César Vallejo. El libro está precedido de una presentación de otro distinguido escritor afroecuatoriano, Nelson Estupiñán Bass. [ORR]

3908 Quiroz Avila, Rubén. El juego de los escondites. Lima: Arteidea Editores, 1997? 47 p.: ill. (Col. de las primicias; 2)

In a brief but interesting note by Marco Martos, he praises Quiroz Avila's interest in the contemplation of apparently casual matters or natural objects that appear to be insignificant but are not. Martos also finds a clear personal and mature voice in this young poet which is expressed in the way Quiroz Avila writes. With originality, he searches for moments of wonder and revelation in spontaneous life encounters. [GP]

3909 Ramírez, Josué. Ulises trivial. México: Ediciones Sin Nombre; Ediciones Casa Juan Pablos, 2000. 62 p. (Col. poesía cuadernos de la salamandra)

Ramírez (Ciudad de México, 1963) continúa en este libro la tradición del poeta y la Ciudad de México (Bernardo de Balbuena, Manuel Maples Arce, Octavio Paz, Efraín Huerta, y David Huerta, entre otros). Este Ulises deja de ser un héroe mitológico y se convierte en personaje mundano que no vacila en retratar la calle por la que transita. Ramírez muestra su manejo de varios tipos de versos (incluyendo la prosa poética), además de que combina un discurso depurado con giros que atacan todo intento de pomposidad. [JS]

3910 Ramos Collado, Lilliana. Reróticas. San Juan: Libros Nómadas, 1998. 107 p. (Libros Nómadas; 3)

Sobre la premisa de que la retórica y el erotismo "comparten los mismos trucos" ("aman la lengua y aman con la lengua"), se aborda en este poemario el amor lesbiano mediante un dinámico conceptismo minimalista que, entre otros, explora la "lógica" del amor a lo idéntico como "un gran amor." [FC]

3911 Restrepo, Juan. El desvaneciente mediodía. Bogotá: Tercer Mundo Editores, 2000. 102 p.

El universo construido por este nuevo poemario de Restrepo se aparta con persistencia de toda referencia familiar o cotidiana; su topografía, semejante a la de los paisajes de Odilon Redon, pertenece al inconsciente o las desrealizaciones a las que la poesía nos tiene acostumbrados a partir del simbolismo. De hecho, podría afirmarse que la tersa musicalidad de estos versos en más de una ocasión substituye todo tipo de tensión dramática. Situada en la historia colombiana reciente, esta alternativa poética resulta, sin embargo, perfectamente inteligible, acaso no como "escape," sino más bien como contrapeso anímico a una realidad difícil e insoslayable. [MG]

3912 Rivas, José Luis. Río. México: Fondo de Cultura Económica, 1998. 106 p. (Letras mexicanas)

Excelente traductor de Rimbaud, Saint-John Perse y Walkott, Rivas (Veracruz, México, 1950) es también un poeta de la densidad de la imagen y de la exploración de la memoria. Adquirió prestigio con *Tierra nativa* (1982) y ahora genera un caudal que hace que su poesía crezca y acumule cada vez más envergadura. Este *Río* (con versos delgados y gruesos) recorre los caminos geográficos y culturales de la rememoración. [JS]

3913 Rivero, Raúl. Herejías elegidas: antología poética. Prefacio y prólogo de José Prats Sariol. Selección del autor y del prologuista. Madrid: Betania, 1998. 172 p. (Col. Antologías)

Dividida en siete partes correspondientes a los siete poemarios que, escritos entre 1969–97, la componen, esta antología reúne el trabajo de quien, además de por la poesía (1969 y 1972), ha sido galardonado por su labor periodística (1997, Cuba Press). Poesía de fino coloquialismo, a la de Rivero le "duele" la patria. [FC]

3914 Rojas, Gonzalo. Obra selecta. Selección, prólogo, cronología, bibliografía y variantes de Marcelo Coddou. Edición revisada por Gonzalo Rojas. Cuidado de la edición de José Ramón Medina. Caracas: Biblioteca Ayacucho; Santiago, Chile: Fondo de Cultura Económica, 1997. 347 p.: bibl. (Biblioteca Ayacucho; 212)

Texto imprescindible para el estudio de la obra de Rojas. En su introducción Coddou inserta esta poesía en el contexto histórico chileno, explica el constante reordenamiento o juego de textos que Rojas lleva a cabo en sus libros, reflexiona sobre todos los índices temáticos en que se dividen los textos de esta selección (entre ellos: lo metapoético, lo erótico, lo elegíaco, y lo político) y sobre las transgresiones sintácticas de esta escritura. La selección de poemas en siete secciones (de la que participó Rojas) incorpora nuevos poemas y es la más inclusiva de las realizadas hasta el momento. Coddou también inserta un detalle de variaciones textuales de los poemas seleccionados, 10 textos en prosa de Rojas donde se expanden los vínculos poéticos y las ideas en torno a la poesía señalados en la introducción, una valiosa cronología de eventos en la vida del poeta que llega hasta 1995 y una bibliografía de las obras del poeta junto con libros, artículos y reseñas dedicados a la poesía de Rojas. [OS]

3915 Rokha, Pablo de. Obras inéditas. Edición a cargo de Naín Nómez. Santiago, Chile: LOM Ediciones; Consejo Nacional del Libro y la Lectura, 1999. 225 p. (Col. Entre mares) (Poesía)

Esta edición de Naín Nómez incluye: poemas en el mejor estilo exuberante de De Rokha; textos de reconocimiento dedicados a figuras como Ho Chi Minh y Regis Debray; ensayos y entrevistas sobre la poética rokhiana; por último, textos polémicos que rescatan la virulencia crítica de De Rokha. [OS]

3916 Romero, Armando. Cuatro líneas. Xalapa, Mexico: Graffiti; Instituto Veracruzano de la Cultura, Editora de Gobierno, 2001. 54 p. (Literatura menor)

Con este poemario, Armando Romero prueba nuevamente su capacidad de transformarse e ir más allá de sus perfiles nadaístas iniciales. Tal como sucede en volúmenes suyos de los últimos años como *Las combinaciones debidas* (1989) o *A rienda suelta* (1991), ningún vestigio de estridencias neovanguardistas se percibe en esta colección de cuartetas libres, que hacen de la discreción tonal y una sencillez cercana a lo clásico sus mayores virtudes. En efecto, el erotismo que da unidad al conjunto oscila entre lo moderno y lo explícitamente helénico, tanto por su expresividad como por el marco "dramático" en el que el lector puede situar las composiciones, que a la par de ciudades modernas como Caracas mencionan "islas," "dioses," y, finalmente, en la fecha de redacción del libro, el "Mar Egeo." El postvanguardismo de Romero, así pues, no implica arcaísmo, sino una atinada recuperación de la tradición que remoza la experiencia del presente. [MG]

3917 Rueda, Manuel. Las metamorfosis de Makandal. Santo Domingo: Banco Central de la República Dominicana, Depto. Cultural, 1998. 221 p.: ill.

"Yo soy uno en extensión de dos. / Yo soy uno replegado en ninguno." Como principio de la unidad en la multiplicidad, del vacío en la presencia, Makandal, el héroe haitiano, supone el proceso del todo a la nada, "de todo lo que había de ser y que no ha sido." [FC]

3918 Ruiz Dueñas, Jorge. Saravá. México: Ediciones Sin Nombre; Juan Pablos Editor, 1997. 61 p. (Cuadernos de la salamandra)

Ganador del Premio Xavier Villaurrutia 1997 por este libro, Ruiz Dueñas (Baja California, México, 1946) explora, fascinado, el territorio cultural de Brasil. La palabra saravá es una "salutación y ensalmo para apartar los malos espíritus y atraer a las potencias bienhechoras." El viaje del poema es un recorrido por la geografía del país, aunado a los encuentros lingüísticos y culturales (con frecuentes referencias al sincretismo religioso afrobrasileño), además de enriquecerse con citas de poetas, como Drummond de Andrade, Ledo Ivo o João Cabral de Melo Neto. [JS]

3919 Salinas, Alicia. Entre el cielo y el fuego. Viña del Mar, Chile: Ediciones Altazor, 1997. 83 p. (Serie divergente)

Textos que dan cuenta de una mirada incisiva de mujer que revisa sigilosamente los paraderos y despeñaderos de su experiencia existencial, cultural y social. [OS]

3920 Sanabria Fernández, Hernando. Romances de mi tierra. Santa Cruz de la Sierra, Bolivia: Fondo Editorial Gobierno Municipal, 1997. 265 p.: ill.

Volumen póstumo publicado 11 años después de la muerte del distinguido historia-

dor y narrador boliviano, Sanabria Fernández (1909–86). La publicación de este volumen no deja de ser un homenaje oficial a su autor pues aparece bajo el sello del Fondo Editorial Municipal de la ciudad de Santa Cruz. Compilado por Marcelino Pérez Fernández, el volumen reúne en orden cronológico 106 romances escritos entre 1924–66 y presenta una obra poco conocida de su autor, quien se distinguió por sus aportes a la investigación histórica y al género narrativo. No obstante, el autor publicó colecciones de versos, como *Poemas provincianos* (1963) y *Figuras de antaño* (1973). Las características estilísticas (preferencia por el romance) y temáticas (personajes y temas del pasado) de esos textos reaparecen ahora diversificadas en la nueva publicación, en la que su autor conjuga sus preocupaciones de historiador, narrador, y poeta. El romance no sólo es la forma preferida de este poeta, como lo demuestra obviamente el libro, sino la forma que le permite introducir relatos de leyendas o episodios de la historia regional de Santa Cruz, Bolivia, y Los Andes. Los motivos de estos textos corresponden a períodos históricos diversos: prehispánico, colonial, de las luchas por la Independencia, o del tiempo contemporáneo. A través de esta preocupación histórica no deja de percibirse un pensamiento sobre la identidad regional. [ORR]

3921 Sauma, Osvaldo. Bitacora del iluso. San José: Agencia Española de Cooperación Internacional, Centro Cultural de España: Ediciones Perro Azul, 2000. 110 p.

Desde su primer poemario, *Las huellas del desencanto* (1982), la poesía de Sauma se caracteriza por el rigor con que propone un nuevo lenguaje para la poesía costarricense contemporánea. Alejado del exteriorismo que desde la década de los 60 determinó el curso de la producción poética centroamericana, Sauma da paso a una poesía que asombra tanto por la fuerza con que dota al lenguaje de un nuevo ritmo, como por la lucidez con que asume el agotamiento de las retóricas del siglo XX. Para el último Sauma la historia y la poesía han salido *calladas* del siglo XX. Sin promesas en el horizonte y obligado a alzar vuelo en medio de la nada, sus poemas responden a lo que ya algunos críticos han señalado como el gesto postutópico de las últimas generaciones de poetas centroamericanos. Destinada a una gran atención en el futuro, la poesía de Sauma empieza a ser percibida como significativa dentro de su tradición nacional. Prueba de ello es su inclusión en una de las mejores antologías que se han hecho recientemente de la poesía costarricense de fin de siglo: *Poesía de fin de siglo: Nicaragua-Costa Rica.* [EM]

3922 Segovia, Tomás. Misma juventud: poemas, 1997–1999. Madrid: Editorial Pre-Textos, 2000. 63 p. (Col. La Cruz del Sur; 481)

Libro que celebra el Premio Octavio Paz, que fue otorgado a Segovia (1927) en 2000. El título es un espejo de Otro invierno, libro de cuentos (ambos referidos a la vejez). Casi como se tratara de un juego de búsqueda, fuga y encuentro, la persona poética refleja y reflexiona con lucidez acerca de la edad y el tiempo. [JS]

3923 Segovia, Tomás. Poesía: 1943–1997. México: Fondo de Cultura Económica, 1998. 771 p. (Col. Tierra firme)

Segunda entrega de la poesía completa de Segovia (España-México, 1927); la primera es de 1980. Aquí se agregan siete libros más, aunque no se incluye *Misma juventud,* que fue publicado inmediatamente después (ver ítem **3922**). Segovia es conocido por su poesía erótica, en la vena surrealista y por *Anagnórisis,* un poema extenso (que incluye, a su vez, otros poemas que aparecen como paréntesis de una frase o imagen verbal) que explora el ámbito del exilio desde diferentes perspectivas: la memoria, el viaje y la orfandad. Las últimas entregas se dedican con mayor vigor al tema de la vejez y la muerte. [JS]

3924 Siempre escrito en el agua: antología. Edición a cargo de Naín Nómez. Santiago, Chile: LOM Ediciones, 1998. 171 p.: ill. (Col. Entre mares)

Precedido por una acertada introducción de Nómez, los poemas de los cinco libros antologados representan fielmente el expresionismo social del poeta desprendido con autonomía de la obra de Pablo de Rokha. [OS]

3925 Silva Acevedo, Manuel. Suma alzada. Prólogo de Adriana Valdés. Santiago: Fondo de Cultura Económica Chile, 1998. 274 p.: bibl. (Tierra firme. Poetas chilenos.)

Excelente antología de textos escritos desde 1967–96. Poemas que oscilan entre el pavor y la resurección de los seres y las cosas y que afirman, de manera persistente, las contradicciones y el quiebre del sujeto dividido entre infierno y paraíso. [OS]

3926 Sin Pega, Lope. No se engañe nadie, no: antología de sonetos y otros poemas. Selección y prólogo de Carlos Alberto Trujillo. Santiago, Chile: Mosquito Comunicaciones, 1999. 196 p.: bibl., ill.

Recopilación de sonetos sarcásticos y textos paródicos escritos por Lope Sin Pega, el alter-ego popular de Trujillo. Se utiliza aquí la jerga chilena para evidenciar una mirada cáustica y carnavalesca de la sociedad chilena bajo la dictadura de Pinochet. [OS]

3927 Sobalvarro, Juan. Unánime. Nicaragua: Nuevo Signo, 1999. 121 p.

El autor de este poemario es el fundador de la prestigiosa revista literaria nicaragüense *400 Elefantes.* Es también co-editor de una excelente muestra poética (ver ítem **3759**). En este volumen Sobalvarro consolida el proyecto cultural de las jóvenes generaciones centroamericanas: cambiarle el rumbo a la poesía, escribir desde una vocación anticanónica, antihegemónica y postutópica. En *Unánime,* Sobalvarro conduce al lector al vértigo de la creatividad, porque si bien se exila de los lugares comunes de la poesía y cultiva un aire cínico, ancla su poética en la desgarradora conciencia de estar viviendo "tiempos propicios para volverse loco." Sin duda este poemario, y su autor, han de convertirse en referentes importantes de la actual poesía centroamericana. [EM]

3928 Sotomayor, Aurea María. Rizoma. San Juan, Puerto Rico: Libros Nómadas, 1998. 86 p. (Libros Nómadas; 2)

En diálogo con la literatura y el cine, con la teoría postestructuralista, este poemario plantea lo poético en el lado "difícil" de la escritura; ese lado en el que se le exige al lector que "diferencie" y "distinga" entre las palabras, las mismas que la poeta ha "igualado" bajo "un solo estilo." [FC]

3929 Tarrab Rivera, Alejandro. Siete cantáridas. México: Ediciones Sin Nombre, 2001. 32 p. (Cuadernos de la salamandra)

Aunque Tarrab Rivera (Ciudad de México, 1972) ya había publicado un par de plaquettes anteriores, este volumen viene a consolidarlo como una de las voces emergentes más interesantes de la poesía mexicana actual. Poemas de iniciación, las cantáridas (insectos que, a su vez, remiten a

Rimbaud y a la vocación por el canto) se construyen como revelaciones que llegan inesperadamente. Destacan, también, las múltiples voces que dialogan en el interior de los poemas. [JS]

3930 Toledo, Aída and **Janet Gold.** The kindness of cybernetics = Bondades de la cibernética. Guatemala?: Univ. Rafael Landívar: Fundación Colloquia, 1998. 90 p.

Publicado en Guatemala por la Univ. Rafael Landívar, este poemario bilingüe es el resultado de la colaboración entre dos artistas: la guatemalteca Toledo y la norteamericana Gold. En el caso de Toledo se publica una selección de libros ya publicados (tres en total); en el de Gold, se da a conocer por primera vez su trabajo poético. En ambos casos el lector se encuentra con poéticas femeninas que abisman la moral patriarcal de las sociedades modernas. [EM]

3931 Tolentino Dipp, Hugo. Vocablos. Ilustraciones de Ada Balcácer. Santo Domingo: Taller, 1998. 147 p.: ill.

Dividido en cinco partes, este poemario incide en una temática muchas veces poética: el pasado-presente, el patriotismo, la amistad, el tiempo, la intimidad. El amor ("algo que latiendo en la cordura / estalla sin saber, inusitado") y la nostalgia ("esa tierna mordida / que es el dolor del alma") lo permean todo. [FC]

3932 Toros en el corazón: antología de poesía eskeletra. Selección e introducción de Pablo Salgado J. Quito: Eskeletra Editorial, 1997. 173 p. (Col. La lulupa. Poesía)

Esta publicación tiene importancia porque corresponde a un grupo de nueve poetas ecuatorianos reunidos bajo el nombre de "Grupo Eskeletra." No es un grupo generacional, pues el mayor tiene 50 años y el menor 32; además, algunos de ellos gozan de prestigio literario en su país y otros son menos conocidos. Por otra parte, la editorial que llevó a cabo esta publicación lleva el mismo nombre del grupo. Los editores definen las características de la compilación como "textos en los que rondan la ironía, la irreverencia, el desenfado; en los que conviven los rastreos postmodernos con lo metafórico, lo intertextual con lo conversacional e incluso con lo realista." Esa caracterización es apropiada a los poemas elegidos. Los autores incluidos son: Jennie Carrasco, Ramiro

Oviedo, Alfredo Pérez, Huilo Ruales, Francisco Torres, Leopoldo Tobar, Alejandro Velasco, Miguel Zambrano y Pablo Salgado, quien es el compilador y autor de una introducción a la antología. [ORR]

3933 Troiano, Marita. Poemas urbanos. Lima: Carpe Diem Editora, 1998. 153 p. (Col. Femmes)

Troiano's second poetry book has a brief prologue by Lady Rojas-Trempe. Troiano's poems are characterized by allegories, symbols, and metaphors, which are used to make spatial references that could be considered local and cosmopolitan. The book is organized into three sections: "Arte poética/De la existencia," "Las ciudades/ La gente," and "Del amor y otros milagros," which gives a sense of the topics Troiano addresses, daring to touch on contemporary cultural issues with intelligence, intensity, and passion. [GP]

3934 Ulate Vázquez, Mario. El beso montaraz de la memoria: poesía. San José: Premià Editores, 1999. 84 p.

Es éste el cuarto poemario de un poeta que desde 1979 publica poesía y participa activamente en talleres y grupos literarios nacionales. Perteneció al "Círculo de Poetas Costarricences" que Jorge Debravo, Marco Aguilar y Laureano Albán fundaron en la década de los 60. Actualmente, es miembro fundador del "Grupo Literario Voz Abierta." En este poemario la poesía de Ulate se declara "heredera del beso montaraz de la memoria," que en es este caso implica en igual medida una memoria histórica, una memoria literaria, y una memoria personal. Ulate las convoca y las recrea para conjurar el olvido. [EM]

3935 Umaña, Helen. Península del viento. Ciudad de Guatemala: Letra Negra Editores, 2000. 54 p. (Poesía centroamericana; 1)

A más de 20 años de la llamada "década perdida" guatemalteca, la escritora y crítica literaria Helen Umaña da claras señas de que el duelo centroamericano no ha concluido. Las composiciones que encontramos en este volumen son poemas de exilio escritos entre 1982–86. En conjunto, registran la escritura del exilio en tres distintos y complejos momentos: la memoria del horror, la experiencia misma del exiliado, y el poder de la palabra poética para recomenzar la vida.

Esto permite que el círculo abierto del duelo sea recorrido en todos sus matices y con todos los lenguajes posibles: el testimonial, el del desastre, el histórico, el documental, pero también el solidario, el que reinstaura la comunicación, el amor y el retorno de la vida. La intensidad y capacidad creativa de estos poemas hacen de Península del viento un aporte significativo a la escritura del exilio en Centroamérica. [EM]

3936 Uribe, Armando. Ataúdes: estamos viejos y no estamos muertos, en un estado incómodo; Erratas. Santiago, Chile: Be-uve-dráis Editores, 1999. 245 p.

Dos secciones: "erratas," ajuste de cuentas en escenas por momentos autobiográficas, y "ataúdes," crónica cáustica de diversos rituales de la muerte. [OS]

3937 Uribe, Armando. Las críticas de Chile. Santiago, Chile: Be-uve-dráis Editores, 1999. 75 p.

El libro se divide en críticas de la vida política, social, sexual, y los rituales del luto. Un "Yo acuso" áspero y directo de los "males" de la sociedad chilena bajo la modernidad postdictatorial. [OS]

3938 Uribe, Armando. A peor vida. Santiago, Chile: LOM Ediciones, 2000. 205 p.: ill. (Col. Entre mares. Poesía)

Segunda parte de Las críticas de Chile (ver ítem **3937**). El libro se divide en críticas de miedo, acríticas, y críticas del amor bestial y hechos reales. A una mirada autoascultadora se conjuga una mirada al grotesco social y sexual. [OS]

3939 Urondo, Francisco. Poemas de batalla: antología poética, 1950–1976. Selección y prólogo de Juan Gelman. Buenos Aires: Seix Barral, 1998. 169 p. (Biblioteca breve)

Esta justa y representativa muestra antológica es un celebrado avance editorial para divulgar la obra de un importante poeta de la llamada "generación del sesenta." El libro incluye tres poemas del libro inédito Cuentos de batalla (1973–76) que sólo habían sido publicados anteriormente en la revista bonaerense Crisis. [LU]

3940 Valdés, Zoé. Cuerdas para el lince. Barcelona: Editorial Lumen, 1999. 78 p. (Poesía; 108)

Dividido en cuatro partes, en este poe-

mario—el cuarto publicado hasta la fecha—la visión filosófica y la urdimbre poética inciden, entre otros, en el paso del tiempo ("El tiempo no es la vida"), en la continuidad de la identidad a través del tiempo ("No soy este ser que soy"). [FC]

3941 Vallejo, César. Poemas completos. Introducción, edición y notas de Ricardo González Vigil. Lima: PETROPERU, Ediciones COPE, 1998. 479 p.: bibl., index.

A popular edition of Vallejo's poetry intended for a large audience, thus the critical references are purposely limited in scope. Based on Obras completas, the critical edition published by González Vigil in 1991. Includes an introductory note and an extensive bibliography. [GP]

3942 Vallejo, César. Poesía completa. v. 1–4. Lima: Pontificia Univ. Católica del Perú, 1997. 4 v.: bibl., ill., indexes.

Critical edition of Vallejo's poetry prepared by a well-known Peruvian literary critic. Contains thorough footnotes, a chronology, and a prologue by the editor. The footnotes are brief but complete. In his "Prologue," Silva-Santisteban discusses his edition compared with four previous editions (Larrea, Hernández Novás, Ferrari, and González Vigil). In addition to the poems, the editor includes many documents intended to help readers understand the discussion of Vallejo's poetry. [GP]

3943 Vargas, Rafael. Se ama tanto el mundo. México: Editorial Aldus, 1997. 102 p.: 1 folded col. ill. (Col. Aldus. Los poetas)

Este libro celebratorio resiste los tiempos de crisis en México. Como en las odas elementales de Neruda, aunque con un estilo muy diferente, Vargas (Ciudad de México, 1954) canta a las cosas del mundo, incluyendo la pintura y la literatura. Resalta aquí su predilección por los surrealistas César Moro, Enrique Molina y Roberto Matta. [JS]

3944 Vargas Ghezzi, Germán. Textículos. Lima: Ediciones El Santo Oficio, 1998. 113 p.

Book of short poems with prologue entitled "Movimiento perpetuo de Germán Vargas Ghezzi" written by the renown Peruvian writer Alfredo Bryce Echenique. In this brief essay, Bryce Echenique refers to Vargas

Ghezzi's humor which he finds similar to Gómez de la Serna's *greguerías*. The book's title is a case in point; beyond the humor, one finds capers and serious word games. [GP]

3945 Vázquez Martín, Eduardo. Naturaleza y hechos. México: Ediciones Era, 1999. 116 p.

Dos temas parecen reverberar en este libro: la poesía urbana y los poemas de amor situados en las playas, frente al mar. En el primer caso, Vázquez Martín (Ciudad de México, 1962) se preocupa por retratar múltiples imágenes de la ciudad más poblada del mundo; en el segundo caso, establece un diálogo entre los amantes que atenúa la autoridad masculina. [JS]

3946 Vicuña, Manuel. Sin pieles ni cebos. Santiago, Chile: C. Porter, 2000. 55 p.

Pesadillas del día a día en que lo erótico se entremezcla con las revelaciones esporádicas de la mortalidad y la insatisfacción existencial del individuo. Lenguaje calibrado con pericia de pintor: "Pálpito de luz / sobre tu cuerpo / esmaltado por las olas." [OS]

3947 Villarreal, José Javier. Bíblica. México: Ediciones Sin Nombre; Juan Pablos Editor; Univ. Autónoma de Nuevo León, 1998. 47 p. (Cuadernos de la salamandra)

Libro que podría haber sido concebido para la red electrónica, puesto que algunas frases de los poemas tienen números (en el sistema del internet, la palabra podría tener un hyperlink) y remiten, a pie de página, a otro texto poético. Villarreal (Tijuana, México, 1959) reúne en su poesía una vocación espiritual combinada con la amorosa y expresada con un lenguaje coloquial que se aproxima al tono de la narración. [JS]

3948 Villegas, Víctor. Ahora no es ahora. Santo Domingo: Dirección de Publicaciones, Editora Universitaria-UASD, 1997. 95 p. (Publicaciones de la Univ. Autónoma de Santo Domingo; 830. Col. Literatura y sociedad; 16)

Miembro de la Generación del 48 ("heredera y afianzadora de la Poesía Sorprendida"), Villegas parte de una negación que, sin embargo, trasciende ("Ahora no es ahora sino mañana"). A la dimensión filosófica ("Ni somos ni estamos"), se le suma una so-

cial ("Sales and purchases, no mas [sic]/alternativas"). [FC]

3949 Villena Alvarado, Marcelo. Pócimas de Madame Orlowska. La Paz: Ediciones del Hombrecito Sentado, 1998? 159 p.: ill.

Es evidente que la intención de este autor es sorprender al lector, a través de un discurso cuya característica principal es la heterogeneidad. Heterogeneidad en los motivos de los enunciados simples o textos más complejos, en el lenguaje apoyado sobre localismos de diversa procedencia regional latinoamericana, en el contexto referencial que aluden a concepciones mitológicas de lugares diferentes, antiguas y modernas, y en los rasgos intertextuales incorporados a sus textos con una intención evidente de practicar la imitación y la parodia, desde la aceptación hasta el rechazo de los mismos textos imitados y parodiados. Dentro de la amplia heterogeneidad discursiva de esta colección, sin embargo, no se puede desconocer aciertos, aunque desiguales, que sin embargo justifican suficientemente para recibir atención crítica. [ORR]

3950 Vitier, Cintio. Antología poética: 1938–1992. Prólogo de Enrique Sainz. Caracas: Monte Avila Editores Latinoamericana, 1998. 421 p. (Altazor)

Más de medio siglo de producción poética incluida (de 1938–92); el propio Vitier escoge lo mejor de su obra; una obra poética que, según Saénz, está entre las grandes del idioma de este siglo. Perseguidor de los silencios, esta antología habla por Vitier; le da su lugar poético. [FC]

3951 Wiethüchter, Blanca. La piedra que labra otra piedra: poesía. La Paz: Ediciones del Hombrecito Sentado, 1998. 295 p.

Este volumen puede ser considerado una antología de la obra literaria de la autora boliviana Blanca Wiethüchter (1947), pues está conformado por las colecciones que la autora publicó anteriormente, excepto la primera que data de 1997. Las colecciones compiladas han sido dispuestas como secciones del volumen, y proporcionan al lector una lectura cronológica retrospectiva del discurso de la autora, pues se inicia en los versos escritos en su madurez, a sus 50 años, y continúa hacia sus ejercicios primigenios. Esas colecciones son las siguientes: "Qantatai" (1997), "La lagarta" (1995), "El rigor de la llama" (1994), "El verde no es un color" (1990), "En los negros labios encantados" (1988), "Madera viva y árbol difunto" (1982), "Huesos de un día" (1996), "Territorial" (1980), "Travesía" (1978), "Asistir al tiempo" (1975). El volumen lleva como prólogo un comentario de Mónica Velásquez Guzmán. [ORR]

3952 Yáñez, Mirta. Algún lugar en ruinas. La Habana: Ediciones Unión, 1997. 76 p. (La rueda dentada. Poesía)

Poesía que, en muchas ocasiones, se refiere a la poesía, a los poetas (Borges, Darío, Sor Juana), en este poemario, que es también un libro de consejos para los futuros poetas, la poeta "intenta salvar de las ruinas" aquello que, a pesar del cambio, fue en su momento un pilar. [FC]

3953 Zonta, José María. Ladrones. San José: Editorial Univ. Nacional, 2001. 213 p.

El poemario que se reseña es el séptimo de un poeta ya imprescindible para dimensionar el proceso político costarricense de las dos últimas décadas. No sólo se trata de una de las expresiones más originales y logradas de las generaciones jóvenes de este país, sino también de una poética que sin renunciar a las posibilidades de un lenguaje intimista (cultivado por las generaciones anteriores) se construye desde una ética de responsabilidad ante la historia. Esto lo distancia de poetas como Jorge Charpentier y lo acerca a las propuestas de Jorge Debravo, por quien Zonta profesa verdadera admiración. Ladrones es un poemario extenso, donde el poema y el proverbio se dan la mano y construyen para nosotros una conciencia del poema como miel oscura, y del poeta como ladrón que se la roba para dársela a los desesperados. Sin duda en la hechura de estos poemas el autor ha sabido incorporar los aciertos de libros anteriores, fundamentalmente *Lobos en la brisa* (Premio Nacional de Poesía, 1998) y *La sonámbula que silba* (Primer lugar en el certamen de la Editorial de la Univ. de Costa Rica, 1999). [EM]

GENERAL STUDIES

3954 Diversa de ti misma: poetas de México al habla. Entrevista de Asunción Horno Delgado. México: Ediciones El Tucán de Virginia, 1997. 374 p.

Horno Delgado entrevista a 19 escritores, delimitando su trabajo a los nacidos entre 1943–56, y a la obra publicada en buena parte entre 1980–95. El volumen está muy bien diseñado, organizado y balanceado; es entretenido y útil para los estudiosos de poesía mexicana. Se incluye a Alejandro Aura, Efraín Bartolomé, Carmen Boullosa, Sandro Cohen, Horácio Costa, Elsa Cross, Antonio Deltoro, Jorge Esquinca, Gloria Gervitz, David Huerta, Elva Macías, Mónica Mansour, Víctor Manuel Mendiola, Eduardo Milán, Fabio Morábito, Myriam Moscona, Vicente Quirarte, Javier Sicilia, y Manuel Ulacia. Incluye, además, una breve selección de poemas. [JS]

3955 Haladyna, Ronald. La contextualización de la poesía postmoderna mexicana: Pedro Salvador Ale, David Huerta y Coral Bracho. Toluca, Mexico: Centro de Investigación en Ciencias Sociales y Humanidades, Univ. Autónoma del Estado de México, 1999. 250 p.: bibl.

Libro que aborda a los tres poetas con un amplio espectro de fuentes teóricas, por lo general asociadas al postestructuralismo. Haladyna analiza, con mayor detalle, *Navegaciones, Incurable,* y *El ser que va a morir,* libros respectivos de estos tres poetas. El volumen se complementa con dos capítulos introductorios sobre la teoría acerca de la posmodernidad y su aplicación a la literatura hispanoamericana. [JS]

3956 Paredes, Alberto. Haz de palabras: ocho poetas mexicanos recientes; Seminario de estilística, 2. México: Coordinación de Difusión Cultural, Dirección de Literatura, UNAM, 1999. 292 p. (Textos de difusión cultural. Serie Diagonal)

Paredes coordina el trabajo crítico de los participantes del Seminario de estilística de la UNAM. El libro recopila poemas y estudios de/sobre poetas nacidos en los 40 y 50 (como Elsa Cross, Francisco Hernández, David Huerta, José Luis Rivas, y Coral Bracho). Aunque los ensayos no son muy extensos, el volumen es de mucha utilidad, puesto que la poesía mexicana reciente apenas comienza a ser estudiada con seriedad. [JS]

3957 Versoconverso: poetas entrevistan poetas. Coordinación de José Angel Leyva. México: Instituto Municipal del Arte y la Cultura; Ediciones Alforja, 2000. 319 p.

Entrevistas a 21 poetas, siete de ellos extranjeros radicados en México. Salvo que los poetas son nacidos entre 1918–40, el coordinador no impuso ningún tipo de formato o restricciones a los entrevistadores, por lo que cada diálogo adopta su propio cauce. Aunque todas las conversaciones se centran en la creación, muchas de ellas permiten que el poeta reflexione acerca de sus experiencias biográficas. [JS]

SPECIAL STUDIES

3958 Aliberti, Antonio. Poesía argentina de fin de siglo: tomos III, IV y V, Estudio preliminar. Buenos Aires: Vinciguerra, 1997. 70 p.: bibl. (Col. Metáfora)

Aunque el criterio de agrupación sea debatible (especialmente el del Tomo III), esta recopilación ofrece un amplio espectro de la producción poética argentina. El Tomo V reúne a los "novísimos" y esto permite una primera aproximación a la obra de las promociones más jóvenes y de menor difusión. [LU]

3959 Barreda, Pedro and **Eduardo C. Béjar.** Poética de la nación: poesía romántica en Hispanoamérica, crítica y antología. Boulder, Colo.: Society of Spanish and Spanish-American Studies, 1999. 707 p.: bibl. (Publications of the Society of Spanish and Spanish-American Studies)

Esta cuidada edición es un indiscutible aporte y un punto de partida indispensable para el estudio de la producción poética del romanticismo hispanoamericano. La selección antológica pone al alcance la obra de autores aún escasamente explorados por la crítica. [LU]

3960 Becerra, Eduardo. Poesía uruguaya del siglo XX. (*Susana Viejos*, 1/2, 1997, p. 371–437, facsims., photos)

La introducción discute en detalle los lineamientos centrales del modernismo, posmodernismo, y vanguardia—o ausencia de ella—en la literatura uruguaya, para luego hacer una revisión más general de las características de promociones más recientes. La muestra antológica es generosa en autores y, por lo mismo, sorprende la ausencia de Rafael Courtoisie. [LU]

3961 Chacón de Umaña, Luz Alba; Luisiana Naranjo; and **Sonia SolArte.** Fuego, tierra, agua— que nunca se enturbia. San

José: Círculo de Escritores Costarricenses, 1999. 242 p.: ill. (Col. Biblioteca Líneas grises; 56)

En la tradición indigenista, este libro reúne el trabajo de tres escritoras que se proponen llevar a la poesía y al cuento los grandes temas de la América indígena: conquista, colonización, desterritorialización, y transculturación. En conjunto, el proyecto del libro quiere ser una denuncia social, pero también el balance de una larga investigación en torno al mundo indígena americano, desde sus expresiones prehispánicas hasta su estado actual. Los límites del libro son evidentemente las coordenadas indigenistas que lo generan y que reproducen una mirada que "traduce" la intimidad del mundo indígena para un lector que la desconoce. Y de esta traducción difícilmente puede el indigenismo salir airoso. Termina siempre convirtiendo al indio en objeto de estudio o en fuente de inspiración. [EM]

3962 "Con tanto tiempo encima": aportes de literatura latinoamericana en homenaje a Pedro Lastra. Recopilación de Elizabeth Monasterios P. La Paz: Plural Editores: Facultad de Humanidades y Ciencias de la Educación, UMSA, 1997. 407 p.: bibl., ill. (Colección Academia; núm. 6)

Volumen de homenaje al crítico chileno Lastra. La primera parte del libro incluye una serie de textos personales en homenaje a Lastra de Miguel Gomes, Rigas Kappatos, y un homenaje en verso a cargo de diversos poetas. La segunda sección es una recopilación de estudios literarios de una veintena de críticos latinoamericanos y norteamericanos. El libro se cierra con facsímiles de cartas de Julio Cortázar y José María Arguedas dirigidas a Lastra. [C. Ferreira]

3963 A cultural history of Latin America: literature, music, and the visual arts in the 19th and 20th centuries. Edited by Leslie Bethell. New York: Cambridge Univ. Press, 1998. 538 p.

El planteo de Jaime Concha muestra con idoneidad el papel central de la poesía en la literatura hispanoamericana de la primera mitad del siglo XX, su importancia como lazo continental e intercontinental, y su relación respecto a los procesos históricos del período en cuestión. La dimensión social del poeta latinoamericano, su mayor o menor participación en los procesos políticos, y su independencia respecto a los vaivenes del mercado económico son el punto de partida de este ensayo sobre la poesía de la segunda mitad del siglo en América Latina. Se centra en los representantes más cabales de cuatro tendencias poéticas: el surrealismo y postsurrealismo, la poesía política, la poesía concreta y neobarroca, y la antipoesía. El artículo adolece de un análisis de las promaciones poéticas de las décadas del 80–90. Para el comentario de especialista en música, ver ítem 4372. [LU]

3964 Friis, Ronald J. José Emilio Pacheco and the poets of the shadows. Lewisburg, Pa.: Bucknell Univ. Press; London: Associated Univ. Presses, 2001. 220 p.: bibl., index. (The Bucknell studies in Latin American literature and theory)

Estudio de los primeros seis libros de poemas de Pacheco. "Los poetas de las sombras" se refiere a los precursores y al diálogo que Pacheco establece con la tradición; particularmente relevantes son Alfonso Reyes, Borges, y Paz. El punto de partida teórico es la "ansiedad de la influencia" de Bloom. Friis logra dar una visión crítica de conjunto de la obra de Pacheco quien, merecidamente, ocupa un lugar de reconocimiento en la poesía mexicana actual. [JS]

3965 Metáfora de la experiencia: la poesía de Antonio Cisneros; ensayos, diálogos y comentarios. Edición de Miguel Angel Zapata. Lima: Pontificia Univ. Católica del Perú, Fondo Editorial, 1998. 445 p.: bibl.

Collection of essays, dialogues, and commentaries on Antonio Cisneros by well-known literary critics such as José Miguel Oviedo, Abelardo Oquendo, Antonio Cornejo Polar, James Higgins, and William Rowe, and writers like Javier Sologuren and Mario Vargas Llosa. Also includes an essay by Cisneros himself. Contains useful bibliographic references compiled by Zapata. Also includes a Prologue written by Luis Jaime Cisneros. The volume represents perhaps the most comprehensive collection of essays on Cisneros to date. [GP]

3966 Monsiváis, Carlos. Las tradiciones de la imagen: notas sobre poesía mexicana. 1. ed., Ariel México. México: Tec de Monterrey; Editorial Ariel, 2001. 150 p.

(Cuadernos de la Cátedra Alfonso Reyes del Tecnológico de Monterrey)

Transcripciones del ciclo de conferencias que Monsiváis dictó en el Instituto Tecnológico de Monterrey en agosto de 2001. Aunque el libro no cuenta con el repertorio crítico del trabajo académico, el autor da muestras de su excelente conocimiento de la poesía mexicana de fines del siglo XIX y de las primeras tres décadas del XX. De especial atención es su conferencia sobre la poesía y la cultura popular. [JS]

3967 Parra Sandoval, Eduardo. Mi hermana Violeta Parra: su vida y obra en décimas. Santiago, Chile: LOM Ediciones, 1998. 166 p. (Col. Entre mares)

Hermoso redescubrimiento de las peripecias sociales y existenciales de Violeta Parra y, por extensión, de la familia Parra, en versos de corte popular. El poeta incorpora de manera directa el humor con la tragedia, el respeto al personaje junto con la iluminación certera de los avatares de su existencia amorosa, creativa, y pública. [OS]

3968 Siebenmann, Gustav. Poesía y poéticas del siglo XX en la América Hispana y el Brasil: historia, movimientos, poetas. Madrid: Gredos, 1997. 506 p.: bibl., index. (Biblioteca románica hispánica. III, Manuales; 79)

Útil recopilación antológica que permite trazar los lineamientos y desarrollo de la poesía en el continente latinoamericano. [LU]

3969 Siete surrealistas argentinos: Ceselli, Latorre, Llinas, Madariaga, Molina, Pellegrini, Vasco. Selección y prólogo de Javier Cofreces. Buenos Aires: Leviatán, 1999. 124 p.: bibl. (Poesía mayor; 22)

La selección de autores y obras aquí reunidos tiene el propósito de mostrar los vínculos que los surrealistas argentinos mantuvieron con el movimiento de vanguardia europeo. El prólogo de Cofreces da cuenta de las principales revistas argentinas de impronta surrealista (*Qué, Ciclo, A partir de cero, Letra y línea, Boa*) y el innegable protagonismo de Aldo Pellegrini en este movimiento. Se incluye también una útil bibliografía y testimonios de los autores. [LU]

3970 Sosa, Víctor. El oriente en la poética de Octavio Paz. Puebla, Mexico: Secretaría de Cultura, Gobierno del Estado de

Puebla, 2000. 96 p.: bibl., ill. (Col. Los nuestros. Serie Cuadrivio)

Breve monografía en la que Sosa estudia los modos en que el tema de Oriente se incorpora en la poesía moderna occidental (las referencias a Tablada son muy pertinentes) para luego revisar el haikú japonés en la poesía temprana de Paz, y el budismo y los ritos del tantrismo en Ladera Este y Blanco. Libro muy útil para los interesados en el tema. [JS]

3971 Stanton, Anthony. Inventores de tradición: ensayos sobre poesía mexicana moderna. México: El Colegio de México; Fondo de Cultura Económica, 1998. 238 p.: bibl. (Serie Estudios de lingüística y literatura; 38) (Vida y pensamiento de México)

Este libro estudia los diálogos de los poetas modernos con sus precursores: la presencia de Sor Juana en los Contemporáneos, la lectura de Alarcón por parte de Henríquez Ureña, Villaurrutia, y Paz; y los diálogos que establece Paz con Quevedo, Alfonso Reyes, y Cernuda. La parte central del libro explora la poética de Reyes, la poesía pura de los Contemporáneos y la poesía de Salvador Novo. Stanton es uno de los ensayistas más lúcidos de poesía actual y este libro consolida un trabajo serio y meticuloso. [JS]

MISCELLANEOUS

3972 Album de poetisas cubanas. Inventario e introducción de Mirta Yáñez. La Habana: Editorial Letras Cubanas, 1997. 159 p.: bibl.

Tras una justificación del término "poetisa," las 16 poetas aquí incluidas, todas pertenecientes al siglo XX, inciden en una sensibilidad femenina que marca la poesía. Entre la preocupación social y la proclividad lírica, esa sensibilidad femenina participa de una poética múltiple, cuyos rostros el album reúne de una manera interesante y dinámica. [FC]

Cano Peláes, Jesús. Identidad y ruptura: notas sobre Latinoamérica y modernidad. See item **4548.**

3973 Chirinos Arrieta, Eduardo. La morada del silencio: una reflexión sobre el silencio en la poesía a partir de las obras de Emilio Adolfo Westphalen, Gonzalo Rojas, Olga Orozco, Javier Sologuren, Jorge Eduardo Eielson y Alejandra Pizarnik. Lima: Fondo de Cultura Económica, 1998. 259 p.: bibl., index. (Col. Tierra firme)

Literary criticism about the multiple meanings of silence in poetry focuses mostly on Peru but also on other major Latin American poets of the second part of the 20th century. Explores the role that the representation of silence plays in relation to the author, the reader, and the text. Chirinos characterizes the relationship between silence and the author as a secular fascination with multiple expressions. Regarding the text, he suggests the possibility of reading silence as a dramatic representation of what takes place during the act of writing. Chirinos conceptualizes silence, however, as something not limited to literary performance. [GP]

3974 Ecología y poesía. Selección y prólogo de Manuel de la Puebla. Fotografías de Eliza Llenza. San Juan, Puerto Rico: Ediciones Mairena, 1998. 154 p.: ill.

Este trabajo reúne una plétora de "poemas ecológicos" escritos a lo largo del siglo XX, sobre todo, aunque no exclusivamente, en el mundo hispanoparlante. Para de la Puebla, "los poetas han sido siempre ecologistas." La actual degradación de la naturaleza justifica la edición. [FC]

3975 Escalante, Evodio. José Gorostiza: entre la redención y la catástrofe. México: Ediciones Casa Juan Pablos; Tabasco, Mexico: Univ. Juárez Autónoma de Tabasco; Durango, Mexico: Instituto Municipal del Arte y la Cultura de Durango; Ciudad Universitaria, México: UNAM, 2001. 317 p.: bibl.

Tal vez el estudio más completo y cuidadoso de *Muerte sin fin* (1939) de Gorostiza. Escalante explora las influencias de Vasconcelos y T.S. Eliot (arguyendo que esta aproximación es más efectiva que la que lo filia con Valéry y la poesía pura), además de que se aboca a la tradición bíblica, dejando de lado los paralelismos que otros críticos habían tratado de trazar con la Cábala o el budismo. De hecho, intenta restituir la vocación religiosa del poema. [JS]

3976 La espina del sueño. Edición de Manuel de la Puebla. San Juan, Puerto Rico: Ediciones Mairena, 1997. 150 p.: bibl., ports.

Con seis poetas puertorriqueñas

(Yvonee Ochart, Etnairis Rivera, Magaly Quiñones, entre otras), todas nacidas a mediados del siglo XX, de la Puebla ofrece un perfil de la poesía femenina de la isla. Además de una selección de poemas, se incluye una entrevista, información bibliográfica, y fragmentos críticos en torno a las poetas. [FC]

3977 Fernández, Pablo Armando. De memoria y anhelos. La Habana: Ediciones Unión, Unión de Escritores y Artistas de Cuba, 1998. 363 p.: bibl. (Contemporáneos)

Perteneciente a la llamada "Generación de los años cincuenta," para Fernández la literatura es mucho más que una actividad intelectual; es también una cuestión vital, afectiva, donde cuenta mucho la amistad. Entre ensayos y poemas, los textos aquí incluidos comentan y celebran la gestión literaria desde la sociabilidad origenista. [FC]

3978 Mullen, Edward J. Afro-Cuban literature: critical junctures. Westport, Conn.: Greenwood Press, 1998. 236 p.: bibl., index. (Contributions to the study of world literature, 91)

En este estudio, que incluye la poesía pero que no se limita a ella, una de las preguntas fundamentales es ésta: ¿de qué manera la literatura de los escritores afrohispánicos llega a convertirse en parte de aquellos textos que, de una manera informal pero autoritativa, son considerados como importantes y valiosos? [FC]

3979 Novísima poesía cubana: antología, 1980–1998. Selección y edición de Jorge Cabezas Miranda. Salamanca, Spain: Ediciones Colegio de España, 1999. 319 p.: bibl. (Col. Patio de escuelas; 4)

Diecinueve poetas cubanos (cuatro mujeres) nacidos entre 1958–74, poetas de las llamadas "Tercera" y "Cuarta" generaciones, conforman esta antología, cuyo propósito es subrayar tanto la continuidad de algunos de estos poetas con las generaciones anteriores, así como también la diferencia, marcada ahora por el retorno de la metáfora. [FC]

3980 Las palabras son islas: panorama de la poesía cubana siglo XX, 1900–1998. Selección, introducción, notas y bibliografía de Jorge Luis Arcos. La Habana: Editorial Letras Cubanas, 1999. 645 p.: bibl.

Como en otras publicaciones de los 90, se incluye la poesía de la diáspora. En tanto que muestra panorámica, ésta es mucho más abarcadora que una antología. Según Arcos, se "aspira a ofrecer una imagen del estado de la crítica y apreciación sobre la poesía cubana en el fin del siglo XX." [FC]

3981 Poesías y canciones a la patria: de cómo los dominicanos han sentido la patria a través de la historia. Autora de la compilación, Fiume Bienvenida Gómez Sánchez. Santo Domingo: Oficina Nacional de Estadística, 1998. 381 p.

Con el fin de "potenciar el amor y la defensa por la patria," esta selección antológica arranca con el primer poema anónimo que, en 1795, se escribió a raíz de la cesión a Francia de la parte occidental de la isla. La invasión norteamericana de 1965 es la última referencia histórica. [FC]

3982 Poetas cubanos marginados. Selección e introducción de Francisco J. Peñas Bermejo. Ferrol, Spain: Sociedad de Cultura Valle-Inclán, 1998. 257 p.: bibl. (Col. Esquío de poesía; 72)

Diez poetas cubanos, entre ellos José Lezama Lima y María Elena Cruz Varela, componen esta antología de poesía marginada, tanto por razones políticas como sociales o literarias, durante la Revolución Cubana. La marginación se basa en estilos de vida, creencias e ideas, preferencia sexual, ritos religiosos, desviación de ideales, disconformidad con el régimen. [FC]

3983 Rosa de cien pétalos. San Juan, Puerto Rico: Ediciones Mairena, 1998. 136 p.: ill.

En esta colección de poemas, que incluye poetas del mundo hispanoparlante, se le rinde tributo a la madre desde las múltiples perspectivas en que se la concibe: como ese llamado íntimo que recibe la mujer desde niña, por el don de fecundidad, por lo psicológico (el cariño, la protección). [FC]

Drama

MARIO A. ROJAS, *Professor of Modern Languages, Catholic University of America*
SANDRA M. CYPESS, *Professor and Chair, Department of Spanish and Portuguese, University of Maryland, College Park*

EL TEATRO HISPANOAMERICANO continúa su movimiento ascendente. Este fenómeno puede observarse no sólo en la producción de textos dramáticos, sino también en la gran cantidad de textos escritos que son llevados a la escena. Un claro ejemplo de este crecimiento es la proliferación de festivales y concursos de dramaturgia locales, nacionales e internacionales de teatro que todos los años se realizan en distintos puntos de Hispanoamérica. De este modo, el teatro ya no llega sólo a un receptor-lector, sino a un receptor-espectador que tiene el privilegio de asistir a espectáculos de bajo costo (y aun gratis como sucede en el Festival Internacional de Teatro que bienalmente se celebra en Santo Domingo), generalmente financiado por las municipalidades y gobiernos que valoran la importancia del teatro no sólo como una expresión artística áurica (en vivo e irrepetible), sino también como un importante vehículo para dar a conocer y reflexionar sobre el entorno social, cultural y político de nuestros pueblos. A través del teatro se puede apreciar la diversidad que atraviesa de norte a sur nuestro continente, pero también los lazos profundos que afianzan un idioma común y varios siglos de historia cultural compartida. En efecto, el teatro es una de las expresiones artísticas más sensibles al registro de acentos y matices culturales e ideológicos que entretejen el multifacético ser hispanoamericano.

Es conveniente destacar un fenómeno singular: a pesar de las crisis económicas que sufren los países de la región, como un mal endémico, y que han recrudecido últimamente, todavía se realizan festivales, simposios, conferencias y foros en que participan dramaturgos, directores y críticos de diversos países. Un caso ejemplar es el del gobierno de Argentina, que en medio de una de sus peores crisis económicas, sigue apoyando el teatro bonaerense y de provincias mediante subvenciones, que aunque mínimas, hacen posible que el teatro continúe vivo, como un medio de entretenimiento, de preservación de tradiciones culturales identitarias y también como un puente que facilita la integración cultural avanzada por el ímpetu globalizador que, cada vez más, conecta apartadas y dispares regiones del planeta. Un caso ejemplar de lo dicho es un encuentro de dramaturgos de toda América Hispana, quienes en noviembre del 2002, se reunieron en Buenos Aires para exponer sus poéticas teatrales y su posición escritural frente al mundo de hoy. También en Argentina se realiza anualmente un congreso iberoamericano de teatro, organizado por la Universidad de Buenos Aires y GETEA, bajo la dirección de Osvaldo Pellettieri, del cual se publica una selección de las ponencias presentadas. En Chile, cada verano se realiza el *Festival Internacional de a mil*, en el cual con un coste de menos de dos dólares, los espectadores tienen fácil acceso a numerosos espectáculos chilenos y extranjeros. En los Estados Unidos, las conferencias de teatro que realiza George Woodyard en The University of Kansas reúnen a académicos de Estados Unidos y Latinoamérica para dialogar sobre el estado actual del teatro hispanoamericano.

A las revistas *GESTOS* (Univ. of California at Irving), *Latin American Theatre Review* (The Univ. of Kansas) y *Ollantay* (Ollantay Press, New York), se suman otras de Latinoamérica como *Conjunto* de Cuba, *Apuntes de Teatro* de Chile, *Teatro XXI* y *Teatro del Sur* de Argentina, *Escenografía* de México, *Escena* de Costa Rica y otras más recientes como *Paso de Gato* de México, y *El monstruo del entremés* de Santo Domingo, que publican ensayos, divulgar obras inéditas, y reseñan importantes eventos teatrales que se realizan en Hispanoamérica y Estados Unidos. El Centro Latinoamericano de Creación e Investigación Teatral (CELCIT) tiene sitio en Internet (*http://www.celcit.org.ar/*) que además de la *Revista de teatrología, técnica y reflexión sobre la práctica teatral iberoamericana*, ofrece una amplia colección textos de dramaturgos latinoamericanos y sendos comentarios, críticas y noticias constantemente actualizados. En otros países, a escala nacional se hace lo mismo. Tal es la gestión iniciada por César de María, Perú, quien tiene un sitio de Internet (*http://www.geocities.com/teatroperuano/*) con obras de dramaturgos de su país. Por su parte, el sitio *http://www.telon.cl/* mantiene al navegante de Internet al día en todo lo que pasa en el mundo teatral chileno, incluyendo reseñas que aparecen en periódicos que generalmente son de difícil acceso cuando se las busca por otros medios.

A escala individual, muchos dramaturgos, directores, y grupos teatrales disponen igualmente de un sitio o página de Internet en la que se puede encontrar un repertorio de obras, de espectáculos y sus respectivas críticas. Sin dudas, la red informática constituye en la actualidad una importante fuente para investigadores que desde Estados Unidos o Europa, buscan contactos o información para sus pesquisas sobre teatro hispanoamericano.

En cuanto a las obras teatrales y estudios críticos publicados en América del Sur hay varias antologías que reúnen las obras de conocidos dramaturgos como Roberto Cossa, Javier Daulte, Carlos Gorostiza, Leopoldo Marechal, Marco Antonio de la Parra, Eduardo Pavlovsky, Carlos Veronese, y Víctor Viviescas (ítems **4002, 4003, 4015, 4027, 4036, 4037, 4067** y **4068**), que compilan textos de dramaturgos de un país (ítems **4053** y **4061**), o antologías que incluyen autores de varios países (ítem **3987**).

Hay dramaturgos establecidos que siguen publicando obras o reeditando otras, como es el caso de Buenaventura (ítem **3995**), Cossa (ítem **4002**), Gorostiza (ítem **4015**), Halac (ítem **4017**), Pavlovsky (ítem **4037**), y Romero (ítem **4049**). Entre los más jóvenes que han sido reconocidos por la crítica por la calidad de su escritura escénica, cabe mencionar a Daulte (ítem **4003**), De la Parra (ítem **4036**), y Veronese (item **4067**).

Mención especial merecen las publicaciones de las obras dramáticas completas del poeta vanguardista peruano César Vallejo (ítem **4065**), cuyo teatro vanguardista no ha sido estudiado como se lo merece, la antología de seis obras de La Candelaria (ítem **4055**), un grupo fundamental en la historia del teatro colectivo hispanoamericano y las obras dramáticas completas de Marechal (ítem **4027**), un destacado novelista argentino que también escribió excelentes obras teatrales.

El teatro hispanoamericano se ha posicionado frente a las ondas expansivas de la globalización, por lo menos, de dos maneras. Primero hay aquellos dramaturgos que, en reacción a la tendencia mundialista que busca lo universal borrando fronteras, cargan sus obras con un fuerte énfasis en aquellos aspectos que consideran parte del patrimonio nacional que dan un sentido de pertenencia y estabilidad. Por otro lado, están los que intentan adaptarse a las demandas de un mercado internacional que les ofrece nuevos espacios más allá de las fronteras de su país, ya sea exportando un teatro folclórico o con matices mágico-realistas, siempre atractivo al imaginario foráneo, o empleando códigos estéticos que responden a un gusto más amplio que el local.

En torno a la crítica teatral sudamericana, se destacan los ensayos de Juan Andrés Piña y Luis Ordaz (ítems **4083** y **4084**) que comentan espectáculos de sus respectivos países y que pueden ser de especial interés para los investigadores cuyo objeto de estudio es la escena del texto dramático o literario. También vale destacar la antología crítica de Jaramillo y Yepes (ítem **3987**). [MR]

En cuanto a México, América Central, y El Caribe, en general, los dramaturgos mexicanos son los que tal vez muestran más audacia en el uso de un lenguaje popular, urbano y sus referencias a temas de la sexualidad (ítems **3996** y **4024**). Otra observación general tiene que ver con la variedad del regionalismo y el uso del inglés en textos tanto de la frontera mexicana con los Estados Unidos como en la Cuba de Castro. A veces es natural, pues así hablan, pero también los dramaturgos quieren enfocar la influencia cultural estadounidense y comentar los peligros del imperialismo cultural (ítem **4001**).

En México como en Cuba, Puerto Rico, la Republica Dominicana, durante estos últimos años los dramaturgos consagrados y prolíficos, como Vicente Leñero, Luisa Josefina Hernández, y Sabina Berman, entre los mexicanos; Nicolas Dorr, Matías Matos Huidobro, entre los cubanos, y en Puerto Rico, Roberto Ramos Perea; siguen escribiendo obras nuevas y ricas. Es importante observar la aparición de un grupo bien nutrido de dramaturgos más jóvenes como Estela Leñero Franco (*Insomnio*, 1993), *Un día en la vida de Catalina* (1994) de Berta Hiriart, y *Las tremendas aventuras de la capitana Gazpacho* (1998) de Gerardo Mancebo del Castillo.

Para ser publicados ya no tienen que venir a estrenarse en DF. sino que pueden participar en concursos teatrales o talleres convocados en otras provincias del país, como Querétaro (ítem **3998**), Guadalajara (ítem **4054**), Tijuana (ítem **4051**), Nuevo León (ítem **4039**) u otras de "tierra adentro," como se ve en la antología de Ricardo Pérez Quitt (ítem **3986**). Otro aspecto que resalta es la tendencia postmodernista de varias piezas que se manifiesta en el empleo de referentes enmarcados en la literatura universal o en la historia (ítems **4009, 4020, 4023, 4026, 4044, 4045, 4052** y **4063**). No se trata de una simple reescritura sino una crítica mordaz que a veces incluye también como personaje al autor de la obra original, como vemos en Vicente Leñero o Fundora Hernández. [SC]

PLAYS

3984 Aceves Azcárate, María Aurora. El serpentario: texto dramático en un acto. Toluca, Mexico: Instituto Mexiquense de Cultura, 2002. 52 p. (El Espejo de amarilis)

Explores the experience of a family of women who can no longer cover up a secret: their grandmother had a lover. Upon the grandmother's death, the lover changes the dynamics in the household when he comes to claim the inheritance. [SC]

3985 Andino, Peky. Kito kon K; Ceremonia con sangre; Ulises y la máquina de perdices: teatro. Quito: Eskeletra Editorial, 1998. 149 p.

En esta obra, a partir del humor negro, la parodia e ironía, el lenguaje alegórico y elementos de la cultura del rock, el autor, en formas teatrales no tradicionales, expresa la frustración juvenil frente al ejercicio del poder político y la implantación de una economía que lanza a muchos a la marginación y violencia. [MR]

3986 Andrade Varas, Aída *et al.* Dramaturgos de tierra adentro. Selección y prólogo de Ricardo Pérez Quitt. México: CONACULTA, 1998. 189 p. (Fondo editorial tierra adentro; 183)

Plays included here are *Secretos* by A. Andrade Varas; *Teoría y práctica de la muerte de una cucaracha (sin dolor)* by B. Colio; *Danzón Xtabay* by G. Espinosa de los Monteros; *Comida para gatos* by M. Lecuona; and *Desierto* by C. López. Topics covered are varied and impressive, from the exploration of adolescent life in *Comida para gatos* to *Desierto*, a psychological study of men lost in the wasteland of the desert, which is heartbreaking in the way it chronicles the meaningless loss of life. [SC]

3987 Antología crítica del teatro breve hispanoamericano: 1948–1993. Edición de María Mercedes Jaramillo y Mario Yepes. Medellín, Colombia: Editorial Univ. de Antioquia, 1997. 533 p.: bibl. (Col. Teatro)

Se reúnen 18 dramaturgos de 12 países hispanoamericanos. Además de la brevedad, las obras se han seleccionados tomando en cuenta una recepción amplia que traspase fronteras locales y la importancia que tienen los autores elegidos en la escena hispanoamericana. Cada obra se acompaña de un ensayo interpretativo. [MR]

3988 Arroyo, Jorge. Dos obras y una más: teatro. San José: Editorial Costa Rica, 2000. 359 p.: ill.

Arroyo began his career in drama in 1985 with *L'anima sola de Chico Muñoz,* a neocostumbristic work similar to *Con la honra en el alambre,* published together here with *El surco entre la flor y el labio* and *La tertulia de los espantos.* These short pieces depict the life of common people, a tradition of popular theater made famous by Samuel Rovinski's *Las fisgonas de Paso ancho* (1971). Arroyo makes use of Costa Rican folklore and regional speech as well as the legends and beliefs of the different provinces of Costa Rica. [SC]

3989 Báez, Rannel. Teatra— la mujer de teatro: obrando en un acto y pico; teatro. Santo Domingo?: Calmoqulp Dominicana S.R.; Cemex Dominicana, 2001. 112 p. (Serie XXX aniversario UCE)

A metatheatrical piece with characters named Teatro, Teatra, Apuntador, and Utilitis, as well as a character referred to as "feminist." The piece is an exploration of the state of "performance" in the theater. [SC]

3990 Barrientos, Alfonso Enrique. El señor embajador: pieza en tres actos. Ciudad de Guatemala: Editorial Oscar de León Palacios, 1998. 140 p. (Col. Títulos de ayer)

Awarded the Quetzaltenango Rama Theater prize in 1965, this edition revives this forgotten three-act play whose themes are still current today. Explores military and political corruption in Latin America vis-à-vis the US and denounces military regimes. It also attacks elitism among social classes, social prejudices, and the instability and sub-

missiveness of the working class, especially in small countries like Guatemala. [SC]

3991 Barroso, Norma. Por no ir a Michigan: ocho piezas teatrales. México: Consejo Nacional para la Cultura y las Artes, 2000. 145 p. (Fondo editorial tierra adentro; 220)

Includes *Virgen la memoria, El ángel, La costurera, La sombra del gato, El Marrakeshito, Romanos 5:8, Por no ir a Michigan,* and *Cuarto No. 7.* Barroso's theater focuses on the world of marginalized peoples and the suffering poor, but her characters occasionally experience good luck. For example, in *Cuarto No. 7,* the protagonist, a poor prostitute, is almost killed by a client, but her fate changes when the client learns that she is the mother of two children and spares her life. [SC]

3992 Berman, Sabina. Molière. México: Plaza y Janés, 2000. 164 p.: ill. (Son de teatro)

An excellent metatheatral piece of four acts in which Berman again demonstrates her talent in the realm of drama. Using the classical figures of Molière and Racine, she explores the meaning of comedy, tragedy, and the role of dramaturgy in life. She shows her fine sense of humor while at the same time effectively uses dramatic techniques. [SC]

3993 Brambilla, Raúl. Teatro. Córdoba, Argentina: Ediciones del Boulevard, 1997. 211 p.

Las tres obras fueron escritas en los años 80 y constituyen la primera publicación del dramaturgo que se ha distinguido también por sus direcciones teatrales. En sus obras confluyen una multiplicidad de elementos artísticos y estéticos, en que se mezclan el guión fílmico, la crónica, la historieta, la tragicomedia, el grotesco, el metateatro, la metáfora, y el esperpento. Por los cruces intertextuales que caracterizan su obra, podría situarse en la estética teatral posmodernista. [MR]

3994 Bruza, Rafael. El encanto de las palabras. Santa Fe, Argentina: Univ. Nacional del Litoral, Centro de Publicaciones, 1997. 55 p. (Col. Sociedad y cultura. Teatro)

El diálogo y su impecable construcción estética constituyen la fuerza dominante de esta obra de gran originalidad. La pulcritud del diálogo, sin embargo, es complementada con otros signos escénicos potenciados en el texto escrito que adquirirán igual estatura en una representación de las complejidades del ser humano y de las respuestas a su entorno. [MR]

3995 Buenaventura, Enrique. Teatro inédito. Bogotá: Presidencia de la República, 1997. 793 p. (Biblioteca familiar de la Presidencia de la República; 24)

Contiene 20 obras inéditas del dramaturgo, creador y director del grupo Teatro Experimental de Cali (TEC) con el que ha trabajado por más de 40 años. Su primera obra importante fue *Cristóbal Colón* (1957). La historia de América es un referente constante de esta producción dramática. *La trampa* alude a la dictadura de Jorge Ubico en Guatemala, y *La denuncia* refiere a la masacre que ocurrió en la zona bananera en 1928. También se incluyen obras inspiradas en la escritura de otros autores, como *El encierro* basada en *Los funerales de la Mama Grande.* Se incluye también la adaptación de *Ubu Rey* de Alfred Jarry, que influirá en la escritura dramática de Buenaventura. [MR]

3996 Cameselle, Yolanda. Entre extraños. Mexicali, Mexico: Instituto de Cultura de Baja California, 1999. 46 p.

Two naive middle-class couples confront sexual problems, emotions, and communication breakdowns. Using a realist treatment, the play openly explores complications of homosexual love, power relations within a couple, and the desire to have children. [SC]

3997 Carballido, Emilio *et al.* Diálogos dramatúrgicos México-Argentina. Felipe Galván, antologador. Puebla, Mexico: Tablado IberoAmericano, 2000. 319 p.

Important anthology reprints the best of two rich dramatic traditions. Includes the plays of the Mexicans Emilio Carballido (*Zorros chinos*), Luisa Josefina Hernández (*El gran parque*), Víctor Hugo Rascón Banda (*La mujer que cayó del cielo*), Edgar Ceballos (*La puerta*), and Felipe Galván (*Icaro Twenty Century*); the selection also includes Argentines Roberto Cossa (*El saludador*), Griselda Gambaro (*Antígona furiosa*), Eduardo Rovner (*Almas gemelas*), Mauricio Kartun (*Rápido nocturno* and *Aire de foxtrot*), and Cristina Escofet (*Los fantasmas del héroe*). [SC]

3998 Ceballos, Edgar *et al.* La puerta. Santiago de Querétaro, Mexico: Q Fondo Editorial, 2000. 295 p. (Dramaturgia)

Anthology brings together the five finalists for the first Manuel Herrera Castañeda national drama contest sponsored by the government of the state of Querétero in 1999. Ceballos' one-act play, *La puerta,* earned first prize. Honorable mention was awarded to *La máquina* by Ignacio Padilla, *Vidas privadas* by Javier Trujillo, *Estrella y su reventador* by Gerardo Luna, *El jugo de tres limones* by Luis E. Gutiérrez, and *De los ojos* by Víctor M. Castillo Bautista. [SC]

3999 Chabaud Magnus, Jaime. Perder la cabeza; Talk show. Zona Río, Mexico: CAEN Editores, 2000. 134 p.: col. ill. (Los inéditos; 9)

Almost farcical in its presentation of the eccentric national life of Mexico, *Perder la cabeza* is also a mystery that takes place in 1940s Mexico City under the government of President Camacho. *Talk Show* mixes fiction with autobiography in dramatizing the experiences of a playwright as a TV scriptwriter. [SC]

4000 Che, sierra adentro. Recopilación de Félix Guerra and Froilán Escobar. Dibujos de José Luis Posada. 4 ed. La Habana, Cuba: Ediciones Unión, 1997. 211 p.: bibl., ill., maps.

A documentary-testimonial form of theater based on the life of Che Guevara, using his own words as well as those of his companions. The drawings of Posada are impressive, and the decision to use a dramatic format to present historic events may have been prompted by the spectacular quality of Che Guevara's life. [SC]

4001 Colio, Bárbara. En la boca del lobo. México: CONACULTA, 2000. 161 p. (Fondo editorial tierra adentro; 222)

Each of the four plays included here (*La boca del lobo, A propósito de Alicia, Ascenso,* and *Ventana amarilla*) explores the violence and ill treatment that characterize interpersonal relationships—whether between women, as in *La boca del lobo,* or within a couple, as in *A propósito de Alicia* and *Ascenso. Ventana amarilla* deals with the nature of identity and stereotypes by depicting a group of North American filmmakers who come to Mexico expecting to find their version of a folkloric Mexican image. [SC]

4002 Cossa, Roberto M. Teatro. v. 5. Buenos Aires: Ediciones de la Flor, 1999. 1 v.

Excelentes obras de uno de los más importantes dramaturgos argentinos del siglo XX. En algunas de las obras, como es el caso en otras obras de Cossa, los conflictos se articulan en función de problemas sociales y morales que afectan el mundo actual. *Lejos de aquí* se refiere específicamente al tema del exilio. [MR]

4003 Daulte, Javier. Martha Stutz: obra de teatro en un acto. Buenos Aires: Ediciones Ultimo Reino, 1997. 62 p.

Excelente obra. Se trata de la desaparición de una chica de nueve años que ocurrió en 1938 en Córdova. El dramaturgo utiliza cartas y fotografías de Lewis Carroll (autor de *Alice in Wonderland* o *Alicia en el país de las maravillas*) para revelar la relación que mantuvo con niñas de temprana edad. El autor da forma a un texto de gran intensidad dramática. [MR]

4004 Dorr, Nicolás. Teatro insólito. La Habana: Ediciones Unión, 2001. 142 p. (Contemporáneos)

Los excéntricos de la noche, a contemporary two-act play with an epilogue, tells the story of two actors who were once friends. On the night the woman is planning to commit suicide because of loneliness, her long-lost friend Arturo visits her. But, Arturo decides to leave the country to find the success which has escaped him thus far in his life. The satirical, almost absurd work could be read as a commentary on Cuban politics. Volume also includes the two-act play *Nenúfares en el techo del mundo* (1996) and *Las pericas* (1961). *Nenúfares* recounts the story of a mother and daughter who find themselves trapped in their penthouse apartment when the elevator stops working. Familiar behavior patterns shape their quarrels and jealousies, especially for the mother, an aging stage actress who cannot come to terms with her status. The play displays Dorr's interest in performance theory. *Las pericas,* the play that guaranteed Dorr's reputation when he was only 14, is considered a classic of Cuban vanguardist theater. [SC]

4005 Drago, Alberto. Teatro. t. 1. Buenos Aires: Nueva Generación, 2000. 129 p. (Col. Teatristas hoy)

Reúne tres piezas. Dos de ellas— *Sábado de vino y gloria* y *Se me murió entre los brazos*—estrenadas en la década de los 70, a través de conflictos individuales, el grotesco y humor negro se alude en último término a la sociedad de la época. La tercera obra, *De no se qué de Libertad* (1997), alude a sucesos recientes de la historia argentina desde Perón hasta la actualidad. Se acompaña de poemas, coros y solistas. Se incluye la partitura musical. [MR]

4006 Drama contemporáneo costarricense, 1980–2000. Recopilación de Carolyn V. Bell y Patricia Fumero Vargas. San José: Editorial de la Univ. de Costa Rica, 2000. 516 p.: bibl. (Col. Identidad cultural)

One of the first anthologies to offer a thorough presentation of Costa Rican theater. Includes 10 plays and 10 essays by various critics. Bell's essay reviews Costa Rican theater in transition and Fumero Vargas' essay discusses theatrical activity in Costa Rica from 1970 onward, including a review of the cultural politics that have influenced the last decades of the 20th century. Each play script is followed by a bibliography of the dramatist's work and a study of the drama itself by a critic. Includes dramas by the more well-known playwrights: *Desempleo* by Guillermo Arriaga; *Sentencia para una aurora* by Jorge Arroyo; *El cristal de mi infancia* by Roxana Campos; *Tarde de granizo y musgo* by Leda Cavallini; *Sobre chapulines y otras langostas* by Wálter Fernández; *Madre nuestra que estás en la tierra* by Ana Istarú; *Eva, sol y sombra* by Mélvin Méndez; *Reflejos de sombra* by Arnoldo Ramos; *Madriguera de ilusiones* by Miguel Rojas; and *Como semillas 'e coyol* by Víctor Valdelomar. [SC]

4007 Feinmann, José Pablo. Dos destinos sudamericanos. Barcelona: Grupo Editorial Norma, 1999. 220 p.

Contiene dos obras. Una se centra en las últimas 16 horas de la vida de Ché Guevara, antes de ser asesinado en una escuela rural de Bolivia. Mediante flashbacks de momentos importantes de la vida del guerrillero, se cuestionan sus ideales revolucionarios. La otra revisita a Evita, presentada en sus flaquezas, ambición personal, su vulgaridad y odio a la oligarquía. Aunque hasta la muerte se la muestra como la protectora de los pobres, el cuadro que surge no es positivo, como tampoco lo es el del Ché Guevara, esto a pesar del equilibrio que busca el autor entre las posiciones adversas de ambos personajes con que los pinta la historia, según sea la ideología que la dibuja. [MR]

4008 Fernández Santana, René. El Gran festín: tres obras de Papalote, una mirada a los ochenta. Matanzas, Cuba: Ediciones Matanzas, 2002. 110 p.: ill. (Col. Milanés)

Fernández Santana, director of the Papalote theater company and one of the most renowned authors of children's theater, is represented here with *Los tres grandes farsantes cazadores de estrellas, El gran festín,* and *Todo comenzó el día en que la isla dejó de ser ordenada y limpia.* [SC]

4009 Fundora Hernández, Carlos. Tres comedias en busca del autor. Santa Clara, Cuba: Ediciones Capiro, 2001. 107 p. (Col. ULAN) (Teatro)

These three plays have well-known literary antecedents. *Los convidados* is a humorous mystery revolving around the death of Don Juan Tenorio in which Zorrilla, Tirso de Molina, Molière, and Pushkin are among the possible suspects of the assassination. *La discordia* is based on Canto 25 of the Iliad and questions aspects of that text as part of the metatheatrical play. Although Lorca does not appear by name in *Se casa Bernarda Alba,* one of the characters is called "the Author," and he enters into a discussion with the characters who appear in the original Bernarda Alba, as well as with other characters created by Fundora, including the Director and the Producer. The plays are entertaining, with a rich thematic development, and show a skillful dramatic technique. [SC]

4010 García Urrea, José Antonio. Que traigan al chucho: teatro chico en un acto para representar y leer. Guatemala: Editorial Cultura, 2000. 73 p. (Colección Manuel Galich. Serie Teatro; 1)

A reprint of four short plays that are part of the dramatic tradition of Guatemala. "Que traigan al chucho," "Felicitaciones, maestro," "El tamal de Nochebuena," and "El mejor regalo" depict episodes from the daily lives of the middle class with a sense of humor and a regional vocabulary. [SC]

4011 Germano, Antonio. Los duendes de Moisés Ville; Cómico. Santa Fe: Univ. Nacional del Litoral, Centro de Publicaciones, c1997. 127 p.

Las dos obras contenidas en este volumen están enmarcadas en un contexto histórico-cultural de gran interés. La que intitula el volumen se inscribe en la temática de la inmigración judía, de los avatares e instalación final de una familia de refugiados en Moisés Ville, un pueblo de la provincia de Santa Fe. *Cómico* tiene como protagonista a Pablo Podestá, un gran actor de comienzos de siglo, miembro de la familia Podestá, de gran importancia en la historia del teatro argentino. [MR]

4012 González Dávila, Jesús. Teatro de frontera 6. Durango, Mexico: Espacio Vacío, 2000. 156 p.

This series publishes plays by writers from Northern Mexico. A number of plays by the prolific playwright, González Dávila, are included in this edition: *Noche de bandidos, Los gatos, Son amores,* and *Quien baila mambo.* [SC]

4013 González Gil, Manuel. Porteños: no se hacen, nacen; el guión. Buenos Aires: Nuevo Extremo, 1999. 122 p.: ill.

Un grupo de amigos, inmigrantes de distintas procedencias, se reúnen en una mesa del café "El Porteño," donde el dueño es un gallego, a jugar al "truco," un juego de naipes o barajas. No tocados por el tiempo, se les presenta en distintos momentos del siglo XX. A través de su conversación, van surgiendo los hechos más importantes de la historia y cultura nacional y mundial y de sus agentes principales. [MR]

4014 González-Pérez, Armando. Presencia negra: teatro cubano de la diáspora; antología crítica. Prólogo de José A. Escarpanter. Prefacio de Kenya C. Dworkin y Méndez. Madrid: Editorial Betania, 1999. 316 p.: bibl., ill. (Col. Antologías)

Critical anthology focusing on the presence of the Afro-Cuban theme in plays by dramatists of the Cuban exile. Includes *La navaja de Olofé* by Matías Montes Huidobro (which premiered at the Coconut Grove Playhouse in Miami in 1986); *Otra historia y Trash* by Pedro R. Monge Rafuls (Off Broadway début in Nov. 1995 by DoGooder Productions in Theatre on Three); *Las hetairas habaneras* by José Corrales/Manuel Pereiras García; *Los hijos de Ochún* by Raúl de Cárdenas; *La eterna noche de Juan Francisco Manzano* by Héctor Santiago; *Rita and Bessie* by Manuel Martin Jr. (which premiered Off Broadway in Aug. 1988 by Duo

Theater); and *E-Motions/E/mociones* by Leandro Soto. Also includes a glossary and a bibliography. [SC]

4015 Gorostiza, Carlos. Teatro. v. 5. Buenos Aires: Ediciones de la Flor, 1998. 1 v.

Reúne tres obras recientes del autor, todas de excelente calidad. El dramaturgo, en lo que es una constante de su producción teatral, continúa profundizando en relaciones humanas particulares, pero siempre con una dimensión universal. De especial interés es *Los otros papeles* en que el autor, a partir del legado de un anarquista/idealista, postula que los grandes ideales/utopías son guías válidas para el hombre. [MR]

4016 Grasso, Ricardo. Teatro. 3, López. Montevideo: Proyección, 1998. 1 v.

El conflicto dramático se desarrolla en torno al cambio súbito experimentado por un cumplido empleado y esposo ejemplar. [MR]

4017 Halac, Ricardo. Teatro. v. 4. Buenos Aires: Corregidor, 1998. 1 v. (Col. Dramaturgos argentinos contemporáneos; 1)

De este dramaturgo argentino de gran trayectoria teatral se incluyen en este breve volumen dos obras, *El destete* y *¡Viva la anarquía!* La primera, una de las obras más conocidas del autor, es interpretada por Osvaldo Pellettieri como una obra farsesca cuyo eje estructurante se perfila como una transgresión realista del vodevil. Además de las acotaciones escénicas intrínsecas al texto, Halac ofrece a un virtual director algunas notas para su montaje. [MR]

4018 Hernández, Luisa Josefina. El galán de ultramar: la amante, Fermento y sueño y tres perros y un gato; teatro. Xalapa, Mexico: Univ. Veracruzana, 2000. 224 p. (Ficción)

The four plays included here form a tetralogy of the interconnected lives of a number of families living on the coast of the Gulf of Mexico between 1862–90. The titles, in chronological order according to the events depicted, are *El galán de ultramar, La amante, Fermento y sueño,* and *Tres perros y un gato.* Characters include Creoles, mestizos, indigenous peoples. As with most plays by Hernández, themes include power relations, feminism, and the complexity of Mexican ethnic interactions. [SC]

4019 Hiriart, Hugo. Minotastasio y su familia; Camille; Casandra. Introducción de David Olguín. México: Ediciones El Milagro: Consejo Nacional para la Cultura y las Artes, 1999. 123 p.: ill. (Teatro)

Known for winning the 1994 Ariel prize for best screenplay for "Novia que te vea," Hiriart has also published and presented a number of plays, three of which are reproduced here. *Minotastasio,* first presented in 1980, and *Casandra,* first presented in 1979, are versions of the Greek myths, while *Camille* tells a version of the life of French sculptress Camille Claudel and her mentor-lover, Rodin. Despite references to literary and historical subtexts, Hiriart offers original dramas that stimulate readers to reconsider these classic tales. In *Minotastasio,* the exchange of human actors and puppets for the same roles helps address ideas of human existence and destiny, while in *Casandra,* four women interchange the role of Casandra, which brings into question what it means to play a part in life as in theater. *Camille* not only raises feminist issues about women in the arts, but also considers the closeness between genius and madness in artistic creation. [SC]

4020 Istarú, Ana. Baby boom en el Paraíso/ Hombres en escabeche: teatro. San José: Editorial Costa Rica, 2001. 165 p. (Teatro/Editorial Costa Rica)

These two plays have received prizes and been produced in a number of countries. The plays show why Istarú has received increasing esteem in the way they explore problems facing Latin American women who live in a patriarchal world; she treats serious topics with humor and theatrical mastery along with feminist ideology. [SC]

4021 La Torre, Alfonso. Vallejo. Lima: Banco Central de Reserva del Perú, Fondo Editorial, 2000. 43 p.: ill.

Obra en un acto en que a partir de un encierro carcelario, el mundo del poeta peruano vanguardista se va llenando de figuras que pasaron por su vida personal o ideológica. En una ambientación surrealista surgen voces o alusiones que refieren a su poesía o a conocidas figuras históricas como Mariátegui y Stalin o la madre y Georgette, compañera del poeta. [MR]

4022 Leis Romero, Raúl Alberto. El puente. Panamá: Instituto Nacional de Cultura, 2001. 71 p. (Col. Ricardo Miró)

A one-act play with eight scenes in

which two characters, Rosalba and Joaquín, inadvertently meet on a bridge, both planning to commit suicide. They did not know each other before this meeting, and we are never sure whether Joaquín arrived there to save the woman or to commit suicide. As they converse and become friends, Rosalba realizes that she does not want to kill herself, despite the difficult life she leads. She lives in a situation of domestic violence; her rural village is beset by the problems of globalization; etc. In spite of the negative portrayal of Panamanian life, the play does end on an optimistic note. [SC]

4023 Leñero, Vicente. Dramaturgia terminal: cuatro obras. México: Editorial Colibrí, 2000. 119 p. (Col. Arco iris)

Of the four one-act plays, *Hace ya tanto tiempo* is the only one that does not include references to historical figures or events. Instead, it deals with the theme of old age, and how aging affects a couple and their reconstruction of the past. *Avaricia*, based on a short story by Vicente Blasco Ibáñez, recreates the political world of 1920 with such historical figures as Blasco Ibáñez himself, along with General Obregón and José de León Toral, among others. It approaches the political theme with humor and cynicism, as in *Todos somos Marcos*, which explores the impact of the Zapatista rebellion of 1994. *Don Juan en Chapultepec* is a metadrama that proposes a conversation between the Spanish dramatist José Zorilla and the monarchs Maximilian and Carlota. [SC]

4024 Leñero Franco, Estela. Paisaje interior norte/sur. México: Ediciones el Milagro; Consejo Nacional para la Cultura y las Artes, 2001. 75 p. (La Centena. Teatro)

With Leticia, a woman from Tijuana, and Maruch, a guerrilla fighter from Chiapas, Leñero tells the story of a Mexico divided by language and region but connected by the similar experience of its marginalized peoples. Although Maruch lives on the border between Mexico and Guatemala and speaks Ttzotzil and Leticia is from the Mexico-US border, at the end of the 22 scenes, their differences and their local identities do not divide them. The two face such similar concerns as fear of police, abuse by authorities, and the search for love as a way to forget sorrow. [SC]

4025 Luna, Isidro. ¿Quieres tomar un café conmigo? Cuenca, Ecuador: Univ. de Cuenca; Casa de la Cultura Ecuatoriana, Núcleo del Azuay; Alianza Francesa, 1999. 108 p. (Honda de David; 5)

Tres obras de tipos existencialista-absurdista con personajes puestos en situaciones límites y en que se rompen fronteras de vida y muerte, ficción y realidad, y las historias adquieren forma mediante la unión de la dispersión y el contrapunto. [MR]

4026 Mancebo del Castillo, Gerardo *et al.* Teatro de La Gruta. Presentación de Luis Mario Moncada. México: CONACULTA; Helénico, 2001. 301 p. (Fondo Editorial Tierra Adentro; 229)

This anthology includes plays that were performed for the first time between 1998–2000. Mancebo del Castillo, in *Las tremendas aventuras de la Capitana Gazpacha (o de cómo los elefantes aprendieron a jugar a las canicas)* (1998), creates a universe marked by a rich sense of humor based on the intertextual references to such classics as *Don Quijote* and *Waiting for Godot. Stabat mater* (1998) by Humberto Leyva (Coahuila) is a study of a dysfunctional family; *Pedro y Lola* by Edward Coward deals with a couple lost in their memories; in *¡Ultimo round!* Edgar Chías uses language characteristic of young people in Mexico City to explore sexual relations and the possible permutations that affect different couples, including a homosexual twosome; *Estrellas enterradas* by Antonio Zúñiga presents some friends who try to adapt to the influences of the modern world without losing their identity. *Y cuando desperté . . . ¡Ya se me había hecho tarde!* by Francisco Olivié is based on the story "El monopolio de la moda" by Britto García, and is a parody of consumer society. [SC]

4027 Marechal, Leopoldo. Obras completas. v. 2, El teatro y los ensayos. Buenos Aires: Perfil Libros, 1998. 1 v.: bibl. (La biblioteca)

Reúne cuatro piezas completas del autor. De ellas las más conocidas son *Antígona Pérez* y *Don Juan.* Se incluyen además *Las batallas de José Luna* y *Las tres caras de Venus* y unos fragmentos de obras. Obras muy bien estructuradas, con toques garcíalorquianos por su lenguaje poético e inclusión de canciones. En ellas retoma mitos literarios y culturales de carácter universal, pero vestidos con un ropaje local. Para el comentario de vols. 1, 3–4 de esta obra, ver ítem **3703**. [MR]

4028 Maslíah, Leo. No juegues con fuego porque lo podés apagar: y otras piezas. Buenos Aires: Ediciones de la Flor, 1998. 191 p.

Las obras de este dramaturgo, cantautor, y novelista uruguayo, aunque sin desmerecer su textualidad escrita, enfatizan su aspecto preformativo. Se podrían situar dentro del discurso teatral del grotesco característico de la región rioplatense. En ellas predomina la anécdota o situación cómica, pero siempre con una intención social fustigante. [MR]

4029 Medina, Roberto Nicolás. Teatro. v. 1. Buenos Aires: Corregidor, 1999. 1 v.: bibl.

Obras breves en que con un buen desarrollo de la tensión dramática, dominio de un lenguaje poético y de variadas estéticas, absurdo, grotesco, y expresionismo, aluden a un referente histórico que mantiene viva la memoria de un pasado de autoritarismo y violencia. No se trata de un teatro denotativo, de lenguaje transparente, sino de uno en que predomina la fineza de la connotación, la ironía, la alegoría, y la metáfora. [MR]

4030 Modern, Rodolfo E. Teatro completo. v. 2. Buenos Aires: Torres Agüero Editor, 1997. 1 v. (Col. Telón abierto)

Obras muy bien escritas y bien estructuradas dramáticamente. En *La mancha de Arequito*, para la creación de la ficción, toma elementos en la historia del Gen. José María Paz. Con la apoyatura de la estética del grotesco rioplatense y situaciones típicas del teatro del absurdo o de la farsa tradicional, el autor da forma a situaciones dramáticas reveladoras del mundo interior de los protagonistas. Incluye también las obras *Saliendo con Clara* y *Noche de ronda*. [MR]

4031 Molino García, Edgardo. En los zapatos ajenos. Panamá: Editorial Portobelo, 1998. 104 p. (Biblioteca de autores panameños; 14. Teatro)

Molino García evokes the work of Osvaldo Dragón or Jorge Díaz in his representation of the dehumanization of the individual and the way in which humans are destroyed by fellow human beings. [SC]

4032 Molino García, Edgardo. La quinta pata del gato. Panamá: Editorial Portobelo, 2000. 93 p. (Biblioteca de autores panameños; 18. Teatro)

Studies the psychology of a group of people in the publishing business who meet in a Chinese restaurant to resolve some work-related problems. Instead of eating, however, they fall into a trance that enables them to reveal their true personalities and prejudices. [SC]

4033 Muñoz, Gloria. Tragedia de la cárcel pública y otras piezas. Asunción: Arandurā Editorial, 2000. 169 p.

El volumen contiene dos obras de un acto y cinco monólogos breves. Continuando con la teatralización de obras narrativas que había iniciado con *Yo el Supremo* de Augusto Roa Bastos, inspirada en otra novela del autor paraguayo, la autora escribe *Almirante de sueños y vigilia*, basada en la vida de Cristóbal Colón. Interesante es también la obra que titula el volumen que también acude a personajes históricos y el monólogo "La confesión," ambientada en la época del dictador Francia y basada en el cuento de Renée Ferrer de Arréllaga. [MR]

4034 Nueva dramaturgia sinaloense. Sinaloa, Mexico?: Dirección de Investigación y Fomento de la Cultura Regional: Fondo Estatal para la Cultura y las Artes; Mexico City: Consejo Nacional para la Cultura y las Artes, 1998. 165 p.

Brings together a selection of dramatists from a Sinaloan drama workshop. Includes works by Dolores Espinosa (*Quinto Mandamiento*), Antonio Martínez (*Páramo para después del reino*), Elmer Mendoza (*El viaje de la tortuga panza rosa*), Ramón Perea (*La hija del R 15*), Miguel Ángel Valencia (*Vuelo de alebrijes*), and Cruz Manuel Villa (*La última sábana*). [SC]

4035 Pais, Carlos and **Américo Torchelli.** Trilogía teatro tango. Buenos Aires: Corregidor, 1997. 125 p.

Inspirados en la letra de los tangos y su afición a ellos, los autores auscultan al hombre de la calle de la gran ciudad, hablan de sus frustraciones, pero también de sus sueños por algo mejor. *Pobre tipo* es una comedia musical que muestra que el tango, en vez de ser la canción triste y quejosa que se le atribuye, es en el fondo una canción de amor.

Muñeca brava es una comedia de humor que destaca la poeticidad del texto de los tangos. [MR]

4036 Parra, Marco Antonio de la. Heroína: teatro repleto de mujeres. Santiago: Editorial Cuarto Propio, 1999. 307 p.: bibl. (Dramaturgia chilena contemporánea) (Serie Teatro)

Contiene seis obras escritas por el autor en la década de los 90. En ellas el dramaturgo chileno retoma mitos clásicos que matiza con símbolos y estéticas posmodernistas. El núcleo de las obras es la indagación psicosocioanalítica del cuerpo e imaginarios femeninos. Se trata de un teatro antropológico con propuestas escénicas en que el cuerpo y lenguaje se convierten en los signos escénicos primarios cuyos significantes más que revelar, buscan y ocultan sentidos. La introducción de Nieves Olcoz, editora del volumen, es iluminadora. [MR]

4037 Pavlovsky, Eduardo A. Teatro completo. v. 1–2. Buenos Aires: Atuel, 1997–2000. 2 v.: bibl. (Col. los argentinos)

El estudio preliminar de Dubatti destaca la importancia que tiene este renombrado dramaturgo argentino en la dramaturgia ríoplatense vanguardista y posmodernista. De cómo en sus obras, a partir de coordenadas psicoanalíticas, histórico-sociales e ideológicas, se profundiza en problemas humanos universales. Se trata de un teatro en que abunda la violencia corporal y psicológica, opresores y oprimidos. Se trata de un teatro que más que hilvanar un argumento, se concentra en la intensidad de lo fragmentario. Vol. 1 contiene siete obras, todas de excelente calidad. Vol. 2 contiene seis obras que se caracterizan por su fuerte apego al conflictivo y violento contexto histórico que se vivió en la Argentina en la época de los 70 y 80. Ellas reflejan un afán crítico y reformador, ideológicamente situado en una militancia de izquierda y promotor de una utopía socialista. Un realismo crítico con visos absurdista permea todas las obras antologadas. [MR]

4038 Perales, Rosalina. Antología de teatro infantil puertorriqueño. San Juan: Editorial de la Univ de Puerto Rico, 2000. 286 p.: bibl.

Consists of 14 plays, beginning with the pleasant *¿Quién preside?* by Eugenio

María de Hostos, with vegetables as characters. Other plays by well-known writers included here are: *Un paisaje marino* by Julia de Burgos, *Las lagrimas de doña Toronja* by Marigloria Palma, and *Honroso, el oso* by Teresa Marichal (1998). [SC]

4039 Pérez Vázquez, Reynol. El tren nuestro de cada día: teatro. Presentación de Vicente Leñero. Monterrey, Mexico: Univ. Autónoma de Nuevo León, 2000. 268 p.: ill.

Anthology includes nine one-act plays by an author from Nuevo León. The prologue by Vicente Leñero praises the plays. He points out their affinities with the work of Elena Garro, especially *El bostezo azul*, but also *Aullidos*, which reminds us of Rulfo as well as Garro. *Ausencia con gato* brings to mind Kafka and Beckett, while two plays are based on a reading of Bulgarian authors: *La vitamina que llegó de América* and *Mocasín*. [SC]

4040 Piñeros Corpas, Joaquín. Teatro colombiano. Bogotá: Patronato Colombiano de Artes y Ciencias, Fundación Joaquín Piñeros Corpas, 1997. 139 p.

Las obras de este reconocido humanista colombiano tienen como referente directo acontecimientos históricos, como sucede con *Muchindote*, que realizan figuras de la guerra de independencia, y situaciones cotidianas típicas. Estructuradas de acuerdo a la convención naturalista apelan a la identificación del receptor con lo presentado, siempre desde una perspectiva positiva. [MR]

4041 Puig, Manuel. Triste golondrina macho; Amor del bueno; Muy señor mío. Edición al cuidado de Graciela Goldchluk y Julia Romero. Rosario, Argentina: Beatríz Viterbo Editora, 1998. 222 p. (Ficciones)

Estas obras muestran el cambio estético que experimentara el autor en su escritura dramática. Aunque en el universo dramático refluyen los mismos deseos e insatisfacciones de obras anteriores, el melodrama, que fue el género preferido del escritor, se matiza aquí con incursiones surrealistas, con la tradición gótica y los cuentos de hadas. [MR]

4042 Quintero, Héctor. Te sigo esperando; Antes de mí, el Sahara. Edición de Juan Antonio Hormigón. Madrid: Publicaciones de la Asociación de Directores de

Escena de España, 1998? 138 p.: bibl. (Serie Literatura dramática iberoamericana; 20)

Te sigo esperando follows the tradition of works using the bolero to discuss themes of national identity. *Antes de mí, el Sahara* is a monologue filled with irony about Cuban life during the Special Period. [SC]

4043 Ramos-Perea, Roberto. Módulo 104: revolución en el purgatorio. 2da. ed. Río Piedras, P.R.: Librería Norberto González, 2000. 112 p.: ill.

A historical drama based on events that occurred during the crisis of the penal system in Puerto Rico in 1980–82. Received the Premio René Marqués del Ateneo Puertorriqueño 1983 and the Premio Nacional de Teatro from the PEN Club 1986. This edition is an enlarged and revised version of the 1983 play that denounces the treatment of political prisoners. [SC]

4044 Rascón Banda, Víctor Hugo. La malinche. México: Plaza y Janés, 2000. 283 p.: ill. (Son de teatro)

This postmodernist, metahistorical play, composed of 37 scenes, caused a scandal when it was first staged in Mexico City in 1998. This edition of the dramatic text includes a chronicle of the mise-en-scène which was directed by the Austrian Johann Kresnik. The work presents a modern-day Malinche, mistreated by prejudice but at the same time a participant in the new conquest of Mexico by its northern neighbor and its commercial products. Rascón Banda makes reference to Mexican history, from the conquest to the present, incorporating references to the chroniclers, texts by Octavio Paz and Carlos Fuentes, and legends about La Llorona. [SC]

4045 Rascón Banda, Víctor Hugo. Sazón de mujer; Table dance. Zona Río, Mexico: CAEN Editores, 2001. 129 p.: ill. (Los inéditos; 10)

In these two plays, Rascón Banda again shows his interest in the lives of women who suffer from violence and whose lives serve as symbols of disorder and social disruption. In *Sazón de mujer*, the kitchen and dining rooms are metaphors demonstrating the need for gender solidarity in spite of superficial differences. In the bar where *Table dance* takes place, the focus is on two women whose poverty forces them to be exploited.

Their interpersonal conflicts prevent them from fostering a sense of solidarity, and national policies clearly affect their lives. The effects of globalization are illustrated by foreign women who come to Mexico and continue to speak their native tongues: Russian and English. [SC]

4046 Rodríguez Barrera, Alberto. Tito quería ser una mujer de la vida pero su mamá era arquitecto: arte dramático cibernético con ñapa. Caracas: FUNDARTE/Alcaldía de Caracas, 1997. 197 p. (Col. Delta; 51)

Este conjunto de obras muestra el talento de este dramaturgo y director de larga trayectoria, pero poco conocido. En las obras el autor asume temas de gran actualidad desde las implicaciones del mundo cibernético en el hombre, los ecológicos que preocupan cada vez más y la exposición de lo marginal. Teatro lúcido que en una violencia llevada a extremos apenas soportable, se revelan escondidas perversidades humanas. Se trata de un teatro digno de conocerse mejor. [MR]

4047 Rodríguez Bécquer, Víctor Hugo. Permanencia voluntaria: teatro. Zacatecas, Mexico: Instituto Zacatecano de Educación para Adultos, 2001. 126 p. (Col. Letras que cuentan; 1)

Rodríguez Bécquer, from Zacatecas, studied with the maestro Alberto Huerta. The plays of this anthology—*Ambivalencia, Permanencia voluntaria, La casa de los espejos, Fotosíntesis,* and *Historia de puntos suspendidos,* are experimental one-act plays, some of which are called "exercises." [SC]

4048 Rojas, Miguel. Hogar, dulce hogar. San José?: Editorial Alma Mater, 2000. 191 p.

Explores the contradictions of family life as a metaphor to analyze globalization and its effect on Costa Rican national identity. [SC]

4049 Romero, Mariela. Nosotros que nos quisimos tanto. Caracas: Alfadil Ediciones; Gente de Teatro, 1998. 141 p.: ill. (Col. Ludens; 8)

Contiene cuatro obras de una buena representante del teatro contemporáneo venezolano. Además de la obra que titula el libro se incluyen: *Tania en cinco movimientos, Esperando al italiano,* y *El regreso del*

Rey Lear. Se trata de dramas existenciales que ahondan en la complejidad psicológica de personajes solitarios, sus triunfos e incumplidas metas. [MR]

4050 Rossell, Levy. El gran libro del teatro rosselliano. Caracas: Fondo Editorial Fundarte, Alcaldía de Caracas, 1998. 396 p.: ill.

Reúne 16 obras del autor, un destacado productor, director, y profesor venezolano. Algunas reflejan el contexto social de su escritura, como es el caso de *Vimazoluleka* de los 60 que expresa el pensamiento juvenil y rebelde del momento; otras tienen un claro referente político-social como *Gran Takamajaka* y *En el limbo.* En otras recurre a la mitología, como en *La Atlántida.* La propuesta, en general, incorpora canciones, coros y músicos populares que la hace muy atractiva a una potencial audiencia. [MR]

4051 Salcedo, Hugo. Teatro de frontera 2. Durango, Mexico: UJED, Espácio Vacío Editorial, 1999. 204 p.

Includes *Bárbara Gandiaga, El árbol del deseo, La estrella del norte, Selena,* and *Asesinato en los parques,* from a talented playwright who explores the lives of marginalized peoples, showing the violence and despair that mark their existence. Aware of the themes of the Borderlands, Salcedo also tries to understand the phenomenon of Selena in the eponymous play. [SC]

4052 Sánchez Mayáns, Fernando. Tres obras de teatro. Presentación de Vicente Leñero. 1. ed. en Lecturas mexicanas. México: CONACULTA, 2000. 146 p. (Lecturas mexicanas. Cuarta serie)

As Leñero comments, Sánchez Mayáns belongs to the Generation of the 50s, along with Carballido, Sergio Magaña, Luisa Josefina Hernández, and reflects some of their interests in realism and themes that dwell on the loss of traditional values, the hypocrisy of contemporary society, and the crisis of modernity. A tragicomedy of three acts, *Las alas del pez* shows the effect on children of their parents fighting in front of them. The well-structured play adheres to the values of its time. Subtitled "obra antimítica en tres actos," *Un extraño laberinto* reexamines the myths of the Minotaur, Theseus, and Ariadne to discuss contemporary Mexican politics. The play explores the lies of official history, creating a Minotaur that is venerable old man, a good host to the Athenian youth who enter his labyrinth. While there are references to Tlatelolco, the dramatist is critical of demagoguery from youth culture. *La bronca,* subtitled "reportaje teatral en dos actos," also alludes to Tlatelolco by exploring the generational conflict between professor and student. The political figures reveal their hypocrisy while the student and the professor try to defend their values. [SC]

4053 Sánchez Salazar, Juan Manuel *et al.* Siete obras de dramaturgia peruana. Lima: Teatro Nacional; Instituto Nacional de Cultura, 1999. 319 p.

Reúne obras de autores que fueron premiados en dos concursos organizados por el Teatro Nacional en que participaron como jurado reconocidos teatristas peruanos y el venezolano Rodolfo Santana. Del primer concurso hacia una dramaturgia joven se incluyen cuatro obras seleccionadas. Del segundo concurso, Solari Swayne se eligió tres obras. De todo el volumen se destaca *Qoyllor ritti* de Delfina Paredes Aparicio, inspirada en la celebración andina de Qoyllor ritti. [MR]

4054 Schmidhuber de la Mora, Guillermo. Trece apuestas al teatro. v. 1–2. Colima, Mexico: Gobierno del Estado de Colima; Univ. de Colima; Guanajuato, Mexico: Instituto Estatal de la Cultura Guanajuato; CONACULTA, 1999. 2 v.

Vol. 1 includes *Dramasutra, o Farsa del diablo dramaturgo, La amistad secreta de Juana y Dorotea, Obituario, El armario de las abuelas, El quinto viaje de Colón, Por las tierras de Colón* (considered by Vicente Leñero to be his best play), and *Fuegos truncos.* Vol. 2 includes *Lacandonia, Los herederos de Segismundo* (winner of the prize from the Nacional de Teatro de INBA 1980), *El robo del penacho de Moctezuma, Todos somos el rey Lear, Los héroes inútiles,* and *Nuestro señor Quetzalcóatl.* All show the diversity of his dramaturgy, which includes historical texts, feminist perpectives, and explorations of personal issues. [SC]

4055 6 obras del Teatro La Candelaria. Bogotá: Ediciones Teatro La Candelaria, 1998. 331 p.: ill.

De la creación colectiva producida por

mucho tiempo, este grupo, formado desde hace más de 20 años por Santiago García, está ahora incursionando en una dramaturgia producida por miembros individuales del grupo. Aunque la obra que titula el libro es de carácter colectivo, las otras cinco que componen el volumen son producto de la autoría de Patricia Ariza, Fernando Peñuela, Nohora Ayala, y del director del grupo, Santiago García, todas creadas bajo el lenguaje escénico que ha caracterizado al grupo. Predomina una línea temática interactiva entre el espacio de la ciudad y los seres marginales que la pueblan. Obras de marcada referencia social. [MR]

4056 Serulle, Haffe. El gran carnaval. Santo Domingo: Fundación Ciencia y Arte, 2000. 113 p.

Using a technique that was already evident in his drama *Duarte* (1976), Serulle creates a collage in which he presents his interpretation of Caribbean history. The cast of characters consists of over 40 people, including pirates, circus performers, giant puppets, deformed figures, etc. Using music, grotesque gestures, and violent scenes, the dramatist tries to recreate his version of life in the Caribbean. [SC]

4057 Sobre el río—y otros historias: ejercicios para actores. Asunción?: Arandurã Editorial, 1998. 110 p.

Contiene 20 textos de autores paraguayos, entre ellos Luis Hernáez, Renée Ferrer, y Agustín Núñez. Se trata de viñetas dramáticas escritas, fundamentalmente, para ser usadas como ejercicios de actuación. [MR]

4058 Solo, Rodrigo. Valta. San Luis Potosí, Mexico: Editorial Ponciano Arriaga; Gobierno del Estado de San Luis Potosí, 1999. 74 p. (Col. Los premios)

Winner of the Manuel José Othon Prize for drama in 1998, this one-act play has two characters: El and Ella. Offers yet another interpretation of the Mexican fascination with death. "Ella," Miss Death, is young, charming, and a master of contemporary and regional vocabulary while she plays with a new victim, "El." [SC]

4059 Solórzano, Carlos. Teatro completo. Presentación de Armando Partida Tayzan. Prólogo de Frank Dauster. 1. ed. en Letras mexicanas. México: CONACULTA,

2002. 281 p.: bibl., ill. (Lecturas mexicanas. Cuarta serie)

Volume includes two critical essays: "Carlos Solórzano, renovador del teatro latinoamericano" and "CS: La libertad sin límites" by Dauster. The republished plays include *Doña Beatriz (la Sin Ventura), El hechicero*, and *Las manos de dios*; and from his one-act plays: "El zapato: Cruce de vías (Vodevil triste)," "El sueño del Ángel," "Mea culpa," "El crucificado," and "Los fantoches." Also presents copies of letters from important writers, including Alfonso Reyes, Albert Camus, and Michel de Ghelderode. Solórzano is known for his existentialist pieces and his exploration of the complex freedom that we enjoy or suffer from as human beings. [SC]

4060 Suárez Durán, Esther. El alma desnuda. La Habana: Ediciones Unión, 2002. 50 p.

Similar to other prize-winning plays by Suárez Durán (such as *Mi amigo Mozart*, Premio La Edad de Oro, 1991; *El libro del orégano*, Premio UNEAC, 1995; *Baños públicos, S.A.*, UNEAC, 1995), *Alma desnuda* was awarded the UNEAC Prize in 2001. This metatheatrical piece, with its imaginative postmodernist vision, rewrites the legend of Pinocchio, but its intertextual richness also includes selections of poems by such Cuban writers as Mirta Aguirre and Dulce María Loynaz, as well as other references to puppet theater in Latin America. [SC]

4061 Teatro: 5 autores. v. 1. Buenos Aires?: Comuna Ediciones; La Plata, Argentina: Subsecretaría de Cultura y Educación de la Municipalidad de La Plata, 1999. 1 v. (Col. Textos del retablo)

Contiene una buena selección de textos de cinco dramaturgos platenses. Entre ellas se destacan *Dos tipos siniestros* de César Genovesi y *La filmación* de Enrique Gaona. [MR]

4062 Tovar, Juan. Las adoraciones: tragedia de don Carlos, cacique de Tezcoco; versión definitiva. México: Ediciones El Milagro; Consejo Nacional para la Cultura y las Artes, 2001. 66 p. (La Centena. Teatro)

The definitive edition of an historical drama published in 1981. It takes place in Tezcoco and México in 1539, and deals with the historical figures of Fray Juan de Zumárraga, Alonso de Molina, and Fray Bernardino de Sahagún. [SC]

4063 Valdivia, Benjamín. Las claves de Eurídice: cuatro piezas teatrales. Guanajuato, Mexico: Univ. de Guanajuato, 2001. 107 p. (Letras versales.) Serie Torre de papel)

El alma del Joel Paredes (written 1979; revised 1981), presents the poverty-stricken situation of a young couple, Joel Paredes and Maru. The action begins with Joel's death and the arrival of his soul as a character who searches for Joel. Throughout the search, various key episodes in his life are presented. *Orfeo y variaciones* deals with a Mexican version of the classical story of Orpheus and Euridice. *El nahual de paramillo* is called a "Mexican ritual for the theater." Composed of one act with nine scenes, it uses the dispute between a witch and a doctor to explore the clash between generations, old traditions versus new technological advances. The fourth and final play, *Luna de hojalata,* is marked by Valdivia's interest in a poetic theater that includes folkloric motifs. [SC]

4064 Valencia, Gerardo. Teatro. Edición y estudio preliminar a cargo de Ernesto Porras Collantes. Bogotá: Instituto Caro y Cuervo, 1998. 367 p.: bibl., ill. (Biblioteca colombiana; 42)

Se reúnen las obras dramáticas del escritor, que también fue poeta y ensayista, quien se dio a conocer en el grupo conocido con el nombre de la revista *Piedra y Cielo* en que publicaban sus textos. Interesado en recoger en sus obras los rasgos nacionales de Colombia, sus obras presentan conflictos familiares y sociales en las cuales, generalmente, el protagonismo está centrado en las figuras femeninas, algunas mulatas, como sucede en *Chonta* y *El poder de Jacinta*. [MR]

4065 Vallejo, César. Teatro completo. v. 1–3. Ed. del Rectorado. Lima: Pontificia Univ. Católica del Perú, 1999. 3 v.: bibl., ill.

Una cuidada edición de todas las obras del poeta peruano cuya escritura dramática no está a la altura de su labor poética, pero que no deja de ser de interés. *De Colacho hermanos* se ofrece la última versión perfeccionada del autor. *La piedra cansada de ambiente incaico* es tal vez la obra en que el autor alcanza una mayor intensidad poética. Estos textos de Vallejos son sin dudas de gran interés no sólo para los estudiosos del teatro

hispanoamericano sino también para un estudio del teatro de exiliados en París, entre los que se cuenta Vicente García Huidobro, y las influencias que allí recibieron. [MR]

4066 Vega Revollo, Oscar. Nuestro teatro costumbrista. Bogotá: Impresos González, 1998. 169 p.

Se incluyen 24 obras breves que dibujan situaciones típicas de personajes populares reconocibles en el contexto colombiano. El apego a la convención realista no sólo se refleja en el mundo representado sino también en expresiones sociolectales. [MR]

4067 Veronese, Daniel. La deriva. Buenos Aires: Adriana Hidalgo Editora, 2000. 315 p.: ill. (La Lengua. Teatro)

Compendia seis textos dramáticos de este dramaturgo que se ha inscripto en el llamado "teatro nuevo," un teatro autorreflexivo que se vuelca a sí mismo, que al mismo tiempo que expresa las instantáneas subjetividades del dramaturgo, evoca un mundo inquietante. Representan estas obras un teatro en que, de la diversidad de todo orden, estético y conceptual, de la unión de lo cotidiano y lo insólito, del objeto inánime y el sujeto convulsionado, aflora un mundo perturbador. Contiene un texto intitulado "Automandamientos," un manifiesto dramático-poético del dramaturgo. Excelente teatro. [MR]

4068 Viviescas, Víctor. Teatro. Medellín, Colombia: Editorial Univ. de Antioquia, 2000. 235 p. (Teatro)

Reúne ocho obras de este importante dramaturgo colombiano. Se destacan por su lenguaje poético y alusivo y situaciones psicológicas muy bien planteadas. Su temática recorre la soledad, el desamor, la incomunicación, el enclaustramiento, y el desarraigo. De especial interés es la trilogía, en torno a la mujer, titulada *Territorios del dolor* que incluye *¡Hello, alejandra . . .!, Hotel California* y *Para el final morir.* [MR]

THEATER CRITICISM AND HISTORY

4069 Ardissone, José Luis. Arlequín Teatro, 1982–1997: primera parte de una historia. Asunción: Fundación Arlequín Teatro; Arandurã Editorial, 1998. 443 p.: ill.

Historia de los 15 años de existencia del Arlequín Teatro, los pormenores de su fundación y demolición. Se pasa revista de todos los espectáculos allí presentados, de reseñas aparecidas en periódicos y ensayos de personalidades del teatro que por él pasaron, como Atahualpa del Cioppo. [MR]

4070 Azparren Giménez, Leonardo. El teatro en Venezuela: ensayos históricos. Caracas: Alfadil Ediciones, 1997. 209 p.: bibl. (Gente de teatro) (Col. Trópicos; 59)

El conocido investigador venezolano entrega un nuevo producto de su investigación y de sus colaboradores. Sin mantener una línea cronológica que considera limitativa, el autor opta por una metodología que permite el cruce de coordenadas temporales y culturales. Para estructurar su historia distingue entre teatralidad y texto dramático, estableciendo formas de periodización diferentes para cada uno. En ambos casos el contexto histórico-social es un importante vector. [MR]

4071 Cacho Palma, Sabatino. Apuntes para lunáticos: el poeta, el pintor, el niño y el actor en el desafío de la puesta en escena. Rosario, Argentina: Homo Sapiens, 1998. 203 p.: ill. (some col.).

Excelente propuesta estética puesta en práctica en el montaje de Hamlet, que colectivamente realizó el psiquiatra, director y actor, Cacho Palma con su grupo. La realidad escénica emprendida como un conjunto polisémico en que la situación dramática está permeada por la fantasía y un profundo andamiaje simbólico-metafórico. Indispensable para creadores de la escena. [MR]

4072 Copi. Habla Copi: homosexualidad y creación. Entrevista de José Tcherkaski. Dibujos de Miguel Rep. Buenos Aires: Galerna, 1998. 160 p.: ill. (Col. Carne y hueso)

Tcherkaski entrevista al genial dramaturgo argentino. El entrevistador plantea preguntas que van develando de modo transparente el proceso creativo Copi y facetas de su personalidad desconocidas por sus críticos o, simplemente, mal interpretadas. [MR]

4073 De Esquilo a Gambaro: teatro, mito y cultura griegos y teatro argentino. Edición de Osvaldo Pellettieri. Buenos Aires: Editorial Galerna, 1997. 126 p.: bibl. (Cuadernos del GETEA; 7)

Contiene una colección de trabajos críticos en que se estudian obras de autores argentinos que se han inspirado directa o indirectamente en mitos del periodo clásico para resemantizarlos de acuerdo a coordenadas contextuales. Entre las obras estudiadas figuran *Antígona Vélez* de Leopoldo Marechal, *La peste viene de Melos* de Osvaldo Dragún, *El reñidero* de Sergio de Cecco, *Antígona furiosa* de Griselda Gambaro, *La oscuridad de la razón* de Ricardo Monti, y *Salto al cielo* de Mauricio Kartún. [MR]

4074 El drama en Venezuela durante los primeros cincuenta años del siglo XIX: antología comentada. Caracas: CELCIT, 1998. 498 p.: bibl. (Col. Estudios; 4)

Se reúnen textos dramáticos reimpresos que reflejan la tendencia estética del momento neoclásica-romántica y la realidad venezolana de ese período. La colección se inicia con una obra de Andrés Bello, *Venezuela consolada*, de carácter alegórico y que constituye una de las primeras creaciones de la dramaturgia venezolana. Entre las obras de esta antología, *Virginia* de Domingo Navas Spinola, inspirada en la tradición de Raciniana, es la que logra una mejor estructura. El volumen es un importante aporte al estudio del teatro venezolano. [MR]

4075 Dramas de mujeres. Dirección de Halima Tahan. Buenos Aires: Biblioteca Nacional; Ediciones Ciudad Argentina, 1998. 387 p.: bibl.

Libro dividido en dos partes. La primera contiene un ensayo, que describe la metodología seguida en la investigación, y una catalogación de 200 dramaturgas argentinas que publicaron sus obras entre 1965–97. La segunda incluye 12 ensayos en que se estudian obras de autoras conocidas como Cristina Escofet, Diana Raznovich, y Susana Torres Molina, y otras menos conocidas pero de gran relevancia. Muy útil. [MR]

4076 Los dramaturgos/as del interior del país: Buenos Aires, 10, 11 y 12 de julio de 1996; actas de las terceras jornadas. Recopilación de Marta Lena Paz. Buenos Aires: Instituto de Artes del Espectáculo, Facultad de Filosofía y Letras, UBA, Programa TEALHI, 1998. 143 p.: bibl.

Valiosa compilación de estudios críticos sobre numerosos dramaturgos cuyas obras son una muestra representativa del interesante movimiento dramatúrgico y teatral que se desarrolla en el país, fuera de la órbita de Buenos Aires que tiende a acaparar la atención crítica. [MR]

4077 Encuentros en cadena: las artes escénicas en Asia, Africa y América Latina. Coordinación de Michiko Tanaka. México: El Colegio de México, Centro de Estudios de Asia y Africa, 1998. 172 p.: bibl., col. ill.

Una valiosa colección de ensayos de perspectivas teóricas influyentes y tendencias teatrales mundiales procedentes del Asia y África que paulatinamente se han incorporado a lo largo de muchos años o más recientemente en el teatro latinoamericano. Entre los temas estudiados figuran las danzas de moros y cristianos, la textualidad híbrida del teatro cubano y brasileño, y el impacto intertextual y preformativo de los cruces teatrales contemporáneos. [MR]

4078 Escenas interiores. Edición de Halima Tahan. Buenos Aires: Instituto Nacional del Teatro; Artes del Sur, 2000. 372 p.: bibl. (Teatro argentino)

Colección de ensayos que dan una visión panorámica de la actividad teatral del interior argentino. En ellos se hace referencia al teatro de las provincias de Buenos Aires, Córdoba, Mendoza, Neuquén, Jujuy, Salta, Santa Fe, San Juan, Santiago del Estero, Santa Cruz, y Tucumán. Tiene una introducción de Halima Tahan, directora de Teatro al Sur de donde se extrajeron algunas de estas notas. [MR]

4079 Gladhart, Amalia. The leper in blue: coercive performance and the contemporary Latin American theater. Chapel Hill: UNC Dept. of Romance Languages: Distributed by Univ. of North Carolina Press, 2000. 245 p.: bibl., index. (North Carolina studies in the Romance languages and literatures; 266)

Se estudian textos teatrales de varios países de Latinoamérica para examinar la manera de cómo representación, coerción y resistencia se interconectan entre sí y con problemas sociales más amplios. El concepto central del pensamiento crítico de la autora es el de la coerción, entendido como las conrestricciones tanto físicas como psicológicas que pueden tomar varias formas, entre ellas convenciones sociales, necesidades económicas, y el abuso físico. Demuestra cómo constantemente fuerzas de poder determinan el proceso de producción y recepción de textos teatrales. [MR]

4080 Lamus Obregón, Marina Bibliografía del teatro colombiano: siglo XIX; índice analítico de publicaciones periódicas. Bogotá: Instituto Caro y Cuervo, 1998. 343 p.: bibl., indexes. (Publicaciones del Instituto Caro y Cuervo. Serie bibliográfica; 16)

El volumen es el resultado de una acuciosa investigación realizada por la autora en que se registran autores, títulos de textos dramáticos y de reseñas o artículos publicados en periódicos que tratan de diversos temas que son de gran interés no solo para aquellos interesados en autores u obras particulares, sino para aquellos que buscan la interacción entre teatro y sociedad. Referencia fundamental para el estudio del teatro decimonónico colombiano. [MR]

4081 Lamus Obregón, Marina. Teatro en Colombia, 1831–1886: práctica teatral y sociedad. Bogotá: Editorial Ariel, 1998. 400 p.: bibl., index. (Ariel historia)

Estudio bien realizado de las tendencias teatrales de Colombia durante este importante periodo del siglo XIX. Más que un estudio de textos dramáticos, la autora centra su atención, dando una amplia información, en la escena teatral misma, en que incluye salas de teatro, compañías, y actores entre los cuales destaca la función del cómico. [MR]

4082 Molinaza, José. Historia del teatro dominicano. Santo Domingo: Editora Universitaria, UASD, 1998. 433 p.: bibl., index. (Publicaciones de la Univ. Autónoma de Santo Domingo; 901. Col. Literatura y sociedad; 25)

In 1984–85, Molinaza published the 2-vol. *Historia crítica del teatro dominicano*, covering the history of Dominican theater from 1492–1930 (see *HLAS 48:6095*). In this updated work, the first four chapters synthesize the earlier volumes. Three additional chapters discuss theatrical events of importance from 1931–85. Appendix includes studies of popular theater, university theater, and children's theater. Although bibliography is incomplete, book is very useful in providing information on the nature of the theatrical experience in the Dominican Republic. [SC]

4083 Ordaz, Luis. Historia del teatro argentino: desde los orígenes hasta la actualidad. Apéndice, "Las tres últimas décadas," por Susana Freire. Buenos Aires: Instituto Nacional del Teatro, 1999. 487 p.: bibl., ill., index. (Homenaje al teatro argentino)

Un excelente volumen de uno de los críticos teatrales más importantes del teatro argentino que recorre los momentos y figuras más relevantes de la trayectoria del teatro argentino. El texto muy bien documentado se acompaña de un ilustrativo material gráfico. Una indispensable referencia para el estudio del teatro argentino. [MR]

4084 Piña, Juan Andrés. 20 años de teatro chileno: 1976–1996. Santiago, Chile: RIL Editores, 1998. 261 p.: bibl., ill., indexes. Contiene un abundante número de

breves ensayos que el autor publicara sobre todo en la revista *Mensaje* y en el diario *El Mercurio* de Santiago. Se trata de análisis de textos importantes en la dramaturgia chilena y de lúcidos comentarios críticos de puestas en escena presentadas en salas de Santiago en el período consignado. [MR]

4085 Teatro argentino del 2000. Edición de Osvaldo Pellettieri. Buenos Aires: Galerna/Fundación Roberto Arlt, 2000. 150 p.: bibl. (Cuadernos del GETEA; 11)

Colección de artículos que estudian las distintas tendencias teatrales experimentadas por el teatro argentino en la década de los 90. Los autores emplean diferentes formas de abordajes a textos que mantienen en vigencia los códigos de la convención teatral realista o la superan total o parcialmente. Los dramaturgos estudiados—entre ellos Ricardo Monti, Eduardo Pavlovsky y Jaime Kogan— son representativos de estéticas teatrales que mancan hitos en la historia escénica de esta década. [MR]

BRAZIL
Novels

REGINA IGEL, *Professor of Spanish and Portuguese, University of Maryland, College Park*

SEVERAL THEMES HAVE EMERGED in Brazilian fiction this biennium, including memories of pain and suffering under the military regime (1964–85); exploitation of rural workers by established forces; early experiences of immigrant groups; pressure and stress caused by urban environments; conflict between indigenous and nonindigenous peoples; and historical events in general. Stimulating works in literary criticism were also published recently, though more should be expected given the abundant production of fictional works.

Although the authoritarian period officially ended two decades ago, it still echoes in much of the fiction in Brazil today. One example is the autobiographical work by Augusto Boal, *Hamlet e o filho do padeiro: memórias imaginadas,* in which the renowned creator of the Theater of the Oppressed recounts his painful experiences during the dictatorship through reminiscences of his life as the son of a baker, then as actor, stage director, and theater professor (item **4091**). Another work that depicts the effects of that regime is *Liv e Tatziu: história de amor incestuoso,* by the psychiatrist Roberto Freire, himself a victim of the military period (item **4095**). Definitely less subtle is the narrative *Liberdade para as estrelas,* by Cleonice Rainho, which describes the atmosphere of the military administration that curbed the natural growth of young dissidents (item **4106**). Frei Betto, although not known as a novelist, wrote *Hotel Brasil,* a mystery that metaphorically incorporates stories of political dissidents who ended up in cemeteries and military dungeons (item **4090**).

Rural workers and their struggle against both repression and oppression are represented in Deonísio da Silva's whimsical novel *Os guerreiros do campo*, which involves an odd encounter of spirits of landless workers killed by the police in Brazil (item **4111**). The novel incorporates many other characters, all involved in some way with the perennial conflict between landowners and workers. *Sassafrás*, by Vicente Ataíde, is a pungent story of another oppressed group (item **4088**); the novel describes the atrocious working conditions of planters of sassafras (a flavoring/thickening agent of the laurel family) in the southern region of Brazil.

Descriptions of descendants of European immigrants to Brazil suggest that their lives were disturbed by the transatlantic relocation. Historian Largman, herself the descendant of an immigrant, in *Tio Kuba nos trópicos* presents an extensive view of the journeys of her predecessors, two European Jewish families (item **4098**). Forced to emigrate, these families selected the state of Bahia to restart their lives as free citizens in a free country. Also addressing difficulties encountered in new territories is the novel *O migrante*, by Frota Neto, which is a fictional rendition of life for migrants traveling from Ceará to the depths of the Amazon forest from 1920–70 (item **4096**). A region not far from the Amazon provides the main landscape of *Saraminda*, a novel by José Sarney, former president of Brazil. The novel is set in French Guiana, where the protagonist, a sensuous, black prostitute, is highly paid by gold diggers who exult in watching the magic tricks she performs during sexual acts (item **4108**).

Set in the backlands of Brazil, the novel *A noite do maracá*, by Marcelo Barros, recalls the indigenous claim for recognition of their identity, in the midst of a mystical atmosphere replenished by the *Kayapós* spiritual rites (item **4089**). Another work with indigenous peoples as the main characters is *Um lugar para Mayra*, by Tadeu França, which is based on real conflicts between the Kaingangue Indians and white explorers in Santa Catarina during the last quarter of the 20th century (item **4094**). Continuing with the setting of the backlands, yet not involving indigenous peoples, is *Fera de Macabu*, a novel that was thoroughly researched by author/journalist Carlos Marchi (item **4101**). Centering on white people and their manipulations, spirit of vengeance, and corruption, the novel conveys one of the major judicial mistakes in Brazil during the Second Empire, which resulted in the hanging of a man accused of a crime that he did not commit. Since that shameful event, in which even Emperor Pedro II was unable to separate lies from truth, the death sentence has been abolished in Brazil.

Urban environments are not exempt from conflict. While rural concerns for land possession do not exist in cities, here conflict stems from the desire for recognition of feelings, emotions, and ultimately, personal identity. These concerns are observed and narrated in *O ponto cego*, by Lya Luft (item **4099**). The novel's main character is a boy who tries to understand, through games of imagination, the drama involving the adult members of his family. Also set in a city is the novel *Lição da noite*, by Esdras do Nascimento, which offers a panoramic view of "carioca" society in the 1990s (item **4103**). In *Subsolo infinito*, by Nelson de Oliveira, São Paulo's underground is explored through the voice of a former teacher who, after losing his memory, lives under a bridge with thieves and vagabonds who pass the time in lofty discussions (item **4104**).

War, both in Brazil and elsewhere, inspired novels such as *Anita*, by Flávio Aguiar, which is a semifictional account of Ana de Jesus Ribeiro's life and passion for Giuseppe Garibaldi, an Italian who fought for the establishment of a republican regime in Brazil (item **4086**). Also set in the southern region, the narrative *A lenda do centauro*, by Antonio Santos, is an epic novel about the *Guerra dos Farrapos*, one of the many struggles forged by Brazilian gauchos to separate their state from Brazil and inaugurate an idealized *República Farroupilha* (item **4107**). In the northeastern region, the well-known Antonio Conselheiro is the main subject of the novel *Os mal-aventurados do Belo Monte: a tragédia de Canudos*, by Eldon D. Canário, which deals mostly with personal aspects of the leader (item **4093**). Very few novels have been written about wars outside Brazilian borders. One example is *Um herói catarinense*, by João Steudel Areão, which is set in Italy and told through the memory of a former Brazilian soldier who served in World War II (item **4087**).

Emotional and sentimental interludes permeate recent literary production: *Clarice*, by Ana Miranda, is a delicate description of some aspects of Clarice Lispector's biography, told in 75 short chapters that reveal Miranda's poetic nuances. (item **4102**). Similarly, Adélia Prado's *Manuscritos de Felipa* is a recollection of thoughts and observations by a present-day woman somewhere in Brazil, who tries to understand her own love and submission to God's will, her love of and boredom with her husband, her faith, and her fear of death (item **4105**). A female protagonist and voice also appears in *A mulher que escreveu a Bíblia*, by Moacyr Scliar (elected to the Brazilian Academy of Letters in 2003), who puts a pen in the hands of a woman and recreates the Bible from her viewpoint (item **4109**).

Among the many works of literary criticism that filled Brazilian bookstores, three should be recognized for their innovative contribution: the first two volumes of *História da literatura brasileira*, organized by Castro (item **4097**); and the short essay by Mário Maestri, *Por que Paulo Coelho teve sucesso* (item **4100**). The collection of Brazilian literature (a third volume has come out since this essay was written) compiles essays by recognized literary critics in Brazil and Portugal, including Castro (the organizer), Fábio Lucas, Gilberto Mendonça Teles, and Samira Mesquita. The approach of most of the essayists to the history of Brazilian literature differs from conventional thought because they do not simply discuss concepts and theories of literary historiography. Rather, they examine fictional, poetic, and theatrical trends and works over the last 500 years of Brazilian literature from a sociocultural perspective. Controversy may surface about some observations regarding the notion that medievalism was the cultural tutor of early Brazilian literature, since most Brazilian scholars believe that those beginnings were the fruits of the Renaissance and baroque movements. Lucas' article on the birth of literature in Brazil is fundamental in clarifying the tensions credited to these different perspectives. Reading this article first will help clarify the thoughts and wise observations of the other critics, such as Castro and Tonini in their study of the testimonial literature by Portuguese chroniclers and travelers, and Teles on the influence of Camões in Brazilian poetry. Castro also contributes two seminal essays in volume 2 on Euclides da Cunha and Machado de Assis. Both volumes—and most likely the third, not yet examined here—are of the utmost importance in reexamining Brazilian literature and its pertinent criticism.

Maestri's essay on Paulo Coelho analyzes the works of one of the most controversial Brazilian writers of the 20th century. Polemics about Coelho stem from his extreme popularity juxtaposed with his extreme shallowness. Maestri delicately deconstructs Coelho's immense verbal web in his esoteric novels with a cool, refreshing, and almost neutral standing. While devoid of bitter criticism, the essay is nevertheless a strong indication that literary critics are correct in determining that

Coelho, who is not a writer by profession, is at best a good narrator, and that his novels, while not literary masterpieces, are at least a source of solace for those who have faith in his esoteric formula for reaching happiness on Earth.

In general, Brazilian literature at the beginning of the 21st century has yet to distinguish itself from earlier years. Most topics represented here were included in novels written over the past two decades. Those that appeared more recently still resound with echoes of past grievances, like the memories of the suffering and losses under the military regime. The same can be observed of fictional works dealing with the stress derived from rapid urbanization and the callousness of members of social classes above the poverty line. With violence as a natural result of these conditions, some writings have begun to explore this aspect of Brazilian society, which probably will be the main topic of the next essay on Brazilian novels.

4086 Aguiar, Flávio. Anita: romance. São Paulo: Boitempo Editorial, 1999. 332 p.: bibl.

Ana de Jesus Ribeiro, known as Anita Garibaldi, is the heroine of this semifictional novel. Led by Giuseppe, her life companion, she became involved in the struggle for the establishment of the Republican regime. In the novel, the couple is faithfully followed by Costa, a Brazilian descendant of Africans to whom the author gives a predominant voice. Anita's life has been the subject of plays, TV series, and movies in Brazil. This novel follows the general tendency to regard Anita as politically savvy, though some see her as merely a woman driven by her passion for her man, Italian Giuseppe Garibaldi.

4087 Areão, João Steudel. Um herói catarinense: a FEB na Itália. Florianópolis, Brazil: Editora Insular, 1999. 213 p.

Very few Brazilian novels address wars in which Brazilians fought. This narrative tells of a Brazilian soldier serving in Italy during WWII. Mixing fiction with historical facts, the narrator recounts several dimensions of the soldier's mind and spirit.

4088 Ataíde, Vicente. Sassafrás. Florianópolis, Brazil: FCC Edições, Governo de Santa Catarina, 1997. 115 p.

Awarded the *Cruz e Sousa Literary Award of the State of Santa Catarina* in 1996, narrative deals with a rare subject in Brazilian literature. In a pungent style, story describes the subhuman conditions of rural workers in the southern region of Brazil at the time when sassafras and other produce were in high demand. Landowners forced peasants to plant the spices that offered abundant financial returns to the farmers, paying the workers just enough to survive, and in some cases nothing at all. Novel is structured on biblical archetypes (Joseph and his brothers), and on an allegorical representation of Brazil as a country devastated by foreign interests, corrupt Brazilian politicians, and a misguided press.

4089 Barros, Marcelo. A noite do maracá: romance. Goiânia, Brazil: Editora Rede: Editora UCG, 1998. 272 p.: ill.

A journalist gets involved with descendants of the *Kayapós*, an indigenous community in the state of Goiás and elsewhere in Brazil. Narrative builds up a mystical scenario, but does not lose sight of the indigenous claim for official recognition of their identity, nor for peoples' respect toward nature.

4090 Betto, Frei. Hotel Brasil: romance. São Paulo: Editora Ática, 1999. 276 p.

Guests in a boarding house are mysteriously killed and their eyes plucked out. As in any good detective story, the killer is actually the last person one would suspect. Novel intricacies can be associated with some political situations in which victims ended up in dungeons or cemeteries during the military dictatorship (1964–85) in Brazil.

4091 Boal, Augusto. Hamlet e o filho do padeiro: memórias imaginadas. Rio de Janeiro: Editora Record, 2000. 347 p.: ill., index.

Autobiography by Boal, the celebrated Brazilian actor, author, stage director, inventor of several stage techniques, and founder of The Theater of the Oppressed. The narrative focuses on his political stands throughout his multiple activities. At the same time, he retraces his own life with well-humored descriptions and examines a full period of Brazilian history with a highly informative recollection of the military period (1964–85), during which he and many of his artistic colleagues were victimized. Arrested, tortured, and finally exiled from Brazil, Boal became emblematic of victims of a political moment that encumbered all cultural activities. The subtitle of the book notwithstanding ("imagined memories"), the novel speaks volumes about a life devoted to the theater as a means of reaching not only the beautiful in art, but also the ugliness of life's contingencies, both transposed on a stage that should be accessible to all layers of society. For comment on English translation, see item **4356.**

4092 Brandão, Adelino. Os invasores: romance. Rio de Janeiro: Editora Record, 1999. 252 p.: bibl.

Historical novel about the Dutch invasion of Bahia. Based on public records, narrative is an extensive verbal panel of a time filled with war, patriots, and traitors from the viewpoint of Christian dogmas and from the perspective of the Portuguese royal establishment.

4093 Canário, Eldon Dantas. Os mal-aventurados do Belo Monte: a tragédia de Canudos. Salvador, Brazil: Editora BDA-Bahia; Aracajú, Brazil: UNIT, 1997. 384 p.

Unlike many novels about the *Guerra de Canudos*, narrative describes personal aspects of Antônio Conselheiro's life, beginning with his birth and following his route as a spiritual leader and war strategist. Focuses on the psychological dimensions of Antônio's personality and charisma. An interesting object of study, Conselheiro built Belo Monte, only to see it destroyed by his government's army, while at the same time becoming the main focus of Euclides da Cunha's Os Sertões. He continues to stimulate the imagination of fictionists and historians alike.

4094 França, Tadeu. Um lugar para Mayra. Maringá, Brazil: EDUEM, 1997. 248 p.: ill.

Novel is mostly based on real conflicts between the Kaingangue indigenous group and white explorers in Santa Catarina, starting in the 1970s. Portrays the Kaingangue as

victims of an aggressive notion of progress, denied rights to lands they occupied for centuries, and, on many occasions, denied their own lives. França denounces FUNAI, a governmental institution, for creating new homes for the indigenous peoples, supposedly to spare them from the white people's greed. The new environment was not appropriate for the indigenous peoples, yet their voices and complaints went unheard.

4095 Freire, Roberto. Liv e Tatziu: uma história de amor incestuoso. São Paulo: Editora Globo, 1999. 303 p.

The author is a renowned psychiatrist who survived the torture chambers of the Brazilian military dictatorship (1964–85). Having written more than 20 novels, he is also known as a pioneer in the field of treating troubled adolescents through "Soma," an anarchist trend of psychiatry. Here, the controversial fictionist deals with an incestuous situation between twins who, after being separated at birth, eventually meet during their adolescent years and fall in love. In this novel Freire's psychoanalytical approach to Eros is complemented by a political dimension. Incidents involving the "Movement of the Landless" (MST) in the state of São Paulo is the second, equally important subject of this novel.

4096 Frota Neto. O migrante. Rio de Janeiro: Francisco Alves, 1998. 159 p.

Two narrators converge to tell the story of a family of migrants who traveled from the state of Ceará to the Amazon forest. The narratives, spanning from the first quarter of the 20th century to the decade of the 1970s, are set in both urban and jungle environments of northern Brazil. One narrator migrated to the tropical Amazonian landscape, expresses himself through the local dialect, which is transposed to a literary vein by another narrator. The two narratives are visually distinctive with different fonts and typefaces. Even without this typographical device, the two would be clearly distinguishable due to their different emotional and poetic voices (as expressed by the experienced migrant and the rational explanations offered by the other one). Though migrant themes are common in Brazilian literature, this novel excels for its deep penetration into the hearts and minds of two representatives of displaced men and women.

4097 História da literatura brasileira. v. 1–2. Lisboa: Publicações Alfa, 1999. 2 v.: bibl., index.

Published in Portugal and directed by a Brazilian scholar (professor at the Univ. of Padova, Italy), the two volumes gather essays on the history of Brazilian literature from 1500 until the premodernist period. (A third volume was subsequently issued.) Written by renowned scholars, the essays are arranged in chronological order with a geographical orientation, and offer a diversified range of interpretations on Brazil's literary history. Among them, Sílvio Castro on cultural and political anthropology; Fábio Lucas on the formative elements of Brazilian culture; Roberto Teixeira Leite on ecology; Jayme Paviani, and J.C. Pozenato on religious ideology; and Samira N. Mesquita on literature itself. Also examined are topics such as the Portuguese literary legacy in Brazil by Gilberto Mendonça Teles; studies on the Romantic theater of Martins Pena by Flávio Wolf Aguiar; and an essay on José de Alencar by Pedro Paulo Montenegro. A bibliographical note on the authors studied is appended to each of the essays.

4098 Largman, Esther. Tio Kuba nos trópicos: romance. Rio de Janeiro: Editora Record, 1999. 286 p.

Semifictional novel portrays generations of two families of Jewish immigrants, the Aders and the Latniks, in Bahia during the 20th century. "Uncle Kuba," whose real name was Iankel Ader, emigrated to Brazil to escape a European life of poverty and terror inflicted by Polish anti-Semites. The Latniks did the same, fleeing the Russian pogroms. Both families are part of the author's ancestral roots, and she tells their stories based on reminiscences and research into documents, photos, and other mementos. Marxists and Zionists contribute to the formation of the new society in the New World. Family members insult and care for each other in alternate behavior patterns. Largman analyzes her own behavior and her sister's experience, as they both attempted to establish their own identities in their native Brazilian society, even though it was a society new for their parents.

4099 Luft, Lya Fett. O ponto cego. São Paulo: Editora Mandarim, 1999. 153 p.

The "blind spot" of the novel's title occurs with a combination of perspectives: at one level, the focus of the narrative is the story of a family through the eyes of a boy. Creative and imaginative, the young narrator constructs and deconstructs stories, highlighting grown-ups' dramatic events. At another level, the episodes interconnect and turn into allegories of literary creativity, including an examination of the hypothetical control that a narrator may have on the written material and on the possible interpretations of the readership.

4100 Maestri Filho, Mário José. Por que Paulo Coelho teve sucesso. Porto Alegre, Brazil: AGE Editora, 1999. 110 p.: bibl.

Examining the complex factors resulting in the extraordinary readership of Coelho's books, Maestri identifies one particular cause: Coelho's books emerged at a time when confusion in the world accompanied emerging neoliberal policies. In view of this analysis, Coelho's "self-help" formula offered a response to increasing global insecurity. Maestri observes that another reason for Coelho's success is his simple writing style, a skill Coelho honed as a journalist and lyricist. His readership is mostly comprised of those who need to understand information quickly, thus he skips metaphors, symbols, and other literary devices in his works. Explaining the success among potentially more demanding readers (such as heads of state), Maestri observes that in times of crisis, people look for the same escapism, that is, stories concocted in a supposedly traditional lore in which esoteric formulas of attaining happiness are readily available. Keeping an objective stance while evaluating Coelho's copious production, Maestri is among the very few to challenge and analyze the most recent product of neoliberalism, globalization, and mediocrity.

4101 Marchi, Carlos. Fera de Macabu: a história e o romance de um condenado à morte. Rio de Janeiro: Editora Record, 1998. 358 p.: bibl., ill., maps.

History and fiction are clearly linked—but not combined—in this novel. Author displays abundant documentation regarding the final days of Brazil's Second Empire and a crime that shook the country at the time. An entire family, except for one of four children, was executed by a small group who invaded their home. Narrative begins with the end of the story, that is, with the hanging by judicial order of a well-known and rich farmer, accused by enemies of ordering the family's assassination. Using realism, author conveys the atmosphere of vengeance, manipulation, and corruption at all levels of the royal administration, as ultimately evidenced by the death sentence ordered for an innocent man.

4102 Miranda, Ana Maria. Clarice: ficção. São Paulo: Companhia das Letras, 1999. 95 p.

Describes events of Clarice Lispector's life through roughly 75 short articles. Embellishes some already-known aspects of Lispector's life with poetic language and imaginative resources. Narrative reflects author's exceptional creative abilities more than Lispector's biographical aspects of her life.

4103 Nascimento, Esdras do. Lição da noite. Rio de Janeiro: Editora Record, 1998. 380 p.

Urban novel provides an extensive view of parts of Rio de Janeiro's middle class society in the 1990s. Psychological conflicts both link and separate the seven characters (four of whom are women) who try to survive their illusions, fantasies, mistakes, and frustrations.

4104 Oliveira, Nelson de. Subsolo infinito: romance. São Paulo: Companhia das Letras, 2000. 213 p.

First novel by Oliveira, a short story writer. This orphic narrative plunges into the underground of the city of São Paulo, through its subway network and along the pipes of the sewage system. Protagonist-narrator, a former teacher who loses his memory after his apartment is destroyed in a fire, ends up living under a bridge with beggars, prostitutes, thieves, and other members of urban society. Searching for an identity, he and his companions become enmeshed in an intricate story that develops into a delirious encounter with a hermaphrodite, then with the devil himself, and ends up in witty dialogues

with angels and other mythological beings about subjects concerning fire as a generator of the soul.

4105 Prado, Adélia. Manuscritos de Felipa. São Paulo: Editora Siciliano, 1999. 161 p. (Literatura brasileira)

Prado conveys a daily register of an intensely perceptive contemporary woman. As if she were praying or talking with God, the protagonist narrates several incidents of her life, from the mutual teasing with her husband, to her conversations with friends and neighbors, to her fear of death. Author completes the fictional autobiography with her recognized poetic vein and mystical allure.

4106 Rainho, Cleonice. Liberdade para as estrelas. Rio de Janeiro: Imago, 1998. 269 p.

Story about the "dark ages"—the decades when a military and authoritarian regime prevailed in Brazil (1964–85). Due to the dictatorship, the political atmosphere was not conducive to the personal growth of young dissidents. Narrator is among those who, at age 30, leaves her beloved country and settles abroad. Returning to her home country, though, she faces a new reality and deals with a new set of challenges and frustrations.

Roland, Ana Maria. Fronteiras da palavra, fronteiras da história: contribuição à crítica da cultura do ensaísmo latino-americano através da leitura de Euclides da Cunha e Octavio Paz. See item **4762.**

4107 Santos, Antonio. A lenda do centauro: romance. Rio de Janeiro: Editora Record, 1999. 223 p.: bibl.

Epic novel stages several episodes related to the *Guerra dos Farrapos* (1835), through which the people of the state of Rio Grande do Sul wanted to separate from the country. The idealized "*República Farroupilha*" was in the minds of the novel's main characters: Artêmio Cruz, who became a symbol for the mythological "centaur," and Helena Romano, who lived a love story through combat and war. Both the "centaur" and Helena are believed dead several times throughout this fictional and realistic narrative, yet they re-emerge almost from the ashes to continue trying to reach their dream of creating a separate state.

4108 Sarney, José. Saraminda. São Paulo: Editora Siciliano, 2000. 250 p.: maps. (Literatura brasileira)

Sarney, former president of Brazil, further advances his career as a writer with this novel, after the successful *O dono do mar* (1995). Saraminda, the protagonist, is a black prostitute who first seduces her owner, a man who buys her with gold bars, and then seduces all the others who come with gold to buy her carnal favors. Written in the style of magical-realism, the male narrator reminisces about the legends of Saraminda, recounting a number of remarkable incidents in the *garimpo* (mine region): Saraminda returns to state of virginity after each sexual encounter, her breasts glow, and her body gleams like gold. Set in the violent goldmining region of French Guiana, the narrative reflects the epic strength of the historical and social conflicts of the Amazonian region. The violence is balanced with a lyrical tonality and the sensual smoothness of the love story between Saraminda and local gold diggers.

4109 Scliar, Moacyr. A mulher que escreveu a Bíblia. São Paulo: Companhia das Letras, 1999. 216 p.

By her own admission (and Scliar's interpretation), the woman who wrote the history of the Jews was no beauty. However, she had a brilliant intellect, was versatile in sexual maneuvers, and tenaciously pursued her dream of becoming one of King Solomon's wives. In this novel, Scliar surpasses himself with a satiric, ironic, and humoresque account of life in the biblical harems and Solomonic royal salons.

4110 Seixas, Heloisa. Através do vidro: amor e desejo. Rio de Janeiro: Editora Record, 2001. 111 p. (Coleção Amores extremos)

Narrated in a dense and oppressive atmosphere, tells the story of a woman and a man who meet again long after their teen years, when they had a short-lived romantic interlude. Intensively erotic, story reveals intimate fantasies that develop even without the participation of the object of desire. Sees love and desire through the glass of time, reflecting of feelings of deviation felt by the protagonist, a married woman looking back for solace.

4111 Silva, Deonísio da. Os guerreiros do campo. São Paulo: Editora Mandarim, 2000. 191, 2 p.

Narrative examines contemporary Brazilian problems resulting from clashes between the oligarchy—as represented by landlords, and the synchronized rural movements—as represented by the Movimento dos Trabalhadores Rurais Sem Terra (MST or Landless Movement). The location is a surreal entrance to heaven, where most of those assassinated by bullets and collective massacres on Brazilian soil meet. Together with victims of repression are some instigators of the civil unrest, such as a landlady who expresses her views about the invaders of her farms. Another dead body with an opportunity to talk freely is a representative of the rightist movement, the Brazilian Society for the Defense of Tradition, Family, and Property. When addressing agrarian reform, a passionate and volatile subject in Brazilian society, Silva utilizes an abundance of historical facts and official statements, quoting from newspapers and other sources. He also exposes readers to other disturbing realities, such as the exploitation of students by unscrupulous landlord's in university cities. Clearly conveying a cry for social justice, the novel's rhythm and ironic tonality emphasize even further the realistic and simultaneously surreal atmosphere.

4112 Valêncio Xavier. Minha mãe morrendo; e, O menino mentido. São Paulo: Companhia das Letras, 2001. 221 p.: bibl., ill. (some col.).

An old man reminisces about his life from his first vision of his nude mother to her death. Innovative and irreverent book retains the format of a box of erotic memories, ranging from events that are personal (death of mother) to social (emergence of Lampião in the Brazilian backlands), to such pleasures as the discovery of sex and the reading of comics. Graphic art including text, collages, newspaper cutouts, old pictures, and drawings have an impact on the novel's presentation.

Short Stories

M. ANGÉLICA GUIMARÃES LOPES, *Associate Professor of Portuguese and Comparative Literature, University of South Carolina, Columbia*

FROM 1997 TO 2000, the period in which the collections examined for *HLAS* 60 were published, Brazil was not only focusing on the end of a millennium, but also on the 500th anniversary of its discovery, on April 22, 1500. Like other artistic and literary productions, the short story reflected such events. Some writers chose historical themes subsumed under "The Discovery of Brazil," and publishers followed the celebratory spirit by reissuing acclaimed books in honor of both historical dates. Other collections were reissued on the occasion of the authors' own anniversaries (Cordovil, item **4121;** Couto, item **4122;** Peregrino Junior, item **4135;** and Viotti, item **4143**). A literary son collected his mother's detective stories (item **4125**), and seasoned authors organized their own anthologies (Aragao, item **4114;** Campos, item **4116;** Kiefer, item **4127;** and Sabino, item **4138**).

The same spirit—both reflective of Brazilian history and anticipatory of the new millennium—had been responsible for philosophical inquiry from the popular press such as the news magazine *Veja* ("Discovering What?," "The Three Brazils," etc.) and academic and professional journals. Concomitant with the reflection on five centuries of Brazilian life were the numerous celebrations of "The Best of the [20th] Century": the best scientists, the best entrepreneurs, the best schools, etc. Together with 1000 and 500, 100 was once again a magic number. Two anthologies organized by Italo Moriconi became best sellers: *Os cem melhores contos brasileiros do século* (item **4119**) and *Os cem melhores poemas brasileiros do século* (2001). These books brought back beloved poems and stories at the same time that they rekindled memories about forgotten ones and introduced new ones.

Most of the collections examined here are by established authors; only a few are by beginners such as Carvalho (item **4118**); Lage (item **4128**); and Oliveira (items **4132** and **4133**). These writers' fiction introduces vibrant voices and unusual narrative viewpoints. Among the most critically and popularly acclaimed authors are Rubem Fonseca (item **4123**) and Dalton Trevisan (item **4142**), who for decades have set their lenses and spotlights on the tortuous and the criminal, each with their own brand of humor. Wolff's stories follow a similar path, although they are closer to journalism than fiction—in this case, and for this critic, not considered a drawback, but simply a different approach (item **4144**).

Fewer women story writers published in this period—a coincidence, perhaps, but one that matches their scarcity in the 1990s section of Moriconi's *Os cem melhores contos brasileiros do século,* in which two stories out of 17 are by women (item **4119**). However, the few women authors examined in *HLAS* 60 (Campello, Colasanti, Lobo, and Tavares) continue to produce notable work.

Among the newer authors, female and male, notwithstanding the prevailing climate of reflections on the 20th century and Brazil's previous 500 years, there are fewer memorialists than in the three earlier decades. Regional fiction is not as evident as in the era of João Guimarães Rosa (1960–80) and neither are magic realism or science fiction. Out of this collection, either because of their skill or new voice, the most satisfying are those by Campello (item **4115**), Campos (item **4116**), Colasanti (item **4120**), Naves (item **4131**), Oliveira (items **4132** and **4133**), Padilha (item **4134**), Trevisan (item **4142**), and Viotti (item **4143**).

4113 Alves, Amil. Contos do Araguaia. Rio de Janeiro: Taurus Editora, 1998. 104 p.: 1 ill.

Fascinating stories recreate legends pertaining to center west Brazil's Karaja cosmogony. By knowledgeable author who dedicates book to Villas Boas brothers. A must read.

4114 Aragão, Adrino. Os filhos da esfinge. Brasília: Da Anta Casa Editora; Rio de Janeiro: Ministério da Cultura, Fundação Biblioteca Nacional, Depto. Nacional do Livro; Mogi das Cruzes, Brazil: Univ. de Mogi das Cruzes, 1998. 240 p.: bibl.

Includes three of the celebrated Amazonas state writer's collections: *Tigre no espelho* (see *HLAS 56:4346*), *As três faces da esfinge* (see *HLAS 52:4575*), and *Inquietação de um feto* (1976).

4115 Campello, Myriam. Sons e outros frutos. Posfácio de Gilberto Mendonça Teles. Rio de Janeiro: Editora Record, 1998. 140 p.

Conveyed in controlled yet metaphorical style, Campello's stories excel in drama and the depiction of passion both sensual and intellectual. "Olho" (Eye) was chosen as one of the best Brazilian stories of the century (see item **4119**). Author of this superb collection has won several other awards and is considered one of the most accomplished living Brazilian story writers.

4116 Campos, Maximiano. O viajante e o horizonte: seleta de contos. Seleção de Antônio Ricardo Campos. Recife, Brazil: Bagaço, 1997. 183 p.

Selections from three short-story collections make up this collection: *As emboscadas da sorte* (see *HLAS 36:6943*); *As sentenças do tempo* (see *HLAS 38:7344*); and *Feras mortas* (1994). Acclaimed by critics, Campos has written "a vast mural of his state of Pernambuco" (Suassuna). His narrative range is broad and style elegant, although never far from popular Portuguese. Tone ranges from comedy to tragedy with perfect pitch. An admirable collection.

4117 Carrascoza, João Anzanello. O vaso azul: contos. São Paulo: Editora Atica, 1998. 95 p.

Several of the stories in "The Blue Vase" focus on a double consciousness: returning son's and old mother's, husband's and wife's, motorcyclist's and pedestrian's. Complex collection evinces masterful pace and tone in its various aspects: dramatic, sensitive, analytical, and meditative.

4118 Carvalho, Fernanda Benevides de. Pequena história marítima: contos. São Paulo: Editora Giordano, 1999. 186 p.

Skillful stories by novice writer are often metaphorical with an oblique approach and occasional hermeticism. Carvalho accumulates details from which characters and situations emerge. "Short Maritime History" is reminscent of 16th-century Portuguese shipwreck narratives; other stories are contemporary with a Brazilian setting.

4119 Os cem melhores contos brasileiros do século. Organização, introdução e referências bibliográficas de Italo Moriconi. Rio de Janeiro: Objetiva, 2000. 618 p.

Anthology of 100 stories which are fairly representive of the production and reception of short fiction in Brazil in the last century. The 1900–30 period and each decade afterwards have short introductions and 13–25 stories each. Beginning with Machado de Assis's famous "Father Against Mother" in 1906 and ending with F. Bonassi's ironic "15 Scenes of Discovering Brazils [sic]." With its exuberant tone, style, and theme, the anthology successfully celebrates 500 years of writing. A few authors are neglected, e.g., Lobato and Maximiano Campos (see item **4116**). Most notable is the absence of João Guimarães Rosa due to his family's refusal to participate.

4120 Colasanti, Marina. O leopardo é um animal delicado. Rio de Janeiro: Rocco, 1998. 150 p.

Elegant and thoughtful stories by celebrated short fiction writer, essayist, journalist, and poet who is also an influential feminist. Her narrative powers are undeniable as she combines sophisticated plots with psychological acumen. Frequently highlights the female characters' consciousness. One story was chosen for *Os cem melhores contos brasileiros do século* (see item **4119**).

4121 Cordovil, Cacy. Ronda de fogo: contos. 2a ed. São Paulo: Musa Editora, 1998. 205 p. (Musa ficção; v. 1)

In 1941, the 29-year-old author, a contemporary of the modernists, published this work—"Wheel of Fire"—to critical acclaim.

The 2nd edition was published 57 years later. Well-constructed stories evince the modernists' psychological focus and concern for the common man and woman, especially the poor and humble. Settings are country ranches.

4122 Couto, Rui Ribeiro. A cidade do vício e da graça: vagabundagem pelo Rio noturno. 2a ed. Rio de Janeiro: Arquivo Público do Estado do Rio de Janeiro, 1998. 80 p.: bibl., ill. (Col. Fluminense; 4)

Short pieces represent conversations between the Poet and his friend, the Provincial, as they stroll through modernized 1920s Rio de Janeiro, then in its glory as the capital of Brazil. Reminiscent of 18th-century philosophical dialogues, these are adept and witty, but less characteristic of 1920s Brazilian modernism (to which its author belonged) than of the preceding Belle Epoque.

4123 Fonseca, Rubem. A confraria dos espadas: contos. São Paulo: Companhia das Letras, 1998. 132 p.

Leitmotiv is death—accidental or planned—in these elegant and ironic stories by Brazil's major thriller author. Fonseca's narrators aspire to Joycean impassivity as they relate conspiracies, murders, fatal strokes, and suicides. A successful collection. Eponymous story was chosen as one of "the best Brazilian stories of the century" in Moriconi's book (see item **4119**).

4124 Franco, Francisco Manoel de Mello. Pêndulo do amor e do crime. Rio de Janeiro: Objetiva, 1998. 236 p.

In this solidly constructed collection, the first two novellas create portraits of obsessed men and their machinations for criminal activities. The third, shorter story takes a new tack with a romantic science fiction adventure of a female astronaut who discovers a novel way to travel backwards in time as she reaches the moon. Mystic vision of Christ's "miraculous fishing(?)" changes the astronaut and her husband.

4125 Galvão, Patrícia. Safra macabra: contos policiais. Introdução de Geraldo Galvão Ferraz. Rio de Janeiro: J. Olympio Editora, 1998. 239 p.: ill.

Well-written, suspenseful stories were first published in 1944 in *Detetive* magazine under pseudonym, King Shelter, by modernist author and muse also known as Pagu. They partake of European setting and Oriental exoticism. Includes an essay on detective fiction in Brazil and an iconography of the author by her son, literary critic and journalist Geraldo Galvão Ferraz, who also chose collection's title.

4126 Gurgel, Tarcísio. Conto por conto. Natal, Brazil: Chegança Editorial, 1998. 102 p.

Dynamic fiction with pun as title focuses on characters viewed from a distance as part of a crowd, involved in daily activities. Some stories deal with Brazilian guerrillas in the 1960s-70s. Most take place in author's Rio Grande do Norte state. By a journalist with an eye for the dramatic who "stitch by stitch" develops a regional tapestry.

4127 Kiefer, Charles. Antologia pessoal: contos. Porto Alegre, Brazil: Mercado Aberto, 1998? 164 p.

Presented in chronological order of publication, Kiefer's stories trace his literary path. Those by young author are solemn and melancholy with a boy or an old man as protagonist. Later, postmodern stories evince irony akin to light cynicism of intrusive narrators. His literary stories cleverly acknowledge influences by Flaubert, Poe, Borges, and Cortázar.

4128 Lage, Claudia. A pequena morte e outras naturezas. Rio de Janeiro: Editora Record, 2000. 222 p.

Critically acclaimed young writer won a R. Janeiro prize with one of these stories. Hers is a powerful and idiosyncratic voice. Characters, situations, and their development point to author's analytical mind. One of the most original collections of the decade.

4129 Lobo, Luiza. Estranha aparição: contos. Rio de Janeiro: Rocco, 2000. 159 p.

Latest story collection evinces author's command of language, cosmopolitan experiences, and a new hermetic style fed by science fiction. Psychologically directed stories examine various instances of unhappy love. Some tales explore the fantastic successfully as they create an oneiric Rio de Janeiro. "Guerra dos Orixas" brilliantly deploys a host of African gods.

4130 Miguel, Salim. Onze de Biguaçu, mais um: ficções. Florianópolis, Brazil: Editora Insular, 1997. 102 p.

By eminent fiction writer, journalist, and cinema script-writer, these memories conveyed as fiction can be read as individual chapters in Bildungsroman. Masterful, sensitive, and many in stream-of-consciousness style, they show immigrant Lebanese family's move and adaptation in new town of Biguaçu. First story from dog's viewpoint renders implicit homage to Graciliano Ramos' canonical Vidas sêcas (see HLAS 04:4241) (English trans. Barren Lives (1965)). Last, separate story, "Balsa" (Raft), told to narrator may be the "extra one" mentioned in the title. "Onze" (11) is, of course, the number of soccer players on a team.

4131 Naves, Rodrigo. O filantropo. São Paulo: Companhia das Letras, 1998. 91 p.

By São Paulo art critic, these very short stories of about one page each often convey reflections and slices of life from a phenomenological angle. Narrators resemble curious and methodical writer of "Experiência" who rejoices at having learned something through uniting disparate materials in a process of self-knowledge akin to a via crucis/way of the cross. Highly recommended.

4132 Oliveira, Nelson de. Naquela época tínhamos um gato: e outros contos. São Paulo: Companhia das Letras, 1998. 100 p.

Recipient of Bahia state's Cultural Literary Prize one year after young author had been awarded the Casa de las Americas Prize, this collection is titled after award-winning story in earlier volume. Outstanding.

4133 Oliveira, Nelson de. Os saltitantes seres da lua: contos. Rio de Janeiro: Relume Dumará, 1997. 86 p.

Oliveira was born in 1966 and in 1995 won a Casa de las Americas Prize. His masterful stories combine everyday occurrences,

such as boys' games and young girls' insomnia, with the fantastic, often told from a child observer's viewpoint. The climate/tone is Kafkian: oneiric, nightmarish in these dramatic and suspenseful stories.

4134 Padilha, João Inácio. Bolha de luzes: contos. São Paulo: Companhia das Letras, 1998. 142 p.

Few short story writers are able to combine literary erudition and good fiction as well as Padilha does. He offers a varied fare: children's memoirs, literary allusions, and recreations (e.g., on blind Borges, and a brilliant one on Machado de Assis's travelling record). Padilha is a Brazilian journalist and diplomat whose literary accomplishments match the extent of his travels.

4135 Peregrino Júnior, João. A mata submersa e outras histórias da Amazônia. Natal, Brazil: EDUFRN, Editora da UFRN, 1998. 335 p.: ill.

Facsimile of celebrated anthology on Amazonian life is from J. Olympio's first edition (1960). It celebrates the centennial of the late physician and Brazilian Academy of Letters president, Peregrino Júnior. Gripping stories have not lost their power: dramatic, realistic, and poetic, they present Amazonian indigenous peoples and immigrants in the forest. A remarkable collection.

4136 Perez, Renard. Creusa, Creusa: contos. Rio de Janeiro: Razão Cultural, 1998? 180 p.

Stories by acclaimed writer evince perception, delicacy, and compassion as they portray the dark side of several characters. Like the eponymous Creusa, they seem to retain their mystery for both author and reader. Two of these stories have received recent awards. Perez is one of writers responsible for the Brazilian boom in short fiction in the 1950s-60s.

4137 Rodrigues, Yone. Caminhos de ontem: relembranças. Rio de Janeiro: Edições Galo Branco, 2000. 114 p.: ill.

Author, an acclaimed poet, children's book writer, pianist and sometime actress, describes these Paths of Yesterday as "an unpretentious diary." Although uneven and occasionally chatty, these pieces are well worth reading. They recreate a happy childhood in the provinces and later years in Rio and abroad among famed artists and intellectuals. Collection gains from author's poems interspersed with the narrative.

4138 Sabino, Fernando Tavares. O galo músico. Rio de Janeiro: Editora Record, 1998. 221 p.: ill.

These "Stories and novellas from youth to maturity, from desire to love" cover several decades of famous *cronista* and novelist's work. Chronologically organized, and with comments by author, the first is a prize-winning story written by Sabino at age 14. At age 17, one of these pieces was acclaimed by none other than Mario de Andrade. Collection exhibits Sabino's skill and makes for pleasant and relaxed reading.

4139 Sodré, Muniz. A lei do santo: contos. Rio de Janeiro: Bluhm, 2000. 142 p.

Starting with the suspenseful story, "Purification" (transl.), based on police brutality and religious fanaticism, book goes on to pay respectful homage to Afro-Brazilian and African legends and popular wisdom. One story is the amusing "A Moda da Bahia" and another has a Cuban setting. A very well-written collection throughout which mystery prevails, it is reflective, poetic, and dramatic.

4140 Spínola, Noênio D. Mariana adeus: cinco histórias paulistas de amor. São Paulo: Editora Mandarim, 1998. 210 p. (Literatura brasileira)

Eponymous novella is a paean to city of São Paulo, and an extended meditation by businessman character who on his way to work meets (and loses) the "woman of his dreams" in metro. His search for her is only part of this competent and witty tale akin to shaggy dog stories in which the city itself is almost a character.

4141 Tavares, Zulmira Ribeiro. Cortejo em abril: ficções. São Paulo: Companhia das Letras, 1998. 83 p.

The *April procession* of the title refers to the funeral for Brazilian President-Elect Tancredo Neves in 1985, the first democratically elected president after 20 years of military dictatorship. Unusual from narrative angles, stories cast oblique look at characters and circumstances. Extremely well-done by writer discovered in her middle years and since then the recipient of prestigious literary prizes for fiction.

4142 Trevisan, Dalton. 234 ministórias. Rio de Janeiro: Editora Record, 1997. 124 p.: ill.

The 234 numbered stories are 7–12 lines long; shorter ones on top of page, often one sentence long, are epigrams used as multiple epigraphs. All develop classic Trevisan fare: assault, adultery, family battering, rape and ensuing pregnancy, pedophilia, murder, suicide, etc. and brilliantly compress them. Another variation on Trevisan's themes with his usual aplomb and irony (and deep down, perhaps compassion).

4143 Viotti, Sérgio. A partida sempre. Prefácio inédito de Jorge de Lima. Rio de Janeiro: Topbooks, 1998. 207 p.

The collection, *Leaving always,* has a story itself. It was published in 1998, 45 years after Viotti showed it to the eminent modernist, Jorge de Lima, who wrote a preface (included here). A prize-winning novelist, Viotti also excels in short fiction, which expectedly echoes WWII era and presents everyday characters through a sensitive and imaginative lens with superb technique.

4144 Wolff, Fausto. O homem e seu algoz: 15 histórias. Rio de Janeiro: Bertrand Brasil, 1998. 285 p.

The title of this work, *Man and his executioner,* aptly fits the stories by this seasoned journalist. Collection is incisive as it examines half a century of social ills in Brazil and cruel or indifferent responses by those who might alleviate or stop them. Stories are depressing perhaps because Wolff develops his narratives so ably.

Crônicas

CHARLES A. PERRONE, *Professor of Portuguese and Luso-Brazilian Literature and Culture, University of Florida*

IN 1999 FERNANDO SABINO RECIEVED the prestigious Machado de Assis Prize for lifetime achievement in literature. Given that half of his more than 40 books are of *crônica* and that his reputation is so closely connected to the genre, Sabino took the award as a sign of official recognition of *crônica* despite its "minor tone and . . . unpretentious spirit." At the same time, he questioned the traditional view of this type of writing as a lesser genre, noting that it was practiced by such luminaries as Machado de Assis himself, Mário de Andrade, and Carlos Drummond de Andrade (acceptance speech cited in introduction of item **4170**).

Writers and critics alike continue to be concerned with the definition of *crônica* and its status in literature. Affonso Romano de Sant'Anna, the poet-*cronista* who assumed Drummond's place in the Rio newspaper upon his retirement, symptomatically asks in "Teoria da *crônica*" why some practitioners are referred to as *cronistas*, while others are considered writers who also wrote *crônica*. He cites various authors who have presented metaphors for writing the widely popular, brief compositions that frequently appear in periodicals. The 19th-century master Machado de Assis pictured the *cronista* as a hummingbird who stops to taste (*beijar*) an issue here and there, while a current leader in the field, Luis Fernando Veríssimo, offers a different zoological explanation: the *cronista* is like a chicken who has to lay an egg with regularity. Sant'Anna himself distinguishes the usual *crônica* writers from columnists and commentators in the press, maintaining that the former still should elaborate language literarily and give it transcendence. The talented *cronista* connotes, though with transparency, while the other journalists denote. Nevertheless, like reporters or opinion editors, *cronistas* write with a deadline; they must be spontaneous and current. They are individuals drenched in their time (item **4173**, p. 272–274).

Beatriz Resende, recognizing the immediacy of *crônica*, stresses that the very sense of being provisional gives the writing its lightness and exceptional authenticity, giving authors a certain courage lost in slower writing (item **4153**, p. 11). Recalling the Romantic legacy of entertaining and informally discussing issues in *crônica*, Leodegário A. de Azevedo Filho conceives of the modern version as an "autonomous literary genre characterized by a lightness of style, quick commentary, poetic tone, and grace in the analysis of people and facts, by being current and thematically varied (item **4163**, p. ix–x). Familiarity with the language and issues of the present, in sum, continue to mark the standard sense of *crônica* and to set it apart from literary fiction. There is, however, somewhat less grief and anxiety about the relationship with *belles-lettres* in the current era of postmodern, postcolonial, cultural and multicultural studies, which have their peculiar manifestations in Brazil as well. It is symptomatic that the category for short story in the Prêmio Jabuti (the national book prizes awarded by the Brazilian publishing industry) now also encompasses *crônica*.

At the turn of the millennium, publications from around Brazil classified as *crônica* increasingly challenge the lines of demarcation of the genre. Thus, there have been numerous titles focused on a specific discipline or profession, including medicine (item **4174**) and even economics. A notable increase in political themes includes both more conventional light moods (items and **4150** and **4175**) and more serious approaches (items **4146** and **4158**). Moving from the collective to the individual, there are recent examples of very personal reflections and diary-like writing that are self-cataloged as *crônica* in view of more flexible notions or for lack of a better technical term (items **4160** and **4165**). As was the case throughout the 1990s, regional works continue to be published in a constant stream, including those from the Northeastern states of Pernambuco (item **4145**), Rio Grande do Norte (item **4166**), and Bahia (item **4151**). While demonstrating a pervasive interest in and identification with the genre, an example from the North comprises brief writings that are closer to oral literature and memoir (item **4161**).

Travel-inspired *crônica,* often reminiscent of travel writing of past centuries, now written for the historically dominant domain of Rio de Janeiro and for the massive market of São Paulo describes sites both in Brazil and abroad, mostly Europe and the US. Examples in late 1990s' publications include recent works (items **4166, 4167,** and **4173**) and noteworthy new editions explicitly about and of travel (item **4164**). Comparisons with situations in other nations color various kinds of *crônica* about cosmopolitan existence and ethics. Both international awareness and an appreciation of tradition (for better or worse) are evident in a series of articles about interpersonal relationships (items **4162, 4167,** and **4176**). Authorship by women, general gender issues, and specifically feminist articulations are important in current *cronistas* with contrasting stances (items **4155, 4157, 4162,** and **4167**) and canonical Modernist names (item **4163**) and, extraordinarily, in historical discoveries (item **4154**). While a given focus often stands out, the sum of these instances show that variety and open-ended thematics are still the rule of this genre.

The body of work under consideration here includes editions in homage to deceased 20th-century writers (items **4147, 4159,** and **4163**) and *crônica* collections of well-established novelists from around the country (items **4146, 4148, 4149, 4167, 4169**). Given the number of literary figures involved, it is no surprise that there should be an abundance of volumes with pieces about the craft of writing, books, authors from Brazil and abroad (items **4146, 4167,** and **4173**), and entire volumes dedicated to language, literature, and authors (items **4148** and **4172**). Given the different roles that writers assume, the words of critic Eduardo Portella about the press pieces of one exceptional, well-recognized novelist-*cronista* are applicable to others: "the sustainable lightness of the *crônica* has recourse both to the taste of the essay and the fluency of narrative. The luck of the texts is cast in solidarity among the chronicler, the essayist, and the narrator" (item **4146,** preface p. xi). Essays and studies about the genre have favored historical approaches, looking back to Machado de Assis and 19th-century contexts, on to 1920s–30s, then to the peaks of the genre in the 1960s (item **4153**). Other sources include brief introductions with biographical information (item **4154**) and academic theses in Brazil (item **4156**) and abroad (both Europe and US). Growth of interest beyond the country's borders is further indicated by the publication of translations, e.g. Caio Fernando Abreu's *Pequenas epifanias* in France, and by the actual writing of *crônica* by foreigners, e.g. Matthew Shirts, in *O Estado de São Paulo.* Resende and Valença are regathering and evaluating the work in periodicals of a key early 20th-century writer ("A crítica emerge das *crônicas* de Lima Barreto" *O Estado de São Paulo,* caderno 2, May 5, 2001).

The growth of the Internet in Brazil has widened opportunities for readers and writers of *crônica.* Major newspapers put scheduled print pieces on line and maintain archives, and amateur writers post their contributions. There have even been *crônica* contests on the Internet resulting in virtual and paper publications (item **4152**). The innovative organizer Mário Prata (item **4168**) noted that the competition demonstrates the resurgence of the genre in the 1990s after a lull (in the 1970s and 1980s) and, to return to the issue of prestige raised above, that the writers who most influenced him were indeed the classic *cronistas* of the 1950s–60s. In overall terms, Brazil is producing more *crônica* than ever. Reading these pieces counterbalances the heaviness of day-to-day news, and subject matter, as the front page of any newspaper illustrates, is everywhere around the country ("A *crônica* volta," Sept. 13, 2000, Caderno 2, *O Estado de São Paulo*). Reflecting the role of *crônica* in the press, the publishing industry, as well as government institutions with book-production capacity, maintain a firm interest in the genre, historically important practitioners of the genre and current talent alike. Authorship and readership continue to make *crônica*, irrespective of any critical bias, Brazil's most popular form of imaginative literature.

The editor would like to acknowledge the assistance of Mary Risner in the preparation of entries for *HLAS 60*.

4145 Borba Filho, Hermilo. Palmares e o coração: crônicas. Palmares, Brazil: Fundação Casa da Cultura Hermilo Borba Filho, 1997. 82 p.: bibl. (Col. Palmares. Crônica; 1)

Better known as a folklorist, playwright, and fiction writer, the author also wrote a series of *crônicas* in the 1970s about the figures and intrigues of his home municipality in southern Pernambuco. Thus these journalistic pieces are often reminiscent of his stories that used real-life personages as points of departure. The longest and most revealing piece here is actually the text of a speech he gave to a graduating class in town.

4146 Callado, Antônio. Crônicas de fim do milênio. Organização de Martha Vianna. Rio de Janeiro: Francisco Alves, 1997. 353 p.

This collection encompasses a greater number of *crônicas* than the common anthology. Volume's size corresponds to the broad intellectual and cultural knowledge of the effusive author (1917–98), known for his informed columns and penetrating novels on the human saga in Brazil. As the end of the millennium approached, this *cronista* reflected on current events and historical legacies in Rio de Janeiro, Brazil as a whole, Latin America, and the world. His reflections on writers and writings from all walks of life reveal that he was clearly troubled by corruption, the disparities of modernity, and insti-

tutional vice. His prose is guided by a fundamental ethical impulse that places human dignity and justice above order and progress. One particularly noteworthy piece addresses the legacy of Gilberto Freyre's *Casa-grande e senzala* (*HLAS 2:1635*), (mis)translated as *The Masters and the Slaves* (*HLAS 12:2832*).

4147 Campos, Paulo Mendes. O amor acaba: crônicas líricas e existenciais. Organização e apresentação de Flávio Pinheiro. Rio de Janeiro: Civilização Brasileira, 1999. 269 p.

The collections of *crônica* that the writer published in his lifetime followed a simple chronological organization; they comprised selected items that had appeared in periodicals during a given time period. The re-edition of that output, projected as eight volumes, will be organized thematically and includes press pieces not included in previous anthologies. Works in this first volume of the series were chosen according to vague stylistic and thematic criteria involving an evident lyricism or reflection upon inner self, as opposed to more objective or outer biases. The lack of bibliographical data detracts from this book's usefulness for historical studies of the author's contribution to the genre.

4148 Campos, Paulo Mendes. Artigo indefinido: crônicas literárias. Organização e apresentação de Flávio Pinheiro. Rio de Janeiro: Civilização Brasileira, 2000. 190 p.

In this continuation of the new edition of the author's work in the genre, the editor has brought together nearly three dozen titles concerning literature itself and its makers, both Brazilian and foreign, including Pessoa, Whitman, and Bernard Shaw. The sophistication and cosmopolitanism of the author are, not surprisingly, much more evident here than in pieces drawn from quotidian realms.

4149 Campos, Paulo Mendes. O gol é necessário: crônicas esportivas. Organização e apresentação de Flávio Pinheiro. Rio de Janeiro: Civilização Brasileira, 2000. 93 p.

This second volume of a series featuring the author's work in the genre features exquisite prose on the world's most popular sport and Brazil's most widely shared passion. The literary approach to soccer is reminiscent of Nelson Rodrigues' forays into the same.

4150 Castelo Branco, Carlos. O caseiro do presidente: e outras notícias de uma chácara quase em estado de sítio. Apresentação de Luis Fernando Verissimo. Ilustrações de Morini. São Paulo: Nova Alexandria, 2001. 135 p.: ill.

These 30 articles combine black humor, vignettes about customs, and political satire to partake in the present-day practice of crônica, with its wide stylistic and thematic parameters. A preface by the renowned Luiz Fernando Veríssimo underlines the original formula of the author, who demonstrates keen senses of textuality and morality, as well as an ability to perceive and filter material in a country rich in absurdities, contradictions, distasteful events, misery, and concomitant beauty. The play on the title's last word (meaning both "siege," and "a place in the country") is suggestive of how the author takes advantage of verbal situations to comment on current affairs.

4151 Costa, Adroaldo Ribeiro. Páginas escolhidas: 200 crônicas e dois contos. Seleção, organização e introdução de Aramis Ribeiro Costa. Salvador, Brazil: Secretaria da Cultura e Turismo, Conselho Estadual de Cultura, 1999. 457 p.: bibl., ill. (Col. Memória; 8)

From the 1950s-80s, the author contributed to *A tarde,* the daily newspaper of the capital of the state of Bahia, thus qualifying as the city's and the state's most widely read *cronista*. His collected pieces represent a conventional contribution from the region to national production in the genre. In a simple and unpretentious speech-like style, the writer discusses urban affairs, state business, public figures, and family life. The substantial volume was edited by a relative explicitly concerned with the publishing legacy of the deceased.

4152 As crônicas dos Anjos de Prata. São Paulo: s.l., 2000. 87 p.

This noncommercial paperback contains the 30 best *crônicas* from an online composition contest conducted in 2000 that yielded 2,357 entries from all over Brazil. Selected contributors range in age from 16–85 years old and reveal a wealth of talent in the nonprofessional ranks.

4153 Cronistas do Rio. Organização de Beatriz Resende. Rio de Janeiro: J. Olympio Editora, 1995. 163 p.: bibl., ill.

Volume of papers prepared in conjunction with an exposition at the Centro Cultural Banco do Brasil in downtown Rio in Oct. 1994. The editor and seven other essayists consider the historical origins of *crônicas* in the 19th century, the long-standing identification of the genre with the former capital city, writers in the 1920s, salient poet-*cronistas*, classics of the 1950s and 1960s, and key women practitioners, notably Clarice Lispector. Given the relative rarity of critical studies and the breadth of this publication, it constitutes an outstanding contribution in the 1990s.

4154 Dolores, Carmen. Crônicas, 1905–1910. Organização e introdução de Eliane Vasconcellos. Rio de Janeiro: Arquivo Público do Estado do Rio de Janeiro, 1998. 154 p.: bibl., ill. (Col. Fluminense; 3)

An admirable example of the critical practice of *resgate* (rescue) of neglected writing by women, this volume resulted from a suggestion by the relatively well-recognized fiction writer Julia Lopes de Almeida. Front-matter contextualizes the author (1852–1910), who published several volumes of short stories in the early 20th century, as well as one of legends and another of *crôni-*

cas. This chronologically organized collection includes 40 of the 270 she wrote for the periodical *O País* in Rio de Janeiro, examining various topics from social activities and cultural life to weather and crime. Yet a range of women's issues clearly prove to be the key concern: access to media, abuse, unequal pay, "the art of motherhood," fashion, moral hypocrisy, education, and especially reading itself, including a sharp critique of Stendhal's suggestion to prohibit women from learning to read. In addition to the evident historical value, several of the feminist points raised in these *crônicas* remain pertinent in the present day.

4155 Felinto, Marilene. Jornalisticamente incorreto. Rio de Janeiro: Editora Record, 2000. 363 p.

A reprint edition of articles that appeared in the *Folha de São Paulo* 1995–99. Inspired somewhat by Virginia Woolf, these *crônicas* often take a resistant, anticommonsense stance in considerations of domestic foibles, social life, current events, media and the arts, and interpersonal relationships. These are seen in "post-modern amorous dialogues" that discuss emotions, courtship, and contemporary differences.

4156 Granja, Lúcia. Machado de Assis, escritor em formação: à roda dos jornais. São Paulo: FAPESP; Campinas, Brazil: Mercado de Letras, 2000. 167 p.: bibl.

Originally a doctoral dissertation at Unicamp, this work offers an account and analysis of the initial phase of the writing career of Brazil's most revered author when he was employed in journalism and produced numerous *crônicas.* A useful bibliography of wider scope accompanies the single-author focused study.

4157 Hilst, Hilda. Cascos e carícias: crônicas reunidas, 1992–1995. São Paulo: Nankin Editorial, 1998. 183 p.: ill.

In the fifth decade of a prolific career in literature, with some 20 books of poetry and 10 of fiction, the controversial author has ventured into the narrative and commentary of *crônica* as well. The present selection displays great stylistic variety, from structured strophes and free verse to some staid presentations and a wealth of prose approaches, often with experimental or humorous aims. The articles from *Correio popular,*

a newspaper in Campinas, often reveal local interests. Notwithstanding derisive or irreverent tones, the writer's critical eye guides a social conscience and concerns for the betterment of life—human, animal, individual, collective, spiritual, domestic, and national.

4158 Kotscho, Ricardo. Coitadinhos e malandrões: flagrantes do fim de feira do Brasil de FHC 10 e 20. Seleção das crônicas de Sérgio Pinto de Almeida. São Paulo: Casa Amarela, 1999. 169 p.

In their original format, these *crônicas* constituted a running account of daily life during the Cardoso presidency. They all appeared in the *Diário Popular* in the years 1997–99. Social conditions and changing times are discussed in human terms that recognize the fall-out of political expediency and economic plans.

4159 Laet, Carlos de. Crônicas. 2a. ed. Rio de Janeiro: Academia Brasileira de Letras, 2000. 452 p.: bibl., ill., index. (Col. Afrânio Peixoto, da Academia Brasileira de Letras; 61)

With a critical introduction and careful thematic selection, this volume is presented as an opportunity to reassess the contributions of this conservative statesman (1847–1927) and active columnist, who wrote over 3,000 items in the Rio press.

4160 Lucchesi, Marco. Saudades do paraíso. Rio de Janeiro: Lacerda Editores, 1997. 142 p.

These compositions did not previously appear in a periodical. The segments of this *sui generis* book could qualify as autonomous, but a sense of continuity also makes them chapters of a self-searching tale, a textual quest for philosophical and religious understanding. They are spiritual meditations, accounts of travel to special sites, profound reflections, and meetings with luminary writers.

4161 Maia, Alvaro. Banco de canoa: cenas de rios e seringais do Amazonas. 2a. ed. rev. Manaus, Brazil: Editora da Univ. do Amazonas, 1997. 394 p.

Accounts of customs and scenes of life on the rivers or in the rubber-tapping areas of the vast northern state, these articles are as often reworked transcriptions of oral literature collected by the author as imaginative original pieces. He calls them "narratives and little stories" (*historietas*) with which he wishes to express the cultural being of the local mestizo population as *caboclitude*, modeled on the operative noun *negritude*. The ethnographic, documentary, and folkloric qualities of the compositions give them particular value for area studies.

4162 Medeiros, Martha. Trem-bala. Porto Alegre, Brazil: L&PM, 1999. 259 p.

The author has a series of books of poetry to her credit, but her approach to the genre of *crônica* is notably unconcerned with figurative or surprising language. In very short and direct pieces, she addresses such normal themes as domestic life, motherhood, dating, gender roles, travel, and the omnipresence of electronic media. The latter aspect is particularly current, as the volume includes pieces first published not only in conventional press vehicles, but also on the Internet.

4163 Meireles, Cecília. Cecília Meireles: obra em prosa. v. 1, Crônicas em geral. Rio de Janeiro: Editora Nova Fronteira, 1998. 1 v.

This first of five volumes of the author's collected titles in this genre covers the period 1941–57. The more than 100 *crônicas* are written in a light language and are relatively long, tending toward commentary rather than anecdote. Themes include religion, public diversions, domestic life, reminiscence, commerce, and the years of WWII. Author's sense of humanity occasionally comes off as social protest. As a bureaucrat her sense of organization often conflicts with her creative writer's eye. While this is an important volume for the task of constitution of the complete works of a major Modernist writer, the prose is not consistently remarkable. See also item **4164.**

4164 Meireles, Cecília. Cecília Meireles: obra em prosa. v. 2, Crônicas de viagem. Rio de Janeiro: Editora Nova Fronteira, 1999. 1 v.

These writings reveal the neosymbolist poet during her time abroad as a midcentury traveler, not a tourist, which she explicitly distinguishes. She writes of Spain, France, India, and Brazil itself, including Rio de Janeiro, a city already starting to show signs of decadence and increased crime in the early 1950s.

4165 Moretzsohn, Virgílio. Cheiro de Cadillac. São Paulo: Scipione Cultural, 1998. 142 p.

Not all *crônicas* collected in books have a journalistic past. In this case the writer published items later in life that had been left in drawers, kept in diaries, or shared only among friends, as a *crônica*-like introduction explains. These pieces, covering the 1970s–90s, are marked by nostalgia and wistfulness; they are more emotional than analytical despite the frequent mention of luminaries of art and literature. The geocultural dimensions range from the privileged *Zona Sul* beachfront districts of Rio de Janeiro to classical Rome.

4166 Navarro, Newton. Obra completa. v. 1–2. Natal, Brazil: FIERN; Fundação José Augusto, 1998. 2 v.

The complete works of this Northeastern writer (1928–91) include a subset comprising a selection of 30 short *crônicas*. They contrast stylistically with the wistful lyrical pieces and philosophical prose of the rest of the first volume. In the chosen examples, the author is rarely partial to his part of the country; rather, he largely approaches European and North American topics and international cultural figures from the point of view of an author who happens to be from a certain region. In a few cases, local sensibility is somewhat more evident.

4167 Piñon, Nélida. Até amanhã, outra vez: crônicas. Rio de Janeiro: Editora Record, 1999. 284 p.

The author distinguished herself as a fiction writer (8 novels, 4 short-story collections) and as the first woman to head the Academia Brasileira de Letras, the national academy of letters (1996). This reprint edition of 121 brief *crônicas* that appeared in the press between 1989–94 displays a careful prose of generally serious tones and a wide variety of conceptual and quotidian issues. As befits someone of her profession, she shows a constant fascination with the instrument of language—names, phrases, usages— and storytelling itself, including historically important and fellow current authors. While there are numerous travel motifs, from European capitals to Miami, where she has a university chair, what proves to be the most compelling topic is contemporary identity, especially national Brazilian character. Half a dozen articles address the formation of personal and collective selves in the context of major cities, affective roles, historical legacies, and literary contributions.

4168 Prata, Mário. Minhas tudo: incluindo sexo, drogas e rock and roll e umas mulheres peladas. Rio de Janeiro: Objetiva, 2001. 178 p.: ill.

These personal chronicles tend to be short but sweet, written by an astute observer who finds the right phrases to expound on individual obsessions and collective manias alike. In the writing of the pains and pleasures of daily modern life, the writer focuses on the body and on revealing objects: clothing, furniture, rubber stamps, bathroom devices. The clichés of the subtitle suggest an abiding and expedient concern with humor and currency.

4169 Ribeiro, João Ubaldo. Arte e ciência de roubar galinha: crônicas. Rio de Janeiro: Editora Nova Fronteira, 1998. 257 p.

Another in a series of anthologies of crônicas by this successful journalist and fiction writer from Bahia whose small-town background provides ample material for the collection. All the present selections appeared in the Rio de Janeiro daily O Globo. The author is an entertainer who here prefers humorous or curious aspects of rural customs, zoological tales (cf. title), human relations colored by local tradition, political foibles, and the Portuguese language itself. A significant subtext in this series is the contrast between provincial existence and modern urban life.

4170 Sabino, Fernando Tavares. Livro aberto. Rio de Janeiro: Editora Record, 2001. 656 p.: 1 ill., index.

Thick volume contains six decades of work (1939–99) by one of the most recognized names in the crônica genre. Covers a wide range of geographical locations, including many where the author was stationed as a reporter, from Minas Gerais and London to Los Angeles and Rio de Janeiro, as well as works from all the newspapers and magazines for which he wrote. Also offers a brief biography, a chronology of works, and a name index that increases the usability of the volume, which may qualify as the largest

and most prestigious collection of crônica to date.

4171 Sant'Anna, Affonso Romano de. Crônicas escolhidas. v. 1. Rio de Janeiro: Luz da Cidade, 2000. 1 computer laser optical disc. (Col. Os Cronistas)

Simple voice readings of 10 selected articles, with no background sound track. Guest appearance by renowned speaker Paulo Autran. First in a collection of recorded crônicas following series in poetry and short fiction by the same production company.

4172 Sant'Anna, Affonso Romano de. A sedução da palavra. Brasília: Letraviva, 2000. 244 p.: ill.

Pt. 1 of this luxury edition is a selection of pieces, originally written between 1984–96, about the art of writing, including journalistic columns and crônicas, and the many sources of inspiration. Pt. 2 concerns encounters with poets and novelists, national and international, and ideas associated with the craft. This is the most concentrated example of an increasingly common practice in late 20th-century crônica: metaliterary articles concerning text-making and text-makers.

4173 Sant'Anna, Affonso Romano de. A vida por viver: crônicas. Rio de Janeiro: Rocco, 1997. 285 p.

The author has been an active figure in poetry and literary criticism of his generation (b. 1936). A transplant from Minas Gerais to Rio de Janeiro, he shows himself to be consistently aware of his dual role as verse-maker and creative columnist, in the mold of Brazil's most beloved poet-cronista, Carlos Drummond de Andrade. This latest volume of crônicas is typically variegated and opinionated, with sections including love and friendships, worldwide travel, beloved people, childhood, daily concerns, art and life, politics, death, and the practice of crônica. The last four entries are about the genre itself, distinctions between types of writers, his own initiation, and the possibilities of representation, both in the sense of mimesis and in that of speaking for local constituencies.

4174 Scliar, Moacyr. A face oculta: inusitadas e reveladoras histórias da medicina. Porto Alegre, Brazil: Artes e Ofícios, 2001. 223 p.: ill.

A selection of the more than 500 *crônicas* this physician-writer has published in the Brazilian newspaper *Zero Hora* between 1993–2001. All items refer to the practice of medicine, including notable cases, popular myths, success stories, and failures. Journalistic tones are counterbalanced by a friendlier language more characteristic of the traditional genre.

4175 Veríssimo, Luís Fernando. Aquele estranho dia que nunca chega. 2 ed. Rio de Janeiro: Objetiva, 1999. 238 p. (Vide Veríssimo; 2. v.)

No critical presentation but an attractive collection of rather short items showing the author's characteristic wit, irony, insight, and good humor in a critical view of the late 1990s and the Fernando Henrique Cardozo regime.

4176 Veríssimo, Luís Fernando. Histórias brasileiras de verão. 2 ed. Rio de Janeiro: Objetiva, 1999. 281 p. (Vide Verissimo)

Compositions about relationships in current society (family, relatives, man-woman), conflicts, and psychological profiles. Again, typical humor and accessible journalistic language.

Poetry

NAOMI HOKI MONIZ, *Director, Brazilian Studies Program, and Professor of Literature, Georgetown University*

AT THE END OF THE MILLENNIUM, the main characteristic of Brazilian poetry was its ability to maintain a uniformly high quality of artistic expression and a capacity for innovation and diversity. Despite a long history of alternating between form and content, Brazilian poets generally have been more focused on reflection and less concerned with self-expression. As a result, the central object of the generational-biographical poetry has been taken over by a problematization of poetry itself—the implied reader and the concept of reality in it. The poetry is more reflexive, ironic, and elliptical.

This style is apparent in the last book published by Affonso Romano de Sant'Anna, *Textamentos* (item **4200**), and in works by others of his generation such as Sebastião Uchoa Leite's *A espreita* (item **4192**) and Affonso Avila's *Código de Minas* (item **4178**). The most common theme is that of the classic voyage, in various forms: Sant'Anna's book is based on his extended stays overseas (in the US and France) and trips to countries such as Italy and Greece; the commemorative 20-year edition of the epic *Grande fala do índio guarani* (1978–98), published together with *A catedral de Colônia* (1985) (item **4199**); and Cirne's *Rio vermelho* works as a *Bildungsroman* of the provincial boy who moved from the Northeastern backlands to Rio de Janeiro (item **4184**). Another variation of this same theme is Cassa's *Bhagavad-Brita: a canção do beco*, which takes the reader on a Joycean voyage through the dead-end streets of São Luís do Maranhão (item **4183**). Finally, Sergio Lemos' *A luz no caleidoscópio* is a maritime odyssey between his carioca Praia da Urca and the classic Aegean (item **4193**).

Another trend among the publications reviewed here is the use of content that echoes themes present since the redemocratization and globalization process in the 1980s, such as land rights, human rights, the environment, gender, ethnicity, and migration. Fernandes' *Terratreme* (item **4187**) and Guimarães' *Canto da Amazonia: vida e morte da floresta* (item **4191**). Both address the Amazon region and its survival, but with different paths: the latter work employs the traditional, 19th-century Indianist style and tone, while the former uses a more contemporary approach, critical of the human and environmental devastation. Moacyr Félix's *Introdução a escombros* is reminiscent of the 1960s belief in the transformative function of collective action (item **4186**); *Amerindia, morte e vida,* coauthored by the bishop Pedro Casaldáliga and Pedro Tierra, the spokespersons for land rights (*Comissão Pastoral de Terras, MST*), examines the survival of indigenous peoples from colonial times to the present plight of the *Pataxós,* indigenous residents in the area of Porto Seguro, Bahia, especially in view of the celebration of 500 years of Brazil's discovery (item **4182**).

Among women poets, there are two representative voices: Alcione Guimarães' *Zuarte* recalls Brazil's rural roots emulating the work of one of the greatest living poets in Brazil today, Adélia Prado, and provides a magical dimension to the intimate details of women's existence (item **4190**). And Chica Xavier is a well-known *filha de santo,* lyricist, and singer of songs and prayers for various *orixas* and figures of Afro-Brazilian religions (item **4206**).

Mass culture is disseminated and distributed through mass media, and this sociocultural form creates complex relations, information crossings, and different interactions encompassing many segments of the population. In recent decades, many lyricists have found their works studied and published in book format. One such example is Paulo César Pinheiro, who has written lyrics for many famous Brazilian singers and composers. His *Atabaques, violas e bambus* is a historical journey, based on oral traditions, of the founding cultures of Brazil (item **4197**). Abel Silva, another lyricist and poet who worked with popular singers such as Ivan Lins, Fagner, and Gal Costa, published *Só uma palavra me devora,* covering three decades of his work (item **4201**). The anthology of *poetas populares* organized by Vicente Salles is an important collection because it illustrates the scope of regional manifestations of this genre, including the Northeastern *cantores* who live in the large migrant communities in two major urban centers in the Southeast (item **4205**).

Finally, it is worthwhile to note the publication of *Poemas* by Ariano Suassuna, one of the most acclaimed Brazilian playwrights. Suassuna combines simple and sophisticated styles taken from popular culture and high culture, oral language, and erudite forms woven into the rich culture of the Northeast with universal motifs and the picaresque humor described as *"astúcia é a coragem do pobre"* ("the cleverness and courage of the poor") (item **4203**).

4177 Alvarez, Reynaldo Valinho. A faca pelo fio: poemas reunidos. Rio de Janeiro: Ministério da Cultura, Fundação Biblioteca Nacional, Depto. Nacional do Livro: Imago, 1999. 403 p.: bibl.

Alvarez' book *Galope do tempo* (1997) received the Jabuti Prize for poetry in 1998. This anthology includes works from books published between 1979–97, including *O continente e a ilha* (1995), *O solitário gesto de viver* (1980), and *Canto em si e outros cantos* (1979). Collection includes a bibliography, a list of contributions to other anthologies, and a list of prizes received in Brazil, Italy, and Portugal. Alvarez is considered an heir of the poet Augusto dos Anjos.

4178 Avila, Affonso. Código de Minas. Nova ed. em texto integral. Rio de Janeiro: Sette Letras, 1997. 122 p.

New edition with complete text. Minas Gerais provides the basis for themes that deal with the historic past, traditions, and the baroque. Avila's poetry mixes satire and science fiction.

4179 Bacellar, Luiz. Satori: haiku, genku, renku & senryü. Manaus, Brazil: Editora Travessia, 1999. 110, 2 p.: bibl., ill.

Includes an introduction about the author and haiku by Renan Freitas Pinto and a short manual by Rogel Samuel on "Satori." Bacellar is familiar with and faithful to the haiku spirit and form, but gives it a Brazilian flavor: "Na laranja e na couve / picada—as cores brasileiras / da feijoada." Or in the delightful pun of "san-to, Basho/baixou" in "Ah! o Satori: Matsuo Basho, San- / to, me baixou na cuca."

4180 Barroso, Ivo. A caça virtual e outros poemas: antologia. Prefácio de Eduardo Portella. Rio de Janeiro: Editora Record, 2001. 222 p.: bibl.

Anthology of poems including: "Caça Virtual," "Nau dos Náufragos," "Concretist Poems," "Papel e Chão," and "Visitações de Alcipe." These impressionist poems employ classic forms in new rhythmic and spatial structures: "Sôbolos rios que vão / salobros rios que não / sãolobos cios oussão / os seios / os sóis / Sal sobre os rios por."

4181 Campos, Maximiano. Lavrador do tempo: poesias. Organização de Antônio Campos and Fátima Borba Campos. Recife, Brazil: Edições Bagaço, 1998? 49 p.

This poet from Recife practices literature as his "calling." In the words of Campos, "Sou um domador de sonho. Sou o guardião de uma loucura mansa, um profeta sem seguidores . . . sou livre porque não temo arriscar a vida. Sou um palhaço que zomba das próprias desventuras. Sou um herói de todas as guerras . . . Sou um rebelado."

4182 Casaldáliga, Pedro and **Pedro Tierra.** Ameríndia, morte e vida. Prefácio de Frei Betto. Petrópolis, Brazil: Editora Vozes, 2000. 109 p.: ill. (some col.).

Casaldáliga is the bishop of São Felix do Araguaia in the state of Mato Grosso, and is famous for his work with the Commissão Pastoral da Terra, an organization that works to benefit campesinos and rural workers. Tierra is from Tocantins in Goais. In this collection of poems, whose title is a pun on the famous Morte e vida severina (1966) by Cabral de Melo Neto, the poets sing about threats to the survival of indigenous peoples in Brazil from colonial times to the 1970s plight of the Pataxós Indians in southern Bahia.

4183 Cassas, Luís Augusto. Bhagavad-Brita: a canção do beco. Rio de Janeiro: Imago, 1999. 78 p.

Considered the best of Cassas' nine books of poems by critics such as A. Carlos Secchinn and Ivan Junqueira. Taking the canon of Hindu religion, the Bhagavad-gita, Cassas transplants it to the cobbblestone streets ("brita") of his São Luís do Maranhão, with references to Manuel Bandeira's "A Ultima Canção do Beco." Introduction by Affonso Ávila "Becomancia," followed by commentaries by poets and critics: "O Ouro das Coisas" by Salgado Maranhão; "Bhagavad-Brita" by Jorge Wanderley; "Bhagavad-Brita" by Foed Castro Chamma; "O Beco Descoberto" by Luís Augusto Cassas; and "A Metáfora da Maturidade" by Cassiano Nunes.

4184 Cirne, Moacy. Rio vermelho. Natal, Brazil: Fundação José Augusto, Depto. Estadual de Imprensa, 1998? 98 p.: ill.

Cirne is one of the founders of the *Poema/Processo* group which started in 1967. His book of poems, divided in three parts, is set up as a movie script with each part depicting a different chronological stage of Cirne's life. The first part, *Rio Seridó*, covers his infancy and early adolescence in Caicó. The poems portray a provincial northeastern life punctuated by movie and comic book heroes—Tarzan, Captain Marvel, Flash Gordon—and the Hollywood siren Esther Williams. The second part, *Rio Potengi*, is set in Natal, where Cirne lived until the age of 25: "Natal / um Potengi e seus crepúsculos / dois filmes aos domingos / e todas as mulheres do Arpège." The third part addresses his life in Rio de Janeiro, with "poemas processos," fragments from Mao Tsetung, ex-libris of Valetin Le Carmon, glimpses of the movie *Imagens*, and the musical inspiration of John Coltrane and Hermeto Paschoal.

4185 Espinheira Filho, Ruy. Poesia reunida e inéditos: 1966–1998. Rio de Janeiro: Editora Record, 1998. 367 p.: index.

Poems from *Heléboro* (1966–73); *As sombras luminosas* (1975–80); *Morte secreta* (1976–84); *A Canção de Beatriz* (1985–90); *Memória da chuva* (1990–96); and *Inéditos* (1996–98). Considered a poet of memory, Espinheira Filho's themes include exile and loneliness.

4186 Félix, Moacyr. Introdução a escombros. Rio de Janeiro: Ministério da Cultura, Fundação Biblioteca Nacional,

Depto. Nacional do Livro: Bertrand Brasil, 1998. 201 p.

Preface by Eduardo Portella titled "A Poesia em Ação." Félix's poetry expresses his outrage at the conditions of the poor and oppressed. He has not lost belief in the utopian concept of collective redemption, summarized in this metaphor from his poetry: "A guitarra elétrica de Jimmy Hendrix é atual: ouvi-la é ouvir o grito que corre entre os fios de qualquer cidade grande deste mundo ocidental."

4187 Fernandes, Ronaldo Costa. Terratreme: poesia. Brasília: Fundação Cultural do Distrito Federal: Governo do Distrito Federal, Secretaria de Cultura, Distrito Federal, 1998. 93 p.

This book was awarded the Literary Production Grant in 1997 by the Cultural Foundation of Brasília. The title echoes T.S. Elliot's *Wasteland* and invokes "the sound and the fury" of little Faulknerian villages in the Amazon region, where the traditional way of life, fauna and flora, and land and water are disappearing. The geometric and sparse style borrows the metaphors of Northeastern writers such as Cabral de Mello Neto and Graciliano Ramos in the poem "No Pântano": "Não se sabe onde / se inicia a terra / onde termina a água / sem margens / o pântano / é mato encharcado / é água barrenta." And in the poem "O Sertão do Mar": "E então penso / nos pescadores como camponeses / lavrando a terra do mar / latifundio de Deus / terra sem cerca / onde os frutos se enterram / e estão vivos."

4188 Franco, Francisco Manoel de Mello. Os Brasis. 2. ed. Rio de Janeiro: Objetiva, 2000. 238 p.

Epic poem celebrating 500 years of Brazil's discovery and the formation of the nation and its people. Chronologically explores Brazil's history from the arrival of Pedro Álvares Cabral (1500) to the government of Fernando Henrique Cardoso (1995–2002) in 10 cantos with stanzas varying in number from 79 (canto 3) to 164 (canto 9).

4189 Geração alternativa: antologia poética potiguar anos 70/80. Compilação de J. Medeiros. Cronologia organizada com Anchieta Fernandes. Natal, Brazil: Amarela Edições, 1997. 339 p.: ill.

As the title explains, this work includes works of 70 poets who go against the canon. Selection is guided by three principles: (1) visual and semiotic similarity to *Poema/Processo* and "arte correio"; (2) audiomusical in the songs and dances of the *sertões,* the Northeast, to urban rock and pop; and (3) self-reflexive or metalinguistic, parody, copy, dadaistic, and intertextual.

4190 Guimarães, Alcione. Zuarte. Goiânia, Brazil: Editora Kelps, 2000. 1 v. (unpaged): ill. (chiefly col.).

Zuarte is a strong rustic textile that the author uses as a metaphor for her rural roots. The broom, a symbol of domesticity and subjugation, becomes a magic and powerful tool by which to metamorphose into a magic angel/witch and flying peasant woman as in the paintings of Klee and Chagall: "muitas bruxas ancestrais andaram por aqui." Also evokes a bucolic tone as in "da flauta a música / do caule de mamão."

4191 Guimarães, Gonçalves. Canto da Amazônia: vida e morte da floresta. Belo Horizonte, Brazil: Armazém de Idéias, 2000. 255 p.: bibl., ill.

Includes 19 cantos of decasyllable quartets that describe the history and riches of the Amazon forest, including plants, animals, and history, with references to biblical and classic myths of Paradise as well as to Indian legends.

4192 Leite, Sebastião Uchoa. A espreita. São Paulo: Editora Perspectiva, 2000. 90 p. (Signos; 27)

Good introduction by João Alexandre Barbosa titled "Raro Entre Raros" analyzes Leite's evolution from his first book, *Dez sonetos* (1960), to the present one that collects 57 poems from 1993–98: ". . . a corrosão da objetividade . . . não é uma saída para a subjetividade mas uma interiorização da marginalidade da pessoa lírica que foi sendo conquistada nos livros sucessivos de Sebastião. . . uma poesia que existe nos interstícios entre a lucidez e a claridade de uma dicção densa e despojada." Considered a must read among those of his generation: Mário Faustino, Décio Pignatari, Paulo Leminski, Affonso Ávila, and Haroldo de Campos.

4193 Lemos, Sergio. A luz no caleidoscópio. Rio de Janeiro: Topbooks, 1998. 163 p.

In reference to the Portuguese poet Camilo Pessanha's Venus: "etérea e venérea," and parodying Brazilian Romantic poets, Lemos states: "pedacinhos nossos / que os anos não trazem mais, Oh a tarde de laranjas bocejando / o papel de pão, as moscas, o café." He also echoes the medieval cantigas de amigo: "Ai ondas do mar de Urca." His Aeneas is "negro, indio, branco" and his circular voyage goes from Urca to the Aegean.

4194 Mourão, Gerardo Mello. Cânon & fuga. Rio de Janeiro: Editora Record, 1999. 141 p.

Born in Ceará, Ipueiras, 1917, Mourão was a journalist, professor, and federal congressman. His epic poem "Invenção do Mar" (1977) won the prestigious Jabuti Prize. His style is classic and biblical, with undertones of Rilke and Leopardi: "Aqui jaz / o que foi poeta, isto é / pregador das rosas, pregou às roas e pregou as rosas." Or, as in the poem "Sopro": "no silen / cinefa / vel da / lua."

4195 Odorizzi, Fortunato. Sacras e profanas. Povoadores de Cotiporã by Sergio Angelo Grando. Organização de Rovílio Costa, Sergio Angelo Grando, and Maria Estela Zonta. Porto Alegre, Brazil: Edições EST, 1998. 320 p.: index. (Col. Italia nel mondo)

Includes an introduction by Moacyr Flores. Provides a compilation of documents of Italian immigrants in Cotiporã, Rio Grande do Sul. Divided into three parts: (1) "Sacras e Profanas," based on the manuscript of Giutinotti de Anaunaia (pseud. of Odorizzi, 1819–98) from the archives of the Curia Metropolitana in Porto Alegre; (2) "Livro de Óbitos 1893–1932"; and (3) "Histórico de Cotiporã," which includes registers, documents of dispensation, blessings, sales, and construction.

4196 Oliveira, Adelmo. Canto mínimo: antologia poética. Salvador, Brazil: Fundação Cultural do Estado da Bahia; Rio de Janeiro: Imago, 2000. 144 p.: bibl. (Bahia: prosa e poesia)

Introduction titled "A Arqueologia do Novo" and organization by Ildasio Tavares. Collection is divided into eight parts and is inspired by poets such as Camões, Gôngora, Quevedo, Gregório de Matos, Bilac, Cruz e Souza, Jorge de Lima, and Vinicius de Morais.

4197 Pinheiro, Paulo César. Atabaques, violas e bambus. Rio de Janeiro: Editora Record, 2000. 254 p.

Born in Rio de Janeiro, Pinheiro started to write poetry and lyrics at 13 years of age. He has written 1,500 songs with some

of the most famous Brazilian composers such as Baden Powell, Edu Lobo, Tom Jobim, and Sivuca, among others. "Canto das três raças," about the suffering and rebellion of the Brazilian masses, is one of his most famous songs. Here, in the style of the Northeastern "cantadores," he presents an epic about the formation of the Brazilian people based on oral tradition (Câmara Cascudo). He combines the languages, rhythms, and cultures of the three roots of Brazilian culture: European traditions, African nations and peoples, and indigenous peoples.

4198 Rezende, Renato. Passeio. Rio de Janeiro: Editora Record, 2001. 105 p.

Introduction by poet Alexei Bueno. Rezende is also a painter and translator. He is a masterful composer of the short poem and classic lines, and knowledgeable about haiku poetry: "o que é verdadeiramente divino / não pode ser escondido; como a luz dentro de cada um de nós / transborda pelo olhi, presa no corpo."

4199 Sant'Anna, Affonso Romano de. A grande fala do índio guarani; e, A catedral de Colônia. Ed. comemorativa. Rio de Janeiro: Rocco, 1998. 181 p.: bibl.

Commemorative edition of the poem published in 1978 which, along with Ferreira Gullars' *Poema Sujo*, became emblematic of the military dictatorship. Includes essays by Tristão de Athayde, "Poesia Planetária"; José Guilherme Merquior, "A Volta do Poema"; Donald Schueler, "A Grande Era da Poesia Terminou"; and Antonio Hohlfeldt, "Mural da Margina(alienação)lidade." Merquior celebrates this volume as a return to the long poem genre and the Indianist theme as Sant'Anna universalizes his thoughts about his identity/identities as the Indian, *mineiro*, and Protestant: "um indio / encontrado na mata / sem passado e escrita / trocando sual alma terna e torta / por qualquer espelho ou faca."

4200 Sant'Anna, Affonso Romano de. Textamentos. Rio de Janeiro: Rocco, 1999. 174 p.

The title seems to be more an allusion to the crepuscular tone of the poems— reflections on aging and death—rather than the end of his writings, which were noted for historical, social, and political issues as in "A Grande Fala do Indio Guarani" and "A

Catedral de Colonia." Also included are previously unpublished poems written during his stays in Los Angeles (1965–67) and in Aix-en-Provence, France (1980), along with poems written on trips to Italy, Greece, Israel, and throughout Latin America.

4201 Silva, Abel. Só uma palavra me devora: poesia reunida e inéditos. Rio de Janeiro: Editora Record, 2000. 252 p.

A collection of poems, some of which are previously unpublished. Includes texts from: *Açougue das almas* (see *HLAS 38: 7408*), *Asas, Mundo delirante* (1992), *Anima*, song lyrics, original poems, and poetic fragments published in magazines and newspapers from 1973–2000. Silva was called "neomodernista surpreendente de cuca voadora" by the director Glauber Rocha. He wrote more than 300 compositions, many of which were songs, in partnership with some of the most famous popular singers such as Sueli Costa, Moraes Moreira, Ivan Lins, Macalé, Fagner, and Menescal, among others. Volume covers three decades of work, including 180 poems, some of which are about Rio and were published in the late 1960s in the underground paper *O Pasquim.*

4202 Sousa, Afonso Félix de. Chamados e escolhidos: reunião de poemas. Rio de Janeiro: Editora Record, 2001. 624 p.

In the preface, Antonio Carlos Secchin writes: "A terra, a mulher, e o divino formam o eixo em torno do qual gira a criação de Afonso." This collection begins with the *Geração de 45*, questioning poetic creation itself and language as the vehicle for poetry. Includes 29 mystic sonnets from *Sonetos aos pés de Deus.*

4203 Suassuna, Ariano. Poemas. Seleção, organização e notas de Carlos Newton Júnior. Recife, Brazil: Editora Universitária UFPE, 1999? 267 p.: bibl.

Careful, scholarly selection, organization, and notes by Newton Jr. This anthology brings together most of the poetic production of Suassuna, known as a writer of novels and plays, and includes more than half of the typed originals from the author's own archives. The poems are collected thematically: (I) "Pasto Incendiado"; (II) "Odes"; (III) "Vida Nova Brasileira"; (IV) "Poemas Iluminogravados"; and (V) "Outros." The first section is the only one organized and selected by Suassuna himself for publication in traditional format.

4204 Tufic, Jorge. Sonetos de Jorge Tufic. Fortaleza, Brazil: UFC Edições, 2000. 128 p.

Tufic, from the state of Acre, is *manauara* by adoption as well as *cearense.* He belongs to the literary group *D'o pão*—Padaria Espiritual. This collection includes 63 sonnets in "Agendário de Sonhos," 15 sonnets in "Retrato da Mãe," and a selection from "Princípios e Fins." Tufic's Middle Eastern roots are present in his poetry: "lentilha, azeite, doce, o acebolado chia na frigideira de lumínio, infância de minha mãe: o ouro, a neve, o monte, o clima raro."

4205 Vicente, Zé. Zé Vicente, poeta popular paraense. Introdução e seleção de Vicente Salles. São Paulo: Hedra, 2000. 139 p.: bibl. (Biblioteca de cordel)

Fifty scholars have chosen 50 renowned *poetas populares.* This work includes an introductory essay and a selection of representative poems by Salles. The volume brings together the work of poets from the Northeast, Rio Grande do Sul, the interior of São Paulo, northeastern Paraná, Mato Grosso, Minas Gerais, Goiás, and the urban centers of Rio de Janeiro and São Paulo where Northeastern migrant groups live.

4206 Xavier, Chica. Chica Xavier canta sua prosa: cantigas, louvações e rezas para os orixás. Prefácio de Miguel Falabella. Ilustrações de Bela D'Oxóssi. Rio de Janeiro: Topbooks, 1999. 124 p.: ill. (some col.).

Includes an introduction by the actor Falabella. Chica Xavier is a theater, television, and movie actress who works in the *terreiro* in Sepetiba and belongs to the sorority *Nossa Senhora do Rosário*, in Salvador. She was born in Bahia, works in *umbanda* in Rio de Janeiro, and considers herself Catholic, "candomblecista, umbandista, espírita, pessoa sincrética." She has written many songs for Zé Pelintra (a type of Exu), Preto Velho (linha das almas), Martim Pescador (son of Oxum and Oxossi), Zumbi, and many "pai, avô, tio" of the line of souls: "Meu rosário tem tantas contas / como tem pedras no meu caminho / nas pedras vou tropeçando / e vou rezando devagarinho / pedindo a Nossa senhora / pra tirar as pedras do meu caminho."

Drama

SEVERINO J. ALBUQUERQUE, *Professor of Portuguese, University of Wisconsin-Madison*

THE TREND TOWARD CATALOGING and historicizing has absorbed drama and theater criticism at the turn of the 20th century, hence the several overviews of the last decade (item **4232**) as well as of the previous one hundred years (items **4226** and **4227**). This historical preoccupation stretches back to include the 19th-century, as demonstrated by an award-winning work by João Roberto Faria (item **4223**) and a new, revised edition of a seminal book that spans the entire period since Anchieta (item **4228**).

Studies of single figures also fared prominently in the years under consideration; excellent examples are books on the contributions of Décio de Almeida Prado (item **4222**), Ademar Guerra (item **4229**), and French director Louis Jouvet during his Brazilian sojourn (item **4231**). One volume, dedicated to the career of Antunes Filho, is of particular importance as it focuses on a stage director who was a key figure in establishing groups as the vital force in contemporary Brazilian theater (item **4225**). Through his work with Grupo Macunaíma and Centro de Pesquisas Teatrais, Antunes Filho has given impetus to the success of theatrical groups thanks to a method that blends experimentation, discipline, and hard work.

Around the country, other groups have both followed in Antunes' tracks and opened new avenues of their own. Paramount among them is Grupo Galpão, which was created in Belo Horizonte in 1982, and burst onto the national scene in the 1990s with their vibrant blend of Brechtian technique, street theater, and the classics (Shakespeare, Molière, Nelson Rodrigues). Just as Antunes Filho has been fortunate in the quality of scholarly work done on his contributions (the names of George, Britton, and Guimarães spring to mind), so has Grupo Galpão figured prominently in the research of Júnia de Castro Magalhães Alves, Marcia Noe, and Lúcia Trindade Valente, whose ongoing, extensive study of Galpão has already produced the series of three articles annotated below (items **4219, 4220,** and **4221**). Other groups and stage directors have not yet found their chroniclers and therein lies a major topic for new and further research in the field.

Thus, while groups are currently at the forefront of Brazilian theater, and *encenadores* like Gerald Thomas are still held in high esteem by a number of critics (although short of the luster and prestige they enjoyed in the 1980s), playwrights are beginning to be noticed again, with strong contributions from established names such as Maria Helena Kühner (item **4215**) as well as from younger playwrights like Clara de Goes (item **4212**) and respected novelists venturing into drama, as is the case of Diogo Mainardi (item **4216**).

Finally, the publication of original plays shows a trend that parallels the cataloging effort referred to above, as several anthologies of note have appeared in the last few years. Some of these books include plays by diverse authors (items **4208** and **4211**), while others have a sole author, as is the case of the complete theater of Caio Fernando Abreu (item **4207**) and the complete verse drama of Carlos Nejar (item **4217**). A serious gap in our field is the study of the type of theater represented in these publications. The work of most of these playwrights is fertile ground for new research but remains virtually unexplored.

ORIGINAL PLAYS

4207 Abreu, Caio Fernando. Teatro completo. Porto Alegre: Editora Sulina: Instituto Estadual do Livro, 1997. 223 p.

The complete dramatic works of the major late-20th-century fiction writer who died in 1996. The present volume does not include short fiction others have adapted to the stage (with Abreu's consent), such as the acclaimed AIDS allegory, *Dama da noite*.

4208 Alvaro de Carvalho. Florianópolis, Brazil: FCC Edições: IOESC, 1997. 259 p.

Volume includes three of the winners of the 1995 state of Santa Catarina drama competition. Checcucci's *Um dia, um sol* won the Children's Drama category, and Pinto's *Cabaré Lupicínio* and Rein's *Éter* took first and second places respectively in the Adult Division. Pontes' play is a moving tribute to the great composer Lupicínio Rodrigues.

4209 Antologia do teatro brasileiro. v. 1, O teatro de inspiração romântica. v. 2, A aventura realista e o teatro musicado. São Paulo: Editora SENAC São Paulo, 1997. v. 1–2.

First ever anthology of 19th-century Brazilian theater, impeccably edited by the noted critic, literature professor, and fiction writer, Flávio Aguiar. A landmark for the study and research of the theater of the period.

4210 César, Murilo Dias. São Bernardo. São Paulo: Imprensa Oficial do Estado, 1997. 64 p.

Stage adaptation of Graciliano Ramos' 1934 novel of the same title. Winner of the 18th Vladimir Herzog Award for theater.

4211 Coleção Teatro brasileiro. Belo Horizonte, Brazil: Hamdan Editora, 1997. 3 v.

The first three volumes in a remarkable effort to distribute free of charge otherwise unavailable copies of works by contemporary dramatists. Each volume is comprised of four plays—dramas and comedies, theater for children or grown-ups—some never before staged and more than half by little-known authors.

4212 Góes, Clara. O cavalo do cão. Rio de Janeiro: Sette Letras, 1997. 53 p.

Goes' short, lyric play focuses on a girl, an old lady, a beggar, and a poor transvestite as they confront a devilish apparition deeply rooted in Brazilian folklore.

4213 Goés, Luiz Carlos. "Nem uma guimba, meu deus! . . ." (*Rev. Teatro/Rio de Janeiro*, 71:497/498, set. 1996, p. 21–36)

Two-act comedy by playwright and stage director Goés, whose career spans over 30 years. Use of nonsense and anarchic humor point to the *teatro besteirol* school so influential in 1980s Brazil.

4214 Jorge, Miguel. Amor: poldro que se doma—fogo de outra chama; e, Décima quarta estação: peças em um ato e vários quadros. Goiânia, Brazil: Editora Kelps, 1997. 175 p.: bibl., ill. (some col.).

Two one-act plays by the prolific author from Goiás, with an afterword by Darcy Denófrio. The first features a chorus that punctuates the work with verses by a number of poets, including Quintana and Drummond, while the second is a surrealist collage of fragments from Jorge's short story collection, *Avarmas* (1978).

4215 Kühner, Maria Helena. O fio de Ariadne: teatro. Rio de Janeiro: Imprinta Express, 1998. 160 p.

Contains three plays (the title work plus *O ouro das facas* and *Encruzilhada*) and an essay ("Apontando para a Lua") by the tireless playwright and activist. *O ouro das facas* focuses on a historical figure, poet Barbara Heliodora, and her role as a participant in the 18th-century Minas Gerais conspiracy.

4216 Mainardi, Diogo. Contra o Brasil. São Paulo: Companhia das Letras, 1998. 214 p.

Antinationalist satire by the controversial literary critic for *Veja* magazine. No icon or myth is left unscathed in antihero Pimenta Bueno's romp through Brazilian history and national identity.

4217 Nejar, Carlos. Teatro em versos: personae-poemas. Rio de Janeiro: Ministério da Cultura, FUNARTE, 1998. 424 p.

The complete verse drama by the distinguished poet, this publication places Nejar in the company of such authors of verse drama as Vinícius de Moraes and João Cabral de Melo Neto. As a collection of autos (which Nejar calls "personae-poemas"), these poems echo the dramatic corpus of Gil Vicente and Lope de Vega.

4218 Porto Alegre, Manuel de Araújo.
Teatro completo de Araújo Porto Alegre. v. 2. Rio de Janeiro: INACEN, 1997. 1 v. (Clássicos do teatro brasileiro; 7)
The second volume (vol. 1 was published in 1988 by Inacen) of the complete works of the underappreciated Romantic playwright. For comment on vol. 1, see *HLAS 54:4924.*

THEATER CRITICISM AND HISTORY

4219 Alves, Júnia de Castro Magalhães and **Lúcia Trinidade Valente.** Grupo Galpão: a volta de Molière ao teatro de rua. (*Aletria/Belo Horizonte,* 7, 2000, p. 69–77)
Part of a series of articles by Alves and collaborators on Grupo Galpão. This particular essay concentrates on the techniques Galpão has used to bring Molière to the streets.

4220 Alves, Júnia de Castro Magalhães and **Marcia Noe.** From the street to the stage: the dialectical theatre practice of Grupo Galpão. (*Luso-Braz. Rev.,* 39:1, Summer 2002, p. 79–93)
As the most thorough and ample of the essays on Grupo Galpão by Alves and collaborators, this article should be read first. An excellent introduction to the most important theater group in turn-of-the-century Brazil.

4221 Alves, Júnia de Castro Magalhães and **Marcia Noe.** Myth and madness in Grupo Galpão's expressionistic production of *Album de família.* (*Lat. Am. Theatre Rev.,* 53:2, Spring 2002, p. 19–36)
Third to appear as part of the ongoing research on Galpão by Alves and collaborators, this piece focuses on the use of expressionistic techniques in one key production of the group from Minas Gerais.

4222 Décio de Almeida Prado: um homem de teatro. Organização de João Roberto Faria, Vilma Sant'Anna Arêas e Flávio Aguiar. São Paulo: FAPESP: Edusp, 1997. 443 p.: bibl., ill. (some col.).
A number of key names in Brazilian theater and literature offer personal reminiscences as well as critical and biographical studies in honor of the renowned critic and drama professor who died in 2000.

4223 Faria, João Roberto. Idéias teatrais: o século XIX no Brasil. São Paulo: FAPESP: Editora Perspectiva, 2001. 685 p.: bibl., ill. (Col. Textos; 15)
Award-winning, definitive study of the theater in 19th-century Brazil by the foremost scholar of the genre. The historical study (Pt. I) is complemented by a superbly researched anthology of often difficult to locate criticism and other relevant documents from the period.

4224 George, David Sanderson. Flash & crash days: Brazilian theater in the post dictatorship period. New York; London: Garland, 1999. 1 v.: bibl., index. (Garland reference library of the humanities; 2153. Latin American studies; 19)
Important study of a variety of theatrical modes appearing after the revocation of censorship and other tools of repression. Special attention (fully one-third of the volume) is dedicated to one practitioner (Gerald Thomas); women authors and general considerations about the period share the other two-thirds of the book.

4225 Guimarães, Carmelinda. Antunes Filho: um renovador do teatro brasileiro. Campinas, Brazil: Editora da Univ. Estadual de Campinas, 1998. 183 p.: bibl., ill. (Coleção Viagens da voz)
Biocritical survey of the lengthy career of one of Brazil's foremost stage directors, from the early days at the TBC (Teatro Brasileiro de Comédia) until the Grupo Macunaíma, Centro de Pesquisas Teatrais, and beyond. Appendices include stills from and detailed information about every one of Antunes' stagings.

4226 Levi, Clovis. Teatro brasileiro: um panorama do século XX. Rio de Janeiro: Ministério da Cultura, FUNARTE; São Paulo: Atração Produções Ilimitadas, 1997. 351 p.: bibl., ill. (História visual; 2)
Short, trilingual (Portuguese, Spanish, English) history of the Brazilian theater in the 20th century followed by a superb, 100-plus page collection of stills from hundreds of plays staged all over Brazil.

4227 **Magaldi, Sábato.** Moderna dramaturgia brasileira. v. 1. São Paulo: Editora Perspectiva, 1998. 1 v. (Col. Estudos; 159. Teatro)

In many ways taking off from where the distinguished critic's earlier *Panorama do teatro brasileiro* ended, this volume includes theater criticism from the past four decades.

4228 **Magaldi, Sábato.** Panorama do teatro brasileiro. 3a ed., rev. e ampliada. São Paulo: Global Editora, 1997. 326 p.

Revised edition of the seminal critical history of the Brazilian theater through the early 1960s. The second of the two appendices surveys the most important developments in the Brazilian stage since then.

4229 **Mendes, Oswaldo.** Ademar Guerra: o teatro de um homem só. São Paulo: Editora SENAC São Paulo, 1997. 262 p.: ill.

Part biography part reference material, this homage to the late director includes testimonies from a number of important names in late 20th-century Brazilian theater and a useful catalog of the plays directed by Guerra from the late 1950s-early 1990s.

4230 **Moura, Carlos Eugênio Marcondes de.** O teatro que o povo cria: cordão de pássaros, cordão de bichos, pássaros juninos do Pará: da dramaturgia ao espetáculo. Belém, Brazil: SECULT/PA, 1997. 404 p.: bibl., ill. (some col.).

Well-researched and highly informative study of popular theater and dance of Brazilian Amazon.

4231 **Pontes, Heloisa.** Louis Jouvet e o nascimento da crítica e do teatro modernos no Brasil. (*Novos Estud. CEBRAP*, 58, nov. 2000, p. 113–129, photos)

A brief study of the Brazilian sojourn of the French actor and director and his company in the early 1940s. Author addresses how Jouvet's interaction with audiences, actors, and directors infuenced the beginnings of modern Brazilian stagecraft.

4232 **Sá, Nelson de.** Divers/idade: um guia para o teatro dos anos 90. São Paulo: Editora HUCITEC, 1997. 479 p.: ill. (some col.), index. (Teatro; 33)

A collection of brief reviews of plays staged in São Paulo from 1990–96 by the theater critic of the influential daily *Folha de São Paulo.*

TRANSLATIONS INTO ENGLISH FROM THE SPANISH AND THE PORTUGUESE

CAROL MAIER, *Professor of Spanish, Kent State University*
DAPHNE PATAI, *Professor of Portuguese, University of Massachusetts, Amherst*
MAUREEN AHERN, *Professor of Spanish, Ohio State University*
KATHLEEN ROSS, *Associate Professor of Spanish, New York University*
STEVEN WHITE, *Professor of Spanish; Chair, Department of Modern Languages, St. Lawrence University*

TRANSLATIONS FROM THE SPANISH

BIENNIA INEVITABLY MARK ARBITRARY DIVISIONS and the biennium under review here is no exception. If, however, one extends the review over several biennia, patterns do emerge, making it possible to speak of tendencies, if not trends, that span longer periods of time. Several of those tendencies in the translation into English of literature from Latin America written in Spanish and Portuguese are sufficiently ongoing and influential that they bear mentioning biennium after biennium.

Fortunately, several of those tendencies are positive, which allows one to begin with the encouraging note that, in general, the quality of translations is increasingly high, thanks to both veteran and new translators. Another encouraging phenomenon is the indefatigable efforts of small independent presses, university presses, and journals that continue to publish literature in translation. Given a national economy and even a national culture whose cultural institutions such as the National Endowments for the Arts and the Humanities, might be said to have "protectionist goals,"[1] the work of such presses as Curbstone, Seven Stories, Four Walls Eight Windows, Cinco Puntos, the University of Texas Press and that of Nebraska is of vital importance. The same is true for periodicals such as *The Times Literary Supplement*, *The Washington Post's Book World*, *The New York Review of Books*, which frequently publish reviews that include more than a passing reference to translation. Less frequent, but nevertheless increasing attention is found in *The Nation*, *The New Yorker*, and *The New York Times Book Review*. Many of those periodicals also publish translations, as do some journals. In fact, Adès's translation of Alfonso Reyes's *Homer in Cuernavaca* (see item **4259**), which won a major translation award, was published during this biennium in *Translation and Literature*.

An additional positive trend, if entries in the Bibliography, Theory, and Practice section can be used as an indication, is that translation criticism by translators and translation scholars continues to increase in quantity and quality. The publication of France's *Oxford Guide to Literature in English Translation* (item **4364**) and Classe's *Encyclopedia of Literary Translation into English* (item **4361**) documents this increase, as do some of the excellent articles reviewed in that section, as well as recent writing by translators about their work. An outstanding example of this is Levine's *Manuel Puig and the Spider Woman: His Life and Fictions* (New York: Farrar, Straus and Giroux, 2000). The translator of several of Puig's novels, Levine proved to be as insightful a biographer as she is skilled a translator.

It is also necessary to mention two closely related negative tendencies and to say that given the persistence of these tendencies, they may be considered trends. The first is the relatively small number of translations published and the increasingly commercial interests of the large multinational houses and what Bromley has described as their "faddish habits and tastes."[2] As Ledbetter has remarked, "The rest of the world reads what Americans write, but rarely vice versa."[3] Or, to cite Palettella with respect to poetry, "a meager diet . . . is available annually in the United States."[4] Palettella feels that one reason for the scarcity of poetry in English translation might be the North American public's "love of the familiar" (p. 55) that results in less than adventuresome reading preferences. It also results, he notes, citing work by Owen, in a growing tendency on the part of poets working in languages other than English "to write verse that is easily translatable into English" in hopes of reaching "the recognition of an English-language audience" (p. 56). Ironically, that same love of the familiar may also result in the need Bromley notes for work in translation to "show off a native exoticism that predates our age of conglomeration" (p. 23). Reading about things exotic, like reading about things familiar, allows readers to remain at a remove, refraining from truly participating in work foreign to their sensibilities and preventing a true understanding of other cultures.

The second negative trend involves the absence from many translations of an introduction or even a short note about the author or the context of the original work. This means that the availability of work in translation is compromised by a lack of the information that would make that work truly accessible to readers in English. Some might argue, of course, that readers would be impatient with such information and disregard it or refuse to purchase a book that seemed too "academic." However, those same readers might welcome some orientation. Consider, for example, the comment by reviewer Frase, who remarked about *Cubana: Contemporary Fiction by Cuban Women* (item **4234**) that "the literary history that

Mirta Yañez surveys in her introduction is pathetically skimpy."[5] Frase is led to write a generally negative review and to ask questions and make assumptions about women's writing in Cuba that a better introduction might have made unnecessary. Here is a reader asking for more, not less, information; and her comments make one speculate about how much more impact Latin American literature might have if it were fully contextualized, well distributed, and widely reviewed.

Fortunately, the high quality of many of the books published this biennium and the appearance of several new series, or several coincidence of titles with similar themes, offer hope that English-language translations of creative work from Latin America will receive increasingly greater recognition. Among the books reviewed here, for example, one finds the first English-language editions of several important primary sources for colonial studies, which appear in annotated editions that will be helpful to scholars and ideal for classroom use. These are Arrom's new critical edition of Pane's *An Account of the Antiquities of the Indias* (1498) (item **1835**); Myers and Powell's selection of Madre María de San José's spiritual journals, *A Wild Country Out in the Garden* in an excellent edition that makes colonial women's life writing available in English-language selection (see items **1294** and **3411**); Peters' and Domeier's *The Divine Narcissus/El Divino Narciso,* which makes Sor Juana's brilliant *Auto sacremental* available in English in its entirety for the first time in a superb translation of script for staging (item **4266**); and Nina Scott's bilingual anthology, *Madres del verbo/Mothers of the Word,* a selection of major texts by early Spanish American women writers that makes them available in an annotated, critical selection, ideal for classroom use (item **4238**).

In the same vein, one appreciates the University of New Mexico's Jewish Latin American series, in which several of the books reviewed here appear, as well as additional titles from other presses about the Jewish immigrant experience in Latin America, specifically in Argentina, Ecuador, Uruguay, and Venezuela. A third coincidence, if not a trend, is the publication of an unusually large number of titles (anthologies and novels) from Cuba. No doubt there are several reasons for this, although Bromley summarizes the recent interest in things Cuban in terms of a new generation of young Cuban writers born after the revolution, whose writing exhibits a renewed vibrancy and sensuality and to a "new generation of foreigners" that "is flocking to Cuba" for those qualities and Cuba's "sun, sea, and (diminishing) socialism" (p. 25).

Although no trends have been discerned among the anthologies, it is important to note in particular the fine work in *Prospero's Mirror: A Translators' Portfolio of Latin American Fiction* (item **4247**), a highly original and creative volume edited by Stavans, and two titles devoted to work from Cuba: *ReMembering Cuba: Legacy of a Diaspora,* edited by O'Reilly (item **4345**); *Dream with No Name: Contemporary Fiction from Cuba,* edited by Ponce de León and Ríos Rivera (item **4235**).

Similarly, in poetry there are no marked trends, but the biennium has seen several outstanding translations. Two of those titles are also anthologies: *Pichka Harawikuna: Five Quechua Poets, an Anthology* with translations by Ahern (item **4244**); and *Ül: Four Mapuche Poets, an Anthology* translated by Bierhorst (item **4250**). In addition to the fine translations they contain, these volumes are important because the poets included (from Peru and Chile respectively) revitalize their indigenous heritage by writing in Quechua and Mapudungun and because both volumes include original texts as well as translations. Three additional titles in poetry must also be mentioned: Franzen's translation of Alicia Borinsky's *Collapsible Couple* (item **4254**); De la Torre's work with Gerardo Deniz's *Poemas/Poems* (item

4255); and Englebert's collaborative work with Sosa on *The Return of the River: The Selected Poems of Roberto Sosa* (item **4260**). In fact, the volume by Englebert and Sosa was recently awarded the 2003 National Translation Award sponsored by the American Literary Translators Association (ALTA).

In neither brief fiction nor drama can one point to a trend, although there seems to be an increase in the number of novellas as opposed to short stories. Outstanding volumes in these two categories are collections of short stories: Hurley's translation of Jorge Luis Borges' *Collected Fictions* and Payne's *She-Calf and other Quechua Folk Tales* (items **4263** and **4248**). Payne's volume includes the original Quechua texts, which makes it an especially rich resource.

Among the novels published during the biennium, in addition to the works from Cuba mentioned above, it is important to note the publication of four major 19th-century novels made available in English for the first time or for the first time in their entirety: Nataniel Aguirre's *Juan de la Rosa: Memoirs of the Last Soldier of the Independence Movement: A Novel,* translated by Waisman (item **4272**); Alberto Blest Gana's *Martín Rivas,* translated by O'Dwyer (item **4282**); Clorinda Matto de Turner's *Aves sin nido,* translated by Polt as *Torn from the Nest* (item **4302**); and *Xicoténcatl: An Anonymous Historical Novel About the Events Leading Up to the Conquest of the Aztec Empire,* translated by Castillo-Feliú (item **4327**). Other titles to note in this genre include: *The Forbidden Stories of Marta Veneranda* (Sonia Rivera Valdés), translated by four translators (item **4270**); *Sirena Silena* (Mayra Santos-Febres), translated by Lytle (item **4309**); and three translations of works long-awaited in English: José María Arguedas' *The Fox from Up Above and the Fox from Down Below,* translated by Horning Barraclough (item **4277**); Julio Cortázar's *Final Exam,* translated by MacAdam (item **4289**); and Elena Poniatowska's *Here's to You, Jesusa!,* translated by Heikkinen (item **4305**).

In the essay category, there were fewer publications than in other years. There are some notable titles, however, and there also seems to be a trend toward memoir and the testimonio, demonstrating a broad range of regional and generational voices. Taking these volumes chronologically, the early 19th-century *Memoirs of Fray Servando,* published by the excellent Library of Latin America series at Oxford UP, brings to English readers the quite astounding journeys of a persecuted Mexican friar just prior to independence (item **4341**); also from Mexico, Octavio Paz's intellectual memoir, *Itinerary,* begins in the early part of the 20th century, following the Mexican Revolution (item **4344**); Alejo Carpentier's *Music in Cuba* explores Cuban music and stands as an important text in his own literary production (item **4333**); Ariel Dorfman (*Heading South, Looking North: A Bilingual Journey,* item **4335**) and Marjorie Agosín (*The Alphabet in My Hands: A Writing Life,* item **4330**), within different time frames, both tell of lives divided between North and South America and the effects of exile on the writer. Finally, three testimonials make important contributions in that genre: María de los Reyes Castillo Bueno presents the life of a Cuban mother, laborer, and activist (item **4334**); and Guatemalans Ignacio Bizarro (*Joseño: Another Mayan Voice Speaks from Guatemala,* item **4331**) and Nobel Prize winner Rigoberta Menchú (*Crossing Borders,* item **4340**) present the controversial question of who speaks most credibly for an oppressed and disenfranchised group. The Menchú volume, it should be noted, has been harshly criticized for failing to credit its original Spanish-language editors. (For a discussion of the response generated by this book, "Rigoberta's History within the Guatemalan Context," edited by Arturo Arias. *The Rigoberta Menchú Controversy.* Univ. of Minnesota Press, 2001.)

Publication in reference works and material about theory, as indicated above, has been strong this biennium. In addition to the valuable contribution made by the volumes edited by France and Classe (items **4361** and **4364**), Juliana de Zavalia's essay on the importance of Spanish-American literature in translation in the context of US Latino literature and Waisman's study of translation in the work of Ricardo Piglia are noteworthy entries (items **4367** and **4368**), as is Ribeiro Pires Vieira's article on Haroldo de Campos (published in item **4366**). In the context of this section, it is also important to note that several online journals regularly publish literature in English-language translation, as well as reviews and other information. Some of these will be discussed in *HLAS 62*. In the meantime, one of the newest and most promising of those journals is *Words Without Borders* hosted by Bard College on Annandale-on-Hudson, N.Y. (*http://www.wordswithoutborders.org/*).

As in past years, each of the annotations is followed by the initials of the contributing editor who prepared it. Most of the annotations in "Essays, Interviews, and Reportage" have been prepared by Kathleen Ross, and Carol Maier has been responsible for those in "Bibliography, Theory, and Practice." New this biennium is the particular attention paid by Maureen Ahern to translations of work from the colonial period and the assignment of most poetry titles to Steven White. White, a noted translator, poet, and scholar (and author most recently of *Escanciador de pócimas*—a bilingual edition of poems—and *El mundo más que humano en la poesía de Pablo Antonio Cuadra: un estudio ecocrítico*) joins the editors of this section with the present volume. It is a pleasure to welcome him. [CM, with MA, KR, and SW]

TRANSLATIONS FROM THE PORTUGUESE

The translation of works by Brazilian writers at the present time involves an oddly paradoxical situation. On the one hand, the number of translations published in the years 2000–02 is smaller than that surveyed in previous volumes of *HLAS*. On the other hand, one of the best known authors in the world these days is the Brazilian Paulo Coelho, whose books have sold more than 46 million copies in 56 languages (see "An Interview with Paulo Coelho: The Coming of Age of a Brazilian Phenomenon," by Glauco Ortolano, in *World Literature Today*, April/June 2003, p. 57–59). Even the Brazilian Academy of Letters finally gave in to the pressure of such success, and in 2002 Coelho was elected as the most recent addition to the 40 "Immortals" (by a slim majority—23 votes). Thus, awareness of Brazil, through the persona of Coelho, is at an all-time high, while simultaneously interest in more challenging practitioners of Brazilian literature seems to be waning.

Still, the situation is not altogether dispiriting. Bloomsbury Publishers, no doubt basking in the success of its *Harry Potter* books, is continuing its commitment to contemporary Brazilian literature, and in the past few years has published translations of recent novels by Patrícia Melo and Milton Hatoum, with more titles underway. And Oxford University Press continues its beautifully produced Library of Latin America series, with translations of Brazilian classics by Alencar, Machado and Azevedo prominent in the present crop.

Despite the absence of large numbers of translations, the quality at this time is high, with talented translators such as Colchie, Frizzi, George, Landers, and Rabassa all contributing to the dissemination of Brazilian literature in English. One problem, however, is the tendency of some translators to use politically correct terminology when lexical problems relating to race, gender, and sexuality appear. Thus "homosexual" (even in dialogue) becomes "gay," and "when someone . . ., he . . ." becomes "when someone . . ., they. . . ." These are unfortunate capitulations that have no place in the translation of fiction. In addition, when rhymed verse, no matter how ordinary and tending toward doggerel, appears in the narratives, many translators seem to feel no need to attempt rhymed versions. The result is, unsurprisingly, a clumsy literalness that impedes the narrative and grossly distorts the original.

In this regard, of special note is the significant contribution made by Landers, who, in addition to his own work as a translator, has produced an excellent book on the practice of translation (item **4362**).

NOTES:

1 Siva Vaidhyanathan, "Cultural Policy and the Art of Commerce," *The Chronicle of Higher Education*, 22 June, 2001, p. B9.
2 Carl Bromley. "Cuba Confidential," *In These Times*, 29 April, 2002, p. 25. See also André Schiffrin's eloquent "Missing Out on a World of Scholarship," *The Chronicle of Higher Education*, 6 Oct., 2000, p. B12.
3 James Ledbetter, "The Culture Blockade," *The Nation*, 4 Nov., 2002, p. 39.
4 John Palattella, "Atlas of the Difficult World: The Problem of Global Poetry," *Lingua Franca* (May/June 1999), p. 57.
5 Brenda Frase, "Gregarious Women," *The Hungry Mind Review*, (Fall 1998), p. 11.

ANTHOLOGIES

4233 Contemporary Argentinean women writers: a critical anthology. Edited by Gustavo G. Fares and Eliana Cazaubon Hermann. Translated by Linda Britt. Gainesville: Univ. Press of Florida, 1998. 250 p.: bibl., ill.

Fourteen writers are included in this expanded version of *Escritoras argentinas contemporáneas* (see *HLAS 54:4203*): Canto, Miguel, Diaconu, Gorodischer, Jurado, Lojo, Loubet, Mercader, Orphée, Pagano, Régoli de Mullen, Roffé, Ulla, Vázquez. Substantial introductory essay contextualizes role of women and construction of their writing and identities in Argentine political and cultural life. Format of each chapter consists of short biography, a bibliography, an interview, and a work selected by the writer herself. A model collection for research as well as classroom use. Expert translation renders orality well. [MA]

4234 Cubana: contemporary fiction by Cuban women. Edited by Mirta Yáñez. Foreword by Ruth Behar. Translated by Dick Cluster and Cindy Schuster. Boston: Beacon Press, 1998. 213 p.

Sixteen stories by both established and newer writers, chosen from groundbreaking Cuban anthology *Estatuas de sal* (see *HLAS 56:3560*). Readers will find some fine work here, even if they question Mirta Yáñez's

explanation of authors' common defense of "Cuban identity" and "the female perspective" ("the woman's voice"). Brief information about each author. Disjuncture between Ruth Behar's Foreword and Yáñez's Introduction is worth exploring. [CM]

4235 Dream with no name: contemporary fiction from Cuba. Edited by Juana Ponce de León and Esteban Ríos Rivera. New York: Seven Stories Press, 1999. 303 p.

Excellent collection of 19 stories by several generations of Cuban writers living both on and off the island who candidly address issues of sexuality, politics, and social conflict. Authors include well-known figures such as Reinaldo Arenas and Alejo Carpentier, as well as important new talent. Good translations by a mix of experienced and new translators. Brief but adequate introduction and information about contributors. [CM]

4236 The fat man from La Paz: contemporary fiction from Bolivia. Edited by Rosario Santos. Introduction by Javier Sanjines. New York: Seven Stories Press, 2000. 314 p.

Collection of 20 stories; emphasis on younger authors. Texts 20 pages or less, excepting Jorge Suárez's novella *The other gamecock* (translated by Gregory Rabassa). Six stories by women. Introduction gives sociohistorical background; bio-bibliographical entries for authors. Stories rich in local detail. Excellent for classroom use. [KR]

Fire from the Andes: short fiction by women from Bolivia, Ecuador, and Peru. See item 3546.

4237 González-Esteva, Orlando. Enigma, old friend: the drawings of Juan Soriano. Translated by Peter Bush and Anne McLean. Prologue by Pierre Schneider. Madrid: Ave del Paraíso Ediciones, 2000. 477 p.: ill. (some col.). (Col. de la aurora)

"Juan Soriano's drawings are my home now," writes Cuban-born Orlando González Esteva in introduction to his poetic meditation on the drawings of Mexican artist Soriano (*Amigo enigma: los dibujos de Juan Soriano*—Madrid: Ave del Paraíso Ediciones, 2000). Present work is a beautiful volume offering both fine reproductions of 451 drawings and a skillful English version of González Esteva's monograph. [CM]

4238 Madres del verbo = Mothers of the word; early Spanish-American women writers; a bilingual anthology. Edited, translated, and with an introduction by Nina M. Scott. Albuquerque: Univ. of New Mexico Press, 1999. 395 p.: bibl., ill., index.

Anthology of writing by nine Spanish-American writers from early colonial times to end of the 19th century: Isabel de Guevara, Catalina de Erauso, Sor Juana Inés de la Cruz, Madre Francisca Josefa de Castillo, Gertrudis Gómez de Avellaneda, Juana Manuel Gorriti, Mercedes Cabello de Carbonera, Teresa González de Fanning, and Soledad Acosta de Samper. Each selection, presented in original Spanish with a graceful English translation by Scott, is introduced by a substantial essay that contextualizes biography with history, literature, and reader reception. Notes and extensive bibliography constitute a model anthology, highly recommended for classroom use. [MA]

4239 Mayan folktales: folklore from Lake Atitlán, Guatemala. Translated and edited by James D. Sexton. Albuquerque: Univ. of New Mexico Press, 1999 265 p.

Reprint of 1992 edition (New York: Anchor Books) offers rich panorama of 35 Quiché-Maya folktales from Lake Atitlán region, collected orally *in situ* in 1987–88 by eminent anthropologist editor and his Quiché collaborator Ignacio Bizarro Ujpán.

Scholarly introduction is a valuable orientation to the tales, and fine translations maintain essential orality of the transmission. Notes, references, and a Spanish-English glossary complete this outstanding collection. Highly recommended for the classroom as well as for the general reader. [MA]

4240 Mutual impressions: writers from the Americas reading one another. Edited by Ilan Stavans. Durham, N.C.: Duke Univ. Press, 1999. 326 p.: bibl., index.

"This is a book about neighbors reading each other," Stavans explains. Those neighbors are well-known writers from North and South America, each of whom has written about a writer "from the opposite hemisphere" whose work he/she admired. Selections have been published previously, but here, in this format, they are read in a new, comparative context that should be of interest to scholars and general readers alike. Translations of South American writers' essays provided by various translators. [CM]

4241 Neruda, Pablo. Full woman, fleshly apple, hot moon: selected poems of Pablo Neruda. Translated by Stephen Mitchell. New York: HarperCollins Publishers, 1997. 261 p.

Collection assembled from eight of Neruda's books. Roughly half of the poems are odes, as Mitchell's goal was not to assemble a representative anthology but to work with the poems that he "loved most." He is drawn to "the poetry of his [Neruda's] ripeness," to the poems in which Neruda felt "at home in the world," rather than to his "restlesssness." Brief introduction in which Mitchell states that he "learned and borrowed from" the work of Neruda's previous translators. No biography or bibliography. [CM]

4242 Oblivion and stone: a selection of contemporary Bolivian poetry and fiction. Selected and edited by Sandra Reyes. Translated by John DuVal *et al.* Fayetteville: Univ. of Arkansas Press, 1998. 273 p.

Collection of work by 22 poets (four are women) and 18 short story writers (two are women) born between 1912–67. Poetry is presented with Spanish *en face*; prose in English only. Schematic three-page introduction by Reyes describes contemporary Bolivian writing as "realistic, sometimes abstract, but always down-to-earth." Notes on contributing authors contain limited bibliographic information. [SFW]

4243 The Picador book of Latin American stories. Edited by Carlos Fuentes and Julio Ortega. London: Picador, 1999. 333 p.

Selection of 39 classic short stories by major writers emphasizes urban, cosmopolitan experience. Authors range from mid-20th century to early 1990s and include Borges, Cortázar, García Márquez, Guimarães Rosa, Lispector, Piñón, Ribeyro, Fuentes, Pacheco, and Puga, but no younger writers from past decade. Distinguished translators, short biographies, and useful introduction by Fuentes and Ortega highly recommend it for general classroom use. [MA]

4244 Pichka harawikuna: five Quechua poets; an anthology. Edited and introduced by Julio Noriega Bernuy. Translated by Maureen Ahern. New York: Americas Society; Pittsburgh, Penn.: Latin American Literary Review Press, 1998. 91 p.: bibl. (Poetry in indigenous languages)

Includes work by five contemporary Peruvian poets (two are women) writing in both Spanish and Quechua due to what editor calls "their dual cultural ties." Spanish text *en face* with English translation; Quechua text follows separately. Brief introduction for each poet with more formal bibliography of poets' works. [SFW]

4245 Poesia Latinoamericana antología bilingüe = Latin-America poetry bilingual anthology. Bogotá: Epsilon Editores, 1998. 215 p.: ill.

Anthology includes 32 contemporary poets (16 are women) from 14 Latin American countries. Original Spanish texts appear on right-hand page. Work by Manoel de Andrade from Brazil appears in English and Spanish but not Portuguese. Translations of introductory material are nonidiomatic and confusing. Biographical notes include no dates of birth. [SFW]

4246 The precarious: the art and poetry of Cecilia Vicuña. Edited by M. Catherine de Zegher. Hanover, N.H.; London: Univ. Press of New England, 1997. 250 p.: bibl., facsims., ill. (some col.), index, ports.

Two-part book that is both visual and verbal. One half of volume is collection of essays about Vicuña's work as poet and visual artist, along with photos by artist and

writer César Peternosto. Other half is Esther Allen's fine translation of Vicuña's *quipoem.* Together, the two parts provide excellent introduction to Vicuña's esthetics. [CM]

4247 Prospero's mirror: a translator's portfolio of Latin American short fiction. Edited and with introduction by Ilan Stavans. Willimantic, Conn.: Curbstone Press, 1998. 319 p.

Unusual and engaging bilingual anthology in which Stavans has collected 16 stories, each selected, translated, and introduced by a different translator. Stories and translations are of high quality, and translators' comments about the stories are witty and informative. Authors include well-known figures as well as writers who will be new to North American readers. Introduction summarizes role of translation in the Americas. [CM]

4248 The she-calf and other Quechua folk tales. Compiled, translated, and edited by Johnny Payne. Albuquerque: Univ. of New Mexico Press, 2000. 271 p.

Bilingual English/Quechua edition of the Spanish/Quechua version originally published as *Cuentos cuzqueños* (Cuzco, Peru: Centro de Estudios Rurales Andinos Bartolomé de las Casas, 1984). Contains 30 stories collected and transcribed by the translator, which narrate the secular and the sacred in sensitive translations that capture orality and humor of original Quechua telling. Payne's insightful memoir of his time among Quechua families in village of San Jerónimo, Cuzco, offers his reflections on being an outsider engaged in collecting, writing, and translating oral popular culture. Recommended for pleasure and research, and as a vehicle for discussion of cultural issues. Highly commendable for bilingual format that provides access to original Quechua. [MA]

4249 Short stories in Spanish. Edited by John R. King. London; New York: Penguin Books, 1999. 233 p. (New Penguin parallel texts)

Ten stories chosen by John R. King as "representative . . . of writing throughout the Hispanic world over the last 25 years or so." Four of the five authors are well-known in English, but Peruvian Julio Ramón Ribeyro is not, and his presence is welcome. Interesting parallel and bilingual format, but, unfortunately, introductory material is scant and almost no information is given about authors or translators. [CM]

4250 Ül: four Mapuche poets; an anthology. Edited and introduced by Cecilia Vicuña. Translated by John Bierhorst. New York: Americas Society; Pittsburgh, Penn.: Latin American Literary Review Press, 1998. 143 p.: bibl. (Poetry in indigenous languages)

In sociohistorical introduction Vicuña explains that Chile has substantial number of indigenous people: "Today, out of a population of 14 million, 1 million are Mapuche." Texts of indigenous language Mapudungan appear for Elicura Chihuailaf and Leonel Lienlaf. Includes thorough introductions for each poet, a glossary, and bibliography on Mapuche culture. [SFW]

4251 Voices from the silence: Guatemalan literature of resistance. Edited by Marc Zimmerman and Raúl Rojas with the collaboration of Patricio Navia. Texts translated by Zimmerman with the collaboration of Robert Scott Curry, Linda Thelma Campos, Preston Browning, Brad Stull, and Anne Woerhle. Athens: Ohio Univ. Center for International Studies, 1998. 545 p.: bibl., index. (Monographs in international studies. Latin American series; 28)

The companion volume to *Literature and resistance in Guatemala* (Athens: Ohio Univ. Center for International Studies, 1995), this book is "almost a direct translation," a revised edition of *Guatemala: voces desde el silencio* (Guatemala: Editorial Oscar de León Palacios; Editorial Palo de Hormigo, 1993), which Zimmerman describes as "the fourth and final 'collage epic'" in a series of Latin American texts. Book offers both an extensive example of genre that Zimmerman finds "encoded" in the work of such poets as Ernesto Cardenal and Roque Dalton, and a thorough explanation of the work and purpose of Zimmerman and his collaborators. [CM]

TRANSLATIONS FROM THE SPANISH
Poetry

4252 Alegría, Claribel. Saudade = Sorrow. Translated by Carolyn Forché. Willimantic, Conn.: Curbstone Press, 1999. 103 p.

This Nicaraguan-born Salvadoran poet has been publishing her poetry and prose for more than 50 years. *Sorrow* pays homage to poet's deceased husband Darwin ("Bud") Flakoll, who translated many of her works into English. Bilingual edition of 47 poems includes long and intimate Translator's Preface in which award-winning Forché speaks of these poems and their "knowledge of the power the living have on behalf of the dead." [SFW]

4253 Alfonso, Rodolfo. Just poetry = Justo poesía. Kearney, Nebr.: Morris Pub., 1998. 154 p.: ill., index.

In rather predictable poetry Cuban-born author addresses "the tyrannical satrap Castro and his hounds," and proclaims that "a man without God is like a heart without a soul." Poet writes in both English and Spanish, and informs reader in a note that original text is placed on the left on even-numbered pages and translation is located on the right. [SFW]

4254 Borinsky, Alicia. The collapsible couple. Translated by Cola Franzen in collaboration with the author. London: Middlesex Univ. Press, 2000. 150 p. (World literature series)

Exemplary bilingual volume. Collaboration between translator and author has rendered *La pareja desmontable* (Buenos Aires: Corregidor, 1994), a humorous and at times satirical but poignant collection of poems, into an equally impressive English volume. Includes review by Saúl Yurkevich of original Spanish, and an interview with Alicia Borinsky by Louisa K. Rol providing information about her writing and work with Franzen. [CM]

4255 Deniz, Gerardo. Poemas = poems. Edición y traducción = Edited and translated by Mónica de la Torre. México: Ditoria/Lost Roads Publishers, 2000. 139 p.: ill. (some col.).

Excellent collection. Mónica de la Torre has chosen several poems from eight books by Deniz (pen name Juan Almela), one of Mexico's most widely read poets. Deniz deserves a wider reading than he has received in US. His work is challenging, but translations render it admirably in English. Together with de la Torre's preliminary note and Josué Ramírez's adulatory but informative afterword, volume provides a good introduction to Deniz's work. [CM]

4256 Huerta, Efraín. 500,000 azaleas: the selected poems of Efraín Huerta. Translated by Jim Normington. Edited by Jack Hirschman. Introduction by Ilan Stavans. Willimantic, Conn.: Curbstone Press, 2001. 201 p.

Stavans describes Mexican poet Efraín Huerta (1914–82) as "very much a political animal: his vision of the urban landscape is fatalistic, of millions of people forming a river of anonymity and indifference." In "Confusion," Huerta claims he doesn't comprehend those who used to teach him Marxism since "Some are/in prison/Others are/in power." Editor includes list of books by the poet, whose work appears amply in English for the first time in this anthology. [SFW]

4257 Maciel, Olivia. Luna de cal: limestone moon. Chicago, Ill.: Black Swan Press, 2000. 1 v.

Collection of 39 poems in three sections, entitled "Limestone Moon," "Geomancy," and "Quince Moon," by contemporary Mexican-born poet. The moon often illuminates landscapes of Mexico and Europe in this poetry. "A Mexican woman intoxicated by that which is holy" appears in "Jerusalem Syndrome." A biographical note mentions that author received the José Martí literary award. [SFW]

4258 Neruda, Pablo. Neruda at Isla Negra: prose poems by Pablo Neruda. Translated by Maria Jacketti, Dennis Maloney, and Clark M. Zlotchew. Photographs by Milton Rogovin. Foreword by Marjorie Agosín. Afterword by Ariel Dorfman. Fredonia, N.Y.: White Pines Press, 1998. 1 v.

Collection of three works by Nobel Prize-winning Chilean author who died in 1973: *The house in the sand* (*HLAS* 52:4950), *The stones of Chile* (*HLAS* 50:4251), and *Seaquake* (*HLAS* 56:4046 and 4543). No supporting materials included in this bilingual edition. [SFW]

4259 Reyes, Alfonso. Homer in Cuernavaca. Translated by Timothy Adès. (*Trans. Lit./Edinburgh*, 9:1, 2000, p. 91–105)

This translation of 30-sonnet sequence by Mexican poet Alfonso Reyes was awarded UK's prestigious Valle-Inclán Prize in 2001. Adès is especially careful to preserve formal

aspects of original Spanish poems in his English versions. In "Homer," poem's speaker relishes the Greek bard who composed *The Iliad:* "He keeps me company for my delight." [SFW]

4260 Sosa, Roberto. The return of the river: the selected poems of Roberto Sosa. Translated by Jo Anne Engelbert. Willimantic, Conn.: Curbstone Press, 2002. 263 p.

En face volume, the result of years of creative teamwork by translator and poet, gathers 30 years of poetic production by Honduras' major poet. Sosa has selected more than 100 compositions from his earliest chapbooks; the prize-winning *Los pobres* (Madrid: Ediciones Rialp, 1969); *Un mundo para todos dividido* (1971 Casa de las Américas Prize—La Habana: Casa de las Américas, 1971); and verse written in Tegucigalpa in 1996. Called a "political poet with a romantic vision" (Hamill), Sosa writes over a wide range of topics, metrics, and forms that combine the personal and political through startling imagery that illuminates even the most ordinary meditations: "In the fullness of its days/the Old Pontiac is a garden in bloom;" "the common grief" of mothers and daughters of the disappeared who wait, "heads unbowed/fused stitch by stitch like a scab to the sutures of a wound;" portraits of hideous generals and dictators, one so swollen with crime that he glistens like a pig, and another a boa constrictor who swallows up Guatemala. Englebert's luminous English texts retain the full force of Sosa's brilliant imagery; the awe he finds in the ordinary; the fusion of pain and beauty; the monsters of oppression; "the tug of sadness" that pervades his life of poetry; exile and the "dream of a society free of the antihuman nightmare and its fabricated image." This definitive collection of an important Central American poet is highly recommended for classroom and scholarly use. For commentary on the 6th edition of *Un mundo para todos dividido,* see *HLAS* 50:3667. [MA]

Brief Fiction and Theater

4261 Basualto, Alejandra. Territorio exclusivo y otros relatos = Exclusive territory and other stories. Translation by Martha J. Manier. Santiago: La Trastienda, 1999. 139 p.

Bilingual *en face* edition of 20 short

stories selected from three collections by this Chilean writer: *Territorio exclusivo* (Santiago: La Trastienda, 1991); *Desacato al bolero* (Santiago: La Trastienda, 1994); and *La mujer de yeso* (see *HLAS 52:3767*). Many stories mix fantastic events and surprise endings in a style reminiscent of Cortázar. No introduction or biography on this author, who is relatively unknown outside Chile. Adequate translation. [MA]

4262 Benítez Rojo, Antonio. A view from the mangrove. Translated by James E. Maraniss. Amherst: Univ. of Massachusetts Press, 1998. 243 p.

Collection of stories, most not published previously in either Spanish or English. Brief introduction by author provides context for each story. Spanish not available for review, but stories read well and Maraniss is known for his fine translation of Benítez Rojo's *La isla que se repite* (*The Repeating Islands*). [CM]

4263 Borges, Jorge Luis. Collected fictions. Translated by Andrew Hurley. New York: Viking, 1998. 565 p.

Hurley's translation of complete collection of Borges' brief fictions represents a major accomplishment and a major contribution. And it has been received as such, albeit with questioning of particular readings and decisions that one would expect in the case of work not only highly influential and revered, but also frequently translated. Hurley provides only a brief "Note" on his translation as a whole, but his notes to individual stories include translation issues as well as textual annotations. [CM]

4264 Casey, Calvert. The collected stories. Translations by John H.R. Polt. Edited and with Introduction by Ilan Stavans. Durham, N.C.: Duke Univ. Press, 1998. 193 p. (Latin America in translation/en traducción/em tradução)

Casey was a Cuban American brought up in Havana, who worked in the US, Rome, and Havana. Known in Cuba as "La Calvita," "Calver," or "Cal," he was part of the circle of Cuban gay writers and intellectuals who worked on the weekly *Lunes de Revolución*, but later became disaffected and went into exile. The 17 stories in this collection date from 1954 to shortly before the writer's death in 1969; his short story "The Walk" is published here for the first time. "Each of his stories is an exploration of the act of survival of the weakest on the margins of society," Stavans points out in his useful introduction. Polt's smooth translations are based on author's final versions and modifications of his manuscripts. [MA]

4265 Five plays in translation from Mexican contemporary theater: a new golden age. Edited by Salvador Rodríguez del Pino. Lewiston, N.Y.: Edwin Mellen Press, 2001. 279 p.: bibl. (Hispanic literature; 42)

These five plays from late 1980s-early 2000s offer a cross-section of contemporary Mexican theater: *On the way to the concert* (*De camino al concierto*) by Marcela del Río; *The dandy of the Savoy* by Carlos Olmos; *Soldiers will be soldiers* by Eduardo Rodríguez Solís; *Picture perfect* (*Las bellas imágenes*) by Pablo Salinas; and *Limited capacity* (*Cupo limitado*) by Tomás Urtusástegui. Four are preceded by interviews with the playwright (three conducted by Rodríguez del Pino), and translated by various translators. Urtusástegui's essay on his own work offers an individual perspective on the Mexican theater scene of this period. Prologue by George Woodyard, a brief introduction by editor, and a short select bibliography supplement the plays. The scripts in translation and their contextual materials are valuable for the growing interest in staging these pieces in the US. [MA]

4266 Juana Inés de la Cruz, Sor. The divine Narcissus = El divino Narciso. Translated and annotated by Patricia A. Peters and Renée Domeier. Albuquerque: Univ. of New Mexico Press, 1998. 202 p.: bibl.

First English translation of Sor Juana's one-act allegorical *auto sacramental* and its interlude, or *loa*, in its entirety. Sor Juana envisions central Catholic mysteries of the Eucharist and the Crucifixion in terms of female experience: the pronoun for Human Nature is *she*; Grace is female; and Satan bears the name of Echo and a woman's costume in the love triangle of Human Nature, Echo, and Narcissus. In the humorous *loa*, the Spanish couple Zeal and Religion debate the nature of the true God—and colonization—with the Aztec prince and princess Occident and America. Peters' and Domier's superb translation respects original Hispanic roots, yet creates graceful, dramatic language that replicates English speech rhythms and uses imagery to convey baroque repetition, producing a delightful dramatic vehicle for English-speaking actors and audiences. *En face* access to baroque original and a critical introduction discussing translation strategies recommend this script for staging as well as reading. For a review of the original Spanish-language version, *El divino Narciso*, see *HLAS 34:3245*. [MA]

4267 López Ortega, Antonio. Moonlit: stories. Translated by Nathan Budoff. Cambridge, Mass.: Lumen Editions, 1998. 224 p.

Translation of Venezuelan writer's *Lunar* (Caracas: Fundarte, Alcaldía de Caracas, 1997), a volume of 75 very brief stories (*microcuentos*). Lyrical tone of stories—many set in Venezuela—combines with sometimes Gothic, violent endings. Skillful translation communicates poetic voice. Not geared for classroom use; no locating materials, notes or biographical information. [KR]

4268 Peri Rossi, Cristina. The museum of useless efforts. Translated by Tobias Hecht. Lincoln: Univ. of Nebraska Press, 2001. 156 p. (European women writers series)

Given these intriguing stories and Tobias Hecht's careful translation of *El museo de esfuerzos inútiles* (Barcelona: Seix Barral, 1983), the first-time reader of Peri Rossi will no doubt regret absence of information about the author or her work. Peri Rossi, a well-known Uruguayan writer-in-exile who now lives in Spain, merits far more attention than she has received in the US, where her themes of politics, sexuality, and language would interest many readers. [CM]

4269 Porzecanski, Teresa. Sun inventions: Perfumes of Carthage; two novellas. Sun inventions translated by Johnny Payne. Perfumes of Carthage translated by Phyllis Silverstein. Introduction by Ilan Stavans. Albuquerque: Univ. of New Mexico Press, 2000. 189 p. (Jewish Latin America)

Two semi-autobiographical narratives by one of Uruguay's most talented writers bring alive experiences of a Jewish family with Sephardim and Ashkenazi roots in River Plate region of 1930s. Skillful translations illuminate Porzecanski's prose, which Stavans calls "an anthropology of the imagination." Recommended for classroom discus-

sion of women and multicultural families in urban Latin America. [MA]

4270 Rivera-Valdés, Sonia. The forbidden stories of Marta Veneranda. Translated by Dick Cluster, Marina Harss, Mark Schafer, and Alan West. New York: Seven Stories Press, 2001. 158 p.

Excellent translation of *Las historias prohibidas de Marta Veneranda* (see item 3522), winner of 1997 Casa de las Américas prize for short stories. Collection also could be considered a novel, since each of the nine stories was told to Marta Veneranda, a fictional narrator who says that she transcribed them all while conducting research for a dissertation that she abandoned in favor of letting protagonists speak for themselves. And speak they do, making it unnecessary for reader to have explanatory material about complex, cross-cultural world in which they live. [CM]

4271 Romero, Denzil. Belated declaration of love to Séraphine Louis: a bilingual, critical edition of Denzil Romero's short stories. Edited and translated by Stephen J. Clark. Critical introduction by Antonio M. Isea. Lanham, Md.: Univ. Press of America, 2000. 132 p.: bibl., index.

Bilingual selection of eight stories that feature surreal erotic episodes set in historical frames, very much in the vein of Cortázar. Long essay by Isea situates Romero's writing within context of modern Venezuelan narrative, and also discusses Romero's historical novels. Translation reads very naturally, and a bibliography of and about Romero's writing is included. [MA]

Novels

4272 Aguirre, Nataniel. Juan de la Rosa: memoirs of the last soldier of the independence movement; a novel. Translated by Sergio Gabriel Waisman. Edited with a foreword by Alba María Paz-Soldán. New York: Oxford Univ. Press, 1998. 329 p.: bibl., maps. (Library of Latin America)

First English translation of the historical novel (*Juan de la Rosa: memorias del último soldado de la independencia*) that constructed Bolivia as a nation. Originally published in *El Heraldo* in Cochabamba in 1885, then as a book in 1909 which this edition closely follows. Col. Juan de la Rosa's memoirs confront 19th-century history of Bolivia and allegorize its passage into modernity. This work was first Bolivian novel that assumed a national reading public that shared the values of the "Bolivian nation." Incisive essay by Paz-Soldán contextualizes Andean politics of independence movement (1809–25). Superb translation captures tone and register of early-19th century speech. Especially valuable for reader orientation are notes prepared by the translator for historical Quechua language references. Highly recommended for classroom and scholarly use. [MA]

4273 Alberto, Eliseo. Caracol Beach. Translated by Edith Grossman. New York: Alfred A. Knopf, 2000. 286 p.

The outgrowth of a fiction workshop directed by Gabriel García Márquez, written at his suggestion, and dedicated to him, *Caracol Beach* could not have found a better translator than Edith Grossman, who has translated much of García Márquez's recent work. Novel's plot, which takes place in Florida over period of two days, is too complex to be summarized quickly; but its tale of a guilt-written Cuban veteran who fought in and survived war in Angola is gripping, and absence of orientation or notes will not be an impediment to readers in English. For comment on original Spanish-language novel, see item **3468.** [CM]

4274 Allende, Isabel. Daughter of fortune: a novel. Translated by Margaret Sayers Peden. New York: HarperCollins, 1999. 399 p.: map.

Translation of *Hija de la fortuna*, romance set in mid-19th-century Chile and California. Historical descriptions of English colony in Chile, gold rush in California, Chinese immigrants, and culture. Touches of magical realism for which Allende is well known. Skillful translation by Peden. For review of original Spanish work, *Hija de la fortuna*, see **3622.** [KR]

4275 Andahazi, Federico. The anatomist. Translated by Alberto Manguel. New York: Doubleday, 1998. 215 p.

In this historical novel (see *HLAS 58:3751* for comment on Spanish-language original), a 16th-century physician who tests scores of prostitutes to discover the organ that governs women's sexuality must clear

his name of charge of heresy to gain his freedom from imprisonment by the Inquisition. Based on an actual historical case, novel caused a scandal in Buenos Aires when it was a awarded a prize that was then revoked (*The New York Times*, May 17, 1997). Manguel captures semilyrical, semisardonic tone of Spanish original, but an introduction for the English-language reader is sorely lacking. [MA]

4276 Andahazi, Federico. The merciful women. Translated by Alberto Manguel. New York: Grove Press, 2000. 188 p.

Translation of *Las piadosas* (see item **3669**). Set in 1816, story reimagines Mary Shelley's invention of the Gothic novel alongside development of competing novel by another character, Byron's manservant Polidori. Andahazi's own framing follows Gothic conventions of violence, sexuality, horror. Complex but engaging plot, elegantly translated to convey 19th-century style. [KR]

4277 Arguedas, José María. The fox from up above and the fox from down below. Translated by Frances Horning Barraclough. Edited by Julio Ortega. Pittsburgh, Penn.: Univ. of Pittsburgh Press, 2000. 326 p.: bibl. (The Pittsburgh editions of Latin American literature) (Col. Archivos)

Long-awaited critical English-language edition of one of the most powerful narratives in modern Latin American literature (see *HLAS 54:3996*). Ortega's incisive introduction analyzes how this text confers "meaning to a dying life and to a vivifying death" on many levels, as interpolation that "gives power to the fiction in the document, to the novel as testimony, and to narrative as autobiographical act." Barraclough's finely nuanced translation meets formidable challenge of hybrid coastal and Andean voices that erupt in visceral mestizo orality that generates "a veritable swarm of discourses" (Rowe). This stunning volume includes glossary for Quechua and Spanish cultural references; critical essays by William Rowe, Christian Fernández, and Sara Castro-Klaren; and bibliography of works by and about Arguedas. Essential text for students and scholars alike. Arguedas' life closed, but his great novel remains open. [MA]

4278 Argueta, Manlio. Little Red Riding Hood in the red light district: a novel. Translated by Edward Waters Hood. Willimantic, Conn.: Curbstone Press, 1998. 237 p.

In translator's note, Hood provides biographical and political background necessary for fuller appreciation of this work by Salvadoran author (see *HLAS 42:5261*). Argueta's novels have a "testimonial format" and reflect conflictive history of his country during 1970s-80s. Here, Argueta creates a mosaic of colliding first-person narratives.

4279 Argueta, Manlio. A place called Milagro de la Paz. Translated by Michael B. Miller. Willimantic, Conn.: Curbstone Press, 2000. 206 p.

Argueta's fifth novel *Milagro de la Paz* (San Salvador: Istmo Editores, 1994) continues his narration of daily life and survival in El Salvador in midst of violence, poverty, and repression. Lyrical story of a widowed mother and her daughters, told in short vignettes. Excellent translation preserves local tone. Includes glossary for Spanish words and author's biography. [KR]

4280 Bencastro, Mario. Odyssey to the north. Translated by Susan Giersbach Rascón. Houston, Tex.: Arte Público Press, 1998. 192 p.

Odisea del norte (Houston, Tex.: Arte Público Press, 1999) examines push and pull factors that explain causes of immigration from Central America to US in 1980s, as well as difficulties faced by the new immigrants once they reach Latino barrios in US urban centers. The Salvadoran author, born in 1949, is also a playwright, which explains this novel's emphasis on dialogue and dramatic courtroom scenes involving political refugees. [SFW]

4281 Berman, Sabina. Bubbeh. Translated by Andrea G. Labinger. Pittsburgh, Penn.: Latin American Literary Review Press, 1998. 90 p. (Series Discoveries)

Taking the title from Yiddish word for grandmother, this novella (*La bobe*—México: Editorial Planeta Mexicana, 1990) by one of Mexico's most distinguished playwrights and directors weaves together the stories of three generations of women in a Jewish community of Mexico City in 1960s. Labinger's translation of colloquial dialogue is smooth, but there is no introductory material. [MA]

4282 Blest Gana, Alberto. Martín Rivas: a novel. Translated by Tess O'Dwyer. Introduction by Jaime Concha. New York: Oxford Univ. Press, 2000. 389 p.

Thanks to a lengthy, comprehensive introduction and a highly readable translation, English-speaking readers now have access to *Martin Rivas* (1862), probably the best-known and most widely-read work of Chilean literature. Concha's introduction provides not only an overview of Blest Gana's life and work, but also a detailed explanation of the period in which the novel's events occur (1851). O'Dwyer's rendition of 19th-century English may make readers wince in places, but her reading of Spanish text is reliable. [CM]

4283 Borinsky, Alicia. Dreams of the abandoned seducer. Translated by Cola Franzen in collaboration with the author. Lincoln: Univ. of Nebraska Press, 1998. 211 p. (Latin American women writers)

Originally published as *Sueños del seductor abandonado: novela vodevil* (Buenos Aires: Corregidor, 1995). Playful, surreal novel told in very short chapters with whimsical, humorous headings. Loosely woven plot involving several female characters; erotic component; colloquial, colorful language. Convincingly translated with author's collaboration. Short translator's note; brief interview with Borinsky following text. [KR]

4284 Boullosa, Carmen. Leaving Tabasco. Translated by Geoff Hargreaves. New York: Grove Press, 2001. 244 p.

Translation of *Treinta años* (México: Alfaguara, 1999). Coming-of-age novel narrates childhood of Delmira, growing up in village of Agustini. Told from child's perspective, tone is alternately magical, ironic, funny, and sad. Translation rather flat; little flavor of original language. No locating material. [KR]

4285 Boullosa, Carmen. They're cows, we're pigs. Translated by Leland H. Chambers. New York: Grove Press, 1997. 180 p.

Translation of *Son vacas, somos puercos: filibusteros del Mar Caribe* (see *HLAS 54:3704*). Although Spanish subtitle is omitted, author has added informative preface to her picaresque novel. There she also explains that book is retelling of widely retold 17th-century account of buccaneer "pigs" and "cows" who were loyal to and represented Spanish monarchy (see *History of the buccaneers of America* by Burney). This is Boullosa's first book to be translated into English, and some material about her and her work would have been appropriate. [CM]

4286 Castellanos, Rosario. The book of lamentations. Translated and with afterword by Esther Allen. Introduction by Alma Guillermoprieto. New York: Penguin Books, 1998. 381 p. (Penguin twentieth-century classics)

Excellent translation of *Oficio de tinieblas* (México: J. Mortiz, 1962), set in Chiapas, Castellanos' home region. Narration of 19th-century indigenous rebellion, reimagined as 1930s event. Unforgiving portrayal of violence and injustice, and their impact on all social and racial groups concerned. Introduction, glossary, translator's afterword locate author and her work. Outstanding. [KR]

4287 Castillo, Roberto. The bugler = El corneta. Translated by Edward Waters Hood. Lanham, Md.: Univ. Press of America, 2000. 134 p.: bibl.

Bilingual edition of 1981 novella (Tegucigalpa: Guaymuras) by Honduran author known for short stories. Picaresque tale of poor boy from Honduran countryside, his travels and mishaps. Colloquial, third-person narration; translation captures local tone, humor. English version of author's 1995 preface (not translated by Hood) unfortunately awkward and inaccurate. Short introduction and bibliography locate author and work. [KR]

4288 Cerda, Carlos. To die in Berlin. Translated by Andrea G. Labinger. Pittsburgh, Penn.: Latin American Literary Review Press, 1999. 176 p.

The characters in this novel (see *HLAS 56:3770* for comment on Spanish original) are Chileans living in East Germany as a result of the 1973 military coup in their country. Particularly chilling are the parallels that the author draws between concentration camps separated by space and time and the general population's unwillingness to acknowledge their existence: "It's Buchenwald and Weimar; it's Chacabuco and Chile." [SFW]

4289 Cortázar, Julio. Final exam. Translated by Alfred Mac Adam. New York: New Directions, 1999. 256 p.

El examen is one of Cortázar's earliest novels, written in 1950 but not published until 1986 (see *HLAS 52:3822*). On the night before their final exam, four young Argentines encounter strange happenings as they wander through the streets and plazas of Buenos Aires. The dense experimental style of this "darkly funny" narrative prefigures Cortázar's later *Blow-Up* and *Hopscotch* (*Rayuela*). The juxtaposition of personal crises of relationships with crisis of Argentine civil society is eerily familiar to 21st-century readers, as are the characters who, even though fiercely *porteño*, "view the nation as pure façade, a fraud." At the border where realism and hallucination blur, Mac Adam's expert rendition of *porteño* vernacular offers the reader the distinctive flavor of Cortázar's hallmark style in the making. [MA]

4290 Demitrópulos, Libertad. River of sorrows. Translated by Mary G. Berg. Buffalo, N.Y.: White Pine Press, 2000. 147 p. (Secret weavers series; 14)

Translation of *Río de congojas* (1981). Translator Berg provides brief but informative preface to the novel, which takes place in 16th-century Argentina in years following Juan de Garay's founding of Santa Fe. She explains, however, that narrative makes clear that "official history" of Argentina at time novel was written closely parallels period in which it is set. [CM]

4291 Domecq, Brianda. The astonishing story of the Saint of Cabora. Translated by Kay S. García. Tempe, Ariz.: Bilingual Press/Editorial Bilingüe, 1998. 362 p.

Translation of *La insólita historia de la Santa de Cabora* (see *HLAS 54:3710*). Fictional re-creation, set in late 19th-century Mexico, of the life of Teresa Urrea, famous for healing powers and work with the poor. Political backdrop of social injustice, oppression under Porfirio Díaz's rule. Narration shifts between Teresa's story and that of woman trying to research it in present time. Clearly translated. Very short glossary; back cover note; no other locating information. [KR]

4292 Estévez, Abilio. Thine is the kingdom: a novel. Translated by David L. Frye. New York: Arcade Pub.; Boston: Little, Brown and Co., 1999. 327 p.

Translation of *Tuyo es el reino* (see **3489**). First novel by well-known Cuban writer of theater and stories. Set in 1950s Marianao (Havana suburb); populated by a large cast of exaggerated, if not fantastic, characters. Frequently changing point of view, time frame, and narrative interventions exposing story as fiction. Many literary, artistic, historical references; some explained in translator's notes. Good translation of challenging prose. [KR]

4293 Feierstein, Ricardo. Mestizo. Translated by Stephen A. Sadow. Introduction by Ilan Stavans. Albuquerque: Univ. of New Mexico Press, 2000. 335 p. (Jewish Latin America)

In this detective novel, first published in Argentina and based on extensive archival research on Jewish immigration (see *HLAS* 52:3827), and set against the story of four generations of a Jewish family, the police try to solve an assassination and a lost man ties to reconstruct his identity. Three parts and an epilogue span a century of cataclysms ranging from WWI, the Russian Revolution, and birth of the state of Israel to military dictatorships in Argentina. The smooth and natural translation includes notes by the translator. Recommended for classroom use. [MA]

4294 Freilich de Segal, Alicia. Cláper. Translated by Joan E. Friedman. Albuquerque: Univ. of New Mexico Press, 1998. 182 p.

Work relates a wide range of Jewish experience in Venezuela through contrasting monologues, one voiced by the father, Max, an Eastern European immigrant; and another by his daughter, a second-generation Venezuelan intellectual. Title is from Yiddish for peddler or "schlepper," as Max describes himself. The brief introduction and smooth translation of the double registers make this a good choice for classroom discussion. For comment on Spanish-language original, see *HLAS* 52:3764. [MA]

4295 Fuentes, Carlos. The crystal frontier: a novel in nine stories. Translated by Alfred Mac Adam. San Diego: Harcourt Brace, 1998. 266 p. (A Harvest book)

La frontera de cristal was published in 1995 (México: Aguilar, Altea, Taurus, Alfaguara) and in a prior English-language edition (New York: Farrar, Strauss and Giroux, 1997). Cultural conflicts between generations and classes on Mexico/US border generate lives of transgression, betrayal, and tragedy linked by their immersion in the web of power spun by business tycoon Leonardo Barroso. A lustful godfather, women in the maquila plants, a chef who returns to Mexico, a gay medical student at Cornell, and service workers in New York City are only a few of the protagonists in these borderland dramas. No introductory material, but Mac Adam's skillful translation of vernacular dialogue makes for engrossing reading. [MA]

4296 Fuentes, Carlos. The years with Laura Díaz. Translated by Alfred J. Mac Adam. New York: Farrar, Straus and Giroux, 2000. 516 p.

Translation of *Los años con Laura Díaz* (Madrid: Alfaguara, 1999). Grand historical novel chronicles life of title character and her descendants through entire sweep of 20th century. Figures from Mexican history, politics, and art populate story, notably Diego Rivera and Frida Kahlo. Relatively short (15–20 p.) chapters, titled by place and date, proceed chronologically. No locating materials. Fine translation. [KR]

4297 González, Gaspar Pedro. Return of the Maya. Translated by Susan Giersbach Rascón with assistance of Fernando Peñalosa and Janet Sawyer. Rancho Palos Verdes, Calif.: Yax Te' Foundation, 1998. 173 p.

Translation of *El retorno de los mayas* (1998), which is sequel to *La otra cara* (see *HLAS* 56:3536; translation: *A Mayan life*— Rancho Palos Verdes, Calif.: Yax Te' Press, 1995). Narrator, a Q'anjob'al-speaking Guatemalan ("the orphan"), warns that his tale is not a happy one because he recounts Mayas' suffering as well as their resistance and resilience. A moving novel for which one wishes there was a far more informative introduction. [CM]

4298 Gutiérrez, Pedro Juan. Dirty Havana trilogy. Translated Natasha Wimmer. New York: Farrar, Straus and Giroux, 2001. 392 p.

Triología sucia de La Habana (see item **3494**), Gutiérrez's novel of 1990s Havana "in the crisis," which must have been quite a challenge to translate, has been described as "down, dirty, and literate" (*Publishers Weekly*). All three adjectives are fitting, although at first the explicitness of the prose might cause a reader to question appropriateness of the last one. There's more than sex, however, in the thoughts of the macho, embittered first-person narrator. Once a journalist, he can no longer find work and now takes whatever he can get, and he no longer writes to "hide the truth." [CM]

4299 Hernández Díaz, Alejandro. The Cuban mile. Translated by Dick Cluster. Pittsburgh, Penn.: Latin American Literary Review Press, 1998. 120 p. (Series Discoveries)

At 24, Hernández Díaz saw his novel *La milla* (La Habana: Editorial Letras Cubanas, 1996) chosen for publication by an Argentine-sponsored project designed to further the work of young Cuban writers. The situation in the novel is not complex: two young men on a raft hoping to reach the Florida coast sail for a week without sighting land. Story is nevertheless poignant because of the "hapless painter" who serves as first-person narrator and records his growing anxiety. Cluster's translation is competent although somewhat too formal. He has included a few footnotes to orient the reader. [CM]

4300 Iparraguirre, Sylvia. Tierra del Fuego. Translated by Hardie St. Martin. Willimantic, Conn.: Curbstone Press, 2000. 199 p.

Iparraguirre is a well-known Argentine human rights advocate and fiction writer. Her gripping novel (Buenos Aires: Alfaguara, 1998), winner of the Sor Juana Inés de la Cruz Prize for 2000, is based on the true story of the Yamana Jemmy Button that was recorded in part in Chapter 10 of Charles Darwin's *The voyage of the Beagle*. Capt. Robert Fitzroy abducts Button from his home in Tierra del Fuego and attempts to "civilize" him in England so that he can return to his country as a bearer of "enlightened society"—an experiment with tragic consequences. Narrating perspective is that of John William Guevara, an Anglo-Argentine who lives between two cultures and can better understand Button and the political

agenda behind the façade of "civilized society." Translation flows seamlessly for a compelling read. Work lacks introduction for context for this fascinating material; however, topic and quality of writing strongly recommend this novel for classroom discussion of 19th-century Argentina. [MA]

4301 Lobo, Tatiana. Assault on paradise: a novel. Translated by Asa Zatz. Willimantic, Conn.: Curbstone press, 1998. 297 p.

Asalto al paraíso (San José: Editorial de la Univ. de Costa Rica, 1992), an historical novel set in 1700s colonial Costa Rica, won the 1995 Sor Juana Inés de la Cruz Prize. Novel takes its cue from León Pinelo's *El paraíso de las Indias* (1650) that situated biblical paradise in America. Spanish rogue Pedro Albarán's romance with an indigenous woman is set against backdrop of Mayan mythology and destruction wreaked by Spanish colonizers and their battles with indigenous peoples. Cast of colorful characters brings Pedro's "education" to a stunning conclusion. Footnotes to translated text offer reader essential historical references, and Zatz's translation flows naturally. [MA]

4302 Matto de Turner, Clorinda. Torn from the nest. Translated by John H.R. Polt. Edited and with foreword and chronology by Antonio Cornejo Polar New York: Oxford Univ. Press, 1998. 174 p.: bibl. (Library of Latin America)

First new translation of *Aves sin nido* (1889) since 1904 translation by J.G Hudson; that work was amended by Naomi Lindstrom and published in 1996 under title *Birds without a nest* (see *HLAS 58:4642*). Present work contains Cornejo Polar's incisive essay on Matto de Turner's writing in terms of development of the novel in Peru, followed by chronology and bibliography of and about her writing. A native of Cuzco who spoke and read Quechua proficiently, Matto's goal was to educate non-Indian readers about native communities, and to contribute to the creation of Peruvian national literature. Her allegory of national life in the persons of two romantic couples reveals the destructive class disparity between *criollo* elites living in Lima and exploited indigenous peoples in Andean communities, and particularly the scandalous abuse of Andean women by corrupt Catholic clergy. Publication in 1889 generated outrage as well as praise. While Polt's explanatory footnotes in translation clarify Quechua terms, toponyms, and other cultural references, reader sorely misses more information about 1889 version since Hudson's version expurgated the text by excising references to the human body, rearranging chapters, and omitting an episode (Lindstrom). Annotated and restored text and valuable supplementary material strongly recommend this new edition for both classroom and scholarly use. [MA]

4303 Peri Rossi, Cristina. Solitaire of love. Translated by Robert S. Rudder and Gloria Chacón de Arjona. Durham, N.C.: Duke Univ. Press, 2000. 111 p.

Peri Rossi's novel, *Solitario de amor* (Barcelona: Grijalbo, 1988), chronicles an addiction: a love for a woman named Aída whom the narrator describes as a "hard drug." This is the fourth book by Peri Rossi to be translated into English, and one wishes that her provocative, absorbing work with language, eroticism, and politics was reaching a wider audience. Perhaps introductions that provided more than brief dust-jacket descriptions (such as offered here) would help. [CM]

4304 Piglia, Ricardo. The absent city. Translated by Sergio Gabriel Waisman. Durham, N.C.: Duke Univ. Press, 2000. 147 p.

Ciudad ausente (Buenos Aires: Editorial Sudamericana, 1992) borrows from genres of detective novel and science fiction to meditate on totalitarianism, role of language in defining reality, history and memory, writers and the city. Many literary and historical references in densely plotted tale set in futuristic Buenos Aires. Skilled, informed translation. Translator's introduction, author's afterword provide frame of reference. [KR]

4305 Poniatowska, Elena. Here's to you, Jesusa! Translated by Deanna Heikkinen. New York: Farrar, Straus and Giroux, 2001. 303 p.

The long-awaited English translation of Poniatowska's classic novel *Hasta no verte, Jesús mío* (see *HLAS 42:5206*) based on testimony of Josefina Bórquez that author tape recorded and recreated as a "testimonial novel." First-person voice of fictional Jesusa Palancares, an indomitable rebel, narrates her

adventures as *soldadera* in the army of General Carranza during the Mexican Revolution, and her violent hardscrabble life as a domestic, factory worker, and member of a spiritualist cult, in feisty vernacular of Mexican popular speech. While her insights reveal both the Revolution's failure to live up to its promises and the brutal life of poor women in 20th-century Mexico, Bórquez never loses her extraordinary sense of humor and humanity. Publication of this unique combination of testimony and fiction marked a profound change in modern Mexican literature and became Poniatowska's hallmark in *Massacre in Mexico* (*La noche de Tlatelolco*, see *HLAS 35:7533*); *Nothing, nobody: voices of the Mexican earthquake* (see *HLAS 52:3495* and *HLAS 56:4613*); and the novels that recreate women's lives: *Dear Diego* (*HLAS 42:5207* and *HLAS 50:4283*) and *Tinísima* (*HLAS 54:3727* and *HLAS 58:4648*). Author's introductory memoir about her relationship with Bórquez and production of fictionalized testimony offer important insights into one of the most important novels of modern Mexico. Heikkinen's translation retains tough orality of Spanish originals and conserves a sprinkling of Mexican phrases that re-enforce sounds of revolution and survival. However, a note about how the translator met those challenges would have been more than welcome. Highly recommended for any discussion of the Revolution and women in Mexico. [MA]

4306 Prieto González, José Manuel. Nocturnal butterflies of the Russian Empire: a novel. Translated by Carol and Thomas Christensen. New York: Grove Press, 2000. 322 p.

Fine translation of challenging but intriguing novel *Livadia* (see item **3521**), in which first-person narrator, a smuggler fascinated by borders and language and interested in optics, journeys to Livadia in search of a rare butterfly and a way to write the letter that will convince his lover to return to him. Cuban-born Prieto González has written work of exile, but here Cuba is present only as allusion, loss. [CM]

4307 Quiroga, Giancarla de. Aurora: a novel. Translated by Kathy S. Leonard. Seattle, Wash.: Women in Translation, 1999. 178 p.

Originally published as *La flor de la Candelaria* (Cochabamba, Bolivia: Editorial Los Amigos del Libro, 1990), this romance of a rebellious young woman and heir to a large hacienda is set amid social unrest in rural Bolivia between 1930–50, at onset of the revolution and 1953 Agrarian Reform Decree that redistributed lands to the peasants. Aurora's struggle to promote literacy among indigenous agricultural workers intersects gender, class, and ethnic conflicts that challenge social change. Short introduction by Alice Weldon, endnote on the Bolivian author, and smooth, natural translation by Leonard make this a good choice for classroom discussion of politics and letters in modern Bolivia. [MA]

4308 Riesco, Laura. Ximena at the crossroads. Translated by Mary G. Berg. Fredonia, N.Y.: White Pine Press, 1998. 1 v. (Secret weavers series; 12)

Narrated by a child but from perspective of an adult, *Ximena de dos caminos* (HLAS 56:3737) in Berg's sensitive if somewhat overly formal translation would be an excellent choice for classes in Latin American and gender studies. Novel is set in La Oroya, where Ximena lives at an Andean crossroads between indigenous world of an encampment and urban world of her family. Introductory material would have been helpful. [CM]

4309 Santos-Febres, Mayra. Sirena Selena. Translated by Stephen A. Lytle. New York: Picador USA, 2000. 214 p.

Stephen Lytle has received richly deserved praise for his impressive translation of *Sirena Selena vestida de pena* (Barcelona: Mondadori, 2000). Except for some brief descriptive information on cover, book contains no introductory material. However, story and situation of Leocadio, the 15-year-old Puerto Rican boy who becomes Sirena Silena speak for themselves and immediately draw the reader into a memorable novel of drag, desire, and exploitation. [CM]

4310 Santos Silva, Loreina. This eye that looks at me: first cycle, memoirs. Translated by Carys Evans-Corrales. Pittsburgh, Penn.: Latin American Literary Review Press, 2000. 106 p.

Translation of lyrical, autobiographical novella (*Este ojo que me mira*—San Juan: Edi-

torial de la Univ. de Puerto Rico, 1996) by Puerto Rican writer and poet. Series of short vignettes; "snapshot" memories of 1940s–50s childhood and adolescence in island countryside. Coming-of-age memoir treats themes of family, sexuality, death, love; translation highly engaging. Short glossary of Puerto Rican vocabulary. Excellent for classroom. [KR]

4311 Scorza, Manuel. The ballad of Agapito Robles. Translated by Anna-Marie Aldaz. New York: Peter Lang, 1999. 175 p. (Wor(l)ds of change; 41)

Cantar de Agapito Robles (Barcelona: Monte Avila, 1978) is fourth among five novels in Scorza's Andean cycle of *La guerra silenciosa* that fuses Andean myth with history to depict armed struggle of Quechua peasants to regain their ancestral lands. Agapito Robles leads his Yanacocha comrades in the invasion of various haciendas and defeat of their archenemy, Judge Montenegro. As they gain political consciousness, the community members come to understand that time and the river never really stood still. Novel concludes with a powerful scene in which Agapito performs a whirlwind dance that sets the world on fire. Short preface by translator, whose version is competent but would have benefited much from notes to explain the many Andean cultural references. Recommended for discussions of modern Peru. [MA]

4312 Scorza, Manuel. Requiem for a lightning bolt. Translated by Anna-Marie Aldaz. New York: Peter Lang, 2000. 208 p. (Wor(l)ds of change; 49)

La tumba del relámpago: quinto cantar (México: Siglo Veintiúno Editores, 1979) was the fifth and final volume of Scorza's cycle *La guerra silenciosa* that chronicled indigenous uprisings in Peruvian Andes in late 1950s-early 1960s. Volume narrates organized insurrection against landholders and the Cerro de Pasco Corporation, opening with a scene inspired by millennial Inkarrí legend of return of the Inka, but quickly shifting to realities of armed revolt by indigenous communities led by Genaro Ledesmo. In final scene, the *llapta*, or lightning, flashes "in the darkness for a brief moment, illuminating the history of the peasants . . . bright moments of hope that vanished all too swiftly." Scorza appears as himself, a committed journalist and social activist of the Movimiento Comunal del Perú who witnessed some of the 1950s uprisings that he fictionalized before his untimely death in a plane crash in 1983. Translator's preface briefly discusses place of this final novel in entire cycle. Occasional inconsistencies and literal renderings in the translation would have benefited substantially from footnotes to clarify the many Andean characters, events, and cultural terms that have been retained in Spanish and Quechua throughout the text. Recommended for discussions of modern Peru. [MA]

4313 Scorza, Manuel. The sleepless rider. Translated by Anna-Marie Aldaz. New York: P. Lang, 1996. 172 p. (Wor(l)ds of change, 1072–334X; 31)

El jinete insome (Barcelona: Monte Avila, 1978) was the third in Scorza's five-novel cycle of indigenous insurrection in Pasco, Peru, that erupted in 1959. Scorza actually witnessed and recorded many of those events and became the spokesperson for peasants, miners, and small landowners that formed the Movimiento Comunal del Perú. In this novel, his fictionalized account of attempts to reclaim community land and establish its boundaries is led by Raymundo Herrera, who also functions as the collective memory of his people, and, like all of Scorza's heroes, is embued with mythic qualities. An informative introduction and competent translation recommend it for classroom use and discussions of modern Peru. [MA]

4314 Serrano, Marcela. Antigua and my life before: a novel. Translated by Margaret Sayers Peden. New York: Doubleday, 2000. 352 p.

Translation of Antigua vida mía (HLAS 56:3797) by accomplished translator Margaret Sayers Peden. Reviews of English version were mixed, but novel established Marcela Serrano as "one of Chile's most important contemporary novelists" (José Promis, HLAS 56:3797). Brief preface added to English translation provides background information about Pinochet's dictatorship and Chile's "problematical" transition to democracy, the period in which this novel of women's friendship and courage is set. [CM]

4315 Sguiglia, Eduardo. Fordlandia. Translated by Patricia J. Duncan. New York: T. Dunne Books/St. Martin's Press, 2000. 245 p.

Narrated by an Argentine who travels to Brazilian Amazon to work at Fordlandia, an actual site established in 1929 by Henry Ford with the hopes of reducing his company's dependence on British-produced rubber. Sguiglia makes detailed use of jungle's flora and fauna. When Ford himself flies in, someone tells the narrator, "Come on, boy, smile. You are about to see God in person." [SFW]

4316 Shua, Ana María. The book of memories. Translated by Dick Gerdes. Introduction by Ilan Stavans. Albuquerque: Univ. of New Mexico Press, 1998. 178 p. (Jewish Latin America)

In this lucid translation of Libro de recuerdos (see HLAS 58:3849), three generations of the Rimetka clan recall life and times of their Eastern European family to produce a "distropian picture of Argentina"(Stavans). A fine sense of humor and irony punctuate this moving exploration of transgenerational experiences of life in Buenos Aires through eyes of Jewish women. Gerdes' translation makes for seamless reading that offers excellent vehicle for classroom discussion of significant Jewish component in modern Argentine culture. [MA]

4317 Solares, Ignacio. Lost in the city: two novels. Translated by Carolyn Brushwood and John Stubbs Brushwood. Austin: Univ. of Texas Press, 1998. 160 p. (The Texas Pan American series)

Translation of 1980s novellas El árbol del deseo and Serafín by Mexican writer Solares. Pre-adolescent protagonists common to both texts. Short locating preface gives useful biographical and literary background; no notes or bibliography. Engaging, colloquial language combined with sometimes fantastic elements. Themes include social class, city vs. rural life, children's problems within the family. [KR]

4318 Stamadianos, Jorge. Beer cans in the Rio de la Plata. Translated by Leland H. Chambers. Pittsburgh, Penn.: Latin American Literary Review Press, 1999. 154 p. (Series Discoveries)

Latas de cerveza en el Río de la Plata (Buenos Aires: Emecé Editores, 1995), by Argentine film director and screenwriter, retells *The Odyssey* while inverting its premise: protagonist (Ulysses) desires to leave home (working-class Buenos Aires) rather than return. Homeric references in text will be understood by informed readers. Black humor; bleak portrayal of human relations. Colloquial, readable translation. Back cover notes; no other locating material. [KR]

4319 Steimberg, Alicia. Musicans & watchmakers. Translated by Andrea G. Labinger. Pittsburgh, Penn.: Latin American Literary Review Press, 1998. 127 p. (Series Discoveries)

Músicos y relojeros (Buenos Aires: Centro Editor de América Latina, 1971) is an affectionate, humorously ironic series of semi-autobiographical vignettes describing eccentric Argentine Jewish family from child's first-person perspective. Set in 1930s-40s. Colloquial translation strikes consistent tone. Short author's note; no other locating material. [KR]

4320 Subercaseaux, Elizabeth. The song of the distant root. Translation and foreword by John J. Hassett. Pittsburgh, Penn.: Latin American Literary Review Press, 2001. 88 p. (Series Discoveries)

In informative introduction translator Hassett likens prose and ambience of *El canto de la raíz lejana* (Santiago: Planeta, 1988), Subercaseaux's first novel, to those of Juan Rulfo. Hassett's own prose is less poetic than that of either Rulfo or journalist and novelist Subercaseaux, but it does convey suggestive, ambiguous nature of this tale about Tapihue, a village dreamed of and sought by visionary protagonist, which stands in sharp contrast to Chile's 1980s political situation. [CM]

4321 Taibo, Paco Ignacio. Just passing through. Translated by Martin Michael Roberts. El Paso, Tex.: Cinco Puntos Press, 2000. 173 p.

Advertised on book jacket as "a true left-wing adventure novel," work oscillates between Mexico City now and 65 years earlier during first decades of Mexican Revolution. Taibo, known for his detective novels, journalistic pieces, and a bestselling biogra-

phy of Che Guevara, is also a character in this purposely disjointed work that includes letters, government memos, and one-paragraph chapters. Originally published as *De paso* (México: Leega, 1986). [SFW]

4322 Torres, Ana Teresa. Doña Inés vs. oblivion: a novel. Translated by Gregory Rabassa. Baton Rouge: Louisiana State Univ. Press, 1999. 243 p. (The Pegasus prize for literature)

Three centuries of Venezuelan history are narrated in the voice of an 18th-century matriarch who refuses to succumb to the oblivion of her own death. Reminiscent of sweeping family sagas of Isabel Allende and of Gabriel García Márquez whose *One hundred years of solitude* was translated by Rabassa to great acclaim in 1970 (see *HLAS* 40:7898). Torres won Pegasus Prize for Literature for this novel. [SFW]

4323 Toscana, David. Tula station: a novel. Translated by Patricia J. Duncan. New York: St. Martin's Press, 2000. 277 p.

Ostensibly based on biography and diary of a missing friend of Toscana, *Estación Tula* (México: Joaquín Mortiz, 1995), with a double narrative, is about the process of writing a novel. A Mexican reader would no doubt recognize the geographical setting of Tula, situated in state of Tamaulipas, and would comprehend references to Mexican history that establish novel's temporal coordinates. The US reader, however, needs more supporting material than English edition provides. [SFW]

4324 Valdés, Zoé. I gave you all I had: a novel. Translated by Nadia Benabid. New York: Arcade Pub., 1999. 238 p.

Readers in both English and Spanish often have divergent reactions to work of Zoé Valdés; response to this translation of *Te di la vida entera* (*HLAS* 56:3590) is no exception. One reviewer found story of Cuca Martínez and 1950s-1990s Havana "an appetizingly rich stew" (*The New York Times*). To another, it was "linguistic razzle-dazzle" that becomes "somewhat tiresome" (*Village Voice*); *HLAS* reviewer agreed. In general, Benabid has met quite well the challenge presented by Valdés' novel, but at times she's added a bit too much razzle-dazzle of her own. [CM]

4325 Valenzuela, Luisa. Clara. Translated by Andrea G. Labinger. Pittsburgh, Penn.: Latin American Literary Review Press, 1999. 159 p. (Series Discoveries)

New translation of *Hay que sonreír* (*HLAS 30:3449*), Valenzuela's first novel. First translation (see *HLAS 40:7929*) now out of print. Story of young, naive prostitute in 1950s Buenos Aires, told in short segments organized into three parts. Cultural commentary; many local details. Short author's preface; no further locating material. [KR]

4326 Vallejo, Fernando. Our Lady of the Assassins. Translated by Paul Hammond. London: Serpent's Tail, 2001. 135 p.

"In . . . Colombia," according to narrator of Vallejo's *La virgen de los sicarios* (Bogotá: Editorial Santillana, 1994), "death has turned into a contagious disease." So narrator takes it upon himself to chronicle that disease, describing life in Medellín's *comunas* where "a soul . . . ascends toward heaven whilst descending toward hell," and by immersing himself in the *comuna's* "capital of hate" with a young hitman. His sarcastic tale filled with violence and affection, and it presents a true challenge to a translator. Hammond's version is accurate and competent, although at least to this reader it seems slightly off-key. North American readers may need to consult a British-North American dictionary for help with words like "trainers" (sneakers). [CM]

4327 Varela, Félix. Xicoténcatl: an anonymous historical novel about the events leading up to the conquest of the Aztec Empire. Translated by Guillermo I. Castillo-Feliú. Austin: Univ. of Texas Press, 1999. 156 p. (Texas Pan American series)

First published in Philadelphia in 1826 as *Jicoténcatl*, authorship has been attributed to Cuban patriot priest Félix Varela. This important historical novel presents events that led to march on Tenochtítlan by Hernán Cortés and his Tlaxcalan allies as idealized view of indigenous heroes and denigrated portraits of Spanish invaders. Xicoténcatl the Younger, captain of the Tlaxcalan troops, is depicted in terms of political and personal morality, good versus evil. Translator's note and brief introduction are complemented by informative footnotes referencing the many extracts from Antonio de Solís' *Historia de la conquista de México* that are woven into

text of the novel. Translation captures 19th-century register and tone of Spanish original without resorting to archaic or artificial expressions. [MA]

4328 Vargas Llosa, Mario. The notebooks of Don Rigoberto. Translated by Edith Grossman. New York: Farrar, Straus and Giroux, 1998. 259 p.: ill.

Nonstop eroticism that erases boundaries between real and imaginery encounters characterizes Vargas Llosa's *Los cuadernos de Don Rigoberto* (*HLAS 58:3690*). Don Rigoberto's obsessive fantasies make their way from his life into his notebook, or perhaps the other way around. The translator faces many challenges with explicit sensuality, dialogue filled with subtle cultural references from a variety of languages, and entertaining humor. [SFW]

4329 Vázquez Díaz, René. The island of Cundeamor. Translated by David E. Davis. Pittsburgh, Penn.: Latin American Literary Review Press, 2000. 231 p.

Readers of Vázquez Díaz's *La isla de Cundeamor* (*HLAS 56:3591*) will be plunged into a Cuba-like island of "sex, wealth, and political and romantic fidelity" (*Publishers Weekly*). This translation contains no introductory material, and novel lacks luster in both languages. [CM]

Essays, Interviews, and Reportage

4330 Agosín, Marjorie. The alphabet in my hands: a writing life. Translated by Nancy Abraham Hall. New Brunswick, N.J.: Rutgers Univ. Press, 2000. 187 p.

Eight chapters made up of very short autobiographical vignettes narrate author's Chilean childhood, immigration to US after 1973 coup, and adult life in New England. Themes of family, Jewishness, exile, language, writing, and literature are main topics treated. Translations capture Agosín's poetic, personal voice. Translator's short introduction gives some locating background. [KR]

4331 Bizarro Ujpán, Ignacio. Joseño: another Mayan voice speaks from Guatemala. Translated and edited by James D. Sexton. Albuquerque: Univ. of New Mexico Press, 2001. 312 p.: bibl., ill., index.

Fourth and final volume of excerpts from diary kept by a Tzutuhil Mayan whom Sexton, an anthropologist, met in 1970; present volume covers period 1987–98. Introduction sets out editorial method, historical background; somewhat tendentious comparison of this life story with Rigoberta Menchú's. Text deals with daily life in a highlands village from a centrist political perspective. Useful notes, bibliography, and glossary. Good for classroom use. [KR]

4332 Borges, Jorge Luis. Selected nonfictions. Edited by Eliot Weinberger. Translated by Esther Allen, Suzanne Jill Levine, and Eliot Weinberger. New York: Viking, 1999. 559 p.: bibl., index.

Translations of 161 texts of various types (essays, reviews, prologues, lectures) and lengths, selected by Weinberger. Detailed methodology of selection, editing, translation explained in Editor's Note. Endnotes provide useful bibliographical, historical references. Elegant, expert translations by all three contributors. Outstanding contribution. [KR]

4333 Carpentier, Alejo. Music in Cuba. Edited and with introduction by Timothy Brennan. Translated by Alan West. Minneapolis: Univ. of Minnesota Press, 2001. 302 p.: ill. (Cultural studies of the Americas; 5)

Almost two books in one, volume contains first English translation of *La música en Cuba*. Original work was first published in 1946 (see *HLAS 12:3396*); however, version used for this translation is third, and posthumous, edition (see *HLAS 54:5221*), with its long introductory study. Univ. of Minnesota Press had good reason to advertise it as a "publishing event." Alejo Carpentier's detailed exploration of Cuban music is essential to both his work and the history of Cuban music. Timothy Brennan's study examines Carpentier's research for and writing of the book, its role in Carpentier's production as a whole, the early 19th- and 20th-century literary and cultural contexts of Europe and Latin America, and book's strengths and weaknesses. His appraisal may not please all readers, but volume makes a true contribution. [CM]

4334 Castillo Bueno, María de los Reyes and **Daisy Rubiera Castillo.** Reyita: the life of a Black Cuban woman in the twentieth century. As told to her daughter, Daisy Rubiera Castillo. Introduction by Eliz-

abeth Dore. Translated by Anne McLean. Durham, N.C.: Duke Univ. Press, 2000. 182 p.: bibl., ill.

Excellent presentation of *Reyita, sencillamente: testimonio de una negra cubana nonagenaria* (La Habana: Instituto Cubano del Libro, Prolibros, 1996), a testimonial by a black Cuban mother, laborer, and activist whose life (1902–97) spanned most of 20th century. McLean's translation is exemplary, and Dore's introduction provides background not only for Reyita's life but also for both history of Afro-Cubans and testimonial literature. [CM]

4335 Dorfman, Ariel. Heading south, looking north: a bilingual journey. New York: Farrar, Straus, and Giroux, 1998. 282 p.

Moving memoir written in separate English and Spanish versions of author's life in both North and South America up to 1973 Chilean coup and its immediate aftermath. Theme of bilingualism and living in two languages is constant throughout. Excellent for students of literature, exile and human rights, and comparative cultures of the Americas. [KR]

4336 Florescano, Enrique. The myth of Quetzalcoatl. Translation by Lysa Hochroth. Illustrations by Raúl Velázquez. Baltimore, Md.: Johns Hopkins Univ. Press, 1999. 287 p.: bibl., ill., index.

Translation of 2nd ed. (1995) of Florescano's *El mito de Quetzalcóatl*, a comparative historical study of multiple interpretations of the Mesoamerican god. Longest section develops author's own new interpretation. Clearly written and translated text accessible to interested readers at different levels. Many line drawings based on scholarly sources. Excellent for classroom use. For comment on first edition of original work, see *HLAS 56:440*. [KR]

4337 Galeano, Eduardo H. Soccer in sun and shadow. Translated by Mark Fried. London; New York: Verso, 1998. 228 p.: bibl., index.

Wonderful translation of *El fútbol a sol y sombra* (Madrid: Siglo Vientiuno de España Editores, 1995). Includes 150 short reflections on culture, politics, historical events associated with soccer around the world since its beginnings. Tone of pieces mixes Uruguayan author's ironic humor with stories both tragic and heroic. Colloquial translations capture Galeano's unique voice. Includes list of informational sources. [KR]

4338 King David's harp: autobiographical essays by Jewish Latin American writers. Edited and with introduction by Stephen A. Sadow. Albuquerque: Univ. of New Mexico Press, 1999. 260 p.: bibl. (Jewish Latin America)

Translations of 15 autobiographical essays by writers from eight countries. Eight essays written or revised for this volume; others previously published. All writers living except one (Gerchunoff); six women. Various translators. Short biographical introduction for each writer; bibliography of published works. Introduction by Sadow includes historical background of Jewish immigration in the region. [KR]

León Portilla, Miguel. Bernardino de Sahagun, first anthropologist. See item **540.**

4339 Ludmer, Josefina. The gaucho genre: a treatise on the motherland. Translated by Molly Weigel. Durham, N.C.: Duke Univ. Press, 2002. 264 p.: index.

Translation of *El género gauchesco* (see *HLAS 54:3661*), treating 19th-century Argentine gaucho poetry in its cultural context. Indispensable volume for students of Argentina, and Latin American literature in general. Includes author's 2000 prologue to second edition; extensive footnotes. Word plays of original sometimes difficult to approximate; translator's footnotes clarify problems. [KR]

María de San José, Madre. A wild country out in the garden: the spiritual journals of a colonial Mexican nun. See item **1294.**

4340 Menchú, Rigoberta. Crossing borders. Translated and edited by Ann Wright. London; New York: Verso, 1998. 242 p.: index, maps.

Volume of 12 autobiographical essays narrates Menchú's experiences inside and outside of Guatemala in 1980s-90s, with an introduction on winning the Nobel Prize in 1992. Maps, glossary, short translator's note. Wright also translated *I, Rigoberta Menchú*, and delineates differences between the two volumes. This volume created controversy regarding authorship (see introductory essay to this chapter). [KR]

4341 Mier Noriega y Guerra, José Servando Teresa de. The memoirs of Fray Servando Teresa de Mier. Translated by Helen R. Lane. Edited and with introduction by Susana Rotker. New York; Oxford: Oxford Univ. Press, 1998. 242 p.: bibl. (Library of Latin America)

Wonderful edition of colorful writings of Mexican friar Mier, who wrote of his various imprisonments, escapes, and travels in Europe at end of colonial period (1795–1805). Excellent translation by Lane, with some footnotes; extensive historico-cultural introduction and endnotes by Rotker. Indispensable for classes on 19th-century Latin American history and literature. [KR]

4342 Moyano, María Elena. The autobiography of María Elena Moyano: the life and death of a Peruvian activist. Edited and annotated by Diana Miloslavich Túpac. Translation, prologue, and afterword by Patricia S. Taylor Edmisten. Gainesville: Univ. Press of Florida, 2000. 110 p.: bibl., index.

This book, as described by editor Miloslavich Túpac, is the "reconstructed testimony" of Peruvian activist María Elena Moyano (1958–92) who was assassinated by Sendero Luminoso guerrillas. A valuable, moving addition to testimonial literature, volume includes translation of *María Elena Moyano: en busca de una esperanza* (see *HLAS 57:3579*); brief preface by translator Edmisten; and lengthy, informative afterword by Miloslavich Túpac about role of women in Peru and the women's movement in that country. [CM]

4343 Neruda, Pablo and Nicanor Parra. Pablo Neruda and Nicanor Parra face to face: a bilingual and critical edition of their speeches on the occasion of Neruda's appointment to the faculty of the University of Chile. Translated and with introduction by Marlene Gottlieb. Lewiston, N.Y.: E. Mellen Press, 1997. 110 p.: bibl. (Hispanic literature; 36)

Brief but valuable volume. As Gottlieb notes, these two speeches from 1962 "capture the essential difference between Neruda the poet and Parra the antipoet;" and "they represent two tendencies which define . . . the trajectory of contemporary Spanish American poetry." Completely bilingual edition includes introduction and notes on speeches. [CM]

Pané, Ramón. An account of the antiquities of the Indians: chronicles of the New World encounter. See item **1835**.

4344 Paz, Octavio. Itinerary: an intellectual journey. Translated by Jason Wilson. New York: Harcourt, 1999. 129 p.: bibl.

Translation of Paz's *Itinerario* (México: Fondo de Cultura Económica, 1993), consisting of two biographical essays: one on the motives for writing *Laberinto de la soledad*; one on his personal political history. Sensitive translation captures Paz's distinctive prose style, with a slightly British diction. Afterword and endnotes by Wilson very helpful for historical and literary references. [KR]

4345 ReMembering Cuba: legacy of a diaspora. Edited by Andrea O'Reilly Herrera. Austin: Univ. of Texas Press, 2001. 325 p.: bibl., col. ill., map.

Handsome volume of more than 100 contributions, organized into eight sections. Wide range of Cuban exile experience reflected, treating several generations. Illustrations from Cuban artists and photographers. Thoughtful introduction by Herrera explains project's complex trajectory and completion. Mixture of pieces originally written in English and translated texts; various translators. [KR]

4346 Tuñón, Julia. Women in Mexico: a past unveiled. Translated by Alan Hynds. Austin: Univ. of Texas Press, Institute of Latin American Studies, 1999. 144 p.: bibl., index. (Translations from Latin America series)

Translation of expanded, updated version of *Mujeres en México* (see item **1198**). Volume informed by feminist historical scholarship covers role of women in Mexico from precolumbian era to 1990s. Introductory-level text; some notes and illustrations; comprehensive bibliography; very useful for classroom. Author's personal involvement and commitment to subject well communicated in translation. [KR]

TRANSLATIONS FROM THE PORTUGUESE
Brief Fiction and Theater

4347 Ribeiro, Edgard Telles. The turn in the river. (*in* Whistler in the nightworld: short fiction from the Latin Americas. Edited by Thomas Colchie. New York: Plume, 2002, p. 207–220)

Ribeiro's superb story is the only Brazilian work in this volume of 21 stories from 11 countries. Brilliantly translated by Margaret Abigail Neves and the author. [DP]

4348 Steen, Edla van. Scent of love. Translated and with foreword by David Sanderson George. Pittsburgh, Penn.: Latin American Literary Review Press, 2001. 110 p. (Series Discoveries)

Cheiro de amor (São Paulo: Global Editora, 1996), Steen's fourth book to be published in English, consolidates her already estimable reputation abroad. The book, which won Brazil's prestigious Nestlé Award for Literature in 1997, is made up of the title novella, followed by two short stories ("Queen of the Abyss" and "Less Than a Dream"), all excellently translated by David Sanderson George. [DP]

Novels

4349 Abreu, Caio Fernando. Whatever happened to Dulce Veiga?: a B-novel. Translated and with afterword and glossary by Adria Frizzi. Austin: Univ. of Texas Press, 2000. 200 p. (Texas Pan American series)

As Frizzi points out in her excellent afterword, Abreu (1948–96) repeatedly dealt with Brazilian urban life in its B-class manifestations—his protagonists always at the periphery, never the center, of power. This complex novel (*Onde andará Dulce Veiga*—São Paulo: Companhia das Letras, 1990), at once concentrated and diffused, depicts protagonist's search for a missing singer and for his own identity. Faithfully translated with energy and style. [DP]

4350 Alencar, José Martiniano de. Iracema: a novel. Translated by Clifford E. Landers. Foreword by Naomi Lindstrom. Afterword by Alcides Villaça. New York: Oxford Univ. Press, 2000. 148 p. (Library of Latin America)

Alencar's Indianist prose-poem, first translated into English by Richard and Isabel Burton in 1886, is given new life by this translation. Landers opts for a far less archaicizing tone and diction than did the Burtons, while attempting to evoke original's poetic flavor and retaining its indigenous terminology. Alencar's explanatory notes are supplemented by a helpful foreword and afterword, and a letter from Alencar about the composition of the book. [DP]

4351 Azevedo, Aluísio. The slum: a novel. Translated by David H. Rosenthal. Foreword by David H. Rosenthal. Afterword by Affonso Romano de Sant'Anna. Oxford: New York: Oxford Univ. Press, 2000. 222 p.: bibl. (Library of Latin America)

The late David Rosenthal has provided a contemporary translation of Azevedo's most famous novel (*O Cortiço*), a naturalist representation of slum life in late-19th-century Rio de Janeiro. Like 1926 translation by Harry W. Brown entitled *A Brazilian Tenement* (New York: R.M. McBride and Co.), this one takes considerable liberties with the original; in particular, it introduces problems in dealing with Brazilian racial terms. Helpful foreword and afterword. [DP]

4352 Hatoum, Milton. The brothers. Translated by John Gledson. New York: Farrar, Straus and Giroux, 2002. 226 p.

Hatoum's second novel (*Dois irmãos—* São Paulo: Companhia das Letras, 2000), published 11 years after his first, won third place in the Jabutí prize's 2001 competition. Work is a dense narrative, exploring a family drama in the Lebanese immigrant community of Manaus. Like Machado in *Esau and Jacob* (see item **4353**), Hatoum depicts an entire social and physical milieu through the story of rivalrous identical twins, Omar and Yaqub. Gledson's translation is a work of beauty and tact. Includes helpful glossary. [DP]

4353 Machado de Assis. Esau and Jacob: a novel. Translated by Elizabeth Lowe. Edited and with foreword by Dain Borges. Afterword by Carlos Felipe Moisés. New York: Oxford Univ. Press, 2000. 276 p. (Library of Latin America)

Machado's fascinating 1904 novel about identical twin brothers whose rivalry starts in the womb and continues in their love for the same woman and their conflicting political ideals. Lowe's new translation avoids some of the errors of Helen Caldwell's 1965 version (Berkeley: Univ. of California Press), but reveals a tone-deaf ear as it vacillates between the too casual and the too literal. Result is a very un-Machadian awkwardness. Accompanying essays are a big plus. [DP]

4354 Melo, Patrícia. Inferno. Translated by Clifford E. Landers. London: Bloomsbury, 1999. 187 p.

Melo's third novel to be translated into English, *Inferno* (São Paulo: Companhia das Letras, 2000) won second place in the 2001 Jabutí Prize competition for best novel in Brazil, adding to her ever-growing reputation. Novel tells story of an ambitious boy and his struggle for survival in violent world (evoked through Melo's insistence on chaotic enumeration) of Rio de Janeiro's slums. Landers' translation is excellent, convincingly adapting register and rhythms of Rio's drug-trafficking *favelas* to an English-language audience. [DP]

4355 Soares, Jô. Twelve fingers: biography of an anarchist. Translated by Clifford E. Landers. New York: Pantheon Books 2001. 303 p.: bibl., ill., maps.

With his second novel (*O Homem que matou Getúlio Vargas: biografia de um anarquista—*São Paulo: Companhia das Letras, 1998), Soares again delivers a comic fictive history, replete with graphics, faux etymologies, and other amusements. Protagonist Dimitri Borja Korozec, a bumbling assassin, is placed, *Zelig*-style, at crucial world events between 1914 and 1954 when he kills Getúlio Vargas. Landers deftly resolves the many problems the original presents to an English-language audience and, through his creative adaptations, produces a highly enjoyable work. [DP]

Essays, Interviews, and Reportage

4356 Boal, Augusto. Hamlet and the baker's son: my life in theatre and politics. Translated by Adrian Jackson and Candida Blaker. London; New York: Routledge, 2001. 366 p.: ill., index.

A fascinating account of an exuberant and exceptional life by Brazil's foremost political dramatist whose theatrical activities ranged from the *favelas* of Rio to the Royal Shakespeare Company. Written in brief vignettes covering decades. One memorable line describes the promise of drama (in this instance, Fernanda Montenegro onstage): "Hope is reborn; perhaps the human being is viable." For comment on original Portuguese version, see item **4091.** [DP]

BIBLIOGRAPHY, THEORY, AND PRACTICE

4357 Balch, Trudy. Pioneer on the bridge of language. (*Source/Alexandria*, 29:1, Winter 1999, p. 10–13)

Although a reprint, this article from newsletter of American Translators Association's Literary Division merits mention here because contribution of Harriet De Onís (1895–1969) has received too little attention. De Onís worked from both Spanish and Portuguese and was responsible for first English-language translation of numerous Latin American writers such as João Guimarães Rosa, Ricardo Güiraldes, and Alejo Carpentier. Balch surveys De Onís' accomplishments thoroughly, and piece makes one wish for similar profiles of other translators whose work has been far more influential than they or others realize. [CM]

4358 Bradu, Fabienne. Octavio Paz Traductor. (*Vuelta/México*, 259, junio 1998, p. 30–37)

In her thoughtful and evaluative discussion of Paz's work as a translator, Bradu focuses her comments primarily on the poet's versions of Apollinaire and Reverdy. However, she also offers clear, concise summary of thoughts about translation articulated by Paz in various contexts. In connection with this article see Paz's *Versiones y diversiones* (Barcelona: Círculo de Lectores; Galaxia Gutenberg, 2000), which includes Paz's complete production as a translator and many of the original poems. [CM]

4359 Bush, Peter. Translating Onetti for Anglo-Saxon others. (*in* Onetti and others: comparative essays on a major figure in Latin American literature. Albany: State Univ. of New York Press, 1999, p. 177–186)

A highly accomplished translator of numerous books from Spain and Latin America, Bush here offers insightful discussion of his work translating Onetti's *Cuando ya no importe* (HLAS 54:4182), entitled *Past caring!* (HLAS 58:4645). He also discusses both his own "dislocation in English" that led him to translation and his close consultations with Dolly Onetti. [CM]

4360 Copia, imitación, manera: cuaderno de traducciones. Compilación de Ricardo H. Herrera. Buenos Aires: Grupo Editor Latinoamericano, 1998. 191 p. (Nuevohacer) (Col. Temas)

Bilingual collection of translations and accompanying commentary (in Spanish) by Argentine translator and poet Ricardo H. Herrera. Two-thirds of volume is focused on work of Italian poets, but translations of work by Robert Frost, Wallace Stevens, Ezra Pound, and others are also included. Commentaries should interest scholars and students of comparative literature. [CM]

4361 Encyclopedia of literary translation into English. Edited by Olive Classe. London; Chicago: Fitzroy Dearborn Publishers, 2000. 2 v.: bibl., indexes.

An ambitious, comprehensive "instrument of record," this two-volume encyclopedia resulted from effort to survey field of translation studies, which Classe identifies as an important, relatively new discipline. Includes more than 600 entries by nearly 300 contributors who address questions of translation history, theory, and practice; provide historical surveys of traditions and trends in translation; and describe and evaluate individual translations and contributions of individual translators. Latin Americanists will find many useful and informative essays on translation in Latin America and translations of Latin American authors' work. [CM]

4362 Landers, Clifford E. Literary translation: a practical guide. Buffalo, N.Y.: Multilingual Matters, 2001. 214 p.: bibl., index. (Topics in translation; 22)

Landers, an experienced translator, has produced a book of immense value. Immune to excesses of theory, he is concerned instead with challenges and problems faced by working translators. He is convinced of the enormous importance of translation, without which our knowledge of the world's riches would be vastly impoverished. Landers attempts to ease the path of other translators, and he succeeds admirably in this engaging and no-nonsense volume, filled with practical examples and thoughtful discussion. [DP]

4363 Nigro, Kirsten. Getting the word out: issues in the translation of Latin American theatre for US audiences. (*in* Moving target: theatre translation and cultural relocation. Manchester, England:, St. Jerome, 2000, p. 115–125)

Important article for scholars and

students interested not only in translation of Latin American literature but also in reception in English of Latin American literature as a whole. Nigro's comments focus specifically on theater, but her observations about factors both within Latin America (for example, the poor circulation of material) and the US (the costly risk of producing works that audiences might find incomprehensible or exotic) are representative of the challenges faced in translation of work in all genres. [CM]

4364 The Oxford guide to literature in English translation. Edited by Peter France. Oxford; New York: Oxford Univ. Press, 2000. 656 p.: bibl., index.

Concise, comprehensive volume provides detailed historical overview and discussion of principal issues in both translation studies and criticism and individual translations themselves. Includes substantial introductory essays by leading translators and translation scholars, as well as pieces focusing on translations from specific languages; a few of those pieces are dedicated to translations of the work of a major canonical writer. Latin Americanists will find particularly useful the entries on Latin American poetry (Susan Bassnett) and fiction (Peter Bush), and the entry on Brazilian literature (Helena Gonçalves Barbosa). [CM]

4365 Post-colonial translation: theory and practice. Edited by Susan Bassnett and Harish Trivedi. London; New York: Routledge, 1999. 201 p.: bibl., index. (Translation studies)

Volume of essays, two of which will be of particular interest to Latin Americanists: Rosemary Arrojo's discussion of Hélène Cixous' "aggressively 'masculine' approach to difference" in her work with Clarice Lispector ("Interpretation as Possessive Love: Hélène Cixous, Clarice Lispector, and the Ambivalence of Fidelity"); and Else Ribeiro Pires Vieira's essay on Haroldo de Campos' provocative, even polemical, translations, his "poetics of transcreation," and anthropophagy as "Brazilian-derived," "disruptive" metaphor likened to Brazilian independence

and experimentation ("Liberating Calibans: Readings of *Antropofagia* and Haroldo de Campos' Poetics of Transgression"). [CM]

4366 Voice-overs: translation and Latin American literature. Edited by Daniel Balderston and Marcy E. Schwartz. Albany: State Univ. of New York Press, 2002. 266 p.: bibl., index. (SUNY series in Latin American and Iberian thought and culture)

Valuable collection of essays by translators, writers, and critics includes contributions by Brazilian writer Nélida Pinon, Portuguese and Spanish translator Gregory Rabassa, and Brazilian translation theorist Else Ribeiro Pires Vieira. [DP]

4367 Waisman, Sergio Gabriel. Ethics and aesthetics North and South: translation in the work of Ricardo Piglia. (*Mod. Lang. Q. /Seattle,* 62:3, 2001, p. 259–283)

Excellent "must-read" article for scholars and students interested in the work of Ricardo Piglia; in the role of translation in Piglia's writing and in Latin American literature as a whole; and in translation of Piglia's writing itself. Waisman bases his comments on his own translations of *Nombre falso* (*Assumed name*—see *HLAS 58:4618*) and *La ciudad ausente* (*The absent city*—see item **4304**). [CM]

4368 Zavalia, Juliana de. The impact of Spanish-American literature in translation on US Latino literature. (*in* Changing the terms: translating in the postcolonial era. Ottawa: Univ. of Ottawa Press, 2000, p. 187–206)

In excellent article Zavalia argues that, thanks to translation of key works that gradually formed a "canon of Spanish-American literatures in translation," Spanish-American literature is an "important component of US Latino literature." Her analysis of this "cultural traffic" is based to a large degree on Itamar Even-Zohar's understanding of polysystems, and Zavalia applies both her own and other translators' ideas eloquently and convincingly. [CM]

MUSIC

GENERAL

4369 Barletta, Victor. Name index of *Renaissance and Baroque musical sources in the Americas.* (*Inter-Am. Music Rev.*, 16:2, Spring/Summer 2000, p. 71–78)

Robert Stevenson's *Renaissance and Baroque Musical Sources in the Americas* (1970) remains an indispensable tool for research in colonial music of the Americas (see *HLAS 36:4516*). The name index provided by Barletta will only increase its utility. [A. Lemmon]

4370 Baumann, Max Peter. Musikalisch-religiöser Synkretismus in Lateinamerika [Musico-religious syncretism in Latin America]. (*Bulletin/Geneva*, 61, 1997, p. 13–24, bibl., table)

An analytical inquiry into the nature of musical "syncretism" in Latin America. Places the commingling of indigenous and European music in the context of colonization and conversion, and examines the myriad ways in which various traditions combined in response to the either/or pattern of religious indoctrination in the context of Andean music and ritual. [W. Clark]

4371 Béjar, Ana María et al. Música, danzas y máscaras en los Andes. Recopilación de Raúl R. Romero. 2. ed. Lima: Pontificia Univ. Católica del Perú, Instituto Riva-Aguero, Proyecto de Preservación de la Música Tradicional Andina, 1998. 411 p.: bibl., ill. (some col.), music.

Romero has assembled a distinguished roster of scholars to treat Andean folk music, dance, and masques, focusing on Peru. Topics include the role of music and dance in the social and religious life of various communities. Amply footnoted and illustrated with musical examples, maps, and color plates. For ethnographer's comment on first edition, see *HLAS 57:1209.* [W. Clark]

Cárdenas, Sergio. Estaciones en la música. See item **4390**.

4372 A cultural history of Latin America: literature, music, and the visual arts in the 19th and 20th centuries. Edited by Leslie Bethell. New York: Cambridge Univ. Press, 1998. 538 p.

The introductory chapters by Gerald Martin focus mostly on literature, but the short section on music provides a useful overall view, especially for students, of music within the larger context of Latin American cultural productions. Gérard Behague's chapter is devoted solely to music and includes general information on both art and popular music. For literature specialist's comment, see item **3963**. [C. Magaldi]

4373 The Garland encyclopedia of world music. v. 2, South America, Mexico, Central America, and the Caribbean. New York: Garland Pub., 1998. 1 v.: bibl., ill., indexes, maps. (v. 2: Garland reference library of the humanities; v. 1169)

An extremely valuable reference source covering a wide array of folk and popular musical styles from all the major geographic areas of Latin America. Pt. 1 profiles the lands and peoples of the diverse regions covered in the book and then treats scholarly approaches to this musical cornucopia. Pt. 2 surveys "issues and processes" in the symbolism and use of musical instruments, musicians in their social context, as well as native and immigrant groups. Pt. 3, section 1, treats South American native peoples and their musics; section 2 examines the many national musical traditions of South America. Sections 3–5 focus on Mexico, Central America, and the Caribbean, respectively. One of the notable and welcome features of this volume is the rich abundance of maps, pictures, and other illustrations, including musical examples. The volume concludes with a glossary as well as guides to publications, recordings, and films/videos. A thoughtful addition is a CD with examples of 39 pieces discussed in the text. While this is but a tiny fraction of the hundreds of musical styles and genres, the sampling is broad and representative of the major regions treated in the book. Helpful notes on these audio examples precede the index. [W. Clark]

4374 Lemmon, Alfred E. La música catedralicia en la América colonial. (*in* Música en España en el siglo XVIII. Edited by Malcolm Boyd and Juan José Carreras. Cambridge: Cambridge Univ. Press, 2000, p. 273–282, bibl.)

Expanded translation of an article that appeared in *Music in Spain During the Eighteenth-Century* (Cambridge: Cambridge Univ. Press, 1998). The essay includes a summary of musical relations between New World cathedrals during the 18th century and an extensive bibliography of sources for the study of cathedral musical life. [A. Lemmon]

4375 Moreno Chá, Ercilia. Music in the Southern Cone: Chile, Argentina, and Uruguay. (*in* Music in Latin American culture: regional traditions. Edited by John M. Schechter. New York: Schirmer Books, 1999, p. 236–301)

Provides a summary of regional traditions from three countries of the Southern Cone with emphasis on the Chilean *tonada* and the Argentine *milonga.* Includes song texts and musical examples. [C. Magaldi]

4376 The new Grove dictionary of music and musicians. Edited by Stanley Sadie with executive editor, John Tyrrell. 2nd ed. New York: Grove, 2001. 26 v.: bibl., ill., index.

Extensive coverage for several Latin American countries, provides much updated information on traditional, popular, and art music; includes illustrations and musical examples of traditional music, but omits musical examples of art music. [C. Magaldi]

4377 Wong, Ketty. Directory of Latin American and Caribbean music theses and dissertations, 1992–1998. (*Lat. Am. Music Rev.,* 20:2, Fall/Winter 1999, p. 253–309)

This compilation includes theses and dissertations from North American and Latin American universities. [C. Magaldi]

MEXICO

JAMES RADOMSKI, *Associate Professor of Music, California State University, San Bernardino*

CATHEDRAL MUSIC OF 17TH- AND 18TH-CENTURY MEXICO continues to attract and challenge scholars. Significant studies of music in the cathedrals of Puebla and Oaxaca have appeared, by Tello (item **4418**) and Kuri Camacho (item **4405**); especially of note is a collection of articles edited by Lizama and Traffano (item **4396**). Another interesting study pertinent to sacred music is the catalog of historic pipe organs in the state of Puebla by Gastellou (item **4399**).

Carredano has provided a useful tool for the study of Mexican classical music in her history and catalog of Mexican editions (item **4391**).

Among several new works dealing with Mexican composers, especially significant are the new biography of Manuel Ponce by Díaz Cervantes and the original approach to analysis of Ponce's style by Miranda (items **4397** and **4408** respectively).

Folk and popular music in Mexico form an enormous area of study that has yet to be conquered. The volume of songs collected by Concha Michel is a useful addition (item **4407**). The history of popular music in Nuevo León is well served by Ayala Duarte's scholarly study (item **4385**).

4378   A tambora batiente. Prólogo, recreación histórica y compilación de Carlos Jesús Gómez Flores. Monterrey, Mexico: Dirección General de Culturas Populares, Unidad Regional Norte; PACMyC, 1997. 142 p.: ill.

Collection of articles revolving around the career of the folk group, "Los Tamborileros de Linares." Photographic essay shows the traditional construction of the tambora (side drum).

4379   Aceves, Laura Alicia. La herencia musical de los Páez. Chihuahua, Mexico: Ediciones del Azar, 1999. 99 p.: bibl., ill.

Aims to make known the lives and works (popular, sacred) of members of the musical Páez family, from the city of Hidalgo del Parral in Chihuahua at the end of the 19th century. Based on an analysis of the scores kept in the archivo musical de la Subdirección de Archivos y Colecciones Especiales del Centro de Información del Estado de Chihuahua. Focuses on the patriarch, Aurelio Páez, Ana de los Dolores Páez, José Rentería Páez, Victoriano Páez. A list of works by Victoriano, Teodoro, Aurelio, and José Rentería Páez is included as well as musical examples (facsimiles) of works by José Rentería Páez, Victoriano Páez, and Aurelio Páez.

4380   Alanís Tamez, Juan. Un barrio lleno de música: historia musical de Santiago, Nuevo León. Monterrey, Mexico: Consejo para la Cultura de Nuevo León, 1998. 254 p.: bibl., ill., photos.

Popular history of soloists and groups (conjuntos, bandas, etc.) in Santiago from 1887-present. Abundant photos, a few musical examples.

4381   Alanís Tamez, Juan. Cronología de el Tigre: grupo de música folklórica popular tradicional 1990–1996. Prólogo de Celso Garza Guajardo. Epílogo de María Eugenia Llamas de Lozano. México: Univ. Autónoma de Nuevo Leon, 1996. 270 p.: bibl., ill.

The group "Tigre," formed at the campus of the Univ. Autónoma de Nuevo León to promote traditional music, was supported by the Depto. de Difusión Cultural from 1990–96. This book is a popular history of the group during this period. Most useful is the annotated list of 100 pieces in the group's repertoire (p. 235–260).

4382   Alcaraz, José Antonio. Carlos Chávez, un constante renacer. México: Instituto Nacional de Bellas Artes, Centro Nacional de Investigación, Documentación e Información Musical, 1996. 188 p.: bibl.

Useful collection of journalistic articles, criticism, program notes by critic José Antonio Alcaraz from the 1960s-90s, grouped by theme: "Personality of Chávez," "Chávez as Director," "Various Works," and "Symphonies."

4383   Alcaraz, José Antonio. En la más honda música de selva. Presentación de Héctor Anaya. 1. ed. en Lecturas Mexicanas México: CONACULTA, 1998. 179 p.: bibl. (Lecturas mexicanas. Cuarta serie)

After introductory essays on the phenomenon of nationalism, presents brief biographies of Mexican nationalist composers: Manuel Ponce, José Rolón, Julián Carillo, Candelario Huízar, Antonio Gomezanda, Carlos Chávez, Silvestre Revueltas, Eduardo Hernández Moncada, Luis Sandi, Blas Galindo, Miguel Bernal Jiménea, José Pablo Moncayo, Carlos Jiménez Mabarak. Concludes with discussion of selected works.

4384   Ayala, Javier. La música de fin de siglo en Nayarit. (*in* Nayarit al final del milenio. Coordinación de Lourdes Pacheco Ladrón de Guevara y Enedina Heredia Quevedo. Recopilación de Francisco Javier Castellón Fonseca. Nayarit, Mexico: Univ. Autónoma de Nayarit, 1998, p. 369–383)

Reviews musical education, performing groups, musical societies in the state of Nayarit from the 1970s to the end of the 20th century.

4385   Ayala Duarte, Alfonso. Músicos y música popular en Monterrey, 1900–1940. Monterrey, Mexico: Univ. Autónoma de Nuevo León, 1998. 190 p.: bibl.

Beginning with a history of military bands in Nuevo León from 1850–1940, surveys various important elements of the popular musical scene: la canción musical guilds; jazz; and music in bars, theater, dance, radio, radio, film. Scholarly, well-documented, useful bibliographical notes. A chapter on "archivos musicales" describes the lamentable state of popular music archives.

4386   Azanza Jiménez, José. Mis vivencias con José Alfredo Jiménez: anécdotas desconocidas, la verdadera historia de sus canciones, una fiel aproximación al genial

compositor. México: Edamex, 1999. 163 p.:
ill. (Vidas que dejan huella; 17)
    Anecdotal remembrances of the mari-
achi legend (1926–73) by his nephew.

4387 **Balderrama Montes, Raúl** and **Roberto
      Francisco Pérez Galindo.** La música
en Chihuahua: 1890–1940. Chihuahua,
Mexico: Univ. Autónoma de Chihuahua:
SPAUACH, 1999. 201 p.: bibl., ill. (Colección Textos universitarios)
    Vol. 1 is divided into two sections: the
first provides a chronological sketch of all
musical activity (organizations, theaters,
persons, programs, musical education) from
the end of the 19th century. The second section provides brief biographies of important
Chihuahuense musicians: José Perches Porras, Guillermo Moye, Guillermo Ramos, Es-
tanislao Urquidi, José Perches Enriquez, Ar-
turo Tolentino, Ernesto Talavera, Antonio
Maguregui, Francisco Moure, Jesús Martínez
González, Lauro Uranga, José María Rico,
Agustín Urquidi Portugal, Hilario Duarte,
José Federico Pérez Márquez, Carlos Pérez
Márquez, Salvador Pérez Márquez. Vol. 2 is
a collection of 13 piano works and songs by
Fortino Contreras, Jesús Martínez González,
Isidro Gómez, Arturo Tolentino Hernández,
Francisco Mourne Holguín, José Perches
Enriquez, Jesús Ignacio Perches Enriquez,
Ernesto Talavera Escandón, Lauro D. Uranga.

4388 **Becerril, Leticia Román de.** Arte y
      artistas: música, teatro y poesía; histo-
ria de la marimba. México: Gernika, 1996.
447 p.: bibl., ill.
    Popular, anecdotal history of the
marimba and marimba players. Author in-
serts 100 p. of irrelevant global music history
before actually focusing on the marimba.

4389 **Bernal, Julio.** Se me reventó el barzón:
      Amparo Ochoa. Culiacán Rosales,
Mexico: Dirección de Investigación y Fomento de Cultura Regional, Univ. Autó-
moma de Sinaloa, 1996. 221 p.: bibl., ill.
    Journalistic biography of Amparo
Ochoa (1946–94), popular singer of Canto
Nuevo as well as Mexican folk music. Includes list of periodical references and
discography.

4390 **Cárdenas, Sergio.** Estaciones en la
      música. Prólogo de Juan Villoro. Mé-
xico: Conaculta, 1999. 152 p.: ill. (Lecturas
mexicanas. Cuarta serie)

    Rhapsodic reflections on major com-
posers and their works. More useful for the
Latin American scholar are chapters on
Julián Carillo, Manuel Esperón, Guadalupe
Parrondo, as well as commentaries on musical education in Mexico and the Filarmónica
de Querétaro.

4391 **Carredano, Consuelo.** Hebert
      Vázquez: cronología, catálogo, referen-
cias documentales. (*Pauta/México*, 18:71,
julio/sept. 1999, p. 74–89, bibl., music,
photos)
    Useful chronology of the composer's
life and of works from 1987–99. Includes
brief discussion of his style.

4392 **Carrizosa, Toño.** La onda grupera: his-
      toria del movimiento grupero. México:
Edamax, 1997. 294 p.: bibl., ill.
    Popular overview of rock groups in
Mexico from 1960s-present.

4393 **Castillo, Roberto et al.** Oye cómo va:
      recuento del rock tijuanense. Coordi-
nación de José Manuel Valenzuela Arce y
Gloria González Fernández. México: Instituto Mexicano de la Juventud, Centro de Investigación y Estudios sobre Juventud; Consejo Nacional para la Cultura y las Artes,
Centro Cultural Tijuana, 1999. 216 p.: bibl.,
ill. (Col. JOVENes; 6)
    Includes glossary of Tijuana rock
slang, biographies of contributors. Collection
of 17 journalistic articles, interviews (including one with Carlos Santana) pertaining to
the Tijuana rock scene from 1960s-present.

4394 **Corridos y canciones de Nuevo León.**
      Recopilación de Silvia Elena Gutiérrez
Islas. Monterrey, Mexico: Univ. Autónoma
de Nuevo León, Centro de Información de
Historia Regional, 1996. 141 p.: bibl.
    After a brief introduction, the author
presents the texts (without music) of 100 *corridos* from the state of Nuevo León, Mexico,
arranged by municipality.

4395 **Cortés, David.** El otro rock mexicano:
      experiencias progresivas, sicodélicas,
de fusión y experimentales. México: Times
Editores; Opción Sónica; Tower Records,
Video, Books, 1999. 277 p.: bibl., ill. (Col. El
legado de Thot)
    Brief history of progressive rock in
Mexico from the late 1970s-90s. Useful bibliography and discography.

Cruz, Eloy. De como una letra hace la diferencia: las obras en náhuatl atribuidas a Don Hernando Franco. See item **460.**

4396 De papeles mudos a composiciones sonoras: la música en la Catedral de Oaxaca, siglos XVII-XX. Coordinación de Jesús Lizama Quijano y Daniela Traffano. Oaxaca, Mexico: Archivo Histórico de la Arquidiócesis de Oaxaca; Fondo Estatal para la Cultura y las Artes, 1998. 76 p.: bibl., ill. (Cuadernos de historia eclesiástica; 2)

Valuable collection of scholarly essays on various aspects of music at the Oaxaca cathedral. Of special note are the Stevenson article on Indian composer Juan Matías and the overview of the catalog by Mejía Torres.

4397 Díaz Cervantes, Emilio and Dolly R. De Díaz. Ponce, genio de México: vida y época, 1882–1948. Durango, Mexico: Secretaría de Educación, Cultura y Deporte, 1998. 374 p.: bibl., ill.

Nicely researched biography and an important contribution to the study of Manuel Ponce. Declares that the majority of biographies of Ponce have been based on the error-filled "Efermérides" published in 1950 by Jesús C. Romero (see *HLAS 16:3195*). In an effort to get to know the "real" Ponce, the author interviewed colleagues, students, and friends of the composer. Owes much to the help provided by Carlos Vásquez Sánchez and his mother (Doña Rosita) who were closest to Ponce and made available never before recorded information and anecdotes, as well as their collection of books, photos, letters, and writings by and about Ponce. Includes catalog of works and useful bibliography.

4398 García López, Abel. Y las manos que hacen de la madera el canto-I. Morelia, Mexico: Morevallado, 1997. 48 p.: bibl., ill.

A brief contribution to the history of guitar construction and tuning in Mexico. Based on a series of interviews with old musicians from the Purépecha people of Michoacán who preserve vestiges of an old music tradition. Includes glossary of terms and color photos of instruments.

4399 Gastellou, Josué and Gustavo Rodríguez Mauleón. Catálogo de órganos tubulares históricos del Estado de Puebla. Puebla, Mexico: Univ. Iberoamericana, Golfo Centro, 1997. 219 p.: bibl., ill. (Col. Lupus inquisitor)

Extremely valuable study of 100 organs dating from the 17th-20th centuries in the state of Puebla. Numerous photos of organs in various states of disrepair, descriptions of the casing and specifications, summary of condition (percentage of original components existing), historical information, and bibliographical references.

4400 González Aktories, Susana and Roberto Kolb. Sensemayá: un juego de espejos entre música y poesía. México: JGH Editores, 1997. 117 p.: bibl., ill. (Bibliotheca litterarum humaniorum. Euterpe; 2)

Scholarly study of the poem "Sensemayá" by Cuban writer Nicolás Guillén and analysis of the musical version by Silvestre Revueltas. Includes a facsimile of Revueltas' 1937 manuscript. An important contribution to the study of Revueltas' music.

4401 Gutiérrez Heras, Joaquín. Notas sobre notas. Recopilación y prólogo de Consuelo Carredano. México: Conaculta, 1998. 517 p.: index. (Sello bermejo)

Collection of program notes written for the Orquesta Filarmónica de la Univ. Nacional Autónoma de México (OFUNAM) between 1971–76 and 1978–81. The first half of the book includes general European classical repertoire; the second half is devoted to Mexican composers. Useful for a cursory glance at standard orchestral repertoire for the concert-goer.

4402 Herrera de la Fuente, Luis. La música no viaja sola. México: Fondo de Cultura Económica, 1998. 274 p. (Vida y pensamiento de México)

Nostalgic and insightful recollections of his life, career, and the classical musical scene in Mexico by the preeminent Mexican conductor.

4403 Huacuz Elías, María Guadalupe. Notas sobre la pauta de las mujeres en la música en el siglo XIX. (*in* Mujeres, género y desarrollo. Michoacán, Mexico: Univ. Michoacana de San Nicolás de Hidalgo, Escuela de Economía; Equipo Mujeres en Acción; Centro Michoacano de Investigación y Formación Vasco de Quiroga; Univ. Autónoma Chapingo; Centro de Investigación y Desarrollo en el Estado de Michoacán, 1998, p. 431–443)

Using literary feminist esthetic theory, discusses the "feminine esthetic" in music.

From the early 19th century: Dolores Munguía, Inesilla (Inés García), a singer by the last name of Ramírez, and a pianist by the last name of Elhuyar. Also discusses women who attended the school connected with the Sociedad Filarmónica de México, founded in 1825: Luz Mosquiera, Guadalupe Espejo, Felícitas González, and María de Jesús Zepeda. From the mid-19th century: the singer Angela Peralta. At the end of the century: Fany Anitúa, María Luisa Meneses, Luz Meneses (harpist), and Alba Herrera y Ogazón. Little information of substance on any of the women mentioned.

4404 Instituto Nacional Indigenista (Mexico). Fonogramas de música indigena mexicana: catalogo nacional. México: Instituto Nacional Indigenista, 1996. 145 p.

Valuable catalog of the 79 recordings (LPs, CDs, cassettes) produced by INI between 1979–96. Contents (1009 individual pieces) and significant data (genre, ethnic group, instrumentation, persons and places, etc.) are included.

4405 Kuri Camacho, Ramón. Los oficios divinos y el espíritu del canto gregoriano en la Puebla de los Angeles, siglos XVII y XVIII. (*Novahispania/México*, 3, 1998, p. 227–260)

Scholarly analysis of reflections on sacred music from a collection of anonymous mid-18th-century manuscripts in the Biblioteca "Lafragua" of the Univ. Autónoma de Puebla. Discusses appropriate use of instruments, relation between music and text, contemporary debates, references to Thomas Aquinas. Valuable for a deeper understanding of liturgical life in Mexico at the time.

4406 Mayer-Serra, Otto. Panorama de la música mexicana: desde la independencia hasta la actualidad. México: CENDIM, 1996. 196 p.: bibl., ill., index.

Reprint of important history by eminent Mexican musicologist (of Catalán origin), first published in 1941. Material is presented in three chapters: "Music and Society in the Nineteenth Century," "Musical Composition in the Nineteenth Century," and "Musical Nationalism." Abundant musical examples. For comment on original edition, see *HLAS 9:4769.*

4407 Mexico en sus cantares. Coleccionados por Concha Michel. Edición y recopilación de Quetzal Rieder Espinoza.

Morelia, Mexico: FONCA; INI; IMC, 1997. 397 p. of music: ill. (some col.).

Valuable collection of over 200 songs (music and lyrics) arranged by region, indigenous group, genre. Brief notes precede each chapter.

4408 Miranda, Ricardo. Exploración y síntesis en la música de Manuel M. Ponce. (*Pauta/México*, 16:67, julio/sept. 1998, p. 36–57, facsim., music, photos)

A scholarly exploration, supported by abundant musical examples, of Ponce's style as a means of refuting previous scholars' attempts to categorize the composer's style by period or genre.

4409 Morales, Melesio. Mi libro verde. Introducción de Karl Bellinghausen. 1. ed. en Memorias mexicanas. México: CONACULTA, 1999. 230 p.: bibl., index. (Memorias mexicanas)

An important contribution to the study of Mexican music. "Mi libro verde de apuntes e impresiones is a document [conserved in the library of the Conservatorio Nacional de Música] without precedent in the history of Mexican culture. In letters and notes which are almost essay-like, in off-the-cuff comments on journal articles that attracted his attention, in reviews of concerts and recitals, in memories and vignettes of his own experience, Melesio Morales reconstructs a life dedicated to music and describes an epoque fundamental for the final development of a national culture" [from the jacket notes]. Includes a biography and useful index of names.

4410 Moreno, Salvador. Detener el tiempo: escritos musicales. Recopilación, selección e introducción por Ricardo Miranda. México: Instituto Nacional de Bellas Artes; Centro Nacional de Investigación, Documentación e Información Musical, 1996. 223 p.: ill.

Valuable collection of writings by and about eminent composer and musicologist Salvador Moreno (b. Orizaba, Veracruz 1916). Useful introduction by Miranda offers overview of Moreno's contribution. Includes chronology of Moreno's life and career, bibliography of articles, catalog of compositions, discography, name index, all compiled by Miranda. Contains previously unedited letters

from Isaac Albéniz and Benito Pérez Galdós
to the pianist Joaquín Malats.

4411 Música prehispánica en las culturas y comunidades del estado de México.
Recopilación del Programa de Investigación Cultural. Toluca, Mexico: Univ. Autónoma del Estado de México, 1997. 103 p.: bibl., ill. (Cuadernos de cultura universitaria; 15)

Collection of articles: "Introducción al Estudio de los Instrumentos Musicales" by Felipe Flores Dorantes; "Los Elementos Prehispánicos en la Música" by Irene Vázquez Valle; "Música de Origen Prehispánico Que Se Sigue Tocando en el Estado de México" by Fernando Nava López; "Transformación y Persistencia en la Música de Bandas Tradicionales en el Estado de México" by Judith Martínez Tapia; "Instrumentos Prehispánicos en la Arqueología y el Vocabulario Indígena" by Alfonso Sánchez Arteche; "Ritos y Mitos en las Danzas Mazahuas" by Edgar Samuel Morales Sales; "Ceremonias y Ritos de la Cultura Náhual" by Geofredo Uriel Valencia; "Los Instrumentos Musicales Prehispánicos de los Mayas."

4412 Olmos Aguilera, Miguel. El sabio de la fiesta: música y mitología en la región cahita-tarahumara. México: Instituto Nacional de Antropología e Historia; CONACULTA, 1998. 172 p.: bibl., ill., music. (Col. Biblioteca del INAH) (Serie Antropología)

Proposes to show similarities among the myths and musics of Yaqui, Mayan, and Tarahumaran peoples. This work focuses on the latter, found in the northwestern part of Mexico, with special emphasis on the figure of Pascola, who dances to the sound of the harp and violin, or violin and guitar, and serves as an intermediary between the spirit world and humankind.

4413 Pareyón, Gabriel. José F. Vásquez: una voz que a los oídos llega. Guadalajara, Mexico: Secretaría de Cultura, Gobierno de Jalisco, 1996. 202 p.: bibl., ill., index, photos.

Detailed scholarly biography of composer/conductor José Francisco Vásquez Cano (b. Arandas, Jalisco 1896; d. Mexico City 1961). Critiques/recollections of the composer by Juan F. Amaya, Manuel M. Bermejo, Gabriel Saldívar, and others. Includes useful evaluation and catalog of works, plot summaries of operas, name index, bibliography, photos.

4414 Pérez-Amador Adam, Alberto. Las óperas mexicanas. (*Pauta/México*, 16:66, abril/junio 1998, p. 47–56, facsims., photos)

After lamenting the lack of serious study of operas by Mexican composers, presents the results of the author's preliminary research, culminating in a list of composers and operas from the 18th-20th centuries.

4415 Ramírez Canul, Marcos. Antología de la música popular quintanarroense. Chetumal?, Mexico: Edición del Gobierno del Estado de Quintana Roo, 1999. 260 p.: ill.

Brief biographies of some 40 popular musicians from the state of Quintana Roo from the early 20th century to the present together with the lyrics of their most popular songs. Four musical examples are included.

4416 Ramos Aguirre, Francisco. Corridos agraristas de Tamaulipas. México: PACMYC, CACREP-Tamaulipas; Culturas Populares, FONCA; Consejo Estatal para la Cultura y las Artes de Tamaulipas, 1996. 42 p.: bibl., ill.

Brief discussion of *corridos* related to the agrarian movement in the state of Tamaulipas (early 20th century). Includes texts of various *corridos* dealing with important events, places and agrarian leaders such as José Silva Sanchez (1896–1924), Conrado Castillo (1894–1935), Juan Báez Guerra (1906–77), and Margarito Alcocer. Complete text and music of "Corrido del Agrarista" (music by Lorenzo Barcelata; lyrics by Ernesto M. Cortazar) and "José Silva Sánchez" (text and music by Reynaldo Martínez Ledesma) are included.

4417 Saavedra, Leonora. Variación contra sinfonía: Eduardo Mata y la historia de la música en México. (*Pauta/México*, 16:66, abril/junio 1998, p. 38–45, photos)

Paper presented at the conference "Eduardo Mata 1942–1995" in Mexico City in 1997. After discussing Mata's study with Carlos Chávez, presents his reflections on the search for a Mexican identity in large musical forms. Mata, apart from being a composer, was head of the Depto. de Música at UNAM and opera conductor of the Instituto Nacional de Bellas Artes.

4418 Tello, Aurelio. La capilla musical de la catedral de Oaxaca en tiempos de Manuel de Sumaya. (*Rev. Music. Venez.*, 16:34, mayo/agosto 1997, p. 111–126, table)

Although it emphasizes Sumaya, this scholarly article also surveys musicians employed in the Cathedral of Oaxaca from the mid-17th century (Juan de Ribeira) through the end of the 18th century (Blas de Peralta) with abundant references from the Actas Capitulares.

4419 Tello, Aurelio. Sor Juana Inés de la Cruz y los maestros de capilla catedralicios o de los ecos concertados y las acordes músicas con que sus villancicos fueron puestos en métrica armonía. (*Data/La Paz*, 7, 1997, p. 7–31, music, table)

Discusses villancicos of Sor Juana and composers who set her texts to music: José de Agurto y Loaysa, Antonio de Salazar,

Miguel Matheo de Dallo y Lana, Matheo Vallados. Only one fragment (by Salazar) of this music remains.

4420 Walker, John L. Música de cámara mexicana para alientos: obras de Kuri-Aldana, Quintanar y Córdoba. (*Pauta/México*, 18:71, julio/sept. 1999, p. 62–71, music, photos)

Brief analyses of four chamber compositions that include oboe: "Candelaria" (1965) and "Xilofonías" (1963) by Mario Kuri-Aldana (b. 1931); "Doble cuarteto" (1964) by Héctor Quintanar (b. 1936); and "A Laura y ellos" (1981) by Jorge Córdoba (b. 1953). Photos of composers and musical examples included.

CENTRAL AMERICA AND THE CARIBBEAN

ALFRED E. LEMMON, *Director, Williams Research Center, The Historic New Orleans Collection*

SEVERAL IMPORTANT TRENDS in the development of Caribbean and Central American musicology are clearly evident in the articles selected for review. Stevenson, in his powerful article, "The Latin American Music Educator's Best Ally: The Latin American Musicologist," (*Inter-American Music Review*, 2:2, Spring/Summer, 1980, p. 117–119) noted the importance of "the conscientious appraisal of popular music purveyed everywhere in Latin America" and that to "codify" the results of such studies is a "proper musicological task." He further notes that the "musical youth of Latin America deserves an opportunity to know their own musical forefathers." Tremendous strides have been taken in fulfilling the vision of Stevenson's now more than 20 year old essay.

First, studies in respected ethnomusicological journals have a greater focus on the region. Likewise, journals such as *Mesoamerica* have been willing to publish articles dealing with music. Second, there is an emerging group of scholars in the region examining their musical past. Finally, through the heroic efforts of the Sociedad Española de Autores y Editores, the monumental *Diccionario de la Música Española e Hispanoamericana* has appeared. Several volumes of the dictionary are cited in the Music chapter of *HLAS 60*.

Produced under the able leadership of Emilio Casares Rodicio, the dictionary is a multivolume work similar in nature to the great dictionaries devoted to the music of England, France, Germany, and Italy. The *Diccionario* has gathered an enormous amount of information, but equally important is its role in developing musicological studies in the region. The vast majority of the articles were written by residents of the region. By periodically gathering contributing editors, selected from each country, a forum for discussion was created. Finally, the importance of the daily contributions of the distinguished Cuban musicologist Eli Rodríguez to the project must be dutifully noted. The contents of the *Diccionario* reflect the varied musical heritage of Spain, Spanish America, and, in this particular case, Central America and the Caribbean. To illustrate this musical heritage, the volumes are enhanced by the presence of maps, facsimiles of music, and illustrations. Articles on the most current popular music "stars," indigenous musical instruments and dance dramas, appear alongside contributions on 19th- and 20th-century musical venues and essays on the great masters of the colonial period. While displaying the scholarly talent of the region, it is noteworthy that many of the authors were born after 1950. Fortunately, the editorial staff included the biographies of many of the contributing musicologists. In essence, within the pages is found a latent "Who's Who of Central American and Caribbean Musicology." Efforts to secure the best authors were not limited by geographic boundaries. The numerous articles on Guatemalan dance drama by Carroll E. Mace of the US reflect the culmination of a lifetime of work.

The articles selected for comment from the *Diccionario* were chosen to demonstrate the tremendous wealth and variety of information contained in this magnificent work. Given the vast scope of the *Diccionario*, it must be on the shelf of every respected music library, but also part of every library's Latin American holdings.

Stevenson, in his 1980 essay, set forth two tasks: "to make more widely known the names of the past musical geniuses of Latin America," and to integrate the music into "the curricula of the national conservatories." In order to accomplish that goal, he felt a "revolution" was needed. The revolution, especially in the case of Central America and the Caribbean, came in the form of this magnificent contribution of the Sociedad Española de Autores y Editores working with its allied institutions. With the goal of systematically gathering and publishing information on the region, and by encouraging the musicological efforts therein, the musical recognition due Central America and the Caribbean has been greatly advanced both outside and within its boundaries.

THE CARIBBEAN (EXCEPT CUBA)

4421 Bilby, Kenneth M. "Roots explosion": indigenization and cosmopolitanism in contemporary Surinamese popular music. (*Ethnomusicology*, 43:2, Spring/Summer 1999, p. 256–296, bibl., photos)

An examination of popular music of Suriname (Dutch Guiana). The author distinguishes between eight styles of popular music currently found in this once-agricultural colony. Boasting a sophisticated recording industry, the music is rarely heard outside of the Republic of Suriname, not even in nearby Caribbean islands, and is dismissed by the Dutch.

4422 Giovannetti Torres, Jorge L. Evolución social, identidades y políticas del reggae en Jamaica. (*Rev. Cienc. Soc./Río Piedras*, 4, enero 1998, p. 174–199, bibl.)

An examination of the social content of reggae in Jamaica. Particularly valuable

analysis of the use of reggae by political parties, giving added insight into a readily indentifiable form of Caribbean music.

Hispanofilia: arquitectura y vida en Puerto Rico, 1900–1950 = Hispanophilia: architecture and life in Puerto Rico, 1900–1950. See item **2063**.

4423 Manuel, Peter. The construction of a diasporic tradition: Indo-Caribbean "local classical music." (*Ethnomusicology*, 44:1, Winter 2000, p. 97–119, bibl., music)

An examination of the musical genre tan-singing practiced by the East Indians of the Caribbean. "Unique and sophisticated," it has remained free of local Creole influences but differs dramatically from its Indian musical sources. As a result, insight is gained into 19th-century Indian performance practices.

McDaniel, Lorna. The Big Drum ritual of Carriacou: praisesongs for re-memory of flight. See *HLAS 59:889.*

Noël, Eric. Saint-Georges: un chevalier de sang-mêlé dans la société des Lumières. See item **1893.**

4424 Rivera, Raquel Z. Cultura y poder en el rap puertorriqueño. (*Rev. Cienc. Soc./Río Piedras,* 4, enero 1998, p. 124–146, bibl.)

Documenting popular music is frequently more difficult than examining art music trends, however, its study is no less important for both sociological and musicological reasons. Rivera provides a valuable model for the study of popular musical forms.

CENTRAL AMERICA

4425 Acevedo, Jorge Luis. Flores, Bernal. (*in* Diccionario de la música española e hispanoamericana. Dirección y coordinación general de Emilio Casares Rodicio. Madrid: Sociedad General de Autores y Editores, 1999, v. 5, p. 166–168, bibl., ill.)

In an excellent biography of the Costa Rican composer/musicologist Bernal Flores (b. 1937), Acevedo traces his career at Eastman School of Music, and the Univs. of Arizona and Kansas. He examines Flores' importance in 20th-century Costa Rican musical life, and includes an extensive bibliography of his musicological writings and a catalog of compositions.

4426 Acevedo, Jorge Luis. Panama. (*in* Diccionario de la música española e hispanoamericana. Dirección y coordinación general de Emilio Casares Rodicio. Madrid: Sociedad General de Autores y Editores, 1999, v. 8, p. 424–430, bibl., ill., maps)

First reviews Panamanean history, then examines colonial music, music during the period when Panama formed part of Colombia, music in the republic of Panama, and folkloric music. The slim documentation for the colonial period indicates the role of the Catholic Church. The development of a local musical identity is based on Indian, African, and European influences. In the 19th century, salon music popular in the US and Europe abounded, with the piano being introduced in 1830. In the 20th century, music education institutions became a greater govern-ment priority. The regional examination of musical folklore reflects Panama's diversity.

4427 Acevedo, Jorge Luis and **Bernal Flores.** Costa Rica. (*in* Diccionario de la música española e hispanoamericana. Dirección y coordinación general de Emilio Casares Rodicio. Madrid: Sociedad General de Autores y Editores, 1999, v. 4, p. 122–135, bibl., ill., maps)

Article places the music history of Costa Rica in the appropriate historical-sociopolitical context by examining indigenous music tradition, Afro-Caribbean heritage, the development of art music in the 19th century, and opera. The presentation of 20th-century music summarizes principal developments by decade. Additional sections are devoted to music education and research and folk music.

4428 Arrivillaga Cortés, Alfonso. Conjunto de arpa, violín y guitarrilla: una reminiscencia hispánica o un producto del sincretismo entre los Maya-Q'eqchi'. (*Bulletin/ Geneva,* 61, 1997, p. 25–33, bibl., photos)

A preliminary study of the music of the Q'eqchi' cultural-linguistic group in Guatemala. Includes historical and anthropological background, discussion of the music in its context and the instruments, with good photographs of the latter. Brief, but useful bibliography. [J. Radomski]

4429 Cáceres, German. La música en El Salvador. (*Cult. Guatem.,* 19:3, sept./dic. 1998, p. 77–92)

Excellent summary article of El Salvador music from the mid-19th century through the 20th century. Included is biographical information on more than a dozen 20th-century composers. Essential study despite lack of bibliography and notes.

4430 Doñas, Oscar Manuel. Alas, Ciriaco de Jesús. (*in* Diccionario de la música española e hispanoamericana. Dirección y coordinación general de Emilio Casares Rodicio. Madrid: Sociedad General de Autores y Editores, 1999, v. 1, p. 165–166, bibl.)

The El Salvadoran composer Ciriaco de Jesús Alas (1866–1962) began his academic career as a medical student, which he abandoned to become a pioneer in El Salvadoran "academic" music. Composing symphonic music, songs, chamber music and arrangements of opera arias, his career demonstrates the country's rich musical heritage.

4431 Duarte, Arturo and **Paulo Alvarado.** Música de Guatemala en el siglo XVIII: los villancicos de Tomás Calvo. (*Mesoamérica/Antigua,* 19:36, dic. 1998, p. 411–498, facsims., music)

A monumental study of the nine villancicos of Tomás Calvo found in a *Vocabulario quiché* of the Princeton Univ. Library (Garret Collection no. 163). The study includes transcripts of the villancicos. The essay is testimony to the contribution of the journal *Mesoamérica* and the research institute Centro de Investigaciones Regionales de Mesoamérica (CIRMA) in the promotion of Guatemalan music.

Horcasitas, Fernando and **Alfred E. Lemmon.** El tratado de Santa Eulalia: un manuscrito musical náhuatl. See item **508.**

4432 Lehnhoff, Dieter. Guatemala. (*in* Diccionario de la música española e hispanoamericana. Dirección y coordinación general de Emilio Casares Rodicio. Madrid: Sociedad General de Autores y Editores, 1999, v. 6, p. 1–11, bibl., ill.)

A masterful article on the development of the diverse musical heritage of Guatemala. It is divided into sections on indigenous and folk music, colonial music, and 19th- and 20th-century music. Particularly important is the review of 20th-century composers, especially the post-1945 generation whose creativity is closely linked to nationalism.

4433 Lemmon, Alfred E. Coello Ramos. (*in* Diccionario de la música española e hispanoamericana. Dirección y coordinación general de Emilio Casares Rodicio. Madrid: Sociedad General de Autores y Editores, 1999, v. 3, p. 791, bibl.)

A prominent family of Honduran musicians, the father Rafael (1877–1967) established the Escuela Nacional de Música and the Orquestra Verdi. His daughter Orfilia, a distinguished pianist, studied in Honduras and France. She eventually became director of the Escuela Nacional de Música.

4434 Lemmon, Alfred E. Honduras. (*in* Diccionario de la música española e hispanoamericana. Dirección y coordinación general de Emilio Casares Rodicio. Madrid: Sociedad General de Autores y Editores, 1999, v. 6, p. 338–340, bibl., ill.)

After summarizing the difficulties (loss of documents from fire and natural disasters) of music research in Honduras, the article demonstrates how surviving documentation can help reconstruct musical life. While "European" music is traced to Cortes' 1524 journey to Honduras, Rafael Manzanares' studies of popular music are basic. Listing numerous composers (of "art" and popular music), and numerous dance-dramas, the riches awaiting researchers are underscored.

4435 Lemmon, Alfred E. and **Dieter Lehnhoff.** Quiroz. (*in* Diccionario de la música española e hispanoamericana. Dirección y coordinación general de Emilio Casares Rodicio. Madrid: Sociedad General de Autores y Editores, 1999, v. 8, p. 1066–1068, bibl.)

The Quiroz family dominated musical activity in Guatemala from 1738–91. Manuel Joseph de Quiroz (Chapelmaster of the Guatemala Cathedral from 1738 to his death in 1765) was succeeded by his nephew, Rafael Antonio Castellanos Quiroz (d. 1791). Manuel Joseph's brother, Francisco, was also a composer. The article contains extensive catalog of compositions by all three.

4436 Mace, Carroll Edward. Algunos apuntes sobre los bailes de Guatemala y de Rabinal. (*Cult. Guatem.,* 19:3, sept./dic. 1998, p. 7–76)

Mace has spent more than 50 years studying the dance-dramas of Guatemala, in particular those of Rabinal and the studies of Brasseur de Bourbourg. In this masterful summary article, he discusses the literary and social contexts of the *Bailes de moros, Los negritos, Rabinal Achi,* and numerous other less well-known dance-dramas.

4437 Mace, Carroll Edward. "Negritos, 1. Guatemala." (*in* Diccionario de la música española e hispanoamericana. Dirección y coordinación general de Emilio Casares Rodicio. Madrid: Sociedad General de Autores y Editores, 1999, vol. 7, p. 1012–1013, bibl., ill.)

The "Baile de los negritos" is one of six dances of precolumbian origin surviving in the Rabinal, Guatemala. Performed between Dec. 18-Jan. 6, rituals begin in Sept. Honoring the infant Jesus and the Three Wise Men, prominent are two small images of negros dressed as Arabs, possibly representing Ek Chuak (a black Maya god) and Ix-tiltón (a black Mexican god).

4438 Marroquín, Salvador. Chapetones. (*in* Diccionario de la música española e hispanoamericana. Dirección y coordinación general de Emilio Casares Rodicio. Madrid: Sociedad General de Autores y Editores, 1999, v. 3, p. 541, bibl.)

An excellent example of Central American dance-drama, the author explains its depiction of an alliance between Turkey and Spain, with 12 representatives from a variety of countries ranging from China to Argentina. Illustrates how these dance-dramas reflect social struggles. Chapetones, performed in Panchilmalco (San Salvador), is unique to El Salvador.

4439 Montenegra, Alvaro. Nicaragua. (*in* Diccionario de la música española e hispanoamericana. Dirección y coordinación general de Emilio Casares Rodicio. Madrid: Sociedad General de Autores y Editores, 1999, v. 7, p. 1021–1023, bibl., ill., maps)

A survey article of Nicaraguan popular and classical music history. It examines the náhuatl influence in Nicaraguan pre-columbian musical instruments, the presence of religious syncretism in the native dance-dramas, and the merging of African, Mesoamerican, and European elements. A discussion of the marimba as the national instrument highlights musical developments of Nicaraguan's Pacific side. The discussion of classical music focuses on the post-1821 period and, in particular, composers José de la Cruz Mena and Alejandro Vega Matus. In the 20th century, Luis Abraham Deladillo, educated in Italy, established the Banda de los Supremos Poseres and conducted studies of Nicaraguan native music.

4440 Rodríguez, Olavo Allén. Caribe. (*in* Diccionario de la música española e hispanoamericana. Dirección y coordinación general de Emilio Casares Rodicio. Madrid: Sociedad General de Autores y Editores, 1999, v. 3, p. 185–188, bibl., maps)

A summary of Caribbean musical history, the author contends "Caribe" refers to a geographical and historical region with a certain homogeneity. It includes an explanation of the linguistic components of the Caribbean—Spanish, French, Dutch, English, African, and native, and musical components

(rhythm, melody, and instruments). The rich musical life is a result of the varied migrations into the region.

4441 Scruggs, T.M. "Let's enjoy as Nicaraguans": the use of music in the construction of a Nicaraguan national consciousness. (*Ethnomusicology*, 43:2, Spring/ Summer 1999, p. 297–321, bibl., photos)

An examination of the development of a Nicaraguan popular music identity. Internal geographical and sociopolitical influences are examined and contrasted with Mexican, Cuban, and US influences.

CUBA

Carpentier, Alejo. Music in Cuba. See item **4333.**

4442 Casanova Oliva, Ana Victoria. María, Cecilia y Amalia: análisis dramatúrgico musical de tres zarzuelas cubanas. (*Rev. Music. Venez.*, 36, 1998, p. 109–127, bibl., facsims., music)

An examination of the libretti of three Cuban zarzuelas (*María la O* by Ernesto Lecuona, 1896–1963; *Celia Valdés* by Gonzalo Roig Rodríguez, 1890–1970; and *Amalia Batista* by Rodrigo Prats, 1909–80) and in particular the musical settings of passages of principle characters.

4443 Escudero Suástegui, Miriam Esther. El archivo de música de la iglesia habanera de La Merced: estudio y catálogo. La Habana: Fondo Editorial Casa de las Américas, 1998. 244 p.: bibl., ill.

An examination of the musical archive of Havana's Iglesia de Nuestra Señora de la Merced. The archive preserves works by Cuban and foreign composers (from 1796–1949). Includes a catalog of the archive, a musical history of La Merced, biographical sketch of 18th-century Catalán organist Cayetano Paqueras, and an analysis of the impact of opera on Cuban sacred music (1855–1924).

4444 Gómez García, Zoila. Cuba. (*in* Diccionario de la música española e hispanoamericana. Dirección y coordinación general de Emilio Casares Rodicio. Madrid: Sociedad General de Autores y Editores, 1999, v. 4, p. 246–274, bibl., ill., maps)

A masterful essay tracing the development of aboriginal music, "European" music in Cuba as a reflection of immigration patterns, and African and Caribbean influences on Cuban music. The authors include an examination of oral music tradition, and art music. After a summary of current popular musical trends, the authors review developments in music education and research.

González Aktories, Susana and **Roberto Kolb.** Sensemayá: un juego de espejos entre música y poesía. See item **4400.**

4445 Linares, María Teresa and **Faustino Núñez.** La música entre Cuba y España. Madrid: Fundación Autor, 1998. 334 p.: bibl., ill., index.

An examination of the musical exchange between Cuba and Spain. Linares, a leader in Cuban musical affairs, examines *música campesina*, the *canción cubana*, the *danzón*, and the *son.*

4446 Rodríguez, Victoria Eli. La Habana. (*in* Diccionario de la música española e hispanoamericana. Dirección y coordinación general de Emilio Casares Rodicio. Madrid: Sociedad General de Autores y Editores, 1999, v. 6, p. 682–686, bibl., ill.)

An excellent review of the development of music in Havana. Succinctly covering colonial religious music, 19th-century musical trends, the development of opera, and the more experimental 20th-century music, alongside that of popular music, abundant information is also given on the development of Havana's musical instruments.

4447 Sáena Coopat, Carmen María and **Laura de Vilar Alvarez.** Nicola. (*in* Diccionario de la música española e hispanoamericana. Dirección y coordinación general de Emilio Casares Rodicio. Madrid:

Sociedad General de Autores y Editores, 1999, v. 7, p. 1024–1026, bibl., ill.)

Nicola family members Clara Amalia de los Reyes Romero (1888–1951), Abel Jorge Nicola Romero (1915–89), and Isaac Noel Nicola Romero (b. 1916) are prominent 19th- and 20th-century Cuban musicians, teachers, and guitarists. Noel Nicola Reyes (b. 1946) is a founder of *La Nueva Trova Cubana.*

4448 Simon, Pedro. Alicia Alonso. (*in* Diccionario de la música española e hispanoamericana. Dirección y coordinación general de Emilio Casares Rodicio. Madrid: Sociedad General de Autores y Editores, 1999, v. 1, p. 315–317, bibl., ill.)

Alicia Alonso (born Alicia Martínez del Hoyo) as ballerina, choreographer, and teacher, had an enormous impact on 20th-century ballet in Cuba, Iberoamerica, the US, and Europe. In an excellent article, the author reviews her international importance. An article on the Alonso family (Fernando and Alberto) provides additional information on ballet in 20th-century Cuba (p. 313–314).

4449 Vinueza González, María Elena. Afrocubanismo. (*in* Diccionario de la música española e hispanoamericana. Dirección y coordinación general de Emilio Casares Rodicio. Madrid: Sociedad General de Autores y Editores, 1999, v. 1, p. 84–85, bibl.)

A superb article on the development of the term "Afrocubanismo" from 1847 (when first used) through the works of Fernando Ortiz (1881–1969). Ortiz's studies examined the African influence on varied aspects of Cuban social and cultural life. The movement became a way to denounce racial discrimination and define Cuba's African heritage.

ANDEAN COUNTRIES

WALTER AARON CLARK, *Professor of Musicology, University of California, Riverside*

THE APPEARANCE OF THE NEW EDITION of *Die Musik in Geschichte und Gegenwart* (Kassel, Germany: Bärenreiter Verlag. 1994–) in most respects fulfills the high expectations held for it. Entries on Latin American countries and topics are detailed and authoritative (the previous edition virtually ignored Latin America), with leading scholars like Stevenson and Béhague contributing many of the entries. The publisher made the decision to divide the encyclopedia into two parts: subjects (Sachteil) and biographies (Personenteil). The first part is now complete; at this writing, the second is halfway finished. The second edition of *The New Grove Dictionary of Music and Musicians* (2001) has appeared in both print and electronic formats and retains its distinction as the foremost reference source on music in English. Articles on Colombia, Ecuador, Peru, and Venezuela are annotated herein (items **4457, 4462, 4463,** and **4468,** respectively).

Of particular importance to the study of music in Latin America is the second volume of the *Garland Encyclopedia of World Music* (1999), which is devoted to Mexico, Central and South America, and the Caribbean (item **4373**). This outstanding volume is an indispensable resource for anyone researching the folk and popular music of those regions. It includes some coverage of the classical heritage as well, insofar as art music has drawn inspiration from the vernacular traditions, especially in the formation of regional styles under the nationalist impulse.

In general, musicological research on Andean countries, especially Ecuador and Bolivia, remains underdeveloped. This is particularly true of the art-music traditions in those countries.

RECENT DOCTORAL DISSERTATIONS

Laura M. Larco, "Ritual Sound: The Mesa Performance in Northern Peru" (Univ. of Maryland College Park, 1996). Focuses on the sounds, chants, and dialogue of the *mesa* ritual. The various texts, both spoken and chanted, offer clues to the community's beliefs and behaviors. Though this is in the field of cultural anthropology, it impinges on issues of concern to ethnomusicologists.

Pamela Bowen Chester, "A Study of the Life and Wind Music of Blas Emilio Atehortua, Including a Critical Edition and Stylistic Analysis of *Cinco piezas a Bela Bartok*" (Univ. of Northern Colorado, 1997). Surveys the Colombian composer's nearly 50 works for band, almost all of which are unpublished. Provides an overview of his life, an analysis of this work, and an assessment of Atehortua's contribution to Latin American music.

Marie Elizabeth Labonville, "Musical Nationalism in Venezuela: The Work of Juan Bautista Plaza (1898–1965)" (Univ. of California, Santa Barbara, 1999). Treats one of the most important figures in the history of Venezuelan art music, who is largely unknown outside his native country. Based on extensive research in Venezuela, the dissertation throws needed light on Plaza's contributions as lecturer, critic, scholar, performer, educator, and composer.

BOLIVIA

4450 Broggini, Norberto. Los manuscritos para teclado de Chiquitos y la música de Domenico Zipoli. (*Data/La Paz*, 7, 1997, p. 133–164, music, tables)

Describes the manuscripts with works for keyboard held at the Concepción de Chiquitos' archive. Includes music by Martin Schmid (1694–1772) and Domenico Zipoli, as well as European works by A. Corelli and Vivaldi. The manuscripts also contain keyboard arrangements of pieces originally written for other instruments. Includes a few transcripts. [C. Magaldi]

4451 Eichmann Oehrli, Andrés and **Carlos Seoane Urioste.** El archivo de San Calixto: informaciones de la vida cultural de Mojos, ss. XVIII-XIX. (*Data/La Paz*, 7, 1997, p. 59–94, music, table)

Describes the musical holdings and documentation related to musical activities in Mojos held in the archives of San Calixto, La Paz. The archive is particularly important for the documentation concerning musical activities after 1811. [C. Magaldi]

4452 Eichmann Oehrli, Andrés and **Carlos Seoane Urioste.** La música en la Audiencia de Charcas: algunos aportes documentales, s. XVII-XIX. (*Anuario/Sucre,* 1998, p. 63–101, bibl.)

Examines the documentation regarding musical activities in the Audiencia de Charcas from the 17th-19th centuries. Reviews the bibliography and reports on the music manuscript holdings in several archives. Argues for a holistic understanding of the region's musical legacy. [C. Magaldi]

4453 Illari, Bernardo. ¿Les *hacen lugar?* ¿Y cómo?: la representación del *indio* en dos villancicos chuquisaqueños de 1718. (*Data/La Paz,* 7, 1997, p. 165–196, bibl., ill., music, tables)

Examines the represenation of "the native" in two villancicos from Chiquisaca cathedral; discusses the relation between music, art, and mestizo culture in the colonial context of 18th-century La Plata. Includes musical excerpts. See also item **4454.** [C. Magaldi]

4454 Illari, Bernardo. No hay lugar para ellos: los indígenas en la capilla musical de La Plata. (*Anuario/Sucre,* 1997, p. 73–108, tables)

This thought-provoking study questions the idea of musical *mestizaje* during the colonial period, particularly during the composer Juan de Araujo's tenure at the cathedral of La Plata. Argues that the "native" had a more active participation in musical activities during an earlier stage of Spanish colonization, when the church had a specific missionary function. For comment on a related article, see item **4453.** [C. Magaldi]

4455 Orías Bleichner, Andrés. Música en la Real Audiencia de Charcas: un perfil de la escuela platense. (*Data/La Paz,* 7, 1997, p. 33–58, facsims., maps)

Brief study reports on documents related to music-making in the Real Audiencia de Charcas, particularly to the "school" of La Plata. [C. Magaldi]

4456 Seoane Urioste, Carlos and **Andrés Eichmann Oehrli.** Algunos hallazgos de música en zonas andinas rurales. (*Data/La Paz,* 7, 1997, p. 95–118, appendix)

It is a rarely acknowledged fact that academic music was composed and performed in churches in rural areas of the Bolivian Andes from the 17th-19th centuries. This article illuminates the venues, repertoires, and manuscript holdings of major rural churches.

COLOMBIA

4457 Béhague, Gerard; Lise Waxer; and **George List.** Colombia. (*in* New Grove dictionary of music and musicians. 2nd ed. Edited by Stanley Sadie. London: Macmillan, 2001, t. 6, p. 134–149, bibl., maps, music, photos)

Excellent coverage of the art music (Béhague); traditional music arranged by region (Waxer/List); and popular music (Waxer) of Colombia. Illustrated with maps, photographs, and musical examples.

4458 Calderón Sáenz, Claudia. Estudio analítico y comparativo sobre la música del joropo, expresión tradicional de Venezuela y Colombia. (*Rev. Music. Venez.,* 19:39, enero/junio 1999, p. 215–256)

A detailed analysis of representative examples of the *joropo,* one of the main genres of folk song and dance in Venezuela and Colombia. Focuses on the harmonic, melodic, and rhythmic characteristics of the *joropo* as well as its characteristic accompaniments.

4459 Espriella Ossío, Alfonso de la. Historia de la música en Colombia: a través de nuestro bolero. Bogotá: Grupo Editorial Norma, 1997. 713 p.: ill. (Col. Biografías y documentos)

Traces the history of music in Colombia, focusing on the bolero. Includes biographies of Colombian composers from 1860-present. Also treats Barranquilla and Cartagena, important locales in the evolution of the Colombian bolero, as well as the development of the music profession and the impact of radio.

4460 Illera Montoya, Carlos Humberto. Clavelitos con amor: la música cantinera; cultura y estética popular. Cauca, Colombia: Fondo Mixto de Promoción de la Cultura y las Artes del Cauca; Popayán, Colombia: Distribución de Elizabeth Ediciones, 1998. 395 p.: bibl., ill., indexes.

Pt. 1 consists of an overview of the

esthetics and culture of cantina music and performance. Pt. 2 provides short biographies of leading performers, while Pt. 3 is a selective list of the best-known cantina songs, giving title, text, rhythmic type (e.g., *pasillo*), performing artist, and record label.

4461 Peñín, José. Decimas cantadas y poetas iletrados. Caracas: Fundación Vicente Emilio Sojo, Consejo Nacional de la Cultura, 1997. 190 p.: bibl., ill. (Cuadernos de musicología; 2)

The author and his team of specialists collected song texts from the Sierra Nevada de Santa Marta region of northeastern Colombia. These texts, by otherwise illiterate authors, consist of 10-line stanzas and are collectively referred to as *décimas*, a poetic form dating back many centuries in the Hispanic world. The volume commences with a brief history of the *décima*, then presents 294 texts. Concludes with an explanation of the system of transcription and analysis of the interface of text and music.

Schwegler, Armin. "Chi ma nkongo": lengua y rito ancestrales en El Palenque de San Basilio, Colombia. See *HLAS 59:1125.*

ECUADOR

4462 Béhague, Gerard and **John Schechter.** Ecuador. (*in* New Grove Dictionary of Music and Musicians. 2nd ed. Edited by Stanley Sadie. London: Macmillan, 2001, t. 7, p. 871–879, bibl., music, photos)

Thorough treatment of the art music of Ecuador (Béhague) as well as traditional music (Schechter), including the highlands (treating genres and instruments), Oriente, and coastal areas. Illustrated with photos and musical examples.

PERU

4463 Béhague, Gerard and **Thomas Turino.** Peru. (*in* New Grove Dictionary of Music and Musicians. 2nd ed. Edited by Stanley Sadie. London: Macmillan, 2001, t. 19, p. 467–477, bibl., music, photos)

Excellent coverage of the art music of Peru (Béhague) as well as traditional styles (Turino), including precolumbian, highlands (indigenous and mestizo), lowlands, and coastal (Afro-Peruvian and criollo) types. Illustrated with photos and musical examples.

4464 Godoy, Enrique Alejandro. Breve semblanza del órgano barroco andino. (*Data/La Paz,* 7, 1997, p. 119–132, photos)

Study of musical organs and organ building in the Peruvian Andes dating back to the 16th century. These instruments display very distinctive traits in their sound and construction.

4465 Rüegg, Daniel and **Gerhard Baer.** Zum Liedrepertoire der *Matsigenka:* Notizen und Analysen [The song repertoire of the *Matsigenka:* notes and analyses]. (*Bulletin/ Geneva,* 61, 1997, p. 71–78, bibl., music, photo)

A thoughtful investigation into poetic and musical structures in the songs of the Matsigenka people in Peru, whose music has not been studied. Analyzes one example from each of the two principal song types.

4466 Yep, Virginia. El valse peruano: análisis musicológico de una de las expresiones más representativas de la música criolla del Perú. Lima: Juan Brito, 1998. 48 p.: bibl., music.

Slender but important volume based on a lecture-recital given by the author in 1994, in Berlin. The Peruvian *valse* (waltz) is one of the most significant manifestations of Creole music in Peru. Her analysis, including musical examples, covers historical and cultural dimensions, as well as accompaniment (she plays guitar), texts, and voice.

VENEZUELA

4467 Balliache, Simón. Jazz en Venezuela. Caracas: Grupo Editorial Ballgrub, 1997. 144 p.: appendices, bibl. (Col. Música)

A narrative account, without pictures or musical examples, of the jazz scene in Venezuela, emphasizing Caracas. Presents a history of the jazz bands, performers, festivals, and clubs that flourished during the 20th century. Useful appendices include lists of Venezuela jazz ensembles and individual performers, as well as appearances by such US artists as Woody Herman, Duke Ellington, and Dave Brubeck.

4468 Béhague, Gerard; Jonathan Hill; and **Walter Guido.** Venezuela. (*in* New Grove Dictionary of Music and Musicians. 2nd ed. Edited by Stanley Sadie. London: Macmillan, 2001, t. 26, p. 386–398, bibl., music, photos)

Excellent coverage of art music (Béhague), Amerindian music (Hill), and Afro-Venezuelan styles (broken down by various groups). Illustrated with photos and musical examples.

Calderón Sáenz, Claudia. Estudio analítico y comparativo sobre la música del joropo, expresión tradicional de Venezuela y Colombia. See item **4458.**

4469   Enciclopedia de la música en Venezuela. v. 1–2. Caracas: Fundación Bigott, 1998. 2 v.

Generally brief entries, although some, such as the one on "nationalism," run to several pages, and no illustrations of any kind. Does include comprehensive works lists for the important composers. Most authoritative reference work to date on the music of Venezuela.

4470   Hemerografía musical venezolana del siglo XX. v. 1, *Revista Elite*, 1925–1992. Caracas: Fundación Vicente Emilio Sojo; Instituto Autónomo Biblioteca Nacional, 1998. 1 v.

Potentially very useful listing of music-related articles in the periodical *Elite*, from 1925–92. Arranged by author with subject and title indices.

4471   Martín, Gloria. El perfume de una época: la nueva canción en Venezuela. Caracas?: Alfadil Ediciones, Secretaría de la Univ. Central de Venezuela, 1998. 188 p.: bibl. (Col. Trópicos)

Pt. 1 lays out the history of the "New Song" movement in Venezuela, including a chronology, and treats the underlying political and social roots of songs of political protest as well as leading figures. Pt. 2 presents interview material with New Song artists. An important contribution to the literature on this topic.

4472   Milanca Guzmán, Mario. Teresa Carreño: manuscrito inéditos y un proyecto para la creación de un Conservatorio de Música y Declamación. (*Rev. Music. Chil.*, 50:186, julio/dic. 1996, p. 13–39)

The legendary piano virtuosa Teresa Carreño played a leading role in promoting music in Latin America, despite her extended residence in Europe. This article investigates her involvement in attempts to establish a Conservatorio de Música y Declamación in Caracas in the 19th century, of which she was to have been the director. The research is based on a cache of letters in the archive of the John Boulton Foundation.

Prieto Soto, Jesús. Mestizaje y cultura costanera. See item **2465.**

4473   Rodríguez Legendre, Fidel. Música, Sojo y caudillismo cultural. Caracas: Fundación Vicente Emilio Sojo; Consejo Nacional de la Cultura, 1998. 193 p.: bibl., ill. (Cuadernos de musicología; no. 2 [i.e. 3])

An intriguing sociocultural study of Emilio Sojo, the leading Venezuelan musician of the 20th century, whose domination of Venezuelan music and culture was so complete that his career bears a marked resemblance to the dictators (*caudillos*) who have plagued the country on its march towards democracy.

4474   Sans, Juan Francisco. Una aproximación analítica a las obras de los compositores de la Escuela Chacao. (*Rev. Music. Venez.*, 14:32/33, 1993, p. 58–77)

Focuses on the Chacao School that flourished in the Caracas area c. 1800. The leader of this group was Juan Bautista Plaza. This study acknowledges the influence of Mozart, Haydn, and Pergolesi that others have observed, but it goes beyond previous research by offering a detailed theoretical analysis of selected works by composers of this school.

SOUTHERN CONE AND BRAZIL

CRISTINA MAGALDI, *Associate Professor of Music, Towson University*

THE ACCESSIBILITY OF INFORMATION ON THE INTERNET is one of the most noteworthy aspects of the recent research on music from the Southern Cone. While well-established music periodicals such as *Latin American Music Review* (University of Texas, Austin) and *Revista Musical Chilena* (Universidad de Chile) now have articles available online (*http://www.utexas.edu/utpress/journals/jlamr.html* and *http://musicologia.uchile.cl/revista/*), new academic online music journals have emerged; one example is the *Revista Eletrônica de Musicologia* (Brazil) (*http://www.humanas.ufpr.br/rem/*), edited by Rogério Budasz, which since 1996 has published online articles on a variety of musical topics, from colonial to electronic music in Latin America.

Several local institutions have also made significant improvements in making their music resources available online. The most comprehensive of these is the *Bibliografia musical Brasileira* (*http://www.abmusica.org.br/*), an extensive online database sponsored by the Academia Brasileira de Música in Rio de Janeiro that lists some 8,000 works about music in Brazil (books, articles, theses and dissertations, annals, and reference works). Since 1999, the Academia Brasileira de Música has also issued the periodical *Brasiliana*, which includes works by renowned Brazilian musicians and scholars, and provides online abstracts of articles in both English and Portuguese (*http://www.abmusica.org.br/*). In addition, the web page of the Museu Villa-Lobos in Rio de Janeiro (*http://www.museuvillalobos.org.br/*) is richly illustrated and provides information in both English and Portuguese about the museum's holdings and cultural promotions, as well as musical samples of some of Villa-Lobos' most popular works. Brazilian colonial music is well represented on the web page *Música Colonial Brasileira* (*http://www.geocities.com/RainForest/9468/musicamg.htm*).

The site for the Argentine Instituto Nacional de Musicología "Carlos Vega" (*http://www.inmuvega.gov.ar/*) also provides valuable information for researchers, including references to back issues of the Instituto's *Revista*, now available on an interactive CD-ROM. One of the most comprehensive web sites on the Argentine tango is *Todo Tango* (*http://www.todotango.com/*), which provides a comprehensive array of information on tango in both English and Spanish, ranging from articles, biographies, videos, and sheet music, to a long list of tango recordings; the music can also be accessed online.

In addition to online sources, a copious number of outstanding publications on music from the Southern Cone have come out in the last few years. Especially noteworthy are reference works, such as the volume on Latin America (1998) in the *Garland Encyclopedia of World Music*, which includes chapters on traditional and popular music of individual countries, as well as chapters on some recent popular musical styles (item **4373**). Gerard Béhague's articles on Latin America and on individual Latin American countries in the revised edition of *New Grove Dictionary of Music and Musicians* (2001) include updated information based on recent research; particularly relevant are his contributions on Afro-Brazilian musical traditions (item **4376**). Leslie Bethell's *A Cultural History of Latin America: Literature, Music, and the Visual Arts in the 19th and 20th Centuries* (1998), although not as up-to-date, provides useful insight into the role of music within the larger context of Latin American culture (item **4372**). The revised edition of the Portuguese language *Enciclopédia da música brasileira: popular, erudita, e folclórica* (1998) is undoubtedly a welcome publication, even though it does not include illustrations or musical examples, and omits much new research (item **4516**). Finally, attesting to academia's general interest in the music of this area, Ketty Wong's compilation (*Latin American Music Review*, 1999) includes no fewer than 40 theses and dissertations about music in the Southern Cone written between 1992–99 in English, Spanish, and Portuguese (item **4377**).

Colonial music has emerged as one of the most researched areas in the Southern Cone. Highlights among them are the articles in the periodical *Anuario* (Sucre, Bolivia) and especially in the 1997 issue of *Data* (La Paz). Noteworthy are Bernardo Illari's seminal articles pioneering colonial music criticism in Latin America (items **4453** and **4454**). Nineteenth-century music continues to receive less attention. Nonetheless, Mario Milanca Guzmán's outstanding historical study on the 19th-century Chilean periodical *El Ferrocarril* is a considerable contribution (item **4501**). A wide majority of publications dealing with the 20th century focus on popular music, especially in Brazil and Argentina, while studies on art music are scarce. Deborah Schwartz-Kates' brilliant article on Felipe Boero is thus particularly appreciated, since the field continues to deserve further scholarly attention (item **4492**).

One welcome feature in the recent music publications is the emergent interest on regional music. Significant regional studies from Brazil are Márcio Leonel Farias Reis Páscoa's book on musical life in 19th-century Manaus (item **4528**), Eurides de Souza Santos' work on music in the city of Canudos, Brazil (item **4531**), and Almerinda Guerreiro's study on Afro-Brazilian popular musical styles in Salvador (item **4518**). Following the trend, Jane Florine's articles on "Cuarteto" music in Córdoba are noteworthy contributions to Argentine regional studies in music (items **4479** and **4480**).

ARGENTINA

4475 Amuchástegui, Irene. Agustín Magaldi: la biografía. Sobra una investigación con Juan José Quiroga y José Luis Benzi. Buenos Aires: Aguilar, 1998. 223 p.: bibl., ill.

Biographical study, shows that the tango singer Magaldi was as famous as his contemporary, Carlos Gardel. Well-documented, the book touches on Magaldi's relationship with Eva Perón. Includes a discography by Juan José Quiroga.

4476 Assunção, Fernando O. El tango y sus circunstancias: 1880–1920. Prólogo de Olga Fernández Latour de Botas. 2a. ed. Buenos Aires: Librería-Editorial El Ateneo, 1998. 179 p.: bibl., ill. (some col.). (Serie Música)

This welcome revised and enlarged second edition provides an excellent historical account of the formation of tango in Buenos Aires at the turn of the 20th century. A CD with musical examples accompanies the publication.

4477 Cambas, Graciela and Jorge Francisco Machón. La música misionera: de la Colonia a la revolución, 1768–1830. Posadas, Argentina: Editora Contemporánea, 1997? 58 p.: bibl., ill., map.

This brief but well-documented study focuses on the music in the Río de la Plata region after the expulsion of the Jesuits, from 1768–1830.

4478 Catholic Church. Conferencia Episcopal Argentina. Delegación para los bienes culturales de la Iglesia. El patrimonio musical de la Iglesia. Textos de Héctor Aguer *et al.* Buenos Aires: Oficina del Libro, Conferencia Episcopal Argentina, 1998. 185 p.: bibl.

Annals of the 1997 national meeting that focused on the musical patrimony of the Church. Musicologist Carmen García Muñoz's article about sacred music in Argentina includes an extensive list of sacred compositions, covering from the late 18th century-20th century.

4479 Florine, Jane L. Carlos Jiménez: reflecting the power of the people in Argentine *cuarteto* music. (*Pop. Music Soc.*, 22:3, Fall 1998, p. 61–113)

Discusses the role of *cuarteto* music as entertainment in the city of Córdoba and as an escape from daily problems. Focuses on the famous pop singer Carlos Jiménez and on how his performances address his fans' hopes for a better life. For comment on related article by same author, see item **4480**.

4480 Florine, Jane L. "Cuarteto" dance-hall entertainment or people's music? (*Lat. Am. Music Rev.*, 19:1, Spring/Summer 1998, p. 31–46)

An outgrowth of the author's PhD dissertation (Florida State Univ., 1996), the article examines the social function of the popular music groups called *cuartetos* in Córdoba. Compares two views of *cuarteto* groups: the first as solely entertainment, and the second as a powerful political tool. See also item **4479.**

4481 Gesualdo, Vicente. Breve historia de la música en la Argentina. Buenos Aires: Claridad, 1998. 410 p.: ill. (Breve historia Claridad)

Abridged version of the author's breathtaking *Historia de la música en la Argentina* (1961). However, this edition lacks bibliographical citations and covers biographies only up to the mid-1980s. For comment on original version, see *HLAS 25:5211*.

4482 Göttling, Jorge. Tango, melancólico testigo. Buenos Aires: Corregidor, 1998. 171 p.

Compilation of short articles dealing with tango lyrics; includes interviews with prominent individuals in the world of Argentine tango.

4483 Judkovski, José. El tango: una historia con judíos. Buenos Aires: IWO, 1998. 233 p.: bibl., ill., index.

Highlights the role of Jewish musicians in the creation, development, and diffusion of the tango in Argentina and abroad. Includes a list of Jewish tango musicians and an index.

4484 Marchi, Sergio. No digas nada: una vida de Charly García. 2a ed. Buenos Aires: Editorial Sudamericana, 1997. 287 p.: ill.

Biographical study of the Argentine rock star Charly García. Not intended as an official biography, the book was written by a close friend with the goal of documenting the first 20 years of García's musical career. Includes accounts by García's contemporaries.

4485 Las mejores letras de tango: antología de doscientas cincuenta letras, cada una con su historia. Selección, prólogo y notas de Héctor Angel Benedetti. Buenos Aires: Seix Barral, 1998. 511 p.: ill., index.

The first part of this book is an anthology of 250 tango lyrics classified by topic; the second part provides a short history of each

song. Includes an index of songs but lacks bibliography.

4486 Napoli, Cristian Gabriel de *et al.* Treinta años de música para jóvenes. Buenos Aires: Fundación Octubre; Ediciones de la Flor, 1998. 271 p.: bibl.

Compilation of articles addressing the appropriation of rock in Argentina and its reinterpretation as a national symbol.

4487 Pérez Bugallo, Rubén. Cancionero popular de Corrientes. Prólogo de Adolfo Colombres. Selección, ordenamiento y supervisión general de Martina Pérez Bugallo. Buenos Aires: Ediciones del Sol: Distribución exclusiva, Ediciones Colihue, 1999. 379 p.: bibl., ill. (Biblioteca de cultura popular; 25)

Compilation of 1,672 song texts from Corrientes, including coplas, décimas, romances, *seguidillas* and *redondillas*.

4488 Pérez Bugallo, Rubén. Katináj: estudios de etno-organología musical chaquense. Buenos Aires: Instituto Nacional Superior del Profesorado de Folklore, 1997. 140 p.: bibl., ill., music, photos, table. (Trabajo del INSPF, 1)

Organological study, reports on some 14 musical instruments from the Chaco region; provides historical background and comments on the instruments' ritual use and symbolic associations. For comments on author's study of instruments in other Argentine regions, see *HLAS 58:4855*.

4489 Pickenhayn, Jorge Oscar. Estudio sobre el tango. Buenos Aires: Editorial Plus Ultra, 1999. 124 p.: bibl.

Compilation of short articles dealing with the origins and development of early tango. Includes biographies of 20 tango musicians and an extensive bibliography.

4490 Portorrico, Emilio Pedro. Diccionario biográfico de la música argentina de raíz folklórica. Buenos Aires: E.P. Portorrico, 1997. 290 p.: bibl., ill., index.

Biographies of traditional and popular Argentine musicians. Includes illustrations and index.

4491 Pujol, Sergio Alejandro. Historia del baile: de la milonga a la disco. Buenos Aires: Emecé, 1999. 411 p., 16 p. of plates: bibl., ill., index.

This excellent book is a panorama of

dance in 20th-century Argentina. Addresses dances from the waltz and the tango to the salsa, and offers a historical and cultural account of the vogue of these dances in Argentina. Briefly reports on the lives of musicians and dancers.

4492 Schwartz-Kates, Deborah. Argentine art music and the search for national identity mediated through a symbolic native heritage: the *tradición gauchesca* and Felipe Boero's El Matrero (1929). (*Lat. Am. Music Rev.*, 20:1, Spring/Summer 1999, p. 1–29)

An outgrowth of the author's PhD dissertation (Univ. of Texas, Austin, 1997), the article focuses on Felipe Boero's opera *El Matrero* and its relationship to Argentine musical nationalism at the beginning of the 20th century. Addresses the work's musical and poetic structures as symbols of national identity.

4493 Selles, Roberto. El origen del tango. Buenos Aires: Academia Porteña del Lunfardo, 1998. 57 p.: bibl., ill.

Brief historical account of the beginnings of tango, focusing on the 19th century.

4494 Tango: magia y realidad: 20 miradas sobre una aventura queno cesa. Buenos Aires: Corregidor, 1998. 334 p.: appendix.

Compilation of articles by 20 tango specialists; covers various aspects of tango, from the music to the lyrics and to the dance. The appendix includes two articles on the Argentine song by musicologists Carlos Vega and Gastón Talamón originally published in 1926 in the magazine *Nosotros*.

4495 Thiers, Walter. El jazz criollo y otras yerbas, 1950–1995. Buenos Aires: Corregidor, 1999. 654 p.: bibl., ill.

Surveys the dissemination of jazz in Argentina; focuses on the biography of Argentine and foreign jazz exponents from the 1950s on. Includes bibliography and discographies.

4496 Valenti Ferro, Enzo. Historia de la ópera argentina. Buenos Aires: Ediciones de Arte Gaglianone, 1997. 314 p.: bibl., ill., indexes, ports.

Provides data on operas written by Argentine composers and foreign musicians active in Buenos Aires from 1877–1997. Includes biographical information, a list of operas by Argentine composers that premiered in Buenos Aires, summaries of plots, index, and bibliography.

4497 Vega, Carlos. Panorama de la música popular argentina: con un ensayo sobre la ciencia del folklore. Ed. facs. Buenos Aires: Instituto Nacional de Musicología Carlos Vega, 1998. 361 p.: bibl., ill., indexes.

Facsimile of the 1944 publication by the leading Argentine musicologist.

4498 Zucchi, Oscar. El tango, el bandoneón y sus intérpretes. v. 1. Buenos Aires: Corregidor, 1998. 1 v.: bibl., indexes.

This excellent study focuses on the development of the bandonéon, its use in tango ensembles, and its performance techniques. Includes information on early composers and performers, list of works, and discography.

CHILE

4499 Lorenz, Ricardo. Orrego-Salas in half a century of sound recordings. (*Lat. Am. Music Rev.*, 21:1, Spring/Summer 2000, p. 9–15)

Reviews and compiles the discography of Chilean composer Orrego-Salas, including LPs and CDs, a total of 29 recorded works spanning 50 years of the composer's life.

4500 Marchant, Guillermo. El libro sesto de Maria Antonia Palacios, c. 1790: un manuscrito musical chileno. (*Rev. Music. Chil.*, 53:192, julio/dic. 1999, p. 27–46, bibl.)

An excerpt from the author's MA thesis (Univ. de Chile, 1997), this study describes a late 18th-century manuscript including instrumental pieces for organ, clavichord, and piano; discusses the provenance of its 165 works.

4501 Milanca Guzmán, Mario. La música en el periódico chileno: *El Ferrocarril*, 1855–1865. (*Rev. Music. Chil.*, 54:193, enero/julio 2000, p. 17–44, bibl.)

In-depth study reports on one decade of music in Chile as chronicled in the 19th-century newspaper *El Ferrocarril;* offers detailed information on musical societies, conservatories, balls, operas, zarzuelas, ballets, bands, singers, performers, orchestras, and music education. Concludes with a useful chronological list of operas and zarzuelas presented in Santiago from 1855–65. Summary of a book published in Caracas by the Instituto Latinoamericano de Investigaciones y Estudios Musicales Vicente Emilio Sojo, Consejo Nacional de la Cultura (CONAC) in 1998. Article also appears in *Rev. Music. Venez.*, no. 37, May/Aug. 1998, p. 1–77.

Moreno Chá, Ercilia. Music in the Southern Cone: Chile, Argentina, and Uruguay. See item **4375**.

4502 Rondón, Victor. Música y cotidianeidad en el Convento de la Recoleta Dominicana de Santiago de Chile en la primera mitad del siglo 19. (*Rev. Music. Chil.*, 53:192, julio/dic. 1999, p. 47–74, bibl., music, photo)

Reports on the musical activities and musical repertory at the Dominican Convent; provides data referent to music making, payments, and musical instruments; examines the historical context that allowed for musical activities in the convent.

PARAGUAY

4503 Szarán, Luis. Diccionario de la música en el Paraguay. Asunción: s.n., 1997. 508 p.: bibl., ill.

This reference work includes a historical introduction on music in Paraguay; a list of musical terms; and biographies of traditional, popular, and art music composers and performers.

URUGUAY

4504 Ferreira, Luis. Los tambores del candombe. Montevideo: Ediciones Colihue-Sepé, 1997. 213 p.: bibl., ill. (some col.), maps. (Col. Peces)

Excellent study provides a historical account of Afro-Uruguayan musical culture, as well as a description of the construction of drums and drumming patterns. Includes an extensive bibliographical list and discography.

4505 Fornaro Bordolli, Marita and **Samuel Sztern.** 1920–1940, música popular e imagen gráfica en Uruguay. Montevideo?: Comisión Sectorial de Investigación Científica; Escuela Universitaria de Música; Escuela Nacional de Bellas Artes, 1997. 150 p.: bibl., ill. (some col.).

Offers an excellent overview of the history of popular music in Uruguay in the first part of the 20th century through images from periodical literature, sheet music publications, and early recordings.

Moreno Chá, Ercilia. Music in the Southern Cone: Chile, Argentina, and Uruguay. See item **4375**.

4506 Pellegrino, Guillermo. Cantares del alma: una biografía definitiva de Alfredo Zitarrosa. Montevideo: Planeta, 1999. 377 p., 32 p. of plates: bibl., ill.

Biographical study based on primary sources, articles in newspapers and magazines, as well as on interviews with contemporaries of the idol of Canto Popular Uruguayo. Includes photos.

BRAZIL

4507 Albin, Ricardo Cravo. MPB: a história de um século. Rio de Janeiro: Ministério da Cultura, FUNARTE; São Paulo: Atração Produções Ilimitadas, 1997. 451 p.: bibl., ill. (História visual; 4)

Part of the series "História visual," this luxurious coffee-table book traces the history of Brazilian popular music through images of its most well-known musicians. Includes a short history of Música Popular Brasileira (MPB) in Portuguese, English, and Spanish, and a short bibliography.

4508 Braga, Sebastião. O lendário Pixinguinha. 2a. ed., rev. e ampliada. Niterói, Brazil: Muiraquitã, 1997. 161 p.: ill.

Short biographical essays based on the author's own acquaintance with composer and performer Pixinguinha. Includes *incipits* for a few works by Pixinguinha.

4509 Brasil: sons e instrumentos populares. Alberto Ikeda, curadoria. São Paulo: Instituto Cultural Itaú, 1997. 54 p.: ill.

This catalog of traditional instruments grew out of the exposition supported by the Itaú Cultural Institute in São Paulo. The publication is richly illustrated and includes background information on each instrument displayed.

4510 Brazilian popular music & globalization. Edited by Charles A. Perrone and Christopher Dunn. Gainesville: Univ. Press of Florida, 2001. 288 p.: bibl., ill., index.

This collection of essays written by scholars from Brazil and the US focuses on the interrelations between national and international trends in 20th-century Brazilian urban popular music; topics range from film music and contemporary carnival, to hip-hop, rock, and heavy metal music. Tropicalia guru Caetano Veloso contributes to this volume with a short essay on Carmen Miranda; he is also the subject of Liv Sovik's discussion on the meaning of the tropicalismo in contemporary Brazil.

4511 Camargo Guarnieri: o tempo e a música. Organização de Flávio Silva. Rio de Janeiro: Ministério da Cultura, FUNARTE; São Paulo: Imprensa Oficial SP, 2001. 671 p.: bibl., ill., indexes.

This monumental publication compiles articles by several Brazilian scholars and includes both biographical essays and analytical studies; closes with Flávio Silva's most-welcome updated catalog of works by Camargo Guarnieri. "Anexo 7" (p. 163), part of a valuable study of Guarnieri's memorable "Carta aberta," also appears in *Lat. Am. Music Rev.*, Vol. 20, no. 2, Fall/Winter 1999, p. 184–212.

4512 Carvalho, José Jorge de. Afro-Brazilian music and rituals: part 1; from traditional genres to the beginnings of samba. Brasília: Univ. de Brasília, Depto. de Antropologia, 1999. 46 p.: bibl. (Série antropologia; 256)

Part of a series of lectures delivered at the Univ. of Wisconsin-Madison in the spring of 1999; outlines various Afro-Brazilian musical traditions, both ritual and secular, addressing their musical texture, lyrics, and social history.

4513 Cazes, Henrique. Choro: do quintal ao Municipal. São Paulo: Editora 34, 1998. 204 p.: ill. (Col. Ouvido musical)

Based on careful analysis of early *choro* recordings, this historical study brings to light fresh data regarding *choro's* early performance practices. Includes discography.

4514 Contier, Arnaldo Daraya. *O ensaio sobre a música brasileira:* estudo das matizes ideológicos do vocabulário social e técnico-estético—Mário de Andrade, 1928. (*Rev. Música,* 6:1/2, maio/nov. 1995, p. 75–121)

Discusses Mário de Andrade's interpretation of Brazilian history and his notion of "national" and "popular" as presented in his acclaimed 1928 publication *Ensaio.* Addresses the impact of Andrade's book on several generations of Brazilian nationalist composers.

4515 Crook, Larry. Northeastern Brazil. (*in* Music in Latin American culture, regional traditions. Edited by John M. Schechter. New York: Schirmer, 1999, p. 192–235)

Within the larger scope of a book devoted to regional traditions in Latin America, this chapter provides information on *zabumbas* and *forrós* in the Brazilian northeast, as well as on black musical traditions from Bahia, including *candomblé* and contemporary pop groups such as *blocos afros.*

4516 Enciclopédia da música brasileira: popular, erudita e folclórica. Edição de Marcos Antônio Marcondes. 2a ed. rev. e atualizada. São Paulo: Art Editora; Publifolha, 1998. 887 p.: bibl.

This publication remains Brazil's most significant reference work in music (1st ed. published in 1977). New articles were added to this second edition and some information from old entries was updated. Nonetheless, recent research was omitted; includes no musical examples or illustrations. Reviewed in *Lat. Am. Music Rev.*, Vol. 22, no. 1, Spring/Summer 2001, p. 108–109.

4517 Galvão, Luiz. Anos 70: novos e baianos. São Paulo: Editora 34, 1997. 285 p.: ill., photos. (Col. Ouvido musical)

Chronicle of the pop/rock group from Bahia as told by one of its members. Includes archival photos and discography.

4518 Guerreiro, Almerinda. A trama dos tambores: a música afro-pop de Salvador. São Paulo: Grupo Pão de Açúcar; Editora 34, 2000. 315 p.: bibl., ill., index, map. (Col. Todos os cantos)

Excellent study traces the emergence of Afro-Brazilian popular musical styles in Salvador (Bahia, Brazil) and describes how this music came to dominate the Brazilian popular musical scene in the 1980s-90s. For comment on related article, see item **4519.**

4519 Guerreiro, Almerinda. As trilhas do samba-reggae: a invenção de um ritmo. (*Lat. Am. Music Rev.*, 20:1, Spring/Summer 1999, p. 105–140)

An outcome of the author's PhD dissertation in anthropology (Univ. de São Paulo, 1999), the article traces the emergence of the *blocos afros* in Salvador (Bahia, Brazil) and their percussion-based samba-reggae rhythms. Discusses the connections of samba-reggae with sacred and secular musical practices in Salvador, as well as with international musical trends. See also item **4518.**

4520 Magaldi, Cristina. Adopting imports: new images and alliances in the Brazilian popular music of the 1990s. (*Pop. Music/Cambridge*, 18:3, Oct. 1999, p. 309–329)

Reports on the appropriation of popular music from the US by Brazilian musicians and audiences in the 1990s. Argues that young Brazilians use the imported music to articulate local social and ethnic issues.

4521 Matos, Maria Izilda Santos de. Dolores Duran: experiências boêmias em Copacabana no anos 50. Rio de Janeiro: Bertrand Brasil, 1997. 158 p.: bibl.

Focuses on the song lyrics by female samba composer Dolores Duran as revealing of the relations between male and female worlds in Rio de Janeiro during the 1950s.

4522 Mattos, Cleofe Person de. José Maurício Nunes Garcia: biografia. Rio de Janeiro: Ministério da Cultura, Fundação Biblioteca Nacional, Depto. Nacional do Livro, 1997. 373 p., 20 p. of plates: bibl., col. ill., index, music.

This biographical study is the result of several years of research on primary sources. Includes a list of works by Garcia, as well as a discography.

4523 Moore, Tom. A visit to pianopolis: Brazilian music for piano at the Biblioteca Alberto Nepomuceno. (*Notes/Middleton*, 57:1, Sept. 2000, p. 59–87)

Reports on the *Album de família* collection: 60-odd volumes of bound sheet music held at the Biblioteca Alberto Nepomuceno, Univ. Federal do Rio de Janeiro. Focuses on music by Brazilian composers published prior to 1920.

4524 Moraes, José Geraldo Vinci de. As sonoridades paulistanas: a música popular na cidade de São Paulo, final do século XIX ao início do século XX. Rio de Janeiro: Ministério da Cultura, FUNARTE; São Paulo: Editora Bienal, 1997. 196 p.: bibl.

Award-winning publication addresses the emergence of urban culture in São Paulo at the turn of the 20th century, with focus on music-making in the streets. Includes a long list of bibliographical sources.

4525 Música sacra mineira: catálogo de obras. Organização e texto final de José Maria Neves. Rio de Janeiro: Ministério da Cultura, FUNARTE, 1997. 137 p.: bibl., ill., indexes.

Neves' scholarly introduction provides invaluable information on the school of Minas Gerais in the 18th-19th centuries; the appended catalog lists 77 sacred works by several composers. A revised edition in electronic format is available at the research and documentation center of FUNARTE. Includes discography, bibliography, and index.

4526 Naves, Santuza Cambraia. O violão azul: modernismo e música popular. Rio de Janeiro: Fundação Getulio Vargas Editora, 1998. 235 p.: bibl.

An outcome of the author's doctoral dissertation in Sociology, this well-documented study focuses on the links between Brazilian popular music and the modernist ideals of the 1920s-30s. Includes a long bibliographical list, but no musical examples.

4527 Páscoa, Márcio Leonel Farias Reis. A música há cem anos no Teatro Amazonas. (*ARTEunesp*, 13, 1997, p. 105–117, bibl.)

Brief overview of the musical milieu in Manaus in the second half of the 19th century and the local impulse to build the famous opera house, the Teatro Amazonas. For an extended study on the topic, see item **4528.**

4528 Páscoa, Márcio Leonel Farias Reis. A vida musical em Manaus na época da borracha, 1850–1910. Manaus, Brazil: Ministério da Cultura, FUNARTE: Secretaria de Estado da Cultura e Estudos Amazônicos, 1997. 363 p.: bibl., ill. (some col.), index.

An outgrowth of the author's MA thesis (Univ. Estadual Paulista, 1996), this study provides a well-documented account of the social and musical milieu in Manaus in the second half of the 19th century, including the vogue for opera and the construction of the Teatro Amazonas. The book adds immensely to the studies on the 19th-century music in Brazil, which are based primarily on the central-south regions. Includes facsimiles of concert programs, illustrations, bibliography, and an index. See also item **4527.**

4529 Paz, Ermelinda Azevedo. Jacob do Bandolim. Rio de Janeiro: Ministério da Cultura, FUNARTE, 1997. 206 p.: bibl., ill., index.

Welcome biographical study on the mandolin "master," this book also adds information on *choro* music and musicians. The 20 appendices include facsimilies of *choro* manuscripts, letters, a catalog of works, and a discography of Jacob do Bandolim.

4530 Piedade, Acácio Tadeu de Camargo. Flautas e trompetes sagrados do noroeste amazônico: sobre gênero e música do Jurupari. (*Horiz. Antropol.*, 5:11, out. 1999, p. 93–118, bibl., music)

Ethnographical study focuses on the ritual Urupari as performed by the Tukanona group from the Northwestern Amazon; analyzes the symbolism of the instruments, having the native cosmology as a point of reference.

4531 Santos, Eurides de Souza. A música de Canudos. Salvador, Brazil: Secretaria da Cultura e Turismo do Estado da Bahia, Fundação Cultural: EGBA, 1998. 190 p.: bibl., ill., photos. (Col. Selo Editorial Letras da Bahia; 34)

An outgrowth of the author's MA thesis (Univ. Federal da Bahia, 1996), the book reports on a wide gamut of music and performance practices in the city of Canudos. Ethnographic study, serves as a starting point for other regional studies. Includes musical transcriptions and photos.

4532 Severiano, Jairo and Zuza Homem de Mello. A canção no tempo: 85 anos de músicas brasileiras. v. 1, 1901–1957. São Paulo: Editora 34, 1997. 1 v.: bibl., ill., indexes. (Col. Ouvido musical)

This first volume classifies 1,083 Brazilian popular songs from 1901–57. Includes historical background on 267 songs, a list of contemporary foreign songs that became popular in Brazil, and a chronology of songs and composers.

4533 Shaw, Lisa. The social history of the Brazilian samba. Aldershot, England; Brookfield, Vt.: Ashgate, 1999. 211 p.: bibl., index.

Insightful study on the Brazilian samba as an urban social and cultural phenomenon in Rio de Janeiro during the 1930s. Focuses on samba's lyrics between 1930–45,

particularly on the sambas by Ataúlfo Alves, Noel Rosa, and Ari Barroso. Reviewed in *Ethnomusicology*, Vol. 44, no. 3, Fall 2000, p. 521–524, and in *Notes*, Vol. 56, no. 4, June 2000, p. 955–957.

4534 Sodré, Muniz. Samba, o dono do corpo. 2a ed. Rio de Janeiro: MAUAD, 1998. 112 p.: bibl.

According to the author, this second edition was revised and expanded; however, a substantial number of recent bibliographical sources were omitted.

4535 Tinhorão, José Ramos. Música popular: um tema em debate. 3a ed. rev. e ampliada. São Paulo: Editora 34, 1997. 188 p.: bibl.

This revised and expanded edition includes a few new essays and continues to focus on social aspects as the basis for musical developments in Brazilian popular music. Includes bibliographical citations, but no musical example. For comment on 1966 edition, see *HLAS 30:4581*.

4536 Travassos, Elizabeth. Os mandarins milagrosos: arte e etnografia em Mário de Andrade e Béla Bartók. Rio de Janeiro: Ministério da Cultura, Funarte; J. Zahar Editor, 1997. 220 p.: ill., index, maps. (Col. Antropologia social)

An outgrowth of the author's PhD dissertation (Anthropology, Univ. Federal do Rio de Janeiro), this stimulating study compares the careers and works of the Brazilian and Hungarian researchers; analyses the historical and cultural contexts from which their work emanates; and highlights the relationship between their ethnographic work and their esthetic ideals.

4537 Veiga, Manuel. O estudo da modinha brasileira. (*Lat. Am. Music Rev.*, 19:1, Spring/Summer 1998, p. 47–91)

Exemplary study, examines a wide range of primary and secondary sources dealing with the Brazilian *modinha*. Traces the origins of this Brazilian lyrical song and discusses its path from the late 18th–20th centuries.

4538 Veloso, Caetano. Verdade tropical. São Paulo: Companhia das Letras, 1997. 524 p.: index.

This book by the leader of the Tropicalia movement reveals his careful attention to, and personal interpretation of, the local and global factors that shaped Brazilian culture and music from the 1960s on. Provides invaluable insights into Brazilian music and musicians in the second half of the 20th century. Includes index.

4539 Volpe, Maria Alice. Irmandades e ritual em Minas Gerais durante o período colonial: o triunfo eucarístico de 1733. (*Rev. Música*, 8:1/2, maio/nov. 1997, p. 5–55, bibl.)

Well-documented study, reports on the feast of the *triunfo eucarístico* and examines the cultural institutions of colonial Minas Gerais of which music was an integral part; analyzes the performance practices and the symbolism that reflected local social relations.

PHILOSOPHY:
LATIN AMERICAN THOUGHT

JUAN CARLOS TORCHIA ESTRADA, *Independent Consultant, Hispanic Division, Library of Congress, Washington, DC*
CLARA ALICIA JALIF DE BERTRANOU, *Professor, Facultad de Filosofía y Letras, Universidad Nacional de Cuyo, Mendoza, Argentina*

EN LA INTRODUCCIÓN DEL *HLAS 58* hemos mostrado los cambios producidos en esta Sección desde su aparición en 1940, en paralelo con el desarrollo de la filosofía latinoamericana durante el mismo período (cf. *HLAS 58*, p. 731–734). Además, una descripción de los materiales de la Sección aparece en la Introducción correspondiente al *HLAS 52*. La principal característica de estos materiales es que se refieren tanto a temas de historia y crítica del pensamiento filosófico latinoamericano propiamente dicho, como a otros asuntos más generales, usualmente de pensamiento político-social, o interpretativos de la historia y el presente de la región. Otra característica es que a veces son estudios, de mayor o menor rigor académico, y otras veces pertenecen al género más amplio del ensayo de opinión, si bien no siempre esas dos modalidades se recortan nítidamente.

El pensamiento latinoamericano no presenta, en cuanto a sus tendencias principales, cambios radicales con respecto a años anteriores. El propósito de la información que sigue a continuación es señalar los aspectos más relevantes del material reseñado. Se organiza según el orden de las correspondientes subsecciones.[1]

GENERAL

Entre los estudios de mayor valor académico se encuentra el volumen colectivo *La Ilustración en América colonial* (ítem **4584**). Por la misma razón de importancia deben señalarse: la obra *Pensamiento europeo y cultura colonial* (ítem **4604**); un libro de Alberto Saladino García dedicado a la literatura científica del siglo XVIII (ítem **4613**); y una contribución de Gregorio Weinberg sobre la ciencia y la idea de progreso (ítem **4622**). En la consideración de temas de pensamiento político-social— en sentido amplio—deben recordarse dos obras colectivas: *Ideologues and Ideologies in Latin America* (ítem **4583**) e *Itinerarios socialistas en América Latina* (ítem **4585**), además de un largo artículo de Torcuato S. di Tella que expone las ideas políticas y sociales en América del Sur durante el siglo XX (ítem **4564**).

La teología de la liberación, como hemos afirmado en otras oportunidades, se toma en cuenta no tanto por su condición de teología, según la cual no correspondería a esta Sección, como por su influencia en la opinión y en la praxis de numerosos grupos e instituciones. Desde el punto de vista doctrinario posiblemente ya no tenga mucho más margen para enriquecerse, pero no por ello disminuye su vigencia en ciertos ambientes. Referente a ella se encontrará aquí un examen de su vinculación con la filosofía de la liberación, como puede verse en el ítem **4569**.

La filosofía de la liberación no tiene la misma presencia que en décadas pasadas, pero esto requiere aclaración. Esta corriente fue en gran medida un programa, un manifiesto que señalaba hacia lo que la filosofía latinoamericana debía ser, y los programas tienden a debilitarse con su reiteración siempre en el plano desiderativo o de plan futuro. El concepto mismo terminó por ser estrecho, al punto de que finalmente se habló de *filosofías* de la liberación. Y, en los casos en que esta tendencia general se concretó en posiciones filosóficas personales, éstas, comprensiblemente, tendieron a diferenciarse según los autores, o a asumir características más allá del programa común. Sería erróneo sin embargo pensar que esta corriente, típica del latinoamericanismo filosófico, ha perdido vigencia o representantes; más bien se ha metamorfoseado en otras direcciones, aunque alimentadas todas por la misma fuente de ideas. La manifestación original, nacida en la década de los 70s era, si se perdona la simplificación, una proyección filosófica de la teoría de la dependencia. Con el nuevo interés intelectual por los problemas de la globalización y, en cierto momento, la apariencia de dominio generalizado del pensamiento neoliberal, la misma antigua orientación tomó diferente forma. El pensamiento neoliberal, acusado, no sin obvia exageración, de "pensamiento único," perdió mucho terreno debido a las dificultades que originó la aplicación de su versión económica en varios países latinoamericanos—por cualesquiera razones que eso haya ocurrido. Y en esta circunstancia, ciertas corrientes, que en términos muy generales podrían denominarse de izquierda, y a las cuales el fin del llamado socialismo real había producido un efecto de confusión y debilitamiento, volvieron a tomar fuerza, no tanto por contener novedades como por su contraposición al experimento neoliberal. Por su parte, la globalización obligaba a replantear uno de los más caros temas del latinoamericanismo filosófico: el de la identidad latinoamericana. Y también revivía la vieja actitud defensiva de América Latina frente a los mayores poderes mundiales, que era parte de la savia que había nutrido desde el principio a la filosofía de la liberación. Por lo tanto, esta mezcla de interés hacia y de reacción contra el fenómeno de la globalización fue una nueva motivación para una vieja inquietud: el de la *interpretación* de América Latina. Esta inquietud interpretativa, que puede asumir las formas del ensayo de opinión, de la filosofía de la historia, de la aplicación de resultados de las ciencias sociales y, por último, también de vestimenta hermenéutica de una visión ideológica, es uno de los campos más prolíficos de la preocupación por la temática latinoamericana. La cual, por otra parte, tiene ilustres antecedentes en el siglo XIX.

Así encontramos varios artículos en que la identidad, la globalización y los reclamos por las diferenciaciones étnicas son el eje de la discusión, como en los casos de los ítems: **4572**, **4592** y **4594**. Y un destacado autor, Tzvi Medin, hace del proceso de globalización un motivo para volver a la afirmación de que el sentido último de la filosofía latinoamericana es el de una "liberación" (ítem **4596**).

Ensayos de interpretación de América Latina se encontrarán en dos obras presentadas por Leopoldo Zea, ambas enfocando a Latinoamérica desde la condición de su cultura (ítem **4587** y **4589**); en un autor clásico como Arturo Uslar Pietri con su *Nuevo mundo, mundo nuevo* (ítem **4621**); y en otra obra que tiene por asunto la mutua percepción de América Latina y Europa y fue coordinada por Patricia Galeana (ítem **4588**). El interés por la postmodernidad aplicado a la realidad latinoamericana vuelve a presentarse. En esta entrega el tema está representado por dos estudios: *Postmodernidad y postcolonialidad: breves reflexiones sobre Latinoamérica* (ítem **4608**) y *New World (Dis)Orders and Peripheral Strains* (ítem **4600**), pero especialmente por la primera. El mismo asunto visto desde una posición marxista se encontrará en el ítem **4611**. La modernidad es asunto de interés permanente porque ha sido el medio en que América Latina se ha desarrollado ya desde el siglo XVIII. Modernidad y modernización en el siglo XX son consideradas en un análisis de Eduardo Devés V. (ítem **4562**) y en dos artículos: ítems **4602** y **4606**. (Sobre modernidad/postmodernidad, *HLAS 58:4928, 4944, 4976*, y *5030*.) La experiencia neoliberal es seriamente cuestionada en un libro de Franz Hinkelammert (ítem **4580**)— que asimismo tiende a reivindicar la teoría de la dependencia—y en una obra colectiva: *Más allá del neoliberalismo: reconstruir la utopía en América Latina* (ítem **4595**). Por último, deben señalarse un libro de varios autores que defiende la permanencia de la concepción marxista (ítem **4561**) y un artículo de Pablo Guadarrama en la misma línea (ítem **4577**). (Sobre marxismo en *HLAS 58*, ver varios ítems en la Introducciòn, p. 736.)

Un fenómeno concomitante es el del multiculturalismo. Este asunto tiene una doble significación. Por un lado, apunta al reconocimiento de que la interdependencia mundial ha aumentado el número de actores y disminuído la brecha de significación cultural (aunque no de poder internacional) entre los países centrales y los periféricos. Por otro, sirve para reivindicar a la segunda clase de países e intentar disminuir (o revalorar con menos énfasis) la llamada "cultura occidental." Lo que se ha venido denominando "filosofía intercultural" puede ponerse dentro de esta línea revalorativa que reclama un escenario más diverso. Y aunque no es de nuestra competencia, expresiones como "estudios postcoloniales" o el cuestionamiento del "canon" tradicional podrían representar el mismo papel en el campo literario, aunque aquí la actitud combativa es a veces más marcada: en los casos extremos, no sólo se reclama atención hacia aspectos oscurecidos por un exceso de visión eurocéntrica, sino que puede llegarse a una posición política o ideológica que no infrecuentemente termina en una nueva parcialidad. Un enfoque, pero en este caso filosófico, de la relación entre la filosofía y el pluralismo cultural puede verse en un artículo de Mauricio Beuchot (ítem **4545**). El multiculturalismo como tema dentro de la filosofía latinoamericana es atendido por Eduard Demenchonok (ítem **4557**). (Asimismo véase *HLAS 58:4970.*)

Siempre están presentes las reflexiones sobre la filosofía latinoamericana. En esta ocasión se destacan tres contribuciones: un número de la *Revista de Occidente* donde varios autores enfocan el tema: "Pensar en español" (item **4610**); el volumen *Semillas en el tiempo: el latinoamericanismo filosófico contemporáneo* (ítem **4618**), conjunto de estudios que contribuye a perfilar esa activa corriente de pensamiento mediante la exposición de un número considerable de sus representantes; y el libro póstumo de Javier Sasso, *La filosofía latinoamericana y las construcciones de su historia* (item **4616**).

Entre las obras colectivas y las actas de congresos y reuniones que no se han mencionado más arriba cabe destacar las ponencias del Congreso Latinoamericano sobre Filosofía y Democracia (ítem **4555**); las presentadas a una reunión especial del Congreso Internacional de Americanistas: *Ideas, cultura e historia en la creación intelectual latinoamericana* (ítem **4581**); y los escritos en homenaje a Gregorio Weinberg, *Del tiempo y de las ideas* (ítem **4556**). Fue omitido anteriormente el volumen *Anverso y reverso de América Latina: estudios desde el fin del milenio*, coordinado por Clara Alicia Jalif de Bertranou y publicado por la Universidad de Cuyo (1995), con un conjunto de casi 70 ponencias correspondientes al IV Congreso Internacional de la Sociedad Latinoamericana de Estudios sobre América Latina y el Caribe (SOLAR).

MÉXICO

Se destaca en la bibliografía sobre este país la traducción inglesa de la *Historia de la filosofía en el México colonial*, de Mauricio Beuchot (ítem **4630**). El pensamiento durante la Colonia tiene abundante representación en esta entrega, con escritos que tratan sobre: libros y censura (ítem **4639**); humanismo mexicano (ítems **4628** y **4629**); Vasco de Quiroga (ítems **4637** y **4640**) (con referencia a esta último asunto, *HLAS 58:5078*); y el obispo Palafox y Mendoza (ítem **4650**). El otro sector con literatura más abundante corresponde al siglo XX. Refiriéndonos solamente a libros, dos se relacionan con el exilio español: el primero es un libro que estudia el marxismo mexicano (ítem **4636**); y el segundo es una apreciación de la contribución de los exiliados españoles a la cultura mexicana (ítem **4647**).[2] Hay también obras sobre autores individuales, como Lombardo Toledano (ítem **4641**) y Octavio Paz (ítem **4646**). Debe recordarse un interesante análisis de las relaciones entre intelectuales mexicanos y norteamericanos (ítem **4627**). Hay asimismo otras contribuciones que se refieren al pensamiento mexicano del siglo XIX y del XX. Por último, no pudo incluirse antes un justificado homenaje al filósofo y educador mexicano Fernando Salmerón: *Filosofía moral, educación e historia. Homenaje a Fernando Salmerón*. León Olivé y Luis Villoro, editores. México: UNAM, 1996. Contiene semblanzas de Salmerón por Alejandro Rossi y Luis Villoro; una lista de publicaciones del autor; y más de 40 contribuciones, seis de ellas dedicadas a la filosofía de Salmerón. En el mismo caso se halla un libro de Mario Magallón Anaya, *Historia de las ideas en México y la filosofía de Antonio Caso*. Toluca: Univ. Autónoma del Estado de México, 1998.

AMÉRICA CENTRAL

En breve tiempo aparecieron en Costa Rica dos libros con escritos de José Figueres: (ítems **4655** y **4656**). Se encontrarán asimismo obras sobre intelectuales de Panamá (Justo Arosemena, ítem **4654** y Diógenes de la Rosa, ítem **4660**); de Honduras (José Cecilio del Valle, item **1665**); y un buen libro sobre el filósofo nicaragüense Alejandro Serrano Caldera (ítem **4658**).

CARIBE INSULAR

Como es habitual, la mayor cantidad de entradas corresponde a Cuba, y de éstas la casi totalidad se dedica a José Martí. La exégesis martiana continúa dividida entre la visión del exilio cubano y la que lo hace antecedente de la Revolución. Entre las contribuciones sobre este tema en forma de libro se destacan los artículos reunidos por Octavio Ramón Costa (ítem **4665**); una tesis doctoral de Paul Estrade (ítem **4667**) y una reunión de escritos de Juan Marinello (ítem **4673**). Debe agregarse, fuera de Cuba, un buen estudio acerca de Ulises Francisco Espaillat y el liberalismo dominicano (ítem **4682**).

VENEZUELA

En el caso de este país, es muy aprovechable el libro de Simón Alberto Consalvi sobre el gran ensayista Mariano Picón Salas (ítem **4685**). Simón Rodríguez es objeto de dos trabajos (ítems **4689** y **4692**), y hay otros dos sobre el pensamiento cristiano de Briceño Iragorry (ítems **4691** y **4696**).[3]

COLOMBIA

Dos buenas contribuciones son los tres volúmenes de Javier Ocampo López, *Colombia en sus ideas* (item **4703**) y el libro de Rubén Jaramillo Vélez, *Colombia: la* *modernidad postergada* (ítem **4700**). Dos antologías de Germán Arciniegas se caracterizan por sendas introducciones de valor: una de Consuelo Triviño (ítem **4698**) y otra de un excelente conocedor de Arciniegas: Juan Gustavo Cobo Borda (item **4697**).

ECUADOR, PERÚ, BOLIVIA

Es escaso el material reunido en este número del *HLAS* para Ecuador y Bolivia. Respecto al primero de estos países se hallará un estudio sobre el liberalismo católico de Antonio Borrero y Cortázar, pensador y político del siglo XIX (ítem **4706**) y una antología de José María Velasco Ibarra (ítem **4707**). En el caso de Bolivia destacamos una obra dedicada a Gabriel René-Moreno (ítem **4723**).

La literatura dedicada al pensamiento peruano es más abundante, con la consabida preponderancia del estudio y el comentario sobre Mariátegui. Seleccionando únicamente libros que se refieren a este último, recordamos: una publicación alemana (ítem **4716**); y una crítica a las ideas de Mariátegui sobre el comunismo indígena (ítem **4717**); además del abundante *Anuario Mariateguiano* de 1997 (ítem **4708**). Es de interés una obra de Osmar Gonzales sobre un grupo de intelectuales socialistas que actuaron en las décadas finales del mismo siglo (ítem **4713**). (El mismo autor había publicado antes *Sanchos fracasados: los arielistas y el pensamiento político peruano* [Lima: PREAL, 1996]). También hay contribuciones que estudian a Pedro Zulen (ítem **4718**) y Manuel González Prada (ítem **4710**).

CHILE

El pensamiento en Chile es estudiado en un número de la revista mexicana *Cuadernos Americanos* (ítem **4725**) y en un libro sobre ese mismo tema en el siglo XX (ítem **4726**). Se destaca también una obra colectiva que estudia al historiador y pensador Jaime Eyzaguirre (ítem **4727**).

BRASIL

De los numerosos materiales que se refieren a Brasil se destaca obviamente la obra excepcional que Antonio Paim ha desarrollado sobre la filosofía brasileña y que, además de otras contribuciones señaladas en oportunidades anteriores, en esta entrega se refleja en las entradas correspondientes a ocho libros: items **4747- 4754.** Un autor al que se vuelve reiteradamente es Gilberto Freyre, como puede verse en los ítems **4731, 4733, 4736, 4742 y 4764**). (Sobre Freyre, *HLAS 58:5207, 5215, 5228.*) En lo que se refiere a la filosofía en Brasil en general, dos obras muy disímiles: *O futuro do pensamento brasileiro* (item **4735**) y *Pensamento original, made in Brazil* (item **4757**), la enfocan con la preocupación de su originalidad. Sobre la realidad de Brasil, su identidad y su cultura, se encuentran varias contribuciones (ítems **4730, 4732, and 4746**) y el libro de Darcy Ribeiro, *O povo brasileiro* (item **4761**). Finalmente, sólo mencionamos algunos de los autores que reciben especial atención: Enio Silveira (item **4739**); Florestán Fernández (item **4741**); Roberto Campos (item **4758**); Sérgio Buarque de Holanda (item **4763**); y Oliveira Viana (item **4768**) (sobre este último, *HLAS 58:5212*).

URUGUAY

D.A. Brading ofrece una visión de Rodó que se sale de lo habitualmente expuesto sobre este autor (ítem **4772**). Un buen trabajo sobre el batllismo como ideología es el de Manuel Antonio Claps (ítem **4773**)[4]. Por último, se encuentra un número especial de la revista *Prisma* dedicado a Francisco Bauzá (ítem **4775**).

ARGENTINA

Es muy alto, en esta ocasión, el número de entradas en el caso de Argentina. En materia de historia y crítica filosóficas se destaca la extensa obra de Alberto Caturelli, *Historia de la filosofía en la Argentina* (ítem **4787**). Siempre en filosofía propiamente dicha, son estudiados en un artículo Juan Carlos Scannone y Enrique Dussel (ítem **4780**). La revista *Cuadernos de Filosofía* recordó el centenario de la Facultad de Filosofía y Letras de Buenos Aires con un número que dedica una docena de artículos a la filosofía argentina del siglo XX (ítem **4790**), y la Universidad Nacional de Mar del Plata organizó un volumen de homenaje al filósofo de la ciencia Mario Bunge (ítem **4838**). La relación de la literatura de Jorge Luis Borges con la filosofía vuelve a presentarse en un excelente libro de Zulma Mateos (ítem **4815**). Olsen Ghirardi reelabora en nueva edición su libro *La filosofía en Alberdi* (ítem **4805**) y Oscar Terán publica una cuidada y bien presentada edición de escritos de ese pensador argentino del siglo XIX (ítem **4777**). Las contribuciones que tienen que ver con la historia de las ideas en un sentido amplio son numerosas, y aquí apenas se destacan algunas: un buen libro de Oscar Terán sobre la vida intelectual en el Buenos Aires de fines del siglo XIX (ítem **4836**); un valioso estudio del socialismo argentino por José Aricó (ítem **4779**); una obra de Hugo Biagini sobre la Reforma Universitaria (ítem **4782**) que debe ponerse en relación con una reunión de escritos de Deodoro Roca, quien fuera líder de ese movimiento universitario (ítem **4829**); y un estudio sobre la revista *Claridad* (ítem **4802**).

Las entradas que llevan las iniciales [CJB] corresponden a Clara Alicia Jalif de Bertranou. Las que no tienen ninguna indicación corresponden a J.C. Torchia Estrada.

NOTES:

1 Recuérdese que la Sección excluye el comentario a la actividad filosófica teórica (lógica, ética, teoría del conocimiento, etc.), y el trabajo crítico sobre la historia de la filosofía. La producción en esos órdenes es hoy muy intensa, y se refleja en numerosos libros y revistas. Algunas de estas últimas recogen colaboraciones no sólo de otros países latinoamericanos sino también de investigadores europeos y norteamericanos.

2 Sobre estos temas puede verse también *En torno a la obra de Adolfo Sánchez Vázquez: filosofía, ética y política* (México: UNAM, 1995). El propio Sánchez Vázquez se ocupó del exilio filosófico español: *HLAS 58:5046.*

3 Una obra anterior de gran valor sobre el positivismo venezolano es la de Elena Plaza, *La tragedia de una amarga convicción: historia y política en el pensamiento de Laureano Vallenilla Lanz* (Caracas: Univ. Central de Venezuela, 1996).

4 Se había omitido anteriormente un excelente estudio, *Krausismo en el Uruguay: algunos fundamentos del Estado tutor* por Susana Monreal (Montevideo: Univ. Católica del Uruguay, 1993).

GENERAL

4540 Abello Trujillo, Ignacio; Sergio de Zubiría Samper; and **Silvio Sánchez Fajardo.** Cultura: teorías y gestión. San Juan de Pasto, Colombia: Ediciones Unariño, 1998. 293 p.: bibl.

Se dedica principalmente a la teoría de la cultura y a problemas de la gestión cultural. Pero hay materiales dedicados a esas cuestiones en América Latina: Sergio de Zubiría Samper, "Momentos de la identidad cultural latinoamericana" e "Identidades modernas y posmodernas en Latinoamérica."

4541 Aguilar Villanueva, Luis F.; César E. Peón; and **Julio Pinto.** La política como respuesta al desencantamiento del mundo: el aporte de Max Weber al debate democrático. Buenos Aires: Eudeba, 1998. 96 p.: bibl. (Temas política)

Cabe destacar el capítulo: "Max Weber

en América Latina: su recepción temprana y algunas claves de lectura."

4542 Ansaldi, Waldo and **Patricia Funes.** Viviendo una hora latinoamericana: acerca de rupturas y continuidades en el pensamiento en los años veinte y sesenta. (*Cuad. CISH*, 3:4, segundo semestre 1998, p. 13–75)

Más allá del evidente interés que despierta la comparación de las dos épocas (los 1920s y los 1960s), el artículo importa para conocer el comportamiento de las ciencias sociales—especialmente durante los 60s— y su relación con los problemas sociales y políticos del momento.

4543 Bastian, Jean-Pierre. Lumières et religion en Amérique latine: réforme religieuse et naissance d'un nouvel acteur social au 19ème siècle. (*Soc. Compass*, 44:2, June 1997, p. 271–282, bibl.)

El tema principal es la relación entre el liberalismo y la religión. Sostiene que la historia contemporánea de América Latina se comprende a partir del contraste entre la modernidad y el arcaísmo social religioso. Se refiere a la situación de los siglos XVIII y XIX y también a la presencia del protestantismo.

4544 Beuchot, Mauricio. Derechos humanos: historia y filosofía. México: Distribuciones Fontamara, 1999. 165 p.: bibl. (Biblioteca de ética, filosofía del derecho y política; 70)

La primera parte es de fundamentación teórica: analiza diversos autores y expone su propia concepción de los derechos humanos en base a un iusnaturalismo tomista renovado que se confronta con ciertas líneas de la filosofía analítica actual. Hay también trabajos de naturaleza histórica, como uno dedicado al iusnaturalismo en México en los siglos XVI al XVIII. Obra valiosa. También ver ítem **4558.**

4545 Beuchot, Mauricio. La filosofía ante el pluralismo cultural. (*Rev. Filos./México*, 30:89, mayo/agosto 1997, p. 237–254)

Se trata de un esfuerzo teórico para lograr la aceptación del multiculturalismo sin caer ni en el exceso de la universalidad ni en el del relativismo. Para tratar el asunto se recurre a un mínimo de racionalidad que el autor llama "analógica."

4546 Biagini, Hugo Edgardo. Espiritualismo y positivismo en Latinoamérica. (*Estud. Leopoldenses Sér. Hist.*, 2:2, julho/dez. 1998, p. 79–98, bibl.)

Panorámico pero útil, en algunos casos con oportunas referencias a autores poco conocidos. Cubre el espiritualismo ecléctico, el krausismo y el positivismo en varios países latinoamericanos.

Biagini, Hugo Edgardo. La Reforma Universitaria: antecedentes y consecuentes. Ver ítem **4782.**

Biagini, Hugo Edgardo. Utopías juveniles: de la bohemia al Che. Ver ítem **4783.**

4547 Bravo, Betulio A. El *Ariel* de José Enrique Rodó en el crepusculo del siglo XIX hispanoamericano. (*Actual/Mérida*, 38, enero/abril 1998, p. 121–134, bibl.)

Breve artículo que se detiene en el siglo XIX para situar el surgimiento de *Ariel*, obra que habría ofrecido a América Latina una visión optimista de sus posibilidades ante un pasado de destrucción y olvido de lo propio. [CJB]

4548 Cano Peláes, Jesús. Identidad y ruptura: notas sobre Latinoamérica y modernidad. (*Relig. Cult.*, 44:207, oct./dic. 1998, p. 795–811, bibl.)

Ensayo referido principalmente al modernismo y Rubén Darío. [CJB]

4549 Capdevila, Nestor. Las Casas, une politique de l'humanité: l'homme et l'empire de la foi. Paris: Cerf, 1998. 380 p.: bibl. (Passages)

Compleja interpretación de Las Casas, explicándolo por lo que el autor denomina la "ideología católica." Busca por ese medio comprender contradicciones como, por ejemplo, la que se da entre la defensa de la soberanía de los pueblos indígenas y la del imperio español. Estima que la interpretación de Las Casas puede depender de que quien juzgue esté situado o no en una posición católica. No es libro de fácil intelección.

4550 Carvalho, Eugênio Rezende de. Idéias e identidade na América: quatro visões. (*Estud. Ibero-Am./Porto Alegre*, 24:2, dez. 1998, p. 7–28, bibl.)

Examina y compara cuatro visiones de América Latina y sus correspondientes proyectos de futuro: las de Sarmiento, Martí, Rodó y Manoel Bomfim. Lo que se dice del último es particularmente aprovechable, por ser escasamente conocido fuera de Brasil.

4551 Castañeda Reyes, José C. El imperialismo de los Estados Unidos en el pensamiento de Martí, Rodó y Haya de la Torre:

pasado y presente. (*Iztapalapa/México*, 18: 43, enero/junio 1998, p. 51–78, bibl., ill.)

Los nombres seleccionados son tomados como una secuencia en la crítica al imperialismo de Estados Unidos. En ese orden temporal, correspondería a Martí el lugar del precursor, a Rodó el del rupturista, y a Haya de la Torre el de la "destrucción y construcción" de las relaciones continentales a la luz del "internacionalismo" expresado en condiciones de igualdad y equidad. [CJB]

4552 Castedo, Leopoldo. Fundamentos culturales de la integración latinoamericana. Santiago?: Banco Interamericano de Desarrollo; Instituto para la Integración de América Latina y el Caribe; Fundación Felipe Herrera Lane; Dolmen Ediciones, 1999. 204 p.: bibl., ill. (Dolmen ensayo)

Utiliza los elementos de la historia del pensamiento y de las artes en América Latina como sustentación de la posible integración regional. Señala también algunas tentativas realizadas para lograr el propósito integracionista, especialmente el pensamiento y la prédica de Felipe Herrera, hombre público chileno que fuera presidente del Banco Interamericano de Desarrollo.

4553 Castellanos Melo, Guillermo. Filosofía y sociología de la cultura: identidad y multiculturalidad en América Latina. (*Rev. Javer./Bogotá*, 136:673, abril 2001, p. 197–212)

En realidad, se trata de una descripción de lo que son (o debieran ser) los llamados "estudios culturales." Expresa bien la compleja estructura interdisciplinaria de esos estudios, y muestra su aplicación al caso de América Latina. Se mantiene en el plano general y programático.

4554 Castro, Augusto. La Guerra de 1898 y su relación con el pensamiento de América Latina. (*Iberoamericana/Tokyo*, 20:1, primer semestre 1998, p. 25–35)

Traza un paralelo entre el pensamiento de la generación española del '98 y el de América Latina en los comienzos del siglo XX. Por distintos motivos y caminos, en ambos extremos geográficos surgieron corrientes de ideas vinculadas con interrogantes que cada realidad planteaba. [CJB]

4555 Congreso Latinoamericano sobre Filosofía y Democracia, Santiago, 1996. Actas. Edición a cargo de Humberto

Giannini y Patricia Bonzi. Santiago?: Cátedra UNESCO de Filosofía, Chile; LOM Ediciones, 1997. 436 p.: bibl. (Col. Sin norte)

Contiene más de 40 intervenciones, muy variadas. Algunas ponencias se refieren directamente al tema del Congreso, expresado en el título de la obra. Otros tratan de la filosofía latinoamericana, bien refiriéndose a ésta como tema general (situación, posibilidades, propuestas para su desarrollo), bien estudiando expresiones históricas específicas de ella. Algunos autores de este segundo grupo: Jorge Acevedo, Pilar Echeverría de Ocariz, Alfredo Joselyn-Holt Letelier, Arturo Roig, María Ester Donoso. Otros trabajos son de interés teórico sobre la democracia, la filosofía, la universidad. Volumen rico, que desafía el resumen.

4556 Del tiempo y de las ideas: textos en honor de Gregorio Weinberg. Recopilación de Agustín Mendoza. Buenos Aires: Fondo de Cultura Económica, 2000. 690 p.: bibl.

Homenaje al historiador de las ideas y humanista contemporáneo Gregorio Weinberg. Contiene artículos sobre Weinberg y expresiones de adhesión al homenaje. Algunos trabajos vinculados con la historia de las ideas que aparecen en el volumen: Arturo Ardao, "Diversidad y unidad en la globalización"; Natalio Botana, "Regeneracionismo español y reformismo argentino: 1896–1930"; Eduardo L. Ortiz, "Una red internacional de científicos extranjeros en Hispanoamérica a comienzos de la era postcolonial"; Arturo A. Roig, "Antonio de León Pinelo y Sor Juana Inés de la Cruz, pensadores de la aurora"; Juan Carlos Torchia Estrada, "Fray Alonso de la Veracruz y la cuestión de la conquista: la teología de un testigo." [CJB]

4557 Demenchonok, Eduard Vasilévich. Latin American philosophy and multiculturalism. (*SECOLAS Ann.*, 30, March 1999, p. 110–121)

Trabajo bien estructurado que plantea la cuestión del multiculturalismo como tema relevante dentro de la filosofía latinoamericana. Desde esa perspectiva se analizan las contribuciones de los filósofos de la liberación acerca de la identidad cultural y la multiplicidad, en tanto ejes de sus aportes. [CJB]

4558 Derechos humanos, filosofía y naturaleza. Compilación de Aurelia Vargas Valencia. México: UNAM, 2000. 171 p.: bibl. (Cuadernos del Instituto de Investigaciones Filológicas; 23)

En esta obra, cuyo tema principal es el derecho natural, hay dos artículos de interés para esta Sección: uno de Mauricio Beuchot sobre Bartolomé de las Casas, el humanismo indígena y los derechos humanos, y otro que toma como referencia principal al mismo Beuchot en su concepción de los derechos humanos. También ver ítem **4544.**

4559 Los desafíos a la sociedad abierta: a fines del siglo XX. Buenos Aires: Ameghino Editora; Fundación Libertad, 1999. 255 p.

Un grupo de economistas e intelectuales liberales, en el sentido político y en el económico, expresan sus opiniones sobre la situación del mundo y especialmente de América Latina. Algunos temas tratados son: globalización y medios de comunicación; corrupción, justicia y sistema político; y reformas sociales.

4560 A descoberta do homem e do mundo. Organização do Adauto Novaes. Rio de Janeiro: MinC, FUNARTE; São Paulo: Companhia das Letras, 1998. 541 p.: bibl., ill. (some col.), index, maps (some col.).

Aunque de variado contenido, el interés de la obra reside en que se enfocan aspectos propios de la conquista y la colonización de América, pero desde la perspectiva de Portugal, lo que permite comparación con la parte española. Así, en el caso del tratamiento de los judíos portugueses, la cuestión de la guerra justa, y aun el tema del derecho natural y de gentes.

4561 Despojados de todo fetiche: la autenticidad del pensamiento marxista en América Latina. Dirección de Pablo Guadarrama González. Bogotá: Univ. INCCA de Colombia; Santa Clara, Cuba: Univ. Central de Las Villas, 1999. 459 p.: bibl.

La declarada motivación de la obra es contradecir cierto consenso de opinión que considera superada la concepción marxista por el hecho del derrumbe de la Unión Soviética. El bosquejo histórico del marxismo en América Latina, a cargo de Guadarrama González, es útil como panorama e inventario. Concluye con reflexiones de relativa ecuanimidad en el balance de la teoría y la acción marxistas en el continente. El cuerpo del libro, con no menos de una docena de trabajos, se ocupa, entre otros temas, de las relaciones entre estado y democracia en el marxismo latinoamericano.

4562 Devés V., Eduardo. El pensamiento latinoamericano en el siglo XX: entre la modernización y la identidad. v. 1, Del Ariel de Rodó a la CEPAL, 1900–1950. Buenos Aires: Biblos; Santiago: Centro de Investigaciones Diego Barros Arana, 2000. 1 v.: bibl., ill., index. (Col. Historias americanas)

Se trata del ambicioso intento de explicar el desarrollo y los cambios del pensamiento latinoamericano por la alternancia de dos tendencias: lo "identitario" (aprecio y valor de lo propio) y lo modernizador (seguimiento del ejemplo de los países más avanzados). La mostración histórica se hace, en este volumen inicial, examinando la primera mitad del siglo XX desde el arielismo hasta el intento modernizador de la CEPAL, pasando por una variada gama de pensamiento (indigenismo, afroamericanismo, positivismo, socialismo y anarquismo, y varios autores individuales en su interpretación de las realidades nacionales de Argentina, México, Brasil, Chile, Venezuela, Ecuador, etc.). [CJB]

4563 Devés V., Eduardo and Ricardo Melgar Bao. Redes teosóficas y pensadores (políticos) latinoamericanos, 1910–1930. (*Cuad. Am./México*, 13:78, nov./dic. 1999, p. 137–152, bibl.)

El tema se construye en torno a diversas hipótesis. Destacamos la que nos parece más controvertida: "el espiritualismo y el idealismo, tan propios de la reacción positivista de comienzos del siglo, tienen que ser comprendidos más bien en relación con la teosofía y el orientalismo, que con la filosofía vitalista o krausista". Como demostración desfilan los nombres de Gabriela Mistral, Raúl Haya de la Torre, César Augusto Sandino, José Vasconcelos y José Santos Chocano, entre otros. [CJB]

4564 Di Tella, Torcuato S. Political and social ideas in twentieth century South America. (*in* Political culture, social movements and democratic transitions in South America in the XXth century. Milano, Italy:

Fondazione Giangiacomo Feltrinelli, 1997, p. 13–45)

El autor intenta la muy difícil tarea de ofrecer, en la extensión de un artículo, una síntesis de las ideas políticas y sociales en Iberamérica durante el siglo XX. A pesar de las limitaciones de espacio, se logra un cuadro que, dando lo esencial, resulta un embargo amplio y representativo. En algunos casos se señalan paralelos entre los distintos países. Se organiza tomando en cuenta, entre otros temas, el efecto de las revoluciones mexicana y rusa, el aprismo y el marxismo, el corporativismo, el populismo y otras recientes experiencias izquierdistas y democráticas.

4565 Domingues, Beatriz Helena. O Medieval e o moderno no mundo ibérico e ibero-americano. (*Estud. Hist. /Rio de Janeiro*, 10:20, 1997, p. 195–216, bibl.)

El *leit motiv* del artículo es que España no se negó a la modernidad, sino que desarrolló una modernidad distinta (una modernidad medieval en lugar de una modernidad moderna). Naturalmente, esto se habría transferido al Nuevo Mundo, donde sin embargo tuvo características especiales. La autora se detiene especialmente en Nueva España, donde trata a Sor Juana y a Sigüenza y Góngora. Es un artículo que como quiera que se consideren sus tesis merece atención.

4566 Estermann, Josef. Filosofía andina: estudio intercultural de la sabiduría autóctona andina. Quito: Ediciones Abya-Yala, 1998. 359 p.: bibl., ill., index.

El objeto del libro es la descripción e interpretación de la "filosofía" (pensamiento, cosmovisión) andina, por ejemplo en su "lógica" correlacional, en su concepción participativa de la realidad, en su ética, su cosmología, etc. El abordaje del asunto no se hace con los elementos de la etnología, sino con un complejo instrumento hermenéutico propio de la filosofía occidental, a la cual, sin embargo, se la acusa por considerarse a sí misma como la única forma válida de pensamiento filosófico. Otra de las consecuencias es apoyar el concepto de una "filosofía intercultural."

4567 Farias, Amy Caldwell de. Reorganizando o passado: Andrés Bello e o Iluminismo na América Latina. (*Estud. Ibero-Am. /Porto Alegre*, 24:2, dez. 1998, p. 29–49)

Intento de explicar la concepción de la historia americana en Andrés Bello utilizando el concepto de "ideología" según es entendido por Althusser. El mismo enfoque ideológico -no muy claro en la exposición- explicaría lo oculto en los poemas americanistas de Bello.

4568 Filippi, Alberto. Para una historia de la difusión de la cultura italiana fuera de Italia: el pensamiento filosófico, jurídico y político de Bobbio en Hispanoamérica y España, 1945–1998. (*Cuad. Am. /México*, 13:77, sept. /oct. 1999, p. 11–63)

Tema de este extenso trabajo es la recepción del pensamiento de Norberto Bobbio (en su dimensión filosófico-jurídica y filosófico-política) en Hispanoamérica y España. Como esa recepción estuvo en muchos casos influida por los vaivenes políticos de la región y de la misma Europa (regímenes dictatoriales, democracia, fascismo, franquismo, postfranquismo . . .), contiene referencias a los casos de Argentina, Chile, México, Colombia, Venezuela y España. [CJB]

4569 Fornet-Betancourt, Raúl. Incidencia de la teología de la liberación en la filosofía latinoamericana. (*Realidad/San Salvador*, 78, nov. /dic. 2000, p. 679–702)

Explora la influencia de la teología de la liberación en la filosofía latinoamericana, especialmente en la filosofía de la liberación y a partir de los años 1968–69. Lo muestra en los siguientes "campos temáticos": "comprensión de la actividad filosófica"; "punto de partida del filosofar"; "función de la filosofía"; "inversión de la racionalidad de las prioridades filosóficas"; la filosofía entendida como "un universo ético"; "comprensión del método"; y "comprensión de la historia de la filosofía". Finalmente, para la interacción entre la teología de la liberación y la filosofía en América Latina señala algunos puntos que formarían una "agenda para un diálogo." [CJB]

4570 Funes, Patricia. El pensamiento latinoamericano sobre la nación en la década de 1920. (*Bol. Am. /Barcelona*, 49, 1999, p. 103–120)

Buen trabajo de síntesis en torno a la idea de "nación" durante los años 20. Recoge sucintamente lo pensado en la Argentina, Brasil y México, después de la etapa positivista. [CJB]

4571 Gabaldón, Eleonora. El discurso de la unidad, 1900–1930: reconciliación y cambio, la paradoja en búsqueda de la síntesis. Caracas: Fundación Centro de Estudios Latinoamericanos Rómulo Gallegos, 1997. 110 p.: bibl. (Col. Cuadernos)

Ensayo sobre el reiterado tema de la unidad hispanoamericana como respuesta al avance de los Estados Unidos. Se revisan las opiniones de autores como César Zumeta, Rodó, Manuel Ugarte, Vasconcelos, Henríquez Ureña, Leopoldo Zea y Angel Rama.

4572 Gallo Armosino, Antonio. La filosofía mesoamericana en un amanecer conflictivo. (*Cult. Guatem.*, 19:1, enero/abril 1998, p. 231–241, bibl.)

El momento actual está atravesado por dos movimientos contrapuestos: "la identidad diferenciada de los pueblos y etnias" en un proceso de desglobalización, por un lado, y por otro, "la unidad globalizada del planeta." Ante ello la tarea de la filosofía, de carácter crítico, "consiste en la mediación entre los dos movimientos contrastantes, para asegurar el derecho a un pensamiento no cosificado ni meramente pragmático." [CJB]

4573 García de la Huerta Izquierdo, Marcos. Reflexiones americanas: ensayos de intra-historia. Santiago, Chile: LOM Ediciones, 1999. 247 p.: bibl. (Col. Sin norte)

Conjunto de reflexiones y opiniones sobre la historia latinoamericana, en tono de ensayo. La lectura resulta, en muchos aspectos, provechosa, pero la obra no llega a organizarse en una estructura con conclusiones definidas.

4574 Gillner, Matthias. Bartolomé de las Casas und die Eroberung des indianischen Kontinents: das friedensethische Profil eines weltgeschichtlichen Umbruchs aus der Perspektive eines Anwalts der Unterdrückten. Stuttgart, Germany: W. Kohlhammer, 1997. 298 p.: bibl. (Theologie und Frieden; 12)

Comenzando por un enfoque biográfico que pone la vida y la obra de Las Casas en su contexto histórico y político, trata con extensión y simpatía hacia el personaje los principales temas, como la justificación de la conquista por las bulas de concesión, la inferioridad de los indios y la guerra justa, siempre comparando a Las Casas con otros comentaristas. La parte final se dedica a la ética "advocatoria" de Las Casas en el horizonte de la evangelización.

4575 Gómez Hurtado, Alvaro. Choque de culturas: síntesis de la Cátedra de Cultura Colombiana dictada en la Universidad Sergio Arboleda durante los años 1994 y 1995. Bogotá?: Fundación Alvaro Gómez Hurtado, 1998. 1 v.

Segundo de tres volúmenes, uno publicado anteriormente y otro por publicarse. Es transcripción de lecciones o conferencias, pero se lee como ensayo y tiene valor más allá de lo didáctico. Se parece a obras como *De la conquista a la Independencia*, de Mariano Picón Salas. Su facilidad de lectura no debe confundirse con simplicidad de contenido. Si hay alguna simpatía hispanista, se expresa muy moderadamente. Aspectos cubiertos panorámicamente: la conquista, la colonización, el mestizaje, el barroco, el fin de la Colonia.

4576 Guadarrama González, Pablo. Balance y perspectiva de la filosofía latinoamericana al final del milenio. (*Islas/Santa Clara*, 41:119, enero/marzo 1999, p. 61–76)

El balance de la filosofía latinoamericana es expresado en 21 puntos, de breve desarrollo. Los mismos se completan con algunas observaciones prospectivas en las que se señala que el futuro de la actividad filosófica en el continente dependerá de una investigación "desprejuiciada," de "la honestidad intelectual" y de "la creatividad." [CJB]

4577 Guadarrama González, Pablo. Humanismo y socialismo en la óptica del pensamiento marxista en América Latina. (*Estud. Av.*, 11:30, maio/agôsto 1997, p. 357–383, photos)

La extensa compulsa de opiniones que realiza el artículo viene a concluir en que, no importa qué haya ocurrido con el marxismo-leninismo clásico, con el DIAMAT y con la desaparición del "socialismo real," el humanismo marxista sigue vigente, y con él la posibilidad de renovar el socialismo, aprendiendo de los errores cometidos. [CJB]

4578 Guadarrama González, Pablo. ¿Qué historia de la filosofía se necesita en América Latina? (*Islas/Santa Clara*, 115, mayo/dic. 1997, p. 90–105)

Reflexiones y comentarios sobre el pasado filosófico latinoamericano y sobre cómo debiera ser una historia de la filosofía [latinoamericana] en América Latina. Son, salvo uno que otro rasgo, consideraciones razonables y amplias, a pesar de la reconocida posición marxista del autor, quien se manifiesta como no identificado con la "manualística filosófica soviética." Pero también afirma que no se deben "estimular actitudes evasivas de academicismo estéril, asepsia ideológica y neutralidad axiológica."

4579 Herrera, Sajid Alfredo. El aporte de la filosofía latinoamericana a los derechos humanos. (*Cult. Guatem.*, 19:1, enero/abril 1998, p. 31–49)

Trabajo de carácter teórico que se articula en torno a tres preguntas: 1) "¿qué puede aún decir la filosofía al problema de los derechos humanos?"; 2) "¿tendrá vigencia su labor eminentemente teórica ante una problemática sumamente práctica?"; 3) "¿qué tiene que decir sobre el tema la filosofía latinoamericana?" La respuesta a esta última cuestión abarca la mayor parte del escrito. [CJB]

4580 Hinkelammert, Franz J. El nihilismo al desnudo: los tiempos de la globalización. Santiago, Chile: LOM Ediciones, 2001. 297 p.: bibl. (Col. Escafandra)

Se trata del intento de reactivar y poner al día concepciones como la teoría de la dependencia que, según el autor, fueron eclipsadas con la generalización del modelo neoliberal. La base de esa posible reactivación sería la observación de los inconvenientes -por lo menos para numerosos países- que ocasionó dicho modelo. Aunque es un reclamo de no considerar muertas ciertas concepciones ideológicas con las que el autor simpatiza, el libro delimita un campo legítimo de discusión.

4581 Ideas, cultura e historia en la creación intelectual latinoamericana, siglos XIX y XX. Compilación de Hugo Cancino Troncoso y Carmen de Sierra. Quito: Ediciones Abya-Yala, 1998. 464 p.: bibl., ill. (Col. Biblioteca Abya-Yala; 56)

Amplia variedad de contenido, como es usual en congresos. Casi la mitad de las ponencias se refieren a Argentina (en general, historia política y cultural). Pero también hay artículos -sin que sea una lista exhaustiva- sobre Brasil (nacionalismo y Estado Novo), Chile (novela), Costa Rica (literatura e identi-

dad), Venezuela (positivismo) y sobre publicaciones como *Marcha* y *Cuadernos Americanos*, y la CEPAL. Algunos autores: Ana Inés Ferreyra, Sandra Gayol, Norma Dolores Riquelme, Cesar Augusto Carneiro Benevides, Hugo Cancino Troncoso, Carmen de Sierra, Javier Pinedo, Eduardo Deves Valdés y Susana Strozzi.

4582 Identity and discursive practices: Spain and Latin America. Edited by Francisco Domínguez. Bern, Switzerland; New York: P. Lang, 2000. 328 p.: bibl., index.

Quiere contribuir al estudio de las relaciones entre España y América Latina mediante trabajos que analizan relaciones económicas y políticas, y también con otros sobre antropología, literatura y cine.

4583 Ideologues and ideologies in Latin America. Edited by Will Fowler. Westport, Conn.: Greenwood Press, 1997. 211 p.: bibl., index. (Contributions in Latin American studies, 9)

En la Introducción se observa (y lamenta) la tendencia contemporánea a abandonar las distinciones ideológicas en aras de un pragmatismo que termina favoreciendo al capitalismo neoliberal, con perjudicales consecuencias para los sectores desfavorecidos de América Latina. Dentro de esta orientación general, algunas contribuciones al volumen son históricas: el anarcosindicalismo; el nacionalismo cubano; las relaciones entre los intelectuales y el Estado; la ideología de la Revolución cubana; la posición de Estados Unidos en América Central durante la Guerra Fría; el régimen de Stroessner en Paraguay. Hay dos artículos sobre la situación de la mujer y el feminismo y dos sobre Chile, especialmente durante la época de Pinochet.

4584 La Ilustración en América colonial: bibliografía crítica. Recopilación de Diana Soto Arango, Miguel Angel Puig Samper y Luis Carlos Arboleda. Madrid: Consejo Superior de Investigaciones Científicas; Ediciones Doce Calles; Colciencias, 1995. 233 p.: bibl., ill., maps. (Col. Actas)

Se trata de una obra importante para la historia de las ideas latinoamericanas en el siglo XVIII. Los trabajos son de análisis historiográfico, lo que le da particular valor para quienes estudien el tema. Hay materiales sobre la región en general (Ilustración, ciencia y técnica; las expediciones botánicas; enseñanza de primeras letras; enseñanza ilustrada en las universidades). También se abordan temas especiales en relación con Argentina, Venezuela, Cuba, Perú y Brasil. Algunos de los autores: Diana Arango, Juan José Saldaña, Celina Lértora Mendoza, Yajaira Freites, Armando García González.

4585 Itinerarios socialistas en América Latina. Compilación de Estela Fernández Nadal. Córdoba, Argentina: Alción Editora, 2001. 223 p.

Las figuras estudiadas son: Simón Rodríguez (como socialista utópico); José Ingenieros; José Carlos Mariátegui; el Che Guevara; Agustín Cueva; Franz Hinkelammert; y Arturo A. Roig. Entre los autores de los trabajos se encuentran: Estela Fernández Nadal, Alejandra Ciriza, Daniela Rawicz, Marisa Muñoz, Dante Ramaglia, Fernanda Beigel y Susana Cuello. A juicio de la compiladora, los autores incluidos son parte de una memoria "en buena medida olvidada o desconocida." La intención del volumen sería oponerse al "discurso opresor y hegemónico" y renovar el sentido de utopía.

4586 Lago Carballo, Antonio. América en la conciencia española de nuestro tiempo. Prólogo de Pedro Laín Entralgo. Madrid: Editorial Trotta, 1997. 198 p.: bibl. (Col. Estructuras y procesos. Serie Ciencias sociales)

Ensayos breves que en su conjunto componen un buen inventario de autores españoles que se han ocupado de América Latina o han estado vinculados cercanamente a ella.

4587 Latinoamérica cultura de culturas. Recopilación de Leopoldo Zea y Mario Magallón. México: Instituto Panamericano de Geografía e Historia; Fondo de Cultura Económica, 1999. 153 p.: photos. (Latinoamérica fin de milenio; 2)

Continuación del anterior (ver ítem **4589**). Como él, tiene una Presentación de Leopoldo Zea ("Integración: el gran desafío para Latinoamérica") y trata los siguientes temas: el indio en la cultura latinoamericana actual (Claudio Malo González); el integracionismo de Lucas Alamán (Salvador Méndez Reyes); la transición chilena a la democracia (Javier Pinedo Castro); y José Martí y la

emancipación cubana (Enrique Ubieta Gómez).

4588 Latinoamérica en la conciencia europea: Europa en la conciencia latinoamericana. Coordinación de Patricia Galeana de Valadés. México: Archivo General de la Nación; Centro Coordinador y Difusor de Estudios Latinoamericanos, UNAM; Facultad de Filosofía y Letras, UNAM; Consejo Nacional para la Cultura y las Artes; Fondo de Cultura Económica, 1999. 229 p.: bibl. (Sección de obras de historia)

Con independencia del valor de muchas contribuciones, el volumen es heterogéneo, aunque todos se refieren, de un modo u otro, a las relaciones entre Latinoamérica y Europa. Los tres grandes campos temáticos abarcados son: cultura, historia y actualidad. Toda selección puede comportar injusticia para otros autores, pero recordamos las contribuciones de Vincenzo Cappelletti, Horacio Cerutti Guldberg, Abelardo Villegas, Liliana Weinberg, Silvio Zavala, Josefina Zoraida Vázquez, Patricia Galeana y Gregorio Weinberg.

4589 Latinoamérica encrucijada de culturas. Recopilación de Leopoldo Zea y Mario Magallón. México: Instituto Panamericano de Geografía e Historia; Fondo de Cultura Económica, 1999. 161 p.: bibl. (Latinoamérica fin de milenio; 1)

En el primer trabajo Leopoldo Zea explica los orígenes institucionales de esta serie de estudios y ofrece reflexiones que dan el marco general del volumen. Luego hay contribuciones de: Héctor G. Alfaro López sobre cultura y liberación en América Latina; de Otto Morales Benítez sobre relaciones entre América Latina y el Caribe; de Miguel A. Sobrino sobre ética de la conflictividad en América Latina; y de Joaquín Santana Castillo sobre integración latinoamericana y caribeña. También ver ítem **4587.**

4590 Lecuna, Vicente. La ciudad letrada en el planeta electrónico: la situación actual del intelectual latinoamericano. Madrid: Pliegos, 1999. 222 p.: bibl. (Pliegos de ensayo; 139)

Este libro puede apreciarse desde dos perspectivas: 1) por su propio contenido, que está constituido por: el examen del "boom" (y el "postboom") de la literatura latinoamericana; las relaciones del intelectual con los programas de organización social y con el Estado; y las críticas a destacados representantes de la intelectualidad latinoamericana: Angel Rama, Antonio Cándido, José Joaquín Brunner, Beatriz Sarlo, Néstor García Canclini, entre otros. Y 2) como una visión generacional más joven, en buena parte desencantada de los productos intelectuales de las décadas de los 60s y los 70s.

4591 Literatura y pensamiento en América Latina. Coordinación de J. Raúl Navarro García. Sevilla, Spain: Escuela de Estudios Hispano-Americanos, Consejo Superior de Investigaciones Científicas, 1999. 204 p.: bibl.

Como indica el título, los estudios presentados se refieren a literatura y pensamiento. Los primeros cubren temas como, entre otros, Rubén Darío, Rosario Castellanos, Borges y las vanguardias y el cuento mexicano del siglo XX. Los de pensamiento se acercan más bien a la historia de las ideas, y sus temas son: José Cecilio del Valle y la visión del indio (artículo de real interés); Rodó y la unidad hispanoamericana; Mariátegui; el movimiento "Iglesia Joven" en Chile; y la obra de Germán Arciniegas.

4592 Luengo, Enrique. La otredad indígena en los discursos sobre la identidad americana. (*Cuad. Am./México,* 12:71, sept./oct. 1998, p. 180–197)

Una de las consecuencias de preguntar por la identidad ha sido desconocer o negar la "heterogeneidad cultural." Lo mismo en el caso del rechazo del Otro (el componente indígena) como factor de atraso (Sarmiento, Alcides Arguedas). El desconocimiento de la heterogeneidad cultural está presente inclusive en Bolívar, Martí, Vasconcelos, Mariátegui y Fernández Retamar, pues todos ellos tienen como rasgo común una "concepción monológica de la identidad latinoamericana." Según el autor, especificar la identidad supone "percibir y verificar las diferencias," lo que lleva a distinguir entre la identidad y la similitud, términos que no son idénticos. [CJB]

4593 Mansilla, H.C.F. La dialécta de lo propio y lo ajeno. (*Rev. Latinoam. Filos.,* 26:2, primavera 2000, p. 333–349)

Reconoce que en los países del Tercer Mundo se da un conflicto entre la preservación de la propia tradición, por un lado, y la

adopción de lo ajeno en el intento de alcanzar la modernidad. Después de examinar diversas propuestas y de atender a realidades étnicas (especialmente del área andina), encuentra que existe la posibilidad de un camino intermedio de mutuo enriquecimiento entre corrientes particularistas y universalistas. [CJB]

4594 Martínez-Echazábal, Lourdes. *Mestizaje* and the discourse of national/cultural identity in Latin America, 1845–1959. (*Lat. Am. Perspect.,* 25:3, May 1998, p. 21–42, bibl.)

Se refiere no tanto al mestizaje en general como a la mezcla que da lugar al mulato ("mulatez," en palabras de la autora). Lo que distingue al artículo es la crítica a la trasculturación y a las interpretaciones que ofrecen un cuadro donde las diferencias no parecieran determinantes. De modo tal que no sólo se critica a los autores que expresan prejuicios raciales (Sarmiento, Carlos Octavio Bunge), sino también a los que, según la autora, al diluir la presencia de la diversidad ocultan relaciones reales de poder. Entre estos últimos se encontrarían José Antonio Saco, José Martí, Nicolás Guillén, Fernando Ortiz, Gilberto Freyre y José Vasconcelos.

4595 Más allá del neoliberalismo: reconstruir la utopía en América Latina. Quito: Ediciones ASEL, 1997. 91 p.

El neoliberalismo, y lo que se consideran sus características y consecuencias, es intensamente criticado, principalmente desde la ética cristiana, pero también en general. El punto de partida y la referencia constante es la actual situación de América Latina.

4596 Medin, Tzvi. La filosofía latinoamericana y el proceso de globalización. (*Universum/Talca,* 12, 1997, p. 131–140)

Simplificando casi injustamente un artículo muy argumentado, la tesis central sería: 1) la filosofía latinoamericana es y debe ser una filosofía de la liberación (en sentido amplio); 2) el proceso real y el discurso de la globalización no son sino una razón más para confirmar a la filosofía latinoamericana en ese destino o función.

4597 Mendoza, Plinio Apuleyo; Carlos Alberto Montaner; and Alvaro Vargas Llosa. Guide to the perfect Latin American idiot. Introduction by Mario Vargas Llosa. Translated by Michaela Lajda Ames. Lanham, Md.: Madison Books, 2000. 218 p.

La obra es periodística, en el sentido de que no tiene el estilo del libro académico. Trata de desmentir lo que para los autores son mitos de la mentalidad estatista, revolucionaria e izquierdista de los años 60s y 70s del siglo pasado, y de promover, en lo político, ideas liberales (en el sentido de la palabra en español) y, en lo económico, el liberalismo económico. Desde el título en adelante, no se caracteriza por un lenguaje respetuoso hacia quienes detentan ideas opuestas (y del mismo tipo ha sido la rea cción contraria al libro). Tomado con muchas precauciones, no deja de resultar saludable para una discusión sobre el asunto, frente a posiciones que se han sostenido con no menos rigidez.

Miller, Nicola. In the shadow of the state: intellectuals and the quest for national identity in twentieth-century Spanish America. See item **1132.**

4598 Mudrovcic, María Eugenia. Mundo nuevo: cultura y guerra fría en la década del 60. Rosario, Argentina: B. Viterbo Editora, 1997. 187 p.: bibl. (Estudios culturales)

El tema es el desarrollo y los antecedentes de la revista *Mundo Nuevo,* que el crítico uruguayo Emir Rodríguez Monegal dirigió entre 1966–68. Expone aspectos de interés como, entre otros, la vinculación del Congress for Cultural Freedom con la CIA; la relación de la revista con el *boom* de la literatura latinoamericana; y las encontradas opiniones de la época sobre la Revolución Cubana. Es una investigación detallada, que ofrece materiales valiosos para la historia intelectual latinoamericana en una época de auge de las posiciones de izquierda y de intensas polémicas; pero los juicios no tienen mayor imparcialidad y, ya en las páginas finales, pierde el carácter investigativo y se convierte en un directo ataque a *Mundo Nuevo* y su director.

4599 Muñoz Rosales, Victórico. Fray Bartolomé de las Casas como paradigma de la filosofía latinoamericana. (*Cuad. Am./ México,* 13:75, mayo/junio 1999, p. 92–101)

Se analiza a Las Casas con el intento de "recuperar al personaje, redimensionando ideológicamente aspectos de su pensamiento." Para ello se alude a las posiciones contradictorias que ha originado, y al uso ideológico de la naturaleza humana en la controversia con Sepúlveda. Se puede considerar a Las Casas como paradigma para la filosofía latinoamericana porque partió de su propia realidad circundante, y porque adaptó sus ideas previas a un nuevo objeto de filosofar—el que estaba indicado por su realidad. [CJB]

4600 New world (dis)orders and peripheral strains: specifying cultural dimensions in Latin American and Latino studies. Edited by Michael Piazza and Marc Zimmerman. Chicago: MARCH/Abrazo Press, 1998. 294 p.: bibl., ill., index. (LACASA Chicago publication series; 2)

La publicación se interesa por los efectos del pensamiento postmoderno en los desarrollos políticos y culturales de América Latina. Entre los autores que toma en cuenta se encuentra Néstor García Canclini (*Culturas híbridas*). También se consideran obras como *Postmodernism, or, The Cultural Logic of Late Capitalism* (Fredric Jameson) y *Hegemony and Socialist Strategy: Towards a Radical Democratic Politics* (Ernesto Laclau and Chantal Mouffe).

4601 O'Meagher, Matthew. Before liberation theology: Catholicism, development, and the *Christian Revolution* in Latin America, 1959–68. (*JILAS/Bundoora,* 3:2, Dec. 1997, p. 55–78, ill.)

Describe el desarrollo del movimiento reformista católico en la primera mitad de la década del 60 y previo al auge de la teología de la liberación. El trabajo muestra que ese movimiento (en buena parte desarrollado en Chile), aunque de corta duración, tuvo una intensidad generalmente no reconocida. Para la visión de una época compleja y no del todo decantada, el artículo es de lectura muy recomendable.

4602 Ortiz, Renato. América Latina: de la modernidad incompleta a la modernidad-mundo. (*Nueva Soc.,* 166, marzo/ abril 2000, p. 44–61, ill.)

Repasa el proceso de constitución de la nacionalidad en América Latina y su unión con las ideas de modernidad y modernización, desde los comienzos del siglo XIX hasta la actualidad. Se trataría de un modelo incompleto que se agravaría en nuestros días con la introducción de las "industrias culturales" y el proceso de globalización, en el que se aprecia una disyunción entre nación y modernidad. [CJB]

The other mirror: grand theory through the lens of Latin America. See *HLAS 59:4.*

4603 Palermo, Vicente. Pensamento político progressista no liberalismo argentino e mexicano do século XIX: Juan Bautista Alberdi e Justo Sierra. (*Estud. Hist./Rio de Janeiro,* 10:20, 1997, p. 295–320, bibl.)

Muy interesante comparación entre Alberdi y Justo Sierra, como representantes del liberalismo modernizador. El doble problema que reflejan esas dos figuras es: 1) el de la necesidad de un estado consolidado para enfrentar el desorden caudillista y lograr el proceso de modernización; y 2) el de las libertades políticas postergadas. Alberdi, situado más al comienzo del proceso, habría acentuado lo primero, en tanto Sierra, avizorando el final del porfiriato, lo segundo. El autor ha escrito un libro sobre el tema, publicado por la Univ. de Salamanca.

4604 Pensamiento europeo y cultura colonial. Recopilación de Karl Kohut y Sonia V. Rose. Frankfurt am Main: Vervuert; Madrid: Iberoamericana, 1997. 409 p.: bibl., ill., index. (Textos y estudios coloniales y de la independencia; 4)

Obra de real interés para la historia de las ideas en la Colonia. Abarca tanto la recepción cultural en América como el efecto americano en Europa. En el primer sentido se incluyen trabajos sobre: el humanismo (Francisco Cervantes de Salazar, Nebrija, el Inca Garcilaso); la neoescolástica (Espinosa Medrano, Fray Francisco del Castillo, Ignacio de Castro); y el neoestoicismo (Sigüenza y Góngora, Sor Juana). Otros dos apartados se refieren a "América en Europa" y "Sociedades Indígenas y Mestizajes."

4605 El pensamiento social latinoamericano en el siglo XX. Coordinación de Ruy Mauro Maríni y Theotonio dos Santos. Recopilación de Francisco López Segrera. Caracas: Fondo de las Naciones Unidas para la Cultura, Educación y Deporte; Unidad Regional de Ciencias Sociales y Humanas para América Latina y el Caribe, 1999. 2 v.: bibl.

Se trata de una especie de "sociología interpretativa," o una concepción de América Latina desde el pensamiento social. De su contenido quedan claramente excluidas las consecuencias interpretativas que pudieran derivarse del neoliberalismo y del funcionalismo sociológico. De la corriente "progresista," que aquí se representa y propugna, se estudian pensadores como Mariátegui, Caio Prado Junior y Silvio Frondizi; también la CEPAL y la relación entre desarrollo y modernización; asimismo la teoría de la dependencia; y las manifestaciones "revolucionarias" (1970–85), para concluir en temas de actualidad. La obra es muy recomendable para el conocimiento de la orientación ideológica que representa y en el mismo sentido lo es el extenso prólogo del editor, Francisco López Segrera.

4606 Pinto M., Gustavo. Una respuesta filosófica a la pregunta: ¿existe o no la modernidad en América Latina? (*Yachay/ Cochabamba,* 15:28, segundo semsetre 1998, p. 89–106, bibl.)

Se analizan algunas respuestas contradictorias a la pregunta que da título al artículo, para luego fijar la posición del autor. Esta incorpora brevemente la consideración de Enrique Dussel de que es preciso acceder a la "trans-modernidad" como un modo de superar las negatividades de la modernidad. [CJB]

4607 Populismo y neopopulismo en América Latina: el problema de la Cenicienta. Recopilación de María Moira Mackinnon y Mario Alberto Petrone. Buenos Aires: Editorial Universitaria de Buenos Aires, 1998. 433 p.: bibl. (Manuales)

Antología de estudios sobre el populismo latinoamericano. Se dedican artículos a Brasil (Vargas), Argentina (peronismo), Perú, Ecuador (Velazco Ibarra), y uno de naturaleza general, a cargo de Alain Touraine. Una segunda parte se dedica al neopopulismo. La Introducción, de índole analítica, es muy útil por el examen del concepto de populismo y de las posiciones de numerosos autores sobre el asunto.

4608 Postmodernidad y postcolonialidad: breves reflexiones sobre Latinoamérica. Recopilación de Alfonso de Toro. Frankfurt: Vervuert; Madrid: Iberoamericana, 1997. 284 p.: bibl., indexes. (Teoría y crítica de la cultura y literatura; 11 = Theorie und Kritik der Kultur und Literatur; 11)

Los conceptos de "postmodernidad" y "postcolonialidad," que ni en su origen ni en su aplicación son exclusivos de América Latina, se analizan sin embargo en relación con ella. Los trabajos se relacionan con la filosofía (especialmente la estética), el teatro, la poesía y la historia. Sobre el asunto (y el consiguiente debate), de complejo desarrollo académico y de perfiles no siempre bien definidos, se encuentra una exposición general en el artículo de Alfonso de Toro y una fundamentación teórica en el de Walter D. Mignolo.

4609 Quijada, Mónica. Sobre el origen y difusión del nombre *América Latina:* o una variación heterodoxa en torno al tema de la construcción social de la verdad. (*Rev. Indias,* 58:214, sept./dic. 1998, p. 595–616)

Las dos principales conclusiones del artículo son: (1) el nombre 'América Latina' fue creado por hispanoamericanos; (2) la motivación fue la preocupación por la expansión de los Estados Unidos. (En esto coincide con las investigaciones de Arturo Ardao, ver *HLAS:44:7501.*) Agrega al tema otros materiales y reflexiones, y la visión que del mismo tuvo la generación del 98. Quizás desestime demasiado la contribución francesa al proceso de formación del mencionado nombre. Para el comentario del historiador, ver ítem **930.**

4610 Revista de Occidente. No. 233, oct. 2000. Madrid: Fundación José Ortega y Gasset.

Parte del número está dedicado al tema "Pensar en español." Artículos sobre el asunto: Javier Muguerza, "La razón y sus patrias." Formula la pregunta: "¿Tiene la razón *patria* o es más bien *cosmopolita*?" y la aplica al universalismo y al particularismo en la filosofía hispanoamericana, lo que hace examinando: la dualidad que al respecto representan José Gaos, el pensamiento de Enrique Dussel y la posición de Lusi Villoro. Guillermo Hoyos Vázquez, "Compromiso vs. dependencia: desafíos de la filosofía latinoamericana." Medita sobre la función de la filosofía en un mundo de violencias e injusticias; busca la convergencia entre ética y política y examina el necesario pluralismo de la sociedad civil. Carlos Thiebaut, "Una mirada cosmopolita a la filosofía hispano-

americana." Señala que lo que más caracteriza a la filosofía son los problemas, y no tanto los "estilos," "lenguajes" o características culturales propias de una región o su idioma. Se requiere la participación de todos y no debe temerse la "dependencia" y la internacionalización. Carlos Pereda, "Luces y sombras de la escritura filosófica en español." Se plantea la "invisibilidad" (desconocimiento) de la filosofía hispanoamericana, fuera y dentro de América Latina. Señala ciertos "vicios:" 1) el "fervor sucursalero" (sucursal doméstica de una escuela extranjera famosa); 2) afán de novedades; 3) como reacción a los dos anteriores: entusiasmo nacionalista. Luego pone en relación estos "vicios" con la tradición latinoamericana del ensayo. Luis Villoro, "¿Pensar en español?" Pregunta si se debe (en filosofía) utilizar "la lengua del imperio." Después de inteligentes consideraciones concluye que, salvo situaciones especiales, lo preferible es utilizar el español pero tratando de crear "un nuevo género de discurso," apto para un pensamiento preciso y riguroso.

4611 Rivero Mendoza, Carmen Irene. Marxismo crítico y postmodernidad: reflexiones epistemológicas, metodológicas y socio-políticas. Los Teques, Venezuela: Fondo Editorial A.L.E.M., 1997. 149 p.: bibl. (Col. Doxa y episteme; 8)

La posición que asume es la de un marxismo crítico afectado por el pensamiento postmoderno, pero donde lo postmoderno funciona como desafío para mantener el marxismo. Algunos trabajos son de naturaleza teórica general. Otros se aplican a América Latina, como, por ejemplo: "A propósito de la incertidumbre postmoderna: nuevos paradigmas alternativos al cambio social latinoamericano."

4612 Rojas Mix, Miguel. La generación del 98 y la idea de América. (*Cuad. Am./México,* 12:72, nov./dic. 1998, p. 43–48)

Según el autor, fue Francisco Bilbao quien por primera vez empleó el nombre "América Latina." Pero el tema es la reacción sobre ese nombre, desde el 98 en adelante. La generación del 98 rechazó la designación de "América Latina," volviendo al de "Hispanoamérica," basado en la unidad de lengua y cultura. Este otro nombre fue usado reiteradamente por posiciones conservadoras, tanto en España como en América.

En cualquier caso, resultó un hispanoamericanismo de unión con España, opuesto al primer hispanoamericanismo de la Independencia, donde España quedaba rechazada. Para el autor, en la actualidad esta idea debería construirse *inter pares*, "de tú a tú," "donde los criterios de protección sean reemplazados por los de sociedad y solidaridad." (Rojas Mix es autor de *Los cien nombres de América* (ver *HLAS 56:4902*). [CJB]

4613 Saladino García, Alberto. Libros científicos del siglo XVIII latinoamericano. México: UNAM, 1998. 340 p.: index.

Se trata de una obra básica de gran utilidad para el estudio de la ciencia en América Latina durante el siglo XVIII. Se ocupa del movimiento de libros, venidos de Europa o publicados en la región, y aun de algunos que se conocen en forma de manuscrito. La vasta nómina se agrupa por temas: ciencias exactas, ciencias experimentales, ciencias naturales, salud, ciencias sociales y humanas (algunas de filosofía). También dedica un capítulo a libros de los siglos XVI y XVII. Todo precedido por una introducción sobre "Política cultural durante el siglo XVIII." Debe mencionarse que el autor lo es también de otra obra igualmente importante: *Ciencia y prensa durante la Ilustración latinoamericana* (Toluca: Univ. Autónoma del Estado de México, 1996).

4614 Sánchez Rubio, David. Filosofía, derecho y liberación en América Latina. Bilbao, Spain: Desclée de Brouwer, 1999. 311 p.: bibl., index. (Palimpsesto, derechos humanos y desarrollo; 3)

Repasa los orígenes y las distintas manifestaciones que ha asumido la filosofía de la liberación—tan variadas que se ha aceptado no poder hablar de esa tendencia en singular—y de las varias clasificaciones que se han dado de sus grupos componentes. Elaborado con un criterio histórico, es útil para el lector que quiera orientarse en las diversas variantes, juicios e interpretaciones que se han dado desde el interior del movimiento que estudia. Una segunda parte del libro se ocupa del análisis del concepto de 'liberación,' su relación con los derechos humanos y la corriente del "derecho alternativo," desarrollada principalmente en Brasil.

4615 Santuc, Vicente. Desafíos actuales de la reflexión filosófica en América Latina. (*Estud. Soc.*/*Santo Domingo*, 32:116, abril/junio 1999, p. 79–90)

La crisis en que se halla sumido el mundo actual, y que alcanza naturalmente a América Latina, requiere relatos emancipatorios que busquen su legitimidad en un futuro apoyado en el principio formal de que "es inmoral todo aquello que no puede ser universalizable." En este sentido, le cabe a la filosofía una tarea que, en lugar de interpretar los hechos ocurridos ("El Buho de Minerva," en la frase de Hegel), sea anticipatoria del mañana, "diciendo el 'hacia dónde' y el 'por qué' de lo humano." [CJB]

4616 Sasso, Javier. La filosofía latinoamericana y las construcciones de su historia. Caracas: Monte Ávila Editores Latinoamericana, 1998. 225 p. (Estudios. Serie ideas)

El autor parte de la dicotomía existente hoy en la filosofía latinoamericana entre: 1) los cultivadores de la filosofía a la manera en que se hace en los restantes países occidentales, llamados también "universalistas"; y 2) lo que puede denominarse el latinoamericanismo filosófico, que pone el énfasis en los problemas y la identidad de la región como forma legítima de hacer *filosofía latinoamericana* (véase la Introducción a esta sección en *HLAS 58*). La obra es una de las pocas en que el latinoamericanismo filosófico es analizado y cuestionado críticamente. La vía para hacerlo es el análisis de cómo se construyó la actual historia de la filosofía latinoamericana. También tiene observaciones sobre cómo los "universalistas" han puesto en práctica la "normalidad filosófica" (concepto acuñado por Francisco Romero). Es un libro muy argumentado al que esta descripción no puede hacer justicia.

4617 Schwenn, Benjamin. Reivindicar la modernidad frente a la posmodernidad en América Latina: el universalismo como base del relativismo cultural. (*Estud. Cult. Contemp.*, 4:7, junio 1998, p. 65–83, bibl., tables)

Las críticas posmodernas que se dan en América Latina tienen su justificación, especialmente cuando se refieren al eurocentrismo y a la versión eurocéntrica de la modernidad, pero el autor propone como tesis la reivindicación de algunos elementos del pensamiento moderno—sobre todo el universalismo—con el fin de fundamentar filosóficamente suposiciones normativas, sin perder de vista aquellas críticas. [CJB]

4618 Semillas en el tiempo: el latino-americanismo filosófico contemporáneo. Presentación y compilación de Clara Alicia Jalif de Bertranou. Mendoza, Argentina: EDIUNC-Editorial de la Univ. Nacional de Cuyo, 2001. 311 p. (América Latina)

Dieciséis autores exponen la obra de 19 representantes del latinoamericanismo filosófico o la historiografía de las ideas realizada dentro de esa corriente, desde Arturo Ardao hasta Leopoldo Zea, pasando, entre otros, por Enrique Dussel, Franz Hinkelammert, Francisco Miró Quesada, Arturo A. Roig, Augusto Salazar Bondy, Alejandro Serrano Caldera, Abelardo Villegas y Gregorio Weinberg. En la Presentación, la compiladora señala etapas del movimiento, al que caracteriza como "una meditación sobre la realidad de América Latina efectuada con instrumental filosófico, pero que incorpora asimismo el aporte de las ciencias sociales." Estima que, por sus objectivos, este movimiento puede considerarse una "filosofia de la liberación."

4619 Sobrino, Miguel Angel. Fray Pedro de Córdoba, precursor de Bartolomé de Las Casas, su vida y su obra. (*Quatrivium/ México*, 8, junio 1997, p. 133–161, ill.)

Traza con detalle y nutrido aporte documental la biografía (acción evangelizadora y defensa de los indios) de Fray Pedro de Córdoba (1482–1521). En sus comienzos, Las Casas colaboró con Fray Pedro, y tuvo siempre gran admiración por él.

4620 Torchia-Estrada, Juan Carlos. Los estudios de filosofía (Artes) en el siglo XVI: México y Perú. (*Rev. Interam. Bibliogr.*, 49:1/2, 1999, p. 69–99)

Expone el contenido de la carrera de Artes (Filosofía), sus materias, los métodos e instituciones de enseñanza, el tipo de alumnos, sus obligaciones y los requerimientos para títulos. Asimismo, se refiere a la función de la escolástica en general. [CJB]

Transformaciones e identidad cultural. Ver ítem **4839**.

4621 Uslar Pietri, Arturo. Nuevo mundo, mundo nuevo. Selección y prólogo de José Ramón Medina. Cronología y bibliografía ensayística de Horacio Jorge Becco. Caracas: Biblioteca Ayacucho; Fundación Cultural Chacao, 1998. 404 p.: bibl. (Biblioteca Ayacucho; 220)

Valiosa reunión de ensayos de un autor clásico en cuyos escritos, más allá de su valor literario, se encuentra siempre una interpretación de la historia, la cultura y la personalidad de Hispanoamérica. Como es usual en la colección a la que el libro pertenece, hay una cronología y una bibliografía.

4622 Weinberg, Gregorio. La ciencia y la idea de progreso en América Latina, 1860–1930. México: Fondo de Cultura Económica, 1998. 129 p.

Precedido de páginas que muestran el estado actual de la historiografía de la ciencia en América Latina, contiene capítulos sobre: 1) la oposición de liberales y conservadores en lo que se refiere a la apreciación de la ciencia; 2) la idea (y la realidad) de progreso, que tiene mucho de crítica a las clases dirigentes del siglo XIX, que encarnaron en su beneficio esa concepción; 3) la actividad científica en el período estudiado; 4) los ferrocarriles. El valor del libro reside en intentar un panorama que, en su pleno desarrollo, no existe.

4623 Weinberg, Gregorio. "Ilustración" y educación superior en Hispanoamérica, siglo XVIII. Buenos Aires: Academia Nacional de Educación, 1997. 95 p.: bibl. (Estudios; 13)

Contiene tres trabajos: 1) "Ilustración y educación superior en Hispanoamérica" (ver *HLAS 54:5374*); 2) "El 'agotamiento' de la universidad latinoamericana del siglo XVIII: perduración y vigencia de algunos de sus problemas," que examina el desfasaje de la universidad frente a la modernidad y el carácter sustitutivo que cumplieron las academias y las sociedades de amigos del país; y 3) "Condorcet y la instrucción pública." Muy buena contribución.

4624 Weiss, Wendy A. Latin American intellectuals and the theoretical trends they promise. (*Anthropol. Q.*, 70:1, Jan. 1997, p. 31–40)

En realidad se trata del examen de dos

obras: *Hybrid Cultures: Strategies for Entering and Exiting Modernity* (*HLAS* 58:4976)—traducción de *Culturas híbridas: estrategias para entrar y salir de la modernidad*—de Néstor García Canclini (Buenos Aires: Editorial Sudamericana, 1992); y *Communication, Culture and Hegemony* (*HLAS* 57:13)—traducción de *De los medios a las mediaciones: comunicación, cultura y hegemonía*—de Jesús Martín-Barbero (1987).

4625 Zorraquín Becú, Ricardo. Errores y omisiones de Francisco de Vitoria. (*in* Congreso del Instituto Internacional de Historia del Derecho Indiano, *11th, Buenos Aires, 1995*. Actas y estudios. Buenos Aires: Instituto de Investigaciones de Historia del Derecho Indiano, 1997, v. 2, p. 55–93)

Contrariamente a los habituales elogios a Francisco de Vitoria, éste es un artículo crítico de ciertos aspectos de su relección *De indis*. Encuentra errónea la posición de Vitoria frente a las bulas alejandrinas y al alcance del poder del papa para evangelizar a los indios. También cuestiona el valor y uso del derecho de gentes, que, como se sabe, es el título de Vitoria como fundador del derecho internacional.

MÉXICO

4626 Aguayo Cruz, Enrique I. La muerte en la filosofía de Agustín Basave. (*Humanitas/Monterrey*, 25, 1998, p. 171–194, bibl.)

Exposición del tema de la muerte en Agustín Basave, filósofo mexicano contemporáneo. Previamente da una idea general del "sistema" filosófico cristiano de este autor.

4627 Aguilar Rivera, José Antonio. La sombra de Ulises: ensayos sobre intelectuales mexicanos y norteamericanos. México: Centro de Investigación y Docencia Económica; Miguel Angel Porrúa, 1998. 197 p.: bibl.

Libro muy recomendable sobre las relaciones intelectuales entre México y Estados Unidos, pero que finalmente apunta a la comparación entre ambos países en general, y termina contribuyendo a la interpretación de México e inclusive, en algunos aspectos, a la de toda América Latina.

4628 Astigueta, Bernardo P. Filósofos humanistas novohispánicos. (*Iberoamericana/Tokyo*, 19:2, segundo semestre 1997, p. 27–50)

Aunque extenso, es un trabajo panorámico, basado en parte en literatura secundaria. Expone las manifestaciones del humanismo renacentista español, y tras las figuras de Vitoria y Las Casas se detiene en la Nueva España: Zumárraga, Vasco de Quiroga, Veracruz y Fray Juan Ramírez.

4629 Beuchot, Mauricio. Escolástica y humanismo en Fray Julián Garcés. (*Novahispania/México*, 3, 1998, p. 7–43)

Examina el contenido filosófico-teológico de la carta que en 1536 Fray Julián Garcés, obispo de Tlaxcala, dirigiera al papa Paulo III defendiendo la racionalidad de los indios (y por lo tanto la validez de su incorporación a la fe). Esta carta dio lugar a la bula *Sublimis Deus*, en concordancia con el pensamiento de Garcés. También da noticias de la vida de este personaje, y estima que la mencionada carta revela elementos del humanismo renacentista.

4630 Beuchot, Mauricio. The history of philosophy in colonial Mexico. Translated by Elizabeth Millán. Foreword by Jorge J.E. Gracia. Washington: Catholic Univ. of America Press, 1998. 204 p.: bibl., index.

Se trata de la obra más completa sobre la filosofía colonial en México, escrita por quien posiblemente sea su mejor conocedor actual. Abarca desde el siglo XVI hasta el XVIII, internándose en los primeros años del XIX. La exposición se estructura en cada siglo según representantes de las distintas órdenes religiosas (y el clero secular). El libro lleva un importante prólogo de Jorge Gracia sobre los orígenes (y el concepto) de la "filosofía hispánica."

4631 Brading, D.A. Edmundo O'Gorman y David Hume. (*Hist. Mex./México*, 46:4, abril/junio 1997, p. 695–704)

Bosquejo de la concepción de la historia del historiador mexicano Edmundo O'Gorman, destacando la influencia de Hume, la crítica a Ranke y su cercanía a Heidegger y Gaos.

4632 Ceballos Ramírez, Manuel. Los jesuitas en en desarrollo del catolicismo social mexicano, 1900–1925. (*in* Coloquio de

Antropología e Historia Regionales, *17th*, *Zamora, Mexico, 1995.* La Iglesia Católica en México. Zamora, Mexico: El Colegio de Michoacán; México: Secretaría de Gobernación, Subsecretaría de Asuntos Jurídicos y Asociaciones Religiosas, Dirección General de Asuntos Religiosos, 1997, p. 211–224)

Se refiere a las tareas de la Compañía de Jesús en el desarrollo de organizaciones sociopolíticas mexicanas inspiradas en la encíclica *Rerum Novarum.* Distingue dos períodos en el lapso estudiado, separados por los efectos de la Revolución Mexicana: 1900–1914 y 1919–1925. En ambos se habría intentado llevar a la práctica un proyecto inspirado en el "catolicismo social" y en "la primera democracia cristiana." [CJB]

4633 Echegollen Guzmán, Alfredo. Antonio Caso y la república bovarista en México. (*Metapolítica/México*, 3:12, oct./dic. 1999, p. 623–635, bibl.)

Reconstruye las ideas filosófico-políticas de Caso sobre México y América Latina. La exposición gira en torno a dos aspéctos: "su análisis del proceso histórico inacabado de estructuración política de México y América Latina; y su crítica del bovarismo político como un elemento constitutivo de las políticas nacional y latinoamericana."

4634 En torno a la obra de Adolfo Sánchez Vázquez: filosofía, ética, estética y política. Recopilación de Gabriel Vargas Lozano. México: UNAM, Facultad de Filosofía y Letras 1995. 640 p.: bibl.

Adolfo Sánchez Vázquez pertenece al grupo de los exiliados españoles en México y representa lo que se ha dado en llamar un "marxismo abierto." Dada la gran cantidad de contribuciones a este volumen, sólo puede decirse que se trata de una obra valiosa, donde se examinan varios aspectos del pensamiento de Sánchez Vázquez y hay contribuciones de este mismo autor. La introducción de Gabriel Vargas Lozano resulta muy útil, y es de particular interés la polémica entre Luis Villoro y Sánchez Vázquez sobre el concepto de ideología. Lo mismo puede decirse de la participación de Javier Muguerza y José Luis Abellán sobre el exilio español. También ver ítem **4636.**

4635 Fernández, Rafael Diego. Influencias y evolución del pensamiento político de Fray Servando Teresa de Mier. (*Hist.*

Mex./México, 48:1, julio/sept. 1998, p. 3–35, bibl.)

Buena y recomendable exposición de conjunto de las ideas políticas de Mier: su posición frente a España y la Independencia, su preferencia por el sistema republicano, y la forma en que entendió el federalismo. [CJB]

4636 Gandler, Stefan. Peripherer Marxismus: kritische Theorie in Mexiko. Hamburg, Germany: Argument Verlag, 1999. 459 p.: bibl. (Argument-Sonderband; 270)

Estudia con amplio detalle la obra de dos pensadores marxistas: Adolfo Sánchez Vázquez, parte del exilio español en México (ver ítem **4634**), y Bolívar Echeverría, de origen ecuatoriano y radicado en México. Uno de los propósitos es mostrar los valores filosóficos que pueden hallarse fuera del "Primer Mundo." Muy amplia bibliografía. También ver ítem **4817.**

4637 Gómez, Fernando. Experimentación social en los albores coloniales de la modernidad: el deseo utópico-reformista de Vasco de Quiroga, 1470–1565. (*Bol. Am./Barcelona*, 50, 2000, p. 101–121)

Critica duramente las experiencias de Vasco de Quiroga en la organización de sus "hospitales-pueblos." Se las considera una expresión de "cultura represiva" y de "una política oficial de segregación racial."

4638 Gonçalves Júnior, Arlindo F. Argumentos éticos na filosofia do direito e sociologia de Recaséns Siches. (*Reflexão/Campinas*, 25:77, maio/agôsto 2000, p. 52–62, bibl.)

Luis Recaséns Siches fue parte del grupo de intelectuales españoles exiliados en México. Aquí se examinan principalmente sus obras *Tratado general de filosofía del derecho* (*HLAS 25:5333*) y *Tratado de sociología* (*HLAS 20:4915*). Se señala la cercanía a las ideas de Ortega y Gasset.

4639 González Rodríguez, Jaime. Lecturas e ideas en Nueva España. (*Rev. Complut. Hist. Am.*, 23, 1997, p. 39–74, bibl.)

Se trata de una exposición muy minuciosa, basada en materiales de archivo y considerable bibliografía, sobre el control de literatura manuscrita e impresa, censura previa, importación y venta de libros, lecturas individuales, participación de la Inquisición y del arzobispo Montúfar, y temas semejantes.

4640 Hurtado López, Juan Manuel. La evangelización en la obra y pensamiento de Vasco de Quiroga. (*in* Coloquio de Antropología e Historia Regionales, *17th, Zamora, Mexico, 1995.* Iglesia Católica en México. Zamora, Mexico: El Colegio de Michoacán; México: Secretaría de Gobernación, Subsecretaría de Asuntos Jurídicos y Asociaciones Religiosas, Dirección General de Asuntos Religiosos, 1997, p. 99–120)

Expone en detalle los aspectos de doctrina y los medios prácticos de la acción evangelizadora llevada a cabo por Vasco de Quiroga. Alude también al aporte del Colegio de San Nicolás, en Michoacán. Aunque está escrito con simpatía de fondo religioso, la documentación utilizada contribuye a la interpretación de Vasco de Quiroga y a la de los problemas de la época en que aquél estuvo involucrado.

4641 Lombardo Toledano, Vicente. Vicente Lombardo Toledano: acción y pensamiento. Estudio introductorio y selección de Martín Tavira Urióstegui. México: Fondo de Cultura Económica, 1999. 297 p.: bibl., ill. (Vida y pensamiento de México)

Antología de Lombardo Toledano (1894–1968), pensador marxista y dirigente sindical mexicano. Reproduce textos cuya reunión es muy oportuna. Lo precede un estudio introductorio escrito con simpatía personal e ideológica, que expone el pensamiento y la acción de Lombardo Toledano y el ambiente de pensamiento en que se formó (discípulo de Antonio Caso, terminó polemizando con él).

4642 López Farjeat, Luis Xavier and Héctor Zagal Arreguín. Dos aproximaciones estéticas a la identidad nacional: una filosofía de la cultura desde el barroco y el surrealismo. Monterrey, Mexico: Univ. Autónoma de Nuevo León, 1998. 121 p.

México visto desde el barroco (siglo XVII) y el surrealismo (siglo XX). En el caso del segundo, se examina la idea que surrealistas como Breton se hicieron de México. En cuanto al primero, lo más importante es la relación entre barroco y conciencia criolla. Con una franca desestima por el pensamiento ilustrado y el positivismo, la conclusión final es que México no se entiende

sin tres componentes: la España de la conquista, los indígenas conquistados y los tres siglos de virreinato.

4643 Magallón Anaya, Mario. El pensamiento filosófico y político de Francisco Severo Maldonado. (*Cuad. Am./México*, 15:85, enero/feb. 2001, p. 193–207, bibl.)

Oportuna presentación de las ideas de Francisco Severo Maldonado (nac. 1775), representante de la Ilustración mexicana, cuyo pensamiento no ha sido mayormente estudiado. [CJB]

4644 Matute, Alvaro. Pensamiento historiográfico mexicano del siglo XX: la desintegración del positivismo, 1911–1935. México: UNAM, Instituto de Investigaciones Históricas; Fondo de Cultura Económica, 1999. 478 p.: bibl., index. (Sección de obras de historia)

Util antología de lo que podría llamarse la concepción o teoría de la historia en México aproximadamente en el primer tercio del siglo XX. Figuran el filósofo Antonio Caso, el bibliógrafo Emeterio Valverde Téllez y otros escritores y profesores de historia (porque también se refiere a la enseñanza de la disciplina). Es de notar la reiterada referencia al filósofo de la historia A.D. Xenopol. El estudio introductorio clarifica aspectos de la historiografía positivista y en general de la época que cubre el libro.

4645 Padilla Hernández, Salvador. El liberalismo mexicano y el pensamiento económico del Dr. José María Luis Mora. (*Probl. Desarro.*, 29:113, abril/junio 1998, p. 137–167)

Examen del liberalismo: en general, en México, y en Mora. De éste se estudia en especial su *Disertación sobre la naturaleza y aplicación de las rentas y bienes eclesiásticos* (1831) y su actuación en los intentos de aplicar las doctrinas liberales en medio de las convulsiones políticas de la época. Concluye con un juicio histórico general sobre el liberalismo, incluyendo el neoliberalismo actual.

4646 Paz, Octavio. Sueño en libertad: escritos políticos. Selección y prólogo de Yvón Grenier. México: Planeta, 2001. 462 p.: bibl. (Seix Barral Biblioteca breve)

Publicación importante para el conocimiento de las opiniones políticas de Octavio Paz, mostrándolas a lo largo de toda su vida de escritor. Naturalmente no se trata de un pensamiento político sistemático, pero sí muy significativo, no sólo para México sino para toda América Latina. Los textos son presentados en orden cronológico. Incluye entrevistas.

4647 Los refugiados españoles y la cultura mexicana: actas de las primeras jornadas, celebradas en la Residencia de Estudiantes en noviembre de 1994. Madrid: Amigos de la Residencia de Estudiantes, 1998. 160 p.: bibl. (Publicaciones de la Residencia de Estudiantes)

En parte por los autores, y en parte por los temas, el libro tiene su lugar propio en la literatura sobre el exilio español en México. Destacamos, por razones temáticas, pero sin desmedro para el resto del libro, los siguientes artículos: de Javier Garciadiego sobre Alfonso Reyes en España; de Francisco Gil Villegas sobre la influencia de Ortega en México; de Juan M. Díaz de Guereño sobre la fundación de la revista *Cuadernos Americanos*; y de Andrés Lira sobre José Gaos, Ramón Iglesia, José Miranda y Juan Antonio Ortega y Medina. Para el comentario sobre *Las segundas jornadas,* ver ítem **1608.**

4648 Rionda Arreguín, Luis. Reflexiones en torno a la historia. Guanajuato, Mexico: Centro de Investigaciones Humanísticas, Univ. de Guanajuato, 1998. 220 p.: bibl.

Junto con artículos sobre filósofos de la historia europeos, hay trabajos útiles sobre los jesuitas novohispanos Clavijero y Alegre, y una comparación entre José María Luis Mora y Lucas Alamán. Otro trabajo se ocupa de "Guanajuato, Barrera y el positivismo."

4649 Seminario Internacional del Pensamiento de Don Efraín González Luna, *Guadalajara, Mexico, 1998.* Ponencias. Guadalajara, Mexico: Partido Acción Nacional, Comité Directivo Estatal Jalisco, 1999. 580 p.: bibl., ill.

Homenaje que realiza el Partido Acción Nacional y un conjunto de investigadores a Efraín González Luna (falleció 1964), donde se estudian y aprecian diversas facetas de su pensamiento político y social.

Skidmore, Thomas E. Onde estava a "Malinche" brasileira?: mitos de origem nacional no Brasil e no México. Ver ítem **4764.**

4650 Torre Villar, Ernesto de la. Don Juan de Palafox y Mendoza, pensador político. México: UNAM, Instituto de Investigaciones Jurídicas, 1997. 108 p. (Serie C— Estudios históricos; 66)

Análisis de la obra *Historia real sagrada, luz de príncipes y súbditos* (1643), de Juan de Palafox y Mendoza (1600–59), obispo de Puebla y figura política de considerable influencia. Traza sus rasgos biográficos, estudia las circunstancias de la creación de esa obra, y expone su contenido y finalidades. Previamente la relaciona con *El gobernador cristiano,* de Fray Juan Márquez (1564–1621), libro que considera antecedente del de Palafox. Buena síntesis que facilita el estudio en mayor profundidad. Para el comentario del historiador, ver ítem **1337.**

Valenzuela Arce, José Manuel. Impecable y diamantina: la deconstrucción del discurso nacional. Ver ítem **1199.**

4651 Vargas Lozano, Gabriel. La filosofía mexicana: las sendas de Gaos. (*Cuad. Am./México,* 15:88, julio/agosto 2001, p. 222–227)

Evoca la figura de José Gaos y su aporte a la cultura filosófica de México y Latinoamérica, a partir de su peculiar idea de la filosofía: "un pensamiento aplicado a problemas inmanentes y no en conexión sistemática, sino en conexión existencial . . ., y este pensamiento se encontraría seguramente unido . . . a las ciencias y a las disciplinas no científicas." [CJB]

4652 Volpi Escalante, Jorge. La imaginación y el poder: una historia intelectual de 1968. México: Ediciones Era, 1998. 455 p.: bibl. (Biblioteca Era)

Crónica circunstanciada y rica en testimonios de los acontecimientos políticos, pero sobre todo culturales, del año en el cual se produjo la matanza de estudiantes en Tlatelolco. En el Epílogo el autor reflexiona sobre la vida de México desde 1968 y sobre el significado del acontecimiento mencionado. Insta a no convertirlo en un mito, a examinar sus fundamentos objetivos y a sumarse a las transformaciones democráticas que el país ha venido acentuando recientemente. Para el comentario del especialista de literatura, ver *HLAS 58:3511.*

4653 Zirión Quijano, Antonio. La fenomenología en Antonio Caso. (*Rev. Filos. / México*, 34:100, enero/abril 2001, p. 27–68, bibl.)

Descripción minuciosa de lo que de fenomenólogia o de Husserl en general puede encontrarse en los escritos de Caso. También se plantean cuestiones como: ¿Fue Caso un fenomenólogo?, a la que se responde negativamente. El artículo se ha desarrollado—sin ser el propósito principal—en diálogo con las apreciaciones de Luis Villoro sobre el mismo tema. [CJB]

AMÉRICA CENTRAL

4654 Che Hassán, Jorge and Gustavo García de Paredes. Filosofía, política y moral de don Justo Arosemena. Panamá: Univ. de Panamá; Editorial Portobelo; Librería El Campus, 1997. 56 p. (Centenario de don Justo Arosemena; 2) (Pequeño formato; 24. Filosofía-historia)

Visión sintética del pensamiento de Justo Arosemena, considerado "el más consistente exégeta de la nacionalidad panameña en el siglo XIX." Se presentan las fuentes de su concepción filosófica, moral y política y su vinculación con el positivismo. Se toma muy en cuenta su obra juvenil *Apuntamientos para la introducción a las ciencias morales y políticas* (1840).

4655 Figueres Ferrer, José. Escritos de José Figueres Ferrer: política, economía y relaciones internacionales. Selección y edición de la Fundación pro Centro Cultural e Histórico José Figueres Ferrer. Prólogo de Eugenio Rodríguez Vega. San José: Fundación pro Centro Cultural e Histórica José Figueres Ferrer; Editorial Univ. Estatal a Distancia, 2000. 603 p.

Oportuna reunión de escritos de una de las principales figuras políticas de Centroamérica. Aunque los temas son ocasionales, se expresa el trasfondo de opiniones e ideas del autor. Interesa por ello para la historia político-ideológica. También ver ítem **4656.**

4656 Figueres Ferrer, José. Obras escogidas. Cartago, Costa Rica: Editorial Tecnológica de Costa Rica, 1997. 581 p.: ill.

Se reúnen aquí tres libros de Figueres (1906–90), tres veces presidente de Costa Rica: *Palabras gastadas* (1943); *Cartas a un ciudadano* (1956); y *La pobreza de las naciones* (1973). Los temas son principalmente nacionales y propios de la sociedad y el gobierno en las circunstancias del momento, pero no faltan las ideas generales en que basaba su acción. Por su estilo Figueres lograba un buen efecto comunicativo con su público. También ver ítem **4655.**

4657 Giglioli, Giovanna *et al.* Arnoldo Mora y la identidad nacional. (*Rev. Filos. Univ. Costa Rica*, 38:94, enero/junio 2000, p. 97–107)

Crítica en la que se cuestionan el fundamento y los contenidos de la obra de Arnoldo Mora, *La identidad nacional en la filosofía costarricense* (San José: EDUCA, 1997).

4658 Pérez Baltodano, Andrés. El derecho a la esperanza: Nicaragua y el pensamiento de Alejandro Serrano Caldera. Managua: Instituto de Investigaciones y Acción Social Martin Luther King, Univ. Politécnica de Nicaragua (UPOLI), 1999. 227 p.: bibl., ill.

Caracteriza a Serrano Caldera (autor de, entre otras obras, *La permanencia de Carlos Marx* (1983); *Entre la nación y el imperio* (1988); *Los dilemas de la democracia* (1995)) la aplicación del ejercicio filosófico a los problemas concretos (nacionales de su país, Nicaragua, o generales de América Latina) y a la meditación sobre la situación actual del mundo en que la región está inmersa. El libro se articula así en tres planos, de lo más general (crisis de la modernidad, globalización, neopragmatismo) a lo más específico (la construcción de la razón en Nicaragua), pasando por la modernidad fragmentada de América Latina. El libro es claro y aprovechable. Concluye con una entrevista a Serrano Caldera, muy iluminadora sobre el pensamiento del autor y que debe considerarse parte integral del libro.

4659 *Revista de Filosofía de la Universidad de Costa Rica.* Vol. 35, No. 87, dic. 1997. Libros filosóficos costarricenses, 1940–1996. San José: Depto. de Filosofía de la Facultad Central de Ciencias y Letras, Univ. de Costa Rica.

Se trata de un instrumento de gran utilidad. Contiene tres índices para el período 1940–96: 1) por autores; 2) por año de las publicaciones; 3) por temas. Es una bibliografía anotada, porque una sección se dedica a proporcionar, para cada libro incluido, una síntesis de su contiendo, y no siempre breve. Se completa con datos biográficos de cada autor. [CJB]

4660 Rosa, Diógenes de la. Diógenes de la Rosa: testigo y protagonista del siglo XX panameño; compilación de su obra. v. 1. Panamá: Academia Panameña de la Lengua, 1999. 1 v.: bibl., ill.

Aunque no de gran envergadura teórica, estos escritos de Rosa (1904–98) contribuyen al conocimiento de las ideas político-sociales de Panamá durante el siglo XX. También ilustran sobre la vida y la acción del autor, quien, en la década de 1930, llegó a proponer la constitución de un Partido Obrero Marxista-Leninista.

4661 Sierra Fonseca, Rolando. La filosofía de la historia de José Cecilio del Valle. Obispado de Choluteca, Honduras: Ediciones Subirana, 1998. 111 p.: bibl. (Col. José Trinidad Reyes; 4)

De los escritos de Valle se destacan los aspectos de interpretación de la historia, y especialmente los que se refieren a América. El fondo del pensamiento de Valle en este aspecto es las ideas de la Ilustración. Para el comentario de historiador, ver ítem **1665.**

Taracena, Luis Pedro. Uso de las palabras "patria" y "patriota" en *El Editor Constitucional* y *El Amigo de la Patria,* Guatemala, 1820–1821. See item **1667.**

4662 Ycaza Tigerino, Julio. Darío y su filosofía política. (*Bol. Nicar. Bibliogr. Doc.,* 101, oct./dic. 1998, p. 21–38)

A pesar de lo específico del título, trata de desentrañar una cosmovisión en Rubén Darío, algunos de cuyos elementos serían una "filosofía de la armonía social universal," el rechazo de la racionalidad moderna, el hispanismo, la reacción contra el socialismo y el anarquismo, el sentido religioso proveniente de la fuente indígena, etc. Interesante en tanto va más allá del habitual enfoque puramente literario.

CARIBE INSULAR

4663 Alvarez Lora, Leonardo. Vigencia de Martí en Panamá. v. 1. Panamá: Editorial Universitaria, 1998. 1 v.

Recoge escritos sobre Martí publicados en Panamá. La gran mayoría, breves.

4664 Anderle, Adám. Cien años de guerra por Martí. (*Anu. Estud. Am.,* 55:1, enero/junio 1998, p. 73–80)

Ante dos interpretaciones antagónicas—representativas de opiniones norteamericanas y cubanas, respectivamente—frente a la obra martiana y su ligamen con la Revolución Cubana, el autor, de nacionalidad húngara, plantea ciertos interrogantes respecto de la ideología fidelista, el Partido Comunista de Cuba y el legado del héroe independentista, cuyas ideas siguen siendo, en su opinión, actuales. [CJB]

4665 Costa, Octavio Ramón. Ser y esencia de Martí. Miami, Fla.: Ediciones Universal, 2000. 253 p. (Col. Formación martiana)

Cuarenta trabajos sobre Martí, escritos a lo largo de 60 años de dedicación al asunto. Es parte de la visión del exilio cubano. Abarca un gran abanico de temas y todos están escritos en un estilo llano que trata de llegar al mayor número de lectores.

4666 Díaz, Esther and **Pedro Luis Sotolongo.** Ernesto Che Guevara: ética y estética de una existencia; "—una voluntad que he cultivado con delectación de artista—." Rosario, Argentina: Laborde Ediciones, 1997. 148 p.: bibl.

Se muestra claramente que la motivación del libro es exaltar la figura del Che. El objetivo propiamente intelectual es utilizar instrumentos filosóficos para describir y defender una forma de ética que se desprendería del pensamiento de Guevara—la ética que daría lugar al "hombre nuevo"—y que se pone en relación con diversas interpretaciones del marxismo, con la filosofía de Foucault y con el tema de la postmodernidad, entre otros asuntos.

4667 Estrade, Paul. José Martí: los fundamentos de la democracia en Latinoamérica. Madrid: Ediciones Doce Calles; Casa de Velázquez, 2000. 794 p.: bibl. (Col. Antilia)

Tesis doctoral. Estudia, con considerable extensión, las ideas económicas, sociales y políticas de Martí, pero sin separarlas de la práctica y de la acción. De los dos hemisferios de apreciación actual de Martí, pertenece al de las simpatías por la Revolución Cubana. Contiene varios apéndices, reseñas bibliográficas y un Complemento Bibliográfico. La principal conclusión es reconocer su condición de fundador, "por el pensamiento y el ejemplo, de una verdadera democracia en Latinoamérica." Esta democracia era de signo distinto de la que Tocqueville vio en la América de su tiempo. La de Martí se distinguiría de la norteamericana de fines del siglo XIX, y por último se colocaría "en la mitad del camino que va de Simón Bolívar a Ernesto Che Guevara, y a la altura de ambos."

4668 García Passalacqua, Juan M. Vate, de la cuna a la cripta: el nacionalismo cultural de Luis Muñoz Marín. San Juan: Editorial LEA, 1998. 340 p.: bibl. (Cuadernos del 98; 7)

Doce trabajos que enfocan diversos aspectos de Luis Muñoz Marín, hombre público puertorriqueño. Se refiere a su actuación política y su época. Podría destacarse especialmente el tema del nacionalismo cultural.

4669 González Serra, Diego Jorge. Martí y la ciencia del espíritu. La Habana: Editorial SI-MAR, 1999. 102 p.: bibl.

El propósito del libro es desentrañar, de numerosos pasajes de Martí, su "pensamiento psicológico," incluida la psicología social.

4670 Juan, Adelaida de. José Martí: imagen, crítica y mercado de arte. La Habana: Editorial Letras Cubanas, 1997. 233 p.: bibl.

Aparentemente sería la única obra que expone e interpreta los escritos de Martí sobre temas de arte, especialmente pintura.

4671 Lewis, Rupert. Walter Rodney's intellectual and political thought. Barbados: Univ. of the West Indies Press; Detroit, Mich.: Wayne State Univ. Press, 1998. 298 p., 4 p. of plates: bibl., ill., ports.

Walter Rodney (1942–80), nacido en Guyana, fue autor de How Europe Underdeveloped Africa. Pan-africanista y marxista, desarrolló una interpretación de las circunstancias de la descolonización del Caribe. Fue activista en defensa de situaciones de racismo y subordinación en Jamaica, Tanzania y Guyana. El presente libro enfoca la obra de Rodney al hilo de su biografía, sus escritos y su actividad política, y toma en cuenta una considerable bibliografía sobre esos temas. El autor de esta obra había estudiado anterior-

mente la ideología y la acción de Marcus Garvey.

4672 Maceo, Antonio. Antonio Maceo: ideología política; cartas y otros documentos. v. 1, 1870–1884. v. 2, 1895–1896. La Habana: Editorial de Ciencias Sociales, 1998. 2 v.: bibl. (Centenario) (Historia)

Se trata de la reedición facsimilar de una obra llevada a cabo, en 1945, por la Sociedad Cubana de Estudios Históricos e Internacionales, que contiene documentos del patriota cubano Antonio Maceo (1845–96), con una introducción de Emilio Roig de Leuchsenring. Para el comentario sobre la obra original, ver *HLAS 17:1737.*

4673 Marinello, Juan. 18 ensayos martianos. La Habana: Ediciones Unión; Centro de Estudios Martianos, 1998. 402 p.: bibl.

Los escritos de Marinello sobre Martí son muy numerosos y exceden los incluidos en este libro que, sin embargo, contiene varios de los más importantes. La obra viene a ser una tercera edición, aumentada, de *Ensayos martianos* (ver *HLAS 26:1497*). La precede un estudio de Roberto Fernández Retamar, coloreado por la identificación con la posición política de Marinello y con la Revolución Cubana, y que quizás sea lo más completo que se ha escrito sobre la obra martiana de Marinello. El estudio también es útil para conocer la evolución intelectual de Marinello. También ver ítem **4674.**

4674 Marinello, Juan. Papeles de Juan Marinello: inéditos o poco conocidos. Recopilación de Sara Molejón Jiménez. La Habana: Editorial SI-MAR, 1998. 126 p.

Como indica el título, recoge escritos de Marinello. Varios se refieren, como era de esperar, a José Martí. Otros tratan de representantes del marxismo en América Latina, especialmente Julio Antonio Mella y Mariátegui. Se agregn algunas cartas dirigidas a Marinello. El pequeño volumen se abre con una apreciación de Fidel Castro. También ver ítem **4673.**

4675 Martí, José. José Martí y el equilibrio del mundo. Estudio introductorio de Armando Hart Dávalos. Selección y notas de Centro de Estudios Martianos. México: Fondo de Cultura Económica, 2000. 282 p. (Tierra firme)

Reunión de escritos de José Martí, en general de carácter político y de comentario periodístico internacional. El estudio introductorio enfoca a Martí desde la óptica de la adhesión a la Revolución Cubana.

4676 Medin, Tzvi. Ideología y conciencia social en la Revolución Cubana. (*Cuad. Am./México,* 11:66, nov./dic. 1997, p. 91–104)

El artículo está basado en un libro previo del autor: *Cuba: The Shaping of Revolutionary Consciousness* (ver *HLAS 52:1936* y *HLAS 53:3658*). Estudia la ideología de la Revolución en sus diversas etapas, desde la democracia reformista inicial hasta el marxismo-leninismo, y trata de mostrar el esfuerzo de la dirigencia cubana—a lo largo de las mencionadas etapas—para formar una conciencia popular acorde con su ideología. Aclarando que no defiende las agresiones sufridas por la Revolución, viene a concluir—dicho muy resumidamente—que el fenómeno revolucionario tomó la forma de un totalitarismo, y que la conciencia revolucionaria que buscó crear fue monolítica y maniquea, entre otras características de igual signo que le atribuye el autor. [CJB]

4677 Mejía, Manuel. La filosofía social en José Ramón Abad: un acercamiento al pensamiento moderno contemporáneo. (*Estud. Soc./Santo Domingo,* 30:108, abril/junio 1997, p. 87–122)

Artículo extenso dedicado a la obra de José Ramón Abad, *La República Dominicana: reseña general geográfico-estadística* (1888). Abad fue representante del positivismo evolucionista. Distinguió entre las "razas" progresistas o civilizadas y las retrasadas, y utilizó las características de las primeras para proponer el desarrollo de su país.

4678 Melgar Bao, Ricardo. Símbolos del tiempo, la identidad y la alteridad en la visión americana de José Martí. (*Convergencia/Toluca,* 8:24, enero/abril 2001, p. 199–221, bibl.)

Para el autor, la dimensión simbólica de la obra martiana ha sido "insuficientemente explorada," por lo cual se propone incursionar en ese campo. Tres son los aspectos que lo ocupan: el tiempo, la identidad, y

la "alteridad," siguiendo el hilo conductor de "Nuestra América" y otros escritos. [CJB]

4679 Monal, Isabel. José de la Luz y Caballero, filósofo de América. (*Cuba Social.,* 18, 2000, p. 57–64)

Clara y ajustada apreciación de José de la Luz y Caballero, quien se caracterizó por su oposición al eclecticismo de Cousin. En el artículo Luz es colocado en el contexto del pensamiento cubano (fue discípulo de Félix Varela) y del latinoamericano de la época en general.

4680 Piña-Contreras, Guillermo. El universo familiar en la formación de Pedro Henríquez Ureña. (*Cuad. Am./México,* 15:90, nov./dic. 2001, p. 143–179)

Escrito biográfico sobre Henríquez Ureña (1884–1946), especialmente referido a su ambiente familiar, desde los primeros años hasta su alejamiento definitivo de la República Dominicana. [CJB]

4681 Portuondo Pajón, Gladys. El problema antropológico y la superación del positivismo en Fernando Ortiz. (*Actual/Mérida,* 37, sept./dic. 1997, p. 163–186)

Examen de la obra socio-antropológica de Fernando Ortiz, considerada como la más importante en la interpretación de la cultura cubana desde el punto de vista antropológico. La autora considera que Ortiz llegó a matizar su indudable pertenencia a la corriente positivista con algunos rasgos historicistas.

4682 Sang, Mu-Kien Adriana. Una utopía inconclusa: Expaillat y el liberalismo dominicano del siglo XIX. Santo Domingo: Instituto Tecnológico de Santo Domingo, 1997. 479 p.: appendices, bibl.

Por el texto y los apéndices, resulta una muy buena contribución al tema, que va más allá del pensamiento y la acción de Ulises Francisco Espaillat (1823–78), pues éste es colocado en el marco de la historia dominicana y en el del liberalismo latinoamericano en general.

4683 Siggins, Jack A. José Martí: political philosophy and the Catholic Church. (*in* Seminar on the Acquisition of Latin American Library Materials, *42nd, Rockville, Maryland, 1997.* Religion and Latin America in the twenty-first century: libraries reacting to social change. Austin: SALALM Secretariat, Univ. of Texas, 1997, p. 15–21)

Desde el punto de vista temático el trabajo consta de dos partes: la primera es un repaso de los principales momentos de la vida del prócer cubano; la segunda resume sus ideas sobre la libertad religiosa en confrontación con la Iglesia Católica y con los extremos dogmáticos de cualquier connotación. [CJB]

4684 Torchia-Estrada, Juan Carlos. Orígenes de la historiografía filosófica en Cuba: José Zacarías González del Valle. (*Rev. Interam. Bibliogr.*, 47:1/4, 1997, p. 57–72)

En 1839 José Zacarías González del Valle publicó un artículo sobre la *Lógica* de José Agustín Caballero, que podría ser la primera manifestación de historiografía filosófica en Hispanoamérica. El presente trabajo discute las características y circunstancias de ese artículo. [CJB]

VENEZUELA

Colombia-Venezuela: historia intelectual. See item **4699.**

4685 Consalvi, Simón Alberto. Profecía de la palabra: vida y obra de Mariano Picón-Salas. Caracas: Tierra de Gracia Editores, 1996. 563 p.: bibl. (Col. Viaje al amanecer)

Busca extraer, de la rica obra de Picón-Salas, un perfil o línea biográfica y una interpretación de su vida y su personalidad. Se trata de una narrativa fluida, siempre en estilo de comentario. Los estudiosos de Picón-Salas encontrarán aquí elementos de valor para su tarea.

4686 Cuñarro Conde, Edith Mabel. El origen del liberalismo en Venezuela: el Acta del Cabildo Extraordinario realizado en la ciudad de Caracas, el 19 de abril de 1810. (*Cuest. Polít.*, 23, julio/dic. 1999, p. 145–171, bibl.)

En el texto del Acta que se estudia se analizan los actos de habla, las funciones de los enunciados lingüísticos, y sus características en los procesos de enunciación. El fin es mostrar que el documento, pese a su aparente espontaneidad, fue pensado con anterioridad en sus menores detalles, preparando el advenimiento de la República. [CJB]

4687 Espriella, Ramiro de la. Las ideas políticas de Bolívar. Bogotá: Editorial Grijalbo, 1999. 299 p.: bibl.

La Carta de Jamaica, el Discurso de Angostura, la Constitución Boliviana, etc., se reproducen y comentan en su contenido y contexto histórico, agregando bibliografía. Util como introducción al asunto.

4688 González Ordosgoitti, Enrique Alí. Educación/filosofía/integración: una proposición para América Latina. (*Apunt. Filos.*, 16, 2000, p. 153–168, tables)

Pese a la generalidad del título, se trata de la organización, experiencia y resultados de la Cátedra de Pensamiento Latinoamericano de la Univ. Central de Venezuela. Es importante porque muestra el creciente interés por esta clase de estudios, que pueden incluir la filosofía, pero que toman en cuenta el ámbito más amplio del "pensamiento," la historia y la cultura, con el ánimo de lograr una "filosofía de la historia" de América Latina y pasar de ella a la propuesta de fórmulas concretas para el futuro. En este caso particular se hace mucho hincapié en la integración regional.

4689 Hérnandez de Sánchez, Rosario. Libertad de opinión y educación en el pensamiento político de Simón Rodríguez. Caracas: Fondo Editorial de Humanidades y Educación, Univ. Central de Venezuela, 2000. 408 p.: bibl. (Col. Estudios. Educación)

El tema de la libertad, de la libertad de opinión, y específicamente de la libertad de imprenta, es analizado en Simón Rodríguez dentro de un amplio contexto de las ideas iluministas y liberales (incluyendo España). Con ello se trata de hacer inteligible al lector el pensamiento del autor estudiado, que se considera un "ilustrado" racionalista y antiliberal. También ver ítem **4692.**

4690 Pérez, Francisco Javier. Lingüística y nación: lo nacional imaginario en las escrituras no políticas del siglo XIX venezolano. (*Montalbán/Caracas*, 31, 1998, p. 65–84, bibl., table)

El artículo versa sobre el concepto de lo nacional en ámbitos culturales, específicamente lingüísticos, fuera del pensamiento convencional. Lo examina a través de discursos que anticipaban o intentaban construir una realidad nacional sobre lo que el autor llama "lo diferencial en materia lingüística," "textos disciplinatorios," y "discursos de la manipulación y discursos de la ilusión." Trata de ver cómo en esos discursos (que pueden ser gramáticas, diccionarios, etc.) se manifiestan ideas no lingüísticas. [CJB]

4691 Presencia y crítica de Mario Briceño-Iragorry. Compilación de Isidoro Requena Torres. Recopilación de Atanasio Alegre. Caracas: Comisión Presidencial para el Centenario del Nacimiento de Mario Briceño-Iragorry; Fundación Mario Briceño-Iragorry, 1997. 379 p.: bibl.

Briceño-Iragorry (1897–1958), ensayista, historiador y político venezolano, es aquí examinado desde muy diversos ángulos por más de 30 autores. Hay dos estudios comparativos, uno con Mariano Picón Salas y otro con Enrique Bernardo Núñez. Varios se ocupan del enfoque histórico de Briceño-Iragorri. También ver ítem **4696**.

Quintero Montiel, Inés Mercedes and **Floreal Contreras.** Antonio José de Sucre: dos ensayos sobre el personaje y su tiempo. Ver ítem **2466**.

4692 Ramírez Fierro, María del Rayo. Simón Rodríguez y su utopia para América. Mexico: UNAM, 1994. 134 p.: bibl., ill. (Col. El ensayo iberoamericano; 2)

Tras exponer nociones generales sobre el concepto de utopía, y sobre la utopía en la historia de América, el libro se dedica al análisis del pensamiento utópico de Simón Rodríguez. El último capítulo trata el tema de la utopía en relación con la situación actual de América Latina. En apéndice se incluyen textos de Simón Rodríguez. También ver ítem **4689**.

4693 Sánchez Macgrégor, Joaquín. Tiempo de Bolívar: una filosofía de la historia latinoamericana. México: Centro Coordinador y Difusor de Estudios Latinoamericanos, Facultad de Filosofía y Letras; M.A. Porrúa, Grupo Editorial, 1997. 159 p.: bibl. (Filosofía de nuestra América)

Comentarios filosóficos a textos de Bolívar, cuyas ideas tratan de proyectarse a una "filosofía de la historia" de América Latina. El eje conceptual es la pareja curso [lo que ocurre en la historia]/discurso, por donde la obra es de las que utilizan como método interpretativo el análisis del discurso. Se desea que las conclusiones vengan "en ayuda del precario tiempo mexicano actual."

4694 Sánchez Marichal, César. Los indios en la correspondencia bolivariana. (*Espac. Temas Cienc. Soc.*, 5:5, 1998, p. 79–113, bibl.)

Contiene una buena selección de cartas y documentos del Libertador donde se hace presente el tema indígena y su representación, con las limitaciones de un "mantuano," que son indicadas puntualmente por el autor. [CJB]

4695 Simón Bolívar: pensamiento político. Recopilación de Enrique Ayala Mora. Sucre, Bolivia: Univ. Andina Simón Bolívar, 1997. 150 p. (Serie Cóndor; 4)

Util como edición popular de los escritos de Bolívar.

4696 Suárez, Wagner Rafael. El pensamiento cristiano de Mario Briceño-Iragorry en el proceso restaurador de la Iglesia venezolana. (*Montalbán/Caracas*, 30, 1997, p. 75–105)

De tono expositivo, destaca en Briceño-Iragorry su llamado al regreso a los valores absolutos, su aprecio por la hispanidad, el valor moral de la formación colonial y su crítica a las consecuencias relativistas de la modernidad. El artículo se cierra con temas especiales como la cuestión del patronato. También ver ítem **4691**.

COLOMBIA

4697 Arciniegas, Germán. Arciniegas polémico. Prólogo de Juan Gustavo Cobo Borda. Bogotá: Espasa, 2001. 286 p. (Espasa selección)

Representativa e interesante reunión de escritos polémicos de Arciniegas. Algunos de sus temas son el Vo. Centenario, la historia y la política colombianas y Bolívar. Lo precede un breve pero excelente prólogo de Juan Gustavo Cobo Borda, quien resalta que, a pesar de su fibra polémica y lo mucho que fue atacado, Arciniegas no siempre reaccionó, o no siempre lo hizo con virulencia. Ver también items **4698** y **4705**.

4698 Arciniegas, Germán. Germán Arciniegas: antología. Recopilación de Consuelo Triviño. Madrid: Ediciones de Cultura Hispánica, 1999. 254 p.: bibl. (Antología del pensamiento político, social y económico de América Latina; 19)

La Introducción es un ensayo muy logrado, donde se presentan los diversos aspectos de Arciniegas en el contexto de acontecimientos políticos y literarios. También es acertada la apreciación de Arciniegas en relación con el tema de América, y las interpretaciones a que ha dado lugar. La antología es amplia, e incluye: sus concepciones "filosóficas;" sus ideas políticas; el concepto de la historia; y varios subtemas de su interpretación de la realidad americana. Ver también items **4697** y **4705**.

4699 Colombia-Venezuela: historia intelectual. Recopilación de Juan Gustavo Cobo Borda. Bogotá: Presidencia de la República, 1997. 495 p.: bibl. (Biblioteca Familiar de la Presidencia de la República)

Antología de autores colombianos y venezolanos, algunos ya "clásicos," como Cecilio Acosta, Carlos Arturo Torres, Rómulo Gallegos, Germán Arciniegas, Mariano Picón Salas, Arturo Uslar Pietri, Miguel Otero Silva, Pedro Grases, Luis Beltrán Guerrero y Gabriel García Márquez. La parte correspondiente a Cecilio Acosta (1818–81) reproduce, de sus *Obras completas*, un largo estudio sobre José María Torres Caicedo, y de su epistolario, numerosas cartas que escribiera a Miguel Antonio Caro y a Rufino José Cuervo.

4700 Jaramillo Vélez, Rubén. Colombia: la modernidad postergada. 2. ed. corr. y aum. Bogotá: G. Rivas Moreno, 1998. 272 p.: bibl. (Argumentos)

Se trata de una segunda edición ampliada. La intención de los artículos reunidos es entender la peculiaridad de Colombia "en su relación con la modernidad." Así, uno de los trabajos centrales es: "La postergación de la experiencia de la modernidad en Colombia." Hay también trabajos sobre el advenimiento de la filosofía moderna en el país. En el aspecto filosófico se hace incapié en el largo predominio de la escolástica.

4701 Landínez Castro, Vicente. Miradas y aproximaciones a la obra multiple de Otto Morales Benítez. Tunja, Colombia: Academia Boyacense de Historia, 1997. 196 p.: bibl., ill. (Biblioteca de la Academia Boyacense de Historia. Serie Obras fundamentales; 19)

Otto Morales Benítez es autor, entre otras obras, de *Liberalismo: destino de la patria* (*HLAS 48:2969*), *Memorias del mestizaje* (*HLAS 50:2138*) y *Colombia y el continente*

(1995). Ha sido también crítico literario y ha escrito sobre figuras de la política y la historia de su país. Este libro es un amplio comentario sobre su personalidad y su obra.

4702 Mejía Mosquera, Juan Fernando. Zuleta, Cruz Vélez y Gómez Dávila: tres lectores colombianos de Nietzsche. (*Univ. Philos.*, 34/35, junio/dic. 2000, p. 257–301, bibl.)

El título es suficientemente expresivo del contenido, y en tal sentido es una contribución al conocimiento de la filosofía colombiana en el siglo XX. Conviene aclarar, sin embargo, que el autor se interesa por formas de pensamiento que no se restringen a la filosofía académica.

4703 Ocampo López, Javier. Colombia en sus ideas. v. 1–3. Bogotá: Fundación Univ. Central; 1999. 3 v.: bibl. (Col. 30 Años Universidad Central 14–16)

Estos tres gruesos volúmenes constituyen una contribución fundamental a la historia de las ideas (y por esa vía, a la historia en general) en Colombia. Los trabajos cubren desde la parte colonial hasta épocas recientes. Sólo a manera de ejemplo señalamos algunos temas: la resistencia indígena ante la conquista; la evangelización de esclavos africanos; eclecticismo y naturalismo en la Ilustración colombiana; la influencia de la independencia de Estados Unidos; ideologías de partidos políticos; las guerras civiles en Colombia; el positivismo colombiano.

4704 Quesada Vanegas, Gustavo Adolfo and **Patricia Illera Pacheco.** Filosofía del descubrimiento y la conquista en Colombia. Bogotá: Univ. Nacional Abierta y a Distancia, Facultad de Ciencias Sociales, Humanas y Educativas, 2000. 385 p.: bibl.

La obra es de carácter didáctico y como tal puede considerarse lograda. Contiene pasajes de Aristóteles, Santo Tomás, Sepúlveda, Vitoria y Las Casas, entre otros, además de variados documentos. La presentación de los autores es extensa, con una introducción sobre los problemas que se presentan en la parte antológica y documental. También contiene una útil cronología.

4705 Tamayo Fernández, Martalucía. Germán Arciniegas: el hombre que nació con el siglo: una autobiografía escrita por otro. Bogotá: Fundación Univ. Central, 1998.

492 p.: ill. (some col.). (Col. 30 años Universidad Central; 11)

Contribución a la biografía intelectual de Arciniegas. Ver también items **4697** y **4698.**

ECUADOR

4706 Borrero Vintimilla, Antonio. Filosofía, política y pensamiento del presidente Antonio Borrero y Cortázar, 1875–1876: aspectos de la política del Ecuador del siglo XIX. Cuenca, Ecuador: Univ. del Azuay; Casa de la Cultura Ecuatoriana, Núcleo del Azuay; Mutualista Azuay, 1999. 261 p.: bibl., ill.

Antonio Borrero y Cortázar (1827–1911) fue presidente de Ecuador entre 1875–76. Como "católico liberal" puede incluirse en la corriente del liberalismo latinoamericano. Este libro lo estudia en su contexto histórico y su acción, pero especialmente en el pensamiento que expresó en el periodismo de la época. Escrito con gran simpatía hacia el personaje, el libro es de todas maneras muy útil, por lo poco frecuente del asunto y algunos anexos documentales y de valor informativo.

4707 Velasco Ibarra, José María. José María Velasco Ibarra: una antología de sus textos. Estudio introductorio y selección de Enrique Ayala Mora. México: Fondo de Cultura Económica, 2000. 486 p.: bibl. (Tierra firme)

Esta reunión de escritos de Velasco Ibarra es muy oportuna porque la larga actuación política del personaje (varias veces presidente de Ecuador), ha dejado en la sombra su pensamiento, el cual es de mayor raigambre intelectual de lo que es usual en los políticos. La antología se ha organizado en base a partes de libros, excluyendo discursos y escritos jurídicos. El estudio preliminar cumple bien su función introductoria. Buena bibliografía.

PERÚ

4708 *Anuario Mariateguiano.* Vol. 9, No. 9, 1997. Lima: Empresa Editora Amuata.

Como textos inéditos se reproducen varias ayuda-memorias que Mariátegui utilizó para el dictado de conferencias. Hay luego ensayos sobre Mariátegui, entre ellos: de Antonio Melis sobre Henríquez Ureña y Mariátegui en la fundación de la historia literaria hispanoamericana; de Francisca da Gamma sobre Mariátegui, la Internacional Comunista y el descubrimiento del indígena; y de Jaime Coronado sobre Mariátegui y la reflexión política en América Latina. Hay además artículos de índole general, como "Colonialidad del poder, cultura y conocimiento en América Latina," de Aníbal Quijano; "Filosofía latinoamericana e interculturalidad," de Arturo Andrés Roig; y "El pensamiento filosófico latinoamericano: filosofías de la identidad, historia y liberación en relación a la dialéctica hegeliana," de Eugene Gogol. Algunos de los restantes contribuyentes al volumen son: Francis Guibal, William W. Stein, Manuel Pantigoso, Yazmin López Lenci, y Edgardo Lander.

4709 Aquino, Emigdio. José Carlos Mariátegui y el problema nacional. México: Unión de Universidades de América Latina, 1997. 236 p.: appendices, bibl., ill. (Idea latinoamericana)

Según indica el autor, la metodología aplicada es la del materialismo histórico. Se presenta primero el marco histórico del Perú desde el fin de la guerra con Chile (1883) hasta 1930. Luego se estudia el problema nacional en Mariátegui, examinando cómo éste enfocó el problema indígena y campesino. Finalmente se buscan las razones de la vigencia de Mariátegui. Contiene dos apéndices documentales y una cronología.

Aricó, José. La hipótesis de Justo: escritos sobre el socialismo en América Latina. Ver ítem **4779.**

4710 Arroyo Reyes, Carlos. Manuel González Prada y la cuestión indígena. (*Cuad. Am./México,* 16:91, enero/feb. 2002, p. 164–179)

Trabajo de síntesis biográfica donde se sitúa la "cuestión indígena" en González Prada (1844–1918), desde sus "baladas peruanas" hasta escritos de madurez en los que el tema adquiere carácter económico y social, según el testimonio de sus artículos aparecidos en el periódico anarquista "Los Parias" (1904–09). [CJB]

4711 Belaúnde, Víctor Andrés. El pensamiento social de Víctor Andrés Belaúnde: antología. Introducción de Pedro Planas Silva. Lima: Instituto de Estudios Social Cristianos, 1997. 183 p.: bibl.

Esta antología de Víctor Andrés Belaúnde (1883–1966), que recoge textos escritos entre 1923–63, expresa el pensamiento social cristiano del autor, aplicado a la situación de Perú. (Belaúnde llegó a polemizar con Mariátegui.) De muy conveniente lectura es la introducción de Pedro Planas.

4712 Bermejo Santos, Antonio. Lugar del marxismo en la meditación filosófica de José Carlos Mariátegui. (*Islas/Santa Clara*, 41:119, enero/marzo 1999, p. 100–113)

Se indica la importancia del materialismo marxista en el pensamiento de Mariátegui, especialmente la teoría de la lucha de clases, el valor del socialismo científico, y la vigencia "universal" de las ideas de Marx. Se refiere también a las influencias de los líderes de la Revolución Rusa (principalmente Lenin, Trotsky, Lunatcharsky y Sinoviev) y a la cuestión del determinismo marxista. [CJB]

4713 Gonzales, Osmar. Señales sin respuesta: los Zorros y el pensamiento socialista en el Perú, 1968–1989. Lima: Ediciones PREAL, 1999. 279 p.

Trata de un grupo de intelectuales peruanos jóvenes, que actuaron entre los 60s y los 80s, y que en 1985 fundaron la revista *El Zorro de Abajo,* la cual fue expresión de un pensamiento—en términos muy amplios—"socialista," que sin embargo no logró plasmarse en una política concreta. Se utilizan testimonios personales de algunos miembros del grupo.

4714 Haya de la Torre, Víctor Raúl. Haya de la Torre, o la política como obra civilizatoria. Estudio introductorio y selección de Jorge Nieto Montesinos. México: Fondo de Cultura Económica, 2000. 373 p.: ill. (Tierra firme)

Selección de escritos de Haya de la Torre, cuya intención es presentar "un panorama lo más completo posible" de las ideas del político peruano. El estudio introductorio sigue la trayectoria de Haya de la Torre en la historia intelectual y política latinoamericana y en el sucesivo desarrollo de sus propias opiniones y, por su amplitud y claridad, es de lectura muy recomendable.

4715 Hintze de Molinari, Gloria. Género e indigenismo. (*Cuad. Am./México*, 13:74, marzo/abril 1999, p. 106–113)

Se refiere a Clorinda Matto de Turner, en cuyo "espacio discursivo se reflejan las problemáticas relacionadas con el género, con la sexualidad y la marginalidad social," dentro de los planteos positivistas de la época. Estos planteos ven "la necesidad de cohesionar la sociedad peruana después de la Guerra del Pacífico." Lugar especial ocupa la cuestión indígena. [CJB]

4716 José Carlos Mariátegui: Gedenktagung zum 100. Geburtstag im Ibero-Amerikanischen Institut Preussischer Kulturbesitz am 10. November 1994 in Berlin. Edited by José Morales Saravia. Frankfurt: Vervuert, 1997. 128 p.: bibl., ill. (Bibliotheca Ibero-Americana; 61)

Conjunto de trabajos sobre Mariátegui, de autores alemanes (con la excepción del editor y de Raúl Fornet Betancourt). Principales temas: el marxismo de Mariátegui; la identidad nacional y el proyecto socialista; el problema indígena; la revista Amauta; la religiosidad de Mariátegui; la recepción de Spengler y Nietzsche; el concepto de vanguardia.

4717 Leibner, Gerardo. El mito del socialismo indígena: fuentes y contextos peruanos de Mariátegui. Lima: Pontificia Univ. Católica del Perú, Fondo Editorial, 1999. 261 p.: bibl.

La tesis central de la obra es que la concepción de Mariátegui sobre el comunismo indígena del incanato era históricamente incorrecta. Pero el libro se refiere también a cómo y a través de cuáles fuentes llegó Mariátegui a esa concepción; qué función ocupa en su proyecto de un socialismo andino o peruano; qué otros antecedentes se habían desarrollado sobre dicha interpretación (y la defensa) del indígena. En la exposición de estos últimos temas radica buena parte del interés de la obra. Una de las conclusiones es que, pese a su indigenismo, Mariátegui representaba el punto de vista criollo-urbano, grupo que anhelaba la conducción del movimiento que se basaría en la fuerza supuestamente revolucionaria del campesinado indígena. Para el comentario del historiador, ver ítem **2599.**

4718 Leibner, Gerardo. Pedro Zulen: del indigenismo paternalista al humanismo radical. (*Rev. Eur. Estud. Latinoam. Caribe*, 63, Dec. 1997, p. 29–47)

Oportuna y amplia exposición del pensamiento y la acción de Pedro Zulen, muerto prematuramente, fundador de la Asociación Pro-Indígena (1909–16), y con algún acercamiento a líderes anarquistas. Significativas las comparaciones con Mariátegui.

4719 López, María Pia and Guillermo Korn. Mariátegui: entre Victoria y Claridad. Buenos Aires: Univ. de Buenos Aires, 1997. 47 p.: bibl. (Hipótesis y discusiones; 14)

El título alude a Victoria Ocampo, fundadora y sostenedora de la revista *Sur*, y a la revista *Claridad* que, como *Sur*, se publicaba en Buenos Aires. Trata un tema poco explorado: las relaciones de Mariátegui con intelectuales argentinos (porteños, más propiamente) y los esfuerzos que se hicieron para que Mariátegui se trasladara a la Argentina, lo que finalmente no se concretó.

4720 Montiel, Edgar. El Inca Garcilaso en el Siglo de las Luces. (*in* Encuentro Internacional de Peruanistas, *1st, Lima, 1996*. Estado de los estudios histórico-sociales sobre el Perú a fines del siglo XX. Lima: UNESCO; Univ. de Lima; Fondo de Cultura Económica, 1998, v. 2, p. 423–431)

Se refiere a la influencia que las obras del Inca Garcilaso ejercieron sobre representantes de la Ilustración europea, en tono de ensayo. [CJB]

4721 Muñoz García, Angel. El derecho colonial en Diego de Avendaño. (*Frónesis/Maracaibo*, 7:3, dic. 2000, p. 77–98, bibl.)

Interesantes comentarios a los Títulos I-III del *Thesaurus Indicus* (1668) del jesuita peruano (nacido en España) Diego de Avendaño, obra de casuística jurídica que sin embargo su autor consideraba como de moral. Muñoz García prepara edición crítica de la obra.

4722 Uriarte, Urpi Montoya. Hispanismo e indigenismo: o dualismo cultural no pensamento social peruano, 1900–1930; uma revisão necessária. (*Rev. Antropol./São Paulo*, 41:1, 1998, p. 151–175, bibl.)

Sostiene que el hispanismo y el indigenismo han creado una dualidad simplificada e irreductible, y que esa posición debe ser revisada, si bien el artículo no ofrece indicaciones para realizar esa superación. El artículo tiene utilidad como descripción de los opuestos señalados.

BOLIVIA

4723 Ovando-Sanz, Guillermo. Gabriel René-Moreno. La Paz: Fundación Humberto Vázquez-Machicado, 1996. 402 p.: bibl., ill., index.

Sobre la vida y la obra de René-Moreno, clásico historiador y bibliógrafo boliviano. La segunda y más extensa parte del libro es de naturaleza bibliográfico-documental y es particularmente útil.

CHILE

4724 Cristi, Renato. El pensamiento político de Jaime Guzmán: autoridad y libertad. Santiago: LOM Ediciones, 2000. 223 p.: bibl. (Col. Sin norte)

Jaime Guzmán, ideólogo conservador que intervino en la redacción de la Constitución chilena de 1980, en la época de Pinochet, es estudiado aquí con intención crítico-filosófica más que histórica. Se estudia la evolución de su pensamiento político y las fuentes en que se inspira, girando en torno a las ideas de autoridad y libertad. En el último capítulo, el autor del presente libro expone su concepción de una democracia republicana desde la cual se organiza su crítica a Jaime Guzmán.

4725 *Cuadernos Americanos.* Año 11, No. 62, marzo/abril 1997. Ideas en Chile. México: UNAM.

Bajo el título general de "Ideas en Chile," aparecen tres artículos: Norman P. Sacks, "Andrés Bello y José Victorino Lastarria: conflicto de generaciones y tensiones intelectuales;" Clara Alicia Jalif de Bertranou, "Francisco Bilbao: de la secularización de las conciencias a la secularización del estado;" Manuel de Jesús Corral C., "Francisco Bilbao: pasión por América." [CJB]

4726 Devés V., Eduardo; Javier Pinedo; and Rafael Sagredo B. El pensamiento chileno en el siglo XX. México: Instituto Panamericano de Geografía e Historia, 1999. 385 p.: bibl.

Conjunto de trabajos sobre autores y temas de historia de las ideas en Chile durante el siglo XX. Entre los autores individuales analizados se encuentran: Enrique Molina, Julio César Jobet, Luis Oyarzún y Félix Schwartzmann. En cuanto a temas de historia del pensamiento, destacamos los siguientes: los orígenes de la sociología profesional en Chile; el pensamiento conservador; la reflexión sobre la cuestión social; el nacionalismo; la ensayística y el problema de la identidad; modernidad, modernización e identidad; ideas políticas (1950–73); y la filosofía en Chile (1973–90). Obra varia pero valiosa.

4727 Jaime Eyzaguirre: historia y pensamiento. Santiago: Editorial Universitaria; Univ. Alonso de Ovalle, 1995. 244 p.: bibl., ill. (Col. Genio y figura)

Jaime Eyzaguirre, historiador chileno de orientación católica (fallecido en 1968), es analizado aquí desde diversos ángulos. Importan, ante todo, los trabajos que lo ven en su obra historiográfica y en su pensamiento, como: "El pensamiento histórico de Jaime Eyzaguirre" (Ricardo Krebs); "Jaime Eyzaguirre, historiografía chilena y conciencia nacional en el siglo XX" (Bernardino Bravo Lira); "Filosofía de la historia en Jaime Eyzaguirre" (José M. Lecaros Sánchez). También se lo enfoca en una semblanza (Walter Hanish Espíndola); en su actividad institucional (Oscar Dávila Campusano); en la historia del derecho (Antonio Donguac Rodríguez); y en sus relaciones con la tradición, la política y la religión (Osvaldo Lira Pérez, Gonzalo Larios Mengotti y Enrique Pérez Silva, respectivamente).

4728 Naranjo, Eduardo. Juan Rivano: un largo contrapunto. (*Convergencia/Toluca,* 8:24, enero/abril 2001, p. 223–266, bibl.)

Exposición de la vida y el pensamiento del filósofo chileno Juan Rivano (nac. 1926) hasta 1960, a la luz de su libro *Un largo contrapunto* (1995), otros escritos y una serie de entrevistas. Aspecto central son las fases de su formación intelectual. [CJB]

4729 Salinas, Augusto. El abate Molina y la ciencia de su época. (*Universum/Talca,* 13, 1998, p. 211–225)

La tesis de este artículo es que Juan Ignacio Molina (1740–1829), primer sabio chileno, sostuvo la idea de la Gran Cadena de los Seres, que niega la existencia real de especies y supone que todos los seres creados se ordenan sin solución de continuidad desde el más superior, el hombre, hasta el organismo más inferior. Este concepto, inscrito en la tradición griega clásica y compatible con la fe cristiana, desvirtúa las afirmaciones que le

adjudican ser un precursor del evolucionismo y el transformismo de las especies. [CJB]

BRASIL

Amory, Frederic. Euclides da Cunha and Brazilian positivism. Ver ítem **3232.**

4730 Barreto, Luiz Antonio. Os vassalos do rei: notas prévias para uma teoria da cultura brasileira, 2a série. Aracajú, Brazil: Sociedade Editorial de Sergipe, 1998. 149 p.: bibl.

Se trata de cuatro ensayos, entre históricos y etnológicos, sobre el Nordeste de Brasil. Principales temas: jesuitas; Inquisición; relaciones de las clases dominantes con los indios y los negros; formas de sincretismo religioso; folclore.

4731 Bastos, Elide Rugai. Viajes de Ganivet a Brasil. (*Fundam. Antropol.,* 8/9, oct. 1998, p. 75–85, bibl., map)

Con cierto grado de detalle muestra la lectura y asimilación que Gilberto Freyre habría hecho de las obras del escritor español Angel Ganivet.

4732 O Brasil no pensamento brasileiro. v. 1. Brasília: Senado Federal; Secretaria de Assuntos Estratégicos, 1998. 1 v.: bibl. (Col. Brasil 500 anos)

Valiosa antología de gran utilidad para el lector general, pero aun para el estudioso cuando el acceso a las fuentes es difícil. Casi 80 textos de autores que se han expresado sobre numerosos aspectos de la realidad brasileña (sociedad, política, población, condiciones de vida, religión, historia, educación, crítica social, entre otros asuntos).

4733 *Cadernos de Estudos Sociais.* Vol. 16, No. 2, julho/dez. 2000. Recife, Brazil: Fundação Joaquim Nabuco, Instituto de Pesquisas Sociais.

Número dedicado a Gilberto Freyre. Artículos: Otamar de Carvalho, "Autoria e compromiso social en Gilberto Freyre." Señala los rasgos de la evolución del capitalismo en Brasil utilizando las obras de Freyre. Renato Duarte, "*Casa-grande e senzala* na leitura de um economista." Destaca los aspectos en que esta obra de Freyre contribuye al conocimiento de la historia económica de Brasil. Fernando da Mota Lima, "Brasileiros de São Paulo e de Pernambuco." La contraposición entre el "modernismo" de São Paulo y el "regionalismo" de Pernambuco sería asimismo la de Mario de Andrade y Freyre, y sus respectivas obras: *Macunaíma* y *Casa-grande e senzala*. Fátima Quintas, "O cristianismo lírico de Gilberto Freyre." *Casa-grande* y la religión en Brasil. Antônio Paulo Rezende, "Gilberto Freyre: o caminho da *Casa-grande*." Se interesa por la actitud tradicionalista y conservadora de Freyre. Maria José Rezende, "A obra *Ordem e progresso* e a mudança social no Brasil." Cómo explica Freyre el cambio social en el paso de la monarquía a la república. Flávio Rabelo Versiani, "Gilberto Freyre, a escravidão benigna e a economia do escravismo." Considera probable la tesis de Freyre en el sentido de que la esclavitud en Brasil podría haber sido más benigna que en otros países.

4734 Carvalho, José Maurício de. Pensando a filosofia brasileira. (*Paradigmas/Londrina*, 3:2, julho 2000, p. 115–120, bibl.)

Texto de una conferencia donde se repasa la historia de la filosofía brasileña, desde los tiempos de la Colonia hasta nuestros días. El autor lo es de un *Curso de introdução à filosofia brasileira*, que utiliza la orientación dada a esos estudios por Miguel Reale. [CJB]

4735 Carvalho, Olavo de. O futuro do pensamento brasileiro: estudos sobre o nosso lugar no mundo. Rio de Janeiro: Faculdade da Cidade Editora, 1997. 203 p.: bibl.

Compuesto de tres trabajos, el que más interesa a esta Sección es el primero: "O pensamento brasileiro no futuro: um apelo à responsabilidade histórica." El común denominador de los tres ensayos es, en palabras del autor, "o lugar do Brasil na história espiritual do mundo, particularmente nesta etapa de sua vida." Es un libro duramente crítico, cuyo propósito es lograr que la intelectualidad brasileña apunte a creaciones que puedan tener valor universal. En ese sentido, encuentra cuatro autores que satisfacen esa exigencia: Gilberto Freyre, Miguel Reale, Otto Maria Carpeaux y Mario Ferreira dos Santos, porque en sus obras "entramos plenamente no diálogo universal dos homens, superando o complexo egocêntrico de uma cultura voltada para si mesma." Lo dicho de ninguna manera agota la variedad, la temática y el contenido crítico del libro.

4736 Ciência & Trópico. Vol. 28, No. 1, jan./junho 2000. Recife, Brazil: Fundação Joaquim Nabuco, Instituto de Pesquisas Sociais.

Número especial dedicado a Gilberto Freyre. Se examinan diversos aspectos de *Casa-grande e senzala*. José Arthur Rios da una visión sintética de la obra de Freyre. Entre los restantes autores se cuentan Vamireh Chacon, Nelson Saldanha y Leonardo Dantas Silva. Al final hay una bibliografía sobre el tema de la tropicología y la obra de Freyre.

4737 Czerna, Renato C. Miguel Reale e a cultura contemporânea. (*Rev. Bras. Filos.*, 47:185, jan./março 1997, p. 27–46)

Examina la obra de Miguel Reale— uno de los más destacados filósofos brasileños del siglo XX—*Paradigmas da cultura contemporânea* (1996).

4738 Desorganizando o consenso: nove entrevistas com intelectuais à esquerda. Organização de Fernando Haddad. São Paulo: Editora Fundação Perseu Abramo; Petrópolis, Brazil: Editora Vozes, 1998. 167 p. (Col. Zero à esquerda)

El contenido está bien expresado en el subtítulo. La intención es una crítica de fondo al capitalismo. La figura de Fernando Henrique Cardoso es casi una constante a lo largo del libro, recordando sus posiciones iniciales y criticando las actuales.

4739 Enio Silveira: arquiteto de liberdades. Organização, seleção e notas de Moacyr Félix. Rio de Janeiro: Bertrand Brasil, 1998. 473 p.

Enio Silveira fue un intelectual de izquierda cuya mayor influencia cultural e ideológica estuvo en la dirección de la editorial Civilização Brasileira. Este libro proporciona numerosas contribuciones para el conocimiento de las opiniones de Enio Silveira y su acción, reproduciendo escritos de y sobre él.

4740 Ferreira, Luiz Otávio. Ciencia pura versus ciencia aplicada: la fuerza de la tradición positivista en la ciencia brasileña a comienzos del siglo XX. (*Secuencia/México*, 41, mayo/agosto 1998, p. 111–123, bibl., facsims., table)

Oportuno enfoque que, para tratar el positivismo en Brasil, se aparta un tanto de los carriles tradicionales. Dentro del mismo ambiente científico positivista brasileño se habría desarrollado una dicotomía entre los que favorecían la ciencia aplicada, y los que sostenían el valor de la ciencia "pura." Estos últimos señalaban que el ideal comtiano de que la ciencia sirviera a un objetivo de reforma social restringía el campo de la ciencia y eliminaba la consideración de doctrinas científicas que se habían desarrollado después de Comte. En otros aspectos confirma la impronta de Comte en Brasil, independientemente de la religión de la humanidad.

4741 Florestan, ou, O sentido das coisas. Organização de Paulo Henrique Martinez. São Paulo: Maria Antonia, USP; Boitempo Editorial, 1998. 263 p.: appendix, bibl., ill.

Florestan Fernandes (1920–95), sociólogo, militante de izquierda, autor de *A revolução burguesa no Brasil* (ver *HLAS 39: 9302*), es evocado y estudiado en este volumen por casi una veintena de autores que atienden distintos aspectos de su biografía, su actuación política y su obra escrita. La simpatía general con que es visto el autor no disminuye el valor testimonial de la obra. El libro contiene también una cronología de Florestan Fernandes, referencias bibliográficas sobre él y un breve apéndice documental.

4742 Freyre, Gilberto. Novo mundo nos trópicos. Prefácio de Wilson Martins. 2a. ed. Rio de Janeiro: Topbooks; Univ. Editora, 2000. 305 p.: bibl., ill. (Gilbertiana)

Obra fundamental de Gilberto Freyre para la interpretación de Brasil. Síntesis posterior a sus grandes estudios sociológicos. En inglés apareció primero *Brazil: An Interpretation* (*HLAS 11:76*), publicado en portugués como *Interpretação do Brasil* (*HLAS 13:2293* y *HLAS 14:686*). Una ampliación, en inglés, fue *New World in the Tropics* (*HLAS 23: 2689, HLAS 23:3907* y *HLAS 45:8387*), que posteriormente fue, en portugués, *Novo mundo nos trópicos* (1971). La presente obra es una segunda edición de la última señalada.

4743 Lima Vaz, Henrique C. de. Leonel Franca e a cultura católica no Brasil. (*Síntese/Belo Horizonte*, 25:82, julho/ set. 1998, p. 317–328)

Leonel Franca, S.J. (1893–1948) es muy recordado por haber sido uno de los primeros en escribir sobre la filosofía en Brasil. Este artículo es importante porque, siendo breve y

claro, muestra la formación de Franca, su actuación en el medio católico brasileño desde la década de 1920 en adelante (situado en el contexto de la cultura católica europea), y su posición frente a la cuestión de la modernidad, reflejada en su libro *A crise do mundo moderno* (*HLAS 6:4303* y *HLAS 8:4906*).

4744 Löwy, Michael and Jesús García-Ruiz. Les sources françaises du christianisme de la libération au Brésil. (*Arch. sci. soc. relig.*, 42:97, jan./mars 1997, p. 9–32)

Muestra cómo, previo al desarrollo de la teología de la liberación, hubo en Brasil clara influencia de pensadores franceses, como Maritain, el P. Lebret, Mounier y la interpretación de Marx por Yves Calvez. La teología de la liberación sería una radicalización de esta etapa.

4745 Montenegro, João Alfredo de Sousa. A historiografia liberal de Tristão de Alencar Araripe. Rio de Janeiro: Tempo Brasileiro, 1998. 185 p.: bibl.

Tristão de Alencar Araripe (1821– 1908), hombre público e historiador cearense, fue autor de una *História da Província do Ceará* (1867). Aquí se examina la modalidad y las fuentes de su historiografía, además de otros de sus escritos.

4746 Naxara, Márcia Regina Capelari. Estrangeiro em sua própria terra: representações do brasileiro, 1870–1920. São Paulo: Annablume; FAPESP, 1998. 159 p.: bibl., ill. (Selo universidade; 84. História)

Contribución al tema de la identidad nacional brasileña, tomando en cuenta manifestaciones de la literatura y el pensamiento social, en la etapa de fines del siglo XIX y comienzos del XX. Destacamos la exposición de las interpretaciones cientificistas de Euclides da Cunha, Sílvio Romero y Manoel Bomfim.

4747 Paim, Antônio. A Escola do Recife. Londrina, Brazil: Editorial Univ. Estadual de Londrina, 1999. 267 p. (Estudos complementares a *História das idéias filosóficas no Brasil*; 5)

Se trata de la reelaboración de la obra anterior, *A filosofia da Escola do Recife* (*HLAS 30:5047*). Se examinan los miembros de la Escuela (Tobias Barreto, Sílvio Romero, Clovis Bevilaqua, etc.) y la doctrina filosófica que desarrollaron (monismo, evolucionismo, diferencias con el positivismo). Contiene varios anexos que enriquecen la edición. También vea ítem **4751**.

4748 Paim, Antônio. A escola eclética. 2a. ed. rev. Londrina, Brazil: Edições CEFIL, 1999. 381 p. (Estudos complementares a *História das idéias filosóficas no Brasil*; 4)

El autor considera que el eclecticismo fue, en Brasil, "la primera corriente filosófica rigurosamente estructurada." El libro tiene mucho de revisión del valor del eclecticismo en general y de la obra de Cousin y su relación con la filosofía alemana. Establece la periodización del eclecticismo brasileño, cubre las etapas de apogeo y declinación, ilustra sobre la presencia del eclecticismo en varios lugares de Brasil, toma en cuenta las publicaciones periódicas y—preocupación típica del autor—trata especialmente la cuestión moral.

4749 Paim, Antônio. Etapas iniciais da filosofia brasileira. Londrina, Brazil: Editorial Univ. Estadual de Londrina, 1998. 272 p. (Estudos complementares a *História das idéias filosóficas no Brasil*; 3)

Este libro es parte de lo que Paim llama "estudos complementares," que lo son a su obra de síntesis, *História das idéias filosóficas no Brasil* (ver ítem **4751**), es decir, ampliaciones a lo que se dice en dicha obra. La expresión "etapas iniciais," que aparece en el título del presente libro, debe tomarse en un sentido amplio, pues llega hasta entrado el siglo XIX. Cubre los no muy desarrollados aspectos escolásticos y contrarreformistas; los moralistas del siglo XVIII; el llamado "empirismo mitigado," relacionado con la reforma de los estudios bajo Pombal; y dos autores tratados con extensión: Silvestre Pinheiro y José da Silva Lisboa. A este último, el autor había dedicado anteriormente un libro especial, aquí reproducido.

4750 Paim, Antônio. As filosofias nacionais. 2a. ed. rev. e amp. Londrina, Brazil: Edições CEFIL, 1999. 159 p. (Estudos complementares a *História das idéias filosóficas no Brasil*; 2)

Se trata aquí primero, en forma teórica, el tema de las filosofías nacionales (como hecho empírico y en su relación con el carácter "universal" de la filosofía). También se busca caracterizar algunas de ellas, como la norteamericana, la portuguesa y la alema-

na. Finalmente se discute la posibilidad de una filosofía luso-brasileña. El tema podría vincularse a la tendencia hispanoamericana de defender la existencia de una "filosofía latinoamericana."

4751 Paim, Antônio. História das idéias filosóficas no Brasil. 5a ed. rev. Londrina, Brazil: Editora Univ. Estadual de Londrina, 1997. 760 p.: bibl.

Esta es la 5a. edición de la obra más completa sobre la filosofía en Brasil, que se ha visto ampliada en sucesivas ediciones. Se inicia con un capítulo en que se examinan los grandes problemas filosóficos que se desarrollaron en el país. Luego cubre las conexiones iniciales con la filosofía portuguesa, siguiendo con el eclecticismo, la filosofía católica en el siglo XIX, la Escola do Recife, Farias Brito, positivismo y marxismo, y la filosofía más reciente. También ver ítem **4747** y **4749**.

Paim, Antônio. História do liberalismo brasileiro. Ver ítem **3311**.

4752 Paim, Antônio. Os intérpretes da filosofia brasileira. Londrina, Brazil: Editorial Univ. Estadual de Londrina, 1999. 235 p. (Estudos complementares a *História das idéias filosóficas no Brasil*; 1)

Este libro es reelaboración de una obra anterior del autor: *O estudo do pensamento filosófico brasileiro* (HLAS 42:7592 y HLAS 50:4681), y es la más importante contribución a una historia de la historiografía filosófica en Brasil.

4753 Paim, Antônio. O krausismo brasileiro. 2a ed. ampliada. Londrina, Brazil: Edições CEFIL; Univ. Estadual de Londrina, 1999. 43 p.: bibl.

Breve trabajo que expone las principales manifestaciones del krausismo en Brasil. Reconoce dos momentos en ese movimiento: el que convive con el predominio del eclecticismo, y un segundo, que hacia 1870 coincide con un cambio en la orientación de las ideas, del que saldrá el positivismo y la Escuela do Recife.

4754 Paim, Antônio. Roteiro para estudo e pesquisa da problemática moral na cultura brasileira. Londrina, Brazil: Editora Univ. Estadual de Londrina, 1996. 115 p.

Aunque el título indica que es una guía, es también una discusión del asunto.

La preocupación principal del autor es la fundamentación de la moral social separada de la religión, partiendo de lo que denomina "la cuestión teórica de la moral moderna." Las etapas históricas que recorre son: las consecuencias de la reforma pombalina; el pensamiento de Silvestre Pinheiro Ferreira (1769–1846) y de José da Silva Lisboa, Vizconde de Cairú (1776–1835); los desarrollos del tema en los seguidores del eclecticismo en Brasil; y, más recientemente, la "moral tolitaria."

4755 Paim, Antônio. Trajetória do liberalismo brasileiro e seus ensinamentos. (*Polít. Comp.*, 2:2, segundo semestre 1998, p. 35–42)

Repaso histórico del liberalismo brasileño y programa para su futuro.

4756 O pensamento de Ignácio Rangel. Organização de Armen Mamigonian e José Marcio Rego. São Paulo: Editora 34, 1998. 174 p.: bibl.

La importancia del autor estudiado radica en su personal interpretación de la historia económica de Brasil, con lo que ello significa para la correspondiente interpretación de la historia en general. De la imagen presentada resultaría una figura menos conocida que Caio Prado Júnior o Celso Furtado, por ejemplo, pero no menos original.

4757 Pensamento original, made in Brazil. Organização de Rosane Araujo Dantas e Aristides Alonso. Rio de Janeiro: Oficina do Autor Editora; UniverCidadeDeDeus, . . . etc.-Estudos Transitivos do Contemporâneo, 1999. 302 p.: bibl., ill. (Série Cena aberta; 7)

La intención es destacar lo que se produjo de original en Brasil, especialmente en los campos científicos y humanísticos. De las figuras escogidas reconocemos tres, según el interés de esta Sección: Newton da Costa, creador de la lógica paraconsistente; Luiz Sergio Cohelo de Sampaio, también lógico, además de ingeniero y economista; y Helio Jaguaribe, filósofo, científico político e intérprete de la realidad brasileña.

4758 Perez, Reginaldo Teixeira. O pensamento político de Roberto Campos: da razão do estado à razão do mercado, 1950–95. Rio de Janeiro: Editora FGV, 1999. 289 p.: bibl.

Excelente como presentación de las ideas económico-políticas de Roberto Cam-

pos (nac. 1917), quien pasó de desarrollista a liberal y tuvo influencia en la política práctica del país. La exposición se da dentro del marco de una visión de la vida económico-política de Brasil en la segunda mitad del siglo XX.

4759 Reale, Miguel. Pluralismo e liberdade. 2. ed. rev. Rio de Janeiro: Editora Expressão e Cultura, 1998. 311 p.: bibl.

El autor es uno de los filósofos más reconocidos fuera de Brasil. El libro es filosófico en un sentido general, pero incluye capítulos sobre la filosofía en Brasil y sobre el filósofo Raymundo de Farias Brito.

4760 *Revista Brasileira de Filosofia.* Vol. 44, Fasc. 186, abril/maio/junho 1997. São Paulo: Instituto Brasileiro de Filosofia.

En este número especial se atiende a la obra de dos autores brasileños contemporáneos: Roque Spencer Maciel de Barros (autor, entre otras obras, de *Introdução à filosofia liberal*—HLAS 34:5315); y Antônio Paim, quien une a su condición de pensador una nutrida obra como historiador de la filosofía en Brasil. Ubiratan de Macedo traza un perfil de Maciel de Barros y varios autores (entre ellos: Eduardo Abranches de Soveral, Ana Maria Moog Rodriguez, Leonardo Prota, Paulo Mercadante y Ricardo Vélez Rodríguez) se refieren a Paim.

4761 Ribeiro, Darcy. O povo brasileiro: a formação e o sentido do Brasil. São Paulo: Companhia das Letras, 1995. 470 p.: bibl., ill. (Estudos de antropologia da civilização)

Aunque este libro viene después de obras clásicas del autor como *O processo civilizatório* (1977), *As Américas e a civilização* (HLAS 33:1622) y *O dilema da América Latina* (1978), tal vez sea aquel en que intentó con más intensidad comprender la realidad de su país, en el marco de una teoría general de la historia y de una interpretación de América Latina. La obra se articula sobre una pregunta clave (posiblemente aplicable a toda Latinoamérica): "Por que o Brasil ainda não deu certo?" El antropólogo pasa a ser aquí filósofo de la historia sin abandonar un cierto compromiso político.

4762 Roland, Ana Maria. Fronteiras da palavra, fronteiras da história: contribuição à crítica da cultura do ensaísmo latino-americano através da leitura de Euclides da Cunha e Octavio Paz. Brasília: Editora UnB, 1997. 267 p.: bibl.

Ambicioso intento, cuyo objetivo es expresado por el subtítulo del libro. No se atiene solamente a la comparación de las obras literarias de Paz y Euclides da Cunha, sino que se extiende también a la interpretación histórica de México y Brasil, en el marco de América Latina en general.

4763 Sérgio Buarque de Holanda e o Brasil. Organização de Antonio Candido. São Paulo: Editora Fundação Perseu Abramo, 1998. 134 p.: bibl., ill.

Libro de real interés, que examina la obra de Buarque de Holanda desde varios ángulos, pero especialmente como historiador e intérprete de Brasil. Se lo relaciona con otros autores brasileños, como Oliveira Vianna, Alberto Torres y Gilberto Freyre, así como con autores europeos. Las obras más examinadas son *Raízes do Brasil* (*HLAS 14:2262* y *5162a*) y *Visão do paraíso* (*HLAS 32:2829a*).

4764 Skidmore, Thomas E. Onde estava a "Malinche" brasileira?: mitos de origem nacional no Brasil e no México. (*Cult. Vozes*, 91:3, maio/junho 1997, p. 107–118)

Se trata principalmente de una crítica a Octavio Paz y Gilberto Freyre como creadores de sendos mitos de origen nacional. Al hilo de ese propósito se trazan paralelos de la historia de ambos países.

4765 Souza, Francisco Martins de. Raízes teóricas do corporativismo brasileiro. Apresentação e adendo de Antônio Paim. Rio de Janeiro: Tempo Brasileiro, 1999. 174 p.: appendix, bibl. (Col. Caminhos brasileiros; 7)

Expone con claridad y buena base documental los fundamentos del corporativismo y el autoritarismo brasileños, a partir de la última década del siglo XIX. Los principales autores estudiados son: Alberto Torres (1865–1917); Azevedo Amaral (1881–1942); Francisco Campos (1891–1968); Plinio Salgado (1895–1975) y Oliveira Viana (1883–1951). Esta obra debiera ponerse en relación, como señala Antônio Paim en el prólogo, con la de Ricardo Vélez Rodríguez sobre el castillismo: *Castilhismo: uma filosofia da República* (*HLAS 50:4687*). El volumen contiene como apéndice el trabajo de Antônio Paim, "Pensamento e ação corporativa no Brasil."

4766 Trindade, Alexandro Dantas. O pensamento conservador e a formação do povo no Brasil. (*Ciênc. Tróp.*, 25:2, julho/dez. 1997, p. 301–314)

Examen de las opiniones sobre la "formação do povo brasileiro" por parte de Oliveira Viana y Gilberto Freyre, a quienes el autor atribuye el rasgo común de ser conservadores.

4767 Vasconcellos, Manoel Luís Cardoso de. O conceito de trabalho no contexto da trajetória intelectual de Alceu Amoroso Lima. (*Cad. ISP*, 10, junho 1997, p. 135–147, bibl.)

Interesa por los trazos de biografía intelectual de Amoroso Lima, especialmente su posición ante los problemas sociales. Muestra etapas de su desarrollo, cuyos principales hitos son el acercamiento a Jackson de Figueiredo y la influencia de Maritain. Analiza la obra *O problema do trabalho* (*HLAS 13:1837*), cuyos conceptos, basados en una posición neotomista, no variaron, en opinión del autor del artículo, a pesar de otros cambios de Alceu de Amoroso Lima.

4768 Vélez Rodríguez, Ricardo. Oliveira Viana e o papel modernizador do estado brasileiro. Londrina, Brazil: Editora Univ. Estadual de Londrina, 1997. 239 p.

La obra quiere mostrar la correspondencia entre la visión histórica del estado en Brasil por parte de Oliveira Viana y las ideas de Max Weber sobre el estado patrimonial. Es parte del tema la aplicación que algunos sociólogos y filósofos brasileños han hecho de esas ideas de Weber (escuela weberiana brasileña). La obra es una seria contribución a la interpretación de Oliveira Viana, pero además, la problemática estudiada y los autores considerados ofrecen interés para el resto de América Latina. Viana (1883–1951), colaborador de Getúlio Vargas durante el Estado Novo, es autor, entre otras obras, de *Populações meridionais do Brasil* (1922) e *Instituições políticas brasileiras* (*HLAS 15:1298*).

4769 Vianna, Luiz Werneck. A revolução passiva: iberismo e americanismo no Brasil. Rio de Janeiro: Editora Revan; IUPERJ, 1997. 222 p.: bibl.

El libro está en la línea del artículo del autor "Americanistas e Iberistas: a polémica de Oliveira Viana con Tavares Bastos," que se reseñó en *HLAS 58:5233*, el cual se reproduce en el libro junto con otros cuatro trabajos, dos de ellos dedicados a Gramsci y a Tocqueville, respectivamente.

4770 Westphalen, Cecília Maria and **Altiva Pilatti Balhana.** Positivismo e os movimentos sociopolíticos do final do século XIX e início do século XX. (*Rev. Inst. Hist. Geogr. Bras.*, 158:395, abril/junho 1997, p. 401–426, bibl.)

La bondad de este artículo reside en señalar, con cierto grado de detalle, la participación de los positivistas brasileños (ortodoxos y heterodoxos) en importantes cuestiones públicas como la abolición de la esclavitud, la constitución de la República y ciertas reformas educacionales. También indica cómo influyeron las ideas liberales en esos procesos. Exposición útil que va más allá de los aspectos puramente filosóficos.

URUGUAY

4771 Ardao, Arturo. Sobre vigencia de Vaz Ferreira. (*Cuad. Marcha*, 11:127, mayo 1997, p. 2–4, ill., photo)

Esta nota fue preparada con motivo del centenario del filósofo uruguayo Carlos Vaz Ferreira, en 1972. Mantiene su valor como equilibrado juicio sobre la vigencia de la obra y el mensaje de dicho filósofo.

4772 Brading, D.A. Marmoreal Olympus: José Enrique Rodó and Spanish American nationalism. Cambridge, England: Centre of Latin American Studies, Univ. of Cambridge, 1998. 22 p. (Working papers; 47)

Entre otras observaciones sostiene que Rodó representó un discurso nacionalista que de hecho procedía del romanticismo alemán y específicamente de Fichte, aunque filtrado a través de autores franceses.

4773 Claps, Manuel Arturo and **Mario Daniel Lamas.** El batllismo como ideología. Montevideo: Cal y Canto, 1999. 132 p.: bibl.

Con una introducción metodológica sobre teoría de las ideologías, se examinan las ideas del batllismo en política, economía, política social y reforma jurídica. La principal conclusión—previsible—es que la ideología batllista no fue socialismo, sino liberalismo reformista.

4774 Mañero Mañero, Salvador. De J.E. Rodó (f. 1917) a J. Ortega y Gasset. (*Relig. Cult.*, 44:207, oct./dic. 1998, p. 775–794)

Capítulo de un trabajo más amplio titulado *A dos voces: un precedente hispanoamericano de Ortega y Gasset.* La parte publicada establece un paralelo donde se señalan las coincidencias entre Rodó y el filósofo español. Puntos de semejanza son: la nueva visión que dan de Goethe, la libertad y la vida como tareas, y el concepto de generación histórica, con los matices diferenciales que es esperable encontrar. [CJB]

4775 *Prisma.* No. 4, mayo 2000. Montevideo: Univ. Católica Dámaso Larrañaga.

El tema central de este número es la exposición y el análisis de la acción y la obra de Francisco Bauzá (1849–99), político e historiador católico, autor de *Historia de la dominación española en el Uruguay* (Montevideo: A. Barreiro y Ramos, 1895–97). Además de una semblanza, se dedican artículos a los estudios constitucionales, a la obra histórica y a sus ideas sobre educación, entre otros temas. En los aspectos educativos se confronta el pensamiento de Bauzá con el de José Pedro Varela.

ARGENTINA

4776 Aguiar de Zapiola, Liliana. Cultura liberal, cultura autoritaria: el Colegio Monserrat, 1943–1955. Córdoba, Argentina: Editorial Univ. Nacional de Córdoba, 1998. 204 p.: bibl., ill. (Col. Nuestras historias)

Los conflictos descritos en el libro corresponden a la época del primer peronismo. Si bien la referencia es a un solo colegio (importante en Córdoba, sin embargo), lo que se narra fue parte de un fenómeno más general. En el examen que realiza de la planta de alumnos y docentes toma la forma de un trabajo sociológico. El libro se hubiera beneficiado de un capítulo final de resumen y conclusiones.

4777 Alberdi, Juan Bautista. Escritos de Juan Bautista Alberdi: el redactor de la ley. Presentación y selección de textos por Oscar Terán. Buenos Aires: Univ. Nacional de Quilmes, 1996. 329 p.: bibl. (La ideología argentina)

Valiosa edición de escritos de Alberdi. Figuran sus trabajos filosóficos juveniles, como *Fragmento preliminar al estudio del derecho* (1837) y otros dos publicados en Montevideo en 1838 y 1840, respectivamente, junto con su obra principal, *Bases* (para la Constitución argentina de 1853). Entre otros escritos se incluyen: *Palabras de un ausente* (1874), *De la anarquía y sus dos causas principales* (1862), y *La República Argentina consolidada en 1880* (1881). La "presentación" de la obra es un extenso estudio que trata de captar el pensamiento de Alberdi en toda su complejidad. Contiene una útil cronología y una bibliografía básica y bien balanceada.

4778 Alori, Laura et al. Reflexiones sobre la Argentina contemporánea. Buenos Aires: Editorial Biblos; Fundación Simón Rodríguez, 1998. 139 p.: bibl. (Col. Cuadernos Simón Rodríguez; 36)

Se compone de dos trabajos: "Organización social, estructura e instituciones: desde la Constitución del Estado Nacional Argentino hasta la crisis de 1930" (Laura Alori, Teodoro Blanco y Angel Cerra); y "Las vicisitudes de la democracia en la Argentina, 1930–83: Entre la confusión y la zozobra" (Mónica Campins, Palmira Dobaño, Horacio Gaggero y Ana Pfeifer). En ambos casos se trata de una descripción de la vida político-social, para culminar en un balance crítico de cada etapa. Es una síntesis aprovechable y de enfoque sereno.

4779 Aricó, José. La hipótesis de Justo: escritos sobre el socialismo en América Latina. Buenos Aires: Editorial Sudamericana, 1999. 203 p. (Col. Historia y cultura)

Se compone de dos trabajos: "La hipótesis de Justo" (1981) y "Mariátegui y los orígenes del marxismo latinoamericano" (1978). El primero es un análisis de cómo se introdujeron y se desarrollaron las ideas socialistas, anarquistas y marxistas en la Argentina, pero va más allá del recuento histórico y es una reflexión y un análisis de ese fenómeno. En el caso particular de Juan Bautista Justo y su intento de formar un partido socialista pero integrado a la corriente democrática, señala sus aciertos y sus limitaciones. Todo el ensayo es valioso como interpretación del socialismo argentino (por lo menos hasta 1930) y contribuye a iluminar las discusiones a que el tema ha dado lugar. El artículo sobre Mariátegui es un estudio de éste y también una lectura de una parte de la literatura sobre el autor peruano. Libro muy recomendable. De sustancia la Introducción de J.C. Portantiero.

4780 Beorlegui, Carlos. La influencia de E. Lévinas en la filosofía de la liberación de J.C. Scannone y de E. Dussel. (*Realidad/San Salvador*, 57, mayo/junio 1997, p. 243–247 and 58, julio/agosto 1997, p. 347–371)

Extenso artículo que sigue con gran detalle la influencia del filósofo francés E. Lévinas en el pensamiento de los filósofos argentinos Juan Carlos Scannone y Enrique Dussel. En una primera etapa (aproximadamente hasta 1975) dicha influencia sería más intensa. Luego toma formas distintas en ambos filósofos, debido a las diferentes vías que sigue cada uno. Pero aunque con variantes según las etapas, la presencia de Lévinas sería, según el autor, constante. [CJB]

4781 Bertoni, Lilia Ana. El surgimiento del nacionalismo en la Argentina de fines del siglo XIX. (*Cuad. Am./México*, 11:66, nov./dic. 1997, p. 179–188)

Se refiere al surgimiento de la preocupación por la nacionalidad y la consiguiente aparición del nacionalismo en la generación del Centenario (1910), como reacción a la inmigración masiva, producida en torno a 1880, y las medidas que se adoptaron para cohesionar la nación. [CJB]

4782 Biagini, Hugo Edgardo. La Reforma Universitaria: antecedentes y consecuentes. Buenos Aires: Leviatán, 2000. 108 p.: bibl. (El hilo de Ariadna)

Ensayos muy elogiosos sobre la Reforma Universitaria, argentina y latinoamericana. Además de ese tema, se recuerdan reuniones y congresos estudiantiles de la primera mitad del siglo XX, en relación con las propuestas de unidad latinoamericana. También se examina la situación actual de la universidad, siempre desde la óptica de los méritos de la Reforma Universitaria, a la que se considera vigente con los ajustes que requieren las nuevas situaciones.

4783 Biagini, Hugo Edgardo. Utopías juveniles: de la bohemia al Che. Buenos Aires: Leviatan, 2000. 106 p.: bibl. (Col. El Hilo de Ariadna)

Se compone de cuatro artículos, cuyos temas son: 1) la utopía y su relación con la juventud; 2) la bohemia en el Río de la Plata (especialmente Rubén Darío); 3) la recepción de Romain Rolland en América Latina. El cuarto es un artículo encomiástico sobre el Che Guevara y su efecto sobre la juventud.

4784 Brizuela, Gabriel Eduardo. Viajes por Europa, Africa y América: su significado en la evolución del pensamiento político de Domingo Faustino Sarmiento. San Juan, Argentina: Andres Lara?, 1998. 269 p.: bibl.

Numerosos comentarios hechos por Sarmiento a lo largo de sus viajes por América del Sur, Europa y Estados Unidos son considerados desde el punto de vista de la posible influencia sobre sus ideas políticas, aunque el autor reconoce el carácter parcial de esa influencia frente a otras fuentes. Reproduce el "Diario de Gastos" del viaje y agrega una extensa bibliografía.

4785 Cárdenas, Eduardo José and **Carlos Manuel Payá.** La Argentina de los hermanos Bunge: 1901–1907. Buenos Aires: Editorial Sudamericana, 1997. 382 p.: bibl., ill.

El interés para esta Sección reside en los aspectos biográficos de Carlos Octavio Bunge (1875–1918), filósofo de orientación positivista. [CJB]

4786 Castellani, Leonardo. Un país de Jauja: reflexiones políticas. Mendoza, Argentina: Ediciones Jauja, 1999. 428 p.: bibl., index.

Entre 1967–69 se publicó en Buenos Aires la revista *Jauja*, dirigida por el Padre Leonardo Castellani (1899–1984), luego expulsado de la Compañía de Jesús. La revista era de orientación nacionalista, y abundan, por lo tanto, las referencias críticas al liberalismo argentino, en tono irreverente, que era propio del Pe. Castellani. El prólogo es una apreciación de Castellani que comparte su orientación política y lo expone especialmente durante su actuación en la década del 60.

4787 Caturelli, Alberto. Historia de la filosofía en la Argentina, 1600–2000. Buenos Aires: Ciudad Argentina; Univ. del Salvador, 2001. 1486 p.: bibl.

La más completa y detallada visión de la filosofía argentina hasta la fecha. Lo mismo puede decirse de la bibliografía, que ocupa un tercio de lo que es un grueso volumen. Es, por lo tanto, instrumento imprescindible para estudiar el tema, aunque no se compartan algunos de los juicios valorativos del autor, basados en una posición católica rigurosa. Esto último explica también la extensión concedida al pensamiento "cristiano."

4788 Cernadas de Bulnes, Mabel Nelida and **Laura Llul.** Lecturas de una elite intelectual argentina: el Colegio Libre de Estudios Superiores, 1930–1959. (*Cuad. Am./México*, 13:74, marzo/abril 1999, p. 241–253)

El Colegio Libre de Estudios Superiores fue creado en 1930, como institución extraestatal y con el fin de "constituirse en un elemento de acción directa para el progreso social," y llevó a cabo una constante labor de enseñanza. Fue órgano suyo la revista *Cursos y Conferencias*, creada en 1931. Las autoras dan cuenta de los más prominentes escritores que aparecieron en sus páginas, cuyo propósito era "eminentemente pedagógico," para reafirmar los valores de la "cultura escrita occidental." [CJB]

4789 Chávez, Fermín. Vico en la Argentina. (*in* Congreso Nacional de Historia Argentina, *Buenos Aires, 1995*. Actas. Buenos Aires: Comisión Post Congreso Nacional de Historia Argentina, 1997, t. 1, p. 311–320)

Repasa la recepción y el estudio de Vico en Argentina, comenzando con Juan Bautista Alberdi y llegando hasta la actualidad. Alguna omisión (Francisco Romero, por ejemplo) no le resta utilidad.

4790 *Cuadernos de Filosofía.* No. 43, otoño 1998. Buenos Aires: Univ. de Buenos Aires, Instituto de Filosofía, Facultad de Filosofía y Letras.

Número especial dedicado al centenario de la Facultad de Filosofía y Letras de la Univ. de Buenos Aires. Fernando Salmerón, en un artículo que se lee con gran provecho, enlaza las posiciones filosóficas de Francisco Romero, Risieri Frondizi, José Gaos y Mario

Bunge, combinando perspectivas mexicanas y argentinas. En otro artículo de gran interés, Ernesto Garzón Valdés se refiere a la filosofía del derecho en Argentina, y en lo que corresponde a la corriente analítica afirma que este movimiento ha hecho una contribución de nivel internacional, que ha sido reconocida fuera del país. Roberto Walton, en uno de los mejores artículos sobre la filosofía de Francisco Romero, se refiere a la posición de este filósofo frente a la fenomenología y al tema de la intencionalidad. Señala anticipaciones de Romero a posiciones filosóficas posteriores. Osvaldo Guariglia realiza una interpretación y crítica de la axiología de Risieri Frondizi y sus consecuencias para la ética, a la luz de los más recientes desarrollos de la ética filosófica actual. Hay también artículos sobre los siguientes temas: Carlos Astrada, Mario Bunge, Carlos Alchourrón, Conrado Eggers Lan, la producción sobre filosofía antigua, la democracia y los derechos humanos, y las revistas filosóficas.

4791 Cúneo, Dardo. Sarmiento y Unamuno. Salamanca, Spain: Ediciones Univ. de Salamanca, 1997. 236 p. (Biblioteca Unamuno; 18)

Esta edición de la Univ. de Salamanca tiene carácter de homenaje a un libro clásico de Dardo Cúneo, que el autor ha venido reelaborando desde su aparición. Para comentario sobre ediciones previas desta obra, ver *HLAS 11:3856* y *HLAS 23:3757*. [CJB]

4792 Cupani, Alberto. Mario Bunge: un estilo polémico de análisis filosófico. (*Rev. Latinoam. Filos.*, 24:2, primavera 1998, p. 237–249, bibl.)

Breve pero bien concebido, este artículo se refiere no tanto al muy extenso contenido de la filosofía científica de Bunge, como a su base conceptual y sus supuestos metodológicos. La principal conclusión del autor es que la ciencia y la filosofía responden a propósitos diferentes. De tal modo, la filosofía que Bunge consideraría de aplicación universal sería solamente un tipo de filosofía. Además de su condición de eminente filósofo, Bunge es un intelectual que gusta de la polémica y encuentra reacciones similares; pero este artículo no tiene ese carácter y respeta el valor filosófico de Mario Bunge.

4793 Cuyo: Anuario de Filosofía Argentina y Americana. Vol. 14, 1997. Mendoza, Argentina: Univ. Nacional de Cuyo, Facultad de Filosofía y Letras, Instituto de Filosofía Argentina y Americana.

Artículos: Eduardo Devés Valdés, "El pensamiento latinoamericano a comienzos del siglo XX: la reivindicación de la identidad"; Daniel Omar de Lucía, "La antorcha del progreso por los caminos del sur: espacios positivistas en la Argentina y su proyección iberoamericana, 1895–1900"; Clara Alicia Jalif de Bertranou, "El hombre como destino de superación en Francisco Romero"; Arturo Andrés Roig, "La recepción del 'giro lingüístico' en Mendoza"; Juan Carlos Torchia Estrada, "La mujer en la filosofía: un texto inédito de Francisco Romero." [CJB]

4794 Cuyo: Anuario de Filosofía Argentina y Americana. Vol. 15, 1998. Mendoza, Argentina: Univ. Nacional de Cuyo, Facultad de Filosofía y Letras, Instituto de Filosofía Argentina y Americana.

Contribuciones de interés para esta Sección: Noemí Girbal-Blacha, "Política, economía y sociedad en la Argentina del siglo XX: una aproximación histórica a sus continuidades y cambios"; Dante Ramaglia, "La formación del espiritualismo nacionalista Argentino: proyecto y discurso en Ricardo Rojas"; Patrice Vermeren y Susana Villavicencio, "Positivismo y ciudadanía: José Ingenieros y la constitución de la ciudadanía por la ciencia y la educación en la Argentina"; María Lucrecia Rovaletti, "Panorama psicológico argentino: antecedentes, constitución, institucionalización y profesionalización de la psicología"; Florencia Ferreira de Cassone, "*Claridad* y la construcción de una izquierda americana"; Marisa A. Muñoz, "José Ingenieros y 'La Historia de una Biblioteca'." [CJB]

4795 Cuyo: Anuario de Filosofía Argentina y Americana. Vol. 16, 1999. Mendoza, Argentina: Univ. Nacional de Cuyo, Facultad de Filosofía y Letras, Instituto de Filosofía Argentina y Americana.

Artículos y textos: H.C.F. Mansilla, "Identidades colectivas y proceso de modernización: los indígenas, el estado y los cambios contemporáneos en el caso boliviano"; Edward Demenchónok, "La globalización y su planteamiento en la filosofía latinoamericana"; Cecilia Sánchez, "Traducción y políticas de la lengua en latinoamérica"; Yamandú Acosta, "Autenticidad, tradición e identidad en Pedro Figari"; Paulina Royo Urrizola, "La pregunta antropológica en la filosofía in-sistencial de Ismael Quiles"; Andy Daitsman, "Ideando contextos: prácticas de lecturas sociales"; Clara Alicia Jalif de Bertranou, "Tres artículos de Francisco Bilbao Aparecidos en *La revista del Nuevo Mundo*"; Gloria Hintze de Molinari, "Clorinda Matto de Turner y dos textos sobre la mujer y la ciencia"; Juan Carlos Torchia Estrada, "Angélica Mendoza en los Estados Unidos: un testimonio epistolar"; Roberto Mora, "Ficha bibliográfica de Carlos Astrada." [CJB]

4796 David, Guillermo. Carlos Astrada: la larga marcha de la filosofía argentina. (*Nombres/Córdoba*, 9:13/14, sept. 1999, p. 67–84)

El título es mucho más amplio que el contenido, pues se refiere exclusivamente a la experiencia de Astrada con temas y figuras de la filosofía alemana durante sus años de residencia europea a partir de 1927. No deja de ser interesante desde esa perspectiva. [CJB]

4797 Dotti, Jorge Eugenio. Carl Schmitt en Argentina. Rosario, Argentina: Homo Sapiens Ediciones, 2000. 929 p.: bibl. (Politeia)

Se trata de una obra muy rica en información, elaborada con seriedad y enfocada desde el punto de vista de la filosofía política. Aunque su pensamiento es mucho más amplio, Schmitt es tenido habitualmente como uno de los contribuyentes a la formación de la ideología nazi. Algunas figuras que, según el autor, representan la "recepción": Eugenio D'Ors (por artículos en la revista argentina *Criterio*), Saúl Taborda, Luis Juan Guerrero, Bruno Jacovella, Ernesto Palacio, Julio Ojea Quintana, Nimio de Anquín, Alberto Caturelli. Entre los abiertamente no simpatizantes: Francisco Ayala, Renato Treves, Carlos Sánchez Viamonte, Sebastián Soler. Dotti da, al final, su propia interpretación de Schmitt.

4798 Encuentro de Historia Argentina y Regional, *4th, Mendoza, Argentina, 1998*. Los hombres y las ideas. v. 1, En la historia de la nación. v. 2, En la historia de Cuyo. Mendoza, Argentina: Editorial de la

Facultad de Filosofía y Letras de la Univ. Nacional de Cuyo, 1999. 2 v.: bibl.

Dos útiles volúmenes, uno dedicado a la Argentina en general, y otro a la región de Cuyo, dentro de ese país. La importancia relativa de los temas abordados es variada, pero combinan figuras clásicas con otras menos conocidas. Suman casi 60 contribuciones, lo que hace imposible dar la lista. Algunos temas: Eduardo Wilde, Enrique del Valle Iberlucea, Ricardo Rojas, Juan Crisóstomo Lafinur, la generación de 1837, Alberdi, Sarmiento, Alfredo Palacios, Carlos Pellegrini, etc., y una serie de asuntos referentes a la vida social, política y económica de la región de Cuyo. [CJB]

Eujanian, Alejandro Claudio. Polémicas por la historia: el surgimiento de la crítica en la historiografía argentina, 1864–1882. See item **2849.**

4799 Feinmann, José Pablo. La sangre derramada: ensayo sobre la violencia política. 3. ed. Buenos Aires: Ariel, 1999. 362 p.: bibl.

No es tanto obra de pensamiento filosófico o político como de opinión sobre muy diversos temas (ejemplos: Hitler y los judíos, Heidegger y el nazismo, Fanon y la guerrilla de los 70s, la teoría del foco, la izquierda peronista, etc.). La primera parte es una especie de crítica de la violencia; la segunda es narrativa de hechos de violencia en las luchas políticas argentinas; y la tercera se titula: "La violencia y el sentido de la historia." El conjunto tiene el carácter señalado de variado comentario, desde una posición "progresista." No deja sin embargo de tener valor testimonial sobre una orientación de pensamiento en Argentina.

4800 Fernández Retamar, Roberto. Desde el Martí de Ezequiel Martínez Estrada. (*Rev. Bibl. Nac. José Martí*, 90:1, enero/marzo 1999, p. 31–42)

Aunque no se indica, se trata de la reimpresión de una conferencia pronunciada en un congreso internacional sobre Martínez Estrada, en Argentina. El texto es en parte memoria de una amistad con el escritor argentino, y en parte apreciación de sus valores, al mismo tiempo que una reflexión sobre su *Martí revolucionario* (ver *HLAS 30: 1675* y *HLAS 36:2305*), que incursiona en los avatares de la edición de dicho libro. [CJB]

4801 Ferraro, Liliana Juana. Reflexiones sobre el pensamiento político de Avellaneda. (*Rev. Hist. Am. Argent.*, 19:37, 1997, p. 215–247, bibl.)

Estudia los escritos de Nicolás Avellaneda (presidente de Argentina, 1874–80), pero en especial las ideas que animaron su acción política en el contexto ideológico-político de la época.

4802 Ferreira de Cassone, Florencia. Claridad y el internacionalismo americano. Buenos Aires: Editorial Claridad, 1998. 309 p.: bibl. (Biblioteca de historia)

Claridad fue una revista de orientación socialista que apareció en Buenos Aires entre 1926–41. Existió también una editorial del mismo nombre. Los datos aportados en este libro sobre la revista (en el marco de otras contemporáneas) llenan un tema no sistemáticamente explorado anteriormente. Asunto especial de la obra es el "internacionalismo" (antiimperialismo, antifascismo e interés—excepcional en aquella época en Argentina—por los problemas de los restantes países hispanoamericanos). La autora considera a la revista como "la empresa ideológica más lograda de la izquierda argentina." Para el comentario del historiador, ver ítem **2852.**

4803 Franceschi, Gustavo Juan. Antología. Buenos Aires: Agencia Informátiva Católica Argentina, 1997. 223 p.

Monseñor Franceschi (falleció 1957) fue director y editorialista de la revista católica *Criterio.* Aquí se reproducen artículos publicados entre 1947–57. Además del interés propiamente religioso, opinó sobre problemas sociales y políticos. Frente a la democracia liberal representó la adhesión al corporativismo. La "Semblanza" que antecede al material, fue introducción a la reunión de escritos de Franceschi, comenzada en 1945, pero que no llegó a término. Escrita con simpatía, y pese a su modesto título, es posiblemente lo más completo que se ha escrito sobre Monseñor Franceschi.

4804 Galasso, Norberto. El Che: revolución latinoamericana y socialismo. Buenos Aires: Ediciones del Pensamiento Nacional, 1997. 104 p.: bibl. (Volver a soñar)

Con profunda simpatía hacia el personaje y en contra de numerosas interpretaciones (especialmente "académicas" y de

"izquierdismo puro"), sigue la trayectoria del Che viéndola desde una óptica de nacionalismo revolucionario, anti-imperialista y proclive al socialismo que el autor ha expresado en otros escritos. Una cuarta parte del libro son documentos (textos breves y cartas). El Che quedaría situado, según el autor, en "la revolución latinoamericana hacia el socialismo."

4805 Ghirardi, Olsen A. La filosofía en Alberdi. 2. ed., aum. Córdoba, Argentina: Academia Nacional de Derecho y Ciencias Sociales de Córdoba, 2000. 248 p.: bibl. (Ediciones de la Academia Nacional de Derecho y Ciencias Sociales de Córdoba; 9)

Esta nueva edición de una cuidadosa investigación de las fuentes filosóficas de Alberdi y su repercusión en la obra del pensador argentino del siglo XIX, se aumenta de tres capítulos: uno sobre Alberdi y Volney, otro sobre la filosofía y el poder constitucional, y un último sobre Alberdi y la generación de 1837. Se trata de un valioso trabajo sobre el Alberdi "filósofo."

4806 Gil Q., Mauricio. El escepticismo de Borges o la filosofía como literatura fantástica. (*Yachay/Cochabamba*, 15:28, segundo semestre 1998, p. 67–88, bibl.)

En diálogo con—entre otros—Ernesto Sábato y Enrique Anderson Imbert, el tema, inteligentemente tratado, es el escepticismo filosófico de Borges según se expresa en su literatura. Un escepticismo, de acuerdo con el autor, que no carece sin embargo de "un gesto de fe." También ver ítem **4815.**

4807 Guevara, Ernesto Che. El pensamiento del Che. Selección de María del Carmen Ariet. La Habana: Editorial Capitán San Luis, 2000. 141 p.: bibl., port. (Col. Pensamiento revolucionario)

Pasajes extractados de los escritos de Guevara. No hay introducción ni notas aclaratorias, pero al final se indican las fuentes de donde salen los textos.

4808 Harris, Jonathan. Bernardino Rivadavia and Benthamite "discipleship." (*LARR*, 33:1, 1998, p. 129–149, bibl., photo)

Con cuidadosa argumentación sostiene que la influencia de Bentham—en general, pero particularmente en el caso especial de Rivadavia—no fue tan intensa como se ha sostenido. Parte de la impresión habría provenido de las expresiones (exageradas) del propio Bentham. Explica cómo las relaciones con Bentham no podían ser independientes de las que se tenían políticamente con el gobierno inglés. Para el comentario del historiador, ver ítem **2894.**

4809 Hernández, Pablo José. Peronismo y pensamiento nacional, 1955–1973. Buenos Aires: Editorial Biblos, 1997. 189 p.: bibl.

Las fechas señaladas en el título comprenden el período en que el peronismo estuvo fuera del poder y en buena parte proscrito. Este "peronismo de la resistencia" dio lugar a expresiones intelectuales (de denuncia, de interpretación histórica de la Argentina, de combate periodístico, etc.), que recibieron el título genérico de "pensamiento nacional." Este libro es una buena crónica y una útil guía para seguir esas manifestaciones. No es un estudio de ese pensamiento, sino una presentación de él en relación con los acontecimientos de la época. La obra tiene, dentro de sus simpatías, una amplitud de juicio y una serenidad de exposición infrecuentes en esta clase de escritos.

4810 Leoni Pinto, Ramón A. Obra y pensamiento historiográfico de Bernardo Canal Feijóo. Tucumán, Argentina: Facultad de Filosofía y Letras-UNT; Santiago del Estero, Argentina: Barco, 1997. 173 p.: bibl. (Col. Estudios)

El propósito es rescatar una obra no suficientemente apreciada, a juicio del autor, o por lo menos no conocida en su integridad. Aunque el estilo tiende al juicio elogioso, es un libro necesario para conocer la obra de interpretación histórica de Canal Feijóo (1898–1982). De no menos utilidad es el aporte bibliográfico que va al final del libro.

4811 López, María Pía and Guillermo Korn. Sábato, o La moral de los argentinos. Buenos Aires: Edita América Libre, 1997. 145 p.: bibl. (Col. Armas de la crítica; 5)

Ernesto Sábato, más allá de su reconocida posición como hombre de letras, es visto en la actualidad, por amplios sectores argentinos, incluida una parte considerable de la juventud, como un maestro en el sentido moral del término. Este libro, cuyas posiciones políticas no se ocultan, es una crítica sistemática a esa interpretación. De hecho viene a resultar también una expresión del debate sobre la vida argentina en los años que corren desde el peronismo hasta la actualidad.

4812 Lucía, Daniel Omar de. Orden y progreso: la utopía positivista iberoamericana en la Argentina finisecular, 1895–1902. (*Desmemoria/Buenos Aires*, 5:18, mayo/agosto 1998, p. 106–121, facsim., photos)

Aporta útil información en base al contenido de dos revistas de difícil acceso: *La Filosofía Positiva*, fundada en Buenos Aires en 1898 por la exiliada peruana Margarita Praxedes Muñoz; y *La Escuela Positiva*, fundada en 1895 y animada por Alfredo J. Ferreira, uno de los más destacados positivistas comteanos del país. [CJB]

4813 Maresca, Silvio Juan. Nuevas bases: Alberdi, Korn, Perón. (*Máscara/s/ Buenos Aires*, 1:3, dic. 1991, p. 59–84, bibl.)

Juan Bautista Alberdi, pensador del siglo XIX; Alejandro Korn (1860–1936), clásico filósofo argentino; y Juan Domingo Perón son colocados en una línea que representaría un pensamiento donde la filosofía estaría al servicio de los problemas nacionales. La semejanza de Alberdi y Korn había sido señalada muchas veces, pero no así con Perón. En cuanto a este último, el autor se basa principalmente en un discurso que pronunciara en 1949 en el Primer Congreso Nacional de Filosofía.

4814 Martínez Heredia, Fernando *et al.* Che, el argentino. Buenos Aires: Ediciones De Mano en Mano, 1997. 329 p.: bibl., ill.

Algunas contribuciones a este volumen son apreciaciones sobre Ernesto Guevara desde el punto de vista político, y expresan simpatía hacia el personaje. Pero aquellas que históricamente más interesan son las de carácter testimonial, y provenientes de representantes de la izquierda peronista, porque ilustran sobre su ideario de pensamiento, siendo reflexiones 30 o 40 años posteriores a la época del Che. Es de particular interés para la influencia del guevarismo en la izquierda político-cultural argentina, el artículo de Néstor Kohan, "Reencontrarnos con el Che."

4815 Mateos, Zulma. La filosofía en la obra de Jorge Luis Borges. Prólogo de Arturo García Astrada. Buenos Aires: Editorial Biblos, 1998. 125 p.: bibl.

Los temas filosóficos (el conocimiento, los universales, el tiempo, Dios, el lenguaje, etc.) y los filósofos a quienes Borges se sintió cercano (Abelardo, Schopenhauer o Hume) se presentan en sus manifestaciones a lo largo de la obra del escritor argentino. Se trata de una de las visiones más claras de un asunto complejo y abordado muchas veces, que pese a su naturaleza académica se lee con facilidad. También ver ítem **4806**.

4816 Miller, Jonathan M. The authority of a foreign talisman: a study of U.S. constitutional practice as authority in nineteenth-century Argentina and the Argentine elite's leap of faith. (*Am. Univ. Law Rev.*, 46:5, p. 1483–1572)

No es en realidad un artículo sino una extensa y detallada monografía. La tesis central, contra la extendida opinión de que una constitución debe ser el resultado de las condiciones propias del país, es que en algunos casos, la adopción de un modelo extraño puede ser muy eficaz debido al prestigio del modelo. No se limita al pensamiento constitucional, sino que revisa también la práctica jurídica argentina en relación con la norteamericana.

4817 Montserrat, Marcelo. Usos de la memoria: razón, ideología e imaginación históricas. Buenos Aires: Editorial Sudamericana; Univ. de San Andrés, 1996. 279 p.: bibl.

El libro se ocupa de teoría de la historia y recoge trabajos sobre historia de las ideas, pero contiene también algunos títulos relacionados con la historia argentina. Así, "La apropiación ideológica en la historiografía argentina reciente;" "El viaje iniciático de Sarmiento;" "La recepción literaria de Darwin en Guillermo Enrique Hudson y Eduardo Holmberg;" y "El pensamiento de Gustavo J. Franceschi y la revista *Criterio* en la cultura política argentina, 1928–1978." También ver ítem **4803**.

4818 Nascimbene, Mario Carlos. El nacionalismo liberal y tradicionalista y la Argentina inmigratoria: Benjamín Villafañe (h.), 1916–1944. Buenos Aires: Editorial Biblos; Fundación Simón Rodríguez, 1997. 161 p.: bibl., ill. (Col. Cuadernos Simón Rodríguez; 34)

El personaje estudiado fue un político que se expresó polémicamente y que aquí es situado en el grupo de los representantes de la derecha nacionalista, autoritaria y negadora de la democracia liberal en la Argentina de la primera mitad del siglo XX. Buena parte del libro está constituido por un apéndice documental. También ver ítem **4843**.

4819 Neiburg, Federico. Los intelectuales y la invención del peronismo: estudios de antropología social y cultural. Buenos Aires: Alianza Editorial, 1998. 290 p.: bibl. (Alianza estudio; 37)

El objetivo es estudiar una serie de interpretaciones que se hicieron del peronismo después de 1955 (cuando Perón pasa al exilio). Con ese propósito se examinan obras de Mario Amadeo, Carlos Strasser, Carlos H. Fayt, Arturo Jauretche, Juan José Hernández Arregui, Ezequiel Martínez Estrada, Gino Germani, Abelardo Ramos, y otros. Estas visiones interpretativas compondrían la "invención" del peronismo, del que habla el título.

4820 Noufouri, Hamurabi. Tinieblas del crisol de razas: ensayos sobre las representaciones simbólicas y espaciales de la noción del "otro" en Argentina. Buenos Aires: Editorial Cálamo de Sumer, 1999. 252 p.: bibl., ill.

A la vez estudio y denuncia de las formas de marginalización y discriminación en la Argentina, desde las poblaciones indígenas originarias hasta expresiones más recientes frente a otros grupos étnicos (antisemitismo, inmigrantes siriolibaneses, etc.).

4821 Osorio Sánchez, Héctor. Che: su concepto revolucionario. Cali, Colombia: Nueva Era Ltda., 1997. 115 p.: bibl.

Expone el concepto de "revolución" en el Che Guevara a lo largo de las etapas de su biografía. Las conclusiones, al final del libro, no recogen los hilos de la exposición sino que resultan ser una caracterización general de Ernesto Guevara.

4822 Ospital, María Silvia. Intelectuales argentinos y cultura española en Buenos Aires: una visión de *Síntesis*, 1927–1930. (*Estud. Soc./Santa Fe*, 7:13, segundo semestre 1997, p. 85–100)

Se refiere a la revista *Síntesis*, publicada en Buenos Aires en las fechas indicadas en el título, y caracterizada por una estrecha relación entre intelectuales argentinos y españoles, y el destaque de los valores hispánicos comunes. [CJB]

4823 Palti, Elías José. Argentina en el espejo: el "pretexto" Sarmiento. (*Prismas/Buenos Aires*, 1, 1997, p. 13–34)

Este extenso artículo cumple la muy útil función de organizar muchas de las poco menos que innumerables visiones sobre Sarmiento que se han dado a lo largo del tiempo y según los distintos enfoques históricos e ideológicos. No es poco mérito del autor haberse manejado con serenidad entre interpretaciones a veces irreconciliables.

Pasolini, Ricardo O. Entre la evasión y el humanismo—lecturas, lectores y cultura de los sectores populares: La Biblioteca Juan B. Justo de Tandil, 1928–1945. Ver ítem **2965.**

4824 Pisarello Virasoro, Roberto Gustavo. Arturo Frondizi: su pensamiento. Prólogo de Roberto Rocca. Buenos Aires: R.G. Pisarello Virasoro, 2000. 429 p.: bibl., ill.

Aunque hay buenos artículos de diversos colaboradores e introducciones aclaratorias a las partes en que se divide el libro, se trata ante todo de una obra documental, que representa buena parte de lo dicho y escrito por Frondizi, intelectual y presidente de Argentina, sobre diversos asuntos públicos. En ese sentido es una contribución útil, toda vez que el pensamiento de Frondizi se ha visto mezclado con las polémicas y los juicios partidarios, y por lo tanto no siempre visto con objetividad, como es frecuente en esos casos.

4825 Pomer, León. La construcción del imaginario histórico argentino. Buenos Aires?: Editores de América Latina, 1998. 117 p.: bibl.

Es una crítica a la concepción de la historia argentina sostenida por los grupos liberales, pero especialmente a la elaboración historiográfica de Bartolomé Mitre, clásico historiador argentino del siglo XIX. La mencionada historiografía, según el autor, "observa con profundo recelo a los grupos sociales subalternos," y sus ideas "les son dadas por la cultura europea occidental."

Propuestas para una antropología argentina. Ver *HLAS 59:1035.*

4826 Puigbó, Raúl. La identidad nacional argentina y la identidad iberoamericana. Buenos Aires: Grupo Editor Latino-

americano, 1998. 404 p.: bibl. (Nuevohacer) (Col. Estudios políticos y sociales)

La obra parte de inquietudes actuales, especialmente las originadas por el fenómeno de la globalización. Expone lo que considera las varias crisis históricas de la identidad argentina y las interpretaciones que se han dado sobre ella (uno de los capítulos más aprovechables). En lo que se refiere a la identidad iberoamericana, se remonta a la colonización, a la obra misional y la aculturación, al mestizaje, y se refiere por último a los precursores de la integración y al indigenismo. Por la información y el estilo expositivo puede ser útil también al lector general.

Rapalo, María Ester. Los empresarios y la reacción conservadora en la Argentina: las publicaciones de la Asociación del Trabajo, 1919–1922. Ver ítem **2990.**

4827 Reigadas, Cristina. Modernización e identidad en el pensamiento argentino contemporáneo. (*Rev. Filos. Latinoam. Cienc. Soc.*, 25:22, oct. 2000, p. 47–72)

Analiza los conceptos enunciados en el título desde el pensamiento crítico actual, para señalar olvidos y ocultamientos, ausencias y reduccionismos. Se toman como ejemplos de esos olvidos dos debates de la segunda mitad del siglo XX: la filosofía de la liberación, en los 70s, y el de la transición democrática, en los 80s, con sus aportes y limitaciones. Resulta interesante el balance del primero que, para la autora, adelantó muchos de los temas discutidos en las décadas siguientes, por lo que cabe pensarlo como "vanguardia de la filosofía posmoderna en Latinoamérica." [CJB]

4828 Revista de filosofía, cultura, ciencias, educación: 1915–1929. Dirección por José Ingenieros y Aníbal Ponce. Prólogo y selección de textos por Luis Alejandro Rossi. Buenos Aires: Univ. Nacional de Quilmes, 1999. 660 p.: bibl. (La ideología argentina)

Muy oportuna reedición de artículos aparecidos en *Revista de Filosofía* que dirigiera José Ingenieros. Los artículos están bien seleccionados, tanto por la amplitud de los temas como por la importancia de los autores. La Introducción, de Alejandro Rossi, "Los proyectos intelectuales de José Ingenieros desde 1915 a 1925: la crisis del positivismo y la filosofía en la Argentina," es de lectura muy recomendable par situar el pensamiento de la época en tanto está relacionado con la *Revista*. [CJB]

4829 Roca, Deodoro. Deodoro Roca, el hereje. Selección y estudio preliminar de Néstor Kohan. Buenos Aires: Editorial Biblos, 1999. 261 p.: bibl.

Oportuna reunión de escritos de uno de los líderes de la Reforma Universitaria de 1918 en Argentina, que el libro muestra también en otras facetas, más allá de aquel movimiento. El estudio preliminar es muy aprovechable, y la simpatía que trasunta lo anima sin privarlo de valor interpretativo. Deodoro Roca es visto en sus orígenes intelectuales, en relación con el modernismo y las figuras de Darío, Ingenieros, el primer Lugones y Rodó, para ser situado luego en los fundamentos de la Reforma, y más tarde en una posición política de izquierda. Se destacan las relaciones con la filosofía de la época y son de interés las similitudes que Kohan encuentra entre Roca y Mariátegui.

4830 Rocca, Carlos José. Juan B. Justo y su entorno. La Plata, Argentina: Editorial Universitaria de La Plata, 1998. 347 p.: bibl., ill. (Historia argentina)

Contribución a la historia del socialismo argentino. Presenta una gran riqueza de noticias biográficas y de acción política de Juan B. Justo (fundador del Partido Socialista Argentino), así como de colaboradores y miembros del Partido, algunos de ellos de relevancia en la política del país, como Alfredo Palacios, Américo Ghioldi, Nicolás Repetto y Antonio de Tomaso, entre otros.

4831 Rubinich, Lucas. Los sociólogos intelectuales: cuatro notas sobre la sociología en los años sesenta. (*Apunt. Invest. CECYP*, 3:4, junio 1999, p. 31–55, bibl.)

Muy útil trabajo que expone el desarrollo de la sociología en la Univ. de Buenos Aires y su alto grado de politización y radicalización en la época que se estudia. Esa radicalización era compartida por la Universidad en general.

4832 Segovia, Gonzalo. Esteban Echeverría: el credo romántico y la heterodoxia política, romanticismo y liberalismo ortodoxo. Mendoza, Argentina: Univ. Nacional de Cuyo, Facultad de Filosofía y Letras, 1997. 92 p.: bibl.

Se compone de dos trabajos. Uno sobre las relaciones de las ideas políticas románticas con la idea de revolución, el liberalismo y el socialismo. El segundo sostiene que en el pensamiento político de Echeverría, el romanticismo es sólo uno de sus componentes.

4833 Suriano, Juan. Las prácticas políticas del anarquismo argentino. (*Rev. Indias*, 57:210, mayo/agosto 1997, p. 421–450)

Buena exposición de las ideas, programas y elementos propagandísticos del anarquismo argentino. El autor tiende a señalar, en último análisis, la ineficacia práctica del movimiento, especialmente después de aprobada la Ley de 1912 que ampliaba la posibilidad de participar en los procesos electorales. Participación que por principio los anarquistas rechazaban. Para el comentario del historiador, ver ítem **3031.**

4834 Szmetan, Ricardo. *Este pueblo necesita* (1934), de Manuel Gálvez: un libro olvidado por la crítica. (*Cuad. Am. /México*, 13:73, enero/feb. 1999, p. 226–242)

El escritor argentino Manuel Gálvez (1882–1962) compuso in 1934, con artículos publicados e inéditos, su libro *Este pueblo necesita.* Este autor, según la descripción del artículo, era admirador del fascismo, ambivalente frente a la cuestión judía, y amante de personalidades fuertes rayanas en lo dictatorial. Szmetan no considera al libro en cuestión como el mejor de Gálvez, pero lo encuentra "importante para conocer su pensamiento en temas que serán recurrentes en él." [CJB]

4835 Terán, Oscar. Carlos Octavio Bunge y la institución filosófica: educando al cacique progresista. (*Estud. Soc. /Santa Fe*, 7:12, primer semestre 1997, p. 9–15)

Expone las ideas conservadoras de Carlos Octavio Bunge (conocido filósofo positivista argentino), con sus rasgos biologistas, su nacionalismo y sus exigencias educativas para la formación de la elite dirigente. Con esto último tiene que ver su apoyo a la fundación de la Facultad de Filosofía y Letras de la Univ. de Buenos Aires. (El subtítulo se explica porque Bunge consideraba a Porfirio Díaz, en sentido elogioso, como "cacique progresista.")

4836 Terán, Oscar. Vida intelectual en el Buenos Aires fin-de-siglo, 1880–1910: derivas de la "cultura científica." Buenos Aires: Fondo de Cultura Económica, 2000. 309 p.: bibl. (Sección Obras de historia)

Contribución valiosa sobre lo que en general se denomina la época "positivista," pero que el autor, con acierto, prefiere llamar de "cultura científica"—que también podría ser, con recaudos, "cientificista." Muy oportuno es que los autores seleccionados no representen exclusivamente el pensamiento *filosófico*, lo que da a la revisión mayor amplitud. La idea básica es apreciar la visión de algunos autores clave para explicar la influencia de las ideas sobre la política y la sociedad. Los autores: Miguel Cané, José María Ramos Mejía, Carlos Octavio Bunge, Ernesto Quesada, José Ingenieros.

4837 Testimonios de vida universitaria: en el 60° aniversario de la creación de la Facultad de Filosofía y Letras de la U.N.T. Compilación y Recopilación de Hilda Naessens y Atilio O. Santillán. Tucumán, Argentina: Facultad de Filosofía y Letras, Univ. Nacional de Tucumán, 1999. 112 p. (Transformaciones del Mundo Contemporáneo Desde la Perspectiva de Ciencias Humanas; 2)

Especie de historia oral de la enseñanza filosófica en la Univ. Nacional de Tucumán, Argentina, en la que varios protagonistas aportan datos para esa historia.

4838 Tópicos actuales en filosofía de la ciencia: homenaje a Mario Bunge en su 80. aniversario. Recopilación de Guillermo M. Denegri y Gladys E. Martínez. Mar del Plata, Argentina: Univ. Nacional de Mar del Plata, Facultad de Ciencias Exactas y Naturales; Editorial Martin, 2000. 265 p.: bibl., ill.

Homenaje al destacado filósofo de la ciencia, de relieve internacional, Mario Bunge (nac. 1919). Bunge nació y se formó en Argentina, pero desde hace mucho tiempo reside en Canadá. Algunos artículos se refieren a su filosofía, y otros a temas que el filósofo cultivó. Muy útil la información sobre publicaciones de Bunge.

4839 Transformaciones e identidad cultural. v. 2, La Argentina ante transformaciones del mundo contemporáneo; desde la perspectiva del NOA [Noroeste Argentina].

Tucumán, Argentina: Univ. Nacional de Tucumán, Facultad de Filosofía y Letras, 1998. 222 p.

Para el interés de esta Sección deben destacarse dos artículos: 1) Lucía Piossek Prebisch, "Filosofía e identidad cultural en la Argentina," que menciona ejemplos de la historia de este país en que se hizo presente la cuestión de la identidad y trata el asunto tomando en cuenta factores como la globalización; 2) Hilda Naessens, "'Identidad cultural' en el pensamiento de Francisco Romero," que tras tratar el tema de la identidad latinoamericana en general, busca su aplicación en el pensamiento de Francisco Romero y en la forma en que este último entendió la naturaleza y el alcance de la filosofía latinoamericana. [CJB]

4840 Tur Donatti, Carlos M. La utopía del regreso y la estética de la barbarie: Vasconcelos, Riva Agüero y los nacionalistas argentinos. (*Cuad. Am./México*, 13:77, set./oct. 1999, p. 167–176)

Severa crítica, dentro de un artículo breve, a José Vasconcelos y José de la Riva Agüero, extendida a nacionalistas argentinos como Hugo Wast (Gustavo Martínez de Zubiría) y Manuel Gálvez, y al populismo peronista de los años 40. Esta tendencia se habría caracterizado por "una militante definición política reaccionaria y una inclinación romántico-arcaizante en los ámbitos del arte." Vasconcelos—pero también los otros autores criticados—es visto, en su etapa de la década de 1930, como "nacionalista reaccionario, hispanófilo y antiindigenista" y proclive al fascismo europeo. [CJB]

4841 Vazeilles, José Gabriel. El fracaso argentino: sus raíces en la ideología oligárquica. 2. ed. Buenos Aires: Editorial Biblos, 1997. 183 p.: bibl.

Existiría una ideología oligárquica, calificada por el autor como "arcaica,"que explicaría el fracaso argentino. Se busca confirmar esta opinión con el examen del curso de la historia argentina del siglo XIX y de la primera parte del XX.

4842 Vieira, Antonio Rufino. Marxismo e filosofia latinoamericana: uma aproximação entre Ernst Bloch e Enrique Dussel. (*Reflexão/Campinas*, 22:67/68, jan./agôsto 1997, p. 132–147)

El título refleja bien el contenido, y

éste no tiene mayores variantes frente a las expresiones desiderativas que son habituales en este tema.

4843 Villafañe, Benjamín. El pensamiento político y económico de Benjamín Villafañe. Compilación de María Silvia Fleitas. San Salvador de Jujuy, Argentina: Univ. Nacional de Jujuy, Unidad de Investigación en Historia Regional, 1997. 256 p.: bibl.

Villafañe (1877–1952) fue un político antiliberal, de rasgos elitistas, corporativistas y nacionalistas. Se reúnen aquí sus escritos políticos y económicos. Una introducción da idea general de su vida, su actuación y sus ideas. A cada parte antológica precede una presentación. La compiladora, sin adherir a las ideas centrales de su personaje, lo rescata, sin embargo, por sus reclamos regionalistas. También ver ítem **4818.**

ABBREVIATIONS AND ACRONYMS

Except for journal abbreviations which are listed: 1) after each journal title in the *Title List of Journals Indexed* (p. 769); and 2) in the *Abbreviation List of Journals Indexed* (p. 783).

ALADI	Asociación Latinoamericana de Integración
a.	annual
ABC	Argentina, Brazil, Chile
A.C.	antes de Cristo
ACAR	Associação de Crédito e Assistência Rural, Brazil
AD	Anno Domini
A.D.	Acción Democrática, Venezuela
ADESG	Associação dos Diplomados de Escola Superior de Guerra, Brazil
AGI	Archivo General de Indias, Sevilla
AGN	Archivo General de la Nación
AID	Agency for International Development
a.k.a.	also known as
Ala.	Alabama
ALALC	Asociación Latinoamericana de Libre Comercio
ALEC	*Atlas lingüístico etnográfico de Colombia*
ANAPO	Alianza Nacional Popular, Colombia
ANCARSE	Associação Nordestina de Crédito e Assistência Rural de Sergipe, Brazil
ANCOM	Andean Common Market
ANDI	Asociación Nacional de Industriales, Colombia
ANPOCS	Associação Nacional de Pós-Graduação e Pesquisa em Ciências Sociais, São Paulo
ANUC	Asociación Nacional de Usuarios Campesinos, Colombia
ANUIES	Asociación Nacional de Universidades e Institutos de Enseñanza Superior, Mexico
AP	Acción Popular
APRA	Alianza Popular Revolucionaria Americana, Peru
ARENA	Aliança Renovadora Nacional, Brazil
Ariz.	Arizona
Ark.	Arkansas
ASA	Association of Social Anthropologists of the Commonwealth, London
ASSEPLAN	Assessoria de Planejamento e Acompanhamento, Recife
Assn.	Association
Aufl.	Auflage (edition, edición)
AUFS	American Universities Field Staff Reports, Hanover, N.H.
Aug.	August, Augustan
aum.	aumentada
b.	born (nació)
B.A.R.	British Archaeological Reports
BBE	Bibliografia Brasileira de Educação
b.c.	indicates dates obtained by radiocarbon methods
BC	Before Christ

bibl(s).	bibliography(ies)
BID	Banco Interamericano de Desarrollo
BNDE	Banco Nacional de Desenvolvimento Econômico, Brazil
BNH	Banco Nacional de Habitação, Brazil
BP	before present
b/w	black and white
C14	Carbon 14
ca.	*circa* (about)
CACM	Central American Common Market
CADE	Conferencia Anual de Ejecutivos de Empresas, Peru
CAEM	Centro de Altos Estudios Militares, Peru
Calif.	California
Cap.	Capítulo
CARC	Centro de Arte y Comunicación, Buenos Aires
CARICOM	Caribbean Common Market
CARIFTA	Caribbean Free Trade Association
CBC	Christian base communities
CBD	central business district
CBI	Caribbean Basin Initiative
CD	Christian Democrats, Chile
CDHES	Comisión de Derechos Humanos de El Salvador
CDI	Conselho de Desenvolvimento Industrial, Brasília
CEB	comunidades eclesiásticas de base
CEBRAP	Centro Brasileiro de Análise e Planejamento, São Paulo
CECORA	Centro de Cooperativas de la Reforma Agraria, Colombia
CEDAL	Centro de Estudios Democráticos de América Latina, Costa Rica
CEDE	Centro de Estudios sobre Desarrollo Económico, Univ. de los Andes, Bogotá
CEDEPLAR	Centro de Desenvolvimento e Planejamento Regional, Belo Horizonte
CEDES	Centro de Estudios de Estado y Sociedad, Buenos Aires; Centro de Estudos de Educação e Sociedade, São Paulo
CEDI	Centro Ecumênico de Documentos e Informação, São Paulo
CEDLA	Centro de Estudios y Documentación Latinoamericanos, Amsterdam
CEESTEM	Centro de Estudios Económicos y Sociales del Tercer Mundo, México
CELADE	Centro Latinoamericano de Demografía
CELADEC	Comisión Evangélica Latinoamericana de Educación Cristiana
CELAM	Consejo Episcopal Latinoamericano
CEMLA	Centro de Estudios Monetarios Latinoamericanos, Mexico
CENDES	Centro de Estudios del Desarrollo, Venezuela
CENIDIM	Centro Nacional de Información, Documentación e Investigación Musicales, Mexico
CENIET	Centro Nacional de Información y Estadísticas del Trabajo, Mexico
CEOSL	Confederación Ecuatoriana de Organizaciones Sindicales LIbres
CEPADE	Centro Paraguayo de Estudios de Desarrollo Económico y Social
CEPA-SE	Comissão Estadual de Planejamento Agrícola, Sergipe
CEPAL	Comisión Económica para América Latina y el Caribe
CEPLAES	Centro de Planificación y Estudios Sociales, Quito
CERES	Centro de Estudios de la Realidad Económica y Social, Bolivia
CES	constant elasticity of substitution
cf.	compare
CFI	Consejo Federal de Inversiones, Buenos Aires
CGE	Confederación General Económica, Argentina
CGTP	Confederación General de Trabajadores del Perú
chap(s).	chapter(s)
CHEAR	Council on Higher Education in the American Republics

Cía.	Compañía
CIA	Central Intelligence Agency
CIDA	Comité Interamericano de Desarrollo Agrícola
CIDE	Centro de Investigación y Desarrollo de la Educación, Chile; Centro de Investigación y Docencias Económicas, Mexico
CIDIAG	Centro de Información y Desarrollo Internacional de Autogestión, Lima
CIE	Centro de Investigaciones Económicas, Buenos Aires
CIEDLA	Centro Interdisciplinario de Estudios sobre el Desarrollo Latinoamericano, Buenos Aires
CIEDUR	Centro Interdisciplinario de Estudios sobre el Desarrollo Uruguay, Montevideo
CIEPLAN	Corporación de Investigaciones Económicas para América Latina, Santiago
CIESE	Centro de Investigaciones y Estudios Socioeconómicos, Quito
CIMI	Conselho Indigenista Missionário, Brazil
CINTERFOR	Centro Interamericano de Investigación y Documentación sobre Formación Profesional
CINVE	Centro de Investigaciones Económicas, Montevideo
CIP	Conselho Interministerial de Preços, Brazil
CIPCA	Centro de Investigación y Promoción del Campesinado, Bolivia
CIPEC	Consejo Intergubernamental de Países Exportadores de Cobre, Santiago
CLACSO	Consejo Latinoamericano de Ciencias Sociales, Secretaría Ejecutiva, Buenos Aires
CLASC	Confederación Latinoamericana Sindical Cristiana
CLE	Comunidad Latinoamericana de Escritores, Mexico
cm	centimeter
CNI	Confederação Nacional da Indústria, Brazil
CNPq	Conselho Nacional de Pesquisas, Brazil
Co.	Company
COB	Central Obrera Boliviana
COBAL	Companhia Brasileira de Alimentos
CODEHUCA	Comisión para la Defensa de los Derechos Humanos en Centroamérica
Col.	Collection, Colección, Coleção
col.	colored, coloured
Colo.	Colorado
COMCORDE	Comisión Coordinadora para el Desarrollo Económico, Uruguay
comp(s).	compiler(s), compilador(es)
CONCLAT	Congresso Nacional das Classes Trabalhadoras, Brazil
CONCYTEC	Consejo Nacional de Ciencia y Tecnología (Peru)
CONDESE	Conselho de Desenvolvimento Econômico de Sergipe
Conn.	Connecticut
COPEI	Comité Organizador Pro-Elecciones Independientes, Venezuela
CORFO	Corporación de Fomento de la Producción, Chile
CORP	Corporación para el Fomento de Investigaciones Económicas, Colombia
Corp.	Corporation, Corporación
corr.	corrected, corregida
CP	Communist Party
CPDOC	Centro de Pesquisa e Documentação, Brazil
CRIC	Consejo Regional Indígena del Cauca, Colombia
CSUTCB	Confederación Sindical Unica de Trabajadores Campesinos de Bolivia
CTM	Confederación de Trabajadores de México
CUNY	City University of New York
CUT	Central Unica de Trabajadores (Mexico); Central Unica dos Trabalhadores (Brazil); Central Unitaria de Trabajadores (Chile; Colombia); Confederación Unitaria de Trabajadores (Costa Rica)

CVG	Corporación Venezolana de Guayana
d.	died (murió)
DANE	Departamento Nacional de Estadística, Colombia
DC	developed country; Demócratas Cristianos, Chile
d.C.	después de Cristo
Dec./déc.	December, décembre
Del.	Delaware
dept.	department
depto.	departamento
DESCO	Centro de Estudios y Promoción del Desarrollo, Lima
Dez./dez.	Dezember, dezembro
dic.	diciembre, dicembre
disc.	discography
DNOCS	Departamento Nacional de Obras Contra as Secas, Brazil
doc.	document, documento
Dr.	Doctor
Dra.	Doctora
DRAE	*Diccionario de la Real Academia Española*
ECLAC	UN Economic Commision for Latin America and the Caribbean, New York and Santiago
ECOSOC	UN Economic and Social Council
ed./éd.(s)	edition(s), édition(s), edición(es), editor(s), redactor(es), director(es)
EDEME	Editora Emprendimentos Educacionais, Florianópolis
Edo.	Estado
EEC	European Economic Community
EE.UU.	Estados Unidos de América
EFTA	European Free Trade Association
e.g.	*exempio gratia* (for example, por ejemplo)
ELN	Ejército de Liberación Nacional, Colombia
ENDEF	Estudo Nacional da Despesa Familiar, Brazil
ERP	Ejército Revolucionario del Pueblo, El Salvador
ESG	Escola Superior de Guerra, Brazil
estr.	estrenado
et al.	*et alia* (and others)
ETENE	Escritório Técnico de Estudos Econômicos do Nordeste, Brazil
ETEPE	Escritório Técnico de Planejamento, Brazil
EUDEBA	Editorial Universitaria de Buenos Aires
EWG	Europaische Wirtschaftsgemeinschaft. *See* EEC.
facsim(s).	facsimile(s)
FAO	Food and Agriculture Organization of the United Nations
FDR	Frente Democrático Revolucionario, El Salvador
FEB	Força Expedicionária Brasileira
Feb./feb.	February, Februar, febrero, febbraio
FEDECAFE	Federación Nacional de Cafeteros, Colombia
FEDESARROLLO	Fundación para la Educación Superior y el Desarrollo
fev./fév.	fevereiro, février
ff.	following
FGTS	Fundo de Garantia do Tempo de Serviço, Brazil
FGV	Fundação Getúlio Vargas
FIEL	Fundación de Investigaciones Económicas Latinoamericanas, Argentina
film.	filmography
fl.	flourished
Fla.	Florida
FLACSO	Facultad Latinoamericana de Ciencias Sociales
FMI	Fondo Monetario Internacional

FMLN	Frente Farabundo Martí de Liberación Nacional, El Salvador
fold.	folded
fol(s).	folio(s)
FPL	Fuerzas Populares de Liberación Farabundo Marti, El Salvador
FRG	Federal Republic of Germany
FSLN	Frente Sandinista de Liberación Nacional, Nicaragua
ft.	foot, feet
FUAR	Frente Unido de Acción Revolucionaria, Colombia
FUCVAM	Federación Unificadora de Cooperativas de Vivienda por Ayuda Mutua, Uruguay
FUNAI	Fundação Nacional do Indio, Brazil
FUNARTE	Fundação Nacional de Arte, Brazil
FURN	Fundação Universidade Regional do Nordeste
Ga.	Georgia
GAO	General Accounting Office, Wahington
GATT	General Agreement on Tariffs and Trade
GDP	gross domestic product
GDR	German Democratic Republic
GEIDA	Grupo Executivo de Irrigação para o Desenvolvimento Agrícola, Brazil
gen.	gennaio
Gen.	General
GMT	Greenwich Mean Time
GPA	grade point average
GPO	Government Printing Office, Washington
h.	hijo
ha.	hectares, hectáreas
HLAS	*Handbook of Latin American Studies*
HMAI	*Handbook of Middle American Indians*
Hnos.	hermanos
HRAF	Human Relations Area Files, Inc., New Haven, Conn.
IBBD	Instituto Brasileiro de Bibliografia e Documentação
IBGE	Instituto Brasileiro de Geografia e Estatística, Rio de Janeiro
IBRD	International Bank for Reconstruction and Development (World Bank)
ICA	Instituto Colombiano Agropecuario
ICAIC	Instituto Cubano de Arte e Industria Cinematográfica
ICCE	Instituto Colombiano de Construcción Escolar
ICE	International Cultural Exchange
ICSS	Instituto Colombiano de Seguridad Social
ICT	Instituto de Crédito Territorial, Colombia
id.	*idem* (the same as previously mentioned or given)
IDB	Inter-American Development Bank
i.e.	*id est* (that is, o sea)
IEL	Instituto Euvaldo Lodi, Brazil
IEP	Instituto de Estudios Peruanos
IERAC	Instituto Ecuatoriano de Reforma Agraria y Colonización
IFAD	International Fund for Agricultural Development
IICA	Instituto Interamericano de Ciencias Agrícolas, San José
III	Instituto Indigenista Interamericana, Mexico
IIN	Instituto Indigenista Nacional, Guatemala
ILDIS	Instituto Latinoamericano de Investigaciones Sociales
ill.	illustration(s)
Ill.	Illinois
ILO	International Labour Organization, Geneva
IMES	Instituto Mexicano de Estudios Sociales
IMF	International Monetary Fund

Impr.	Imprenta, Imprimérie
in.	inches
INAH	Instituto Nacional de Antropología e Historia, Mexico
INBA	Instituto Nacional de Bellas Artes, Mexico
Inc.	Incorporated
INCORA	Instituto Colombiano de Reforma Agraria
Ind.	Indiana
INEP	Instituto Nacional de Estudios Pedagógicos, Brazil
INI	Instituto Nacional Indigenista, Mexico
INIT	Instituto Nacional de Industria Turística, Cuba
INPES/IPEA	Instituto de Planejamento Econômico e Social, Brazil
INTAL	Instituto para la Integración de América Latina
IPA	Instituto de Pastoral Andina, Univ. de San Antonio de Abad, Seminario de Antropología, Cusco, Peru
IPEA	Instituto de Pesquisa Econômica Aplicada, Brazil
IPES/GB	Instituto de Pesquisas e Estudos Sociais, Guanabara, Brazil
IPHAN	Instituto de Patrimônio Histórico e Artístico Nacional, Brazil
ir.	irregular
IS	Internacional Socialista
ITESM	Instituto Tecnológico y de Estudios Superiores de Monterrey
ITT	International Telephone and Telegraph
Jan./jan.	January, Januar, janeiro, janvier
JLP	Jamaican Labour Party
Jr.	Junior, Júnior
JUC	Juventude Universitária Católica, Brazil
JUCEPLAN	Junta Central de Planificación, Cuba
Kan.	Kansas
KITLV	Koninklijk Instituut voor Tall-, Land- en Volkenkunde (Royal Institute of Linguistics and Anthropology)
km	kilometers, kilómetros
Ky.	Kentucky
La.	Louisiana
LASA	Latin American Studies Association
LDC	less developed country(ies)
LP	long-playing record
Ltd(a).	Limited, Limitada
m	meters, metros
m.	murió (died)
M	mille, mil, thousand
M.A.	Master of Arts
MACLAS	Middle Atlantic Council of Latin American Studies
MAPU	Movimiento de Acción Popular Unitario, Chile
MARI	Middle American Research Institute, Tulane University, New Orleans
MAS	Movimiento al Socialismo, Venezuela
Mass.	Massachusetts
MCC	Mercado Común Centro-Americano
Md.	Maryland
MDB	Movimiento Democrático Brasileiro
MDC	more developed countries
Me.	Maine
MEC	Ministério de Educação e Cultura, Brazil
Mich.	Michigan
mimeo	mimeographed, mimeografiado
min.	minutes, minutos
Minn.	Minnesota

MIR	Movimiento de Izquierda Revolucionaria, Chile and Venezuela
Miss.	Mississippi
MIT	Massachusetts Institute of Technology
ml	milliliter
MLN	Movimiento de Liberación Nacional
mm.	millimeter
MNC	multinational corporation
MNI	minimum number of individuals
MNR	Movimiento Nacionalista Revolucionario, Bolivia
Mo.	Missouri
MOBRAL	Movimento Brasileiro de Alfabetização
MOIR	Movimiento Obrero Independiente y Revolucionario, Colombia
Mont.	Montana
MRL	Movimiento Revolucionario Liberal, Colombia
ms.	manuscript
M.S.	Master of Science
msl	mean sea level
n.	nació (born)
NBER	National Bureau of Economic Research, Cambridge, Massachusetts
N.C.	North Carolina
N.D.	North Dakota
NE	Northeast
Neb.	Nebraska
neubearb.	neubearbeitet (revised, corregida)
Nev.	Nevada
n.f.	neue Folge (new series)
NGO	nongovernmental organization
NGDO	nongovernmental development organization
N.H.	New Hampshire
NIEO	New International Economic Order
NIH	National Institutes of Health, Washington
N.J.	New Jersey
NJM	New Jewel Movement, Grenada
N.M.	New Mexico
no(s).	number(s), número(s)
NOEI	Nuevo Orden Económico Internacional
NOSALF	Scandinavian Committee for Research in Latin America
Nov./nov.	November, noviembre, novembre, novembro
NSF	National Science Foundation
NW	Northwest
N.Y.	New York
OAB	Ordem dos Advogados do Brasil
OAS	Organization of American States
OCLC	Online Computer Library Center
Oct./oct.	October, octubre, octobre
ODEPLAN	Oficina de Planificación Nacional, Chile
OEA	Organización de los Estados Americanos
OECD	Organisation for Economic Cooperation and Development
OIT	Organización Internacional del Trabajo
Okla.	Oklahoma
Okt.	Oktober
ONUSAL	United Nations Observer Mission in El Salvador
op.	opus
OPANAL	Organismo para la Proscripción de las Armas Nucleares en América Latina

OPEC	Organization of Petroleum Exporting Countries
OPEP	Organización de Países Exportadores de Petróleo
OPIC	Overseas Private Investment Corporation, Washington
Or.	Oregon
OREALC	Oficina Regional de Educación para América Latina y el Caribe
ORIT	Organización Regional Interamericana del Trabajo
ORSTOM	Office de la recherche scientifique et technique outre-mer (France)
ott.	ottobre
out.	outubro
p.	page(s)
Pa.	Pennsylvania
PAN	Partido Acción Nacional, Mexico
PC	Partido Comunista
PCCLAS	Pacific Coast Council on Latin American Studies
PCN	Partido de Conciliación Nacional, El Salvador
PCP	Partido Comunista del Perú
PCR	Partido Comunista Revolucionario, Chile and Argentina
PCV	Partido Comunista de Venezuela
PD	Partido Democrático
PDC	Partido Demócrata Cristiano, Chile
PDS	Partido Democrático Social, Brazil
PDT	Partido Democrático Trabalhista, Brazil
PDVSA	Petróleos de Venezuela S.A.
PEMEX	Petróleos Mexicanos
PETROBRAS	Petróleo Brasileiro
PIMES	Programa Integrado de Mestrado em Economia e Sociologia, Brazil
PIP	Partido Independiente de Puerto Rico
PLN	Partido Liberación Nacional, Costa Rica
PMDB	Partido do Movimento Democrático Brasileiro
PNAD	Pesquisa Nacional por Amostra Domiciliar, Brazil
PNC	People's National Congress, Guyana
PNM	People's National Movement, Trinidad and Tobago
PNP	People's National Party, Jamaica
pop.	population
port(s).	portrait(s)
PPP	purchasing power parities; People's Progressive Party of Guyana
PRD	Partido Revolucionario Dominicano
PREALC	Programa Regional del Empleo para América Latina y el Caribe, Organización Internacional del Trabajo, Santiago
PRI	Partido Revolucionario Institucional, Mexico
Prof.	Professor, Profesor(a)
PRONAPA	Programa Nacional de Pesquisas Arqueológicas, Brazil
prov.	province, provincia
PS	Partido Socialista, Chile
PSD	Partido Social Democrático, Brazil
pseud.	pseudonym, pseudónimo
PT	Partido dos Trabalhadores, Brazil
pt(s).	part(s), parte(s)
PTB	Partido Trabalhista Brasileiro
pub.	published, publisher
PUC	Pontifícia Universidade Católica
PURSC	Partido Unido de la Revolución Socialista de Cuba
q.	quarterly
rev.	revisada, revista, revised
R.I.	Rhode Island

s.a.	semiannual
SALALM	Seminar on the Acquisition of Latin American Library Materials
SATB	soprano, alto, tenor, bass
sd.	sound
s.d.	*sine datum* (no date, sin fecha)
S.D.	South Dakota
SDR	special drawing rights
SE	Southeast
SELA	Sistema Económico Latinoamericano
SEMARNAP	Secretaria de Medio Ambiente, Recursos Naturales y Pesca, Mexico
SENAC	Serviço Nacional de Aprendizagem Comercial, Rio de Janeiro
SENAI	Serviço Nacional de Aprendizagem Industrial, São Paulo
SEP	Secretaría de Educación Pública, Mexico
SEPLA	Seminario Permanente sobre Latinoamérica, Mexico
Sept./sept.	September, septiembre, septembre
SES	socioeconomic status
SESI	Serviço Social da Indústria, Brazil
set.	setembro, settembre
SI	Socialist International
SIECA	Secretaría Permanente del Tratado General de Integración Económica Centroamericana
SIL	Summer Institute of Linguistics (Instituto Lingüístico de Verano)
SINAMOS	Sistema Nacional de Apoyo a la Movilización Social, Peru
S.J.	Society of Jesus
s.l.	*sine loco* (place of publication unknown)
s.n.	*sine nomine* (publisher unknown)
SNA	Sociedad Nacional de Agricultura, Chile
SPP	Secretaría de Programación y Presupuesto, Mexico
SPVEA	Superintendência do Plano de Valorização Econômica da Amazônia, Brazil
sq.	square
SSRC	Social Sciences Research Council, New York
STENEE	Empresa Nacional de Energía Eléctrica. Sindicato de Trabajadores, Honduras
SUDAM	Superintendência de Desenvolvimento da Amazônia, Brazil
SUDENE	Superintendência de Desenvolvimento do Nordeste, Brazil
SUFRAMA	Superintendência da Zona Franca de Manaus, Brazil
SUNY	State University of New York
SW	Southwest
t.	tomo(s), tome(s)
TAT	Thematic Apperception Test
TB	tuberculosis
Tenn.	Tennessee
Tex.	Texas
TG	transformational generative
TL	Thermoluminescent
TNE	Transnational enterprise
TNP	Tratado de No Proliferación
trans.	translator
UABC	Universidad Autónoma de Baja California
UCA	Universidad Centroamericana José Simeón Cañas, San Salvador
UCLA	University of California, Los Angeles
UDN	União Democrática Nacional, Brazil
UFG	Universidade Federal de Goiás
UFPb	Universidade Federal de Paraíba
UFSC	Universidade Federal de Santa Catarina

UK	United Kingdom
UN	United Nations
UNAM	Universidad Nacional Autónoma de México
UNCTAD	United Nations Conference on Trade and Development
UNDP	United Nations Development Programme
UNEAC	Unión de Escritores y Artistas de Cuba
UNESCO	United Nations Educational, Scientific and Cultural Organization
UNI/UNIND	União das Nações Indígenas
UNICEF	United Nations International Children's Emergency Fund
Univ(s).	university(ies), universidad(es), universidade(s), université(s), universität(s), universitá(s)
uniw.	uniwersytet (university)
Unltd.	Unlimited
UP	Unidad Popular, Chile
URD	Unidad Revolucionaria Democrática
URSS	Unión de Repúblicas Soviéticas Socialistas
UNISA	University of South Africa
US	United States
USAID	*See* AID.
USIA	United States Information Agency
USSR	Union of Soviet Socialist Republics
UTM	Universal Transverse Mercator
UWI	Univ. of the West Indies
v.	volume(s), volumen (volúmenes)
Va.	Virginia
V.I.	Virgin Islands
viz.	*videlicet* (that is, namely)
vol(s).	volume(s), volumen (volúmenes)
vs.	versus
Vt.	Vermont
W.Va.	West Virginia
Wash.	Washington
Wis.	Wisconsin
WPA	Working People's Alliance, Guyana
WWI	World War I
WWII	World War II
Wyo.	Wyoming
yr(s).	year(s)

TITLE LIST OF JOURNALS INDEXED

For journal titles listed by abbreviation, see *Abbreviation List of Journals Indexed*, p. 783

A ALFA A: Europa-Latinoamérica, coope-
ración en estudios sociales aplicados. Beat-
riz Viterbo Editora: Red Interuniversitaria
Europea-Latinoamericana para los
Estudios Sociales Aplicados. Rosario,
Argentina. (ALFA/Rosario)

Acervo. Arquivo Nacional. Rio de Janeiro.
(Acervo/Rio de Janeiro)

Actual. Univ. de Los Andes, Dirección General de Cultura y Extensión. Mérida, Venezuela. (Actual/Mérida)

Afro-Asia. Univ. Federal da Bahia, Faculdade
de Filosofia e Ciências Humanas, Centro
de Estudos Afro-Orientais. Salvador,
Brazil. (Afro-Asia/Salvador)

Aletria: Revista de Estudos de Literatura.
Univ. Federal de Minas Gerais. Centro de
Estudos Literários. Belo Horizonte, Brazil.
(Aletria/Belo Horizonte)

Allpanchis. Instituto de Pastoral Andina.
Cuzco, Peru. (Allpanchis/Cuzco)

América. Centro de Estudos Hispanoamericanos. Santa Fe, Argentina. (América/
Santa Fe)

América Latina en la Historia Económica:
Boletín de Fuentes. Instituto de Investiga-
ciones Dr. José Luis Mora, Proyecto de
Historia Económica. México. (Am. Lat.
Hist. Econ. Bol. Fuentes)

América Negra. Expedición Humana, Insti-
tuto de Genética Humana, Facultad de
Medecina, Pontificia Univ. Javeriana.
Bogotá. (Am. Negra)

American Anthropologist. American Anthropological Assn. Washington. (Am.
Anthropol.)

The American Historical Review. Indiana
Univ. at Bloomington. Bloomington, Ind.
(Am. Hist. Rev.)

American Journal of Sociology. Univ. of
Chicago Press. Chicago, Ill. (Am. J.
Sociol.)

The American University Law Review.
American Univ., Washington College of
Law. Washington. (Am. Univ. Law Rev.)

The Americas: A Quarterly Review of Inter-
American Cultural History. Catholic
Univ. of America, Academy of American
Franciscan History; Catholic Univ. of
America Press. Washington. (Americas/
Washington)

Anais da . . . Reunião. Sociedade Brasileira de
Pesquisa Histórica. São Paulo. (Anais/São
Paulo)

Anais do Museu Histórico Nacional. Museu
Histórico Nacional, Instituto do Patri-
mônio Histórico e Artístico Nacional,
Ministério da Cultura. Rio de Janeiro.
(An. Mus. Hist. Nac.)

Anais do Museu Paulista: História e Cultura
Material. Museu Paulista. São Paulo. (An.
Mus. Paul.)

Anales del Instituto de Historia Militar
Argentina. Instituto de Historia Militar
Argentina. Buenos Aires. (An. Inst. Hist.
Mil. Argent.)

Anales del Instituto de Investigaciones Estéticas. UNAM, Instituto de Investigaciones Estéticas. México. (An. Inst. Invest.
Estét.)

Anales del Instituto de la Patagonia: Serie
Ciencias Humanas. Univ. de Magallanes,
Instituto de la Patagonia. Punta Arenas,
Chile. (An. Inst. Patagon. Ser. Cienc.
Hum.)

Anales Literarios. Matías and Yara Montes
Foundation. Honolulu. (An. Lit./Hono-
lulu)

Análisis Político. Univ. Nacional de Colombia, Instituto de Estudios Políticos y Relaciones Internacionales. Bogotá. (Anál.
Polít./Bogotá)

Ancient Mesoamerica. Cambridge Univ.
Press. Cambridge, England; New York.
(Anc. Mesoam.)

ANDES: Antropología e Historia. Univ. Nacional de Salta, Facultad de Humanidades,
Centro Promocional de las Investigaciones
en Historia y Antropología. Salta, Argentina. (ANDES Antropol. Hist.)

Annuarium Historiae Conciliorum. Ferdinand Schoningh. Paderborn, Germany. (Annu. Hist. Concil./Paderborn)

Anos 90: Revista do Programa de Pós-Graduação em História. Univ. Federal do Rio Grande do Sul, Programa de Pós-Graduação em História. Porto Alegre, Brazil. (Anos 90)

Anthropologica del Departamento de Ciencias Sociales. Pontificia Univ. Católica del Perú, Depto. de Ciencias Sociales. Lima. (Anthropol. Dep. Cienc. Soc.)

Anthropological Quarterly. Catholic Univ. Press of America. Washington. (Anthropol. Q.)

Antiquity. Antiquity Publications Ltd. Cambridge, England. (Antiquity/Cambridge)

Antropológica. Fundación La Salle, Instituto Caribe de Antropología y Sociología. Caracas. (Antropológica/Caracas)

Anuario. Archivo y Biblioteca Nacionales de Bolivia. Sucre, Bolivia. (Anuario/Sucre)

Anuario Colombiano de Historia Social y de la Cultura. Depto. de Historia, Facultad de Ciencias Humanas, Univ. Nacional de Colombia. Bogotá. (Anu. Colomb. Hist. Soc. Cult.)

Anuario de Espacios Urbanos. Univ. Autónoma Metropolitana—Unidad Azcapotzalco. División de Ciencias y Artes para el Diseño, Depto. de Evaluación del Diseño en el Tiempo. México. (Anu. Espacios Urbanos)

Anuario de Estudios Americanos. Consejo Superior de Investigaciones Científicas, Escuela de Estudios Hispano-Americanos. Sevilla, Spain. (Anu. Estud. Am.)

Anuario de Estudios Centroamericanos. Univ. de Costa Rica. San José. (Anu. Estud. Centroam.)

Anuario de Estudios Indígenas. Univ. Autónoma de Chiapas, Instituto de Estudios Indígenas. San Cristóbal de las Casas, Mexico. (Anu. Estud. Indíg.)

Anuario de la Historia de la Iglesia en Chile. Arzobispado de Santiago, Seminario Pontificio Mayor; Sociedad de Historia de la Iglesia en Chile. Santiago. (Anu. Hist. Iglesia Chile)

Anuario del Centro de Estudios Gallegos. Univ. de la República, Facultad de Humanidades y Ciencias de la Educación, Centro de Estudios Gallegos. Montevideo. (Anu. Cent. Estud. Gallegos)

Anuario IEHS. Univ. Nacional del Centro de la Provincia de Buenos Aires, Facultad de Ciencias Humanas, Instituto de Estudios Histórico-Sociales. Tandil, Argentina. (Anu. IEHS)

Anuario Mariateguiano. Empresa Editora Amauta. Lima. (Anu. Mariateg.)

Anuario ... Estudios Sociales. El Colegio de Puebla. México. (Anu. Estud. Soc.)

Apuntes de Investigación del CECYP. Centro de Estudios en Cultura y Política, Fundación del Sur. Buenos Aires. (Apunt. Invest. CECYP)

Apuntes Filosóficos. Univ. Central de Venezuela, Escuela de Filosofía. Caracas. (Apunt. Filos.)

Arbor. Consejo Superior de Investigaciones Científicas. Madrid. (Arbor/Madrid)

Archaeology. Archaeological Institute of America. New York. (Archaeology/New York)

Archaeology and Anthropology. Walter Roth Museum of Anthropology, Ministry of Culture. Georgetown, Guyana. (Archaeol. Anthropol.)

Archives de sciences sociales des religions. Presses universitaires de France. Paris. (Arch. sci. soc. relig.)

Archivo Ibero-Americano: Revista Franciscana de Estudios Históricos. Franciscanos Españoles. Madrid. (Arch. Ibero-Am.)

Archivum Historicum Societatis Iesu. Institutum Historicum Societatis Iesu. Rome. (Arch. Hist. Soc. Iesu)

Arqueología Mexicana. Instituto Nacional de Antropología e Historia; Editorial Raíces. México. (Arqueol. Mex.)

ARTEunesp. Univ. Estadual Paulista. São Paulo. (ARTEunesp)

Asclepio: Revista de Historia de la Medicina y de la Ciencia. Consejo Superior de Investigaciones Científicas, Instituto de Historia. Madrid. (Asclepio/Madrid)

Atenea. Univ. de Concepción. Concepción, Chile. (Atenea/Concepción)

Atti e Memorie dell'Ateneo di Treviso. L'Ateneo. Treviso, Italy. (Atti Memorie Ateneo Treviso)

Auriga: Revista de Filosofía, Antropología e Historia. Univ. Autónoma de Querétaro, Facultad de Filosofía. Querétaro, Mexico. (Auriga/Querétaro)

Bahamas: Journal of Science. Media Enterprises Ltd. Nassau, The Bahamas. (Bahamas J. Sci.)

Biography. Univ. Press of Hawaii for the Biographical Research Center. Honolulu. (Biography/Honolulu)

Boletín Americanista. Univ. de Barcelona. Barcelona. (Bol. Am./Barcelona)

Boletín Antropológico. Univ. de los Andes, Facultad de Humanidades y Educación, Centro de Investigaciones Etnológicas y Museo Arqueológico Gonzalo Rincón Gutiérrez. Mérida, Venezuela. (Bol. Antropol./Mérida)

Boletín Cultural y Bibliográfico. Banco de la República, Biblioteca Luis-Angel Arango. Bogotá. (Bol. Cult. Bibliogr.)

Boletín de Antropología Americana. Instituto Panamericano de Geografía e Historia. México. (Bol. Antropol. Am.)

Boletín de Arqueología. Fundación de Investigaciones Arqueológicas Nacionales, Banco de la República. Bogotá. (Bol. Arqueol./Bogotá)

Boletín de Arqueología PUCP. Pontificia Univ. Católica del Perú, Depto. de Humanidades, Sección de Arqueología. Lima. (Bol. Arqueol. PUCP)

Boletín de Historia y Antigüedades. Academia Colombiana de Historia. Bogotá. (Bol. Hist. Antig.)

Boletín de la Academia Nacional de la Historia. Academia Nacional de la Historia. Caracas. (Bol. Acad. Nac. Hist./Caracas)

Boletín de la Academia Puertorriqueña de la Historia. Academia Puertorriqueña de la Historia. San Juan. (Bol. Acad. Puertorriq. Hist.)

Boletín de la Biblioteca Artiguista. Círculo Militar General Artigas. Montevideo. (Bol. Bibl. Artiguista)

Boletín de Lima: Revista Cultural Científica. Asociación Cultural Boletín de Lima A.C. Lima. (Bol. Lima)

Boletín del Fideicomiso Archivos Plutarco Elías Calles y Fernando Torreblanca. Fideicomiso Archivos Plutarco Elías Calles y Fernando Torreblanca. México. (Boletín/México)

Boletín del Instituto Riva-Agüero: BIRA. Pontificia Univ. Católica del Perú, Instituto Riva-Agüero. Lima. (Bol. Inst. Riva-Agüero)

Boletín Histórico del Ejército. República Oriental del Uruguay, Comando General del Ejército, Estado Mayor del Ejército, Depto. de Estudios Históricos. Montevideo. (Bol. Hist. Ejérc.)

Boletín Nicaragüense de Bibliografía y Documentación. Banco Central de Nicaragua, Biblioteca Dr. Roberto Incer Barquero. Managua. (Bol. Nicar. Bibliogr. Doc.)

Bulletin. Société suisse des américanistes = Schweizerische Amerikanisten Gesellschaft; Musée et institut d'éthnographie. Geneva. (Bulletin/Geneva)

Bulletin de l'Institut français d'études andines. Lima. (Bull. Inst. fr. étud. andin.)

Bulletin de la Société d'histoire de la Guadeloupe. Archives départamentales avec le concours du Conseil général de la Guadeloupe. Basse-Terre, Guadeloupe. (Bull. Soc. hist. Guadeloupe)

Bulletin du Centre d'histoire des espaces atlantiques. Talence-Cedex, France. (Bull. Cent. hist. atl.)

Bulletin hispanique. Éditions Bière. Bordeaux, France. (Bull. hisp./Bordeaux)

Bulletin of Latin American Research. Blackwell Publishers. Oxford, England; Malden, Mass. (Bull. Lat. Am. Res.)

Caderno de Filosofia e Ciências Humanas. Depto. de Filosofia e Ciências Humanas, Faculdade de Ciências Humanas e Letras, Centro Universitário Newton Paiva. Belo Horizonte, Brazil. (Cad. Filos. Ciênc. Hum.)

Cadernos de Antropologia e Imagem. Univ. do Estado do Rio de Janeiro, Programa de Pós-Graduação em Ciências Sociais, Núcleo de Antropologia e Imagem. Rio de Janeiro. (Cad. Antropol. Imagem)

Cadernos de Estudos Sociais. Fundação Joaquim Nabuco, Instituto de Pesquisas Sociais. Recife, Brazil. (Cad. Estud. Sociais)

Cadernos de História Social. Campinas, Brazil. (Cad. Hist. Soc.)

Cadernos do ISP. Univ. Federal de Pelotas, Instituto de Sociologia e Política. Pelotas, Brazil. (Cad. ISP)

Les Cahiers d'Outre-Mer. Faculté des lettres de Bordeaux, Institut de géographie; Institut de la France d'Outre-Mer; Société de géographie de Bordeaux. Bordeaux, France. (Cah. Outre-Mer)

Cahiers des Amériques latines. Univ. de la Sorbonne nouvelle—Paris III, Institut des haute études de l'Amérique latine. Paris. (Cah. Am. lat.)

Les cahiers du patrimoine. Conseil régional de la Martinique, Bureau du patrimoine. Fort-de-France, Martinique. (Cah. patrim.)

Caleidoscopio. Univ. Autónoma de Aguascalientes, Centro de Artes y Humanidades.

Aguascalientes, Mexico. (Caleidoscopio/
Aguascalientes)

California History. California Historical Society. San Francisco, Calif. (Calif. Hist.)

**Canadian Journal of Latin American and Ca-
ribbean Studies = Revue canadienne des
études latino-américaines et caraïbes.**
Univ. of Calgary Press. Calgary, Canada.
(Can. J. Lat. Am. Caribb. Stud.)

Caribbean Quarterly: CQ. Univ. of the West
Indies, Vice Chancellery, Cultural Studies
Initiative. Mona, Jamaica. (Caribb. Q. /
Mona)

Caribbean Studies. Univ. of Puerto Rico, Institute of Caribbean Studies. Río Piedras.
(Caribb. Stud.)

Casa de la Libertad. Fundación Cultural;
Banco Central de Bolivia. Sucre, Bolivia.
(Casa Lib.)

Chiapas. UNAM, Instituto de Investigaciones Económicas. México. (Chiapas/
México)

**Church History: Studies in Christianity and
Culture.** American Society of Church History. Red Bank, N.J. (Church Hist.)

**Ciclos en la Historia, Economía y la So-
ciedad.** Univ. de Buenos Aires, Facultad de
Ciencias Económicas, Instituto de Investigaciones de Historia Económica y Social.
Buenos Aires. (Ciclos Hist. Econ. Soc.)

Ciência & Trópico. Ministério de Educação,
Fundação Joaquim Nabuco; Editora Massangana. Recife, Brazil. (Ciênc. Tróp.)

Ciência e Cultura. Sociedade Brasileira para
o Progresso da Ciência. São Paulo. (Ciênc.
Cult.)

Ciudad y Territorio Estudios Territoriales.
Ministerio de Fomento, Centro de Publi-
caciones. Madrid. (Ciudad Territ. Estud.
Territ.)

Colonial Latin American Historical Review.
Univ. of New Mexico, Spanish Colonial
Research Center. Albuquerque. (CLAHR)

Colonial Latin American Review. City Univ.
of New York (CUNY), City College, Dept.
of Foreign Languages and Literatures, Simon H. Rifkind Center for the Humanities. New York; Carfax Publishing, Taylor
& Francis, Ltd. Abingdon, England; Philadelphia, Penn. (Colon. Lat. Am. Rev.)

Comparative Studies in Society and History.
Society for the Comparative Study of Soci-
ety and History; Cambridge Univ. Press.
London. (Comp. Stud. Soc. Hist.)

Contracorriente: Revista de Historia. Ponti-
ficia Univ. Católica del Perú, Servicios
Universitarios. Lima. (Contracorriente/
Lima)

**Contribuciones Científicas y Tecnológicas:
Area Ciencias Sociales y Humanidades.**
Univ. de Santiago de Chile, Vicerrectoría
de Investigación y Desarrollo, Depto. de
Investigaciones Científicas y Tecnológicas.
Santiago. (Contrib. Cient. Tecnol. Cienc.
Soc. Humanid.)

Convergencia: Revista de Ciencias Sociales.
Univ. Autónoma del Estado de México,
Facultad de Ciencias Políticas y Administración Pública. Toluca, Mexico. (Conver-
gencia/Toluca)

Critique of Anthropology. Sage Publications.
London. (Crit. Anthropol.)

Cuadernos Americanos. UNAM. México.
(Cuad. Am./México)

Cuadernos de Antropología. Univ. de Costa
Rica, Depto. de Antropología, Laboratorio
de Etnología. San José. (Cuad. Antropol./
San José)

**Cuadernos de Arte de la Universidad de
Granada.** Univ. de Granada, Depto. de
Historia de Arte. Granada, Spain. (Cuad.
Arte/Granada)

Cuadernos de Desarrollo Rural. Pontificia
Univ. Javeriana, Facultad de Estudios Am-
bientales y Rurales, Instituto de Estudios
Rurales, Depto. de Procesos Sociales y De-
sarrollo, Depto. de Tecnologías para la
Conservación y la Producción. Bogotá.
(Cuad. Desarro. Rural)

Cuadernos de Filosofía. Univ. de Buenos
Aires, Instituto de Filosofía, Facultad de
Filosofía y Letras. Buenos Aires. (Cuad.
Filos.)

**Cuadernos de Historia. Serie Economía y So-
ciedad.** Univ. Nacional de Córdoba, Facultad de Filosofía y Humanidades, Centro
de Investigaciones. Córdoba, Argentina.
(Cuad. Hist. Ser. Econ. Soc.)

Cuadernos de Historia. Serie Población. Centro de Investigaciones, Facultad de Filosofía y Humanidades. Univ. Nacional de
Córdoba. Córdoba, Argentina. (Cuad. Hist.
Ser. Poblac.)

Cuadernos de Marcha. Centro de Estudios
Uruguay-América Latina. Montevideo.
(Cuad. Marcha)

Cuadernos del CIESAL. Univ. Nacional de
Rosario, Facultad de Ciencia Política y
Relaciones Internacionales, Centro Inter-
disciplinario de Estudios Sociales Argenti-

nos y Latinoamericanos. Rosario, Argentina. (Cuad. CIESAL)

Cuadernos del CISH. Univ. Nacional de La Plata, Facultad de Humanidades y Ciencias de la Educación, Centro de Investigaciones Socio Históricas. La Plata, Argentina. (Cuad. CISH)

Cuadernos del Instituto Nacional de Antropología y Pensamiento Latinoamericano. Presidencia de la Nación, Secretaria de Cultura, Instituto Nacional de Antropología y Pensamiento Latinoamericano. Buenos Aires. (Cuad. Inst. Nac. Antropol. Pensam. Latinoam.)

Cuadernos del Sur: Historia. Univ. Nacional del Sur, Depto. de Humanidades. Bahía Blanca, Argentina. (Cuad. Sur Hist./Bahía Blanca)

Cuba Socialista. Comité Central del Partido Comunista de Cuba. La Habana. (Cuba Social.)

Cuestiones Políticas. Univ. de Zulia, Facultad de Ciencias Jurídicas, Instituto de Estudios Políticos y Derecho Público. Maracaibo, Venezuela. (Cuest. Polít.)

Cultura de Guatemala. Univ. Rafael Landívar. Guatemala. (Cult. Guatem.)

Cultura Vozes. Editôra Vozes. Petrópolis, Brazil. (Cult. Vozes)

Cuyo: Anuario de Historia del Pensamiento Argentino. Univ. Nacional de Cuyo, Instituto de Filosofía, Sección de Historia del Pensamiento Argentino. Mendoza, Argentina. (Cuyo/Mendoza)

Dados. Instituto Universitários de Pesquisas do Rio de Janeiro. Rio de Janeiro. (Dados/Rio de Janeiro)

Data: Revista del Instituto de Estudios Andinos y Amazónicos. Instituto de Estudios Andinos y Amazónicos. La Paz. (Data/La Paz)

Debates Americanos. Casa de Altos Estudios Don Fernado Ortíz. La Habana. (Debates Am.)

Decursos: Revista de Ciencias Sociales. Univ. Mayor de San Simón, Centro de Estudios Superiores Universitarios. Cochabamba, Bolivia. (Decursos/Cochabamba)

A Defesa Nacional: Revista de Assuntos Militares e Estudo de Problemas Brasileiros. Palácio Duque de Caxias, Biblioteca do Exército. Rio de Janeiro. (Def. Nac./Rio de Janeiro)

Desarrollo Económico: Revista de Ciencias Sociales. Instituto de Desarrollo Económico y Social. Buenos Aires. (Desarro. Econ.)

Desmemoria. Buenos Aires. (Desmemoria/Buenos Aires)

Diálogo y Debate de Cultura Política. Centro de Estudios para la Reforma del Estado. México. (Diálogo Debate Cult. Polít.)

Diogenes. Blackwell Publishers. Oxford, England. (Diogenes/Oxford)

Eco Andino. Centro de Ecología y Pueblos Andinos. Oruro, Bolivia. (Eco Andin.)

En Otras Palabras: Mujeres, Amores y Desamores. Univ. Nacional de Colombia, Grupo Mujer y Sociedad; Corporación Casa de la Mujer. Bogotá. Fundación Promujer. Bogotá? (En Otras Palabras)

Entorno Urbano: Revista de Historia. Univ. Autónoma Metropolitana—Iztapalapa; Instituto de Investigaciones Dr. José María Luis Mora. México. (Entorno Urbano)

Entrepasados: Revista de Historia. Buenos Aires. (Entrepasados/Buenos Aires)

Espacio, Tiempo y Forma: Revista de la Facultad de Geografía e Historia; Serie V, Historia Contemporánea. Univ. Nacional de Educación a Distancia, Facultad de Geografía e Historia. Madrid. (Espac. Tiempo Forma Ser. V Hist. Contemp.)

Espacio: Temas de Ciencias Sociales. Univ. Católica Andrés Bello, Escuela de Ciencias Sociales. Caracas. (Espac. Temas Cienc. Soc.)

Estudios Bolivianos. Univ. Mayor de San Andrés, Facultad de Humanidades y Ciencias de la Educación, Instituto de Estudios Bolivianos. La Paz. (Estud. Boliv.)

Estudios de Asia y Africa. El Colegio de México. México. (Estud. Asia Afr.)

Estudios de Cultura Náhuatl. UNAM, Instituto de Investigaciones Históricas. México. (Estud. Cult. Náhuatl)

Estudios de Historia Moderna y Contemporánea de México. UNAM, Instituto de Investigaciones Históricas. México. (Estud. Hist. Mod. Contemp. Méx.)

Estudios de Historia Novohispana. UNAM, Instituto de Investigaciones Históricas. México. (Estud. Hist. Novohisp.)

Estudios de Historia Social y Económica de América. Univ. de Alcalá de Henares. Madrid. (Estud. Hist. Soc. Econ. Am.)

Estudios del Hombre. Univ. de Guadalajara, Depto. de Estudios del Hombre. Guadalajara, Mexico. (Estud. Hombre)

Estudios: Filosofía, Historia, Letras. Instituto

Tecnológico Autónomo de México, División Académica de Estudios Generales y Estudios Internacionales, Depto. Académico de Estudios Generales. México. (Estud. Filos. Hist. Let.)

Estudios Geográficos. Instituto de Economía y Geografía Aplicadas. Madrid. (Estud. Geogr./Madrid)

Estudios Internacionales. Univ. de Chile, Instituto de Estudios Internacionales. Santiago. (Estud. Int./Santiago)

Estudios Internacionales: Revista del IRIPAZ. Instituto de Relaciones Internacionales y de Investigaciones para la Paz. Guatemala. (Estud. Int./Guatemala)

Estudios Jaliscienses. El Colegio de Jalisco. Zapopan, Mexico. (Estud. Jalisc.)

Estudios Michoacanos. El Colegio de Michoacán. Zamora, Mexico. (Estud. Michoac.)

Estudios Migratorios Latinoamericanos. Centro de Estudios Migratorios Latinoamericanos. Buenos Aires. (Estud. Migr. Latinoam.)

Estudios: Revista de Antropología, Arqueología e Historia. Univ. de San Carlos de Guatemala, Escuela de Historia, Instituto de Investigaciones Históricas, Antropológicas, y Arqueológicas. Guatemala. (Estudios/Guatemala)

Estudios: Revista del Centro de Estudios Avanzados. Univ. Nacional de Córdoba, Centro de Estudios Avanzados. Córdoba, Argentina. (Estudios/Córdoba)

Estudios sobre las Culturas Contemporáneas. Univ. de Colima, Centro Universitario de Investigaciones Sociales. Colima, Mexico. (Estud. Cult. Contemp.)

Estudios Sociales. Centro de Estudios Sociales P. Juan Montalvo, SJ. Santo Domingo. (Estud. Soc./Santo Domingo)

Estudios Sociales: Revista Universitaria Semestral. Univ. Nacional del Litoral, Secretaría de Extensión, Centro de Publicaciones. Santa Fe, Argentina. (Estud. Soc./Santa Fe)

Estudos Afro-Asiáticos. Centro de Estudos Afro-Asiáticos. Rio de Janeiro. (Estud. Afro-Asiát.)

Estudos Avançados. Univ. de São Paulo, Instituto de Estudos Avançados. São Paulo. (Estud. Av.)

Estudos de História. Univ. Estadual Paulista, Faculdade de História, Direito e Serviço Social, Curso de Pós-Graduação em História. Franca, Brazil. (Estud. Hist./Franca)

Estudos Econômicos. Univ. de São Paulo, Faculdade de Economia, Administração e Contabilidade, Fundação Instituto de Pesquisas Econômicas. São Paulo. (Estud. Econ./São Paulo)

Estudos Históricos. Fundação Getulio Vargas, Centro de Pesquisa e Documentação de História Contemporânea do Brasil. Rio de Janeiro. (Estud. Hist./Rio de Janeiro)

Estudos Ibero-Americanos. Pontifícia Univ. Católica do Rio Grande do Sul, Faculdade de Filosofia e Ciências Humanas, Depto. de História, Programa Pós-Graduação em História. Porto Alegre, Brazil. (Estud. Ibero-Am./Porto Alegre)

Estudos Leopoldenses: Série História. Univ. do Vale do Rio Dos Sinos, Centro de Ciências Humanas, Programa de Pós-Graduação em História. São Leopoldo, Brazil. (Estud. Leopoldenses Sér. Hist.)

Estudos: Revista da Universidade Católica de Goiás. Univ. Católica de Goiás. Goiânia, Brazil. (Estudos/Goiânia)

Estudos Sociedade e Agricultura. Univ. Federal Rural do Rio de Janeiro, Instituto de Ciências Humanas e Sociais, Curso de Pós-Graduação em Desenvolvimento, Agricultura e Sociedade, Depto. de Letras e Ciências Sociais. Rio de Janeiro. (Estud. Soc. Agric.)

Ethnohistory: the Bulletin of the Ohio Valley Historic Indian Conference. American Society for Ethnohistory, Columbus, Ohio. (Ethnohistory/Columbus)

Ethnomusicology. Univ. of Illinois Press. Champaign, Ill. (Ethnomusicology)

FACES: Revista de la Facultad de Ciencias Económicas y Sociales. Univ. Nacional de Mar del Plata, Facultad de Ciencias Económicas y Sociales. Mar del Plata, Argentina. (FACES/Mar del Plata)

Feminist Studies. Univ. of Maryland. College Park. (Fem. Stud.)

Folia Histórica del Nordeste. Univ. Nacional del Nordeste, Facultad de Humanidades, Instituto de Historia; CONICET, Instituto de Investigaciones Geohistóricas; FUNDANORD. Resistencia, Argentina. (Folia Hist. Nordeste)

French Historical Studies. Society for French Historical Studies. Raleigh, N.C. (Fr. Hist. Stud.)

Frónesis: Revista de Filosofía Jurídica, Social y Política. Univ. de Zulia, Facultad de Ciencias Jurídicas y Políticas, Instituto de Filosofía del Derecho Dr. José Manuel Delgado Ocando. Maracaibo, Venezuela. (Frónesis/Maracaibo)

Frontera Norte. El Colegio de la Frontera Norte. Tijuana, Mexico. (Front. Norte)

Fundamentos de Antropología. Centro de Investigaciones Etnológicas Angel Ganivet. Granada, Spain. (Fundam. Antropol.)

Généalogie et histoire de la Caraïbe. Assn. de la généalogie et histoire de la Caraïbe. Le Pecq, France. (Généal. hist. Caraïbe)

Geographical Review. American Geographical Society. New York. (Geogr. Rev.)

Hastings International and Comparative Law Review. Univ. of California, Hastings College of the Law. San Francisco, Calif. (Hastings Int. Comp. Law Rev.)

Hispania. Consejo Superior de Investigaciones Científicas, Instituto de Historia, Depto. de Medieval Moderna y Contemporánea. Madrid. (Hispania/Madrid)

Hispania. American Assn. of Teachers of Spanish and Portuguese; Mississippi State Univ. Mississippi State, Miss. (Hispania/University)

Hispanic American Historical Review. Duke Univ. Press. Durham, N.C. (HAHR)

Hispanic Journal. Indiana Univ. of Pennsylvania, Dept. of Foreign Languages. Indiana, Penn. (Hisp. J.)

Hispanic Review. Univ. of Pennsylvania, Dept. of Romance Languages. Philadelphia, Penn. (Hisp. Rev./Philadelphia)

Hispanófila. Univ. of North Carolina, Dept. of Romance Languages. Chapel Hill. (Hispanófila/Chapel Hill)

Historia. Pontificia Univ. Católica de Chile, Facultad de Historia, Geografia y Ciencia Política, Instituto de Historia. Santiago. (Historia/Santiago)

História & Perspectivas: Revista dos Cursos de Graduação e do Programa de Pós-Graduação em História. Editora da Univ. Federal de Uberlândia. Uberlândia, Brazil. (Hist. Perspect./Uberlândia)

Historia Agraria. Univ. Autónoma de Barcelona, Facultad de CC.EE., Depto. de Economía e Historia Económica, Seminario de Historia Agraria. Barcelona. (Hist. Agrar.)

Historia Antropología y Fuentes Orales.
Univ. de Barcelona, Depto. de Historia Contemporánea, Seminario de Historia Oral; Arxiu Històric de la Ciutat; Centro Investigaciones Etnológicas Ángel Ganivet. Barcelona. (Hist. Antropol. Fuentes Orales)

História Ciências Saúde: Manguinhos. Fundação Oswaldo Cruz, Casa de Oswaldo Cruz. Rio de Janeiro. (Hist. Ciênc. Saúde Manguinhos)

Historia Contemporánea. Univ. del País Vasco, Depto. de Historia Contemporánea. Bilbao, Spain. (Hist. Contemp.)

Historia Crítica. Univ. Nacional Autónoma de Honduras. Tegucigalpa. (Hist. Crít./Tegucigalpa)

História em Revista. Univ. Federal de Pelotas, Núcleo de Documentação Histórica, Instituto de Ciências Humanas. Pelotas, Brazil. (Hist. Rev./Pelotas)

Historia Mexicana. El Colegio de México, Centro de Estudios Históricos. México. (Hist. Mex./México)

História: Questões e Debates. Univ. Federal do Paraná, Programa de Pós-Graduação em História, Associação Paraense de História. Curitiba, Brazil. (Hist. Quest. Debates)

Historia y Cultura. Museo Nacional de Arqueología, Antropología e Historia. Lima. (Hist. Cult./Lima)

Historia y Grafía. Univ. Iberoamericana, Depto. de Historia. México. (Hist. Graf./México)

Historia y Sociedad. Univ. de Puerto Rico, Depto. de Historia. Río Piedras. (Hist. Soc./Río Piedras)

Historia y Sociedad. Univ. Nacional de Colombia—Sede Medellín, Facultad de Ciencias Humanas y Económicas, Depto. de Historia. Medellín, Colombia. (Hist. Soc./Medellín)

Histórica. Pontificia Univ. Católica del Perú, Depto. de Humanidades. Lima. (Histórica/Lima)

Historical Reflections. Univ. of Waterloo, Dept. of History. Waterloo, Canada. (Hist. Reflect./Waterloo)

Históricas: Boletín del Instituto de Investigaciones Históricas. UNAM, Instituto de Investigaciones Históricas. México. (Históricas/México)

History of Religions. Univ. of Chicago. Chicago, Ill. (Hist. Relig./Chicago)

History Workshop. Ruskin College. Oxford, England. (Hist. Workshop)

Horizontes. Pontificia Univ. Católica de Puerto Rico. Ponce. (Horizontes)

Horizontes Antropológicos. Univ. Federal do Rio Grande do Sul, Instituto de Filosofia e Ciências Humanas, Programa de Pós-Graduação em Antropologia Social. Porto Alegre, Brazil. (Horiz. Antropol.)

Huellas: Revista de la Universidad del Norte. Univ. del Norte. Barranquilla, Colombia. (Huellas/Barranquilla)

Human Biology. Wayne State Univ. Press. Detroit, Mich. (Hum. Biol.)

Humanitas: Anuario del Centro de Estudios Humanísticos. Centro de Estudios Humanísticos, Secretaría de Extensión y Cultura, Univ. Autónoma de Nuevo León. Monterrey, Mexico. (Humanitas/Monterrey)

Ibero-Amerikanisches Archiv: Zeitschrift für Sozialwissenschaften und Geschichte. Ibero-Amerikanisches Institut. Berlin. (Ibero-Am. Arch.)

Iberoamericana. Madrid. (Iberoamericana/Madrid)

Iberoamericana = Ibero Amerika Kenkyu. Univ. Sofia, Instituto Iberoameriano. Tokyo. (Iberoamericana/Tokyo)

Iconos: Revista Peruana de Conservación Arte y Arqueología. Yachay Wasi: Instituto Superior de Conservación, Restauración y Turismo. Lima. (Iconos/Lima)

Inter-American Music Review. Theodore Front Musical Literature, Inc. Van Nuys, Calif. (Inter-Am. Music Rev.)

The International History Review. Simon Fraser Univ., Dept. of History. Burnaby, British Columbia. (Int. Hist. Rev./Burnaby)

International Journal. Canadian Institute of International Affairs. Toronto, Canada. (Int. J./Toronto)

International Studies Quarterly. Blackwell Publishers. Malden, Mass.; Oxford, England. (Int. Stud. Q./Oxford)

Internationale Spectator. Nederlandsch Genootschap voor Internationale Zaken. The Hague. (Int. Spect./Hague)

Investigaciones Geográficas. Univ. de Alicante, Instituto Universitario de Geografía. Alicante, Spain. (Invest. Geogr./Alicante)

Investigaciones y Ensayos. Academia Nacional de Historia. Buenos Aires. (Invest. Ens.)

Islas. Univ. Central de Las Villas, Facultad de Ciencias Sociales y Humanísticas, Depto. de Letras. Santa Clara, Cuba. (Islas/Santa Clara)

Iztapalapa. Univ. Autónoma Metropolitana—Unidad Iztapalapa, División de Ciencias Sociales y Humanidades. México. (Iztapalapa/México)

Jahrbuch für Geschichte Lateinamerikas. Böhlau Verlag. Köln, Germany. (Jahrb. Gesch. Lat.am.)

Jahrbuch für Geschichte von Staat, Wirtschaft und Gesellschaft Lateinamerikas. Böhlau Verlag. Köln, Germany. (Jahrb. Gesch. Staat Wirtsch. Ges. Lat.am.)

Jamaica Journal. Institute of Jamaica. Kingston. (Jam. J.)

The Jamaican Historical Review. The Jamaican Historical Society. Kingston. (Jam. Hist. Rev.)

JILAS: Journal of Iberian and Latin American Studies. Assn. of Iberian and Latin American Studies of Australasia; La Trobe Univ., School of History. Bundoora, Australia. (JILAS/Bundoora)

Journal de la Société des américanistes. Paris. (J. Soc. am.)

Journal of Anthropological Research. Univ. of New Mexico. Albuquerque. (J. Anthropol. Res.)

The Journal of Caribbean History. Univ. of the West Indies Press; Univ. of the West Indies, Dept. of History. Mona, Jamaica. (J. Caribb. Hist.)

Journal of Church and State. Baylor Univ., J.M. Dawson Studies in Church and State. Waco, Tex. (J. Church State)

Journal of Family History. Sage Periodicals Press. Thousand Oaks, Calif. (J. Fam. Hist.)

Journal of Interamerican Studies and World Affairs. Univ. of Miami, School of Interamerican Studies. Coral Gables, Fla. (J. Interam. Stud. World Aff.)

The Journal of Interdisciplinary History. The MIT Press. Cambridge, Mass. (J. Interdiscip. Hist.)

Journal of Latin American Anthropology. American Anthropological Assn., Society of Latin American Anthropologists. Arlington, Va. (J. Lat. Am. Anthropol.)

Journal of Latin American Studies. Cambridge Univ. Press. Cambridge, England. (J. Lat. Am. Stud.)

The Journal of Mississippi History. Mississippi Historical Society; Mississippi Dept. of Archives and History. Jackson, Miss. (J. Miss. Hist.)

Journal of Social History. George Mason Univ. Press. Fairfax, Va. (J. Soc. Hist.)

Journal of the Bahamas Historical Society. Bahamas Historical Society. Nassau, Bahamas. (J. Bahamas Hist. Soc.)

Journal of the Early Republic. Society for Historians of the Early American Republic. Indianapolis, Ind. (J. Early Repub.)

Journal of the History of Sexuality. Univ. of Chicago Press. Chicago, Ill. (J. Hist. Sex.)

Journal of the Southwest. Univ. of Arizona, Southwest Center. Tucson. (J. Southwest)

Journal of Women's History. Indiana Univ. Press. Bloomington, Ind.; Johns Hopkins Univ. Press. Baltimore, Md. (J. Women's Hist.)

Latin American Indian Literatures. Geneva College, Dept. of Foreign Languages. Beaver Falls, Penn. (Lat. Am. Indian Lit.)

Latin American Indian Literatures Journal. Geneva College, Dept. of Foreign Languages. Beaver Falls, Penn. (Lat. Am. Indian Lit. J.)

Latin American Music Review (LAMR) = Revista de Música Latinoamericana. Univ. of Texas Press. Austin. (Lat. Am. Music Rev.)

Latin American Perspectives. Sage Publications, Inc. Thousand Oaks, Calif. (Lat. Am. Perspect.)

Latin American Research Review. Latin American Studies Assn.; Univ. of New Mexico, Latin American Institute. Albuquerque. (LARR)

Latin American Theatre Review. Univ. of Kansas, Center of Latin American Studies. Lawrence. (Lat. Am. Theatre Rev.)

Leituras: Revista da Biblioteca Nacional. Biblioteca Nacional. Lisboa. (Leituras/ Lisboa)

Literatura Mexicana. UNAM, Instituto de Investigaciones Filológicas, Centro de Estudios Literarios. México. (Lit. Mex.)

LOCUS: Revista de História. Univ. Federal de Juiz de Fora, Instituto de Ciências Humanas e de Letras, Depto. de História; NHR (Núcleo de História Regional); Arquivo Histórico. Juiz de Fora, Brazil. (LOCUS Rev. Hist.)

Luso-Brazilian Review. Univ. of Wisconsin Press. Madison. (Luso-Braz. Rev.)

Mapocho. Dirección de Bibliotecas, Archivos y Museos. Santiago, Chile. (Mapocho/ Santiago)

Mar Oceana: Revista del Humanismo Español e Iberoamericano. Univ. Francisco de Vitoria, Asociación López de Gómara. Madrid. (Mar Oceana)

Máscara/s: Revista de Pensamiento Político. Fundación de Relaciones Internacionales. Buenos Aires. (Máscara/s/Buenos Aires)

Memoria. Sociedad Ecuatoriana de Investigaciones Históricas y Geográficas. Quito. (Memoria/Quito)

Memoria Americana. Univ. de Buenos Aires, Facultad de Filosofía y Letras, Instituto de Ciencias Antropológicas. Buenos Aires. (Mem. Am.)

Memoria del Museo Nacional de Arte. Museo Nacional de Arte. México. (Mem. Mus. Nac. Arte)

Mesoamérica. Plumsock Mesoamerican Studies. South Woodstock, Vt.; Centro de Investigaciones Regionales de Mesoamérica. Antigua, Guatemala. (Mesoamérica/Antigua)

Metapolítica: Revista Trimestral de Teoría y Ciencia de la Política. Centro de Estudios de Política Comparada. México. (Metapolítica/México)

Mexican Studies/Estudios Mexicanos. Univ. of California Press. Berkeley. (Mex. Stud.)

Milenio: Revista de Artes y Ciencias. Univ. de Puerto Rico, Colegio Universitario Tecnológico de Bayamón. Bayamón. (Milenio/ Bayamón)

Military History of the West. Univ. of North Texas, Dept. of History; National Guard Assn. of Texas. Denton, Tex. (Mil. Hist. West)

MLN: Modern Language Notes. Johns Hopkins Univ. Press. Baltimore, Md. (MLN/ Baltimore)

Modern Language Quarterly. University of Washington. Seattle. (Mod. Lang. Q/ Seattle)

Montalbán. Univ. Católica Andrés Bello, Facultad de Humanidades y Educación, Institutos Humanísticos de Investigación. Caracas. (Montalbán/Caracas)

Mora: Revista del Area Interdisciplinaria de

Estudios de la Mujer. Univ. de Buenos Aires, Facultad de Filosofía y Letras. Buenos Aires. (Mora/Buenos Aires)

New Mexico Historical Review. Univ. of New Mexico; Historical Society of New Mexico. Albuquerque. (N.M. Hist. Rev.)

Nomadías. Univ. de Chile, Facultad de Filosofía y Humanidades, Programa Género y Cultura en América Latina. Santiago. (Nomadías/Santiago)

Nombres. Univ. Nacional de Córdoba, Facultad de Filosofía y Humanidades, Centro de Investigaciones, Area de Filosofía. Córdoba, Argentina. (Nombres/Córdoba)

Notes. Music Library Assn., Inc. Middleton, Wisc. (Notes/Middleton)

Novahispania. UNAM, Instituto de Investigaciones Filológicas. México. (Novahispania/México)

Novos Estudos CEBRAP. Centro Brasileiro de Análise e Planejamento. São Paulo. (Novos Estud. CEBRAP)

Nuestra Historia: Revista de Historia de Occidente. Fundación Nuestra Historia. Buenos Aires. (Nuestra Hist./Buenos Aires)

Nueva Sociedad. Fundación Friedrich Ebert. Caracas. (Nueva Soc.)

NWIG: New West Indian Guide/Nieuwe West Indische Gids. Royal Institute of Linguistics and Anthropology, KITLV Press. Leiden, The Netherlands. (NWIG)

Opción: Revista de Ciencias Humanas y Sociales. Univ. de Zulia, Facultad Experimental de Ciencias, Depto. de Ciencias Humanas. Maracaibo, Venezuela. (Opción/Maracaibo)

Osiris. History of Science Society; Univ. of Chicago Press. Chicago, Ill. (Osiris/Chicago)

Pagara. Société des amis des archives et de histoire de la Guyane. Cayenne, French Guiana. (Pagara/Cayenne)

Paradigma. Univ. Pedagógica Nacional Francisco Morazán, Dirección de Investigación. Tegucigalpa. (Paradigma/Tegucigalpa)

Paradigmas: Revista de Filosofía. Univ. Estadual de Londrina, Centro de Estudos Filosóficos; Editora da Univ. Estadual de Londrina. Londrina, Brazil. (Paradigmas/Londrina)

Paramillo. Univ. Católica de Táchira, Centro de Estudios Interdisciplinarios. San Cristóbal, Venezuela. (Paramillo/San Cristóbal)

Paraninfo. Instituto de Ciencias del Hombre Rafael Heliodoro Valle. Tegucigalpa. (Paraninfo/Tegucigalpa)

Past & Present. Oxford Univ. Press. Oxford, England; New York; Past and Present Society. Oxford, England. (Past Present)

Pauta: Cuadernos de Teoría y Crítica Musical. Consejo Nacional para la Cultura y las Artes, Dirección General de Publicaciones, Instituto Nacional de Bellas Artes. México. (Pauta/México)

Pesquisas História. Instituto Anchietano de Pesquisas. São Leopoldo, Brazil. (Pesqui. Hist.)

Plantation Society in the Americas. Univ. of New Orleans, Dept. of History. New Orleans, La. (Plant. Soc. Am.)

Política Comparada: Revista Brasilense de Políticas Comparadas. Arko Advice Editorial. Brasília. (Polít. Comp.)

População e Família. Univ. de São Paulo, Faculdade de Filosofia, Letras e Ciências Humanas, Centro de Estudos de Demografia Histórica da América Latina, Humanitas Publicações. São Paulo. (Popul. Fam./São Paulo)

Popular Music. Cambridge Univ. Press. England. (Pop. Music/Cambridge)

Popular Music and Society. Taylor & Francis Group, Routledge Press. London; New York. (Pop. Music Soc.)

Population. Institut national d'études démographiques. Paris. (Population/Paris)

Pós-História. Univ. Estadual Paulista, Faculdade de Ciências e Letras, Programa de Pós-Graduação em Historia. São Paulo. (Pós-Hist.)

Prisma. Univ. Católica del Uruguay. Montevideo. (Prisma/Montevideo)

Prismas: Revista de Historia Intelectual. Univ. Nacional de Quilmes, Centro de Estudios e Investigaciones, Programa de Historia Intelectual. Buenos Aires. (Prismas/Buenos Aires)

Problemas del Desarrollo: Revista Latinoamericana de Economía. UNAM, Instituto de Investigaciones Económicas. México. (Probl. Desarro.)

Procesos. Corporación Editora Nacional. Quito. (Procesos/Quito)

Quantum. Univ. de la República, Facultad de Ciencias Económicas y de Administración. Montevideo. (Quantum/Montevideo)

Quatrivium. Univ. Autónoma del Estado de México, Centro de Investigación en Cien-

cias Sociales y Humanidades. México.
(Quatrivium/México)

Quinto Sol. Univ. Nacional de La Pampa,
Facultad de Ciencias Humanas, Instituto
de Estudios Socio-Históricos. Santa Rosa,
Argentina. (Quinto Sol/Santa Rosa)

Quipu. Sociedad Latinoamericana de Historia
de las Ciencias y la Tecnología. México.
(Quipu/México)

Radical History Review. Duke Univ. Press.
Durham, N.C. (Radic. Hist. Rev.)

Realidad Económica. Instituto Argentino
para el Desarrollo Económico. Buenos
Aires. (Real. Econ./Buenos Aires)

Realidad: Revista de Ciencias Sociales y Humanidades. Univ. Centroamericana José
Simeón Cañas. San Salvador. (Realidad/
San Salvador)

Reflexão. Instituto de Filosofia, Pontifícia
Univ. Católica de Campinas. Campinas,
Brazil. (Reflexão/Campinas)

**Región y Sociedad: Revista de El Colegio de
Sonora.** El Colegio de Sonora. Hermosillo,
Mexico. (Reg. Soc./Hermosillo)

Relaciones. El Colegio de Michoacán.
Zamora, Mexico. (Relaciones/Zamora)

**Relaciones de la Sociedad Argentina de
Antropología.** Buenos Aires. (Relac. Soc.
Argent. Antropol.)

Religión y Cultura. Padres Agustinos.
Madrid. (Relig. Cult.)

Res Gesta. Pontificia Univ. Católica Argentina, Facultad de Derecho y Ciencias Sociales del Rosario, Instituto de Historia.
Rosario, Argentina. (Res Gesta)

Research in Economic Anthropology. JAI
Press. Greenwich, Conn. (Res. Econ.
Anthropol.)

Revista Andina. Centro Bartolomé de las
Casas. Cuzco, Peru. (Rev. Andin.)

Revista Bimestre Cubana. Sociedad
Económica de Amigos del País. La Habana. (Rev. Bimest. Cuba.)

Revista Brasileira de Estudos de População.
Associação Brasileira de Estudos Populacionais. São Paulo. (Rev. Bras. Estud.
Popul.)

Revista Brasileira de Filosofia. Instituto
Brasileiro de Filosofia. São Paulo. (Rev.
Bras. Filos.)

Revista Brasileira de História. Associação
Nacional de História. São Paulo. (Rev.
Bras. Hist./São Paulo)

Revista Canadiense de Estudios Hispánicos.
Asociación Canadiense de Hispanistas;

Univ. of Alberta, Dept. of Modern Languages and Cultural Studies. Edmonton,
Canada. (Rev. Can. Estud. Hisp.)

Revista Catarinense de História. Univ. Federal de Santa Catarina, Centro de Filosofia
e Ciências Humanas, Depto. de História.
Florianópolis, Brazil. (Rev. Catarin. Hist.)

Revista Chilena de Historia y Geografía. Sociedad Chilena de Historia y Geografía.
Santiago. (Rev. Chil. Hist. Geogr.)

Revista Colombiana de Antropología. Ministerio de Educación Nacional, Instituto
Colombiano de Antropología. Bogotá.
(Rev. Colomb. Antropol.)

**Revista Complutense de Historia de
América.** Univ. Complutense de Madrid,
Facultad de Geografía e Historia, Depto.
de Historia de América I. Madrid. (Rev.
Complut. Hist. Am.)

Revista da APG. Pontifícia Univ. Católica de
São Paulo, Associação de Pós-Graduados.
São Paulo. (Rev. APG)

Revista da SBPH. Sociedade Brasileira de
Pesquisa Histórica. Curitiba, Brazil. (Rev.
SBPH)

Revista de Antropologia. Univ. de São Paulo,
Faculdade de Filosofia, Letras e Ciências
Humanas, Depto. de Antropologia. São
Paulo. (Rev. Antropol./São Paulo)

Revista de Arqueologia. Sociedade de Arqueologia Brasileira. São Paulo. (Rev.
Arqueol./São Paulo)

Revista de Arqueología Americana. Instituto
Panamericano de Geografía e Historia.
México. (Rev. Arqueol. Am./México)

Revista de Ciências Históricas. Univ. Portucalense. Porto, Portugal. (Rev. Ciênc. Hist.)

Revista de Ciencias Sociales. Editorial Univ.
de Costa Rica. San José. (Rev. Cienc.
Soc./San José)

Revista de Ciencias Sociales. Univ. de Puerto
Rico, Recinto de Río Piedras, Facultad de
Ciencias Sociales, Centro de Investigaciones Sociales. Río Piedras. (Rev. Cienc.
Soc./Río Piedras)

Revista de Crítica Literaria Latinoamericana.
Latinoamericana Editores. Lima. (Rev.
Crít. Lit. Latinoam.)

**Revista de Economia Política = Brazilian
Journal of Political Economy.** Centro de
Economia Política. São Paulo. (Rev. Econ.
Polít.)

Revista de Filosofía. Univ. Iberoamericana,
Depto. de Filosofía. México. (Rev. Filos./
México)

Revista de Filosofía de la Universidad de Costa Rica. Editorial de la Univ. de Costa Rica. San José. (Rev. Filos. Univ. Costa Rica)

Revista de Filosofía Latinoamericano y Ciencias Sociales. Asociación de Filosofía Latinoamericana y Ciencias Sociales. Buenos Aires. (Rev. Filos. Latinoam. Cienc. Soc.)

Revista de Historia. Depto. de Ciencias Históricas y Sociales, Univ. de Concepción, Chile. (Rev. Hist./Concepción)

Revista de Historia. Univ. Centroamericana, Instituto de Historia de Nicaragua y Centroamérica. Managua. (Rev. Hist./Managua)

Revista de Historia. Univ. Nacional, Escuela de Historia. Heredia, Costa Rica; Univ. de Costa Rica, Centro de Investigaciones Históricas de América Central. San José. (Rev. Hist./Heredia)

Revista de História. Univ. de São Paulo, Faculdade de Filosofia, Letras e Ciências Humanas, Depto. de História. São Paulo. (Rev. Hist./São Paulo)

Revista de Historia Americana y Argentina. Univ. Nacional de Cuyo, Instituto de Historia. Mendoza, Argentina. (Rev. Hist. Am. Argent.)

Revista de Historia de América. Instituto Panamericano de Geografía e Historia. Comisión de Historia. México. (Rev. Hist. Am./México)

Revista de Historia del Derecho Ricardo Levene. Univ. de Buenos Aires, Facultad de Derecho y Ciencias Sociales; Instituto de Investigaciones Jurídicas y Sociales Ambrosio L. Gioja. Buenos Aires. (Rev. Hist. Derecho Ricardo Levene)

Revista de Historia Naval. Ministerio de Defensa, Armada Española, Instituto de Historia y Cultura Naval. Madrid. (Rev. Hist. Nav.)

Revista de História Regional. Univ. Estadual de Ponta Grossa, Depto. de História. Ponta Grossa, Brazil. (Rev. Hist. Reg.)

Revista de Humanidades: Tecnológico de Monterrey. Depto. de Humanidades, División de Ciencias y Humanidades, Instituto Tecnológico y de Estudios Superiores de Monterrey. Monterrey, Mexico. (Rev. Humanid./Monterrey)

Revista de Indias. Consejo Superior de Investigaciones Científicas, Instituto de Historia, Depto. de Historia de América. Madrid. (Rev. Indias)

Revista de la Biblioteca Nacional José Martí. Biblioteca Nacional José Martí. La Habana. (Rev. Bibl. Nac. José Martí)

Revista de la Inquisición. Univ. Complutense, Instituto de Historia de la Inquisición. Madrid. (Rev. Inquis.)

Revista de la Junta de Estudios Históricos de Mendoza. Mendoza, Argentina. (Rev. Junta Estud. Hist. Mendoza)

Revista de la Junta Provincial de Estudios Históricos de Santa Fe. Santa Fe, Argentina. (Rev. Junta Prov. Estud. Hist. Santa Fe)

Revista de la Universidad. Univ. Nacional de La Plata. La Plata, Argentina. (Rev. Univ./La Plata)

Revista de la Universidad Nacional de Río Cuarto. Univ. Nacional de Río Cuarto. Río Cuarto, Argentina. (Rev. Univ. Nac. Río Cuarto)

Revista de Occidente. Fundación José Ortega y Gasset. Madrid. (Rev. Occident.)

Revista de Teatro. Sociedade Brasileira de Autores Teatrais. Rio de Janeiro. (Rev. Teatro/Rio de Janeiro)

Revista del Archivo General de la Nación. Ministerio de Justicia, Instituto Nacional de Cultura. Lima. (Rev. Arch. Gen. Nac./Lima)

Revista del Archivo Regional del Cusco. Cuzco, Peru. (Rev. Arch. Reg. Cusco)

Revista del Museo Nacional de Etnografía y Folklore. MUSEF Editores. La Paz. (Rev. Mus. Nac. Etnogr. Folk.)

Revista do Instituto Histórico e Geográfico Brasileiro. Instituto Histórico e Geográfico Brasileiro. Rio de Janeiro. (Rev. Inst. Hist. Geogr. Bras.)

Revista do Patrimônio Histórico e Artístico Nacional. Ministério da Cultura, Secretaria de Patrimônio, Museus e Artes Plásticas, Instituto do Patrimônio, Histórico e Artístico Nacional. Rio de Janeiro. (Rev. Patrim. Hist. Artíst. Nac.)

Revista Española de Antropología Americana. Univ. Complutense de Madrid, Facultad de Geografía e Historia, Depto. de Historia de América II (Antropología de América). Madrid. (Rev. Esp. Antropol. Am.)

Revista Europea de Estudios Latinoamericanos y del Caribe = European Review of Latin American and Caribbean Studies. Center for Latin American Research and Documentation = Centro de Estudios y

Documentación Latinoamericanos. Amsterdam. (Rev. Eur. Estud. Latinoam. Caribe)

Revista Iberoamericana. Instituto Internacional de Literatura Iberoamericana; Univ. de Pittsburgh. Pittsburgh, Penn. (Rev. Iberoam.)

Revista Instituto de Historia Marítima. Instituto de Historia Marítima. Guayaquil, Ecuador. (Rev. Inst. Hist. Marít.)

Revista Interamericana de Bibliografía = Review of Inter-American Bibliography. Organization of American States (OAS). Washington. (Rev. Interam. Bibliogr.)

Revista Interamericana de Planificación. Sociedad Interamericana de Planificación. Bogotá. (Rev. Interam. Planif.)

Revista Javeriana. Provincia Colombiana de la Compañía de Jesús. Bogotá. (Rev. Javer./Bogotá)

Revista Latinoamericana de Filosofía. Centro de Investigaciones Filosóficas. Buenos Aires. (Rev. Latinoam. Filos.)

Revista Mexicana de Ciencias Políticas y Sociales. UNAM, Facultad de Ciencias Políticas y Sociales. México. (Rev. Mex. Cienc. Polít. Soc.)

Revista Mexicana del Caribe. Chetumal, Mexico. (Rev. Mex. Caribe)

Revista Música. Univ. de São Paulo, Depto. de Música. São Paulo. (Rev. Música)

Revista Musical Chilena. Univ. de Chile, Facultad de Artes, Sección de Musicología. Santiago. (Rev. Music. Chil.)

Revista Musical de Venezuela. Consejo Nacional de la Cultura, Fundación Emilio Sojo. Caracas. (Rev. Music. Venez.)

Revista Paraguaya de Sociología. Centro Paraguayo de Estudios Sociológicos. Asunción. (Rev. Parag. Sociol.)

Revista/Review Interamericana. Univ. Interamericana de Puerto Rico/Inter-American Univ. of Puerto Rico. San Germán. (Rev. Interam.)

Revista Uruguaya de Ciencia Política. Univ. de la República, Facultad de Ciencias Sociales, Instituto de Ciencia Política; Fundación de Cultura Universitaria. Montevideo. (Rev. Urug. Cienc. Polít.)

Revista USP. Univ. de São Paulo, Coordenadoria de Comunicação Social. São Paulo. (Rev. USP/São Paulo)

Revue de la Société française d'histoire des hôpitaux. Paris. (Rev. Soc. fr. hist. hôp.)

Revue de l'Agenais et des anciennes provinces du sudouest. Société des sciences, lettres et arts d'Agen. Agen, France. (Rev. Agen.)

Revue française d'histoire d'Outre-mer. Société française d'histoire d'Outre-mer. Paris. (Rev. fr. hist. Outre-mer)

Revue historique. Presses Univ. de France. Paris. (Rev. hist./Paris)

Romance Philology. Univ. of California Press. Berkeley and Los Angeles, Calif. (Roman. Philol.)

Sarance. Instituto Otavaleño de Antropología. Otavalo, Ecuador. (Sarance/Otavalo)

SECOLAS Annals: Journal of the Southeastern Council on Latin American Studies. Southeastern Council on Latin American Studies; Georgia Southern Univ. Statesboro, Ga. (SECOLAS Ann.)

Secuencia: Revista de Historia y Ciencias Sociales. Instituto de Investigaciones Dr. José María Luis Mora. México. (Secuencia/México)

Semata. Univ. de Santiago de Compostela, Servicio de Publicacións e Intercambio Científico. Santiago de Compostela, Spain. (Semata)

Silabario. Univ. Nacional de Córdoba, Facultad de Filosofia y Humanidades, Centro de Investigaciones. Córdoba, Argentina. (Silabario/Córdoba)

Síntese: Revista de Filosofia. Companhia de Jesus, Centro de Estudos Superiores, Faculdade de Filosofia. Belo Horizonte, Brazil. (Síntese/Belo Horizonte)

Slavery and Abolition. Frank Cass & Co. Ltd. London. (Slavery Abolit.)

Social Compass: Revue Internationale de Sociologie de la Religion (International Review of Sociology of Religion. Sage. London. (Soc. Compass)

Socialismo y Participación. Centro de Estudios para el Desarrollo y Participación. Lima. (Social. Particip.)

Sociétés, espaces, temps. Dakar, Senegal. (Soc. espaces temps)

Sociológica. Univ. Autónoma Metropolitana—Unidad Azcapotzalco, División de Ciencias Sociales y Humanidades, Depto. de Sociología. México. (Sociológica/México)

Sólo Historia. Instituto Nacional de Estudios Históricos de la Revolución Mexicana, Secretaría de Gobernación. México. (Sólo Hist.)

Source. Literary Division of the American Translators Assn. Alexandria, Va. (Source/Alexandria)

Stromata. Univ. del Salvador, Filosofía y Teología. San Miguel, Argentina. (Stromata/San Miguel)

Studia Histórica: Historia Contemporánea. Ediciones Univ. de Salamanca. Salamanca, Spain. (Stud. Hist. Hist. Contemp.)

Studia Zamorensia. Ediciones Univ. de Salamanca. Salamanca, Spain. (Stud. Zamorensia)

Susana y Los Viejos. Editorial SIAL (Sociedad Internacional de Amigos de la Literatura); Univ. Autónoma de Madrid. Madrid. (Susana Viejos)

Taller: Revista de Sociedad, Cultura y Política. Asociación de Estudios de Cultura y Sociedad. Buenos Aires. (Taller/Buenos Aires)

Temas Americanistas. Univ. de Sevilla, Servicio de Publicaciones. Sevilla, Spain. (Temas Am.)

Temas: Cultura, Ideología, Sociedad. Instituto Cubano del Libro. La Habana; Univ. of New Mexico, Latin American Institute, Cuban Project. Albuquerque. (Temas/Habana)

Tempo. Univ. Federal Fluminense, Depto. de História. Rio de Janeiro. (Tempo/Rio de Janeiro)

Tempo Brasileiro. Edições Tempo Brasileiro Ltda. Rio de Janeiro. (Tempo Bras.)

Textos de História. Univ. de Brasília, Instituto de Ciências Humanas, Depto. de História, Programa de Pós-Graduação em História. Brasília. (Textos Hist.)

Tiempo y Espacio. Univ. Pedagógica Experimental Libertador, Instituto Pedagógico de Caracas, Depto. de Geografía e Historia, Centro de Investigaciones Históricas Mario Briceño Iragorry. Caracas. (Tiempo Espacio/Caracas)

Tiempos de América. Univ. Jaume I—

Campus de Borriol, Centros de Investigación de América Latina. Castellón, Spain. (Tiempos Am./Castellón)

Tierra Firme. Editorial Tierra Firme. Caracas. (Tierra Firme/Caracas)

Tlalocan. UNAM, Instituto de Investigaciones Históricas; Instituto de Investigaciones Antropológicas. México. (Tlalocan/México)

Todo es Historia. Buenos Aires. (Todo es Hist.)

TRACE. Centre d'études mexicaines et centraméricaines. México. (TRACE/México)

Translation and Literature. Edinburgh Univ. Press. Edinburgh, Scotland. (Trans. Lit./Edinburgh)

El Trimestre Económico. Fondo de Cultura Económica. México. (Trimest. Econ.)

Universitas Philosophica. Pontificia Univ. Javeriana, Facultad de Filosofía. Bogotá. (Univ. Philos.)

Universum. Univ. de Talca. Talca, Chile. (Universum/Talca)

Varia História. Univ. Federal de Minas Gerais, Faculdade de Filosofia e Ciencias Humanas, Depto. de História. Belo Horizonte, Brazil. (Varia Hist.)

Vuelta. México. (Vuelta/México)

The William and Mary Quarterly. College of William and Mary. Williamsburg, Va. (William Mary Q.)

World Archaeology. Routledge & Kegan Paul. London. (World Archaeol.)

World Policy Journal. World Policy Institute. New York. (World Policy J.)

World Politics. Johns Hopkins Univ. Press. Baltimore, Md. (World Polit.)

Yachay. Univ. Católica Boliviana, Deptos. de Filosofía y Letras y Ciencias Religiosas. Cochabamba, Bolivia. (Yachay/Cochabamba)

Yaxkin. Instituto Hondureño de Antropología e Historia. Tegucigalpa. (Yaxkin/Tegucigalpa)

ABBREVIATION LIST OF
JOURNALS INDEXED

For journal titles listed by full title, see *Title List of Journals Indexed*, p. 769

Acervo/Rio de Janeiro. Acervo. Arquivo Nacional. Rio de Janeiro.

Actual/Mérida. Actual. Univ. de Los Andes, Dirección General de Cultura y Extensión. Mérida, Venezuela.

Afro-Asia/Salvador. Afro-Asia. Univ. Federal da Bahia, Faculdade de Filosofia e Ciências Humanas, Centro de Estudos Afro-Orientais. Salvador, Brazil.

Aletria/Belo Horizonte. Aletria: Revista de Estudos de Literatura. Univ. Federal de Minas Gerais. Centro de Estudos Literários. Belo Horizonte, Brazil.

ALFA/Rosario. A ALFA A: Europa-Latinoamérica, cooperación en estudios sociales aplicados. Beatriz Viterbo Editora: Red Interuniversitaria Europea-Latino-americana para los Estudios Sociales Aplicados. Rosario, Argentina.

Allpanchis/Cuzco. Allpanchis. Instituto de Pastoral Andina. Cuzco, Peru.

Am. Anthropol. American Anthropologist. American Anthropological Assn. Washington.

Am. Hist. Rev. The American Historical Review. Indiana Univ. at Bloomington. Bloomington, Ind.

Am. J. Sociol. American Journal of Sociology. Univ. of Chicago Press. Chicago, Ill.

Am. Lat. Hist. Econ. Bol. Fuentes. América Latina en la Historia Económica: Boletín de Fuentes. Instituto de Investigaciones Dr. José Luis Mora, Proyecto de Historia Económica. México.

Am. Negra. América Negra. Expedición Humana, Instituto de Genética Humana, Facultad de Medecina, Pontificia Univ. Javeriana. Bogotá.

Am. Univ. Law Rev. The American University Law Review. American Univ., Washington College of Law. Washington.

América/Santa Fe. América. Centro de Estudios Hispanoamericanos. Santa Fe, Argentina.

Americas/Washington. The Americas: A Quarterly Review of Inter-American Cultural History. Catholic Univ. of America, Academy of American Franciscan History; Catholic Univ. of America Press. Washington.

An. Inst. Hist. Mil. Argent. Anales del Instituto de Historia Militar Argentina. Instituto de Historia Militar Argentina. Buenos Aires.

An. Inst. Invest. Estét. Anales del Instituto de Investigaciones Estéticas. UNAM, Instituto de Investigaciones Estéticas. México.

An. Inst. Patagon. Ser. Cienc. Hum. Anales del Instituto de la Patagonia: Serie Ciencias Humanas. Univ. de Magallanes, Instituto de la Patagonia. Punta Arenas, Chile.

An. Lit./Honolulu. Anales Literarios. Matías and Yara Montes Foundation. Honolulu.

An. Mus. Hist. Nac. Anais do Museu Histórico Nacional. Museu Histórico Nacional, Instituto do Patrimônio Histórico e Artístico

Nacional, Ministério da Cultura. Rio de Janeiro.

An. Mus. Paul. Anais do Museu Paulista: História e Cultura Material. Museu Paulista. São Paulo.

Anais/São Paulo. Anais da ... Reunião. Sociedade Brasileira de Pesquisa Histórica. São Paulo.

Anál. Polít./Bogotá. Análisis Político. Univ. Nacional de Colombia, Instituto de Estudios Políticos y Relaciones Internacionales. Bogotá.

Anc. Mesoam. Ancient Mesoamerica. Cambridge Univ. Press. Cambridge, England; New York.

ANDES Antropol. Hist. ANDES: Antropología e Historia. Univ. Nacional de Salta, Facultad de Humanidades, Centro Promocional de las Investigaciones en Historia y Antropología. Salta, Argentina.

Annu. Hist. Concil./Paderborn. Annuarium Historiae Conciliorum. Ferdinand Schoningh. Paderborn, Germany.

Anos 90. Anos 90: Revista do Programa de Pós-Graduação em História. Univ. Federal do Rio Grande do Sul, Programa de Pós-Graduação em História. Porto Alegre, Brazil.

Anthropol. Dep. Cienc. Soc. Anthropologica del Departamento de Ciencias Sociales. Pontificia Univ. Católica del Perú, Depto. de Ciencias Sociales. Lima.

Anthropol. Q. Anthropological Quarterly. Catholic Univ. Press of America. Washington.

Antiquity/Cambridge. Antiquity. Antiquity Publications Ltd. Cambridge, England.

Antropológica/Caracas. Antropológica. Fundación La Salle, Instituto Caribe de Antropología y Sociología. Caracas.

Anu. Cent. Estud. Gallegos. Anuario del Centro de Estudios Gallegos. Univ. de la República, Facultad de Humanidades y Ciencias de la Educación, Centro de Estudios Gallegos. Montevideo.

Anu. Colomb. Hist. Soc. Cult. Anuario Colombiano de Historia Social y de la Cultura. Depto. de Historia, Facultad de Ciencias Humanas, Univ. Nacional de Colombia. Bogotá.

Anu. Espacios Urbanos. Anuario de Espacios Urbanos. Univ. Autónoma Metropolitana—Unidad Azcapotzalco. División de Ciencias y Artes para el Diseño, Depto. de Evaluación del Diseño en el Tiempo. México.

Anu. Estud. Am. Anuario de Estudios Americanos. Consejo Superior de Investigaciones Científicas, Escuela de Estudios Hispano-Americanos. Sevilla, Spain.

Anu. Estud. Centroam. Anuario de Estudios Centroamericanos. Univ. de Costa Rica. San José.

Anu. Estud. Indíg. Anuario de Estudios Indígenas. Univ. Autónoma de Chiapas, Instituto de Estudios Indígenas. San Cristóbal de las Casas, Mexico.

Anu. Estud. Soc. Anuario ... Estudios Sociales. El Colegio de Puebla. México.

Anu. Hist. Iglesia Chile. Anuario de la Historia de la Iglesia en Chile. Arzobispado de Santiago, Seminario Pontificio Mayor; Sociedad de Historia de la Iglesia en Chile. Santiago.

Anu. IEHS. Anuario IEHS. Univ. Nacional del Centro de la Provincia de Buenos Aires, Facultad de Ciencias Humanas, Instituto de Estudios Histórico-Sociales. Tandil, Argentina.

Anu. Mariateg. Anuario Mariateguiano. Empresa Editora Amauta. Lima.

Anuario/Sucre. Anuario. Archivo y Biblioteca Nacionales de Bolivia. Sucre, Bolivia.

Apunt. Filos. Apuntes Filosóficos. Univ. Central de Venezuela, Escuela de Filosofía. Caracas.

Apunt. Invest. CECYP. Apuntes de Investigación del CECYP. Centro de Estudios en Cultura y Política, Fundación del Sur. Buenos Aires.

Arbor/Madrid. Arbor. Consejo Superior de Investigaciones Científicas. Madrid.

Arch. Hist. Soc. Iesu. Archivum Historicum Societatis Iesu. Institutum Historicum Societatis Iesu. Rome.

Arch. Ibero-Am. Archivo Ibero-Americano: Revista Franciscana de Estudios Históricos. Franciscanos Españoles. Madrid.

Arch. sci. soc. relig. Archives de sciences sociales des religions. Presses universitaires de France. Paris.

Archaeol. Anthropol. Archaeology and Anthropology. Walter Roth Museum of Anthropology, Ministry of Culture. Georgetown, Guyana.

Archaeology/New York. Archaeology. Archaeological Institute of America. New York.

Arqueol. Mex. Arqueología Mexicana. Instituto Nacional de Antropología e Historia; Editorial Raíces. México.

ARTEunesp. ARTEunesp. Univ. Estadual Paulista. São Paulo.

Asclepio/Madrid. Asclepio: Revista de Historia de la Medicina y de la Ciencia. Consejo Superior de Investigaciones Científicas, Instituto de Historia. Madrid.

Atenea/Concepción. Atenea. Univ. de Concepción. Concepción, Chile.

Atti Memorie Ateneo Treviso. Atti e Memorie dell'Ateneo di Treviso. L'Ateneo. Treviso, Italy.

Auriga/Querétaro. Auriga: Revista de Filosofía, Antropología e Historia. Univ. Autónoma de Querétaro, Facultad de Filosofía. Querétaro, Mexico.

Bahamas J. Sci. Bahamas: Journal of Science. Media Enterprises Ltd. Nassau, The Bahamas.

Biography/Honolulu. Biography. Univ. Press of Hawaii for the Biographical Research Center. Honolulu.

Bol. Acad. Nac. Hist./Caracas. Boletín de la Academia Nacional de la Historia. Academia Nacional de la Historia. Caracas.

Bol. Acad. Puertorriq. Hist. Boletín de la Academia Puertorriqueña de la Historia.

Academia Puertorriqueña de la Historia. San Juan.

Bol. Am./Barcelona. Boletín Americanista. Univ. de Barcelona. Barcelona.

Bol. Antropol. Am. Boletín de Antropología Americana. Instituto Panamericano de Geografía e Historia. México.

Bol. Antropol./Mérida. Boletín Antropológico. Univ. de los Andes, Facultad de Humanidades y Educación, Centro de Investigaciones Etnológicas y Museo Arqueológico Gonzalo Rincón Gutiérrez. Mérida, Venezuela.

Bol. Arqueol./Bogotá. Boletín de Arqueología. Fundación de Investigaciones Arqueológicas Nacionales, Banco de la República. Bogotá.

Bol. Arqueol. PUCP. Boletín de Arqueología PUCP. Pontificia Univ. Católica del Perú, Depto. de Humanidades, Sección de Arqueología. Lima.

Bol. Bibl. Artiguista. Boletín de la Biblioteca Artiguista. Círculo Militar General Artigas. Montevideo.

Bol. Cult. Bibliogr. Boletín Cultural y Bibliográfico. Banco de la República, Biblioteca Luis-Angel Arango. Bogotá.

Bol. Hist. Antig. Boletín de Historia y Antigüedades. Academia Colombiana de Historia. Bogotá.

Bol. Hist. Ejérc. Boletín Histórico del Ejército. República Oriental del Uruguay, Comando General del Ejército, Estado Mayor del Ejército, Depto. de Estudios Históricos. Montevideo.

Bol. Inst. Riva-Agüero. Boletín del Instituto Riva-Agüero: BIRA. Pontificia Univ. Católica del Perú, Instituto Riva-Agüero. Lima.

Bol. Lima. Boletín de Lima: Revista Cultural Científica. Asociación Cultural Boletín de Lima A.C. Lima.

Bol. Nicar. Bibliogr. Doc. Boletín Nicaragüense de Bibliografía y Documentación. Banco Central de Nicaragua, Biblioteca Dr. Roberto Incer Barquero. Managua.

Boletín/México. Boletín del Fideicomiso Archivos Plutarco Elías Calles y Fernando Torreblanca. Fideicomiso Archivos Plutarco Elías Calles y Fernando Torreblanca. México.

Bull. Cent. hist. atl. Bulletin du Centre d'histoire des espaces atlantiques. Talence-Cedex, France.

Bull. hisp./Bordeaux. Bulletin hispanique. Éditions Bière. Bordeaux, France.

Bull. Inst. fr. étud. andin. Bulletin de l'Institut français d'études andines. Lima.

Bull. Lat. Am. Res. Bulletin of Latin American Research. Blackwell Publishers. Oxford, England; Malden, Mass.

Bull. Soc. hist. Guadeloupe. Bulletin de la Société d'histoire de la Guadeloupe. Archives départamentales avec le concours du Conseil général de la Guadeloupe. Basse-Terre, Guadeloupe.

Bulletin/Geneva. Bulletin. Société suisse des américanistes = Schweizerische Amerikanisten Gesellschaft; Musée et institut d'éthnographie. Geneva.

Cad. Antropol. Imagem. Cadernos de Antropologia e Imagem. Univ. do Estado do Rio de Janeiro, Programa de Pós-Graduação em Ciências Sociais, Núcleo de Antropologia e Imagem. Rio de Janeiro.

Cad. Estud. Sociais. Cadernos de Estudos Sociais. Fundação Joaquim Nabuco, Instituto de Pesquisas Sociais. Recife, Brazil.

Cad. Filos. Ciênc. Hum. Caderno de Filosofia e Ciências Humanas. Depto. de Filosofia e Ciências Humanas, Faculdade de Ciências Humanas e Letras, Centro Universitário Newton Paiva. Belo Horizonte, Brazil.

Cad. Hist. Soc. Cadernos de História Social. Campinas, Brazil.

Cad. ISP. Cadernos do ISP. Univ. Federal de Pelotas, Instituto de Sociologia e Política. Pelotas, Brazil.

Cah. Am. lat. Cahiers des Amériques latines. Univ. de la Sorbonne nouvelle—Paris III, Institut des haute études de l'Amérique latine. Paris.

Cah. Outre-Mer. Les Cahiers d'Outre-Mer. Faculté des lettres de Bordeaux, Institut de géographie; Institut de la France d'Outre-Mer; Société de géographie de Bordeaux. Bordeaux, France.

Cah. patrim. Les cahiers du patrimoine. Conseil régional de la Martinique, Bureau du patrimoine. Fort-de-France, Martinique.

Caleidoscopio/Aguascalientes. Caleidoscopio. Univ. Autónoma de Aguascalientes, Centro de Artes y Humanidades. Aguascalientes, Mexico.

Calif. Hist. California History. California Historical Society. San Francisco, Calif.

Can. J. Lat. Am. Caribb. Stud. Canadian Journal of Latin American and Caribbean Studies = Revue canadienne des études latino-américaines et caraïbes. Univ. of Calgary Press. Calgary, Canada.

Caribb. Q./Mona. Caribbean Quarterly: CQ. Univ. of the West Indies, Vice Chancellery, Cultural Studies Initiative. Mona, Jamaica.

Caribb. Stud. Caribbean Studies. Univ. of Puerto Rico, Institute of Caribbean Studies. Río Piedras.

Casa Lib. Casa de la Libertad. Fundación Cultural; Banco Central de Bolivia. Sucre, Bolivia.

Chiapas/México. Chiapas. UNAM, Instituto de Investigaciones Económicas. México.

Church Hist. Church History: Studies in Christianity and Culture. American Society of Church History. Red Bank, N.J.

Ciclos Hist. Econ. Soc. Ciclos en la Historia, Economía y la Sociedad. Univ. de Buenos Aires, Facultad de Ciencias Económicas, Instituto de Investigaciones de Historia Económica y Social. Buenos Aires.

Ciênc. Cult. Ciência e Cultura. Sociedade Brasileira para o Progresso da Ciência. São Paulo.

Ciênc. Tróp. Ciência & Trópico. Ministério de Educação, Fundação Joaquim Nabuco; Editora Massangana. Recife, Brazil.

Ciudad Territ. Estud. Territ. Ciudad y Territorio Estudios Territoriales. Ministerio de Fomento, Centro de Publicaciones. Madrid.

CLAHR. Colonial Latin American Historical Review. Univ. of New Mexico, Spanish Colonial Research Center. Albuquerque.

Colon. Lat. Am. Rev. Colonial Latin American Review. City Univ. of New York (CUNY), City College, Dept. of Foreign Languages and Literatures, Simon H. Rifkind Center for the Humanities. New York; Carfax Publishing, Taylor & Francis, Ltd. Abingdon, England; Philadelphia, Penn.

Comp. Stud. Soc. Hist. Comparative Studies in Society and History. Society for the Comparative Study of Society and History; Cambridge Univ. Press. London.

Contracorriente/Lima. Contracorriente: Revista de Historia. Pontificia Univ. Católica del Perú, Servicios Universitarios. Lima.

Contrib. Cient. Tecnol. Cienc. Soc. Humanid. Contribuciones Científicas y Tecnológicas: Area Ciencias Sociales y Humanidades. Univ. de Santiago de Chile, Vicerrectoría de Investigación y Desarrollo, Depto. de Investigaciones Científicas y Tecnológicas. Santiago.

Convergencia/Toluca. Convergencia: Revista de Ciencias Sociales. Univ. Autónoma del Estado de México, Facultad de Ciencias Políticas y Administración Pública. Toluca, Mexico.

Crit. Anthropol. Critique of Anthropology. Sage Publications. London.

Cuad. Am./México. Cuadernos Americanos. UNAM. México.

Cuad. Antropol./San José. Cuadernos de Antropología. Univ. de Costa Rica, Depto. de Antropología, Laboratorio de Etnología. San José.

Cuad. Arte/Granada. Cuadernos de Arte de la Universidad de Granada. Univ. de Granada, Depto. de Historia de Arte. Granada, Spain.

Cuad. CIESAL. Cuadernos del CIESAL. Univ. Nacional de Rosario, Facultad de Ciencia Política y Relaciones Internacionales, Centro Interdisciplinario de Estudios Sociales Argentinos y Latinoamericanos. Rosario, Argentina.

Cuad. CISH. Cuadernos del CISH. Univ. Nacional de La Plata, Facultad de Humanidades y Ciencias de la Educación, Centro de Investigaciones Socio Históricas. La Plata, Argentina.

Cuad. Desarro. Rural. Cuadernos de Desarrollo Rural. Pontificia Univ. Javeriana, Facultad de Estudios Ambientales y Rurales, Instituto de Estudios Rurales, Depto. de Procesos Sociales y Desarrollo, Depto. de Tecnologías para la Conservación y la Producción. Bogotá.

Cuad. Filos. Cuadernos de Filosofía. Univ. de Buenos Aires, Instituto de Filosofía, Facultad de Filosofía y Letras. Buenos Aires.

Cuad. Hist. Ser. Econ. Soc. Cuadernos de Historia. Serie Economía y Sociedad. Univ. Nacional de Córdoba, Facultad de Filosofía y Humanidades, Centro de Investigaciones. Córdoba, Argentina.

Cuad. Hist. Ser. Poblac. Cuadernos de Historia. Serie Población. Centro de Investigaciones, Facultad de Filosofía y Humanidades. Univ. Nacional de Córdoba. Córdoba, Argentina.

Cuad. Inst. Nac. Antropol. Pensam. Latinoam. Cuadernos del Instituto Nacional de Antropología y Pensamiento Latinoamericano. Presidencia de la Nación, Secretaria de Cultura, Instituto Nacional de Antropología y Pensamiento Latinoamericano. Buenos Aires.

Cuad. Marcha. Cuadernos de Marcha. Centro de Estudios Uruguay-América Latina. Montevideo.

Cuad. Sur Hist./Bahía Blanca. Cuadernos del Sur: Historia. Univ. Nacional del Sur, Depto. de Humanidades. Bahía Blanca, Argentina.

Cuba Social. Cuba Socialista. Comité Central del Partido Comunista de Cuba. La Habana.

Cuest. Polít. Cuestiones Políticas. Univ. de Zulia, Facultad de Ciencias Jurídicas, Instituto de Estudios Políticos y Derecho Público. Maracaibo, Venezuela.

Cult. Guatem. Cultura de Guatemala. Univ. Rafael Landívar. Guatemala.

Cult. Vozes. Cultura Vozes. Editôra Vozes. Petrópolis, Brazil.

Cuyo/Mendoza. Cuyo: Anuario de Historia del Pensamiento Argentino. Univ. Nacional de Cuyo, Instituto de Filosofía, Sección de Historia del Pensamiento Argentino. Mendoza, Argentina.

Dados/Rio de Janeiro. Dados. Instituto Universitários de Pesquisas do Rio de Janeiro. Rio de Janeiro.

Data/La Paz. Data: Revista del Instituto de Estudios Andinos y Amazónicos. Instituto de Estudios Andinos y Amazónicos. La Paz.

Debates Am. Debates Americanos. Casa de Altos Estudios Don Fernado Ortíz. La Habana.

Decursos/Cochabamba. Decursos: Revista de Ciencias Sociales. Univ. Mayor de San Simón, Centro de Estudios Superiores Universitarios. Cochabamba, Bolivia.

Def. Nac./Rio de Janeiro. A Defesa Nacional: Revista de Assuntos Militares e Estudo de Problemas Brasileiros. Palácio Duque de Caxias, Biblioteca do Exército. Rio de Janeiro.

Desarro. Econ. Desarrollo Económico: Revista de Ciencias Sociales. Instituto de Desarrollo Económico y Social. Buenos Aires.

Desmemoria/Buenos Aires. Desmemoria. Buenos Aires.

Diálogo Debate Cult. Polít. Diálogo y Debate de Cultura Política. Centro de Estudios para la Reforma del Estado. México.

Diogenes/Oxford. Diogenes. Blackwell Publishers. Oxford, England.

Eco Andin. Eco Andino. Centro de Ecología y Pueblos Andinos. Oruro, Bolivia.

En Otras Palabras. En Otras Palabras: Mujeres, Amores y Desamores. Univ. Nacional de Colombia, Grupo Mujer y Sociedad; Corporación Casa de la Mujer. Bogotá. Fundación Promujer. Bogotá?.

Entorno Urbano. Entorno Urbano: Revista de Historia. Univ. Autónoma Metropolitana—Iztapalapa; Instituto de Investigaciones Dr. José María Luis Mora. México.

Entrepasados/Buenos Aires. Entrepasados: Revista de Historia. Buenos Aires.

Espac. Temas Cienc. Soc. Espacio: Temas de Ciencias Sociales. Univ. Católica Andrés Bello, Escuela de Ciencias Sociales. Caracas.

Espac. Tiempo Forma Ser. V Hist. Contemp. Espacio, Tiempo y Forma: Revista de la Facultad de Geografía e Historia; Serie V, Historia Contemporánea. Univ. Nacional de Educación a Distancia, Facultad de Geografía e Historia. Madrid.

Estud. Afro-Asiát. Estudos Afro-Asiáticos. Centro de Estudos Afro-Asiáticos. Rio de Janeiro.

Estud. Asia Afr. Estudios de Asia y Africa. El Colegio de México. México.

Estud. Av. Estudos Avançados. Univ. de São Paulo, Instituto de Estudos Avançados. São Paulo.

Estud. Boliv. Estudios Bolivianos. Univ. Mayor de San Andrés, Facultad de Humanidades y Ciencias de la Educación, Instituto de Estudios Bolivianos. La Paz.

Estud. Cult. Contemp. Estudios sobre las Culturas Contemporáneas. Univ. de Colima, Centro Universitario de Investigaciones Sociales. Colima, Mexico.

Estud. Cult. Náhuatl. Estudios de Cultura Náhuatl. UNAM, Instituto de Investigaciones Históricas. México.

Estud. Econ./São Paulo. Estudos Econômicos. Univ. de São Paulo, Faculdade de Economia, Administração e Contabilidade, Fundação Instituto de Pesquisas Econômicas. São Paulo.

Estud. Filos. Hist. Let. Estudios: Filosofía, Historia, Letras. Instituto Tecnológico Autónomo de México, División Académica de Estudios Generales y Estudios Internacionales, Depto. Académico de Estudios Generales. México.

Estud. Geogr./Madrid. Estudios Geográficos. Instituto de Economía y Geografía Aplicadas. Madrid.

Estud. Hist./Franca. Estudos de História. Univ. Estadual Paulista, Faculdade de História, Direito e Serviço Social, Curso de Pós-Graduação em História. Franca, Brazil.

Estud. Hist. Mod. Contemp. Méx. Estudios de Historia Moderna y Contemporánea de México. UNAM, Instituto de Investigaciones Históricas. México.

Estud. Hist. Novohisp. Estudios de Historia Novohispana. UNAM, Instituto de Investigaciones Históricas. México.

Estud. Hist./Rio de Janeiro. Estudos Históricos. Fundação Getulio Vargas, Centro de Pesquisa e Documentação de História Contemporânea do Brasil. Rio de Janeiro.

Estud. Hist. Soc. Econ. Am. Estudios de Historia Social y Económica de América. Univ. de Alcalá de Henares. Madrid.

Estud. Hombre. Estudios del Hombre. Univ. de Guadalajara, Depto. de Estudios del Hombre. Guadalajara, Mexico.

Estud. Ibero-Am./Porto Alegre. Estudos Ibero-Americanos. Pontificia Univ. Católica do Rio Grande do Sul, Faculdade de Filosofia e Ciências Humanas, Depto. de História, Programa Pós-Graduação em História. Porto Alegre, Brazil.

Estud. Int./Guatemala. Estudios Internacionales: Revista del IRIPAZ. Instituto de Relaciones Internacionales y de Investigaciones para la Paz. Guatemala.

Estud. Int./Santiago. Estudios Internacionales. Univ. de Chile, Instituto de Estudios Internacionales. Santiago.

Estud. Jalisc. Estudios Jaliscienses. El Colegio de Jalisco. Zapopan, Mexico.

Estud. Leopoldenses Sér. Hist. Estudos Leopoldenses: Série História. Univ. do Vale do Rio Dos Sinos, Centro de Ciências Humanas, Programa de Pós-Graduação em História. São Leopoldo, Brazil.

Estud. Michoac. Estudios Michoacanos. El Colegio de Michoacán. Zamora, Mexico.

Estud. Migr. Latinoam. Estudios Migratorios Latinoamericanos. Centro de Estudios Migratorios Latinoamericanos. Buenos Aires.

Estud. Soc. Agric. Estudos Sociedade e Agricultura. Univ. Federal Rural do Rio de Janeiro, Instituto de Ciências Humanas e Sociais, Curso de Pós-Graduação em Desenvolvimento, Agricultura e Sociedade, Depto. de Letras e Ciências Sociais. Rio de Janeiro.

Estud. Soc./Santa Fe. Estudios Sociales: Revista Universitaria Semestral. Univ. Nacional del Litoral, Secretaría de Extensión, Centro de Publicaciones. Santa Fe, Argentina.

Estud. Soc./Santo Domingo. Estudios Sociales. Centro de Estudios Sociales P. Juan Montalvo, SJ. Santo Domingo.

Estudios/Córdoba. Estudios: Revista del Centro de Estudios Avanzados. Univ. Nacional de Córdoba, Centro de Estudios Avanzados. Córdoba, Argentina.

Estudios/Guatemala. Estudios: Revista de Antropología, Arqueología e Historia. Univ. de San Carlos de Guatemala, Escuela de Historia, Instituto de Investigaciones Históricas, Antropológicas, y Arqueológicas. Guatemala.

Estudos/Goiânia. Estudos: Revista da Universidade Católica de Goiás. Univ. Católica de Goiás. Goiânia, Brazil.

Ethnohistory/Columbus. Ethnohistory: the Bulletin of the Ohio Valley Historic Indian Conference. American Society for Ethnohistory, Columbus, Ohio.

Ethnomusicology. Ethnomusicology. Univ. of Illinois Press. Champaign, Ill.

FACES/Mar del Plata. FACES: Revista de la Facultad de Ciencias Económicas y Sociales. Univ. Nacional de Mar del Plata, Facultad de

Ciencias Económicas y Sociales. Mar del Plata, Argentina.

Fem. Stud. Feminist Studies. Univ. of Maryland. College Park.

Folia Hist. Nordeste. Folia Histórica del Nordeste. Univ. Nacional del Nordeste, Facultad de Humanidades, Instituto de Historia; CONICET, Instituto de Investigaciones Geohistóricas; FUNDANORD. Resistencia, Argentina.

Fr. Hist. Stud. French Historical Studies. Society for French Historical Studies. Raleigh, N.C.

Frónesis/Maracaibo. Frónesis: Revista de Filosofía Jurídica, Social y Política. Univ. de Zulia, Facultad de Ciencias Jurídicas y Políticas, Instituto de Filosofía del Derecho Dr. José Manuel Delgado Ocando. Maracaibo, Venezuela.

Front. Norte. Frontera Norte. El Colegio de la Frontera Norte. Tijuana, Mexico.

Fundam. Antropol. Fundamentos de Antropología. Centro de Investigaciones Etnológicas Angel Ganivet. Granada, Spain.

Généal. hist. Caraïbe. Généalogie et histoire de la Caraïbe. Assn. de la généalogie et histoire de la Caraïbe. Le Pecq, France.

Geogr. Rev. Geographical Review. American Geographical Society. New York.

HAHR. Hispanic American Historical Review. Duke Univ. Press. Durham, N.C.

Hastings Int. Comp. Law Rev. Hastings International and Comparative Law Review. Univ. of California, Hastings College of the Law. San Francisco, Calif.

Hisp. J. Hispanic Journal. Indiana Univ. of Pennsylvania, Dept. of Foreign Languages. Indiana, Penn.

Hisp. Rev./Philadelphia. Hispanic Review. Univ. of Pennsylvania, Dept. of Romance Languages. Philadelphia, Penn.

Hispania/Madrid. Hispania. Consejo Superior de Investigaciones Científicas, Instituto de Historia, Depto. de Medieval Moderna y Contemporánea. Madrid.

Hispania/University. Hispania. American Assn. of Teachers of Spanish and Portuguese; Mississippi State Univ. Mississippi State, Miss.

Hispanófila/Chapel Hill. Hispanófila. Univ. of North Carolina, Dept. of Romance Languages. Chapel Hill.

Hist. Agrar. Historia Agraria. Univ. Autónoma de Barcelona, Facultad de CC.EE., Depto. de Economía e Historia Económica, Seminario de Historia Agraria. Barcelona.

Hist. Antropol. Fuentes Orales. Historia Antropología y Fuentes Orales. Univ. de Barcelona, Depto. de Historia Contemporánea, Seminario de Historia Oral; Arxiu Històric de la Ciutat; Centro Investigaciones Etnológicas Ángel Ganivet. Barcelona.

Hist. Ciênc. Saúde Manguinhos. História Ciências Saúde: Manguinhos. Fundação Oswaldo Cruz, Casa de Oswaldo Cruz. Rio de Janeiro.

Hist. Contemp. Historia Contemporánea. Univ. del País Vasco, Depto. de Historia Contemporánea. Bilbao, Spain.

Hist. Crít./Tegucigalpa. Historia Crítica. Univ. Nacional Autónoma de Honduras. Tegucigalpa.

Hist. Cult./Lima. Historia y Cultura. Museo Nacional de Arqueología, Antropología e Historia. Lima.

Hist. Graf./México. Historia y Grafía. Univ. Iberoamericana, Depto. de Historia. México.

Hist. Mex./México. Historia Mexicana. El Colegio de México, Centro de Estudios Históricos. México.

Hist. Perspect./Uberlândia. História & Perspectivas: Revista dos Cursos de Graduação e do Programa de Pós-Graduação em História. Editora da Univ. Federal de Uberlândia. Uberlândia, Brazil.

Hist. Quest. Debates. História: Questões e Debates. Univ. Federal do Paraná, Programa de Pós-Graduação em História, Associação Paraense de História. Curitiba, Brazil.

Hist. Reflect./Waterloo. Historical Reflections. Univ. of Waterloo, Dept. of History. Waterloo, Canada.

Hist. Relig./Chicago. History of Religions. Univ. of Chicago. Chicago, Ill.

Hist. Rev./Pelotas. História em Revista. Univ. Federal de Pelotas, Núcleo de Documentação Histórica, Instituto de Ciências Humanas. Pelotas, Brazil.

Hist. Soc./Medellín. Historia y Sociedad. Univ. Nacional de Colombia—Sede Medellín, Facultad de Ciencias Humanas y Económicas, Depto. de Historia. Medellín, Colombia.

Hist. Soc./Río Piedras. Historia y Sociedad. Univ. de Puerto Rico, Depto. de Historia. Río Piedras.

Hist. Workshop. History Workshop. Ruskin College. Oxford, England.

Historia/Santiago. Historia. Pontificia Univ. Católica de Chile, Facultad de Historia, Geografia y Ciencia Política, Instituto de Historia. Santiago.

Histórica/Lima. Histórica. Pontificia Univ. Católica del Perú, Depto. de Humanidades. Lima.

Históricas/México. Históricas: Boletín del Instituto de Investigaciones Históricas. UNAM, Instituto de Investigaciones Históricas. México.

Horiz. Antropol. Horizontes Antropológicos. Univ. Federal do Rio Grande do Sul, Instituto de Filosofia e Ciências Humanas, Programa de Pós-Graduação em Antropologia Social. Porto Alegre, Brazil.

Horizontes. Horizontes. Pontificia Univ. Católica de Puerto Rico. Ponce.

Huellas/Barranquilla. Huellas: Revista de la Universidad del Norte. Univ. del Norte. Barranquilla, Colombia.

Hum. Biol. Human Biology. Wayne State Univ. Press. Detroit, Mich.

Humanitas/Monterrey. Humanitas: Anuario del Centro de Estudios Humanísticos. Centro de Estudios Humanísticos, Secretaría de Extensión y Cultura, Univ. Autónoma de Nuevo León. Monterrey, Mexico.

Ibero-Am. Arch. Ibero-Amerikanisches Archiv: Zeitschrift für Sozialwissenschaften und Geschichte. Ibero-Amerikanisches Institut. Berlin.

Iberoamericana/Madrid. Iberoamericana. Madrid.

Iberoamericana/Tokyo. Iberoamericana = Ibero Amerika Kenkyu. Univ. Sofia, Instituto Iberoameriano. Tokyo.

Iconos/Lima. Iconos: Revista Peruana de Conservación Arte y Arqueología. Yachay Wasi: Instituto Superior de Conservación, Restauración y Turismo. Lima.

Int. Hist. Rev./Burnaby. The International History Review. Simon Fraser Univ., Dept. of History. Burnaby, British Columbia.

Int. J./Toronto. International Journal. Canadian Institute of International Affairs. Toronto, Canada.

Int. Spect./Hague. Internationale Spectator. Nederlandsch Genootschap voor Internationale Zaken. The Hague.

Int. Stud. Q./Oxford. International Studies Quarterly. Blackwell Publishers. Malden, Mass.; Oxford, England.

Inter-Am. Music Rev. Inter-American Music Review. Theodore Front Musical Literature, Inc. Van Nuys, Calif.

Invest. Ens. Investigaciones y Ensayos. Academia Nacional de Historia. Buenos Aires.

Invest. Geogr./Alicante. Investigaciones Geográficas. Univ. de Alicante, Instituto Universitario de Geografía. Alicante, Spain.

Islas/Santa Clara. Islas. Univ. Central de Las Villas, Facultad de Ciencias Sociales y Humanísticas, Depto. de Letras. Santa Clara, Cuba.

Iztapalapa/México. Iztapalapa. Univ. Autónoma Metropolitana—Unidad Iztapalapa, División de Ciencias Sociales y Humanidades. México.

J. Anthropol. Res. Journal of Anthropological Research. Univ. of New Mexico. Albuquerque.

J. Bahamas Hist. Soc. Journal of the Bahamas Historical Society. Bahamas Historical Society. Nassau, Bahamas.

J. Caribb. Hist. The Journal of Caribbean History. Univ. of the West Indies Press; Univ. of the West Indies, Dept. of History. Mona, Jamaica.

J. Church State. Journal of Church and State. Baylor Univ., J.M. Dawson Studies in Church and State. Waco, Tex.

J. Early Repub. Journal of the Early Republic. Society for Historians of the Early American Republic. Indianapolis, Ind.

J. Fam. Hist. Journal of Family History. Sage Periodicals Press. Thousand Oaks, Calif.

J. Hist. Sex. Journal of the History of Sexuality. Univ. of Chicago Press. Chicago, Ill.

J. Interam. Stud. World Aff. Journal of Interamerican Studies and World Affairs. Univ. of Miami, School of Interamerican Studies. Coral Gables, Fla.

J. Interdiscip. Hist. The Journal of Interdisciplinary History. The MIT Press. Cambridge, Mass.

J. Lat. Am. Anthropol. Journal of Latin American Anthropology. American Anthropological Assn., Society of Latin American Anthropologists. Arlington, Va.

J. Lat. Am. Stud. Journal of Latin American Studies. Cambridge Univ. Press. Cambridge, England.

J. Miss. Hist. The Journal of Mississippi History. Mississippi Historical Society; Mississippi Dept. of Archives and History. Jackson, Miss.

J. Soc. am. Journal de la Société des américanistes. Paris.

J. Soc. Hist. Journal of Social History. George Mason Univ. Press. Fairfax, Va.

J. Southwest. Journal of the Southwest. Univ. of Arizona, Southwest Center. Tucson.

J. Women's Hist. Journal of Women's History. Indiana Univ. Press. Bloomington, Ind.; Johns Hopkins Univ. Press. Baltimore, Md.

Jahrb. Gesch. Lat.am. Jahrbuch für Geschichte Lateinamerikas. Böhlau Verlag. Köln, Germany.

Jahrb. Gesch. Staat Wirtsch. Ges. Lat.am. Jahrbuch für Geschichte von Staat, Wirtschaft und Gesellschaft Lateinamerikas. Böhlau Verlag. Köln, Germany.

Jam. Hist. Rev. The Jamaican Historical Review. The Jamaican Historical Society. Kingston.

Jam. J. Jamaica Journal. Institute of Jamaica. Kingston.

JILAS/Bundoora. JILAS: Journal of Iberian and Latin American Studies. Assn. of Iberian and Latin American Studies of Australasia; La Trobe Univ., School of History. Bundoora, Australia.

LARR. Latin American Research Review. Latin American Studies Assn.; Univ. of New Mexico, Latin American Institute. Albuquerque.

Lat. Am. Indian Lit. Latin American Indian Literatures. Geneva College, Dept. of Foreign Languages. Beaver Falls, Penn.

Lat. Am. Indian Lit. J. Latin American Indian Literatures Journal. Geneva College, Dept. of Foreign Languages. Beaver Falls, Penn.

Lat. Am. Music Rev. Latin American Music Review (LAMR) = Revista de Música Latinoamericana. Univ. of Texas Press. Austin.

Lat. Am. Perspect. Latin American Perspectives. Sage Publications, Inc. Thousand Oaks, Calif.

Lat. Am. Theatre Rev. Latin American Theatre Review. Univ. of Kansas, Center of Latin American Studies. Lawrence.

Leituras/Lisboa. Leituras: Revista da Biblioteca Nacional. Biblioteca Nacional. Lisboa.

Lit. Mex. Literatura Mexicana. UNAM, Instituto de Investigaciones Filológicas, Centro de Estudios Literarios. México.

LOCUS Rev. Hist. LOCUS: Revista de História. Univ. Federal de Juiz de Fora, Instituto de Ciências Humanas e de Letras, Depto. de História; NHR (Núcleo de História Regional); Arquivo Histórico. Juiz de Fora, Brazil.

Luso-Braz. Rev. Luso-Brazilian Review. Univ. of Wisconsin Press. Madison.

Mapocho/Santiago. Mapocho. Dirección de Bibliotecas, Archivos y Museos. Santiago, Chile.

Mar Oceana. Mar Oceana: Revista del Humanismo Español e Iberoamericano. Univ. Francisco de Vitoria, Asociación López de Gómara. Madrid.

Máscara/s/Buenos Aires. Máscara/s: Revista de Pensamiento Político. Fundación de Relaciones Internacionales. Buenos Aires.

Mem. Am. Memoria Americana. Univ. de Buenos Aires, Facultad de Filosofía y Letras, Instituto de Ciencias Antropológicas. Buenos Aires.

Mem. Mus. Nac. Arte. Memoria del Museo Nacional de Arte. Museo Nacional de Arte. México.

Memoria/Quito. Memoria. Sociedad Ecuatoriana de Investigaciones Históricas y Geográficas. Quito.

Mesoamérica/Antigua. Mesoamérica. Plumsock Mesoamerican Studies. South Woodstock, Vt.; Centro de Investigaciones Regionales de Mesoamérica. Antigua, Guatemala.

Metapolítica/México. Metapolítica: Revista Trimestral de Teoría y Ciencia de la Política. Centro de Estudios de Política Comparada. México.

Mex. Stud. Mexican Studies/Estudios Mexicanos. Univ. of California Press. Berkeley.

Mil. Hist. West. Military History of the West. Univ. of North Texas, Dept. of History; National Guard Assn. of Texas. Denton, Tex.

Milenio/Bayamón. Milenio: Revista de Artes y Ciencias. Univ. de Puerto Rico, Colegio Universitario Tecnológico de Bayamón. Bayamón.

MLN/Baltimore. MLN: Modern Language Notes. Johns Hopkins Univ. Press. Baltimore, Md.

Mod. Lang. Q./Seattle. Modern Language Quarterly. University of Washington. Seattle.

Montalbán/Caracas. Montalbán. Univ. Católica Andrés Bello, Facultad de Humanidades y Educación, Institutos Humanísticos de Investigación. Caracas.

Mora/Buenos Aires. Mora: Revista del Area Interdisciplinaria de Estudios de la Mujer. Univ. de Buenos Aires, Facultad de Filosofía y Letras. Buenos Aires.

N.M. Hist. Rev. New Mexico Historical Review. Univ. of New Mexico; Historical Society of New Mexico. Albuquerque.

Nomadías/Santiago. Nomadías. Univ. de Chile, Facultad de Filosofia y Humanidades, Programa Género y Cultura en América Latina. Santiago.

Nombres/Córdoba. Nombres. Univ. Nacional de Córdoba, Facultad de Filosofia y Humanidades, Centro de Investigaciones, Area de Filosofia. Córdoba, Argentina.

Notes/Middleton. Notes. Music Library Assn., Inc. Middleton, Wisc.

Novahispania/México. Novahispania. UNAM, Instituto de Investigaciones Filológicas. México.

Novos Estud. CEBRAP. Novos Estudos CEBRAP. Centro Brasileiro de Análise e Planejamento. São Paulo.

Nuestra Hist./Buenos Aires. Nuestra Historia: Revista de Historia de Occidente. Fundación Nuestra Historia. Buenos Aires.

Nueva Soc. Nueva Sociedad. Fundación Friedrich Ebert. Caracas.

NWIG. NWIG: New West Indian Guide/Nieuwe West Indische Gids. Royal Institute of Linguistics and Anthropology, KITLV Press. Leiden, The Netherlands.

Opción/Maracaibo. Opción: Revista de Ciencias Humanas y Sociales. Univ. de Zulia, Facultad Experimental de Ciencias, Depto. de Ciencias Humanas. Maracaibo, Venezuela.

Osiris/Chicago. Osiris. History of Science Society; Univ. of Chicago Press. Chicago, Ill.

Pagara/Cayenne. Pagara. Société des amis des archives et de histoire de la Guyane. Cayenne, French Guiana.

Paradigma/Tegucigalpa. Paradigma. Univ. Pedagógica Nacional Francisco Morazán, Dirección de Investigación. Tegucigalpa.

Paradigmas/Londrina. Paradigmas: Revista de Filosofia. Univ. Estadual de Londrina, Centro de Estudos Filosóficos; Editora da Univ. Estadual de Londrina. Londrina, Brazil.

Paramillo/San Cristóbal. Paramillo. Univ. Católica de Táchira, Centro de Estudios Interdisciplinarios. San Cristóbal, Venezuela.

Paraninfo/Tegucigalpa. Paraninfo. Instituto de Ciencias del Hombre Rafael Heliodoro Valle. Tegucigalpa.

Past Present. Past & Present. Oxford Univ. Press. Oxford, England; New York; Past and Present Society. Oxford, England.

Pauta/México. Pauta: Cuadernos de Teoría y Crítica Musical. Consejo Nacional para la Cultura y las Artes, Dirección General de Publicaciones, Instituto Nacional de Bellas Artes. México.

Pesqui. Hist. Pesquisas História. Instituto Anchietano de Pesquisas. São Leopoldo, Brazil.

Plant. Soc. Am. Plantation Society in the Americas. Univ. of New Orleans, Dept. of History. New Orleans, La.

Polít. Comp. Política Comparada: Revista Brasilense de Políticas Comparadas. Arko Advice Editorial. Brasília.

Pop. Music/Cambridge. Popular Music. Cambridge Univ. Press. England.

Pop. Music Soc. Popular Music and Society. Taylor & Francis Group, Routledge Press. London; New York.

Popul. Fam./São Paulo. População e Família. Univ. de São Paulo, Faculdade de Filosofia, Letras e Ciências Humanas, Centro de Estudos de Demografia Histórica da América Latina, Humanitas Publicações. São Paulo.

Population/Paris. Population. Institut national d'études démographiques. Paris.

Pós-Hist. Pós-História. Univ. Estadual Paulista, Faculdade de Ciências e Letras, Programa de Pós-Graduação em Historia. São Paulo.

Prisma/Montevideo. Prisma. Univ. Católica del Uruguay. Montevideo.

Prismas/Buenos Aires. Prismas: Revista de Historia Intelectual. Univ. Nacional de Quilmes, Centro de Estudos e Investigaciones, Programa de Historia Intelectual. Buenos Aires.

Probl. Desarro. Problemas del Desarrollo: Revista Latinoamericana de Economía. UNAM, Instituto de Investigaciones Económicas. México.

Procesos/Quito. Procesos. Corporación Editora Nacional. Quito.

Quantum/Montevideo. Quantum. Univ. de la República, Facultad de Ciencias Económicas y de Administración. Montevideo.

Quatrivium/México. Quatrivium. Univ. Autónoma del Estado de México, Centro de Investigación en Ciencias Sociales y Humanidades. México.

Quinto Sol/Santa Rosa. Quinto Sol. Univ. Nacional de La Pampa, Facultad de Ciencias Humanas, Instituto de Estudios Socio-Históricos. Santa Rosa, Argentina.

Quipu/México. Quipu. Sociedad Latinoamericana de Historia de las Ciencias y la Tecnología. México.

Radic. Hist. Rev. Radical History Review. Duke Univ. Press. Durham, N.C.

Real. Econ./Buenos Aires. Realidad Económica. Instituto Argentino para el Desarrollo Económico. Buenos Aires.

Realidad/San Salvador. Realidad: Revista de Ciencias Sociales y Humanidades. Univ. Centroamericana José Simeón Cañas. San Salvador.

Reflexão/Campinas. Reflexão. Instituto de Filosofia, Pontifícia Univ. Católica de Campinas. Campinas, Brazil.

Reg. Soc./Hermosillo. Región y Sociedad: Revista de El Colegio de Sonora. El Colegio de Sonora. Hermosillo, Mexico.

Relac. Soc. Argent. Antropol. Relaciones de la Sociedad Argentina de Antropología. Buenos Aires.

Relaciones/Zamora. Relaciones. El Colegio de Michoacán. Zamora, Mexico.

Relig. Cult. Religión y Cultura. Padres Agustinos. Madrid.

Res. Econ. Anthropol. Research in Economic Anthropology. JAI Press. Greenwich, Conn.

Res Gesta. Res Gesta. Pontificia Univ. Católica Argentina, Facultad de Derecho y Ciencias Sociales del Rosario, Instituto de Historia. Rosario, Argentina.

Rev. Agen. Revue de l'Agenais et des anciennes provinces du sudouest. Société des sciences, lettres et arts d'Agen. Agen, France.

Rev. Andin. Revista Andina. Centro Bartolomé de las Casas. Cuzco, Peru.

Rev. Antropol./São Paulo. Revista de Antropologia. Univ. de São Paulo, Faculdade de Filosofia, Letras e Ciências Humanas, Depto. de Antropologia. São Paulo.

Rev. APG. Revista da APG. Pontificia Univ. Católica de São Paulo, Associação de Pós-Graduados. São Paulo.

Rev. Arch. Gen. Nac./Lima. Revista del Archivo General de la Nación. Ministerio de Justicia, Instituto Nacional de Cultura. Lima.

Rev. Arch. Reg. Cusco. Revista del Archivo Regional del Cusco. Cuzco, Peru.

Rev. Arqueol. Am./México. Revista de Arqueología Americana. Instituto Panamericano de Geografía e Historia. México.

Rev. Arqueol./São Paulo. Revista de Arqueologia. Sociedade de Arqueologia Brasileira. São Paulo.

Rev. Bibl. Nac. José Martí. Revista de la Biblioteca Nacional José Martí. Biblioteca Nacional José Martí. La Habana.

Rev. Bimest. Cuba. Revista Bimestre Cubana. Sociedad Económica de Amigos del País. La Habana.

Rev. Bras. Estud. Popul. Revista Brasileira de Estudos de População. Associação Brasileira de Estudos Populacionais. São Paulo.

Rev. Bras. Filos. Revista Brasileira de Filosofia. Instituto Brasileiro de Filosofia. São Paulo.

Rev. Bras. Hist./São Paulo. Revista Brasileira de História. Associação Nacional de História. São Paulo.

Rev. Can. Estud. Hisp. Revista Canadiense de Estudios Hispánicos. Asociación Canadiense de Hispanistas; Univ. of Alberta, Dept. of Modern Languages and Cultural Studies. Edmonton, Canada.

Rev. Catarin. Hist. Revista Catarinense de História. Univ. Federal de Santa Catarina, Centro de Filosofía e Ciências Humanas, Depto. de História. Florianópolis, Brazil.

Rev. Chil. Hist. Geogr. Revista Chilena de Historia y Geografía. Sociedad Chilena de Historia y Geografía. Santiago.

Rev. Ciênc. Hist. Revista de Ciências Históricas. Univ. Portucalense. Porto, Portugal.

Rev. Cienc. Soc./Río Piedras. Revista de Ciencias Sociales. Univ. de Puerto Rico, Recinto de Río Piedras, Facultad de Ciencias Sociales, Centro de Investigaciones Sociales. Río Piedras.

Rev. Cienc. Soc./San José. Revista de Ciencias Sociales. Editorial Univ. de Costa Rica. San José.

Rev. Colomb. Antropol. Revista Colombiana de Antropología. Ministerio de Educación Nacional, Instituto Colombiano de Antropología. Bogotá.

Rev. Complut. Hist. Am. Revista Complutense de Historia de América. Univ. Complutense de Madrid, Facultad de Geografía e Historia, Depto. de Historia de América I. Madrid.

Rev. Crít. Lit. Latinoam. Revista de Crítica Literaria Latinoamericana. Latinoamericana Editores. Lima.

Rev. Econ. Polít. Revista de Economia Política = Brazilian Journal of Political Economy. Centro de Economia Política. São Paulo.

Rev. Esp. Antropol. Am. Revista Española de Antropología Americana. Univ. Complutense de Madrid, Facultad de Geografia e Historia, Depto. de Historia de América II (Antropología de América). Madrid.

Rev. Eur. Estud. Latinoam. Caribe. Revista Europea de Estudios Latinoamericanos y del Caribe = European Review of Latin American and Caribbean Studies. Center for Latin American Research and Documentation = Centro de Estudios y Documentación Latinoamericanos. Amsterdam.

Rev. Filos. Latinoam. Cienc. Soc. Revista de Filosofía Latinoamericano y Ciencias Sociales. Asociación de Filosofía Latinoamericana y Ciencias Sociales. Buenos Aires.

Rev. Filos./México. Revista de Filosofía. Univ. Iberoamericana, Depto. de Filosofía. México.

Rev. Filos. Univ. Costa Rica. Revista de Filosofía de la Universidad de Costa Rica. Editorial de la Univ. de Costa Rica. San José.

Rev. fr. hist. Outre-mer. Revue française d'histoire d'Outre-mer. Société française d'histoire d'Outre-mer. Paris.

Rev. Hist. Am. Argent. Revista de Historia Americana y Argentina. Univ. Nacional de Cuyo, Instituto de Historia. Mendoza, Argentina.

Rev. Hist. Am./México. Revista de Historia de América. Instituto Panamericano de Geografía e Historia. Comisión de Historia. México.

Rev. Hist./Concepción. Revista de Historia. Depto. de Ciencias Históricas y Sociales, Univ. de Concepción, Chile.

Rev. Hist. Derecho Ricardo Levene. Revista de Historia del Derecho Ricardo Levene. Univ. de Buenos Aires, Facultad de Derecho y Ciencias Sociales; Instituto de Investigaciones Jurídicas y Sociales Ambrosio L. Gioja. Buenos Aires.

Rev. Hist./Heredia. Revista de Historia. Univ. Nacional, Escuela de Historia. Heredia, Costa Rica; Univ. de Costa Rica, Centro de Investigaciones Históricas de América Central. San José.

Rev. Hist./Managua. Revista de Historia. Univ. Centroamericana, Instituto de Historia de Nicaragua y Centroamérica. Managua.

Rev. Hist. Nav. Revista de Historia Naval. Ministerio de Defensa, Armada Española, Instituto de Historia y Cultura Naval. Madrid.

Rev. hist./Paris. Revue historique. Presses Univ. de France. Paris.

Rev. Hist. Reg. Revista de História Regional. Univ. Estadual de Ponta Grossa, Depto. de História. Ponta Grossa, Brazil.

Rev. Hist./São Paulo. Revista de História. Univ. de São Paulo, Faculdade de Filosofia, Letras e Ciências Humanas, Depto. de História. São Paulo.

Rev. Humanid./Monterrey. Revista de Humanidades: Tecnológico de Monterrey. Depto. de Humanidades, División de Ciencias y Humanidades, Instituto Tecnológico y de Estudios Superiores de Monterrey. Monterrey, Mexico.

Rev. Iberoam. Revista Iberoamericana. Instituto Internacional de Literatura Iberoamericana; Univ. de Pittsburgh. Pittsburgh, Penn.

Rev. Indias. Revista de Indias. Consejo Superior de Investigaciones Científicas, Instituto de Historia, Depto. de Historia de América. Madrid.

Rev. Inquis. Revista de la Inquisición. Univ. Complutense, Instituto de Historia de la Inquisición. Madrid.

Rev. Inst. Hist. Geogr. Bras. Revista do Instituto Histórico e Geográfico Brasileiro. Instituto Histórico e Geográfico Brasileiro. Rio de Janeiro.

Rev. Inst. Hist. Marít. Revista Instituto de Historia Marítima. Instituto de Historia Marítima. Guayaquil, Ecuador.

Rev. Interam. Bibliogr. Revista Interamericana de Bibliografía = Review of Inter-American Bibliography. Organization of American States (OAS). Washington.

Rev. Interam. Planif. Revista Interamericana de Planificación. Sociedad Interamericana de Planificación. Bogotá.

Rev. Javer./Bogotá. Revista Javeriana. Provincia Colombiana de la Compañía de Jesús. Bogotá.

Rev. Junta Estud. Hist. Mendoza. Revista de la Junta de Estudios Históricos de Mendoza. Mendoza, Argentina.

Rev. Junta Prov. Estud. Hist. Santa Fe. Revista de la Junta Provincial de Estudios Históricos de Santa Fe. Santa Fe, Argentina.

Rev. Latinoam. Filos. Revista Latinoamericana de Filosofía. Centro de Investigaciones Filosóficas. Buenos Aires.

Rev. Mex. Caribe. Revista Mexicana del Caribe. Chetumal, Mexico.

Rev. Mex. Cienc. Polít. Soc. Revista Mexicana de Ciencias Políticas y Sociales. UNAM, Facultad de Ciencias Políticas y Sociales. México.

Rev. Mus. Nac. Etnogr. Folk. Revista del Museo Nacional de Etnografía y Folklore. MUSEF Editores. La Paz.

Rev. Music. Chil. Revista Musical Chilena. Univ. de Chile, Facultad de Artes, Sección de Musicología. Santiago.

Rev. Music. Venez. Revista Musical de Venezuela. Consejo Nacional de la Cultura, Fundación Emilio Sojo. Caracas.

Rev. Música. Revista Música. Univ. de São Paulo, Depto. de Música. São Paulo.

Rev. Occident. Revista de Occidente. Fundación José Ortega y Gasset. Madrid.

Rev. Parag. Sociol. Revista Paraguaya de Sociología. Centro Paraguayo de Estudios Sociológicos. Asunción.

Rev. Patrim. Hist. Artíst. Nac. Revista do Patrimônio Histórico e Artístico Nacional. Ministério da Cultura, Secretaria de Patrimônio, Museus e Artes Plásticas, Instituto do Patrimônio, Histórico e Artístico Nacional. Rio de Janeiro.

Rev. Rev. Interam. Revista/Review Interamericana. Univ. Interamericana de Puerto Rico/Inter-American Univ. of Puerto Rico. San Germán.

Rev. SBPH. Revista da SBPH. Sociedade Brasileira de Pesquisa Histórica. Curitiba, Brazil.

Rev. Soc. fr. hist. hôp. Revue de la Société française d'histoire des hôpitaux. Paris.

Rev. Teatro/Rio de Janeiro. Revista de Teatro. Sociedade Brasileira de Autores Teatrais. Rio de Janeiro.

Rev. Univ./La Plata. Revista de la Universidad. Univ. Nacional de La Plata. La Plata, Argentina.

Rev. Univ. Nac. Río Cuarto. Revista de la Universidad Nacional de Río Cuarto. Univ. Nacional de Río Cuarto. Río Cuarto, Argentina.

Rev. Urug. Cienc. Polít. Revista Uruguaya de Ciencia Política. Univ. de la República, Facultad de Ciencias Sociales, Instituto de Ciencia Política; Fundación de Cultura Universitaria. Montevideo.

Rev. USP/São Paulo. Revista USP. Univ. de São Paulo, Coordenadoria de Comunicação Social. São Paulo.

Roman. Philol. Romance Philology. Univ. of California Press. Berkeley and Los Angeles, Calif.

Sarance/Otavalo. Sarance. Instituto Otavaleño de Antropología. Otavalo, Ecuador.

SECOLAS Ann. SECOLAS Annals: Journal of the Southeastern Council on Latin American Studies. Southeastern Council on Latin American Studies; Georgia Southern Univ. Statesboro, Ga.

Secuencia/México. Secuencia: Revista de Historia y Ciencias Sociales. Instituto de Investigaciones Dr. José María Luis Mora. México.

Semata. Semata. Univ. de Santiago de Compostela, Servicio de Publicacións e Intercambio Científico. Santiago de Compostela, Spain.

Silabario/Córdoba. Silabario. Univ. Nacional de Córdoba, Facultad de Filosofia y Humanidades, Centro de Investigaciones. Córdoba, Argentina.

Síntese/Belo Horizonte. Síntese: Revista de Filosofia. Companhia de Jesus, Centro de Estudios Superiores, Faculdade de Filosofia. Belo Horizonte, Brazil.

Slavery Abolit. Slavery and Abolition. Frank Cass & Co. Ltd. London.

Soc. Compass. Social Compass: Revue Internationale de Sociologie de la Religion (International Review of Sociology of Religion). Sage. London.

Soc. espaces temps. Sociétés, espaces, temps. Dakar, Senegal.

Social. Particip. Socialismo y Participación. Centro de Estudios para el Desarrollo y Participación. Lima.

Sociológica/México. Sociológica. Univ. Autónoma Metropolitana—Unidad Azcapotzalco, División de Ciencias Sociales y Humanidades, Depto. de Sociología. México.

Sólo Hist. Sólo Historia. Instituto Nacional de Estudios Históricos de la Revolución Mexicana, Secretaría de Gobernación. México.

Source/Alexandria. Source. Literary Division of the American Translators Assn. Alexandria, Va.

Stromata/San Miguel. Stromata. Univ. del Salvador, Filosofía y Teología. San Miguel, Argentina.

Stud. Hist. Hist. Contemp. Studia Histórica: Historia Contemporánea. Ediciones Univ. de Salamanca. Salamanca, Spain.

Stud. Zamorensia. Studia Zamorensia. Ediciones Univ. de Salamanca. Salamanca, Spain.

Susana Viejos. Susana y Los Viejos. Editorial SIAL (Sociedad Internacional de Amigos de la Literatura); Univ. Autónoma de Madrid. Madrid.

Taller/Buenos Aires. Taller: Revista de Sociedad, Cultura y Política. Asociación de Estudios de Cultura y Sociedad. Buenos Aires.

Temas Am. Temas Americanistas. Univ. de Sevilla, Servicio de Publicaciones. Sevilla, Spain.

Temas/Habana. Temas: Cultura, Ideología, Sociedad. Instituto Cubano del Libro. La Habana; Univ. of New Mexico, Latin American Institute, Cuban Project. Albuquerque.

Tempo Bras. Tempo Brasileiro. Edições Tempo Brasileiro Ltda. Rio de Janeiro.

Tempo/Rio de Janeiro. Tempo. Univ. Federal Fluminense, Depto. de História. Rio de Janeiro.

Textos Hist. Textos de História. Univ. de Brasília, Instituto de Ciências Humanas, Depto. de História, Programa de Pós-Graduação em História. Brasília.

Tiempo Espacio/Caracas. Tiempo y Espacio. Univ. Pedagógica Experimental Libertador, Instituto Pedagógico de Caracas, Depto. de Geografía e Historia, Centro de Investigaciones Históricas Mario Briceño Iragorry. Caracas.

Tiempos Am./Castellón. Tiempos de América. Univ. Jaume I—Campus de Borriol, Centros de Investigación de América Latina. Castellón, Spain.

Tierra Firme/Caracas. Tierra Firme. Editorial Tierra Firme. Caracas.

Tlalocan/México. Tlalocan. UNAM, Instituto de Investigaciones Históricas; Instituto de Investigaciones Antropológicas. México.

Todo es Hist. Todo es Historia. Buenos Aires.

TRACE/México. TRACE. Centre d'études mexicaines et centraméricaines. México.

Trans. Lit./Edinburgh. Translation and Literature. Edinburgh Univ. Press. Edinburgh, Scotland.

Trimest. Econ. El Trimestre Económico. Fondo de Cultura Económica. México.

Univ. Philos. Universitas Philosophica. Pontificia Univ. Javeriana, Facultad de Filosofia. Bogotá.

Universum/Talca. Universum. Univ. de Talca. Talca, Chile.

Varia Hist. Varia História. Univ. Federal de Minas Gerais, Faculdade de Filosofia e Ciencias Humanas, Depto. de História. Belo Horizonte, Brazil.

Vuelta/México. Vuelta. México.

William Mary Q. The William and Mary Quarterly. College of William and Mary. Williamsburg, Va.

World Archaeol. World Archaeology. Routledge & Kegan Paul. London.

World Policy J. World Policy Journal. World Policy Institute. New York.

World Polit. World Politics. Johns Hopkins Univ. Press. Baltimore, Md.

Yachay/Cochabamba. Yachay. Univ. Católica Boliviana, Deptos. de Filosofía y Letras y Ciencias Religiosas. Cochabamba, Bolivia.

Yaxkin/Tegucigalpa. Yaxkin. Instituto Hondureño de Antropología e Historia. Tegucigalpa.

SUBJECT INDEX

Abad, José Ramón, 4677.

Abandoned Children. Mexico, 1262. Viceroyalty of Río de la Plata, 2405.

Abarca, Agustín, 249.

Abolition (slavery), 1073, 1907. Brazil, 3148, 3235, 3306. Chile, 2326. Ecuador, 2551. France, 1950, 1966, 2002. French Caribbean, 1898, 2003, 2009–2010. French Guiana, 1849. Guadeloupe, 1862. Haiti, 1865. Martinique, 1972, 1985. Puerto Rico, 1977. Saint-Domingue, 1886. Uruguay, 3110. Women, 1985.

Abramo, Lívio, 53.

Abreu, Caio Fernando, 4207.

Abreu, João Capistrano de, 3132.

Abreu, José de, 3085.

Abstract Art. Argentina, 229–230, 243. Brazil, 374. Chile, 256–257. Colombia, 275. Exhibitions, 374. Mexico, 121, 155.

Academia Nacional de la Historia (Argentina), 2909.

Acapulco, Mexico (city). Maritime History, 1324.

Acarete, *du Biscay*, 2291.

Acculturation, 444, 896, 986, 4624. Argentina, 2945. Colonial History, 1001, 1251. Indigenous Peoples, 1005. Indigenous/Non-Indigenous Relations, 1680. Marriage, 1314. Mexico, 1342. Nahuas, 473. Puerto Rico, 2042. Spanish Conquest, 956. Tarasco, 640.

Adams, Lewis Brian, 302.

Admiral Graf Spee (battleship), 1117.

Adolescents. *See* Youth.

Advertising. Brazil, 3268. Mexico, 1463, 1530. Venezuela, 2426.

African Influences. Barbados, 2030. Brazil, 3129, 3178, 3224, 4512, 4515, 4518. Brazilians, 3299. Costa Rica, 1685. Cuba, 4449. Guyana, 1786. Haiti, 1796. Mexico, 1191. Musical History, 4426–4427. Peru, 2581. Popular Music, 4439, 4518. Uruguay, 4504. Venezuela, 4468.

African-Americans. *See* Africans; Blacks.

Africans. Argentina, 2768, 3004. Brazil, 3210, 3214. Cultural Identity, 1302. Ethnic Groups and Ethnicity, 3217. Haiti, 1796. Mexico, 1279, 1302. Paraguay, 3073. Religious Life and Customs, 1315. Saint-Domingue, 1796. Uruguay, 3104, 3110.

Afrikaners. Argentina, 2830.

Afro-Americans. *See* Africans; Blacks.

Agosín, Marjorie, 4330.

Agrarian Reform. *See* Land Reform.

Agricultural Colonization, 2494. Chile, 2752. Puerto Rico, 1833. *See Also* Land Settlement.

Agricultural Development. Ecuador, 2553. French Caribbean, 1840, 1897. Jamaica, 1900. Land Tenure, 1748. Mexico, 1501. Puerto Rico, 1833. Venezuela, 2126.

Agricultural Development Projects. *See* Development Projects.

Agricultural Ecology. Central America, 1755. Honduras, 1774.

Agricultural Industries. *See* Agroindustry.

Agricultural Labor. Audiencia of Charcas, 2311. Brazil, 3298. French Guiana, 1965. Haiti, 1864–1865. Mayas, 446. Mexico, 1327, 1484. Trinidad and Tobago, 1987. Viceroyalty of Río de la Plata, 2377, 2379.

Agricultural Policy. Argentina, 2867. Chile, 2741. Guadeloupe, 2036. Mexico, 1501, 1520.

Agricultural Production. Haciendas, 1318. Viceroyalty of New Spain, 1308.

Agricultural Productivity. Colonial History, 1225. Venezuela, 2126. Viceroyalty of New Spain, 1230. Viceroyalty of Río de la Plata, 2377, 2379.

Agricultural Systems. Indigenous Peoples, 694. Jamaica, 1901. Slaves and Slavery, 1902.

Agricultural Technology. Venezuela, 766.

Agriculture. Archives, 1184. European Influences, 480.

Agroindustry. Venezuela, 766.

Aguascalientes, Mexico (state). Autonomy, 1238. Cabildos, 1238. Haciendas, 1430. Landowners, 1430. Political History, 1419.

1948. Guadeloupe, 2021. Honduras, 1756. Indigenous Peoples, 613, 4549. Judicial Process, 3204. Labor Movement, 1494. Manuscripts, 1148. Mesoamerica, 415. Mestizos and Mestizaje, 1029. Mexico, 1151, 1153, 1207, 1268, 1315, 1478, 1493–1494, 1535. Missionaries, 1946. Musical History, 4454, 4525. Nuns, 1243. Puerto Rico, 1844. Religious Music, 4478. Social Change, 1321. Social Conditions, 4711. Socialism and Socialist Parties, 2713. Venezuela, 2463. Viceroyalty of New Spain, 1352, 4629. Viceroyalty of Río de la Plata, 714, 2364. Wealth, 1350–1351. Zoque, 417.

Catholicism, 4601. African Influences, 3129, 3178. Argentina, 2783, 3005. Criollos, 1793. Cultural Identity, 1777. Indigenous Peoples, 555, 584, 1295. Martinique, 1793. Mexico, 4632. Nahuas, 415, 610. Puerto Rico, 2097. Quechua, 2263. Social Movements, 1478. Viceroyalty of New Spain, 1291.

Cattle Raising and Trade, 2401. Brazil, 3239. Colonial History, 733, 1052. Land Tenure, 1693. Mexico, 1145, 1541. Paraguay, 3060. Saint-Domingue, 1831. Viceroyalty of Río de la Plata, 2377.

Catunda, Leda, 347.

Caudillos. Argentina, 2812, 2833, 2853. Bolivia, 2676, 2678. Folklore, 2833. Uruguay, 2812, 3100, 3114.

Cautiverio feliz, 2321.

Caves. Chile, 810.

Cayambe, Ecuador (town). Indigenous Peoples, 798. Schools, 798.

Cayapo (indigenous group), 4089.

Ceará, Brazil (state). Historiography, 4745.

Cena, Juan Carlos, 2813.

Censorship. Brazil, 3233.

Censuses. Peru, 863. Viceroyalty of New Spain, 1339.

Central-Local Government Relations, 1079. Argentina, 2973. Brazil, 3242. Chile, 2732. Mexico, 1456, 1492, 1544. *See Also* Federal-State Relations; Municipal Government.

Ceremonies. *See* Rites and Ceremonies.

Cerro de Pasco, Peru (city). Local History, 2620–2622.

Cevallos, Pedro Fermín, 2552.

Chacao School, 4474.

Chachapoya (indigenous group). Ethnohistory, 712. Iconography, 720.

Chaco, Argentina (prov.). Colonial History, 809. Human Geography, 811. Indigenous Peoples, 809, 811. Military Occupation, 2939. Musical Instruments, 4488.

Chaco War (1932–1935), 2666, 2677, 2696, 3083.

Chamacoco (indigenous group). Pictorial Works, 719.

Chamberlain, Joseph, 1866.

Chamie, Emilie, 345.

Charnay, Désiré, 1409.

Chávez, Carlos, 4382.

Chávez Morado, José, 158.

Che Guevara. *See* Guevara, Ernesto Che.

Chiapas, Mexico (state). Art, 97. Art History, 101. Colonial Architecture, 10. Colonial History, 1203, 1346. Confraternities, 557. Description and Travel, 1312. Elites, 1545. Indigenous Peoples, 1346. Indigenous/Non-Indigenous Relations, 1495. Insurrections, 1346, 1607. Land Tenure, 1495. Mayas, 1239. Religious Life and Customs, 1203, 1346. Social Classes, 1545.

Chibcha (indigenous group). Colonial History, 818, 835, 2148. Elites, 829. Food, 804. Historical Demography, 799. Human Ecology, 799. Medicine, 804. Nutrition, 804. Relations with Spaniards, 829, 835. Rites and Ceremonies, 805. Sacred Space, 805. Social Life and Customs, 818. Time, 805.

Chichén Itzá Site (Mexico), 551, 592.

Chichimecs (indigenous group). Sources, 479.

Chihuahua, Mexico (state). Economic History, 1551. Education, 1356. Historiography, 1491. Labor and Laboring Classes, 1551. Musical History, 4387.

Chilam Balam de Chumayel, 545.

Chilcuautla, Mexico (town). Religious Life and Customs, 1154.

Child Labor. Colombia, 2507.

Childbirth. Chile, 2761. Colonial History, 689. Mesoamerica, 414. Mexico, 1262.

Children. Brazil, 3330. Mexico, 1428. Refugees, 2108.

Chile. Armada, 2731.

Chileans. Bolivia, 2679.

Chiloé, Chile (prov.). Migration, 759.

Chimalpahin Cuauhtlehuanitzin, Domingo Francisco de San Antón Muñón, 449.

Chinese. Caribbean Area, 1936. Cuba, 1943. Panama, 1750. Peru, 2588.

Chinese Influences. Mexico, 11.

Chiquinquirá Díaz, María, 2175.

Chiquito (indigenous group). Audiencia of Charcas, 2311. Ethnohistory, 709.

Cojo (Firm), 2426.
Colegio de Propaganda Fide (Tarija, Bolivia), 2296.
Colegio Libre de Estudios Superiores (Argentina), 4788.
Colegio Nacional de Monserrat (Córdoba, Argentina), 3048, 4776.
Coliqueo, Ignacio, 734.
Colla (indigenous group). History, 793.
Collection Aubin-Goupil a la Bibliotheque nationale de France, 527.
Collective Memory. Andean Region, 808. Aymara, 655. Brazil, 918. Costa Rica, 865. French Guiana, 1801. Land Tenure, 576. Martinique, 1940. Mesoamerica, 474, 476. Mexico, 475. Nicaragua, 865. Peru, 2274. Slaves and Slavery, 1940. Spanish Conquest, 838.
Colonia del Sacramento, Argentina (port). Colonial History, 2394.
Colonial Administration, 949, 982, 990, 1002, 1020, 1056, 1071, 1087, 1373. Audiencia de Quito, 2218. Belize, 1757. Bolivia, 2300. Brazil, 661, 3141, 3145, 3157, 3200, 3213, 3216, 3221, 3228. British Caribbean, 1863. Chile, 2332, 2337, 2340–2341. Colombia, 824. Cuba, 1922, 1933–1934, 1986, 1992–1993, 1998. Elites, 2153. Encomiendas, 1047. Finance, 1681. French Caribbean, 1822, 1967, 2003. French Guiana, 1878, 1965. Guadeloupe, 1862, 1956. Guatemala, 1697. Honduras, 1674, 1676. Indigenous Influences, 749. Jews, 1041. Labor Supply, 2165. Law and Legislation, 614. Markets, 994. Martinique, 1972, 2020. Mesoamerica, 537, 634. Mexico, 1216, 1238, 1309, 1389. Mosquito, 1691. Netherlands, 2071. Nueva Granada, 2164. Puerto Rico, 1832, 1935, 2090. Saint-Domingue, 1000, 1841, 1867, 1886. Suriname, 1860. Venezuela, 2134, 4686. Viceroyalty of New Spain, 539, 1245. Viceroyalty of Peru, 2242, 2269. Viceroyalty of Río de la Plata, 2347.
Colonial Architecture, 2. Andean Region, 72–73. Argentina, 2404. Bolivia, 69. Brazil, 319–322, 325, 327. Colombia, 2157. Ecuador, 2189. Historiography, 74. Mexico, 7, 9, 28, 36–37. Peru, 64, 74, 76, 78, 82–84. South America, 1. Viceroyalty of Peru, 78.
Colonial Art, 5. Andean Region, 72. Bolivia, 71. Brazil, 3149. Colombia, 62. Ecuador, 65. Mexico, 6, 8, 18, 21, 31, 62, 145. Peru, 64, 70. South America, 1. Venezuela, 61.
Colonial Discourse, 2166, 4604.

Colonial History, 823, 989. Brazil, 3185, 3207. Guatemala, 1658, 1675. Honduras, 1652.
Colonial Literature. Brazil, 3139. Suriname, 1803.
Colonial Painting. Mexico, 11–12. Peru, 80.
Colonization, 858, 1002. Argentina, 2345, 2951. Bolivia, 2652. Brazil, 661, 3141. Caribbean Area, 1836. Chile, 2334. French Caribbean, 1801, 1824, 1842. French Guiana, 1801. Honduras, 1709. Indigenous Peoples, 1253. Mexico, 1385. Paraguay, 664. Venezuela, 779.
Coloquios y doctrina cristiana, 563.
Columbus, Christopher, 512, 1062, 1072.
Comisión Plebiscitaria de Tacna y Arica, 2624.
Commerce. Argentina, 2950, 3020. Bolivia, 2678. Brazil, 3171. Caribbean Area, 1692. Chile, 2332. Colonial History, 743, 1051. Guatemala, 1694. Indigenous Peoples, 1684. Jews, 1006. Merchants, 1333. Mexico, 1156, 1332. Pacific Area, 1331. Spain, 859, 975.
Commercial Policy. *See* Trade Policy.
Communism and Communist Parties, 4585. Archives, 2824. Argentina, 2824, 2981. Brazil, 3316. Chile, 2739. Mexico, 1573. Venezuela, 2460.
Community Development. Ecuador, 4846. Indigenous Peoples, 734.
Compadrazgo. Peru, 2574. Slaves and Slavery, 3343.
Compagnie sucrière de la Pointe-à-Pitre, 2006.
Compañía Accesoria del Tránsito (Nicaragua), 1742.
Compañía de Salitres de Chile (COSACH), 2751.
Compañía del Ferrocarril de Guayaquil a Quito, 2554.
Composers, 4376. Argentina, 4475, 4484, 4496. Bolivia, 4454. Brazil, 4508, 4511, 4514, 4522–4523, 4538. Chile, 4499–4500. Colombia, 4459. Costa Rica, 4425. El Salvador, 4429–4430. Guatemala, 4432, 4435. Mexico, 4382–4383, 4386, 4390–4391, 4397, 4400, 4408–4410, 4413–4414, 4417, 4419–4420. Paraguay, 4503. Peru, 2600. Venezuela, 4469, 4474.
Comuneros. *See* Insurrection of the Comuneros (Colombia, 1781).
Concepción, Chile (city). Rural-Urban Migration, 2734.
Concepción, Chile (prov.). Economic Development, 2730. Economic History, 2728,

Coyohua Italatollo, 543.
Crafts. *See* Artisanry.
Craon et les trois opprimés, 1850.
Crime. *See* Crime and Criminals.
Crime and Criminals, 932. Argentina, 995,
2407, 2803, 3014. Bolivia, 995. Brazil,
3325. Colonial Administration, 1242.
Martinique, 2091. Mexico, 1270, 1393,
1467, 1597. Peru, 2582. Women, 3134.
Criminals. *See* Crime and Criminals.
Criollos. Catholicism, 1793. Cultural Iden-
tity, 1808. Elites, 996. French Guiana,
1805. Guadeloupe, 1939. Mexico, 1272.
Popular Music, 4466. Puerto Rico, 1944.
Viceroyalty of New Spain, 1208.
Crise do mundo moderno, 4743.
Cristalerías de Chile, 2744.
Cristero Rebellion (Mexico, 1926–1929),
1518, 1604, 1609. Women, 1631.
Criterio, 4803.
Crítica (Buenos Aires), 3012.
Crónicas, 957.
Cronistas, 654, 777, 957. Colombia, 731. In-
cas, 815. Mesoamerica, 544. Viceroyalty of
Peru, 700, 728.
Cruz Vélez, Danilo, 4702.
Cuadros Caldas, Julio, 1592.
Cuautinchán, Mexico (village). Land Tenure,
513.
Cuban Revolution (1959), 1144, 2057, 2088,
4676.
Cuenca, Ecuador (city), 2225. Colonial Archi-
tecture, 2189. Colonial History, 788, 2199,
2210, 2225. Economic History, 2209. Eth-
nic Groups and Ethnicity, 2209. Historical
Demography, 2209. Social History, 2199,
2209.
Cuevas, José Luis, 105–106.
Cuiabá, Brazil (city). Children, 3315. Family
and Family Relations, 3315. Social History, 3315.
Cultural Adaptation. *See* Acculturation.
Cultural Assimilation. *See* Acculturation.
Cultural Collapse. Mayas, 453. *See Also* Cultural Destruction.
Cultural Contact. Argentina/Spain, 4822. Ar-
gentina/US, 3055. Chiquito/Europeans,
709. Criollos/Mapuche, 682. Haiti/US,
2095. Indigenous Peoples/Europeans, 694,
722, 821. Latin America/Europe, 4588.
Latin America/Spain, 4582. Mexico/US,
1625, 4627. Puerto Rico/Spain, 2063.
Spaniards/Taino, 1835. Spanish Conquest,
1002. Tarasco/Spaniards, 640.
Cultural Destruction, 869. Bahamas, 2101.

Indigenous Peoples, 911. Modernization,
4593. *See Also* Cultural Collapse.
Cultural Development, 886, 4587, 4589,
4624, 4826. Mesoamerica, 458. Otomi,
650. Puerto Rico, 2064. Viceroyalty of
Peru, 2273.
Cultural Geography. Brazil, 3157, 3292. Colombia, 2536. Mesoamerica, 435. South
America, 773. *See Also* Human Geography.
Cultural History, 840, 851, 873, 898, 903,
905, 914, 971, 981, 1109, 1132, 3963, 4372,
4575, 4587, 4589. Argentina, 4839. Bolivia, 2669, 2692. Brazil, 3140. Chile,
2338. Colombia, 2527, 2530. Honduras,
1660. Incas, 2260. Indigenous Peoples, 773.
Mesoamerica, 506, 558. Mexico, 987,
1170, 1319, 1476, 1547, 1561, 1568, 1623,
1633. Nahuas, 421. Peru, 2576. Puerto
Rico, 1798. Suriname, 1803. Uruguay,
3102. Viceroyalty of Peru, 2244, 2284.
Cultural Identity, 861, 873, 912, 919, 929–
930, 947, 1081, 1120, 4540, 4547, 4550,
4594, 4609, 4617, 4621. Argentina, 4781,
4820, 4826, 4839. Blacks, 906, 2014. Bolivia, 2681. Brazil, 918, 3135, 3140, 3290,
3292, 3335, 4746, 4764. British, 1876. Caribbean Area, 2014. Chile, 2320, 2709. Colombia, 2497, 2511. Colonial History, 514,
1001. Costa Rica, 4657. Cuba, 4681. Dominican Republic, 1991. French, 1891.
Globalization, 4572. Guadeloupe, 2069,
2069. Incas, 685. Indigenous Peoples, 691,
831, 4592. Linguistics, 4690. Mass Media,
4624. Mesoamerica, 458. Mestizos and
Mestizaje, 747. Mexico, 475, 1321, 1566,
1598, 4764. Modernization, 4593. Peru,
4722. Philosophy, 4545, 4557. Political
Philosophy, 4553. Puerto Rico, 1798, 1944,
1989, 2042, 2060, 2078, 2092. Regional Integration, 4552. Venezuela, 4690. Zoque,
417.
Cultural Policy, 4540. Brazil, 395. Venezuela,
4473.
Cultural Property. Brazil, 395. Dominican
Republic, 51. Mexico, 17, 1409.
Cultural Relations. Audiencia of
Quito/Chile, 2193. Brazil/Portugal, 3171.
Cuba/Spain, 4445. Latin America/France,
1140. Mexico/Spain, 1608, 4647.
Cultural Studies, 4553. Mexico, 1547, 1561,
1568, 1623, 1633.
Cumaná, Venezuela (city). Local History,
2449.
Cuna (indigenous group), 178. Insurrections,
1745.

Educational Reform. Colombia, 2522. Ecuador, 2572. Mexico, 1299.

Educational Sociology. Argentina, 4776. Brazil, 3330. Mexico, 1635. Suriname, 1797.

Eguiara y Eguren, Juan José de, 1272.

Ejército Popular Revolucionario (Mexico), 1517.

Ejército Revolucionario del Pueblo (Argentina), 2839.

Ejército Zapatista de Liberación Nacional (Mexico), 1517, 1524, 1607, 1634.

El Angel, Ecuador (town). History, 2190.

Election Fraud. Colombia, 2485.

Elections. Argentina, 2838, 2929. Chile, 2711. Colonial Administration, 1226. Mexico, 1265, 1414, 1554, 1558, 1619. Nicaragua, 1746. Peru, 2609, 2619.

Electric Industries. Bolivia, 2688.

Elementary Education. Ecuador, 798. French Caribbean, 1948. *See Also* Education.

Elites. Argentina, 2778, 2815, 2864, 3000. Bolivia, 2308, 2674, 2685, 2692. Brazil, 3336. Chile, 2325, 2328. Colombia, 2486, 2503. Colonial Administration, 996. Costa Rica, 1669, 1685. Cuba, 1922. Cultural Identity, 1077, 1944. Economic Development, 2503. El Salvador, 1752. Guatemala, 1695–1696. Historiography, 1143, 1159. Honduras, 1687. Indigenous Peoples, 574. Landowners, 1693. Marriage, 1210. Mexico, 1173, 1231, 1276, 1304, 1422, 1513. Nahuas, 610. Nationalism, 1778, 2681. Nicaragua, 1707, 1732. Peru, 2574, 2591. Political Participation, 1712. Political Parties, 1945. Puerto Rico, 1957, 2078. Uruguay, 3115. Viceroyalty of New Spain, 1287. Women, 2516.

Elso, Juan Francisco, 200.

Embera (indigenous group), 3559.

Emigration and Immigration. *See* Migration.

Employment. Argentina, 2897, 2943. Puerto Rico, 1888. Women, 1888, 2943.

Encomiendas. Argentina, 809. Audiencia of Charcas, 2311. Audiencia of Quito, 740. Bolivia, 2316. Chile, 2343. Guatemala, 430. Indigenous Peoples, 2419. Mexico, 1278. Paraguay, 2419. Viceroyalty of Peru, 2233.

Encyclopedias. Dominican Republic, 1794. Music, 4516.

Ender, Thomas, 334.

Engineers. Brazil, 3341.

Engraving. Argentina, 216. Cuba, 197. Mexico, 1281.

Enlightenment, 4623, 4661, 4720. Brazil, 3167. Colonial History, 4584. Historiography, 4584. Mexico, 4643. Saint-Domingue, 1875. Venezuela, 2129, 4689.

Enríquez, Miguel, 1887.

Ensaio, 4514.

Ensenada, Mexico (city). History, 1528.

Entrepreneurs. Argentina, 2791. Atlantic Trade, 1331. Brazil, 3243. Chile, 2722–2723. Haiti, 1941. Mexico, 1407. Viceroyalty of Río de la Plata, 2376.

Environmental Degradation. Brazil, 3199. Cattle Raising and Trade, 1541. Colonial History, 3199. Paraguay, 3075.

Environmental Policy. Argentina, 2798.

Environmental Protection. Colonial History, 3199.

Epidemics. Argentina, 2798, 2885. Colonial History, 984. Costa Rica, 1683. Mexico, 1266. Peru, 2586. *See Also* Diseases.

EPR. *See* Ejército Popular Revolucionario (Mexico).

Erauso, Catalina de, 2117–2118.

Escola do Recife (Brazil), 4747, 4751, 4753.

Escola Tropicalista Bahiana (Brazil), 3313.

Escuela Nacional de Música, 4433.

Escuela Positiva, 4812.

Espaillat y Quiñones, Ulises Francisco, 4682.

España, José María, 2127, 2132, 2139.

Esperón, Manuel, 4390.

Espinosa, José María, 60.

Espírito Santo, Brazil (state). Architecture, 332, 399. Art History, 332. Italians, 399.

Estado de São Paulo, 3233.

Estancias. Uruguay, 2382. Viceroyalty of Río de la Plata, 2382. *See Also* Haciendas.

Este pueblo necesita, 4834.

Esthetics, 91.

Estrada Ycaza, Julio, 2183.

Ethics. Brazil, 4754. Venezuela, 2457.

Ethnic Groups and Ethnicity, 879, 955, 972, 978. Argentina, 2386, 2796, 2901, 2912, 4820. Brazil, 3290. California, 1359. Caribbean Area, 1812, 2027. Central America, 1759. Confraternities, 2236. Dominican Republic, 2065. Ecuador, 2569. French Guiana, 1805. Haiti, 1941. Honduras, 1717. Indigenous Peoples, 831, 1026. International Relations, 723. Mexico, 475, 1209, 1256, 1342. Montserrat, 1819. Nicaragua, 1737. Peru, 2598, 2605. Puerto Rico, 2092. Slaves and Slavery, 1821. Spain, 855.

Ethnic Groups. *See* Ethnic Groups and Ethnicity.

Planning, 1817. Colonial Administration, 1822, 1967, 2003. Colonization, 1801, 1824, 1842. Criollos, 1808. Demography, 1815. East Indians, 1947. Economic History, 1790, 1828. Elementary Education, 1948. Freedmen, 2003. Genealogy, 1808. Historiography, 1808. Jesuits, 1839. Jews, 1820. Judicial Power, 1967. Maroons, 1853. Migration, French, 1824, 1842. Missionaries, 1839. Money, 2018. Notaries, 1859. Ports, 2094. Protestantism, 1883. Racism, 1967. Slaves and Slavery, 1791, 1796, 1830, 1853, 2002, 2009–2010. Social History, 1790, 1824. Statistics, 1815. Sugar Industry and Trade, 1816.

French Influences, 1140. Argentina, 4780. Brazil, 4743–4744. Colombia, 2544. Mexico, 1420, 1454, 1464. Theater, 4231.

French Revolution (1789–1799), 1863, 1873, 1880, 1905. Educational Models, 1870. Exiles, 1891. French Guiana, 1849. Guadeloupe, 1862.

Frente Amplio (Uruguay), 3098.

Frente Farabundo Martí para la Liberación Nacional (El Salvador), 1782.

Frente Justicialista de Liberación (Argentina), 2810.

Frente Nacional (Colombia), 2488.

Freud, Sigmund, 2975.

Freyre, Gilberto, 4731, 4733, 4736, 4764, 4766.

Friendship. See Interpersonal Relationships.

Frondizi, Arturo, 4824.

Frontier and Pioneer Life, 1373. Argentina, 2907, 3054. Brazil, 3157. Colonial History, 733. Income Distribution, 2907. Indigenous Peoples, 1366. Mexican-American Border Region, 1381. Missions, 1385. Paraguay, 3061. Patagonia, 716. Spanish Conquest, 886. Tlaxcalans, 1391. Viceroyalty of Río de la Plata, 2420.

Frontiers. Andean Region, 2667. Argentina, 746, 2967, 2979. Brazil, 737. Chile, 2742. Mexico, 1457. Paraguay, 3074, 3079.

Fruit Trade. Argentina, 2941.

Frutos, Juan Manuel, 3076.

Fuentes Mares, José, 1491.

Fuerzas Armadas Revolucionarias de Colombia, 2484.

Fujimori, Alberto, 2628.

Fukushima, Tikashi, 354.

Gaitán, Jorge Eliécer, 2537, 2548.

Galápagos Islands. See Galápagos Islands, Ecuador.

Galápagos Islands, Ecuador. Discovery and Exploration, 684. Historical Geography, 2563. Human Geography, 2563. Land Settlement, 2564.

Galeria Witcomb, 234.

Galicians. Argentina, 2802, 2823. Genealogy, 2823. Mexico, 1386, 1488. Uruguay, 2355.

Gallegans. See Galicians.

Gallegos, Rómulo, 2461.

Gálvez, José de, 1389.

Gálvez, Manuel, 4834.

Gálvez, Mariano, 1705.

Gama, Vasco da, 3168.

Gamboa, Francisco, 1470.

Gana, Andrés, 251.

Ganivet, Angel, 4731.

Gaos, José, 4651.

Garcés, Julián, 4629.

García, Charly, 4484.

Garcia, José Maurício Nunes, 4522.

García, Pedro Andrés, 2951.

García Bustos, Arturo, 157.

García de León y Pizarro, Ramón, 2201.

García Elgueta, Manuel, 450.

García M8, 530.

García Márquez, Gabriel, 3540.

Gardel, Carlos, 3687.

Garibaldi, Anita, 4086.

Garifuna (indigenous group). See Black Carib (indigenous group).

Garrido Canabal, Tomás, 1509.

Garvey, Marcus, 1740, 1814.

Gasca, Pedro de la, 2300.

Gauchos, 4339. Argentina, 2860, 4492. Poetry, 3755.

Geber, Roma, 245.

Gelbard, José B., 3024.

Geldner, Karl Friedrich, 2473.

Gender Relations, 907. Aztecs, 529. Bolivia, 2656. Caribbean Area, 1800. Central America, 1664. Colombia, 2501, 2521. Colonial History, 976, 1981. Cuba, 1981. East Indians, 1994. Haiti, 2015. History, 889. Mesoamerica, 484, 528, 567. Mexico, 1490. Mosquitia, 1679. Nahuas, 495. Nicaragua, 1715. Peru, 2603, 2611. Precolumbian Civilizations, 484. Puerto Rico, 1800, 1954. Religious Life and Customs, 567. Saint-Domingue, 1868–1869. Textiles and Textile Industry, 2501. Viceroyalty of Peru, 2287.

Généalogie et histoire de la Caraïbe, 1813.

Genealogy. Argentina, 56, 2823. Bolivia, 2638. Caribbean Area, 1899. Ecuador, 2190. Free Blacks, 1807, 1813. Freedmen, 1813. French Caribbean, 1808. Guade-

Incas, 729, 1067. Agricultural Technology, 710. Archeoastronomy, 665. Argentina, 806. Commerce, 803. Cosmology, 750. Deities, 765. Discovery and Exploration, 684. Economic Anthropology, 822. Elites, 685. Engineering, 710. Genealogy, 736. Historiography, 772, 793, 803, 815. History, 800, 2227. Iconography, 713. Indigenous Languages, 688. Intellectual History, 2260. Kings and Rulers, 736, 772, 795. Mathematics, 668, 749, 827. Mortuary Customs, 720, 725. Myths and Mythology, 748, 750, 765, 803, 828. Oral Tradition, 828. Relations with Spaniards, 795, 2268. Religious Life and Customs, 677, 795. Rites and Ceremonies, 677. Rock Art, 786. Sex and Sexual Relations, 471. Social Structure, 803, 819, 837. Sources, 736. State-Building, 814. Vernacular Architecture, 683. Warfare, 819. Writing, 827.

Income Distribution. Argentina, 2907.

Indentured Servants. Caribbean Area, 1812. East Indians, 1984. Indochinese, 2008. *See Also* Debt Bondage.

Independence Movements, 902, 964, 1082, 1107. Bolivia, 2694. Brazil, 3151. Colombia, 2142. Ecuador, 2570. Elites, 1697. Guatemala, 1667. Historiography, 1162. Mass Media, 2315. Mexico, 1162, 1201, 1246, 1484, 1486. Peru, 2607. Venezuela, 2127, 2132, 2139, 2448. Women, 1111. *See Also* Wars of Independence.

Indians. *See* East Indians; Indigenous Peoples; West Indians.

Indigenismo and Indianidad. Bolivia, 2668. Brazil, 831. Guatemala, 1730. Mexico, 1527. Musical History, 4454. Peru, 4718, 4722.

Indigenous Architecture. *See* Vernacular Architecture.

Indigenous Art. Argentina, 235. Brazil, 333. Cuna, 178. Dominican Republic, 207. Franciscan Influences, 55. Mayas, 509. Mexico, 270. Viceroyalty of New Spain, 598.

Indigenous Influences. Brazil, 3159. Musical History, 4426.

Indigenous Languages, 1789. Amazon Basin, 726. Andean Region, 688. Audiencia of Quito, 2178, 2186. Brazil, 678, 3180. Colonial Administration, 1260. Ecuador, 2178, 2186. Guatemala, 1688. Manuscripts, 564. Mayas, 549, 603. Mexico, 438, 536, 547, 1260. Viceroyalty of New Spain, 538, 1328.

Indigenous Literature. Aztecs, 605. Mexico, 438, 547. Suriname, 1803.

Indigenous Music, 4370. Aztecs, 605. Brazil, 4530. Costa Rica, 4427. Cuba, 4444. Guatemala, 4432. Mesoamerica, 508. Mexico, 4404, 4407, 4411. Migration, 508. Peru, 4371, 4463, 4465. Venezuela, 4468.

Indigenous Peoples, 557, 1024, 1166, 2343. Acculturation, 614, 747, 1250, 2322, 2425, 2704. Agricultural Development, 2553. Agricultural Labor, 1300. Alcohol and Alcoholism, 1730. Amazon Basin, 3260. Argentina, 698, 715, 734, 2992. Bolivia, 792, 2668–2669. Brazil, 686, 732, 775, 778, 789, 831, 3159, 3191. Cannibalism, 1038. Caribbean Area, 1684. Catholicism, 514, 555, 702, 1295, 2234. Chile, 2120. Citizenship, 2664, 2676. Collective Memory, 476, 599. Colonial History, 1003, 1648. Commerce, 913. Confraternaties, 1353. Congresses, 726. Cultural Destruction, 2203. Cultural Identity, 1387, 4592. Demography, 1026, 1663. Diseases, 984, 1266. Domestics, 2309. Educational Policy, 2671. Elites, 1296, 1671. Evangelicalism, 563, 2233. Guatemala, 1688. Historical Demography, 1657, 1683, 2396. Historiography, 686, 787, 894. Honduras, 1687, 1709. Influences on, 694. Inquisition, 2293, 2307. Intellectual History, 1199. International Law, 4625. Kings and Rulers, 707. Labor Supply, 1241. Land Tenure, 778, 1174, 2667. Land Use, 2342. Law and Legislation, 1004, 1014, 2550. Literacy and Illiteracy, 1053. Mesoamerica, 621. Metal-Work, 1070. Metallurgy, 1010, 1070. Mexico, 1278, 1527. Minerals and Mining Industry, 2683. Money, 596. Names, 762. National Characteristics, 1775. Nicaragua, 1723, 1737. Origins, 654. Peru, 2605, 2610. Political Participation, 1226, 1703. Relations with Spaniards, 956. Religious Life and Customs, 702, 948, 1213, 4412. Rites and Ceremonies, 1042. Slaves and Slavery, 911. Social Life and Customs, 744. Social Mobility, 1314. Social Structure, 715, 1005. Socialism and Socialist Parties, 2599. Viceroyalty of New Spain, 653, 1334. Views of, 446, 654, 734, 742, 752, 787, 815, 820, 1050, 1527, 2508, 2553, 2736, 3191, 4549, 4574. Warfare, 741. Wars of Independence, 1246. Women, 1287.

Indigenous Policy. Amazon Basin, 3160. Argentina, 742, 791, 2789, 2801, 2985. Bolivia, 792. Brazil, 661, 775, 778, 3160,

International Economic Relations. Bolivia/ Chile, 2642. Brazil, 3230. Brazil/Portugal, 3200. Central America/Great Britain, 1766. Chile/Europe, 2328. Chile/Great Britain, 2729, 2751. Chile/US, 2712. Cuba/Spain, 1998. Latin America/US, 1137, 1139. Mexico, 1590. Mexico/Great Britain, 1553. Mexico/US, 1408, 1469, 1480, 1483, 1553. Peru/Great Britain, 926. Peru/US, 926.

International Law. Indigenous Peoples, 4625.

International Migration. *See* Migration.

International Relations, 912. Argentina, 2842, 2883, 2902, 2997, 3015, 3023. Argentina/Brazil, 2944. Argentina/Chile, 2111. Argentina/Ecuador, 2557. Argentina/France, 2916. Argentina/Germany, 2882, 2898. Argentina/Great Britain, 2889. Argentina/Mexico, 3056. Argentina/ Paraguay, 2799. Argentina/US, 2898. Brazil, 885, 3322. Brazil/France, 3155. Brazil/Paraguay, 3085. Caribbean Area/ Great Britain, 1866. Caribbean Area/Mexico, 1460. Caribbean Area/US, 2093. Central America/US, 2093. Chile/Germany, 2743. Chile/Peru, 2615, 2624, 2714. Chile/ Spain, 1089, 1123. Chile/US, 3015. Colombia, 2495. Colombia/Cuba, 2512. Colombia/Germany, 2505. Colombia/US, 2505, 2541. Costa Rica/Nicaragua, 1723. Costa Rica/Spain, 1768. Cuba/Mexico, 1952. Cuba/Spain, 1922, 2088. Cuba/US, 1074, 2047, 2088, 2106, 2108. Dominican Republic/Haiti, 1991, 2065. Ecuador/Peru, 2561. Ecuador/Spain, 2555. Germany, 1133. Great Britain/US, 2054. Guatemala/ US, 1776. Guyana/US, 2054. Haiti/ France, 1925. Haiti/Jamaica, 2013. Haiti/ US, 2038, 2095, 2109. Latin America/ Europe, 1037. Latin America/France, 1091. Latin America/Spain, 861, 1082, 1102, 4582. Latin America/US, 883, 930, 940, 1116, 2568, 4551, 4609. Mexico/ France, 1416, 1454, 1580. Mexico/Great Britain, 1406. Mexico/South America, 1639. Mexico/Spain, 1565, 1570, 1580. Mexico/US, 1163, 1413, 1421, 1431, 1434, 1470, 1475, 1543, 1559, 1563, 1584, 1596, 1612, 1614, 1625, 1628. Netherlands/ Aruba, 2071. Netherlands/Netherlands Antilles, 2071. Panama/US, 1763. Paraguay, 3088. Peru/France, 2626. Peru/Japan, 2628. Portugal/Spain, 3179. Puerto Rico/ US, 2042. Río de la Plata/France, 2777.

Río de la Plata/Great Britain, 2777. Saint Kitts and Nevis/US, 1866. South America, 891, 2763. South America/Great Britain, 1125. Spain/US, 1075, 1094. Uruguay/ France, 3106. Venezuela, 2442. Venezuela/ Spain, 2478. Venezuela/US, 1121, 2467, 2475.

International Trade, 843. Costa Rica, 1751. Mexico, 1637.

International Trade Relations. Argentina/ Chile, 2790. Audiencia of Quito/Chile, 2193. Brazil, 3230. French Caribbean/ France, 1816. Mexico/European Union, 1617. Venezuela/Spain, 2141. Viceroyalty of Río de la Plata/Spain, 2349.

Interpersonal Relationships. Aztecs, 605. Mayas, 509.

Interpretation. *See* Translating and Interpreting.

Interpreting. *See* Translating and Interpreting.

Intervention. *See* Foreign Intervention.

Investments. Minerals and Mining Industry, 2641. *See Also* Foreign Investment.

Iommi, Enio, 230.

Iquitos, Peru (city). Ethnic Groups and Ethnicity, 2630.

Irigoyen, Bernardo de, 2790.

Irigoyen, Hipólito, 2877.

Irish. Montserrat, 1819.

Iron Industry and Trade. Architecture, 330.

Isabella I, *Queen of Spain*, 1030.

Islamic Influences. Jamaica, 1787. Maroons, 1787.

Islas Malvinas. *See* Falkland Islands.

Italian Influences. Brazil, 3280. Colombia, 2539. Uruguay, 3092, 3108. Venezuela, 309.

Italians. Argentina, 2781, 2836, 2964, 3253. Brazil, 399, 3253, 3280, 3283, 3342. Catholic Church, 935. Peru, 2629. Uruguay, 3092.

Itza (indigenous group). Spanish Conquest, 525.

Ivo, Gonçalo, 362.

Iwan, Llwyd Ap, 2872.

Jalisco, Mexico (state). Church Architecture, 36. Historical Demography, 1400.

Japanese. Peru, 797.

Japanese Influences. Peru, 2628.

Jauja, 4786.

Javouhey, Anne-Marie, 1930, 1946.

Jazz. Argentina, 4495. Festivals, 4467. Musical History, 4467, 4495. Venezuela, 4467.

Jesuits. Architecture, 394. Archives, 2159. Argentina, 2412. Audiencia of Charcas,

2304. Baja California, 1380. Brazil, 394, 751, 3142, 3152, 3154, 3197. Chile, 739. Church Architecture, 57. French Caribbean, 1839. Guaraní, 656, 670, 708. Incas, 700, 728. Indigenous Languages, 3180. Indigenous Peoples, 3152. Land Tenure, 1358, 2371, 2412–2413. Mexico, 1177, 1248, 1258, 1317, 1365, 1372, 4632. Military, 3197. Missions, 2422. Paraguay, 58, 656, 670, 2396, 2403. Patagonia, 2335. Peru, 2165. Social Life and Customs, 1374. Venezuela, 2135. Viceroyalty of New Spain, 1374. Viceroyalty of Peru, 2227, 2265.

Jews, 855, 879. Argentina, 2910, 3037, 4483. Authors, 4338. Bolivia, 2650. Colombia, 2502. Colonial Administration, 1041. Colonial History, 978. Cultural History, 1006. Cultural Identity, 1122. French Caribbean, 1820. Haiti, 1810. Mexico, 1602, 1641. Oral History, 2910. Peru, 2630. Saint-Domingue, 1867. Spain, 855. Uruguay, 4269.

Jiménez, Carlos, 4479.

Jiménez, José Alfredo, 4386.

Jiménez, Luz, 133.

Jiménez, Marcos Pérez. See Pérez Jiménez, Marcos.

Jobs. See Employment.

Jocotitlán, Mexico (municipality). Colonial History, 1280.

Johan Maurits *Prince of Nassau-Siegen*, 3222.

Journalism. Argentina, 3041. Brazil, 3273. Guatemala, 1646. Haiti, 2061. Mexico, 1444. Peru, 2576. Public Health, 1444. South America, 938. *See Also* Mass Media; Newspapers.

Journalists. Argentina, 2397, 2969.

Jouvet, Louis, 4231.

Juárez, Mexico (city). See Ciudad Juárez, Mexico (city).

Juan, Jorge, 2116, 2280.

Juana Inés de la Cruz, *Sor*, 4419.

Juarros, Domingo, 1656.

Judges. Mexico, 1464. Saint-Domingue, 1875.

Judicial Power. French Caribbean, 1967.

Judicial Process. Brazil, 3228. Colonial History, 3204. French Influences, 1464. Haiti, 1976. Mexico, 1464. Portuguese Influences, 3228. Puerto Rico, 1832. Viceroyalty of New Spain, 1311.

Jujuy, Argentina (prov.). Incas, 806. Local History, 3027.

Justo, Juan Bautista, 2908, 4779, 4830.

Juston, Adolphe, 1967.

Juzgado de Bienes de Difuntos (Chile), 2329.

Kahlo, Frida, 113, 131.

Kaingang (indigenous group). Ethnohistory, 678–679.

Kaingangue (indigenous group), 4094.

Kalinya (indigenous group). *See* Carib (indigenous group).

Katz, Renina, 359.

Kemble, Kenneth, 228.

Kennedy, John Fitzgerald, 1139.

Kings. *See* Kings and Rulers.

Kings and Rulers, 1066. Aztecs, 497. Brazil, 3331. Festivals, 2340. Mayas, 469, 602. Mexico, 1284.

Kinship. Mexico, 1407. Slaves and Slavery, 3343.

Korn, Alejandro, 4813.

Krause, Karl Christian Friedrich, 4753.

Kubitschek, Juscelino, 3302.

Kuélap Site (Peru), 712.

K'ulta, Bolivia (town). Ethnohistory, 655.

Kuna (indigenous group). *See* Cuna (indigenous group).

La Azucena de Quito, 2202.

La Ceiba, Honduras (town). Oral History, 1709.

La Condamine, Charles-Marie de, 2167.

La Guajira, Colombia (dept.). Colonial History, 2152. Fish and Fishing, 2152.

La Habana, Cuba (city). Church Architecture, 48. Historic Sites, 50. Military History, 1854, 1895. Musical History, 4446. Social History, 1924. Social Life and Customs, 1924.

La leyenda de los soles, 489.

La música en Cuba, 4333.

La Pampa, Argentina (prov.). Social Conditions, 2775, 2847.

La Paz, Bolivia (city). Archives, 4451. Colonial History, 2701. Commerce, 2701. Domestics, 2309. Economic History, 2637. Elites, 2305, 2694. Musical History, 4451. Women, 2666, 2685.

La Rioja, Argentina (city). Censuses, 2368. Historical Demography, 2368.

La Rioja, Argentina (prov.). Colonial History, 2412–2413. Inheritance and Succession, 2356. Jesuits, 2413. Land Tenure, 2413. Political Ideology, 2810.

La Romana, Dominican Republic (prov.). History, 1802.

La Vega, Dominican Republic (prov.). History, 1795. Social Life and Customs, 1795.

Liberalism. Argentina, 3003. Brazil, 3311, 4755. Central America, 1705. Mexico, 1403, 1432, 4645.

Liberation Theology, 702, 4601. Brazil, 4744. French Influences, 4744. Honduras, 1756. Philosophy, 4557, 4569.

Libraries. Argentina, 2963, 2965, 3039. Bolivia, 2661. Brazil, 3125, 3139. Convents, 1148. Mexico, 1254. Peru, 2255. Viceroyalty of New Spain, 1219.

Library Resources. Colombia, 2160. The Netherlands, 3175.

Lienzo de Carapan, 599–600.

Lienzo de Jucutácato, 599.

Lienzo de Tlaxcala, 502, 631.

Liga de Comunidades Agrarias y Sindicatos Campesinos del Estado de Tamaulipas (Mexico), 1560.

Liga del Sur (Argentina), 2929.

Lima, Alceu Amoroso, 4767.

Lima, Peru (city). Church Architecture, 83–84. City Planning, 2597. Colonial Administration, 2275. Colonial Architecture, 75. Colonial Theater, 76. Elites, 2612. Exhibitions, 81. Guidebooks, 2601. History, 2584. Inquisition, 2252–2253, 2261–2262, 2278. Photography, 2595. Race and Race Relations, 2239. Social History, 2597. Women, 2603.

Limantour, José Yves, 1440, 1448.

Lincogur, Santiago, 707.

Linguistic Geography, 912, 930, 4609, 4612.

Linguistics. Cultural Identity, 4690. Venezuela, 4690.

Lispector, Clarice, 4365.

Literacy. *See* Literacy and Illiteracy.

Literacy and Illiteracy. Colonial History, 1053.

Literary Criticism, 852, 3963, 4372, 4590–4591, 4762. History, 908.

Livestock. Jamaica, 1901. Mexico, 1145, 1360.

Llanos Orientales Region (Colombia and Venezuela). Indigenous/Non-Indigenous Relations, 2508. Land Settlement, 2508.

Local Elections. Mexico, 1558, 1572.

Local Government. *See* Municipal Government.

Local History, 898. Mexico, 1542. Venezuela, 2449.

Lockouts. *See* Strikes and Lockouts.

Lombardo Toledano, Vicente, 4641.

Longa, Rita, 181.

Longinos Martínez, José, 1293.

López, Evaristo, 2988.

López, José Hilario, 2513.

López, Telmo, 3698.

López, Vicente Fidel, 2849.

López Antay, Joaquín, 289.

López de Casas, Alonso, 2257.

López Jordán, Ricardo, 2845.

Los Angeles, US (city). Riots, 1543.

Louisiana, US (state). Colonial History, 1905.

Loynaz, Dulce María, 3537.

Lunardi, Federico, 1727.

Luz y Caballero, José de la, 4679.

Lynch, Grayston L., 2079.

Macas, Ecuador (town). History, 693.

Maceo, Antonio, 4672.

Machado, Gustavo, 2429.

Machado de Assis, 4156.

Machiganga (indigenous group). *See* Machiguenga (indigenous group).

Machiguenga (indigenous group). Indigenous Music, 4465.

Machismo. *See* Sex Roles.

Madero, Francisco I., 1500, 1567.

Madre de Díos, Peru (dept.). Archeology, 786.

Madres de Plaza de Mayo (Argentina), 2881.

Maestro Rural, 1593.

Magaldi, Agustín, 4475.

Magallanes, Chile (prov.). Excavations, 810. Indigenous Peoples, 758. Migration, 759. Precolumbian Civilizations, 776.

Magariños D., Víctor, 231.

Magdalena, Colombia (dept.). Colonial History, 2161. Election Fraud, 2485. Slaves and Slavery, 2161.

Magdalena, Mexico (town). Historical Demography, 1400.

Magellan Strait. Climatology, 2410. Geographical History, 2410.

Magic. Argentina, 2851.

Magón, Ricardo Flores. *See* Flores Magón, Ricardo.

Maids. *See* Domestics.

Maine (battleship), 1995.

Mainero Alvarado, Carlos Guadalupe, 1435.

Maitland, Thomas, *Sir*, 3035.

Malaria. Peru, 2586.

Maldonado, Francisco Severo, 4643.

Mallku (indigenous group). Political Culture, 763. Social Structure, 763.

Malvinas, Islas. *See* Falkland Islands.

Mam (indigenous group). Land Tenure, 1653.

Manatí, Puerto Rico (town). History, 1799.

Manaus, Brazil (city). Architecture, 3301. European Influences, 3301. Labor and Laboring Classes, 3255. Mass Media, 3255.

Musical History, 4527–4528. Opera, 4527. Public Works, 3301.

Mando, Alonso, 1844.

Manet, Eduardo, 3538.

Mannerism (architecture), 3.

Manso, Juana, 2772.

Manuscripts. Aztecs, 630. Colonial History, 703. Forgery, 526. Mayas, 581. Meso-america, 455–456, 466–467, 474, 489, 530, 533, 541, 649. Mexico, 599. Migra-tion, 644. Mixtec, 617. Music, 4450. Peru, 721.

Manuscrito quechua de Huarochirí, 673.

Maps and Cartography. Argentina, 2956. Brazil, 397, 3208, 3223. Colonial History, 1049. Mexico, 1415. Paraguay, 2367. Rail-roads, 844. South America, 2112. Viceroy-alty of Río de la Plata, 2385.

Mapuche (indigenous group). Colonial His-tory, 696, 2322. Cultural Development, 682. Cultural History, 2322–2324. Cul-tural Identity, 682. European Influences, 2323. Indigenous Policy, 2704. Indige-nous Resistance, 735. Indigenous/Non-Indigenous Relations, 2736. Relations with Spaniards, 836. Spanish Conquest, 2323–2324.

Mar del Plata, Argentina (city). Employment, 2943.

Marín, Luis Muñoz. *See* Muñoz Marín, Luis.

Maracaibo, Venezuela (city). Colonial His-tory, 2140. Elites, 2140. History, 2450. Marriage, 2140. Social History, 2140.

Maracaibo, Venezuela (prov.). Abolition, 2474.

Maranhão, Brazil (state). Indigenous Peoples, 667. Political History, 3249. Politicians, 3249. Sources, 667.

Marginalization. *See* Marginalized Peoples; Social Marginality.

Marginalized Peoples. Central America, 1744. *See Also* Social Marginality.

María de San José, *madre*, 1294, 3411.

Mariana de Jesús *Beata*, 2202.

Mariátegui, José Carlos, 2599, 2631, 4708–4709, 4712, 4716–4719, 4779.

Marie-Galante (island). Fish and Fishing, 2034. Social Life and Customs, 2034.

Marimba. Mexico, 4388.

Marina, 502.

Marinello, Juan, 4673–4674.

Maritime History. Costa Rica, 1751. Falkland Islands, 2807. Martinique, 1918. Patago-nia, 2807. Peru, 2617. Venezuela, 2141. *See Also* Naval History.

Maritime Law, 1017.

Maritime Policy. Spain, 860.

Markets. Economic History, 994. Mexico, 1181. Women, 1449.

Maroons. Barbados, 1827. French Caribbean, 1853. Islamic Influences, 1787. Jamaica, 1787. Suriname, 1860.

Márquez, Juan, 1337, 4650.

Marranos. Brazil, 3195.

Marriage. Audiencia of Charcas, 2310. Cen-tral America, 1664. Chile, 2327, 2703. Co-lombia, 2542. Mexico, 1256, 1288. Social History, 2386. Viceroyalty of Peru, 2239.

Martí, José, 4663–4665, 4667, 4669–4670, 4673–4675, 4678, 4683, 4800.

Martí revolucionario, 4800.

Martínez de Arizala, Pedro, 2208, 2216, 2218–2219.

Martínez Estrada, Ezequiel, 4800.

Martínez Peláez, Severo, 1662, 1662.

Martńez Compañon y Bujanda, Baltasar Jaime, 2279.

Marulanda Vélez, Manuel, 2484.

Marxism, 4577, 4611, 4674, 4842. Argentina, 4779. Intellectual History, 4561. Mexico, 4634, 4636. Peru, 4712.

Masons. *See* Freemasonry.

Mass Media. Argentina, 2936, 3041, 3059. Brazil, 358, 412, 3335. Cultural Identity, 4624. Mexico, 1463, 1481. Modern Art, 412. Peru, 2576. US, 1497–1498. Venezu-ela, 2478. *See Also* Journalism.

Mata, Eduardo, 4417.

Mate (tea). Paraguay, 3074, 3079.

Material Culture, 927. Brazil, 3337. South America, 773.

Mathematics. Aztecs, 597. Mayas, 606.

Matiauda, Vicente Antonio, 2926.

Matiauda y Marzola, Manuel, 3089.

Matlatzinca (indigenous group). Land Tenure, 454.

Mato Grosso, Brazil (state). Historical Geog-raphy, 3156. Indigenous Peoples, 789. Land Settlement, 3286.

Mato Grosso do Sul, Brazil (state). Artifacts, 3314. Historical Geography, 3156. Indige-nous Peoples, 3329. Missions, 3314, 3329.

Matrero, 4492.

Matsigenka (indigenous group). *See* Machiguenga (indigenous group).

Matta Echaurren, Roberto Sebastián, 252–253.

Matto de Turner, Clorinda, 4715.

Maturana Family, 2325.

Populism, 1138, 4607. Argentina, 2996. Costa Rica, 1765. Peru, 2593.

Por la pendiente del sacrificio, 2561.

Port-au-Prince, Haiti (city). Description and Travel, 1970. History, 1970. Pictorial Works, 2068. Urban History, 2068.

Portes Gil, Emilio, 1532.

Porto Alegre, Brazil (city). Architecture, 392. Modern Architecture, 406. Social History, 3337. Urban History, 3337.

Porto Alegre, Manuel de Araújo, 4218.

Portraits. Mexico, 129, 138, 149, 166. Venezuela, 302.

Ports. Venezuela, 2443.

Portuguese. Brazil, 3245, 3321. Ecuador, 2225. Paraguay, 2359. Slaves and Slavery, 2361. Viceroyalty of Río de la Plata, 2359.

Portuguese Conquest, 880, 1011, 3206, 4560. Exiles, 3201. Sources, 3136.

Portuguese Influences. Brazil, 4751.

Positivism, 4546. Argentina, 2938, 4785, 4812, 4836. Brazil, 3232, 4740, 4753, 4770. Mexico, 4644. Political Development, 4770. Women, 2938.

Post-Modernism. *See* Postmodernism.

Postal Cards. *See* Postcards.

Postcards. El Salvador, 1739. Haiti, 2068.

Postmodernism, 305. Mexico, 3955.

Potosí, Bolivia (city). Archives, 2314. Basques, 2297. Books, 2661. Civil War, 2297. Colonial Administration, 2298. Colonial History, 2297. Description and Travel, 2291. Indigenous Policy, 2298. Markets, 743. Minerals and Mining Industry, 2314. Mita, 2298, 2300. Religious Life and Customs, 2313.

Potosí, Bolivia (dept.). Indigenous/Non-Indigenous Relations, 2682.

Pottery. Mexico, 160.

Powles, L.D., 2019.

Prado, Décio de Almeida, 4222.

Prado, Mariano Ignacio, 2583.

Precolumbian Architecture. Peru, 772.

Precolumbian Art, 4. Chile, 704. *See Also* Iconography.

Precolumbian Civilizations. Agricultural Technology, 710. Chile, 704. Colombia, 705, 799, 2494. Cultural Development, 659. Cultural History, 659. Cultural Identity, 660, 1003. Dance, 4437. Easter Island, 817. Ecuador, 662. Engineering, 710. Food, 776. Gender Relations, 484. Guatemala, 4437. Iconography, 701. Inter-Tribal Relations, 730. Mesoamerica, 621. Metallurgy,

705. Mexico, 506. Mortuary Customs, 738. Music, 4411. Nicaragua, 4439. Peru, 660, 701, 729, 738, 771, 2626.

Precolumbian Land Settlement Patterns. Brazil, 813.

Precolumbian Trade. South America, 730.

Pregnancy. Colonial History, 689.

Prehistory. *See* Archeology.

Presidential Systems. *See* Political Systems.

Presidents. Argentina, 2111, 2785, 2811, 2859, 2914, 2930, 2935, 3018, 3025. Bolivia, 2639, 2647, 2649. Brazil, 3302. Chile, 2111, 2718–2719. Colombia, 2535, 2538. Costa Rica, 4655–4656. Cuba, 2106. Ecuador, 2558, 4706–4707. Haiti, 2039. Mexico, 1414, 1487, 1510, 1567, 1621. Paraguay, 3082. Venezuela, 2458, 2472, 2477.

Press. *See* Mass Media.

Prestes, Luís Carlos, 3316–3317.

Prices. Colonial History, 969.

Primary Education. *See* Elementary Education.

Prime Ministers. Trinidad and Tobago, 2073.

Printers. *See* Printing Industry.

Printing Industry. Argentina, 2876. Strikes and Lockouts, 2876.

Prints. Argentina, 238, 246. Brazil, 355, 364. Colombia, 267. Mexico, 20, 124, 132. Peru, 81.

PRI. *See* Partido Revolucionario Institucional (Mexico).

Prisoners. Argentina, 2868. Brazil, 3325.

Prisons. Argentina, 2787, 2803, 2868. Brazil, 3339.

Problema do trabalho, 4767.

Professional Education. Colonial History, 4620.

Propaganda. Brazil, 3233, 3312. Mexico, 1497. Newspapers, 1092. Venezuela, 2475.

Prostitution. Argentina, 2773, 2946. Brazil, 338. Mexico, 1504, 1506. Puerto Rico, 1954.

Protestant Churches. British Caribbean, 1792.

Protestantism. French Caribbean, 1883. Nicaragua, 1754.

Protestants. Colonial History, 1012.

Protests. Colombia, 2483. Martinique, 1940. Puerto Rico, 2085. Viceroyalty of New Spain, 1307.

Proyecto económico, 446.

PSB. *See* Partido Socialista Brasileiro.

Psychiatry. Guadeloupe, 2025.

Silver, 917, 1031. Bolivia, 2642, 2680, 2684, 2689. Viceroyalty of New Spain, 1313.
Silverwork. Ecuador, 79. Peru, 66–67.
Sinaloa, Mexico (state). Cultural History, 1263. Political History, 1567.
Síntesis, 4822.
Slavery. *See* Slaves and Slavery.
Slavery, 20th Century. Venezuela, 2454.
Slaves. *See* Slaves and Slavery.
Slaves and Slavery, 897, 936, 1030, 1073. Acculturation, 1821. Agricultural Systems, 1902. Argentina, 3004. Artisans, 3183. Audiencia of Quito, 2175, 2223. Bahamas, 2001. Barbados, 1847–1848, 1908. Brazil, 871, 939, 3133, 3148, 3177, 3181, 3183, 3186, 3215–3217, 3234, 3240, 3247, 3271–3272, 3298, 3300, 3318–3319, 3343, 3348–3350. British, 1876. British Caribbean, 1931. Capitalism, 988. Caribbean Area, 871, 1829, 1848, 1873, 1905, 1942. Catholicism, 3178, 3343. Chile, 2326, 2339. Colombia, 2196, 2514. Costa Rica, 1669, 1672, 1685. Cuba, 2004. Cultural Identity, 1302. Ecuador, 2196, 2551. Ethnic Groups and Ethnicity, 3217. Family and Family Relations, 3272. French Caribbean, 1791, 1796, 1830, 1853, 1861, 2002, 2009–2010. French Guiana, 1855, 1965. Guadeloupe, 1951, 2050. Guatemala, 1682. Haiti, 1976. Historiography, 1942, 2004. Indigenous Peoples, 2120, 3148. Insurrections, 1880, 1905, 2050. Jamaica, 1821, 1890, 1900, 1902–1903. Judicial Process, 1931. Kinship, 3272. Land Use, 1902. Law and Legislation, 1015–1016, 3247. Marriage, 2339. Martinique, 1937, 1972, 1979. Medical Care, 1903. Mexico, 1279. Peru, 2625. Puerto Rico, 1977, 2004. Saint Barthélemy, 1830. Saint-Domingue, 1864, 1871–1872. Sex and Sexual Relations, 2339. Sex Roles, 1908, 3177. Social History, 1043, 3319. Social Life and Customs, 3318. Social Mobility, 3178. Social Structure, 1848, 3318. Sources, 2123. Spanish Caribbean, 2005. Sugar Industry and Trade, 1327, 1872. Suriname, 1834. Urban Areas, 1903. Uruguay, 3104, 3110. US, 1829. Venezuela, 2123, 2464, 2474. Viceroyalty of Peru, 2228, 2282. Viceroyalty of Río de la Plata, 2358, 2361, 2401. Women, 1890, 2174, 2339.
Small Business. Colonial History, 1249.
Smith, Robert Chester, 411.
Smuggling. Mosquitia, 1692. Shipping, 1324.
Smyley, William H., 2807.

Soap Operas. Peru, 2634.
Soccer, 4337.
Social Change, 968, 4547. Chile, 2735. Historiography, 1108. Mexico, 1321, 4652. Modern Art, 352. Nongovernmental Organizations, 1115. Popular Music, 4526. Positivism, 4770. Venezuela, 2126.
Social Classes, 2573. Argentina, 2406, 2864. Bolivia, 2692. Colombia, 2501–2502. Colonial History, 1296. Cuba, 1933–1934. Mesoamerica, 505. Mexico, 1173, 1180, 1217, 1603. Peru, 2574, 2598, 2618.
Social Conflict, 959. Argentina, 2775, 3049. Brazil, 3161. Colombia, 2488.
Social Customs. *See* Social Life and Customs.
Social Development. Dominican Republic, 4677. Panama, 1758. Suriname, 1797.
Social History, 858, 903, 927, 931, 955, 968, 1127, 2893, 4543. Argentina, 2345, 2778, 2818, 2828, 2864, 2893, 2923, 2945, 2955. Bahamas, 2019. Bolivia, 2640, 2673, 2697. Brazil, 334, 3157, 3215, 3294, 3336. Caribbean Area, 1968, 2027. Chile, 2318–2319, 2327, 2703. Colombia, 2496, 2507, 2516, 2542. Cuba, 1923, 1981, 1993. Ecuador, 2551–2552. French Caribbean, 1790, 1824. French Guiana, 1878. Guadeloupe, 1939. Guatemala, 1658, 1662. Guyana, 1786. Haiti, 1881. Jamaica, 1814, 1904. Martinique, 1838. Medicine, 1647. Mexico, 987, 1163, 1170, 1423, 1459, 1476, 1482, 1490, 1505, 1545. Paraguay, 3084, 3086. Peru, 2610–2611, 4715. Puerto Rico, 1811, 1818, 1889, 1957, 1978, 2000. Saint-Domingue, 1882. Slaves and Slavery, 1016. Textbooks, 857, 1116. Venezuela, 2130, 2440.
Social Life and Customs, 595, 878, 905, 928, 966. Argentina, 791, 2818, 2840, 2895. Brazil, 331, 334, 3277–3279, 3294. Central America, 1759. Chile, 2703. Colombia, 2499, 2516. Colonial History, 979, 990, 1210. Costa Rica, 1735. Danish Caribbean, 1856. Elites, 1304. French Guiana, 1878. French Influences, 1140. Frontier and Pioneer Life, 886. Martinique, 2096. Mayas, 416. Mesoamerica, 528. Mexico, 1481–1482, 1490, 4385. Peru, 2595, 4371. Puerto Rico, 1889. Venezuela, 2136. Viceroyalty of Peru, 2239. Viceroyalty of Río de la Plata, 2347. West Indians, 2105.
Social Marginality, 2040. Argentina, 4820. Carib, 2053. Martinique, 2091. *See Also* Marginalized Peoples.

AUTHOR INDEX

Asturias, Miguel Angel, 3773
Asturias Montenegro, Gonzalo, 1706
Ataíde, Vicente, 4088
Atán, Adriana, 2776
Atlantic history: history of the Atlantic system 1580–1830, 843
Aulestia, Carlos, 3567
Auletta, Estela, 58
Austin, Robert, 1115
Avances historiográficos en el estudio de Venustiano Carranza, 1499
Avellaneda, Mercedes, 670
Avendaño, Santiago, 671
Avendaño Rojas, Xiomara, 1707
Avenel, Jean-David, 2777
Aveni, Anthony F., 420
Avila, Affonso, 4178
Avila Espinosa, Felipe Arturo, 1500
Avila Hernández, Julieta, 11
Ayala, Ernesto, 3627
Ayala, Gabriel de, 421
Ayala, Javier, 4384
Ayala, Walmir, 313
Ayala Calderón, Kristhian, 2576
Ayala Diago, César Augusto, 2489
Ayala Duarte, Alfonso, 4385
Ayala Loayza, Juan Luis, 672
Ayala Mora, Enrique, 4707
Aycart Luengo, Carmen, 844
Ayrolo, Valentina, 2778
Azanza Jiménez, José, 4386
Azaretto, Roberto A., 2779
Azcona Cranwell, Elizabeth, 3774
Azevedo, Aluísio, 4351
Azevedo, Celia Maria Marinho de, 3235
Azevedo, Francisca L. Nogueira de, 931
Azevedo Filho, Leodegário Amarante de, 4163–4164
Azougarh, Abdeslam, 3410
Azparren Giménez, Leonardo, 4070
Azpúrua E., Miguel, 2429
Azulejos na cultura luso-brasileira, 321

Bacacorzo, Gustavo, 63
Bacardí Moreau, Emilio, 3472
Bacellar, Carlos de Almeida Prado, 3143
Bacellar, Luiz, 4179
Backal, Alicia Gojman de, 1122
Baer, Gerhard, 4465
Baer, James A., 856, 2780
Baetens, Jan, 385
Báez, Marcelo, 3775–3776
Báez, Myrna, 184, 205
Báez, Rannel, 3989
Báez-Jorge, Félix, 458, 1213

Baggio, Kátia Gerab, 2031
Bahamón, Astrid, 174
Bähr, Aida, 3473
Bailón Corres, Jaime, 1622
Baily, Samuel L., 2781
Bakewell, Peter John, 845, 917
Balbi, Mariella, 284
Balbis, Jorge, 3094
Balch, Trudy, 4357
Balderrama Montes, Raúl, 4387
Balderston, Daniel, 4366
Baldi Salas, Norberto, 4844
Baldrich, Juan José, 1921
Balhana, Aliva Pilatti, 4770
Bali, Jaime, 30
Balliache, Simón, 4467
Ballina, Osvaldo, 4061
Ballón Aguirre, Enrique, 673, 3362
Ballón Lozada, Héctor, 2608
Balsera, Viviana Díaz, 422
Balta, Aída, 2577
Banco Central de Reserva del Perú, 2578–2579
Banco Central del Ecuador, 2181
Banco de la Ciudad de Buenos Aires, 233
Banco Real (São Paulo), 3149
Bandeira, Júlio, 334
Banko, Catalina, 846
Baptiste, Fitzroy Andre, 2032
Baralt, Guillermo A., 2033
Baranda, María, 3851
Baratti, Danilo, 3063
Baraya, Aristides, 796
Barbero, María Inés, 2782–2783
Barbosa, Rubens Antonio, 3126
Barbotin, Maurice, 2034
Barceló, Tomás, 3485
Barcia, Pedro Luis, 4027
Barcia Zequeira, María del Carmen, 1922–1924
Bardach, Ann Louise, 3484
Bardi, Pietro Maria, 338
Bareiro Saguier, Rubén, 3727
Bargellini, Clara, 1274
Barickman, B.J., 3236
Barletta, Victor, 4369
Barman, Roderick J., 3237
Barnadas, Josep María, 3404
Barón Ortega, Julio, 2490
Baroni Boissonas, Ariane, 1357
Barraclough, Frances Horning, 4277
Barrado Barquilla, José, 862
Barragán Romano, Rossana, 2295, 2685, 2697
Barrán, José Pedro, 3095–3096
Barreda, Pedro, 3959

Cobo del Arco, Teresa, 1715

Coddou, Marcelo, 3914

Códice Techialoyan de San Pedro Tototepec, Estado de México, 454

Códices y documentos sobre México: segundo simposio, 455

Códices y documentos sobre México: tercer simposio, 456

Coelho, Geraldo Mártires, 3154

Coelho, Gustavo Neiva, 322

Cófreces, Javier, 3969

Cohen, M. Lorena, 2390

Cohen, Mario Eduardo, 855, 978

Colasanti, Marina, 4120

Colberg Pérez, Antonio, 3901

Coleção Teatro brasileiro, 4211

La colección Bernard y Edith Lewin: del Museo de Arte del Condado de Los Ángeles: vivencias para ser exhibidas: autobiografía de una galerista Bernard Lewin, 103

Colección del centenario salesiano: salesianos, 100 años en Paraguay, 3067–3072

Colectivo Neosaurios (Mexico), 1524

Colegio de México. Centro de Estudios Lingüísticos y Literarios, 1152

Colegio de Misioneros de Propaganda Fide de la Santa Cruz (Querétaro, Mexico), 41

Colegio de Propaganda Fide (Tarija, Bolivia), 2296

Colegio Mexiquense, 492

Colina, José de la, 3419

Colio, Bárbara, 4001

Collado, Lipe, 3482

Collazos, Oscar, 268, 3558

Colloque de l'Institut de recherches sur les civilisations de l'Occident moderne, 20th, Paris, 1997, 3155

Collyer, Jaime, 3633

Colmenares, Germán, 1081, 2147–2148

Colombia-Venezuela: historia intelectual, 4699

The colonial Caribbean in transition: essays on Post-Emancipation social and cultural history, 1938

Colonial legacies: the problem of persistence in Latin American history, 858

Colonial lives: documents on Latin American history, 1550–1850, 979

Colonial Spanish America: a documentary history, 980

Colonialism past and present: reading and writing about colonial Latin America today, 3361

Las colonias del Nuevo Mundo: discursos imperiales, 981

Coloquio de Historia de Lima, 6th, Lima, 1999, 2584

Coloquio de Historia Regional de Orizaba, 2nd, México, 1998, 639

Coloquio Internacional "Buenos Aires 1910: El Imaginario para una Gran Capital," Buenos Aires, 1995, 2800

Coloquio Internacional El Siglo de la Revolución Mexicana, México, 2000, 1622

Coloquio "La Producción Cultural en las Colonias del Nuevo Mundo," San Miguel de Tucumán, Argentina, 1994, 981

Coloquio sobre Avances Historiográficos en el Estudio de Venustiano Carranza, Saltillo, Mexico, 1995, 1499

Coloquio sobre la lengua y la etnohistoria purépecha: homenaje a Benedict Warren, Morelia, Mexico, 1994, 536

Colson, Audrey Butt, 1858

El comercio de vinos y aguardientes andaluces con América, siglos XVI-XX, 859

Comercio marítimo colonial: nuevas interpretaciones y últimas fuentes, 1156

Comisión Chilena de Derechos Humanos, 2733

Comunidades: tierra, instituciones, identidad, 691

"Con tanto tiempo encima": aportes de literatura latinoamericana en homenaje a Pedro Lastra, 3962

Conaghan, Catherine M., 2618

Concurso Banco Provincia, Buenos Aires, 1997, 238

Concurso Nacional de Dramaturgia—Alvaro de Carvalho, 1st, Florianópolis, Santa Catarina, Brazil, 1995, 4208

Confederación Nacional Campesina (Mexico), 1560

La conformación de las identidades políticas en la Argentina del siglo XX, 2821

Congrès national des sociétés historiques et scientifiques, 123rd, Fort-de-France, 1998, 1801, 1816

Congreso Centroamericano de Historia, 5th, San Salvador, 2000, 1651

Congreso Cincuenta Años de Investigación Histórica de México, Guanajuato, Mexico, 1996, 1523

Congreso de Historia de Colombia, 9th, Tunja, Colombia, 1995, 2496

Congreso de Historia de Colombia, 10th, Medellín, Colombia, 1997, 2530

Congreso de Historia de los Pueblos de la

Estrella, Ulises, 3817
Estudios: Filosofía, Historia, Letras, 1424
Estudios sobre historia y ambiente en
América, 877
Estupiñán Viteri, Tamara, 2180–2181
Esvertit Cobes, Natàlia, 2559–2560
Etchenique, Jorge, 2775, 2847
Etchepare Jensen, Jaime, 2711
Eujanian, Alejandro Claudio, 2848–2849
Euraque, Darío A., 1654, 1726–1727
Evans-Corrales, Carys, 4310
Evolução física de Salvador, 1549 a 1800, 397
Ewen, Charles Robin, 1912
Expo '98, *Lisbon, 1998*, 982
Extractos de escrituras públicas: Archivo
General de Centroamérica, 1675

Fábio Penteado: ensaios de arquitetura, 398
Fabris, Annateresa, 376
The faces of honor: sex, shame, and violence
in colonial Latin America, 992
Faces of pre-Columbian Chile, 704
Fahsen, Federico, 638
Fajardo Ortiz, Guillermo, 993
Fajardo Sánchez, Luis Alfonso, 2500
Falchetti, Ana María, 705
Falcón, Ricardo, 2953
Falconí Almeida, Patricio, 3818
Falla, Juan José, 1675
Familias iberoamericanas: historia, identidad
y conflictos, 878
Faraone, Roque, 3102
Farberman, Judith, 2369
Farcau, Bruce W., 1085
Fares, Gustavo C., 4233
Faria, João Roberto, 4222–4223
Faria, Sheila Siqueira de Castro, 3166
Farias, Amy Caldwell de, 4567
Farnsworth-Alvear, Ann, 2501
The fat man from La Paz: contemporary
fiction from Bolivia, 4236
Faulhaber, Priscila, 706
Fausto, Boris, 879
Favaro, Orietta, 2850, 2949
Favela Fierro, María Teresa, 110
Favier Orendáin, Claudio, 22
Fawcett, Louise, 2502
Fazer a América: a imigração em massa para
a América Latina, 879
Fee, Nancy H., 1244
Feierstein, Ricardo, 4293
Feinmann, José Pablo, 4007, 4799
Feldman, Lawrence H., 553
Felguérez, Manuel, 169
Felinto, Marilene, 4155

Félix, Loiva Otero, 918
Félix, Moacyr, 4186, 4739
Fermandois Huerta, Joaquín, 1123, 2712
Fernandes, Anchieta, 4189
Fernandes, Eliane Moury, 3222
Fernandes, Orlandino Seitas, 326
Fernandes, Ronaldo Costa, 4187
Fernández, Adriana, 3719
Fernández, Alejandro E., 2901
Fernández, Claudia, 1529
Fernández, Eva Balbina, 3025
Fernández, Jorge, 707
Fernández, Mauro A., 2851
Fernández, Miguel Angel, 281
Fernández, Nona, 3639
Fernández, Pablo Armando, 3977
Fernández, Rafael Diego, 4635
Fernández, Rodolfo, 1212
Fernández Bulete, Virgilio, 1245
Fernández Fe, Gerardo, 3490
Fernández Fernández, David, 2713
Fernández Ferrer, Antonio, 3459
Fernández García, Ana María, 225
Fernández García, Martha, 14
Fernández Hernández, Bernabé, 1676
Fernández Moreno, Baldomero, 3819
Fernández Moreno, César, 3820
Fernández Moreno, Inés, 3688
Fernández Nadal, Estela, 4585
Fernández Pagliano, Alvaro, 3736
Fernández Pintado, Mylene, 3491
Fernández Rasines, Paloma, 2182
Fernández Retamar, Roberto, 4800
Fernández Santalices, Manuel, 48
Fernández Santana, René, 4008
Fernández Spencer, Antonio, 3492
Fernández Torres, Moisés, 2744
Fernández Valdés, Juan José, 2714
Fernández Zeballos Correcha, Pedro, 2177
Ferrari, Marcela P., 2838
Ferraro, Liliana Juana, 4798, 4801
Ferré, Rosario, 3493
Ferreira, Aurélio Buarque de Holanda, 382
Ferreira, Lúcio M., 3266
Ferreira, Luis, 4504
Ferreira, Luiz Otávio, 3267, 4740
Ferreira de Cassone, Florencia, 2852, 4802
Ferrer, Ada, 1953
Ferrer Benimeli, José Antonio, 949
Ferrer Muñoz, Manuel, 1246
Ferrer Rodríguez, Eulalio, 1530
Ferrero, Mary, 3612
Ferrero, Roberto A., 2853
Ferreyra, Aleida, 1531
Ferrigni Varela, Yoston, 2126